# DISCRIMINATION IN EMPLOYMENT

**Fourth Edition**

**Unit Three**
**of**

**Labor Relations and Social Problems**
**A Course Book**

# LABOR RELATIONS AND SOCIAL PROBLEMS

# DISCRIMINATION IN EMPLOYMENT

**Fourth Edition**

**Unit Three**
**of**

**Labor Relations and Social Problems**
**A Course Book**

Prepared by

**William P. Murphy,** Chairman, Unit Three
University of North Carolina

**Julius G. Getman**
Yale University

**James E. Jones, Jr.**
University of Wisconsin

for

**The Labor Law Group**

The Bureau of National Affairs, Inc., Washington, D.C.

**Library of Congress Cataloging in Publication Data**

Murphy, William P., 1919-
  Discrimination in employment.

  (Labor relations and social problems; unit 3)
  Previous editions of unit 3 written by R. N. Covington, J. G. Getman,
and J. E. Jones.
  Includes index.
  1. Discrimination in employment—Law and legislation—United
States. I. Getman, Julius G., joint author. II. Jones, James E., joint author.
III. Covington, Robert N. Discrimination in employment. IV. Labor Law
Group Trust. V. Title. VI. Series.
        KF3369.A1L26 unit 3, 1979 [KF3464]        344′.73′01s
        ISBN 0-87179-306-7        [344′.73′01133]        79-15283
                                                              Rev.

Printed in the United States of America
International Standard Book Number: 0-87179-306-7

# LABOR LAW GROUP

# Foreword

Starting in 1971, the Labor Law Group made a sharp break from the traditional format and content of law school teaching materials in the area of labor relations and social problems.

The Group had its genesis in a paper delivered at the 1946 meeting of the Association of American Law Schools by Willard Wirtz, then a professor of law at Northwestern University. Inspired by the vision of this address, a group of law teachers obtained a grant from the Carnegie Corporation of New York. With the cooperation of the University of Michigan Law School, the group held, at Ann Arbor in June of 1947, a two-week "Conference on the Training of Law Students in Labor Relations."

After the conference, the law teachers began the preparation of teaching materials. Eventually, the materials were published in 1953 by Little, Brown and Co. under the title LABOR RELATIONS AND THE LAW. All of the preparation of the preliminary drafts and the first published edition were under the general editorship of Professor Robert E. Mathews.

The law teachers soon thereafter established a common law trust, obtained recognition of tax-exempt status, and assumed the name "Labor Law Group." The original membership was 31. Over the years some teachers have dropped out and others have become members. Altogether almost 70 persons, including some practitioners and government officials, have been members of the Group. Three of the original members—Benjamin Aaron, Donald H. Wollett, and Edwin R. Teple—are still active. All royalties from Group publications have gone into a trust fund to finance the Group's planning and editorial activities. No member of the Group has ever received personal financial remuneration.

In 1958 Professor Mathews, to whom we continue to pay honor as the foremost of our founding fathers, resigned as head of the group, and he was succeeded by Professors Benjamin Aaron and Donald H. Wollett as co-chairmen and co-editors of the second edition of LABOR RELATIONS AND THE LAW, which appeared in 1960. They in turn were succeeded by Professor Jerre Williams, who was general editor of the third edition in 1965 and Group chairman through 1967. The Group has also published EMPLOYMENT RELATIONS AND THE LAW (1957, Benjamin Aaron, Editor) and READINGS IN LABOR LAW (1955). From 1967 to 1972, Professor William P. Murphy served as chairman of the Group's Executive and Editorial Committees. He was succeeded by Professor Herbert L. Sherman, Jr., who was Group chairman from 1973 to 1977. Since January 1978, Professor James E. Jones, Jr., has served as chairman of these committees.

The Group reexamined the teaching of labor law at a one-week conference held at Boulder, Colo., in 1969. The conference was attended by law teachers, academic authorities from other disciplines, and management and labor spokesmen. As a result of this meeting and others, the Group decided to publish a series of books on LABOR RELATIONS AND SOCIAL PROBLEMS. Between 1971 and 1977 ten books, and subsequent editions of several of these books, were published by the Group.

In 1976 the Group decided to reorganize the materials for future books (starting in 1978), and to publish six books, including a substantial amount of nondoctrinal material, on the following subject matter: Collective Bargaining in Private Employment, Social Legislation, Discrimination in Employment, Collective Bargaining in Public Employment, Negotiation, and Arbitration and Conflict Resolution. Each of these books is designed so that it may be used by itself, but two or more of these books may be used in the same course or seminar.

The following characteristics distinguish this series of books from standard labor law casebooks:

1. The format of separate units (each dealing with a separate topic in the general field) in recognition of the fact that it is impossible to teach all of these subjects in one course.

2. For each subject a book which is shorter in length than a standard casebook, thus making it more practical to use in a typical course.

3. Frequent updating of units to keep abreast of a fast-changing field of law.

4. Inclusion of a separate unit on social legislation.

5. Coverage of matters not covered in standard casebooks, *e.g.*, the art and techniques of negotiation and the myth of expertise.

6. Inclusion of material on professional responsibility and comparative law.

7. A blending of legal and nondoctrinal materials so that a greater appreciation of the "law" can be achieved.

8. Meeting of the need for materials for seminars and advanced courses.

9. Meeting of the need for legal materials in the labor-management area for use in undergraduate courses.

10. Greater flexibility for the law teacher in putting together a course or courses of the teacher's own liking.

It is our hope that these books will give students an idea of industrial relations law and practices, and also shed light on the variety of techniques which are available for the peaceful resolution of significant social disputes.

THE EDITORIAL POLICY COMMITTEE

# Summary Table of Contents

# Detailed Table of Contents

# 1. Introduction

## A.  SCOPE AND ORGANIZATION OF THE UNIT

The cost of discrimination in employment in the United States has been variously estimated. In dollars and cents, one must include the loss of income due to greater unemployment and to discriminatory wage rates, as well as the heavy expense required in some industrial facilities for construction of additional rest rooms, maintaining separate employee rosters, and the like. More significant in the long run, however, is the loss of social and political stability attendant upon the inevitable change in the status of disadvantaged workers.

In the employment sphere, regulation or prohibition of discrimination is a recent phenomenon, dating only from the Second World War. The variety of weapons now in the arsenal of those waging a legal battle against arbitrary discrimination is surprising when thought of as the product of less than three decades. In dealing with these statutes, one major problem is their newness, since this means so little guidance is available in court decisions. However, all these laws borrow heavily from somewhat older statutes, especially with regard to coverage and techniques of enforcement, so that analogies are not difficult to find. Some provisions have no counterpart, however, in other protective statutes, particularly those provisions identifying what constitutes prescribed misconduct. A great deal of interpretation will have to take place before these sections acquire that certainty of meaning essential to evenhanded enforcement and adequate evaluation.

This chapter continues with a brief overview of modern EEO law and a listing of some of the major sources of antidiscrimination law. It also includes data on the earnings of minority and women workers.

Chapter 2 examines the basics of discrimination—disparate impact and disparate treatment, seniority, sex, and religion. Chapter 3 covers enforcement litigation; Chapter 4, affirmative action and the Executive order. Chapter 5 discusses EEO and labor relations law. Chapters 6, 7, 8, and 9, respectively, deal with equal pay, age, national origin and alienage, and the handicapped. Chapter 10 covers EEO and the Constitution.

## B.  THE DEVELOPMENT OF MODERN EEO LAW—A BRIEF*

It is both historically defensible, and convenient, to date the development of modern equal employment law from 1941. At that time, A. Philip

* The substance of these comments is taken largely from Jones, James E., Jr., *The*

Randolph, president of the predominantly black Brotherhood of Sleeping Car Porters, convened a conference of top black leaders, from which emerged the organization of the march-on-Washington movement.[1] America was preparing for World War II and its employment practices, as well as other aspects of life in America, revealed a most embarrassing contradiction—a tight labor market and a great need for skilled workers while employment discrimination prohibited the complete utilization of black workers in war industries.

In response to a threatened massive march on Washington, President Franklin D. Roosevelt issued Executive Order 8802,[2] establishing a Fair Employment Practice Committee (FEPC) in the Office of Production and Management.

The significant thing about the FEPC, established by that Executive order, was perhaps more its existence than its accomplishments. It was unpopular with the Congress, which was dominated by southern Democrats elected on anti-black political platforms; and Congress was not long in challenging the executive authority to proceed in that fashion and in limiting the program through the use of budgetary constraints.

Executive orders of the President, validly issued, have the force and effect of law, and they remain on the books until repealed or amended by a succeeding president, unless they go out of business pursuant to their own terms. Although there have been periods in which the programs have been rather inactive, and certainly periods in which they have been ineffective, succeeding presidents since Roosevelt have either left on the books the Executive order on the subject which they inherited or issued others in their own names directed to the same or similar ends.

The most significant innovation in such an Executive order was in the one issued by John F. Kennedy in April 1961.[3] It is the John F. Kennedy order which contains the affirmative action obligation that has emerged in the 1970s as the most controversial of the modern civil rights concepts.

Between the late 1930s and the mid-1940s we saw an increase in the activities of civil rights lawyers, predominantly black lawyers, seeking constitutional vindication of equal rights. While most of the cases which went to the U.S. Supreme Court were school, transportation, or housing cases with a clear constitutional nexus, in 1944 the Supreme Court decided *Steele* v. *Louisville & Nashville R.R. Co.*[4] and *Wallace Corp.* v. *NLRB*,[5] in which the Court, by interpretations of the Railway Labor Act and the National Labor Relations Act, concluded that unions had a duty of fair representation which prohibited invidious discrimination against

---

*Development of Modern Equal Employment Opportunity and Affirmative Action Law: A Brief Chronological Overview,* 20 HOWARD L. J. 1, pp. 74-99 (1977).

[1] Sumner Rosen, *The CIO Era, 1935-55,* in THE NEGRO AND THE AMERICAN LABOR MOVEMENT (J. Jacobsen, ed., (1968)).

[2] 6 Fed. Reg. 3109 (June 25, 1941).

[3] Executive Order 10925, 26 Fed. Reg. 1977 (1961).

[4] 323 U.S. 192 (1944).

[5] 323 U.S. 248 (1944).

members of the groups which they were authorized to represent under the law.

These decisions while statutory in declaration were constitutional in concept. However, they required that there be a union-management relationship established under the law for any protection to be forthcoming. Moreover, the effectiveness of such a cumbersome device to deal with racial discrimination is somewhat suspect.[6]

Also during the 1940s, perhaps reflecting demographic shifts of blacks from the South to more hospitable northern areas as well as their political potential, a number of states enacted little fair employment practice commission laws. Although Congress made an effort to pass such legislation, its efforts did not bear fruit until 1964. Like the duty of fair representation, the effectiveness of state administrative agencies in dealing with race discrimination has been questioned.[7]

It is known to most school children that in 1954, in *Brown* v. *Board of Education,* the Supreme Court declared that school segregation was inherently unequal; the radiations of that declaration permeated all aspects of society in America and gave impetus to increased efforts to eradicate the vestiges of racial discrimination. The period following *Brown* was marked by intensive civil rights activities. Marches, boycotts, sit-ins, freedom rides, and other tactics proliferated and focused the attention of the nation and the world on the status of civil rights of blacks in America.

Without attempting to assert that such activity was the total cause, or to establish the extent of the causal relationship, it seems apparent that the responses of the government agencies were related to this endeavor as well as to the increased political activism of the black population.

Beginning with Executive Order 10925, issued by John F. Kennedy in 1961, there was a steady proliferation of civil rights endeavors, court interpretations, and other administrative developments resulting in a multiplicity of laws and forums addressing invidious discrimination.

We saw emerging in July 1, 1964, the assertion by the NLRB of jurisdiction to deal with racial discrimination as an unfair labor practice under the National Labor Relations Act in *Hughes Tool Co.*[8] The next day Congress passed Title VII of the Civil Rights Act of 1964, prohibiting job discrimination on the basis of race, religion, national origin, and sex, and for the first time in modern history we had a rather widespread federal law applying to this area.

In 1968, the Supreme Court breathed life into the Reconstruction Era civil rights statutes as applied to private acts of discrimination. It had previously concluded that 42 U.S.C. §§ 1981, 1982, and 1983 required state action to prohibit discrimination, because they were based upon

---

[6] Herring, *The Fair Representation Doctrine: An Effective Weapon in Union Discrimination?,* 24 MARYLAND L. R. 113 (1964).

[7] Herbert Hill, *20 Years of State Fair Employment Practice Commissions: A Critical Analysis With Recommendations,* 14 BUFFALO L. R. 22 (1964).

[8] 147 NLRB 66; see also *Jubilee Manufacturing Co.,* 202 NLRB 2 (1973), applying the duty of fair representation to sex.

the Fourteenth Amendment of the U.S. Constitution.[9] In 1968, in *Jones v. Alfred Mayer Co.*,[10] the Supreme Court declared that the authority for the enactment of 42 U.S.C. §§ 1982 and 1981 was rooted in the Thirteenth Amendment and did not require state action and therefore was applicable to private employment discrimination.

In consequence of the multiplicity of activitites, equal employment law includes a multiplicity of statutes, executive orders, administrative agencies, and programs.

In 1972 Congress returned to the drawing board and substantially amended the major vehicle, the Civil Rights Act of 1964, expanding coverage by including state and local entities, by limiting the number and the extent of the exemptions, by dropping the numerical requirement substantially, and by specifically including the federal executive branches and the administrative agencies in the prohibitions against invidious discrimination.

Since the thrust of the federal law under Title VII, contrary to the National Labor Relations Act, was to add protections for the affected class without excluding (preempting the field) other laws and programs designed to achieve the same end, we are now faced with an increasing proliferation of laws under which persons may seek redress for the same actions. The wisdom of such a proliferation of tribunals and laws has been increasingly questioned; and, in the reorganization plan of the president of 1978, we see evidence, perhaps, of the first effort to consolidate programs leading in the distant future to a single federal agency with jurisdiction over the equal or human rights subject matter.[11]

## C.  AN INVENTORY OF LAWS PROHIBITING DISCRIMINATION

The source of antidiscrimination doctrine with which this book is most concerned is Title VII of the Civil Rights Act of 1964, 42 U.S.C. § 2000 *et seq.* In many settings, however, other sources may be turned to in addition to or instead of Title VII. The following list illustrates the variety of possibilities which counsel must consider:*

---

[9] See the *Slaughterhouse Cases*, 83 U.S. 36 (1873); the *Civil Rights Cases*, 109 U.S. 3 (1883); see also *Hodge* v. *U.S.*, 203 U.S. 1 (1905).

[10] 392 U.S. 419 (1908).

[11] For a more elaborate discussion of the overview, see Chapter 7 of the Industrial Relations Research Association's Series, 1976, FEDERAL POLICIES AND WORKER STATUS SINCE THE 30's, ed. Joseph P. Goldberg, *et. al.,* "The Transformation of Fair Employment Practices Policies," by James E. Jones, Jr., p. 159 (1976); see also Jones, *The Development of the Law Under Title VII Since 1965: Implications of the New Law,* 30 RUTGERS L. REV. 1 (1976).

* For more detailed, though slightly dated, reviews of the multiplicity of legal remedies for discrimination see Peck, *Remedies for Discrimination in Employment: A Comparative Evaluation of Forums,* 46 WASH. L. REV. 455 (1971); Cohen & Fried, *Multiple Jeopardy in Employment Discrimination Cases,* 31 MD. L. REV. 101 (1971); Herbert & Reischel, *Title VII and the Multiple Approaches to Employment Discrimination,* 46 N.Y.U.L. REV. 449 (1971).

## (1) *The Federal Constitution*

The Due Process Clause of the Fifth Amendment and the Due Process and Equal Protection Clauses of the Fourteenth Amendment have been interpreted to forbid invidious discrimination in government employment. Enforcement of these prohibitions by litigation is illustrated in *Ambach* v. *Norwick, infra* (national origin and alienage); *Cleveland Board of Education* v. *La Fleur, infra* (pregnant women); *Ethridge* v. *Rhodes, infra* (race discrimination by government contractors). See Das, *Discrimination Against Aliens,* 35 U. PITT. L. REV. 499 (1974).

## (2) *The Early Civil Rights Acts*

These statutes, now codified at 42 U.S.C. §§ 1981, 1983, and 1985 (insofar as they are relevant to the employment context), were long given a restrictive interpretation by the courts, but recent reinterpretations, such as that in the *Johnson* case, *infra,* make them important sources of antidiscrimination doctrine insofar as race and alienage are concerned. Whether they will be applied in sex, age, or other types of discrimination cases is less clear. Compare *Cohen* v. *Illinois Institute of Technology,* 524 F.2d 818 (7th Cir. 1975), with *McLellan* v. *Mississippi Power & Light Co.,* 545 F.2d 919 (5th Cir. 1976). Enforcement is through litigation. The discriminatory act is treated as a type of economic tort. See Larson, *The Development of Section 1981 as a Remedy for Racial Discrimination in Private Employment,* 7 HARV. CIV. RIGHTS—CIV. LIB. L. REV. 56 (1972). See also *The Expanding Scope of § 1981: Assault on Private Discrimination and a Cloud on Affirmative Action,* 90 HARV. L. REV. 412-52 (1977).

## (3) *The Civil Rights Act of 1964*

This is the most important single source of antidiscrimination doctrine. Title VII forbids discrimination on the basis of race, color, creed, national origin, and sex (age is not mentioned) by employment agencies, labor organizations, and private and public employers. The statute creates the Equal Employment Opportunity Commission, which investigates complaints and seeks to negotiate settlements in cases in which discrimination is found by the EEOC to have occurred. If conciliation fails, either the EEOC or the individual may bring an action in federal court in the case of private employers, employment agencies, and labor organizations. The Attorney General rather than the EEOC brings the action in the case of state government employers. If federal employees are involved after October 1978, enforcement is through the EEOC rather than the Civil Service Commission, with the individual suits permitted following pursuit of the administrative remedy. Title VI forbids discrimination by recipients of federal financial assistance.

### (4) *Presidential Executive Orders*

The major executive orders dealing with discrimination in employment are: Executive Order 11246 (discrimination on the basis of race, color, religion, sex, or national origin by federal contractors); Executive Order 11141 (age discrimination by contractors); Executive Order 11764 (making the Attorney General responsible for coordinating enforcement of Title VI of the Civil Rights Act of 1964 so far as recipients of federal financial assistance are concerned); and Executive Order 11478 (discrimination on the basis of race, color, religion, sex, or national origin in Federal Government employment).

### (5) *Equal Pay Act\**

This statute appears as Section 6(d) of the Fair Labor Standards Act. (29 U.S.C. § 206(d)) It requires equal pay for equal work without regard to sex. The statute is administered by the Department of Labor. Remedies include suits by the Secretary of Labor or by the discriminatee.

### (6) *Age Discrimination in Employment Act\**

This statute (29 U.S.C. § 621 *et seq.*) forbids employers (including the state and federal governments), labor organizations, and employment agencies to discriminate against individuals between the ages of 40 and 70 on the basis of age. Enforcement is through the Department of Labor, and the remedies include suits by the Secretary of Labor or by the discriminatee (except in the case of the Federal Government in which case enforcement is through the Civil Service Commission and the right of suit extends only to a discriminatee who has properly exhausted administrative remedies). A new statute, the Age Discrimination Act of 1975, applies to those employers receiving federal financial assistance.

### (7) *State Fair Employment Practice Laws*

Most states and many local jurisdictions have fair employment practice laws applying to employers, unions, and employment agencies. Many states also provide that government agencies, political subdivisions, and contractors doing business with the state are obligated to provide equal employment opportunity.

State agencies process charges brought by claimants, and claims deferred to the agencies by the EEOC. As of fall 1978, the EEOC was deferring more than 60 percent of its job discrimination charges for initial action to 77 state and local fair employment practice agencies that have enforcement standards comparable to those of the EEOC.

---

\* But see Reorganization Plan No. 1, *infra,* at p. 14.

State fair employment practice laws include bans against discrimination on the basis of sex, age, handicap, or marital status. When state laws extend beyond federal statutes, employers are bound by the more comprehensive requirements of state laws as well as the requirements of Title VII.

State laws often cover smaller employers. While Title VII applies to employers with 15 or more employees, state legislation may specify that an employer need have only one employee, or make no provision for the minimum number of employees needed to determine coverage.

## EEOC: PROCEDURAL REGULATIONS

*29 Code of Federal Regulations 1601, issued July 1, 1965, as last amended effective February 20, 1979, 44 Federal Register 6095 (1979)*

§ 1601.74 Designated 706 and notice agencies.

(a) The designated 706 Agencies are:

Alaska Commission for Human Rights
Alexandria (Virginia) Human Rights Office
Allentown (Pennsylvania) Human Relations Commission
Arizona Civil Rights Division
Augusta Richmond County (Georgia) Human Relations Commission
Austin (Texas) Human Relations Commission
Baltimore (Maryland) Community Relations Commission
Bloomington (Indiana) Human Rights Commission
California Fair Employment Practices Commission
Charleston (West Virginia) Human Rights Commission
Colorado Civil Rights Commission
Commonwealth of Puerto Rico Department of Labor
Connecticut Commission on Human Rights and Opportunities
Dade County (Florida) Fair Housing and Employment Commission
Delaware Department of Labor
District of Columbia Office of Human Rights
East Chicago (Indiana) Human Relations Commission
Evansville (Indiana) Human Relations Commission
Fairfax County (Virginia) Human Relations Commission
Florida Commission of Human Relations
Fort Wayne (Indiana) Metropolitan Human Relations Commission
Fort Worth (Texas) Human Relations Commission
Gary (Indiana) Human Relations Commission
Howard County (Maryland) Human Rights Commission
Hawaii Department of Labor and Industrial Relations
Idaho Commission on Human Rights
Illinois Fair Employment Practices Commission
Indiana Civil Rights Commission

Iowa Commission on Civil Rights
Kansas Commission on Civil Rights
Kentucky Commission on Human Rights
Lexington-Fayette (Kentucky) Urban County Human Rights Commission
Lincoln (Nebraska) Commission on Human Rights
Madison (Wisconsin) Equal Opportunities Commission
Maine Human Rights Commission
Maryland Commission on Human Relations
Massachusetts Commission Against Discrimination
Michigan Civil Rights Commission
Minneapolis (Minnesota) Department of Civil Rights
Minnesota Department of Human Rights
Missouri Commission on Human Rights
Montana Commission for Human Rights
Montgomery County (Maryland) Human Relations Commission
Nebraska Equal Opportunity Commission
Nevada Commission on Equal Rights of Citizens
New Hampshire Commission for Human Rights
New Jersey Division on Civil Rights, Department of Law and Public
  Safety
New York City (New York) Commission on Human Rights
New York State Division on Human Rights
Ohio Civil Rights Commission
Oklahoma Human Rights Commission
Omaha (Nebraska) Human Relations Department
Oregon Bureau of Labor
Orlando (Florida) Human Relations Department
Pennsylvania Human Relations Commission
Philadelphia (Pennsylvania) Commission on Human Relations
Pittsburgh (Pennsylvania) Commission on Human Relations
Prince Georges County (Maryland) Human Relations Commission
Rhode Island Commission for Human Rights
Rockville (Maryland) Human Rights Commission
St. Paul (Minnesota) Department of Human Rights
Seattle (Washington) Human Rights Commission
Sioux Falls (South Dakota) Human Relations Commission
South Bend (Indiana) Human Rights Commission
South Carolina Human Affairs Commission
South Dakota Division of Human Rights
Springfield (Ohio) Human Relations Department
Tacoma (Washington) Human Rights Commission
Utah Industrial Commission
Vermont Attorney General's Office, Civil Rights Division
Virgin Islands Department of Labor
Washington State Human Rights Commission
West Virginia Human Rights Commission
Wheeling (West Virginia) Human Rights Commission

Wichita (Kansas) Commission on Civil Rights
Wisconsin Equal Rights Division, Department of Industry, Labor and
   Human Relations
Wyoming Fair Employment Practices Commission

(b) The designated notice agencies are:

Arkansas Governor's Committee on Human Resources
Georgia Office of Fair Employment Practices
North Dakota Commission on Labor
Ohio Director of Industrial Relations
Raleigh (North Carolina) Human Resources Department, Civil Rights
   Unit

## (8) *Labor Relations Laws*

Both the Railway Labor Act (45 U.S.C. § 151 *et seq.*) and the National
Labor Relations Act (29 U.S.C. § 151 *et seq.*) have been held to impose
on labor organizations a duty to represent all members of relevant bargaining units fairly without regard to race, religion, national origin, and
sex. This duty is enforceable by suit by a discriminatee. In addition, certain types of discriminatory acts by labor organizations or employers may
constitute unfair labor practices, for which remedies are available through
the administrative processes of the NLRB, or may constitute a basis for
objecting to the selection of a labor organization as an exclusive bargaining representative. See generally Herring, *The Fair Representation Doctrine: An Effective Weapon Against Union Racial Discrimination,* 24 MD.
L. REV. 113 (1964); Leiken, *The Current and Potential Equal Employment Role of the NLRB,* 1971 DUKE L. J. 833.

## (9) *Vocational Rehabilitation Act of 1973*

Section 503 of this statute (29 U.S.C. § 793) requires federal contractors
to take special steps to provide employment opportunities for handicapped individuals. Enforcement is through the Department of Labor.

## (10) *Vietnam Era Veterans Readjustment Act of 1974*

38 U.S.C. § 2012 requires federal contractors to seek to promote employment opportunities for "qualified disabled veterans and veterans of
the Vietnam era." Enforcement is through the Department of Labor.
38 US.C. § 2014 requires special consideration to be given such veterans
in federal employment, with enforcement responsibility lodged in the
Civil Service Commission.

## (11) *Title IX of the Higher Education Amendments of 1972*

This Act, the principal section being 20 U.S.C. § 1681, forbids sex discrimination by educational institutions. It extends to matters other than

employment and has received the greatest attention with respect to providing for rights of participation in physical education activities by women. The Act also amends Title IV of the Civil Rights Act of 1964 to include sex as a forbidden basis of discriminatiton. Administration is for the most part through the Department of Health, Education and Welfare. Its direct applicability to employment is being challenged in the courts. See, e.g., *Isleboro School Committee* v. *Califano,* 19 FEP Cases 172 (CA 1 1979). See also *Cannon* v. *University of Chicago,* 99 S.Ct. 1946, 47 USLW 4549 (1979), in which the Supreme Court affirms a private right of action to enforce Title IX.

## (12) *Collective Bargaining Agreements*

In 400 representative union contracts in effect in 1973-74, 69 percent had bans on discrimination by the employer, union, or both. Among the prohibitions was discrimination based on race, creed, color, national origin, sex, union membership, and union activity. BASIC PATTERNS IN UNION CONTRACTS, BNA BOOKS (1975).

Enforcement is through grievance procedures, often culminating in arbitration. Arbitrators' attitudes concerning their responsibilities and powers with regard to invidious discrimination vary. A good survey appears in M. STONE & E. BADERSCHNEIDER, ARBITRATION OF DISCRIMINATION GRIEVANCES (1974). See also the widely debated decision in the *Gardner-Denver* case.

In an attempt to provide for better coordination of the federal efforts to combat discrimination, the Congress in 1972 established the Equal Employment Opportunity Coordinating Council (EEOCC). EEOCC is composed of the chief officers (or their delegates) of the Departments of Labor and Justice, the EEOC, the Civil Rights Commission, and the Civil Service Commission. EEOCC's success has thus far been limited, as illustrated by ongoing disagreement among the agencies with regard to uniform employee selection guidelines. The Reorganization Plan of 1978 abolished the Council and transferred its functions to the EEOC.

The bulk of the antidiscrimination laws listed have come into force within the past dozen or so years. Have they had any impact? No one simple answer to that query would be either honest or complete.

## (13) *Pregnancy Disability*

### CONFERENCE REPORT (H.R. REP. NO. 95-1786)
*95th Cong., 2d Sess. (1978)*

The committee of conference on the disagreeing votes of the two Houses on the amendment of the House to the bill (S. 995) to amend title VII of the Civil Rights Act of 1964 to prohibit sex discrimination on the basis of pregnancy, having met, after full and free conference, have agreed to recommend and do recommend to their respective Houses as follows:

That the Senate recede from its disagreement to the amendment of the House and agree to the same with an amendment as follows:

In lieu of the matter proposed to be inserted by the House amendment insert the following:

*That section 701 of the Civil Rights Act of 1964 is amended by adding at the end thereof the following new subsection:*

*"(k) The terms 'because of sex' or 'on the basis of sex' include, but are not limited to, because of or on the basis of pregnancy, childbirth or related medical conditions; and women affected by pregnancy, childbirth, or related medical conditions shall be treated the same for all employment-related purposes, including receipt of benefits under fringe benefit programs, as other persons not so affected but similar in their ability or inability to work, and nothing in section 703(h) of this title shall be interpreted to permit otherwise. This subsection shall not require an employer to pay for health insurance benefits for abortion, except where the life of the mother would be endangered if the fetus were carried to term, or except where medical complications have arisen from an abortion: Provided, That nothing herein shall preclude an employer from providing abortion benefits or otherwise affect bargaining agreements in regard to abortion."*

SEC. 2. *(a) Except as provided in subsection (b), the amendment made by this Act shall be effective on the date of enactment.*

*(b) The provisions of the amendment made by the first section of this Act shall not apply to any fringe benefit program or fund, or insurance program which is in effect on the date of enactment of this Act until 180 days after enactment of this Act.*

SEC. 3. *Until the expiration of a period of one year from the date of enactment of this Act or, if there is an applicable collective-bargaining agreement in effect on the date of enactment of this Act, until the termination of that agreement, no person who, on the date of enactment of this Act is providing either by direct payment or by making contributions to a fringe benefit fund or insurance program, benefits in violation with this Act shall, in order to come into compliance with this Act, reduce the benefits or the compensation provided any employee on the date of enactment of this Act, either directly or by failing to provide sufficient contributions to a fringe benefit fund or insurance program: Provided, That where the costs of such benefits on the date of enactment of this Act are apportioned between employers and employees, the payments or contributions required to comply with this Act may be made by employers and employees in the same proportion: And provided further, That nothing in this section shall prevent the readjustment of benefits or compensation for reasons unrelated to compliance with this act.*

And the House agree to the same.

CARL D. PERKINS,
AUGUSTUS F. HAWKINS,
JOHN H. DENT,
EDWARD P. BEARD,
MICHAEL O. MYERS,

JOSEPH A. LE FANTE,
BALTASAR CORRADA,
ALBERT H. QUIE,
RONALD A. SARASIN,
JAMES M. JEFFORDS,
CARL D. PURSELL,
*Managers on the Part of the House.*
HARRISON WILLIAMS,
JENNINGS RANDOLPH,
CLAIBORNE PELL,
GAYLORD NELSON,
DON RIEGLE,
J. JAVITS,
RICHARD S. SCHWEIKER,
ROBERT T. STAFFORD,
*Managers on the Part of the Senate.*

D.    THE "NEW" CIVIL RIGHTS PROGRAM FOR EMPLOYMENT

## PRESIDENT CARTER'S REORGANIZATION OF FEDERAL EQUAL EMPLOYMENT ENFORCEMENT ACTIVITIES*

Howard A. Glickstein**

### I. INTRODUCTION

On February 23, 1978, President Carter announced his plan to reorganize the Federal government's equal employment opportunity enforcement programs. Speaking at a ceremony in the East Room of the White House, the president said: "We are here today to announce a comprehensive series of measures to consolidate and streamline the enforcement of equal employment laws in our country. I believe that this is the single most important action to improve civil rights in the last decade."

The equal employment reorganization plan grew out of the President's interest in improving government efficiency and ensuring strong enforcement of our civil rights laws. Early in his term, the President directed that a reorganization project be established in the Office of Management and Budget to make a comprehensive study of all government programs and agencies and determine what steps could be taken to eliminate overlap and duplication and improve performance. As part of the President's Reorganization Project, a Task Force on Civil Rights Reorganiza-

* Reprinted with permission from EQUAL EMPLOYMENT PRACTICE GUIDE, ed. Katherine Savers McGovern, copyright © 1978 by the Federal Bar Association.
** Professor of Law, Howard University, Former Director, Task Force on Civil Rights Reorganization, President's Reorganization Project, Office of Management and Budget.

tion was created. The Task Force has as its mandate a review of all of the Federal government's civil rights programs.

## II.  THE PROCESS FOLLOWED BY THE TASK FORCE

The first set of programs selected for study by the Task Force were the equal employment enforcement programs. The Task Force collected and analyzed existing studies and supplemented those studies where necessary. Great emphasis also was placed on carrying out the President's directive to solicit a wide range of public participation in the development of the reorganization proposals. For example, option papers discussing all the major alternatives for reorganization of the equal employment opportunity agencies were circulated to a cross-section of hundreds of individuals and groups, and comments were solicited. Nearly 200 responses were received and analyzed. Personal interviews were held with over 100 individuals. Members of the Task Force had consultations and meetings with many interested groups, including representatives of the various Federal agencies with responsibilities in this field

The development of a reorganization plan requires different techniques than those employed in the normal legislative process. The legislative process generally involves the building of a consensus after the legislative proposal is submitted to Congress. Reorganization plans, however, become effective within 60 legislative days of their submission to Congress if neither House votes to disapprove. This fast time schedule leaves little opportunity for consensus building after a plan is submitted. Accordingly, a major part of the Task Force's effort involved discussions with the various interest groups concerned with equal employment enforcement. The Task Force attempted to meet the concerns of these groups or to persuade them of the desirability of alternatives they did not necessarily favor. At the same time, the Task Force had been directed by the President not to make political compromises before plans were presented to him. The President wanted submitted to him the plan the Task Force regarded as most effective, but he wanted to be advised of who opposed and supported the plan so he could assess the political implications. The President regarded it as his responsibility to make political compromises where necessary.

The Task Force also was directed to concentrate its efforts on reforms that could be achieved pursuant to the President's authority under the Reorganization Act of 1977 or through the issuance of Executive orders. Either of these two courses of action is likely to achieve reforms more rapidly than the normal legislative process. The Task Force was aware, however, that some of the deficiencies of the equal employment enforcement effort only could be remedied by legislation. We noted legislative changes that might be desirable. Our hope is that after the results of the reorganization can be assessed, legislative changes will be considered and proposed.

### III. THE EQUAL EMPLOYMENT REORGANIZATION PLAN

#### A. The Plan's Underlying Structure

The equal employment reorganization plan involves a number of steps, some to be taken within a few months and still others not to be acted upon for over a year. The Plan lays the foundation of a single coherent Federal structure to combat job discrimination in all its forms. The incremental implementation of the Plan will allow the affected agencies to continue with their internal reforms as well as to accept new responsibilities without becoming bogged down in their own bureaucracies. The Plan moves toward the ultimate consolidation of all Federal equal employment opportunity programs into one agency.

Full consolidation of equal employment programs has many advantages. It is likely to remedy most of the serious deficiencies of the Government's equal employment effort. It will end the problems of inconsistent standards for compliance, duplicative investigations, and excessive reporting and data demands. It also will reduce the number of enforcement actions that could be involved based on a single set of circumstances. Full consolidation will result in a more efficient and effective effort to enforce the equal employment laws. Complainants would have one contact point; scarce resources would be directed to the most severe problems; and sanctions could be utilized in a consistent fashion.

The President's reorganization proposal places in the EEOC the responsibility as the principal Federal agency in fair employment enforcement. The EEOC has developed expertise in the employment discrimination field since Congress created it by the Civil Rights Act of 1964. It has played a pioneer role both in defining the meaning of employment discrimination and the appropriate remedies for it. Its size, years of experience, and the broad scope of its activities makes it suitable to assume the role as the lead Federal equal employment agency. Although the reorganization does not consolidate all equal employment enforcement programs in the EEOC, continued improvement in the performance of the EEOC should lead to such a consolidation.

#### B. The Main Component of the Plan

There are two major aspects of the reorganization proposal. The first involves steps to be taken pursuant to the President's reorganization authority and are incorporated in Reorganization Plan No. 1 of 1978. These include transferring to the EEOC responsibility for enforcing the Equal Pay Act and the Age Discrimination in Employment Act and the authority to insure equal employment opportunity for Federal employees. Responsibility to coordinate equal employment programs that reside in agencies other than the EEOC also would be assigned to the EEOC, and the Equal Employment Opportunity Coordinating Council would be abolished. The Reorganization Plan also clarifies the Attorney General's authority to initiate "pattern or practice" suits under Title VII against State or local governments. The second aspect of the reorganization proposal will be accomplished by Executive order. It involves centralizing in the Department of Labor all contract compliance activities.

1. *Contract Compliance.* Contract compliance consolidation is scheduled to occur on October 1, 1978. Eleven government agencies now have responsibility for insuring that government contractors adhere to the equal employment provisions of their contracts. The activities of these agencies are supervised by the Office of Federal Contract Compliance Programs in the Department of Labor. Consolidation will relieve these agencies of their contract compliance responsibilities. The resources scattered among these agencies will be transferred to the Department of Labor where full responsibility and accountability for the success or failure of the program will rest.

This consolidation will promote consistent standards, procedures, and reporting requirements and relieve many contractors of the burden of being subject to the jurisdiction of multiple agencies. It removes the basis of the major complaint of business groups. As a result, cooperation with the intent and provisions of the contract compliance program should be achieved more readily.

The transfer, in addition, will eliminate the current conflict of interest between the procurement and and construction objectives of government agencies and their equal employment enforcement objectives. This conflict arises when agency officials find that if civil rights responsibilities are strictly enforced, it might be difficult, if not impossible, to enter into a desirable contract. Even in situations where top management has the best of intentions, civil rights concerns that are in conflict with procurement goals, tend to be brushed aside. The consolidation, moreover, by unifying planning, staff training, and the use of sanctions, also should facilitate the development of a better organized and more efficient enforcement program.

2. *The Equal Pay Act and the Age Discrimination in Employment Act.* Reorganization Plan No. 1 provides for the transfer of authority to enforce the Equal Pay Act and to enforce the Age Discrimination in Employment Act to the EEOC. This transfer is scheduled to occur on July 1, 1979. The EEOC, following the transfer, will continue to utilize the enforcement procedures of the Equal Pay Act and the Age Act.

The Equal Pay Act and Title VII are essentially duplicative. While Title VII covers a broader range of discriminatory wage practices based on sex, such as different rates of pay for work of comparable value, any violation of the Equal Pay Act also is a violation of Title VII. The transfer of the enforcement of the Act will minimize overlap and centralize Federal enforcement of the absolute statutory prohibitions against sex discrimination in employment. EEOC, moreover, will be provided with important additional enforcement authority and remedies with which to strengthen its efforts against sex discrimination in employment. For example, EEOC will be able to conduct self-initiated investigations without a Commissioner having to file a sworn charge against an employer, and to file suit in Federal court on equal pay matters without first being required to engage in prolonged negotiations. The transfer also will facilitate imposing monetary liabilities on labor unions that participate in an Equal Pay Act violation. Where the EEOC finds that a union is jointly responsible with an employer, it could file a Title VII Commissioner charge against the union.

More efficient and effective enforcement also is likely to result from transfer of the enforcement of the Age Discrimination Act from the Department of Labor to the EEOC. There is virtually complete overlap in the coverage of employers, employment agencies, and labor organizations under Title VII and the Age Act. The Age Act was modeled on Title VII and the standards of the two Acts are compatible. Many of the issues which relate to age cases, moreover, are similar to those the EEOC has faced in the context of sex discrimination, e.g., participation in pension plans and requirements of specific types of jobs. It also will promote the enforcement of the Age Act to remove it from an agency with a multiplicity of responsibilities and place it in a single purpose antidiscrimination agency.

*3. Equal Employment for Federal Employees.* The Reorganization Plan transfers from the Civil Service Commission to the EEOC the authority to ensure equal employment opportunities for Federal employees. This transfer is scheduled to take effect on October 1, 1978. At present, the Civil Service Commission is responsible for enforcement of the nondiscrimination and affirmative action in Federal employment requirements of Section 717 of Title VII and Executive Order 11478 of August 12, 1969. Federal employees who wish to challenge the resolution of their equal employment complaints by the head of their agencies may appeal to the Civil Service Commission. Each Federal department and agency also is required to develop and submit to the Civil Service Commission annually an affirmative action program. For Federal employees, the Civil Service Commission also enforces the Equal Pay Act and the Age Discrimination in Employment Act as well as Section 501 of the Rehabilitation Act of 1973 covering discrimination on the basis of handicap in the Federal government. Thus, unlike private employees and the employees of State and local governments, Federal employees must look to their own agencies and to the Civil Service Commission for the vindication of their equal employment rights under Title VII and similar equal employment statutes.

The Civil Service Commission has been a recalcitrant and reluctant enforcer of the Title VII rights of Federal employees. The Commission adheres to weaker substantive Title VII standards than those imposed on private employers. Burdens imposed on job applicants and employees alleging individual acts of discrimination in the Federal sector are significantly greater than those imposed by the EEOC in the case of complaints filed against private employers and State and local governments. Only recently, and as a result of a court order, did the Civil Service Commission issue regulations allowing the filing of class action complaints, and these regulations are highly restrictive. Nor has the Commission been aggressive in promoting affirmative action. The instructions that the Commission provides to agencies on affirmative action are substantially weaker than the requirements imposed on Federal contractors by the Department of Labor.

The transfer prescribed by Reorganization Plan No. 1 will achieve three important objectives:

(a) Federal employees will have the same rights and remedies and be subject to the same rules and procedures as private employees and employees of State and local governments;

(b) Federal agencies will be required to meet the same standards of equal employment opportunity as are private employers and State and local governments. Private employers who are government contractors, for example, are *required* to have goals and timetables for remedying underutilization in employment. Federal agencies only are *encouraged* to set goals and timetables. If anything, the Federal government should set an example for the private sector since discrimination by a private employer or labor union violates a statute, while discrimination by the Federal government violates the Constitution.

(c) Enforcement of equal employment opportunity and affirmative action will be administered separately from personnel management functions to avoid possible conflicts of interest.

The proposed reforms of the Civil Service system have provided an opportunity for those opposed to broadening the jurisdiction of the EEOC to cover Federal employment to continue to advocate separate treatment for Federal employees. They contend that the creation of an independent Merit Systems Protection Board will insure that Federal employees will have an impartial tribunal before which to take their equal employment complaints. But this Board does not cure the problem. The Board's orientation will be toward personnel management. It will not possess the EEOC's sensitivity and experience for dealing with equal employment questions. And many of the same people who have resisted the equal employment claims of Federal employees will be conducting the business of the new Board. Most significantly, failure to accomplish the transfer prescribed by Reorganization Plan No. 1 will continue the existing anomaly of lodging in the EEOC the responsibility of interpreting Title VII as it applies to private employees and employees of State and local governments but giving this responsibility for Federal employees to another agency.

*4. Centralization of Equal Employment Coordinating Responsibility.* The Reorganization Plan abolishes the Equal Employment Opportunity Coordinating Council and transfers its responsibilities to the EEOC effective July 1, 1978. The Coordinating Council was established by the 1972 amendments to Title VII of the Civil Rights Act of 1964. The Council is responsible for developing and implementing agreements, policies and practices designed to maximize enforcement efforts and promote efficiency.

The Council also is responsible for eliminating conflict, competition, duplication and inconsistency among the various departments, agencies and branches of the Federal Government responsible for ensuring equal employment opportunity. The Act requires the Council to report annually to the President and to Congress on its activities and to make recommendations for legislative or administrative changes.

The Council is composed of the Attorney General, the Secretary of Labor, the Chairpersons of the Equal Employment Opportunity Commission, the Civil Service Commission, and the Civil Rights Commission. Title VII gave the Council no specific enforcement authority. Implementation of policies or procedures developed by the Council is dependent on the acceptance of each of the members. The Council has made its decisions by consensus rather than by majority vote.

For the most part, the Council has been a failure. The problems in equal employment enforcement coordination which prompted Congress to establish the Council have grown worse in the last five years. The Council's decision to operate by consensus has contributed to its ineffectiveness.

The abolition of the Council and the transfer of its responsibilities to the EEOC will provide the Commission with significant new duties and will make it the "lead agency" in the government's equal employment program. The responsibilities which the EEOC will assume include the development of substantive equal employment opportunity standards applicable to the entire Federal government, standardization of Federal data collection procedures, creation of joint training programs, establishment of requirements to ensure that information is shared among the enforcement agencies, and development of governmentwide complaint and compliance review methodologies. This transfer also will decrease the widespread duplication, overlap and inconsistency among the equal employment programs. For example, the EEOC will be able to work out arrangements with the Department of Labor so that it will not conduct an investigation of a pattern and practice of discrimination by an employer if that employer were found in compliance under the contract compliance program. Similarly, the EEOC will be responsible for ensuring that the equal employment provisions which are applicable to recipients of Federal grants are applied in a uniform manner so that a State or local government need not file different equal employment data with each grant agency or have the same complaint subject to investigation by more than one agency.

These changes will result in a fairer and more efficient enforcement program. Effective use of the coordination and leadership role granted by this transfer should enhance the coherence and thus the credibility of the entire Federal compliance effort.

*5. Clarification of the Right of the Department of Justice to Bring Pattern or Practice Suits Under Title VII Against State and Local Governments.* The Plan clarifies the right of the Attorney General to bring pattern or practice suits under Title VII against State and local governments. Some courts have read Title VII as precluding the Attorney General from bringing such suits or as requiring that he receive a referral from the EEOC before doing so. The Reorganization Plan makes clear that the Attorney General has the authority under Title VII to insure equal employment opportunity of State and local governments through independent investigations and the initiation of litigation.

IV. PROGRAMS NOT PRESENTLY AFFECTED BY THE REORGANIZATION PLAN

The President's plan does not call for the total consolidation of all equal employment enforcement programs. A number of programs have not been restructured. The President, however, has indicated that by 1981 he will take another look at the equal employment programs to determine whether further consolidations are desirable. The principal programs that will be reviewed are these:

*The Contract Compliance Program.* The contract compliance program was not transferred to the EEOC primarily because it was feared that the consolidation of two such significant programs would jeopardize the successful implementation of major internal reforms by OFCCP and the EEOC. In addition, there are a number of unresolved legal questions concerning the standards applicable to both programs that might be confused if the programs were merged at this time. The eventual merger of the programs, however, would insure the elimination of all overlapping jurisdiction, inconsistent standards, duplication of effort and would increase the leverage for insuring compliance with Title VII.

*Section 503 of the Rehabilitation Act of 1973 and Section 402 of the Vietnam Era Veteran's Readjustment Assistance Act of 1974.* OFCCP also has responsibility for enforcement of these statutes. They require government contractors to take affirmative action to employ and advance in employment qualified handicapped individuals, disabled veterans and veterans of the Vietnam Era.

Although there are some differences between the Executive Order 11246 program and the Veterans' and Handicapped programs, all are based upon the Federal government's procurement powers and require compliance only by those who are Federal contractors. Because of these important similarities, these programs can be enforced best within the same government agency. Therefore, the Task Force recommended that these programs remain in the Department of Labor as long as that agency has responsibility for the Executive order program.

*Equal Employment Litigation Authority of the Department of Justice.* The Task Force considered recommending transfer to the EEOC of the Justice Department's authority to litigate equal employment matters against State and local governments. In light of the record and expertise of the Department of Justice, however, the Task Force concluded that it would not enhance civil rights enforcement to relieve the Department of its present authority at this time. While the EEOC is strengthening its ability to litigate against Title VII violations by private employers, the

Department of Justice can help create new law in the difficult area of public employment.

For similar reasons, the Task Force recommended that the Department retain its responsibility for enforcing the provisions of Executive Order 11246 and for filing pattern or practice suits authorized by several Federal grant statutes.

*The Equal Employment Responsibilities of Federal Grant-Making Agencies.* There are at least 14 agencies which enforce over 30 nondiscrimination and/or affirmative action requirements which are applicable only to the employment practices of organizations and entities which participate in specific agency programs. Some examples of such provisions are: The State and Local Fiscal Assistance Act of 1972 (Revenue Sharing), which prohibits discrimination on the basis of race, color, religion, sex, national origin, handicap or age, and is enforced by the Department of the Treasury; and the Housing and Community Development Act of 1974 which prohibits discrimination on the basis of race, color, national origin, or sex and is enforced by the Department of Housing and Urban Development.

The Task Force evaluated the possibility of transferring to the EEOC the equal employment responsibilities of Federal grant-making agencies. Such a step could eliminate the duplication of effort, inconsistency in standards and investigative findings, and excessive and unproductive reporting requirements that now hinder the effort to bring State and local governments into compliance. The consolidation of authority approach was rejected in favor of assigning to the EEOC a coordination and leadership role for the whole Federal equal employment program. Among the principal reasons for this decision is that the multiplicity of statutes involved, and diverse regulations and investigative procedures, and the large number of personnel would have caused management problems of major proportions. In some instances, moreover, it is difficult to separate an agency's responsibility to insure equality in the provision of services from its responsibility to insure equal employment opportunity.

## V. CONCLUSION

In 1957, Congress enacted the first civil rights law since Reconstruction. Prior to that time, civil rights advocates had placed principal reliance on the courts, especially the Supreme Court. In the 1960's, however, increasing attention was paid to legislative actions and to enforcement by the Executive. Additional civil rights laws were enacted, and Presidents Kennedy and Johnson used the authority of their offices to add to the civil rights protections available to our citizens. But toward the end of the 60's it became clear that historic court decisions, comprehensive legislation and forceful Executive action was not enough to guarantee the enjoyment of civil rights. What also was important was the way our civil rights programs were organized and the way our laws were enforced by those civil servants charged with that responsibility.

Adequate resources, strong commitment and good management are now recognized as essential ingredients of an effective civil rights program. The proliferation of civil rights responsibilities among government agencies also suggests that some reorganziation of programs is required. The reorganization has begun. Its impact on strong, efficient and effective enforcement is yet to be seen.

## E.   Economic Consequences of Discrimination

Selection of materials illustrative of the "problem" for the Labor Law Group's first edition of "Discrimination in Employment" was substantially easier than our chore in late 1978 for the fourth edition.

Had we started this endeavor in 1961, we could have safely ignored everything not related to Negroes. Using the reports of the U.S. Civil Rights Commission as an indicator of the problem with which the nation was concerned, except for a short chapter on American Indians, most of the report of that commission on employment in 1961 was devoted to the Negro problem.

Despite the recognition in FEPC laws since the 1940s of religion, ancestry, and national origin, the priority remained race (black) until the mid-1960s. It would seem fair to infer that both the appearance of success of the civil rights movement and the response of Congress in enacting the Civil Rights Act of 1964 encouraged other groups to insist upon attention to their problems and that their demands sparked action. There is, of course, a more cynical inference that governmental attention to these other affected classes, such as sex, persons of Spanish or Oriental origin, age, handicapped, and so forth was a Machiavellian effort to divide otherwise natural allies and set them fighting among themselves, thus neutralizing their potential.

Whichever choice one makes regarding causal factors, it is true that in 1978 we have both proliferation of statutory and administrative provisions granting protection to a multiplicity of groups and a concomitant proliferation of studies and data attempting to illustrate or otherwise portray the conditions of the affected classes compared with those of a more favored group. No doubt the next decade will see the emergence of charts, graphs, studies, and so forth which will compare all such groups.

The following materials include a disproportionate number of black-white comparisons because of the greater availability of such data, particularly for temporal comparisons. It is evident that the key problem has not been solved.

The references in the charts and tables relating to sex, Spanish-surname Americans, Orientals, handicapped, Native Americans, aged, and the like permit the student to consult data specific to these classes, which cannot be included in a book whose objective is to be as comprehensive as possible within a manageable number of pages.

## EXCERPTS FROM USDL 78-842*

### *October 21, 1978*

#### WEEKLY EARNINGS

Large differences persist in the weekly earnings of the various groups, as shown below:

The median weekly earnings of all men who usually work full time was $272 in May 1978, while the median of women in full-time jobs was $166, or about 61 percent of the earnings of men. This ratio has shown little change since 1967 (table 1).

Usual weekly earnings of white men were $279, while those of men of black and other minority races were $218, or 22 percent less. Black and other minority women earned $158, or 5 percent less than the $167 earned by white women. Eleven years ago, the earnings gaps were considerably larger—31 percent for men and 20 percent for women.

. . .

Earnings trends for older and younger workers also differ substantially. Real weekly earnings of both men and women 25 years of age and over working full time show increases of about 14 percent since 1967. However, real earnings for workers 16 to 24, who have been entering the labor force in large numbers over this 11-year period, have not increased.

Over the 5-year period since May 1973, the rise in earnings for most groups failed to match the 47 percent increase in the Consumer Price Index. Thus, real earnings in May 1978 were still below their peak levels of 1973. For all full-time workers, real weekly earnings in May 1973 were 10 percent above the 1967 level; in May 1978 they were only 7 percent above the 1967 level.

Data on the weekly and hourly earnings of black workers (exclusive of other minority races) and of workers of Hispanic origin were tabulated for the first time for May 1978. They show that usual weekly earnings averaged $181 for blacks and $174 for Hispanics, compared with $232 for whites (table 2).

About 30 percent of all full-time workers reported earnings of $300 or more per week in May 1978, up from 25 percent a year earlier. This proportion varied widely among different groups of workers—ranging from 44 percent for white men, 22 percent for black men, and 9 percent for both white and black women. Among Hispanic workers, about 21 percent of the men and 4 percent of the women had earnings of $300 or more.

In every major occupation group, median weekly earnings of women were well below those of men. Earnings of blacks and Hispanics were very similar in most occupations, and below those of whites . . . .

---

* This study, by the Bureau of Labor Statistics of the U.S. Department of Labor in May 1978, shows that the real earnings of blacks and other minorities have risen 22 percent since May 1967. However, large differences persist in the weekly earnings of various groups.

## HOURLY EARNINGS

. . .
White men had median hourly earnings of $5.40 per hour, 18 percent above the $4.58 rate for black men. The hourly earnings of white women ($3.31) were not significantly different from those of black women ($3.23). The hourly wage for Hispanic workers averaged $4.55 for men and $3.14 for women, nearly the same as the averages for black men and women.

By broad occupation group, the highest hourly wage rates were reported for workers in craft, professional and technical, and transport equipment operative occupations. For most of the occupation groups for which comparisons can be made between black and Hispanic workers, there was either little or no difference in reported hourly earnings. . . .

## TABLE 1. MEDIAN USUAL WEEKLY EARNINGS OF WAGE AND SALARY WORKERS BY SELECTED CHARACTERISTICS, IN CURRENT DOLLARS, MAY 1967-MAY 1978*

| Characteristic | May 1967 | May 1969 | May 1970 | May 1971 | May 1972 | May 1973 | May 1974 | May 1975 | May 1976 | May 1977 | May 1978 | Annual average percent change[1] |
|---|---|---|---|---|---|---|---|---|---|---|---|---|
| **ALL WAGE AND SALARY WORKERS** | | | | | | | | | | | | |
| Total | $100 | $111 | $118 | $124 | $130 | $140 | $151 | $161 | $169 | $180 | $195 | 6.3 |
| **FULL-TIME WAGE AND SALARY WORKERS** | | | | | | | | | | | | |
| Total | 109 | 121 | 130 | 138 | 144 | 159 | 169 | 185 | 197 | 212 | 227 | 6.9 |
| Sex and age: | | | | | | | | | | | | |
| Men, 16 years and over | 125 | 142 | 151 | 162 | 168 | 188 | 204 | 221 | 234 | 253 | 272 | 7.3 |
| 16 to 24 years | 97 | 108 | 112 | 114 | 118 | 136 | 146 | 149 | 159 | 168 | 185 | 6.1 |
| 25 years and over | 131 | 148 | 160 | 172 | 178 | 203 | 219 | 235 | 251 | 273 | 294 | 7.6 |
| Women, 16 years and over | 78 | 86 | 94 | 100 | 106 | 116 | 124 | 137 | 145 | 156 | 166 | 7.1 |
| 16 to 24 years | 74 | 82 | 88 | 91 | 96 | 103 | 111 | 117 | 125 | 133 | 142 | 6.1 |
| 25 years and over | 79 | 88 | 96 | 103 | 110 | 121 | 131 | 146 | 154 | 165 | 175 | 7.5 |
| Race, Hispanic origin, and sex: | | | | | | | | | | | | |
| White | 113 | 125 | 134 | 142 | 149 | 162 | 173 | 190 | 202 | 217 | 232 | 6.8 |
| Men | 130 | 146 | 157 | 168 | 172 | 193 | 209 | 225 | 239 | 259 | 279 | 7.2 |
| Women | 79 | 88 | 95 | 102 | 108 | 117 | 125 | 138 | 147 | 157 | 167 | 7.0 |
| Black and other | 79 | 90 | 99 | 107 | 115 | 129 | 140 | 156 | 162 | 171 | 186 | 8.1 |
| Men | 90 | 104 | 113 | 123 | 129 | 149 | 160 | 173 | 187 | 201 | 218 | 8.4 |
| Women | 63 | 73 | 81 | 87 | 99 | 107 | 117 | 130 | 138 | 147 | 158 | 8.7 |
| Black[2] | — | — | — | — | — | — | — | — | — | — | 181 | — |
| Men | — | — | — | — | — | — | — | — | — | — | 213 | — |
| Women | — | — | — | — | — | — | — | — | — | — | 156 | — |

|  |  |  |  |  |  |  |  |  |  |  |  |  |
|---|---|---|---|---|---|---|---|---|---|---|---|---|
| Hispanic[2] | — | — | — | — | — | — | — | — | — | — | 174 | — |
| Men | — | — | — | — | — | — | — | — | — | — | 201 | — |
| Women | — | — | — | — | — | — | — | — | — | — | 141 | — |
| **Sex and marital status:** |  |  |  |  |  |  |  |  |  |  |  |  |
| Men: |  |  |  |  |  |  |  |  |  |  |  |  |
| Never married | 95 | 108 | 113 | 116 | 119 | 134 | 144 | 153 | 161 | 173 | 190 | 6.5 |
| Husbands | 131 | 148 | 159 | 172 | 177 | 200 | 216 | 234 | 248 | 272 | 293 | 7.6 |
| Other marital status | 113 | 125 | 139 | 148 | 153 | 171 | 194 | 205 | 224 | 239 | 263 | 8.0 |
| Women: |  |  |  |  |  |  |  |  |  |  |  |  |
| Never married | 79 | 87 | 95 | 97 | 104 | 114 | 120 | 132 | 141 | 150 | 159 | 6.6 |
| Wives | 79 | 88 | 95 | 101 | 107 | 117 | 126 | 139 | 147 | 158 | 167 | 7.0 |
| Other marital status | 75 | 85 | 91 | 100 | 106 | 115 | 123 | 138 | 146 | 158 | 168 | 7.6 |
| **Occupation:** |  |  |  |  |  |  |  |  |  |  |  |  |
| Professional and technical workers | 145 | 167 | 181 | 189 | 192 | 212 | 228 | 246 | 256 | 277 | 294 | 6.6 |
| Managers and administrators, except farm | 164 | 178 | 190 | 200 | 214 | 238 | 250 | 274 | 289 | 302 | 323 | 6.4 |
| Sales workers | 113 | 123 | 133 | 141 | 151 | 163 | 172 | 189 | 198 | 225 | 232 | 6.8 |
| Clerical workers | 91 | 102 | 109 | 115 | 121 | 130 | 140 | 150 | 158 | 167 | 175 | 6.2 |
| Craft and kindred workers | 131 | 146 | 157 | 167 | 172 | 195 | 211 | 223 | 239 | 259 | 279 | 7.1 |
| Operatives, except transport[3] | — | — | — | — | 119 | 132 | 141 | 157 | 162 | 171 | 191 | 8.2 |
| Transport equipment operatives[3] | — | — | — | — | 152 | 169 | 180 | 198 | 214 | 231 | 249 | 8.6 |
| Nonfarm laborers | 93 | 106 | 110 | 117 | 122 | 138 | 149 | 154 | 161 | 181 | 193 | 6.9 |
| Private household workers | 32 | 34 | 38 | 38 | 40 | 39 | 50 | 54 | 60 | 59 | 59 | 5.7 |
| Other service workers | 75 | 82 | 87 | 96 | 104 | 112 | 117 | 123 | 134 | 142 | 152 | 6.6 |
| Farm workers | 58 | 66 | 71 | 74 | 80 | 96 | 107 | 111 | 120 | 127 | 139 | 8.3 |

* USDL 78-842

[1] Reflects annually compounded rates of change for the 1967-1978 period.

[2] Data for blacks (exclusive of other races) and Hispanic origin workers are not available prior to 1978. Data on persons of Hispanic origin are tabulated separately without regard to race, which means they are also included in the data for white and black workers. At the time of the 1970 census, approximately 96 percent of their population was white.

[3] Data for these two groups are not available prior to 1972. Average annual percent change is for the 1972-1978 period.

TABLE 2. DISTRIBUTION OF USUAL WEEKLY EARNINGS OF FULL-TIME WAGE AND SALARY WORKERS, BY SELECTED CHARACTERISTICS, MAY 1978*

| Characteristics | Total reporting in thousands[1] | Percent distribution by weekly earnings | | | | | | | | | $ Median |
| --- | --- | --- | --- | --- | --- | --- | --- | --- | --- | --- | --- |
| | | Total | Under $80 | $80 to 99 | $100 to 149 | $150 to 199 | $200 to 249 | $250 to 299 | $300 to 399 | $400 or more | |
| **RACE, HISPANIC ORIGIN AND SEX** | | | | | | | | | | | |
| All races: | | | | | | | | | | | |
| Both sexes | 53,773 | 100.0 | 1.3 | 1.8 | 19.5 | 18.2 | 16.8 | 12.7 | 16.9 | 12.8 | $227 |
| Men | 33,680 | 100.0 | .7 | .7 | 11.0 | 13.9 | 16.9 | 15.0 | 22.9 | 18.9 | 272 |
| Women | 20,092 | 100.0 | 2.4 | 3.6 | 33.7 | 25.4 | 16.6 | 8.8 | 6.9 | 2.7 | 166 |
| White: | | | | | | | | | | | |
| Both sexes | 47,499 | 100.0 | 1.3 | 1.6 | 18.3 | 17.8 | 16.8 | 12.9 | 17.5 | 13.8 | 232 |
| Men | 30,179 | 100.0 | .6 | .6 | 9.9 | 13.3 | 16.7 | 15.1 | 23.6 | 20.2 | 279 |
| Women | 17,321 | 100.0 | 2.4 | 3.4 | 33.0 | 25.7 | 17.1 | 9.0 | 6.8 | 2.6 | 167 |
| Black: | | | | | | | | | | | |
| Both sexes | 5,343 | 100.0 | 2.1 | 3.2 | 29.0 | 22.0 | 16.2 | 11.2 | 11.6 | 4.6 | 181 |
| Men | 2,963 | 100.0 | 1.6 | 1.7 | 21.6 | 20.2 | 18.7 | 14.3 | 15.9 | 6.1 | 213 |
| Women | 2,379 | 100.0 | 2.7 | 5.1 | 38.3 | 24.3 | 13.0 | 7.4 | 6.4 | 2.8 | 156 |
| Hispanic origin[2]: | | | | | | | | | | | |
| Both sexes | 2,905 | 100.0 | 1.8 | 2.8 | 31.0 | 24.5 | 15.9 | 8.6 | 11.0 | 4.3 | 174 |
| Men | 1,915 | 100.0 | 1.0 | 1.4 | 22.9 | 24.2 | 18.6 | 11.0 | 14.9 | 6.3 | 201 |
| Women | 989 | 100.0 | 3.4 | 5.6 | 46.9 | 25.2 | 10.8 | 3.9 | 3.6 | .4 | 141 |

Age:

| | | | | | | | | | | |
|---|---|---|---|---|---|---|---|---|---|---|
| 16 to 19 years | 2,343 | 100.0 | 3.8 | 7.6 | 56.3 | 19.6 | 6.4 | 3.2 | 1.9 | 1.1 | 128 |
| 20 to 24 years | 8,625 | 100.0 | 1.3 | 2.5 | 30.7 | 27.1 | 18.6 | 9.8 | 7.3 | 2.7 | 173 |
| 25 years and over | 42,804 | 100.0 | 1.2 | 1.3 | 15.2 | 16.3 | 17.0 | 13.8 | 19.7 | 15.5 | 246 |

## MARITAL STATUS AND SEX

Men:

| | | | | | | | | | | |
|---|---|---|---|---|---|---|---|---|---|---|
| Never married | 6,162 | 100.0 | 1.7 | 2.2 | 26.8 | 22.9 | 17.7 | 10.9 | 11.7 | 6.0 | 190 |
| Husbands | 24,878 | 100.0 | .4 | .3 | 6.9 | 11.6 | 16.7 | 16.0 | 25.7 | 22.3 | 293 |
| Other marital status | 2,640 | 100.0 | 1.1 | .9 | 12.8 | 14.6 | 16.6 | 14.7 | 22.5 | 16.7 | 263 |

Women:

| | | | | | | | | | | |
|---|---|---|---|---|---|---|---|---|---|---|
| Never married | 4,502 | 100.0 | 2.8 | 4.6 | 36.9 | 23.3 | 14.4 | 8.3 | 6.9 | 2.7 | 159 |
| Wives | 11,160 | 100.0 | 1.8 | 3.3 | 33.1 | 26.1 | 17.2 | 9.0 | 6.9 | 2.5 | 167 |
| Other marital status | 4,430 | 100.0 | 3.4 | 3.4 | 31.7 | 25.6 | 17.3 | 9.1 | 6.6 | 3.0 | 168 |

* USDL 78-842

[1] These numbers, which have been weighted up from raw sample data, exclude that proportion of each universe for which earnings data could not be obtained through the sample.

[2] Data on persons of Hispanic origin are tabulated separately, without regard to race, which means that they are also included in the data for white and black workers. At the time of the 1970 census, approximately 96 percent of their population was white.

NOTE: Due to rounding, sums of individuals may not equal totals.

TABLE 3. MEDIAN MONEY WAGE OR SALARY INCOME OF ALL WORKERS WITH WAGE OR SALARY INCOME, AND OF YEAR-ROUND FULL-TIME WORKERS, BY SEX, RACE, AND MAJOR OCCUPATION GROUP: 1939-1970

All male workers

| Year | Race [1] | | Major occupation group [2] | | | | | | | | | |
| | White | Negro and other races | Professional, technical, and kindred workers | Farmers and farm managers | Managers, officials, and proprietors, except farm | Clerical and kindred workers | Sales workers | Craftsmen, foremen, and kindred workers | Operatives and kindred workers | Service workers, except private household | Farm laborers and foremen | Laborers, except farm and mine |
| | 372 | 373 | 374 | 375 | 376 | 377 | 378 | 379 | 380 | 381 | 382 | 383 |
| 1970 | $8,254 | $5,485 | $10,722 | $1,105 | $11,430 | $7,585 | $7,992 | $8,580 | $6,671 | $5,027 | $1,911 | $4,337 |
| 1969 | 7,859 | 5,237 | 10,257 | 1,151 | 10,874 | 7,135 | 7,570 | 8,231 | 6,473 | 4,545 | 1,855 | 4,091 |
| 1968 | 7,291 | 4,839 | 9,368 | 1,215 | 9,904 | 6,755 | 7,245 | 7,581 | 6,066 | 4,462 | 1,775 | 3,850 |
| 1967 | 6,833 | 4,369 | 8,882 | 968 | 9,357 | 6,193 | 6,644 | 7,142 | 5,702 | 4,251 | 1,432 | 3,764 |
| 1966 | 6,510 | 3,864 | 8,204 | 1,179 | 8,730 | 5,893 | 6,337 | 6,819 | 5,528 | 3,830 | 1,454 | 3,323 |
| 1965 | 6,188 | 3,563 | 7,798 | 696 | 8,444 | 5,617 | 6,097 | 6,493 | 5,258 | 3,864 | 1,284 | 3,234 |
| 1964 | 5,853 | 3,426 | 7,460 | 710 | 7,560 | 5,549 | 5,620 | 6,133 | 4,985 | 3,684 | 1,128 | 3,126 |
| 1963 | 5,663 | 3,217 | 7,182 | 703 | 7,411 | 5,318 | 5,581 | 5,875 | 4,830 | 3,581 | 1,051 | 2,869 |
| 1962 | 5,462 | 3,023 | 6,870 | 486 | 7,099 | 5,187 | 5,267 | 5,737 | 4,601 | 3,372 | 1,205 | 2,895 |
| 1961 | 5,287 | 3,015 | 6,716 | 521 | 6,957 | 4,990 | 5,122 | 5,527 | 4,344 | 3,238 | 1,002 | 2,730 |
| 1960 | 5,137 | 3,075 | 6,343 | 500 | 6,864 | 4,800 | 4,742 | 5,443 | 4,275 | 3,155 | 893 | 2,559 |
| 1959* | 4,902 | 2,844 | 6,287 | 645 | 6,670 | 4,691 | 4,660 | 5,272 | 4,101 | 3,192 | 968 | 2,834 |
| 1958 | 4,569 | 2,652 | 5,956 | 498 | 6,034 | 4,398 | 4,291 | 4,970 | 3,909 | 3,090 | 750 | 2,486 |
| 1957 | 4,396 | 2,436 | 5,601 | 469 | 5,872 | 4,252 | 4,379 | 4,777 | 3,984 | 2,894 | 940 | 2,763 |
| 1956 | 4,260 | 2,396 | 5,465 | 455 | 5,589 | 4,150 | 4,275 | 4,619 | 3,824 | 2,946 | 892 | 2,635 |
| 1955 | 3,986 | 2,342 | 5,055 | 461 | 5,290 | 3,870 | 4,315 | 4,356 | 3,586 | 2,778 | 971 | 2,387 |
| 1954 | 3,754 | 2,131 | 4,905 | 577 | 5,234 | 3,735 | 3,823 | 4,246 | 3,349 | 2,818 | 923 | 2,358 |
| 1953 | 3,760 | 2,233 | 4,816 | 493 | 5,071 | 3,766 | 3,716 | 4,156 | 3,415 | 2,806 | 817 | 2,406 |
| 1952 | 3,507 | 2,038 | 4,691 | 479 | 4,696 | 3,421 | 3,576 | 3,756 | 3,216 | 2,374 | 847 | 2,244 |
| 1951 | 3,345 | 2,060 | 4,071 | 482 | 4,143 | 3,366 | 3,539 | 3,601 | 3,064 | 2,426 | 982 | 2,170 |
| 1950 | 2,982 | 1,828 | 3,874 | 711 | 4,171 | 3,002 | 3,148 | 3,405 | 2,736 | 2,299 | 986 | 1,850 |
| 1939 | 1,112 | 460 | 1,809 | 373 | 2,136 | 1,421 | 1,277 | 1,309 | 1,007 | 833 | 309 | 673 |

All female workers

| Year | Race[1] | | Major occupation group[2] | | | | | | | |
|---|---|---|---|---|---|---|---|---|---|---|
| | White | Negro and other races | Professional, technical, and kindred workers | Managers, officials, and proprietors, except farm | Clerical and kindred workers | Sales workers | Craftsmen, foremen, and kindred workers | Operatives and kindred workers | Private household workers | Service workers, except private household |
| | 384 | 385 | 386 | 387 | 388 | 389 | 390 | 391 | 392 | 393 |
| 1970 | $3,870 | $3,285 | $6,589 | $5,741 | $4,467 | $1,972 | $4,053 | $3,637 | $527 | $2,248 |
| 1969 | 3,640 | 2,884 | 6,012 | 5,469 | 4,124 | 1,896 | 4,358 | 3,544 | 513 | 2,053 |
| 1968 | 3,465 | 2,497 | 5,564 | 4,840 | 3,882 | 2,073 | 4,040 | 3,383 | 546 | 2,029 |
| 1967 | 3,254 | 2,288 | 5,225 | 4,724 | 3,719 | 1,870 | 3,717 | 3,088 | 512 | 1,904 |
| 1966 | 3,079 | 1,981 | 4,801 | 4,151 | 3,515 | 1,896 | 3,432 | 2,839 | 526 | 1,696 |
| 1965 | 2,994 | 1,722 | 4,720 | 3,830 | 3,444 | 1,933 | 3,408 | 2,764 | 555 | 1,588 |
| 1964 | 2,841 | 1,652 | 4,374 | 3,675 | 3,420 | 1,761 | 3,074 | 2,630 | 518 | 1,449 |
| 1963 | 2,723 | 1,448 | 4,163 | 3,370 | 3,285 | 1,521 | 3,008 | 2,518 | 477 | 1,369 |
| 1962 | 2,630 | 1,396 | 4,150 | 3,640 | 3,190 | 1,606 | 3,141 | 2,430 | 476 | 1,378 |
| 1961 | 2,538 | 1,302 | 3,991 | 3,182 | 3,112 | 1,528 | 3,095 | 2,322 | 458 | 1,384 |
| 1960 | 2,537 | 1,276 | 3,868 | 3,500 | 3,039 | 1,359 | (3) | 2,368 | 473 | 1,427 |
| 1959* | 2,422 | 1,289 | 3,615 | 3,556 | 2,955 | 1,474 | (3) | 2,267 | 502 | 1,287 |
| 1958 | 2,364 | 1,055 | 3,501 | 3,313 | 2,943 | 1,304 | (3) | 2,075 | 467 | 1,255 |
| 1957 | 2,240 | 1,019 | 3,344 | 3,118 | 2,802 | 1,442 | (3) | 2,130 | 459 | 1,249 |
| 1956 | 2,179 | 970 | 3,114 | 2,976 | 2,699 | 1,504 | (3) | 2,130 | 486 | 1,151 |
| 1955 | 2,065 | 894 | 2,963 | 3,158 | 2,597 | 1,582 | (3) | 2,048 | 502 | 1,135 |
| 1954 | 2,046 | 914 | 3,008 | (3) | 2,468 | 1,548 | (3) | 1,852 | 495 | 1,154 |
| 1953 | 2,049 | 994 | 2,929 | 2,548 | 2,420 | 1,558 | (3) | 1,901 | 554 | 1,223 |
| 1952 | 1,976 | 814 | 2,695 | 2,705 | 2,270 | 1,675 | 2,075 | 1,908 | 433 | 1,128 |
| 1951 | 1,855 | 781 | 2,495 | 2,679 | 2,147 | 1,176 | (3) | 1,739 | 447 | 996 |
| 1950 | 1,698 | 626 | 2,264 | 2,089 | 2,064 | 1,118 | (3) | 1,616 | 448 | 895 |
| 1939 | 676 | 246 | 1,023 | 1,107 | 966 | 646 | 827 | 582 | 296 | 493 |

See footnotes at end of table.

## TABLE 3. MEDIAN MONEY WAGE OR SALARY INCOME OF ALL WORKERS WITH WAGE OR SALARY INCOME, AND OF YEAR-ROUND FULL-TIME WORKERS BY SEX, RACE, AND MAJOR OCCUPATION GROUP: 1939-1970 (CONT'D)

Male year-round full-time workers

| Year | Race [1] | | Major occupation group [2] | | | | | | | | | | |
|---|---|---|---|---|---|---|---|---|---|---|---|---|
| | White | Negro and other races | Professional, technical, and kindred workers | Farmers and farm managers | Managers, officials, and proprietors, except farm | Clerical and kindred workers | Sales workers | Craftsmen, foremen, and kindred workers | Operatives and kindred workers | Service workers, except private household | Farm laborers and foremen | Laborers, except farm and mine |
| | 394 | 395 | 396 | 397 | 398 | 399 | 400 | 401 | 402 | 403 | 404 | 405 |
| 1970 | $9,373 | $6,598 | $11,806 | $1,260 | $12,117 | $8,617 | $9,790 | $9,254 | $7,623 | $6,955 | $3,519 | $6,563 |
| 1969 | 8,876 | 6,158 | 11,266 | 1,180 | 11,467 | 7,966 | 9,135 | 8,757 | 7,307 | 6,373 | 2,985 | 6,150 |
| 1968 | 8,014 | 5,603 | 10,151 | 1,275 | 10,340 | 7,351 | 8,549 | 7,978 | 6,738 | 6,058 | 3,069 | 5,504 |
| 1967 | 7,512 | 5,069 | 9,523 | 993 | 9,817 | 6,757 | 7,744 | 7,484 | 6,316 | 5,439 | 2,489 | 5,182 |
| 1966 | 7,164 | 4,528 | 8,945 | 1,229 | 9,103 | 6,487 | 7,569 | 7,197 | 6,112 | 5,078 | 2,489 | 4,946 |
| 1965 | 6,814 | 4,367 | 8,464 | 750 | 8,856 | 6,231 | 7,188 | 6,877 | 5,830 | 4,986 | 2,458 | 4,445 |
| 1964 | 6,497 | 4,285 | 8,004 | 754 | 7,870 | 6,134 | 6,733 | 6,538 | 5,659 | 4,701 | 2,160 | 4,436 |
| 1963 | 6,277 | 4,104 | 7,713 | 750 | 7,639 | 5,838 | 6,493 | 6,315 | 5,480 | 4,399 | 1,655 | 4,449 |
| 1962 | 6,025 | 3,799 | 7,357 | 587 | 7,454 | 5,889 | 6,193 | 6,251 | 5,319 | 4,406 | 1,984 | 4,380 |
| 1961 | 5,880 | 3,883 | 7,339 | 558 | 7,343 | 5,387 | 6,163 | 6,067 | 5,108 | 4,203 | 1,793 | 4,330 |
| 1960 | 5,662 | 3,789 | 6,848 | 499 | 7,241 | 5,247 | 5,755 | 5,868 | 4,977 | 4,089 | 1,731 | 3,872 |
| 1959* | 5,456 | 3,339 | 6,835 | 683 | 6,910 | 5,130 | 5,545 | 5,654 | 4,607 | 4,002 | 1,637 | 3,930 |
| 1958 | 5,186 | 3,368 | 6,513 | 490 | 6,431 | 4,839 | 5,332 | 5,365 | 4,460 | 3,898 | 1,406 | 3,672 |
| 1957 | 4,950 | 3,137 | 5,990 | 454 | 6,110 | 4,564 | 5,143 | 5,216 | 4,397 | 3,605 | 1,518 | 3,710 |
| 1956 | 4,710 | 2,912 | 5,847 | 479 | 5,967 | 4,388 | 5,005 | 4,981 | 4,235 | 3,521 | 1,526 | 3,410 |
| 1955 | 4,458 | 2,831 | 5,382 | 414 | 5,584 | 4,162 | 4,937 | 4,712 | 4,046 | 3,565 | (3) | 3,105 |
| 1939 | 1,419 | 639 | 2,100 | 430 | 2,254 | 1,564 | 1,451 | 1,562 | 1,268 | 1,019 | 365 | 991 |

Female year-round full-time workers

| Year | Race [1] | | Major occupation group [2] | | | | | | | |
|---|---|---|---|---|---|---|---|---|---|---|
| | White | Negro and other races | Professional, technical, and kindred workers | Managers, officials, and proprietors, except farm | Clerical and kindred workers | Sales workers | Craftsmen, foremen, and kindred workers | Operatives and kindred workers | Private household workers | Service workers, except private household |
| | 406 | 407 | 408 | 409 | 410 | 411 | 412 | 413 | 414 | 415 |
| 1970 | $5,490 | $4,674 | $7,878 | $6,834 | $5,551 | $4,788 | $5,089 | $4,510 | $2,101 | $3,953 |
| 1969 | 5,168 | 4,231 | 7,309 | 6,091 | 5,187 | 3,904 | 4,992 | 4,317 | 1,851 | 3,755 |
| 1968 | 4,700 | 3,677 | 6,691 | 5,635 | 4,789 | 3,661 | 4,625 | 3,991 | 1,523 | 3,332 |
| 1967 | 4,394 | 3,363 | 6,307 | 5,341 | 4,537 | 3,283 | 4,284 | 3,649 | 1,298 | 3,071 |
| 1966 | 4,152 | 2,949 | 5,826 | 4,919 | 4,316 | 3,103 | 4,345 | 3,416 | 1,297 | 2,815 |
| 1965 | 3,960 | 2,713 | 5,634 | 4,593 | 4,154 | 2,561 | 4,023 | 3,327 | 1,150 | 2,607 |
| 1964 | 3,859 | 2,674 | 5,150 | 4,369 | 4,060 | 2,719 | (3) | 3,271 | 1,082 | 2,525 |
| 1963 | 3,723 | 2,368 | 4,998 | 4,219 | 3,951 | 2,531 | (3) | 3,143 | 1,108 | 2,528 |
| 1962 | 3,601 | 2,278 | 4,863 | 4,311 | 3,832 | 2,699 | (3) | 3,157 | 1,107 | 2,283 |
| 1961 | 3,480 | 2,325 | 4,961 | 3,910 | 3,743 | 2,409 | (3) | 2,925 | 1,045 | 2,357 |
| 1960 | 3,410 | 2,372 | 4,384 | 4,173 | 3,586 | 2,428 | (3) | 2,970 | 1,133 | 2,418 |
| 1959* | 3,306 | 2,196 | 4,385 | 3,934 | 3,493 | 2,340 | (3) | 2,916 | 1,146 | 2,241 |
| 1958 | 3,225 | 1,988 | 4,146 | 3,771 | 3,388 | 2,333 | (3) | 2,745 | 1,161 | 2,073 |
| 1957 | 3,107 | 1,866 | 3,810 | 3,890 | 3,287 | 2,239 | (3) | 2,611 | 980 | 1,995 |
| 1956 | 2,958 | 1,637 | 3,650 | 3,525 | 3,145 | 2,030 | (3) | 2,632 | 879 | 1,950 |
| 1955 | 2,870 | 1,637 | 3,500 | (3) | 3,065 | (3) | (3) | 2,489 | (3) | 1,759 |
| 1939 | 863 | 327 | 1,277 | 1,218 | 1,072 | 745 | 995 | 742 | 339 | 607 |

Source: U.S. Bureau of the Census, HISTORICAL STATISTICS OF THE UNITED STATES, COLONIAL TIMES TO 1970, Bicentennial Edition, Part 1 (Washington, D.C.: U.S. Government Printing Office, 1976), pp. 304-305.

* Denotes first year for which figures include Alaska and Hawaii.

[1] For wage or salary workers at time of survey.

[2] For experienced civilian labor force. 1939 excludes public emergency workers and persons having less than $100 of wage or salary income, but includes members of the Armed Forces; 1950 excludes persons having less than $100 of wage or salary income.

[3] Fewer than 100 cases in the sample reporting with $1 or more of wage or salary income.

## TABLE 4. UNEMPLOYMENT RATES FOR SELECTED GROUPS IN THE LABOR FORCE: 1947 to 1970

| Year | All civilian workers | | | White | | | Negro and other races | | | Both sexes, 16–19 years old | Men, 20 years and over | Women, 20 years and over | Unemployed 15 weeks and over, total | Average duration of unemployment, weeks | State insured unemployment |
| | Total | Male | Female | Total | Male | Female | Total | Male | Female | | | | | | |
| | 87 | 88 | 89 | 90 | 91 | 92 | 93 | 94 | 95 | 96 | 97 | 98 | 99 | 100 | 101 |
| 1970 | 4.9 | 4.4 | 5.9 | 4.5 | 4.0 | 5.4 | 8.2 | 7.3 | 9.3 | 15.2 | 3.5 | 4.8 | 0.8 | 8.8 | 3.4 |
| 1969 | 3.5 | 2.8 | 4.7 | 3.1 | 2.5 | 4.2 | 6.4 | 5.3 | 7.8 | 12.2 | 2.1 | 3.7 | .5 | 8.5 | 2.2 |
| 1968 | 3.6 | 2.9 | 4.8 | 3.2 | 2.6 | 4.3 | 6.7 | 5.6 | 8.3 | 12.7 | 2.2 | 3.8 | .5 | 8.5 | 2.2 |
| 1967 | 3.8 | 3.1 | 5.2 | 3.4 | 2.7 | 4.6 | 7.4 | 6.0 | 9.1 | 12.9 | 2.3 | 4.2 | .6 | 8.8 | 2.5 |
| 1966 | 3.8 | 3.2 | 4.8 | 3.3 | 2.8 | 4.3 | 7.3 | 6.3 | 8.6 | 12.8 | 2.5 | 3.8 | .7 | 10.4 | 2.4 |
| 1965 | 4.5 | 4.0 | 5.5 | 4.1 | 3.6 | 5.0 | 8.1 | 7.4 | 9.2 | 14.8 | 3.2 | 4.5 | 1.0 | 11.8 | 3.0 |
| 1964 | 5.2 | 4.6 | 6.2 | 4.6 | 4.1 | 5.5 | 9.6 | 8.9 | 10.6 | 16.2 | 3.9 | 5.2 | 1.3 | 13.3 | 3.7 |
| 1963 | 5.7 | 5.2 | 6.5 | 5.0 | 4.7 | 5.8 | 10.8 | 10.5 | 11.0 | 17.2 | 4.5 | 5.4 | 1.5 | 14.0 | 4.3 |
| 1962 | 5.5 | 5.2 | 6.2 | 4.9 | 4.6 | 5.5 | 10.9 | 10.9 | 11.0 | 14.7 | 4.6 | 5.4 | 1.6 | 14.7 | 4.4 |
| 1961 | 6.7 | 6.4 | 7.2 | 6.0 | 5.7 | 6.5 | 12.4 | 12.8 | 11.8 | 16.8 | 5.7 | 6.3 | 2.2 | 15.6 | 5.7 |
| 1960 | 5.5 | 5.4 | 5.9 | 4.9 | 4.8 | 5.3 | 10.2 | 10.7 | 9.4 | 14.7 | 4.7 | 5.1 | 1.4 | 12.8 | 4.8 |
| 1959 | 5.5 | 5.3 | 5.9 | 4.8 | 4.6 | 5.3 | 10.7 | 11.5 | 9.4 | 14.6 | 4.7 | 5.2 | 1.5 | 14.4 | 4.4 |
| 1958 | 6.8 | 6.8 | 6.8 | 6.1 | 6.1 | 6.2 | 12.6 | 13.8 | 10.8 | 15.9 | 6.2 | 6.1 | 2.1 | 13.9 | 6.3 |
| 1957 | 4.3 | 4.1 | 4.7 | 3.8 | 3.6 | 4.3 | 7.9 | 8.3 | 7.3 | 11.6 | 3.6 | 4.1 | .8 | 10.5 | 4.3 |
| 1956 | 4.1 | 3.8 | 4.8 | 3.6 | 3.4 | 4.2 | 8.3 | 7.9 | 8.9 | 11.1 | 3.4 | 4.2 | .8 | 11.3 | 3.4 |
| 1955 | 4.4 | 4.2 | 4.9 | 3.9 | 3.7 | 4.3 | 8.7 | 8.8 | 8.4 | 11.0 | 3.8 | 4.4 | 1.1 | 13.0 | 3.5 |
| 1954 | 5.5 | 5.3 | 6.0 | 5.0 | 4.8 | 5.6 | 9.9 | 10.3 | 9.3 | 12.6 | 4.9 | 5.5 | 1.3 | 11.8 | 5.1 |
| 1953 | 2.9 | 2.8 | 3.3 | 2.7 | 2.5 | 3.1 | 4.5 | 4.8 | 4.1 | 7.6 | 2.5 | 2.9 | .3 | 8.0 | 2.8 |
| 1952 | 3.0 | 2.8 | 3.6 | 2.8 | 2.5 | 3.3 | 5.4 | 5.2 | 5.7 | 8.5 | 2.4 | 3.2 | .4 | 8.4 | 3.0 |
| 1951 | 3.3 | 2.8 | 4.4 | 3.1 | 2.6 | 4.2 | 5.3 | 4.9 | 6.1 | 8.2 | 2.5 | 4.0 | .5 | 9.7 | 3.0 |
| 1950 | 5.3 | 5.1 | 5.7 | 4.9 | 4.7 | 5.3 | 9.0 | 9.4 | 8.4 | 12.2 | 4.7 | 5.1 | 1.3 | 12.1 | 4.8 |
| 1949 | 5.9 | 5.9 | 6.0 | 5.6 | 5.6 | 5.7 | 8.9 | 9.6 | 7.9 | 13.4 | 5.4 | 5.3 | 1.1 | 10.0 | 6.0 |
| 1948 | 3.8 | 3.6 | 4.1 | 3.5 | 3.4 | 3.8 | 5.9 | 5.8 | 6.1 | 9.2 | 3.2 | 3.6 | .5 | 8.6 | 3.1 |
| 1947 | 3.9 | 4.0 | 3.7 | — | — | — | — | — | — | — | — | — | — | — | — |

Source: U.S. Bureau of the Census, *id.* at 135.

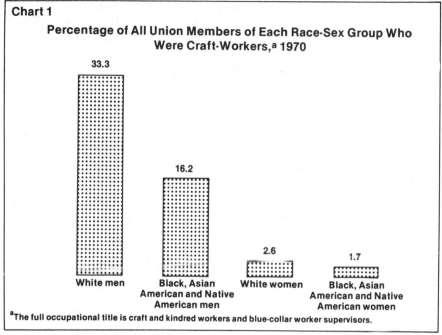

**Chart 1**

## Percentage of All Union Members of Each Race-Sex Group Who Were Craft-Workers,[a] 1970

33.3 — White men

16.2 — Black, Asian American and Native American men

2.6 — White women

1.7 — Black, Asian American and Native American women

[a]The full occupational title is craft and kindred workers and blue-collar worker supervisors.

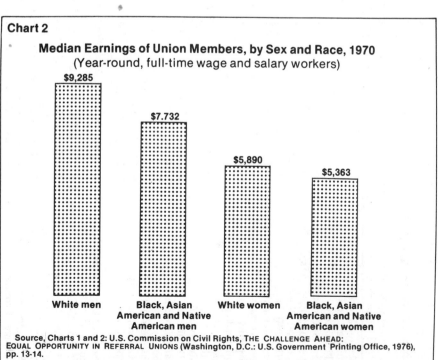

**Chart 2**

## Median Earnings of Union Members, by Sex and Race, 1970
(Year-round, full-time wage and salary workers)

$9,285 — White men

$7.732 — Black, Asian American and Native American men

$5,890 — White women

$5,363 — Black, Asian American and Native American women

Source, Charts 1 and 2: U.S. Commission on Civil Rights, THE CHALLENGE AHEAD: EQUAL OPPORTUNITY IN REFERRAL UNIONS (Washington, D.C.: U.S. Government Printing Office, 1976), pp. 13-14.

TABLE 5.  MINORITIES AND WOMEN IN BUILDING TRADES UNIONS
AND AVERAGE WAGE RATES, 1972

| International union | Male minority membership, percent* | Female nonminority membership, percent* | Female minority membership, percent* | Average wage rate of a trade represented by union** |
|---|---|---|---|---|
| Asbestos Workers | 3.7 | 0 | 0 | $8.83 |
| Plumbers and Pipefitters | 4.4 | —a | —a | 9.67 |
| Elevator Constructors | 5.6 | 0 | 0 | 8.87 |
| Operating Engineers | 6.1 | 0.5 | —a | —c |
| Electrical Workers (IBEW) | 6.5 | 1.4 | 0.9 | 9.07 |
| Sheet Metal Workers | 6.7 | 0.1 | 0.3 | 9.07 |
| Iron Workers | 9.3 | —a | —a | 8.98 |
| Carpenters | 11.2 | 0.5 | —a | 8.61 |
| Boilermakers | 11.3 | 0.2 | —a | 9.02 |
| Bricklayers | 13.1 | —a | 0 | 9.12 |
| Lathers | 14.2 | 0 | 0 | 8.47 |
| Painters and Decorators | 14.7 | 0.5 | 0.1 | 7.85 |
| Marble Polishers | 15.2 | 0 | 0 | 8.11 |
| Roofers | 23.4 | —a | 0 | 8.13b |
| Plasterers and Cement Masons | 32.5 | —a | 0 | 8.39 |
| Laborers | 42.9 | 0.5 | 0.5 | 6.55 |

Source: U.S. Commission on Civil Rights, *id* at 25. Minorities include blacks, persons of Spanish origin, Asian Americans, and Native Americans.

* U.S., EEOC, News Release, June 30, 1974; based on Local Union EEO-3 Reports for 1972.

** U.S., Department of Labor, BLS, *Union Wages and Hours: Building Trades, July 1, 1972*, Bulletin 1807 (1974), p. 10.

a. Less than 0.05 percent.

b. Wages include employer contributions to insurance and pension funds and vacation payments. The wage rates refer to specific trades, while several international unions represent two or more trades. For example, the wage of $8.13 listed for roofers is the wage of composition roofers, while slate and tile roofers earned $7.97.

c. Not available.

## TABLE 6. ESTIMATES OF THE EXTENT OF UNIONIZATION AMONG BLACK AND WHITE WORKERS, 1886-1970, SELECTED YEARS

| Year | (1) Total union members | (2) Black union members | (3) Percentage of black labor force unionized | (4) White union members | (5) Percentage of white labor force unionized | (6) Black union members as a percentage of total union members |
|---|---|---|---|---|---|---|
| 1886 | 960,241 | 60,000 | 2.4 | 900,241 | 4.2 | 6.3 |
| 1890 | 540,454 | 3,523 | .1 | 536,931 | 2.8 | 0.7 |
| 1900 | 868,000 | 32,619 | .9 | 853,381 | 3.5 | 3.8 |
| 1910 | 2,140,000 | 68,753 | 1.4 | 2,071,247 | 6.4 | 3.2 |
| 1926-28 | 3,500,000 | 61,000 | 1.1 | 3,439,000 | 7.9 | 1.7 |
| 1930 | 3,416,000 | 56,000 | 1.0 | 3,360,000 | 7.9 | 1.6 |
| 1940 | 8,717,000 | 600,000 | 10.7 | 8,117,000 | 17.3 | 6.9 |
| 1944 | 14,146,000 | 1,250,000 | 21.4 | 12,896,000 | 25.8 | 8.8 |
| 1955 | 16,802,000 | 1,500,000 | 21.3 | 15,302,000 | 26.0 | 8.9 |
| 1967 | 17,790,070 | 1,989,270 | 23.0 | 15,800,770 | 23.0 | 10.7 |
| 1970 | 17,192,000 | 2,130,000 | 21.8 | 15,062,000 | 20.2 | 12.4 |

Source: U.S. Commission on Civil Rights, id at 279. Figures for 1886 to 1967 from Orley Ashenfelter and Lamond Godwin, "Some Evidence on the Effect of Unionism on the Average Wage of Black Workers Relative to White Workers, 1900-1967," *Proceedings of the Twenty-fourth Winter Annual Meeting of the Industrial Relations Research Association*, no. 2 (May 1972), p. 219. These statistics came from a variety of sources, some of doubtful reliability, and were not compiled on a uniform basis from year to year. Figures for 1970, which include Asian American and Native American as well as black union members, are from U.S. Department of Labor, Bureau of Labor Statistics, *Selected Earnings and Demographic Characteristics of Union Members, 1970* (1972).

## TABLE 7. BLACK MEMBERSHIP IN SELECTED CRAFT UNIONS, 1967 AND 1972, AND BLACK EMPLOYMENT IN SELECTED CRAFTS, 1890

| International union (short name) | (1) Black membership as percentage of total membership 1972[a] | (2) Black membership as percentage of total membership 1967 | (3) Black employment as percentage of total employment 1890 |
|---|---|---|---|
| Carpenters ...... | 3.7 | 1.6 | 3.6 |
| Painters ......... | 4.9 | 3.7 | 2.0 |
| Bricklayers ....... | 9.7 | 9.6 | 6.1 |
| Plasterers ........ | 16.0 | 14.0 | 10.3 |
| Plumbers ........ | 1.5 | 0.2 | 1.1 |
| Electricians ...... | 2.6 | 0.6 | 0.0 |
| Common Laborers . | 29.1 | 30.5 | 20.0 |
| Sheet Metal Workers ....... | 1.1 | 0.2 | 1.2 |
| Boilermakers and Blacksmiths[b] ... | 4.6 | 3.9 | 5.2 |
| Printing Pressmen and Lithographers and Photoengravers ...... | 3.8[c] | 3.0 | 0.8 |
| Printing Pressmen .......... | 5.8 | 4.4 | —[d] |
| Lithographers and Photoengravers | 2.2[c] | 1.3 | —[d] |
| All reporting building trades (including Laborers) ...... | 8.3 | 8.4 | —[d] |
| All reporting referral unions ... | 10.6[c] | 9.7 | —[d] |

Source: U.S. Commission on Civil Rights, *id* at 281. Col. 1: 1972 figures are from U.S. Equal Employment Opportunity Commission, News Release, June 30, 1974, except for Printing Pressmen. The 1972 figure for Printing Pressmen and the 1970 figures (see ftn. c) were supplied directly by EEOC. Col. 2 and 3: Orley Ashenfelter, *Racial Discrimination and Trade Unionism*, JOURNAL OF POLITICAL ECONOMY, vol. 80, no. 3, pt. 1 (May/June 1972), p. 444. Ashenfelter obtained these figures from an EEOC publication and from the Bureau of the Census report on the 1890 census.

a. Most statistics are preliminary.

b. The inclusion of Blacksmiths in the third column renders the figures in this row of doubtful comparability.

c. 1970 statistics.

d. Not available.

# RESEARCH SUMMARY OF EEOC REPORT*

## MINORITY MEMBERSHIP IMPROVES IN JOB-REFERRAL UNIONS

. . .

Since 1970, minority membership has been slowly increasing in unions that refer members to employers (referral unions). In 1974, total membership was 2 million in the 2,907 local unions participating in the Equal Employment Opportunity Commission survey—23 percent were members of racial minorities, and nearly 12 percent were women. In a group of locals which reported in both years, total membership was 5 percent higher than in 1970, with minority membership up by 17 percent and that of women, 18 percent.

Minorities were more commonly found in lower paying trades outside construction (35 percent of the workers), rather than in the generally better paying building trades (16 percent, half of whom were laborers). About 1 of 5 building trade unions had no black members, compared with 1 of 10 of the other trades. Hispanics were also underrepresented in the better paying trades.

Asian Americans represented 1.3 percent of referral union members, compared with 0.8 percent of the labor force. However, they too were concentrated in lower paying, nonbuilding trades. About half were either hotel and restaurant employees or ladies' garment workers.

American Indians representation in referral unions was three times greater than their participation in the civilian labor force (1 percent and 0.3 percent, respectively). Also, their participation was higher in building than other trades, even though 1 of 4 was a construction laborer.

Female membership was less than 1 percent in 8 of 10 reporting locals. More than two-thirds of the building trades unions had no women members. Inasmuch as only 0.2 percent of construction apprentices are women, little improvement is expected in this industry.

* MONTHLY LABOR REVIEW, Vol. 101, No. 2 (1978).

## TABLE 8. LABOR FORCE PARTICIPATION AND NATIONAL UNION AND ASSOCIATION MEMBERSHIP OF WOMEN, SELECTED YEARS, 1956-76

[Numbers in millions]

| Year | Civilian labor force | | | Membership[1] | | | Women membership as a percent of all women in labor force |
|---|---|---|---|---|---|---|---|
| | Total | Total, women | Percent, women | Total | Total, women | Percent, women | |
| **Unions and associations[2]** | | | | | | | |
| 1970 | 82.7 | 31.5 | 38.1 | 21.1 | 5.0 | 23.9 | 16.0 |
| 1972 | 86.5 | 33.3 | 38.5 | 21.5 | 5.3 | 24.9 | 16.0 |
| 1974 | 91.0 | 35.8 | 39.4 | 22.9 | 5.7 | 25.0 | 15.8 |
| 1976 | 94.8 | 38.4 | 40.5 | 22.8 | 6.1 | 26.8 | 15.9 |
| **Unions** | | | | | | | |
| 1956 | 66.6 | 21.5 | 32.2 | 17.2 | 3.2 | 18.5 | 14.9 |
| 1958 | 67.6 | 22.1 | 32.7 | 16.8 | 3.1 | 18.2 | 13.8 |
| 1960 | 69.6 | 23.2 | 33.4 | 16.9 | 3.1 | 18.3 | 13.3 |
| 1962 | 70.6 | 24.0 | 34.0 | 16.4 | 3.1 | 18.6 | 12.8 |
| 1964 | 73.1 | 25.4 | 34.8 | 16.7 | 3.2 | 19.1 | 12.5 |
| 1966 | 75.8 | 27.3 | 36.0 | 17.8 | 3.4 | 19.3 | 12.6 |
| 1968 | 78.7 | 29.2 | 37.1 | 18.8 | 3.7 | 19.5 | 12.5 |
| 1970 | 82.7 | 31.5 | 38.1 | 19.2 | 4.0 | 20.7 | 12.6 |
| 1972 | 86.5 | 33.3 | 38.5 | 19.3 | 4.2 | 21.7 | 12.6 |
| 1974 | 91.0 | 35.8 | 39.4 | 20.0 | 4.3 | 21.3 | 11.9 |
| 1976 | 94.8 | 38.4 | 40.5 | 19.5 | 4.3 | 22.2 | 11.3 |

[1] Membership data are limited to the United States.
[2] Associations were first surveyed in 1970. That survey covered 23 associations. The 1976 survey covered 35 associations.

# WOMEN IN LABOR ORGANIZATIONS: THEIR RANKS ARE INCREASING*

## Linda H. LeGrande**

. . . Some 1.1 million women joined labor unions between 1956 and 1976. . . . As indicated in table 8, although the overall increase in union membership was sluggish, rising only 13 percent, the number of women on union rolls rose 34 percent.

The proportion of women who joined trade unions was outpaced by the accelerated rate at which women entered the labor force. Female labor force participants who also had union cards fell from almost 15 percent of women workers in 1956, to about 11 percent in 1976. At the same time, the ratio of women workers to all labor force participants rose 8.3 percentage points, compared with the 3.6-percentage-point decline for all union members.

### OCCUPATIONS, INDUSTRIES INFLUENCE MEMBERSHIP

Occupational and industrial choices by women explain, in part, the more rapid growth of women as labor force participants and the smaller proportion of women workers who join unions. According to the May 1975 Current Population Survey women are concentrated in occupations that unions have traditionally found difficult to organize. Almost two-thirds of all women wage and salary workers who had full-time jobs in May 1975 were employed in white-collar occupations, compared with two-fifths of all men. (See table 9). Reflecting the low degree of unionization among white-collar jobholders, only 13 percent of the women and 14 percent of the men had union cards.

Blue-collar workers, in contrast, traditionally have been the most highly unionized occupational group, and a predominantly male group—63 percent of full-time wage earners were male blue-collar workers in May 1975. Fewer than one-fifth of the women workers had blue-collar jobs. Among these, 34 percent belonged to unions; 45 percent of the men had both blue-collar jobs and union cards.

* MONTHLY LABOR REVIEW, Vol. 101, No. 8 (1978).

** Linda H. LeGrande is an economist in the Division of Industrial Relations, Bureau of Labor Statistics.

## TABLE 9. DISTRIBUTION OF FULL-TIME WAGE AND SALARY WORKERS IN THE LABOR FORCE AND IN LABOR UNIONS, BY OCCUPATION AND INDUSTRY, MAY 1975[1]

[In percent]

| Occupation and industry | Labor force | | Labor unions | |
|---|---|---|---|---|
| | Men | Women | Men | Women |
| All occupations .............. | 100.0 | 100.0 | 31.1 | 16.3 |
| White-collar workers .............. | 39.5 | 63.5 | 14.2 | 12.5 |
| Professional, technical, and kindred ................... | 14.7 | 17.5 | 12.3 | 18.4 |
| Managers and administrators, except farm ................ | 12.5 | 4.8 | 7.4 | 4.5 |
| Clerical and kindred .......... | 7.2 | 36.7 | 36.0 | 11.5 |
| Sales ....................... | 5.1 | 4.5 | 5.3 | 6.2 |
| Blue-collar workers .............. | 51.0 | 18.9 | 45.3 | 34.1 |
| Craft and kindred ............ | 23.1 | 1.7 | 43.1 | 23.2 |
| Operatives and kindred ....... | 20.1 | 16.1 | 50.3 | 35.4 |
| Nonfarm laborers ............. | 7.8 | 1.1 | 39.3 | 32.8 |
| Service workers, including private household workers .............. | 7.7 | 17.2 | 29.7 | 11.0 |
| All industries .............. | 100.0 | 100.0 | 31.1 | 16.5 |
| Agriculture ...................... | 2.3 | .7 | 4.2 | 4.8 |
| Mining ......................... | 1.7 | — | 35.3 | — |
| Construction .................... | 9.9 | .7 | 39.5 | 6.2 |
| Manufacturing .................. | 32.3 | 22.1 | 42.5 | 28.0 |
| Transportation, communication, and public utilities ................. | 9.2 | 4.2 | 51.5 | 58.7 |
| Trade ......................... | 16.9 | 27.7 | 14.3 | 8.5 |
| Finance, insurance, and real estate ... | 4.2 | 6.7 | 6.7 | 1.8 |
| Service ......................... | 16.1 | 39.9 | 16.8 | 15.8 |
| Public administration ............. | 7.5 | 5.6 | 34.8 | 19.6 |

[1] "Earnings and Demographic Characteristics of Union Members, May 1975," unpublished, Bureau of Labor Statistics.

# 2. The Basics of Discrimination

## A. DISPARATE IMPACT AND DISPARATE TREATMENT

### (1) Order of Allocation of Proof

### GRIGGS v. DUKE POWER COMPANY

*Supreme Court of the United States, 1971*
**401 U.S. 424, 3 FEP Cases 175**

MR. CHIEF JUSTICE BURGER delivered the opinion of the Court.

We granted the writ in this case to resolve the question whether an employer is prohibited by the Civil Rights Act of 1964, Title VII, from requiring a high school education or passing of a standard general intelligence test as a condition of employment in or transfer to jobs when (a) neither standard is shown to be significantly related to successful job performance, (b) both requirements operate to disqualify Negroes at a substantially higher rate than white applicants, and (c) the jobs in question formerly had been filled only by white employees as part of a longstanding practice of giving preference to whites.

Congress provided, in Title VII of the Civil Rights Act of 1964, for class actions for enforcement of provisions of the Act and this proceeding was brought by a group of incumbent Negro employees against Duke Power Company. All the petitioners are employed at the Company's Dan River Steam Station, a power generating facility located at Draper, North Carolina. At the time this action was instituted, the Company had 95 employees at the Dan River Station, 14 of whom were Negroes; 13 of these are petitioners here.

The District Court found that prior to July 2, 1965, the effective date of the Civil Rights Act of 1964, the Company openly discriminated on the basis of race in the hiring and assigning of employees at its Dan River plant. The plant was organized into five operating departments: (1) Labor, (2) Coal Handling, (3) Operations, (4) Maintenance, and (5) Laboratory and Test. Negroes were employed only in the Labor Department where the highest paying jobs paid less than the lowest paying jobs in the other four "operating" departments in which only whites were employed.[2] Promotions were normally made within each depart-

---

2 [Footnotes numbered as in original—Ed.] A Negro was first assigned to a job in an operating department in August 1966, five months after charges had been filed with the Equal Employment Opportunity Commission. The employee, a high school graduate who had begun in the Labor Department in 1953, was promoted to a job in the Coal Handling Department.

41

ment on the basis of job seniority. Transferees into a department usually began in the lowest position.

In 1955 the Company instituted a policy of requiring a high school education for initial assignment to any department except Labor, and for transfer from the Coal Handling to any "inside" department (Operations, Maintenance, or Laboratory). When the Company abandoned its policy of restricting Negroes to the Labor Department in 1965, completion of high school also was made a prerequisite to transfer from Labor to any other department. From the time the high school requirement was instituted to the time of trial, however, white employees hired before the time of the high school education requirement continued to perform satisfactorily and achieve promotions in the "operating" departments. Findings on this score are not challenged.

The Company added a further requirement for new employees on July 2, 1965, the date on which Title VII became effective. To qualify for placement in any but the Labor Department it became necessary to register satisfactory scores on two professionally prepared aptitude tests, as well as to have a high school education. Completion of high school alone continued to render employees eligible for transfer to the four desirable departments from which Negroes had been excluded if the incumbent had been employed prior to the time of the new requirement. In September 1965 the Company began to permit incumbent employees who lacked a high school education to qualify for transfer from Labor or Coal Handling to an "inside" job by passing two tests— the Wonderlic Personnel Test, which purports to measure general intelligence, and the Bennett Mechanical Aptitude Test. Neither was directed or intended to measure the ability to learn to perform a particular job or category of jobs. The requisite scores used for both initial hiring and transfer approximated the national median for high school graduates.[3]

The District Court had found that while the Company previously followed a policy of overt racial discrimination in a period prior to the Act, such conduct had ceased. The District Court also concluded that Title VII was intended to be prospective only and, consequently, the impact of prior inequities was beyond the reach of corrective action authorized by the Act.

The Court of Appeals was confronted with a question of first impression, as are we, concerning the meaning of Title VII. After careful analysis a majority of that court concluded that a subjective test of the employer's intent should govern, particularly in a close case, and that in this case there was no showing of a discriminatory purpose in the adoption of the diploma and test requirements. On this basis, the Court of Appeals concluded there was no violation of the Act.

The Court of Appeals reversed the District Court in part, rejecting the holding that residual discrimination arising from prior employment prac-

---

[3] The test standards are thus more stringent than the high school requirement, since they would screen out approximately half of all high school graduates.

tices was insulated from remedial action.[4] The Court of Appeals noted, however, that the District Court was correct in its conclusion that there was no finding of a racial purpose of invidious intent in the adoption of the high school diploma requirement or general intelligence test and that these standards had been applied fairly to whites and Negroes alike. It held that, in the absence of a discriminatory purpose, use of such requirements was permitted by the Act. In so doing, the Court of Appeals rejected the claim that because these two requirements operated to render ineligible a markedly disproportionate number of Negroes, they were unlawful under Title VII unless shown to be job-related.[5] We granted the writ on these claims. 399 U.S. 926.

The objective of Congress in the enactment of Title VII is plain from the language of the statute. It was to achieve equality of employment opportunities and remove barriers that have operated in the past to favor an identifiable group of white employees over other employees. Under the Act, practices, procedures, or tests neutral on their face, and even neutral in terms of intent, cannot be maintained if they operate to "freeze" the status quo of prior discriminatory employment practices.

The Court of Appeals' opinion, and the partial dissent, agreed that, on the record in the present case, "whites fare far better on the Company's alternative requirements" than Negroes.[6] This consequence would appear to be directly traceable to race. Basic intelligence must have the means of articulation to manifest itself fairly in a testing process. Because they are Negroes, petitioners have long received inferior education in segregated schools and this Court expressly recognized these differences in *Gaston County* v. *United States,* 395 U.S. 285 (1969). There, because of the inferior education received by Negroes in North Carolina, this Court barred the institution of a literacy test for voter registration on the ground that the test would abridge the right to vote indirectly on account of race. Congress did not intend by Title VII, however, to guarantee a job to every person regardless of qualifications.

---

[4] The Court of Appeals ruled that Negroes employed in the Labor Department at a time when there was no high school or test requirement for entrance into the higher paying departments could not now be made subject to those requirements, since whites hired contemporaneously into those departments were never subject to them. The Court of Appeals also required that the seniority rights of those Negroes be measured on a plantwide, rather than a departmental, basis. However, the Court of Appeals denied relief to the Negro employees without a high school education or its equivalent who were hired into the Labor Department after institution of the educational requirement.

[5] One member of that court disagreed with this aspect of the decision, maintaining, as do the petitioners in this Court, that Title VII prohibits the use of employment criteria which operate in a racially exclusionary fashion and do not measure skills or abilities necessary to performance of the jobs for which those criteria are used.

[6] In North Carolina, 1960 census statistics show that, while 34% of white males had completed high school, only 12% of Negro males had done so. U.S. Bureau of the Census, U.S. Census of Population: 1960, Vol. 1, Part 35, Table 47.

Similarly, with respect to standardized tests, the EEOC in one case found that the use of a battery of tests, including the Wonderlic and Bennett tests used by the Company in the instant case, resulted in 58% of whites passing the tests, as compared with only 6% of the blacks. Decision of EEOC, CCH Empl. Prac. Guide, ¶ 17,304.53 (Dec. 2, 1966). See also Decision of EEOC 70-552, CCH Empl. Prac. Guide, ¶ 6139 (Feb. 19, 1970).

In short, the Act does not command that any person be hired simply because he was formerly the subject of discrimination, or because he is a member of a minority group. Discriminatory preference for any group, minority or majority, is precisely and only what Congress has proscribed. What is required by Congress is the removal of artificial, arbitrary, and unnecessary barriers to employment when the barriers operate invidiously to discriminate on the basis of racial or other impermissible classification.

Congress has now provided that tests or criteria for employment or promotion may not provide equality of opportunity only in the sense of the fabled offer of milk to the stork and the fox. On the contrary, Congress has now required that the posture and condition of the job seeker be taken into account. It has—to resort again to the fable—provided that the vessel in which the milk is proffered be one all seekers can use. The Act proscribes not only overt discrimination but also practices that are fair in form, but discriminatory in operation. The touchstone is business necessity. If an employment practice which operates to exclude Negroes cannot be shown to be related to job performance, the practice is prohibited.

On the record before us, neither the high school completion requirement nor the general intelligence test is shown to bear a demonstrable relationship to successful performance of the jobs for which it was used. Both were adopted, as the Court of Appeals noted, without meaningful study of their relationship to job-performance ability. Rather, a vice president of the Company testified, the requirements were instituted on the Company's judgment that they generally would improve the overall quality of the work force.

The evidence, however, shows that employees who have not completed high school or taken the tests have continued to perform satisfactorily and make progress in departments for which the high school and test criteria are now used.[7] The promotion record of present employees who would not be able to meet the new criteria thus suggests the possibility that the requirements may not be needed even for the limited purpose of preserving the avowed policy of advancement within the Company. In the context of this case, it is unnecessary to reach the question whether testing requirements that take into account capability for the next succeeding position or related future promotion might be utilized upon a showing that such long range requirements fulfill a genuine business need. In the present case the Company has made no such showing.

The Court of Appeals held that the Company had adopted the diploma and test requirements without any "intention to discriminate against Negro employees." We do not suggest that either the District Court or the Court of Appeals erred in examining the employer's intent; but good intent or absence of discriminatory intent does not redeem employ-

---

[7] For example, between July 2, 1965, and November 14, 1966, the percentage of white employees who were promoted but who were not high school graduates was nearly identical to the percentage of nongraduates in the entire white work force.

ment procedures or testing mechanisms that operate as "built-in head-winds" for minority groups and are unrelated to measuring job capability.

The Company's lack of discriminatory intent is suggested by special efforts to help the undereducated employees through Company financing of two-thirds the cost of tuition for high school training. But Congress directed the thrust of the Act to the *consequences* of employment practices, not simply the motivation. More than that, Congress has placed on the employer the burden of showing that any given requirement must have a manifest relationship to the employment in question.

The facts of this case demonstrate the inadequacy of broad and general testing devices as well as the infirmity of using diplomas or degrees as fixed measures of capability. History is filled with examples of men and women who rendered highly effective performance without the conventional badges of accomplishment in terms of certificates, diplomas, or degrees. Diplomas and tests are useful servants, but Congress had mandated the common-sense proposition that they are not to become masters of reality.

The Company contends that its general intelligence tests are specifically permitted by § 703(h) of the Act.[8] That section authorizes the use of "any professionally developed ability test" that is not "designed, intended, *or used* to discriminate because of race . . . ." (Emphasis added.)

The Equal Employment Opportunity Commission, having enforcement responsibility, has issued guidelines interpreting § 703(h) to permit only the use of job-related tests.[9] The administrative interpretation of the Act by the enforcing agency is entitled to great deference. See, *e. g., United States* v. *City of Chicago,* —U.S.— (No. 386, O. T. 1970); *Udall* v. *Tallman,* 380 U.S. 1 (1965); *Power Reactor Co.* v. *Electricians,* 367 U.S. 396 (1961). Since the Act and its legislative history support the Commission's construction, this affords good reason to treat the Guidelines as expressing the will of Congress.

Section 703(h) was not contained in the House version of the Civil Rights Act but was added in the Senate during extended debate. For a period, debate revolved around claims that the bill as proposed would prohibit all testing and force employers to hire unqualified persons simply

---

[8] Section 703(h) applies only to tests. It has no applicability to the high school diploma requirements.

[9] EEOC Guidelines on Employment Testing Procedures, issued August 24, 1966, provide:
"The Commission accordingly interprets 'profesionally developed ability test' to mean a test which fairly measures the knowledge or skills required by the particular job or class of jobs which the applicant seeks, or which fairly affords the employer a chance to measure the applicant's ability to perform a particular job or class of jobs. The fact that a test was prepared by an individual or organization claiming expertise in test preparation does not, without more, justify its use within the meaning of Title VII." The EEOC position has been elaborated in the new Guidelines on Employee Selection Procedures, 35 Fed. Reg. 12333 (August 1, 1970). These Guidelines demand that employers using tests, have available "data demonstrating that the test is predictive of or significantly correlated with important elements of work behavior comprising or relevant to the job or jobs for which Guidelines are being evaluated." *Id.* at § 1607.4(c).

because they were part of a group formerly subject to job discrimination.[10] Proponents of Title VII sought throughout the debate to assure the critics that the Act would have no effect on job-related tests. Senators Case of New Jersey and Clark of Pennsylvania, comanagers of the bill on the Senate floor, issued a memorandum explaining that the proposed Title VII "expressly protects the employer's right to insist that any prospective applicant, Negro or white, *must meet the applicable job qualifications.* Indeed, the very purpose of Title VII is to promote hiring on the basis of job qualifications, rather than on the basis of race or color." (Emphasis added.) 110 Cong. Rec. 7247.[11] Despite these assurances, Senator Tower of Texas introduced an amendment authorizing "professionally developed ability tests." Proponents of Title VII opposed the amendment because, as written, it would permit an employer to give any test, "whether it was a good test or not, so long as it was professionally designed. Discrimination could actually exist under the guise of compliance with the statute." Remarks of Senator Case, 110 Cong. Rec. 13504.

The amendment was defeated and two days later Senator Tower offered a substitute amendment which was adopted verbatim and is now the testing provision of § 703(h). Speaking for the supporters of Title VII, Senator Humphrey, who had vigorously opposed the first amendment, endorsed the substitute amendment, stating: "Senators on both sides of the aisle who were deeply interested in Title VII have examined the text of this amendment and have found it to be in accord with the intent and purpose of that title." 110 Cong. Rec. 13724. The amendment was then adopted.[12] From the sum of the legislative history relevant in this

---

[10] The congressional discussion was prompted by the decision of a hearing examiner for the Illinois Fair Employment Commission in *Myart* v. *Motorola Co.* (The decision is reprinted at 110 Cong. Rec. 5662 (1964).) That case suggested that standardized tests on which whites performed better than Negroes could never be used. The decision was taken to mean that such tests could never be justified even if the needs of the business required them. A number of Senators feared that Title VII might produce a similar result. See remarks of Senators Ervin, 110 Cong. Rec. 5614-5616; Smathers, *id.*, at 5999-6000; Holland, *id.*, at 7012-7013; Hill, *id.*, at 8447; Tower, *id.*, at 9024; Talmadge, *id.*, at 9025-9026; Fulbright, *id.*, at 9599-9690; and Ellender, *ibid.*

[11] The Court of Appeals majority, in finding no requirement in Title VII that employment tests be job-related, relied in part on a quotation from an earlier Clark-Case interpretative memorandum addressed to the question of the constitutionality of Title VII. The Senators said in that memorandum:
"There is no requirement in Title VII that employers abandon bona fide qualification tests where, because of differences in background and education, members of some groups are able to perform better on these tests than members of other groups. An employer may set his qualifications as high as he likes, he may test to determine which applicants have these qualifications, and he may hire, assign, and promote on the basis of test performance." 110 Cong. Rec. 7213.
However, nothing there stated conflicts with the later memorandum dealing specifically with the debate over employer testing. 110 Cong. Rec. 7247 (quoted from in the text above), in which Senators Clark and Case explained that tests which measure "applicable job qualifications" are permissible under Title VII. In the earlier memorandum Clark and Case assured the Senate that employers were not to be prohibited from using tests that determine *qualifications.* Certainly a reasonable interpretation of what the Senators meant, in light of the subsequent memorandum directed specifically at employer testing, was that nothing in the Act prevents employers from requiring that applicants be fit for the job.

[12] Senator Tower's original amendment provided in part that a test would be permis-

case, the conclusion is inescapable that the EEOC's construction of § 703(h) to require that employment tests be job-related comports with congressional intent.

Nothing in the Act precludes the use of testing or measuring procedures; obviously they are useful. What Congress has forbidden is giving these devices and mechanisms controlling force unless they are demonstrably a reasonable measure of job performance. Congress has not commanded that the less qualified be preferred over the better qualified simply because of minority origins. Far from disparaging job qualifications as such, Congress has made such qualifications the controlling factor, so that race, religion, nationality, and sex become irrelevant. What Congress has commanded is that any tests used must measure the person for the job and not the person in the abstract.

The judgment of the Court of Appeals is, as to that portion of the judgment appealed from, reversed.

MR. JUSTICE BRENNAN took no part in the consideration or decision of this case.

## STRANGERS IN PARADISE: *GRIGGS* V. *DUKE POWER CO.* AND THE CONCEPT OF EMPLOYMENT DISCRIMINATION*

*71 Michigan Law Review 59 (1972)*

Alfred W. Blumrosen

. . .

[*Griggs* v. *Duke Power*] provided the first occasion for the high court to determine the nature and scope of the prohibition on racial discrimination in employment under the Civil Rights Act of 1964. Although issued without fanfare, *Griggs* is in the tradition of the great cases of constitutional and tort law which announce and apply fundamental legal principles to the resolution of basic and difficult problems of human relationships. The decision has poured decisive content into a previously vacuous conception of human rights. It shapes the statutory concept of "discrimination" in light of the social and economic facts of our society. The decision restricts employers from translating the social and economic subjugation of minorities into a denial of employment opportunity, and makes practical a prompt and effective nationwide assault by both administrative agencies and the courts on patterns of discrimination.

---

sible "if . . . in the case of any individual who is an employee of such employer, such test is designed to determine or predict whether such individual is suitable or trainable with respect to his employment in the particular business or enterprise involved. . . ." 110 Cong. Rec. 13492. This language indicates that Senator Tower's aim was simply to make certain that job-related tests would be permitted. The opposition to the amendment was based on its loose wording which the proponents of Title VII feared would be susceptible to misinterpretation. The final amendment, which was acceptable to all sides, could hardly have required less of a job relation than the first.

The assumption underlying *Griggs* is that the Civil Rights Act of 1964 protects the interests of minority groups and their members in securing and improving employment opportunities. *Griggs* views discrimination not only as an isolated act by an aberrant individual wrongdoer that affects only an individual complainant, but also as the operation of industrial-relations systems that adversely affect minority group members. Title VII law thus focuses on the harm to both the group and the individual.

*Griggs* redefines discrimination in terms of consequence rather than motive, effect rather than purpose. This definition is new to the field of employment discrimination, in which a subjective test had previously been used. The Court applied this new definition to invalidate hiring standards based upon education and testing, and in the process gave strong legal sanction to the EEOC's statutory interpretations.

Significantly, the *Griggs* opinion was written by Chief Justice Burger, and concurred in by seven of his brethren (Justice Brennan absented himself from the case). The case was decided during a time in which the Supreme Court appeared to be shifting toward a cautious approach to constitutional issues. Yet, it is a sensitive, liberal interpretation of Title VII. It has the imprimatur of permanence and may become a symbol of the Burger Court's concern for equal opportunity. Although the Court may take a more cautious approach to constitutional rights of minorities, *Griggs* makes clear that sympathetic interpretation of *statutory* rights is the order of the day. This dichotomy accords with the notion that the legislature rather than the courts should be the prime policy maker in this field. The recognition of legislative suzerainty in this area should be, in the long run, desirable. At this point in our history, many important civil rights have received statutory recognition from Congress. It is more important, today, that we be concerned about the broad and practical implementation of these rights than about their constitutional foundation. A judge may feel more comfortable in rendering a liberal interpretation of a statute than in interpreting the Constitution since a decision based on the Constitution is less easily revised.

## McDONNELL DOUGLAS CORP. v. GREEN

*Supreme Court of the United States, 1973*
*411 U.S. 792, 5 FEP Cases 965*

MR. JUSTICE POWELL delivered the opinion of the Court.

The case before us raises significant questions as to the proper order and nature of proof in actions under Title VII of the Civil Rights Act of 1964.

. . .

In remanding, the Court of Appeals attempted to set forth standards to govern the consideration of respondent's claim. The majority noted that respondent had established a prima facie case of racial discrimination; that petitioner's refusal to rehire respondent rested on "subjective" criteria which carried little weight in rebutting charges of discrimination; that though respondent's participation in the unlawful demonstrations might indicate a lack of a responsible attitude toward performing work for that employer, respondent should be given the opportunity to demonstrate that petitioner's reasons for refusing to rehire him were merely pretextual.[7] In order to clarify the standards governing the disposition of an action challenging employment discrimination, we granted certiorari, 409 U.S. 1036 (1972).

. . .

II. The critical issue before us concerns the order and allocation of proof in a private, single-plaintiff action challenging employment discrimination. The language of Title VII makes plain the purpose of Congress to assure equality of employment opportunities and to eliminate those discriminatory practices and devices which have fostered racially stratified job environments to the disadvantage of minority citizens. . . .

"Congress did not intend Title VII, however, to guarantee a job to every person regardless of qualifications. In short, the Act does not command that any person be hired simply because he was formerly the subject of discrimination, or because he is a member of a minority group. Discriminatory preference for any group, minority or majority, is precisely and only what Congress has proscribed. What is required by Congress is the removal of artificial, arbitrary, and unnecessary barriers to employment when the barriers operate invidiously to discriminate on the basis of racial or other impermissible classification." *Id.,* at 430, 3 FEP Cases at 177.

There are societal as well as personal interests on both sides of this equation. The broad, overriding interest shared by employer, employee, and consumer, is efficient and trustworthy workmanship assured through fair and racially neutral employment and personnel decisions. In the implementation of such decisions, it is abundantly clear that Title VII tolerates no racial discrimination, subtle or otherwise.

In this case respondent, the complainant below, charges that he was denied employment "because of his involvement in civil rights activities" and "because of his race and color." [11] Petitioner denied discrimination of any kind, asserting that its failure to re-employ respondent was based upon and justified by his participation in the unlawful conduct against it. Thus, the issue at the trial on remand is framed by those opposing factual contentions. The two opinions of the Court of Appeals and the several opinions of the three judges of the court attempted, with a notable lack of harmony, to state the applicable rules as to burden of proof and

---

[7] [Footnotes numbered as in original.—Ed.] All references here are to Part V of the revised opinion of the Court of Appeals, 463 F.2d, at 352, which superseded Part V of the Court's initial opinion with respect to the order and nature of proof.

[11] The respondent initially charged petitioner in his complaint filed April 15, 1968 with discrimination because of his "involvement in civil rights activities." Appendix 7, 8. In his amended complaint, filed March 20, 1969, plaintiff broadened his charge to include denial of employment because of race in violation of § 703(a)(1). Appendix 27.

how this shifts upon the making of a prima facie case.[12] We now address this problem.

The complainant in a Title VII trial must carry the initial burden under the statute of establishing a prima facie case of racial discrimination. This may be done by showing (i) that he belongs to a racial minority; (ii) that he applied and was qualified for a job for which the employer was seeking applicants; (iii) that, despite his qualifications, he was rejected; and (iv) that, after his rejection, the position remained open and the employer continued to seek applicants from persons of complainant's qualifications.[13] In the instant case, we agree with the Court of Appeals that respondent proved a prima facie case. — F.2d, at —. Petitioner sought mechanics, respondent's trade, and continued to do so after respondent's rejection. Petitioner, moreover, does not dispute respondent's qualifications[14] and acknowledges that his past work performance in petitioner's employ was "satisfactory."[15]

The burden then must shift to the employer to articulate some legitimate, nondiscriminatory reason for respondent's rejection. We need not attempt in the instant case to detail every matter which fairly could be recognized as a reasonable basis for a refusal to hire. Here petitioner has assigned respondent's participation in unlawful conduct against it as the cause for his rejection. We think that this suffices to discharge petitioner's burden of proof at this stage and to meet respondent's prima facie case of discrimination.

The Court of Appeals intimated, however, that petitioner's stated reason for refusing to rehire respondent was a "subjective" rather than objective criterion which "carries little weight in rebutting charges of discrimination," — F.2d, at —, 5 FEP Cases, at 178. This was among the statements which caused the dissenting judge to read the opinion as taking "the position that such unlawful acts as Green committed against McDonnell would not legally entitle McDonnell to refuse to rehire him, even though no racial motivation was involved. . . ." F.2d, at —, 5 FEP Cases, at 180. Regardless of whether this was the intended import of the opinion, we think the court below seriously under-estimated the rebuttal

[12] See original opinion of the majority of panel which heard the case, 463 F. 2d, at 338; the concurring opinion of Judge Lay, id., at 344; the first opinion of Judge Johnsen, dissenting in part, id., at 346; the revised opinion of the majority, id., at 352; and the supplemental dissent of Judge Johnsen, id., at 353. A petition for rehearing en banc was denied by an evenly divided Court of Appeals.

[13] The facts necessarily will vary in Title VII cases, and the specification above of the prima facie proof required from respondent is not necessarily applicable in every respect to differing factual situations.

[14] We note that the issue of what may properly be used to test qualifications for employment is not present in this case. Where employers have instituted employment tests and qualifications with an exclusionary effect on minority applicants, such requirements must be "shown to bear a demonstrable relationship to successful performance of the jobs" for which they were used, Griggs v. Duke Power Co., 401 U. S. 424, 431 (1971). Castro v. Beecher, 459 F. 2d 725 (CA1 1972); Chance v. Board of Examiners, 458 F. 2d 1167 (CA2 1972).

[15] Tr. of Oral Arg. 3; 463 F.2d, at 353.

weight to which petitioner's reasons were entitled. Respondent admittedly had taken part in a carefully planned "stall-in," designed to tie up access and egress to petitioner's plant at a peak traffic hour.[16] Nothing in Title VII compels an employer to absolve and rehire one who has engaged in such deliberate, unlawful activity against it.[17] In upholding, under the National Labor Relations Act, the discharge of employees who had seized and forcibly retained an employer's factory buildings in an illegal sit-down strike, the Court noted pertinently:

"We are unable to conclude that Congress intended to compel employers to retain persons in their employ regardless of their unlawful conduct—to invest those who go on strike with an immunity from discharge for acts of trespass or violence against the employer's property. . . . Apart from the question of the constitutional validity of an enactment of that sort, it is enough to say that such a legislative intention should be found in some definite and unmistakable expression." *NLRB v. Fansteel Corp.,* 306 U.S. 240, 255, 4 LRRM 515, 519 (1939).

Petitioner's reason for rejection thus suffices to meet the prima facie case, but the inquiry must not end here. While Title VII does not, without more, compel rehiring of respondent, neither does it permit petitioner to use respondent's conduct as a pretext for the sort of discrimination prohibited by § 703(a)(1). On remand, respondent must, as the Court of Appeals recognized, be afforded a fair opportunity to show that petitioner's stated reason for respondent's rejection was in fact pretext. Especially relevant to such a showing would be evidence that white employees involved in acts against petitioner of comparable seriousness to the "stall-in" were nevertheless retained or rehired. Petitioner may justifiably refuse to rehire one who was engaged in unlawful, disruptive acts against it, but only if this criterion is applied alike to members of all races.

Other evidence that may be relevant to any showing of pretextuality includes facts as to the petitioner's treatment of respondent during his prior term of employment, petitioner's reaction, if any, to respondent's legitimate civil rights activities, and petitioner's general policy and practice with respect to minority employment.[18] On the latter point, statistics

---

[16] The trial judge noted that no personal injury or property damage resulted from the "stall-in" due "solely to the fact that law enforcement officials had obtained notice in advance of plaintiff's [here respondent's] demonstration and were at the scene to remove plaintiff's car from the highway." 318 F. Supp. 846, 851.

[17] The unlawful activity in this case was directed specifically against petitioner. We need not consider or decide here whether, or under what circumstances, unlawful activity not directed against the particular employer may be a legitimate justification for refusing to hire.

[18] We are aware that some of the above factors were, indeed, considered by the District Judge in finding under § 704(a), that "defendant's [here petitioner's] reasons for refusing to rehire the plaintiff were motivated solely and simply by the plaintiff's participation in the 'stall in' and 'lock in' demonstrations." 318 F. Supp., at 850. We do not intimate that this finding must be overturned after consideration on remand of respondent's § 703(a)(1) claim. We do, however, insist that respondent under § 703(a)(1) must be given a full and fair opportunity to demonstrate by competent

as to petitioner's employment policy and practice may be helpful to a determination of whether petitioner's refusal to rehire respondent in this case conformed to a general pattern of discrimination against blacks. *Jones* v. *Lee Way Motor Freight, Inc.*, 421 F.2d 245, 2 FEP Cases 895 (CA 10 1970); Blumrosen, *Strangers in Paradise: Griggs v. Duke Power Co., and the Concept of Employment Discrimination*, 71 MICH. L. REV. 59, 91-94 (1972).[19] In short, on the retrial respondent must be given a full and fair opportunity to demonstrate by competent evidence that the presumptively valid reasons for his rejection were in fact a coverup for a racially discriminatory decision.

The court below appeared to rely upon *Griggs* v. *Duke Power Co., supra*, in which the Court stated: "If an employment practice which operates to exclude Negroes cannot be shown to be related to job performance, the practice is prohibited." *Id.*, at 431, 3 FEP Cases at 178.[20] But *Griggs* differs from the instant case in important respects. It dealt with standardized testing devices which, however, neutral on their face, operated to exclude many blacks who were capable of performing effectively in the desired positions. *Griggs* was rightly concerned that childhood deficiencies in the education and background of minority citizens, resulting from forces beyond their control, not be allowed to work a cumulative and invidious burden on such citizens for the remainder of their lives. *Id.*, at 430. Respondent, however, appears in different clothing. He had engaged in a seriously disruptive act against the very one from whom he now seeks employment. And petitioner does not seek his exclusion on the basis of a testing device which overstates what is necessary for competent performance, or through some sweeping disqualification of all those with any past record of unlawful behavior, however remote, insubstantial or unrelated to applicant's personal qualifications as an employee. Petitioner assertedly rejected respondent for unlawful conduct against it and in the absence of proof of pretextual or discriminatory application of such a reason, this cannot be thought the kind of "artificial, arbitrary, and unnecessary barrier to employment" which the Court found to be the intention of Congress to remove. *Griggs*, p. 431.

III.  In sum, respondent should have been allowed to amend his complaint to include a claim under § 703(a)(1). If the evidence on retrial is substantially in accord with that before us in this case, we think that respondent carried his burden of establishing a prima facie case of racial discrimination and that petitioner successfully rebutted that case. But

---

evidence that whatever the stated reasons for his rejection, the decision was in reality racially premised.

[19] The District Court may, for example, determine, after reasonable discovery that "the [racial] composition of defendant's labor force is itself reflective of restrictive or exclusionary practices." See Blumrosen, *supra*, at 92. We caution that such general determinations, while helpful, may not be in and of themselves controlling as to an individualized hiring decision, particularly in the presence of an otherwise justifiable reason for refusing to rehire. See generally *United States* v. *Bethlehem Steel Corp.*, 312 F. Supp. 977, 992 (WDNY 1970), *order modified*, 446 F. 2d 652 (CA2 1971). Blumrosen, *supra*, n. 19, at 93.

[20] See 463 F. 2d, at 352.

this does not end the matter. On retrial respondent must be afforded a fair opportunity to demonstrate that petitioner's assigned reason for refusing to re-employ was pretextual or discriminatory in its application. If the District Judge so finds, he must order a prompt and appropriate remedy. In the absence of such a finding, petitioner's refusal to rehire must stand.

The case is hereby remanded to the District Court for reconsideration in accordance with this opinion.

## McDONALD v. SANTE FE TRAIL TRANSPORTATION CO.

*Supreme Court of the United States, 1976*
*427 U.S. 273, 12 FEP Cases 1577*

MR. JUSTICE MARSHALL delivered the opinion of the Court.

Petitioners, L. N. McDonald and Raymond L. Laird, brought this action in the United States District Court for the Southern District of Texas seeking relief against Santa Fe Trail Transportation Co. (Santa Fe) and International Brotherhood of Teamsters Local 988 (Local 988), which represented Santa Fe's Houston employees, for alleged violations of the Civil Rights Act of 1866, 42 U.S.C. § 1981, and of Title VII of the Civil Rights Act of 1964, 42 U.S.C. § 2000e *et seq.,* in connection with their discharge from Santa Fe's employment. The District Court dismissed the complaint on the pleadings. The Court of Appeals for the Fifth Circuit affirmed. In determining whether the decisions of these courts were correct, we must decide, first, whether a complaint alleging that white employees charged with misappropriating property from their employer were dismissed from employment, while a black employee similarly charged was not dismissed, states a claim under Title VII. Second, we must decide whether § 1981, which provides that "[a]ll persons . . . shall have the same right . . . to make and enforce contracts . . . as is enjoyed by white citizens . . ." affords protection from racial discrimination in private employment to white persons as well as nonwhites.

I

Because the District Court dismissed this case on the pleadings, we take as true the material facts alleged in petitioners' complaint. . . . On September 26, 1970, petitioners, both white, and Charles Jackson, a Negro employee of Santa Fe, were jointly and severally charged with misappropriating 60 one-gallon cans of antifreeze which was part of a shipment Santa Fe was carrying for one of its customers. Six days later, petitioners were fired by Santa Fe, while Jackson was retained. A grievance was promptly filed with Local 988, pursuant to the collective-bargaining agreement between the two respondents, but grievance proceedings secured no relief. The following April, complaints were filed with the Equal Employment Opportunity Commission (EEOC) charging that

Santa Fe had discriminated against both petitioners on the basis of their race in firing them, and that Local 988 had discriminated against McDonald on the basis of his race in failing properly to represent his interests in the grievance proceedings, all in violation of Title VII of the Civil Rights Act of 1964. Agency process proved equally unavailing for petitioners, however, and the EEOC notified them in July 1971 of their right under the Act to initiate a civil action in district court within 30 days. This suit followed, petitioners joining their § 1981 claim to their Title VII allegations.

. . .

## II

Title VII of the Civil Rights Act of 1964 prohibits the discharge of "any individual" because of "such individual's race," § 703(a)(1), 42 U.S.C. § 2000e–2(a)(1). Its terms are not limited to discrimination against members of any particular race. Thus, although we were not there confronted with racial discrimination against whites, we described the Act in *Griggs* v. *Duke Power Co.*, 401 U.S. 424, 431, 91 S.Ct. 849, 853, 28 L.Ed.2d 158 (1971), as prohibiting "[d]iscriminatory preference for *any* [racial] group, *minority* or *majority*" (emphasis added). Similarly the EEOC, whose interpretations are entitled to great deference, *id.*, at 433–34, 91 S.Ct., at 854–55, has consistently interpreted Title VII to proscribe racial discrimination in private employment against whites on the same terms as racial discrimination against nonwhites, holding that to proceed otherwise would

"constitute a derogation of the Commission's Congressional mandate to eliminate all practices which operate to disadvantage the employment opportunities of any group protected by Title VII, including Caucasians." EEOC Decision No. 74–31, 7 FEP 1326, 1328, CCH EEOC Decisions ¶ 6404, p. 4084 (1973).

This conclusion is in accord with uncontradicted legislative history to the effect that Title VII was intended to "cover white men and white women and all Americans," 110 Cong. Rec. 2578 (1964) (remarks of Rep. Celler), and create an "obligation not to discriminate against whites," *id.*, at 7218 (memorandum of Sen. Clark). See also *id.*, at 7213 (memorandum of Sens. Clark and Case); *id.*, at 8912 (remarks of Sen. Williams). We therefore hold today that Title VII prohibits racial discrimination against the white petitioners in this case upon the same standards as would be applicable were they Negroes and Jackson white.

. . .

## III

Title 42 U.S.C. § 1981 provides in pertinent part: "All persons within the jurisdiction of the United States shall have the same right in every State and Territory to make and enforce contracts . . . as is enjoyed by white citizens. . . ." [15] We have previously held, where discrimination against Negroes was in question, that § 1981 affords a federal remedy against discrimination in private employment on the basis of race, and respondents do not contend otherwise. *Johnson* v. *Railway Express Agency,* 421 U.S. 454, 459–460, 95 S.Ct. 1716, 1719–1720, 44 L.Ed.2d 295 (1975). See also *Runyon* v. *McCrary,* 427 U.S. 160, 168, 96 S.Ct. 2586, 2593, 49 L.Ed.2d 415; *Jones* v. *Alfred H. Mayer Co.,* 392 U.S. 409, 88 S.Ct. 2186, 20 L.Ed.2d 1189 (1968). The question here is whether § 1981 prohibits racial discrimination in private employment against whites as well as nonwhites.[16]

While neither of the courts below elaborated its reasons for not applying § 1981 to racial discrimination against white persons, respondents suggest two lines of argument to support that judgment. First, they argue that by operation of the phrase "as is enjoyed by white citizens," § 1981 unambiguously limits itself to the protection of nonwhite persons against racial discrimination. Second, they contend that such a reading is consistent with the legislative history of the provision, which derives its operative language from § 1 of the Civil Rights Act of 1866, Act of Apr, 9, 1866, c. 31, § 1, 14 Stat. 27. See *Runyon* v. *McCrary, supra,* 427 U.S., at 168–170, n. 8, 96 S.Ct., at 2593; *Tillman* v. *Wheaton-Haven Recreation Assn.,* 410 U.S. 431, 439, 93 S.Ct. 1090, 1094, 35 L.Ed.2d 403 (1973). The 1866 statute, they assert, was concerned predominantly with assuring specified civil rights to the former Negro slaves freed by virtue of the Thirteenth Amendment, and not at all with protecting the corresponding civil rights of white persons.

We find neither argument persuasive. Rather, our examination of the language and history of § 1981 convinces us that § 1981 is applicable to racial discrimination in private employment against white persons.

First, we cannot accept the view that the terms of § 1981 exclude its application to racial discrimination against white persons. On the contrary, the statute explicitly applies to *"all* persons" (emphasis added), including white persons. See, *e.g., United States* v. *Wong Kim Ark,* 169 U.S. 649, 675–676, 18 S.Ct. 456, 467–468, 42 L.Ed. 890 (1898). While a mechanical reading of the phrase "as is enjoyed by white citizens" would seem to lend support to respondents' reading of the statute, we have previously described this phrase simply as emphasizing "the racial character of the rights being protected," *Georgia* v. *Rachel,* 384 U.S. 780, 791, 86 S.Ct. 1783, 1789, 16 L.Ed.2d 925 (1966). In any event, whatever ambiguity there may be in the language of § 1981, see cases cited *supra* at 2581 n. 16, is clarified by an examination of the legislative history of §

---

[15] [Footnotes numbered as in original.—Ed.] The statute provides in full:
"All persons within the jurisdiction of the United States shall have the same right in every State and Territory to make and enforce contracts, to sue, be parties, give evidence, and to the full and equal benefit of all laws and proceedings for the security of persons and property as is enjoyed by white citizens, and shall be subject to like punishment, pains, penalties, taxes, licenses, and exactions of every kind, and to no other."

[16] The lower federal courts have divided on the applicability of § 1981 to racial discrimination against white persons. [Citations omitted.]

1981's language as it was originally forged in the Civil Rights Act of 1866. *Tidewater Oil Co.* v. *United States,* 409 U.S. 151, 157, 93 S.Ct. 408, 412, 34 L.Ed.2d 375 (1972); *Immigration Service* v. *Errico,* 385 U.S. 214, 218, 87 S.Ct. 473, 476, 17 L.Ed.2d 318 (1966). It is to this subject that we now turn. [Discussion of legislative history omitted.]

This cumulative evidence of congressional intent makes clear, we think, that the 1866 statute, designed to protect the "same right . . . to make and enforce contracts" of "citizens of every race and color" was not understood or intended to be reduced by Representative Wilson's amendment, or any other provision, to the protection solely of nonwhites. Rather, the Act was meant, by its broad terms, to proscribe discrimination in the making or enforcement of contracts against, or in favor of, any race. Unlikely as it might have appeared in 1866 that white citizens would encounter substantial racial discrimination of the sort proscribed under the Act, the statutory structure and legislative history persuade us that the 39th Congress was intent upon establishing in the federal law a broader principle than would have been necessary simply to meet the particular and immediate plight of the newly freed Negro slaves. And while the statutory language has been somewhat streamlined in re-enactment and codification, there is no indication that § 1981 is intended to provide any less than the Congress enacted in 1866 regarding racial discrimination against white persons. *Runyon* v. *McCrary,* 427 U.S. 168, and n. 8, 96 S.Ct. 2586, 49 L.Ed.2d 415. Thus, we conclude that the District Court erred in dismissing petitioners' claims under § 1981 on the ground that the protections of that provision are unavailable to white persons.

The judgment of the Court of Appeals for the Fifth Circuit is reversed, and the case is remanded for further proceedings consistent with this opinion.

*So ordered.*

Mr. Justice White and Mr. Justice Rehnquist join Parts I and II of the Court's opinion, but for the reasons stated in Mr. Justice White's dissenting opinion in *Runyon* v. *McCrary,* 427 U.S. 160, 192, 96 S.Ct. 2586, 2604, 49 L.Ed.2d 415, cannot join Part III since they do not agree that § 1981 is applicable in this case. To that extent they dissent.

## NOTE

Title 42 U.S.C. § 1983 provides:

"Civil action for deprivation of rights. Every person who, under color of any statute, ordinance, regulation, custom, or usage, of any State or Territory, subjects, or causes to be subjected, any citizen of the United States or other persons within the jurisdiction thereof to the deprivation of any rights, privileges or immunities secured by the Constitution laws, shall be liable to the person injured in an action of law, suit in equity, or other proper proceedings for redress."

In *Monroe* v. *Pape,* 365 U.S. 167 (1961), the Supreme Court held that municipalities were not "persons" under the above statute. In *Monell* v. *Department of Social Services of the City of New York*, 436 U.S. 658 (1978), the Court overruled *Monroe* v. *Pape*. The Court made plain, however, that a municipality could not be held liable on a respondeat superior theory solely because of acts of its employees, but only where the action of the municipality "that is alleged to be unconstitutional implements or executes a policy statement, ordinance, regulation, or decision officially adopted and promulgated by that body's officers."

In *Novotny* v. *Great American Federal Savings & Loan Ass'n.*, 584 F.2d 1235, 17 FEP 1252 (1978), *cert.* granted, 47 USLW 3449 (1979), a male employee claimed that he was discharged because his actions and advocacy hindered a conspiracy among the corporation's directors and officers to deprive women of equal employment rights. The cause of action was sustained under 42 U.S.C. § 1985 (3) which provides:

"Conspiracy to interfere with civil rights. . . . If two or more persons in any State or Territory conspire or go in disguise on the highway or on the premises of another, for the purpose of depriving, either directly or indirectly, any person or class of persons of the equal protection of the laws, or of equal privileges and immunities under the laws; . . . the party so injured or deprived may have an action for the recovery of damages, occasioned by such injury or deprivation, against any one or more of the conspirators."

The court of appeals' decision sustaining the cause of action was reversed by the Supreme Court on June 11, 1979, 47 USLW 4681.

(2) *Use of Statistics*

## THE NUMBERS GAME IS THE ONLY GAME IN TOWN*

*20 Howard Law Journal 374 (1977)*

David Copus**

The guarantee of equal employment opportunity for all regardless of sex, race, color, religion or national origin is a national goal of the "highest priority." No person "should be deprived of the right to earn his industrial way on free and equal terms." This reasoning is basic to our heritage: "[t]he ethic which permeates the American dream is that a person may advance as far as his talents and his merit will carry him."

To attain the goal of equal employment there have been a number of federal enactments, the most comprehensive and far-reaching of which is Title VII of the Civil Rights Act of 1964, as amended. Section 703(a) of that Title provides that:

"It shall be an unlawful employment practice for an employer—(1) to fail or refuse to hire or to discharge an *individual*, or otherwise to

* Copyright © 1977 by Howard University. Used with permission.
** B.A., Northwestern University 1963; LL.B., Harvard University 1966. At the time this article was written, the author was Director of the Special Investigation and Conciliation Division of the EEOC.

discriminate against any *individual* with respect to his compensation, terms, conditions or pivileges of employment because of such *individual's* race, color, religion, sex, or national origin; or (2) to limit, segregate, or classify his employees in any way which would deprive or tend to deprive any *individual* of employment opportunities or otherwise adversely affect his status as an employee, because of such *individual's* race, color, religion, sex, or national origin."

While section 703(a) speaks in terms of *individuals,* the real problem of discrimination in employment is not one of isolated cases of bigotry directed toward particular persons. Most unlawful discrimination is the result of *institutionalized practices and policies,* such as testing procedures, subjective selection standards, sex-role stereotypes, or seniority rules, which systematically exclude women, Blacks, Asians, Spanish-surnamed and Native Americans from the work force or from certain job classifications.

The Senate Committee on Labor and Public Welfare, in its 1970 report recommending amendments to strengthen the enforcement of Title VII, said it could not "stress too much the importance of the 'pattern and practice' approach" to the problem of employment discrimination. The Committee outlined the reasons for this recommendation as follows:

"In 1964, employment discrimination tended to be viewed as a series of isolated and distinguishable events, for the most part due to ill-will on the part of some identifiable individual or organization. . . . Employment discrimination, as viewed today, is a far more complex and pervasive phenomenon. Experts familiar with the subject generally describe the problem in terms of 'systems' and 'effects' rather than simply intentional wrongs. . . . In short, the problem is one whose resolution in many instances requires not only expert assistance, but also the technical perception that a problem exists in the first place, and that the system complained of is unlawful."

Title VII is mainly concerned with these institutionalized policies and practices that deny women and minorities their rightful place in the employment process. Although Congress appears not to have understood this when it enacted Title VII in 1964, the Federal courts, particularly in the South, because of their extensive experience with other forms of discrimination, realized almost immediately that employment discrimination was inherently *class,* rather than *individual* discrimination:

"[A]lthough the actual effects of a discriminatory policy may . . . vary throughout the class, the existence of the discriminatory policy threatens the entire class. And whether the Damoclean threat of a racially discriminatory policy hangs over the racial class is a question of fact common to all members of a class." [9]

Thus, a basic body of Title VII law developed which holds that Title VII suits are "perforce" class actions and that an individual plaintiff is cloaked with the responsibilities of a "private attorney general" in seek-

---

[9] [Footnotes numbered as in original.—Ed.] *Hall* v. *Werthan Bag Corp.,* 251 F. Supp. 184, 186 (N.D. Tenn. 1966).

ing to eradicate systematic discrimination.[10] It is now generally agreed that "the objectives of Title VII can be obtained only by eliminating widespread, institutionalized discrimination" through private class actions or EEOC "pattern and practice" suits.[11]

This conclusion has important implications in terms of the evidence necessary to establish a Title VII violation. Proof of acts of individual overt discrimination would necessarily involve evidence relating primarily to the particular incident.[13] But proof of the discrimination inherent in institutionalized practices requires a much broader approach—an approach which relies almost exclusively on statistics. In the area of institutional discrimination, "statistics often tell much, and courts listen." [14]

### A. USE OF STATISTICS—GENERALLY

Statistical proofs have been widely used in jury, school, voting, and more recently in housing and age discrimination cases. These cases have relied primarily on the so-called *"prima facie* rule" or "rule of exclusion" which originated in 1881 in *Neal* v. *Delaware*.[20] Under this rule, the plaintiff is required to show a substantial disparity between the percentage which his or her class represents in the relevant population sample and the percentage which the class represents on the jury panel, in a given school, in the electorate, or in a given housing area.

Such a demonstration of a substantial statistical disparity constitutes a *prima facie* showing of unlawful exclusion and shifts the burden of proof to the defendant. This burden is a heavy one and cannot be over-

---

[10] See, e.g., *Jenkins* v. *United Gas Corp.,* 400 F.2d 28, 33 (5th Cir. 1968); *Oatis* v. *Crown Zellerbach,* 398 F.2d 496 (5th Cir. 1968); *Bowe* v. *Colgate-Palmolive Co.,* 416 F.2d 711 (7th Cir. 1969).

[11] Note, *Federal Employment Discrimination: Scope of Inquiry and the Class Action Under Title VII,* 22 U.C.L.A. L. REV. 1288 (1975). . . .

[13] Statistics, in some situations, can be used in Title VII cases involving primarily individual discrimination. The Supreme Court has outlined the manner in which statistics could be used to aid an individual's case. *McDonnell-Douglas Corp.* v. *Green,* 411 U.S. 792 (1973). . . . See also, Dorsaneo, *Statistical Evidence in Employment Discrimination Litigation: Selection of the Available Population, Problems and Proposals,* 29 Sw. L.J. 859, 861-864 (1975). Individual cases almost always depend on proof of individual acts of disparate treatment and the plaintiff has the initial burden of proving such different treatment. Frequently, this initial burden is difficult to sustain because statistics are of little help in identifying whether any particular isolated historical event was discriminatory. Note, *Beyond the Prima Facie Case in Employment Discrimination Law: Statistical Proofs and Rebuttal,* 89 HARV. L. REV. 387, 417 n.142 (1975). As the discussion *infra* indicates, plaintiffs in a class action suit base their case on statistical evidence of disparate impact and, consequently, have a much lighter burden of proof. Hence, the burden of proof standards laid down in *McDonnell-Douglas Corp.* v. *Green,* are *not* applicable in cases challenging patterns and practices of discrimination. . . .

[14] *State of Alabama* v. *United States,* 304 F.2d 583, 586 (5th Cir. 1962), aff'd *per curiam,* 371 U.S. 37 (1962). . . .

[20] 103 U.S. 397 (1880). In *Neal* the Supreme Court stated the principle as follows: "The showing thus made, including as it did, the fact that (so generally known that the court felt obliged to take judicial notice of it) that no colored citizen had ever been summoned as a juror in the courts of the state—although its colored population exceeded twenty-six thousand . . . in a total population of less than one hundred and fifty thousand—presented a *prima facie* case of denial, by the officers charged with the selection of grand and petit jurors, of that equality of protection which has been secured by the Constitution and laws of the United States." 103 U.S. at 397.
. . .

come by "mere generalities" or "general assertions" of non-discrimination. In the face of statistics which "cry out 'discrimination' with unmistakeable clarity," only the most compelling evidence can rebut the presumption of discrimination.

The same principles of statistical proof, long used in jury, school, and voting cases have, quite naturally, been used in employment discrimination cases. As the Fifth Circuit has declared, "[W]e reject the district court's conclusion that statistics have a lesser role in employment discrimination cases than these other types of litigation. . . ."[23] Other Courts have agreed: "[T]he often-cited aphorism, 'statistics often tell much and Courts listen,' has particular application in Title VII cases."

The courts have approved the heavy reliance on statistics for three reasons. First, and most obviously, the one inevitable consequence of systematic discrimination is the consistent underrepresentation of females and minorities in jobs from which they have been excluded. Underrepresentation is the *inexorable* result of unlawful exclusion.[25] Second, statistics are frequently the best available evidence of employer or union discrimination. Discrimination "will seldom be admitted by any em-

---

[23] *Pettway* v. *American Cast Iron Pipe Co.*, 494 F.2d 211 n.41 (5th Cir. 1974). The Fifth Circuit had previously held that experience with statistical proofs in other types of discrimination cases "have led us to rely heavily in Title VII cases" on statistics. *Burns* v. *Thiokol*, 483 F.2d 300, 305 (5th Cir. 1973). Even earlier, the Fifth Circuit declared, " 'Figures speak and when they do, Courts listen.' " *Rowe* v. *General Motors Corp.*, 457 F.2d 348, 357 (5th Cir. 1972). See generally Note, *Employment Discrimination: Statistics and Preferences Under Title VII*, 59 VA. L. REV. 463 (1973); Montlack, *Using Statistical Evidence to Enforce the Laws Against Discrimination*, 32 CLEV. ST. L. REV. 259 (1973); Note, *The Supreme Court, 1974 Term*, 89 HARV. L. REV. 47, 395 (1975).

[25] It is an "indisputable proposition" that the "one necessary *consequence* of racial discrimination is racial imbalance. If the employer discriminates against Negroes on the basis of race, there will be no Negroes or very few." Fiss, *A Theory of Fair Employment Laws*, 38 U. CHI. L. REV. 235, 269 (1971); Fiss, *The Fate of an Idea Whose Time Has Come: Antidiscrimination Laws in the Second Decade After Brown v. Board of Education*, 41 U. CHI. L. REV. 742, 761 (1974).

Defendants frequently argue that § 703(j) of Title VII, 42 U.S.C. § 2000e-2(j) (1970), which prohibits "preferential treatment" on the basis of disparity between the race, sex or ethnic composition of an employer's jobs and the local community, also prohibits reliance on such disparities to establish a prima facie violation of Title VII or the imposition of numerical goals and timetables. Such arguments have been uniformly rejected. See, e.g., *Carter* v. *Gallagher*, 452 F.2d 315, 330 (8th Cir. 1972) (*en banc*), *cert. denied*, 406 U.S. 950 (1972); *Contractors Ass'n of Eastern Pennsylvania* v. *Shultz*, 442 F.2d 159 (3d Cir. 1971), *cert. denied*, 404 U.S. 854 (1971); *Davis* v. *County of Los Angeles*, 12 Empl. Prac. Dec. ¶ 11,219 (9th Cir. 1976). See also the Interpretive Memorandum, written by Senators Clark and Case, Floor Managers of the House Bill, which states:

"[T]he presence or absence of other members of the same minority group in the workforce may be a relevant factor in determining whether in a given case a decision to hire was based on race, color, etc. . . ." 110 CONG. REC. 7213 (April 8, 1964).

. . .

In addition, the legislative history of the 1972 amendments to Title VII is replete with arguments supporting the amendments based on statistical disparities. For example, Senator Javits urged the extension of Title VII to educational institutions because of "tremendous disproportion—the courts have held that that is a perfectly proper item of evidence—between the percentages of positions held by blacks and other minorities and the percentage which they represent in the population." LEGISLATIVE HISTORY OF THE EQUAL EMPLOYMENT OPPORTUNITY ACT OF 1972, at 1253. See also S. Rep. No. 92-415, 13-14 (1971).

ployer." In many cases, "the only available avenue of proof" is the use of statistics.

Third, Title VII is mainly concerned with the effect of employment systems, not the subjective motivation behind such systems. As the Supreme Court has declared, "good intent or absence of discriminatory intent does not redeem employment procedures" which "operate as 'built-in headwinds' " for females and minorities; "Congress directed the thrust of the Act to the *consequences* of employment practices, not simply the motivation." Statistics obviously play a critical role in evaluating the impact of a defendant's employment systems.

Hence it is not surprising that virtually every decision involving institutionalized discrimination has relied primarily on statistics. Only cases solely involving questions of law, such as an employer's obligation to make a reasonable accommodation to an employee's religious convictions, have not relied on statistics. The reliance on statistics has become so complete and developed so rapidly that the most "radical change" in antidiscrimination law since Title VII was passed has been the "legitimation of measuring compliance in terms of numbers."

## DOTHARD v. RAWLINSON

*Supreme Court of the United States, 1977*
*433 U.S. 321, 15 FEP Cases 10*

MR. JUSTICE STEWART delivered the opinion of the Court.

Appellee Dianne Rawlinson sought employment with the Alabama Board of Corrections as a prison guard, called in Alabama a "correctional counselor." After her application was rejected, she brought this class suit under Title VII of the Civil Rights Act of 1964, 78 Stat. 253, as amended, 42 U.S.C. § 2000e *et seq.* (1970 ed. and Supp. V), and under 42 U.S.C. § 1983, alleging that she had been denied employment because of her sex in violation of federal law. A three-judge Federal District Court for the Middle District of Alabama decided in her favor. *Mieth* v. *Dothard,* 418 F. Supp. 1169. We noted probable jurisdiction of this appeal from the District Court's judgment. 429 U.S. 976.[1]

### I

At the time she applied for a position as correctional counselor trainee, Rawlinson was a 22-year-old college graduate whose major course of study had been correctional psychology. She was refused employment because she failed to meet the minimum 120-pound weight requirement

---

[1] [Footnotes numbered as in original.—Ed.] The appellants sought to raise for the first time in their brief on the merits the claim that Congress acted unconstitutionally in extending Title VII's coverage to state governments. See the Equal Employment Opportunity Act of 1972, 86 Stat. 103, effective date, Mar. 24, 1972, 42 U. S. C. §§2000e (a), (b), (f), (h) (1970 ed., Supp. V). Not having been raised in the District Court, that issue is not before us. See *Adickes* v. *Kress & Co.,* 398 U. S. 144, 147 n. 2; *Irvine* v. *California,* 347 U. S. 128, 129.

established by an Alabama statute. The statute also establishes a height minimum of 5 feet, 2 inches.[2]

After her application was rejected because of her weight, Rawlinson filed a charge with the Equal Employment Opportunity Commission, and ultimately received a right-to-sue letter. She then filed a complaint in the District Court on behalf of herself and other similarly situated women, challenging the statutory height and weight minima as violative of Title VII and the Equal Protection Clause of the Fourteenth Amendment. A three-judge court was convened. . . .

## II

In enacting Title VII, Congress required "the removal of artificial, arbitrary, and unnecessary barriers to employment when the barriers operate invidiously to discriminate on the basis of racial or other impermissible classification." *Griggs* v. *Duke Power Co.,* 401 U.S. 424, 431. The District Court found that the minimum statutory height and weight requirements that applicants for employment as correctional counselors must meet constitute the sort of arbitrary barrier to equal employment opportunity that Title VII forbids. The appellants assert that the District Court erred both in finding that the height and weight standards discriminate against women, and in its refusal to find that, even if they do, these standards are justified as "job related."

## A

The gist of the claim that the statutory height and weight requirements discriminate against women does not involve an assertion of purposeful discriminatory motive. It is asserted, rather, that these facially neutral qualification standards work in fact disproportionately to exclude women from eligibility for employment by the Alabama Board of Corrections. We dealt in *Griggs* v. *Duke Power Co., supra,* and *Albemarle Paper Co.* v. *Moody,* 422 U.S. 405, with similar allegations that facially neutral employment standards disproportionately excluded Negroes from employment, and those cases guide our approach here.

Those cases make clear that to establish a prima facie case of discrimination, a plaintiff need only show that the facially neutral standards in question select applicants for hire in a significantly discriminatory pattern. Once it is thus shown that the employment standards are discriminatory in effect, the employer must meet "the burden of showing that any given requirement [has] . . . a manifest relationship to the em-

---

[2] The statute establishes minimum physical standards for all law enforcement officers. In pertinent part, it provides:

"(d) *Physical qualifications.*—The applicant shall be not less than five feet two inches nor more than six feet ten inches in height, shall weigh not less than 120 pounds nor more than 300 pounds and shall be certified by a licensed physician designated as satisfactory by the appointing authority as in good health and physically fit for the performance of his duties as a law-enforcement officer. The commission may for good cause shown permit variances from the physical qualifications prescribed in this subdivision." Ala. Code, Title 55, § 373 (109) (Supp. 1973).

ployment in question." *Griggs* v. *Duke Power Co., supra,* at 432. If the employer proves that the challenged requirements are job related, the plaintiff may then show that other selection devices without a similar discriminatory effect would also "serve the employer's legitimate interest in 'efficient and trustworthy workmanship.' " *Albemarle Paper Co.* v. *Moody, supra,* at 425, quoting *McDonnell Douglas Corp.* v. *Green,* 411 U.S. 792, 801.

Although women 14 years of age or older compose 52.75 percent of the Alabama population and 36.89 percent of its total labor force, they hold only 12.9 percent of its correctional counselor positions. In considering the effect of the minimum height and weight standards on this disparity in rate of hiring between the sexes, the District Court found that the 5′2″-requirement would operate to exclude 33.29 percent of the women in the United States between the ages of 18–79, while excluding only 1.28 percent of men between the same ages. The 120-pound weight restriction would exclude 22.29 percent of the women and 2.35 percent of the men in this age group. When the height and weight restrictions are combined, Alabama's statutory standards would exclude 41.13 percent of the female population while excluding less than 1 percent of the male population.[12] Accordingly, the District Court found that Rawlinson had made out a prima facie case of unlawful sex discrimination.

The appellants argue that a showing of disproportionate impact on women based on generalized national statistics should not suffice to establish a prima facie case. They point in particular to Rawlinson's failure to adduce comparative statistics concerning actual applicants for correctional counselor positions in Alabama. There is no requirement, however, that a statistical showing of disproportionate impact must always be based on analysis of the characteristics of actual applicants. See *Griggs* v. *Duke Power Co., supra,* at 430. The application process itself might not adequately reflect the actual potential applicant pool, since otherwise qualified people might be discouraged from applying because of a self-recognized inability to meet the very standards challenged as being discriminatory. See *Teamsters* v. *United States,* 431 U.S. 324, 365–67. A potential applicant could easily determine her height and weight and conclude that to make an application would be futile. Moreover, reliance on general population demographic data was not misplaced where there was no reason to suppose that physical height and weight characteristics of Alabama men and women differ markedly from those of the national population.

---

[12] Affirmatively stated, approximately 99.76% of the men and 58.87% of the women meet both these physical qualifications. From the separate statistics on height and weight of males it would appear that after adding the two together and allowing for some overlap the result would be to exclude between 2.35% and 3.63% of males from meeting Alabama's statutory height and weight minima. None of the parties has challenged the accuracy of the District Court's computations on this score, however, and the discrepancy is in any event insignificant in light of the gross disparity between the female and male exclusions. Even under revised computations the disparity would greatly exceed the 34% to 12% disparity that served to invalidate the high school diploma requirement in the *Griggs* case. 401 U.S., at 430.

For these reasons, we cannot say that the District Court was wrong in holding that the statutory height and weight standards had a discriminatory impact on women applicants. The plaintiffs in a case such as this are not required to exhaust every possible source of evidence, if the evidence actually presented on its face conspicuously demonstrates a job requirement's grossly discriminatory impact. If the employer discerns fallacies or deficiencies in the data offered by the plaintiff, he is free to adduce countervailing evidence of his own. In this case no such effort was made.

## B

We turn, therefore, to the appellants' argument that they have rebutted the prima facie case of discrimination by showing that the height and weight requirements are job related. These requirements, they say, have a relationship to strength, a sufficient but unspecified amount of which is essential to effective job performance as a correctional counselor. In the District Court, however, the appellants produced no evidence correlating the height and weight requirements with the requisite amount of strength thought essential to good job performance. Indeed, they failed to offer evidence of any kind in specific justification of the statutory standards.[14]

If the job-related quality that the appellants identify is bona fide, their purpose could be achieved by adopting and validating a test for applicants that measures strength directly.[15] Such a test, fairly administered, would fully satisfy the standards of Title VII because it would be one that "measure[s] the person for the job and not the person in the abstract." *Griggs* v. *Duke Power Co.,* 401 U.S., at 436. But nothing in the present record even approaches such a measurement.

For the reasons we have discussed, the District Court was not in error in holding that Title VII of the Civil Rights Act of 1964, as amended, prohibits application of the statutory height and weight requirements to Rawlinson and the class she represents.
. . .[24]

---

[14] In what is perhaps a variation on their constitutional challenge to the validity of Title VII itself, see n. 1, *supra,* the appellants contend that the establishment of the minimum height and weight standards by statute requires that they be given greater deference than is typically given private employer-established job qualifications. The relevant legislative history of the 1972 amendments extending Title VII to the States as employers does not, however, support such a result. Instead, Congress expressly indicated the intent that the same Title VII principles be applied to governmental and private employers alike. See H. R. Rep. No. 92–238, p. 17 (1971); S. Rep. No. 92–415, p. 10 (1971). See also *Schaeffer* v. *San Diego Yellow Cabs,* 462 F. 2d 1002 (CA9). Thus for both private and public employers, "[t]he touchstone is business necessity," *Griggs,* 401 U. S., at 431; a discriminatory employment practice must be shown to be necessary to safe and efficient job performance to survive a Title VII challenge.

[15] Cf. EEOC Guidelines on Employee Selection Procedures, 29 CFR § 1607 (1976). See also *Washington* v. *Davis,* 426 U. S. 229, 246–247; *Albemarle Paper Co.* v. *Moody,* 422 U. S. 405; *Officers for Justice* v. *Civil Service Comm'n,* 395 F. Supp. 378 (ND Cal.).

[24] The record shows, by contrast, that Alabama's minimum-security facilities, such as work-release centers, are recognized by their inmates as privileged confinement situations not to be lightly jeopardized by disobeying applicable rules of conduct. Inmates

MR. JUSTICE REHNQUIST, with whom THE CHIEF JUSTICE and MR. JUSTICE BLACKMUN join, concurring in the result and concurring in part. . . . While I . . . agree with the Court's conclusion in Part II of its opinion, holding that the District Court was "not in error" in holding the statutory height and weight requirements in this case to be invalidated by Title VII, . . . the issues with which that Part deals are bound to arise so frequently that I feel obliged to separately state the reasons for my agreement with its result. I view affirmance of the District Court in this respect as essentially dictated by the peculiarly limited factual and legal justifications offered below by appellants on behalf of the statutory requirements. For that reason, I do not believe—and do not read the Court's opinion as holding—that all or even many of the height and weight requirements imposed by States on applicants for a multitude of law enforcement agency jobs are pretermitted by today's decision.

I agree that the statistics relied upon in this case are sufficient, absent rebuttal, to sustain a finding of a prima facie violation of § 703(a)(2), in that they reveal a significant discrepancy between the numbers of men, as opposed to women, who are automatically disqualified by reason of the height and weight requirements. The fact that these statistics are national figures of height and weight, as opposed to statewide or pool-of-labor-force statistics, does not seem to me to require us to hold that the District Court erred as a matter of law in admitting them into evidence. See *Hamling* v. *United States,* 418 U.S. 87, 108, 124–125 (1974); cf. *Zenith Corp.* v. *Hazeltine,* 395 U.S. 100, 123–25 (1969). It is for the District Court, in the first instance, to determine whether these statistics appear sufficiently probative of the ultimate fact in issue—whether a given job qualification requirement has a disparate impact on some group protected by Title VII. *Hazelwood School Dist.* v. *United States* . . . ; see *Hamling* v. *United States, supra,* at 108, 124–125; *Mayor* v. *Educational Equality League,* 415 U.S. 605, 621 n. 20 (1974); see also *McAllister* v. *United States,* 348 U.S. 19 (1954); *United States* v. *Yellow Cab Co.,* 338 U.S. 338, 340–342 (1949). In making this determination, such statistics are to be considered in light of all other relevant facts and circumstances. Cf. *Teamsters* v. *United States,* 431 U.S. 324, 340 (1977). The statistics relied on here do not suffer from the obvious lack of relevancy of the statistics relied on by the District Court in *Hazelwood School Dist.* v. *United States.* . . . A reviewing court cannot say as a matter of law that they are irrelevant to the contested issue or so lacking in reliability as to be inadmissible.

If the defendants in a Title VII suit believe there to be any reason to discredit plaintiffs' statistics that does not appear on their face, the opportunity to challenge them is available to the defendants just as in any other lawsuit. They may endeavor to impeach the reliability of the statistical evidence, they may offer rebutting evidence, or they may

---

assigned to these institutions are thought to be the "cream of the crop" of the Alabama prison population.

disparage in arguments or in briefs the probative weight which the plaintiffs' evidence should be accorded. Since I agree with the Court that appellants made virtually no such effort, . . . I also agree with it that the District Court cannot be said to have erred as a matter of law in finding that a prima facie case had been made out in the instant case.

While the District Court's conclusion is by no means *required* by the proffered evidence, I am unable to conclude that the District Court's finding in that respect was clearly erroneous. In other cases there could be different evidence which could lead a district court to conclude that height and weight are in fact an accurate enough predictor of strength to justify, under all the circumstances, such minima. Should the height and weight requirements be found to advance the job-related qualification of strength sufficiently to rebut the prima facie case, then, under our cases, the burden would shift back to appellee Rawlinson to demonstrate that other tests, *without* such disparate effect, would also meet that concern. *Albemarle Paper Co.* v. *Moody*, 422 U.S. 405, 425 (1975). But, here, the District Court permissibly concluded that appellants had not shown enough of a nexus even to rebut the inference.

Appellants, in order to rebut the prima facie case under the statute, had the burden placed on them to advance job-related reasons for the qualification. *McDonnell Douglas Corp.* v. *Green*, 411 U.S. 792, 802 (1973). This burden could be shouldered by offering evidence or by making legal arguments not dependent on any new evidence. The District Court was confronted, however, with only one suggested job-related reason for the qualification—that of strength. Appellants argued only the job-relatedness of actual physical strength; they did not urge that an equally job-related qualification for prison guards is the *appearance* of strength. As the Court notes, the primary job of correctional counselor in Alabama prisons "is to maintain security and control of the inmates . . . ," *ante,* a function that I at least would imagine is aided by the psychological impact on prisoners of the presence of tall and heavy guards. If the appearance of strength had been urged upon the District Court here as a reason for the height and weight minima, I think that the District Court would surely have been entitled to reach a different result than it did. For, even if not perfectly correlated, I would think that Title VII would not preclude a State from saying that anyone under 5'2" or 120 pounds, no matter how strong in fact, does not have a sufficient appearance of strength to be a prison guard.

But once the burden has been placed on the defendant, it is then up to the defendant to articulate the asserted job-related reasons underlying the use of the minima. *McDonnell Douglas Corp.* v. *Green, supra,* at 802; *Griggs* v. *Duke Power Co.,* 401 U.S. 424, 431 (1971); *Albemarle Paper Co.* v. *Moody, supra,* at 425. Because of this burden, a reviewing court is not ordinarily justified in relying on arguments in favor of a job qualification that were not first presented to the trial court. Cf. *United States* v. *Arnold, Schwinn & Co.,* 388 U.S. 365, 374 n. 5 (1967); *Thomas* v. *Taylor,* 224 U.S. 73, 84 (1912); *Bell* v. *Bruen,* 1 How. 169, 187 (1843). As appellants did not even present the "appearance of strength" contention to the District Court as an asserted job-related reason for the qualification requirements, I agree that their burden was not met. The District Court's holding thus did not deal with the question of whether such an assertion could or did rebut appellee Rawlinson's prima facie case.

## HAZELWOOD SCHOOL DISTRICT v. UNITED STATES

*Supreme Court of the United States, 1977*
*433 U.S. 299, 15 FEP Cases 1*

MR. JUSTICE STEWART delivered the opinion of the Court.

The petitioner Hazelwood School District covers 78 square miles in the northern part of St. Louis County, Mo. In 1973 the Attorney General brought this lawsuit against Hazelwood and various of its officials, alleging that they were engaged in a "pattern or practice" of employment discrimination in violation of Title VII of the Civil Rights Act of 1064, as amended, 12 U.S.C. § 2000e *et seq.* (1970 ed. and Supp. V).[1] The complaint asked for an injunction requiring Hazelwood to cease its discriminatory practices, to take affirmative steps to obtain qualified Negro faculty members, and to offer employment and give backpay to victims of past illegal discrimination.

Hazelwood was formed from 13 rural school districts between 1949 and 1951 by a process of annexation. By the 1967–1968 school year, 17,550 students were enrolled in the district, of whom only 59 were Negro; the number of Negro pupils increased to 576 of 25,166 in 1972–1973, a total of just over 2 percent.

From the beginning, Hazelwood followed relatively unstructured procedures in hiring its teachers. Every person requesting an application for a teaching position was sent one, and completed applications were submitted to a central personnel office, where they were kept on file.[2] During the early 1960's the personnel office notified all applicants whenever a teaching position became available, but as the number of applications on file increased in the late 1960's and early 1970's, this practice was no longer considered feasible. The personnel office thus began the practice of selecting anywhere from 3 to 10 applicants for interviews at the school

1 [Footnotes numbered as in original.—Ed.] Under 42 U.S.C. § 2000e–6 (a), the Attorney General was authorized to bring a civil action "[w]henever [he] has reasonable cause to believe that any person or group of persons is engaged in a pattern or practice of resistance to the full enjoyment of any of the rights secured by [Title VII], and that the pattern or practice is of such a nature and is intended to deny the full exercise of [those rights]." The 1972 amendments to Title VII directed that this function be transferred as of March 24, 1974, to the Equal Employment Opportunity Commission, at least with respect to private employers. § 2000e–6 (c) (1970 ed., Supp. V); see also § 2000e–5 (f)(1) (1970 ed., Supp. V). The present lawsuit was instituted more than seven months before that transfer.

2 Before 1954 Hazelwood's application forms required designation of race, and those forms were in use as late as the 1962–1963 school year.

where the vacancy existed. The personnel office did not substantively screen the applicants in determining which of them to send for interviews, other than to ascertain that each applicant, if selected, would be eligible for state certification by the time he began the job. Generally, those who had most recently submitted applications were most likely to be chosen for interviews.[3]

Interviews were conducted by a department chairman, program co-ordinator, or the principal at the school where the teaching vacancy existed. Although those conducting the interviews did fill out forms rating the applicants in a number of respects, it is undisputed that each school principal possessed virtually unlimited discretion in hiring teachers for his school. The only general guidance given to the principals was to hire the "most competent" person available, and such intangibles as "personality, disposition, appearance, poise, voice, articulation, and ability to deal with people" counted heavily. The principal's choice was routinely honored by Hazelwood's Superintendent and the Board of Education.

In the early 1960's Hazelwood found it necessary to recruit new teachers, and for that purpose members of its staff visited a number of colleges and universities in Missouri and bordering States. All the institutions visited were predominantly white, and Hazelwood did not seriously recruit at either of the two predominantly Negro four-year colleges in Missouri.[4] As a buyer's market began to develop for public school teachers, Hazelwood curtailed its recruiting efforts. For the 1971–1972 school year, 3,127 persons applied for only 234 teaching vacancies; for the 1972–1973 school year, there were 2,373 applications for 282 vacancies. A number of the applicants who were not hired were Negroes.[5]

Hazewood hired its first Negro teacher in 1969. The number of Negro faculty members gradually increased in successive years: six of 957 in the 1970 school year; 16 of 1,107 by the end of the 1972 school year; 22 of 1,231 in the 1973 school year. By comparison, according to 1970 census figures, of more than 19,000 teachers employed in that year in the St. Louis area, 15.4 percent were Negro. That percentage figure included the St. Louis City School District, which in recent years has followed a policy of attempting to maintain a 50 percent Negro teaching staff. Apart from that school district, 5.7 percent of the teachers in the county were Negro in 1970.

Drawing upon these historic facts, the Government mounted its "pattern or practice" attack in the District Court upon four different fronts. It adduced evidence of (1) a history of alleged racially discriminatory practices, (2) statistical disparities in hiring, (3) the standardless and largely subjective hiring procedures, and (4) specific instances of alleged

---

[3] Applicants with student or substitute teaching experience at Hazelwood were given preference if their performance had been satisfactory.

[4] One of those two schools was never visited even though it was located in nearby St. Louis. The second was briefly visited on one occasion, but no potential applicant was interviewed.

[5] The parties disagree whether it is possible to determine from the present record exactly how many of the job applicants in each of the school years were Negroes.

discrimination against 55 unsuccessful Negro applicants for teaching jobs. Hazelwood offered virtually no additional evidence in response, relying instead on evidence introduced by the Government, perceived deficiencies in the Government's case, and its own officially promulgated policy "to hire all teachers on the basis of training, preparation and recommendations, regardles of race, color, or creed." [6]

The District Court ruled that the Government had failed to establish a pattern or practice of discrimination. The court was unpersuaded by the alleged history of discrimination, noting that no dual school system had ever existed in Hazelwood. The statistics showing that relatively small numbers of Negroes were employed as teachers were found nonprobative, on the ground that the percentage of Negro pupils in Hazelwood was similarly small. The court found nothing illegal or suspect in the teacher hiring procedures that Hazelwood had followed. Finally, the court reviewed the evidence in the 55 cases of alleged individual discrimination, and after stating that the burden of proving intentional discrimination was on the Government, it found that this burden had not been sustained in a single instance. Hence, the court entered judgment for the defendants *United States v. Hazelwood School District,* 392 F. Supp. 1276, 12 FEP Cases 1150 (ED Mo.).

The Court of Appeals for the Eighth Circuit reversed. After suggesting that the District Court had assigned inadequate weight to evidence of discriminatory conduct on the part of Hazelwood before the effective date of Title VII, the Court of Appeals rejected the trial court's analysis of the statistical data as resting on an irrelevant comparison of Negro teachers to Negro pupils in Hazelwood. The proper comparison, in the appellate court's view, was one between Negro teachers in Hazelwood and Negro teachers in the relevant labor market area. Selecting St. Louis County and St. Louis City as the relevant area,[8] the Court of Appeals compared the 1970 census figures, showing that 15.4 percent of teachers in that area were Negro, to the racial composition of Hazelwood's teaching staff. In the 1972–1973 and 1973–1974 school years, only 1.4 percent and 1.8 percent, respectively, of Hazelwood's teachers were Negroes. This statistical disparity, particularly when viewed against the background of the teacher-hiring procedures that Hazelwood had followed, was held to constitute a prima facie case of a pattern or practice of racial discrimination.

In addition, the Court of Appeals reasoned that the trial court had erred in failing to measure the 55 instances in which Negro applicants were denied jobs against the four-part standard for establishing a prima facie case of individual discrimination set out in this Court's opinion in

---

[6] The defendants offered only one witness, who testified to the total number of teachers who had applied and were hired for jobs in the 1971-1972 and 1972-1973 school years. They introduced several exhibits consisting of a policy manual, policy book, staff handbook, and historical summary of Hazelwood's formation and relatively brief existence.

[8] The city of St. Louis is surrounded by, but not included in, St. Louis County. Mo. Ann. Stat. § 46.145 (1966).

*McDonnell Douglas Corp.* v. *Green,* 411 U.S. 792, 802. Applying that standard, the appellate court found 16 cases of individual discrimination,[10] which "buttressed" the statistical proof. Because Hazelwood had not rebutted the Government's prima facie case of a pattern or practice of racial discrimination, the Court of Appeals directed judgment for the Government and prescribed the remedial order to be entered.[11]

We granted certiorari, 429 U.S. 1037, to consider a substantial question affecting the enforcement of a pervasive federal law.

The petitioners primarily attack the judgment of the Court of Appeals for its reliance on "undifferentiated work force statistics to find an unrebutted prima facie case of employment discrimination." [12] The question they raise, in short, is whether a basic component in the Court of Appeals' finding of a pattern or practice of discrimination—the comparatively small percentage of Negro employees on Hazelwood's teaching staff—was lacking in probative force.

This Court's recent consideration in *Teamsters* v. *United States,* 431 U.S. 324, of the role of statistics in pattern-or-practice suits under Title VII provides substantial guidance in evaluating the arguments advanced by the petitioners. In that case we stated that it is the Government's burden to "establish by a preponderance of the evidence that racial discrimination was the [employer's] standard operating procedure—the regular rather than the unusual practice." *Id.,* at 336. We also noted that statistics can be an important source of proof in employment discrimination cases, since

"absent explanation, it is ordinarily to be expected that nondiscriminatory hiring practices will in time result in a work force more or less representative of the racial and ethnic composition of the population in

10 The Court of Appeals held that none of the 16 prima facie cases of individual discrimination had been rebutted by the petitioners. See 534 F. 2d, at 814.

11 The District Court was directed to order that the petitioners cease from discriminating on the basis of race or color in the hiring of teachers, promulgate accurate job descriptions and hiring criteria, recruit Negro and white applicants on an equal basis, give preference in filling vacancies to the 16 discriminatorily rejected applicants, make appropriate backpay awards, and submit periodic reports to the Government on its progress in hiring qualified Negro teachers. *Id.,* at 819–20.

12 In their petition for certiorari and brief on the merits, the petitioners have phrased the question as follows:

"Whether a court may disregard evidence that an employer has treated actual job applicants in a nondiscriminatory manner and rely on undifferentiated workforce statistics to find an unrebutted prima facie case of employment discrimination in violation of Title VII of the Civil Rights Act of 1964."

Their petition for certiorari and brief on the merits did raise a second question: "Whether Congress has authority under Section 5 of the Fourteenth Amendment to prohibit by Title VII of the Civil Rights Act of 1964 employment practices of an agency of a state government in the absence of proof that the agency purposefully discriminated against applicants on the basis of race." That issue, however, is not presented by the facts in this case. The Government's opening statement in the trial court explained that its evidence was designed to show that the scarcity of Negro teachers at Hazelwood "is the result of purpose" and is attributable to "deliberately continued employment policies." Thus here, as in *Teamsters* v. *United States,* 431 U.S. 324, "[t]he Government's theory of discrimination was simply that the [employer], in violation of § 703 (a) of Title VII, regularly and purposefully treated Negroes . . . less favorably than white persons." *Id.,* at 335 (footnote omitted).

the community from which employees are hired. Evidence of longlasting and gross disparity between the composition of a work force and that of the general population thus may be significant even though § 703(j) makes clear that Title VII imposes no requirement that a work force mirror the general population." *Id.*, at 340 n. 20.

See also *Arlington Heights* v. *Metropolitan Housing Dev. Corp.*, 429 U.S. 252, 266; *Washington* v. *Davis*, 426 U.S. 229, 241–242. Where gross statistical disparities can be shown, they alone may in a proper case constitute prima facie proof of a pattern or practice of discrimination. *Teamsters, supra,* at 339.

There can be no doubt, in light of the *Teamsters* case, that the District Court's comparison of Hazelwood's teacher work force to its student population fundamentally misconceived the role of statistics in employment discrimination cases. The Court of Appeals was correct in the view that a proper comparison was between the racial composition of Hazelwood's teaching staff and the racial composition of the qualified public school teacher population in the relevant labor market.[13] See *Teamsters, supra,* at 337–338, and n. 17. The percentage of Negroes on Hazelwood's teaching staff in 1972–1973 was 1.4 percent, and in 1973–1974 it was 1.8 percent. By contrast, the percentage of qualified Negro teachers in the area was, according to the 1970 census, at least 5.7 percent.[14] Although

---

[13] In *Teamsters*, the comparison between the percentage of Negroes on the employer's work force and the percentage in the general areawide population was highly probative, because the job skill there involved—the ability to drive a truck—is one that many persons possess or can fairly readily acquire. When special qualifications are required to fill particular jobs, comparisons to the general population (rather than to the smaller group of individuals who possess the necessary qualifications) may have little probative value. The comparative statistics introduced by the Government in the District Court, however, were properly limited to public school teachers, and therefore this is not a case like *Mayor* v. *Educational Equality League*, 415 U.S. 605, in which the racial-composition comparisons failed to take into account special qualifications for the position in question. *Id.*, at 620–21.

Although the petitioners concede as a general matter the probative force of the comparative work-force statistics, they object to the Court of Appeals' heavy reliance on these data on the ground that applicant-flow data, showing the actual percentage of white and Negro applicants for teaching positions at Hazelwood, would be firmer proof. As we have noted, see n. 5, *supra*, there was not clear evidence of such statistics. We leave it to the District Court on remand to determine whether competent proof of those data can be adduced. If so, it would, of course, be very relevant. Cf. *Dothard* v. *Rawlinson, post*, at 330.

[14] As is discussed below, the Government contends that a comparative figure of 15.4%, rather than 5.7%, is the appropriate one. See *infra*, at 310–12. But even assuming, *arguendo*, that the 5.7% figure urged by the petitioners is correct, the disparity between that figure and the percentage of Negroes on Hazelwood's teaching staff would be more than fourfold for the 1972–1973 school year, and threefold for the 1973–1974 school year. A precise method of measuring the significance of such statistical disparities was explained in *Castaneda* v. *Partida*, 430 U.S. 482, 496–97, n. 17. It involves calculation of the "standard deviation" as a measure of predicted fluctuations from the expected value of a sample. Using the 5.7% figure as the basis for calculating the expected value, the expected number of Negroes on the Hazelwood teaching staff would be roughly 63 in 1972–1973 and 70 in 1973–1974. The observed number in those years was 16 and 22, respectively. The difference between the observed and expected values was more than six standard deviations in 1972–1973 and more than five standard deviations in 1973–1974. The Court in *Castaneda* noted that "[a]s a general rule for such large samples, if the difference between the expected value and the observed number is greater than

these differences were on their face substantial, the Court of Appeals erred in substituting its judgment for that of the District Court and holding that the Government had conclusively proved its "pattern or practice" lawsuit.

The Court of Appeals totally disregarded the possibility that this prima facie statistical proof in the record might at the trial court level be rebutted by statistics dealing with Hazelwood's hiring after it became subject to Title VII. Racial discrimination by public employers was not made illegal under Title VII until March 24, 1972. A public employer who from that date forward made all its employment decisions in a wholly nondiscriminatory way would not violate Title VII even if it had formerly maintained an all-white work force by purposefully excluding Negroes.[15] For this reason, the Court cautioned in the *Teamsters* opinion that once a prima facie case has been established by statistical work-force disparities, the employer must be given an opportunity to show that "the claimed discriminatory pattern is a product of pre-Act hiring rather than unlawful post-Act discrimination." 431 U.S., at 360.

The record in this case showed that for the 1972–1973 school year, Hazelwood hired 282 new teachers, 10 of whom (3.5 percent) were Negroes; for the following school year it hired 123 new teachers, five of whom (4.1 percent) were Negroes. Over the two-year period, Negroes constituted a total of 15 of the 405 new teachers hired (3.7 percent). Although the Court of Appeals briefly mentioned these data in reciting the facts, it wholly ignored them in discussing whether the Government had shown a pattern or practice of discrimination. And it gave no consideration at all to the possibility that post-Act data as to the number of Negroes hired compared to the total number of Negro applicants might tell a totally different story.[16]

What the hiring figures prove obviously depends upon the figures to which they are compared. The Court of Appeals accepted the Government's argument that the relevant comparison was to the labor market area of St. Louis County and the city of St. Louis, in which, according to the 1970 census, 15.4 percent of all teachers were Negro. The propriety of that comparison was vigorously disputed by the petitioners, who urged that because the city of St. Louis has made special attempts to maintain a 50 percent Negro teaching staff, inclusion of that school district in the relevant market area distorts the comparison. Were that argument ac-

---

two or three standard deviations," then the hypothesis that teachers were hired without regard to race would be suspect. 430 U.S., at 497 n. 17.

[15] This is not to say that evidence of pre-Act discrimination can never have any probative force. Proof that an employer engaged in racial discrimination prior to the effective date of Title VII might in some circumstances support the inference that such discrimination continued, particularly where relevant aspects of the decisionmaking process had undergone little change. Cf. Fed. Rule E id. 406; *Arlington Heights* v. *Metropolitan Housing Dev. Corp.*, 429 U.S. 252, 267; 1 J. Wigmore, Evidence § 92; 2 *id.*, §§ 302–305, 371, 375 (3d ed. 1940). And, of course, a public employer even before the extension of Title VII in 1972 was subject to the command of the Fourteenth Amendment not to engage in purposeful racial discrimination.

[16] See n. 13, *supra*, and n. 21, *infra*. But cf. *Teamsters*, 431 U.S., at 364–67.

cepted, the percentage of Negro teachers in the relevant labor market area (St. Louis County alone) as shown in the 1970 census would be 5.7 percent rather than 15.4 percent.

The difference between these figures may well be important; the disparity between 3.7 percent (the percentage of Negro teachers hired by Hazelwood in 1972–1973 and 1973–1974) and 5.7 percent may be sufficiently small to weaken the Government's other proof, while the disparity between 3.7 percent and 15.4 percent may be sufficiently large to reinforce it.[17] In determining which of the two figures—or, very possibly, what intermediate figure—provides the most accurate basis for comparison to the hiring figures at Hazelwood, it will be necessary to evaluate such considerations as (i) whether the racially based hiring policies of the St. Louis City School District were in effect as far back as 1970, the year in which the census figures were taken; [18] (ii) to what extent those policies have changed the racial composition of that district's teaching staff from what it would otherwise have been; (iii) to what extent St. Louis' recruitment policies have diverted to the city, teachers who might otherwise have applied to Hazelwood; [19] (iv) to what extent Negro teachers employed by the city would prefer employment in other districts such as Hazelwood; and (v) what the experience in other school districts in St. Louis County indicates about the validity of excluding the City School District from the relevant labor market.

---

[17] Indeed, under the statistical methodology explained in *Castaneda* v. *Partida, supra,* at 496–97, n. 17, involving the calculation of the standard deviation as a measure of predicted fluctuations, the difference between using 15.4% and 5.7% as the areawide figure would be significant. If the 15.4% figure is taken as the basis for comparison, the expected number of Negro teachers hired by Hazelwood in 1972–1973 would be 43 (rather than the actual figure of 10) of a total of 282, a difference of more than five standard deviations; the expected number in 1973–1974 would be 19 (rather than the actual figure 5) of a total of 123, a difference of more than three standard deviations. For the two years combined, the difference between the observed number of 15 Negro teachers hired (of a total of 405) would vary from the expected number of 62 by more than six standard deviations. Because a fluctuation of more than two or three standard deviations would undercut the hypothesis that decisions were being made randomly with respect to race, 430 U.S., at 497 n. 17, each of these statistical comparisons would reinforce rather than rebut the Government's other proof. If, however, the 5.7% areawide figure is used, the expected number of Negro teachers hired in 1972–1973 would be roughly 16, less than two standard deviations from the observed number of 10; for 1973–1974, the expected value would be roughly seven, less than one standard deviation from the observed value of 5; and for the two years combined, the expected value of 23 would be less than two standard deviations from the observed total of 15. A more precise method of analyzing these statistics confirms the results of the standard deviation analysis. See F. Mosteller, R. Rourke, & G. Thomas, PROBABILITY WITH STATISTICAL APPLICATIONS 494 (2d ed. 1970).

These observations are not intended to suggest that precise calculations of statistical significance are necessary in employing statistical proof, but merely to highlight the importance of the choice of the relevant labor market area.

[18] In 1970 Negroes constituted only 42% of the faculty in St. Louis city schools, which could indicate either that the city's policy was not yet in effect or simply that its goal had not yet been achieved.

[19] The petitioners observe, for example, that Harris Teachers College in St. Louis, whose 1973 graduating class was 60% Negro, is operated by the city. It is the petitioners' contention that the city's public elementary and secondary schools occupy an advantageous position in the recruitment of Harris graduates.

It is thus clear that a determination of the appropriate comparative figures in this case will depend upon further evaluation by the trial court. As this Court admonished in *Teamsters:* "[S]tatistics . . . come in infinite variety. . . . [T]heir usefulness depends on all of the surrounding facts and circumstances." 431 U.S., at 340. Only the trial court is in a position to make the appropriate determination after further findings. And only after such a determination is made can a foundation be established for deciding whether or not Hazelwood engaged in a pattern or practice of racial discrimination in its employment practices in violation of the law.[20]

We hold, therefore, that the Court of Appeals erred in disregarding the post-Act hiring statistics in the record, and that it should have remanded the case to the District Court for further findings as to the relevant labor market area and for an ultimate determination of whether Hazelwood engaged in a pattern or practice of employment discrimination after March 24, 1972.[21] Accordingly, the judgment is vacated, and the case is remanded to the District Court for further proceedings consistent with this opinion.

MR. JUSTICE BRENNAN, concurring: I join the Court's opinion. Similarly to our decision in *Dayton Board of Education* v. *Brinkman, post,* p. 406, today's opinion revolves around the relative factfinding roles of district courts and courts of appeals. It should be plain, however, that the liberal substantive standards for establishing a Title VII violation, including the usefulness of statistical proof, are reconfirmed.

In the present case, the District Court had adopted a wholly inappropriate legal standard of discrimination, and therefore did not evaluate the factual record before it in a meaningful way. This remand in effect orders it to do so. It is my understanding, as apparently it is MR. JUSTICE STEVENS', *post,* at 318 n. 5, that the statistical inquiry mentioned by the Court, *ante,* at 311 n. 17, and accompanying text, can be of no help to the Hazelwood School Board in rebutting the Government's evidence of discrimination. Indeed, even if the relative comparison market is found to be 5.7 percent rather than 15.4 percent black, the applicable statistical analysis at most will not serve to bolster the Government's case. This obviously is of no aid to Hazelwood in meeting *its* burden of proof. Nonetheless I think that the remand directed by the Court is appropriate and will allow the parties to address these figures and calculations with greater care and precision. I also agree that given the misapplication of governing legal principles by the District Court, Hazelwood reasonably

---

[20] Because the District Court focused on a comparison between the percentage of Negro teachers and Negro pupils in Hazelwood, it did not undertake an evaluation of the relevant labor market, and its casual dictum that the inclusion of the city of St. Louis "distorted" the labor market statistics was not based upon valid criteria. 392 F. Supp. 1276, 1287 (ED Mo.).

[21] It will also be open to the District Court on remand to determine whether sufficiently reliable applicant-flow data are available to permit consideration of the petitioners' argument that those data may undercut a statistical analysis dependent upon hirings alone.

should be given the opportunity to come forward with more focused and specific applicant-flow data in the hope of answering the Government's prima facie case. If, as presently seems likely, reliable applicant data is found to be lacking, the conclusion reached by my Brother STEVENS will inevitably be forthcoming.

MR. JUSTICE STEVENS, dissenting: The basic framework in a pattern-or-practice suit brought by the Government under Title VII of the Civil Rights Act of 1964 is the same as that in any other lawsuit. The plaintiff has the burden of proving a prima facie case; if he does so, the burden of rebutting that case shifts to the defendant.[1] In this case, since neither party complains that any relevant evidence was excluded, our task is to decide (1) whether the Government's evidence established a prima facie case; and (2) if so, whether the remaining evidence is sufficient to carry Hazelwood's burden of rebutting that prima facie case.

## I

The first question is clearly answered by the Government's statistical evidence, its historical evidence, and its evidence relating to specific acts of discrimination.

One-third of the teachers hired by Hazelwood resided in the city of St. Louis at the time of their initial employment. As MR. JUSTICE CLARK explained in his opinion for the Court of Appeals, it was therefore appropriate to treat the city, as well as the county, as part of the relevant labor market.[2] In that market, 15 percent of the teachers were black. In the Hazelwood District at the time of trial less than 2 percent of the teachers were black. An even more ·telling statistic is that after Title VII became

[1] "At the initial, 'liability' stage of a pattern-or-practice suit the Government is not required to offer evidence that each person for whom it will ultimately seek relief was a victim of the employer's discriminatory policy. Its burden is to establish a prima facie case that such a policy existed. The burden then shifts to the employer to defeat the prima facie showing of a pattern or practice by demonstrating that the Government's proof is either inaccurate or insignificant. An employer might show, for example, that the claimed discriminatory pattern is a product of pre-Act hiring rather than unlawful post-Act discrimination, or that during the period it is alleged to have pursued a discriminatory policy it made too few employment decisions to justify the inference that it had engaged in a regular practice of discrimination." *Teamsters* v. *United States,* 431 U.S. 324, 360.

[2] "We accept the Government's contention that St. Louis City and County is the relevant labor market area for our consideration. The relevant labor market area is that area from which the employer draws its employees. *United States* v. *Ironworkers Local 86,* 443 F. 2d 544, 551 n. 19 (9th Cir. 1971). Of the 176 teachers hired by Hazelwood between October, 1972, and September, 1973, approximately 80 percent resided in St. Louis City and County at the time of their initial employment. Approximately one-third of the teachers hired during this period resided in the City of St. Louis and 40 percent resided in areas of St. Louis County other than the Hazelwood District." 534 F. 2d 805, 811–12, n. 7 (1976).

It is noteworthy that in the Court of Appeals, Chief Judge Gibson, in dissent, though urging—as Hazelwood had in the District Court—that the labor market was even broader than the Government contended, *id.,* at 821, did not question the propriety of including the City in the same market as the County, see Defendants' Brief and Memorandum in Support of Its Proposed Findings of Fact and Conclusions of Law, filed on Aug. 21, 1974, in Civ. Act. No. 73–C–553(A) (ED Mo.), p. 24. In this Court, petitioners had abandoned any argument similar to that made below.

applicable to it, only 3.7 percent of the new teachers hired by Hazelwood were black. Proof of these gross disparities was in itself sufficient to make out a prima facie case of discrimination. See *Teamsters* v. *United States,* 431 U.S. 324, 339; *Castaneda* v. *Partida,* 430 U.S. 482, 494–498.

As a matter of history, Hazelwood employed no black teachers until 1969. Both before and after the 1972 amendment making the statute applicable to public school districts, Hazelwood used a standardless and largely subjective hiring procedure. Since "relevant aspects of the decisionmaking process had undergone little change," it is proper to infer that the pre-Act policy of preferring white teachers continued to influence Hazelwood's hiring practices.[3]

The influence of discrimination was corroborated by post-Act evidence that Hazelwood had refused to hire 16 qualified black applicants for racial reasons. Taking the Government's evidence as a whole, there can be no doubt about the sufficiency of its prima facie case.

## II

Hazelwood "offered virtually no additional evidence in response," *ante,* at 303. It challenges the Government's statistical analysis by claiming that the city of St. Louis should be excluded from the relevant market and pointing out that only 5.7 percent of the teachers in the county (excluding the city) were black. It further argues that the city's policy of trying to maintain a 50 percent black teaching staff diverted teachers from the county to the city. There are two separate reasons why these arguments are insufficient: they are not supported by the evidence; even if true, they do not overcome the Government's case.

The petitioners offered no evidence concerning wage differentials, commuting problems, or the relative advantages of teaching in an inner-city school as opposed to a suburban school. Without any such evidence in the record, it is difficult to understand why the simple fact that the city was the source of a third of Hazelwood's faculty should not be sufficient to demonstrate that it is a part of the relevant market. The city's policy of attempting to maintain a 50/50 ratio clearly does not undermine that conclusion, particularly when the record reveals no shortage of qualified black applicants in either Hazelwood or other suburban school districts.[4]

---

[3] Proof that an employer engaged in racial discrimination prior to the effective date of the Act creates the inference that such discrimination continued "particularly where relevant aspects of the decisionmaking process [have] undergone little change. Cf. Fed. Rule Evid. 406; *Arlington Heights* v. *Metropolitan Housing Dev. Corp.,* 429 U.S. 252, 267; 1 J. Wigmore, Evidence § 92; 2 *id.,* §§ 302–305, 371, 375 (3d ed. 1940). And, of course, a public employer even before the extension of Title VII in 1972 was subject to the command of the Fourteenth Amendment not to engage in purposeful racial discrimination." *Ante,* at 309–310, n. 15.

Since Hazelwood's hiring before 1972 was so clearly discriminatory, there is some irony in its claim that "Hazelwood continued [after 1972] to select its teachers on the same careful basis that it had relied on before in staffing its growing system." Brief for Petitioners 29–30.

[4] "Had there been evidence obtainable to contradict and disprove the testimony offered by [the Government], it cannot be assumed that the State would have refrained from introducing it." *Pierre* v. *Louisiana,* 306 U.S. 354, 361–62.

Surely not *all* of the 2,000 black teachers employed by the city were un-available for employment in Hazelwood at the time of their initial hire.

But even if it were proper to exclude the city of St. Louis from the market, the statistical evidence would still tend to prove discrimination. With the city excluded, 5.7 percent of the teachers in the remaining market were black. On the basis of a random selection, one would there-fore expect that 5.7 percent of the 405 teachers hired by Hazelwood in the 1972–1973 and 1973–1974 school years to have been black. But instead of 23 black teachers, Hazelwood hired only 15, less than two-thirds of the expected number. Without the benefit of expert testimony, I would hesitate to infer that the disparity between 23 and 15 is great enough, in itself, to prove discrimination.[5] It is perfectly clear, however, that whatever probative force this disparity has, it tends to prove discrimina-tion and does absolutely nothing in the way of carrying Hazelwood's burden of overcoming the Government's prima facie case.

Absolute precision in the analysis of market data is too much to expect. We may fairly assume that a nondiscriminatory selection process would have resulted in the hiring of somewhere between the 15 percent sug-gested by the Government and the 5.7 percent suggested by petitioners, or perhaps 30 or 40 black teachers, instead of the 15 actually hired.[6] On that assumption, the Court of Appeals' determination that there were 16 individual cases of discriminatory refusal to hire black applicants in the post-1972 period seems remarkably accurate.

In sum, the Government is entitled to prevail on the present record. It proved a prima facie case, which Hazelwood failed to rebut. Why, then, should we burden a busy federal court with another trial? Hazelwood had an opportunity to offer evidence to dispute the 16 examples of racially motivated refusals to hire; but as the Court notes, the Court of Appeals has already "held that none of the 16 prima facie cases of individ-ual discrimination had been rebutted by the petitioners. See 534 F. 2d 805, 814 (CA8) ." *Ante,* at 306 n. 10. Hazelwood also had an opportunity to offer any evidence it could muster to show a change in hiring practices or to contradict the fair inference to be drawn from the statistical evi-dence. Instead, it "offered virtually no additional evidence in response," *ante,* at 303.

Perhaps "a totally different story" might be told by other statistical evidence that was never presented, *ante,* at 310. No lawsuit has ever been tried in which the losing party could not have pointed to a similar possi-bility.[7] It is always possible to imagine more evidence which could have been offered, but at some point litigation must come to an end.

[5] After I had drafted this opinion, one of my law clerks advised me that, given the size of the two-year sample, there is only about a 5% likelihood that a disparity this large would be produced by a random selection from the labor pool. If his calculation (which was made using the method described in H. Blalock, SOCIAL STATISTICS 151–173 (1972)) is correct, it is easy to understand why Hazelwood offered no expert testimony.

[6] Some of the other school districts in the county have a 10% ratio of blacks on their faculties. See Plaintiff's Exhibit 54 in Civ. Act. No. 73–C–553 (A) (ED Mo. 1975); Brief for United States 30 n. 30.

[7] Since Hazelwood failed to offer any "applicant-flow data" at the trial, and since it

Rather than depart from well-established rules of procedure, I would affirm the judgment of the Court of Appeals.[9] Since that judgment reflected a correct appraisal of the record, I see no reason to prolong this litigation with a remand neither side requested.[10]

## FURNCO CONSTRUCTION CORP. v. WATERS

*Supreme Court of the United States, 1978*
*438 U.S. 567, 17 FEP Cases 1062*

MR. JUSTICE REHNQUIST delivered the opinion of the Court.

Respondents are three black bricklayers who sought employment with petitioner Furnco Construction Corporation. Two of the three were never offered employment. The third was employed only long after he initially applied. Upon adverse findings entered after a bench trial, the District Court for the Northern District of Illinois held that respondents had not proved a claim under either the "disparate treatment" theory of *McDonnell Douglas Corp.* v. *Green,* 411 U.S. 792, 93 S.Ct. 1817, 36 L.Ed.2d 668 (1973), or the "disparate impact" theory of *Griggs* v. *Duke Power Co.,* 401 U.S. 424, 91 S.Ct. 849, 28 L.Ed.2d 158 (1971). The Court of Appeals for the Seventh Circuit, concluding that under *McDonnell Douglas* respondents had made out a prima facie case which had not been effectively rebutted, reversed the judgment of the District Court. We granted certiorari to consider important questions raised by this case regarding the exact scope of the prima facie case under *McDonnell Douglas* and the nature of the evidence necessary to rebut such a case. 434 U.S. 996, 98 S.Ct. 632, 54 L.Ed.2d 490 (1977). Having concluded that the Court of Appeals erred in its treatment of the latter question, we

---

does not now claim to have any newly discovered evidence, I am puzzled by MR. JUSTICE BRENNAN's explanation of the justification for a remand. Indeed, after the first trial was concluded, Hazelwood emphasized the fact that no evidence of this kind had been present; it introduced no such evidence itself. It stated:
"There is absolutely no evidence in this case that provides any basis for making a comparison between black applicants and white applicants and their treatment by the Hazelwood School District relative to hiring or not being hired for a teaching position." Defendants' Brief and Memorandum in Support of Its Proposed Findings of Fact and Conclusions of Law, *supra*, n. 2, at 22.

9 It is interesting to compare the disposition in this case with that in *Castaneda* v. *Partida*, 430 U.S. 482. In *Castaneda*, as in this case, "[i]nexplicably, the State introduced practically no evidence," *id.*, at 498. But in *Castaneda*, unlike the present case, the Court affirmed the finding of discrimination, rather than giving the State a second chance at trying its case. (It should be noted that the *Castaneda* Court expressly stated that it was possible that the statistical discrepancy could have been explained by the State). *Id.*, at 499.

10 Hazelwood's brief asks only for a remand "for reconsideration of the alleged individual cases of discrimination . . . ." Brief for Petitioners 78. Hazelwood explains: "[The question raised in its petition for certiorari is] a question of law. It is a question of what sort of evidentiary showing satisfies Title VII. . . . The question is whether on the evidence of record an unrebutted prima facie case was established." Reply Brief for Petitioners 2.

reverse and remand to that court for further proceedings consistent with this opinion.

# I

A few facts in this case are not in serious dispute. Petitioner Furnco, an employer within the meaning of §§ 701 (b) and (h) of Title VII of the 1964 Civil Rights Act, specializes in refractory installation in steel mills and, more particularly, the rehabilitation or relining of blast furnaces with what is called in the trade "firebrick." Furnco does not, however, maintain a permanent force of bricklayers. Rather, it hires a superintendent for a specific job and then delegates to him the task of securing a competent work force. In August 1971, Furnco contracted with Interlake, Inc., to reline one of its blast furnaces. Joseph Dacies, who had been a job superintendent for Furnco since 1965, was placed in charge of the job and given the attendant hiring responsibilities. He did not accept application at the jobsite, but instead hired only persons whom he knew to be experienced and competent in this type of work or persons who had been recommended to him as similarly skilled. He hired his first four bricklayers, all of whom were white, on two successive days in August, the 26th and 27th, and two in September, the 7th and 8th. On September 9 he hired the first black bricklayer. By September 13, he had hired eight more bricklayers, one of whom was black; by September 17, seven more had been employed, another of whom was black; and by September 23, 17 more were on the payroll, again with one black included in that number.[1] Between October 12 to 18, he hired six bricklayers, all of whom were black, including respondent Smith, who had worked for Dacies previously and had applied at the jobsite somewhat earlier. Respondents Samuels and Nemhard were not hired, though they were fully qualified and had also attempted to secure employment by appearing at the jobsite gate. Out of the total of 1819 man-days worked on the Interlake job, 242, or 13.3 percent were worked by black bricklayers.

Many of the remaining facts found by the District Court and the inferences to be drawn therefrom are in some dispute between the parties, but none was expressly found by the Court of Appeals to be clearly erroneous. The District Court elaborated at some length as to the "critical" necessity of insuring that only experienced and highly qualified fire-bricklayers were employed. Untimely work would result in substantial losses both to Interlake, which was forced to shut down its furnace and lay off employees during the relining job, and to Furnco, which was paid for this work at a fixed price and for a fixed time period. In addition, not only might shoddy work slow this work process down, but it also might necessitate costly future maintenance work with its attendant loss

---

[1] [Footnotes numbered as in original.—Ed.] Respondents contend that two of these four blacks were not actually "hired," but merely "transferred" from another Furnco job. Brief for Respondents 7–8. Both the District Court and the Court of Appeals spoke only of "hiring" bricklayers, however, and those parts of the record to which respondents point do not persuade us that this is a mischaracterization.

of production and employee layoffs; diminish Furnco's reputation and ability to secure similar work in the future; and perhaps even create serious safety hazards, leading to explosions and the like. Pet. for Cert. A13–A15. These considerations justified Furnco's refusal to engage in on-the-job training or to hire at the gate, a hiring process which would not provide an adequate method of matching qualified applications to job requirements and assuring that the applicants are sufficiently skilled and capable. *Id.,* at A18–A19. Furthermore, there was no evidence that these policies and practices were a pretext to exclude black bricklayers or were otherwise illegitimate or had a disproportionate impact or effect on black bricklayers. Pet. for Cert. A17–A18. From late 1969 through late 1973, 5.7 percent of the bricklayers in the relevant labor force were minority group members, see 41 CFR § 60–11 *et seq.,*[2] while, as mentioned before, 13.3 percent of the man-days on Furnco's Interlake job were worked by black bricklayers.

Because of the above considerations and following the established practice in the industry, most of the fire-bricklayers hired by Dacies were persons known by him to be experienced and competent in this type of work. The others were hired after being recommended as skilled in this type of work by his general foreman, an employee (a black), another Furnco superintendent in the area, and Furnco's General Manager John Wright. Wright had not only instructed Dacies to employ, as far as possible, at least 16 percent black bricklayers, a policy due to Furnco's self-imposed affirmative action plan to insure that black bricklayers were employed by Furnco in Cook County in numbers substantially in excess of their percentage in the local union,[3] but he had also recommended, in an effort to show good faith, that Dacies hire several specific bricklayers, who had previously filed a discrimination suit against Furnco, negotiations for the settlement of which had only recently broken down, see n.3, *supra.*

From these factual findings, the District Court concluded that respondents had failed to make out a Title VII claim under the doctrine

[2] Respondents attempted to introduce a study conducted in late 1973 by the local union which matched members' names and race in an effort to show what percentage of the union membership was black. The study concluded that approximately 500 of the 3,800 union members were black. The District Court excluded this evidence because the study had been conducted two years after Furnco completed its job. Pet. for Cert. A16 n.1. The Court of Appeals thought rejection of this evidence was an abuse of discretion, but in dealing with the merits did not rely on the racial proportions in the labor force, so did not remand the case to permit introduction of that testimony. The Court of Appeals also noted that in any event respondents suffered no prejudice by the court's refusal to admit the study because it would not have demonstrated discrimination. The study showed that 13.7% of the membership of the union was black, while the evidence demonstrated that 13.3% of the man-days were worked by black bricklayers, Furnco had set a goal of 16% black bricklayers, and 20% of the individuals hired were black. 551 F.2d, at 1090.

[3] According to the District Court, this affirmative action program was initiated by Furnco following a job performed in 1969–1970 from which charges of racial discrimination in hiring were filed by several black bricklayers. These claims are apparently still pending on appeal in the Illinois courts and the merits of a parallel federal action remain to be adjudicated. See Pet. for Cert. A15; *Batiste* v. *Furnco,* 503 F.2d 447 (CA7 1974).

of *Griggs v. Duke Power Co., supra*. Furnco's policy of not hiring at the gate was racially neutral on its face and there was no showing that it had a disproportionate impact or effect. Pet. for Cert. A20–A21. It also held that respondents had failed to prove a case of discrimination under *McDonnell Douglas, supra*. Pet. for Cert. A21. It is not entirely clear whether the court thought respondents had failed to make out a prima facie case of discrimination under *McDonnell Douglas, supra*, see Pet. for Cert. A20–A21, but the court left no doubt that it thought Furnco's hiring practices and policies were justified as a "business necessity" in that they were required for the safe and efficient operation of Furnco's business, and were "not used as a pretext to exclude Negroes." Thus, even if a prima facie case had been made out, it had been effectively rebutted. *Id.*, at A21.

"Not only have Plaintiffs entirely failed to establish that Furnco's employment practices on the Interlake job discriminated against them on the basis of race or constituted retaliatory conduct but Defendant has proven what it was not required to. By its cross-examination and direct evidence, Furnco has proven beyond all reasonable doubt that it did not engage in either racial discrimination or retaliatory conduct in its employment practices in regard to bricklayers on the Interlake job." Pet. for Cert. A22.

The Court of Appeals reversed, holding that respondents had made out a prima facie case under *McDonnell Douglas, supra*, 411 U.S. at 802, 93 S.Ct. 1817, which Furnco had not effectively rebutted. Because of the "historical inequality of treatment of black workers" [5] and the fact that the record failed to reveal that any white persons had applied at the gate, the Court of Appeals rejected Furnco's argument that discrimination had not been shown because a white appearing at the jobsite would have fared no better than respondents. That court also disagreed with Furnco's contention, which the District Court had adopted, "that the importance of selecting people whose capability had been demonstrated to defendant's brick superintendent is a 'legitimate, nondiscriminatory reason' for defendant's refusal to consider plaintiffs." *Id.*, at 1088. Instead, the appellate court proceeded to devise what it thought would be an appropriate hiring procedure for Furnco, saying "[i]t seems to us that there is a reasonable middle ground between immediate hiring decisions on the spot and seeking out employees from among those known to the superintendent." *Ibid.* This middle course, according to the Court of Appeals, was to take written applications, with inquiry as to qualifications and experience, and then check, evaluate and compare those claims against the qualifications and experience of other bricklayers with whom the superintendent was already acquainted. We granted certiorari to consider

---

[5] The court stated:
"The historical inequality of treatment of black workers seems to us to establish that it is *prima facie* racial discrimination to refuse to consider the qualifications of a black job seeker before hiring from an approved list containing only the names of white bricklayers. How else will qualified black applicants be able to overcome the racial imbalance in a particular craft, itself the result of past discrimination." 551 F.2d, at 1089.

whether the Court of Appeals had gone too far in substituting its own
judgment as to proper hiring practices in the case of an employer which
claimed the practices it had chosen did not violate Title VII.[6] 434 U.S.
996, 98 S.Ct. 632, 54 L.Ed.2d 490 (1977).

## II

### A

We agree with the Court of Appeals that the proper approach was the
analysis contained in *McDonnell Douglas, supra*.[7] We also think the
Court of Appeals was justified in concluding that as a matter of law
respondents made out a prima facie case of discrimination under *Mc-
Donnell Douglas*. In that case we held that a plaintiff could make out a
prima facie claim by showing:
"(i) that he belongs to a racial minority; (ii) that he applied and was
qualified for a job for which the employer was seeking applicants; (iii)
that, despite his qualifications, he was rejected; and (iv) that, after his
rejection, the position remained open and the employer continued to
seek applicants from persons of complainant's qualifications." 411 U.S.,
at 802, 93 S.Ct., at 1824 (footnote omitted).
This, of course, was not intended to be an inflexible rule, as the Court
went on to note that "[t]he facts necessarily will vary in Title VII cases,
and the specification . . . of the prima facie proof required from respondent is not necessarily applicable in every respect to differing factual
situation." *Id.*, at 802 n. 13, 93 S.Ct., at 1824. See *International Brotherhood of Teamsters* v. *United States, supra*, 431 U.S., at 358, 97 S.Ct., at
1866. But *McDonnell Douglas* did make clear that a Title VII plaintiff
carries the initial burden of showing actions taken by the employer from
which one can infer, if such actions remain unexplained, that it is more
likely than not that such actions were "based on a discriminatory criterion
illegal under the Act." *International Brotherhood of Teamsters* v. *United*

6 The petition for certiorari set out three questions:
"1. Whether the Seventh Circuit, in reversing the judgment of the District Court,
erred in finding as irrelevant to the issue of racial discrimination in hiring, statistics
demonstrating that in hiring highly skilled bricklayers, the employer hired Negroes in a
percentage far in excess of their statistical presence in the relevant labor force.
"2. Whether a court may find an employer guilty of racial discrimination in employment due to alleged disparate treatment in hiring without a finding of discriminatory
intent or motive.
"3. Whether a hiring practice not shown to result in disparate impact or treatment
of prospective minority employees and found by the District Court to be justified by
business necessity and legitimate business reasons may be found to be racially discriminatory by the Court of Appeals merely because it is subjective and because the Court of
Appeals substitutes its judgment for that of the District Court as to what constitutes
legitimate business reasons." Pet. for Cert. 2.
7 This case did not involve employment tests, which we dealt with in *Griggs* v. *Duke
Power Co., supra*, and in *Albemarle Paper Co.* v. *Moody*, 422 U.S. 405, 412–413, 95 S.Ct.
2362, 2369–2370, 45 L.Ed.2d 280 (1975), nor particularized requirements such as the
height and weight specifications considered in *Dothard* v. *Rawlinson*, 433 U.S. 321, 329,
97 S.Ct. 2720, 2727, 53 L.Ed.2d 786 (1977), and it was not a "pattern or practice" case
like *International Brotherhood of Teamsters* v. *United States*, 431 U.S. 324, 358, 97 S.Ct.
1843, 1866, 52 L.Ed.2d 396 (1977).

*States, supra,* 431 U.S., at 358, 97 S.Ct., at 1866. See also *id.,* at 335 n. 15, 97 S.Ct., at 1854. And here respondents carried that initial burden by proving they were members of a racial minority; they did everything within their power to apply for employment; Furnco has conceded that they were qualified in every respect for the jobs which were about to be open;[8] they were not offered employment, although Smith later was; and the employer continued to seek persons of similar qualifications.

### B

We think the Court of Appeals went awry, however, in apparently equating a prima facie showing under *McDonnell Douglas* with an ultimate finding of fact as to discriminatory refusal to hire under Title VII; the two are quite different and that difference has a direct bearing on the proper resolution of this case. The Court of Appeals, as we read its opinion, thought Furnco's hiring procedures not only must be reasonably related to the achievement of some legitimate purpose, but also must be the method which allows the employer to consider the qualifications of the largest number of minority applicants. We think the imposition of that second requirement simply finds no support either in the nature of the prima facie case or the purpose of Title VII.

The central focus of the inquiry in a case such as this is always whether the employer is treating "some people less favorably than others because of their race, color, religion, sex, or national origin." *International Brotherhood of Teamsters* v. *United States, supra,* at 335 n. 15, 97 S.Ct., at 1854. The method suggested in *McDonnell Douglas* for pursuing this inquiry, however, was never intended to be rigid, mechanized, or ritualistic. Rather, it is merely a sensible, orderly way to evaluate the evidence in light of common experience as it bears on the critical question of discrimination. A prima facie case under *McDonnell Douglas* raises an inference of discrimination only because we presume these acts, if otherwise unexplained, are more likely than not based on the consideration of impermissible factors. See *International Brotherhood of Teamsters* v. *United States, supra,* 431 U.S., at 358 n. 44, 97 S.Ct., at 1866. And we are willing to presume this largely because we know from our experience that more often than not people do not act in a totally arbitrary manner, without any underlying reasons, especially in a business setting. Thus, when all legitimate reasons for rejecting an applicant have been eliminated as possible reasons for the employer's actions, it is more likely than not the employer, whom we generally assume acts only with *some* reason, based his decision on an impermissible consideration such as race.

When the prima facie case is understood in the light of the opinion in

---

[8] We note that this case does not raise any questions regarding exactly what sort of requirements an employer can impose upon any particular job. Furnco has conceded that for all its purposes respondents were qualified in every sense. Thus, with respect to the *McDonnell Douglas* prima facie case, the only question it places in issue is whether its refusal to consider respondents' applications at the gate was based upon legitimate, nondiscriminatory reasons and therefore permissible.

*McDonnell Douglas,* it is apparent that the burden which shifts to the employer is merely that of proving that he based his employment decision on a legitimate consideration, and not an illegitimate one such as race. To prove that, he need not prove that he pursued the course which would both enable him to achieve his own business goal *and* allow him to consider the *most* employment applications. Title VII forbids him from having as a goal a work force selected by any proscribed discriminatory practice, but it does not impose a duty to adopt a hiring procedure that maximizes hiring of minority employees. To dispel the adverse inference from a prima facie showing under *McDonnell Douglas,* the employer need only "articulate some legitimate nondiscriminatory reason for the employee's rejection." *McDonnell Douglas, supra,* 411 U.S., at 802, 93 S.Ct., at 1824.

The dangers of embarking on a course such as that charted by the Court of Appeals here, where the court requires businesses to adopt what it perceives to be the "best" hiring procedures, are nowhere more evident than in the record of this very case. Not only does the record not reveal that the court's suggested hiring procedure would work satisfactorily, but there is nothing in the record to indicate that it would be any less "haphazard, arbitrary, and subjective" than Furnco's method, which the Court of Appeals criticized as deficient for exactly those reasons. Courts are generally less competent than employers to restructure business practices, and unless mandated to do so by Congress they should not attempt it.

This is not to say of course that proof of a justification which is reasonably related to the achievement of some legitimate goal necessarily ends the inquiry. The plaintiff must be given the opportunity to introduce evidence that the proffered justification is merely a pretext for discrimination. And as we noted in *McDonnell Douglas, supra,* at 804–805, 93 S.Ct., at 1825–1826, this evidence might take a variety of forms. But the Court of Appeals, although stating its disagreement with the District Court's conclusion that the employer's hiring practices were a "legitimate, nondiscriminatory reason" for refusing to hire respondents, premised its disagreement on a view which we have discussed and rejected above. It did not conclude that the practices were a pretext for discrimination, but only that different practices would have enabled the employer to at least consider, and perhaps to hire, more minority employees. But courts may not impose such a remedy on an employer at least until a violation of Title VII has been proven, and here none had been under the reasoning of either the District Court or the Court of Appeals.

## C

The Court of Appeals was also critical of petitioner's effort to employ statistics in this type of case. While the matter is not free from doubt, it appears the court thought once a *McDonnell Douglas* prima facie showing had been made out, statistics of a racially balanced work force were totally irrelevant to the question of motive. See 551 F.2d, at 1089. That would undoubtably be a correct view of the matter if the *McDonnell Douglas* prima facie showing were the equivalent of an ultimate finding by the trier of fact that the original rejection of the applicant was racially motivated: a racially balanced work force cannot immunize an employer from liability for specific acts of discrimination. As we said in *International Brotherhood of Teamsters* v. *United States, supra,* 431 U.S. at 341–343, 97 S.Ct., at 1857:

"the District Court and the Court of Appeals found upon substantial evidence that the company had engaged in a course of discrimination that continued well after the effective date of Title VII. The company's later changes in its hiring and promotion policies could be of little comfort to the victims of the earlier post-Act discrimination, and could not erase its previous illegal conduct or its obligation to afford relief to those who suffered because of it."

See also *Albemarle Paper Co.* v. *Moody,* 422 U.S. 405, 412–413, 95 S.Ct. 2362, 2369–2370, 45 L.Ed.2d 280 (1975). It is clear beyond cavil that the obligation imposed by Title VII is to provide an equal opportunity for *each* applicant regardless of race, without regard to whether members of the applicant's race are already proportionately represented in the work force. See *Griggs* v. *Duke Power Co., supra,* 401 U.S., at 430, 91 S.Ct., at 853; *McDonald* v. *Santa Fe Trail Transportation Co.,* 427 U.S. 273, 279, 96 S.Ct. 2574, 2578, 49 L.Ed.2d 493 (1976).

A *McDonnell Douglas* prima facie showing is not the equivalent of a factual finding of discrimination, however. Rather, it is simply proof of actions taken by the employer from which we infer discriminatory animus because experience has proved that in the absence of any other explanation it is more likely than not those actions were bottomed on impermissible considerations. When the prima facie showing is understood in this manner, the employer must be allowed some latitude to introduce evidence which bears on his motive. Proof that his work force was racially balanced or that it contained a disproportionately high percentage of minority employees is not wholly irrelevant on the issue of intent when that issue is yet to be decided. We cannot say that such proof would have absolutely no probative value in determining whether the otherwise unexplained rejection of the minority applicants was discriminatorily motivated. Thus, although we agree with the Court of Appeals that in this case such proof neither was nor could have been sufficient to *conclusively* demonstrate that Furnco's actions were not discriminatorily motivated, the District Court was entitled to *consider* the racial mix of the work force when trying to make the determination as to motivation. The Court of Appeals should likewise give similar consideration to the proffered statistical proof in any further proceedings in this case.

## III

The parties also press upon the Court a large number of alternative theories of liability and defense,[9] none of which were directly addressed by the Court of Appeals as we read its opinion. Given the present posture of this case, however, we think those matters which are still preserved for review are best decided by the Court of Appeals in the first instance. Accordingly, we declined to address them as an original matter here. The judgment of the Court of Appeals is reversed and remanded for further proceedings consistent with this opinion.

MR. JUSTICE MARSHALL, with whom MR. JUSTICE BRENNAN joins, concurring in part and dissenting in part.

It is well established under Title VII that claims of employment discrimination because of race may arise in two different ways. *International Brotherhood of Teamsters* v. *United States,* 431 U.S. 324, 335–336, n. 15, 97 S.Ct. 1843, 1854, 52 L.Ed.2d 396. An individual may allege that he has been subjected to "disparate treatment" because of his race, or that he has been the victim of a facially neutral practice having a "disparate impact" on his racial group. The Court today concludes that the Court of Appeals was correct in treating this as a disparate treatment case controlled by *McDonnell Douglas Corp.* v. *Green,* 411 U.S. 792, 93 S.Ct. 1817, 36 L.Ed.2d 668 (1973).

Under *McDonnell Douglas,* a plaintiff establishes a prima facie case of employment discrimination through disparate treatment by showing: "(i) that he belongs to a racial minority; (ii) that he applied and was qualified for a job for which the employer was seeking applicants; (iii) that, despite his qualifications, he was rejected; and (iv) that, after his

[9] Respondents, for example, argue that regardless of the propriety of Furnco's general refusal to hire at the gate or of a general policy of hiring only bricklayers known to the superintendent or referred to him by an insider, a foreman or another bricklayer, Dacies' particular method of hiring was discriminatory. Thus, the general hiring practice, though perhaps legitimate in the abstract, was discriminatorily applied in this case, and cannot be used to rebut the prima facie case. Brief for Respondents 19–26. In particular, respondents argue that the evidence proved that Dacies hired from a "list" he had prepared, which allegedly included competent fire-bricklayers with whom he had worked, but in fact included only white fire-bricklayers with whom he had worked. Exclusion from this list of competent blacks with whom he had worked, such as respondents Smith and Samuels, was itself discriminatory and thus cannot be used to rebut respondents' prima facie case.

Furnco, on the other hand, vigorously disputes that Dacies hired only from this list and that the hiring process can be as neatly broken down into various components as respondents would like. It argues that even if most of the people with whom Dacies was familiar were white, Dacies made a concerted effort to speak with people who were familiar with competent black bricklayers and then hired a large number of black bricklayers. In fact, argues Furnco, the statistics indicate that he hired a disproportionately large number of blacks, thus clearly indicating that his so-called "list" certainly could not have been the exclusive source of potential employees even if it had been all white. It further disputes the notion that Furnco or Dacies had in any way put some sort of ceiling on the maximum number of blacks they were willing to hire. It asserts there is absolutely nothing in the record to support such a conclusion.

The District Court made no findings which would support respondents' view of the evidence. The Court of Appeals mentioned the existence of such a list, 551 F.2d, at 1086, but we do not read its opinion as expressly relying on this point either. Rather, as we read its opinion, the court found only that respondents had made out a prima facie case under *McDonnell Douglas* and that, for the reasons outlined in the text, Furnco had failed to rebut that prima facie case. On remand, respondents are of course free to pursue any such contentions which have been properly preserved.

rejection, the position remained open and the employer continued to seek applicants from persons of complainant's qualifications." 411 U.S., at 802, 93 S.Ct., at 1824 (footnote omitted).

Once a plaintiff has made out this prima facie case, the burden shifts to the employer who must prove that he had a "legitimate, nondiscriminatory reason for the [plaintiff's] rejection." *Ibid.*

The Court of Appeals properly held that respondents had made out a prima facie case of employment discrimination under *McDonnell Douglas.* Once respondents had established their prima facie case, the question for the court was then whether petitioner had carried its burden of proving that respondents were rejected on the basis of legitimate nondiscriminatory considerations. The court, however, failed properly to address that question and instead focused on what other hiring practices petitioner might employ. I therefore agree with the Court that we must remand the case to the Court of Appeals so that it can address, under the appropriate standards, whether petitioner had rebutted respondents' prima facie showing of disparate treatment. I also agree that on remand the Court of Appeals is to address the other theories of liability which respondents have presented. See *ante,* at 2051, and n. 9.

Where the Title VII claim is that a facially neutral employment practice actually falls more harshly on one racial group, thus having a disparate impact on that group, our cases establish a different way of proving the claim. See, e.g., *Teamsters,* 431 U.S., at 336 n. 15, 349, 97 S.Ct., at 1854 n. 15, 1861; *Dothard* v. *Rawlinson,* 433 U.S. 321, 329, 97 S.Ct. 2720, 53 L.Ed.2d 786 (1977); *General Electric* v. *Gilbert,* 429 U.S. 125, 137, 97 S.Ct. 401, 408, 50 L.Ed.2d 343 (1976); *Albemarle Paper Co.* v. *Moody,* 422 U.S. 405, 422, 425, 95 S.Ct. 2362, 2373, 2375, 45 L.Ed.2d 280 (1975); *Griggs* v. *Duke Power Co.,* 401 U.S. 424, 430–32, 91 S.Ct. 849, 853–854, 28 L.Ed.2d 158 (1971). As set out by the Court in *Griggs* v. *Duke Power Co., supra,* to establish a prima facie case on a disparate impact claim, a plaintiff need not show that the employer had a discriminatory intent but need only demonstrate that a particular practice in actuality "operates to exclude Negroes." 401 U.S., at 431, 91 S.Ct., at 853.

Once the plaintiff has established the disparate impact of the practice, the burden shifts to the employer to show that the practice has "a manifest relationship to the employment in question." *Id.,* at 432, 91 S.Ct., at 854. The "touchstone is business necessity," *id.,* at 431, 91 S.Ct., at 853, and the practice "must be shown to be necessary to safe and efficient job performance to survive a Title VII challenge." *Dothard* v. *Rawlinson,* 433 U.S., at 332, n. 14, 97 S.Ct., at 2728. Under this principle, a practice of limiting jobs to those with prior experience working in an industry or for a particular person, or to those who hear about jobs by word of mouth would be invalid if the practice in actuality impacts more harshly on a group protected under Title VII, unless the practice can be justified by business necessity.

There is nothing in today's opinion that is inconsistent with this approach or with our prior decisions. I must dissent, however, from the Court's apparent decision, see *ante*, at 2948, to foreclose on remand further litigation on the *Griggs* question of whether petitioner's hiring practices had a disparate impact. Respondents claim that petitioner's practice of hiring from a list of those who had previously worked for the foreman foreclosed Negroes from consideration or the vast majority of jobs. Although the foreman also hired a considerable number of Negroes through other methods, respondents assert that the use of other methods to augment the representation of Negroes in the work force does not answer whether the primary hiring practice is discriminatory.

It is clear that an employer cannot be relieved of responsibility for past discriminatory practices merely by undertaking affirmative action to obtain proportional representation in his work force. As the Court said in *Teamsters,* and reaffirms today, a "company's later changes in its hiring and promotion policies could be of little comfort to the victims of the earlier . . . discrimination, and could not erase its previous illegal conduct or its obligation to afford relief to those who suffered because of it." *Teamsters,* 431 U.S., at 341–42, 97 S.Ct., at 1857; *ante,* at 2951. Therefore, it is at least an open question whether the hiring of workers primarily from a list of past employees would, under *Griggs,* violate Title VII where the list contains no Negroes but the company uses additional methods of hiring to increase the numbers of Negroes hired.*

The Court today apparently assumes that the Court of Appeals affirmed the District Court's findings that petitioner's hiring practice had no disparate impact. I cannot agree with that assumption. Because the Court of Appeals disposed of this case under the *McDonnell Douglas* analysis, it had no occasion to address those findings of the District Court pertaining to disparate impact. Although the Court of Appeals did discuss *Griggs* in its opinion, 551 F.2d 1085, 1089–1090, as I read that discussion the Court was merely rejecting petitioner's argument that it could defeat respondents' *McDonnell Douglas* claim by showing that the work force had a large percentage of Negro members. I express no view on the issue of whether respondents' claim should prevail on the facts presented here since that question is not presently before us, but I believe that respondents' opportunity to make their claim should not be foreclosed by this Court.

## NOTE

For a more recent Supreme Court discussion of the use of statistics, see *NYC Transit Authority* v. *Beazer, infra,* page 833.

---

* Of course, the Court leaves open on remand the issue of whether Furnco's use of the list violated Title VII under a disparate treatment theory. See *ante,* at 2951 n. 9.

## BOARD OF TRUSTEES OF
## KEENE STATE COLLEGE v. SWEENEY

*Supreme Court of the United States, 1978*
*438 U.S. _____, 18 FEP Cases 520*

PER CURIAM.

The petition for a writ of certiorari is granted. In *Furnco Construction Co.* v. *Waters,* 438 U.S. 567, 98 S.Ct. 2943, 57 L.Ed.2d 957 (1978), we stated that "[t]o dispel the adverse inference from a prima facie showing under *McDonnell Douglas,* the employer need only 'articulate some legitimate, nondiscriminatory reason for the employee's rejection.'" *Id.,* at _____, 98 S.Ct., at 2950 quoting *McDonnell Douglas Corp.* v. *Green,* 411 U.S. 792, 802, 93 S.Ct. 1817, 1824, 36 L.Ed.2d 668 (1973). We stated in *McDonnell Douglas, supra,* that the plaintiff "must . . . be afforded a fair opportunity to show that [the employer's] stated reason for [the plaintiff's] rejection was in fact pretext." 411 U.S., at 804, 93 S.Ct., at 1825. The Court of Appeals in the present case, however, referring to *McDonnell Douglas, supra,* stated that "in requiring the defendant to *prove absence of discriminatory motive,* the Supreme Court placed the burden squarely on the party with the greater access to such evidence." *Sweeney* v. *Board of Trustees of Keene State College,* 569 F.2d 169, 177 (CA1 1978) (emphasis added).[1]

While words such as "articulate," "show," and "prove," may have more or less similar meanings depending upon the context in which they are used, we think that there is a significant distinction between merely "articulat[ing] some legitimate, nondiscriminatory reason" and "prov[ing] absence of discriminatory motive." By reaffirming and emphasizing the *McDonnell Douglas* analysis in *Furnco Construction Co.* v. *Waters, supra,* we made it clear that the former will suffice to meet the employee's prima facie case of discrimination. Because the Court of Appeals appears to have imposed a heavier burden on the employer than *Furnco* warrants, its judgment is vacated and the case is remanded for reconsideration in the light of *Furnco, supra,* at _____, 98 S.Ct., at 2950.[2]

---

[1] [Footnotes numbered as in original.—Ed.]
While the Court of Appeals did make the statement that the dissent quotes, *post,* at _____, it also made the statement quoted in the text above. These statements simply contradict one another. The statement quoted in the text above would make entirely superfluous the third step in the *Furnco—McDonnell Douglas* analysis, since it would place on the employer at the second stage the burden of showing that the reason for rejection was not a pretext, rather than requiring such proof from the employee as a part of the third step. We think our remand is warranted both because we are unable to determine which of the two conflicting standards the Court of Appeals applied in reviewing the decision of the District Court in this case, and because of the implication in its opinion that there is no difference between the two standards. We of course intimate no view as to the correct result if the proper test is applied in this case.

[2] We quite agree with the dissent that under *Furnco* and *McDonnell Douglas* the employer's burden is satisfied if he simply "explains what he has done" or "produc[es] evidence of legitimate nondiscriminatory reasons." *Post,* at 297. But petitioners clearly did produce evidence to support their legitimate nondiscriminatory explanation for refusing to promote respondent during the years in question. See 569 F.2d 172–73, 178;

MR. JUSTICE STEVENS, with whom MR. JUSTICE BRENNAN, MR. JUSTICE STEWART, and MR. JUSTICE MARSHALL join, dissenting.

Whenever this Court grants certiorari and vacates a Court of Appeals judgment in order to allow that court to reconsider its decision in the light of an intervening decision of this Court, the Court is acting on the merits. Such action always imposes an additional burden on Circuit Judges who—more than any other segment of the Federal Judiciary—are struggling desperately to keep afloat in the flood of federal litigation. For that reason, such action should not be taken unless the intervening decision has shed new light on the law which, if it had been available at the time of the Court of Appeals' decision, might have led to a different result.

In this case, the Court's action implies that the recent opinion in *Furnco Construction Corp.* v. *Waters*, 438 U.S. _____, 98 S.Ct. 2943, 57 L.Ed.2d 957 (1978), made some change in the law as explained in *McDonnell Douglas Corp.* v. *Green*, 411 U.S. 792, 93 S.Ct. 1817, 36 L.Ed.2d 668. When I joined the *Furnco opinion*, I detected no such change and I am still unable to discern one. In both cases, the Court clearly stated that when the complainant in a Title VII trial establishes a prima facie case of discrimination, "the burden which shifts to the employer is merely that of proving that he based his employment decision on a legitimate consideration, and not an illegitimate one such as race." [1]

The Court of Appeals' statement of the parties' respective burdens in this case is wholly faithful to this Court's teachings in *McDonnell Douglas*. The Court of Appeals here stated:

"As we understand those cases [*McDonnell Douglas* and *International Brotherhood of Teamsters*, 431 U.S. 324], a plaintiff bears the initial

---

Pet. for Cert. B–2 to B–24. Nonetheless, the Court of Appeals held that petitioners had not met their burden because the proffered legitimate explanation did not "rebut" or "disprove" respondent's prima facie case or "prove absence of nondiscriminatory motive." 569 F.2d, at 177–79; see Pet. for Cert. B–25. This holding by the Court of Appeals is further support for our belief that the court appears to have imposed a heavier burden on the employer than *Furnco*, and the dissent here, requires.

[1] This language is quoted from the following paragraph in *Furnco*:

"When the prima facie case is understood in the light of the opinion in *McDonnell Douglas*, it is apparent that the burden which shifts to the employer is merely that of proving that he based his employment decision on a legitimate consideration, and not an illegitimate one such as race. To prove that, he need not prove that he pursued the course which would both enable him to achieve his own business goal *and* allow him to consider the *most* employment applications. Title VII forbids him from having as a goal a work force selected by any proscribed discriminatory practice, but it does not impose a duty to adopt a hiring procedure that maximizes hiring of minority employees. To dispel the adverse inference from a prima facie showing under *McDonnell Douglas*, the employer need only 'articulate some legitimate nondiscriminatory reason for the employee's rejection.'" 438 U.S., at _____, 98 S.Ct., at 2950 (emphasis in original).

The comparable passage in *McDonnell Douglas* reads as follows:

"The burden then must shift to the employer to articulate some legitimate, nondiscriminatory reason for the employee's rejection. We need not attempt in the instant case to detail every matter which fairly could be recognized as a reasonable basis for a refusal to hire. Here petitioner has assigned respondent's participation in unlawful conduct against it as the cause for his rejection. We think that this suffices to discharge petitioner's burden of proof at this stage and to meet respondent's prima facie case of discrimination." 411 U.S., at 802–803, 93 S.Ct., at 1824.

burden of presenting evidence sufficient to establish a prima facie case of discrimination. *The burden then shifts to the defendant to rebut the prima facie case by showing that a legitimate, nondiscriminatory reason accounted for its actions.* If the rebuttal is successful, the plaintiff must show that the stated reason was a mere pretext for discrimination. *The ultimate burden of persuasion on the issue of discrimination remains with the plaintiff who must convince the court by a preponderance of the evidence that he or she has been the victim of discrimination."* Swee- ney v. *Board of Trustees of Keene State College,* 569 F.2d 169, 177 (CA1 1978) (emphasis added).

This statement by the Court of Appeals virtually parrots this Court's statements in *McDonnell Douglas* and *Furnco.* Nonetheless, this Court vacates the judgment on the ground that "the Court of Appeals appears to have imposed a heavier burden on the employer than *Furnco* war- rants." *Post,* at 295. As its sole basis for this conclusion, this Court relies on a distinction drawn for the first time in this case "between merely 'articulat[ing] some legitimate, nondiscriminatory reason' and 'prov[ing] absence of discriminatory motive.' " *Post,* at 295.[2] This novel distinction has two parts, both of which are illusory and unequivocally rejected in *Furnco* itself.

First is a purported difference between "articulating" and "proving" a legitimate motivation. Second is the difference between affirming a non- discriminatory motive and negating a discriminatory motive.

With respect to the first point, it must be noted that it was this Court in *Furnco,* not the Court of Appeals in this case, that stated that the employer's burden was to "*prov[e]* that he based his employment decision on a legitimate consideration." [3] Indeed, in the paragraph of this Court's opinion in *Furnco* cited earlier, the words "prove" and "articulate" were used interchangeably,[4] and properly so. For they were descriptive of the defendant's burden in a trial context. In litigation the only way a defendant can "articulate" the reason for his action is by adducing evidence that explains what he has done; when an executive takes the witness stand to "articulate" his reason, the litigant for whom he speaks is thereby proving those reasons. If the Court intends to authorize a

[2] The Court also suggests that "further support" for its decision is derived from the Court of Appeals' "holding" that "respondent had not met its burden because the proffered legitimate explanation did not 'rebut' or 'disprove' petitioners prima facie case . . . 569 F.2d, at 177–79." *Post* at 296 n. 2. The actual "holding" of the Court of Appeals was that "the trial court's finding that sex discrimination impeded the plaintiff's second promotion was not clearly erroneous." 569 F.2d, at 179. The Court of Appeals reached this conclusion by considering all of the evidence presented by both parties to determine whether the evidence of discrimination offered by the plaintiff was "sufficient evidence to sustain the district court's finding" in light of the counter evidence offered by the employer. *Ibid.* Such factual determinations by two federal courts are entitled to a strong presumption of validity.

[3] 438 U.S., at _____, 98 S.Ct., at 2950 (emphasis added). Quoted in n. 1, *supra.* It should also be noted that the Court of Appeals did not state that the petitioner's burden here was to "prove" anything; rather, the burden which shifted to the defendants was to "show" a legitimate reason for its action.

[4] See n. 1, *supra.*

method of articulating a factual defense without proof, surely the Court should explain what it is.

The second part of the Court's imaginative distinction is also rejected by *Furnco*. When an employer shows that a legitimate nondiscriminatory reason accounts for his action, he is simultaneously demonstrating that the action was not motivated by an illegitimate factor such as race. *Furnco* explicitly recognized this equivalence when it defined the burden on the employer as "that of proving that he based his employment decision on a legitimate consideration, and not an illegitimate one such as race." [5] Whether the issue is phrased in the affirmative or in the negative, the ultimate question involves an identification of the real reason for the employment decision. On that question—as all of these cases make perfectly clear—it is only the burden of producing evidence of legitimate nondiscriminatory reasons which shifts to the employer; the burden of persuasion, as the Court of Appeals properly recognized, remains with the plaintiff.

In short, there is no legitimate basis for concluding that the Court of Appeals erred in this case—either with or without the benefit of *Furnco*.

### (3) Objective Hiring Standards

## ALBEMARLE PAPER CO. v. MOODY

*Supreme Court of the United States, 1975*
*422 U.S. 405, 10 FEP Cases 1181*

MR. JUSTICE STEWART delivered the opinion of the Court.

These consolidated cases raise two important questions under Title VII of the Civil Rights Act of 1964, 78 Stat. 253, as amended by the Equal Employment Opportunity Act of 1972. . . . Second: What must an employer show to establish that preemployment tests racially discriminatory in effect, though not in intent, are sufficiently "job related" to survive challenge under Title VII?

. . .

### III

In *Griggs* v. *Duke Power Co.*, 401 U.S. 424 (1971), this Court unanimously held that Title VII forbids the use of employment tests that are discriminatory in effect unless the employer meets "the burden of showing that any given requirement [has] . . . a manifest relationship to the employment in question." *Id.*, at 432.[21] This burden arises, of course,

---

5 438 U.S., at _____, 98 S.Ct., at 2950.

21 [Footnotes numbered as in original.—Ed.] In *Griggs*, the Court was construing 42 U.S.C. § 2000e–2 (h), which provides in pertinent part that it shall not "be an unlawful employment practice for an employer to give and to act upon the results of any professionally developed ability test provided that such test, its administration or action upon the results is not designed, intended, or used to discriminate because of race, color, religion, sex, or national origin."

only after the complaining party or class has made out a prima facie case of discrimination, *i.e.*, has shown that the tests in question select applicants for hire or promotion in a racial pattern significantly different from that of the pool of applicants. See *McDonnell Douglas Corp.* v. *Green*, 411 U.S. 792, 802 (1973). If an employer does then meet the burden of proving that its tests are "job related," it remains open to the complaining party to show that other tests or selection devices, without a similarly undesirable racial effect, would also serve the employer's legitimate interest in "efficient and trustworthy workmanship." *Id.*, at 801. Such a showing would be evidence that the employer was using its tests merely as a "pretext" for discrimination. *Id.*, at 804–805. In the present case, however, we are concerned only with the question whether Albemarle has shown its tests to be job related.

. . .

Like the employer in *Griggs*, Albemarle uses two general ability tests, the Beta Examination, to test nonverbal intelligence, and the Wonderlic Test (Forms A and B), the purported measure of general verbal facility which was also involved in the *Griggs* case. Applicants for hire into various skilled lines of progress at the plant are required to score 100 on the Beta Exam and 18 on one of the Wonderlic Test's two, alternate forms.[22]

The question of job relatedness must be viewed in the context of the plant's operation and the history of the testing program. The plant, which now employs about 650 persons, converts raw wood into paper products. It is organized into a number of functional departments, each with one or more distinct lines of progression, the theory being that workers can move up the line as they acquire the necessary skills. The number and structure of the lines has varied greatly over time. For many years, certain lines were themselves more skilled and paid higher wages than others, and until 1964 these skilled lines were expressly reserved for white workers. In 1968, many of the unskilled "Negro" lines were "end-tailed" on to skilled "white" lines, but it apparently remains true that at least the top jobs in certain lines require greater skills than the top in other lines. In this sense, at least, it is still possible to speak of relatively skilled and relatively unskilled lines.

In the 1950's while the plant was being modernized with new and more sophisticated equipment, the company introduced a high school diploma requirement for entry into the skilled lines. Though the company soon concluded that this requirement did not improve the quality of the labor force, the requirement was continued until the District Court enjoined its use. In the late 1950's, the company began using the Beta Examination and the Bennett Mechanical Comprehension Test (also involved in the *Griggs* case) to screen applicants for entry into the skilled lines. The

---

[22] Albemarle has informed us that it has now reduced the cut-off score to 17 on the Wonderlic Test.

Bennett test was dropped several years later, but use of the Beta test continued.[23]

The company added the Wonderlic Test in 1963, for the skilled lines, on the theory that a certain verbal intelligence was called for by the increasing sophistication of the plant's operations. The company made no attempt to validate the test for job relatedness,[24] and simply adopted the national "norm" score of 18 as a cutoff point for new job applicants. After 1964, when it discontinued overt segregation of the lines of progression, the company allowed Negro workers to transfer to the skilled lines if they could pass Beta and Wonderlic Tests, but few succeeded in doing so. Incumbents in the skilled lines, some of whom had been hired before adoption of the tests, were not required to pass them to retain their jobs or their promotion rights. The record shows that a number of white incumbents in high ranking job groups could not pass the tests.[25]

Because departmental reorganization continued up to the point of trial, and has indeed continued since that point, the details of the testing program are less than clear from the record. The District Court found that, since 1963, the Beta and Wonderlic tests have been used in 13 lines of progression, within eight departments. Albemarle contends that at present the tests are used in only eight lines of progression, within four departments.

Four months before this case went to trial, Albemarle engaged an expert in industrial psychology to "validate" the job relatedness of its testing program. He spent a half day at the plant and devised a "concurrent validation" study, which was conducted by plant officials, without his supervision. The expert then subjected the results to statistical analysis. The study dealt with 10 job groupings, selected from near the top of

[23] While the Company contends that the Bennett and Beta Tests were "locally validated" when they were introduced no record of this validation was made. Plant officials could recall only the barest outlines of the alleged validation. Job relatedness cannot be proven through vague and insubstantiated hearsay.

[24] As explained by the responsible plant official, the Wonderlic Test was chosen in rather casual fashion.

"I had had experience with using the Wonderlic before, which is a short form Verbal Intelligence Test, and knew that it had, uh, probably more validation studies behind it than any other short form Verbal Intelligence Test. So, after consultation we decided to institute the Wonderlic, in addition to the Beta, in view of the fact that the mill had changed quite a bit and it had become exceedingly more complex in operation. . . . We did not, uh, validate it, uh, locally, primarily, because of the, the expense of conducting such a validation, and there were some other considerations, such as, uh, we didn't know whether we would get the co-operation of the employees that we'd need to validate it against in taking the test, and we certainly have to have that, so we used National Norms and on my suggestion after study of the Wonderlic and Norms had been established nationally for skilled jobs, we developed a, uh, cut-off score of eighteen (18)."

[25] In the course of a 1971 validation effort, . . . test scores were accumulated for 105 incumbent employees (101 of whom were white) working in relatively high ranking jobs. Some of these employees apparently took the tests for the first time as part of this study. The Company testified that the test cutoff scores originally used to screen these incumbents for employment or promotion "couldn't have been . . . very high scores because some of these guys tested very low, as low as 8 on the Wonderlic test and as low as 95 in the Beta. They couldn't have been using very high cut-off scores or they wouldn't have these low testing employees."

the nine of the lines of progression.[26] Jobs were grouped together solely by their proximity in the line of progression; no attempt was made to analyze jobs in terms of the particular skills they might require. All, or nearly all, employees in the selected groups participated in the study— 105 employees in all, but only four Negroes. Within each job grouping, the study compared the test scores of each employee with an independent "ranking" of the employee, relative to each of his coworkers, made by two of the employee's supervisors. The supervisors, who did not know the test scores, were asked to

"determine which ones they felt irrespective of the job that they were actually doing, but in their respective jobs, did a better job than the person they were rating against. . . .[27]

For each job grouping, the expert computed the "Phi coefficient" of statistical correlation between the test scores and an average of the two supervisorial rankings. Consonant with professional conventions, the expert regarded as "statistically significant" any correlation that could have occurred by chance only five times, or less, in 100 trials.[28] On the basis of these results, the District Court found that "[t]he personnel tests administered at the plant have undergone validation studies and have been proven to be job related." Like the Court of Appeals, we are constrained to disagree.

The EEOC has issued "Guidelines" for employers seeking to determine, through professional validation studies, whether their employment tests are job related. 29 CFR Part 1607 (1974). These Guidelines draw upon and make reference to professional standards of test validation established by the American Psychological Association.[29] The EEOC Guidelines are not administrative "regulations" promulgated pursuant to formal procedures established by the Congress. But, as this Court has heretofore noted, they do constitute "[t]he administrative interpretation of the Act by the enforcing agency," and consequently they are "entitled to great deference." *Griggs* v. *Duke Power Co., supra,* 401 U.S., at 433-434, 3 FEP Cases, at 179. See also *Espinoza* v. *Farah Mfg. Co.,* 414 U.S. 86, 94, 6 FEP Cases 933.

The message of these Guidelines is the same as that of the *Griggs* case —that discriminatory tests are impermissible unless shown, by professionally acceptable methods, to be "predictive of or significantly correlated with important elements of work behavior which comprise or are relevant to the job or jobs for which candidates are being evaluated." 29 CFR § 1607.4(c).

---

[26] See the charts appended to this opinion. It should be noted that testing is no longer required for some of the job groups tested.

[27] This "standard" for the ranking was described by the plant official who oversaw the conduct of the study.

[28] The results of the study are displayed on Chart A appended to this opinion.

[29] American Psychological Association Standards for Educational and Psychological Tests and Manuals (1966). A volume of the same title, containing modifications, was issued in 1974. The EEOC Guidelines refer to the APA Standards at 29 C.F.R. § 1607.5(a). Very similar guidelines have been issued by the Secretary of Labor for the use of federal contractors. 41 CFR § 60-3.1 *et seq.* (1974).

Measured against the Guidelines, Albemarle's validation study is materially defective in several respects:

(1) Even if it had been otherwise adequate, the study would not have "validated" the Beta and Wonderlic test battery for all of the skilled lines of progression for which the two sets are, apparently, now required. The study showed significant correlations for the Beta Exam in only three of the eight lines. Though the Wonderlic Test's Form A and Form B are in theory identical and interchangeable measures of verbal facility, significant correlations for one Form but not for the other were obtained in four job groupings. In two job groupings neither Form showed a significant correlation. Within some of the lines of progression, one Form was found acceptable for some job groupings but not for others. Even if the study were otherwise reliable, this odd patchwork of results would not entitle Albemarle to impose its testing program under the Guidelines. A test may be used in jobs other than those for which it has been professionally validated only if there are "no significant differences" between the studied and unstudied jobs. 29 CFR § 1607.4(c)(2). The study in this case involved no analysis of the attributes of, or the particular skills needed in, the studied job groups. There is accordingly no basis for concluding that "no significant differences" exist among the lines of progression, or among distinct job groupings within the studied lines of progression. Indeed, the study's checkered results appear to compel the opposite conclusion.

(2) The study compared test scores with subjective supervisorial rankings. While they allow the use of supervisorial rankings in test validation, the Guidelines quite plainly contemplate that the rankings will be elicited with far more care than was demonstrated here.[30] Albemarle's supervisors were asked to rank employees by a "standard" that was extremely vague and fatally open to divergent interpretations. Each "job grouping" contained a number of different jobs, and the supervisors were asked, in each grouping, to

"determine which ones [employees] they felt irrespective of the job that they were actually doing, but in their respective jobs, did a better job than the person they were rating against. . . ."[31]

[30] The Guidelines provide, at CFR § 1607.5(b)(3) and (4):

"(3) The work behaviors or other criteria of employee adequacy which the test is intended to predict or identify must be fully described; and, additionally, in the case of rating techniques, the appraisal form(s) and instructions to the rater(s) must be included as a part of the validation evidence. Such criteria may include measures other than actual work proficiency, such as training time, supervisory ratings, regularity of attendance and tenure. Whatever criteria are used they must represent major or critical work behaviors as revealed by careful job analyses.

"(4) In view of the possibility of bias inherent in subjective evaluations, supervisory rating techniques should be carefully developed, and the ratings should be closely examined for evidence of bias. In addition, minorities might obtain unfairly low performance criterion scores for reasons other than supervisor's prejudice, as when, as new employees, they have had less opportunity to learn job skills. The general point is that all criteria need to be examined to insure freedom from factors which would unfairly depress the scores of minority groups."

[31] See n. 27, *supra*.

There is no way of knowing precisely what criteria of job performance the supervisors were considering, whether each of the supervisors was considering the same criteria—or whether, indeed, any of the supervisors actually applied a focused and stable body of criteria of any kind.[32] There is, in short, simply no way to determine whether the criteria *actually* considered were sufficiently related to the Company's legitimate interest in job-specific ability to justify a testing system with a racially discriminatory impact.

(3) The company's study focused, in most cases, on job groups near the top of the various lines of progression. In *Griggs* v. *Duke Power Co., supra,* the Court left open "the question whether testing requirements that take into account capability for the next succeeding position or related future promotion might be utilized upon a showing that such long-range requirements fulfill a genuine business need." 401 U.S., at 432, 3 FEP Cases at 178. The Guidelines take a sensible approach to this issue, and we now endorse it:

"If job progression structures and seniority provisions are so established that new employees will probably, within a reasonable period of time and in a great majority of cases, progress to a higher level, it may be considered that candidates are being evaluated for jobs at that higher level. However, where job progression is not so nearly automatic, or the time span is such that higher level jobs or employees' potential may be expected to change in significant ways, it shall be considered that candidates are being evaluated for a job at or near the entry level." 29 CFR § 1607.4(c)(1).

The fact that the best of those employees working near the top of a line of progression score well on a test does not necessarily mean that that test, or some particular cutoff score on the test, is a permissible measure of the minimal qualifications of new workers, entering lower level jobs. In drawing any such conclusion, detailed consideration must be given to the normal speed of promotion, to the efficacy of on-the-job training in the scheme of promotion, and to the possible use of testing as a promotion device, rather than as a screen for entry into low-level jobs. The District Court made no findings on these issues. The issues take on special importance in a case, such as this one, where incumbent employees are permitted to work at even high-level jobs without passing the company's test battery. See 29 CFR § 1607.11.

(4) Albemarle's validation study dealt only with job-experienced, white workers; but the tests themselves are given to new job applicants, who are younger, largely inexperienced, and in many instances nonwhite. The Standards of the American Psychological Association state that it is "essential" that

"[t]he validity of a test should be determined on subjects who are at the

---

[32] It cannot escape notice that Albemarle's study was conducted by plant officials, without neutral, on-the-scene oversight, at a time when this litigation was about to come to trial. Studies so closely controlled by an interested party in litigation must be examined with great care.

age or in the same educational or vocational situation as the persons for whom the test is recommended in practice." [33]

The EEOC Guidelines likewise provide that "[d]ata must be generated and results separately reported for minority or non-minority groups wherever technically feasible." 29 CFR § 1607.5(b)(5). In the present case, such "differential validation" as to racial groups was very likely not "feasible," because years of discrimination at the plant have insured that nearly all of the upper level employees are white. But there has been no clear showing that differential validation was not feasible for lower-level jobs. More importantly, the Guidelines provide:

"If it is not technically feasible to include minority employees in validation studies conducted on the present work force, the conduct of a validation study without minority candidates does not relieve any person of his subsequent obligation for validation when inclusion of minority candidates becomes technically feasible." 29 CFR § 1607.5(b)(1).

. . .

"[E]vidence of satisfactory validity based on other groups will be regarded as only provisional compliance with the guidelines pending separate validation of the test for the minority groups in question." 29 CFR § 1607.5(b)(5).

For all these reasons, we agree with the Court of Appeals that the District Court erred in concluding that Albemarle had proved the job relatedness of its testing program and that the respondents were consequently not entitled to equitable relief. The outright reversal by the Court of Appeals implied that an injunction should immediately issue against all use of testing at the plant. Because the particular circumstances of this case, however, it appears that the more prudent course is to leave to the District Court the precise fashioning of the necessary relief in the first instance. During the appellate stages of this litigation, the plant has apparently been amending its departmental organization and the use made of its tests. The appropriate standard of proof for job relatedness has not been clarified until today. Similarly, the respondents have not until today been specifically apprised of their opportunity to present evidence that even validated tests might be a "pretext" for discrimination in light of alternative selection procedures available to the company. We also note that the Guidelines authorize provisional use of tests, pending new validation efforts, in certain very limited circumstances. 29 CFR § 1607.9. Whether such circumstances now obtain is a matter best decided, in the first instance, by the District Court. That court will be free to take such new evidence, and to exercise such control of the company's use and validation of employee selection procedures, as are warranted by the circumstances and by the controlling law.

Accordingly, the judgment is vacated, and these cases are remanded to the District Court for proceedings consistent with this opinion.

It is so ordered.

---

[33] APA Standards, *supra*, n. 29 at ¶ C 5.4.

. . .

MR. CHIEF JUSTICE BURGER, concurring in part and dissenting in part.
. . .

The Court's treatment of the testing issue is equally troubling. Its entire analysis is based upon a wooden application of EEOC Guidelines which, it says, are entitled to "great deference" as an administrative interpretation of Title VII under *Griggs* v. *Duke Power Co.,* 401 U.S. 424, 3 FEP Cases 175 (1971). The Court's reliance upon *Griggs* is misplaced. There we were dealing with Guidelines which state that a test must be demonstrated to be job-related before it can qualify for the exemption contained in § 703 (h) of Title VII as a device not "designed, intended or used to discriminate. . . ." Because this interpretation of specific statutory language was supported by both the Act and its legislative history, we observed that there was "good reason to treat the guidelines as expressing the will of Congress." 401 U.S., at 434, 3 FEP Cases, at 179. See also *Espinoza* v. *Farah Mfg. Co.,* 414 U.S. 86, 93-95, 6 FEP Cases 933 (1973).

In contrast, the Guidelines upon which the Court now relies relate to methods for *proving* job-relatedness; they interpret no section of Title VII and are nowhere referred to in its legislative history. Moreover, they are not federal regulations which have been submitted to public comment and scrutiny as required by the Administrative Procedure Act.[3] Thus, slavish adherence to the EEOC Guidelines regarding test validation should not be required; those provisions are, as their title suggests, guides entitled to the same weight as other well-founded testimony by experts in the field of employment testing.

The District Court so considered the Guidelines in this case and resolved any conflicts in favor of Albemarle's experts. For example, with respect to the question whether validating tests for persons at or near the top of a line of progression "is a permissible measure of the minimal qualifications of new workers," *ante,* at 27, the District Court found:

"The group tested was typical of employees in the skilled lines of progression. They were selected from the top and middle of various lines. Professional studies have shown that when tests are validated in such a narrow range of competence, there is a greater chance that the test will validate even a broader range, that is, if job candidates as well as present employees are tested." App., at 490-491.

Unless this Court is prepared to hold that this and similar factual findings are clearly erroneous, the District Court's conclusion that Albemarle had sustained its burden of showing that its tests were job-related is entitled to affirmance, if we follow traditional standards of review. At the very least, the case should be remanded to the Court of Appeals with instructions that it reconsider the testing issue, giving the District Court's findings of fact the deference to which they are entitled.

[3] Such comment would not be a mere formality in light of the fact that many of the EEOC Guidelines are not universally accepted. For example, the Guideline relating to "differential validation," upon which the Court relies in this case, *ante,* at 27-28, 10 FEP Cases, at 1194, has been questioned by the American Psychological Association. See *United States* v. *Georgia Power Co.,* 474 F.2d 906, 914 n. 8, 5 FEP Cases 587, 592 (CA5 1974).

## WASHINGTON v. DAVIS

*Supreme Court of the United States, 1976*
*426 U.S. 229, 12 FEP Cases 1415*

MR. JUSTICE WHITE delivered the opinion of the Court.

This case involves the validity of a qualifying test administered to applicants for positions as police officers in the District of Columbia Metropolitan Police Department. The test was sustained by the District Court but invalidated by the Court of Appeals. We are in agreement with the District Court and hence reverse the judgment of the Court of Appeals.

I

This action began on April 10, 1970, when two Negro police officers filed suit against the then Commissioner of the District of Columbia, the Chief of the District's metropolitan Police Department and the Commissioners of the United States Civil Service Commission.[1] An amended complaint, filed December 10, alleged that the promotion policies of the Department were racially discriminatory and sought a declaratory judgment and an injunction. The respondents Harley and Sellers were permitted to intervene, their amended complaint asserting that their applications to become officers in the Department had been rejected, and that the Department's recruiting procedures discriminated on the basis of race against black applicants by a series of practices including, but not limited to, a written personnel test which excluded a disproportionately high number of Negro applicants. These practices were asserted to violate respondents' rights "under the due process clause of the Fifth Amendment to the United States Constitution, under 42 U.S.C. § 1981 and under D. C. Code § 1-320."[2] Defendants answered,

---

[1] [Footnotes numbered as in original.—Ed.] Under § 4-103 of the District of Columbia Code, appointments to the Metropolitan police force were to be made by the Commissioner subject to the provisions of Title 5 of the United States Code relating to the classified civil service. The District of Columbia Council and the Office of Commissioner of the District of Columbia, established by Reorganization Plan No. 37 of 1967, were abolished as of January 2, 1975, and replaced by the Council of the District of Columbia and the Office of Mayor of the District of Columbia.

[2] Title 42 U.S.C. § 1981 provides:

"All persons within the jurisdiction of the United States shall have the same right in every State and Territory to make and enforce contracts, to sue, be parties, give evidence, and to the full and equal benefit of all laws and proceedings for the security of persons and property as is enjoyed by white citizens, and shall be subject to like punishment, pains, penalties, taxes, licenses, and exactions of every kind, and to no other."

Section 1-320 of the District of Columbia Code provides:

"In any program of recruitment or hiring of individuals to fill positions in the government of the District of Columbia, no officer or employee of the government of the District of Columbia shall exclude or give preference to the residents of the District of Columbia or any State of the United States on the basis of residence, religion, race, color, or national origin."

One of the provisions expressly made applicable to the Metropolitan police force by § 4-103 is 5 U.S.C. § 3304(a) which provides: "§ 3304. Competitive service; examinations.

and discovery and various other proceedings followed.[3] Respondents then filed a motion for partial summary judgment with respect to the recruiting phase of the case, seeking a declaration that the test administered to those applying to become police officers is "unlawfully discriminatory and therefore in violation of the Due Process Clause of the Fifth Amendment. . . ." No issue under any statute or regulation was raised by the motion. The District of Columbia defendants, petitioners here, and the federal parties also filed motions for summary judgment with respect to the recruiting aspects of the case asserting that respondents were entitled to relief on neither constitutional nor statutory grounds.[4] The District Court granted petitioners' and denied respondents' motions. *Davis* v. *Washington,* 348 F.Supp. 15, 4 FEP Cases 1132 (DC 1972).

According to the findings and conclusions of the District Court, to be accepted by the Department and to enter an intensive 17-week training program, the police recruit was required to satisfy certain physical and character standards, to be a high school graduate or its equivalent and to receive a grade of at least 40 on "Test 21," which is "an examination that is used generally throughout the federal service," which "was developed by the Civil Service Commission not the Police Department" and which was "designed to test verbal ability, vocabulary, reading and comprehension." 348 F.Supp., at 16, 4 FEP Cases, at 1132.

The validity of Test 21 was the sole issue before the court on the motions for summary judgment. The District Court noted that there was no claim of "an intentional discrimination or purposeful discriminatory actions" but only a claim that Test 21 bore no relationship to job performance and "has a highly discriminatory impact in screening out black candidates." 348 F.Supp., at 16, 4 FEP Cases, at 1133. Petitioners' evidence, the District Court said, warranted three conclusions: "(a) The number of black police officers, while substantial, is not proportionate to the population mix of the city. (b) A higher percentage of blacks fail the Test than whites. (c) The Test has not been validated to establish its reliability for measuring subsequent job performance." *Ibid.* This showing was deemed sufficient to shift the burden of proof to

"(a) The President may prescribe rules which shall provide, as nearly as conditions of good administration warrant, for—
"(1) open, competitive examinations for testing applicants for appointment in the competitive service which are practical in character and as far as possible relate to matters that fairly test the relative capacity and fitness of the applicants for the appointment sought; and
"(2) noncompetitive examinations when competent applicants do not compete after notice has been given of the existence of the vacancy."
The complaint asserted no claim under § 3304.
[3] Those proceedings included a hearing on respondents' motion for an order designating the case as a class action. A ruling on the motion was held in abeyance and was never granted insofar as the record before us reveals.
[4] In support of the motion, petitioners and the federal parties urged that they were in compliance with all applicable constitutional, statutory and regulatory provisions, including the provisions of the Civil Service Act which since 1883 were said to have established a "job relatedness" standard for employment.

the defendants in the action, petitioners here; but the court nevertheless concluded that on the undisputed facts respondents were not entitled to relief. The District Court relied on several factors. Since August 1969, 44% of new police force recruits had been black; that figure also represented the proportion of blacks on the total force and was roughly equivalent to 20-29-year-old blacks in the 50-mile radius in which the recruiting efforts of the Police Department had been concentrated. It was undisputed that the Department had systematically and affirmatively sought to enroll black officers many of whom passed the test but failed to report for duty. The District Court rejected the assertion that Test 21 was culturally slanted to favor whites and was "satisfied that the undisputable facts prove the test to be reasonably and directly related to the requirements of the police recruit training program and that it is neither so designed nor operated to discriminate against otherwise qualified blacks." 348 F.Supp., at 17, 4 FEP Cases, at 1133. It was thus not necessary to show that Test 21 was not only a useful indicator of training school performance but had also been validated in terms of job performance—"the lack of job performance validation does not defeat the test given its direct relationship to recruiting and the valid part it plays in this process." The District Court ultimately concluded that "the proof is wholly lacking that a police officer qualifies on the color of his skin rather than ability" and that the Department "should not be required on this showing to lower standards or to abandon efforts to achieve excellence." 348 F.Supp., at 18, 4 FEP Cases, at 1134.

Having lost on both constitutional and statutory issues in the District Court, respondents brought the case to the Court of Appeals claiming that their summary judgment motion, which rested on purely constitutional grounds, should have been granted. The tendered constitutional issue was whether the use of Test 21 invidiously discriminated against Negroes and hence denied them due process of law contrary to the commands of the Fifth Amendment. The Court of Appeals, addressing that issue, announced that it would be guided by *Griggs* v. *Duke Power Co.,* 401 U.S. 424, 3 FEP Cases 175 (1971), a case involving the interpretation and application of Title VII of the Civil Rights Act of 1964, and held that the statutory standards elucidated in that case were to govern the due process question tendered in this one.[6] 168 U.S. App. D.C. 42, 512 F.2d 956, 10 FEP Cases 105 (1975). The court went on to declare that lack of discriminatory intent in designing and administering Test 21 was irrelevant; the critical fact was rather that a far greater proportion of blacks—four times as many—failed the test than did whites. This

---

[6] "Although appellants' complaint did not allege a violation of Title VII of the Civil Rights Act of 1964, which then was inapplicable to the Federal Government, decisions applying Title VII furnish additional instruction as to the legal standard governing the issues raised in this case. The many decisions disposing of employment discrimination claims on constitutional grounds have made no distinction between the constitutional standard and the statutory standard under Title VII." Footnote 2 of the Court of Appeals opinion, 168 U.S. App. D.C., at 44 n. 2, 512 F.2d, at 958, 10 FEP Cases, at 105-106.

disproportionate impact, standing alone and without regard to whether it indicated a discriminatory purpose, was held sufficient to establish a constitutional violation, absent proof by petitioners that the test was an adequate measure of job performance in addition to being an indicator of probable success in the training program, a burden which the court ruled petitioners had failed to discharge. That the Department had made substantial efforts to recruit blacks was held beside the point and the fact that the racial distribution of recent hirings and of the Department itself might be roughly equivalent to the racial makeup of the surrounding community, broadly conceived, was put aside as a "comparison [not] material to this appeal." 168 U.S. App. D.C., at 46 n.24; 512 F.2d, at 960 n.24, 10 FEP Cases, at 107. The Court of Appeals, over a dissent, accordingly reversed the judgment of the District Court and directed that respondents' motion for partial summary judgment be granted. We granted the petition for certiorari, 423 U.S. 820 (1975), filed by the District of Columbia officials.[7]

## II

Because the Court of Appeals erroneously applied the legal standards applicable to Title VII cases in resolving the constitutional issue before it, we reverse its judgment in respondents' favor. Although the petition for certiorari did not present this ground for reversal,[8] our Rule 40 (1)(d)(2) provides that we "may notice a plain error not presented";[9] and this is an appropriate occasion to invoke the rule.

As the Court of Appeals understood Title VII,[10] employees or applicants proceeding under it need not concern themselves with the employer's possibly discriminatory purpose but instead may focus solely on the racially differential impact of the challenged hiring or promotion practices. This is not the constitutional rule. We have never held that

---

[7] The Civil Service Commissioners, defendants in the District Court, did not petition for writ of certiorari but have filed a brief as respondents. See our Rule 25 (4). We shall at times refer to them as the "federal parties."

[8] Apparently not disputing the applicability of the *Griggs* and Title VII standards in resolving this case, petitioners presented issues going only to whether *Griggs* had been misapplied by the Court of Appeals.

[9] See, e.g., *Silber* v. *United States,* 370 U.S. 717 (1962); *Brotherhood of Carpenters* v. *United States,* 330 U.S. 395, 412, 19 LRRM 2406 (1947); *Sibbach* v. *Wilson & Co.,* 312 U.S. 1, 16 (1941); *Mahler* v. *Eby,* 264 U.S. 32, 45 (1924); *Weems* v. *United States,* 217 U.S. 349, 362 (1910).

[10] Although Title VII standards have dominated this case, the statute was not applicable to federal employees when the complaint was filed; and although the 1972 amendments extending the title to reach government employees were adopted prior to the District Court's judgment, the complaint was not amended to state a claim under that title, nor did the case thereafter proceed as a Title VII case. Respondents' motion for partial summary judgment, filed after the 1972 amendments, rested solely on constitutional grounds; and the Court of Appeals ruled that the motion should have been granted.

At the oral arguments before this Court, when petitioners' counsel was asked whether "this is just a purely Title VII case as it comes to us from the Court of Appeals without any constitutional overtones," counsel responded: "My trouble honestly with that proposition is the procedural requirements to get into court under Title VII and this case has not met them." Tr. of Oral. Arg., at 66.

the constitutional standard for adjudicating claims of invidious racial discrimination is identical to the standards applicable under Title VII, and we decline to do so today.

The central purpose of the Equal Protection Clause of the Fourteenth Amendment is the prevention of official conduct discriminating on the basis of race. It is also true that the Due Process Clause of the Fifth Amendment contains an equal protection component prohibiting the United States from invidiously discriminating between individuals or groups. *Bolling* v. *Sharpe,* 347 U.S. 497 (1954). But our cases have not embraced the proposition that a law or other official act, without regard to whether it reflects a racially discriminatory purpose, is unconstitutional *solely* because it has a racially disproportionate impact.

Almost 100 years ago, *Strauder* v. *West Virginia,* 100 U.S. 303 (1879), established that the exclusion of Negroes from grand and petit juries in criminal proceedings violated the Equal Protection Clause, but the fact that a particular jury or a series of juries does not statistically reflect the racial composition of the community does not in itself make out an invidious discrimination forbidden by the Clause. "A purpose to discriminate must be present which may be proven by systematic exclusion of eligible jurymen of the prescribed race or by an unequal application of the law to such an extent as to show intentional discrimination." *Akins* v. *Texas,* 325 U.S. 398, 403-404 (1945). A defendant in a criminal case is entitled "to require that the State not deliberately and systematically deny to the members of his race the right to participate as jurors in the administration of justice." See also *Carter* v. *Jury Commission,* 396 U.S. 320, 335-337, 339 (1970); *Cassell* v. *Texas,* 339 U.S. 282, 287-290 (1950); *Patton* v. *Mississippi,* 332 U.S. 463, 468-469 (1947).

The rule is the same in other contexts. *Wright* v. *Rockefeller,* 376 U.S. 52 (1964), upheld a New York congressional apportionment statute against claims that district lines had been racially gerrymandered. The challenged districts were made up predominantly of whites or of minority races, and their boundaries were irregularly drawn. The challengers did not prevail because they failed to prove that the New York legislature "was either motivated by racial considerations or in fact drew the districts on racial lines"; the plaintiffs had not shown that the statute "was the product of a state contrivance to segregate on the basis of race or place of origin." 376 U.S., at 56, 58. The dissenters were in agreement that the issue was whether the "boundaries . . . were purposefully drawn on racial lines." 376 U.S., at 67.

The school desegregation cases have also adhered to the basic equal protection principle that the invidious quality of a law claimed to be racially discriminatory must ultimately be traced to a racially discriminatory purpose. That these are both predominantly black and predominantly white schools in a community is not alone violative of the Equal Protection Clause. The essential element of *de jure* segregation is "a current condition of segregation resulting from intentional state action . . . the differentiating factor between *de jure* segregation and so-called *de facto* segregation . . . is *purpose* or *intent* to segregate." *Keyes* v. *School District No. 1*, 413 U.S. 189, 205, 208 (1973). See also *id.*, at 199, 211, 213. The Court has also recently rejected allegations of racial discrimination based solely on the statistically disproportionate racial impact of various provisions of the Social Security Act because "the acceptance of appellant's constitutional theory would render suspect each difference in treatment among the grant classes, however lacking the racial motivation and however rational the treatment might be." *Jefferson* v. *Hackney*, 406 U.S. 535, 548 (1972). And compare *Hunter* v. *Erickson*, 393 U.S. 385 (1969), with *James* v. *Valtierra* 402 U.S. 137 (1971).

This is not to say that the necessary discriminatory racial purpose must be expressed or appear on the face of the statute, or that a law's disproportionate impact is irrelevant in cases involving Constitution-based claims of racial discrimination. A statute, otherwise neutral on its face, must not be applied so as invidiously to discriminate on the basis of race. *Yick Wo* v. *Hopkins*, 118 U.S. 356 (1886). It is also clear from the cases dealing with racial discrimination in the selection of juries that the systematic exclusion of Negroes is itself such an "unequal application of the law . . . as to show intentional discrimination." *Akins* v. *Texas, supra*, at 404. *Smith* v. *Texas*, 311 U.S. 128 (1940); *Pierre* v. *Louisiana*, 306 U.S. 354 (1939); *Neal* v. *Delaware*, 103 U.S. 370 (1881). A prima facie case of discriminatory purposes may be proved as well by the absence of Negroes on a particular jury combined with the failure of the jury commissioners to be informed of eligible Negro jurors in a community, *Hill* v. *Texas*, 316 U.S. 400, 404 (1942), or with racially non-neutral selection procedures, *Alexander* v. *Louisiana*, 405 U.S. 625 (1972); *Avery* v. *Georgia*, 345 U.S. 559 (1953); *Whitus* v. *Georgia*, 385 U.S. 545 (1967). With a prima facie case made out "the burden of proof shifts to the State to rebut the presumption of unconstitutional action by showing that permissible racially neutral selection criteria and procedures have produced the monochromatic result." *Alexander, supra*, at 632. See also *Turner* v. *Fouche*, 396 U.S. 346, 361 (1970); *Eubanks* v. *Louisiana*, 356 U.S. 584, 587 (1958).

Necessarily, an invidious discriminatory purpose may often be inferred from the totality of the relevant facts, including the fact, if it is true, that the law bears more heavily on one race than another. It is also not infrequently true that the discriminatory impact—in the jury cases for example, the total or seriously disproportionate exclusion of Negroes from jury venires—may for all practical purposes demonstrate unconstitutionality because in various circumstances the discrimination is very difficult to explain on nonracial grounds. Nevertheless we have not held that a law, neutral on its face and serving ends otherwise within the power of government to pursue, is invalid under the Equal Protection Clause simply because it may affect a greater proportion of one race than of another. Disproportionate impact is not irrelevant, but it is not the sole touchstone of an invidious racial discrimination forbidden by the Constitution. Standing alone, it does not trigger the rule,

*McLaughlin* v. *Florida*, 379 U.S. 184 (1964), that racial classifications are to be subjected to the strictest scrutiny and are justifiable only by the weightiest of considerations.

There are some indications to the contrary in our cases. [Discussion omitted.]

As an initial matter, we have difficulty understanding how a law establishing a racially neutral qualification for employment is nevertheless racially discriminatory and denies "any person equal protection of the laws" simply because a greater proportion of Negroes fail to qualify than members of other racial or ethnic groups. Had respondents, along with all others who had failed Test 21, whether white or black, brought an action claiming that the test denied each of them equal protection of the laws as compared with those who had passed with high enough scores to qualify them as police recruits, it is most unlikely that their challenge would have been sustained. Test 21, which is administered generally to prospective government employees, concededly seeks to ascertain whether those who take it have acquired a particular level of verbal skill; and it is untenable that the Constitution prevents the government from seeking modestly to upgrade the communicative abilities of its employees rather than to be satisfied with some lower level of competence, particularly where the job requires special ability to communicate orally and in writing. Respondents, as Negroes, could no more successfully claim that the test denied them equal protection than could white applicants who also failed. The conclusion would not be different in the face of proof that more Negroes than whites had been disqualified by Test 21. That other Negroes also failed to score well would, alone, not demonstrate that respondents individually were being denied equal protection of the laws by the application of an otherwise valid qualifying test being administered to prospective police recruits.

Nor on the facts of the case before us would the disproportionate impact of Test 21 warrant the conclusion that it is a purposeful device to discriminate against Negroes and hence an infringement of the constitutional rights of respondents as well as other black applicants. As we have said, the test is neutral on its face and rationally may be said to serve a purpose the government is constitutionally empowered to pursue. Even agreeing with the District Court that the differential racial effect of Test 21 called for further inquiry, we think the District Court correctly held that the affirmative efforts of the Metropolitan Police Department to recruit black officers, the changing racial composition of the recruit classes and of the force in general, and the relationship of the test to the training program negated any inference that the Department discriminated on the basis of race or that "a police officer qualifies on the color of his skin rather than ability." 348 F.Supp., at 18, 4 FEP Cases, at 1134.

Under Title VII, Congress provided that when hiring and promotion practices disqualifying substantially disproportionate numbers of blacks are challenged, discriminatory purpose need not be proved, and that it is an insufficient response to demonstrate some rational basis for the challenged practices. It is necessary, in addition, that they be "validated" in terms of job performance in any one of several ways, perhaps by ascertaining the minimum skill, ability or potential necessary for the position at issue and determining whether the qualifying tests are appropriate for the selection of qualified applicants for the job in question.[13] However this process proceeds, it involves a more probing judicial review of, and less deference to, the seemingly reasonable acts of administrators and executives than is appropriate under the Constitution where special racial impact, without discriminatory purpose is claimed. We are not disposed to adopt this more rigorous standard for the purposes of applying the Fifth and the Fourteenth Amendments in cases such as this.

A rule that a statute designed to serve neutral ends is nevertheless invalid, absent compelling justification, if in practice it benefits or burdens one race more than another would be far reaching and would raise serious questions about, and perhaps invalidate, a whole range of tax, welfare, public service, regulatory, and licensing statutes that may be more burdensome to the poor and to the average black than to the more affluent white.[14]

Given that rule, such consequences would perhaps be likely to follow. However, in our view, extension of the rule beyond those areas where it is already applicable by reason of statute, such as in the field of public employment, should await legislative prescription.

As we have indicated, it was error to direct summary judgment for respondents based on the Fifth Amendment.

---

[13] It appears beyond doubt by now that there is no single method for appropriately validating employment tests for their relationship to job performance. Professional standards developed by the American Psychological Association in its Standards for Educational and Psychological Tests and Manuals (1966), accept three basic methods of validation: "empirical" or "criterion" validity (demonstrated by identifying criteria that indicate successful job performance and then correlating test scores and the criteria so identified), "construct" validity (demonstrated by examination structured to measure the degree to which job applicants have identifiable characteristics that have been determined to be important in successful job performance), and "content" validity (demonstrated by tests whose content closely approximates tasks to be performed on the job by the applicant). These standards have been relied upon by the Equal Employment Opportunity Commission in fashioning its Guidelines on Employment Selection procedures, 29 CFR pt. 1607, and have been judicially noted in cases where validation of employment tests has been in issue. See, e.g., *Albemarle Paper Co.* v. *Moody*, 422 U.S. 405, 431, 10 FEP Cases 1181, 1192 (1975); *Douglas v. Hampton* 168 U.S. App. D.C. 62, 512 F.2d 976, 984, 10 FEP Cases 91, 96 (1975); *Vulcan Society* v. *Civil Service Comm'n*, 490 F.2d 387, 394, 6 FEP Cases 1045 (CA2 1973).

[14] Goodman, *De facto School Segregation: Constitutional and Empirical Analysis,* 60 CAL L. REV. 275, 300 (1972), suggests that disproportionate impact analysis might invalidate "tests and qualifications for voting, draft deferment, public employment, jury service and other government-conferred benefits and opportunities . . .; [s]ales taxes, bail schedules, utility rates, bridge tolls, license fees, and other state-imposed charges." It has also been argued that minimum wage and usury laws as well as professional licensing requirements would require major modifications in light of the unequal impact rule. Silverman, *Equal Protection Economic Legislation and Racial Discrimination*, 25 VAND. L. REV. 1183 (1972). See also Demsetz, *Minorities in the Market Place,* 43 N.C.L. REV. 271.

## III

We also hold that the Court of Appeals should have affirmed the judgment of the District Court granting the motions for summary judgment filed by petitioners and the federal parties. Respondents were entitled to relief on neither constitutional nor statutory grounds.

The submission of the defendants in the District Court was that Test 21 complied with all applicable statutory as well as constitutional requirements; and they appear not to have disputed that under the statutes and regulations governing their conduct standards similar to those obtaining under Title VII had to be satisfied.[15] The District Court also assumed that Title VII standards were to control the case, identified the determinative issue as whether Test 21 was sufficiently job related and proceeded to uphold use of the test because it was "directly related to a determination of whether the applicant possesses sufficient skills requisite to the demands of the curriculum a recruit must master at the police academy." 348 F.Supp., at 17, 4 FEP Cases, at 1133. The Court of Appeals reversed because the relationship between Test 21 and training school success, if demonstrated at all, did not satisfy what it deemed to be the crucial requirement of a direct relationship between performance on Test 21 and performance on the policeman's job.

We agree with petitioners and the federal respondents that this was error. The advisability of the police recruit training course informing the recruit about his upcoming job, acquainting him with its demands and attempting to import a modicum of required skills seems conceded. It is also apparent to us, as it was to the District Judge, that some minimum verbal and communicative skill would be very useful, if not essential, to satisfactory progress in the training regimen. Based on the evidence before him, the District Judge concluded that Test 21 was directly related to the requirements of the police training program and that a positive relationship between the test and training course performance was sufficient to validate the former, wholly aside from its possible relationship to actual performance as a police officer. This conclusion of the District Judge that training-program validation may itself be sufficient is supported by regulations of the Civil Service Commis-

---

15 In their memorandum supporting their motion for summary judgment the federal parties argued:
"In *Griggs, supra,* the Supreme Court set a job-relationship standard for the private sector employees which has been a standard for federal employment since the passage of the Civil Service Act in 1883. In that act Congress has mandated that the federal government must use '. . . examinations for testing applicants for appointment . . . which . . . as far as possible relate to matters that fairly test the relative capacity and fitness of the applicants for the appointments sought.' 5 U.S.C. § 3304(a)(1). Defendants contend that they have been following the job-related standards of *Griggs, supra,* for the past eighty-eight years by virtue of the enactment of the Civil Service Act which guaranteed open fair competition for jobs."
They went on to argue that the *Griggs* standard had been satisfied. In granting the motions for summary judgment filed by petitioners and the federal parties, the District Court necessarily decided adversely to respondents the statutory issues expressly or tacitly tendered by the parties.

sion, by the opinion evidence placed before the District Judge and by the current views of the Civil Service Commissioners who were parties to the case.[16] Nor is the conclusion foreclosed by either *Griggs* or *Albemarle Paper Co.* v. *Moody,* 422 U.S. 405, 10 FEP Cases 1181 (1975); and it seems to us the much more sensible construction of the job relatedness requirement.

The District Court's accompanying conclusion that Test 21 was in fact directly related to the requirements of the police training program was supported by a validation study, as well as by other evidence of record;[17] and we are not convinced that this conclusion was erroneous.

The federal parties, whose views have somewhat changed since the decision of the Court of Appeals and who still insist that training-program validation is sufficient, now urge a remand to the District Court for the purpose of further inquiry into whether the training program test scores, which were found to correlate with Test 21 scores, are themselves an appropriate measure of the trainee's mastership of the material taught in the course and whether the training program itself is sufficiently related to actual performance of the police officer's task. We think a

[16] See n. 17, *infra.* Current instructions of the Civil Service Commission on "Examining, Testing, Standards, and Employment Practices" provide in pertinent part:
"S2-2—Use of applicant appraisal procedures
"a. *Policy.* The Commission's staff develops and uses applicant appraisal procedures to assess the knowledges, skills, and liabilities of persons for jobs and persons in the abstract.
"(1) Appraisal procedures are designed to reflect real, reasonable, and necessary qualifications for effective job behavior.
"(2) An appraisal procedure must, among other requirements, have a demonstrable and rational relationship to important job-related performance objectives identified by management, such as:
"(a) Effective job performance;
"(b) Capability;
"(c) Success in training;
"(d) Reduced turnover; or
"(e) Job satisfaction." 37 Fed. Reg. 21557 (Oct. 12, 1972).
See also *Equal Employment Opportunity Commission Guidelines on Employment Selection Procedures,* 29 CFR § 1607.5(b)(3), discussed in *Albemarle Paper Co.* v. *Moody,* 422 U.S. 405, 430-435, 10 FEP Cases 1181 (1975).
[17] The record includes a validation study of Test 21's relationship to performance in the recruit training program. The study was made by D. L. Futransky of the Standards Division, Bureau of Policies and Standards, United States Civil Service Commission. Appendix, at 99-109. Findings of the study included data "support[ing] the conclusion that T[est] 21 is effective in selecting trainees who can learn the material that is taught at the Recruit School." App. 103. Opinion evidence, submitted by qualified experts examining the Futransky study and/or conducting their own research, affirmed the correlation between scores on Test 21 and success in the training program. E.g., Affidavit of Dr. Donald R. Schwartz (personnel research psychologist, U.S. Civil Service Commission), Appendix, at 178, 183 ("It is my opinion . . . that Test 21 has a significant positive correlation with success on the MPD Recruit School for both Blacks and whites and is therefore shown to be job related . . ."); affidavit of Diane E. Wilson (personnel research psychologist, U.S. Civil Service Commission), Appendix at 185, 186 ("It is my opinion that there is a direct and rational relationship between the content and difficulty of Test 21 and successful completion of recruit school training.").
The Court of Appeals was "willing to assume for the purposes of this appeal that appellees have shown that Test 21 is predictive of further progress in Recruit School." 512 F.2d, at 962, 10 FEP Cases, at 109.

remand is inappropriate. The District Court's judgment was warranted by the record before him, and we perceive no good reason to reopen it, particularly since we were informed at oral argument that although Test 21 is still being administered, the training program itself has undergone substantial modification in the course of this litigation. If there are now deficiencies in the recruiting practices under prevailing Title VII standards, those deficiencies are to be directly addressed in accordance with the appropriate procedures mandated under that section.

The judgment of the Court of Appeals accordingly is reversed.

*So ordered.*

Mr. Justice Stewart joins Parts I and II of the Court's opinion.

Mr. Justice Stevens, concurring:

While I agree with the Court's disposition of this case, I add these comments on the constitutional issue discussed in Part II and the statutory issue discussed in Part III of the Court's opinion.

The requirement of purposeful discrimination is a common thread running through the cases summarized in Part II. These cases include criminal convictions which were set aside because blacks were excluded from the grand jury, a reapportionment case in which political boundaries were obviously influenced to some extent by racial considerations, a school desegregation case, and a case involving the unequal administration of an ordinance purporting to prohibit the operating of laundries in frame buildings. Although it may be proper to use the same language to describe the constitutional claim in each of these contexts, the burden of proving a prima facie case may well involve differing evidentiary considerations. The extent of deference that one pays to the trial court's determination of the factual issue, and indeed, the extent to which one characterizes the intent issue as a question of fact or a question of law, will vary in different contexts.

Frequently the most probative evidence of intent will be objective evidence of what actually happened rather than evidence describing the subjective state of mind of the actor. For normally the actor is presumed to have intended the natural consequences of his deeds. This is particularly true in the case of governmental action which is frequently the product of compromise, of collective decisionmaking and of mixed motivation. It is unrealistic, on the one hand, to require the victim of alleged discrimination to uncover the actual subjective intent of the decisionmaker or, conversely, to invalidate otherwise legitimate action simply because an improper motive affected the deliberation of a participant in the decisional process. A law conscripting clerics should not be invalidated because an atheist voted for it.

My point in making this observation is to suggest that the line between discriminatory purpose and discriminatory impact is not nearly as bright, and perhaps not quite as critical, as the reader of the Court's opinion might assume. I agree, of course, that a constitutional issue does not arise every time some disproportionate impact is shown. On the other hand, when the disproportion is as dramatic as in *Gomillion* or *Yick Wo,* it really does not matter whether the standard is phrased in terms of purpose or effect. Therefore, although I accept the statement of the general rule in the Court's opinion, I am not yet prepared to indicate how that standard should be applied in the many cases which have formulated the governing standard in different language.

My agreement with the conclusion reached in Part II of the Court's opinion rests on a ground narrower than the Court describes. I do not rely at all on the evidence of good-faith efforts to recruit black police officers. In my judgment, neither those efforts nor the subjective good faith of the District administration, would save Test 21 if it were otherwise invalid.

There are two reasons why I am convinced that the challenge to Test 21 is insufficient. First, the test serves the neutral and legitimate purpose of requiring all applicants to meet a uniform minimum standard of literacy. Reading ability is manifestly relevant to the police function, there is no evidence that the required passing grade was set at an arbitrarily high level, and there is sufficient disparity among high schools and high school graduates to justify the use of a separate uniform test. Second, the same test is used throughout the federal service. The applicants for employment in the District of Columbia Police Department represent such a small fraction of the total number of persons who have taken the test that their experience is of minimal probative value in assessing the neutrality of the test itself. That evidence, without more, is not sufficient to overcome the presumption that a test which is this widely used by the Federal Government is in fact neutral in its effect as well as its "purpose" as that term is used in constitutional adjudication.

My study of the statutory issue leads me to the same conclusion reached by the Court in Part III of its opinion. Since the Court of Appeals set aside the portion of the District Court's summary judgment granting the defendants' motion, I agree that we cannot ignore the statutory claims even though, as the Court's n. 10 makes clear, there is no Title VII question in this case. The actual statutory holdings are limited to 42 U.S.C. § 1981 and § 1–320 of the District of Columbia Code, to which regulations of the Equal Employment Opportunity Commission have no direct application.

The parties argued the case as though Title VII standards were applicable. In a general way those standards shed light on the issues, but there is sufficient individuality and complexity to that statute, and to the regulations promulgated under it, to make it inappropriate simply to transplant those standards in their entirety into a different statutory scheme having a different history. Moreover, the subject matter of this case—the validity of qualifications for the law enforcement profession—is one in which federal district judges have a greater expertise than in many others. I therefore do not regard this as a case in which the District Court was required to apply Title VII standards as strictly as would be necessary either in other contexts or in litigation actually arising under that statute.

The Court's specific holding on the job relatedness question contains, I believe, two components. First, as a matter of law, it is permissible for the police department to use a test for the purpose of predicting ability to master a training program even if the test does not otherwise predict ability to perform on the job. I regard this as a reasonable proposition and not inconsistent with the Court's prior holdings, although some of its prior language obviously did not contemplate this precise problem. Second, as a matter of fact, the District Court's finding that there was a correlation between success on the test and success in the training program has sufficient evidentiary support to withstand attack under the "clearly erroneous" standard mandated by Fed. Rule Civ. Proc. 52A. Whether or not we would have made the same finding of fact, the opinion evidence identified in n. 17 of the Court's opinion—and indeed the assumption made by the Court of Appeals quoted therein—is surely adequate to support the finding under the proper standard of appellate review.

On the understanding that nothing which I have said is inconsistent with the Court's reasoning, I join the opinion of the Court except to the extent that it expresses an opinion on the merits of the cases cited in n. 12.

MR. JUSTICE BRENNAN, with whom MR. JUSTICE MARSHALL joins, dissenting.

The Court holds that the job qualification examination (Test 21) given by the District of Columbia Metropolitan Police Department does not unlawfully discriminate on the basis of race under either constitutional or statutory standards.

Initially, it seems to me that the Court should not pass on the statutory questions, because they are not presented by this case. The Court says that respondents' summary judgment motion "rested on purely constitutional grounds," *ante,* at 5, 12 FEP Cases, at 1417, and that "the Court of Appeals erroneously applied the legal standards applicable to Title VII cases in resolving the constitutional issue before it," *ante,* at 7, 12 FEP Cases, at 1418. There is a suggestion, however, that petitioners are entitled to prevail because they met the burden of proof imposed by 5 U.S.C. § 3304. *Ante,* at 18 and n. 15, 12 FEP Cases, at 1422–1423. As I understand the opinion, the Court therefore holds that Test 21 is job-related under § 3304, but not necessarily under Title VII. But that provision, by the Court's own analysis, is no more in the case than Title VII; respondents' "complaints asserted no claim under § 3304." *Ante,* at 3 n. 2, 12 FEP Cases, at 1416. Compare *id.,* at 7–8 n. 10, 12 FEP Cases, at 1418. If it was "plain error" for the Court of Appeals to apply a statutory standard to this case, as the Court asserts, *ante,* at 7, 12 FEP Cases, at 1418, then it is unfortunate that the Court does not recognize that it is also plain error to address the statutory issues in Part II of its opinion.

Nevertheless, although it appears unnecessary to reach the statutory question, I will accept the Court's conclusion that respondents were entitled to summary judgment if they were correct in their statutory arguments, and I would affirm the Court of Appeals because petitioners have failed to prove that Test 21 satisfies the applicable statutory standards.

All parties' arguments and both lower court decisions were based on Title VII standards. In this context, I think it wrong to focus on § 3304 to the exclusion of the Title VII standards, particularly because the Civil Service Commission views the job-relatedness standards of Title VII and § 3304 as identical.[2] See also pp. 7–8, *infra,* 12 FEP Cases, p. 1418.

In applying a Title VII test,[3] both the District Court and the Court of Appeals held that respondents had offered sufficient evidence of discriminatory impact to shift to petitioners the burden of proving job-relatedness. 168 U.S. App. D.C., at 45–47, 512 F.2d, at 959–961, 10 FEP Cases, at 107–109; 348 F. Supp., at 16, 4 FEP Cases, at 1133. The Court does not question these rulings, and the only issue before us is what petitioners were required to show and whether they carried their burden. The Court agrees with the District Court's conclusion that Test 21 was validated by a positive relationship between Test 21 scores and performance in police training courses. This result is based upon the Court's reading of the record, its interpretation of instructions governing testing practices issued by the Civil Service Commission (CSC), and "the current views of the Civil Service Commissioners who were parties to the case." We are also assured that today's result is not foreclosed by *Griggs* v. *Duke Power Co.,* 401 U.S. 424, 3 FEP Cases 175 (1971), and *Albemarle Paper Co.* v. *Moody,* 422 U.S. 405, 10 FEP Cases 1181 (1975). Finally, the Court asserts that its conclusion is "the much more sensible construction of the job-relatedness requirement." *Ante,* at 20, 12 FEP Cases, at 1423.

But the CSC instructions cited by the Court do not support the District Court's conclusion. More importantly, the brief filed in this Court by the CSC takes the position that petitioners did not satisfy the burden of proof imposed by the CSC guidelines. It also appears that longstanding regulations of the Equal Employment Opportunity Commission (EEOC)—previously endorsed by this Court—require a result contrary to that reached by the Court. Furthermore, the Court's conclusion is inconsistent with my understanding of the interpretation of Title VII in *Griggs* and *Albemarle.* I do not find this conclusion "much more sensible," and with all respect I suggest that today's decision has the potential of significantly weakening statutory safeguards against discrimination in employment.

## I

On October 12, 1972, the CSC issued a supplement to the Federal Personnel Manual containing instructions for compliance with its general

[2] The only administrative authority relied on by the Court in support of its result is a regulation of the Civil Service Commission construing the civil service employment standards in Title 5 of the United States Code. *Ante,* at 19-20 n.16, 12 FEP Cases, at 1423. I note, however, that 5 U.S.C. § 3304 was brought into this case by the CSC, not by respondents, and the CSC's only reason for referring to that provision was to establish that petitioners had been "following the job-related standards of *Griggs* [v. *Duke Power Co.,* 401 U.S. 424, 3 FEP Cases 175 (1971)] for the past eighty-eight years." *Ante,* at 18 n. 15, 12 FEP Cases, at 1422-1423.

[3] The provision in Title VII on which petitioners place principal reliance is 42 U.S.C. § 2000e-2(h). See *Griggs* v. *Duke Power Co., supra,* at 433-436, 3 FEP Cases, at 178-179 (1971).

regulations concerning employment practices.[4] The provision cited by the Court requires that Test 21 "have a demonstrable and rational relationship to important job-related performance objectives identified by management." "Success in training" is one example of a possible objective. The statistical correlation established by the Futransky validity study, *ante,* at 20 n.17, 12 FEP Cases, at 1423, was between applicants' scores on Test 21 and recruits' average scores on final examination given during the police training course.

It is hornbook law that the Court accords deference to the construction of an administrative regulation when that construction is made by the administrative authority responsible for the regulation. E.g., *Udall* v. *Tallman,* 380 U.S. 1, 16 (1965). It is worthy of note, therefore, that the brief filed by the CSC in this case interprets the instructions in a manner directly contrary to the Court, despite the Court's claim that its result is supported by the Commissioners' "current views."

"Under Civil Service Commission regulations and current professional standards governing criterion-related test validation procedures, the job-relatedness of an entrance examination may be demonstrated by proof that scores on the examination predict properly measured success in job-relevant training (regardless of whether they predict success on the job itself).

"The documentary evidence submitted in the district court demonstrates that scores on Test 21 are predictive of Recruit School Final Averages. There is little evidence, however, concerning the relationship between the Recruit School tests and the substance of the training program, and between the substance of the training program and the post-training job of a police officer. *It cannot be determined, therefore, whether the Recruit School Final Averages are a proper measure of success in training and whether the training program is relevant.*" Brief for CSC 14–15 (emphasis added).

The CSC maintains that a positive correlation between scores on entrance examinations and the criterion of success in training may establish the job-relatedness of an entrance test—thus relieving an employer from the burden of providing a relationship to job performance after training—but only subject to certain limitations.

"Proof that scores on an entrance examination predict scores on training school achievement tests, however, does not, by itself, satisfy the burden of demonstrating the job-relatedness of the entrance examination. There must also be evidence—the nature of which will depend on the particular circumstances of the case—showing that the achievement test scores are

---

4 See 5 CFR § 300.101 *et seq.* These instructions contain the "regulations" that the Court finds supportive of the District Court's conclusion, which was reached under Title VII, but neither the instructions nor the general regulations are an interpretation of Title VII. The instructions were issued "under authority of sections 3301 and 3302 of title 5, United States Code, and E.O. 10577, 3 CFR 1954-58 Comp., p. 218." 37 Fed. Reg. 21552. The pertinent regulations of the Civil Service Commission in 5 CFR § 300.101 *et seq.* were promulgated pursuant to the same authorities, as well as 5 U.S.C. §§ 7151, 7154 and Exec. Order 11478, 3 CFR (1969 Comp.).

an appropriate measure of the trainee's mastery of the material taught in the training program and that the training program imparts to a new employee knowledge, skills, or abilities required for performance of the post-training job." *Id.,* at 24–25.

Applying its standards [5] the CSC concludes that none of the evidence presented in the District Court established "the appropriateness of using Recruit School Final Averages as the measure of training performance or the relationship of the Recruit School program to the job of a police officer." *Id.,* at 30.[6]

The CSC's standards thus recognize that Test 21 can be validated by a correlation between Test 21 scores and recruits' averages on training examinations only if (1) the training averages predict job performance or (2) the averages are proven to measure performance in job-related training. There is no proof that the recruits' average is correlated with job performance after completion of training. See n. 10, *infra.* And although a positive relationship to the recruits' average might be sufficient to validate Test 21 if the average were proven to reflect mastery of material on the training curriculum that was in turn demonstrated to be relevant to job performance, the record is devoid of proof in this regard. First, there is no demonstration by petitioners that the training course examinations measure comprehension of the training curriculum; indeed, these examinations do not even appear in the record. Furthermore, the Futransky study simply designated an average of 85 on the examination as a "good" performance and assumed that a recruit with such an average learned the material taught in the training course.[7] Without any further proof of the significance of a score of 85, and there is none in the record, I cannot agree that Test 21 is predictive of "success in training."

## II

Today's decision is also at odds with EEOC regulations issued pursuant to explicit authorization in Title VII. 42 U.S.C. § 2000e–12(a). Although

---

[5] The CSC asserts that certain of its guidelines have some bearing on Test 21's job relationship. Under the CSC instructions, "criterion-related validity," see *Douglas v. Hampton,* 168 U.S. D.C. 62, 70 n. 60, 512 F.2d 976, 984 n. 60, 10 FEP Cases 91, 96 (1975), can be established by demonstrating a correlation between entrance examination scores and "a criterion which is legitimately based on the needs of the Federal Government." ¶ S3-2(a)(2), 37 Fed. Reg. 21558. Further, to prove validity, statistical studies must demonstrate that Test 21, "to a significant degree, measures performance or qualification requirements which are relevant to the job or jobs for which candidates are being evaluated." ¶ S3-3(a), 37 Fed. Reg. 21558. There provisions are ignored in the Court's opinion.

[6] On this basis, the CSC argues that the case ought to be remanded to enable petitioners to try to make such a demonstration, but this resolution seems to me inappropriate. Both lower courts recognized that petitioners had the burden of proof, and as this burden is yet unsatisfied, respondents are entitled to prevail.

[7] The finding in the Futransky study on which the Court relies, *ante,* at 20 n. 17, 12 FEP Cases, at 1423, was that Test 21 "is effective in selecting trainees who can learn the material that is taught at the Recruit School," because it predicts averages over 85. On its face, this would appear to be an important finding, but the fact is that *everyone* learns the material included in the training course. The study noted that all recruits pass the training examinations; if a particular recruit has any difficulty, he is given assistance until he passes.

the dispute in this case is not within the EEOC's jurisdiction, as I noted above, the proper construction of Title VII nevertheless is relevant. Moreover, the 1972 extension of Title VII to public employees gave the same substantive protection to those employees as had previously been accorded in the private sector, *Morton* v. *Mancari,* 417 U.S. 535, 546–547, 8 FEP Cases 105, 109–110 (1974), and it is therefore improper to maintain different standards in the public and private sectors. *Chandler* v. *Roudebush,* _____ U.S. _____, _____, 12 FEP Cases 1368 (1976). See n.2, *supra.*

As with an agency's regulation, the construction of a statute by the agency charged with its administration is entitled to great deference. *Trafficante* v. *Metropolitan Life Ins. Co.,* 409 U.S. 205, 210 (1972); *Udall* v. *Tallman,* 380 U.S., at 16; *Power Reactor Dev. Co.* v. *Electrical Workers,* 367 U.S. 396, 408 (1961). The deference due the pertinent EEOC regulations is enhanced by the fact that they were neither altered nor disapproved when Congress extensively amended Title VII in 1972.[8] *Chemehuevi Tribe of Indians* v. *FPC,* 420 U.S. 395, 410 (1975); *Cammarano* v. *United States,* 358 U.S. 498, 510 (1959); *Allen* v. *Grand Central Aircraft Co.,* 347 U.S. 535, 547 (1954); *Massachusetts Mutual Life Ins. Co.* v. *United States,* 288 U.S. 269, 273 (1933). These principles were followed in *Albemarle*—where the Court explicitly endorsed various regulations no fewer than eight times in its opinion, 422 U.S., at 431–436, 10 FEP Cases, at 1192–1194 [9]— and *Griggs,* 401 U.S., at 433–434, 3 FEP Cases, at 179.

The EEOC regulations require that the validity of a job qualification test be proven by "empirical data demonstrating that the test is predictive of or significantly correlated with important elements of work behavior which comprise or are relevant to the job or jobs for which candidates are being evaluated." 29 CFR § 1607.4(c). This construction of Title VII was approved in *Albemarle,* where we quoted this provision and remarked that "[t]he message of these Guidelines is the same as that of the *Griggs* case." 422 U.S., at 431, 10 FEP Cases at 1192. The regulations also set forth minimum standards for validation and delineate the criteria that may be used for this purpose.

"The work behaviors or other criteria of employee adequacy which the test is intended to predict or identify must be fully described; and, additionally, in the case of rating techniques, the appraisal form[s] and instructions to the rater[s] must be included as a part of the validation

---

[8] Still another factor mandates deference to the EEOC regulations. The House and Senate committees considering the 1972 amendments to Title VII recognized that discrimination in employment, including the use of testing devices, is a "complex and pervasive phenomenon." S. Rep. No. 92-415, 92d Cong., 1st Sess., p. 5 (1971); H.R. Rep. No. 92-238, 92nd Cong., 1st Sess., p. 8 (1971). As a result, both committees noted the need to obtain "expert assistance" in this area. S. Rep. No. 92-415, *supra,* at 5; H.R. Rep. No. 92-238, *supra,* at 8.

[9] Indeed, two Justices asserted that the Court relied too heavily on the EEOC guidelines. *Albemarle Paper Co.* v. *Moody,* 422 U.S. 405, 10 FEP Cases 1181, 1197 (BLACKMUN, J., concurring in the judgment): *id.,* at 451, 10 FEP Cases, at 1200 (BURGER, C.J., concurring in part and dissenting in part).

evidence. Such criteria may include measures other than actual work proficiency, such as training time, supervisory ratings, regularity of attendance and tenure. Whatever criteria are used they must represent major or critical work behaviors as revealed by careful job analyses." 29 CFR § 1607.5(b)(3).

This provision was also approved in *Albemarle*, 422 U.S., at 432 and n. 30, 10 FEP Cases, at 1193.

If we measure the validity of Test 21 by this standard, which I submit we are bound to do, petitioners' proof is deficient in a number of ways similar to those noted above. First, the criterion of final training examination averages does not appear to be "fully described." Although the record contains some general discussion of the training curriculum, the examinations are not in the record, and there is no other evidence completely elucidating the subject matter tested by the training examinations. Without this required description we cannot determine whether the correlation with training examination averages is sufficiently related to petitioners' need to ascertain "job-specific ability." See *Albemarle*, 422 U.S., at 433, 10 FEP Cases, at 1193. Second, the EEOC regulations do not expressly permit validation by correlation to training performance, unlike the CSC instructions. Among the specified criteria the closest to training performance is "training time." All recruits to the Metropolitan Police Department, however, go through the same training course in the same amount of time, including those who experience some difficulty. See n. 5, *supra*. Third, the final requirement of §1607.5(b)(3) has not been met. There has been no job analysis establishing the significance of scores on training examinations, nor is there any other type of evidence showing that these scores are of "major or critical" importance.

Accordingly, EEOC regulations that have previously been approved by the Court set forth a construction of Title VII that is distinctly opposed to today's statutory result.

## III

The Court also says that its conclusion is not foreclosed by *Griggs* and *Albemarle*, but today's result plainly conflicts with those cases. *Griggs* held that "[i]f an employment practice which operates to exclude Negroes cannot be shown to be *related to the job performance*, the practice is prohibited." 401 U.S., at 431, 3 FEP Cases, at 178 (emphasis added). Once a discriminatory impact is shown, the employer carries the burden of proving that the challenged practice "bear[s] *a demonstrable relationship to successful performance of the jobs* for which it was used." *Ibid.* (emphasis added). We observed further:

"Nothing in the Act precludes the use of testing or measuring procedures; obviously they are useful. What Congress has forbidden is giving these devices and mechanisms controlling force unless they are demonstrably a reasonable measure of job performance. . . .

"What Congress has commanded is that any tests used must measure the person for the job and not the person in the abstract." *Id.*, at 436, 10 FEP Cases at 180.

*Albemarle* read *Griggs* to require that a discriminatory test be validated through proof "by professionally acceptable methods" that it is "'predictive of or significantly correlated with *important* elements of work behavior *which comprise or are relevant to the job or jobs* for which candidates are being evaluated.'" 422 U.S., at 431, 10 FEP Cases, at 1192 (emphasis added), quoting 29 CFR § 1607.4(c). Further, we rejected the employer's attempt to validate a written test by proving that it was related to supervisors' job performance ratings, because there was no demonstration that the ratings accurately reflected job performance. We were unable "to determine whether the criteria *actually* considered were sufficiently related to the [employer's] legitimate interest in job-specific ability to justify a testing system with a racially discriminatory impact." 422 U.S., at 433, 10 FEP Cases, at 1193 (emphasis in original). To me, therefore, these cases read Title VII as requiring proof of a significant relationship to job performance to establish the validity of a discriminatory test. See also *McDonnell-Douglas Corp.* v. *Green,* 411 U.S. 792, 802 and n. 14, 5 FEP Cases 965, 969 (1973). Petitioners do not maintain that there is a demonstrated correlation between Test 21 scores and job performance. Moreover, their validity study was unable to discern a significant positive relationship between training averages and job performance.[10] Thus, there is no proof of a correlation—either direct or indirect—between Test 21 and performance of the job of being a police officer.

It may well be that in some circumstances, proof of a relationship between a discriminatory qualification test and training performance is an acceptable substitute for establishing relationship to job performance. But this question is not settled, and it should not be resolved by the minimal analysis in the Court's opinion. Moreover, it is particularly inappropriate to decide the question on this record. "Professionally acceptable standards" apparently recognize validation by proof of a correlation with training performance, rather than job performance, if (1) the training curriculum includes information proven to be important to job performance and (2) the standard used as a measure of training performance is shown to reflect the trainees' mastery of the material included in the training curriculum. See Brief for CSC 24–29; Brief for the Executive Committee of Division 14 of the American Psychological Assn. 37–43. But no authority, whether professional, administrative, or judicial, has accepted the sufficiency of a correlation with training performance in the absence of such proof. For reasons that I have stated above, the record does not adequately establish either factor. As a result, the Court's conclusion cannot be squared with the focus on job performance in *Griggs* and *Albemarle,* even if this substitute showing is reconcilable with the holdings in those cases.

[10] Although the validity study found that Test 21 predicted job performance for white officers, but see *Albemarle,* 422 U.S., at 433, 10 FEP Cases at 1193, no similar relationship existed for black officers. The same finding was made as to the relationship between training examination averages and job performance. See *id.,* at 435, 10 FEP Cases, at 1194.

Today's reduced emphasis on a relationship to job performance is also inconsistent with clearly expressed congressional intent. The Conference Report on the 1972 amendments to Title VII states as follows:

"In any area where the new law does not address itself, or in any areas where a specific contrary intention is not indicated, it was assumed that the present case law as developed by the courts would continue to govern the applicability and construction of Title VII." 118 Cong. Rec. 7166.

The pre-1972 judicial decisions dealing with standardized tests used as job qualification requirements uniformly follow the EEOC regulations discussed above and insist upon proof of a relationship to job performance to prove that a test is job-related. Furthermore, the Court ignores Congress' explicit hostility towards the use of written tests as job-qualification requirements; Congress disapproved the CSC's "use of general ability tests which are not aimed at any direct relationship to specific jobs." H.R. Rep. No. 92–238, 92d Cong., 1st Sess., p. 24 (1971). See S. Rep. No. 92–415, 92d Cong., 1st Sess., pp. 14–15 (1971). Petitioners concede that Test 21 was devised by the CSC for general use and was not designed to be used by police departments.

Finally, it should be observed that every federal court, except the District Court in this case, presented with proof identical to that offered to validate Test 21 has reached a conclusion directly opposite to that of the Court today. Sound policy considerations support the view that, at a minimum, petitioners should have been required to prove that the police training examinations either measure job-related skills or predict job performance. Where employers try to validate written qualification tests by proving a correlation with written examinations in a training course, there is a substantial danger that people who have good verbal skills will achieve high scores on both tests due to verbal ability, rather than "job-specific ability." As a result, employers could validate any entrance examination that measures only verbal ability by giving another written test that measures verbal ability at the end of a training course. Any contention that the resulting correlation between examination scores would be evidence that the initial test is "job-related" is plainly erroneous. It seems to me, however, that the Court's holding in this case can be read as endorsing this dubious proposition. Today's result will prove particularly unfortunate if it is extended to govern Title VII cases.

---

On the constitutional requirement of discriminatory intent, see *Personnel Administrator of Massachusetts* v. *Feeney, infra,* page 783.

## UNITED STATES v. STATE OF SOUTH CAROLINA

*United States District Court, South Carolina, 1977*
*445 F. Supp. 1094, 15 FEP Cases 1196*

Before HAYNSWORTH and RUSSELL, Circuit Judges and SIMONS, District Judge: . . .

The United States brought this action on September 15, 1975, against the State of South Carolina, the South Carolina State Board of Education, the South Carolina State Retirement System, the South Carolina Budget and Control Board, and three local school boards in their individual capacities and as representatives of a defendant class of all local school boards in the State. The defendants are charged with violations of the Fourteenth Amendment to the Constitution of the United States and Title VII of the Civil Rights Act of 1964, as amended, 42 U.S.C. § 2000e, *et. seq.* (1970), through the use of minimum score requirements on the National Teacher Examinations (hereinafter "NTE") to certify and determine the pay levels of teachers within the State.

On September 17, 1975, the South Carolina Education Association (SCEA), the National Education Association (NEA), and nine named individuals as class plaintiffs brought another suit against the same defendants in their official and individual capacities, seeking substantially the same relief sought by the U.S. Attorney General's suit, basing their actions also upon the Fourteenth Amendment and Title VII of the Civil Rights Act of 1964, as amended; and, in addition, alleging violations of Sections 1981 and 1983 of Title 42 of the United States Code.

These plaintiffs moved to intervene in the Attorney General's action. This motion was granted on January 6, 1976, and they became the plaintiff-intervenors, and their separate action was stayed.

For over 30 years the State of South Carolina and its agencies have used scores on the NTE to make decisions with respect to the certification of teachers and the amount of state aid payable to local school districts. Local school boards within the State use scores on the NTE for selection and compensation of teachers. From 1969 to 1976, a minimum score of 975 was required by the State for its certification and state aid decisions. In June, 1976, after an exhaustive validation study by Educational Testing Service (ETS), and, after a critical review and evaluation of this study by the Board of Education's Committee on Teacher Recruitment, Training and Compensation and the Department Staff, the State established new certification requirements involving different minimum scores in various areas of teaching specialization that range from 940 to 1198. The court holds that these regulations are properly before it since the plaintiffs were undoubtedly aware that the validity study by ETS upon which these regulations were based was well under way when the suits were filed.

The local boards are required by the State to hire only certified teachers, S.C. Code §§ 21–45, 21–371, 21–375, but there are no uniform standards with respect to test scores used by the local school boards in selecting from among the pool of certified applicants.

Plaintiffs challenge each of the uses of the NTE. They contend that more blacks than whites historically have failed to achieve the required minimum score, and that this result creates a racial classification in violation of the constitutional and statutory provisions cited in their complaints. Each complaint seeks declaratory and injunctive relief with respect to the use of the minimum score requirement in certifying and determining the pay levels of teachers, injunctive relief to upgrade the certification levels of teachers adversely affected by the minimum score requirement, and monetary relief for alleged financial losses of teachers, together with costs. Plaintiff-intervenors also asked for attorneys' fees.

. . .

*Review of the Order permitting examination by written questions:* Plaintiffs asked the three-judge panel to review and overturn the order entered by the district judge (acting for the three-judge panel in all preliminary and prehearing matters) granting a motion by the State defendants to make certain written questions propounded during discovery and the answers thereto a part of the record.

This dispute arose during the deposition of Dr. Winton H. Manning, a Vice President of ETS which administers the NTE. The plaintiffs deposed Dr. Manning for several days resulting in nearly 2000 pages of transcript. ETS being concerned with plaintiffs' inability to conclude the deposition of this senior officer offered to answer written questions in lieu of continuing the deposition by oral questioning.[3] Plaintiffs agreed and submitted 188 written questions on cross-examination. ETS answered these questions promptly. Thereafter, Dr. Manning submitted to another day of oral cross-examination. Defendants then submitted 174 written questions in lieu of redirect examination by oral questions. ETS answered those questions. Plaintiffs then submitted 54 written questions in lieu of oral re-cross examination which ETS answered.

Plaintiffs objected to the admission into evidence of the answers to the questions on redirect examination. They urge that the procedure is not permitted by the Federal Rules, or authorized by any agreement of the parties. We hold that the agreement of the parties did not give plaintiffs the exclusive right to use written questions in this regard, and such agreed to procedure is not inconsistent with the Federal Rules, and did not adversely affect the plaintiffs. It would be unfair to deny the defendants the same opportunity to use written questions as was afforded to plaintiffs. Plaintiffs' motion is therefore denied.

. . .

The remaining claims under Title VII must be tested under statutory standards. In *Washington* v. *Davis*, 426 U.S. 229, 96 S.Ct. 2040, 48 L.Ed.2d 597 (1976), the Supreme Court summarized the order of proof:

"Under Title VII, Congress provided that when hiring and promotion practices disqualifying substantially disproportionate numbers of blacks are challenged, discriminatory purpose need not be proved, and that it is an insufficient response to demonstrate some rational basis for the challenged practices. It is necessary, in addition, that they be 'validated' in terms of job performance in any one of several ways, perhaps by ascertaining the minimum skill, ability or potential necessary for the

---

[3] [Footnotes numbered as in original.—Ed.] Because ETS is not a party, it could not be subjected to discovery through written interrogatories except by its consent. Rule 33, Federal Rules of Civil Procedure.

position at issue and determining whether the qualifying tests are appropriate for the selection of qualified applicants for the job in question." (*Id.* at 246, 96 S.Ct. at 2051).

Thus, it was held not sufficient for the governmental entity to prove that the classification resulting from the test scores had a rational basis, that is, that it differentiated between persons who did and did not have some minimum verbal and communication skill. It was necessary, in addition, for the governmental entity to demonstrate that the minimum verbal and communication skill, in turn, had some rational relationship to the legitimate employment objectives of the employer. And *Washington* v. *Davis* left intact the holding in *Griggs* v. *Duke Power Co.,* 401 U.S. 424, 91 S.Ct. 849, 28 L.Ed.2d 158 (1971), that the employment practice must be a "business necessity." *Id.* at 431, 91 S.Ct. 849.

A. CERTIFICATION

Plaintiffs have proved that the use of NTE scores by the State in its certification decisions disqualifies substantially disproportionate numbers of blacks. The burden of proof was thereby shifted to the defendants, and in an effort to meet this burden the State commissioned an extensive validity study by ETS. The design of this study is novel, but consistent with the basic requirements enunciated by the Supreme Court, and we accordingly hold such study sufficient to meet the burden placed on defendants under Title VII.

The study seeks to demonstrate content validity by measuring the degree to which the content of the tests matches the content of the teacher training programs in South Carolina. It also seeks to establish a minimum score requirement by estimating the amount of knowledge (measured by the ability to answer correctly test questions that have been content validated) that a minimally qualified teacher candidate in South Carolina would have.

To conduct the study, all 25 of the teacher training institutions in South Carolina were canvassed for experienced teacher educators in the various specialty fields tested in the NTE program. A group of 456 persons with the requisite professional credentials was assembled including representative numbers from each institution and both races. All were volunteers nominated by the colleges themselves. These 456 participants were divided into two general groups. One group was assigned the task of assessing the content validity of the NTE as compared to the curriculum in South Carolina institutions. The other was assigned the task of establishing the minimum score requirement. The two large groups were then each subdivided into panels of about 10 participants assigned to each test in the Common Examinations and each of the Area Examinations. The panelists were given the questions and answers on two current forms of the NTE and asked to record certain judgments about the tests.

Each content review panel member was asked to decide whether each question on the tests involved subject matter that was a part of the curriculum at his or her teacher training institution, and therefore could be judged to be appropriate for use in South Carolina. Each minimum score panel member was asked to look at each of the questions on the test and estimate the percentage of minimally qualified students in teacher education programs in South Carolina who would know the correct answer. Each test was evaluated by teacher educators specializing in the field or one of the major fields covered by the test. Art education teachers evaluated the test in Art Education; French teachers evaluated the test in French, and so on.

The content review panels determined that from 63 percent to 98 percent of the questions on the various tests were content valid for use in South Carolina. The panel members' overview of the tests as a whole also found the NTE to be sufficiently closely related to the curriculum in South Carolina to be an appropriate measure of achievement with respect to that curriculum.

The estimates made by the minimum score panel members (as to the percentage of minimally qualified students who would answer the question correctly) were combined statistically and analyzed to generate scaled scores that reflected, for each test, the level that would be achieved by the minimally knowledgeable candidate. Only test questions that had been determined by a majority of the content review panel members to be content appropriate for use in South Carolina were used in making the minimum score estimates. These scores were 548 on the Common Examinations and a range from 458 (Agriculture) to 690 (Media Specialist) on the Area Examinations.

| Test | State's New Scores | ETS Study Scores | SEM* Units |
|---|---|---|---|
| Agriculture | 940 | 1006 | 2 |
| Art Education | 1040 | 1104 | 2 |
| Biology and General Science | 1115 | 1196 | 3 |
| Business Education | 1071 | 1167 | 3 |
| Chemistry, Physics, and Gen. Science | 1100 | 1158 | 2 |
| Early Childhood Education | 1052 | 1124 | 2 |
| Education in the Elementary School | 1132 | 1194 | 2 |
| Education of the Mentally Retarded | 1120 | 1234 | 3 |
| English Language and Literature | 1041 | 1069 | 1 |
| French | 1144 | 1210 | 2 |
| Home Economics Education | 1075 | 1143 | 2 |
| Industrial Arts Education | 1100 | 1162 | 2 |
| Mathematics | 1113 | 1203 | 3 |
| Librarian-Media Specialist | 1178 | 1238 | 2 |
| Music Education | 1020 | 1086 | 2 |
| Physical Education | 1125 | 1195 | 2 |
| Social Studies | 1086 | 1148 | 2 |
| Spanish | 1132 | 1163 | 1 |
| Common Examinations | 510** | 548 | 2 |

\* Standard error of measurement.
\*\* The score from the Common Examinations alone is used to certify teachers in specialty fields for which there is no Area Examination under the NTE program.

After receiving the recommended minimum scores the State Board considered a variety of statistical and human factors. Among these considerations were the standard error of measurement of the NTE, the possibility of sampling error in the study, the consistency of the results (internal comparisons of panel results), the supply of and demand for teachers in each specialty field, and the racial composition of the teacher force. It decided to *lower* the minimum scores by one, two, or three standard errors of measurement.

The design of the validity study is adequate for Title VII purposes. The Supreme Court made clear once again in *Washington* v. *Davis* that a content validity study that satisfies professional standards also satisfies Title VII. 426 U.S. at 247, n. 13, 96 S.Ct. 2040. The defendants called as an expert witness Dr. Robert M. Guion, the principal author of STANDARDS FOR EDUCATIONAL AND PSYCHOLOGICAL TESTS published by the American Psychological Association and a nationally recognized authority in the field of testing and measurement who testified in an unqualified fashion that in his expert opinion the ETS study design met all of the requirements of the APA Standards, the Division 14 Principles,[19] and the EEOC Guidelines.[20] Two other experts testified similarly, and ETS sought and obtained favorable opinions on the study design, before its implementation, from another two independent experts. The ETS decision to validate against the academic training program rather than job performance is specifically endorsed in principle in *Davis, supra:*

"[A] positive relationship between the test and training-course performance was sufficient to validate the former, *wholly aside from its possible relationship to actual [job] performance as a police officer. . . .* Nor is the conclusion foreclosed by either *Griggs* or *Albemarle Paper Co.* v. *Moody,* 422 U.S. 405, 95 S.Ct. 2362, 45 L.Ed.2d 280 (1975); and it seems to us the much more sensible construction of the job-relatedness requirement." 426 U.S. at 250–251, 96 S.Ct. at 2053." (Emphasis added.)

The principal issue raised by plaintiffs in attacking the validity study is whether the execution of the design was such that the results can be trusted. Plaintiffs deposed 81 of the 456 panel members selected at random and, on the basis of those depositions, claim that the panel members did not prepare for the tasks they were asked to undertake, and did not understand or follow the instructions.

Admittedly, there is a showing from these depositions which indicates some misunderstanding did exist; however, our review of these depositions shows that the misunderstandings were much less extensive than claimed by plaintiffs. When so many people are involved some misunderstanding and failure adequately to follow instructions are inevitable.

---

[19] Division of Industrial Organizational Psychology (Division 14), American Psychological Association, PRINCIPLES FOR THE VALIDATION AND USE OF PERSONNEL SELECTION PROCEDURES (1975).

[20] Guidelines for Employee Selection Procedures, 29 CFR 160, (1970). To the extent that the EEOC Guidelines conflict with well-grounded expert opinion and accepted professional standards, they need not be controlling. *General Electric Co.* v. *Gilbert,* 429 U.S. 125, 97 S.Ct. 401, 50 L.Ed.2d 343 (1976).

The new cutoff scores adopted by the State which are substantially below the scores recommended by ETS after completion of its validation study provide a substantial margin of error.

It appears that most of the deposed panel members recalled receiving the instructions sent in advance of the panel meetings, but did not recall doing any of the preparation suggested by the instructions. We are asked to find that this lack of preparation requires a finding that the results are untrustworthy. It is evident from the design of the study that the panel members were selected on the basis of their professional experience, and it was this experience that they were asked to apply to the task of content review and minimum score determination, not the results of current research in college catalogues or interviews of teaching colleagues. For many, the preparation suggested by the instructions may have been unnecessary. In order to support the allegation of untrustworthiness, plaintiffs would have to offer some evidence as to the necessity of preparation, the reasons why the panel members did not prepare and the effect of the lack of preparation on the panel members' judgments.

We find that the results of the validity study are sufficiently trustworthy to sustain defendants' burden under Title VII. First, the possible error rate was not high. Second, the key question is not whether some of the panel members failed to understand the instructions or for other reasons failed to follow the instructions, but whether they would have reached any different result if they had understood and followed the instructions. Plaintiffs misconceive their burden once defendants have made a reasonable showing that the study was executed in a responsible, professional manner designed to produce trustworthy results. In order to rebut the presumption that trustworthy results were indeed produced, plaintiffs must not only show that the study was not executed as intended, but also that the results were adversely affected.

Our findings with respect to the validity study end the inquiry for purposes of injunctive relief with respect to the certification system because the regulations now in effect are based on the validity study, and the actions of the State Board in lowering the scores recommended by the study to account for various statistical and human factors were reasonable, and, as before stated, provide and compensate for a substantial margin of error.

However, an ancillary inquiry remains with respect to the 975 minimum score requirement in effect from 1969 through 1976 and not specifically validated. Plaintiff-intervenors' claims for damages bring the legality of that requirement into question. There is nothing in the record to indicate that the requirements of the teaching profession changed substantially from 1969 to 1976 so that what was judged to be the minimum amount of knowledge to graduate from a teacher training program or to teach effectively would have been higher or lower in 1976 than it was in 1969. The State has offered some evidence to the contrary, indicating that the expectations with respect to teacher capability remained about the same during this period.

The 975 minimum score requirement in effect during these years is substantially below the State's new minimum score requirements in every field except in Agriculture, which has been reduced to 940. It is reasonable to conclude, based on the present validity study, that the 975 minimum score excluded only those who did not have the requisite minimum knowledge. The only discrimination question raised is with respect to the classification of those who do *not* have minimum knowledge. During the years 1969 through 1976 some of those who lacked minimum knowledge were denied a professional certificate because their scores were below 975, while others who also lacked minimum knowledge but whose scores were above 975 but below the 1976 minimum score requirements, were certified.

In any decision-making process that relies on a standardized test, there is some risk of error. The risk of excluding a truly qualified candidate whose low test score does not reflect his or her real ability can be decreased by lowering the minimum score requirement. That also increases the risk of including an unqualified candidate whose low test score does reflect his or her real ability. The State must weigh many facets of the public interest in making such a decision. If there is a teacher shortage, a relatively high minimum score requirement may mean that some classrooms will be without teachers, and it may be better to provide a less than fully competent teacher than no teacher at all. But to the extent that children are exposed to incompetent teachers, education suffers. It may be that education suffers less than would be the case if classrooms were overcrowded due to lack of teachers. We think it is within the prerogative of the State to accept some unqualified teachers under circumstances where that is judged by the State to be on balance in the public interest, and that such an action by the State is not a violation of Title VII.

There remains, however, the question whether the State has satisfied the "business necessity" requirement set out in *Griggs* v. *Duke Power Co.,* 401 U.S. 424, 91 S.Ct. 849, 28 L.Ed.2d 158 (1971). This "business necessity" doctrine appears neither in the explicit language nor the legislative history of Title VII. The Court in *Griggs* and subsequent Title VII cases did not establish judicial standards for determining whether a particular practice is a business necessity. The EEOC Guidelines are of little assistance because they were published before *Griggs* and have not been updated since that time.[21]

---

21 The EEOC re-published these regulations, without change, on November 24, 1976, 41 Fed. Reg. 51985 (1976). The EEOC evidently equates the concept of business necessity with the measurement concepts of statistical and practical significance. 29 CFR § 1607.5(c) provides:
"In assessing the utility of a test the following considerations will be applicable:
"(1) The relationship between the test and at least one relevant criterion must be statistically significant.
"(2) In addition to statistical significance, the relationship between the test and criterion should have practical significance."
By their terms, these regulations are applicable only to a criterion-related validity study. The EEOC sets out no analogous requirements for a content validity study.

We think that *Griggs* did not import into Title VII law the concept of "compelling interest" developed as a part of the "strict scrutiny" standard for assessing certain classifications under the Fourteenth Amendment. Under this concept, the Court would balance the disparate impact on blacks against the business purpose of the employer and uphold the business practice only if it were sufficiently "compelling" to overcome the disparate impact. It is our view that the Supreme Court intended an examination of the alternatives available with respect to the legitimate employment objective identified by the employer to determine whether there is available to the employer an alternative practice that would achieve his business purpose equally well but with a lesser disparate impact by race. In examining alternatives, the risk and cost to the employer are relevant.

Here, plaintiffs have suggested only one alternative to the use of the NTE for certification purposes. Plaintiffs contend that mere graduation from an approved program should be sufficient and would have a lesser disparate impact on blacks. We cannot find that this alternative will achieve the State's purpose in certifying minimally competent persons equally well as the use of a content-validated standardized test. The record amply demonstrates that there are variations in admissions requirements, academic standards and grading practices at the various teacher training institutions within the State. The approval that the State gives to the teacher training program is to general subject matter areas covered by the program, not to the actual course content of the program, and not to the means used within the program to measure whether individual students have actually mastered the course content to which they have been exposed. The standardized test scores do reflect individual achievement with respect to specific subject matter content, which is directly relevant to (although not sufficient in itself to assure) competence to teach, and thus the use of these scores for certification purposes survives the business necessity test under Title VII.

### B. PAY SCALES

There remains, finally, the question whether the uses of the NTE for salary purposes are a violation of Title VII.[22] Where the salary system was linked to the certification system, some salary benefits were available only by improving the grade of the certificate; and that, in turn, could be done only by achieving certain minimum NTE scores. That system continued in effect after March 24, 1972, when Title VII was made applicable to states, and in 1976, the distribution of teachers within the four grades of the pay scale system showed a substantial disparate impact by race. A higher proportion of whites (98 percent) were classified in the two higher grades (*A* and *B*) and a higher proportion of blacks (51 percent) were classified in the lower grades (*C* and *D*). By such showing

---

[22] These uses, enacted by the Legislature, have remained the same since 1944 and were not changed in 1957, 1969, or 1976, when the certification system was changed by the State Board.

plaintiffs have satisfied their burden of proof under Title VII to shift the burden of proof to the defendants to show a rational relationship to a legitimate employment objective and to show business necessity. The State identifies its legitimate employment objective as providing an incentive for improvement, so that teachers without adequate knowledge to teach effectively will upgrade their capability; and the State offers the same evidence of a rational relationship between its pay scales and this objective as it did with respect to the constitutional challenges. We think that evidence is sufficient to establish the relationship.

We believe that a distinction for pay purposes between those who are qualified as well as between those who are not qualified survives the business necessity test. There appears to be no alternative available to the State, within reasonable limits of risk and cost, for providing the incentive necessary to motivate thousands of persons to acquire, generally on their own time and at their own expense, the necessary additional academic training so that they will be minimally competent teachers. Having made the investment of four years in an undergraduate education, it seems reasonable to try to upgrade the talent of unqualified teachers where possible, rather than rejecting them altogether.

In accordance with the foregoing findings and conclusions, we conclude that plaintiff and plaintiff-intervenors have failed to establish their right to any of the relief sought in their respective complaints. It is, therefore, ORDERED that judgment be entered in favor of the defendants.


## NATIONAL EDUCATION ASS'N v. SOUTH CAROLINA

*United States Supreme Court, 1978*

*434 U.S. 1026, 16 FEP Cases 501*


MR. JUSTICE WHITE, with whom MR. JUSTICE BRENNAN joins, dissenting.

For many years, South Carolina has used the National Teachers' Examination (NTE) in hiring and classifying teachers, despite the advice of its authors that it should not be used as the State uses it and despite the fact that it serves to disqualify a greater proportion of black applicants than white and to place a greater percentage of black teachers in lower paying classifications. For example, the new test score requirements contained in the 1976 revision of the State's plan will disqualify 83 percent of black applicants, but only 17.5 percent of white applicants; and 96 percent of the newly certified candidates permitted to teach will be white teachers.

This litigation began when the United States brought suit challenging the use of the NTE under both the Constitution and Title VII. The District Court upheld the State's use of the test and rejected both claims.

Not only had plaintiffs failed to prove a racially discriminatory purpose in the State's use of the NTE but, in view of the District Court, the State had carried its burden of justifying the test despite its disparate racial impact.

The State's evidence in this regard consisted of a validation study prepared by the authors of the test at the request of the State. The District Court deemed the study sufficient to validate the NTE, even though the validation was not in relation to job performance and showed at best that the test measured the familiarity of the candidate with the content of certain teacher training courses.

*Washington* v. *Davis,* 426 U.S. 229 (1976), was thought by the District Court to have warranted validating the test in terms of the applicant's training rather than against job requirements; but *Washington* v. *Davis,* in this respect, held only that the test there involved, which sought to ascertain whether the applicant had the minimum communication skills necessary to understand the offerings in a police training course, could be used to measure eligibilty to enter that program. The case did not hold that a training course, the completion of which is required for employment, need not itself be validated in terms of job relatedness. Nor did it hold that a test that a job applicant must pass and that is designed to indicate his mastery of the materials or skills taught in the training course, can be validated without reference to the job. Tests supposedly measuring an applicant's qualifications for employment, if they have differential racial impact, must bear "some manifest relationship to the employment in question," *Griggs* v. *Duke Power Co.,* 401 U.S. 424, 432 (1971), and it is insufficient for the employer "to demonstrate some rational basis for the challenged provisions." *Washington* v. *Davis,* 426 U.S., at 247.

The District Court here held that no other measures would satisfy the State's interest in obtaining qualified teachers and paying them fairly. But only two other States use the NTE for initial certification and South Carolina is the only State which uses the NTE in determining pay. Furthermore, the authors of the test themselves advise against using it for determining the pay for experienced teachers and believe that the NTE should not be the sole criterion for initial certification.

The question here is not merely whether the District Court, applying correct legal standards, reached the correct conclusion on the record before it, but whether the Court was legally correct in holding that the NTE need not be validated against job performance and that the validation requirement was satisfied by a study which demonstrated only that a trained person could pass the test.

I therefore dissent from the Court's summary affirmance and would set the case for oral argument.

Mr. Justice Marshall and Mr. Justice Blackmun took no part in the consideration or decision of these appeals.

# ISSUES IN SELECTION, TESTING, AND THE LAW *

## Sheldon Zedeck and Mary L. Tenopyr **

The Civil Rights Act of 1964 provided a significant impetus to the fields of personnel psychology and industrial relations. Increased concern for possible ethnic and racial bias in psychological testing was evinced by those involved with educational and employment testing and by those in federal, state, and local governments who were responsible for implementing the Civil Rights Act.

. . .

### VALUE OF TESTS

Given the extensiveness of the guidelines' coverage and the inclusiveness of the employment devices which can be considered as tests, and which consequently are subject to scrutiny as potential unfair discriminators, one reaction for industry and others is to eliminate the use of such devices. Rather than contend with regulatory agencies, their audits, their demands for recordkeeping and reporting, etc., and eventually face the possibility of lawsuits, damages, back-pay awards, and most likely, poor public relations, industry can decide to eliminate formal test programs. (Informal decision devices are also subject to guidelines adherence if they have potential for discriminating, but the problems with these devices are more subtle.)

In fact, a relatively recent article in the *Wall Street Journal* (September 3, 1975) indicated that industries were decreasing their reliance on tests. According to the *Journal* staff reporter, "The use of testing is declining sharply in American business for reasons that have little to do with its accuracy. . . . Many employers feel that the guidelines applied to testing are so rigorous, expensive and time-consuming that they have decided to just chuck it all and go back to the seat-of-the-pants approach to hiring and promotion."

Despite the prevailing attitudes toward testing persons, the general evidence is that there is really no alternative that does as well. Ghiselli (1966) reviewed and summarized the literature on the effectiveness of different types of tests in the selection and placement of personnel in a wide spectrum of jobs. His general conclusion was that tests can have a sufficiently high degree of predictive power and can be of considerable practical value in the selection of personnel.

We echo Ghiselli's conclusion. Tests that are properly administered, are reliable, and are demonstrated to be related to performance or job

---

* Reprinted with permission from Equal Rights and Industrial Relations, eds. L. J. Hansman et al. Copyright © 1977 by Industrial Relations Research Association, Madison, Wis.
** Sheldon Zedeck, University of California, Berkeley, and Mary L. Tenopyr, American Telephone and Telegraph Company.

behavior are more efficient hiring devices than anything else. Then why has industry reacted so strongly and tended to cease testing?

The answer to this question may be fear and some misinterpretation of guidelines and court decisions. Many seem to believe that all testing is illegal, especially when there are differences on average scores between a majority group and a minority group. On the contrary, the intention of the Civil Rights Act was that the process of testing was legal and encouraged.

. . .

## JOB ANALYSIS

Job analysis is one of the first steps in most validation efforts. All government guidelines and orders refer to job analysis in more or less detail. Some persons have construed the *Albemarle* v. *Moody* decision as requiring job analysis. The employer, therefore, is well advised to con-duct thorough job analyses in conjunction with most validation studies of selection procedures. Job analysis is an unnecessary procedure in those cases in which criteria are to be actual employee outputs, such as sales, units produced, or days absent.

The basic practical problem with job analysis is that it is an art rather than a science (Cronbach, 1970). It is difficult to define except in the broadest terms. Textbook definitions are often of little help in informing the employer of what constitutes an acceptable job analysis. For example, Tiffin and McCormick (1965) define job analysis as "the collection and analysis of any type of job-related information, by any method, for any purpose."

In seeking assistance in job analysis, the employer will find that there are many ways to go about it. For example, McCormick and Tiffin (1974) list nine ways of collecting job information. After job information is collected, it may be analyzed and assembled in any number of ways.

Already there have been legal arguments over what constitutes the proper conduct of a job analysis. The psychological profession quite appropriately has no standards for job analysis, and unfortunately stand-ards will probably subsequently be set by courts or government agencies.

As a usual thing the employer should develop, in any validation effort, a catalogue of duties done by job incumbents. Each of these tasks should be somehow evaluated as to their importance, broadly defined, for efficient and safe job behavior. Evaluations may be done in terms of ratings of importance or difficulty, in duration of time spent on duties, frequency of performance, or consequences of error in duty performance. The employer also should be prepared to show that these evaluations are reliable. This is generally done by showing that at least two observers agree on the degree of duty importance.

The typical job description resulting from a wage and salary evaluation program usually does not meet the requirements for a job analysis. Many employers are, therefore, faced with the prospect of duplicating efforts in job analysis. Consolidating wage and salary job analysis and employ-ment job analysis is a possible course of action, but there may be prob-lems with any unions involved.

In a criterion-related study, except where actual employee outputs are the criteria, there should be a direct relationship between job analysis results and the criterion one is attempting to predict. Also, if job analysis is to be the main basis for developing a predictor test, as it would be in content validity (to be discussed later), there should be close correspond-ence between the job analysis results and the test. Thus, job analysis is not a free standing technique; it cannot be done in a vacuum. It must be related to the appropriate aspect of whatever validation process is chosen.

## VALIDATION MODELS

There are three professionally and legally recognized models of test validation. These go under the headings of the criterion-related, the content, and construct model.

The criterion-related model is the one preferred in both the 1970 EEOC guidelines, but it is not preferred in the EEOCC guidelines. The U.S. Supreme Court decision in *Washington* v. *Davis* specifically did not grant any preference to this model.

There are generally two types of procedure accepted under the cri-terion-related model: (1) the predictive procedure, which involves testing job applicants, not using their scores, and obtaining a measure of job or training success later, and (2) the concurrent procedure in which present employees are tested and measures of job success are obtained at approxi-mately the same time. Both procedures involve the use of statistics, especially the regression and correlation analyses mentioned earlier in this chapter.

The predictive procedure has more to recommend it scientifically; however, both the predictive and the concurrent procedure are acceptable under government orders and guidelines. There is one legal problem attendant upon the concurrent model; the present employees used in the validation study may be quite different from the normal job applicant population. For example, they may be older or less well educated. At least one U.S. District Court has taken issue with the concurrent model because of these differences.

There are a number of practical problems in complying with the government guidelines and legal procedures regarding criterion-related validation. The first of these is obtaining a suitable sample of persons for the validation study. It normally takes a considerable number of persons in the sample so that results can be statistically meaningful. It is impossible to specify the number of persons needed in each case; however, in most cases this number is upward of 100 or so. The small employer, or even the larger employer who has jobs fractionated so that there are small numbers in each job class, faces considerable difficulty in obtaining enough persons to do a study. The small employer has the option of using a different validation model, where it is appropriate, or using criterion-related validation data generated by others, or entering into a cooperative validation study with other employers with similar jobs.

A second problem is developing a criterion. Here is where the job analysis comes in. Unless the criterion is an actual work outcome such as sales, days absent, or number of units produced, the criterion should reflect the results of the job analysis. One often sees studies with both job analyses and criteria and yet no demonstrable relationship between the two. It is often extremely difficult to translate job analysis data into performance measures. For example, a job analysis shows that coding is an important duty of a clerk's job, and one wants to build a measure of coding ability. Should one have the clerk memorize the codes? Should the codes be visible at all times during this coding task? How numerous and complicated should the codes be?

Even more difficult is developing supervisors' rating forms on the basis of job analysis and being certain that the supervisors actually rate the characteristics shown by the job analysis to be important. Not only do definitions of characteristics to be rated have to be unequivocal, but also the rating forms have to be developed according to the best psychological principles, and the raters have to be properly trained and instructed.

From the foregoing, it may be inferred that developing a criterion is neither simple nor inexpensive. However, if one is going to conduct validation at all, it is only good common and business sense to have the criterion against which tests are to be validated as refined as feasible. The employer planning a validation study is advised to expend as much time, effort, and expense developing the criterion as is spent on all of the rest of the study.

Possibly the most serious obstacle of conducting criterion-related studies in compliance with government guidelines is the requirement for test fairness studies. The problem of not having enough comparable persons in each ethnic, race, and sex group is a particular hindrance. Even when there is a sufficient number of each group in a particular job class, the groups may not be comparable. For example, there may be differences in age, education, or length of service. Sometimes there are subtle differences in job assignment for different groups.

In addition to the problem of obtaining comparable groups, as discussed earlier, there are the serious difficulties imposed by the competing and sometimes conflicting definitions of test fairness. The employer contemplating a differential validation or test bias study is advised to obtain the services of an expert psychologist well trained in statistics.

The criterion-related validation model, thus, is not easy to apply. The simple concurrent validation study involving giving tests to present employees and correlating test results with hastily developed supervisors' ratings has until recently been the most common type of criterion-related study. This unsophisticated type of study will probably no longer meet the various legal requirements. Furthermore, such studies were never really good business practice. Employers planning criterion-related validation of tests must be prepared for sufficient effort to ensure the tests are fair and are legally defensible. Such effort, in addition, is merely sensible business procedure.

The content validation model is, according to the 1970 EEOC guidelines, acceptable in most instances only when criterion-related validation is not technically feasible. However, as has been mentioned, the U.S. Supreme Court (*Washington* v. *Davis*) apparently has granted equal status to content and criterion-related validation, and the EEOCC guidelines do likewise. Even so, most psychologists agree that content validation is by itself not sufficient when one is attempting in an employment situation to measure abstract traits like verbal comprehension or initiative. Content validation is more appropriate for skill tests like typing or welding work samples or for job knowledge tests.

The employer seeking information on content validation will find little in the way of guidance in the professional literature. Most writings on the subject have been prepared in the context of education settings. One source of information is PRINCIPLES FOR THE VALIDATION AND USE OF PERSONNEL SELECTION PROCEDURES (American Psychological Association, Division of Industrial and Organizational Psychology, 1974).

Although job analysis is not always needed for a criterion-related validation study, it is the very foundation of content validity. A test may be said to be content valid when the content of the test reflects the content of the job. In conducting a content validation effort, the job's content, called a content domain, should be defined. This domain does not have to cover all job duties. For example, a content domain for a clerk's job may include only typing, although the clerk may have other duties such as answering the telephone, filing, or making coffee.

The content domain should ordinarily be defined in terms of tasks, activities, or responsibilities. It may be useful at times to define the domain in terms of specific knowledge or skill, so that one can have the basis for a knowledge or skill test. However, there have been major problems when persons have attempted to define the domain in terms of abstract traits such as dominance, leadership, or spatial reasoning.

The test is then developed on the basis of the content domain. The problems of developing test tasks that reflect the results of the job analysis are very much like those in criterion development. Test development must be done in a rigorous manner, and the steps in development must be carefully documented.

Questions of sample size, utility, and differential validation do not arise when content validation is the method employed. A content valid test may be developed for a job with a small number of incumbents. There is no way of assessing utility as part of the content validation procedure, and significantly, a test which is content valid is valid for all racial, ethnic, and sex groups.

Construct validation is deemed by the 1970 EEOC guidelines to be permissible only when criterion-related validation is not technically feasible. Yet construct validation was granted parity with the other two validation models by the Supreme Court in *Washington* v. *Davis* and is also given parity in the EEOC guidelines. The methodology of construct validation has been discussed far more than it has been applied in an employment setting. In fact, there have not been enough applications of construct validation in employment settings so that it can be said that there is any professional agreement on proper methodology. One thing construct validation is *not,* for example, is the mere designation of a test as measuring "intelligence" and then arguing that people have to be intelligent to do the job concerned. It may be said that construct validation is a difficult and arduous undertaking. A criterion-related study is a simple undertaking in comparison with a construct validation effort. Employers, particularly those with limited resources, are advised to view construct validation with caution until its methodology is better developed.

. . .

The statistical criterion-related model has been predominant in government guidelines. There are various ways of conducting criterion-related studies and a number of problems with the method. Among the latter is the difficulty in developing a reliable and relevant criterion. Content validation is appropriate for situations in which the job applicant brings developed skills and knowledge to the job. Construct validation is a method under development for employment settings.

As a result of Title VII of the Civil Rights Act of 1964, various orders and guidelines on testing have emerged. In addition there have been numerous lower court cases on testing. There have been three U.S. Supreme Court decisions on testing, and it is probably best to think of the law as being in its formative stages. However, it is clear the federal law requires tests to be related to job behavior.

Employers are urged to do careful validation studies on employment selection procedures. These studies are not only necessary for compliance with the law, they are also good business.

Finally, testing is still in its formative stages. The state of the situation is that testing and validation is still an art. Until more research is done and more is learned about the generalizability of the abilities, aptitudes, skills, etc., which are measured by tests, testing will remain an art. It is our hope that research on abilities needed to perform jobs by industry, the public sector, and unions will result in testing becoming a science.

### NOTE

In *Robinson* v. *Lorillard Corp.,* 444 F.2d 791, 3 FEP Cases, *cert. denied,* 404 U.S. 1006 (1971), the Fourth Circuit noted:
"Collectively these cases conclusively establish that the applicable test

is not merely whether there exists a business purpose for adhering to a challenged practice. The test is whether there exists an overriding legitimate business purpose such that the practice is necessary to the safe and efficient operation of the business. Thus, the business purpose must be sufficiently compelling to override any racial impact; the challenged practice must effectively carry out the business purpose it is alleged to serve; and there must be available no acceptable alternative policies or practices which would better accomplish the business purpose advanced, or accomplish it equally well with a lesser differential racial impact."

(4) *Other Hiring Standards*

## GREEN v. MISSOURI PACIFIC RAILROAD CO.

*United States Court of Appeals, Eighth Circuit, 1975*
*523 F.2d 1290, 10 FEP Cases 1409*

BRIGHT, Circuit Judge: The Missouri Pacific Railroad Company (MoPac) follows an absolute policy of refusing consideration for employment to any person convicted of a crime other than a minor traffic offense. Appellant-Buck Green, who is black, raises the principal question of whether this policy violates Title VII of the Civil Rights Act of 1964, as amended, 42 U.S.C. § 2000e *et seq.* (Supp. II, 1972) and 42 U.S.C. § 1981 (1970), because this practice allegedly operates to disqualify blacks for employment at a substantially higher rate than whites and is not job related.

Green on his own behalf and as a class action filed this suit November 7, 1972, seeking declaratory and injunctive relief as well as back pay. The district court denied Green relief on his individual claim and that of the class.[3] Green brings this timely appeal. We outline the undisputed facts.

On September 29, 1970, Green, then 29 years of age, applied for employment as a clerk at MoPac's personnel office in the corporate headquarters in St. Louis, Missouri.[4] In response to a question on an application form, Green disclosed that he had been convicted in December 1967 for refusing military induction. He stated that he had served 21 months in prison until paroled on July 24, 1970.[5] After reviewing the application form, MoPac's personnel officer informed Green that he

---

[3] [Footnotes numbered as in original.—Ed.] The district court opinion is reported at 381 F. Supp. 992 (E.D. Mo. 1974). The district court defined the class as those blacks denied employment at MoPac's corporate headquarters in St. Louis, Missouri, because of the company's refusal to consider persons with a criminal record other than minor traffic offenses.

[4] MoPac employs about 2,000 people at its corporate headquarters.

[5] Prior to Green's prosecution he had unsuccessfully sought classification as a conscientious objector by his draft board. Green did not appeal his conviction but sought post-conviction review. In proceedings which reached this court, the court, in a divided opinion, refused to review appellant's challenge to the alleged constitutional invalidity of his draft classification. *Cassidy* v. *United States*, 428 F.2d 585 (8th Cir. 1970) (Green's legal name at the time of these proceedings was Cassidy).

was not qualified for employment at MoPac because of his conviction and prison record. Green, thereafter, sought relief under Title VII, and, when administrative conciliation failed, he brought this action.

Since 1948, MoPac has followed the policy of disqualifying for employment any applicant with a conviction for any crime other than a minor traffic offense.[6] Prior to 1972, MoPac also investigated an applicant's arrest record, but after the decision in *Gregory* v. *Litton Systems, Inc.*, 472 F.2d 631 (9th Cir. 1972), MoPac eliminated any arrest inquiry from its application form and ceased using arrest records as an employment criterion.

Green makes the following contentions on this appeal: (1) MoPac's policy of not hiring any person convicted of a criminal offense has a racially discriminatory effect and violates Title VII; (2) this policy is not justified by any business necessity; and (3) the district court erred in restricting the class only to black persons denied employment consideration because of a conviction record.

## I.   *Whether Green proved a prima facie case of discrimination.*

Although the employment practice in question is facially neutral, an employment test or practice which operates to exclude a disproportionate percentage of blacks violates Title VII unless the employer can establish that the practice is justified as a business necessity. *Griggs* v. *Duke Power Co.*, 401 U.S. 424, 431, 91 S.Ct. 849, 28 L.Ed.2d 158 (1971); see *Boston Chapter N.A.A.C.P., Inc.* v. *Beecher*, 504 F.2d 1017, 1019 (1st Cir. 1974); *Wallace* v. *Debron Corp.*, 494 F.2d 674, 675 (8th Cir. 1974); *United States* v. *Georgia Power Co.*, 474 F.2d 906, 911 (5th Cir. 1973); *Gregory* v. *Litton Systems, Inc.*, 316 F. Supp. 401, 403 (C.D. Cal. 1970), *aff'd*, 472 F.2d 631 (9th Cir. 1972). Once a prima facie case of substantially disparate impact is made the burden shifts to the employer to justify the employment practice or test as a business necessity. *McDonnell Douglas Corp.* v. *Green*, 411 U.S. 792, 802, 93 S.Ct. 1817, 36 L.Ed.2d 668 (1973); *Rogers* v. *International Paper Co.*, 510 F.2d 1340, 1348–49 (8th Cir. 1975); *Rodriguez* v. *East Texas Motor Freight*, 505 F.2d 40, 54 (5th Cir. 1974); *Hester* v. *Southern Ry. Co.*, 497 F.2d 1374, 1381 (5th Cir. 1974).

Thus, we examine the threshold question of whether Green has presented a prima facie case. A disproportionate racial impact may be established statistically in any of three ways. The first procedure considers whether blacks as a class (or at least blacks in a specified geographical area) are excluded by the employment practice in question at a substantially higher rate than whites. See *Griggs* v. *Duke Power Co., supra*, 401 U.S. at 430 n. 6, 91 S.Ct. 849, 28 L.Ed.2d 158 (on the requirement of a

---

[6] MoPac's personnel manager testified that this stringent policy occasionally has been relaxed. For example, one current employee has been convicted of disturbing the peace while another employee has been convicted of possession of intoxicants by a minor. Nevertheless, as a policy matter, MoPac denies employment to any person with a conviction record for a felony or misdemeanor (excepting minor traffic offenses).

high school diploma, the Court cited statistics from the U.S. Census Bureau that in North Carolina only 12 percent of black males had completed high school while 34 percent of white males had done so); *United States* v. *Georgia Power Co.*, 474 F.2d 906, 918 (5th Cir. 1973) (the court cited statistics from the South and from the Atlanta area showing that a substantially higher percentage of whites had completed high school than blacks); *Gregory* v. *Litton Systems, Inc.*, 316 F. Supp. 401, 403 (C.D. Cal. 1970), *aff'd*, 472 F.2d 631 (9th Cir. 1972) (the court cited national arrest statistics showing that blacks suffered a disproportionately high percentage of arrests); *Johnson* v. *Pike Corp.*, 332 F. Supp. 490, 494 (C.D. Cal. 1971) (the court cited general studies indicating that blacks' wages were garnished at a disproportionately high rate).

The second procedure focuses on a comparison of the percentage of black and white job applicants actually excluded by the employment practice or test of the particular company or governmental agency in question. See *Griggs* v. *Duke Power Co., supra*, 401 U.S. at 430 n. 6, 91 S.Ct. 849, 28 L.Ed.2d 158; *Vulcan Society of the New York City Fire Dept.* v. *Civil Service Comm. of the City of New York*, 490 F.2d 387, 392 (2d Cir. 1973); *Bridgeport Guard, Inc.* v. *Members of the Bridgeport Civil Service Comm.*, 482 F.2d 1333, 1335 (2d Cir. 1973); *cf. Rogers* v. *International Paper Co., supra*, 510 F.2d at 1348–49.

Finally, a third procedure examines the level of employment of blacks by the company or governmental agency in comparison to the percentage of blacks in the relevant geographical area. See *Bridgeport Guard, Inc.* v. *Members of the Bridgeport Civil Service Comm., supra.*, 482 F.2d at 1335–36; *United States* v. *Georgia Power Co., supra*, 474 F.2d at 910; *Butts* v. *Nichols*, 381 F. Supp. 573, 579 (S.D. Ia. 1974) (three-judge court); *cf. Rodriguez* v. *East Texas Motor Freight, supra*, 505 F.2d at 54–55.

Although Green alleged that MoPac discriminates against blacks generally in its employment practices, the district court focused only on whether a disparate impact could be statistically demonstrated by MoPac's policy of automatically rejecting all applicants with a conviction for an offense other than minor traffic infractions. Here, we consider a sweeping disqualification of all persons with a past record of some unlawful behavior, see *McDonnell Douglas Corp.* v. *Green, supra*, 411 U.S. at 806, 93 S.Ct. 1817, 36 L.Ed.2d 668, rather than a test directed at a precise measurement of intelligence or skills. The disparity of impact, if any, will be disclosed by an examination of how that policy affects applicants and potential applicants. We agree with the approach taken by the district court and primarily limit our statistical analysis to the effect of MoPac's policies against both blacks and whites in the general population in the area from which employees are drawn (metropolitan St. Louis), and the effect of this policy upon black and white applicants for employment with MoPac.

Initially, we note that the district court recognized statistical data and treatises offered into evidence by the plaintiff which indicate that blacks are convicted of crimes at a rate at least two to three times greater than the percentage of blacks in the populations of certain geographical areas. Dr. Ronald Christensen, a qualified expert witness for the plaintiff, concluded that it is between 2.2 and 6.7 times as likely that a black person will have a criminal conviction record during his lifetime than that a white person will have such a record. He further concluded that in urban areas from 36.9 percent to 78.1 percent of all black persons would incur a conviction during their lifetimes, but that from only 11.6 percent to 16.8 percent of all white persons would acquire a conviction.

MoPac's records of employment applications at its corporate headquarters during the period from September 1, 1971, through November 7, 1973,[7] disclose that 3,282 blacks and 5,206 whites applied for employment. Of these individuals, 174 blacks (5.3 percent of the black applicants) and 118 whites (2.23 percent of the white applicants) were rejected because of their conviction records. Thus, statistically, the policy operated automatically to exclude from employment 53 of every 1,000 black applicants but only 22 of every 1,000 white applicants. The rejection rate for blacks is two and one-half times that of whites under this policy.

Although the district court recognized that these statistics denote a disparate impact, the court further compared the number of blacks rejected (174) to the total pool of applicants (8,488) and deemed the resulting figure of 2.05 percent as showing a *"de minimis discriminatory effect"* when compared to the percentage of blacks (16 percent) in the St. Louis metropolitan area.

The trial court's use of additional statistics supporting a conclusion of a *de minimis* discriminatory effect suffers from two principal defects. First, comparing the number of black applicants rejected because of a conviction record to the total number of applicants does not reflect a disparity of impact separately against each race. Moreover, because more whites than blacks applied for employment (3,282 blacks and 5,206 whites) a comparison of the rejected blacks to the total number of applicants serves to dilute the actual discriminatory impact against blacks.

Second, comparing the resulting percentage of 2.05 against the percent of blacks in the relevant population area is of no assistance for the issue in Title VII cases focuses on whether an employer has discriminated against any individual "because of such individual's race, color, religion, sex, or national origin." 42 U.S.C. § 2000e–2(a)(1). The issue to be examined statistically is whether the questioned employment practice operates in a disparate manner upon a minority race or group, not whether the individuals actually suffering from a discriminatory practice are statistically large in number.

An employment criterion must be examined for its operation on a racially exclusionary basis—thus its effect must be measured upon blacks

---

[7] These figures reflect the only available data.

separately and upon whites separately. See *Griggs* v. *Duke Power Co.,* *supra,* 401 U.S. at 430 n. 6, 91 S.Ct. 849, 28 L.Ed.2d 158; *United States* v. *Georgia Power Co., supra,* 474 F.2d at 918; *Gregory* v. *Litton Systems, Inc., supra,* 316 F. Supp. at 403; *Johnson* v. *Pike Corp., supra,* 332 F. Supp. at 494; *cf.* Note, *Employment Discrimination: Statistics and Preferences Under Title VII,* 59 Va.L.Rev. 463, 468 (1973).

The statistics established that MoPac's employment practice under consideration disqualifies black applicants or potential black applicants for employment at a substantially higher rate than whites. Thus, Green has established a prima facie case of discrimination.

## II.  *Is MoPac's employment practice justified by "Business Necessity?"*

Once a prima facie case of discrimination has been established, the defendants must show that the employment practice in question is justified by "business necessity." The seminal decision for business necessity, of course, is *Griggs* v. *Duke Power Co.,* 401 U.S. 424, 91 S.Ct. 849, 28 L.Ed.2d 158 (1971), where the Court, in discussing the reach and intent of equal employment opportunity cases under Title VII said:

"[Title VII] proscribes not only overt discrimination but also practices that are fair in form, but discriminatory in operation. The touchstone is business necessity. If an employment practice which operates to exclude Negroes cannot be shown to be related to job performance, the practice is prohibited. . . .

. . .

"What is required by Congress is the removal of artificial, arbitrary, and unnecessary barriers to employment when the barriers operate invidiously to discriminate on the basis of racial or other impermissible classification. [*Id.* at 431, 91 S.Ct. at 853.]

. . .

"What Congress has commanded is that any tests used must measure the person for the job and not the person in the abstract." [*Id.* at 436, 91 S.Ct. at 856.]

In *Griggs,* the Court considered professionally prepared aptitude tests and a requirement of a high school diploma by which the employer sought to measure the skills of the prospective employee to perform the required work. Here, the employment requirement does not seek to measure technical aptitude or ability but serves as an absolute bar to employment because of some prior unlawful act committed by the applicant. The Supreme Court, in *McDonnell Douglas Corp.* v. *Green,* 411 U.S. 792, 93 S.Ct. 1817, 36 L.Ed.2d 668 (1973), acknowledged a distinction between the employment tests struck down in *Griggs*—standardized testing devices which, however neutral on their face, were not job related and operated to exclude a disproportionate percentage of blacks—and the qualification asserted in the *McDonnell Douglas* case where the applicant for employment, Green, had engaged in a seriously disruptive act against his prospective employer. *Id.* at 806, 93 S.Ct. 1817, 1826, 36 L.Ed.2d 668. But, JUSTICE POWELL's opinion for a unanimous court added a caveat to its holding in these words:

"[P]etitioner [McDonnell Douglas] does not seek his [Green's] exclusion on the basis of a testing device which overstates what is necessary for competent performance, or through some *sweeping disqualification of all those with any past record of unlawful behavior, however remote, insubstantial, or unrelated to applicant's personal qualifications as an employee."* [*Id.* (emphasis added).]

We perceive this comment to suggest that a sweeping disqualification for employment resting solely on past behavior can violate Title VII where that employment practice has a disproportionate racial impact and rests upon a tenuous or insubstantial basis. Although the Supreme Court has not directly addressed this type of employment qualification, similar employment criteria have been examined and struck down by the courts as discriminatory.

In *Carter* v. *Gallagher,* 452 F.2d 315 (8th Cir. 1971), *cert. denied,* 406 U.S. 950, 92 S.Ct. 2045, 32 L.Ed.2d 338 (1972), an *en banc* court reviewed a decree of the district court relating to the recruitment, examination, and hiring practices in the Minneapolis, Minnesota, Fire Department, which allegedly discriminated against blacks and other minority groups.

The City of Minneapolis had routinely disqualified applicants for the position of fire fighter for a prior felony or misdemeanor conviction. The district court decree in pertinent part had limited the disqualification to a time period of five years, after a felony conviction or after incarceration had ended and a time period of two years after a misdemeanor conviction or two years after incarceration for such conviction had ended. The decree had provided further that any rejection of an applicant for employment because of a crime must be based on a finding that the applicant's behavior giving rise to the conviction furnished an inference that the applicant could not fulfill the duties of a fire fighter. *Id.* at 321.

On appeal, the parties agreed that a conviction for a felony or misdemeanor should not "per se constitute an absolute bar to employment." *Id.* at 326. In reviewing this part of the decree, we said:
"The trial court in its discretion may require the defendants to submit to it for approval a rule with respect to the consideration to be given to an applicant's conviction record, which at a minimum should not treat conviction as an absolute bar to employment. We would not consider any rule giving fair consideration to the bearing of the conviction upon applicant's fitness for the fire fighter job to be inappropriate." [*Id.*]
. . .

The court in *Gregory* v. *Litton Systems, Inc.,* 316 F. Supp. 401 (C.D. Cal. 1970), *aff'd,* 472 F.2d 631 (9th Cir. 1972), determined that defendant's policy of barring from employment consideration anyone arrested on "a number of occasions" violated Title VII.

In *Wallace* v. *Debron Corp.,* 494 F.2d 674 (8th Cir. 1974), we reviewed an employer's policy of automatically discharging those individuals whose wages had been garnished more than once in a 12-month period. In remanding the factual question of whether this policy was justified by the business necessity test,[11] we observed that all "artificial, arbitrary, and unnecessary racial barriers to employment" should be removed. *Id.* at 676. See also *Johnson* v. *Pike Corp.,* 332 F. Supp. 490 (C.D. Cal. 1971).

These cases suggest that MoPac's procedure now at issue does not meet the requirements of the business necessity test. This test has been articulated in this circuit as follows: "It is likewise apparent that a neutral policy, which is inherently discriminatory, may be valid if it has overriding business justification. . . . However, this doctrine of business necessity, which has arisen as an exception to the amenability of discriminatory practices, 'connotes an irresistible demand.' The system in question must not only *foster* safety and efficiency, but must be *essential* to that goal. . . . In other words, there must be no acceptable alternative that will accomplish that goal 'equally well with a lesser differential racial impact.' " [*United States* v. *St. Louis-San Francisco Ry. Co.,* 464 F.2d 301, 308 (8th Cir. 1972), *cert. denied,* 409 U.S. 1116, 93 S.Ct. 900, 34 L.Ed.2d 687 (1973) (emphasis in original).]
See also *Rodriguez* v. *East Texas Motor Freight, supra,* 505 F. 2d at 55–56; *Wallace* v. *Debron Corp., supra,* 494 F.2d at 677; *United States* v. *N. L. Industries, Inc.,* 479 F.2d 354, 364–65 (8th Cir. 1973); *Robinson* v. *Lorillard Corp.,* 444 F.2d 791, 798 (4th Cir.), *cert. denied,* 404 U.S. 1006, 92 S.Ct. 573, 30 L.Ed.2d 655 (1971); Note, *Business Necessity Under Title VII of the Civil Rights Act of 1964: A No-Alternative Approach,* 84 YALE L.J. 98 (1974); Wilson, *A Second Look at Griggs* v. *Duke Power Company: Ruminations on Job Testing, Discrimination, and the Role of the Federal Courts,* 58 VA.L.REV. 844, 859–73 (1972).

Although this circuit's articulation of the business necessity test emphasizes the ability of a prospective employee to do the work, the second part of the test, that of "no acceptable alternative that will accomplish the goal equally well with a lesser differential racial impact," constitutes a general test which applies to an employment practice such as that in this case. See *Wallace* v. *Debron Corp., supra,* 494 F.2d at 677.

MoPac proffers a number of reasons for claiming that its policy is a business necessity: 1) fear of cargo theft, 2) handling company funds, 3) bonding qualifications, 4) possible impeachment of an employee as a witness, 5) possible liability for hiring persons with known violent tendencies, 6) employment disruption caused by recidivism, and 7) alleged lack of moral character of persons with convictions. But, as recognized by the district court, MoPac has not empirically validated its policy with respect to conviction records, 381 F. Supp. at 996, nor shown that a less restrictive alternative with a lesser racial impact would not serve as well.

---

[11] The defendant conceded for purposes of the appeal that its garnishment policy would subject a disproportionate number of blacks to discharge. 494 F.2d at 676.

MoPac's witness, Dr. Robert N. McMurry, a consulting industrial psychologist to MoPac, testified that not every ex-offender will be a poor employee and that it would be preferable for a company to consider ex-offenders on an individual basis.[12] He further acknowledged that an employment practice which excludes ex-offenders accentuates recidivism. Although the reasons MoPac advances for its absolute bar can serve as relevant considerations in making individual hiring decisions, they in no way justify an absolute policy which sweeps so broadly.

We cannot conceive of any business necessity that would automatically place every individual convicted of any offense, except a minor traffic offense, in the permanent ranks of the unemployed. This is particularly true for blacks who have suffered and still suffer from the burdens of discrimination in our society. To deny job opportunities to these individuals because of some conduct which may be remote in time or does not significantly bear upon the particular job requirements is an unnecessarily harsh and unjust burden.

Accordingly, we hold that appellant-Green and all other blacks who have been summarily denied employment by MoPac on the basis of conviction records have been discriminated against on the basis of race in violation of Title VII and that the district court should enjoin MoPac's practice of using convictions as an absolute bar to employment.[13] With respect to appellant-Green, the district court should determine whether on the date of his application his background and experience qualified him for any position for which he applied with MoPac.[14] If the court so finds, it should award him back pay. See *Albemarle Paper Co. v. Moody,* 422 U.S. 405, 95 S.Ct. 2362, 45 L.Ed.2d 280 (1975). The record does not disclose whether other members of the class also disqualified by their criminal record would have otherwise been eligible for employment with the company. Under these circumstances, we do not feel that MoPac is obligated for any back pay for the class. On remand, the court should also award the plaintiff appropriate attorney's fees for proceedings in the

[12] The district court also specifically noted that not all ex-offenders will be poor employees and that the employment of ex-offenders should be encouraged. 381 F. Supp. at 997.

[13] The EEOC guidelines require validation and evidence of a high degree of utility of employment tests. 29 CFR § 1607 (1974). These include standardized tests as well as qualifying or disqualifying personal history or background requirements. 29 CFR § 1607.2. The district court rejected these guidelines as inappropriate for MoPac's employment practice here in question. The application of these guidelines to the use of conviction data in a less restrictive way is not now before us and, therefore, we need not resolve that question.

[14] We note that Green's conviction was for refusal to submit to military induction after he had been denied conscientious objector status. He has paid his debt to society for a nonviolent crime. It is difficult to view this conviction as related to any job qualification except in a most remote way. Although one of MoPac's witnesses, Dr. McMurry, expressed some reservations about Green, we note that Green worked as a clerk during his 21 months of imprisonment and at the time of trial in this case was employed by the Lead Poisoning Control Service of the City of St. Louis and had received a "superior" rating from his supervisor. The supervisor testified that "superior" ratings are given very infrequently.

district court and on appeal. 42 U.S.C. § 2000e–5(k); see *Parham* v. *Southwestern Bell Telephone Co.*, 433 F.2d 421, 430 (8th Cir. 1970).

. . .

### ORDER DENYING PETITION FOR REHEARING EN BANC

The petition for rehearing *en banc* in the above case is denied by four of the judges voting in favor of the denial. JUDGE WEBSTER is ineligible to vote, having sat in the district court on preliminary matters in this case. Three of the judges vote in favor of the rehearing en banc.

GIBSON, Chief Judge, joined by JUDGES STEPHENSON and HENLEY, would grant the petition for rehearing en banc for the following reasons.

The rule enforced by Missouri Pacific Railroad Co. (MoPac) in the present case which prohibited the employment of those with criminal records is not racially discriminatory. Rather, it discriminates against both blacks and whites on the basis of their criminal records.

Title VII, which proscribes covert discrimination, requires a showing of a disparate effect upon a protected class. *Griggs* v. *Duke Power Co.*, 401 U.S. 424, 91 S.Ct. 849, 28 L.Ed.2d 158 (1971), found an adequate disparate effect when it was shown that the aptitude tests used there disqualified 94 percent of blacks, while only 42 percent of whites were excluded because of inability to pass the tests. The disparity in the present case was a ratio of 5.3 percent blacks excluded to 2.23 percent whites. As found by the District Court, this appears to be *de minimus* in light of the total number employed by MoPac. In 1970, the year that Green was rejected, 29 percent of the employees hired by MoPac in the St. Louis Metropolitan area were black, although blacks comprised only 16.4 percent of that area. *Green* v. *Missouri Pac. Ry.*, 381 F. Supp. 992, 998–1000 (E.D. Mo. 1974). Contrary to the panel holding in the instant case, it does not appear that black applicants were disqualified at a "substantially higher" rate than whites.

Title VII is remedial in nature, not punitive. It is intended to ensure nondiscriminatory and fair employment practices, not to invade every province normally reserved for the employers' business judgment. MoPac's policy disqualified a very small percentage of *all* applicants and affected only 3 percent more blacks than whites. It is conceivable that *any* qualification for employment or promotion can be shown by statistics or otherwise to have *some* effect, however minimal, on blacks, women or other protected groups. This is not to say that these qualifications are "built-in headwinds" for the protected groups. *Griggs* v. *Duke Power Co.*, *supra*, 401 U.S. at 432, 91 S.Ct. 849. Title VII should be construed in a manner to preserve the employers' right to make reasonable business judgments in these matters based upon the exigencies of the particular business.

The evidence in the above case, as was that presented in *Butts* v. *Nichols*, 381 F. Supp. 573 (S.D. Ia. 1974), is too "inconclusive" to show racial discrimination. In effect, the present case has judicially created a new Title VII protected class persons with conviction records. This extension, if wise, is a legislative responsibility and should not be done under the guise of racial discrimination.

In view of the impact of this decision and the apparent division in our court on this issue, we feel an en banc hearing would be of further illumination in this evolving field of the law.

## YUHAS v. LIBBEY-OWENS-FORD CO.

*United States Court of Appeals, Seventh Circuit, 1977*
*562 F. 2d 496, 16 FEP Cases 891, cert. denied, 435 U.S. 934,*
*17 FEP Cases 87 (1978)*

SWYGERT, Circuit Judge: We must decide whether an employer's rule that a present employee's spouse may not be hired in a similar capacity violates the antidiscrimination provisions of Title VII of the Civil Rights Act of 1964, as amended, 42 U.S.C. §§ 2000e *et seq.* The district court found a violation. We take a contrary view and reverse.

### I

Defendant Libbey-Owens-Ford Company operates two plants in Ottawa, Illinois. The Company has a rule against hiring an hourly employee at these plants when the applicant's spouse is already employed there in the same capacity. The rule was promulgated at the Ottawa plants on July 1, 1968 as an extension of a company policy which has been in effect since before 1953. The rule is directed only to the hiring of new employees, whether male or female. It does not require discharging either spouse of couples already married on July 1, 1968, and does not require terminating an employee who marries a fellow employee.

On June 30, 1969, plaintiff Dorothy I. Yuhas applied for employment as an hourly employee at defendant's Ottawa plants. Her application was denied, pursuant to the no-spouse rule, because her husband was then employed as an hourly employee at one of those plants.

Contending that she was the victim of sexual discrimination, Yuhas filed charges against defendant with the Equal Employment Opportunity Commission on August 15, 1969. The gravamen of her claim was that the no-spouse rule had a discriminatory effect because since its inception seventy-one women, compared to three men, had been denied employment for the reason that their spouses were already employed as hourly employees. Yuhas obtained a right-to-sue letter from the EEOC on June 2, 1972, and filed this action in the District Court for the Northern District of Illinois on August 22, 1972. The court permitted Nancy Anderson, who was denied employment pursuant to the no-spouse rule in August 1972 and received a right-to-sue letter on May 23, 1973, to join the action as a party-plaintiff on May 30, 1973. Plaintiffs maintained the action on behalf of themselves and the class of all similarly situated women.

After discovery and the reassignment of the case to a new district judge, each side moved for summary judgment on January 12, 1976. The district court found that although the no-spouse rule was sexually neutral on its face, it had "a greatly disparate impact" under *Griggs* v. *Duke Power Co.*, 401 U.S. 424, 91 S.Ct. 849, 28 L.Ed.2d 158 (1971). The court held plaintiffs had therefore made out a prima facie case for relief. This prima facie case could be rebutted only if defendant could show that the rule was job-related. The court found that there was a question of fact as to whether the rule was job-related which could only be resolved by a trial. 411 F. Supp. 77 (N.D. Ill. 1976).

At a bench trial, defendant attempted to demonstrate that the no-spouse rule served a legitimate, business-related function. It introduced evidence that hourly workers who are married to each other are absent from work or tardy in appearing for work more often than other workers. It also tried to show that the employment of both partners in a marriage led to problems in the scheduling of vacations and work assignments because both partners often wanted the same vacation and work assignment. Finally, it presented testimony that the employment of both spouses undermined employee moral and efficiency because the relationship between the spouses interfered with the ordinary relationships workers have with each other and with their supervisors.

On December 15, 1976, the district court held that the evidence introduced by defendant was insufficient to rebut plaintiffs' prima facie case. It found the statistical evidence of absenteeism and tardiness to be unconvincing, and rejected the validity of the other testimony presented by defendant on the ground that there was "no hard information as to what specific production problems were ever caused in any particular case." Accordingly, the court enjoined defendant from continuing to maintain its no-spouse rule.

Defendant now appeals. It contends both that the district court erred in holding that plaintiffs had made out a prima facie case of employment discrimination and that, in any event, the no-spouse rule is job-related.

## II

Defendant's argument that the district court erred in holding that plaintiffs had established a prima facie case is based on the claim that *Griggs*, which was a case of racial discrimination, should not be extended to cases of sexual discrimination. It contends, relying on *General Electric* v. *Gilbert*, 429 U.S. 125, 97 S.Ct. 401, 50 L.Ed.2d 343 (1976), that an employment rule which is not based on gender is not sexually discriminatory within the meaning of Title VII, regardless of whether the rule has a discriminatory impact.

We cannot accept this argument. In the recent case of *Dothard* v. *Rawlinson*, _____ U.S. _____, 97 S.Ct. 2720, 53 L.Ed.2d 786 (1977), the Supreme Court expressly extended *Griggs* to a case of sexual discrimination. Alabama had a rule requiring all state prison guards to be at least five feet, two inches tall and to weigh at least 120 pounds. The rule excluded 41.13 percent of the female population in the United States while excluding less than one percent of the male population. The Court held that these statistics alone, without a showing of discriminatory intent, were sufficient to make out a prima facie case of unlawful sexual discrimination. It stated:

"The gist of the claim that the statutory height and weight requirements discriminate against women does not involve an assertion of purposeful discriminatory motive. It is asserted rather, that these facially neutral qualification standards work in fact disproportionately to exclude women from eligibility for employment by the Alabama Board of Corrections. We dealt in *Griggs* v. *Duke Power Co., supra,* and *Albemarle Paper Co.* v. *Moody,* 422 U.S. 405, 95 S.Ct. 2362, 45 L.Ed.2d 280, with similar allegations that facially neutral employment standards disproportionately excluded Negroes from employment, and those cases guide our approach here.

"Those cases make clear that to establish a prima facie case of discrimination, a plaintiff need only show that the facially neutral standards in question select applicants for hire in a significantly discriminatory pattern. Once it is thus shown that the employment standards are discriminatory in effect, the employer must meet 'the burden of showing that any given requirement [has] . . . a manifest relation to the employment in question.' " *Griggs* v. *Duke Power Co.,* 401 U.S. at 432 [91 S.Ct. 849, at 854], 97 S.Ct. at 2726 (footnote omitted).

*Dothard* governs the case at bar. Like the Alabama rule, defendant's no-spouse rule is not gender-based and does not intentionally discriminate against women. But again like the Alabama rule, the no-spouse rule has a substantial discriminatory impact which is demonstrated by the statistic that seventy-one of the last seventy-four people disqualified under it were women. It therefore is invalid under Title VII unless defendant can show that it is job-related. See also *United States* v. *City of Chicago,* 549 F.2d 415, 427 (7th Cir. 1977).

We do not find this result to be at odds with *General Electric* v. *Gilbert.* The plaintiffs in *General Electric* challenged the validity of the company's disability plan which excluded disability benefits arising from pregnancies. The Court held that the plan did not violate Title VII for two reasons: first, because it was not gender-based and therefore did not intentionally discriminate against women; and second, because plaintiffs had not made a showing that the plan would have a discriminatory impact. 429 U.S. at 133–40, 97 S.Ct. 401. The Court in no way intimated that *Griggs* would not be applicable if plaintiffs had been able to demonstrate that the plan had a discriminatory impact. Moreover, even if isolated language in the *General Electric* opinion could be read as *sub silentio* overruling *Griggs* or restricting it to cases of racial discrimination, see 429 U.S. at 153, 97 S.Ct. 401 (BRENNAN, J., dissenting), the Court's square holding in the more recent *Dothard* case prohibits such an interpretation.

## III

We therefore turn to a determination of whether the no-spouse rule is job-related. The district court held that defendant failed to satisfy its burden of proof on this issue. The court first found that defendant failed to demonstrate by statistical evidence that its rule was necessary to prevent excessive absenteeism or tardiness, or that without the rule the scheduling of vacation and work assignments would be more difficult. This finding is not clearly erroneous and we affirm it on appeal.

The court also rejected defendant's assertion that the rule prevented situations which could undermine employee morale and efficiency. The court found that defendant had not proved this assertion because it had not shown that production would fall if the rule were discarded. We cannot argue with the factual predicate of this statement, for there is no evidence in the record linking the rule and production in defendant's Ottawa plants.

However, unlike the district court, we do not find that these facts conclusively demonstrate that the rule was not job-related. The no-spouse rule is predicated on the assumption that it is generally * a bad idea to have both partners in a marriage working together. There are a number of reasons why this assumption is plausible. First, the marital relationship often generates intense emotions which would interfere with a worker's job performance. The typical employee is often able to temporarily put aside these emotional feelings when he or she goes to work because the work environment is sharply differentiated from the home environment. This distinction becomes impossible if the employee's spouse is also his or her coworker.

Second, if an employee who works with his or her spouse became involved in a grievance with the employer or another worker, the two spouses might be expected to take the same side in the dispute. This factor could hamper the expeditious resolution of grievances.

Third, if both partners in a marriage were employed together, and one spouse was promoted to a supervisory position, numerous problems could arise. One spouse might resent the other's promotion, preventing the promoted worker from efficiently performing his or her new job. The person in the supervisory position might have a great deal of difficulty in imposing discipline on or otherwise exercising authority over his or her spouse. Moreover, the other workers who were placed under the authority of the higher-ranking partner might resent the "advantage," which his or her spouse received, whether or not the supervisor in fact favored his or her spouse.

Finally, a no-spouse rule eliminates the possibility of the already-employed marriage partner intervening in the hiring process on behalf of

---

* Plaintiffs argue that we should not permit defendant to maintain the no-spouse rule because it has not extended the rule to its executives. We cannot accept this reasoning. Defendant is under no obligation to be consistent in its company policy. By not extending the no-spouse rule to executives, defendant loses whatever benefits the rule confers. But that is a matter of policy for defendant to decide.

his or her spouse, to the detriment of the employer and any more qualified persons who did not obtain the job because of this intervention.

It would be hard to prove that any of these reasons for maintaining a no-spouse rule are valid in the sense that, without the rule, production would fall. Our devices for measuring industrial efficiency and morale are not so finely tuned that they can easily make such a determination. On the other hand, these reasons are far from frivolous. They correspond to the reasons which have led a number of institutions to conclude that family members should not work in the same environment. The movement to a sharp dichotomy between the workplace and the home may not in the long run prove to be a fruitful one, but it has become widely prevalent in our society.

We are therefore left in a difficult situation. Defendant cannot statistically prove that its rule increases production, but its arguments that the rule "improves" the workplace are convincing. In our judgment the solution to this problem lies in examining the animating spirit behind the *Griggs* rule. The *Griggs* Court stated: "We do not suggest that either the District Court or the Court of Appeals erred in examining the employer's intent, but good intent or absence of discriminatory intent does not redeem employment procedures or testing mechanisms that operate as 'built-in headwinds' for minority groups and are unrelated to measuring job capability." 401 U.S. at 432, 91 S.Ct. at 854. The rule which *Griggs* laid down later in the opinion—that an employment practice with a discriminatory impact is invalid unless it is job-related—must be examined in light of this earlier statement.

The no-spouse rule in this case does not operate as a "built-in headwind" for women. It is unlike the requirement in *Griggs* that an employee have a high school diploma, or a rule that only the top-ranking contestants on a standardized test will be selected for employment, see *United States* v. *City of Chicago*, 549 F.2d 415 (7th Cir. 1977), or the rule in *Dothard* that only people of a certain size may be hired. These employment tests all had a discriminatory impact because they focused on personal characteristics which members of a minority group were not as likely to possess, given their environmental or genetic background, as other job applicants. The no-spouse rule, on the other hand, does not place women at a disadvantage because they failed to develop certain personal characteristics as a consequence of their environmental or genetic backgrounds. Rather, the rule's discriminatory impact is the result of the historical fact that in the past far more men than women chose to work in defendant's Ottawa plants, with the result that substantially more than half of the employees in those plants are now men. Defendant asserts, and there is nothing in the record contradicting its assertion, that in some of its other plants historical circumstances operated differently and there is a majority of female workers. In those plants, the no-spouse rule, which is in effect on a company-wide basis, has a discriminatory impact on men.

This would be a different case if plaintiffs had shown that defendant historically employed more men than women in its Ottawa plants because it intentionally discriminated against women. There is no evidence in the record supporting such a finding, however, and we must assume that the present disparity between men and women in the Ottawa plants was the result of noninvidious factors.

Because the no-spouse rule plausibly improves the work environment, and because it does not penalize women on the basis of their environmental or genetic background, we hold that the rule is job-related. We therefore conclude that it does not violate Title VII.

(5) *Constitutional-Statutory Relationships*

## DAVIS v. COUNTY OF LOS ANGELES

*United States Court of Appeals, Ninth Circuit, 1977*
*566 F.2d 1334, 16 FEP Cases 396*

TUTTLE, Circuit Judge: This Court entered its original opinion in this case on October 20, 1976. The Court thereafter granted defendants-cross-appellants' motion for rehearing, and the case was regularly set down for rehearing and oral argument. Although the principal basis for the rehearing motion was the Supreme Court's decision in *Washington* v. *Davis*, 426 U.S. 229, 96 S.Ct. 2040, 48 L.Ed.2d 597 (1976), the parties were permitted to brief and argue all other issues as well.

We now withdraw the original opinion and decision, and this opinion and decision are announced in their stead.

This suit was brought on behalf of all present and future black and Mexican-American applicants for positions as firemen with the Los Angeles County Fire Department, alleging that the defendants Los Angeles County, the County Board of Supervisors and the County Civil Service Commission had been guilty of racial discrimination in hiring in violation of the Fourteenth Amendment, 42 U.S.C. §§ 1981, 1983 and Title VII of the Civil Rights Act of 1964, 42 U.S.C. § 2000e *et seq.*

The district court found that the Los Angeles County Fire Department employed blacks and Mexican-Americans grossly out of proportion to their number in the population of Los Angeles County. The court further found that the Fire Department, despite its admitted knowledge of its prior discriminatory practices and its bad reputation as an employer in the minority community, failed to undertake any effective positive steps to eradicate the effects of prior discrimination. Accordingly, the court ordered accelerated hiring of racial minorities in a ratio of one black and one Mexican-American applicant for each three white applicants until the effects of past discrimination had been erased.[3]

---

[3] [Footnotes numbered as in original.—Ed.] Data introduced by the plaintiffs showed that this 1–1–3 ratio, given the present rate of hiring, would produce a work force of minority firemen in proportion to the number of minority persons in the community by 1979 for blacks and 1983 for Mexican-Americans.

Despite the fact that the Mexican-American population of Los Angeles County was approximately double the size of the black population, the district court ordered identical accelerated hiring for both groups due to its finding that the Fire Department's 5'7" height requirement for job applicants was a valid requirement for employment and that this height requirement had the effect of eliminating 41 percent of the otherwise eligible Mexican-American applicants from consideration.

The plaintiffs appeal the trial court's finding that the 5'7" height requirement is valid and could therefore be used in limiting the relief available to the Mexican-American members of the plaintiff class. The defendants cross-appeal the trial court's order of accelerated hiring. We affirm the district court's finding of a current violation of the rights of members of this class by the improper post-1971 use of an unvalidated written test as a selection device for entry level positions and its order of accelerated hiring to cure past racial discrimination; we disagree with the court's findings that plaintiffs have standing to challenge defendants' pre-1971 use of an unvalidated written test as a selection device and that the 5'7" height requirement has been sufficiently validated by the defendants. Accordingly, we reverse and remand for reconsideration of the proper ratio of accelerated racial hiring to be ordered.

## I. WRITTEN EXAMINATION PROCEDURES

Despite a minority population of approximately 29.1 percent in Los Angeles County, only 3.3 percent of the firemen employed by the defendants at the time of trial were black or Mexican-American. Plaintiffs alleged, and the trial court found, that this severe racial imbalance resulted in part from the defendants' utilization of unvalidated written examinations to rank applicants for positions as firemen. The defendants do not, and indeed cannot, dispute that these verbal aptitude tests, administered to applicants in August 1969 and in January 1972, had a discriminatory impact on minority applicants. Of the 244 blacks who took the 1969 examination, 5 were hired; of the 100 Mexican-Americans, 7 were hired, while of the 1080 whites taking the test, 175 were hired. Thus, while approximately 25 percent of the 1969 applicants were black or Mexican-American, based on the results of this test only 6.4 percent of the hires were minorities. Black and Mexican-American applicants fared no better on the 1972 examination. Specifically, while 25.8 percent of the white applicants were among the top 544 scorers on the test, only 5.1 percent of the black applicants were included in that group. Applying the now-familiar standards announced in *Griggs* v. *Duke Power Co.,* 401 U.S. 424, 91 S.Ct. 849, 28 L.Ed.2d 158 (1971), the district court concluded that such statistical data alone established a prima facie case of racial discrimination in employment, thereby shifting the burden to the defendants to establish that the tests were job-related.[4] We agree that defendants failed to satisfy their burden.[5]

Defendants have challenged the plaintiffs' standing to complain of the use of the unvalidated 1969 written test. In light of the fact that plaintiffs' class did not include any prior unsuccessful applicants, it follows that plaintiffs neither suffered nor were threatened with any injury in fact from the use of the 1969 examination. No firemen were hired on the basis of success on this test after plaintiffs became applicants in October 1971. The parties stipulated that approximately 100 vacancies occur in the ranks of firemen each year, and testimony at trial established that 187 applicants were placed on an eligibility list following the 1969 test. Based on these facts, we must conclude that the 1969 list was depleted before plaintiffs applied for employment as firemen.

In the absence of a statute expressly conferring standing, it is well settled that in order to have standing a plaintiff must suffer some actual or threatened injury as a result of the alleged unlawful conduct. See, e.g., *Linda S.* v. *Richard D.,* 410 U.S. 614, 617, 93 S.Ct. 1146, 35 L.Ed.2d 536 (1973); *Moose Lodge No. 107* v. *Irvis,* 407 U.S. 163, 166–67, 92 S.Ct. 1965, 32 L.Ed.2d 627 (1972); *Flast* v. *Cohen,* 392 U.S. 83, 101, 88 S.Ct. 1942, 20 L.Ed.2d 947 (1968); *Baker* v. *Carr,* 369 U.S. 186, 204–208, 82 S.Ct. 691, 7 L.Ed.2d 663 (1962). It is thus clear that plaintiffs lacked standing to challenge defendants' prior use of the test in 1969.[6]

As previously indicated, the district court reached the conclusion that defendants' use of unvalidated written examinations was an illegal employment practice through application of the principles announced in *Griggs,* a Title VII case. Subsequent to trial on the merits in this case, the Supreme Court in *Washington* v. *Davis,* 426 U.S. 229, 96 S.Ct. 2040, 48 L.Ed.2d 597 (1976), held that to establish a prima facie case of *unconstitutional* employment discrimination, discriminatory intent or purpose must be shown rather than or in addition to a statistical showing of disproportionate impact. Defendants interpret *Washington* to require similar proof in cases alleging employment discrimination under § 1981. Accordingly, defendants urge us to reverse the decision of the district court, since no showing was made that defendants administered the 1972

[4] The cases holding that statistics alone may prove a prima facie case of employment discrimination, thereby shifting the burden to the defendants to justify the racial imbalance, are by this time legion. See, e.g., *United States* v. *Masonry Contractors Ass'n of Memphis, Inc.,* 497 F.2d 871, 875 (6th Cir. 1974); *Pettway* v. *American Cast Iron Pipe Co.,* 494 F.2d 211, 225 (5th Cir. 1974); *United States* v. *N. L. Indus., Inc.,* 479 F.2d 354, 368 (8th Cir. 1973); *United States* v. *Hayes Int'l Corp.,* 456 F.2d 112, 120 (5th Cir. 1972); *United States* v. *Ironworkers Local 86,* 443 F.2d 544, 550–51 (9th Cir.), *cert. denied,* 404 U.S. 984, 92 S.Ct. 447, 30 L.Ed.2d 367 (1971).

[5] Defendants conceded that no studies establishing the validity of the written employment tests have been conducted in accordance with "professionally acceptable methods." See *Albemarle Paper Co.* v. *Moody,* 422 U.S. 405, 95 S.Ct. 2362, 45 L.Ed.2d 280 (1975).

[6] Our holding on this point makes it unnecessary to discuss defendants' contention that the recent decision in *East Texas Motor Freight Sys., Inc.* v. *Rodriguez,* 431 U.S. 395, 97 St.Ct. 1891, 52 L.Ed.2d 453 (1977), precludes plaintiffs from attacking the defendants' pre-1971 hiring procedures.

It is equally clear that defendants' decision to employ the 1972 written test as a selection device was an unlawful employment practice which had adverse impact on the racial class of plaintiffs. The plaintiffs thus have standing to litigate the lawfulness of the 1972 test.

examination with any intent or purpose to discriminate against minority applicants. The issue presented is one of first impression in this Circuit.[7] We have carefully reviewed the Court's opinion in *Washington* and the post-*Washington* cases brought to our attention by the parties. We must reject defendants' argument.

[Summary of *Washington* v. *Davis* omitted.]

It is significant that throughout this discussion of "constitutional standards" and "Constitution-based claims," the Court mentioned neither § 1981 nor cases construing that statute.[9] Nor can it be said that in resolving the equal protection question before it, the Court necessarily resolved the § 1981 claim on the same basis.

During recent history, every court which has considered the question has construed § 1981 to bar discrimination in employment. See *Long* v. *Ford Motor Co.*, 496 F.2d 500 (6th Cir. 1974); *Macklin* v. *Spector Freight Sys., Inc.*, 156 U.S. App. D.C. 69, 478 F.2d 979 (1973); *Brady* v. *Bristol-Meyers, Inc.*, 459 F.2d 621 (8th Cir. 1972); *Brown* v. *Gaston County Dye-*

[7] Only four other Courts of Appeals have had occasion to apply or construe the decision in *Washington*. The Court of Appeals for the D.C. Circuit has stated that a plaintiff proceeding under Title VII and § 1981 need not show the type of purposeful or intentional discrimination required to establish a violation of the Equal Protection Clause. *Kinsey* v. *First Regional Securities, Inc.*, 557 F.2d 830 (D.C. Cir. 1977) (dictum).

In *United States* v. *City of Chicago*, 549 F.2d 415 (7th Cir. 1977), the court reversed the trial court's finding that the defendants' written examination violated the Fourteenth Amendment solely because the plaintiffs failed to satisfy the purposeful discrimination requirement of *Washington*. *Id.* at 435. The *City of Chicago* plaintiffs also had alleged that the examination violated § 1981, and defendants here contend that the appeals court equated § 1981 with the Fourteenth Amendment for purposes of determining the burden of proof applicable to non-Title VII actions. The *City of Chicago* court, however, made no mention of § 1981 in reversing the district court's ruling but specifically held that the defendants' hiring and promotion policies "did not violate *the Constitution*." *Id.* (emphasis added).

In *Chicano Police Officer's Ass'n* v. *Stover*, 526 F.2d 431 (10th Cir. 1975), an employment discrimination action alleging violations of the Equal Protection Clause, §§1981, 1983 and 1985, the court held that "the measure of a claim under the Civil Rights Act is in essence that applied in a suit under Title VII . . . ." *Id.* at 438 (citations omitted). Subsequently, the Supreme Court granted certiorari, vacated the judgment and remanded for reconsideration in light of *Washington* v. *Davis*. *Stover* v. *Chicano Police Officer's Ass'n*, 426 U.S. 944, 96 S.Ct. 3161, 49 L.Ed.2d 1181 (1976). Defendants here argue that had the Supreme Court intended the adverse impact rule of Title VII to apply to § 1981 actions after *Washington*, the Court simply would have denied certiorari in *Stover* and allowed the judgment to stand on the basis of a violation of § 1981 alone. However, neither the district court nor the court of appeals in *Stover* ever found that defendants had violated § 1981. Further, it is clear that the Supreme Court's action was necessitated by the court of appeal's failure to distinguish causes of action under §§ 1981 and 1983 in equating the "Civil Rights Act" and Title VII. And although the case was eventually remanded to the district court, *Chicano Police Officer's Ass'n* v. *Stover*, 552 F.2d 918 (10th Cir. 1977), the issue before this Court was not expressly decided.

Finally, in *Arnold* v. *Ballard*, 12 E.P.D. ¶ 11,224 (6th Cir. 1976) (per curiam), the court vacated an earlier decision and remanded for reconsideration in light of *Washington*. The per curiam opinion, however, did not discuss the issue now before us and did not explain the rationale underlying the court's decision.

[9] Defendants contend that the *Washington* majority "specifically refer[red] to several § 1981 cases and note[d] their disagreement with the appellate court's reliance upon the Title VII standards of proof." The Court did note its disapproval of several cases but explained that it was in disagreement only "to the extent that those cases rested on or expressed the views that proof of discriminatory racial purpose is unnecessary in making out *an equal protection violation*." 426 U.S. at 245, 96 S.Ct. at 2050 (emphasis added). Furthermore, each case cited in this context involved, in addition to a § 1981 claim, a claim under either the Equal Protection Clause or § 1983.

*ing Mach. Co.*, 457 F.2d 1377 (4th Cir.), *cert. denied*, 409 U.S. 982, 93 S.Ct. 319, 34 L.Ed.2d 246 (1972); *Young* v. *International Tel. & Tel. Co.*, 438 F.2d 757 (3d Cir. 1971); *Sanders* v. *Dobbs Houses, Inc.*, 431 F.2d 1097 (5th Cir. 1970), *cert. denied*, 401 U.S. 948, 91 S.Ct. 935, 28 L.Ed.2d 231 (1971); *Waters* v. *Wisconsin Steel Works of Int'l Harvester Co.*, 427 F.2d 476 (7th Cir.), *cert. denied*, 400 U.S. 911, 91 S.Ct. 137, 27 L.Ed.2d 151 (1970). The courts consistently have employed Title VII principles as a benchmark not only in cases involving alleged discriminatory impact, see *Wade* v. *Mississippi Coop. Extension Serv.*, 528 F.2d 508, 516–17 (5th Cir. 1976); *King* v. *Yellow Freight Sys., Inc.*, 523 F.2d 879, 882 (8th Cir. 1975); *Kirkland* v. *New York State Dept. of Correctional Servs.*, 520 F.2d 420, 425 (2d Cir. 1975), *cert. denied*, 429 U.S. 823, 97 S.Ct. 73, 50 L.Ed.2d 84 (1976); *Barnett* v. *W. T. Grant Co.*, 518 F.2d 543, 549 (4th Cir. 1975), but in other contexts as well. See, e.g., *Flowers* v. *Crouch-Walker Corp.*, 552 F.2d 1277, 1281 & n. 3 (7th Cir. 1977) (discriminatory discharge of employee); *McCormick* v. *Attala County Bd. of Educ.*, 541 F.2d 1094, 1095 (5th Cir. 1976) (per curiam) (available remedies). Indeed, the Supreme Court has recognized that Title VII and § 1981 embrace "parallel or overlapping remedies against discrimination." *Alexander* v. *Gardner-Denver Co.*, 415 U.S. 36, 47 & n. 7, 94 S.Ct. 1011, 1019, 39 L.Ed.2d 147 (1973). In the absence of any express pronouncement from the Supreme Court—a pronouncement not delivered in *Washington*—we are unwilling to deviate from this established practice. Any unnecessary deviation not only could produce undesirable substantive law conflicts, see *Waters* v. *Wisconsin Steel Works of Int. Harvester Co.*, 502 F.2d 1309, 1316 (7th Cir. 1974), *cert. denied*, 425 U.S. 997, 96 S.Ct. 2214, 48 L.Ed.2d 823 (1976), but also would dilute what has been a potent remedy for the ills of countless minority employees subjected to the unlawful discriminatory conduct of their employers. Thus, we cannot conclude that *Washington* embraced a ruling that a showing of disproportionate impact no longer will suffice to establish a prima facie case of employment discrimination under § 1981.[10] In our view, there remains no operational distinction in this context between liability based upon Title VII and § 1981.

. . .

In summary, we believe the district court properly found defendants' use of the 1972 written examination as a selection device to be a violation of § 1981. Plaintiffs produced overwhelming statistical data to establish the test's disproportionate impact upon minority applicants, and the defendants were unable to validate the test in terms of job-relatedness.[13]

---

[10] *Accord, League of Latin American Citizens* v. *City of Santa Ana*, 410 F. Supp. 873 (C.D. Cal. 1976). But see *Ortiz* v. *Bach*, 14 FEP Cases 1019 (D.Colo. 1977); *Johnson* v. *Hoffman*, 424 F. Supp. 490 (E.D. Mo. 1977); *Resident Advisory Bd.* v. *Rizzo*, 425 F. Supp. 987 (E.D. Pa. 1976).

[13] In Part III of the opinion in *Washington* v. *Davis*, the majority agreed with the district court's conclusion that Test 21 had been sufficiently validated by a validation study and other evidence showing a nexus between success on the test and success in

Defendants' decision, prompted solely by the filing of this lawsuit, to abandon the written exam as a selection device does not moot the claim. *United States* v. *W. T. Grant Co.,* 345 U.S. 629, 632–33, 73 S.Ct. 894, 97 L.Ed. 1303 (1953).[14]

## II.   THE 5 FOOT, 7 INCH HEIGHT REQUIREMENT

Among the other of defendants' practices challenged by the plaintiffs was the 5′7″ height requirement. In *Dothard* v. *Rawlinson,* _____ U.S. _____, 97 S.Ct. 2720, 53 L.Ed.2d 786 (1977), the Supreme Court held that Title VII forbids the use of height requirements which have discriminatory effect unless the employer meets "the burden of showing that [the] requirement [has] . . . a manifest relation to the employment in question." *Id.* at 2726, quoting *Griggs* v. *Duke Power Co.,* 401 U.S. 424, 432, 91 S.Ct. 849, 28 L.Ed.2d 158 (1971).

Here there can be no question that the 5′7″ height requirement has discriminatory impact. The parties stipulated that 41 percent of the otherwise eligible Mexican-American applicants are excluded by the requirement.[15] The defendants further conceded that no scientifically approved test has been utilized to determine whether the height requirement is in fact job-related. The only testimony in the record on point is that of Chief Stanley E. Barlow, himself only 5′8″, who testified that he believed a small man might have difficulty working with taller men in removing long ladders and other equipment and might have a slower reaction time in climbing on and off equipment. Chief Barlow conceded that in the past firemen under 5′7″ have been able to function without impairment due to their height.[16]

It seems clear to us that this testimony falls far short of validating a height requirement which has a serious impact in restricting Mexican-American employment in the County Fire Department.[17] The district court did not have the benefit of *Dothard, supra,* and, therefore, did not apply the standard of proof required by that case. The evidence introduced was inadequate to meet the *Dothard* requirement that the height

---

police training school. 426 U.S. at 250–51 & n. 17, 96 S.Ct. 2040. It is at least arguable that by not requiring the defendants to meet the job-relatedness standards of Title VII, the Court implicitly held that employers sued under § 1981 may escape liability by showing something less than job-relatedness. We need not address that question here, since defendants' proof not only is insufficient under *Griggs,* but also falls far short of the quality and quantity of proof offered in *Washington.*

14 Of course, this continued threat to use the 1972 test as part of the selection process right up to the filing of the complaint in this case is admittedly a violation of Title VII.

15 We accordingly note that the continuing use of this height requirement constitutes a continuing violation of Title VII and provides a basis for relief in addition to § 1981.

16 These shorter firemen were employed during World War II when the standard was relaxed, and when firemen of other cities automatically joined the L.A. County Fire Department when their employing cities were annexed by L.A. County.

17 Our earlier comments with respect to validation of employment criterion challenged under § 1981 are equally applicable in this context. See note 15, *supra.*

restriction was manifestly related to employment by the Fire Department. Accordingly, the district court's finding of job-relatedness must be reversed.

## III. AFFIRMATIVE RELIEF

The defendants contest the affirmative relief ordered by the district court. However, as this Court has noted,

"[t]here can be little doubt that where a violation of Title VII is found, the court is vested with broad remedial power to remove the vestiges of past discrimination and eliminate present and assure the nonexistence of future barriers to the full enjoyment of equal job opportunities by qualified black workers."

*United States* v. *Ironworkers Local 86,* 443 F.2d 544, 553 (9th Cir.), *cert. denied,* 404 U.S. 984, 92 S.Ct. 447, 30 L.Ed.2d 367 (1971) (citations omitted). We do not believe the court lacks equal power under § 1981 to order relief. Indeed, "[i]n fashioning an appropriate remedy for employment discrimination, Congress has granted courts plenary equitable power under both Title VII . . . and section 1981." *Pettway* v. *American Cast Iron Pipe Co.,* 494 F.2d 211, 243 (5th Cir. 1974) (footnotes omitted). Although the decided cases have primarily involved either Title VII or § 1983, and not § 1981, we feel the extensive case law under both sections approving affirmative relief is directly applicable here. We see no reason to limit the relief available under § 1981 merely because in the past § 1981 and Title VII have been read in tandem. See, e.g., *Boston Chapter, NAACP, Inc.* v. *Beecher,* 504 F.2d 1017 (1st Cir. 1974), *cert. denied,* 421 U.S. 910, 95 S.Ct. 1561, 43 L.Ed.2d 775 (1975); *Franks* v. *Bowman Transp. Co.,* 495 F.2d 398 (5th Cir. 1974) *modified,* 424 U.S. 747, 96 S.Ct. 1251, 47 L.Ed.2d 444 (1976); *Pettway* v. *American Cast Iron Pipe Co.,* 494 F.2d 211 (5th Cir. 1974); *Johnson* v. *Goodyear Tire &Rubber Co.,* 491 F.2d 1364 (5th Cir. 1974). Similarly, we note that Title VII and § 1983 cases frequently have been cited as involving analogous principles in fashioning equitable relief, see *Rios* v. *Enterprise Ass'n Steamfitters Local 638,* 501 F.2d 622, 628 (2d Cir. 1974); *Carter* v. *Gallagher,* 452 F.2d 315, 329 (8th Cir. 1971) (en banc), *cert. denied,* 406 U.S. 950, 92 S.Ct. 2045, 32 L.Ed.2d 338 (1972), and cases involving one statute have been cited in support of the relief ordered in cases involving the other.

Eight Courts of Appeals, including this one, have considered and approved the use of accelerated hiring goals or quotas to eradicate the effects of past discrimination. See *Boston Chapter, NAACP, Inc.* v. *Beecher,* 504 F.2d 1017 (1st Cir. 1974), *cert. denied,* 421 U.S. 910, 95 S.Ct. 1561, 43 L.Ed.2d 775 (1975) (§§ 1981 & 1983, Title VII); *Rios* v. *Enterprise Ass'n Steamfitters Local 638,* 501 F.2d 622 (2d Cir. 1974) (Title VII); *United States* v. *Masonry Contractors Ass'n of Memphis, Inc.,* 497 F.2d 871 (6th Cir. 1974) (Title VII); *Franks* v. *Bowman Transp. Co.,* 495 F.2d 398 (5th Cir. 1974), *modified,* 424 U.S. 747, 96 S.Ct. 1251, 47 L.Ed.2d 444 (1976) (Title VII); *Morrow* v. *Crisler,* 491 F.2d 1053 (5th Cir.) (en banc), *cert. denied,* 419 U.S. 895, 95 S.Ct. 173, 42 L.Ed.2d 139 (1974) (§ 1983); *Vulcan Society* v. *Civil Serv. Comm'n,* 490 F.2d 387 (2d Cir. 1973) (§ 1983); *Associated Gen. Contractors of Mass., Inc.* v. *Altshuler,* 490 F.2d 9 (1st Cir. 1973), *cert. denied,* 416 U.S. 957, 94 S.Ct. 1971, 40 L.Ed.2d 307 (1974) (Title VII); *Bridgeport Guardians, Inc.* v. *Civil Serv. Comm'n,* 482 F.2d 1333 (2d Cir. 1973) (§§ 1981, 1983); *United States* v. *N. L. Indus., Inc.,* 479 F.2d 354 (8th Cir. 1973) (en banc) (§ 1983); *Pennsylvania* v. *O'Neill,* 473 F.2d 1029 (3d Cir. 1973) (en banc) (§ 1983); *United States* v. *Local 212, IBEW,* 472 F.2d 634 (6th Cir. 1973) (Title VII); *United States* v. *Wood Lathers Local 46,* 471 F.2d 408 (2d Cir.), *cert. denied,* 412 U.S. 939, 93 S.Ct. 2773, 37 L.Ed.2d 398 (1973) (Title VII); *Castro* v. *Beecher,* 459 F.2d 725 (1st Cir. 1972) (§ 1983); *United States* v. *Carpenters Local 169,* 457 F.2d 211 (7th Cir.), *cert. denied,* 409 U.S. 851, 93 S.Ct. 63, 34 L.Ed.2d 94 (1972) (Title VII); *Carter* v. *Gallagher,* 452 F.2d 315 (8th Cir. 1971) (en banc), *cert. denied,* 406 U.S. 950, 92 S.Ct. 2045, 32 L.Ed.2d 338 (1972) (§ 1983); *United States* v. *Ironworkers Local 86,* 443 F.2d 544 (9th Cir.), *cert. denied,* 404 U.S. 984, 92 S.Ct. 447, 30 L.Ed.2d 367 (1971) (Title VII); *Contractors Ass'n of Eastern Pa.* v. *Secretary of Labor,* 442 F.2d 159 (3d Cir.), *cert. denied,* 404 U.S. 854, 92 S.Ct. 98, 30 L.Ed.2d 95 (1971) (Title VII); *United States* v. *Local 38, IBEW,* 428 F.2d 144 (6th Cir.), *cert. denied,* 400 U.S. 943, 91 S.Ct. 245, 27 L.Ed.2d 248 (1970) (Title VII); *Local 53, Asbestos Workers* v. *Vogler,* 407 F.2d 1047 (5th Cir. 1969) (Title VII).[18] While the defendants argue § 703(j) of Title VII forbids the imposition of racial quota hiring, even were this to be an order premised solely on Title VII, we note this view has been uniformly rejected by the many courts which have considered the question.

We believe the district court properly exercised its discretion in ordering affirmative action to be undertaken to erase the effects of past discrimination. We do not believe that such relief may be limited to the identifiable persons denied employment in the past—for "the presence of identified persons who have been discriminated against is not a necessary prerequisite to ordering affirmative relief in order to eliminate the present effects of past discrimination." *Carter* v. *Gallagher,* 452 F.2d at 330.

"Nor are remedial goals limited to any specific or prescribed form. The precise method of remedying past misconduct is left largely to the broad discretion of the district court. Goals have been expressed in terms of specific numbers or ratios . . . or percentages. . . ."
*Rios* v. *Steamfitters Local 638,* 501 F.2d at 631 (citations omitted).

While we remand because the district court expressly stated that the reason it ordered identical accelerated hiring of blacks and Mexican-Americans in equal ratios was because of the validity of the 5'7" height requirement, we do not necessarily believe a 1–1–3 ratio was incorrect.

---

[18] *Harper* v. *Kloster,* 486 F.2d 1134 (4th Cir. 1973) did not hold to the contrary, but upheld the district court's refusal to impose quotas within the facts of that case as not being an abuse of discretion.

The court, however, should reconsider its order in light of our decision that the 5'7" height requirement is invalid and that plaintiffs lacked standing to challenge defendants' use of the 1969 written examination.

The defendants finally argue that the imposition of an affirmative order to hire minority applicants is unnecessary. They argue in effect that they have already commenced and that they can be relied upon further to improve their hiring practices without the added impetus of a court order. The experience of the Court of Appeals for the Fifth Circuit is useful in this regard—"protestations or repentance and reform aimed to anticipate or blunt the force of a lawsuit offer insufficient assurance that the practices sought to be enjoined will not be repeated." *Rowe* v. *General Motors Corp.*, 457 F.2d 348, 359 (5th Cir. 1972). . . . Here the record shows that the defendants had decided to use an unvalidated verbal aptitude test to hire new candidates in 1973 and that the *only* reason the test was not used was notice of this suit. The personnel director of the defendants testified at length at the trial and acknowledged that he was aware of the discriminatory impact such a test would have. Further, the trial judge found that defendants had failed and refused to take necessary affirmative steps to overcome the department's bad reputation in black and Mexican-American communities. We emphasize that this was not a close case—in a community of 29.1 percent minority population, only 3.3 percent of the firemen employed by defendants were black or Mexican-American. These factors are hardly persuasive evidence of the defendants' good faith, even were such good faith relevant in fashioning relief.[19] We agree with the district court that an accelerated hiring order is the only way "to overcome the presently existing effects of past discrimination within a reasonable period of time."

In sum, we believe the district court was wholly justified in deciding to impose affirmative hiring orders upon the defendants.[20]

While it should be obvious to all, we nevertheless repeat the admonition that nothing said by this Court is to be taken as a requirement that the defendants hire any unqualified applicant for the performance of these essential jobs.

*Affirmed* in part, *reversed* in part and *remanded* for further proceedings not inconsistent with this opinion.

WALLACE, Circuit Judge, dissenting: I respectfully dissent.

Discrimination in employment based upon race, creed or color is a practice inconsistent with the views and aspirations of nearly all Americans and clearly repugnant to the principles upon which our society is built. But even in rooting out such an evil practice, we are bound by

[19] In *Griggs* v. *Duke Power Co.*, 401 U.S. 424, 91 S.Ct. 849, 28 L.Ed.2d 158 (1971), a Title VII case, the Supreme Court rejected good faith as a defense. "Congress directed the thrust of the Act to the *consequences* of employment practices, not simply the motivation." *Id.* at 432, 91 S.Ct. at 854. We believe good faith is equally inapplicable to § 1981.

[20] We do not read *United Air Lines* v. *Evans*, 431 U.S. 553, 97 S.Ct. 1885, 52 L.Ed.2d 571 (1977) to restrict in any way the affirmative relief ordered in this case.

certain procedural and jurisdictional limitations which may serve to protect the rights of others.

I think it is clear from the record that the plaintiffs' challenges to two of the three allegedly illegal employment practices are barred by such a jurisdictional limitation. The majority concedes that the named plaintiffs have no standing to attack the defendants' pre-1971 hiring procedures. I agree. I believe it equally plain that they lack standing to challenge the height limitation.

As to the remedy, I conclude that while the plaintiffs may well have standing to challenge the post-1971 hiring procedures, there is a critical issue as to whether the imposition of minority hiring quotas is now warranted given the limited scope of this issue and the circumstances under which the defendants' objectionable conduct occurred. Because the district court imposed quotas based on conduct which in large part has been rejected by the majority as a basis for remedial action, the district judge may well now believe that mandatory quotas are no longer appropriate. Because the question should be resolved in the first instance by the trial judge, I would reverse and remand for reconsideration of the appropriate remedy in light of the limited standing of the plaintiffs and the nature of the defendants' conduct within the new, limited time frame adopted by the majority in this case.

## B. LIABILITY FOR THE ATTEMPTED USE OF THE 1972 EXAMINATION

In deciding that the attempted use of the 1972 written examination was illegal, the majority relies almost exclusively upon 42 U.S.C. § 1981. Only in a footnote is it mentioned that this same conduct also constitutes a Title VII violation.[2] I agree with the majority that under *United States v. W. T. Grant Co.,* 345 U.S. 629, 632–33, 73 S.Ct. 894, 97 L.Ed. 1303 (1953), the defendants' decision, prompted by the commencement of this lawsuit, not to use improperly the 1972 examination as a selection device, does not shield them from liability. But I would base that liability on Title VII, not section 1981. The majority's extensive discussion of section 1981 is not only incorrect, but in this case it is wholly unnecessary.

The district judge found as a matter of fact that "neither the defendants nor their officials had engaged in employment practices with a willful or conscious purpose of excluding blacks and Mexican-Americans from

---

[2] Even if they had had proper standing, the plaintiffs could not have attacked defendants' pre-1972 procedures under Title VII since that statute first became applicable to state public employers on March 24, 1972. Since a stipulation states that the defendants abandoned their plan to make a discriminatory use of the 1972 exam on January 8, 1972, Title VII is arguably unavailable to the plaintiffs as a basis of liability in this case. In that event, and in light of the subsequent analysis in the text, the defendants would be absolved of all liability whatsoever. It appears, however, that the stipulated date may be in error, and in addition it seems to me that a persuasive argument can be made that the threat to use the 1972 examination in a discriminatory manner can fairly be construed as continuing after March 24, 1972, thus providing a legitimate basis for some relief to the plaintiffs.

employment." Since a prima facie case under Title VII clearly does not require proof of an improper purpose when a discriminatory impact is alleged, *Griggs* v. *Duke Power Co.,* 401 U.S. 424, 91 S.Ct. 849, 28 L.Ed.2d 158 (1971), this finding does not put defendants beyond the reach of Title VII.

The majority's decision that section 1981 similarly requires no proof of intentional discrimination is both unnecessary and unfortunate. The potential scope of section 1981 is exceptionally broad, going far beyond the Title VII realm of employment, and conceivably reaching virtually all private contractual arrangements. See *Runyon* v. *McCrary,* 427 U.S. 160, 168–71, 96 S.Ct. 2586, 49 L.Ed.2d 415 (1976). Since the relief available under Title VII is extensive enough to include the remedy approved by the majority in this case,[3] the wiser course would be to base the finding of liability on that statute and to wait for a more appropriate opportunity to consider the reaches of section 1981. Since the majority does choose to rely upon section 1981, however, I wish to make it clear that I cannot accept its easy conclusion that a prima facie case under that statute does not require proof of discriminatory intent.

The majority asserts that the Supreme Court's opinion in *Washington* v. *Davis,* 426 U.S. 229, 96 S.Ct. 2040, 48 L.Ed.2d 597 (1976), does not address the question of whether cases brought under section 1981—like those brought directly under the Fourteenth Amendment—always require proof of discriminatory intent, or whether—as in Title VII cases—proof of discriminatory impact alone may be sufficient. I agree. But *Washington* v. *Davis* serves at least to remind us that improper intent may be an essential ingredient in some discrimination cases where the lower courts have heretofore thought otherwise. When it is necessary to decide such cases on the basis of authority other than Title VII or the Fourteenth Amendment, therefore, a most careful reconsideration of the role of discriminatory intent is in order.

The majority reasons that because both Title VII and section 1981 apply to employment discrimination cases, because the remedies available under these two statutes are "parallel or overlapping," *Alexander* v. *Gardner-Denver Co.,* 415 U.S. 36, 47 & n. 7, 94 S.Ct. 1011, 39 L.Ed.2d 147 (1974), and because *Washington* v. *Davis* does not decide that intentional discrimination is required under section 1981, "there remains no operational distinction in this context between liability based upon Title VII and section 1981." This analysis is inadequate.[5]

---

[3] "[T]he remedies available to the individual under Title VII are co-extensive with the indiv[i]dual's right to sue under the provisions of the Civil Rights Act of 1866, 42 U.S.C. § 1981 . . . ." *Johnson* v. *Railway Express Agency, Inc.,* 421 U.S. 454, 459, 95 S.Ct. 1716, 1719, 44 L.Ed.2d 295 (1975), *quoting* H.R.Rep. No. 92–238, 92nd Cong., 1st Sess. 19 (1971).

[5] The majority's analysis is not helped by the string of citations offered in support of the propositions that section 981 has been applied "to bar discrimination in employment," and that Title VII principles are a "benchmark" in discrimination cases. The burden of these cases is that section 1981 provides a cause of action for private acts of employment discrimination and that it was not implicitly repealed by Title VII. I do

That both statutes can apply to the same facts and that both may afford similar remedies is beside the point. The same can be said of Title VII and the Fourteenth Amendment, yet, after *Washington* v. *Davis,* there remains an essential "operational distinction" between them. The proper inquiry is whether the legislative history of section 1981 indicates that it *should* track the Fourteenth Amendment's standards of proof rather than those of Title VII. I believe that the history of section 1981 strongly suggests precisely that.

Because section 1981 is peculiarly linked to the Fourteenth Amendment, the standards pertaining to that amendment should also control section 1981. Of course, Title VII also depends in part upon the Fourteenth Amendment for its validity.[6] Title VII, however, was intentionally structured to rest upon as many other constitutional bases as possible. It is otherwise with section 1981. Section 1981 originated in two earlier statutes: section 1 of the Civil Rights Act of 1866, 14 Stat. 27, and section 16 of the Voting Rights Act of 1870, 16 Stat. 144. *Runyon* v. *McCrary, supra,* 427 U.S. at 168–70 n. 8, 96 S.Ct. 2586. The 1866 Act is generally regarded as a "Thirteenth Amendment statute," see *Jones* v. *Alfred H. Mayer Co.,* 392 U.S. 409, 422, 437–38, 88 S.Ct. 2186, 20 L.Ed.2d 1189 (1968), but it has also been found to rely upon the Fourteenth Amendment. In fact, part of the motivation behind the congressional support of the Fourteenth Amendment was to eliminate doubts about the constitutionality of the 1866 Act. *Id.* at 436, 88 S.Ct. 2186. The second root of section 1981, section 16 of the Voting Rights Act of 1870, is clearly a "Fourteenth Amendment statute," *Runyon* v. *McCrary, supra,* 427 U.S. at 195–202, 96 S.Ct. 2586 (White, J. dissenting); its legislative history demonstrates that its precise purpose was to implement the congressional powers created by that Amendment. *Id.*

---

not disagree. If any of these decisions arguably imply that section 1981 and Title VII are equivalent with respect to the required elements of a prima facie case, it should be noted that all but two of them were rendered prior to *Washington* v. *Davis,* and of those, none offers any analysis of the critical issue of discriminatory intent which the opinion in that case revived as a major factor in discrimination law. The two post-*Washington* v. *Davis* decisions, *Flowers* v. *Crouch-Walker Corp.,* 552 F.2d 1277 (7th Cir. 1977) and *McCormick* v. *Attala County Bd. of Educ.,* 541 F.2d 1094 (5th Cir. 1976), make no reference to *Washington* v. *Davis* or to the issues it discussed. Thus, none of these cases contributes much to the resolution of the issue at hand.

Actually, one of the Fifth Circuit cases relied upon by the majority, *Wade* v. *Mississippi Coop. Extension Serv.,* 528 F.2d 508 (5th Cir. 1976), undermines the majority's position. *Wade* specifically rejected the lower court's application to section 1981 of "the standard of proof established by the regulations implementing Title VII" and held that "[u]nder the law of this circuit, . . . *public employment tests are to be judged under a constitutional standard in suits brought under 42 U.S.C.A. §§ 1981, 1983.*" *Id.* at 518 (emphasis added). The court in *Wade,* although it had the foresight to recognize that *Washington* v. *Davis,* then pending before the Supreme Court, could affect its understanding of the issues in the case before it, *id.* at 518 n.7, unavoidably lacked the wisdom later supplied by *Washington* v. *Davis* that purposeful discrimination is one element of the constitutional standard. But of interest here is the Fifth Circuit's recognition that section 1981 tracks the Constitution, not Title VII, in its standards of proof.

[6] E.g., *Fitzpatrick* v. *Bitzer,* 427 U.S. 445, 447–48, 96 S.Ct. 2666, 49 L.Ed.2d 614 (1976) (1972 amendments to Title VII rely upon Fourteenth Amendment). With respect to section 1981, see subsequent text.

The significance of this is that section 1981 enjoys a unique historical and conceptual relationship to the Fourteenth Amendment which is not shared by Title VII. Consequently, it is quite proper to assume, absent a contrary holding by the Supreme Court, that the standards for establishing a prima facie case of discrimination under section 1981 and the Equal Protection Clause of the Fourteenth Amendment should be the same: there must be proof of discriminatory intent.

Other factors reinforce this conclusion. Interpreting section 1981 to require discriminatory intent is consistent with the Supreme Court's statement in *Jones* v. *Alfred H. Mayer Co., supra,* that Congress intended section 1 of the Civil Rights Act of 1866—the source of what is now section 1982 as well as one source of section 1981—"to prohibit *all racially motivated* deprivations of the rights enumerated in the statute. . . ." *Id.* 392 U.S. at 426, 88 S.Ct. at 2196 (emphasis partly added). That racial motivation was originally meant by Congress to be a requirement in actions under the 1866 Act is further suggested by section 2 of the Act which imposes criminal penalities upon anyone who, under color of law, deprives another of the rights protected by section 1 "by reason of his color or race." 14 Stat. 27.

In addition, there are practical reasons for requiring proof of discriminatory intent in section 1981 cases, but not in Title VII cases. Title VII is part of a complex statute; together with its accompanying administrative regulations it identifies with particularity the conduct it proscribes and imposes a course of administrative remedies that must be exhausted before the jurisdiction of the courts may be invoked. 42 U.S.C. §2000e–5; 29 C.F.R. §§ 1601.1 *et seq.* Because these barriers tend to eliminate claims that are frivolous or suffering from obvious legal or factual defects, it is not unreasonable to provide that a prima facie case may be established without a showing of discriminatory intent.

Section 1981 is a very different statute. Its language is both brief and sweeping in scope, and it does not have the screening mechanism provided by a requirement of the exhaustion of administrative remedies. The section 1981 screening mechanism, as in actions proceeding directly under the Fourteenth Amendment, is the required demonstration of discriminatory intent.

Indeed, because section 1981 can probably be invoked in a great many cases brought directly under the Fourteenth Amendment, the consequence of judicially creating a less demanding standard for section 1981 than for the Fourteenth Amendment might often be to circumvent the holding in *Washington* v. *Davis* altogether. In the vast array of cases such as the one before us now and *Washington* v. *Davis* itself, where Title VII does not apply but Section 1981 and the Fourteenth Amendment do, one could easily avoid the intent requirement of the Amendment by simply pleading section 1981. See *Croker* v. *Boeing Co.,* 437 F. Supp. 1138 (E.D. Pa. 1977).

. . .

For these reasons I would base defendants' liability for the use of the

1972 examination on Title VII alone. The majority's reliance on section 1981 is ill-advised because it is both unnecessary and incorrect.

## NOTE

The Supreme Court, 5-to-4, vacated the judgment on the ground of mootness in that the use of an unvalidated written examination had been discontinued and was unlikely to recur. *County of Los Angeles* v. *Davis,* 99 S. Ct. 1379, 19 FEP Cases 282 (1979). The Court noted that its action deprived the opinion of the Court of Appeals of any precedential effect. Justices Stewart and Rehnquist would have found a Title VII violation but did not believe the Section 1981 question was properly presented. Justices Powell and Burger would have passed on the Section 1981 question. All four dissenters thought that the remedy was excessive in light of the violation.

## FITZPATRICK v. BITZER

*Supreme Court of the United States, 1976*
*427 U.S. 445, 12 FEP Cases 1586*

MR. JUSTICE REHNQUIST delivered the opinion of the Court.

In the 1972 Amendments to Title VII of the Civil Rights Act of 1964, Congress, acting under § 5 of the Fourteenth Amendment, authorized federal courts to award money damages in favor of a private individual against a state government found to have subjected that person to employment discrimination on the basis of "race, color, religion, sex, or national origin." The principal question presented by these cases is whether, as against the shield of sovereign immunity afforded the State by the Eleventh Amendment, *Edelman* v. *Jordan,* 415 U.S. 651 (1974), Congress has the power to authorize federal courts to enter such an award against the State as a means of enforcing the substantive guarantees of the Fourteenth Amendment. The Court of Appeals for the Second Circuit held that the effect of our decision in *Edelman* was to foreclose Congress' power. We granted certiorari to resolve this important constitutional question. 423 U.S. 1031 (1975). We reverse.

. . .

## II

In *Edelman* this Court held that monetary relief awarded by the District Court to welfare plaintiffs, by reason of wrongful denial of benefits which had occurred previous to the entry of the District Court's determination of their wrongfulness, violated the Eleventh Amendment. Such an award was found to be indistinguishable from a monetary award against the State itself which had been prohibited in *Ford Motor Co.* v.

*Department of Treasury,* 323 U.S. 459, 464 (1945). It was therefore controlled by that case rather than by *Ex parte Young,* 209 U.S. 123 (1908), which permitted suits against state officials to obtain prospective relief against violations of the Fourteenth Amendment.

*Edelman* went on to hold that the plaintiffs in that case could not avail themselvse of the doctrine of waiver expounded in cases such as *Parden* v. *Terminal R. Co.,* 377 U.S. 184 (1964), and *Employees* v. *Missouri Public Health Dept.,* 411 U.S. 279 (1973), because the necessary predicate for that doctrine was congressional intent to abrogate the immunity conferred by the Eleventh Amendment. We concluded that none of the statutes relied upon by plaintiffs in *Edelman* contained any authorization by Congress to join a State as defendant. . . .

Our analysis begins where *Edelman* ended, for in this Title VII case the "threshold fact of congressional authorization," *id.,* at 672, to sue the State as employer is clearly present. This is, of course, the prerequisite found present in *Parden* and wanting in *Employees.* We are aware of the factual differences between the type of state activity involved in *Parden* and that involved in the present case, but we do not think that difference is material for our purposes. The congressional authorization involved in *Parden* was based on the power of Congress under the Commerce Clause; here, however, the Eleventh Amendment defense is asserted in the context of legislation passed pursuant to Congress' authority under § 5 of the Fourteenth Amendment.[9]

As ratified by the States after the Civil War, that Amendment quite clearly contemplates limitations on their authority. In relevant part, it provides:

"Section 1. . . . No State shall make or enforce any law which shall abridge the privileges or immunities of citizens of the United States; nor shall any State deprive any person of life, liberty, or property, without due process of law; nor deny to any person within its jurisdiction the equal protection of the laws.

. . .

"Section 5. The Congress shall have power to enforce, by appropriate legislation, the provisions of this article."

The substantive provisions are by express terms directed at the States. Impressed upon them by those provisions are duties with respect to their treatment of private individuals. Standing behind the imperatives is Congress' power to "enforce" them "by appropriate legislation."

The impact of the Fourteenth Amendment upon the relationship between the Federal Government and the States, and the reach of congressional power under § 5, were examined at length by this Court in *Ex parte Virginia,* 100 U.S. 339 (1880). A state judge had been arrested

---

9 [Footnotes numbered as in original.—Ed.] There is no dispute that in enacting the 1972 Amendments to Title VII to extend coverage to the States as employers, Congress exercised its power under § 5 of the Fourteenth Amendment. See, e.g., H. R. Rep. No. 92–238, p. 19 (1971); S. Rep. No. 92–415, pp. 10–11 (1971). Cf. *National League of Cities* v. *Usery,* 426 U.S. 833 (1976).

and indicted under a federal criminal statute prohibiting the exclusion on the basis of race of any citizen from service as a juror in a state court. The judge claimed that the statute was beyond Congress' power to enact under either the Thirteenth [10] or the Fourteenth Amendment. The Court first observed that these Amendments "were intended to be, what they really are, limitations of the power of the States and enlargements of the power of Congress." Id., at 345. It then addressed the relationship between the language of § 5 and the substantive provisions of the Fourteenth Amendment:

"The prohibitions of the Fourteenth Amendment are directed to the States, and they are to a degree restrictions of State power. It is these which Congress is empowered to enforce, and to enforce against State action, however put forth, whether that action be executive, legislative, or judicial. Such enforcement is no invasion of State sovereignty. No law can be, which the people of the States have, by the Constitution of the United States, empowered Congress to enact. . . . It is said the selection of jurors for her courts and the administration of her laws belong to each State; that they are her rights. This is true in the general. But in exercising her rights, a State cannot disregard the limitations which the Federal Constitution has applied to her power. Her rights do not reach to that extent. Nor can she deny to the general government the right to exercise all its granted powers, though they may interfere with the full enjoyment of rights she would have if those powers had not been thus granted. Indeed, every addition of power to the general government involves a corresponding diminution of the governmental powers of the States. It is carved out of them.

. . .

"The argument in support of the petition for a *habeas corpus* ignores entirely the power conferred upon Congress by the Fourteenth Amendment. Were it not for the fifth section of that amendment, there might be room for argument that the first section is only declaratory of the moral duty of the State. . . . But the Constitution now expressly gives authority for congressional interference and compulsion in the cases embraced within the Fourteenth Amendment. It is but a limited authority, true, extending only to a single class of cases; but within its limits it is complete." Id., at 346–48.

*Ex parte Virginia's* early recognition of this shift in the federal-state balance has been carried forward by more recent decisions of this Court. See, *e.g., South Carolina* v. *Katzenbach*, 383 U.S. 301, 308 (1966); *Mitchum* v. *Foster*, 407 U.S. 225, 238–39 (1972).

There can be no doubt that this line of cases has sanctioned intrusions by Congress, acting under the Civil War Amendments, into the judicial,

---

[10] "Section 1. Neither slavery nor involuntary servitude, except as a punishment for crime whereof the party shall have been duly convicted, shall exist within the United States, or any place subject to their jurisdiction.

"Section 2. Congress shall have power to enforce this article by appropriate legislation."

executive, and legislative spheres of autonomy previously reserved to the States. The legislation considered in each case was grounded on the expansion of Congress' powers—with the corresponding diminution of state sovereignty—found to be intended by the Framers and made part of the Constitution upon the States' ratification of those Amendments, a phenomenon aptly described as a "carv[ing] out" in *Ex parte Virginia, supra*, at 346.

It is true that none of these previous cases presented the question of the relationship between the Eleventh Amendment and the enforcement power granted to Congress under § 5 of the Fourteenth Amendment. But we think that the Eleventh Amendment, and the principle of state sovereignty which it embodies, see *Hans* v. *Louisiana*, 134 U.S. 1 (1890), are necessarily limited by the enforcement provisions of § 5 of the Fourteenth Amendment. In that section Congress is expressly granted authority to enforce "by appropriate legislation" the substantive provisions of the Fourteenth Amendment, which themselves embody significant limitations on state authority. When Congress acts pursuant to § 5, not only is it exercising legislative authority that is plenary within the terms of the constitutional grant, it is exercising that authority under one section of a constitutional Amendment whose other sections by their own terms embody limitations on state authority. We think that Congress may, in determining what is "appropriate legislation" for the purpose of enforcing the provisions of the Fourteenth Amendment, provide for private suits against States or state officials which are constitutionally impermissible in other contexts.[11] See *Edelman* v. *Jordan*, 415 U.S. 651 (1974); *Ford Motor Co.* v. *Department of Treasury*, 323 U.S. 459 (1945).

## B. SENIORITY

### (1) *Introduction*

## REFLECTIONS ON THE LEGAL NATURE AND ENFORCEABILITY OF SENIORITY RIGHTS *

*75 Harvard Law Review 1532, 1534-35 (1961)*
Benjamin Aaron

#### THE NATURE OF SENIORITY RIGHTS

Seniority is a system of employment preference based on length of service; employees with the longest service are given the greatest job security

---

11 Apart from their claim that the Eleventh Amendment bars enforcement of the remedy established by Title VII in this case, respondent state officials do not contend that the substantive provisions of Title VII as applied here are not a proper exercise of congressional authority under § 5 of the Fourteenth Amendment.

and the best opportunities for advancement. Neither by law nor by custom has seniority become an essential ingredient of the employment relationship. The employer who operates an unorganized plant is free to ignore relative length of service in laying off, recalling, promoting, or assigning his employees, and he usually does so. Yet the seniority principle is so important that it is embodied in virtually every collective agreement. It is thus the product of collective bargaining; it owes its very existence to the collective agreement.

Seniority provisions assume an almost infinite variety and are constantly being altered and reinterpreted to meet changing or unforeseen situations. For the purposes of this discussion it is unnecessary to review the different types, which range from absolute rigidity to great flexibility, and from relative simplicity to extreme complexity. It is sufficient to note that every seniority provision reduces, to a greater or lesser degree, the employer's control over the work force and compels the union to participate to a corresponding degree in the administration of the system of employment preferences which pits the interests of each worker against those of all the others.

More than any other provision of the collective agreement, including union security provisions under existing law, seniority affects the economic security of the individual employee covered by its terms. In industries characterized by a steady reduction in total employment the employee's length of service is his principal protection against the loss of his job. In cases of mass layoffs his chances of being retained or recalled will very likely depend upon such factors as the basis for determining seniority preference (*e.g.*, plant, departmental, or craft), the provision for trial periods to "make out" on a new job, and the extent to which "bumping" is permitted.

The role of the union in negotiating a seniority system thus becomes a matter of key importance to the membership. A debate among the members over whether the union should seek craft or departmental seniority, as opposed to district or plant seniority, for example, is not likely to be prompted simply by a desire to consider objectively the merits of competing theories; more probably, it represents a power struggle between the highly-skilled and the semi-skilled, between the older members and the younger, or between other rival groups within the union. Similarly, the union's role in administering the seniority system provides the opportunity for discriminating in favor of some individuals and groups and against others, not only within its own membership, but also as between members and non-members within the bargaining unit represented by the union. Whatever the union's practice may be in this regard, it usually is jealous of its own right to decide between the conflicting claims of the employees whom it represents, and is quick to challenge settlements of seniority grievances between individual employees and employer representatives to which it has not been a party. [Footnotes omitted.]

**(2)   *Layoffs, Recalls, and Promotions—The Critical Problems
of Seniority and Civil Rights***

The critical role of seniority in determining who should work and its
priority position in trade union ideology insured that efforts would be
made by its supporters to immunize it from the emerging EEO law and
the attempts of civil rights advocates to curb its effect. It is no wonder
that the AFL-CIO's legislative support of the Civil Rights Act of 1964
included efforts to insure that precious seniority rights would not be
adversely affected by the new civil rights. That the trade union objectives
in this regard were less than clearly successful is attested to by two
factors: (1) the ambiguity of §§ 703(h) and (j) of the Civil Rights Act of
1964, and (2) extensive litigation of seniority issues over the past 12 years.

The cases which are included in this chapter illustrate the evolution
of EEO seniority law. Before turning to these cases, examine the following
excerpt, which shows the conflict between civil rights objectives and the
effects of seniority systems.

## LAST HIRED, FIRST FIRED—LAYOFFS AND CIVIL RIGHTS

### *U.S. Commission on Civil Rights, February 1977*

Layoffs in the United States economy are generally based on seniority,
or "the last hired, first fired" principle. Seniority involves a set of rules
which gives workers with longer years of continuous service a prior claim
to a job over others with fewer years of service. What is referred to here is
"competitive status seniority" as opposed to "benefit seniority." Competitive status seniority determines priorities for promotion, job security, shift
preference, and other employment advantages. By contrast, benefit seniority, earned without regard to the status of other employees, determines
the eligibility for certain types of fringe benefits, such as paid vacations
or sick leave.

In applying competitive status seniority, companies differ as to the
unit within which seniority operates. In some, length of service may be
measured by total length of employment with employer ("plant" or
"mill" seniority). In others, length of service in a department ("department" seniority) or length of service in a job ("job" seniority) are the
units used for applying seniority.

By itself a seniority system is racially and sexually nondiscriminatory.
It applies equally to whites and nonwhites, men and women, allocating
jobs on the length of service in the unit in which seniority operates.
Indeed, it is the "facially neutral" feature that gave rise to its introduction. Unions demanded the establishment of the seniority system to replace the foreman's complete authority over promotion and layoff. Seniority is one of the union organizer's principal and more effective appeals in
unionizing a plant's work force.

For union officials or nonunion employers, the length-of-service seniority rule is an objective internal device for allocating job opportunities
among members. It helps to immunize the union or the employers from
the criticisms of disgruntled employees denied promotion or laid off.
Yet seniority systems have been significant instruments of racial and sex
discrimination, as part III of this report will demonstrate.

A 1975 survey of major collective bargaining agreements in the United
States found that 90 percent contained layoff provisions; in 85 percent
of these contracts, seniority was a factor. More than 42 percent of the
agreements provided for layoffs based on seniority alone, and 30 percent
provided for seniority as the "determining factor" in layoffs (*i.e.,* more
senior employees are retained during a reduction in force only if they
are qualified for available jobs). Other factors are given equal consideration with seniority in less than 1 percent of the contracts. Seniority is the
sole or determining factor in at least two-thirds of the contracts in all
manufacturing industries except printing and in most nonmanufacturing
industries except maritime, services, construction, and insurance and
finance.

Most agreements also provide for eventual loss of seniority and recall
rights in a long layoff. Seniority retention periods may last from 6 months
or less to 5 years; one year is the most common term.

Always a vital concern, seniority becomes decisive during periods of
economic downturn when jobs are scarce. In an industrial or other employment setting, a worker's place in the seniority "pecking order" can
mean the difference between having a job and being unemployed.

The implications of the "last in, first out" rule for new workers, whether
minorities, women, or youth generally, are obvious. The disproportionately high rates of job loss among minorities have already been noted.
In some areas where minorities represented only 10 to 12 percent of the
work force, they accounted for 60 to 70 percent of those being laid off in
1974. Many companies which had only recently hired significant numbers
of minority and women employees have laid off workers. A *Business
Week* survey of companies that have undergone layoffs failed to find a
single employer who refrained from using the "last in, first out" approach
in order to retain minority or women workers.

For example, at the Norton Company, an abrasives manufacturer in
Worcester, Mass., the percentage of minority workers on the firm's total
work force dropped from 3.7 percent in 1973 (up from 1.9 percent in
1971) to 2.7 percent in 1974—"a countrywide pattern that varies only in
timing and degree." Elsewhere:
"A Pittsburgh-based conglomerate that recently followed seniority in
laying off 15 percent of its 30,000 member work force reports that 26
percent of its black employees and an even larger percentage of its women
lost their jobs. In the auto industry . . . layoffs of 215,000 out of 750,000
production workers have removed large numbers of minority workers
from some plants and all women from others."

Layoffs of employees by State and local government agencies have also
been based on "last in, first out," with disparate effects on minorities and

women. For example, layoffs in mid-1975 of 371 female officers appointed since January 1973 by the New York City Police Department ended their brief tenure with the previously overwhelmingly male police force. Over half of all Hispanic city workers in New York lost their jobs between July 1974 and November 1975. In a number of school districts in California and the Southwest, Mexican American teachers were disproportionately threatened by layoffs because of their low seniority. Some 300 Asian American employees of the California Department of Transportation faced layoffs in September 1975. A spokesperson for these workers described the problems created for this minority group:

"There is an extraordinary multiplying effect when Asians are laid off . . . not only does it affect their families so much more by creating unmanageable financial hardships, but you have to consider how much harder it is for them to find new jobs. Asians aren't as mobile as Caucasians, many have a language difficulty, [and] recent affirmative action policies have been so delayed that few have the seniority to hold on to positions. . . ."

While seniority does generally determine which employees are to be laid off first, it is not uniformly or always given exclusive weight. In 11 percent of labor contracts, seniority is a secondary factor to be considered only when factors such as ability and physical fitness are equal. Forty-six percent of the contracts allow for exceptions from seniority in layoffs, and union representatives are given superseniority for layoff purposes in more than three-fourths of these provisions. About 19 percent of layoff provisions in manufacturing contracts afford similar protection to specially skilled employees whom management desires to retain. Still other contracts exclude older or handicapped workers from the seniority provisions for layoffs.

Some agreements provide for payment of supplemental unemployment benefits (SUB) to buttress unemployment compensation for job losers. Contracts providing such plans differ as to the amount a worker can receive and the duration of such payments.

These are the mechanics of layoffs by seniority. The Commission wishes to stress the fact that while seniority usually determines who is to be laid off first, there are various exceptions to "last hired, first fired"—applied to groups or categories of workers. [Footnotes omitted.]

## NOTES

1. Who has the greater stake in a seniority system, the employer or the union?

2. Does seniority serve a business purpose? Can you make a case for it as necessary to the safe and efficient operation of a business activity?

3. If seniority were a "vested right," would not that suggest that there is a "property right" in a job? Is the concept of a property right in a job consistent with current U.S. law regarding the nature of the employment contract or of collective bargaining?

4. What effect would the adoption of a vested- or property-right concept have upon the union's duty of fair representation?

5. These and other questions should be kept in mind as you study the materials and cases on the evolution of EEO law as it relates to seniority.

(3) *Phase I—The Present Effects of Past Discrimination as a Violation of Title VII*

## ASBESTOS WORKERS, LOCAL 53 v. VOGLER

*United States Court of Appeals, Fifth Circuit, 1969*
*407 F.2d 1047, 1 FEP Cases 577*

DYER, Circuit Judge: Local 53 appeals from a temporary injunction entered against it, which prohibits the union's admitted discrimination in acts and policies of membership, referrals for employment, and training, in violation of Title VII of the Civil Rights Act of 1964, 42 U.S.C.A. § 2000e et seq. We affirm.

The facts are relatively undisputed. Local 53 is a labor organization which is the exclusive representative in negotiating terms and conditions of employment for those engaged in the asbestos and insulation trade in southeastern Louisiana, including the metropolitan areas of New Orleans and Baton Rouge and some counties of Mississippi. Local 53 effectively controls employment and training opportunities in the asbestos and insulation trade in the area. It is by contract the exclusive bargaining agent for all asbestos workers employed by every major firm in that territory, and, in practice although not by contract, it operates a referral system at the union office through which it either furnishes or approves each journeyman and helper hired by asbestos contractors.[1]

In order to be admitted into Local 53 at the top rating of journeyman mechanic, the union requires that the applicant be a physically fit citizen under 30 years of age, obtain written recommendations from three members, and obtain the approval of a majority of the members voting by secret ballot at a union meeting. Additionally, the applicant must have had four years of experience as an "improver" or "helper" member of the union, but improver membership in the union is restricted to sons or close relatives living in the households of members.[2] Aside from the citi-

---

[1] [Footnotes numbered as in original.—Ed.] Generally, workmen are sent to employers by the defendant [Local 53] in accordance with the fluctuating needs of the contractors in the area. When workmen are not available through the Union, contractors solicit men on their own but must send them to the Union before placing them on the job. Finding of Fact No. 3.

[2] It is the policy of the defendant Local 53 to restrict its membership to the sons or close relatives of other members. Local 53 does not admit new men as mechanics, regardless of their qualifications. In the past four years the defendant has accepted 72 first-year improvers as members. Sixty-nine of these are sons or stepsons of members; each of the other three is a nephew who was raised by a member as his son. Only such sons are even considered for membership. Finding of Fact No. 4(f).

zenship, age and physical fitness requirements, the union has imposed no qualifications or standards related to the trade upon persons seeking membership or referral for work.

Despite its dominance of employment and training opportunities in the asbestos trade and an increasing industry need for insulation tradesmen, Local 53 intentionally limited membership until by the time this action was instituted union members constituted less than one-fourth of the labor force in the industry. In the two years prior to the commencement of this suit the industry's labor needs had tripled,[3] yet in the four years prior to that time, Local 53 admitted but 72 improver members and no new mechanic members.[4] By the time of this suit, out of the 1,200 man insulation tradesman labor force of those contractors required by contract to recognize Local 53 as the exclusive bargaining agent for such employees, only 282, including 64 improvers, were actually members of Local 53.

In pursuing its exclusionary and nepotistic policies, Local 53 engaged in a pattern and practice of discrimination on the basis of race and national origin both in membership and referrals. It was found to be Local 53's practice to refer white persons of limited experience and white journeymen of other trade unions as mechanic asbestos workers. It was also found to be its practice to refuse to consider negroes or Mexican-Americans for membership and to refuse to refer negroes for employment or to accept negroes for referral for employment. This policy and various acts of discrimination, both prior to and after the effective date of the Civil Rights Act of 1964,[5] were admitted at trial and on this appeal.[6]

On February 25, 1966, March 9, 1966, and April 9, 1966, Paul M. Vogler, Jr., Juan Galaviz and Casimere Joseph, III, respectively filed complaints with the Equal Employment Opportunity Commission alleging that they had been denied membership in and referral for work by Local 53 in violation of Title VII of the Civil Rights Act of 1964. On November 19, 1966, the EEOC found reasonable cause to believe that the violations had occurred but was unable to secure voluntary union compliance with the Act.

---

[3] "In July of 1965, men affiliated with Local 53 worked a total of 58,690 hours; by November of 1966, that number had reached 160,548." Finding of Fact No. 4(c).

[4] See note 2 supra.

[5] Local 53 has more than 100 members and is engaged in the representation of employees of employers in an industry affecting commerce. Thus it was amenable to the Act on July 2, 1965. See 42 U.S.C.A. § 2000e(e).

[6] Brief of Appellant Local 53:
"At the time of the filing of this suit in November, 1966, there was [sic] on file with the union in excess of 200 applications for membership by white mechanic [sic] and improvers, some of which had been pending for more than ten years. In November and December, 1965, and January and February, 1966, seven (7) negroes applied for referral for employment as improvers or helpers. All were denied referral admittedly because they were negroes. Three (3) negroes, qualified members of the Plasterers Union, applied for referral for employment as mechanics in September, 1966, and were refused referral because they were negroes. At the time, the three individuals being members of the Plasterers Union were not seeking membership but only job referrals.
. . .
"Appellant . . . acknowledges the existence of evidence warranting the propriety of an order prohibiting in forceful terms discrimination on the basis of race in referrals for employment and in admission to membership."

On November 25, 1966, Vogler, Galaviz and Joseph instituted this action in the District Court and on the same day filed a motion for a temporary restraining order, entered that day by the court,[7] and a preliminary injunction. On December 15, 1966, the United States filed a complaint under 42 U.S.C.A. § 2000e—5(a) and (b) alleging a pattern or practice of discrimination and a motion for a preliminary injunction. The two cases were consolidated, and following an evidentiary hearing the District Court on May 31, 1967, entered an injunction.

The injunction prohibits discrimination in excluding persons from union membership or referring persons for work; prohibits use of members' endorsements, family relationship or elections as criteria for membership; ordered that four individuals be admitted to membership and nine others be referred for work; ordered the development of objective membership criteria and prohibited new members other than the four until developed; and ordered continuation of chronological referrals for work, with alternating white and negro referrals until objective membership criteria are developed.

The union argues that the preliminary injunction has retrospective effect and penalizes the union for pre-Act discriminatory policies in violation of the intent of Congress; that the injunction violates the Act's prohibitions against preferential racial treatment or establishing a quota system to correct racial imbalance; that the injunction is inconsistent with other Congressional labor legislation; and that the order exceeds the District Court's discretion by interfering with the scheme of the Civil Rights Act. The union also argues that despite its emphasis of the importance of this case and the necessity for guidance by this Court,[8] it should be permitted to withdraw its appeal, or alternatively that the appeal should be dismissed without prejudice, contending that little remains to be done and that future action could better be sought in the District Court by motion.

We agree with none of the union's contentions.

Local 53 admits that the evidence warrants "an order prohibiting in forceful terms discrimination on the basis of race in referral for employment and in admission to membership," [9] and indeed it does, but the union apparently would limit any relief to a "forceful," but formless, order. If Local 53 wishes to read a forceful prohibition against discrimination, it need look no further than the Civil Rights Act itself.

---

[7] The restraining order enjoined Local 53 from voting on any new members, tabulating any votes upon new members, or accepting any new members. The union had a meeting scheduled for that night at which 20 members were to be admitted from a ballot of 257 names, including the names of two negroes.

[8] Brief of Appellant:
"The proper adjudication and formulation of remedies in this case is important to the individuals the Government and the defendant unions in guidance in compliance with the Act and their future survival as an agent protecting and promoting the rights of the laboring man. The newness of the statute and the uniqueness of its administration either through private suits or a governmental officer not normally concerned with labor problems make a clear mandate and directional guidance from this court imperative."

[9] See note 6, *supra*.

Section 703(c) and (d) of the Act, 42 U.S.C.A. § 2000e—2(c) and (d), declares that it is an unlawful employment practice for a labor organization within the purview of the Act to discriminate on the basis of race or national origin in membership, employment referrals or training programs,[10] and section 706(g), 42 U.S.C.A. § 2000e—5(g), authorizes appropriate judicial relief from unlawful discriminatory practices.[11] In formulating relief from such practices the courts are not limited to simply parroting the Act's prohibitions but are permitted, if not required, to "order such affirmative action as may be appropriate."[12] See *United States* v. *Louisiana,* E.D. La. 1963, 225 F. Supp. 353, 393, *aff'd,* 1965, 380 U.S. 145, 154, 85 S.Ct. 817, 13 L.Ed.2d 709.[13] The District Court was invested with a large measure of discretion in modeling its decree to ensure compliance with the Act, *Mitchell* v. *Robert DeMario Jewelry Co.,* 1965, 361 U.S. 288, 291, 80 S.Ct. 332, 4 L.Ed.2d 323; *International Salt Co.* v. *United States,* 1947, 332 U.S. 392, 400–401, 68 S.Ct. 12, 92 L.Ed. 20, and this Court will not interfere with that discretion except for an abuse thereof. *United States* v. *Crescent Amusement Co.,* 1944, 323 U.S.

---

[10] Section 703 provides as follows:

"(c) It shall be an unlawful employment practice for a labor organization—

"(1) to exclude or to expel from its membership, or otherwise to discriminate against, any individual because of his race, color, religion, sex, or national origin;

"(2) to limit, segregate, or classify its membership, or to classify or fail or refuse to refer for employment any individual, in any way which would deprive or tend to deprive any individual of employment opportunities, or would limit such employment opportunities or otherwise adversely affect his status as an employee or as an applicant for employment, because of such individual's race, color, religion, sex, or national origin; or

"(3) to cause or attempt to cause an employer to discriminate against an individual in violation of this section.

"(d) It shall be an unlawful employment practice for any employer, labor organization, or joint labor-management committee controlling apprenticeship or other training or retraining, including on-the-job training programs to discriminate against any individual because of his race, color, religion, sex, or national origin in admission to, or employment in, any program established to provide apprenticeship or other training."

[11] Section 706(g) provides as follows:

"(g) If the court finds that the respondent has intentionally engaged in or is intentionally engaging in an unlawful employment practice charged in the complaint, the court may enjoin the respondent from engaging in such unlawful employment practice, and order such affirmative action as may be appropriate, which may include reinstatement or hiring of employees, with or without back pay (payable by the employer, employment agency, or labor organization, as the case may be, responsible for the unlawful employment practice). Interim earnings or amounts earnable with reasonable diligence by the person or persons discriminated against shall operate to reduce the back pay otherwise allowable. No order of the court shall require the admission or reinstatement of an individual as a member of a union or the hiring, reinstatement, or promotion of an individual as an employee, or the payment to him of any back pay, if such individual was refused admission, suspended, or expelled or was refused employment or advancement or was suspended or discharged for any reason other than discrimination on account of race, color, religion, sex or national origin or in violation of section 2000e—3(a) of this title."

[12] *Id.*

[13] Cf. also *United States* v. *Loew's Inc.,* 1962, 371 U.S. 38, 83 S.Ct. 97, 9 L.Ed.2d 11; *United States* v. *United States Gypsum Co.,* 1948, 340 U.S. 76, 71 S.Ct. 160, 95 L.Ed. 89; *International Salt Co.* v. *United States,* 1947, 332 U.S. 392, 68 S.Ct. 12, 92 L.Ed. 20; *Hartford-Empire Co.* v. *United States,* 1944, 323 U.S. 386, 65 S.Ct. 373, 89 L.Ed. 322; *United States* v. *Bausch & Lomb Optical Co.,* 1944, 321 U.S. 707, 64 S.Ct. 805, 88 L.Ed. 1024; *Ethyl Gasoline Corp.* v. *United States,* 1940, 309 U.S. 436, 60 S.Ct. 618, 84 L.Ed. 852.

THE BASICS OF DISCRIMINATION

173, 185, 65 S.Ct. 254, 89 L.Ed. 160.[14] Where necessary to ensure compliance with the Act. the District Court was fully empowered to eliminate the present effects of past discrimination. *United States* v. *Local 189, United Papermakers & Paperworkers,* E.D. La. 1968, 282 F. Supp. 39, 45; *Quarles* v. *Philip Morris, Inc.,* E.D. Va. 1968, 279 F. Supp. 505, 516. See also *Louisiana* v. *United States,* 1965, 380 U.S. 145, 154, 85 S.Ct. 817, 13 L.Ed.2d 709.

The District Court properly ordered the immediate admission into membership of four individuals, including three negro members of another union, Plasterers Local 93, and a Mexican-American, who had applied for and were refused consideration for membership in Local 53. The union contends that this was error because the three negroes had not applied for membership,[15] and because these individuals were refused membership for reasons other than race or national origin. Because we are bound by the District Court's finding, amply supported by the evidence, that the three negroes had been refused consideration for membership, the union's first attack fails. Rule 52(a), Fed. R. Civ. P. Neither is the second attack of avail to the union, because its exclusionary membership policies were invalid as applied to these individuals. We fully agree with the District Court's finding that the three negroes were refused membership solely because they are negro and that the Mexican-American equally effectively was denied membership because of his national origin. The same reasoning applies to the District Court's order that nine individuals be immediately referred for employment as first year asbestos helpers, as the union unlawfully discriminated against them following the effective date of the Civil Rights Act.[16]

In addition to rectifying Local 53's discriminatory admission and referral practices as applied to the thirteen individuals, the injunction ordered affirmative action to prevent future discrimination. The court ordered the development of objective, trade-related membership criteria and procedures, excluding as criteria relationship to or recommendation by present members or other persons employed in the trade, and excluding also any membership vote. The order additionally required Local 53 to objectively determine the size of its membership with reference to the number of skilled asbestos workers reasonably calculated to meet present and future industry needs in its geographic area. The order further provided for implementation of the criteria and procedures through a

---

[14] Cf. also *Federal Trade Comm'n* v. *Colgate-Palmolive Co.,* 1964, 380 U.S. 374, 85 S.Ct. 1035, 13 L.Ed.2d 904; *Phelps Dodge Corp.* v. *NLRB,* 1940, 313 U.S. 177, 61 S.Ct. 845, 85 L.Ed. 1271; *Triple "AAA" Co.* v. *Wirtz,* 10 Cir. 1967, 378 F.2d 884.

[15] See note 6 *supra.*

[16] See note 7 *supra.*

In its Motion to Withdraw Appeal, Local 53 has assured this Court that it has complied with those portions of the injunction ordering it to admit or refer the thirteen individuals against whom it had discriminated. The union states that it "began effectuating compliance" by "offering" membership or referral to the named individuals. Because we are unsure from this terminology that there has been and will continue to be full compliance in this regard, we here expressly affirm this portion of the injunction. Cf. *Bailey* v. *Patterson,* 5 Cir. 1963, 323 F.2d 201, 205, *cert. denied sub nom., City of Jackson* v. *Bailey,* 1964, 376 U.S. 910, 84 S.Ct. 666, 11 L.Ed.2d 609.

report by the union, an opportunity for objections to it, hearings, and an effective date, since extended. The injunction suspended the admission of new members until such objective criteria are developed.

The union asserts that it was error to eliminate its policy of excluding persons not related to present members by blood or marriage because it is a "penalty" for pre-Act discrimination and because it establishes a quota system to correct racial imbalance in violation of section 703(j) of the Civil Rights Act, 42 U.S.C.A. § 2000e—2(j).[17] We disagree.

The District Court did no more than prevent *future* discrimination when it prohibited a continuing exclusion of negroes through the application of an apparently neutral membership provision which was *originally* instituted at least in part because of racial discrimination and which served no significant trade-related purpose. While the nepotism requirement is applicable to black and white alike and is not on its face discriminatory, in a completely white union the present effect of its continued application is to forever deny to negroes and Mexican-Americans any real opportunity for membership. See *Ross* v. *Dyer*, 5 Cir. 1963, 312 F.2d 191, 196; *State Comm'n for Human Rights* v. *Farrel*, 43 Misc.2d 958, 252 N.Y.S.2d 649 (1964). See also *Quarles* v. *Philip Morris, Inc.*, E.D. Va. 1968, 279 F. Supp. 505, 516, 518–19; *United States* v. *Local 189, United Papermakers & Paperworkers*, E.D. La. 1968, 282 F. Supp. 39, 44–45. See M. I. Sovern, LEGAL RESTRAINTS ON RACIAL DISCRIMINATION IN EMPLOYMENT 181–82 (1966). In view of the general policies of racial discrimination in Louisiana, *United States* v. *State of Louisiana*, E.D. La. 1963, 225 F. Supp. 353, 363–81, aff'd, 1965, 380 U.S. 145, 85 S.Ct. 817, 13 L.Ed.2d 709, and Local 53's admitted policy of racial discrimination both prior to and following the effective date of the Act, the union cannot salvage the invalidity of this requirement by convincing us that it did not arise at least in part from racial bases. Neither can Local 53 show retroactive application of the Act by superimposing its practices upon the facts of *United States* v. *Sheet Metal Workers Int'l Ass'n*, E.D. Mo. 1968, 280 F. Supp. 719. The district court in *Sheet Metal Workers* apparently held that because there was absolutely no evidence of acts of discrimination following the Civil Rights Act, a referral seniority system rewarding pre-Act employment from which Negroes were excluded is permissible. Regardless of the validity of the referral seniority systems involved there,[18] they are not analogous to the exclusion of negroes from an all

[17] Section 703(j) reads in pertinent part:
"(j) Nothing . . . shall be interpreted to require any . . . labor organization to grant preferential treatment to any individual or to any group because of the race . . . or national origin of such individual or group on account of an imbalance which may exist with respect to the total number or percentage of persons of any race . . . or national origin . . . referred or classified for employment by any . . . labor organization, or admitted to, or employed in, any apprenticeship or other training program, in comparison with the total number or percentage of persons of such race . . . or national origin in any community, State, section, or other area, or in the available work force . . . ."

[18] We express no opinion as to whether the elimination of either of the referral seniority systems in *Sheet Metal Workers* would constitute an abuse of discretion by retroactively penalizing pre-Act discrimination, by destroying "vested" seniority rights or by giving preferential treatment to negroes or whether either's use constituted a pattern or practice of discrimination violative of the Act.

white union by a system of nepotism. While the former might for a limited time operate to exclude negroes, the latter probably would do so interminably.

The requirements of Local 53 that applicants for membership obtain recommendations from present members and receive a favorable vote of a majority of its members were applied in a discriminatory manner, see *Hawkins* v. *North Carolina Dental Soc'y*, 4 Cir. 1966, 355 F.2d 718, 723; *United States* v. *Logue*, 5 Cir. 1965, 344 F.2d 290, 292–293; *Hunt* v. *Arnold*, N.D. Ga. 1959, 172 F. Supp. 847, and hence it was permissible to eliminate them. It is immaterial that they were required by the union's constitution or contracts, as Congress under the Commerce Clause may invalidate private agreements. See *J. I. Case Co.* v. *NLRB*, 1944, 321 U.S. 332, 337, 64 S. Ct. 576, 88 L.Ed. 762; *Philadelphia, B. & W.R.R. Co.* v. *Schubert*, 1912, 224 U.S. 603, 613–614, 32 S.Ct. 589, 56 L.Ed. 911; *Louisville & N.R.R. Co.* v. *Mottley*, 1911, 219 U.S. 467, 482–83, 31 S.Ct. 265, 55 L.Ed. 297. Neither did the District Court abuse its discretion by eliminating as a membership criterion work experience gained prior to the date of the injunction. Until that date negroes were prevented from gaining such experience due to the union's racial discrimination, and this lack of experience would disadvantage them were pre-order experience allowed to be used. If a racially exclusionary practice originating from pre-Act discrimination cannot be *continued* following the Act, certainly such a racial disadvantage cannot be *instituted*.

It is clear that by ordering Local 53 to develop objective criteria for membership, including a method by which union size based on industry need could objectively be determined, and by temporarily suspending admissions, the District Court did no more than ensure that the injunction against further racial discrimination would be fairly administered. Absent objective criteria regarding admissions and union size, covert subversion of the purpose of the injunction could occur. The same administrative reasons support alternating white and negro referrals, particularly in view of the union business agent's testimony that "every now and then" referral application forms tend to "run out." The court was authorized to "order such affirmative action as may be appropriate," 42 U.S.C.A. § 2000e—5(g), and nothing convinces us that it did not do so. In no manner did the injunction interfere with other labor legislation, usurp National Labor Relations Board jurisdiction, or constitute an abuse of discretion. See *Local Union No. 12, United Rubber, C., L. & P. Wkrs. of America, A.F.L.–C.I.O.* v. *NLRB*, 5 Cir. 1966, 368 F.2d 12, 24.

We view with a jaundiced eye Local 53's assertion that cessation of its illegal conduct is sufficient reason to allow it to withdraw this appeal. Cf. *United States* v. *W. T. Grant Co.*, 1953, 345 U.S. 629, 73 S.Ct. 894, 97 L.Ed. 1303. Therefore the motion to withdraw its appeal from the temporary injunction entered by the District Court is denied. The District Court's entry of a temporary injunction is

Affirmed.

---

The foregoing case was back before the Court of Appeals in 1972:

## VOGLER v. McCARTY, INC.

*United States Court of Appeals, Fifth Circuit, 1971*
*451 F.2d 1236, 4 FEP Cases 12*

THORNBERRY, Circuit Judge: This appeal concerns the district court's equity jurisdiction to fashion remedies pursuant to Sections 706 and 707 of Title VII of the Civil Rights Act of 1964 [42 U.S.C.A. § 2000e-5 to -6].

Although the decision is simple, the facts are somewhat complex. We therefore begin by setting them out.

On May 31, 1967, the district court, based on its finding that the Union [2] had denied to Negroes opportunities for both employment referral and Union membership, ordered the Union to effectuate a system of alternate referrals of Negro and white workers and required it to develop a plan for the admission of new members based on factors other than race.

The parties to the original action were unable to agree on criteria for membership in the Union, and the referral system originally set up did not succeed in furnishing more than limited employment opportunities to Negroes. In order to resolve these problems, the district court, pursuant to proposals by the government, on February 19, 1970, entered a new order.

The February order provided in part that separate hiring books were to be maintained for four categories of employees: (1) White mechanics, (2) black mechanics, (3) white improvers, and (4) black improvers. As before, the Union was to alternate referrals between Negro and white workers on a one-for-one basis. The order further provided that the Union could set up so-called "A" and "B" books for the white mechanics. Workers listed in the "A" book were to be those men with more than five 1200-hour years experience in the trade; workers listed in the "B" book were to be those men with less than five years of such experience. Referral preference could be given to workers listed in the "A" book.

The Union, on December 9, 1970, sought to modify the court order because of its alleged failure to accomplish the desired results in certain respects. Due to the influx of Negroes into the trade, along with a depressed economy which substantially affected overall employment opportunity in the building and trades industry, the system established by the court had created a substantial backlog of persons who were potential employees, but who had not been employed for long periods of time, or not at all. Full employment, because of the large number of employees in each seniority book, was thus impossible for a substantial number of workers. As a result of prolonged layoffs, many of the applicants appearing on the white mechanic lists had lost their eligibility for hospitalization and pension benefits.

To remedy this unstable employment situation and the accompanying effects on the white mechanics, the district court on January 25, 1971

---

[2] [Footnotes numbered as in original.—Ed.] Local 53 of the International Association of Heat and Frost Insulators and Asbestos Workers.

entered the order involved in the instant case. This order substituted three lists of white mechanics, cited as groups A, B, and C, based on different periods of experience, in place of the previous two lists. This resulted in increased employment opportunity for the more experienced white employees at the expense of those white employees with less experience, and thus provided stable employment for at least some white workers. The order admittedly had no effect on the Negro workers because the one-for-one referral system was preserved.

Appellant (Association) [3] contends that the district court had no discretion to enter this order, which affects only white Union members and which imposes on the Association terms of employment subject to collective bargaining between the Union and the Association.

We note at the outset that district courts are possessed of broad discretionary power under Title VII of the Civil Rights Act to fashion remedies which prevent future discrimination and remedy the effects of past discrimination.

"In formulating relief from such practices the courts are not limited to simply parroting the Act's prohibitions but are permitted, if not required, to 'order such affirmative action as may be appropriate.'" *Local 53 of the International Association of Heat and Frost Insulators and Asbestos Workers* v. *Vogler, Jr., et al.,* 5th Cir., 407 F.2d 1047. See also *Louisiana* v. *United States,* 380 U.S. 145, 85 S.Ct. 817, 13 L.Ed.2d 709 (1965). The district court's discretion in preventing discriminatory practices and violations of federal law may even include orders affecting private agreements, including those under collective bargaining. *J. I. Case Company* v. *NLRB,* 321 U.S. 332, 64 S.Ct. 576, 88 L.Ed. 762 (1944); *Philadelphia, B. & W. R. R. Co.* v. *Schubert,* 224 U.S. 603, 32 S.Ct. 589, 56 L.Ed. 911 (1912); *Local 189, United Papermakers and Paperworkers* v. *United States,* 5th Cir. 1969, 416 F.2d 980; *Local Union No. 12, United Rubber, Cork, Linoleum & Plastic Workers* v. *NLRB,* 5th Cir. 1966, 368 F.2d 12.

Adequate protection of Negro rights under Title VII may necessitate, as in the instant case, some adjustment of the rights of white employees. The Court must be free to deal equitably with conflicting interests of white employees in order to shape remedies that will most effectively protect and redress the rights of the Negro victims of discrimination. We hold, therefore, that the district court, under the circumstances of the instant case, did not abuse its discretion in making reasonable adjustments between the various classes of white employees.

The Association further contends that the district court order will eventually harm Negro employment opportunity. For present purposes the order will cause no disadvantage to Negroes because referrals will continue to be made on a one-for-one basis. It may, however, affect the Negro workers when the Negro and white mechanics' lists merge, as is contemplated. If the seniority basis for referral is continued, it is feared

[3] Master Insulator's Association of New Orleans and Baton Rouge, La., of which the defendant in the original district court action, McCarty, Inc., is a member.

that the "super-seniority" accorded the most senior white workers under the most recent court order might be used to give white workers hiring preference over the relatively new Negro workers.

Our disposition of the Association's first contention also takes care of this contention. Any harm to Negroes resulting in the future from the district court plan can be remedied by the district court's further exercise of the rather broad discretionary power with which it is endowed under Title VII. There is no indication at this time that such prejudice will occur or is likely to go without remedy.

Accordingly, we affirm.

CLARK, Circuit Judge (dissenting): [omitted].

## UNITED STATES v. SHEET METAL WORKERS INTERNATIONAL ASSOCIATION, LOCAL 36

*U.S. Court of Appeals, Eighth Circuit, 1969*
*416 F.2d 123, 2 FEP Cases 127*

Before BLACKMUN, MEHAFFY and HEANEY, Circuit Judges.

HEANEY, Circuit Judge: The Attorney General brought an action on February 4, 1966, against Local 1 and Local 36 charging them with engaging in a "pattern or practice" of discrimination against Negroes on account of their race in violation of Title VII of the Civil Rights Act of 1964. 42 U.S.C. §§ 2000e to 2000e-15.

The trial court found: (1) that both Locals excluded Negroes prior to 1964; (2) that the record was devoid of specific instances of discrimination by either Local after July 2, 1965, the effective date of the Act; (3) that both Locals made a post-Act effort to recruit Negroes and to advise them of their rights to membership and related benefits; and (4) that no complaints of discrimination by either Local had been made to any governmental agency. The court concluded:

"The Civil Rights Act of 1964 was not intended to penalize unions or others for their sins prior to the effective date of the Act. It is prospective only. Neither was it passed to destroy seniority rights in unions or in business. The Act specifically forbids a union or a business from giving preferential treatment to Negroes to correct an existing imbalance of whites. In order to be a violation of this Act, there must be an intentional pattern and practice of discrimination and not an isolated instance of discrimination. There is no pattern or practice of discrimination in this case since the effective date of the Act." *United States* v. *Sheet Metal Wkrs. Ass'n, L. U. No. 36*, 280 F.Supp. 719, 730 (E.D. Mo. 1968).

The government asks this Court to reverse the trial court. It argues that it is not necessary to prove that a number of Negroes sought and were denied union membership or related benefits to establish a pattern or practice of discrimination. It asserts that the Act casts upon those subject to its provisions not merely the duty to follow racially neutral employment policies in the future but an obligation to correct or revise practices which would perpetuate racial discrimination. It specifically requests that we find: (1) that both locals are continuing to discriminate against Negroes in the operation of their employment referral systems, (2) that both Locals are continuing to discriminate against Negroes in their admission policies, and (3) that both Locals had failed to publicize their abandonment of racially discriminatory policies and that they have an affirmative obligation to do so.

It asks that the matter be remanded to the District Court for the entry of an appropriate remedial order.

We first consider the general question of whether it was necessary for the government to prove that the Locals have refused membership or work referral to Negroes since the effective date of the Act. We answer this question in the negative. . . . [The referral systems involved exclusive hiring hall arrangements. Persons seeking work were classified into four priority groups, according to criteria including experience in the industry, passing of examinations, and employment under an agreement involving the local union. Group I is the most desirable priority group for each local.]

. . .

It is clear that Local 1's referral system was operated on a discriminatory (exclusionary) basis prior to 1966. Negroes were barred from using the hiring hall, they were denied the right to take a journeyman's examination, and they were prohibited from joining the Local. As a result of these discriminatory practices, they were unable to gain experience under the collective bargaining agreement. Furthermore, it was very difficult for them to gain experience elsewhere in the electrical construction industry because Local 1 controlled most of the work.

Local 1 contends that it now accepts Negroes into membership. It has accepted two (both were formerly members of a nonconstruction division of the Local). It contends that it now permits Negroes to take a journeyman's examination. It has permitted two. It contends that Negroes are now permitted to use the facilities of the hiring hall. Two have used it. The Local has also organized two Negro contractors (who had previously sought and have been denied membership) with fourteen Negro employees.[14] Their employees have been accepted as members, and presumably will be permitted to use the facilities of the hiring hall. Even if it is assumed that Negroes have been permitted since the passage of the Act to take a journeyman's examination, to join the Local and to use the hiring hall, the highest priority group in which a Negro can expect to be placed if he takes and passes a journeyman's examination and joins the Local is Group IV. Under the collective bargaining agreement, he would still lack the experience required for a higher classification. Furthermore, he would have to have at least one year of experience to be placed in Group IV. It is clear that employment opportunities for

14 [Footnotes numbered as in original—Ed.] Frank Witt, one of the Negro contractors testified that a union representative told him that "it was about time the organization was going to move to get a Negro into the organization and that I had the first shot."

persons in Group IV, or the lower unnumbered group, are substantially less than for persons in the higher groups. Indeed, the referral system was established to assist in preserving work opportunities for those who had worked in the trade for a union contractor over a period of time. It also follows, however, that Negroes qualified to do the work customarily performed by a journeyman electrician are deprived of an opportunity to be placed in a priority group in which they would have a reasonable opportunity to make a living. And they are so deprived because they were denied the opportunity to gain experience under the collective bargaining agreement or in the industry before the Act was passed.

It is equally clear that Local 36 did not permit Negroes to take a journeyman's examination, to join the Local, or to use its hiring hall prior to 1967. The Local built the discriminatory practices into its employment referral system by negotiating a new system of referring persons for employment by priority groups, and by giving preference to those who had an opportunity to gain experience under the collective bargaining agreement and in the industry prior to its effective date.

In our view, neither Local can be permitted to continue to operate its employment referral systems without change. Both plans effectively operate to deprive qualified Negroes of an equal opportunity for employment as journeymen electricians or as sheet metal workers. Because the plans carry forward the effects of former discriminatory practices, they result in present and future discrimination and are violative of Title VII of the Act.[15]

. . .

If the Locals desire to retain the referral systems, modifications must be made in the collective bargaining agreements [16] and in the referral systems to permit Negroes who are reasonably qualified (capable of performing that work ordinarily required of a journeyman craftsman) to

---

[15] *Local 189, United Papermakers and Paperworkers, AFL.-CIO, United Papermakers and Paperworkers, AFL-CIO, CLC;* and *Crown Zellerbach Corporation* v. *United States of America,* 416 F.2d 980 (5th Cir. July 28, 1969), aff'g, *United States by Clark* v. *Local 189, United Papermakers and Paperworkers,* 282 F.Supp. 39 (D.C.La.1968); *Local 53 of Int. Ass'n of Heat & Frost I.&A. Wkrs.* v. *Vogler,* 407 F.2d 1047 (5th Cir. 1969), aff'g *Vogler* v. *McCarty, Inc.,* 294 F.Supp. 368 (E.D.La.1968); *N.L.R.B.* v. *Local 269, Internat'l Bro. of Electrical Wkrs.,* 357 F.2d 51 (3rd Cir. 1966); *Dobbins* v. *Local 212, International Bro. of Elec. Wkrs.,* 292 F.Supp. 413 (S.D. Ohio 1968); *Quarles* v. *Philip Morris, Incorporated,* 279 F.Supp. 505 (E.D.Va. 1968). *Contra, Griggs* v. *Duke Power Company,* 292 F.Supp. 243 (M.D.N.C. 1968); *U.S.* v. *International Brotherhood of Electrical Workers, Local 39,* 71 L.R.R.M. 2087 (1969); *U.S.* v. *International Brotherhood of Electrical Workers, Local 38,* 70 L.R.R.M. 3019 (1969). The *Dobbins* Court, at 445, said:
"A policy of giving priority in work referral to persons who have experience under the Local's Collective Bargaining Agreement is discriminatory when competent [Negroes] have previously been denied the opportunity to work under the referral agreement by reason of their race. . . ."
[16] We recognize that the employers with whom the Locals have collective bargaining agreements are not parties to this lawsuit and that the employers' agreement will be necessary if modification to the collective bargaining agreements is to be made. See Note, *Title VII, Seniority Discrimination and the Incumbent Negro,* 80 HARV. L.REV. 1260, 1280, n. 97 (1967). In the light of this record, we assume that an agreement with the employers, which will meet the conditions laid by this opinion, can be met. If no new agreement is possible, the union must nonetheless discontinue those practices which have been found to be in violation of Title VII by this Court.

register for employment at the Locals' hiring halls and to be placed in the highest group for which they qualify. The specific modifications shall be worked out by the parties and shall be approved by the trial court. They shall generally conform to the following standards:

(1) The residency requirements of both Locals are nondiscriminatory and need not be changed.

(2) The experience requirements must be modified:

(a) Experience under the collective bargaining agreement shall not be required of Negroes meeting the requirements set forth in (b) and (c) of this section.

(b) Negroes with the requisite years of experience in the construction industry (five years for electricians and four years for sheet metal workers) who desire to register for employment shall be permitted to do so within a reasonable time and shall be placed in Group I. They shall be referred for employment from this group. After being employed, they shall be permitted to take a journeyman's examination. The examination shall be an objective one designed to determine whether the applicants are reasonably qualified. If they pass the examination, they shall have a continuing right to be referred for employment from Group I. Negroes who do not have the requisite experience as of the date of this opinion, but who acquire such experience within the next five (Local 1) and four (Local 36) years shall be given the same opportunity. Experience under the collective bargaining agreement shall not be required of Negroes meeting the qualifications noted above.

(c) Negroes without construction experience who are beyond the apprenticeship age and who have as of the date of this opinion been residents of the area for at least five (Local 1) and four (Local 36) years shall, on request to the Local, if they are qualified to be a journeyman by other than construction experience, be given a reasonable opportunity to take a journeyman's examination under the conditions set forth in (b) and placed in Group I if they pass the examination. The parties shall, under the trial court's supervision, develop a procedure for determining, from written applications, whether a resident Negro applicant has that experience and training which appears to qualify him to take the examination. Negroes who do not have the requisite experience as of the date of this opinion but who acquire it during the next five years shall be given the same opportunity.

(3) Negroes without construction experience who are beyond the apprenticeship age shall, on request to the Local, if they are shown to have other reasonably comparable experience, be given an opportunity for work referral in Group IV (Local 1) or Group III (Local 36).

(4) Reasonable steps shall be taken to make it known to the Negro community that all persons are now permitted to use the referral system without respect to race, color or creed.

In requiring the modifications, we impose no quotas, we grant no preferences.

Nor do we deprive any non-Negro craftsman of bona fide seniority rights. Each such craftsman will remain in the group to which he is now assigned and will move to a higher group when he has satisfied the elegibility requirements. We do make it possible, however, for qualified Negroes—those who have been deprived of the opportunity to gain experience in the construction industry or to gain experience under the collective bargaining agreement—to be placed in the group where they will have an equal opportunity to be referred for work.

### THE ADMISSIONS POLICIES OF THE LOCALS

We next consider the government's contention that both Locals are continuing to discriminate against Negroes in determining their eligibility for membership, and that Local 36 discriminates against Negroes with reference to initiation fees.

A brief résumé of the policies of both Locals governing the admission of members will be helpful in understanding the government's contentions.

To be eligible for membership in the construction division of Local 1, an applicant must: (1) be at least sixteen years of age, (2) be of good character, (3) pass an examination, and (4) be a resident of the area, be employed at the electrical trade within the jurisdiction of the Local, and be working under a Local 1 collective bargaining agreement. The name of each applicant is required to be read at a regular meeting of the Local. Thereafter, the executive board of the Local reviews the applicant's qualifications and reports to the membership. If this report is favorable, the members of the Local vote upon the admission of the applicant. Every member in attendance at a regular membership meeting votes on all applications for membership. Applicants may be submitted to the voting procedure individually or as a group.

The minutes of the Local's regular meetings, from February 1, 1952, to September 1, 1966, disclose only thirteen instances in which the membership denied admission to an applicant. No reasons for the denials are recorded, but there is no cause to believe that race or color was a factor.

Membership in Local 1 may be obtained in four ways: (1) by application, (2) by completing the apprenticeship training program, (3) by transfer from a nonconstruction classification (an applicant must have at least five years experience in the nonconstruction classification), and (4) by admission through an organizational campaign.

To be eligible for admission to Local 36, an applicant must (1) have good moral character and (2) be employed in the sheet metal trade within the jurisdiction of the Local.

Admission to membership in Local 36 can be obtained in three ways: (1) by application (including those situations where employees of nonunion contractors are organized), (2) by completion of the apprenticeship training program, and (3) by transfer from another Local.

An applicant is required to file an application for a journeyman sheet metal worker examination and an application for membership. It must be countersigned by "two good standing members of the Local." In practice, this requirement is routinely fulfilled by members of the executive board. The application for the examination elicits information which tends to reflect his experience in the trade. The applicant is then scheduled to take a test which is administered by the apprentice instructor, Edward Schultz—a Local 36 member. The examination consists of three sets of written questions—the Purdue Sheet Metal Test, a layout problem and a welding test. The testing time varies from one to four hours. Schultz notes the scores on the test sheets and adds personal comments as to why a person is or is not qualified. No passing score is established. Neither the test sheets nor the scores on them are forwarded to anyone. Schultz simply notifies the Business Agent that the applicant is qualified or that he is not qualified.

The applicant is required to pay an initiation fee equal to one hundred times the hourly rate or somewhat more than $500 at the time of trial. When the initiation fee is paid in full, the applicant is initiated into membership. No vote by the membership is required.

No examination is required of persons who are selected for membership during an organizational campaign. The initiation fee for such applicants is reduced from a sum in excess of $500 to a range of $50 to $150.

The government contends that the membership vote requirement of Local 1 and the practice in Local 36 of relying on the judgment of Edward Schultz to determine whether an applicant has passed the journeyman's examination are violative of Title VII of the Act. It contends that each procedure is defective "because it vests absolute discretion in a body or individual which has, in the past, shown a tendency to racial discrimination and which is not prevented from exercising that same bent today."

. . .

The government's contention that Local 36 continues to violate Title VII by permitting a single member of the Local, Mr. Schultz, to conduct and grade journeymen's examinations in the manner he does is well taken:

(1) The examinations are a prerequisite to employment. A passing grade is essential to all who are required to take them. A person's very right to earn a living in the trade of his choice is involved.

(2) As long as the examinations are partially subjective in nature and are graded "pass" or "fail," with no established standard for either grade, there is no practical way in which the judgment of the examiner can be reviewed.

(3) In the light of Local 36's pre-1967 record of excluding Negroes and a post-1967 record of discriminating against them as to membership and related benefits, it is essential that journeymen's examinations be objective in nature, that they be designed to test the ability of the applicant to do that work usually required of a journeyman and that they be given and graded in such a manner as to permit review. (The Local gives such an examination to apprentices.) Compare, *Dobbins* v. *Local 212, International Bro. of Elec. Wkrs.*, 292 F.Supp. 413, 447, 464, 465 (S.D. Ohio 1968).

In reaching this conclusion, we do not necessarily accept the government's contention that Mr. Schultz, as an individual, would, because of his past participation in the exclusionary policies of the Local, discriminate against Negroes in giving and grading journeymen's examinations. We are not here concerned with the individual who gives and grades the examination. We are concerned rather with the system, the nature of the examination, its objectivity and its susceptibility to review.

The government also contends that Local 36 discriminates against Negroes with respect to initiation fees. It argues that Local 36 had a pre-Act policy of limiting its organizational efforts to white contractors employing white journeymen; that this policy has continued since the passage of the Act; that the journeymen accepted in the organizing campaigns are given the benefit of special initiation fees ranging from $50 to $150, compared with the regular initiation fee of more than $500; that these policies permit the Local to maintain effective control over its membership and are discriminatory as to Negroes. It asserts that the District Court should have enjoined the practice and directed that initiation fees be equalized.

. . .

The effectiveness, thoroughness and frequency of the efforts of the Locals to inform Negroes that the apprenticeship training programs were at long last being operated in a nondiscriminatory manner must be viewed in the light of (1) the fact that Negroes were excluded from membership in the Locals until 1966, (2) the fact that both Locals historically gave preference to those related to members, and (3) the fact that individual union members will inevitably continue to talk with their sons about opportunities available to them in the trades.

When so viewed, the efforts of the Locals fall short of what is necessary. While it is not the intention of this Court to minimize what has been accomplished by the Joint Committees and the Locals in making the public aware of the now nondiscriminatory character of the program, we cannot believe that what has been done is all that can be reasonably expected. The school appearances do not appear to have been conducted on a regular basis. Only two meetings were held with high school counsellors. The A.I.C. bulletins did not indicate that the programs were open to persons of every race and color.

We recognize that the best of publicity programs will not fully convince Negroes that they now have the opportunity to attempt to qualify for apprenticeship training. We also recognize that no such program can hope to be as effective as parental guidance, but a good public information program can help to persuade the doubtful and the skeptical that the discriminatory bars have been removed. Such a program is mandatory. It shall be worked out by the parties and submitted to the District Court for approval.

Finally, we note that we are not here concerned with the question of whether a labor organization which discriminated against Negroes prior to the Act but discontinued such discrimination when the Act became effective must, at the risk of being held to have violated the Act, publicize the fact that it has abandoned its discriminatory policies and practices. See, *Dobbins v. Local 212, International Bro. of Elec. Wkrs.*, 292 F. Supp. at 444, 445. Here, the discriminatory policies and practices continued after July 2, 1965. The question thus is whether the courts are authorized, under § 707(a)(3) of the Act, to require unions to publicize the fact that membership and related benefits have been opened to all persons. We hold that they can be so required. In our view, the Court's authority is not limited by § 703(j) which provides that nothing in the Act "shall be interpreted to require any . . . labor organization . . . to grant preferential treatment to any individual or to any group because of race, [or] color." See, Rachlin, *Title VII: Limitations and Qualifications*, 7 B.C. IND. & COM.L.REV. 473, 491-492 (1966). In the light of this holding, it is obviously unnecessary to discuss further the right of the District Court to require the Locals to institute a public information program with respect to membership and employment referral similar in context to that required with respect to the apprenticeship program. It has the right and should exercise it in a manner consistent with the views expressed herein.

. . .

## PAPERMAKERS, LOCAL 189 v. UNITED STATES

*United States Court of Appeals, Fifth Circuit, 1969*
*416 F.2d 980, 1 FEP Cases 875*

WISDOM, Circuit Judge: Title VII of the Civil Rights Act of 1964 prohibits discrimination in all aspects of employment.[1] In this case we deal with one of the most perplexing issues troubling the courts under Title VII:[2] how to reconcile equal employment opportunity *today* with

[1] [Footnotes numbered as in original.—Ed.] Pub.L. No. 88–352, 78 Stat. 241, 42 U.S.C. §§ 2000e to 2000e–15. For the legislative history, see Bureau of National Affairs, THE CIVIL RIGHTS ACT OF 1964; Vass, *Title VII: Legislative History*, 7 B.C.IND. & COM.L.REV. 431 (1966). Section 703(a) provides that:
"It shall be an unlawful employment practice for an employer—
"(1) to fail or refuse to hire or to discharge any individual, or otherwise to discriminate against any individual with respect to his compensation, terms, conditions, or privileges of employment, because of such individual's race, color, religion, sex or national origin; or
"(2) to limit, segregate, or classify his employees in any way which would deprive or tend to deprive any individual of employment opportunities or otherwise adversely affect his status as an employee, because of such individual's race, color, religion, sex, or national origin."
[2] In the last two or three years there has been a burst of writing on Title VII and seniority rights. See, for example, Gould, *Seniority and the Black Worker: Reflections on Quarles and its Implications*, 47 TEX.L.REV. 1039 (1969); Cooper & Sobol, *Seniority and Testing Under Fair Employment Laws: A General Approach to Objective Criteria of Hiring and Promotion*, 82 HARV.L.REV. 1598 (1969) (The authors are of counsel in the case before the court and in some of the other cases mentioned in this opinion); Jenkins, *A Study of Federal Effort to End Job Bias: A History, A Status Report and a Prognosis*, 14 HOW.L.J. 259 (1968); Gould, *Employment Security, Seniority and Race: The Role of Title VII of the Civil Rights Act of 1964*, 13 HOW.L.J. 1 (1967); Walker, *Title VII: Complaint and Enforcement Procedures and Relief and Remedies*, 7 B.C.IND. & COM. L.REV. 495, 518 (1966); Vaas, *Title VII: Legislative History*, 7 B.C.IND. & COM.L.REV. 431

seniority expectations based on *yesterday's* built-in racial discrimination. May an employer continue to award formerly "white jobs" on the basis of seniority attained in other formerly white jobs, or must the employer consider the employee's experience in formerly "Negro jobs" as an equivalent measure of seniority? We affirm the decision of the district court. We hold that Crown Zellerbach's job seniority system in effect at its Bogalusa Paper Mill prior to February 1, 1968, was unlawful because by carrying forward the effects of former discriminatory practices the system results in present and future discrimination. When a Negro applicant has the qualifications to handle a particular job, the Act requires that Negro seniority be equated with white seniority.

## I

A. The parties stipulated most of the basic facts. Crown Zellerbach (Crown) runs a paper mill at Bogalusa, Louisiana. The Company employs about 950 white workers and 250 Negro workers. Jobs there have always been organized hierachically within "lines of progression." The jobs within each line for the most part are related functionally so that experience in one job serves as training for the next.

Until May 1964, the Company segregated the lines of progression by race, reserving some lines to white employees and others to Negroes. Local 189 of the United Papermakers and Paperworkers, the white local, had jurisdiction over the more desirable lines; Local 189–A, the Negro local, had jurisdiction over the left-overs. With very few exceptions, the lowliest white jobs paid more and carried greater responsibility than the most exalted Negro jobs. Promotion within each line was determined by "job seniority"; when a vacancy occurred, the workers in the slot below it could bid for the job, and the one who had worked the longest *in the job slot below* had priority.

The Company put new employees on "extra boards." These boards were labor pools used to fill temporary vacancies within the lines of progression. The senior men had first call on vacancies in the entry jobs at the bottom of the various lines. When lay-offs occurred, those at the bottom of the line were bumped back to the extra board. They had first claim, however, on any vacancies in their old jobs under "rights of recall." Crown segregated its extra boards, like its lines of progression, by race, one for Negroes and one for whites.

The Company merged the extra boards in May 1964. Whoever, regardless of race, had the longest term on the board now gained priority to bid on entry jobs in the white lines. Merger opened up the lines to Negro entrants, and helped the relatively recent Negro employees on the board. It did not help more senior Negroes already in the lines of

(1966); Note, *Civil Rights-Racially Discriminatory Employment Practices under Title VII*, 46 N.C.L.REV. 891 (1968) (The note is on *Quarles*); Note, *Title VII, Seniority Discrimination, and the Incumbent Negro*, 80 HARV.L.REV. 1260 (1967) (The court in *Quarles* v. *Philip Morris, Inc.*, D.C., 279 F. Supp. 505, heavily relied on this note. In this case we draw heavily on *Quarles* and the note.)

progression. Moreover, the rights of recall gave any white who had served in a white line preference over others on the board in bidding on his old job. That fact slowed the advance of even newer Negro employees. A "transfer provision" added in 1965 enabled Negroes already in black lines of progression to bid on the bottom jobs in white lines on the basis of their "mill seniority," or time worked at the mill. This change meant that they did not have to become junior men on the extra board in order to bid on the starting job in previously white lines. It also meant that they did not have to surrender certain benefits accruing to mill seniority when they made the transfer.

Title VII went into effect with regard to Crown on July 2, 1965. Section 703(a)(2) makes it unlawful for an employer

"to limit, segregate, or classify his employees in any way which would deprive or tend to deprive any individual of employment opportunities or otherwise adversely affect his status as an employee, because of such individual's race, color, religion, sex, or national origin." 42 U.S.C. § 2000e–(a)(2).

Later in 1965 the Equal Employment Opportunity Commission discussed with the Company and the Papermakers the effect of Title VII on seniority arrangements. A letter from Herman Edelsberg, the Executive Director of the EEOC, stated that the Commission would be satisfied by the "non-discriminatory application of the seniority agreement established by collective bargaining," i.e. job seniority, provided that Crown discontinue segregation of the progression lines. The Chairman of the Commission, Franklin D. Roosevelt, Jr., met with representatives of the Company and the unions in December 1965 and declared that "application of the seniority system established by collective bargaining" would comply with the statute.

In January 1966 the unions and the Company amended the collective bargaining agreement so as to merge the progression lines within each department on the basis of existing pay rates. Except for one job in the plant, merger by pay rates merely meant tacking the Negro lines to the bottom of white lines. Whites on the extra boards who had rights of recall to jobs formerly entry jobs retained those rights to the same jobs, even though the positions were now in the middle of the merged lines. More importantly, Crown continued to award promotions according to job seniority: the man with the most years in the job slot below the vacancy had first call. Time worked in the mill counted for nothing as such. As a necessary result, Negroes had no seniority in bidding for formerly white jobs except as against each other and new white employees. They could not have such seniority, since the Company had not allowed them into the white progression lines. Crown gave no recognition to years spent in the Negro lines, and continued to make years spent in formerly white jobs the determinative factor in awarding all former white jobs except those previously at the entry level. The system conditioned job advancement upon a qualification that the Company itself had limited racially, *regardless of whether the qualification*—seniority in previously white jobs—*was necessary to do the work*. The legality of that arrangement is the main issue here.

In February 1967, more than a year after the merger of the lines, the Office of Federal Contract Compliance entered the picture. That agency has responsibility for overseeing compliance with Executive Order 11246 requiring non-discrimination assurances from all employers who contract with the federal government.[3] The OFCC attacked what the EEOC had previously seemed to approve, Crown Zellerbach's system of job seniority. In place of job seniority the OFCC proposed an "A + B" system which would combine an employee's time in the job below the vacancy and his total time at the mill in computing seniority. The Company accepted this compromise and tried to get the Papermakers to go along with it. The two locals, 189 and 189–A, both refused, although for different reasons. Crown thus faced a strike if it went ahead with the "A + B" system and the loss of future federal contracts if it did not.[4] In January it notified the unions that it would install the "A + B" system unilaterally on February 1, 1968. Local 189, the white union, responded by voting to strike on that date. Local 189–A, the Negro union, refused to join in the strike warning, calling the "A + B" system "a step in the right direction."

The Government filed this suit on January 30, 1968, to enjoin the strike as an effort "to perpetuate a seniority and recall system which discriminates against Negro employees." The district court granted the injunction the next day. The United States then asked the courts to strike down the "A + B" system as illegal, and to require that mill experience alone become the standard of seniority. The Government now was asking the court to set aside job seniority in any form, a stronger measure than the one requested earlier by the OFCC, which in turn had gone beyond the original position of the EEOC.[5] Local 189–A and two Negro employees intervened as plaintiffs on behalf of all Negro employees at the mill.

After a three-day hearing on job seniority, the district court issued an order on March 26, 1968, dealing with two issues that had been stipulated by the parties as severable from the eleven others in the case. The court continued in effect the injunction of January 31. It also held that job

[3] Section 202 of the order in part reads as follows:
". . . During the performance of this contract, the contractor agrees as follows: '(1) The contractor will not discriminate against any employee or applicant for employment because of race, creed, color, or national origin. The contractor will take affirmative action to ensure that applicants are employed, and that employees are treated during employment, without regard to their race, creed, color, or national origin. Such action shall include, but not be limited to the following: employment, upgrading, demotion, or transfer, recruitment or recruitment advertising; layoff or termination; rates of pay or other forms of compensation; and selection for training, including apprenticeship. The contractor agrees to post in conspicuous places, available to employees and applicants for employment, notices to be provided by the contracting officer setting forth the provisions of this nondiscrimination clause.' " (3 CFR 1965 Supp. p. 168).
[4] Crown obtained an injunction from a district court in December restraining the Secretary of Labor from barring the company from federal contracts without a prior hearing. *Crown Zellerbach Corp.* v. *Wirtz*, D.D.C. 1968, 281 F. Supp. 337.
[5] See Section VI of this opinion.

seniority "presently discriminate[s] against Negro employees at the mill whenever Negroes hired prior to January 1965 [when progression lines were merged] compete against white employees for promotion, demotion or selection for training." The court also found that job seniority, as a matter of fact, "is not necessitated by safety or efficiency factors. . . ." It ordered the abolition of job seniority in favor of mill seniority "in all circumstances in which one or more competing employees is a Negro employee hired prior to January 16, 1966." The decree did not, by its terms, upset the use of job seniority in bidding that involved only whites or Negroes hired after the merger of the lines of progression.

In explaining its order, the court pointed out that the abolition of job seniority did not mean that affected Negro employees would be able to bid on any job in the mill solely on the basis of their years with the Company. They would still have to move up the lines of progression job-by-job. Among the competitors within the slot below a vacancy, however, time in the mill rather than time in the job would define seniority. As a further qualification of its order, the court disavowed any intention "to deny Crown the right to require that competing employees have the fundamental qualifications necessary to fill the vacant position."

A month after issuing its order, the district court heard testimony and argument on the remaining eleven issues stipulated as severable from the issue of job seniority. The court disposed of one issue by ordering the merger of Local 189 and Local 189–A. The court decided the remaining ten issues on June 26, 1969.[6]

B. The stipulated issues are: "whether, under the facts and circumstances of this case, the job seniority system which was in effect at the Bogalusa paper mill prior to February 1, 1968, was unlawful" and, if so, "what is the necessary or appropriate standard or guideline for identifying the seniority of employees for purposes of promotion or demotion?"

The plaintiffs maintain that Crown's practice of awarding jobs on the basis of *job* seniority rather than *mill* seniority discriminates against Negroes, since they had no way of attaining job seniority in "white" slots until the recent desegregation of the plant. When Negroes bid for jobs above the former entry level of white lines of progression, Crown in

---

6 On June 26, 1969 the district court issued its findings of fact and conclusions of law on the remaining issues. (1) The court found that Crown had continued to discriminate in job assignments by appointing whites to traditionally white jobs and Negroes to traditionally Negro jobs. The court added to the aggrieved class Negroes hired since the merger of the progression lines (1966), except for the six Negroes hired since then "who in fact bid for and received formerly white jobs from the Extra Board." (2) The court concluded that a six-months residency requirement was not necessary to train employees for the next higher job in every instance. The parties, it noted, had stipulated which residency requirements were justified by need. (3) The court also found that certain jobs provide no training for the next higher levels. It therefore held that Negroes within the aggrieved class could skip those jobs in bidding on higher jobs in the merged lines of progression. (4) Finally, the court found that 64 hours of temporary assignment to a job per month provided training equivalent to permanent assignment to the job and should be treated as such for the purposes of bidding. The disposition of these and other issues in the district court's decision of June 26 does not affect our consideration of its earlier findings of fact and conclusions of law.

effect penalized them for not having what it denied them on account of their race until a short time ago—"white" job seniority. Crown's system gives renewed effect to the old racial distinctions without, the plaintiffs say, *the justification of business necessity*. The practice of awarding jobs by job seniority would, the plaintiffs assert, amount to present and prospective racial discrimination.

Crown and Local 189, the white union, maintain that Crown ceased to discriminate in 1966 when it merged the white and Negro lines of progression. That change, coupled with the merger of the extra boards in 1964 and the transfer provisions of 1965 removed all explicit racial classification at the Bogalusa mill. What remains, the defendants say, is a racially neutral system of job seniority. The fact that the system continues to prefer whites over previously hired Negroes in filling certain vacancies does not in itself show racial discrimination. That effect, the defendants argue, is merely an ineradicable consequence of extinct racial discrimination. They point to evidence that Congress meant Title VII to apply prospectively only. Competitive seniority has an honorable place in the history of labor,[7] and portions of the legislative history of the Act seem to immunize accrued rights of seniority against remedial measures. Thus Title VII § 703(h) specifically protects "bona fide seniority systems" from the operation of the Act. The defendants also maintain that insistence upon mill seniority would effectively bestow preferential treatment upon one race, which the Act by its terms positively forbids.

## II

No one can quarrel with the board proposition that Title VII operates only prospectively. By specific provision, the Act did not become effective at all until one year after the date of enactment. The central operative provision, § 703(a), declares that "it *shall* be an unlawful employment practice" for an employer to discriminate. (Emphasis added.) Section 701(b) and (e) provide that for staggered effective dates: The Act applied on July 2, 1965, only to employers of 100 employees or more, extending to employers of 75, 50, and 25 at successive yearly intervals. The dispute is whether a seniority system based on pre-Act work credit constitutes present discrimination.

---

[7] Cooper and Sobol, 82 HARV.L.REV. 1601, fn. 2: "The use of competitive status seniority to govern promotions, demotions, and layoffs is a fundamental aspect of industrial relations in this country. In nearly all businesses of significant size whose employees are organized, a seniority system plays some role in determining the allocation of the work. Such systems are commonly accompanied by lines of progression or promotional ladders which establish an order of jobs through which employees normally are promoted.

"Seniority may be measured by total length of employment with the employer ('employment,' 'mill,' or 'plant' seniority), length of service in a department, ('departmental seniority'), length of service in a line of progression ('progression line' seniority), or length of service in a job ('job' seniority). Different measures of seniority sometimes are used in the same plant for different purposes. The variations and combinations of seniority principles are very great, but in all cases the basic measure is length of service, with preference accorded to the senior worker. Similarly, construction craft unions, which control the allocation of local work in their craft, have adopted referral rules based on length of service."

Although the effect of Title VII provoked considerable debate in Congress, the legislative history of the title is singularly uninstructive on seniority rights. Opponents of the Act warned that Title VII would destroy hard-earned seniority rights; proponents responded that it would not affect accrued seniority.[8] In *Quarles* v. *Philip Morris, Inc.*, E.D. Va. 1968, 279 F. Supp. 505, after a careful review of the legislative history, Judge John D. Butzner, Jr. concluded:

"Several facts are evident from the legislative history. First, it contains no express statement about departmental seniority. Nearly all of the references are clearly to employment seniority. None of the excerpts upon which the company and the union rely suggests that as a result of past discrimination a Negro is to have employment opportunities inferior to those of a white person who has less employment senority. Second, the legislative history indicates that a discriminatory seniority system established before the act cannot be held lawful under the act. The history leads the court to conclude that Congress did not intend to require "reverse discrimination"; that is, the act does not require that Negroes be preferred over white employees who possess employment seniority. It is also apparent that Congress did not intend to freeze an entire generation of Negro employees into discriminatory patterns that existed before the act.

Perhaps the strongest argument for the *Quarles* construction of the Act is § 703(h):

"Section 703(h) expressly states the seniority system must be *bona fide*. The purpose of the act is to eliminate racial discrimination in covered employment. Obviously one characteristic of a *bona fide* seniority system must be lack of discrimination. Nothing in § 703(h), or in its legislative history suggests that a racially discriminatory seniority system established before the act is a *bona fide* seniority system under the act." *Quarles* v. *Philip Morris, Incorporated*, E.D. Va. 1968, 279 F. Supp. 505, 517. We agree with this view.

---

[8] "Title VII would have no effect on seniority rights existing at the time it takes effect" Justice Department statement. Cong. Record, April 8, 1964, p. 6986. "If a rule were to state that all Negroes must be laid off before any white man, such a rule could not serve as a basis for a discharge subsequent to the effective date of the title . . . but, in the ordinary case, assuming that seniority rights were built up over a period of time during which Negroes were not hired, these rights would not be set aside by taking effect of Title VII. Employer and labor organizations would simply be under a duty not to discriminate against Negroes because of their race. Any differences in treatment based on established seniority rights would not be based on race and would not be forbidden by the title." *Ibid.* "Title VII would have no effect on established seniority rights. Its effect is prospective and not retrospective. Thus, for example, if a business has been discriminating in the past and as a result has an all-white working force, when the Title comes into effect, the employer's obligation would be simply to fill future vacancies on a non-discriminatory basis. He would not be obliged—or indeed, permitted—to fire whites in order to hire Negroes, or to prefer Negroes for future vacancies, or, once Negroes are hired, to give them special seniority rights at the expense of the white workers hired earlier." Memorandum by Senators Clark and Case. Bureau of National Affairs Operations Manual, THE CIVIL RIGHTS ACT OF 1964, p. 320. See Cooper and Sobol, fn. 2, 82 HARV.L.REV. 1607–1609.

## III

The defendants assert, paradoxically, that even though the system conditions future employment opportunities upon a previously determined racial status the system is itself racially neutral and not in violation of Title VII. The translation of racial status to job-seniority status cannot obscure the hard, cold fact that Negroes at Crown's mill will lose promotions which, *but* for their race, they would surely have won. Every time a Negro worker hired under the old segregated system bids against a white worker in his job slot, the old racial classification reasserts itself, and the Negro suffers anew for his employer's previous bias. It is not decisive therefore that a seniority system may appear to be neutral on its face if the inevitable effect of tying the system to the *past* is to cut into the employees *present* right not to be discriminated against on the ground of race. The crux of the problem is how far the employer must go to undo the effects of past discrimination. A complete purge of the "but-for" effects of previous bias would require that Negroes displace white incumbents who hold jobs that, but for discrimination, the Negroes' greater mill seniority would entitle them to hold. Under this *"freedom now"* theory,[9] allowing junior whites to continue in their jobs constitutes an act of discrimination.

Crown and Local 189 advance a *"status quo"* theory: the employer may satisfy the requirements of the Act merely by ending explicit racial discrimination.[10] Under that theory, whatever unfortunate effects there might be in future bidding by Negroes luckless enough to have been hired before desegregation would be considered merely as an incident of now extinguished discrimination.

A *"rightful place"* theory [11] stands between a complete purge of "but-for" effects maintenance of the status quo. The Act should be construed to prohibit the *future awarding* of vacant jobs on the basis of a seniority system that "locks in" prior racial classification. White incumbent workers should not be bumped out of their *present* positions by Negroes with greater plant seniority; plant seniority should be asserted only with respect to new job openings. This solution accords with the purpose and history of the legislation.

Not all "but-for" consequences of pre-Act racial classification warrant relief under Title VII. For example, unquestionably Negroes, as a class, educated at all-Negro schools in certain communities have been denied skills available to their white contemporaries. That fact would not, however, prevent employers from requiring that applicants for secretarial positions know how to type, even though this requirement might prevent Negroes from becoming secretaries.

This Court recently struck down a nepotism membership requirement of a "white" union which shortly before had ceased overt discrimination.

9 See Note, 80 HARV.L.REV., 1268 fn. 2.
10 Id.
11 Id.

*Local 53 of the International Association of Heat and Frost Insulators and Asbestos Workers* v. *Vogler,* 5 Cir. 1969, 407 F.2d 1047. Under the nepotism rule, only the sons of members or close relatives living with members could become "improvers," and only "improvers" could be accepted into the union. Relationship to a member as a prerequisite to admission had the necessary effect of locking non-whites out of the union. The union argued that the desire to provide family security was a rational non-racial basis for the rule and that since the nepotism requirement excluded all persons unrelated to members, regardless of their race, it could not, therefore, be called a racial classification. This court held that the rule served no purpose related to ability to perform the work in the asbestos trade and that it violated Title VII:

"The District Court did no more than prevent *future* discrimination when it prohibited a continuing exclusion of Negroes through the application of an apparently neutral membership provision which was *originally* instituted at least in part because of racial discrimination and which served no significant trade-related purpose. While the nepotism requirement is applicable to black and white alike and is not on its face discriminatory, in a completely white union the present effect of its continued application is to forever deny to negroes and Mexican-Americans any real opportunity for membership."

In *Vogler* this Court made the point, citing *Quarles,* that "where necessary to insure compliance with the Act, the District Court was fully empowered to eliminate the present effects of past discrimination." *Vogler,* however, does not mesh completely with the facts in this case. The nepotism rule there, as the court pointed out, had scant relation to the operation of the business. It also had the inevitable effect of assuring the lily-white status of the union for all time. Nevertheless, the decision does support the position that reliance on a standard, neutral on its face, is no defense under the Act when the effect of the standard is to lock the victims of racial prejudice into an inferior position.

The controlling difference between the hypothetical typing requirement and the nepotism rule rejected in *Vogler* is *business necessity.* When an employer or union has discriminated in the past and when its present policies renew or exaggerate discriminatory effects, those policies must yield, unless there is an overriding legitimate, non-racial business purpose. Secretaries must be able to type. There is no way around that necessity. A nepotism rule, on the other hand, while not unrelated to the training of craftsmen,[12] is not essential to that end. To be sure, skilled workers may gain substantial benefits from having grown up in the home of a members of the trade. It is clear, nonetheless, that the benefits secured by nepotism must give way because of its effective continuation and renewal of racial exclusion. That much was decided in *Vogler.*

The decisive question then is whether the job seniority standard, as it is now functioning at the Bogalusa plant, is so necessary to Crown

[12] See *Kotch* v. *Board of River Port Pilot Commrs.*, 1947, 330 U.S. 552, 67 S.Ct. 910, 91 L.Ed. 1093.

Zellerbach's operations as to justify locking Negroes, hired before 1966, into permanent inferiority in their terms and conditions of employment. The record supports the district court's holding that job seniority is not essential to the safe and efficient operation of Crown's mill. The defendants' chief expert witness, Dr. Northrup, made it clear that he considered mill seniority "disastrous" only to the extent that it allowed *all* men in a slot to bid on the basis of their time at the mill. He stated that mill seniority in that sense would create labor unrest because its main effect would be to allow whites to "jump" other whites and Negroes to "jump" other Negroes. He also expressed fears about allowing anyone to bid on any vacancy in a line of progression, without requiring that he first advance job-by-job through the various levels below it. That problem might be solved, he stated, by imposing a residency requirement for training purposes. Dr. Northrup explicity stated that job seniority does *not* provide the only safe or efficient system for governing promotions. He suggested, in fact, an alternative "job credit" system that would give certain fractional seniority credit to victims of discrimination for the years in which they had been excluded from the white progression lines.

The court took account of Dr. Northrup's apprehensions in fashioning its decree. In place of job security the court ordered the institution of a mill seniority system carefully tailored to assure that no employee would have a right to a job that he could not perform properly. The court's decision put the emphasis where it belongs: absent a showing that the worker has the ability to handle a particular job, the entry job is the proper beginning for any worker. Under the court's decree, employees still must move up through the various lines of progression job-by-job.[13] As a further restraint, if a certain minimum time is needed in one job to train an employee for the next, a residency requirement may be imposed that will slow the rise of Negro employees. Under the system that is in effect at the mill now, and that is unaffected by the decree, that residency period is six months. To meet the problem of labor unrest that might result from "jumping" unrelated to racial issues, the court specifically limited its decree to instances in which Negroes hired before 1966 were among the bidders. Finally, and most importantly, both the court's decree and the existing collective bargaining agreement give Crown Zellerbach the right to deny promotions to employees who lack the ability or qualification to do the job properly.

All these precautions, we think, bear out the plaintiffs' assertion that there are satisfactory alternatives to job seniority at the Bogalusa mill. They lead us to conclude that the imposition of a system that perpetuates and renews the effects of racial discrimination in the guise of job seniority is not necessary or justified at Bogalusa. Job seniority, embodying as it does, the racially determined effects of a biased past, constitutes a form of present racial discrimination.

---

[13] See footnote 6.

This case is not the first case to present to courts in this circuit the problem of dealing with a change in system that is apparently fair on its face but in fact freezes into the system advantages to whites and disadvantages to Negroes. In *United States* v. *State of Louisiana,* E.D. La. 1963, 225 F. Supp. 353, a three-judge court had before it a new citizenship test adopted by the State Board of [Voters] Registration. The test was fair on its face and, perhaps, capable of fair administration. But it was a test that white voters, almost all of whom were registered, had not had to take. It was a difficult test for eligible Negroes, most of whom were not registered. The court enjoined the State from administering the test. "The promise of evenhanded justice in the future does not bind our hands in undoing past injustices." 225 F. Supp. at 396. The court said:

"The cessation of prior discriminatory practices cannot justify the imposition of new and onerous requirements, theoretically applicable to all, but practically affecting primarily those who bore the brunt of previous discrimination. An appropriate remedy therefore should undo the results of past discrimination as well as prevent future inequality of treatment. A court of equity is not powerless to eradicate the effects of former discrimination. If it were, the State could seal into permanent existence the injustices of the past."

The Supreme Court affirmed, adding: "the court has not merely the power but the duty to render a decree which will so far as possible eliminate the discriminatory effects of the past as well as bar like discrimination in the future." *Louisiana* v. *United States,* 1965, 380 U.S. 145, 85 S.Ct. 817, 13 L.Ed.2d 709. See also *Meredith* v. *Fair,* 5 Cir. 1962, 298 F.2d 696, 702, *cert. denied; United States* v. *Dogan,* 5 Cir. 1963, 314 F.2d 767; *United States* v. *Atkins,* 5 Cir. 1963, 323 F.2d 733; *United States* v. *Penton,* M.D. Ala. 1962, 212 F. Supp. 193. Cf. *Guinn* v. *United States,* 1915, 238 U.S. 347, 35 S.Ct. 926, 59 L.Ed. 1340; *Lane* v. *Wilson,* 1939, 307 U.S. 268, 59 S.Ct. 872, 83 L.Ed. 1281; *Goss* v. *Board of Education,* 1963, 373 U.S. 683, 688, 83 S.Ct. 1405, 1409, 10 L.Ed.2d 632, 636.

It might be said that in these cases the courts focussed on the unlawfulness of the prior discrimination. In *Gaston County* v. *United States,* 1969, 395 U.S. 285, 89 S.Ct. 1720, 23 L.Ed.2d 309, however, the Court's refusal to approve a voter literacy test was based on the inferior education inherent in segregated schooling. The automatic "triggering" provisions of the 1965 Voting Rights Act of 1965 had suspended Gaston County's literacy test because certain indicia chosen by Congress raised the presumption that the tests were being used to discriminate against Negroes seeking to register. In order to reinstate its test under the Act, Gaston County had to show that it had not used the test in the preceding five years "for the purpose or with the effect of denying or abridging the right to vote on account of race or color." The district court found, as a fact, that Gaston County's Negro schools had not provided educational opportunities equal to those available to whites. That alone, said the Supreme Court, would make the imposition of a literacy test an act of continuing discrimination. Neither the fair administration of the test, nor its legitimate public purpose could save it from condemnation under the Act.

## IV

With specific regard to employment opportunities under Title VII, decisions by at least two district courts support our conclusion that facially neutral but needlessly restrictive tests may not be imposed where they perpetuate the effects of previous racial discrimination.

In *Quarles* v. *Philip Morris, Inc.*, E.D. Va. 1968, 279 F. Supp. 505, the first case to challenge the legality of a promotion system under Title VII, the employer had segregated the races by departments at its plant. The employer desegregated the plant but prohibited transfers from one department to another. It also required that the transferor bid on vacancies according to his departmental seniority, rather than his seniority at the plant. The effect was to deny to Negroes promotion into the better paying jobs, because they could not accumulate seniority in the fabrication and warehouse departments, where the better jobs lay. Quarles, a Negro employed in the prefabrication department, could not become a truck driver, a higher-rung position in an all-white department. The court held that the new arrangement violates the statute (279 F. Supp. at 513, 519):

"The present discrimination resulting from historically segregated departments is apparent from consideration of the situation of a Negro who has worked for ten years in the prefabrication department. . . . [He is required] to sacrifice his employment seniority and take new departmental seniority based on his transfer date. Thus a Negro with ten years employment seniority transferring . . . from the prefabrication department to the fabrication department takes an entry level position with departmental seniority lower than a white employee with years less employment seniority. These restrictions upon the present opportunity for Negroes result from the racial pattern of the company's employment practices prior to January 1, 1966. The restrictions do not result from lack of merit or qualification. A transferee under any plan must satisfy ability and merit requirements regardless of his seniority.

. . .

"The court finds that the defendants have intentionally engaged in unlawful employment practices by discriminating on the ground of race against Quarles, and other Negroes similarly situated. This discrimination, embedded in seniority and transfer provisions of collective bargaining agreements, adversely affects the conditions of employment and opportunities for advancement of the class."

In *Dobbins* v. *Local 212, IBEW*, S.D. Ohio 1968, 292 F. Supp. 413, the union had formerly excluded nonwhites from membership. The effects of this practice had been doubly serious, since the union controlled hiring referrals within a certain geographic area. After opening its apprenticeship programs and membership to Negroes the union continued to prefer applicants who had previously worked under union contracts. This preferential referral system contained no explicit racial classification or discriminatory purpose. The court looked, nonetheless, to its inevitable discriminatory effect:

"A policy of giving priority in work referral to persons who have experience under the Local's Collective Bargaining Agreement is discriminatory when competent N[egroe]s have previously been denied the opportunity to work under the referral agreement by reason of their race." 292 F. Supp. at 445.

When the defendant's conduct evidences an "economic purpose" there is no discrimination under Title VII: "The limitation of either union or apprentice membership to a number far below the number necessary for the particular trade would be a discriminatory practice and pattern in a context involving an all W[hite] union membership with a previous history of discrimination. *Louisiana* v. *United States,* 380 U.S. 145, 85 S.Ct. 817, 13 L.Ed.2d 709 (1965). However, on a showing by a defendant that the limitation has nothing to do with any discriminatory intention but is related to reasonable economic purpose, the limitation in number is not unlawful." The court went on to hold the referral system illegal: "Preference to union members in work referral is a violation of Title VII if that preference operates, after July, 1965, to continue to restrict the employment opportunities of N's who have been excluded from membership and work under union auspices because of their race. *United States by Clark* v. *Local 189, United Papermakers and Paperworkers,* 282 F. Supp. 39 (D.C. La., 1968); *Quarles* v. *Philip Morris, Inc.,* 279 F. Supp. 505 (D.C. Va., 1968)." 292 F. Supp. at 446.

Nothing that we said in *Whitfield* v. *United Steelworkers, Local 2708,* 5 Cir. 1958, 263 F.2d 546, *cert. denied,* 360 U.S. 902, 79 S.Ct. 1285, 3 L.Ed.2d 1254, compels a different result. In that case Negro workers challenged a plan, negotiated through collective bargaining, purporting to do away with segregated lines of progression in a steel mill. There was no issue in *Whitfield* as to the measure of promotion from one job to another. *Quarles* distinguishes *Whitfield* (279 F. Supp. at 518):

"*Whitfield* does not stand for the proposition that present discrimination can be justified simply because it was caused by conditions in the past. Present discrimination was allowed in *Whitfield* only because it was rooted in the Negro employees' lack of ability and training to take skilled jobs on the same basis as white employees. The fact that white employees received their skill and training in a discriminatory progression line denied to the Negroes did not outweigh the fact that the Negroes were unskilled and untrained. Business necessity, not racial discrimination, dictated the limited transfer privileges under the contract."

In *Whitfield* the company had organized functionally-related jobs into two separate lines of progression, Line 1 (the skilled jobs) for whites and Line 2 (the unskilled jobs) for Negroes. Advancement in a line was based on knowledge and experience acquired in the next lower job. The company opened both lines on a non-racial basis, and added that Negroes in Line 2 would in the future have preference over new whites in apply-ing for vacancies in Line 1. Except for variations in pay, the change had the effect of merging the lines into one, with the formerly white line on top. In *Whitfield,* unlike the present case, the two lines were not so functionally related that experience at the top of the formerly black line could provide adequate training for the bottom jobs in the white line. The company therefore required that men moving into the formerly all-white Line 1 take a qualification test, one that the white incumbents had not been required to take. (The company had previously required 260 hours "probationary" experience instead.) Negroes objected to the test requirement on the ground that whites already working in Line 1 did not have to take the test to advance or remain in the line. The com-pany also required, as we have said, that employees bidding into Line 1 from Line 2 start at the bottom job. Negroes in Line 2 protested that this requirement also discriminated against them because it meant that Negroes would have to take a wage cut in moving from the top job in Line 2 to the bottom job in Line 1. The plaintiffs brought the complaint under the *Steele* doctrine,[14] which requires certified unions to represent members of the bargaining unit on a non-discriminatory basis.

This Court rejected both of the plaintiffs' objections. We held that the qualification test was the " 'minimum assurance' the Company could have of efficient operations," and that the company and union had gone "about as far as they could go in giving negroes a preference in filling Number 1 line vacancies, consistent with being *fair to incumbents and consistent with efficient management.*" 263 F.2d at 550 (emphasis added). The requirement that entrants into Line 1 start at the bottom job was justified as a business necessity:

"*Such a system was conceived out of business necessity,* not out of racial discrimination. An employee without proper training and with no proof of potential ability to rise higher, cannot expect to start in the middle of the ladder, regardless of plant seniority. It would be unfair to the skilled, experienced, and deserving employee to give a top or middle job to an unqualified employee. It would also destroy the whole system of lines of progression, *to the detriment of efficient management* and to the disadvantage of negro as well as white employees having a stake in orderly promotion." 263 F.2d at 550.

In *United States by Clark* v. *H. K. Porter Co.,* N.D. Ala. 1968, 296 F. Supp. 40, 90, the court rejected an attack by the Government upon "the procedure that the first man to [get] a job is the first to advance," *i.e.,* job seniority, super-imposed, as here, upon a history of racial discrimination. The court found, as a matter of fact, that it was not "permissible" to assume "on the record in this case" that

"with less than the amount of on-the-job training now acquired by

---

[14] See *Steele* v. *Louisville & Nashville R.R. Co.,* 323 U.S. 192, 65 S.Ct. 226, 89 L.Ed. 173, and *Syres* v. *Oil Workers International Union, Local 23,* 1955, 350 U.S. 892, 76 S.Ct. 152, 100 L.Ed. 785.

reason of the progression procedure, employees could move into the jobs in the progression lines and perform those jobs satisfactorily and—more importantly—without danger of physical injury to themselves and their fellow employees." 296 F. Supp. at 91.

In other words, the record in that case, as the district court viewed it, showed that safety and efficiency, the component factors of business necessity, would not allow relaxation of the job seniority system. We see no necessary conflict between *Porter's* holding on this point and our holding in the present case.

We have also considered two district court decisions cited by the defendants, *United States* v. *Sheet Metal Workers,* E.D. Mo. 1968, 280 F. Supp. 719, and *Griggs* v. *Duke Power Co.,* M.D.N.C. 1968, 292 F.2d 243. In *Sheet Metal Workers,* the defendant white unions had adopted a referral system giving priority to men with previous referrals. They had also discriminated racially before the effective date of the Act as had the union in Dobbins. On the other hand, they had adopted positive measures to encourage minority-group membership. The district court could find no person who had actually suffered on account of his race under the referral preference system and no "pattern or practice" of discrimination. (The sole plaintiff was the United States.) On the contrary, it found that "in every instance, qualified Negroes applying for union membership and/or apprenticeship training since July 2, 1965, have been admitted therein." 280 F. Supp. 729. Among union members, of course, the referral preference system might well have had the effect of favoring whites, since they would have had a greater chance to amass time under the collective bargaining agreement. On the other hand, if there was more than enough work to go around, the discriminatory tendency inherent in the referral rule might not have asserted itself. The opinion is silent on that critical fact, noting only that "the record is devoid of any specific instance of discrimination." 280 F. Supp. 730.

In *Griggs* the defendant employer had in the past limited Negroes to jobs in the labor department, excluding them from better work in other departments. The plaintiffs sought to overturn a requirement of ten years standing that any employee transferring into one of the formerly white departments have a high school education or passing marks on a qualification test. The court found that both the tests and the education requirements were not racially motivated, but were part of the company's effort to upgrade its work force. It took note of a specific provision in Title VII, § 703(h), that exempts from the operation of the Act the use of "any professionally developed ability test . . . not designed . . . to discriminate because of race" and went on to strike down an EEOC interpretation of that provision which would limit the exemption to tests that measure ability *"required* by *the particular job* or class of jobs which the applicant seeks."* (Emphasis added.) The court concluded that the defendant had not violated the Act, since it had not discriminated after July 2, 1965.

When an employer adopts a system that necessarily carries forward the incidents of discrimination into the present, his practice constitutes on-going discrimination, unless the incidents are limited to those that safety and efficiency require. That appears to be the premise for the Commission's interpretation of § 703(h). To the extent that *Griggs* departs from that view, we find it unpersuasive.

V

The defendants maintain that Congress specifically exempts seniority systems such as Crown's from the operation of Title VII. In support of their assertion the defendants cite that portion of § 703(h) which allows an employer to "apply different standards of compensation, or different terms, conditions, or privileges of employment *pursuant to a bona fide seniority* or merit system . . . provided that such differences are not the result of an intention to discriminate because of race, color, religion, sex, or national origin."

No doubt, Congress, to prevent "reverse discrimination" meant to protect certain seniority rights that could not have existed but for previous racial discrimination. For example a Negro who had been rejected by an employer on racial grounds before passage of the Act could not, after being hired, claim to outrank whites who had been hired before him but after his original rejection, even though the Negro might have had senior status but for the past discrimination. As the court pointed out in *Quarles,* the treatment of "job" or "department seniority" raises problems different from those discussed in the Senate debates: "a department seniority system that has its genesis in racial discrimination is not a bona fide seniority system." 279 F. Supp. at 517.

It is one thing for legislation to require the creation of *fictional* seniority for newly hired Negroes, and quite another thing for it to require that time *actually worked* in Negro jobs be given equal status with time worked in white jobs. To begin with, requiring employers to correct their pre-Act discrimination by creating fictional seniority for new Negro employees would not necessarily aid the actual victims of the previous discrimination. There would be no guaranty that the new employees had actually suffered exclusion at the hands of the employer in the past, or, if they had, there would be no way of knowing whether, after being hired, they would have continued to work for the same employer. In other words, creating fictional employment time for newly-hired Negroes would comprise preferential rather than remedial treatment. The clear thrust of the Senate debate is directed against such preferential treatment on the basis of race. That sentiment was codified in an important portion of Title VII, § 703(j):

"(j) Nothing contained in this subchapter shall be interpreted to require any employer, employment agency, labor organization, or joint labor-management committee subject to this subchapter to grant preferential treatment to any individual or to any group because of the race, color, religion, sex, or national origin of such individual or group on account of an imbalance which may exist with respect to the total number or percentage of persons of any race, color, religion, sex, or national origin employed by any employer, referred or classified for employment by any employment agency or labor organization, admitted to membership or classified by any labor organization, or admitted to, or employed in, any apprenticeship or other training program, in comparison with the total number or percentage of persons of such race, color, religion, sex, or national origin in any community, State, section, or other area, or in the available work force in any community, State, section, or other area." 42 U.S.C. § 2000e-2(j).

No stigma of preference attaches to recognition of time actually worked in Negro jobs as the equal of white time. The individual victims of prior discrimination in this case would necessarily be the ones—the only ones—to benefit by the institution of mill seniority, as modified in the decree. We conclude, in agreement with *Quarles,* that Congress exempted from the anti-discrimination requirements only those seniority rights that gave white workers preference over junior Negroes. This is not to say that *Whitfield* and *Quarles* and Title VII prohibit an employer from giving compensatory training and help to the Negro workers who have been discriminated against. Title VII's imposition of an affirmative duty on employers to undo past discrimination permits compensatory action for those who have suffered from prior discrimination.

## VI

We find unpersuasive the argument that, whatever its operational effects, job seniority is immune under the statute because not imposed with the *intent* to discriminate. Section 703(h), quoted earlier, excludes from the strictures of Title VII different working terms dictated by "bona fide" seniority systems "provided that such differences are *not the result of an intention to discriminate because of race. . . .*" [15] Here, how-

---

[15] "In determining the meaning of 'intentional,' resort must be had almost entirely to legislative history. In its original form, 706(g) contained no such requirement; it was amended by Senator Dirksen's proposal, probably in response to opposition pressure. The first draft of the amendment contained the word 'willfully' instead of 'intentionally'; interpretative material was introduced into the record by Senator Dirksen:

'The words "willful and willfully" as ordinarily employed, mean nothing more than that the person, of whose actions or default the expressions are used, knows what he is doing, intends what he is doing, and is a free agent. . . .

'The terms are also employed to denote an intentional act . . . as distinguished from an accidental act . . .

'This is precisely the situation which might exist if the words are not added. . . . Accidental, inadvertent, heedless, unintended acts could subject an employer to charges under the present language.'

"For reasons that are not apparent, this version was not enacted, and not until some time later was the amendment with the present language passed. The only significant difference between the two versions is the substitution of 'intentionally' for "willfully' and there is no indication that any strengthening of the requirement was meant. It may be concluded that the Dirksen Amendment does not greatly narrow the coverage of section 706(g)." Note, *Legal Implications of the Use of Standardized Ability Tests in Employment and Education,* 68 COL.L.REV. 691, 713 (1968).

ever, if Crown did not intend to punish Negroes as such by reinstituting job seniority, the differences between the job status of Negroes hired before 1966 and whites hired at the same time would have to be called the "result" of Crown's earlier, intentional discrimination. *Quarles* put it this way:

"The differences between the terms and conditions of employment for white [sic] and Negroes about which plaintiffs complain are the result of an intention to discriminate in hiring policies on the basis of race before January 1, 1966. The differences that originated before the act are maintained now. The act does not condone present differences that are the result of intention to discriminate before the effective date of the act, although such a provision could have been included in the act had Congress so intended. The court holds that the present differences in departmental seniority of Negroes and white [sic] that result from the company's intentional, racially discriminatory hiring policy before January 1, 1966 are not validated by the *proviso* of § 703(h)." 279 F. Supp. 517–18.

Section 706(g) limits injunctive (as opposed to declaratory) relief to cases in which the employer or union has *"intentionally engaged in"* an unlawful employment practice. Again, the statute, read literally, requires only that the defendant meant to do what he did, that is, his employment practice was not accidental. The relevant legislative history, quoted in the margin, bears out the language of the statute on that point.

Section 707(a) allows the Attorney General to enforce the Act only where there is a "pattern or practice of resistance to the full enjoyment of any of the rights secured by this subchapter" and where the pattern or practice "is *intended* to deny the full exercise of the rights herein described." Defendants contend that no such condition existed here. The same point arose in *Dobbins*. The court rejected it (292 F. Supp. at 448): "In reviewing statutes, rules or conduct which result in the effective denial of equal rights to Negroes or other minority groups, intention can be inferred from the operation and effect of the statute or rule or from the conduct itself. The conduct of defendant in the present case 'by its very nature' contains the implications of the required intent. *Local 357, Intern. Broth. of Teamsters, etc.* v. *National Labor Relations Board, 365* U.S. 667 at 675, 81 S.Ct. 835, 6 L.Ed.2d 11 (1961) citing *Radio Officers' Union, etc.* v. *National Labor Relations Board, 347* U.S. 17, 45, 74 S.Ct. 323, 98 L. Ed. 455 (1954). See also the remarks of then Senator Humphrey, 110 Cong. Rec. 14270 in reference to Title VII, 'Intention could be proved by or inferred from words, conduct or both.' Thus the Attorney General has a cause of action when the conduct of a labor organization in relation to N's or other minority groups has the effect of creating and preserving employment opportunities for W's only. Section 707(a) of the Civil Rights Act of 1964."

Here, as in *Dobbins*, the conduct engaged in had racially-determined effects. The requisite intent may be inferred from the fact that the defendants persisted in the conduct after its racial implications had become known to them. Section 707(a) demands no more.

## VII

The defendants contend that the letters and statements made by EEOC officials approving the merger of Crown's progression lines acted as a bar under § 713(b) of the Act to suit by either the Government or by the private plaintiffs Johnson, Hill, and Local 189–A. The relevant portion of § 713(b) reads as follows: "In any action or proceeding based on any alleged unlawful employment practice, no person shall be subject to any liability or punishment for or on account of (1) the commission by such person of an unlawful employment practice if he pleads and proves that the act or omission complained of was in good faith, in conformity with, and in reliance on any written interpretation or opinion of the Commission."

The key phrase in this provision is "written opinion or interpretation of the Commission." The EEOC published its own interpretation of the phrase in the *Federal Register* in June 1965, *before Title VII took effect and some six months before the public statements at issue here.* "Only (a) a letter entitled 'opinion letter' and signed by the General Counsel on behalf of the Commission or (b) matter published and so designated in the *Federal Register* may be considered a 'written interpretation or opinion of the Commission' within the meaning of section 713 of Title VII." 29 CFR § 1601.30.

The statements that Crown relied upon to its supposed detriment in this case do not fall within either of the defined categories. They appeared neither as portions of the *Federal Register* or as designated "opinion letters" over the signature of the General Counsel. We have merely a letter from Mr. Edelsberg, Executive Director, and a statement of Mr. Roosevelt, the Chairman of the Commission. Mr. Edelsberg was not General Counsel, nor did his letter bear the "opinion letter" label. Mr. Roosevelt issued his statement orally. The regulation clearly requires more.

Courts give great weight to an agency's interpretation of the statute that it administers.[16] The regulation here gives reasonable scope to the statutory provision. A broader reading might bind the Commission to informal or unapproved opinions volunteered by members of its staff.

We cannot help sharing Crown Zellerbach's bewilderment at the twists and turns indulged in by government agencies in this case. We feel compelled to hold, however, that neither the statement by Chairman Roosevelt nor the letter by Executor Director Edelsberg provides a legal defense to the present suit.

---

[16] *Zemel* v. *Rusk,* 1965, 381 U.S. 1, 85 S.Ct. 1271, 14 L.Ed.2d 179; *Udall* v. *Tallman,* 1965, 380 U.S. 1, 85 S.Ct. 792, 13 L.Ed.2d 616; *Power Reactor Development Corp.* v. *Int. U. of Elec.,* 1960, 367 U.S. 396, 81 S.Ct. 1529, 6 L.Ed.2d 924.

## VIII

Our main conclusions may be summarized as follows: (1) Crown's job seniority system carries forward the discriminatory effects integral to the company's former employment practices. (2) The safe and efficient operation of the Bogalusa mill does not depend upon maintenance of the job seniority system. (3) To the extent that Crown and the white union insisted upon carrying forward exclusion of a racially-determined class, *without business necessity,* they committed, with the requisite intent, in the statutory sense, an unfair employment practice as defined by Title VII.

The district court thoughtfully worked a decree studded with provisos to protect the employer from the imposition of unsafe or inefficient practices and at the same time prevent racial discrimination. The decree also specifically provides that job seniority may still apply to bidding between one white employee and other. By making the decree applicable only to bidding that involves Negroes hired before 1966, the district court limited the remedy to the scope of the illegal conduct. The judgment of the district court is affirmed.

### ON PETITION FOR REHEARING AND PETITION FOR REHEARING EN BANG

PER CURIAM: The Petition for Rehearing is denied and no member of this panel nor Judge in regular active service on the Court having requested that the Court be polled on rehearing en banc, (Rule 35 Federal Rules of Appellate Procedure; Local Fifth Circuit Rule 12) the Petition for Rehearing En Banc is denied.

## TITLE VII, SENIORITY AND THE SUPREME COURT: CLARIFICATION OR RETREAT? *

*26 Kansas Law Review, 1, 12-19 (1977)*
James E. Jones, Jr.

### II.  SENIORITY IN THE SUPREME COURT IN OCTOBER TERM, 1975-1976

In order that we may have a frame of reference against which to evaluate the implications of the Supreme Court's decision in *Franks* v. *Bowman Transportation Co.* we need first to examine the cases pending before the Supreme Court contemporaneously with *Bowman,* and then to search the disposition of those cases by the Supreme Court after *Bowman* for such implications as might appear. The departmental seniority and job seniority cases had settled into a generally predictable pattern for the incumbent Black following the *Quarles* and *Local 189* analyses.

* Reprinted by permission. Copyright © 1977 by the Kansas Law Review.

The presiding seniority issue in the Supreme Court at October Term 1975, concerned the problems of layoffs. It is curious that even in the Fifth Circuit the promotion cases that have been suggested as providing a bridge to challenging plant-wide seniority cases have not received the same attention as the layoff cases. Perhaps this result is dictated by economic conditions.

A.   *Seniority Cases Pending Before the Court*

The *Waters* v. *Wisconsin Steel Works* case was the first contemporary of *Bowman* to seek Supreme Court review. Wisconsin Steel Works is an International Harvester plant in Chicago that hired its first Black bricklayers in its bricklaying department in 1964. Waters, one of the five Blacks hired, had applied to the company earlier and had been turned down. A change in the steelmaking process motivated the company to cut back in its bricklaying department, and by March 1965 more than thirty bricklayers had been laid off, including all five of the Blacks. Plaintiff Waters and three others had been laid off pursuant to the last hired, first fired seniority system, even before completing their three month probationary period. The company viewed the cutback as permanent and, along with the union, changed the collective bargaining agreement to provide severance pay for long-service bricklayers. The contract provided, however, that by opting for severance pay, the two-year right to recall under the contract was forfeited. A number of the white bricklayers with long service accepted the severance pay option. When it turned out the company's estimate of its long term labor needs was wrong, the severance pay agreement was amended to permit recall of the white bricklayers. Several white workers who had accepted severance pay were returned to work with Wisconsin Steel Works, despite the pendency of reapplication by Waters and an application by Samuels, a new Black applicant. Waters, who had no recall right because of his failure to complete the probationary period, was later rehired for two months in 1967.

Plaintiffs filed a complaint with the Equal Employment Opportunity Commission (EEOC) challenging the company's hiring and layoff policies as discriminatory under Title VII. At first, the Commission found no probable cause, but subsequent evidence, particularly the severance agreement, caused the Commission to change its mind and determine that plaintiffs did have cause to sue. The district court found that both the seniority system and the severance agreement violated Title VII and 42 U.S.C. § 1981. The Seventh Circuit Court of Appeals, however, reversed on the seniority system, but affirmed the illegality of the severance agreement as it applied to Waters. While agreeing with the lower court that the company had discriminated in hiring prior to 1964, the Seventh Circuit nevertheless held that the last hired, first fired seniority system was not itself racially discriminatory, nor did it have the effect of perpetuating prior racial discrimination in violation of Title VII. The court found

the seniority system to be bona fide and supported by the distinction between departmental and plant-wide seniority that emerged from the
dicta in *Local 189*. The court felt that to alter these rights earned by
length of service would be placing the burden of past discrimination
created by the employer upon the shoulders of the innocent white employees. In addition, the court held that the seniority system that it
determined to be acceptable under Title VII was lawful under 42 U.S.C.
§ 1981. This determination was made in the face of the uniformly affirmed
position that the equal employment provisions of Title VII do not super-
sede the provisions of section 1981. Moreover, the remedies fashioned by
Congress in Title VII were not intended to preempt the general remedial
language of the older law.

Meanwhile, the Third Circuit Court of Appeals was faced with a
rather novel procedural situation in 1974 in *Jersey Central Power &
Light Co.* v. *IBEW Local 327*. The Jersey Central Power and Light Company was anticipating layoffs and brought an action against the unions
representing its employees and the EEOC for declaratory judgment to
resolve an apparent conflict between obligations imposed by an EEOC
conciliation agreement and the collective bargaining agreement. The
company also sought to broaden the declaratory judgment to include
its obligation under Title VII and under Executive Order No. 11,246,
but the district court apparently excluded consideration of these broader
laws and restricted its consideration to construing what the judge called
two contracts.

The EEOC conciliation agreement provided for a five year affirmative
action hiring program to increase the percentages of minorities and
women in Jersey Central's work force. The collective bargaining agreement provided for layoffs in inverse order of employment date. Obviously, if the collective bargaining agreement operated in the normal
last hired, first fired procedure, there would be substantial decrease in
the percentage of minorities and females remaining in Jersey Central's
work force if the planned layoffs came about. In viewing the potential
conflict between these two agreements, the lower court ruled that to the
extent the terms of the contracts were inconsistent, the EEOC agreement
should prevail. To carry this out, the court ordered the use of three
seniority lists—one for minorities, one for women, and one for other
employees. Layoffs were to be apportioned among them so that when
they were completed the percentage that had been achieved by the
affirmative action plan would be maintained.

The Third Circuit Court of Appeals reversed and held that the collective bargaining agreement controlled the order of layoffs despite the
disproportionate impact on minorities and female workers. While the
court agreed that the controversy was a matter of contract law, the court
interpreted the conciliation agreement of the EEOC as not being in
conflict with or frustrated by the collective bargaining agreement. In its
view, the conciliation agreement was directed solely to hiring and explicitly incorporated the collective bargaining agreement for other aspects

of employment. The court went on to consider whether the seniority clause was invalid as contrary to public policy and to delineate the type of evidence the district court could entertain on remand or in a related case. The majority held that a seniority clause providing for layoffs by reverse order of seniority was not contrary to public policy and welfare, and consequently was not subject to modification by court decree. Moreover, the court, relying on *Waters* and *Local 189* for support, concluded that "Congress intended to bar proof of the 'perpetuating' effect of a plant-wide seniority system as it regarded such systems as 'bona fide'" although it recognized that these systems might well perpetuate past discriminatory practices. "[T]he only evidence probative in a challenge to a plant-wide seniority system would be evidence directed to its bona fide character; that is, evidence directed either to the neutrality of the seniority system or evidence directed to ascertaining an intent or design to disguise discrimination."

A concurring opinion in the *Jersey Central* case rejected the view that only proof of subjective intent could warrant relief from the use of a plant-wide seniority system that had a disparate impact. Judge Van Dusen found persuasive the analysis in *Watkins* v. *USW Local 2369* that legislative history did not preclude the alteration of the plant-wide seniority that perpetuates discrimination. He opined that the consequences test expressed in *Griggs* v. *Duke Power Co.*, as well as the rationale of the departmental seniority cases, applied equally to plant-wide seniority systems when the plant formally hired on a white-only basis.

The Third Circuit need not have addressed the reverse layoff issue so expansively. It could have restricted its views to the question of conflict between the EEOC conciliation agreement and the collective bargaining agreement, and accepted the limited legal problem presented by the district court's disposition of the matter. The position in *Waters* already noted, the discussion of Judge Van Dusen that brings *Watkins* into focus, and the *Jersey Central* case present more difficult problems to be resolved in the seniority layoff cases than that which is squarely presented in *Bowman*.

The *Watkins* case does not precisely belong in an article seeking to explore the implications of the Supreme Court's position on layoff/seniority cases before it in October Term 1975. Although this case has been much commented upon in most of the layoff and seniority articles, Supreme Court review of the Fifth Circuit's decision was not sought in *Watkins*. As noted in the discussion of *Jersey Central*, however, the concurring opinion relying on the lower court's reasoning in *Watkins* justifies attention to that case in this Article, particularly in view of the Supreme Court's disposition of *Jersey Central*.

In *Watkins* v. *USW Local 2369*, defendant Continental Can Company had operated a plant in Harvey, Louisiana for many years. With the exception of two Blacks hired during World War II, only whites were hired at this plant until 1965. By the end of 1966 there were only three Blacks—including the original two—out of four hundred ten hourly employees. In 1967 and 1968 the company began hiring Blacks and at one point in 1971 there were over fifty Blacks among a total of four hundred hourly employees. In 1971, however, substantial cutbacks in employment began at the Harvey plant and by April 1973 there were only one hundred fifty-two hourly employees left. The collective bargaining agreement required layoffs to be made on the basis of total employment seniority with the last man to be hired, the first to be laid off. Laid-off employees were on a recall list to be reemployed, as needed, in the reverse order of the layoff. The contract provisions were followed in the layoffs, and employees hired as early as 1951 were affected. Necessarily, all the Blacks hired after 1965 were laid off and, except for the two Blacks hired in the 1940s, the company's work force was all white. Moreover, the first 138 positions on the recall list belonged to whites, and of a total of 172 names on these lists, there were 13 Blacks between positions 139 to 172. Under the recall provisions it would be many years before the company could be expected to employ another Black. Not only did the company concede racial discrimination up to 1962, but the court concluded that plaintiffs had sustained the burden of proving discrimination by the company prior to 1963. Consequently there was no disputing prior discrimination in this case.

Judge Cassibry decided that plaintiffs were entitled to the relief sought. The court held that on the facts of the case, defendant's layoffs and recall practices discriminated on the grounds of race in violation of Title VII of the Civil Rights Act of 1964 and in violation of the Civil Rights Act of 1866.

The judge ordered defendants to refrain from discriminating, to determine the percentage of Blacks in the work force in 1971 when the layoffs commenced, and to identify and reinstate with back pay a number of Blacks sufficient to regain the proportion employed by the company on the 1971 date. Moreover, no incumbent white workers were to be laid off at the time of the reinstatement and no employee's weekly pay was to be reduced. The order was temporary, in that any employee offered immediate recall who declined to return to work forfeited any rights under the decree and could exercise only those rights spelled out in the contract. The order required, in the event of future layoffs after the ratio had been returned to the 1971 status, that these future layoffs be allocated between white employees and Black employees so that the percentage prevailing would be maintained. Concerning future recalls, the names on the existing lists were to be divided on a racial basis and recalled on a one-white-one-Black basis using the separate lists until all persons on the Black list had been recalled to work. Subsequently, the company could fill existing vacancies from the white list until all the names on that list were recalled or until recall rights were lost. Then the company was required exclusively to hire Black persons available until the then current percentage of Black employment in the work force equaled the percentage of Black employees on active nonprobationary status on the last date in 1971 on which a new employee was hired.

Judge Cassibry correctly viewed *Watkins* as a case of first impression, but he found strong support for his disposition of the case in two lines of related cases. The first series of cases involved the legality of departmental or job seniority systems in the context of industrial plants that formerly maintained segregated work forces. The other related line of cases relied upon by the court concerned work referral rules in previously all-white craft unions.

The Fifth Circuit reversed Judge Cassibry, holding that "[R]egardless of an earlier history of employment discrimination, when present hiring practices are nondiscriminatory and have been for over ten years, an employer's use of a long-established seniority system for determining who will be laid off, and who will be rehired, adopted without intent to discriminate, is not a violation of Title VII or § 1981, even though the use of the seniority system results in the discharge of more blacks than whites to the point of eliminating blacks from the work force, where the individual employees who suffer layoff under the system have not themselves been the subject of prior employment discrimination."

The Fifth Circuit viewed its decision as being in line with the Third and Seventh Circuits in *Waters* and *Jersey Central,* respectively. The court specifically noted, however, that it did not "decide the rights of a laid-off employee who could show that, . . . but for his failure to obtain earlier employment because of exclusion of minority employees from the work force, he would have sufficient seniority to be insulated against layoff."

The Fifth Circuit relied heavily upon its own opinion in *Local 189,* regarding the bona fide nature of the seniority system when a plant seniority system was in effect and its view that granting "fictional seniority" was prohibited under Title VII. The court concluded that in the *Watkins* layoff situation there was a bona fide seniority system in operation that was protected by section 703(h) of Title VII. The court pointed out that its position was anticipated in its own decision in *Local 189.*

Before turning to the discussion of *Bowman,* a brief mention of *Meadows* v. *Ford Motor Co.* is appropriate. Dolores Marie Meadows brought a class action under Title VII of the Civil Rights Act of 1964 for back pay and injunctive relief, alleging sex discrimination in hiring. The district court granted partial summary judgment in finding defendant liable, but denied back pay and retroactive seniority. Plaintiffs established that between April 1971 and April 1973 the Ford Motor Company, at its new truck plant near Louisville, Kentucky, had hired nine hundred men. On the basis of a 150-pound weight requirement for production job eligibility, however, the company had hired no women. On review, the Sixth Circuit held that both back pay and date of application seniority would be permissible remedies under Title VII. Rejecting the argument that the equitable discretion of the court was somehow restricted, the court declared that "[i]f eligibility and discriminatory refusal are established, then back pay should be fully awarded, including compen-

sation for fringe benefits then enjoyed by employees." On the seniority issue, the court recognized that there were even greater problems involved in an award of retroactive job seniority than in determining matters of back pay and other fringe benefits. The court opined as follows:
"Seniority is a system of job security calling for a reduction of work forces in periods of low production by layoff first of those employees with the most recent dates of hire. It is justified among workers by the concept that the older workers in point of service have earned their retention of jobs by the length of prior services for the particular employer. From the employer's point of view, it is justified by the fact that it means retention of the most experienced and presumably most skilled of the work force. Obviously, the grant of fully retroactive seniority would collide with both of these principles."
The court noted that while the burden of retroactive pay would fall upon the party who violated the law, the burden of retroactive seniority for layoff purposes would be borne by other workers who were innocent of any wrongdoing. The court determined, however, that there was no provision to be found in the statute that prohibited retroactive seniority, and held that the remedy for the wrong of discriminatory refusal to hire lay in the first instance with the district judge. For the trial court's guidance on this issue it observed, however, that a grant of retroactive seniority would not depend solely upon the existence of a record sufficient to justify back pay under the standards of the back pay section of its opinion. The court would also need to consider the interests of the workers who might be displaced and the interests of the employer in retaining an experienced work force. "We do not assume, as our brethren in the Fifth Circuit appeared to (*Local 189, AFL-CIO, CLC* v. *United States*, 416 F.2d 980, *cert. denied*, 397 U.S. 919, 90 S.Ct. 926, 25 L.Ed.2d 100 (1970)), that such reconciliation is impossible, but as is obvious, we certainly do foresee genuine difficulties."

Thus, the Sixth Circuit bluntly asserted that given discriminatory hiring, the federal judges at the district court level have the authority in an appropriate case to grant retroactive seniority as a part of make-whole relief.

It was significant at the time, with so many cases following the lead of the Fifth Circuit in *Local 189*, that this court declared its disagreement with the limited view of the equitable powers of the district courts. The *Meadows* case was pending certiorari when *Bowman* was decided. [Footnotes omitted—Ed.]

(4)  *Fictional Seniority and the Limits of Remedy*

## FRANKS v. BOWMAN TRANSPORTATION CO.

*Supreme Court of the United States, 1976*
*427 U.S. 747, 12 FEP Cases 549*

MR. JUSTICE BRENNAN delivered the opinion of the Court.
This case presents the question whether identifiable applicants who

were denied employment because of race after the effective date and in violation of Title VII of the Civil Rights Act of 1964, 42 U.S.C. § 2000e *et seq.,* may be awarded seniority status retroactive to the dates of their employment applications.[1]

Petitioner Franks brought this class action in the United States District Court for the Northern District of Georgia against his former employer, respondent Bowman Transportation Company, and his unions, the International Union of District 50, Allied and Technical Workers of the United States and Canada and its local, No. 13600, alleging various racially discriminatory employment practices in violation of Title VII. Petitioner Lee intervened on behalf of himself and others similarly situated alleging racially discriminatory hiring and discharge policies limited to Bowman's employment of over-the-road (OTR) truck drivers. Following trial, the District Court found Bowman had engaged in a pattern of racial discrimination in various company policies, including the hiring, transfer, and discharge of employees, and found further that the discriminatory practices were perpetrated in Bowman's collective-bargaining agreement with the unions. The District Court certified the action as a proper class action under Fed. Rule Civ. Proc. 23(b)(2) and, of import to the issues before this Court, found that petitioner Lee represented all black applicants who sought to be hired or to transfer to OTR driving positions prior to January 1, 1972. In its final order and decree, the District Court subdivided the class represented by petitioner Lee into a class of black nonemployee applicants for OTR positions prior to January 1, 1972 (class 3), and a class of black employees who applied to transfer to OTR positions prior to the same date (class 4).

In its final judgment entered July 14, 1972, the District Court permanently enjoined the respondents from perpetuating the discriminatory practices found to exist, and, in regard to the black applicants for OTR positions, ordered Bowman to notify the members of both subclasses within 30 days of their right to priority considerations for such jobs. The District Court declined, however, to grant to the unnamed members of classes 3 and 4 any other specific relief sought, which included an award of backpay and seniority status retroactive to the date of individual application for an OTR position.

On petitioners' appeal to the Court of Appeals for the Fifth Circuit, raising for the most part claimed inadequacy of the relief ordered respecting unnamed members of the various subclasses involved, the Court of Appeals affirmed in part, reversed in part, and vacated in part. 495 F.2d 398, 8 FEP Cases 66. The Court of Appeals held that the District Court had exercised its discretion under an erroneous view of law insofar as it failed to award backpay to the unnamed class members of both classes 3 and 4, and vacated the judgment in that respect. The judgment was reversed insofar as it failed to award any seniority remedy to the members

---

[1] [Footnotes numbered as in original.—Ed.] Petitioners also alleged an alternative claim for relief for violations of 42 U.S.C. § 1981. In view of our decision we have no occasion to address that claim.

of class 4 who after the judgment of the District Court sought and obtained priority consideration for transfer to OTR positions.[3] As respects unnamed members of class 3—nonemployee black applicants who applied for and were denied OTR prior to January 1, 1972—the Court of Appeals affirmed the District Court's denial of any form of seniority relief. Only this last aspect of the Court of Appeals' judgment is before us for review under our grant of the petition for certiorari. 420 U.S. 989 (1975).

## I

[The Court first determined that the claim of Petitioner Lee was not moot, even though Lee had been discharged for cause.]

## II

In affirming the District Court's denial of seniority relief to the class 3 groups of discriminatees, the Court of Appeals held that the relief was barred by § 703(h) of Title VII, 42 U.S.C. § 2000e-2(h). We disagree. Section 703(h) provides in pertinent part that:

"Notwithstanding any other provision of this title it shall not be an unlawful employment practice for an employer to apply different standards of compensation, or different terms, conditions, or privileges of employment pursuant to a bona fide seniority or merit system . . . provided that such differences are not the result of an intention to discriminate because of race, color, religion, sex, or national origin. . . ."

The Court of Appeals reasoned that a discriminatory refusal to hire "does not affect the bona fides of the seniority system. Thus, the differences in the benefits and conditions of employment which a seniority system accords to old and newer employees is protected as 'not an unlawful employment practice' [by § 703(h)]." 495 F.2d, at 417, 8 FEP Cases, at 800. Significantly, neither Bowman nor the unions undertake to defend the Court of Appeals judgment on that ground. It is clearly erroneous.

The black applicants for OTR positions composing class 3 are limited to those whose applications were put in evidence at the trial.[10] The underlying legal wrong affecting them is not the alleged operation of a racially

---

[3] In conjunction with its directions to the District Court regarding seniority relief for the members of other subclasses not involved in the issues presently confronting this Court, the Court of Appeals directed that class 4 members who transferred to OTR positions under the District Court's decree should be allowed to carry over all accumulated company seniority for all purposes in the OTR department. 495 F.2d, at 417, 8 FEP Cases, at 79.

[10] By its terms, the judgment of the District Court runs to all black applicants for OTR positions prior to January 1, 1972, and is not qualified by a limitation that the discriminatory refusal to hire must have taken place after the effective date of the Act. However, only post-Act victims of racial discrimination are members of class 3. Title VII's prohibition on racial discrimination in hiring became effective on July 2, 1965, one year after the date of its enactment. Pub. L. 88-352, § 716(a)-(b); 78 Stat. 253. Petitioners sought relief in this case for identifiable applicants for OTR positions "whose applications were put in evidence at the trial." App., at 20a. There are 206 unhired black applicants prior to January 1, 1972, whose written applications are summarized in the record and none of the applications relates to years prior to 1970. App., at 52a, Table VA.

discriminatory seniority system but of a racially discriminatory hiring system. Petitioners do not ask modification or elimination of the existing seniority system, but only an award of the seniority status they would have individually enjoyed under the present system but for the illegal discriminatory refusal to hire. It is this context that must shape our determination as the meaning and effect of § 703(h).

On its face, § 703(h) appears to be only a definitional provision; as with the other provisions of § 703, subsection (h) delineates which employment practices are illegal and thereby prohibited and which are not. Section 703(h) certainly does not expressly purport to qualify or proscribe relief otherwise appropriate under the remedial provisions of Title VII, § 706(g), 42 U.S.C. § 2000e-5(g) in circumstances where an illegal discriminatory act or practice is found. Further, the legislative history of § 703(h) plainly negates its reading as limiting or qualifying the relief authorized under § 706(g). The initial bill reported by the House Judiciary Committee as H.R. 7152 and passed by the full House on February 10, 1964, did not contain § 703(h). Neither the House bill nor the majority Judiciary Committee Report even mentioned the problem of seniority. That subject thereafter surfaced during the debate of the bill in the Senate. This debate prompted Senators Clark and Case to respond to criticism that Title VII would destroy existing seniority systems by placing an Interpretive Memorandum in the Congressional Record. The Memorandum stated that "Title VII would have no effect on established seniority rights. Its effect is prospective and not retrospective." 110 Cong. Rec. 7213 (1964). Senator Clark also placed in the Congressional Record a Justice Department statement concerning Title VII which stated that "it has been asserted that Title VII would undermine vested rights of seniority. This is not correct. Title VII would have no effect on seniority rights existing at the time it takes effect." 110 Cong. Rec. 7207 (1964).[16] Several weeks thereafter, following several informal conferences among the Senate leadership, the House leadership, the Attorney General and others, see Vass, *Title VII: Legislative History,* 7 B.C. IND. & COM. L. REV. 431, 445 (1966), a compromise substitute bill prepared by Senators Mansfield and Dirksen, Senate majority and minority leaders respectively, containing § 703(h) was introduced on the Senate floor. Although the Mansfield-Dirksen substitute bill, and hence § 703(h), was not the subject of a committee report, see generally Vass, *supra,* Senator Humphrey, one of the informal conferees, later stated during debate on the substitute that

---

[16] The full text of the Statement introduced by Senator Clark pertinent to seniority states:

"First, it has been asserted that title VII would undermine vested rights of seniority. This is not correct. Title VII would have no effect on seniority rights existing at the time it takes effect. If, for example, a collective bargaining contract provides that in the event of layoffs, those who were hired last must be laid off first, such a provision would not be affected in the least by title VII. This would be true even in the case where owing to discrimination prior to the effective date of the title, white workers had more seniority than Negroes. Title VII is directed at discrimination based on race, color, religion, sex, or national origin. It is perfectly clear that when a worker is laid

§ 703(h) was not designed to alter the meaning of Title VII generally but rather "merely clarifies its present intent and effect." 110 Cong. Rec. 12,723 (1964) (remarks of Sen. Humphrey). Accordingly, whatever the exact meaning and scope of § 703(h) in light of its unusual legislative history and the absence of the usual legislative materials, see Vass, *supra,* at 457-458, it is apparent that the thrust of the section is directed toward defining what is and what is not an illegal discriminatory practice in instances in which the post-Act operation of a seniority system is challenged as perpetuating the effects of discrimination occurring prior to the effective date of the Act. There is no indication in the legislative materials that § 703(h) was intended to modify or restrict relief otherwise appropriate once an illegal discriminatory practice occurring after the effective date of the Act is proved—as in the instant case, a discriminatory refusal to hire. This accords with the apparently unanimous view of commentators, see Cooper and Sobol, *Seniority and Testing Under Fair Employment Laws: A General Approach to Objective Criteria of Hiring and Promotion,* 82 HARV. L. REV. 1598, 1632 (1969); Stacy, *Title VII Seniority Remedies in a Time of Economic Downturn,* 28 VAND. L. REV. 487, 506 (1975).[18] We therefore hold that the Court of Appeals erred in concluding that, as a matter of law, § 703(h) barred the award of seniority relief to the unnamed class 3 members.

---

off or denied a chance for promotion because under established seniority rules he is "low man on the totem pole" he is not being discriminated against because of his race. Of course, if the seniority rule itself is discriminatory, it would be unlawful under title VII. If a rule were to state that all Negroes must be laid off before any white man, such a rule could not serve as the basis for a discharge subsequent to the effective date of the title. I do not know how anyone could quarrel with such a result. But, in the ordinary case, assuming that seniority rights were built up over a period of time during which Negroes were not hired, these rights would not be set aside by the taking effect of title VII. Employers and labor organizations would simply be under a duty not to discriminate against Negroes because of their race. Any differences in treatment based on established seniority rights would not be based on race and would not be forbidden by the title." 110 Cong. Rec. 7207 (1964).

Senator Clark also introduced into the Congressional Record a set of answers to a series of questions propounded by Senator Dirksen. Two of these questions and answers are pertinent to the issue of seniority:

"Question. Would the same situation prevail in respect to promotions, when that management function is governed by a labor contract calling for promotion on the basis of seniority? What of dismissals? Normally, labor contracts call for 'last hired, first fired.'

"If the last hired are Negroes, is the employer discriminating if his contract requires they be first fired and the remaining employees are white?

"Answer. Seniority rights are in no way affected by the bill. If under a 'last hired, first fired' agreement a Negro happens to be the 'last hired,' he can still be 'first fired' as long as it is done because of his status as 'last hired' and not because of his race.

"Question. If an employer is directed to abolish his employment list because of discrimination what happens to seniority?

"Answer. The bill is not retroactive, and it will not require an employer to change existing seniority lists." 110 Cong. Rec. 7217 (1964).

[18] Cf. Gould, *Employment Security, Seniority and Race: The Role of Title VII of the Civil Rights Act of 1964,* 13 How. L. J. 1, 8-9, and n. 32 (1967); see also *Jurinko* v. *Edwin L. Weigand Company,* 477 F.2d 1038, 5 FEP Cases 925 (CA3), *vacated and remanded on other grounds,* 414 U.S. 970, 6 FEP Cases 795 (1973), wherein the court awarded back seniority in a case of discriminatory hiring after the effective date of Title VII without any discussion of the impact of § 703 (h) on the propriety of such a remedy.

## III

There remains the question whether an award of seniority relief is appropriate under the remedial provisions of Title VII, specifically, § 706 (g).

We begin by repeating the observation of earlier decisions that in enacting Title VII of the Civil Rights Act of 1964, Congress intended to prohibit all practices in whatever form which create inequality in employment opportunity due to discrimination on the basis of race, religion, sex, or national origin. *Alexander* v. *Gardner-Denver Co.,* 415 U.S. 36, 44, 7 FEP Cases 81, 84 (1974); *McDonnell Douglas Corp.* v. *Green,* 411 U.S. 792, 800, 5 FEP Cases 965, 969 (1973); *Griggs* v. *Duke Power Co.,* 401 U.S. 424, 429-430, 3 FEP Cases 175, 178 (1971), and ordained that its policy of outlawing such discrimination should have the "highest priority," *Alexander, supra,* at 47, 7 FEP Cases at 85; *Newman* v. *Piggie Park Enterprises, Inc.,* 390 U.S. 400, 402 (1968). Last Term's *Albemarle Paper Company* v. *Moody,* 422 U.S. 405, 10 FEP Cases 1181 (1975), consistently with the congressional plan, held that one of the central purposes of Title VII is "to make persons whole for injuries suffered on account of unlawful employment discrimination." *Id.,* at 418, 10 FEP Cases at 1189. To effectuate this "make-whole" objective, Congress in § 706(g) vested broad equitable discretion in the federal courts to "order such affirmative action as may be appropriate, which may include, but is not limited to, reinstatement or hiring of employees, with or without backpay . . ., or any other relief as the court deems appropriate." *Ibid.* The legislative history supporting the 1972 Amendments of § 706(g) of Title VII [20] affirms the breadth of this discretion. "The provisions of [Section 706(g)] are intended to give the courts wide discretion exercising their equitable powers to fashion the most complete relief possible. . . . [T]he Act is intended to make the victims of unlawful employment discrimination whole and . . . the attainment of this objective . . . requires that persons aggrieved by the consequences and effects of the unlawful employment practice be, so far as possible, restored to a position where they would have been were it not for the unlawful discrimination." Section by Section Analysis of H. R. 1746, accompanying The Equal Employment Opportunity Act of 1972—Conference Report, 118 Cong. Rec. 7166, 7168 (1972). This is emphatic confirmation that federal courts are empowered to fashion such relief as the particular circumstances of a case may require to effect restitution, making whole insofar as possible the victims of racial discrimination in hiring.[21] Adequate relief may well be denied

[20] Equal Employment Opportunity Act of 1972, Pub. L. No. 92-261, 86 Stat. 104, amending 42 U.S.C. § 2000e *et seq.*

[21] It is true that backpay is the only remedy specifically mentioned in § 706(g). But to draw from this fact and other sections of the statute, 12 FEP Cases at 564, any implicit statement by Congress that seniority relief is a prohibited, or at least less available form of remedy is not warranted. Indeed, any such contention necessarily disregards the extensive legislative history underlying the 1972 Amendments to Title VII. The 1972 Amendments added the phrase speaking to "other equitable relief" in § 706 (g). The Senate Report manifested an explicit concern with the "earnings gap" presently

in the absence of a seniority remedy slotting the victim in that position in the seniority system that would have been his had he been hired at the time of his application. It can hardly be questioned that ordinarily such relief will be necessary to achieve the "make-whole" purposes of the Act.

Seniority systems and the entitlements conferred by credits earned thereunder are of vast and increasing importance in the economic employment system of this Nation. S. Slichter, J. Healy, and E. Livernash, THE IMPACT OF COLLECTIVE BARGAINING ON MANAGEMENT, 104-115 (1960). Seniority principles are increasingly used to allocate entitlements to scarce benefits among competing employees ("competitive status" seniority) and to compute noncompetitive benefits earned under the contract of employment ("benefit" seniority). *Ibid.* We have already said about "competitive status" seniority that it "has become of overriding importance, and one of its major functions is to determine who gets or who keeps an available job." *Humphrey* v. *Moore,* 375 U.S. 335, 346-347, 55 LRRM 2031 (1964). "More than any other provision of the collective [bargaining] agreement . . . seniority affects the economic security of the individual employee covered by its terms." Aaron, *Reflections on the Legal Nature and Enforceability of Seniority Rights,* 75 HARV. L. REV. 1532, 1535 (1962). "Competitive status" seniority also often plays a broader role in modern employment systems, particularly systems operated under collective bargaining agreements:

---

existing between black and white employees in American society. S. Rep. No. 415, 92d Cong., 1st Sess., 6 (1971). The Reports of both Houses of Congress indicated that "rightful place" was the intended objective of Title VII and the relief accorded thereunder. *Ibid.;* H. R. Rep. No. 238, 92d Cong., 1st Sess., 4 (1971). As indicated, *infra,* n. 28, 12 FEP Cases at 556, rightful place seniority, implicating an employee's *future* earnings, job security and advancement prospects, is absolutely essential to obtaining this congressionally mandated goal.

The legislative history underlying the 1972 Amendments completely answers the argument that Congress somehow intended seniority relief to be less available in pursuit of this goal. In explaining the need for the 1972 Amendments, the Senate Report stated: "Employment discrimination as viewed today is a . . . complex and pervasive phenomenon. Experts familiar with the subject now generally describe the problem in terms of 'systems' and 'effects' rather than simply intentional wrongs, and the literature on the subject is replete with discussions of, for example, the mechanics of seniority and lines of progression, perpetuation of the present effect of pre-act discriminatory practices through various institutional devices, and testing and validation requirements." S. Rep., *supra,* at 5. See also H.R. Rep., *supra,* at 8. In the context of this express reference to seniority, the Reports of both Houses cite with approval decisions of the lower federal courts which granted forms of retroactive "rightful place" seniority relief. S. Rep., *supra,* at 5 n. 1; H. Rep., *supra,* at 8 n. 2. (The dissent, *post,* at n. 18, 12 FEP Cases at 568, would distinguish these lower federal court decisions as not involving instances of discriminatory *hiring.* Obviously, however, the concern of the entire thrust of the dissent—the impact of rightful place seniority upon the expectations of other employees—is in no way a function of the specific type of illegal discriminatory practice upon which the judgment of liability is predicated.) Thereafter, in language that could hardly be more explicit, the Conference Report stated:

"In any area where the new law does not address itself, or in any areas where a specific contrary intention is not indicated, it was assumed *that the present case law as developed by the courts would continue to govern the applicability and construction of Title VII.*" Section-by-Section Analysis of H. R. 1746, accompanying The Equal Opportunity Act of 1972—Conference Report, 118 Cong. Rec. 7166 (1972) (emphasis added).

"Included among the benefits, options, and safeguards affected by competitive status seniority, are not only promotion and layoff, but also transfer, demotion, rest days, shift assignments, prerogative in scheduling vacation, order of layoff, possibilities of lateral transfer to avoid layoff, "bumping" possibilities in the face of layoff, order of recall, training opportunities, working conditions, length of layoff endured without reducing seniority, length of layoff recall rights will withstand, overtime opportunities, parking privileges, and in one plant, a preferred place in the punch-out line." Stacy, 28 VAND. L. REV., at 490 (footnotes omitted).

Seniority standing in employment with respondent Bowman, computed from the departmental date of hire, determines the order of layoff and recall of employees. Further, job assignments for OTR drivers are posted for competitive bidding and seniority is used to determine the highest bidder. As OTR drivers are paid on a per-mile basis, earnings are therefore to some extent a function of seniority. Additionally, seniority computed from the company date-of-hire determines the length of an employee's vacation and pension benefits. Obviously merely to require Bowman to hire the class 3 victim of discrimination falls far short of a "make whole" remedy.[27] A concomitant award of the seniority credit he presumptively would have earned but for the wrongful treatment would also seem necessary in the absence of justification for denying that relief. Without an award of seniority dating from the time at which he was discriminatorily refused employment, an individual who applies for and obtains employment as an OTR driver pursuant to the District Court's order will never obtain his rightful place in the hierarchy of seniority according to which these various employment benefits are distributed. He will perpetually remain subordinate to persons who, but for the illegal discrimination, would have been in respect to entitlement to these benefits his inferiors.[28]

The Court of Appeals apparently followed this reasoning in holding that the District Court erred in not granting seniority relief to class 4 Bowman employees who were discriminatorily refused transfer to OTR positions. Yet the class 3 discriminatees in the absence of a comparable

[27] Further, at least in regard to "benefit"-type seniority such as length of vacation leave and pension benefits in the instant case, any general bar to the award of retroactive seniority for victims of illegal hiring discrimination serves to undermine the mutually reinforcing effect of the dual purposes of Title VII; it reduces the restitution required of an employer at such time as he is called upon to account for his discriminatory actions perpetrated in violation of the law. See *Albemarle Paper*, 422 U.S., at 417-418, 10 FEP Cases at 1187-1188.

[28] Accordingly, it is clear that the seniority remedy which petitioners seek does not concern only the "make-whole" purposes of Title VII. The dissent errs in treating the issue of seniority relief in implicating only the "make-whole" objective of Title VII and in stating that "Title VII's 'primary objective' of eradicating discrimination is not served at all. . . ." 12 FEP Cases at 564-565. Nothing could be further from the reality—the issue of seniority relief cuts to the very heart of Title VII's primary objective of eradicating present and future discrimination in a way that backpay, for example, can never do. "[S]eniority, after all, is a right which a worker exercises in each job movement in the future, rather than a simple one-time payment for the past." Poplin, *Fair Employment in a Depressed Economy: The Layoff Problem*, 23 U.C.L.A. L. REV. 177, 225 (1975).

seniority award would also remain subordinated in the seniority system to the class 4 discriminatees. The distinction plainly finds no support anywhere in Title VII or its legislative history. Settled law dealing with the related "twin" areas of discriminatory hiring and discharges violative of National Labor Relations Act, 29 U. S. C. § 151 *et seq.*, provides a persuasive analogy. "[I]t would indeed be surprising if Congress gave a remedy for the one which it denied for the other." *Phelps Dodge Corp.* v. *NLRB*, 313 U. S. 177, 187, 8 LRRM 439 (1941). For courts to differentiate without justification between the classes of discriminatees "would be a differentiation not only without substance but in defiance of that against which the prohibition of discrimination is directed." *Id.*, at 188, 8 FEP Cases at 443.

Similarly, decisions construing the remedial section of the National Labor Relations Act, § 10(c), 29 U. S. C. § 160(c)—the model for § 706(g), *Albemarle Paper*, 405 U. S., at 419 [29]—make clear that remedies constituting authorized "affirmative action" include an award of seniority status, for the thrust of "affirmative action" redressing the wrong incurred by an unfair labor practice is to make "the employees whole, and thus restor[e] the economic status quo that would have obtained but for the company's wrongful [act]." *NLRB* v. *J. H. Rutter-Rex Manufacturing Company*, 396 U. S. 258, 263, 72 LRRM 2881 (1969). The task of the NLRB in applying § 10(c) is "to take measures designed to recreate the conditions and relationships that would have been had there been no unfair labor practice." *Local 60, United Brotherhood of Carpenters and Joiners of America, AFL-CIO* v. *NLRB*, 365 U.S. 651, 657, 47 LRRM 2900 (1961) (Harlan, J., concurring). And the NLRB has often required that the hiring of employees who had been discriminatorily refused employment be accompanied by an award of seniority equivalent to that which they would have enjoyed but for the illegal conduct. See, e. g., *In re Phelps Dodge Corp.*, 19 NLRB 547, 600 & n. 39, 603-604, 5 LRRM 526 (1940), *modified on other grounds*, 313 U.S. 177, 8 LRRM 439 (1941) (ordering persons discriminatorily refused employment hired "without prejudice to their other rights and privileges"); *In re Nevada Consolidated Copper Corp.*, 26 NLRB 1182, 1235, 7 LRRM 33 (1940), *enforced*, 316 U.S. 105, 10 LRRM 607 (1942) (ordering persons discriminatorily refused employment hired with "any seniority or other rights and privileges which they would have acquired, had the respondent not unlawfully discriminated against them"). Plainly the "affirmative action injunction of § 706(g) has no lesser reach in the district courts. "Where racial discrimination is concerned, 'the district court has not merely the

---

[29] To the extent that there is difference in the wording of the respective provisions, § 706(a) grants, if anything, broader discretionary powers than those granted the NLRB. Section 10(c) of the NLRA authorizes "such affirmative action including reinstatement of employees with or without back pay, as will effectuate the policies of this subchapter," 29 U.S.C. § 160(c), whereas §706(g) as amended in 1972 authorizes "such affirmative action as may be appropriate, which may include, *but is not limited to,* reinstatement *or hiring* of employees, with or without back pay . . ., *or any other equitable relief as the court deems appropriate.*" 42 U.S.C. § 2000-e5(g) (emphasis added).

power but the duty to render a decree which will so far as possible eliminate the discriminatory effects of the past as well as bar like discrimination in the future.' " *Albemarle Paper, supra,* at 418, 10 FEP Cases at 1187-1188.

## IV

We are not to be understood as holding that an award of seniority status is requisite in all circumstances. The fashioning of appropriate remedies invokes the sound equitable discretion of the district courts. Respondent Bowman attempts to justify the District Court's denial of seniority relief for petitioners as an exercise of equitable discretion, but the record is its own refutation of the argument.

*Albemarle Paper, supra,* at 416, 10 FEP Cases at 1187, made clear that discretion imports not the Court's "inclination, but . . . its judgment; and its judgment is to be guided by sound legal principles." Discretion is vested not for purposes of "limit[ing] appellate review of trial courts, or . . . invit[ing] inconsistency and caprice," but rather to allow the most complete achievement of the objectives of Title VII that is attainable under the facts and circumstances of the specific case. *Id.,* at 421, 10 FEP Cases at 1188-1189. Accordingly, the District Court's denial of any form of seniority remedy must be reviewed in terms of its effect on the attainment of the Act's objectives under the circumstances presented by this record. No less than with the denial of the remedy of backpay, the denial of seniority relief to victims of illegal racial discrimination in hiring is permissible "only for reasons which, if applied generally, would not frustrate the central statutory purposes of eradicating discrimination throughout the economy and making persons whole for injuries suffered through past discrimination." *Ibid.*

The District Court stated two reasons for its denial of seniority relief for the unnamed class members.[30] The first was that those individuals had not filed administrative charges under the provisions of Title VII with the Equal Employment Opportunity Commission and therefore class relief of this sort was not appropriate. We rejected this justification for denial of class-based relief in the context of backpay awards in *Albemarle Paper,* and for the same reasons reject it here. This justification for denying class-based relief in Title VII suits has been unanimously rejected by the courts of appeals, and Congress ratified that construction by the 1972 Amendments. *Albemarle Paper, supra,* at 414 n.8, 10 FEP Cases at 1186.

The second reason stated by the District Court was that such claims "presuppose a vacancy, qualification, and performance by every member.

---

[30] Since the Court of Appeals concluded that an award of retroactive seniority to the non-named members of class 3 was barred by § 703(h), a conclusion which we today reject, the Court did not address specifically the District Court's stated reasons for refusing the relief. The Court of Appeals also stated, however, that the District Court did not "abuse its discretion" in refusing such relief, 495 F.2d, at 418, 8 FEP Cases at 80, and we may therefore appropriately review the validity of the District Court's reasons.

There is no evidence on which to base these multiple conclusions." The Court of Appeals rejected this reason insofar as it was the basis of the District Court's denial of backpay, and of its denial of retroactive seniority relief to the unnamed members of class 4. We hold that it is also an improper reason for denying seniority relief to the unnamed members of class 3.

We read the District Court's reference to the lack of evidence regarding a "vacancy, qualification and performance" for every individual member of the class as an expression of concern that some of the unnamed class members (unhired black applicants whose employment applications were summarized in the record) may not in fact have been actual victims of racial discrimination. That factor will become material however only when those persons reapply for OTR positions pursuant to the hiring relief ordered by the District Court. Generalizations concerning such individually applicable evidence cannot serve as a justification for the denial of relief to the entire class. Rather, at such time as individual class members seek positions as OTR drivers, positions for which they are presumptively entitled to priority hiring consideration under the District Court's order,[31] evidence that particular individuals were not in fact victims of racial discrimination will be material. But petitioners here have carried their burden of demonstrating the existence of a discriminatory hiring pattern and practice by the respondents and, therefore, the burden will be upon respondents to prove that individuals who reapply were not in fact victims of previous hiring discrimination. Cf. *Mc-Donnell Douglas Corp.* v. *Green,* 411 U. S., at 802, *Baxter* v. *Savannah Sugar Refining Corp.,* 495 F.2d 437, 443-444, 8 FEP Cases 84 (CA5), *cert. denied,* 419 U.S. 1033, 8 FEP Cases 1142 (1974).[32] Only if this burden is met may retroactive seniority—if otherwise determined to be an appropriate form of relief under the circumstances of the particular case—be denied individual class members.

Respondent Bowman raises an alternative theory of justification. Bowman argues that an award of retroactive seniority to the class of discriminatees will conflict with the economic interests of other Bowman

---

[31] The District Court order is silent whether applicants to OTR positions who were previously discriminatorily refused employment must be presently qualified for those positions in order to be eligible for priority hiring under that order. The Court of Appeals, however, made it plain that they must be. 495 F.2d at 417, 8 FEP Cases at 79. We agree.

[32] Thus Bowman may attempt to provide that a given individual member of class 3 was not in fact discriminatorily refused employment as an OTR driver in order to defeat the individual's claim to seniority relief as well as any other remedy ordered for the class generally. Evidence of a lack of vacancies in OTR positions at the time the individual application was filed, or evidence indicating the individual's lack of qualification for the OTR positions—under nondiscriminatory standards *actually applied* by Bowman to individuals who in fact hired—would of course be relevant. It is true of course that obtaining the third category of evidence with which the District Court was concerned—what the individual discriminatee's job performance would have been but for the discrimination—presents great difficulty. No reason appears, however, why the victim rather than the perpetrator of the illegal act should bear the burden of proof on this issue.

employees. Accordingly, it is argued the District Court acted within its discretion in denying this form of relief as an attempt to accommodate the competing interest of the various groups of employees.[33]

We reject this argument for two reasons. First, the District Court made no mention of such considerations in its order denying the seniority relief. As we noted in *Albemarle Paper, supra,* at 421 n.14, 10 FEP Cases at 1189, if the District Court declines due to the peculiar circumstances of the particular case to award relief generally appropriate under Title VII, "[i]t is necessary . . . that . . . it carefully articulate its reasons" for so doing. Second and more fundamentally, it is apparent that denial of seniority relief to identifiable victims of racial discrimination on the sole ground that such relief diminishes the expectations of other, arguably innocent, employees would if applied generally frustrate the central "make-whole" objective of Title VII. These conflicting interests of other employees will of course always be present in instances where some scarce employment benefit is distributed among employees on the basis of their status in the seniority hierarchy. But, as we have said, there is nothing in the language of Title VII, or in its legislative history, to show that Congress intended generally to bar this form of relief to victims of illegal discrimination, and the experience under its remedial model in the National Labor Relations Act points to the contrary.[34] Accordingly, we find

[33] Even by its terms, this argument could apply only to the award of retroactive seniority for purposes of "competitive status" benefits. It has no application to a retroactive award for purposes of "benefit" seniority—extent of vacation leave and pension benefits. Indeed, the decision concerning the propriety of this latter type of seniority relief is analogous, if not identical, to the decision concerning an award of backpay to an individual discriminatee hired pursuant to an order redressing previous employment discrimination.

[34] With all respect, the dissent does not adequately treat with and fails to distinguish, 12 FEP Cases at 568, the standard practice of the National Labor Relations Board granting retroactive seniority relief under the National Labor Relations Act to persons discriminatorily discharged or refused employment in violation of the Act. The Court in *Phelps Dodge Corp.* v. *NLRB,* 313 U.S. 177, 196, 8 LRRM 439 (1941), of course made reference to "restricted judicial review" as that case arose in the context of review of the policy determinations of an independent administrative agency, which are traditionally accorded a wide-ranging discretion under accepted principles of judicial review. "Because the relation of remedy to policy is peculiarly a matter for administrative competence, courts must not enter the allowable area of the Board's discretion." *Id.,* at 194. As we made clear in *Albemarle Paper,* however, the pertinent point is that in utilizing the NLRA as the remedial model for Title VII, reference must be made to actual operation and experience as it has evolved in administering the Act. E.g, "We may assume that Congress was aware that the Board, since its inception, has awarded backpay as a matter of course." 422 U.S., at 419-420, 10 FEP Cases at 1188. "[T]he Board has from its inception pursued 'a practically uniform policy with respect to these orders requiring affirmative action.'" *Id.,* at n. 12.

The dissent has cited no case, and our research discloses none, wherein the Board has ordered hiring relief and yet withheld the remedy of retroactive seniority status. Indeed, the Court of Appeals for the First Circuit has noted that a Board order requiring hiring relief "without prejudice to . . . seniority and other rights and privileges" is "language . . . in the standard form which has long been in use by the Board." *NLRB* v. *Draper Corp.,* 159 F.2d 294, 296-297, 19 LRRM 2267 (CA1 1947). The Board "routinely awards both back pay and retroactive seniority in hiring discrimination cases." Poplin, *supra,* n. 28, at 223. See also Edwards & Zaretsky, *Preferential Remedies for Employment Discrimination,* 74 MICH. L. REV. 1, 45 n. 224 (1975) (a "common remedy"); *Last Hired, First Fired Seniority, Layoffs and Title VII, supra,* n. 11, at 377 ("traditionally and uniformly required"). This also is a "presumption" in favor of this form

untenable the conclusion that this form of relief may be denied merely because the interests of other employees may thereby be affected. "If relief under Title VII can be denied merely because the majority group of employees, who have not suffered discrimination, will be unhappy about it, there will be little hope of correcting the wrongs to which the Act is directed." *United States* v. *Bethlehem Steel Corp.*, 446 F.2d 652, 663, 3 FEP Cases 589, 596 (CA2 1971).[35]

With reference to the problems of fairness or equity respecting the conflicting interests of the various groups of employees, the relief which petitioners seek is only seniority status retroactive to the date of individual application, rather than some form of arguably more complete relief.[36] No claim is asserted that nondiscriminatee employees holding OTR positions they would not have obtained but for the illegal discrimination should be deprived of the seniority status they have earned. It is therefore clear that even if the seniority relief petitioners seek is awarded, most if not all discriminatees who actually obtain OTR jobs under the court order will not truly be restored to the actual seniority that would have existed in the absence of the illegal discrimination. Rather, most discriminatees even under an award of retroactive seniority status will still remain subordinated in the hierarchy to a position inferior to that of a greater total number of employees than would have been the case in the absence of discrimination. Therefore, the relief which petitioners seek, while a more complete form of relief than that which the District Court accorded, in no sense constitutes "complete relief."[37] Rather, the burden of the past discrimination in hiring is with respect to competitive status benefits divided among discriminatee and nondiscriminatee employees under the form of relief sought. The dissent criticizes the Court's

---

of seniority relief. If victims of racial discrimination are under Title VII to be treated differently and awarded less protection than victims of unfair labor practice discrimination under the National Labor Relations Act, some persuasive justification for such disparate treatment should appear. That no justification exists doubtless explains the position of every union participant in the proceedings before the Court in the instant case arguing for the conclusion we have reached.

[35] See also *Volger* v. *McCarty Inc.*, 451 F.2d 1238-1239, 4 FEP Cases 12, 14 (CA 1971): "Adequate protection of Negro rights under Title VII may necessitate, as in the instant case, some adjustment of the rights of white employees. The courts must be free to deal equitably with conflicting interests of white employees in order to shape remedies that will most effectively protect and redress the rights of the Negro victims of discrimination."

[36] Another countervailing factor in assessing the expected impact on the interests of other employees actually occasioned by an award of the seniority relief sought is that it is not probable in instances of class-based relief that all of the victims of the past racial discrimination in hiring will actually apply for and obtain the prerequisite hiring relief. Indeed, in the instant case, there appear in the record the rejected applications of 166 black applicants who claimed at the time of application to have had the necessary job qualifications. However, the Court was informed at oral argument that only a small number of those individuals have to this date actually been hired pursuant to the District Court's order ("five, six, seven, something in that order"), Tr. of Oral Arg., at 23, although ongoing litigation may ultimately determine more who desire the hiring relief and are eligible for it. *Id.*, at 15.

[37] In no way can the remedy established as presumptively necessary be characterized as "total restitution," *post* n. 9, 12 FEP Cases at 566, or as deriving from an "absolutist concep[tion] of 'make-whole' " relief. 12 FEP Cases at 566.

result as not sufficiently cognizant that it will "directly implicate the rights and expectations of perfectly innocent employees." 12 FEP Cases at 565. We are of the view, however, that the result which we reach today —which, standing alone,[38] establishes that a sharing of the burden of the past discrimination is presumptively necessary—is entirely consistent with any fair characterization of equity jurisdiction,[39] particularly when considered in light of our traditional view that "[a]ttainment of a great national policy . . . must not be confined within narrow cannons for equitable relief deemed suitable by chancellors in ordinary private controversies." *Phelps Dodge Corp.* v. *NLRB,* 313 U.S., at 188, 8 LRRM at 443.

Certainly there is no argument that the award of retroactive seniority to the victims of hiring discrimination in any way deprives other employees of indefeasibly vested rights conferred by the employment contract. This Court has long held that employee expectations arising from a seniority system agreement may be modified by statutes furthering a strong public policy interest.[40] *Tilton* v. *Missouri Pacific Railroad Co.,* 376 U.S. 169, 55 LRRM 2369 (1964) (construing §§ 9(c)(1) and 9(c)(2) of the Universal Military Training and Service Act of 1948, 50 U.S.C. §§ 459 (c)(1)–(2), which provided that a reemployed returning veteran should enjoy the seniority status he would have acquired but for his absence in military service); *Fishgold* v. *Sullivan Drydock & Repair Corp.,* 328 U.S. 275, 18 LRRM 2075 (1946) (construing the comparable provision of the Selective Training and Service Act of 1940). The Court has also held that a collective-bargaining agreement may go further, enhancing the seniority status of certain employees for purposes of furthering public policy interests beyond what is required by statute, even though this will to some extent be detrimental to the expectations acquired by other employees under

---

[38] In arguing that an award of the seniority relief established as presumptively necessary does nothing to place the burden of the past discrimination on the wrongdoer in most cases—the employer—the dissent of necessity addresses issues not presently before the Court. Further remedial action by the district courts, having the effect of shifting to the employer the burden of the past discrimination in respect to competitive status benefits raises such issues as the possibility of an injunctive "hold harmless" remedy respecting all affected employees in a layoff situation. Brief of *Amicus Curiae* for Local 862, United Automobile Workers, the possibility of an award of monetary damages (sometimes designated "front pay") in favor of each employee and discriminatee otherwise bearing some of the burden of the past discrimination, *ibid.;* Brief for the United States and the Equal Employment Opportunity Commission as *Amici Curiae,* and the propriety of such further remedial action in instances wherein the union has been adjudged a participant in the illegal conduct. Such issues are not presented by the record before us, and we intimate no view regarding them.

[39] "The qualities of mercy and practicality have made equity the instrument for nice adjustment and reconciliation between the public interest and private needs as well as between competing private claims." " 'Moreover, . . . equitable remedies are a special blend of what is necessary, what is fair, and what is workable. . . .

" 'In equity, as nowhere else courts eschew rigid absolutes and looking to the practical realities and necessities inescapably involved in reconciling competing interests. . . .' " 12 FEP Cases at 565.

[40] "[C]laims under Title VII involve the vindication of a major public interest. . . ." Section-By-Section Analysis, accompanying The Equal Employment Opportunity Act of 1972—Conference Report, 118 Cong. Rec. 7166, 7168 (1972).

the previous seniority agreement. *Ford Motor Company* v. *Huffman,* 345 U.S. 330 (1953). And the ability of the union and employer voluntarily to modify the seniority system to the end of ameliorating the effects of past racial discrimination, a national policy objective of the "highest priority," is certainly no less than in other areas of public policy interests. *Pellicer* v. *Brotherhood of Railway and Steamship Clerks,* 217 F.2d 205, 9 FEP Cases 423 (CA5 1954), *cert. denied,* 349 U.S. 912, 9 FEP Cases 1407 (1955). See also Cooper and Sobol, 82 HARV. L. REV., at 1605.

## V

In holding that class-based seniority relief for identifiable victims of illegal hiring discrimination is a form of relief generally appropriate under § 706(g), we do not in any way modify our previously expressed view that the statutory scheme of Title VII "implicitly recognizes that there may be cases calling for one remedy but not another, and—owing to the structure of the federal judiciary—these choices are of course left in the first instance to the district courts." *Albemarle Paper, supra,* at 416, 10 FEP Cases at 1187. Circumstances peculiar to the individual case may of course justify the modification or withholding of seniority relief for reasons that would not if applied generally undermine the purposes of Title VII.[41] In the instant case it appears that all new hirees establish seniority only upon completion of a 45-day probationary period, although upon completion seniority is retroactive to the date of hire. Certainly any seniority relief ultimately awarded by the district court could properly be cognizant of this fact. Amici and the respondent union point out that there may be circumstances where an award of full seniority should be deferred until completion of a training or apprenticeship program, or other preliminaries required of all new hirees. We do not undertake to delineate all such possible circumstances here. Any enumeration must await particular cases and be determined in light of the trial courts' "keen appreciation" of peculiar facts and circumstances. *Albemarle Paper, supra,* at 421-422, 10 FEP Cases at 1189.

Accordingly, the judgment of the Court of Appeals affirming the District Court's denial of seniority relief to class 3 is reversed, and the case remanded to the District Court for further proceedings consistent with this opinion.

*It is so ordered.*

MR. JUSTICE STEVENS took no part in the consideration of this case.

MR. CHIEF JUSTICE BURGER, concurring in part and dissenting in part.

---

[41] Accordingly, to no "significant extent" do we "[strip] the district court of [their] equitable powers." 12 FEP Cases, at 564. Rather our holding is that in exercising their equitable powers, district courts should take as their starting point the presumption in favor of rightful place seniority relief, and proceed with further legal analysis from that point; and that such relief may not be denied on the abstract basis of adverse impact upon interests of other employees but rather only on the basis of unusual adverse impact arising from facts and circumstances that would not be generally found in Title VII cases. To hold otherwise would be to shield "inconsisten[t] and capri[cious]" denial of such relief from "thorough appellate review." *Albemarle Paper,* 422 U.S., at 416, 421, 10 FEP Cases at 1189.

I concur in the judgment in part and generally with MR. JUSTICE POWELL, but I would stress that although retroactive benefit-type seniority relief may sometimes be appropriate and equitable, competitive-type seniority relief at the expense of wholly innocent employees can rarely, if ever, be equitable if that term retains traditional meaning. More equitable would be a monetary award to the person suffering the discrimination. An award such as "front pay" could replace the need for competitive-type seniority relief. See, *ante,* at 28, n. 38. (Majority opinion.) Such monetary relief would serve the dual purpose of deterring the wrongdoing employer or union—or both—as well as protecting the rights of innocent employees. In every respect an innocent employee is comparable to a "holder-in-due-course" of negotiable paper or a bona fide purchaser of property without notice of any defect in the seller's title. In this setting I cannot join in judicial approval of "robbing Peter to pay Paul."

I would stress that the Court today does not foreclose claims of employees who might be injured by this holding from petitioning the District Court for equitable relief on their own behalf.

MR. JUSTICE POWELL, with whom MR. JUSTICE REHNQUIST joins, concurring in part and dissenting in part: [omitted].

(5)   *The New Law of Seniority*

## TEAMSTERS v. UNITED STATES

*Supreme Court of the United States, 1977*
*431 U.S. 324, 14 FEP Cases 1514*

MR. JUSTICE STEWART delivered the opinion of the Court.

This litigation brings here several important questions under Title VII of the Civil Rights Act of 1964, 78 Stat. 253, as amended, 42 U.S.C. § 2000e et seq. (1970 ed. and Supp. V). The issues grow out of alleged unlawful employment practices engaged in by an employer and a union. The employer is a common carrier of motor freight with nationwide operations, and the union represents a large group of its employees. The District Court and the Court of Appeals held that the employer had violated Title VII by engaging in a pattern and practice of employment discrimination against Negroes and Spanish-surnamed Americans, and that the union had violated the Act by agreeing with the employer to create and maintain a seniority system that perpetuated the effects of past racial and ethnic discrimination. In addition to the basic questions presented by these two rulings, other subsidiary issues must be resolved if violations of Title VII occurred—issues concerning the nature of the relief to which aggrieved individuals may be entitled.

I

The United States brought an action in a Tennessee federal court against the petitioner T.I.M.E.-D.C., Inc. (the company) pursuant to

§ 707 (a) of the Civil Rights Act of 1964, 42 U.S.C. § 2000e-6(a).[1] The complaint charged that the company had followed discriminatory hiring, assignment, and promotion policies against Negroes at its terminal in Nashville, Tenn.[2] The Government brought a second action against the company almost three years later in a federal district court in Texas, charging a pattern and practice of employment discrimination against Negroes and Spanish-surnamed persons throughout the company's transportation system. The petitioner International Brotherhood of Teamsters (the union) was joined as a defendant in that suit. The two actions were consolidated for trial in the Northern District of Texas.

The central claim in both lawsuits was that the company had engaged in a pattern or practice of discriminating against minorities in hiring so-called line drivers. Those Negroes and Spanish-surnamed persons who had been hired, the Government alleged, were given lower paying, less desirable jobs as servicemen or local city drivers, and were thereafter discriminated against with respect to promotions and transfers.[3] In this connection the complaint also challenged the seniority system established by the collective-bargaining agreements between the employer and the union. The Government sought a general injunctive remedy and specific "make whole" relief for all individual discriminatees, which would allow them an opportunity to transfer to line-driver jobs with full company seniority for all purposes.

---

[1] [Footnotes numbered as in original.—Ed.] At the time of suit the statute provided as follows:

"(a) Whenever the Attorney General has reasonable cause to believe that any person or group of persons is engaged in a pattern or practice of resistance to the full enjoyment of any of the rights secured by this subchapter, and that the pattern or practice is of such a nature and is intended to deny the full exercise of the rights herein described, the Attorney General may bring a civil action in the appropriate district court of the United States by filing with it a complaint (1) signed by him (or in his absence the Acting Attorney General), (2) setting forth facts pertaining to such pattern or practice, and (3) requesting such relief, including an application for a permanent or temporary injunction, restraining order or other order against the person or persons responsible for such pattern or practice, as he deems necessary to insure the full enjoyment of the rights herein described."

Section 707 was amended by § 5 of the Equal Employment Opportunity Act of 1972, 86 Stat. 107, 42 U.S.C. §200e-6(c) (Supp. V.), to give the Equal Employment Opportunity Commission, rather than the Attorney General, the authority to bring "pattern or practice" suits under that section against private-sector employers. In 1974, an order was entered in this action substituting the EEOC for the United States but retaining the United States as a party for purposes of jurisdiction, appealability, and related matters. See 42 U.S.C. § 2000e-6(d) (Supp. V).

[2] The named defendant in this suit was T.I.M.E. Freight, Inc., a predecessor of T.I.M.E.-D.C., Inc. T.I.M.E.-D.C., Inc., is a nationwide system produced by 10 mergers over a 17-year period. See *United States* v. *T.I.M.E.-D.C., Inc.*, 517 F.2d 299, 304, and n. 6, 11 FEP Cases 66, 69 (CA5). It currently has 51 terminals and operates in 26 States and three Canadian provinces.

[3] *Line drivers*, also known as over-the-road drivers, engage in long-distance hauling between company terminals. They compose a separate bargaining unit at T.I.M.E.-D.C. Other distinct bargaining units include *servicemen*, who service trucks, unhook tractors and trailers, and perform similar tasks; and *city operations*, composed of dockmen, hostlers, and city drivers who pick up and deliver freight within the immediate area of a particular terminal. All of these employees were represented by the petitioner International Brotherhood of Teamsters.

The cases went to trial [4] and the District Court found that the Government had shown "by a preponderance of the evidence that T.I.M.E.-D.C. and its predecessor companies were engaged in a plan and practice of discrimination in violation of Title VII. . . ." [5] The court further found that the seniority system contained in the collective-bargaining contracts between the company and the union violated Title VII because it "operate[d] to impede the free transfer of minority groups into and within the company." Both the company and the union were enjoined from committing further violations of Title VII.

With respect to individual relief the court accepted the Government's basic contention that the "affected class" of discriminatees included all Negro and Spanish-surnamed incumbent employees who had been hired to fill city operations or serviceman jobs at every terminal that had a line-driver operation.[6] All of these employees, whether hired before or after the effective date of Title VII, thereby became entitled to preference over all other applicants with respect to consideration for future vacancies in line-driver jobs.[7] Finding that members of the affected class had been injured in different degrees, the court created three subclasses. Thirty persons who had produced "the most convincing evidence of discrimination and harm" were found to have suffered "severe injury." The court ordered that they be offered the opportunity to fill line-driver jobs with competitive seniority dating back to July 2, 1965, the effective date

[4] Following the receipt of evidence, but before decision, the Government and the company consented to the entry of a Decree in Partial Resolution of Suit. The consent decree did not constitute an adjudication on the merits. The company agreed, however, to undertake a minority recruiting program; to accept applications from all Negroes and Spanish-surnamed Americans who inquired about employment, whether or not vacancies existed, and to keep such applications on file and notify applicants of job openings; to keep specific employment and recruiting records open to inspection by the Government and to submit quarterly reports to the District Court; and to adhere to certain uniform employment qualifications respecting hiring and promotion to line driver and other jobs.

The decree further provided that future job vacancies at any T.I.M.E.-D.C. terminal would be filled first "[b] those persons who may be found by the Court, if any, to be individual or class discriminatees suffering the present effects of past discrimination because of race or national origin prohibited by Title VII of the Civil Rights Act of 1964." Any remaining vacancies could be filled by "any other persons," but the company obligated itself to hire one Negro or Spanish-surnamed person for every white person hired at any terminal until the percentage of minority workers at that terminal equaled the percentage of minority group members in the population of the metropolitan area surrounding the terminal. Finally, the company agreed to pay $89,500 in full settlement of any backpay obligations. Of this sum, individual payments not exceeding $1,500 were to be paid to "alleged individual and class discriminatees" identified by the Government.

The Decree in Partial Resolution of Suit narrowed the scope of the litigation, but the District Court still had to determine whether unlawful discrimination had occurred. If so, the Court had to identify the actual discriminatees entitled to fill future job vacancies under the decree. The validity of the collective-bargaining contract's seniority system also remained for decision, as did the question whether any discriminatees should be awarded additional equitable relief such as retroactive seniority.

[5] The District Court's Memorandum Decision in *United States* v. *T.I.M.E.-D.C., Inc.*, Civ. No. 5-368 (Oct. 19, 1972), is not officially reported. It is unofficially reported at 6 FEP Cases 690 and 6 EPD ¶ 8979.

[6] The Government did not seek relief for Negroes and Spanish-surnamed Americans hired at a particular terminal after the date on which that terminal first employed a minority group member as a line driver.

[7] See *supra*, at 3-4, n. 4.

of Title VII.[8] A second subclass included four persons who were "very possibly the objects of discrimination" and who "were likely harmed," but as to whom there had been no specific evidence of discrimination and injury. The court decreed that these persons were entitled to fill vacancies in line-driving jobs with competitive seniority as of January 14, 1971, the date on which the Government had filed its system-wide lawsuit. Finally, there were over 300 remaining members of the affected class as to whom there was "no evidence to show that these individuals were either harmed or not harmed individually." The court ordered that they be considered for line-driver jobs [9] ahead of any applicants from the general public but behind the two other subclasses. Those in the third subclass received no retroactive seniority; their competitive seniority as line drivers would begin with the date they were hired as line drivers. The court further decreed that the right of any class member to fill a line-driver vacancy was subject to the prior recall rights of laid-off line drivers, which under the collective-bargaining agreements then in effect extended for three years.[10]

The Court of Appeals for the Fifth Circuit agreed with the basic conclusions of the District Court: that the company had engaged in a pattern or practice of employment discrimination and that the seniority system in the collective-bargaining agreements violated Title VII as applied to victims of prior discrimination. *United States* v. *T.I.M.E.-D.C., Inc.,* 517 F.2d 299, 11 FEP Cases 66. The appellate court held, however, that the relief ordered by the District Court was inadequate. Rejecting the District Court's attempt to trisect the affected class, the Court of Appeals held that all Negro and Spanish-surnamed incumbent employees were entitled to bid for future line-driver jobs on the basis of their company seniority, and that once a class member had filled a job, he could use his full company seniority—even if it predated the effective date of Title VII— for all purposes, including bidding and layoff. This award of retroactive seniority was to be limited only by a "qualification date" formula, under which seniority could not be awarded for periods prior to the date when

---

[8] If an employee in this class had joined the company after July 2, 1965, then the date of his initial employment rather than the effective date of Title VII was to determine his competitive seniority.

[9] As with the other subclasses, there were a few individuals in the third group who were found to have been discriminated against with respect to jobs other than line driver. There is no need to discuss them separately in this opinion.

[10] This provision of the decree was qualified in one significant respect. Under the Southern Conference Area Over-the-Road Supplemental Agreement between the employer and the union, line drivers employed at terminals in certain southern States work under a "modified" seniority system. Under the modified system an employee's seniority is not confined strictly to his home terminal. If he is laid off at his home terminal he can move to another terminal covered by the Agreement and retain his seniority, either by filling a vacancy at the other terminal or by "bumping" a junior line driver out of his job if there is no vacancy. The modified system also requires that any new vacancy at a covered terminal be offered to laid-off line drivers at all other covered terminals before it is filled by any other person. The District Court's final decree, as amended slightly by the Court of Appeals, 517 F.2d, at 323, 11 FEP Cases, at 83, altered this system by requiring that any vacancy be offered to all members of all three subclasses before it may be filled by laid-off drivers from other terminals.

(1) a line-driving position was vacant,[11] *and* (2) the class member met (or would have met, given the opportunity) the qualifications for employment as a line driver.[12] Finally, the Court of Appeals modified that part of the District Court's decree that had subjected the rights of class members to fill future vacancies to the recall rights of laid-off employees. Holding that the three-year priority in favor of laid-off workers "would unduly impede the eradication of past discrimination," *id.*, at 322, 11 FEP Cases at 83, the Court of Appeals ordered that class members be allowed to compete for vacancies with laid-off employees on the basis of the class members' retroactive seniority. Laid-off line drivers would retain their prior recall rights with respect only to "purely temporary" vacancies. *Ibid.*[13]

The Court of Appeals remanded the case to the District Court to hold the evidentiary hearing necessary to apply these remedial principles. We granted both the company's and the union's petitions for certiorari to consider the significant questions presented under the Civil Rights Act of 1964, 425 U.S. 990.

## II

In this Court the company and the union contend that their conduct did not violate Title VII in any respect, asserting first that the evidence introduced at trial was insufficient to show that the company engaged in a "pattern or practice" of employment discrimination. The union further contends that the seniority system contained in the collective-bargaining agreements in no way violated Title VII. If these contentions are correct, it is unnecessary, of course, to reach any of the issues concerning remedies that so occupied the attention of the Court of Appeals.

## A

Consideration of the question whether the company engaged in a pattern or practice of discriminatory hiring practices involves controlling legal principles that are relatively clear. The Government's theory of discrimination was simply that the company, in violation of § 703(a) of

[11] Although the opinion of the Court of Appeals in this case did not specifically mention the requirement that a vacancy exist, it is clear from earlier and later opinions of that court that this requirement is a part of the Fifth Circuit's "qualification date" formula. See, *e.g., Rodriguez* v. *East Texas Motor Freight*, 505 F.2d 40, 63 n. 29, 8 FEP Cases 1246, 1262 (CA5), rev'd on other grounds, *ante*, at _____, 14 FEP Cases, at 1505, cited in *United States* v. *T.I.M.E.-D.C.*, 517 F.2d, at 318 n. 35, 11 FEP Cases, at 79; *Sagers* v. *Yellow Freight System, Inc.*, 529 F.2d 721, 731-34, 12 FEP Cases 961, 968-69 (CA5 1976).

[12] For example, if a class member began his tenure with the company on January 1, 1966, at which time he was qualified as a line driver and a line-driving vacancy existed, his competitive seniority upon becoming a line driver would date back to January 1, 1966. If he became qualified or if a vacancy opened up only at a later date, then that later date would be used.

[13] The Court of Appeals also approved (with slight modification) the part of the District Court's order that allowed class members to fill vacancies at a particular terminal ahead of line drivers laid off at other terminals. See *supra*, at 6-7 n. 10, 14 FEP Cases, at 1518.

Title VII,[14] regularly and purposefully treated Negroes and Spanish-surnamed Americans less favorably than white persons. The disparity in treatment allegedly involved the refusal to recruit, hire, transfer, or promote minority group members on an equal basis with white people, particularly with respect to line-driving positions. The ultimate factual issues are thus simply whether there was a pattern or practice of such disparate treatment and, if so, whether the differences were "racially premised." *McDonnell Douglas Corp.* v. *Green,* 411 U.S. 792, 805 n. 18, 5 FEP Cases 965, 970.[15]

As the plaintiff, the Government bore the initial burden of making out a prima facie case of discrimination. *Albemarle Paper Co.* v. *Moody,* 422 U.S. 405, 425, 10 FEP Cases 1181, 1190; *McDonnell Douglas Corp.* v. *Green, supra,* at 802, 5 FEP Cases, at 969. And, because it alleged a system-wide pattern or practice of resistance to the full enjoyment of Title VII rights, the Government ultimately had to prove more than the mere occurrence of isolated or "accidental" or sporadic discriminatory acts. It had to establish by a preponderance of the evidence that racial discrimination was the company's standard operating procedure—the regular rather than the unusual practice.[16]

---

[14] Section 703(a) of Title VII, 42 U.S.C. §2000e-2(a) (1970 ed. and Supp. V), provides:
"(a) It shall be an unlawful employment practice for an employer—
"(1) to fail or refuse to hire or to discharge any individual, or otherwise to discriminate against any individual with respect to his compensation, terms, conditions, or privileges of employment, because of such individual's race, color, religion, sex, or national origin; or
"(2) to limit, segregate, or classify his employees or applicants for employment in any way which would deprive or tend to deprive any individual of employment opportunities or otherwise adversely affect his status as an employee, because of such individual's race, color, religion, sex, or national origin."

[15] "Disparate treatment" such as alleged in the present case is the most easily understood type of discrimination. The employer simply treats some people less favorably than others because of their race, color, religion, sex, or national origin. Proof of discriminatory motive is critical, although it can in some situations be inferred from the mere fact of differences in treatment. See, *e.g., Village of Arlington Heights* v. *Metropolitan Housing Dev. Corp.,* 429 U.S. 252, 265-66. Undoubtedly disparate treatment was the most obvious evil Congress had in mind when it enacted Title VII. See, *e.g.,* 110 Cong. Rec. 13088 (1964) (remarks of Sen. Humphrey) ("What the bill does . . . is simply to make it an illegal practice to use race as a factor in denying employment. It provides that men and women shall be employed on the basis of their qualifications, not as Catholic citizens, not as protestant citizens, not as Jewish citizens, not as colored citizens, but as citizens of the United States").
Claims of disparate treatment may be distinguished from claims that stress "disparate impact." The latter involve employment practices that are facially neutral in their treatment of different groups but that in fact fall more harshly on one group than another and cannot be justified by business necessity. See *infra,* at 22, 14 FEP Cases, at 1524. Proof of discriminatory motive, we have held, is not required under a disparate impact theory. Compare, *e.g., Griggs* v. *Duke Power Co.,* 401 U.S. 424, 430-32, 3 FEP Cases 175, 177-78, with *McDonnell Douglas Corp.* v. *Green,* 411 U.S. 792, 802-806, 5 FEP Cases 965, 969-70. See generally Schlei & Grossman, Employment Discrimination Law 1-12 (1976); Blumrosen, *Strangers in Paradise: Griggs* v. *Duke Power Co. and the Concept of Employment Discrimination,* 71 Mich. L. Rev. 59 (1972). Either theory may, of course, be applied to a particular set of facts.

[16] The "pattern or practice" language in § 707(a) of Title VII, *supra,* at 2 n. 1, was not intended as a term of art, and the words reflect only their usual meaning. Senator Humphrey explained:
"[A] pattern or practice would be present only where the denial of rights consists of

We agree with the District Court and the Court of Appeals that the Government carried its burden of proof. As of March 31, 1971, shortly after the Government filed its complaint alleging systemwide discrimination, the company had 6,472 employees. Of these, 314 (5 percent) were Negroes and 257 (4 percent) were Spanish-surnamed Americans. Of the 1,828 line drivers, however, there were only 8 (0.4 percent) Negroes and 5 (0.3 percent) Spanish-surnamed persons, and all of the Negroes had been hired after the litigation had commenced. With one exception—a man who worked as a line driver at the Chicago terminal from 1950 to 1959—the company and its predecessors *did not employ a Negro on a regular basis as a line driver until 1969.* And, as the Government showed, even in 1971 there were terminals in areas of substantial Negro population where all of the companys' line drivers were white.[17] A great majority of the Negroes (83 percent) and Spanish-surnamed Americans (78 percent) who did work for the company held the lower paying city operations and serviceman jobs,[18] whereas only 39 percent of the nonminority employees held jobs in those categories.

The Government bolstered its statistical evidence with the testimony of individuals who recounted over 40 specific instances of discrimination. Upon the basis of this testimony the District Court found that "[n]umerous qualified black and Spanish-surnamed American applicants who sought line-driving jobs at the company over the years had their requests

---

something more than an isolated, sporadic incident, but is repeated, routine, or of a generalized nature. There would be a pattern or practice if, for example, a number of companies or persons in the same industry or line of business discriminated, if a chain of motels or restaurants practiced racial discrimination throughout all or a significant part of its system, or if a company repeatedly and regularly engaged in acts prohibited by the statute.

. . .

"The point is that single, insignificant, isolated acts of discrimination by a single business would not justify a finding of a pattern or practice. . . ." 110 Cong. Rec. 14270 (1964).

This interpretation of "pattern or practice" appears throughout the legislative history of § 707(a), and is consistent with the understanding of the identical words as used in similar federal legislation. See *id.,* at 12946 (remarks of Sen. Magnuson) (referring to § 206 (a) of the Civil Rights Act of 1964, 42 U.S.C. § 206(a)); *id.,* at 13081 (remarks of Sen. Case); *id.,* at 14239 (remarks of Sen. Humphrey); *id.,* at 15895 (remarks of Rep. Celler). See also *United States* v. *Jacksonville Terminal Co.,* 451 F.2d 418, 438, 441, 3 FEP Cases 862, 878, 881 (CA5); *United States* v. *Ironworkers Local 86,* 443 F.2d 544, 552. 3 FEP Cases 496, 501-502 (CA9); *United States* v. *West Peachtree Tenth Corp.,* 437 F.2d 221, 327 (CA5); *United States* v. *Mayton,* 335 F.2d 153, 158-59 (CA5).

17 In Atlanta, for instance, Negroes composed 22.35% of the population in the surrounding metropolitan area and 51.31% of the population in the city proper. The company's Atlanta terminal employed 57 line drivers. All were white. In Los Angeles, 10.84% of the greater metropolitan population and 17.88% of the city population were Negro. But at the company's two Los Angeles terminals there was not a single Negro among the 374 line drivers. The proof showed similar disparities in San Francisco, Denver, Nashville, Chicago, Dallas, and at several other terminals.

18 Although line-driver jobs pay more than other jobs, and the District Court found them to be "considered the most desirable of the driving-jobs," it is by no means clear that all employees, even driver employees, would prefer to be line drivers. See *infra,* at 42-43, and n. 55, 14 FEP Cases, at 1533. Of course, Title VII provides for equal opportunity to compete for *any* job, whether it is thought better or worse than another. See, *e.g., United States* v. *Hayes Internat'l Corp.,* 456 F.2d 112, 118, 4 FEP Cases 411, 415 (CA5); *United States* v. *National Lead Co.,* 438 F.2d 935, 939, 3 FEP Cases 211, 214 (CA8).

ignored, were given false or misleading information about requirements, opportunities, and application procedures or were not considered and hired on the same basis that whites were considered and hired." Minority employees who wanted to transfer to line-driver jobs met with similar difficulties.[19]

The company's principal response to this evidence is that statistics can never in and of themselves prove the existence of a pattern or practice of discrimination, or even establish a prima facie case shifting to the employer the burden of rebutting the inference raised by the figures. But, as even our brief summary of the evidence shows, this was not a case in which the Government relied on "statistics alone." The individuals who testified about their personal experiences with the company brought the cold numbers convincingly to life.

In any event, our cases make it unmistakably clear that "[s]tatistical analyses have served and will continue to serve an important role" in cases in which the existence of discrimination is a disputed issue. *Mayor of Philadelphia* v. *Educational Equality League,* 415 U.S. 605, 620. See also *McDonnell Douglas Corp.* v. *Green, supra,* at 805, 5 FEP Cases, at 970. Cf. *Washington* v. *Davis,* 426 U.S. 229, 241-42, 12 FEP Cases 1415, 1422. We have repeatedly approved the use of statistical proof, where it reached proportions comparable to those in this case, to establish a prima facie case of racial discrimination in jury selection cases, see, *e.g., Turner* v. *Fouche,* 396 U.S. 346; *Hernandez* v. *Texas,* 347 U.S. 475; *Norris* v. *Alabama,* 294 U.S. 587. Statistics are equally competent in proving employment discrimination.[20] We caution only that statistics are not irrefu-

---

[19] Two examples are illustrative:

George Taylor, a Negro, worked for the company as a city driver in Los Angeles, beginning late in 1966. In 1968, after hearing that a white city driver had transferred to a line-driver job, he told the terminal manager that he also would like to consider line driving. The manager replied that there would be "a lot of problems on the road . . . with different people, Caucasian, et cetera," and stated "I don't feel the company is ready for this right now. . . . Give us a little time. It will come around, you know." Mr. Taylor made similar requests some months later and got similar responses. He was never offered a line-driving job or an application.

Feliberto Trujillo worked as a dockman at the company's Denver terminal. When he applied for a line-driver job in 1967, he was told by a personnel officer that he had one strike against him. He asked what that was and was told: "You're a Chicano, and as far as we know, there isn't a Chicano driver in the system."

[20] Petitioners argue that statistics, at least those comparing the racial composition of an employer's work force to the composition of the population at large, should never be given decisive weight in a Title VII case because to do so would conflict with § 703 (j) of the Act, 42 U.S.C. § 2000(e)-2(j). That section provides:

"Nothing contained in this subchapter shall be interpreted to require any employer . . . to grant preferential treatment to any individual or to any group because of the race . . . or national origin of such individual or group on account of an imbalance which may exist with respect to the total number or percentage of persons of any race . . . or national origin employed by any employer . . . in comparison with the total number or percentage of persons of such race . . . or national origin in any community, State, section, or other area, or in the available work force in any community, State, section, or other area."

The argument fails in this case because the statistical evidence was not offered or used to support an erroneous theory that Title VII requires an employer's work force to be racially balanced. Statistics showing racial or ethnic imbalance are probative in a case such as this one only because such imbalance is often a telltale sign of purposeful discrimination; absent explanation, it is ordinarily to be expected that nondiscrimi-

table; they come in infinite variety and, like any other kind of evidence, they may be rebutted. In short, their usefulness depends on all of the surrounding facts and circumstances. See, *e.g., Hester* v. *Southern R. Co.,* 497 F.2d 1374, 1379-81, 8 FEP Cases 646, 650-52 (CA5).

In addition to its general protest against the use of statistics in Title VII cases, the company claims that in this case the statistics revealing racial imbalance are misleading because they fail to take into account the company's particular business situation as of the effective date of Title VII. The company concedes that its line drivers were virtually all white in July 1965, but it claims that thereafter business conditions were such that its work force dropped. Its argument is that low personnel turnover, rather than post-Act discrimination, accounts for more recent disparities. It points to substantial minority hiring in later years, especially after 1971, as showing that any pre-Act patterns of discrimination were broken.

The argument would be a forceful one if this were an employer who, at the time of suit, had done virtually no new hiring since the effective date of Title VII. But it is not. Although the company's total number of employees apparently dropped somewhat during the late 1960's, the record shows that many line drivers continued to be hired throughout this period, and that almost all of them were white.[21] To be sure, there were improvements in the company's hiring practices. The Court of Appeals commented that "T.I.M.E.-D.C.'s recent minority hiring progress stands as a laudable good faith effort to eradicate the effects of past discrimination in the area of hiring and initial assignment."[22] 517 F.2d,

---

natory hiring practices will in time result in a work force more or less representative of the racial and ethnic composition of the population in the community from which employees are hired. Evidence of longlasting and gross disparity between the composition of a work force and that of the general population thus may be significant even though § 703(j) makes clear that Title VII imposes no requirement that a work force mirror the general population. See, *e.g., United States* v. *Sheet Metal Workers Local 36,* 416 F.2d 123, 127 n. 7, 2 FEP Cases 127, 130. Considerations such as small sample size may, of course, detract from the value of such evidence, see, *e.g., Mayor of Philadelphia* v. *Educational Equality League,* 415 U.S. 605, 620-621, and evidence showing that the figures for the general population might not accurately reflect the pool of qualified job applicants would also be relevant. Ibid. See generally Schlei & Grossman, EMPLOYMENT DISCRIMINATION LAW, 1161-93 (1976).

"Since the passage of the Civil Rights Act of 1964, the courts have frequently relied upon statistical evidence to prove a violation. . . . In many cases the only available avenue of proof is the use of racial statistics to uncover clandestine and covert discrimination by the employer or union involved." *United States* v. *Ironworkers Local 86,* 443 F.2d 544, 551, 3 FEP Cases 496, 500-501 (CA9). See also, *e.g., Pettway* v. *American Cast Iron Pipe Co.,* 494 F.2d 211, 225 n. 34, 7 FEP Cases 1115, 1126-27 (CA5); *Brown* v. *Gaston County Dyeing Mach. Co.,* 457 F.2d 1377, 1382, 4 FEP Cases 514, 518 (CA4); *United States* v. *Jacksonville Terminal Co.,* 451 F.2d 418, 442, 3 FEP Cases 862, 881-82 (CA5); *Parham* v. *Southwestern Bell Tel. Co.,* 433 F.2d 421, 426, 2 FEP Cases 1017, 1021 (CA8); *Jones* v. *Lee Way Motor Freight, Inc.,* 431 F.2d 245, 247, 2 FEP Cases 895, 897 (CA10).

21 Between July 2, 1965, and January 1, 1969, hundreds of line drivers were hired systemwide, either from the outside or from the ranks of employees filling other jobs within the company. None was a Negro. Government Exh. 204.

22 For example, in 1971 the company hired 116 new line drivers, of whom 16 were Negro or Spanish-surnamed Americans. Minority employees composed 7.1% of the company's systemwide work force in 1967 and 10.5% in 1972. Minority hiring increased greatly in 1972 and 1973, presumably due at least in part to the existence of the consent decree. See 517 F.2d, at 316 n. 31, 11 FEP Cases, at 78.

at 316, 11 FEP Cases, at 78. But the District Court and the Court of Appeals found upon substantial evidence that the company had engaged in a course of discrimination that continued well after the effective date of Title VII. The company's later changes in its hiring and promotion policies could be little comfort to the victims of the earlier post-Act discrimination, and could not erase its previous illegal conduct or its obligation to afford relief to those who suffered because of it. Cf. *Albemarle Paper Co.* v. *Moody, supra,* at 413-23, 10 FEP Cases, at 1186-89.[23]

The District Court and the Court of Appeals, on the basis of substantial evidence, held that the Government had proved a prima facie case of systematic and purposeful employment discrimination, continuing well beyond the effective date of Title VII. The company's attempts to rebut that conclusion were held to be inadequate.[24] For the reasons we have summarized, there is no warrant for this Court to disturb the findings of the District Court and the Court of Appeals on this basic issue. See *Blau* v. *Lehman,* 368 U.S. 403, 408-409; *Faulkner* v. *Gibbs,* 338 U.S. 267; *United States* v. *Dickinson,* 331 U.S. 745, 751; *United States* v. *Commercial Credit Co.,* 286 U.S. 63, 67; *United States* v. *Chemical Foundation,*

---

[23] The company's narrower attacks upon the statistical evidence—that there was no precise delineation of the areas referred to in the general population statistics, that the Government did not demonstrate that minority populations were located close to terminals or that transportation was available, that the statistics failed to show what portion of the minority population was suited by age, health, or other qualifications to hold trucking jobs, etc.—are equally lacking in force. At best, these attacks go only to the accuracy of the comparison between the composition of the company's work force at various terminals and the general population of the surrounding communities. They detract little from the Government's further showing that Negroes and Spanish-surnamed Americans who were hired were overwhelmingly excluded from line-driver jobs. Such employees were willing to work, had access to the terminal, were healthy and of working age, and often were at least sufficiently qualified to hold city-driver jobs. Yet they became line drivers with far less frequency than whites. See, *e.g.,* Pre-trial Stipulation 14, summarized at 517 F.2d, at 312 n. 24, 11 FEP Cases, at 75 (of 2,919 whites who held driving jobs in 1971, 1,802 (62%) were line drivers and 1,117 (38%) were city drivers; of 180 Negroes and Spanish-surnamed Americans who held driving jobs, 13 (7%) were line drivers and 167 (93%) were city drivers).

In any event, fine tuning of the statistics could not have obscured the glaring absence of minority line drivers. As the Court of Appeals remarked, the company's inability to rebut the inference of discrimination came not from a misuse of statistics but from "the inexorable zero." 517 F.2d at 315, 11 FEP Cases, at 77.

[24] The company's evidence, apart from the showing of recent changes in hiring and promotion policies, consisted mainly of general statements that it hired only the best qualified applicants. But "affirmations of good faith in making individual selections are insufficient to dispel a prima facie case of systematic exclusion." *Alexander* v. *Louisiana,* 405 U.S. 625, 632.

The company also attempted to show that all of the witnesses who testified to specific instances of discrimination either were not discriminated against or suffered no injury. The Court of Appeals correctly ruled that the trial judge was not bound to accept this testimony and that it committed no error by relying instead on the other overpowering evidence in the case. 517 F.2d, at 315, 11 FEP Cases, at 77. The Court of Appeals was also correct in the view that individual proof concerning each class member's specific injury was appropriately left to proceedings to determine individual relief. In a suit brought by the Government under § 707(a) of the Act the District Court's initial concern is in deciding whether the Government has proved that the defendant has engaged in a pattern or practice of discriminatory conduct. See *infra,* at 31-35, 14 FEP Cases, at 1528-30.

*Inc.*, 272 U.S. 1, 14; *Baker* v. *Schofield*, 243 U.S. 114, 118; *Towson* v. *Moore*, 173 U.S. 17, 24.

## B

The District Court and the Court of Appeals also found that the seniority system contained in the collective-bargaining agreements between the company and the union operated to violate Title VII of the Act.

For purposes of calculating benefits, such as vacations, pensions, and other fringe benefits, an employee's seniority under this system runs from the date he joins the company, and takes into account his total service in all jobs and bargaining units. For competitive purposes, however, such as determining the order in which employees may bid for particular jobs, are laid off, or are recalled from layoff, it is bargaining-unit seniority that controls. Thus, a line driver's seniority, for purposes of bidding for particular runs [25] and protection against layoff, takes into account only the length of time he has been a line driver at a particular terminal.[26] The practical effect is that a city driver or serviceman who transfers to a line-driver job must forfeit all the competitive seniority he has accumulated in his previous bargaining unit and start at the bottom of the line-drivers' "board."

The vice of this arrangement, as found by the District Court and the Court of Appeals, was that it "locked" minority workers into inferior jobs and perpetuated prior discrimination by discouraging transfers to jobs as line drivers. While the disincentive applied to all workers, including whites, it was Negroes and Spanish-surnamed persons who, those courts found, suffered the most because many of them had been denied the equal opportunity to become line drivers when they were initially hired, whereas whites either had not sought or were refused line-driver positions for reason unrelated to their race or national origin.

The linchpin of the theory embraced by the District Court and the Court of Appeals was that a discriminatee who must forfeit his competitive seniority in order finally to obtain a line-driver job will never be able to "catch up" to the seniority level of his contemporary who was not subject to discrimination.[27] Accordingly, this continued, built-in

[25] Certain long-distance runs, for a variety of reasons, are more desirable than others. The best runs are chosen by the line drivers at the top of the "board"—a list of drivers arranged in order of their bargaining-unit seniority.

[26] Both bargaining-unit seniority and company seniority rights are generally limited to service at one particular terminals, except as modified by the Southern Conference Area Over-the-Road Supplemental Agreement. See *supra*, at 6-7, n. 10, 14 FEP Cases, at 1518.

[27] An example would be a Negro who was qualified to be a line driver in 1958 but who, because of his race, was assigned instead a job as a city driver, and is allowed to become a line driver only in 1971. Because he loses his competitive seniority when he transfers jobs, he is forever junior to white line drivers hired between 1958 and 1970. The whites, rather than the Negro, will henceforth enjoy the preferable runs and the greater protection against layoff. Although the original discrimination occurred in 1958— before the effective date of Title VII—the seniority system operates to carry the effects of the discrimination into the present.

disadvantage to the prior discriminatee who transfers to a line-driver job was held to constitute a continuing violation of Title VII, for which both the employer and the union who jointly created and maintain the seniority system were liable.

The union, while acknowledging that the seniority system may in some sense perpetuate the effects of prior discrimination, asserts that the system is immunized from a finding of illegality by reason of § 703(h) of Title VII, 42 U.S.C. § 2000e-2(h), which provides in part:

"Notwithstanding any other provision of this subchapter, it shall not be an unlawful employment practice for an employer to apply different standards of compensation, or different terms, conditions, or privileges of employment pursuant to a bona fide seniority . . . system, . . . provided that such differences are not the result of an intention to discriminate because of race . . . or national origin. . . ."

It argues that the seniority system in this case is "bona fide" within the meaning of § 703(h) when judged in light of its history, intent, application, and all of the circumstances under which it was created and is maintained. More specifically, the union claims that the central purpose of § 703(h), is to ensure that mere perpetuation of *pre-Act* discrimination is not unlawful under Title VII. And, whether or not § 703(h) immunizes the perpetuation of *post-Act* discrimination, the union claims that the seniority system in this case has no such effect. Its position in this Court, as has been its position throughout this litigation, is that the seniority system presents no hurdle to post-Act discriminatees who seek retroactive seniority to the date they would have become line drivers but for the company's discrimination. Indeed, the union asserts that under its collective-bargaining agreements the union will itself take up the cause of the post-Act victim and attempt, through grievance procedures, to gain for him full "make whole" relief, including appropriate seniority.

The Government responds that a seniority system that perpetuates the effects of prior discrimination—pre-or post-Act—can never be "bona fide" under § 703(h); at a minimum Title VII prohibits those applications of a seniority system that perpetuate the effects on incumbent employees of prior discriminatory job assignments.

The issues thus joined are open ones in this Court.[28] We considered

---

28 Concededly, the view that § 703(h) does not immunize seniority systems that perpetuate the effects of prior discrimination has much support. It was apparently first adopted in *Quarles* v. *Philip Morris, Inc.*, 279 F. Supp. 505, 1 FEP Cases 260, 67 LRRM 2098 (ED Va.). The court there held that "a departmental seniority system *that has its genesis in racial discrimination* is not a *bona fide* seniority system." *Id.*, at 517, 1 FEP Cases, at 270 (first emphasis added). The *Quarles* view has since enjoyed wholesale adoption in the Courts of Appeals. See, *e.g.*, *Local 189, United Paperworks* v. *United States*, 416 F.2d 980, 987-88, 1 FEP Cases 875, 880, 71 LRRM 3070 (CA5); *United States* v. *Sheet Metal Workers Local 36*, 416 F.2d 123, 133-34, n. 20, 2 FEP Cases 127, 135 (CA8); *United States* v. *Bethlehem Steel Corp.*, 446 F.2d 652, 658-59, 3 FEP Cases 589, 593 (CA2); *United States* v. *Chesapeake & Ohio R. Co.*, 471 F.2d 582, 587-88, 5 FEP Cases 308, 312 (CA4). Insofar as the result in *Quarles* and in the cases that followed it depended upon findings that the seniority systems were themselves "racially discriminatory" or had their "genesis in racial discrimination," 279 F. Supp., at 517, 1 FEP Cases, at 270, the decisions can be viewed as resting upon the proposition that a seniority system that per-

§ 703(h) in *Franks* v. *Bowman Transportation Co.*, 424 U.S. 747, 12 FEP Cases 549; but there decided only that § 703(h) does not bar the award of retroactive seniority to job applicants who seek relief from an employer's post-Act hiring discrimination. We stated that "the thrust of [§ 703(h)] is directed toward defining what is and what is not an illegal discriminatory practice in instances in which the post-Act operation of a seniority system is challenged as perpetuating the effects of discrimination occurring prior to the effective date of the Act." 424 U.S., at 761, 12 FEP Cases, at 554-55. Beyond noting the general purpose of the statute, however, we did not undertake the task of statutory construction required in this case.

## (1)

Because the company discriminated both before and after the enactment of Title VII, the seniority system is said to have operated to perpetuate the effects of both pre- and post-Act discrimination. Post-Act discriminatees, however, may obtain full "make whole" relief, including retroactive seniority under *Franks* v. *Bowman, supra,* without attacking the legality of the seniority system as applied to them. *Franks* made clear and the union acknowledges that retroactive seniority may be awarded as relief from an employer's discriminatory hiring and assignment policies even if the seniority system agreement itself makes no provision for such relief.[29] 424 U.S., at 778-79, 12 FEP Cases, at 559. Here the Government has proved that the company engaged in a post-Act pattern of discriminatory hiring, assignment, transfer, and promotion policies. Any Negro or Spanish-surnamed American injured by those policies may receive all appropriate relief as a direct remedy for this discrimination.[30]

---

petuates the effects of pre-Act discrimination cannot be bona fide if an intent to discriminate entered into its very adoption.

[29] Article 38 of the National Master Freight Agreement between T.I.M.E.-D.C. and the International Brotherhood of Teamsters in effect as of the date of the systemwide lawsuit provided:

"The Employer and the Union agree not to discriminate against any individual with respect to his hiring, compensation, terms or conditions of employment because of such individual's race, color, religion, sex, or national origin, nor will they limit, segregate or classify employees in any way to deprive any individual employee of employment opportunities because of his race, color, religion, sex, or national origin."

Any discrimination by the company would apparently be a grievable breach of this provision of the contract.

[30] The legality of the seniority system insofar as it perpetuates post-Act discrimination nonetheless remains at issue in this case, in light of the injunction entered against the union. See *supra*, at 4, 14 FEP Cases, at 1517. Our decision today in *United Air Lines* v. *Evans, post*, at _____, 14 FEP Cases, at 1510, is largely dispositive of this issue. *Evans* holds that the operation of a seniority system is not unlawful under Title VII even though it perpetuates post-Act discrimination that has not been the subject of a timely charge by the discriminatee. Here, of course, the Government has sued to remedy the post-Act discrimination directly and there is no claim that any relief would be time-barred. But this is simply an additional reason not to hold the seniority system unlawful, since such a holding would in no way enlarge the relief to be awarded. See *Franks* v. *Bowman*, 424 U.S., at 778-79, 12 FEP Cases, at 559. Section 703(h) on its face immunizes all bona fide seniority systems, and does not distinguish between the perpetuation of pre- and post-Act discrimination.

(2)

What remains for review is the judgment that the seniority system unlawfully perpetuated the effects of *pre-Act* discrimination. We must decide, in short, whether § 703(h) validates otherwise bona fide seniority systems that afford no constructive seniority to victims discriminated against prior to the effective date of Title VII, and it is to that issue that we now turn.

The primary purpose of Title VII was "to assure equality of employment opportunities and to eliminate those discriminatory practices and devices which have fostered racially stratified job environments to the disadvantage of minority citizens." *McDonnell Douglas Corp.* v. *Green, supra,* at 800, 5 FEP Cases, at 969.[31] See also *Albemarle Paper Co.* v. *Moody, supra,* at 417-18; *Alexander* v. *Gardner-Denver Co.,* 415 U.S. 36, 44, 7 FEP Cases 81, 84; *Griggs* v. *Duke Power Co., supra,* at 429-31, 3 FEP Cases, at 177-78. To achieve this purpose, Congress "proscribe[d] not only overt discrimination but also practices that are fair in form, but discriminatory in operation." *Griggs,* 401 U.S., at 431, 3 FEP Cases, at 178. Thus, the Court has repeatedly held that a prima facie Title VII violation may be established by policies or practices that are neutral on their face and in intent but that nonetheless discriminate in effect against a particular group. *General Electric Co.* v. *Gilbert,* 429 U.S. 125, 137, 13 FEP Cases 1657, 1662; *Washington* v. *Davis,* 426 U.S. 229, 246-247, 12 FEP Cases 1415, 1422; *Albemarle Paper Co.* v. *Moody, supra,* at 422, 425, 10 FEP Cases, at 1189, 1190; *McDonnell Douglas Corp.* v. *Green, supra,* at 802 n. 14, 5 FEP Cases, at 969, *Griggs* v. *Duke Power Co., supra.*

One kind of practice "fair in form, but discriminatory in operation" is that which perpetuates the effects of prior discrimination.[32] As the Court held in *Griggs, supra:* "Under the Act, practices, procedures, or tests neutral on their face, and even neutral in terms of intent, cannot be maintained if they operate to 'freeze' the status quo of prior discriminatory employment practices." 401 U.S., at 430, 3 FEP Cases, at 177.

Were it not for § 703(h), the seniority system in this case would seem to fall under the *Griggs* rationale. The heart of the system is its allocation

---

[31] We also noted in *McDonnell Douglas* that:
"There are societal as well as personal interests on both sides of the [employer-employee] equation. The broad, overriding interest, shared by employer, employee, and consumer, is efficient and trustworthy workmanship assured through fair and racially neutral employment and personnel decisions. In the implementation of such decisions, it is abundantly clear that Title VII tolerates no racial discrimination, subtle or otherwise," 411 U.S., at 801, 5 FEP Cases, at 969.

[32] *Asbestos Workers Local 53* v. *Vogler,* 407 F.2d 1047, 1 FEP Cases 577, 70 LRRM 2257 (CA5), provides an apt illustration. There a union had a policy of excluding persons not related to present members by blood or marriage. When in 1966 suit was brought to challenge this policy, all of the union's members were white, largely as a result of pre-Act, intentional racial discrimination. The court observed: "While the nepotism requirement is applicable to black and white alike and is not on its face discriminatory, in a completely white union the present effect of its continued application is to forever deny to negroes and Mexican-Americans any real opportunity for membership." 407 F.2d, at 1054, 1 FEP Cases, at 581.

of the choicest jobs, the greatest protection against layoffs, and other advantages to those employees who have been line drivers for the longest time. Where, because of the employer's prior intentional discrimination, the line drivers with the longest tenure are without exception white, the advantages of the seniority system flow disproportionately to them and away from Negro and Spanish-surnamed employees who might by now have enjoyed those advantages had not the employer discriminated before the passage of the Act. This disproportionate distribution of advantages does in a very real sense "operate to 'freeze' the status quo of prior discriminatory employment practices." *Ibid.* But both the literal terms of § 703(h) and the legislative history of Title VII demonstrate that Congress considered this very effect of many seniority systems and extended a measure of immunity to them.

Throughout the initial consideration of H. R. 7152, later enacted as the Civil Rights Act of 1964, critics of the bill charged that it would destroy existing seniority rights.[33] The consistent response of Title VII's congressional proponents and of the Justice Department was that seniority rights would not be affected, even where the employer had discriminated prior to the Act.[34] An interpretative memorandum placed in the Congressional Record by Senators Clark and Case stated:
"Title VII would have no effect on established seniority rights. Its effect is prospective and not retrospective. Thus, for example, *if a business has been discriminating in the past and as a result has an all-white working force, when the title comes into effect the employer's obligation would be simply to fill future vacancies on a non-discriminatory basis.* He would not be obliged—or indeed, permitted—to fire whites in order to hire Negroes, or to prefer Negroes for future vacancies, or, once Negroes are hired, to give them special seniority rights at the expense of the white workers hired earlier." 110 Cong. Rec. 7213 (1964) (emphasis added).[35]
A Justice Department statement concerning Title VII, placed in the Congressional Record by Senator Clark voiced the same conclusion:
"Title VII would have no effect on seniority rights existing at the time it takes effect. If for example, a collective bargaining contract provides that in the event of layoffs, those who were hired last must be laid off first, such a provision would not be affected in the least by Title VII. *This would be true even in the case where owing to discrimination prior to the*

---

[33] *E.g.,* H. R. Rep. No. 914, 88th Cong., 1st Sess., 65-66, 71 (1963) (minority report); 110 Cong. Rec. 486-488 (1964) (remarks of Sen. Hill); *id.,* at 2726 (remarks of Rep. Dowdy); *id.,* at 7091 (remarks of Sen. Stennis).

[34] In addition to the material cited in *Franks* v. *Bowman,* 424 U.S., at 759-62, 12 FEP Cases, at 554, see 110 Cong. Rec. 1518 (1964) (remarks of Rep. Celler); *id.,* at 6549 (remarks of Sen. Humphrey); *id.,* at 6564 (remarks of Sen. Kuchel).

[35] Senators Clark and Case were the "bipartisan captains" responsible for Title VII during the Senate debate. Bipartisan captains were selected for each title of the Civil Rights Act by the leading proponents of the Act in both parties. They were responsible for explaining their title in detail, defending it, and leading discussion on it. See 110 Cong. Rec. 6528 (1964) (remarks of Sen. Humphrey); Vass, *Title VII: Legislative History,* 7 B. C. IND. & COM. L. REV. 431, 444-445 (1966).

*effective date of the title, white workers had more seniority than Negroes."*
*Id.,* at 7207 (emphasis added).[36]

While these statements were made before § 703(h) was added to Title VII, they are authoritative indicators of that section's purpose. Section 703(h) was enacted as part of the Mansfield-Dirksen compromise substitute bill that cleared the way for the passage of Title VII.[37] The drafters of the compromise bill stated that one of its principal goals was to resolve the ambiguities in the House-passed version of H. R. 7152. See, *e.g., id.,* at 11935-937 (remarks of Sen. Dirksen); *id.,* at 12707 (remarks of Sen. Humphrey). As the debates indicate, one of those ambiguities concerned Title VII's impact on existing collectively bargained seniority rights. It is apparent that § 703(h) was drafted with an eye toward meeting the earlier criticism on this issue with an explicit provision embodying the understanding and assurances of the Act's proponents: namely, that Title VII would not outlaw such differences in treatment among employees as flowed from a bona fide seniority system that allowed for full exercise of seniority accumulated before the effective date of the Act. It is inconceivable that § 703(h), as part of a compromise bill, was intended to vitiate the earlier representations of the Act's supporters by increasing Title VII's impact on seniority systems. The statement of Senator Humphrey, noted in *Franks, supra,* at 761, 12 FEP Cases, at 554, confirms that the addition of § 703(h) "merely clarifies [Title VII's] present intent and effect." 110 Cong. Rec. 12723 (1964).

In sum, the unmistakable purpose of § 703(h) was to make clear that the routine application of a bona fide seniority system would not be unlawful under Title VII. As the legislative history shows, this was the intended result even where the employer's pre-Act discrimination resulted in whites having greater existing seniority rights than Negroes. Although a seniority system inevitably tends to perpetuate the effects of pre-Act discrimination in such cases, the congressional judgment was that Title VII should not outlaw the use of existing seniority lists and thereby destroy or water down the vested seniority rights of employees simply because their employer had engaged in discrimination prior to the passage of the Act.

To be sure, § 703(h) does not immunize all seniority systems. It refers only to "bona fide" systems, and a proviso requires that any differences in

36 The full text of the statement is set out in *Franks* v. *Bowman,* 424 U.S., at 760 n. 16, 12 FEP Cases, at 554. Senator Clark also introduced a set of answers to questions propounded by Senator Dirksen, which included the following exchange:
"Question. Would the same situation prevail in respect to promotions, when the management function is governed by a labor contract calling for promotions on the basis of seniority? What of dismissals? Normally, labor contracts call for 'last hired, first fired.' If the last hired are Negroes, is the employer discriminating if his contract requires they be first fired and the remaining employees are white?
"Answer. Seniority rights are in no way affected by the bill. If under a 'last hired, first fired' agreement a Negro happens to be the 'last hired,' he can still be 'first fired' as long as it is done because of his status as 'last hired' and not because of his race." 110 Cong. Rec. 7217 (1964). See *Franks, supra,* at 760 n. 16, 12 FEP Cases, at 554.

37 See *Franks* v. *Bowman,* 424 U.S. at 761, 12 FEP Cases, at 554; Vass, *Title VII: Legislative History,* 7 B. C. IND. & COM. L. REV. 431, 435 (1966).

treatment not be "the result of an intention to discriminate because of race . . . or national origin. . . ." But our reading of the legislative history compels us to reject the Government's broad argument that no seniority system that tends to perpetuate pre-Act discrimination can be "bona fide." To accept the argument would require us to hold that a seniority system becomes illegal simply because it allows the full exercise of the pre-Act seniority rights of employees of a company that discriminated before Title VII was enacted. It would place an affirmative obligation on the parties to the seniority agreement to subordinate those rights in favor of the claims of pre-Act discriminatees without seniority. The consequence would be a perversion of the congressional purpose. We cannot accept the invitation to disembowel § 703(h) by reading the words "bona fide" as the Government would have us do.[38] Accordingly, we hold that an otherwise neutral, legitimate seniority system does not become unlawful under Title VII simply because it may perpetuate pre-Act discrimination. Congress did not intend to make it illegal for employees with vested seniority rights to continue to exercise those rights, even at the expense of pre-Act discriminatees.[39]

That conclusion is inescapable even in a case, such as this one, where the pre-Act discriminatees are incumbent employees who accumulated seniority in other bargaining units. Although there seems to be no explicit reference in the legislative history to pre-Act discriminatees already employed in less desirable jobs, there can be no rational basis for distinguishing their claims from those of persons initially denied *any* job but hired later with less seniority than they might have had in the absence of pre-Act discrimination.[40] We rejected any such distinction in *Franks*, finding

[38] For the same reason, we reject the contention that the proviso in § 703(h), which bars differences in treatment resulting from "an intention to discriminate," applies to any application of a seniority system that may perpetuate past discrimination. In this regard the language of the Justice Department memorandum introduced at the legislative hearings, see *supra*, at 24, 14 FEP Cases, at 1525, is especially pertinent: "It is perfectly clear that when a worker is laid off or denied a chance for promotion because he is 'low man on the totem pole' he is not being discriminated against because of his race. . . . Any differences in treatment based on established seniority rights would not be based on race and would not be forbidden by the title." 110 Cong. Rec. 7207 (1964).

[39] The legislative history of the 1972 amendments to Title VII, summarized and discussed in *Franks, supra*, at 764-65, n. 21, 12 FEP Cases, at 556 *id.*, at 796-97, n. 18, 12 FEP Cases, at 568 (opinion of POWELL, J.), in no way points to a different result. As the discussion in *Franks* indicates, that history is itself susceptible of different readings. The few broad references to perpetuation of pre-Act discrimination or "*de facto* segregated job ladders," see, *e.g.*, S. Rep. No. 92-415, pp. 5, 9 (1971); H. R. Rep. No. 92-238, pp. 8, 17 (1971), did not address the specific issue presented by this case. And the assumption of the authors of the Conference Report that "the present case law as developed by the courts would continue to govern the applicability and construction of Title VII," see *Franks, supra*, at 765 n. 21, 12 FEP Cases, at 556, of course does not foreclose our consideration of that issue. More importantly, the section of Title VII that we construe here, § 703(h), was enacted in 1964, not 1972. The views of members of a later Congress, concerning different sections of Title VII, enacted after this litigation was commenced, are entitled to little if any weight. It is the intent of the Congress that enacted § 703(h) in 1964, unmistakable in this case, that controls.

[40] That Title VII did not proscribe the denial of fictional seniority to pre-Act discriminatees who got no job was recognized even in *Quarles* v. *Phillip Morris, Inc.*, 279 F. Supp. 505, 1 FEP Cases 260, 67 LRRM 2098 (ED Va.), and its progeny. Quarles

that it had "no support anywhere in Title VII or its legislative history," 424 U.S., at 768, 12 FEP Cases, at 557. As discussed above, Congress in 1964 made clear that a seniority system is not unlawful because it honors employees' existing rights, even where the employer has engaged in pre-Act discriminatory hiring or promotion practices. It would be as contrary to that mandate to forbid the exercise of seniority rights with respect to discriminatees who held inferior jobs as with respect to later-hired minority employees who previously were denied any job. If anything, the latter group is the more disadvantaged. As in *Franks*, " '[i]t would indeed be surprising if Congress gave a remedy for the one [group] which it denied for the other.' " *Id.*, quoting *Phelps Dodge Corp.* v. *NLRB*, 313 U.S. 177, 187, 8 LRRM 439.[41]

(3)

The seniority system in this case is entirely bona fide. It applies equally to all races and ethnic groups. To the extent that it "locks" employees into nonline-driver jobs, it does so for all. The city drivers and servicemen who are discouraged from transferring to line-driver jobs are not all Negroes or Spanish-surnamed Americans; to the contrary, the overwhelming majority are white. The placing of line drivers in a separate bargaining unit from other employees is rational, in accord with the industry practice, and consistent with NLRB precedents.[42] It is conceded that the seniority system did not have its genesis in racial discrimination, and that it was negotiated and has been maintained free from any illegal purpose. In these circumstances, the single fact that the system extends

---

stressed the fact that the references in the legislative history were to employment seniority rather than departmental seniority. 279 F. Supp., at 516, 1 FEP Cases, at 269. In *Local 189, United Paperworks* v. *United States*, 416 F.2d 980, 1 FEP Cases 875, 71 LRRM 3070 (CA5), another leading case in this area, the court observed: "No doubt, Congress, to prevent 'reverse discrimination' meant to protect certain seniority rights that could not have existed but for previous racial discrimination. For example a Negro who had been rejected by an employer on racial grounds before passage of the Act could not, after being hired, claim to outrank whites who had been hired before him but after his original rejection, even though the Negro might have had senior status but for the past discrimination." 416 F.2d, at 994, 1 FEP Cases, at 886.

41 In addition, there is no reason to suppose that Congress intended in 1964 to extend less protection to legitimate departmental seniority systems than to plant-wide seniority systems. Then as now, seniority was measured in a number of ways, including length of time with the employer, in a particular plant, in a department, in a job, or in a line of progression. See Aaron, *Reflections on the Legal Nature and Enforceability of Seniority Rights*, 75 HARV. L. REV. 1532, 1534 (1962); Cooper & Sobol, *Seniority and Testing under Fair Employment Laws: A General Approach to Objective Criteria of Hiring and Promotion*, 82 HARV. L. REV. 1598, 1602 (1969). The legislative history contains no suggestion that any one system was preferred.

42 See *Georgia Highway Express*, 150 NLRB 1649, 1651, 58 LRRM 1319: "The Board has long held that local drivers and over-the-road drivers constitute separate appropriate units where they are shown to be clearly defined, homogeneous, and functionally distinct groups with separate interests which can effectively be represented separately for bargaining purposes. . . . In view of the different duties and functions, separate supervision, and different bases of payment, it is clear that the over-the-road drivers have divergent interests from those of the employees in the [city operations] unit . . . and should not be included in that unit."

no retroactive seniority to pre-Act discriminatees does not make it unlawful.

Because the seniority system was protected by § 703(h), the union's conduct in agreeing to and maintaining the system did not violate Title VII. On remand, the District Court's injunction against the union must be vacated.[43]

### III

Our conclusion that the seniority system does not violate Title VII will necessarily affect the remedy granted to individual employees on remand of this litigation to the District Court. Those employees who suffered only pre-Act discrimination are not entitled to relief, and no person may be given retroactive seniority to a date earlier than the effective date of the Act. Several other questions relating to the appropriate measure of individual relief remain, however, for our consideration.

The petitioners argue generally that the trial court did not err in tailoring the remedy to the "degree of injury" suffered by each individual employee, and that the Court of Appeals' "qualification date" formula sweeps with too broad a brush by granting a remedy to employees who were not shown to be actual victims of unlawful discrimination. Specifically, the petitioners assert that no employee should be entitled to relief until the Government demonstrates that he was an actual victim of the company's discriminatory practices; that no employee who did not apply for a line-driver job should be granted retroactive competitive seniority; and that no employee should be elevated to a line-driver job ahead of any current line driver on layoff status. We consider each of these contentions separately.

### A

The petitioners' first contention is in substance that the Government's burden of proof in a pattern or practice case must be equivalent to that outlined in *McDonnell Douglas* v. *Green, supra.* Since the Government introduced specific evidence of company discrimination against only some 40 employees, they argue that the District Court properly refused to award retroactive seniority to the remainder of the class of minority incumbent employees.

In *McDonnell Douglas* the Court considered "the order and allocation of proof in a private, non-class action challenging employment discrimination." 411 U.S., at 800, 5 FEP Cases, at 968. We held that an individual Title VII complainant must carry the initial burden of proof by establishing a prima facie case of racial discrimination. On the specific facts there involved, we concluded that this burden was met by showing that a

---

[43] The union will properly remain in this litigation as a defendant so that full relief may be awarded the victims of the employer's post-Act discrimination, Fed. Rule Civ. Proc. 19(a). See *EEOC* v. *MacMillan Bloedel Containers, Inc.,* 503 F.2d 1086, 1095, 8 FEP Cases 897, 904 (CA6).

qualified applicant, who was a member of a racial minority group, had unsuccessfully sought a job for which there was a vacancy and for which the employer continued thereafter to seek applicants with similar qualifications. This initial showing justified the inference that the minority applicant was denied an employment opportunity for reasons prohibited by Title VII, and therefore shifted the burden to the employer to rebut that inference by offering some legitimate nondiscriminatory reason for the rejection. *Id.*, at 802, 5 FEP Cases, at 969.

The company and union seize upon the *McDonnell Douglas* pattern as the *only* means of establishing a prima facie case of individual discrimination. Our decision in that case, however, did not purport to create an inflexible formulation. We expressly noted that "[t]he facts necessarily will vary in Title VII cases, and the specification . . . of the prima facie proof required from [a plaintiff] is not necessarily applicable in every respect to differing factual situations." 411 U.S., at 802 n. 13, 5 FEP Cases, at 969. The importance of *McDonnell Douglas* lies not in its specification of the discrete elements of proof there required, but in its recognition of the general principle that any Title VII plaintiff must carry the initial burden of offering evidence adequate to create an inference that an employment decision was based on a discriminatory criterion illegal under the Act.[44]

In *Franks* v. *Bowman Transportation Co.* the Court applied this principle in the context of a class action. The Franks' plaintiffs proved, to the satisfaction of a district court, that Bowman Transportation Company "had engaged in a pattern of racial discrimination in various company policies, including the hiring, transfer, and discharge of employees." 424 U.S., at 751, 12 FEP Cases, at 550-51. Despite this showing, the trial court denied seniority relief to certain members of the class of discriminatees because not every individual had shown that he was qualified for the job he sought and that a vacancy had been available. We held that the trial court had erred in placing this burden on the individual plaintiffs. By "demonstrating the existence of a discriminatory hiring pattern and practice" the plaintiffs had made out a prima facie case of discrimination against the individual class members; the burden therefore shifted to the employer "to prove that individuals who reapply were not in fact victims of previous hiring discrimination." 424 U.S., at 772, 12 FEP Cases, at 559. The *Franks* case thus illustrates another means by which a Title VII plaintiff's initial burden of proof can be met. The class there alleged a broad-based policy of employment discrimination; upon

---

[44] The *McDonnell Douglas* case involved an individual complainant seeking to prove one instance of unlawful discrimination. An employer's isolated decision to reject an applicant who belongs to a racial minority does not show that the rejection was racially based. Although the *McDonnell Douglas* formula does not require direct proof of discrimination, it does demand that the alleged discriminatee demonstrate at least that his rejection did not result from the two most common legitimate reasons on which an employer might rely to reject a job applicant: an absolute or relative lack of qualifications or the absence of a vacancy in the job sought. Elimination of these reasons for the refusal to hire is sufficient, absent other explanation, to create an inference that the decision was a discriminatory one.

proof of that allegation there were reasonable grounds to infer that individual hiring decisions were made in pursuit of the discriminatory policy and to require the employer to come forth with evidence dispelling that inference.[45]

Although not all class actions will necessarily follow the *Franks* model, the nature of a pattern or practice suit brings it squarely within our holding in *Franks*. The plaintiff in a pattern or practice action is the Government, and its initial burden is to demonstrate that unlawful discrimination has been a regular procedure or policy followed by an employer or group of employers. See pp. 9-10, and n. 16, *supra*, 14 FEP Cases, at 1519. At the initial, "liability" stage of a pattern or practice suit the Government is not required to offer evidence that each person for whom it will ultimately seek relief was a victim of the employer's discriminatory policy. Its burden is to establish a prima facie case that such a policy existed. The burden then shifts to the employer to defeat the prima facie showing of a pattern or practice by demonstrating that the Government's proof is either inaccurate or insignificant. An employer might show, for example, that the claimed discriminatory pattern is a product of pre-Act hiring rather than unlawful post-Act discrimination, or that during the period it is alleged to have pursued a discriminatory policy it made too few employment decisions to justify the inference that it had engaged in a regular practice of discrimination.[46]

If an employer fails to rebut the inference that arises from the Government's prima facie case, a trial court may then conclude that a violation has occurred and determine the appropriate remedy. Without any future evidence from the Government, a court's finding of a pattern or practice justifies an award of prospective relief. Such relief might take the form

[45] The holding in *Franks* that proof of a discriminatory pattern and practice creates a rebuttable presumption in favor of individual relief is consistent with the manner in which presumptions are created generally. Presumptions shifting the burden of proof are often created to reflect judicial evaluations of probabilities and to conform with a party's superior access to the proof. See C. McCormick, HANDBOOK OF THE LAW OF EVIDENCE §§ 337, 343 (E. Cleary ed. 1972); James, *Burdens of Proof*, 47 VA. L. REV. 51, 61 (1961). See also *Keyes* v. *School Dist. No. 1*, 413 U.S. 189, 208-209. These factors were present in *Franks*. Although the prima facie case did not conclusively demonstrate that all of the employer's decisions were part of the proven discriminatory pattern and practice, it did create a greater likelihood that any single decision was a component of the overall pattern. Moreover, the finding of a pattern or practice changed the position of the employer to that of a proven wrongdoer. Finally, the employer was in the best position to show why any individual employee was denied an employment opportunity. Insofar as the reasons related to available vacancies or the employer's evaluation of the applicant's qualifications, the company's records were the most relevant items of proof. If the refusal to hire was based on other factors, the employer and its agents knew best what those factors were and the extent to which they influenced the decision-making process.

[46] The employer's defense must, of course, be designed to meet the prima facie case of the Government. We do not mean to suggest that there are any particular limits on the type of evidence an employer may use. The point is that at the liability stage of a pattern or practice trial the focus often will not be on individual hiring decisions, but on a pattern of discriminatory decisionmaking. While a pattern might be demonstrated by examining the discrete decisions of which it is composed, the Government's suits have more commonly involved proof of the expected result of a regularly followed discriminatory policy. In such cases the employer's burden is to provide a nondiscriminatory explanation for the apparently discriminatory result. See n. 20, and cases cited therein, *supra*.

of an injunctive order against continuation of the discriminatory practice, an order that the employer keep records of its future employment decisions and file periodic reports with the court, or any other order "necessary to ensure the full employment of the rights" protected by Title VII.[47]

When the Government seeks individual relief for the victims of the discriminatory practice, a district court must usually conduct additional proceedings after the liability phase of the trial to determine the scope of individual relief. The petitioners' contention in this case is that if the Government has not, in the course of proving a pattern or practice, already brought forth specific evidence that each individual was discriminatorily denied an employment opportunity, it must carry that burden at the second, "remedial" stage of trial. That basic contention was rejected in the *Franks* case. As was true of the particular facts in *Franks*, and as is typical of Title VII pattern or practice suits, the question of individual relief does not arise until it has been proved that the employer has followed an employment policy of unlawful discrimination. The force of that proof does not dissipate at the remedial stage of the trial. The employer cannot, therefore, claim that there is no reason to believe that its individual employment decisions were discriminatorily based; it has already been shown to have maintained a policy of discriminatory decisionmaking.

The proof of the pattern or practice supports an inference that any particular employment decision, during the period in which the discriminatory policy was in force, was made in pursuit of that policy. The Government need only show that an alleged individual discriminatee unsuccessfully applied for a job [48] and therefore was a potential victim of the proven discrimination. As in *Franks*, the burden then rests on the employer to demonstrate that the individual applicant was denied an employment opportunity for lawful reasons. See 424 U.S., at 773 n. 32, 12 FEP Cases, at 559.

In Part II-A, supra, we have held that the District Court and Court of Appeals were not in error in finding that the Government had proved a systemwide pattern and practice of racial and ethnic discrimination on the part of the company. On remand, therefore, every post-Act minority group applicant [49] for a line-driver position will be presumptively entitled to relief, subject to a showing by the company that its earlier refusal to place the applicant in a line-driver job was not based on its policy of discrimination.[50]

---

[47] The federal courts have freely exercised their broad equitable discretion to devise prospective relief designed to assure that employers found to be in violation of § 707 (a) eliminate their discriminatory practices and the effects therefrom. See, *e.g.*, cases cited in n. 51, *infra*. In this case prospective relief was incorporated in the parties' consent decree. See *supra*, at 3-4, n. 4, 14 FEP Cases at 1517.

[48] Nonapplicants are discussed in Part III-B, *infra*.

[49] Employees who initially applied for line-driver jobs and were hired in other jobs before the effective date of the Act, and who did not later apply for transfer to line-driver jobs, are part of the group of nonapplicants discussed infra.

[50] Any nondiscriminatory justification offered by the company will be subject to

## B

The Court of Appeals' "qualification date" formula for relief did not distinguish between incumbent employees who had applied for line-driver jobs and those who had not. The appellate court held that where there has been a showing of classwide discriminatory practices coupled with a seniority system that perpetuates the effects of that discrimination, an individual member of the class need not show that he unsuccessfully applied for the position from which the class had been excluded. In support of its award of relief to all non-applicants, the Court suggested that "as a practical matter . . . a member of the affected class may well have concluded that an application for transfer to an all White position such as [line driver] was not worth the candle." 517 F.2d, at 320, 11 FEP Cases, at 81.

The company contends that a grant of retroactive seniority to these nonapplicants is inconsistent with the make-whole purpose of a Title VII remedy and impermissibly will require the company to give preferential treatment to employees solely because of their race. The thrust of the company's contention is that unless a minority-group employee actually applied for a line-driver job, either for initial hire or for transfer, he has suffered no injury from whatever discrimination might have been involved in the refusal of such jobs to those who actually applied for them.

The Government argues in response that there should be no "immutable rule" that nonapplicants are nonvictims, and contends that a determination whether nonapplicants have suffered from unlawful discrimination will necessarily vary depending on the circumstances of each particular case. The Government further asserts that under the specific facts of this case, the Court of Appeals correctly determined that all qualified nonapplicants were likely victims and were therefore presumptively entitled to relief.

The question whether seniority relief may be awarded to nonapplicants was left open by our decision in *Franks*, since the class at issue in that case was limited to "identifiable applicants who were denied employment . . . after the effective date . . . of Title VII." 424 U.S., at 750, 12 FEP Cases, at 550. We now decide that an incumbent employee's failure to apply for a job is not an inexorable bar to an award of retroactive seniority. Individual nonapplicants must be given an opportunity to undertake their difficult task of proving that they should be treated as applicants and therefore are presumptively entitled to relief accordingly.

## (1)

Analysis of this problem must begin with the premise that the scope of a district court's remedial powers under Title VII is determined by the

---

further evidence by the Government that the purported reason for an applicant's rejection was in fact a pretext for unlawful discrimination. *McDonnell Douglas* v. *Green, supra*, at 804-806, 5 FEP Cases, at 970.

purposes of the Act. *Albemarle Paper Co.* v. *Moody, supra,* at 417, 10
FEP Cases, at 1187. In *Griggs* v. *Duke Power Co., supra,* and again in
*Albemarle,* the Court noted that a primary objective of Title VII is
prophylactic: to achieve equal employment opportunity and to remove
the barriers that have operated to favor white male employees over other
employees. 401 U.S., at 429-30, 3 FEP Cases, at 177; 422 U.S., at 417, 10
FEP Cases, at 1187. The prospect of retroactive relief for victims of
discrimination serves this purpose by providing the " 'spur or catalyst
which causes employers and unions to self-examine and to self-evaluate
their employment practices and to endeavor to eliminate, so far as possible, the last vestiges' " of their discriminatory practices. *Albemarle, supra,*
at 417-18, 10 FEP Cases, at 1187. An equally important purpose of the
Act is "to make persons whole for injuries suffered on account of unlawful employment discrimination." *Id.,* at 418, 10 FEP Cases, at 1187. In
determining the specific remedies to be afforded, a district court is "to
fashion such relief as the particular circumstances of a case may require
to effect restitution." *Franks, supra,* at 764, 12 FEP Cases, at 556.

Thus, the Court has held that the purpose of Congress in vesting broad
equitable powers in Title VII courts was "to make possible the 'fashion-
[ing] [of] the most complete relief possible,' " and that the district courts
have " 'not merely the power but the duty to render a decree which will
so far as possible eliminate the discriminatory effects of the past as well
as bar like discrimination in the future.' " *Albemarle, supra,* at 421, 418,
10 FEP Cases, at 1189, 1187-88. More specifically, in *Franks* we decided
that a court must ordinarily award a seniority remedy unless there exist
reasons for denying relief " 'which, if applied generally, would not
frustrate the central statutory purposes of eradicating discrimination . . .
and making persons whole for injuries suffered.' " 424 U.S., at 771, 12
FEP Cases, at 559, quoting *Albemarle, supra,* at 421, 10 FEP Cases, at
1189.

Measured against these standards, the company's assertion that a person who has not actually applied for a job can *never* be awarded seniority
relief cannot prevail. The effects of and the injuries suffered from discriminatory employment practices are not always confined to those who
were expressly denied a requested employment opportunity. A consistently
enforced discriminatory policy can surely deter job applications from
those who are aware of it and are unwilling to subject themselves
to the humiliation of explicit and certain rejection.

If an employer should announce his policy of discrimination by a sign
reading "Whites Only" on the hiring-office door, his victims would not
be limited to the few who ignored the sign and subjected themselves to
personal rebuffs. The same message can be communicated to potential
applicants more subtly but just as clearly by an employer's actual practices—by his consistent discriminatory treatment of actual applicants, by
the manner in which he publicizes vacancies, his recruitment techniques,
his responses to casual or tentative inquiries, and even by the racial or
ethnic composition of that part of his work-force from which he has

discriminatorily excluded members of minority groups.[51] When a person's desire for a job is not translated into a formal application solely because of his unwillingness to engage in a futile gesture he is as much a victim of discrimination as is he who goes through the motions of submitting an application.

In cases decided under the National Labor Relations Act, the model for Title VII's remedial provisions, *Albemarle, supra,* at 419, 10 FEP Cases, at 1188; *Franks, supra,* at 769, 12 FEP Cases, at 557, the National Labor Relations Board, and the courts in enforcing its orders, have recognized that the failure to submit a futile application does not bar an award of relief to a person claiming that he was denied employment because of union affiliation or activity. In *NLRB* v. *Nevada Consolidated Copper Corp.,* 316 U.S. 105, 10 LRRM 607, this Court enforced an order of the Board directing an employer to hire, with retroactive benefits, former employees who had not applied for newly available jobs because of the employer's well-known policy of refusing to hire union members. See *In re Nevada Consolidated Copper Corp.,* 26 NLRB 1182, 1208, 1231, 7 LRRM 33. Similarly, when an application would have been no more than a vain gesture in light of employer discrimination, the Courts of Appeals have enforced Board orders reinstating striking workers despite the failure of individual strikers to apply for reinstatement when the strike ended. *E.g., NLRB* v. *Park Edge Sheridan Meats, Inc.,* 323 F.2d 956, 54 LRRM 2411 (CA2); *NLRB* v. *Valley Die Cast Corp.,* 303 F.2d 64, 50 LRRM 2281 (CA6); *Eagle-Picher Mining & Smelting Co.,* v. *NLRB,* 119 F.2d 903, 8 LRRM 824 (CA8). See also *Piasecki Aircraft Corp.* v. *NLRB,* 280 F.2d 575, 46 LRRM 2469, 3169 (CA3); *NLRB* v. *Anchor Rome Mills,* 228 F.2d 775, 37 LRRM 2367 (CA5); *NLRB* v. *Lummus Co.,* 210 F.2d 377, 33 LRRM 2513 (CA5). Consistent with the NLRA model, several Courts of Appeals have held in Title VII cases that a nonapplicant can be a victim of unlawful discrimination entitled to make-whole relief when an application would have been a useless act serving only to confirm a discriminatee's knowledge that the job he wanted was unavailable to him. *Acha* v. *Beame,* 531 F.2d 648, 656, 12 FEP Cases 257, 263 (CA2); *Hairston* v. *McLean Trucking Co.,* 520 F.2d 226, 231-233, 11 FEP Cases 91, 95-96 (CA4); *Bing* v. *Roadway Express, Inc.,* 485 F.2d 441, 451, 6 FEP Cases 677, 685 (CA5); *United States* v. *N. L. Industries, Inc.,* 479 F.2d 354, 369, 5 FEP Cases 823, 834 (CA8).

---

[51] The far-ranging effects of subtle discriminatory practices have not escaped the scrutiny of the federal courts, which have provided relief from practices designed to discourage job applications from minority-group members. See, *e.g., Franks* v. *Bowman Transportation Co.,* 495 F.2d 398, 418-19, 8 FEP Cases 66, 80-81 (CA5) (public recruitment and advertising), *rev'd on other grounds,* 424 U.S. 747, 12 FEP Cases 549; *Carter* v. *Gallagher,* 452 F.2d 315, 319, 3 FEP Cases 900, 903 (CA8) (recruitment); *United States* v. *Jacksonville Terminal Co.,* 451 F.2d 418, 458, 3 FEP Cases 862, 895 (CA5) (posting of job vacancies and job qualification requirements); *United States* v. *Local No. 8, IAB, S. O. & R. I.,* 315 F. Supp. 1202, 1238, 1245-46, 2 FEP Cases 741, 773-74, 779 (WD Wash.) (dissemination of information), *aff'd,* 443 F.2d 544, 3 FEP Cases 496 (CA9). While these measures may be effective in preventing the deterrence of future applicants, they afford no relief to those persons who in the past desired jobs but were intimidated and discouraged by employment discrimination.

The denial of the Title VII relief on the ground that the claimant had not formally applied for the job could exclude from the Act's coverage the victims of the most entrenched forms of discrimination. Victims of gross and pervasive discrimination could be denied relief precisely because the unlawful practices had been so successful as totally to deter job applications from members of minority groups. A *per se* prohibition of relief to nonapplicants could thus put beyond the reach of equity the most invidious effects of employment discrimination—those that extend to the very hope of self-realization. Such a *per se* limitation on the equitable powers granted to courts by Title VII would be manifestly inconsistent with the "historic purpose of equity to 'secur[e] complete justice' " and with the duty of courts in Title VII cases " ' to render a decree which will so far as possible eliminate the discriminatory effects of the past.' " *Albemarle Paper Co.* v. *Moody, supra,* at 418, 10 FEP Cases, at 1187-88.

## (2)

To conclude that a person's failure to submit an application for a job does not inevitably and forever foreclose his entitlement to seniority relief under Title VII is a far cry, however, from holding that nonapplicants are always entitled to such relief. A nonapplicant must show that he was a potential victim of unlawful discrimination. Because he is necessarily claiming that he was deterred from applying for the job by the employer's discriminatory practices, his is the not always easy burden of proving that he would have applied for the job had it not been for those practices. Cf. *Mt. Healthy City School District Board of Education* v. *Doyle,* 229 U.S. 274. When this burden is met, the nonapplicant is in a position analogous to that of an applicant and is entitled to the presumption discussed in Part III-A, supra.

The Government contends that the evidence it presented in this case at the liability stage of the trial identified all nonapplicants as victims of unlawful discrimination "with a fair degree of specificity," and that the Court of Appeals' determination that qualified nonapplicants are presumptively entitled to an award of seniority should accordingly be affirmed. In support of this contention the Government cites its proof of an extended pattern and practice of discrimination as evidence that an application from a minority employee for a line-driver job would have been a vain and useless act. It further argues that since the class of nonapplicant discriminatees is limited to incumbent employees, it is likely that every class member was aware of the futility of seeking a line-driver job and therefore deterred from filing both an initial and a followup application.[52]

---

[52] The limitation to incumbent employees is also said to serve the same function that actual job applications served in *Franks:* providing a means of distinguishing members of the excluded minority group from minority members of the public at large. While it is true that incumbency in this case and actual applications in *Franks* both serve to narrow what might otherwise be an impossible task, the status of nonincumbent applicant and nonapplicant incumbent differ substantially. The refused applicants in *Franks* had been denied an opportunity they clearly sought, and the only issue to be

We cannot agree. While the scope and duration of the company's discriminatory policy can leave little doubt that the futility of seeking line-driver jobs was communicated to the company's minority employees, that in itself is insufficient. The known prospect of discriminatory rejection shows only that employees who wanted line-driving jobs may have been deterred from applying for them. It does not show which of the non-applicants actually wanted such jobs, or which possessed the requisite qualifications.[53] There are differences between city and line-driving jobs,[54] for example, but the desirability of the latter is not so self-evident as to warrant a conclusion that all employees would prefer to be line drivers if given a free choice.[55] Indeed, a substantial number of white city drivers who were not subjected to the company's discriminatory practices were apparently content to retain their city jobs.[56]

resolved was whether the denial was pursuant to a proven discriminatory practice. Resolution of the nonapplicant's claim, however, requires two distinct determinations: that he would have applied but for discrimination and that he would have been discriminatorily rejected had he applied. The mere fact of incumbency does not resolve the first issue, although it may tend to support a nonapplicant's claim to the extent that it shows he was willing and competent to work as a driver, that he was familiar with the tasks of line drivers, etc. An incumbent's claim that he would have applied for a line-driver job would certainly be more superficially plausible than a similar claim by a member of the general public who may never have worked in the trucking industry or heard of T.I.M.E.-D.C. prior to suit.

[53] Inasmuch as the purpose of the nonapplicant's burden of proof will be to establish that his status is similar to that of the applicant, he must bear the burden of coming forward with the basic information about his qualifications that he would have presented in an application. As in *Franks*, and in accord with Part III-A, *supra*, the burden then will be on the employer to show that the nonapplicant was nevertheless not a victim of discrimination. For example, the employer might show that there were other, more qualified persons who would have been chosen for a particular vacancy, or that the nonapplicant's stated qualifications were insufficient. See *Franks, supra*, at 773 n. 32, 12 FEP Cases, at 559.

[54] Of the employees for whom the Government sought transfer to line-driving jobs, nearly one-third held city-driver positions.

[55] The company's line drivers generally earned more actually than its city drivers, but the difference varied from under $1,000 to more than $5,000 depending on the terminal and the year. In 1971 city drivers at two California terminals, "LOS" and San Francisco, earned substantially more than the line drivers at those terminals. In addition to earnings, line drivers have the advantage of not being required to load and unload their trucks. City drivers, however, have regular working hours, are not required to spend extended periods away from home and family, and do not face the hazards of long-distance driving at high speeds. As the Government acknowledged at argument, the jobs are in some sense "parallel"—some may prefer one job and some may prefer another. The District Court found generally that line-driver jobs "are considered the most desirable of the driving jobs." That finding is not challenged here, and we see no reason to disturb it. We observe only that the differences between city and line driving were not such that it can be said with confidence that all minority employees free from the threat of discriminatory treatment would have chosen to give up city for line driving.

[56] In addition to the futility of application, the Court of Appeals seems to have relied on the minority employees' accumulated seniority in nonline-driver positions in concluding that nonapplicants had been unlawfully deterred from applying. See 517 F.2d, at 318, 320, 11 FEP Cases, at _____, _____. The Government adopts that theory here, arguing that a nonapplicant who has accrued time at the company would be unlikely to have applied for transfer because he would have had to forfeit all of his competitive seniority and the job security that went with it. In view of our conclusion in Part II-B, *supra*, this argument detracts from rather than supports a nonapplicant's entitlement to relief. To the extent that an incumbent was deterred from applying by his desire to retain his competitive seniority, he simply did not want a line-driver job requiring him

In order to fill this evidentiary gap, the Government argues that a non-applicant's current willingness to transfer into a line-driver position confirms his past desire for the job. An employee's response to the court-ordered notice of his entitlement to relief [57] demonstrates, according to this argument, that the employee would have sought a line-driver job when he first became qualified to fill one, but for his knowledge of the company's discriminatory policy.

This assumption falls short of satisfying the appropriate burden of proof. An employee who transfers into a line-driver unit is normally placed at the bottom of the seniority "board." He is thus in jeopardy of being laid off and must, at best, suffer through an initial period of bidding on only the least desirable runs. See *supra,* at 17, and n. 25, 14 FEP Cases, at 1522. Nonapplicants who chose to accept the appellate court's *post hoc* invitation, however, would enter the line-driving unit with retroactive seniority dating from the time they were first qualified. A willingness to accept the job security and bidding power afforded by retroactive seniority says little about what choice an employee would have made had he previously been given the opportunity freely to choose a starting line-driver job. While it may be true that many of the nonapplicant employees desired and would have applied for line-driver jobs but for their knowledge of the company's policy of discrimination, the Government must carry its burden of proof, with respect to each specific individual, at the remedial hearings to be conducted by the District Court on remand.[58]

## C

The task remaining for the District Court on remand will not be a simple one. Initially, the court will have to make a substantial number of individual determinations in deciding which of the minority employees were actual victims of the company's discriminatory practices. After the victims have been identified, the court must, as nearly as possible, " 're-create the conditions and relationships that would have been had there been no' " unlawful discrimination. *Franks, supra,* 424 U.S., at 769, 12 FEP Cases, at 557. This process of recreating the past will necessarily involve a degree of approximation and imprecision. Because the class of victims may include some who did not apply for line-driver jobs as well

---

to start at the bottom of the "board." Those nonapplicants who did not apply for transfer because they were unwilling to give up their previously acquired seniority suffered only from a lawful deterrent imposed on all employees regardless of race or ethnicity. The nonapplicant's remedy in such cases is limited solely to the relief, if any, to which he may be entitled because of the discrimination he encountered at a time when he wanted to take a starting line-driver job.

57 The District Court's final order required that the company notify each minority employee of the relief he was entitled to claim. The employee was then required to indicate, within 60 days, his willingness to accpet the relief. Under the decision of the Court of Appeals, the relief would be qualification date seniority.

58 While the most convincing proof would be some overt act such as a pre-Act application for a line-driver job, the District Court may find evidence of an employee's informal inquiry, expression of interest, or even unexpressed desire credible and convincing. The question is a factual one for determination by the trial judge.

as those who did, and because more than one minority employee may have been denied each line-driver vacancy, the court will be required to balance the equities of each minority employee's situation in allocating the limited number of vacancies that were discriminatorily refused to class members.

Moreover, after the victims have been identified and their rightful place determined, the District Court will again be faced with the delicate task of adjusting the remedial interests of discriminatees and the legitimate expectations of other employees innocent of any wrongdoing. In the prejudgment consent decree, see *supra*, at 3-4, n. 4, 14 FEP Cases, at 1517, the company and the Government agreed that minority employees would assume line-driver positions that had been discriminatorily denied to them by exercising a first-priority right to job vacancies at the company's terminals. The decree did not determine what constituted a vacancy, but in its final order the trial court defined "vacancy" to exclude any position that became available while there were laid-off employees awaiting an opportunity to return to work. Employees on layoff were given a preference to fill whatever openings might occur at their terminals during a three-year period after they were laid-off.[59] The Court of Appeals

[59] Paragraph 9(a) of the trial court's final order provided:
"A 'vacancy' as used in this Order, shall include any opening which is caused by the transfer or promotion to a position outside the bargaining unit, death, resignation or final discharge of an incumbent, or by an increase in operations or business where, ordinarily, additional employees would be put to work. A vacancy shall not exist where there are laid off employees on the seniority roster where the opening occurs. Such laid off employees shall have a preference to fill such laid off positions when these again become open without competition from the individuals granted relief in this case.
"However, if such layoff continues for three consecutive years the position will be deemed as 'vacant' with the right of all concerned to compete for the position, using their respective seniority dates, including those provided for in this Order."

The trial court's use of a three-year recall right is apparently derived from provisions in the collective bargaining agreements. Article 5 of the National Master Freight Agreement ("NMFA") establishes the seniority rights of employees covered by the Agreement. Under Art. 5, "[s]eniority rights for employees shall prevail. . . . Seniority shall be broken by discharge, voluntary quit, [or] more than a three (3) year layoff." § 1. As is evident, the three-year layoff provision in the Master Agreement determines only when an employee shall lose *all* of his accumulated seniority; it does not determine either the order of layoff or the order of recall. Subject to other terms of the Master Agreement, NMFA Art. 2, § 2, "the extent to which seniority shall be applied as well as the methods and procedures of such application" are left to the Supplemental Agreements. *Id.*, § 1. The Southern Conference Area Over-the-Road Supplemental Agreement, covering line drivers in the Southern Conference, also provides for a complete loss of seniority rights after a three-year layoff, Art. 42, § 1, and further provides that in the event of a reduction in force "the last employee hired shall be laid off first and when the force is again increased, the employees are to be returned to work in the reverse order in which they were laid off," *id.*, § 3.

This order of layoff and recall, however, is limited by the Master Agreement in at least two situations involving an influx of employees from outside a terminal. NMFA Art. 5, § 3(a)(1) (merger with a solvent company), § 5(b)(2) (branch closing with transfer of operations to another branch). In these cases the Master Agreement provides for "dovetailing" the seniority rights of active and laid-off employees at the two facilities involved. *Ibid.*; see also NMFA Art. 15 (honoring Military Selective Service Act of 1967). The Master Agreement also recognizes that "questions of accrual, interpretation or application of seniority rights may arise which are not covered by the general rules set forth," and provides a procedure for resolution of unforeseen seniority problems. NMFA Art. 5, § 7. Presumably § 7 applies to persons claiming discriminatory denial of jobs and seniority in violation of Art. 38, which prohibits discrimination in hiring as well as clas-

rejected the preference and held that all but "purely temporary" vacancies were to be filled according to an employee's seniority, whether as a member of the class discriminated against or as an incumbent line driver on layoff. 517 F.2d at 322-32, 11 FEP Cases, at 83.

As their final contention concerning the remedy, the company and the union argue that the trial court correctly made the adjustment between the competing interests of discriminatees and other employees by granting a preference to laid-off employees, and that the Court of Appeals erred in disturbing it. The petitioners therefore urge the reinstatement of that part of the trial court's final order pertaining to the rate at which victims will assume their rightful places in the line-driver hierarchy.[60]

Although not directly controlled by the Act,[61] the extent to which the legitimate expectations of nonvictim employees should determine when victims are restored to their rightful place is limited by basic principles of equity. In devising and implementing remedies under Title VII, no less than in formulating any equitable decree, a court must draw on the "qualities of mercy and practicality [that] have made equity the instrument for nice adjustment and reconciliation between the public interest and private needs as well as between competing private claims." *Hecht Co.* v. *Bowles,* 321 U.S. 321, 329-30. Cf. *Phelps Dodge Corp.* v. *NLRB,* 313 U.S. 177, 195-96, 8 LRRM 439, *modifying and remanding In re Phelps Dodge Corp.,* 19 NLRB 547, 600, 5 LRRM 526; *Franks, supra,* at 798-99, 12 FEP Cases, at 565. Especially when immediate implementation of an equitable remedy threatens to impinge upon the expectations of innocent parties, the courts must "look to the practical realities and necessities inescapably involved in reconciling competing interests," in order to determine the "special blend of what is necessary, what is fair, and what is workable." *Lemon* v. *Kurtzman,* 411 U.S. 192, 201, 200 (opinion of BURGER, C. J.).

Because of the limited facts now in the record, we decline to strike

---

sification of employees so as to deprive them of employment opportunities on account of race or national origin. See *supra,* at 20-21, n. 29. The District Court apparently did not consider these provisions when it determined the recall rights of employees on layoff.

60 In their briefs the petitioners also challenge the trial court's modification of the interterminal transfer rights of line drivers in the Southern Conference. See *supra,* at 6-7, n. 10, 14 FEP Cases, at 1518. This question was not presented in either petition for certiorari and therefore is not properly before us. Rules of the Supreme Court 23.1(c). Our disposition of the claim that is presented, however, will permit the trial court to reconsider any part of the balance it struck in dealing with this issue.

61 The petitioners argue that to permit a victim of discrimination to use his rightful place seniority to bid on a line-driver job before the recall of all employees on layoff would amount to a racial or ethnic preference in violation of § 703(j) of the Act. Section 703(j) provides no support for this argument. It provides only that Title VII does not require an employer to grant preferential treatment to any group in order to rectify an imbalance between the composition of the employer's workforce and the make-up of the population at large. See *supra,* at 13 n. 20, 14 FEP Cases, at 1520-21. To allow identifiable victims of unlawful discrimination to participate in a layoff recall is not the kind of "preference" prohibited by § 703(j). If a discriminatee is ultimately allowed to secure a position before a laid-off line driver, a question we do not now decide, he will do so because of the bidding power inherent in his rightful place seniority, and not because of a preference based on race. See *Franks, supra,* at 792, 12 FEP Cases, at 567 (POWELL, J., concurring in part and dissenting in part).

the balance in this Court. The District Court did not explain why it subordinated the interests of class members to the contractual recall expectations of other employees on layoff. When it made that determination, however, it was considering a class of more than 400 minority employees, all of whom had been granted some preference in filling line-driver vacancies. The overwhelming majority of these were in the District Court's subclass three, composed of those employees with respect to whom neither the Government nor the company had presented any specific evidence on the question of unlawful discrimination. Thus, when the court considered the problem of what constituted a line-driver "vacancy" to be offered to class members, it may have been influenced by the relatively small number of proven victims and the large number of minority employees about whom it had no information. On the other hand, the Court of Appeals redefined "vacancy" in the context of what it believed to be a class of more than 400 employees who had actually suffered from discrimination at the behest of both the company and the union, and its determination may well have been influenced by that understanding. For the reasons discussed in this opinion, neither court's concept was completely valid.

After the evidentiary hearings to be conducted on remand, both the size and the composition of the class of minority employees entitled to relief may be altered substantially. Until those hearings have been conducted and both the number of identifiable victims and the consequent extent of necessary relief have been determined, it is not possible to evaluate abstract claims concerning the equitable balance that should be struck between the statutory rights of victims and the contractual rights of nonvictim employees. That determination is best left, in the first instance, to the sound equitable discretion of the trial court.[62] See *Franks v. Bowman, supra,* at 779, 12 FEP Cases, at 561; *Albemarle Paper Co. v. Moody, supra,* at 416, 10 FEP Cases, at 1187. We observe only that when the court exercises its discretion in dealing with the problem of laid-off employees in light of the facts developed at the hearings on remand, it should clearly state its reason so that meaningful review may be had on appeal. See *Franks, supra,* at 774, 12 FEP Cases, at 559; *Albemarle Paper Co. v. Moody, supra,* at 421 n. 14, 10 FEP Cases, at 1189.

For all the reasons we have discussed, the judgment of the Court of Appeals is vacated, and the cases are remanded to the District Court for further proceedings consistent with this opinion.

*It is so ordered.*

MR. JUSTICE MARSHALL, with whom MR. JUSTICE BRENNAN joins, concurring in part and dissenting in part.

I agree with the Court that the United States proved that petitioner T.I.M.E.-D.C. was guilty of a pattern or practice of discriminating against

---

[62] Other factors, such as the number of victims, the number of nonvictim employees affected and the alternatives available to them, and the economic circumstances of the industry may also be relevant in the exercise of the District Court's discretion. See *Franks, supra,* 424 U.S., at 796 n. 17, 14 FEP Cases, at 568 (POWELL, J., concurring and dissenting).

blacks and Spanish-speaking Americans in hiring line drivers. I also agree that incumbent minority-group employees who show that they applied for a line-driving job or that they would have applied but for petitioner's unlawful acts are presumptively entitled to the full measure of relief set forth in our decision last Term in *Franks* v. *Bowman Transportation Co.,* 424 U.S. 747, 12 FEP Cases 549 (1976).[1] But I do not agree that Title VII permits petitioners to treat non-Anglo line drivers differently from Anglo drivers who were hired by the company at the same time simply because the non-Anglo drivers were prevented by the company from acquiring seniority over the road. I therefore dissent from that aspect of the Court's holding, and from the limitations on the scope of the remedy that follow from it.

As the Court quite properly acknowledges, *ante,* at 23, 14 FEP Cases, at 1525, the seniority provision at issue here clearly would violate Title VII absent § 703(h), 42 U.S.C. § 2000e-2(h), which exempts at least some seniority systems from the reach of the Act, Title VII prohibits an employer from "classify[ing] his employees . . . in any way which would deprive or tend to deprive any individual of employment opportunities or otherwise adversely affect his status as an employee, because of such individual's race, color, religion, sex or national origin." 42 U.S.C. § 2000e-2(a)(2). "Under the Act, practices, procedures or tests neutral on their face and even neutral in terms of intent, cannot be maintained *if they operate to 'freeze' the status quo of prior discriminatory employment practices.*" *Griggs* v. *Duke Power Co.,* 401 U.S. 424, 429, 3 FEP Cases 175, 178 (1971) (emphasis added). Petitioners' seniority system does precisely that: it awards the choicest jobs and other benefits to those possessing a credential—seniority—which, due to past discrimination, blacks and Spanish-speaking employees were prevented from acquiring. Consequently, "Every time a Negro worker hired under the old segregated system bids against a white worker in his job slot, the old racial classification reasserts itself, and the Negro suffers anew for his employer's previous bias." *Local 189, United Papermakers & Paperworkers* v. *United States,* 416 F.2d 980, 1 FEP Cases 875, 71 LRRM 3070 (CA5 1969) (WISDOM, J.), *cert. denied,* 397 U.S. 919, 2 FEP Cases 426 (1970).

As the Court also concedes, with a touch of understatement, "the view that § 703(h) does not immunize seniority systems that perpetuate the

---

[1] In stating that the task nonapplicants face in proving that they should be treated like applicants is "difficult," *ante,* at 37, 14 FEP Cases, at 1531, I understand the Court simply to be addressing the facts of this case. There may well be cases in which the jobs that the nonapplicants seek are so clearly more desirable than their present jobs that proving that but for the employer's discrimination the nonapplicants previously would have applied will be anything but difficult.

Even in the present case, however, I believe the Court unnecessarily adds to the nonapplicants' burden. While I agree that proof of a nonapplicant's current willingness to accept a line-driver job is not dispositive of the question of whether petitioner's discrimination deterred the nonapplicant from applying in the past, I do not agree that current willingness "says little," see *ante,* at 44, 14 FEP Cases, at 1534, about past willingness. In my view, we would do well to leave questions of this sort concerning the weight to be given particular pieces of evidence to the district courts, rather than attempting to resolve them through overly broad and ultimately meaningless generalizations.

effects of prior discrimination has much support." *Ante,* at \_\_\_\_\_, n. 28, 14 FEP Cases, at 1523. Without a single dissent, six courts of appeals have so held in over 30 cases,[2] and two other courts of appeals have indicated their agreement, also without dissent.[3] In an unbroken line of cases, the EEOC has reached the same conclusion.[4] And the overwhelming weight

[2] *Acha* v. *Beame,* 531 F.2d 648, 12 FEP Cases 257 (CA2 1976); *United States* v. *Bethlehem Steel Corp.,* 446 F.2d 652, 3 FEP Cases 589 (CA2 1971); *Nance* v. *Union Carbide Corp.,* 540 F.2d 718, 13 FEP Cases 231 (CA4 1976), *petitions for cert. pending,* Nos. 76-824, 76-838; *Patterson* v. *American Tobacco Co.,* 535 F.2d 257, 12 FEP Cases 314 (CA4 1976), *cert. denied,* 425 U.S. 944, 13 FEP Cases 1808 (1976); *Russell* v. *American Tobacco Co.,* 528 F.2d 357, 11 FEP Cases 395 (CA4 1975), *cert. denied,* 425 U.S. 935, 12 FEP Cases 1090 (1976); *Hairston* v. *McLean Trucking Co.,* 520 F.2d 226, 11 FEP Cases 91 (CA4 1975); *United States* v. *Chesapeake & Ohio Ry. Co.,* 471 F.2d 582, 5 FEP Cases 308 (CA4 1972), *cert. denied,* 411 U.S. 939, 5 FEP Cases 862 (1973); *Robinson* v. *Lorillard Corp.,* 444 F.2d 791, 3 FEP Cases 653 (CA4), *cert. dismissed,* 404 U.S. 1006 (1971); *Griggs* v. *Duke Power Co.,* 420 F.2d 1225, 2 FEP Cases 310 (CA4 1970), *rev'd on other grounds,* 401 U.S. 424, 3 FEP Cases 175 (1971); *Swint* v. *Pullman-Standard,* 539 F.2d 77, 13 FEP Cases 604 (CA5 1976); *Sagers* v. *Yellow Freight System,* 529 F.2d 721, 12 FEP Cases 961 (CA5 1976); *Sabala* v. *Western Gillette, Inc.,* 516 F.2d 1251, 11 FEP Cases 98 (CA5 1975), *petitions for cert. pending,* Nos. 75-788, 76-1060; *Gamble* v. *Birmingham Southern RR,* 514 F.2d 678, 10 FEP Cases 1148 (CA5 1975); *Resendis* v. *Lee Way Motor Freight, Inc.,* 505 F.2d 69, 8 FEP Cases 1268 (CA5 1974), *cert. denied,* 425 U.S. 991, 12 FEP Cases 1335 (1976); *Herrera* v. *Yellow Freight System, Inc.,* 505 F.2d 66, 8 FEP Cases 1266 (CA5 1974), *cert. denied,* 425 U.S. 991, 12 FEP Cases 1335 (1976); *Carey* v. *Greyhound Bus Co.,* 500 F.2d 1372, 8 FEP Cases 1184 (CA5 1974); *Pettway* v. *American Cast Iron Pipe Co.,* 494 F.2d 211, 7 FEP Cases 1115 (CA5 1974); *Johnson* v. *Goodyear Tire & Rubber Co.,* 491 F.2d 1364, 7 FEP Cases 627 (CA5 1974); *Bing* v. *Roadway Express, Inc.,* 485 F.2d 441, 6 FEP Cases 677 (CA5 1973); *United States* v. *Georgia Power Co.,* 474 F.2d 906, 5 FEP Cases 587 (CA5 1973); *United States* v. *Jacksonville Terminal Co.,* 451 F.2d 418, 3 FEP Cases 862 (CA5 1971), *cert. denied,* 406 U.S. 906, 4 FEP Cases 661 (1972); *Long* v. *Georgia Kraft Co.,* 450 F.2d 557, 3 FEP Cases 1222 (CA5 1971); *Taylor* v. *Armco Steel Corp.,* 429 F.2d 498, 2 FEP Cases 820 (CA5 1970); *Local 189, United Papermakers & Paperworkers* v. *United States,* 416 F.2d 980, 1 FEP Cases 875, 71 LRRM 3070 (CA5 1969), *cert. denied,* 397 U.S. 919, 2 FEP Cases 426 (1970); *EEOC* v. *Detroit Edison Co.,* 515 F.2d 301, 10 FEP Cases 239, 1063 (CA6 1975), *petitions for cert. pending,* 75-220, 75-221, 75-239, 75-393; *Palmer* v. *General Mills, Inc.,* 513 F.2d 1040, 10 FEP Cases 465 (CA6 1975); *Head* v. *Timken Roller Bearing Co.,* 486 F.2d 870, 6 FEP Cases 813 (CA6 1973); *Bailey* v. *American Tobacco Co.,* 462 F.2d 160, 4 FEP Cases 916 (CA6 1972); *Rogers* v. *International Paper Co.,* 510 F.2d 1340, 10 FEP Cases 404 (CA8), *vacated,* 423 U.S. 809, 11 FEP Cases 576 (1975); *United States* v. *N. L. Industries, Inc.,* 479 F.2d 354, 5 FEP Cases 823 (CA8 1973); *Gibson* v. *Longshoremen Local 40,* 543 F.2d 1259, 12 FEP Cases 1349 (CA9 1976); *United States* v. *Navajo Freight Lines, Inc.,* 525 F.2d 1318, 11 FEP Cases 787 (CA9 1975).
The leading case in this line is a district court decision, *Quarles* v. *Phillip Morris, Inc.,* 279 F. Supp. 505, 1 FEP Cases 260, 67 LRRM 2098 (E.D. Va. 1968).

[3] *Bowe* v. *Colgate Palmolive Co.,* 489 F.2d 896, 6 FEP Cases 1132 (CA7 1973); *Jones* v. *Lee Way Motor Freight, Inc.,* 431 F.2d 245, 2 FEP Cases 895 (CA10 1970), *cert. denied,* 401 U.S. 954, 3 FEP Cases 193 (1971).
I agree with the Court, *ante,* at 19-20, n. 28, 14 FEP Cases, at 1523, that the results in a large number of the *Quarles* line of cases can survive today's decision. That the instant seniority system "is rational, in accord with the industry practice, . . . consistent with NLRB precedents[,] . . . did not have its genesis in racial discrimination, and . . . was negotiated and has been maintained free from any illegal purpose," *ante,* at 29, 14 FEP Cases, at 529 distinguishes the facts of this case from those in many of the prior decisions.

[4] No. 75-031, CCH Employment Prac. Guide ¶ 6481 (Sept. 29, 1974); No. 75-251, *id.,* ¶ 6448 (May 8, 1975); No. 75-047, *id.,* ¶ 6441, 10 FEP Cases 286 (Oct. 21, 1974); No. 74-25, *id.,* ¶ 6400 (Sept. 10, 1973); No. 74-28, *id.,* ¶ 6399 (Sept. 17, 1973); No. 72-2179, *id.,* ¶ 6395 (June 30, 1972); No. 72-1089, *id.,* ¶ 6382 (Feb. 2, 1972); No. 73-0479, *id.,* ¶ 6381 (Feb. 14, 1973); No. 72-1931, 1973 CCH EEOC Decisions ¶ 6373 (July 7, 1972); No. 72-1919, *id.,* ¶ 6370, 4 FEP Cases 1163 (June 6, 1972); No. 72-2062, *id.,* ¶ 6366 (June 22, 1972); No. 72-1704, *id.,* ¶ 6365 (April 26, 1972); No. 72-1390, *id.,* ¶ 6355, 4 FEP Cases 848 (March 17, 1972); No. 72-1000, *id.,* ¶ 6334 (Feb. 3, 1972); No. 72-0599, *id.,* ¶ 6313 (Dec. 22, 1971); No.

of scholarly opinion is in accord.[5] Yet for the second time this Term, see *General Electric Co.* v. *Gilbert,* 429 U.S. 125, 12 FEP Cases 1335 (1976), a majority of this Court overturns the unanimous conclusion of the courts of appeals and the EEOC concerning the scope of Title VII. Once again, I respectfully disagree.

## I

Initially, it is important to bear in mind that Title VII is a remedial statute designed to eradicate certain invidious employment practices. The evils against which it is aimed are defined broadly: "to fail . . . to hire or to discharge . . . *or otherwise to discriminate* . . . with respect to . . . compensation, terms, conditions, or privileges of employment," and "to limit, segregate, or classify . . . *in any way* that would deprive *or tend to deprive* any individual of employment opportunities *or otherwise adversely affect his status.*" 42 U.S.C. § 2000e-2(a) (emphasis added). Section 703(h) carves out an exemption from these broad prohibitions. Accordingly, under longstanding principles of statutory construction, the Act should "be given a liberal interpretation . . . [and] exemptions from its sweep should be narrowed and limited to effect the remedy intended." *Piedmont & Northern R. Co.* v. *ICC,* 286 U.S. 290, 311-12 (1932); see also *Spokane & Inland R. Co.* v. *United States,* 241 U.S. 344, 350 (1916); *United States* v. *Dickinson,* 15 Pet. 141, 165 (1841) (STORY, J.). Unless a seniority system that perpetuates discrimination falls "plainly and unmistakably within [the] terms and spirit" of § 703(h), *A. H. Phillips, Inc.* v. *Walling,* 324 U.S. 490, 493, 5 WH Cases 186 (1945), the system should be deemed unprotected. I submit that whatever else may be true of the

71-1876, *id.*, ¶ 6272, 3 FEP Cases 1023 (April 22, 1971); No. 71-1418, *id.*, ¶ 6223, 3 FEP Cases 580 (March 17, 1971); No. 71-1447, *id.*, ¶ 6217 (March 18, 1971); No. 71-1325, *id.*, ¶ 6214 (March 2, 1971); No. 71-1250, *id.*, ¶ 6211, 3 FEP Cases 389 (Jan. 21, 1971); No. 71-1100, *id.*, ¶ 6197, 3 FEP Cases 272 (Dec. 31, 1970); No. 71-1010, *id.*, ¶ 6195 (Dec. 29, 1970); No. 71-786, *id.*, ¶ 6188, 3 FEP Cases 262 (Dec. 21, 1970); No. 71-484, *id.*, ¶ 6176 (Nov. 16, 1970); No. 71-362, *id.*, ¶ 6169, 2 FEP Cases 1086 (Oct. 22, 1970); No. 70-47, *id.*, ¶ 6044 (July 24, 1969).
[5] Blumrosen, *Seniority & Equal Employment Opportunity: A Glimmer of Hope,* 23 RUTGERS L. REV. 268 (1969); Cooper & Sobol, *Seniority and Testing Under Fair Employment Laws: A General Approach to Objective Criteria of Hiring and Promotion,* 82 HARV. L. REV. 1598 (1969); Fine: *Plant Seniority and Minority Employees: Title VII's Effect on Layoffs,* 47 U. COLO. L. REV. 73 (1975); Gould, *Seniority and the Black Worker: Reflections on* Quarles *and its Implications,* 47 TEX. L. REV. 1039 (1969); Poplin, *Fair Employment in a Depressed Economy: The Layoff Problem,* 23 U.C.L.A. L. REV. 177 (1975); Ross, *Reconciling Plant Seniority with Affirmative Action and Anti-Discrimination,* 28 N.Y.U. CONF. LABOR 231 (1976); *Developments in the Law—Employment Discrimination and Title VII of the Civil Rights Act of 1964,* 84 HARV. L. REV. 1109, 1157-64 (1971); Comment, *Last Hired, First Fired Seniority Layoffs and Title VII: Questions of Liability and Remedy,* 11 COLUM. J. LAW & SOC. Prob. 343 (1975): Note, *The Problem of Last Hired, First Fired: Retroactive Seniority as a Remedy Under Title VII,* 9 GA. L. REV. 611 (1975); Note, *Last Hired, First Fired Layoffs and Title VII,* 88 HARV. L. REV. 1544 (1975); Note, *Title VII, Seniority Discrimination, and the Incumbent Negro,* 80 HARV. L. REV. 1260 (1967); Comment, *Title VII and Seniority Systems: Back to the Foot of the Line?* 64 KY. L .REV. 114 (1975); Comment, *Layoffs and Title VII: The Conflict Between Seniority and Equal Employment Opportunities,* 1975 WIS. L. REV. 791; 1969 DUKE L. J. 1091; 46 N.C. L. REV. 891 (1968).

section, its applicability to systems that perpetuate past discrimination is not "plainly and unmistakably" clear.

The language of § 703(h) provides anything but clear support for the Court's holding. That section provides, in pertinent part:

"[I]t shall not be an unlawful employment practice for an employer to apply different standards of compensation, or different terms, conditions or privileges of employment pursuant to a bona fide seniority . . . system . . . *provided that such differences are not the result of an intention to discriminate because of race, color, religion, sex, or national origin. . . .*" (Emphasis added.)

In this case, however, the different "privileges of employment" for Anglos and non-Anglos produced by petitioners' seniority system are precisely the result of prior, intentional discrimination in assigning jobs; but for that discrimination, non-Anglos would not be disadvantaged by the system. Thus if the proviso is read literally, the instant case falls squarely within it, thereby rendering § 703(h) inapplicable. To avoid this result the Court is compelled to reconstruct the proviso to read: "provided that such a seniority system did not have its genesis in racial discrimination, and that it was negotiated and has been maintained free from any illegal purpose." *Ante*, at 29, 14 FEP Cases, at 1527.

There are no explicit statements in the legislative history of Title VII that warrant this radical reconstruction of the proviso. The three documents placed in the Congressional Record by Senator Clark concerning seniority all were authored many weeks before the Mansfield-Dirksen amendment containing § 703(h) was introduced. Accordingly, they do not specifically discuss the meaning of the proviso.[6] More importantly, none of the documents addresses the general problem of seniority systems that perpetuate discrimination. Not surprisingly, Congress simply did not think of such subtleties in enacting a comprehensive, pathbreaking civil rights act.[7] To my mind, this is dispositive. Absent unambiguous statutory language or an authoritative statement in the legislative history legalizing seniority systems that continue past wrongs, I do not see how it can be said that the § 703(h) exemption "plainly and unmistakably" applies.

[6] The three documents, quoted in full in *Franks* v. *Bowman Transportation, supra*, 424 U.S., at 759-61, nn. 15-16, 12 FEP Cases, at 567-68, and in substantial part in today's decision, *ante*, at 24-25, and n. 36, are (1) the Clark-Case Interpretative Memorandum, 110 Cong. Rec. 7212-15 (1964); (2) the Justice Department Reply to Arguments Made by Senator Hill, *id.*, 7207; and (3) Senator Clark's Response to Dirksen Memorandum, *id.*, 7216-18. They were all placed in the Congressional Record of April 8, 1964, but were not read aloud during the debates. The Mansfield-Dirksen amendment was presented by Senator Dirksen on May 26, 1964. *Id.*, at 11926.

A few general statements also were made during the course of the debates concerning Title VII's impact on seniority, but these statements add nothing to the analysis contained in the documents. See *id.*, at 1518 (Rep. Cellar); *id.*, at 6549, 11848, (Sen. Humphrey); *id.*, at 6563-64 (Sen. Kuchel); *id.*, at 9113 (Sen. Keating); *id.*, at 15893 (Rep. McCulloch).

[7] In amending Title VII in 1972, Congress acknowledged its own prior naivete:

"In 1964, employment discrimination tended to be viewed as a series of isolated and distinguishable events, for the most part due to ill-will on the part of some identifiable individual or organization. . . . Experience has shown this view to be false." S. Rep. No. 92-415, 92nd Cong., 1st Sess., 5 (1971); see H. R. Rep. No. 92-238, 92nd Cong., 1st Sess., 8 (1971).

## II

Even if I were to agree that this case properly can be decided on the basis of inferences as to Congress' intent, I still could not accept the Court's holding. In my view, the legislative history of the 1964 Civil Rights Act does not support the conclusion that Congress intended to legalize seniority systems that perpetuate discrimination, and administrative and legislative developments since 1964 positively refute that conclusion.

## A

The Court's decision to uphold seniority systems that perpetuate post-Act discrimination—that is, seniority systems that treat non-Anglos who become line drivers as new employees even though, after the effective date of Title VII, these non-Anglos were discriminatorily assigned to city-driver jobs where they accumulated seniority—is explained in a single foot note. *Ante,* at _____ n. 30, 14 FEP Cases, at 1524. That footnote relies almost entirely on *United Air Lines* v. *Evans, post,* at _____, 14 FEP Cases at 1510. But like the instant decision, *Evans* is devoid of any analysis of the legislative history of § 703(h); it simply asserts its conclusion in a single paragraph. For the Court to base its decision here on the strength of *Evans* is sheer bootstrapping.

Had the Court objectively examined the legislative history, it would have been compelled to reach the opposite conclusion. As we stated just last Term, "it is apparent that the thrust of [§ 703(h)] is directed toward defining what is and what is not an illegal discriminatory practice in instances in which the post-Act operation of a seniority system is challenged as perpetuating the effects of discrimination *occurring prior to the effective date of the Act.*" [8] *Franks* v. *Bowman Transportation Co., supra,* 424 U.S., at 761, 12 FEP Cases, at 556 (emphasis added). Congress was concerned with seniority expectations that had developed prior to the enactment of Title VII, not with expectations arising thereafter to the extent that those expectations were dependent on whites benefiting from unlawful discrimination. Thus, the paragraph of the Clark-Case Interpretive Memorandum dealing with seniority systems begins:

"Title VII would have no effect on established seniority rights. *Its effect is prospective and not retrospective.*" 110 Cong. Rec. 7213 (emphasis added).

Similarly, the Justice Department memorandum that Senator Clark introduced explains:

"Title VII would have no effect on seniority rights existing *at the time it takes effect.* If, for example, a collective bargaining contract provides that in the event of layoffs, those who were hired last must be laid off first, such a provision would not be affected . . . by title VII. This would be

---

[8] This understanding of § 703(h) underlies *Franks'* holding that constructive seniority is the presumptively correct remedy for discriminatory refusals to hire, even though awarding such seniority necessarily disrupts the expectations of other employees.

true even in the case where *owing to discrimination prior to the effective date of the title,* white workers had more seniority than Negroes. . . . Any difference based on *established* seniority rights would not be based on race and would not be forbidden by the title." *Id.,* at 7202 (emphasis added).

Finally, Senator Clark's prepared answers to questions propounded by Senator Dirksen stated:

"Question. If an employer is directed to abolish his employment list because of discrimination what happens to seniority?

"Answer. *The bill is not retroactive,* and it will not require an employer to change existing seniority lists." *Id.,* at 7217 (emphasis added).

For the Court to ignore this history while reaching a conclusion contrary to it is little short of remarkable.

## B

The legislative history of § 703(h) admittedly affords somewhat stronger support for the Court's conclusion with respect to seniority systems that perpetuate pre-Act discrimination—that is, seniority systems that treat non Anglos who become line drivers as new employees even though these non-Anglos were discriminatorily assigned to city-driver jobs where they accumulated seniority before the effective date of Title VII. In enacting § 703(h), Congress intended to extend at least some protection to seniority expectations that had developed prior to the effective date of the Act. But the legislative history is very clear that the only threat to these expectations that Congress was seeking to avert was nonremedial, fictional seniority. Congress did not want minority group members who were hired after the effective date of the Act to be given superseniority simply because they were members of minority groups, nor did it want the use of seniority to be invalidated whenever it had a disparate impact on newly hired minority employees. These are the evils—and the only evils—that the opponents of Title VII raised [9] and that the Clark-Case Interpretive Memorandum addressed.[10] As the Court acknowledges, "there seems to

[9] The most detailed attack on Title VII's effect on seniority rights was voiced in the minority report to the House Judiciary Committee report, No. 914, 88th Cong., 1st Sess. (1963):

"*The provisions of this act grant the power to destroy union seniority.* . . . [T]*he extent of actions which would be taken to destroy the seniority system is unknown and unknowable.*

". . . Under the power granted in this bill, if a carpenters' hiring hall, say, had 20 men awaiting call, the first 10 in seniority being white carpenters, the union could be forced to pass them over in favor of carpenters beneath them in seniority, but of the stipulated race." *Id.,* at 717 (emphasis in original). The Senate opponents of the bill who discussed its effects on workers generally followed this line, although the principal argument advanced in the Senate was that Title VII would require preferential hiring of minorities. See 110 Cong. Rec. 487 (1964) (Sen. Hill); *id.,* at 7091 (Sen. Stennis); *id.,* at 7878 (Sen. Russell).

[10] The Clark-Case Memorandum states:

"Title VII would have no effect on established seniority rights. . . . Thus, for example, if a business has been discriminating in the past and as a result has an all-white working force, when the title come into effect the employers obligation would be simply to fill future vacancies on a nondiscriminatory basis. He would not be obliged—or indeed,

be no explicit reference in the legislative history to pre-Act discriminatees already employed in less desirable jobs." *Ante,* at 28, 14 FEP Cases, at 1527.

Our task, then, assuming still that the case properly can be decided on the basis of imputed legislative intent, is "to put to ourselves the question, which choice is it more likely that Congress would have made," *Burnet* v. *Guggenheim,* 288 U.S. 280, 285 (1933) (CARDOZO, J.), had it focused on the problem: would it have validated or invalidated seniority systems that perpetuate pre-Act discrimination? To answer that question, the devastating impact of today's holding validating such systems must be fully understood. Prior to 1965 blacks and Spanish-speaking Americans who were able to find employment were assigned the lowest paid, most menial jobs in many industries throughout the Nation but especially in the South. In many factories, blacks were hired as laborers while whites were trained and given skilled positions; [11] in the transportation industry blacks could only become porters; [12] and in steel plants blacks were assigned to the coke ovens and blasting furnaces, "the hotter and dirtier" places of employment. [13] The Court holds, in essence, that while after 1965 these incumbent employees are entitled to an equal opportunity to advance to more desirable jobs, to take advantage of that opportunity they must pay a price: they must surrender the seniority they have accumulated in their old jobs. For many, the price will be too high, and they will be locked in to their previous positions. [14] Even those willing to

---

permitted—to fire whites in order to hire Negroes, or to prefer Negroes for future vacancies, or, once Negroes are hired, to give them special seniority rights at the expense of the white workers." 110 Cong. Rec. 7213 (1972).

The remaining documents, see n. 6, supra, while phrased more generally, are entirely consistent with the focus of Senators Clark and Case.

[11] *E.g., Johnson* v. *Goodyear Tire & Rubber Co., supra,* n. 2; *United States* v. *N. L. Industries, Inc., supra,* n. 2; *Griggs* v. *Duke Power Co., supra,* n. 2.

[12] *E.g., Carey* v. *Greyhound Bus Co., supra,* n. 2; *United States* v. *Jacksonville Terminal Co., supra,* n. 2.

[13] *United States* v. *Bethlehem Steel Corp.,* 446 F.2d 652, 655, 3 FEP Cases 589, 590 (CA2 1971).

[14] This "lock-in" effect explains why, contrary to the Court's assertion, *ante,* at 28, there is a "rational basis for distinguishing . . . claims [of persons already employed in less desirable jobs] from those of persons initially denied *any* job." Although denying constructive seniority to the latter group will prevent them from assuming the position they would have occupied but for the pre-Act discrimination, it will not deter them from moving into higher paying jobs.

In comparing incumbent employees with pre-Act discriminatees who were refused jobs, however, the Court assumes that § 703(h) must mean that the latter group need not be given constructive seniority if they are later hired. The only clear effect of § 703(h), however, is to prevent persons who were *not* discriminated against from obtaining special seniority rights because they are members of minority groups. See _____, and n. 10, *supra,* 14 FEP Cases, at 1518. Although it is true, as the Court notes, *ante,* at 27 n. 39, 14 FEP Cases, at 1526-27, that in *Quarles* and *United Paperworkers* the courts concluded that persons refused jobs prior to the Act need not be given fictional seniority, the EEOC, Decision No. 71-1447, 1973 CCH EEOC Decisions ¶ 6217 (March 18, 1971), and several commentators, *e.g.,* Cooper & Sobol, *supra,* n. 5; Note, *Last Hired, First Fired Layoffs and Title VII,* 88 HARV. L. REV. 1544 (1975), have rejected this conclusion, and more recent decisions have questioned it, *e.g., Watkins* v. *United Steel Workers Local 2369,* 516 F.2d 41, 10 FEP Cases 1297 (CA5 1975).

pay the price will have to reconcile themselves to being forever behind subsequently hired whites who were not discriminatorily assigned. Thus equal opportunity will remain a distant dream for all incumbent employees.

I am aware of nothing in the legislative history of the 1964 Civil Rights Act to suggest that if Congress had focused on this fact it nonetheless would have decided to write off an entire generation of minority group employees. Nor can I believe that the Congress that enacted Title VII would have agreed to postpone for one generation the achievement of economic equality. The backers of that Title viewed economic equality as both a practical necessity and a moral imperative.[15] They were well aware of the corrosive impact employment discrimination has on its victims, and on the society generally.[16] They sought, therefore, "to eliminate those discriminatory practices and devices which have fostered racially stratified job environments to the disadvantage of minority citizens"; *McDonnell Douglas Corp.* v. *Green,* 411 U.S. 792, 800, 5 FEP Cases 965, 969 (1973); see also *Griggs* v. *Duke Power Co., supra,* 401 U.S., at 429-30, 431, 3 FEP Cases, at 177, 178; *Alexander* v. *Gardner-Denver Co.,* 415 U.S. 36, 44, 7 FEP Cases 81, 84 (1974); and "to make persons whole for injuries suffered on account of unlawful employment discrimination," *Albemarle Paper Co.* v. *Moody,* 422 U.S. 405, 418, 10 FEP Cases 1181, 1187 (1975). In short, Congress wanted to enable black workers to assume their rightful place in society.

It is of course true that Congress was not willing to invalidate seniority systems on a wholesale basis in pursuit of that goal.[17] But the United States, as the plaintiff suing on behalf of the incumbent minority group employees here, does not seek to overturn petitioners' seniority system. It seeks only to have the "time actually worked in [non-Anglo] jobs [recognized] as the equal of [Anglo] time." *Local 189, United Papermakers & Paperworkers* v. *United States, supra,* 416 F.2d, at 995, 1 FEP Cases, at 886, within the existing seniority system. Admittedly, such recognition would impinge on the seniority expectations white employees had developed prior to the effective date of the Act. But in enacting Title VII, Congress manifested a willingness to do precisely that. For example, the Clark-Case Interpretative Memorandum, see n. 6, *supra,* makes clear that Title VII prohibits unions and employers from using discriminatory waiting lists, developed prior to the effective date of the Title, in making selections for jobs or training programs after that date. 110 Cong. Rec. 7213 (1964). Such a prohibition necessarily would disrupt the expectations

---

[15] See, e.g., 110 Cong. Rec. 6547 (1946) (remarks of Sen. Humphrey); *id.,* at 6562 (remarks of Sen. Kuchel); *id.,* at 7203-04 (remarks of Sen. Clark); H. R. Rep. No. 88-914 Pt. 2, 88th Cong., 1st Sess., 26-29 (1963).

[16] See sources cited n. 15, *supra.*

[17] As one commentator has stated:
"[T]he statute conflicts with itself. While on the one hand Congress did wish to protect established seniority rights, on the other it intended to expedite black integration into the economic mainstream and to end once and for all, the *de facto* discrimination which replaced slavery at the end of the Civil War." Poplin, *supra,* n. 5, at 191.

of those on the lists. More generally, the very fact that Congress made Title VII effective shortly after its enactment demonstrates that expectations developed prior to passage of the Act were not considered sacrosanct, since Title VII's general ban on employment discrimination inevitably interfered with the pre-existing expectations of whites who anticipated benefiting from continued discrimination. Thus I am in complete agreement with Judge BUTZNER's conclusion in his seminal decision in *Quarles* v. *Philip Morris, Inc.,* 279 F. Supp. 505, 516, 1 FEP Cases 260, 269, 67 LRRM 2098 (ED Va. 1968): "It is . . . apparent that Congress did not intend to freeze an entire generation of Negro employees into discriminatory patterns that existed before the Act." [18]

## C

If the legislative history of § 703(h) leaves any doubt concerning the section's applicability to seniority systems that perpetuate either pre- or post-Act discrimination, that doubt is entirely dispelled by two subsequent developments. The Court all but ignores both developments; I submit they are critical.

First, in more than a score of decisions beginning at least as early as 1969, the Equal Employment Opportunities Commission has consistently held that seniority systems that perpetuate prior discrimination are unlawful.[19] While the Court may have retreated, see *General Electric* v. *Gilbert,* 429 U.S. 125, 141-42, 13 FEP Cases 1657, 1664 (1976), from its prior view that the interpretations of the EEOC are " 'entitled to great deference,' " *Albemarle Paper Co.* v. *Moody,* 422 U.S. 405, 431, 10 FEP Cases 1181, 1192 (1975), quoting, *Griggs* v. *Duke Power Co., supra,* 401 U.S., at 433, 3 FEP Cases, at 179, I have not. Before I would sweep aside the EEOC's consistent interpretation of the statute it administers, I would require " 'compelling indications that it is wrong.' " *Espinoza* v. *Farah Manufacturing Co.,* 414 U.S. 86, 94-95, 6 FEP Cases 933, 960 (1973), quoting *Red Lion Broadcasting Co.* v. *FCC,* 395 U.S. 367, 381 (1969). I find no such indications in the Court's opinion.

Second, in 1972 Congress enacted the Equal Employment Opportunities Act of 1972, Pub. L. 92-261, 86 Stat. 103, amending Title VII. In so doing,

---

[18] See also Gould, *supra,* n. 5, at 1042:
"If Congress intended to bring into being an integrated work force, . . . and not merely to create a paper plan meaningless to Negro workers, the only acceptable legislative intent on past discrimination is one that requires unions and employers to root out the past discrimination embodied in presently nondiscriminatory seniority arrangements so that black and white workers have equal job advancement rights."

[19] See cases cited n. 4, *supra.*
The National Labor Relations Board has reached a similar conclusion in interpreting the National Labor Relations Act, 29 U.S.C. § 141 *et seq.* In *Local 269, Electrical Workers,* 149 NLRB 769, 57 LRRM 1372 (1964), *enforced,* 357 F.2d 51, 61 LRRM 2371 (CA3 1966), the Board held that a union hiring hall commits present acts of discrimination when it makes referrals based on experience if, in the past, the union has denied nonunion members the opportunity to develop experience. See also *Houston Maritime Assn.,* 168 NLRB 615, 66 LRRM 1337 (1967), *enforcement denied,* 426 F.2d 584, 74 LRRM 2200, 9 FEP Cases 336 (CA5, 1970).

Congress made very clear that it approved of the lower court decisions invalidating seniority systems that perpetuate discrimination. That Congress was aware of such cases is evident from the Senate and House Committee reports which cite the two leading decisions, as well as several prominent law review articles. S.Rep. No. 92-415, 92d Cong., 1st Sess., 5 n. 1 (1971); H. R. Rep. No. 92-238, 92d Cong., 1st Sess., 8 n. 2 (1971). Although Congress took action with respect to other lower court opinions with which it was dissatisfied,[20] it made no attempt to overrule the seniority cases. To the contrary, both the Senate and House reports expressed approval of the "perpetuation principle" as applied to seniority systems [21] and invoked the principle to justify the committee's recommendations to extend Title VII's coverage to state and local government employees,[22] and to expand the powers of the EEOC.[23] Moreover, the Section-by-

---

[20] For example, the 1972 Act added to the definitional section of Title VII, 42 U.S.C. § 2000e a new subsection (j) defining "religion" to include "religious observance and practice, as well as belief." This section was added "to provide the statutory basis for EEOC to formulate guidelines on discrimination because of religion such as those challenged in *Dewey* v. *Reynolds Metal Co.*, 429 F.2d 325, 2 FEP Cases 687, 869 (6th Cir. 1970), *affirmed by an equally divided court*, 402 U.S. 689, 3 FEP Cases 508 (1971)." 118 Cong. Rec. 7167 (1972) (Section-by-Section Analysis of H.R. 1746, The Equal Employment Opportunity Act by 1972, prepared by Sens. Williams and Javits). Dewey had questioned the authority of the EEOC to define "religion" to encompass religious practices. 429 F.2d, at 331 n. 1, 334-35, 2 FEP Cases at _____, _____.

[21] After acknowledging the naive assumptions of the 1964 Civil Rights Act, see n. 7, *supra*, both committee reports went on to state:
"Employment discrimination as viewed today is a far more complex and pervasive phenomenon. Experts familiar with the subject now generally describe the problem in terms of 'systems' and 'effects' rather than simply intentional wrongs, and the literature on the subject is replete with discussions of, for example, the mechanics of seniority and lines of progression, [and] perpetuation of the present effect of pre-act discriminatory practices through various institutional devices. . . . In short, the problem is one whose resolution in many instances requires not only expert assistance, but also the technical perception that the problem exists in the first instance, and that the system complained of is unlawful."
S. Rep. No. 92-415, 92d Cong., 1st Sess., 5 (1971); see H. R. Rep. No. 92-238, 92d Cong., 1st Sess., 8 (1971).
In addition, in discussing "pattern or practice" suits and the recommendation to transfer the power to bring them to the EEOC, the House report singled out several seniority cases, including *United Papermakers*, as examples of suits that "have contributed significantly to the Federal effort to combat employment discrimination." *Id.*, at 13, and n. 4.
It is difficult to imagine how Congress could have better "address[ed] the specific issue presented by this case, *ante*, at _____ n. 39, 14 FEP Cases at 1526-27, than by referring to "the mechanics of seniority . . . [and] perpetuation of the present effect of pre-act discriminatory practices" and by citing *Quarles* and *United Papermakers*.

[22] Both reports stated that state and local governments had discriminated in the past and that "the existence of this discrimination is perpetuated by both institutional and overt discriminatory practices . . . [such as] *de facto* segregated job ladders." S. Rep., at 10; H. R. Rep., at 17. The same points [were] made in the debate in the House and Senate. 110 Cong. Rec. 1815 (1972) (remarks of Sen. Williams); *id.*, at 31961 (remarks of Rep. Perkins).

[23] The Senate stated:
"It is expected that through the administrative process, the Commission will continue to define and develop the approaches to handling serious problems of discrimination that are involved in the area of employment . . . (including seniority systems)." S. Rep., at 18.
The House report argued:
"Administrative tribunals are better equipped to handle the complicated issues involved in employment discrimination cases. . . . Issues that have perplexed courts include plant-

Section Analysis of the Conference Committee bill, which was prepared and placed in the Congressional Record by the floor managers of the bill, stated in "language that could hardly be more explicit," *Franks* v. *Bowman Transportation Co., supra,* 424 U.S., at 765 n. 21, 12 FEP Cases, at 556, that, "in any areas where a specific contrary intention is not indicated, it was assumed that the present case law . . . would continue to govern the applicability and construction of Title VII." 118 Cong. Rec. 7166, 7564 (1972). And perhaps most important, in explaining the section of the 1972 Act that empowers the EEOC "to prevent any person from engaging in any unlawful employment practice as set forth in section 703 or 704," 42 U.S.C. § 2000e-5(a), the Section-by-Section Analysis declared that:

"The unlawful employment practices encompassed by sections 703 and 704 which were enumerated in 1964 by the original Act, *and as defined and expanded by the courts* remain in effect." *Id.,* at 7167, 7564 (emphasis added).[24]

We have repeatedly held that "[w]hen several acts of Congress are passed touching the same subject matter, subsequent legislation may be considered to assist in the interpretation of prior legislation upon the same subject." *Tiger* v. *Western Investment Co.,* 221 U.S. 286, 309 (1911); see *NLRB* v. *Bell Aerospace Co.,* 416 U.S. 267, 275, 85 LRRM 2945 (1974) (subsequent legislation entitled to "significant weight"): *Red Lion Broadcasting Co.* v. *FCC,* 395 U.S. 367, 380 (1969); *United States* v. *Stafoff,* 260 U.S. 477, 480 (1923) (HOLMES, J.); *New York & Norfolk R. Co.* v. *Peninsula Exchange,* 240 U.S. 34, 39 (1916) (HUGHES, J.); *United States* v. *Weeks,* 5 Cranch 1, 8 (1809). Earlier this Term, we implicitly followed this canon in using a statute passed in 1976 to conclude that the Administrative Procedure Act, 5 U.S.C. §§ 701-706, enacted in 1946, was not intended as an independent grant of jurisdiction to the federal courts. *Califano* v. *Sanders,* _____ U.S. _____ (1977). The canon is particularly applicable here for two reasons. First, because there is no explicit legislative history discussing seniority systems that perpetuate discrimination, we are required to " 'seize everything from which aid can be derived. . . .' " *Brown* v. *GSA,* 425 U.S. 820, 825, 12 FEP Cases 1361, 1362 (1976), quoting, *United States* v. *Fisher,* 2 Cranch 358, 386 (1805), if we are to reconstruct congressional intent. Second, because petitioners' seniority system was readopted in a collective bargaining agreement signed after the 1972 Act took effect, any retroactivity problems that ordinarily inhere in using a later act to interpret an earlier one are not present here. Cf.

---

wide restructuring of pay-scales and progression lines, seniority rosters, and testing." H. R. Rep., at 10.

[24] By enacting a new section defining the EEOC's powers with reference to §§ 703 and 704 of the 1964 Act, Congress in 1972 effectively re-enacted those sections, and the judicial gloss that had been placed upon them. See 2A C. Sands, SUTHERLAND'S STATUTES AND STATUTORY CONSTRUCTION § 49.10 and cases cited (1973); cf. *Albemarle Paper Co.* v. *Moody,* 422 U.S. 405, 414 n. 8, 10 FEP Cases 1181, 1186 (1975) (finding that re-enactment in 1972 of backpay provision of 1964 Act "ratified" courts of appeals decisions awarding backpay to unnamed class members who had not filed charges with the EEOC).

*Stockdale* v. *Insurance Companies,* 20 Wall. 323, 331-32 (1873). Thus, the Court's bald assertion that the intent of the Congress that enacted the 1972 Act is "entitled to little if any weight," *ante,* at _____ n. 39, 14 FEP Cases at 1527, in construing § 703(h) is contrary to both principle and precedent.

Only last Term, we concluded that the legislative materials reviewed above "completely answer the argument that Congress somehow intended seniority relief to be less available" than backpay as a remedy for discrimination. *Franks* v. *Bowman Transportation Co., supra,* at 765 n. 21, 12 FEP Cases, at 556. If anything, the materials provide an even more complete answer to the argument that Congress somehow intended to immunize seniority systems that perpetuate past discrimination. To the extent that today's decision grants immunity to such systems, I respectfully dissent.

## UNITED AIR LINES v. EVANS

*Supreme Court of the United States, 1977*
*431 U.S. 553, 14 FEP Cases 1510*

MR. JUSTICE STEVENS delivered the opinion of the Court.

Respondent was employed by United Air Lines as a flight attendant from November 1966 to February 1968. She was rehired in February 1972. Assuming, as she alleges, that her separation from employment in 1968 violated Title VII of the Civil Rights Act of 1964,[1] the question now presented is whether the employer is committing a second violation of Title VII by refusing to credit her with seniority for any period prior to February 1972.

Respondent filed charges with the Equal Employment Opportunity Commission in February 1973, alleging that United discriminated and continues to discriminate against her because she is a female. After receiving a letter granting her the right to sue, she commenced this action in the United States District Court for the Northern District of Illinois. Because the District Court dismissed her complaint, the facts which she has alleged are taken as true. They may be simply stated.

During respondent's initial period of employment, United maintained a policy of refusing to allow its female flight attendants to be married.[2] When she married in 1968, she was therefore forced to resign. Although it was subsequently decided that such a resignation violated Title VII, *Sprogis* v. *United Air Lines,* 444 F.2d 1194, 3 FEP Cases 621 (CA7 1971), *cert. denied,* 404 U.S. 991, 4 FEP Cases 37, respondent was not a party

---

[1] [Footnotes numbered as in original.—Ed.] 78 Stat. 253, Title VII, as amended, is codified in 42 U.S.C. § 2000e et seq. (1970 ed. and Supp V).

[2] At that time United required that all flight attendants be female, except on flights between the mainland and Hawaii and on overseas military charter flights. See *Sprogis* v. *United Air Lines,* 444 F.2d 1194, 1203, 3 FEP Cases 621, 627-28 (CA7 1971) (Stevens, J., dissenting); *cert. denied,* 404 U.S. 991, 4 FEP Cases 37.

to that case and did not initiate any proceedings of her own in 1968 by filing a charge with the EEOC within 90 days of her separation.[3] A claim based on that discriminatory act is therefore barred.[4]

In November 1968, United entered into a new collective-bargaining agreement which ended the pre-existing "no marriage" rule and provided for the reinstatement of certain flight attendants who had been terminated pursuant to that rule. Respondent was not covered by that agreement. On several occasions she unsuccessfully sought reinstatement; on February 16, 1972, she was hired as a new employee. Although her personnel file carried the same number as it did in 1968, for seniority purposes she has been treated as though she had no prior service with United.[5] She has not alleged that any other rehired employees were given credit for prior service with United, or that United's administration of the seniority system has violated the collective-bargaining agreement covering her employment.[6]

Informal requests to credit her with pre-1972 seniority having been denied, respondent commenced this action.[7] The District Court dismissed the complaint, holding that the failure to file a charge within 90 days of her separation in 1968 caused respondent's claim to be time-barred, and foreclosed any relief under Title VII.[8]

---

[3] Section 706 (d), 42 U.S.C. § 2000e-5 (d), then provided in part:
"A charge under subsection (a) shall be filed within ninety days after the alleged unlawful employment practice occurred . . . ." 78 Stat. 260.
The 1972 amendments to Title VII added a new subsection (a) to § 706. Consequently, subsection (d) was redesignated as subsection (e). At the same time it was amended to enlarge the limitations period to 180 days. See 86 Stat. 103, 105.

[4] Timely filing is a prerequisite to the maintenance of a Title VII action. *Alexander* v. *Gardner-Denver Co.*, 415 U.S. 36, 47, 7 FEP Cases 81, 85. See *Electrical Workers* v. *Robbins & Myers, Inc.*, 429 U.S. 229, 239-40, 13 FEP Cases 1813, 1817.

[5] Respondent is carried on two seniority rolls. Her "company" or "system" seniority dates from the day she was rehired, February 16, 1972. Her "Stewardess" or "pay" seniority dates from the day she completed her flight attendant training, March 16, 1972. One or both types of seniority determine a flight attendant's wages; the duration and timing of vacations; rights to retention in the event of layoffs and rights to re-employment thereafter; and rights to preferential selection of flight assignments, App. 5-6, 10.

[6] Under the provisions of the collective-bargaining agreement between United and the Air Line Stewardesses and Flight Stewards as represented by the Air Line Pilots Association, International for the period 1972-1974, seniority is irrevocably lost or broken after the separation from employment of a flight attendant "who resigns or whose services with the Company are permanently severed for just cause." Resp. Brief, at 6.

[7] The relief requested in respondent's complaint included an award of seniority to the starting date of her initial employment with United, and back pay "lost as a result of the discriminatory employment practices of [United]," App., at 8. In her brief in this Court, respondent states that she seeks back pay only since her date of rehiring, February 16, 1972, which would consist of the increment in pay and benefits attributable to her lower seniority since that time. Resp. Brief, at 4.

[8] The District Court recited that the motion was filed pursuant to Fed. Rule Civ. Proc. 12(b)(1) and dismissed the complaint on the ground that it had no jurisdiction of a time-barred claim. The District Court also held, however, that the complaint did not allege any continuing violation. For that reason, the complaint was ripe for dismissal under Rule 12(b)(6). The District Court stated:
"Plaintiff asserts that by defendant's denial of her seniority back to the starting date of her original employment in 1966, United is currently perpetuating the effect of past discrimination.
"Plaintiff, however, has not been suffering from any 'continuing' violation. She is

A divided panel of the Court of Appeals initially affirmed; then, after our decision in *Franks* v. *Bowman Transportation Co.*, 424 U.S. 747, 12 FEP Cases 549, the panel granted respondent's petition for rehearing and unanimously reversed, 534 F.2d 1247, 12 FEP Cases 1105 (CA7 1976). We granted certiorari, 419 U.S. 917, and now hold that the complaint was properly dismissed.

Respondent recognizes that it is now too late to obtain relief based on an unlawful employment practice which occurred in 1968. She contends, however, that United is guilty of a present, continuing violation of Title VII and therefore that her claim is timely.[9] She advances two reasons for holding that United's seniority system illegally discriminates against her: first, she is treated less favorably than males who were hired after her termination in 1968 and prior to her reemployment in 1972; second, the seniority system gives present effect to the past illegal act and therefore perpetuates the consequences of forbidden discrimination. Neither argument persuades us that United is presently violating the statute.

It is true that some male employees with less total service than respondent have more seniority than she. But this disparity is not a consequence of their sex, or of her sex. For females hired between 1968 and 1972 also acquired the same preference over respondent as males hired during that period. Moreover, both male and female employees who had service prior to February 1968, who resigned or were terminated for a nondiscriminatory reason (or for an unchallenged discriminatory reason), and who were later re-employed, also were treated as new employees receiving no seniority credit for their prior service. Nothing alleged in the complaint indicates that United's seniority system treats existing female employees differently from existing male employees, or that the failure to credit prior service differentiates in any way between prior service by males and prior services by females. Respondent has failed to allege that United's seniority system differentiates between similarly situated males and females on the basis of sex.

Respondent is correct in pointing out that the seniority system gives present effect to a past act of discrimination. But United was entitled to treat that past act as lawful after respondent failed to file a charge of discrimination within the 90 days then allowed by § 706(d). A discriminatory act which is not made the basis for a timely charge is the legal equivalent of a discriminatory act which occurred before the statute was

seeking to have this court merely reinstate her November, 1966 seniority date which was lost solely by reason of her February, 1968 resignation. The fact that that resignation was the result of an unlawful employment practice is irrelevant for purposes of these proceedings because plaintiff lost her opportunity to redress that grievance when she failed to file a charge within ninety days of February, 1968. United's subsequent employment of plaintiff in 1972 cannot operate to resuscitate such a time-barred claim." App. 18.

[9] Respondent cannot rely for jurisdiction on the single act of failing to assign her seniority credit for her prior service at the time she was rehired, for she filed her discrimination charge with the Equal Employment Opportunity Commission on February 21, 1973, more than one year after she was rehired on February 16, 1972. The applicable time limit in February 1972, was 90 days; effective March 24, 1972, this time was extended to 180 days, see n. 3, *supra*.

passed. It may constitute relevant background evidence in a proceeding in which the status of a current practice is at issue, but separately considered, it is merely an unfortunate event in history which has no present legal consequences.

Respondent emphasizes the fact that she alleged a *continuing* violation. United's seniority system does indeed have a continuing impact on her pay and fringe benefits. But the emphasis should not be placed on mere continuity; the critical question is whether any present *violation* exists. She has not alleged that the system discriminates against former female employees or that it treats former employees who were discharged for a discriminatory reason any differently than former employees who resigned or were discharged for a nondiscriminatory reason. In short, the system is neutral in its operation.[10]

Our decision in *Franks* v. *Bowman Transportation Co.*, 424 U.S. 747, 12 FEP Cases 549, does not control this case. In *Franks* we held that retroactive seniority was an appropriate remedy to be awarded under § 706(g) of Title VII, 42 U.S.C. § 2000e-5(g) after an illegal discriminatory act or practice had been proved, *id*, at 762-68. When that case reached this Court, the issues relating to the timeliness of the charge [11] and the violation of Title VII [12] had already been decided; we dealt only with a question of remedy. In contrast, in the case now before us we do not reach any remedy issue because respondent did not file a timely charge based on her 1968 separation and she has not alleged facts establishing a violation since she was rehired in 1972.[13]

The difference between a remedy issue and a violation issue is highlighted by the analysis of § 703(h) of Title VII in *Franks*.[14] As we held in that case, by its terms that section does not bar the award of retroactive seniority after a violation has been proved. Rather, § 703(h) "delineates

---

[10] This case does not involve any claim by respondent that United's seniority system deterred her from asserting any right granted by Title VII. It does not present the question raised in the so-called departmental seniority cases. See, *e.g.*, *Quarles* v. *Phillip Morris*, 279 F. Supp. 505, 1 FEP Cases 260, 67 LRRM 2098 (ED Va. 1968).

[11] The Court of Appeals had disposed of the timeliness issues in Franks, 495 F.2d 398, 405, 8 FEP Cases 66, 70 (CA5 1974).

[12] This finding at the District Court was unchallenged in the Court of Appeals, 495 F.2d 398, 402, 403, 8 FEP Cases 66, 68, and was assumed in this Court, 424 U.S., at 750, 12 FEP Cases, at 550.
In any event we noted in *Franks*, "[t]he underlying legal wrong affecting [the class] is not the alleged operation of a racially discriminatory seniority system but of a racially discriminatory hiring system." *Id.*, at 758, 12 FEP Cases, at 553.

[13] At the time she was rehired in 1972, respondent had no greater right to a job than any other applicant for employment with United. Since she was in fact treated like any other applicant when she was rehired, the employer did not violate Title VII in 1972. And if the employer did not violate Title VII in 1972 by refusing to credit respondent with back seniority, its continued adherence to that policy cannot be illegal.

[14] Section 703 (h), 42 U.S.C. § 2000e-2 (h), provides:
"Notwithstanding any other provision of this title, it shall not be an unlawful employment practice for an employer to apply different standards of compensation, or different terms, conditions, or privileges of employment pursuant to a bona fide seniority or merit system . . . provided that such differences are not the result of an intention to discriminate because of race, color, religion, sex, or national origin. . . ."

which employment practices are illegal and thereby prohibited and which are not," *id.,* at 758, 12 FEP Cases, at 553.

That section expressly provides that it shall not be an unlawful employment practice to apply different terms of employment pursuant to a bona fide seniority system, provided that any disparity is not the result of intentional discrimination. Since respondent does not attack the bona fides of United's seniority system, and since she makes no charge that the system is intentionally designed to discriminate because of race, color, religion, sex, or national origin, § 703(h) provides an additional ground for rejecting her claim.

The Court of Appeals read § 703(h) as intended to bar an attack on a seniority system based on the consequences of discriminatory acts which occurred prior to the effective date of Title VII in 1965,[15] but having no application to such attacks based on acts occurring after 1965. This reading of § 703(h) is too narrow. The statute does not foreclose attacks on the current operation of seniority systems which are subject to challenge as discriminatory. But such a challenge to a neutral system may not be predicated on the mere fact that a past event which has no present legal significance has affected the calculation of seniority credit, even if the past event might at one time have justified a valid claim against the employer. A contrary view would substitute a claim for seniority credit for almost every claim which is barred by limitations. Such a result would contravene the mandate of § 703(h).

The judgment of the Court of Appeals is reversed.

MR. JUSTICE MARSHALL, with whom MR. JUSTICE BRENNAN joins, dissenting.

But for her sex, respondent Carolyn Evans presently would enjoy all of the seniority rights that she seeks through this litigation. Petitioner United Air Lines has denied her those rights pursuant to a policy that perpetuates past discrimination by awarding the choicest jobs to those possessing a credential married women were unlawfully prevented from acquiring: continuous tenure with United. While the complaint respondent filed in the District Court was perhaps inartfully drawn,[1] it adequately draws into question this policy of United's.

For the reasons stated in the Court's opinion and in my separate, dissenting opinion in *International Brotherhood of Teamsters* v. *United States, ante,* at ____, 14 FEP Cases at 1536, I think it indisputable that absent § 703(h), the seniority system at issue here would constitute an "unlawful employment practice" under Title VII, 42 U.S.C. § 2000e-

---

[15] 534 F.2d, at 1251, 12 FEP Cases, at 1108.

[1] Although the District Court dismissed respondent's complaint for lack of jurisdiction pursuant to Fed. Rule Civ. Proc. 12(b)(1), the basis for his ruling was that the complaint was time barred. Thus, the dismissal closely resembles a dismissal for failure to state a claim upon which relief can be granted, and the only issue before us is whether "it appears beyond doubt that the plaintiff can prove no set of facts in support of [her] claim which would entitle [her] to relief." *Conley* v. *Gibson,* 355 U.S. 41, 45-46, 9 FEP Cases 439, 442 (1957).

2(a)(2). And for the reasons developed at length in my dissenting opinions in Teamsters, *ante,* at _____, 14 FEP Cases at 1536, I believe § 703(h) does not immunize seniority systems that perpetuate post-Act discrimination.

The only remaining question is whether Ms. Evans' complaint is barred by the applicable statute of limitations, 42 U.S.C. § 2000e-5(e). Her cause of action accrued, if at all, at the time her seniority was recomputed after she was rehired. Although she apparently failed to file a charge with the EEOC within 180 days after her seniority was determined, Title VII recognizes that certain violations, once commenced, are continuing in nature. In these instances, discriminatees can file charges at any time up to 180 days after the violation ceases. (They can, however, receive backpay only for the two years preceding the filing of charge with the EEOC. 42 U.S.C. § 2000e-5(g).) In the instant case, the violation—treating respondent as a new employee even though she was wrongfully forced to resign—is continuing to this day. Respondent's charge therefore was not time barred, and the Court of Appeals judgment reinstating her complaint should be affirmed.[2]

## JAMES v. STOCKHAM VALVES & FITTINGS CO.

*United States Court of Appeals, Fifth Circuit, 1977*
*559 F.2d 310, 15 FEP Cases 827*

WISDOM, Circuit Judge: This appeal presents issues of segregated facilities and programs that were long ago resolved in the courts of this country. The case also raises issues related to job assignment, transfer, promotion, training, recruitment, seniority, and testing; some of the answers to these questions seem clear, but others are still being formulated by legal processes. All of the issues, the settled and the unsettled, are intertwined.

### I.

#### STATEMENT OF THE CASE

On October 5, 1966, the named plaintiffs, Patrick James, Howard Harville and Louis Winston, black employees at Stockham's Birmingham facilities, filed charges of discrimination with the Equal Employment Opportunity Commission ("EEOC") against Stockham Valves and Fit-

---

[2] It is of course true that to establish her entitlement to relief, respondent will have to prove that she was unlawfully forced to resign more than 180 days prior to filing her charge with the EEOC. But if that is sufficient to defeat her claim, then discriminatees will never be able to challenge "practices, procedures, or tests . . . [which] operate to 'freeze' the status quo of prior discriminatory employment practices," *Griggs* v. *Duke Power Co.*, 401 U.S. 424, 430, 3 FEP Cases 175, 177 (1971), even though *Griggs* holds that such practices are impermissible, and the legislative history of the Equal Employment Opportunity Act of 1972, Pub. L. 92-261, 86 Stat. 103, indicates that Congress agrees, see *International Brotherhood of Teamsters* v. *United States, post,* at _____, _____, 14 FEP Cases at 1542-43 (MARSHALL, J., dissenting). The consequence of Ms. Evans' failure to file charges after she was discharged is that she has lost her right to backpay, not her right to challenge present wrongs.

tings, Inc. ("Stockham" or "company"), alleging that the company maintained racially segregated facilities; discriminated against black employees in job assignment, promotion, training, and transfer; and employed discriminatory testing, education, and age requirements. The EEOC found "reasonable cause" to believe that Stockham engaged in discriminatory practices and issued the plaintiffs a "right to sue" notice in February 1970.

The plaintiffs brought this class action suit on March 16, 1970, within the 30-day statutory period, against Stockham under the Civil Rights Act of 1866, 42 U.S.C. § 1981, and Title VII of the Civil Rights Act of 1964, 42 U.S.C. § 2000e *et seq.* The plaintiffs filed an amended charge of discrimination with the EEOC on June 8, 1970, against the United Steelworkers of America, AFL–CIO ("Steelworkers") and its Local 3036 ("Local" or "Union"), and later amended its complaint by adding the Steelworkers and the Local as defendants. The union defendants are alleged to have violated Title VII and 29 U.S.C. §§ 151 *et seq.* ("the duty of fair representation"). The district court referred the case to the EEOC for conciliation until June 1973 when the district court granted the plaintiffs' motion to set aside the stay order. The court certified the class represented by the named plaintiffs under Rule 23(b)(1), F.R. Civ. P., to include all black hourly production and maintenance employees of Stockham who are currently employed and all black persons who have been so employed at Stockham from July 2, 1965, to the date of trial. The trial was held from February 4 through February 22, 1974.

The district court rendered final judgment March 19, 1975. Relying heavily on the proposed findings of fact and conclusions of law filed by the defendant Stockham,[1] the court found that, except for those segre-

---

[1] [Footnotes numbered as in original.—Ed.] In Appendix A to their initial brief filed in this Court the plaintiffs tabulated a page-by-page comparison between the district court's findings of fact and conclusions of law and those proposed by the defendant Stockham. The analysis reveals that 92 percent of the district court's factual findings are identically or substantially the same as those the defendant Stockham suggested; while, 98.2 percent of the district court's conclusions of law are identically or substantially the same as conclusions proposed by Stockham. The plaintiffs concede that in this Circuit the "clearly erroneous" standard of Rule 52(a), F. R. Civ. P., applies to a trial judge's factual findings whether he prepared them or they were developed by one of the parties and mechanically adopted by the judge. *Volkswagen of America, Inc.* v. *Jahre,* 5 Cir. 1973, 472 F.2d 557; *Railex Corp.* v. *Speed Check Co.,* 5 Cir. 1972, 457 F.2d 1040, *cert. denied,* 409 U.S. 876, 93 S.Ct. 125, 34 L.Ed.2d 128; *George W. Bennett Bryson & Co., Ltd.* v. *Norton Lilly & Co., Inc.,* 5 Cir. 1974, 502 F.2d 1045. Nevertheless, under *Louis Dreyfus and Cie.* v. *Panama Canal Co.,* 5 Cir. 1962, 298 F.2d 733, this Court can take into consideration the district court's lack of personal attention to factual findings in applying the "clearly erroneous" rule. This Court has expressed its disapproval of a district court's mechanical adoption of the proposed findings of fact of a party. *See Lorenz* v. *General Steel Products Co.,* 5 Cir. 1964, 337 F.2d 726, 727 n. 3; *George W. Bennett Bryson & Co., Ltd.* v. *Norton Lilly & Co.;* Wright and Miller, FEDERAL PRACTICE AND PROCEDURE § 2578 at pp. 705–708 (1971). As we observed in *Louis Dreyfus,* "the appellate court can feel slightly more confident in concluding that important evidence has been overlooked or inadequately considered" when factual findings were not the product of personal analysis and determination by the trial judge. "The findings also will carry more of a badge of personal determination when the trial judge has selected certain of the proposed findings but written others himself or when he has revised and edited the proposed findings, than they will when he has adopted a slate of findings verbatim. It must be remembered, however, that . . . [w]hen substantial

gated facilities maintained by Stockham and resolved in a conciliation agreement between the EEOC and Stockham two weeks before the trial, Stockham had engaged in no employment discrimination.[2] The plaintiffs appeal from the district court's judgment in favor of the defendants.[3]

## II.

### FACTS

### A. *Introduction*

Stockham is engaged in the manufacture of cast iron valves; malleable fittings; bronze, iron and steel valves; and other industrial valves and fittings at its facilities in Birmingham, Alabama. The product diversity and overall capacity of the company have gradually increased since Stockham was founded in 1903. By 1973 Stockham's work force in Birmingham was comprised of more than two thousand employees. Although the district court found that "[h]istorically, approximately two-thirds of Stockham's employees have been black," 394 F. Supp. at 443, the record reveals that the two-thirds figure applies to production and maintenance workers during the years from 1966 to 1973. Approximately 56 percent of the entire work force at Stockham's Birmingham facility was black during that same period, a figure larger than the percentage of blacks in the Birmingham area.

The district court found that Stockham has a multi-plant complex in Birmingham that is, in effect, six plants in one, comprised of a cast iron fittings plant, a malleable iron fittings plant, a bronze valve plant, an iron valve plant, a steel valve plant, and a butterfly valve plant. That finding is overstated, for at least four of the 22 seniority departments at Stockham, valve machining and assembly, electrical, machine shop, and construction, extend over all or virtually all of the "plants."

The defendant unions, the Steelworkers and its Local, have been the bargaining unit representatives for the production and maintenance

---

evidence supports a finding it will not be found clearly erroneous merely because the expression of the finding was adopted from a proposal by counsel."
*Louis Dreyfus & Cie.* v. *Panama Canal Co., supra,* 298 F.2d at 738–39.

Of course, the clearly erroneous standard does not apply to findings made under an erroneous view of controlling legal principles. *United States* v. *Jacksonville Terminal Co.,* 5 Cir. 1971, 451 F.2d 418, 423–24, *cert. denied,* 1972, 406 U.S. 906, 92 S.Ct. 1607, 31 L.Ed.2d 815; *Rowe* v. *General Motors Corp.,* 5 Cir. 1972, 457 F.2d 348, 365 n. 15. In addition, "findings of 'ultimate' fact such as whether *a series of acts* did or did not establish the existence of a violation of Title VII was a legal conclusion and not controlled by the 'clearly erroneous' rule." (emphasis in original) *Bolton* v. *Murray Envelope Corp.,* 5 Cir. 1974, 493 F.2d 191, 195, *citing United States* v. *Jacksonville Terminal,* 451 F.2d at 423.

[2] The district court's findings of fact and conclusions of law are reported at 394 F. Supp. 434.

[3] The Equal Employment Opportunity Commission filed a brief as *amicus curiae* in support of the plaintiffs-appellants, contending that the district court's factual findings relevant to the discrimination allegations are clearly erroneous, that the failure of the court to enjoin the maintenance of segregated facilities is an abuse of discretion, and that the court's refusal to award backpay constitutes a disregard of well-established legal principles.

hourly employees at Stockham since 1944. A majority of the local union's members have been black since World War II, and a majority of the members of the Local's grievance committee and of its officers have been black since 1967. Plaintiffs James and Winston have been officers of the Local and participated in collective bargaining negotiations. The Steelworkers' staff representative who has aided the Local in contract negotiations is black.

All the plaintiffs were black hourly employees of Stockham. Patrick James, a high school graduate and a graduate of Booker T. Washington Business College, was hired as a laborer at Stockham in 1950 and 24 years later at the time of trial was still working in that capacity. Howard Harville was hired in 1946 and worked as an arbor molder in the grey foundry until 1970 when he retired on a medical disability. Louis Winston was hired as a laborer for the galvanizing department in 1964, was transferred to the electrical department as a laborer in 1965, and in 1971 became one of the first blacks enrolled in the apprenticeship program.

## B.  Organization

### 1.  Departments

By agreement with the Local, Stockham has maintained a formal departmental seniority system since 1949. There are 22 seniority departments. The foundry departments produce the basic materials and molds for Stockham's products (e.g. grey iron foundry, bronze foundry, and malleable foundry); other departments assemble, finish, and machine products (e.g. tapping room and valve machining and assembly); and another group of departments perform maintenance functions (e.g. electrical shop, machine shop, valve tool room, and construction).

Since 1965 the company has regularly employed approximately 200 office and clerical personnel. In addition, the work force includes 22 non-union, salaried timekeepers. As of June 1973, there were also 32 plant guards. The Stockham sales department in Birmingham included 22 employees at the time of trial. At that time a total of 46 salesmen were employed by Stockham throughout the country.

### 2.  Wage Determinants

Within each seniority department bargaining unit jobs are divided into twelve job classes in ascending order of hourly wage from JC 2 to JC 13. These classifications reflect the increasingly complex nature of the jobs and the level of skill necessary to perform them. An employee's job classification determines his base pay rate. Other factors such as incentive earnings and merit raises also determine actual earnings. For each job classification there are different gradations of pay for non-incentive employees. Under Stockham's incentive system employees in highly repetitive jobs can add to their base pay if their work output reaches a sufficiently high level. A direct incentive worker's earnings averages approximately 25 percent above his base pay rate. Indirect incentive workers provide support services to direct incentive workers and receive incentive pay based on the output of the incentive workers. Non-incentive workers advance from one grade of pay to the next within a job classification if they achieve a predetermined score under a formal merit rating system. Although incentive workers are not eligible for merit pay raises, all employees receive merit ratings from their foremen every six months.

### 3.   Advancement and Transfers

The merit scores received by both incentive and non-incentive employees become part of their personnel records; such ratings constitute one of the factors considered in promotion and training selection.[4]

Job vacancies have never been posted at Stockham and the company does not have a formal bidding system. In 1965 Stockham instituted a "timely application" procedure that received a formal blessing in the 1970 collective bargaining agreement. An employee may ask his supervisor to prepare an application on his behalf for any job at Stockham, whether or not a vacancy for that job exists at the time of the application. The application is considered "timely" regardless of when the vacancy occurs. In filling vacancies company officials are not restricted to those employees who have filed timely applications. In practice many promotion and training selections are made in favor of employees who have not filed such applications.

Stockham administered the Wonderlic Test (discussed later in this opinion) to job applicants and employees seeking promotions and transfers from August 1965 until April 1971. To be considered for a position an employee was required to attain the Wonderlic score designated for the job. An employee seeking a job in a new department, another department from the one in which he was working, was required to obtain the higher "norm" score on the test; a worker seeking promotion within his own department was eligible for the job if he achieved the lower "minimum" score on the test, provided that he had attained "basic departmental job skills."

Under the seniority system at Stockham a senior employee is entitled to preference only when two or more competing workers possess the same degree of qualifications. An employee's foreman decides whether he meets this test and is entitled to promotion or training opportunities. This decision is totally within the discretion of the foreman and is not subject to review.

---

4 The supervising foreman rates an individual employee using the "personnel rating" form which requires an evaluation of seven factors: quantity and quality of work, job or trade knowledge, ability to learn, cooperation, dependability, industry, and attendance. The employee is rated on each factor as "unsatisfactory," "poor," "average," "superior," and "exceptional." Stockham's wage and salary administrator scores the form by assigning point values to each rating in each category. The defendant's expert testified that in 1973 blacks averaged 71.3 in merit ratings, whereas, whites averaged 79.5.

## C.  Employment Practices

### 1.  Initial Job Assignments

According to company officials, it has been and still is the practice at Stockham for the initial job assignments of new employees to be made by the supervisors, both superintendents and foremen, of the departments containing the vacancies. The personnel office at Stockham serves as a recruiting agency and interviews and screens job applicants. The supervisor of a department advises the personnel office of any need for additional employees, and he is informed when suitable applications are available for review. In some cases the supervisor will request a particular individual whom he knows has filed an application. In other cases the personnel office will present the supervisor with a group of applications for examination. The supervisor, either the foreman or superintendent depending on the department, makes the hiring decision, which is totally discretionary and without written guidelines. Supervisors usually accept approximately 75 percent of the applicants recommended by the personnel department.

### 2.  Seniority System

As stated, a Stockham employee seeking a new job in his existing department or desiring to transfer to a position in another department may file a timely application. A supervisor fills the vacancy within his department from employees who have filed timely applications, other employees, and applicants from outside the company. If two Stockham applicants are about equal in qualifications, the collective bargaining agreement requires that the employee with the most departmental seniority be selected.

If other factors are equal, departmental seniority determines not only promotions but also lay-offs and recalls. A worker who transfers between departments is a new employee for purposes of promotion and regression in the transferee department. Before June 1970 if a worker transferred departments he immediately lost all seniority in his old department. In 1970 this requirement was modified in the collective bargaining agreement. An employee was given 18 months after transfer to the new department to decide if he wanted to return to his old department. If within that time he decided to return, he would be permitted to reenter his old department within 24 months of his transfer with his accumulated seniority. The 1973 collective agreement further modified these seniority provisions. If after 18 months an employee elected to remain in the transferee department, then he would be allowed to retain his seniority in his old department solely for lay-offs, but only until he had been in the new department as long as he had been in the old. If he was laid-off during this period, he would be permitted to return to his old department with his accumulated seniority.

The basic features of Stockham's seniority system have remained unchanged: (1) an employee who transfers between departments forfeits his accumulated seniority at some point; (2) an employee who transfers between departments is a new employee for all promotion and regression purposes; and (3) a departmental employee has preference over employees from other departments for promotion to all vacancies within his department.

. . .

## III.

### DISCRIMINATION, ADVERSE IMPACT, AND THE BUSINESS NECESSITY DOCTRINE

The plaintiffs-appellants raise a broad spectrum of issues in this appeal, challenging every aspect of the district court's finding that Stockham and the unions were not guilty of discriminatory employment practices.

### A. Segregated Facilities

Segregation of many of Stockham's facilities and programs continued into the 1970s and, in some cases, until a few weeks before trial. In 1965 the system of total segregation extended to the entrance gates of the plant, employee identification numbers, pay windows, toilet facilities, the cafeteria, drinking fountains, the locker rooms, and bathhouses. In addition, the company-sponsored Young Men's Christian Association ("YMCA") had two boards and separate Bible classes; one board and one Bible class was composed of white members and the other board and Bible class of black members. In addition, there were racially separate company baseball and bowling teams.

Until 1969 all black hourly employees at Stockham had badge identification numbers ranging from 300 to 2999, while all white employees had badge numbers above 2999. Employees with numbers up to 2999, that is, the blacks, used one set of pay windows for cash payments; whereas, white employees with numbers greater than 2999 used another set of windows. In 1969 the company began to assign badge identification numbers by departments and in 1972 abandoned cash payments and the use of pay windows.

The partitions in the cafeteria,[7] toilets, and bathhouse,[8] the racial as-

---

[7] The segregation in the cafeteria after 1965 was not total although the vast majority of white and black employees continued to eat on separate sides of the partition. The testimony of one black employee, Claude Chapman, Jr., who attempted to cross the barrier with a few fellow black employees in 1967 suggests the nature of the pressure exerted on blacks who failed to conform to custom:
"Q [Plaintiffs' attorney] Have you had any experience with segregated facilities at Stockham?
"A [Chapman] Yes. I've had some experience with the cafeteria that we have at Stockham.
"Q What years—what year or years did you have that—
"A In 1967, I believe, I was working at night at Stockham on Number One Unit as a Molder. I was one of the first to go in the cafeteria on the white side. We had two sides, white and colored.
"Q What do you mean one of the first? One of the first coloreds—
"A To go on the white side. I went in the cafeteria that night; about ten of us went in.

signment of lockers, and the racially separate YMCA boards were the subjects of a conciliation agreement between Stockham and the EEOC entered into January 21, 1974. In addition, the plaintiffs adduced testimony at trial on the existence of racially separate toilet facilities for the seven female employees in the dispensary at Stockham.[9]

. . .

The plaintiff in an action under Title VII has the burden of establishing a prima facie case of discrimination in employment practices. That burden may be met with statistical proof when it reaches proportions

---

"Q    Ten of us, black or white?
"A    Ten blacks went in the cafeteria. We were served. We sat and we ate. And as we left, the guards followed us back to the plant. He didn't—they didn't say anything to us. He didn't say anything. He just walked up and down the line looking at all of us and we was at work. The next night the money sheets came out and they had a red X by everybody's name that participated in going in the cafeteria. So we went back in the cafeteria that night. So some of the fellows began to get annoyed about the X's. They started to ask me questions, 'What's the X for?' I say, 'Well, the X is nothing but something to annoy you. They're not going to say anything to you.' So this went on for about a week. The superintendent at the time, his name was Mr. Stone. So after going in the cafeteria for a week, the next week we started again, still going in the cafeteria eating. So the foreman came down one night after we had came back to the cafeteria and said, 'Well, Mr. Stone wants to see you in his office,' say, 'He wants all the fellows that participated in going in the cafeteria.' So he say, 'Now, you're not—you don't have to say anything,' say, 'I just merely want to talk with you fellows.' So I told him, 'Okay, I'll go.' The rest of us fellows, we all went to his office. When we got in Mr. Stone's office, Mr. Stone say, 'Fellows,' say, 'I don't want you to say anything,' say, 'I just merely want to talk with you fellows.' Well, he didn't say fellows. 'Boys,' say, 'I want to talk with you boys.' So he say, 'is there anything wrong with the food on the other side?' He say, 'If there is, let me know.' We didn't say anything. He says, 'You know, fellows,' say, 'Mr. Stockham been good to you people,' says, 'do you know Mr. Stockham has the only company that has had black boys around skid trucks and things for years?' He say, 'I would just hate to see you fellows tear down overnight what took us 65 years to build.' And after he said it, he started crying. He reared back and tears came out of his eyes. We still didn't say anything. He say, 'If any of you fellows have anything you want to tell me about food or facilities that you think is different, let me know; other than that, I'm through. I just hate to see you boys tear down what it took 65 years to build out here.' So after then a few of them stopped going. But they never tried to stop us from going then.'
The cafeteria partition was finally removed one week before trial.
    8 Claude Chapman, Jr. also testified that the bathhouse partition was still in place at the time of trial:
"Q    [Plaintiffs' attorney] All right. Mr. Chapman, have you had any other experience with segregated facilities at Stockham?
"A    [Chapman] Well, the bathhouse is segregated.
    . . .
"THE COURT: Now?
"A    Yes, now. I had a—my committee chairman is white and he changed in a different side of the bathhouse. I had to go over one evening to see my committeeman and as I came out of the bathhouse I saw one of the guards standing looking at me real hard. He didn't say anything. They are still segregated now.
"THE COURT: Do they have any signs on them?
"A    No sir, they don't have any signs on them.
"THE COURT: They just have the facilities that have been traditionally used by the two different races?
"A    That's right."
    9 Mrs. Lola Short, a black dental hygienist, testified that when she started working at Stockham in 1971, she was instructed to share one of the women's bathrooms with her black co-worker. The five white female employees shared the other bathroom. Mrs. Short stated that this practice was continuing at the time of trial.

comparable to those in this case. *Wade* v. *Mississippi Cooperative Extension Service,* 5 Cir. 1976, 528 F.2d 508, 516–17; *United States* v. *Hayes International Corp.* ("Hayes II"), 5 Cir. 1972, 456 F.2d 112, 120. See also *Pettway* v. *American Cast Iron Pipe Co.,* 5 Cir. 1974, 494 F.2d 211, 225 n. 34;*United States* v. *Jacksonville Terminal Co.,* 5 Cir. 1971, 451 F.2d 418, 442, 446, *cert. denied,* 1972, 406 U.S. 906, 92 S.Ct. 1607, 31 L.Ed.2d 815. Indeed the Supreme Court has recently approved the use of statistical proof in establishing a prima facie case of racial discrimination in the trucking industry. "Statistics are equally competent in proving employment discrimination. . . . Statistics showing racial or ethnic imbalance are probative in a case such as this one only because such imbalance is often a telltale sign of purposeful discrimination; absent explanation, it is ordinarily to be expected that nondiscriminatory hiring practices will in time result in a work force more or less representative of the racial and ethnic composition of the population in the community from which employees are hired." *International Brotherhood of Teamsters* v. *United States,* 431 U.S. 324, 339 and n. 20, 97 S.Ct. 1843, 1856, 52 L.Ed.2d 396 (1977) (*Teamsters*).

Here the plaintiffs have produced evidence of gross disparities in job allocations at Stockham on the basis of race. All but two of the seniority departments were either predominantly white or predominantly black at Stockham at the time of trial in 1973. Only sixteen percent of the hourly jobs were integrated by that time.[27] In 1973 the overwhelming majority of both incentive and non-incentive white workers were employed in jobs with the highest job classifications.

Blacks earn, on the average, $0.37 less per hour than whites, including overtime and incentive pay.[28] Seventy percent of all black employees work in the monotonous, pressurized conditions of the incentive system, and 94 percent of all workers subject to the hot, dusty, dirty conditions of the foundry departments are black. The disparities revealed by the statistics on job allocations at Stockham are gross and the statistical evidence compelling; they establish a clear prima facie case of purposeful discrimination.

*The statistical patterns do not complete the plaintiffs' case.* In addition, they offer persuasive evidence of total job segregation prior to 1965 and the intransigent retention of segregated facilities and programs at Stockham until at least 1974.

. . .

---

[27] In *Pettway* this Court reversed a finding of no discrimination by the district court in partial reliance on statistics revealing that "[a]s late as 1971, only fifty-nine of 232 jobs were integrated—only 25% of the total." *Pettway* v. *American Cast Iron Pipe Co.,* 494 F.2d at 230.

[28] In *Watkins* v. *Scott Paper Co.,* 5 Cir. 1976, 530 F.2d 1159, 1165, this Court found a pay differential of $0.47 an hour for white and black employees a persuasive element of the plaintiffs' prima facie case on employment discrimination. See also the discussion of the relevance of interracial wage comparisons in Title VII cases in *Baxter* v. *Savannah Sugar Refining Corp.,* 5 Cir. 1974, 495 F.2d 437.

## F. *Seniority System*

The plaintiffs and the EEOC contend that Stockham's departmental seniority system, when combined with the company's discriminatory job assignment practices, unlawfully reinforces and perpetuates prior discrimination. According to the EEOC, the seniority system operates to "freeze in" the effects of discriminatory job assignments in two ways:

"(1) by conditioning transfer on the sacrifice of seniority, it inevitably inhibits black employees from seeking to escape to departments to which they were assigned because of race, and

"(2) by refusing to recognize after transfer seniority acquired in black departments, or departments with particular jobs open to blacks, it continues to penalize them for their initial, racially-based assignments."

We discussed Stockham's job assignment practices in subsection "III.B." of this opinion and concluded that the company has unlawfully allocated jobs on the basis of race both before and after the effective date of Title VII, at least until 1973. The issue here is whether Stockham's departmental seniority system, which is neutral on its face, is unlawful because it accentuates the effects of Stockham's discriminatory job assignment practices.

The seniority system at Stockham has been modified twice since 1970. Until June 10, 1970, an employee who voluntarily transferred to a new department lost all of his accumulated seniority at the time of the transfer. He was treated for promotion and regression purposes as a new employee. With the 1970 modification to the system, an employee transferring to a new department was given 18 months from the date of the transfer to decide whether he wanted to return to his old department. If he decided to return, the employee was permitted to reenter his old department with his accumulated seniority within 24 months of his transfer. If he stayed in the new department, the employee lost the seniority he had accumulated in his old department. In 1973 the collective bargaining agreement effected a further modification of the seniority system at Stockham. If after 18 months an employee elected to remain in the department to which he transferred, he was permitted to retain his seniority in the old department for layoff purposes, but only until he had been in the new department as long as he had been in the old department. If during that period the employee was laid off from the new department, he was allowed to return to his old department with his accumulated seniority. Even after the 1970 and 1973 modifications to the seniority system several features remained unchanged: (1) at some point after an employee transfers to a new department, he forfeits his accumulated seniority; (2) an employee who transfers between departments is a new employee for all promotion and regression purposes in his new department; and (3) a departmental employee has the first opportunity to promote to all vacancies within his department.

Seniority systems such as the one at Stockham consistently have been condemned by the courts because black employees must choose to commit "seniority suicide" to enter departments from which they were previously excluded unlawfully on account of race. In addition, the plaintiffs argue, the Stockham system also "locks" such employees into their old depart- ments by not providing for pay rate retention, thereby forcing transferring employees to take a short-term pay cut to receive potentially greater earnings in the future.

According to the district court, "the record does not support the con- clusion that Stockham's departmental seniority system locks black em- ployees into particular jobs, pay categories or departments." 394 F. Supp. at 454. The court's determination was based on two sets of findings. On the issue of the comparative desirability of predominantly black and predominantly white departments, the court found:

"The relatively high earning opportunities in the foundries (malleable, brass, and grey iron) suggest that the high number of blacks in these departments results from voluntary choices by these employees to work in those departments where the most money can be made. . . .

". . . The evidence introduced by plaintiffs failed to establish that there are demonstrably superior working conditions in certain departments, and this Court finds that the working conditions in various departments at Stockham are generally the same."

394 F. Supp. at 453–54. As to the number of interdepartmental transfers made by black and white employees the court found:

"At all relevant times black employees have accounted for the large majority of all inter-departmental transfers. Black employees accounted for a low of 59.4 percent in 1965 and a high of 89.7 percent in 1968 of all inter-departmental transfers."

394 F. Supp. at 452.

The district court's conclusion that blacks have no incentive to transfer at Stockham because the departments to which they have been assigned are no less desirable than those with predominantly white employees is clearly erroneous. We have already discussed [55] the evidence on the work- ing conditions of predominantly black and white departments. The record shows that black employees at Stockham tend to work in the hottest, dustiest, and dirtiest departments. In addition, the vast majority of blacks work in lower classified jobs under the company's incentive system. Even if some black employees earn as much as whites working in higher job classes, the evidence shows they do so only under the great pressure of the "racetrack" while performing numbingly repetitive tasks. Further, the evidence does not establish that the earnings opportunities are the same in these departments. Thirty-three percent or 174 of all whites work in the seven departments with the highest earnings oppor- tunities while only 4 percent of the blacks are employed in those depart- ments. And, 70 percent or 836 of all black employees work in the seven departments with the lowest earnings opportunities; whereas, 23 percent of all white workers are employed in those departments. Therefore, the district court's first set of findings does not support its conclusion that

[55] See subsection "III.B." and the text and note at footnotes 21 and 23.

blacks remain in the departments to which they are assigned because they have no incentive to leave.

The statistics cited by the court on the percentage of interdepartmental transfers by black employees do not include the actual number of inter-departmental transfers. It is impossible, therefore, to judge the magnitude of the transfers at Stockham. Because some blacks are willing to transfer to new departments even though they will lose seniority and suffer a cut in pay as a result does not mean that many more blacks are deterred from transferring because of these disadvantages. In addition, we would expect a larger percentage of blacks than whites to transfer where, as in this case, whites already work in jobs with better earnings potential, less pressure, and more satisfactory working conditions; and the statistics cited by the district court support this thesis. Finally, the figures cited by the district court are not accompanied by information on the seniority of transferring blacks. The more junior the employee, the less inhibition to transfer there is from the system. The evidence cited by the district court, therefore, does not support its conclusion that the seniority system at Stockham does not "lock" blacks into jobs discriminatorily assigned to them.

The district court's conclusion that the seniority system at Stockham had no "locking-in effect" because there was no incentive for black employees to transfer to new departments and because a higher per-centage of blacks than whites changed departments after 1965 is clearly erroneous. In *Pettway* v. *American Cast Iron Pipe Co.*, 494 F.2d at 223–24, this Court evaluated a departmental seniority system. In that case a transferring employee retained his former seniority for purposes of re-turning to his old department in case of layoff from his new department, but did not carry over any of his accumulated seniority for purposes of departmental promotion. Under that system an employee who transferred to a new department to enhance his chances for eventual advancement, higher pay, or better working conditions was required to endure a loss of seniority and a wage cut as a condition of transfer. We concluded in *Pettway* that the present effect of such a system was to lock black em-ployees into jobs and departments to which they had originally been assigned on account of race. In so doing this Court rejected the district court's eight reasons for finding that blacks were not being "locked-in." Those reasons included voluntary refusal of blacks to accept training and promotion opportunities, their failure to request promotions, poor job performances by black employees, lack of job vacancies, and the lack of motivation on the part of blacks at the company. This Court deter-mined that critical examination of those variables led to the conclusion that they did not weigh heavily enough to overcome the plaintiffs' em-pirical evidence of racial stratification in departments, jobs, and pay rates.

Here too we reject the reasons given by the district court for finding no locking-in effect. The continued stratification of blacks in the least de-sirable departments and jobs, in terms of working conditions and earnings potential, is clear from the plaintiffs' statistics.[56] "Once it has been determined that blacks have been discriminatorily assigned to a particular department within a plant, departmental seniority cannot be utilized to freeze those black employees into a discriminatory case." (Footnote omitted.) *Johnson* v. *Goodyear Tire & Rubber Co.*, 491 F.2d at 1373. Under the seniority system in effect at Stockham before 1970 blacks who transferred between departments lost all accumulated seniority for promotion and regression purposes. Blacks transferring to new departments after 1970 have been required to start as new employees for job promotion and regression in the new department. After a period of time in the new department a new employee is forced to forfeit all his accumulated seniority even for layoff back to his former department.

In *United States* v. *Jacksonville Terminal Co.*, 451 F.2d at 453, we dealt with a craft and class seniority system in which an employer who gained a position in a new craft or class could not retain his accumulated seniority in his former craft or class. In finding the system unlawful we commented: "In any industry loss of seniority is a critical inhibition to transfer." That statement applies here too. Further, from 1965 to 1971 the company required a lower score on the Wonderlic test for an employee transferring to a job within his department than for an employee transferring from another department. This procedure operated more decisively to freeze in past discrimination than the three-day preferential bidding period for departmental employees condemned in *Pettway*. See *Pettway* v. *American Cast Iron Pipe Co.*, 494 F.2d at 240. Finally, Stockham's seniority system does not provide for rate retention for an employee who transfers to a lower paying job in a new department as a first step to reaping long range job and earnings rewards. These factors compel us to conclude that the departmental seniority system at Stockham, even as modified in 1970 and 1973, locks in the effects of pre- and post-Act discriminatory employment practices at Stockham. See *Johnson* v. *Goodyear Tire & Rubber Co.*, 491 F.2d at 1373–74 and cases cited at 1373 n. 27; *United States* v. *Georgia Power Co.*, 5 Cir. 1973, 474 F.2d 906, 926–27; *United States* v. *Jacksonville Terminal Co.*, 451 F.2d at 452–53.

The defendant Stockham contends that even if the seniority system operates to lock in the effects of past discrimination, the system is justified by business necessity. Although this contention is not detailed in the defendant's brief, its essentials seem to be that the seniority system is a necessary element of the "unique multi-plant complex" operated by Stockham in Birmingham. A company official testified that the six "plants" are composed of the following seniority units: cast iron fittings, malleable fittings, bronze valve, iron valve, steel valve, and butterfly valve. He asserted that interdepartmental, or "cross-plant," transfers will create substantial difficulties for Stockham.

The business necessity defense, as the defendant applies it here, has no substance. First, at least four of the 22 seniority departments at Stockham extend over more than one "plant." The valve machining and assembly

---

[56] See subsection "III.B."

department extends over several of the six "plants" and the electrical, machine shop, and construction departments extend over all of the "plants." Thus, the functional separation of the company's manufacturing operations does not reach the proportions suggested by Stockham's contention that it effectively operates six different plants at its Birmingham facility. Second, Stockham's statement that it has not discouraged interdepartmental transfers is inconsistent with its assertion that there are difficulties associated with so-called "cross-plant" transfers.

To be justifiable under the business necessity doctrine a seniority system must be essential to the goals of safety and efficiency. *United States v. Bethlehem Steel Corp.*, 446 F.2d at 662; *Pettway v. American Cast Iron Pipe Co.*, 494 F.2d at 245. The defendant has failed to satisfy that heavy burden. There has been no showing that departmental seniority is essential to safety and efficiency at Stockham.

In its recent opinion in *Teamsters*, _____ U.S. at _____, 97 S.Ct. 1843, the Supreme Court stated that a seniority system, not justified by business necessity, that operates to freeze the status quo of prior discriminatory employment practices would seem to be unlawful under the rationale of *Griggs v. Duke Power Co.* Nevertheless, the Court concluded that such a system is legally valid under section 703(h) of Title VII, 42 U.S.C. § 2000e–2(h), if it is a bona fide seniority system within the meaning of that section.[57] In reaching this result the Court refused to distinguish between seniority systems that perpetuate pre- and post-Act discrimination. *Id.* at _____ n. 30, 97 S.Ct. 1843. As to relief, however, the Court differentiated between pre- and post-Act discriminatory acts, pointing to the holding in *Franks v. Bowman Transportation Co.*, 1976, 424 U.S. 747, 96 S.Ct. 1251, 47 L.Ed.2d 444, that:

"§ 703(h) does not bar the award of retroactive seniority to job applicants who seek relief from an employer's post-Act hiring discrimination."
*Id.* at _____, 97 S.Ct. at 1860. Thus, according to the Court,
"[p]ost-Act discriminatees . . . may obtain full 'make whole' relief, including retroactive seniority under *Franks v. Bowman, supra,* without attacking the legality of the seniority system as applied to them."
*Id.* at _____, 97 S.Ct. at 1860. See EEOC; Interpretative Memorandum, 7/12/77, 46 L.W. 2028.

In this case the plaintiffs have proved that Stockham engaged in post-Act discriminatory employment practices in job allocation, testing, craft training and selection, and promotion. Any black injured by these practices is entitled to relief, including retroactive seniority. The issue whether the seniority system at Stockham is bona fide under section 703(h) of Title VII is relevant to this case only if the district court concludes that

---

[57] Section 703(h), 42 U.S.C. § 2000e–2(h), provides in part:
"Notwithstanding any other provision of this subchapter, it shall be an unlawful employment practice for an employer to apply different standards of compensation, or different terms, conditions, or privileges of employment pursuant to a bona fide seniority . . . system . . . provided that such differences are not the result of an intention to discriminate because of race."

the class of black employees represented by the plaintiffs consists of some blacks who suffered only from pre-Act discrimination. The following comments are intended to guide the district court's analysis of that issue.

In *Teamsters* the Court focused on whether a seniority system, contained in collective bargaining agreements between the employer, a nationwide common carrier of motor freight, and the unions was bona fide. Under that system an employee's seniority for competitive purposes was his bargaining unit seniority, which controlled the order in which he was laid off or recalled and the order in which he could bid for a particular job. Line drivers were in one bargaining unit and city drivers and servicemen were in another. The practical effect of the seniority arrangement was that a city driver or serviceman who transferred to a line-driver job forfeited all the competitive seniority he had accumulated in his previous bargaining unit and started at the bottom of the line-driver's roster. The Court found that the system locked-in the effects of the employer's past intentional discrimination; nevertheless, the system was bona fide. The Court explained:

"[The seniority system] applies equally to all races and ethnic groups. To the extent that it 'locks' employees into nonline-driver jobs, it does so for all. The city drivers and servicemen who are discouraged from transferring to line-driver jobs are not all Negroes or Spanish-surnamed Americans; to the contrary, the overwhelming majority are white. The placing of line drivers in a separate bargaining unit from other employees is rational, in accord with the industry practice, and consistent with NLRB precedents. It is conceded that the seniority system did not have its genesis in racial discrimination, and that it was negotiated and has been maintained free from any illegal purpose. In these circumstances, the single fact that the system extends no retroactive seniority to pre-Act discriminatees does not make it unlawful." (Footnote omitted.)
*International Brotherhood of Teamsters* v. *United States*, _____ U.S. at _____, 97 S.Ct. at 1865.

As we read the *Teamsters* opinion, the issue whether there has been purposeful discrimination in connection with the establishment or continuation of a seniority system is integral to a determination that the system is or is not bona fide. See also *United Air Lines, Inc.* v. *Evans*, _____ U.S. _____, 97 S.Ct. 1885, 52 L.Ed.2d 571 (1977). The Court's analysis suggests that the totality of the circumstances in the development and maintenance of the system is relevant to examining that issue. See also *Washington* v. *Davis,* 426 U.S. 229, 96 S.Ct. 2040, 48 L.Ed.2d at 608–609. In *Teamsters* the Court focused on four factors:

(1) whether the seniority system operates to discourage all employees equally from transferring between seniority units;

(2) whether the seniority units are in the same or separate bargaining units (if the latter, whether that structure is rational and in conformance with industry practice);

(3) whether the seniority system had its genesis in racial discrimination; and

(4) whether the system was negotiated and has been maintained free from any illegal purpose.

The Court analyzed the context in which the seniority system developed. In discussing the relationship of seniority units to bargaining units, the Court quoted a National Labor Relations Board opinion that emphasized the rationality of separate bargaining units in the case of over-the-road and city drivers "where they are shown to be clearly defined, homogeneous, and functionally distinct groups with separate interests." *Id.*, _____ U.S. at _____, n. 42, 97 S.Ct. at 1865. Thus, the facts of a particular seniority unit are critical to a determination whether the system is bona fide; and a case-by-case analysis of seniority systems in light of section 703(h) is necessary.

In *Teamsters* the plaintiffs conceded that the seniority system did not have its genesis in racial discrimination and that it was negotiated and maintained free from any illegal purpose. There is no such concession here. The seniority system at Stockham was adopted in a collective bargaining agreement in 1949, when segregation in the South was standing operating procedure. The history of the negotiations associated with Stockham's seniority system is clouded. Since 1967 the local union has sought major revisions in the departmental seniority system through contract negotiations with the defendant Stockham.[58] In 1970 the union

---

[58] E. Reeves Sims, the company's manager of employee and public relations, gave the following testimony on the 1970 negotiations:

"Q   Isn't it a fact that the Union wanted and has tried to get job posting and job bidding at the plant, Mr. Sims?
"A   They have proposed that, yes, sir.
"Q   Isn't that—that would take the place of this timely application procedure?
"A   Yes.
"Q   Now, a job posting, isn't it true that the Union has sought posting throughout the plants so all employees would know what jobs are open; isn't that correct?
"A   That's correct.
"Q   And what's the Company position? Why do you or have you and the Company opposed this job posting?
"A   We've never agreed on it because we felt that timely application was the best.
"Q   Wouldn't job posting provide better information to all of the employees?
"A   We've never agreed on that.
"Q   All right. Now, job bidding and job posting, you've never agreed on. The Union has continually sought to get that, have they not?
"A   They have proposed it, yes, sir.
"Q   I think that was part of the package that was on the table in 1970 when you had a five months strike, was it not, Mr. Sims?
"A   As I remember it, it was in the proposal, yes, sir.
"Q   Now, the Union in 1970 in one of its proposals was seeking plantwide seniority. If I understand it correctly, the Company opposed that, is that correct?
"A   We didn't agree on it, yes, sir."
In addition, Edward D. Coleman, Stockham's superintendent of quality assurance and a participant in the 1970 negotiations, stated: "All of the discussions we had with the union were in issue during this [1970] strike."
Finally, the president of the Local, Joseph E. Robbins, confirmed that the subject of plantwide seniority was included in the 1973 contract negotiations:
"Q   In the '73 contract negotiations in the meetings that—and you attended them, I assume—do you recall the mention of a Bethlehem Steel Decision at Lackawanna, New York?
"A   The name doesn't—I know what it pertains to, I mean what it—
"Q   All right. What—
"A   What it's all about.

struck for five months seeking the company's agreement with its proposals, including plant-wide seniority. Stockham's failure to go along
with revisions in the seniority system must be evaluated in the context
of the company's extensive unlawful employment practices during the
period of the negotiations and its intransigent adherence to wide-spread
segregated facilities at the plant, at least until 1974. In addition, Stockham's resistance to revisions in the seniority system must be considered
in light of the union's firm support for such changes and its willingness
to strike for the proposed modifications in 1970. Finally, unlike the facts
of *Teamsters,* here the seniority units do not reflect existing separate and
distinct bargaining units that conform to industry practice. The district
court should give careful consideration to the negotiations involving the
seniority system at Stockham and to the employment practices of the
company underlying such negotiations. Because the issue whether the
seniority system is bona fide was not legally relevant when this case was
tried, on remand the district court should allow the parties to present
additional evidence on the question.

## IV

### UNION LIABILITY

As to the defendant unions, Local 3036 and the United States Steelworkers of America, AFL–CIO, the district court concluded:

"Since this Court finds that there has been no violation of the Act, there
is of course no liability on the part of the defendant unions. However,
in the interest of judicial economy, this Court concludes that if liability
existed, and since the contract between Stockham and the unions is the
product of negotiation, the defendant unions would also be liable in
their roles as bargaining agent in the collective bargaining process. . . ."
394 F. Supp. at 499. We remand the question of the unions' liability to
the district court. The court clearly erred in finding no liability for any
defendant under Title VII. Thus, the determination that the unions
are not liable because the employer is not liable cannot stand. The alternative finding that the unions violated Title VII if the employer did also
must fall. The Supreme Court's decision in *Teamsters* may require a
determination whether the seniority system at Stockham is bona fide. If

---

"Q   All right, sir. In what context was that raised, if you remember?
"A   By the Union prior to going into our written statements on the table.
"Q   All right, sir.
"A   We had discussed plant-wide seniority.
"Q   And is it in that context that a reference was made to some lawsuit?
"A   Yes.
"Q   Now, when you say prior to your written proposals do you orally go through some
particular sections of the contract or some—pick out some items and talk about these
orally before you go into your written proposals sections by section?
"A   Yes.
"Q   And it was this occasion that you had an oral discussion of plant-wide seniority?
"A   Right.
"Q   In 1973?
"A   '73."

the system is found to be protected under section 703(h) or if the court does not reach that question, the unions could not have violated Title VII in agreeing to and maintaining the system. *Teamsters,* _____ U.S. at _____, 97 S.Ct. 1843. If, on the other hand, the district court concludes that the seniority system is not bona fide, it must consider the question whether the unions' role in ratifying collective bargaining agreements containing the various seniority provisions compels a finding of liability.

The plaintiffs in this case assert that the findings of the district court on the unions' role in negotiating the seniority system are not supported by the evidence. The court found:

"While other forms of seniority may have been discussed from time to time, the basic (*i.e.,* written) bargaining proposals submitted to Stockham by the Unions have never requested a change from the existing departmental seniority system and have instead reflected an intention on the part of the unions to preserve the present seniority system."

394 F. Supp. at 451. The plaintiffs contend that the record reveals that from 1967 to 1973 the unions sought major revisions in the departmental seniority system through negotiations.[59] Union segregation is not an issue in this case, as it was recently in *Myers* v. *Gilman Paper Corp.*, 5 Cir. 1977, 544 F.2d 837. Since World War II a majority of the local union's members have been black, and a majority of the members of the grievance committee and the officers have been black since 1967. On remand, the district court should evaluate these facts in light of *Teamsters* and *Evans* in determining whether the unions must bear legal responsibility in the event the seniority system is not bona fide.

. . .

# VI

## CONCLUSION

The record in this case reveals that the defendant Stockham is guilty of unlawful racial discrimination in the segregation of facilities and programs, the allocation of jobs, craft training and selection, promotion, and supervisory recruitment and training. We have discussed the broad remedies available to the district court under Title VII for rectifying such practices. Except for backpay relief, nothing the courts can do will change the past. On remand, the future of blacks at Stockham is at issue.

*Reversed and Remanded.*

# NOTE

For other examples of the courts' efforts to apply the intentional-discrimination or genesis-in-discrimination standard see *Chrapliwy* v. *Uniroyal*, 15 FEP Cases 795 (N.D. Ind. 1977). Compare *Nickel* v. *Highway Industries*, 441 F. Supp. 477 (W.D. Wisc. 1977). See also *Younger* v.

59 [Omitted.]

*Glamorgan Pipe & Foundry Co.*, 561 F.2d 563 (4th Cir. 1977); *Recent Developments—Title VII, Seniority—The Relevant Scope of Inquiry for Determining the Legality of a Seniority System*, 31 VAND. L. REV. 151 (1978); and *Sears* v. *Atchison, Topeka & Sante Fe Ry.*, 17 FEP Cases, 1138 (D. Kan 1978).

(6)  *Relief From Discriminatory Seniority Under Other Laws*

## JOHNSON v. RYDER TRUCK LINES, INC.

*United States Court of Appeals, Fourth Circuit, 1978*

*575 F.2d 471, 17 FEP Cases 571, cert. denied, _____ U.S. _____,*
*19 FEP Cases 467 (1979)*

BUTZNER, Circuit Judge: After affirming the district court's grant of injunctive relief, retroactive seniority, and back pay in this class action brought under Title VII of the Civil Rights Act of 1964 [42 U.S.C. § 2000e *et seq.*] and § 16 of the Civil Rights Act of 1870 [42 U.S.C. § 1981], we granted rehearing to consider the effect of *International Brotherhood of Teamsters* v. *United States*, 431 U.S. 324, 97 S.Ct. 1843, 52 L.Ed.2d 396 (1977).[1] The principal question to emerge on rehearing is whether some employees can obtain relief under § 1981 that is not available to them under Title VII. We hold that in this instance they cannot, and we modify our initial opinion and remand the case for further proceedings.

### I

Incumbent black employees who were discriminated against when hired before the effective date of Title VII in 1965 were subsequently prevented by the company's bargaining agreement from obtaining jobs as line drivers while maintaining their full company seniority. The district court's order provided relief to employees who suffered in this way from the present effects of pre-Act discrimination. Rehearing disclosed that the relevant provisions of the bargaining contract involved in this case and the one considered in *Teamsters* are virtually identical. Both contracts provided that employees could not carry their full company seniority for all purposes with them when they transferred to line driver positions.

In *Teamsters* the Court considered the effects of § 703(h) of the 1964 Act [42 U.S.C. § 2000e–2(h)] on the contract's seniority system.[2] It said:

---

[1] [Footnotes numbered as in original.—Ed.] Our initial decision is reported as *Johnson* v. *Ryder Truck Lines, Inc.*, 555 F.2d 1181 (4th Cir. 1977).

[2] Section 703(h) of the 1964 Act [42 U.S.C. § 2000e–2(h)] provides in part:

"Notwithstanding any other provision of this subchapter, it shall not be unlawful employment practice for an employer to apply different standards of compensation, or different terms, conditions, or privileges of employment pursuant to a bona fide seniority or merit system, . . . provided that such differences are not the result of an intention to discriminate because of race . . . ."

"[W]e hold that an otherwise neutral, legitimate seniority system does not become unlawful under Title VII simply because it may perpetuate pre-Act discrimination. Congress did not intend to make it illegal for employees with vested seniority rights to continue to exercise those rights, even at the expense of pre-Act discriminatees." 431 U.S. at 353–54, 97 S.Ct. at 1864.

Therefore, *Teamsters* invalidates our affirmance of the district court's conclusion that the company's seniority system violated Title VII.

The employees assert, however, that § 703(h) is expressly limited to Title VII and that it should not be construed as a restriction on § 1981. They therefore insist that the seniority system violates their rights secured by § 1981 and that they are entitled to relief under that statute. It is this issue that we now address.

## II

Title 42 U.S.C. § 1981, provides:

"All persons within the jurisdiction of the United States shall have the same right in every State and Territory to make and enforce contracts, to sue, be parties, give evidence, and to the full and equal benefit of all laws and proceedings for the security of persons and property as is enjoyed by white citizens, and shall be subject to like punishment, pains, penalties, taxes, licenses, and exactions of every kind, and to no other." The Civil Rights Act of 1964 did not repeal by implication any part of § 1981. This is firmly established by both the legislative history of the 1964 Act and its 1972 amendments. *Johnson* v. *Railway Express Agency, Inc.,* 421 U.S. 454, 457–61, 95 S.Ct. 1716, 44 L.Ed.2d 295 (1975); cf. *Jones* v. *Alfred H. Mayer Co.,* 392 U.S. 409, 416 n. 20, 88 S.Ct. 2186, 20 L.Ed.2d 1189 (1968). Section 1981 affords a federal remedy against racial discrimination in private employment that is "separate, distinct, and independent" from the remedies available under Title VII of the 1964 Act. *Johnson* v. *Railway Express Agency, Inc., supra,* 421 U.S. at 461, 95 S.Ct. 1716. Thus an employee "who establishes a cause of action under § 1981 is entitled to both equitable and legal relief, including compensatory and, under certain circumstances, punitive damages." 421 U.S. at 460, 95 S.Ct. at 1770.

This case therefore presents the question of whether the incumbent employees who were discriminatorily hired before 1965 when Title VII became effective have a cause of action under § 1981 because the bargaining contract's restriction of carryover seniority perpetuates the pre-1965 hiring discrimination.[3] Of course, each pre-1965 incumbent black employee had a cause of action under § 1981 because of the company's discriminatory hiring practices. But all parties recognize that this cause

---

[3] Applicants refused jobs after 1965 on account of their race are entitled to an award of seniority retroactive to the date of application. *Franks* v. *Bowman Transportation Co.,* 424 U.S. 747, 762–70, 96 S.Ct. 1251, 47 L.Ed.2d 444 (1976). Theoretically, the same measure of retroactive seniority would be available to pre-1965 incumbents who sought linehaul jobs, but it would be of less value to them because they could not carry over their full employment seniority to their new job assignment.

of action is barred by North Carolina's three year statute of limitations, N.C. Gen. Stat. § 1–52(1), which is made applicable to the § 1981 claim. *Johnson* v. *Railway Express Agency, Inc., supra,* 421 U.S. at 462, 95 S.Ct. 1716.

The seniority provision of the bargaining contract was facially neutral, applying to both white and black employees if they transferred to the higher paying position of a line driver. Both black and white employees were subject to loss of their former departmental seniority and had to start at the bottom of the seniority list for line drivers even though they may have had more employment seniority than line drivers higher on the ladder. Consequently, § 1981 does not afford the black employees relief, because this statute confers on black persons only the same rights possessed by white persons.

Moreover, the application of 42 U.S.C. § 1988 does not lead to a different conclusion. Section 1988 directs federal courts to enforce § 1981 "in conformity with the laws of the United States, so far as such laws are suitable. . . ." [4] Section 1988 in itself does not create any cause of action, but it "instructs federal courts as to what law to apply in causes of action arising under federal civil rights acts." *Moor* v. *County of Alameda,* 411 U.S. 693, 703–06, 93 S.Ct. 1785, 1792, 36 L.Ed.2d 596 (1973); *Scott* v. *Vandiver,* 476 F.2d 238, 242 (4th Cir. 1973).

In *Griggs* v. *Duke Power Co.,* 401 U.S. 424, 430, 91 S.Ct. 849, 853, 28 L.Ed.2d 158 (1971), the Court held: "Under the [1964] Act, practices, procedures, or tests neutral on their face, and even neutral in terms of intent, cannot be maintained if they operate to 'freeze' the status quo of prior discriminatory employment practices." This concept is essential to the employees' suit. However, in *Teamsters* v. *United States, supra,* 431 U.S. at 349, 97 S.Ct. 1843, the Court held that the *Griggs* rationale is not applicable to a seniority system that is lawful under § 703(h). Ordinarily, § 1988 enables a district court to utilize *Griggs'* interpretation of Title VII in a § 1981 employment discrimination suit, but the court cannot transgress the limitation placed on the *Griggs* rationale in *Teamsters* with respect to § 703(h). A ruling that a seniority system which is lawful under Title VII is nevertheless unlawful under § 1981 would disregard the precepts of § 1988. An analogous situation concerning the application of § 1988 is presented by *Moor* v. *County of Alameda,* 411 U.S. 693, 93 S.Ct. 1785, 36 L.Ed.2d 596 (1973), dealing with the enforcement of a § 1983 claim by utilization of a state law which made municipalities vicariously liable for the acts of their employees.[5] The Court held that such a state law could not be utilized to enforce the rights secured by § 1983 because it was inconsistent with federal law that ex-

---

[4] Title 42 U.S.C. § 1988 provides in part:
"The jurisdiction in civil . . . matters conferred on the district courts by the provisions of this chapter . . . shall be exercised and enforced in conformity with the laws of the United States, so far as such laws are suitable to carry the same into effect . . . ."

[5] Section 1988 also authorizes resort to state laws for enforcement of the civil rights acts if they are not "inconsistent with the Constitution and laws of the United States."

cludes municipal corporations from liability under § 1983. 411 U.S. at 706, 93 S.Ct. 1785.

Our conclusion accords with decisions that have held, although in different context, that § 1981 does not invalidate bona fide seniority provisions. See, e.g., *Chance* v. *Board of Examiners*, 534 F.2d 993, 998 (2d Cir. 1976); *Watkins* v. *United Steel Workers Local 2369*, 516 F.2d 41, 49–50 (5th Cir. 1975); *Waters* v. *Wisconsin Steel Works*, 502 F.2d 1309, 1320 n. 4 (7th Cir. 1974); cf. *Patterson* v. *American Tobacco Co.*, 535 F.2d 257, 270 (4th Cir. 1976). It is also consistent with the Supreme Court's opinion in *Johnson* v. *Railway Express Agency, Inc.*, 421 U.S. 454, 95 S.Ct. 1716, 44 L.Ed.2d 295 (1975). *Johnson* emphasized that a party proceeding under § 1981 is not restricted by the administrative and procedural requirements of Title VII, but nothing in *Johnson* suggests that a practice lawful under Title VII can be held unlawful under § 1981. On the contrary, *Johnson* recognizes that Congress noted that Title VII and § 1981 are "co-extensive" and that they "augment each other and are not mutually exclusive." 421 U.S. at 459, 95 S.Ct. at 1719. *Johnson* gives no indication, however, that Congress intended to create conflicting and contradictory standards for determining what constitutes illegal discrimination.

We therefore withdraw our mandate and direct that a new judgment issue consistent with this opinion. We remand the case to the district court for reconsideration of the claims made by those employees who were afforded relief on the basis of the seniority system that *Teamsters* later held to be lawful. The parties suggest that additional evidence may be necessary, and the district court should reopen the proceedings for this purpose. Although the union did not appeal from the entry of the injunction against it, we direct the district court to permit it to move for relief from this order. Fed. R. Civ. P. 60(b)(6). The union's conduct in agreeing to the seniority system violated neither Title VII nor § 1981. Therefore, the judgment against it should be vacated. See, *Teamsters* v. *United States, supra*, 431 U.S. at 356, 97 S.Ct. 1843. In all other respects we affirm the district court for the reasons stated in our initial opinion.

WINTER, Circuit Judge, concurring specially: I concur in the judgment of the court and in parts of its opinion; but since my concurrence rests in part on grounds different from those assigned by the majority, I append this statement of my separate views.

I have no doubt that *Teamsters* invalidates our affirmance of the district court's conclusion that the company's seniority system violated Title VII, and that we must vacate this portion of our judgment and remand, giving to affected employees the right to present additional evidence and giving to the union the right to have the judgment against it vacated. Where my reasoning differs from that of the majority is with respect to plaintiff's alleged cause of action under § 1981.

I readily agree that under § 1981, standing alone, the plaintiffs' only cause of action was their initial discriminatory employment. Unlike Title VII (42 U.S.C. § 2000e–2(a)(1)), which proscribes discriminatory hiring or firing of an employee *and* other discrimination with respect to "compensation, terms, conditions, or privileges of employment," [1] § 1981 merely guarantees the black employee the same right to contract for his services "as is enjoyed by white citizens." The right guaranteed by § 1981 was denied when black employees were denied the right to be hired in certain classifications of jobs because of their race. But having obtained initial employment in classifications in which they were acceptable, I find no subsequent violation of § 1981 by reason of the seniority provisions of the bargaining contract. After initial employment, the right of blacks to contract was not abridged by reason of their race.

. . .

In summary, my reason for denying plaintiffs' recovery under § 1981 is that the only causes of action which plaintiffs have under § 1981 are time-barred.

## BOLDEN v. PENNSYLVANIA STATE POLICE

*United States Court of Appeals, Third Circuit, 1978*
*578 F.2d 912, 17 FEP Cases 687*

Gibbons, Circuit Judge: This is an appeal from an order denying three applications to intervene as parties-defendants for the purpose of seeking temporary relief from and permanent modification of a final judgment. The final judgment at issue was entered by consent on June 20, 1974, and modified by the district court on November 29, 1976. It disposed of a complaint by William H. Bolden, III, and others charging the Commonwealth of Pennsylvania with racial discrimination in the hiring and promotion practices of the State Police, in violation of the Thirteenth and Fourteenth Amendments and of 42 U.S.C. §§ 1981, 1983, 1985(3), and 1988.[1] The consent judgment was entered after substantial discovery and after the completion of the plaintiffs' case, which consisted in part of a detailed stipulation by the defendants admitting discriminatory practices in selection and promotion by the State Police. The defendants at that time were the Pennsylvania State Police, a legislatively created agency of the Commonwealth, and a number of government officials responsible for its operations. The judgment mandated class action relief.

The present applicants for intervention do not contend that the discrimination charged in the complaint, and shown by the evidence in the

---

[1] Section 2000e–2(a)(2) also proscribes the limitation, segregation or classification of employees or applicants for employment in any way which would deprive or tend to deprive them of employment opportunities or adversely affect their status as employees because of their race.

---

[1] [Footnotes numbered as in original.—Ed.] Although the complaint was filed on November 16, 1973, it did not allege a violation of Title VII of the Civil Rights Act of 1964, Pub. L. No. 88–352, 78 Stat. 255, 42 U.S.C. § 2000e *et seq.* Apparently, the reason for this was the exemption for state and local governments originally incorporated in Title VII and not removed until March 24, 1972, the effective date of the Equal Employment Opportunity Act of 1972, Pub. L. No. 92–261, 86 Stat. 103.

plaintiffs' case, did not occur. They seek modification only of the remedial provisions of the judgment. Each motion for intervention seeks to modify the judgment in four respects:

(1) to establish a mandatory schedule for the defendants to submit validated hiring and promotion criteria for court approval (the validation claim);

(2) to terminate the hiring and promotion quotas immediately, or at the latest when valid hiring and promotion criteria are adopted (the quota claim);

(3) to restore seniority as a criterion for promotion and to grant retroactive seniority to any person shown to have been an actual victim of racially discriminatory employment or promotion practices (the seniority credit claim);

(4) to adjust the work force statistics to reflect a lower representation of minorities in the work force from which the State Police draws its employees (the minority goal claim).
. . .

The second proposed modification concerns seniority credits. This time the FOP's theory is that the law has changed since the consent decree. Since what is before us is an order denying relief *pendente lite,* our initial inquiry must be whether the FOP has shown a likelihood of ultimate success on the merits. The FOP argues that the decisions in *Franks* v. *Bowman Transportation Co.,* 424 U.S. 747, 96 S.Ct. 1251, 47 L.Ed.2d 444 (1976), *International Brotherhood of Teamsters* v. *United States,* 431 U.S. 324, 97 S.Ct. 1843, 52 L.Ed.2d 396 (1977), and *United Airlines, Inc.* v. *Evans,* 431 U.S. 553, 97 S.Ct. 885, 52 L.Ed.2d 571 (1977), have made illegal the elimination of seniority as a criterion for promotion. In *Mayberry* v. *Maroney,* 558 F.2d 1159 (3d Cir. 1977), this court referred to the heavy burden imposed on a party seeking relief from a final judgment on the ground of precedential evolution. The burden of obtaining *pendente lite* relief on that ground is even heavier.

We are not dealing in this case with a judgment enforcing an unconstitutional statute. In such a case, the applicant's burden is necessarily lighter. See *Neely* v. *United States,* 546 F.2d 1059 (3d Cir. 1976). The FOP does not suggest that the facts which justified the injunction have changed. See *United States* v. *Swift & Co.,* 286 U.S. 106, 52 S.Ct. 460, 76 L.Ed. 999 (1932). Nor does it attempt to analogize this case to a case in which, by virtue of other decisions, one firm in an industry is subject to more rigorous requirements than are imposed on its competitors. See *American Iron and Steel Institute* v. *Environmental Protection Agency,* 560 F.2d 589 (3d Cir. 1977). Instead, the FOP's argument amounts to no more than a claim that the Supreme Court has made a non-constitutional decision which interprets a remedial statute in a manner inconsistent with prior decisions of this court. But the statute involved in the three recent decisions, Title VII of the Civil Rights Act of 1964, was not the predicate for relief in this case. Before we could find those three cases relevant here, we would have to impute to the second session of the Eighty-eighth

Congress the intention to circumscribe the remedial powers of the federal courts under §§ 1981, 1983, 1985, and 1988. We find nothing in *Franks* v. *Bowman Transportation Co., International Brotherhood of Teamsters* v. *United States,* or *United Airlines, Inc.* v. *Evans* to support such a construction of § 703(h) of Title VII. Nothing in the legislative history of that section supports it. Moreover, the settled law in this circuit is that there is a distinction, when relief is sought under Title VII, between violations of § 703(h) and remedies under § 703(g). *Equal Employment Opportunity Commission* v. *American Tel. & Tel.,* 556 F.2d 167 (3d Cir. 1977), *cert. denied,* _____ U.S. _____, 98 S.Ct. 3145, 56 L.Ed.2d _____ (1978); *United States* v. *International Union of Elevator Constructors,* 538 F.2d 1012 (3d Cir. 1976). Viewing all these obstacles to the requested relief, we conclude that there was so little likelihood of success on the merits that the district court properly denied *pendente lite* relief from the provision in the decree eliminating seniority credits in promotion.

. . .

GARTH, Circuit Judge, concurring in part and dissenting in part: [omitted].

## NOTE

The relationship of E.O. 11246 to seniority is discussed in Chapter 4. See particularly *United States* v. *East Texas Motor Freight; Steelworkers* v. *Weber;* and *EEOC* v. *American Telephone & Telegraph Co., supra.*

## C.  SEX

(1) *The Basic Concept*

### PHILLIPS v. MARTIN MARIETTA CORP.

*Supreme Court of the United States, 1971*
*400 U.S. 542, 3 FEP Cases 40*

PER CURIAM.
Petitioner Mrs. Ida Phillips commenced an action in the United States District Court for the Middle District of Florida under Title VII of the Civil Rights Act of 1964 * alleging that she had been denied employment

---

* Section 703 of the Act, 78 Stat. 255, 42 U.S.C. § 2000e-2, provides as follows:
"(a) It shall be an unlawful employment practice for an employer—
"(1) to fail or refuse to hire or to discharge any individual, or otherwise to discriminate against any individual with respect to his compensation, terms, conditions, or privileges of employment, because of such individual's race, color, religion, sex, or national origin. . . .
"(e) Notwithstanding any other provision of this title, (1) it shall not be an unlawful employment practice for an employer to hire and employ employees . . . on the basis

because of her sex. The District Court granted summary judgment for Martin Marietta Corp. (Martin) on the basis of the following showing: (1) in 1966 Martin informed Mrs. Phillips that it was not accepting job applications from women with pre-school-age children; (2) as of the time of the motion for summary judgment, Martin employed men with pre-school-age children; (3) at the time Mrs. Phillips applied, 70-75% of the applicants for the position she sought were women; 75-80% of those hired for the position, assembly trainee, were women, hence no question of bias against women as such was presented.

The Court of Appeals for the Fifth Circuit affirmed, 411 F.2d 1, and denied a rehearing *en banc,* 416 F.2d 1257 (1969). We granted certiorari. 397 U.S. 960 (1970).

Section 703(a) of the Civil Rights Act of 1964 requires that persons of like qualifications be given employment opportunities irrespective of their sex. The Court of Appeals therefore erred in reading this section as permitting one hiring policy for women and another for men—each having pre-school-age children. The existence of such conflicting family obligations, if demonstrably more relevant to job performance for a woman than for a man, could arguably be a basis for distinction under § 703(e) of the Act. But that is a matter of evidence tending to show that the condition in question "is a bona fide occupational qualification reasonably necessary to the normal operation of that particular business or enterprise." The record before us, however, is not adequate for resolution of these important issues. See *Kennedy* v. *Silas Mason Co.,* 334 U.S. 249, 256-257 (1948). Summary judgment was therefore improper and we remand for fuller development of the record and for further consideration.

*Vacated and remanded.*

MR. JUSTICE MARSHALL, concurring.

While I agree that this case must be remanded for a full development of the facts, I cannot agree with the Court's indication that a "bona fide occupational qualification reasonably necessary to the normal operation of" Martin Marietta's business could be established by a showing that some women, even the vast majority, with pre-school-age children have family responsibilities that interfere with job performance and that men do not usually have such responsibilities. Certainly, an employer can require that all of his employees, both men and women, meet minimum performance standards, and he can try to insure compliance by requiring parents, both mothers and fathers, to provide for the care of their children so that job performance is not interfered with.

But the Court suggests that it would not require such uniform standards. I fear that in this case, where the issue is not squarely before us, the Court has fallen into the trap of assuming that the Act permits ancient

of . . . religion, sex, or national origin in those certain instances where religion, sex, or national origin is a bona fide occupational qualification reasonably necessary to the normal operation of that particular business or enterprise. . . ."

canards about the proper role of women to be a basis for discrimination. Congress, however, sought just the opposite result.

By adding [1] the prohibition against job discrimination based on sex to the 1964 Civil Rights Act Congress intended to prevent employers from refusing "to hire an individual based on stereotyped characterizations of the sexes." Equal Employment Opportunity Commission, Guidelines on Discrimination Because of Sex, 29 CFR § 1604.1(a)(1)(ii). See *Bowe* v. *Colgate-Palmolive Co.*, 416 F.2d 711 (CA7 1969); *Weeks* v. *Southern Bell Tel. & Tel. Co.*, 408 F.2d 228 (CA5 1969). Even characterizations of the proper domestic roles of the sexes were not to serve as predicates for restricting employment opportunity. [2] The exception for a "bona fide occupational qualification" was not intended to swallow the rule.

That exception has been construed by the Equal Employment Opportunity Commission, whose regulations are entitled to "great deference," *Udall* v. *Tallman*, 380 U.S. 1, 16 (1965), to be applicable only to job situations that require specific physical characteristics necessarily possessed by only one sex. Thus the exception would apply where necessary "for the purpose of authenticity or genuineness" in the employment of actors or actresses, fashion models, and the like. If the exception is to be limited as Congress intended, the Commission has given it the only possible construction.

When performance characteristics of an individual are involved, even when parental roles are concerned, employment opportunity may be limited only by employment criteria that are neutral as to the sex of the applicant.

## (2) *The Bona Fide Occupational Qualification Exception*

### DIAZ v. PAN AMERICAN WORLD AIRWAYS, INC.

*United States Court of Appeals, Fifth Circuit, 1971*
*442 F.2d 385, 3 FEP Cases 337*

TUTTLE, Circuit Judge: This appeal presents the important question of whether Pan American Airlines' refusal to hire appellant and his class of males solely on the basis of their sex violates § 703(a)(1) of Title VII of the 1964 Civil Rights Act. Because we feel that being a female is not a "bona fide occupational qualification" for the job of flight cabin attendant, appellee's refusal to hire appellant's class solely because of their sex, does constitute a violation of the Act.

The facts in this case are not in dispute. Celio Diaz applied for a job as flight cabin attendant with Pan American Airlines in 1967. He was re-

---

[1] [Footnotes numbered as in original.—Ed.] The ban on discrimination based on sex was added to the Act by an amendment offered during the debate in the House by Rep. Smith of Virginia. 110 Cong. Rec. 2577.

[2] See *Neal* v. *American Airlines, Inc.*, 1 CCH Employment Practices Guide ¶ 6002 (EEOC 1968); *Colvin* v. *Piedmont Aviation, Inc.*, 1 CCH Employment Practices Guide ¶ 6003 (EEOC 1968); 110 Cong. Rec. 2578 (remarks of Rep. Bass).

jected because Pan Am had a policy of restricting its hiring for that position to females. He then filed charges with the Equal Employment Opportunity Commission (EEOC) alleging that Pan Am had unlawfully discriminated against him on the grounds of sex. The Commission found probable cause to believe his charge but was unable to resolve the matter through conciliation with Pan Am. Diaz next filed a class action in the United States District Court for the Southern District of Florida on behalf of himself and others similarly situated, alleging that Pan Am had violated Section 703 of the 1964 Civil Rights Act by refusing to employ him on the basis of his sex; he sought an injunction and damages.

Pan Am admitted that it had a policy of restricting its hiring for the cabin attendant position to females. Thus, both parties stipulated that the primary issue for the District Court was whether, for the job of flight cabin attendant, being a female is a "bona fide occupational qualification (heretofore BFOQ) reasonably necessary to the normal operation" of Pan American's business.

The trial court found that being a female was a BFOQ. Before discussing its findings in detail, however, it is necessary to set forth the framework within which we view this case.

Section 703(a) of the 1964 Civil Rights Act provides, in part:

"(a) It shall be an unlawful employment practice for an employer—

"(1)  to fail or refuse to hire or to discharge any individual, or otherwise to discriminate against any individual with respect to his compensation, terms, conditions, or privileges of employment, because of such individual's race, color, religion, sex or national origin. . . ."

The scope of this section is qualified by § 703(e) which states:

"(e)  Notwithstanding any other provision of this subchapter,

"(1)  it shall not be unlawful employment practice for an employer to hire and employ employees . . . on the basis of his religion, sex, or national origin in those certain instances where religion, sex or national origin is a bona fide occupational qualification reasonably necessary to the normal operation of that particular business or enterprise . . ."

Since it has been admitted that appellee has discriminated on the basis of sex, the result in this case, turns, in effect, on the construction given to this exception.

We note, at the outset, that there is little legislative history to guide our interpretation. The amendment adding the word "sex" to race, color, religion and national origin was adopted one day before House passage of the Civil Rights Act. It was added on the floor and engendered little relevant debate. In attempting to read Congress' intent in these circumstances, however, it is reasonable to assume, from a reading of the statute itself, that one of Congress' main goals was to provide equal access to the job market for both men and women. Indeed, as this court in *Weeks* v. *Southern Bell Telephone and Telegraph Co.*, 408 F.2d 228 at 235, 1 FEP Cases 656, 70 LRRM 2843, clearly stated, the purpose of the Act was to provide a foundation in the law for the principle of nondiscrimination. Construing the state as embodying such a principle is based on the assumption that Congress sought a formula that would not only achieve the optimum use of our labor resources, but and more importantly, would enable individuals to develop as individuals.

Attainment of this goal, however, is, as stated above, limited by the bona fide occupational qualification exception in section 703(e). In construing this provision, we feel, as did the court in *Weeks supra,* that it would be totally anomalous to do so in a manner that would, in effect, permit the exception to swallow the rule. Thus, we adopt the EEOC guidelines which state that "the Commission believes that the bona fide occupational qualification as to sex should be interpreted narrowly." 29 CFR 1604.1(a) Indeed, close scrutiny of the language of this exception compels this result. As one commentator has noted:

"The sentence contains several restrictive adjectives and phrases: it applies only *'in those certain instances'* where there are *'bona fide'* qualifications *'Reasonably necessary'* to the operation of that *'particular'* enterprise. The care with which Congress has chosen the words to emphasize the function and to limit the scope of the exception indicates that it had no intention of opening the kind of enormous gap in the law which would exist if [for example] an employer could legitimately discriminate against a group solely because his employees, customers, or clients discriminated against that group. Absent much more explicit language, such a broad exception should not be assumed for it would largely emasculate the act." (emphasis added) 65 MICH. L. REV. (1966).

Thus, it is with this orientation that we now examine the trial court's decision. Its conclusion was based upon (1) its view of Pan Am's history of the use of flight attendants; (2) passenger preference; (3) basic psychological reasons for the preference; and (4) the actualities of the hiring process.

Having reviewed the evidence submitted by Pan American regarding its own experience with both female and male cabin attendants it had hired over the years, the trial court found that Pan Am's current hiring policy was the result of a pragmatic process, "representing a judgment made upon adequate evidence acquired through Pan Am's considerable experience, and designed to yield under Pan Am's current operating conditions better *average* performance for its passengers than would a policy of mixed male and female hiring." (emphasis added) The Performance of female attendants was *better* in the sense that they were *superior* in such non-mechanical aspects of the job as "providing reassurance to anxious passengers, giving courteous personalized service and, in general, making flights as pleasurable as possible within the limitations imposed by aircraft operations."

The trial court also found that Pan Am's passengers overwhelmingly preferred to be served by female stewardesses. Moreover, on the basis of the expert testimony of a psychiatrist, the court found that an airplane cabin represents a unique environment in which an air carrier is required to take account of the special psychological needs of its passengers. These psychological needs are better attended to by females. This is not to say that there are no males who would not have the necessary qualities to perform these non-mechanical functions, but the trial court found that the actualities of the hiring process would make it more difficult to find these few males. Indeed, "the admission of men to the hiring process, in the present state of the art of employment selection, would have increased the number of unsatisfactory employees hired, and reduced the average levels of performance of Pan Am's complement of flight attendants. . . ." In what appears to be a summation of the difficulties which the trial court found would follow from admitting males to this job the court said "that to eliminate sex qualification would simply eliminate the *best* available tool for screening out applicants *likely* to be unsatisfactory and thus reduce the *average* level of performance." (emphasis added)

Because of the narrow reading we give to section 703(e), we do not feel that these findings justify the discrimination practiced by Pan Am.

We begin with the proposition that the use of the word "necessary" in section 703(e) requires that we apply a business *necessity test,* not a business *convenience* test. That is to say, discrimination based on sex is valid only when the *essence* of the business operation would be undermined by not hiring members of one sex exclusively.

The primary function of an airline is to transport passengers safely from one point to another. While a pleasant environment, enhanced by the obvious cosmetic effect that female stewardesses provide as well as, according to the finding of the trial court, their apparent ability to perform the non-mechanical functions of the job in a more effective manner than most men, may all be important, they are tangential to the essence of the business involved. No one has suggested that having male stewards will so seriously affect the operation of an airline as to jeopardize or even minimize its ability to provide safe transportation from one place to another. Indeed the record discloses that many airlines including Pan Am have utilized both men and women flight cabin attendants in the past and Pan Am, even at the time of this suit, has 283 male stewards employed on some of its foreign flights.

We do not mean to imply, of course, that Pan Am cannot take into consideration the ability of *individuals* to perform the non-mechanical functions of the job. What we hold is that because the non-mechanical aspects of the job of flight cabin attendant are not "reasonably necessary to the normal operation" of Pan Am's business, Pan Am cannot exclude *all* males simply because *most* males may not perform adequately.

Appellees argue, however, that in so doing they have complied with the rule in *Weeks.* In that case, the court stated:

"We conclude that the principle of nondiscrimination requires that we hold that in order to rely on the bona fide occupational qualification exception an employer has the burden of proving that he had reasonable cause to believe, that is, a factual basis for believing, that all or substantially all women would be unable to perform safely and efficiently the duties of the job involved." *Id.* at 235.

We do not agree that in this case "all or substantially all men" have been shown to be inadequate and, in any event, in *Weeks,* the job that most women supposedly could not do was necessary to the normal operation of the business. Indeed, the inability of switchman to perform his or her job could cause the telephone system to break down. This is of an entirely different magnitude than a male steward who is perhaps not as soothing on a flight as a female stewardess.

Appellees also argue, and the trial court found, that because of the actualities of the hiring process, "the *best* available initial test for determining whether a particular applicant for employment is likely to have the personality characteristics conducive to high-level performance of the flight attendant's job as currently defined is consequently the applicant's biological sex." Indeed, the trial court found that it was simply not practicable to find the few males that would perform properly.

We do not feel that this alone justifies discriminating against all males. Since, as stated above, the basis of exclusion is the ability to perform non-mechanical functions which we find to be tangential to what is "reasonably *necessary*" for the business involved, the exclusion of *all* males because this is the *best* way to select the kind of personnel Pan Am desires simply cannot be justified. Before sex discrimination can be practiced, it must not only be shown that it is impracticable to find the men that possess the abilities that most women possess, but that the abilities are *necessary* to the business, not merely tangential.

Similarly, we do not feel that the fact that Pan Am's passengers prefer female stewardesses should alter our judgment. On this subject, EEOC guidelines state that a BFOQ ought not be based on "the refusal to hire an individual because of the preferences of coworkers, the employer, clients or customers. . . ." 29 CFR § 1604.1 (iii).

As the Supreme Court stated in *Griggs* v. *Duke Power Co.,* 400 U.S. 424, 3 FEP Cases 175 (1971), "the administration interpretation of the Act by the enforcing agency is entitled to great deference." . . . Indeed, while we recognize that the public's expectation of finding one sex in a particular role may cause some initial difficulty, it would be totally anomalous if we were to allow the preferences and prejudices of the customers to determine whether the sex discrimination was valid. Indeed, it was, to a large extent, these very prejudices the Act was meant to overcome. Thus, we feel that customer preference may be taken into account only when it is based on the company's inability to perform the primary function or service it offers.

Of course, Pan Am argues that the customers' preferences are not based on "stereotyped thinking," but the ability of women stewardesses to better provide the non-mechanical aspects of the job. Again, as stated above, since these aspects are tangential to the business, the fact that customers prefer them cannot justify sex discrimination.

The judgment is REVERSED and the case is REMANDED for proceedings not inconsistent with this opinion.

## NOTE

One of the questions which is suggested by *Diaz* is whether an employer can ever make sexual appeal to one sex a BFOQ. For example, can a nightclub owner insist that scantily clad women with certain measurements can serve as waitresses if they take the position that they are primarily selling sex appeal?

## DOTHARD v. RAWLINSON

*Supreme Court of the United States, 1977*
*433 U.S. 321, 15 FEP Cases 10*

MR. JUSTICE STEWART delivered the opinion of the Court.

The appellee, Dianne Rawlinson, sought employment with the Alabama Board of Corrections as a prison guard, called in Alabama a "correctional counselor." After her application was rejected, she brought this class suit under Title VII of the Civil Rights Act of 1964, 78 Stat. 253, as amended, 42 U.S.C. § 2000e *et seq.* (1970 ed. and Supp. V), and under 42 U.S.C. § 1983, alleging that she had been denied employment because of her sex in violation of federal law. A three-judge Federal District Court for the Middle District of Alabama decided in her favor. *Mieth* v. *Dothard*, 418 F. Supp. 1169, 13 FEP Cases 1412. We noted probable jurisdiction of this appeal from the District Court's judgment, *sub nom. Dothard* v. *Mieth*, _____ U.S. _____.

### I

At the time she applied for a position as correctional counselor trainee, Rawlinson was a 22-year-old college graduate whose major course of study had been correctional psychology. She was refused employment because she failed to meet the minimum 120-pound weight requirement established by an Alabama statute. The statute also establishes a height minimum of 5 feet and 2 inches.

After her application was rejected because of her weight, Rawlinson filed a charge with the Equal Employment Opportunity Commission, and ultimately received a right to sue letter. She then filed a complaint in the District Court on behalf of herself and other similarly situated women, challenging the statutory height and weight minima as violative of Title VII and the Equal Protection Clause of the Fourteenth Amendment. A three-judge court was convened. While the suit was pending, the Alabama Board of Corrections adopted Administrative Regulation 204, establishing gender criteria for assigning correctional counselors to maximum security institutions for "contact positions," that is, positions requiring continual close physical proximity to inmates of the institution. Rawlinson amended her class-action complaint by adding a challenge to

Regulation 204 as also violative of Title VII and the Fourteenth Amendment.

. . .

A correctional counselor's primary duty within these institutions is to maintain security and control of the inmates by continually supervising and observing their activities. To be eligible for consideration as a correctional counselor, an applicant must possess a valid Alabama driver's license, have a high school education or its equivalent, be free from physical defects, be between the ages of 20½ years and 45 years at the time of appointment, and fall between the minimum height and weight requirements of five feet and two inches and 120 pounds, and the maximum of six feet and 10 inches and 300 pounds. Appointment is by merit, with a grade assigned each applicant based on experience and education. No written examination is given.

At the time this litigation was in the District Court, the Board of Corrections employed a total of 435 people in various correctional counselor positions, 56 of whom were women. Of those 56 women, 21 were employed at the Julia Tutwiler Prison for Women, 13 were employed in noncontact positions at the four male maximum security institutions, and the remaining 22 were employed at the other institutions operated by the Alabama Board of Corrections. Because most of Alabama's prisoners are held at the four maximum security male penitentiaries, 336 of the 435 correctional counselor jobs were in those institutions, a majority of them concededly in the "contact" classification. Thus, even though meeting the statutory height and weight requirements, women applicants could under Regulation 204 compete equally with men for only about 25 percent of the correctional counselor jobs available in the Alabama prison system.

## II

In enacting Title VII, Congress required "the removal of artificial, arbitrary, and unnecessary barriers to employment when the barriers operate invidiously to discriminate on the basis of racial or other impermissible classification." *Griggs* v. *Duke Power Co.*, 401 U.S. 424, 431, 3 FEP Cases 175, 177. The District Court found that the minimum statutory height and weight requirements that applicants for employment as correctional counselors must meet constitute the sort of arbitrary barrier to equal employment opportunity that Title VII forbids.[10] The

10 [Footnotes numbered as in original.—Ed.] Section 703(a) of Title VII, 42 U.S.C. § 2000e 2(a) (1970 ed. and Supp. V), provides:
"(2) Employers practices. It shall be an unlawful employment practice for an employer—
"(1) to fail to refuse to hire or to discharge any individual or otherwise to discriminate against any individual with respect to his compensation, terms, conditions, or privileges of employment, because of such individual's race, color, religion, sex, or national origin; or
"(2) to limit, segregate, or classify his employees or applicants for employment in any way which would deprive or tend to deprive any individual of employment opportunities or otherwise adversely affect his status as an employee, because of such individual's race, color, religion, sex, or national origin."

appellants assert that the District Court erred both in finding that the height and weight standards discriminate against women, and in its refusal to find that, even if they do, these standards are justified as "job related."

## A

The gist of the claim that the statutory height and weight requirements discriminate against women does not involve an assertion of purposeful discriminatory motive.

. . .

## B

We turn . . . to the appellants' argument that they have rebutted the prima facie case of discrimination by showing that the height and weight requirements are job related. These requirements, they say, have a relationship to strength, a sufficient but unspecified amount of which is essential to effective job performance as a correctional counselor. In the District Court, however, the appellants produced no evidence correlating the height and weight requirements with the requisite amount of strength thought essential to good job performance. Indeed, they failed to offer evidence of any kind in specific justification of the statutory standards.

If the job-related quality that the appellants identify is bona fide, their purpose could be achieved by adopting and validating a test for applicants that measures strength directly. Such a test, fairly administered, would fully satisfy the standards of Title VII because it would be one that "measure[s] the person for the job and not the person in the abstract." *Griggs* v. *Duke Power Co.*, 401 U.S., at 436, 3 FEP Cases, at 180. But nothing in the present record even approaches such a measurement.

. . .

## III

Unlike the statutory height and weight requirements, Regulation 204 explicitly discriminates against women on the basis of their sex. In defense of this overt discrimination, the appellants rely on § 703e of Title VII, which permits sex-based discrimination "in those certain instances where . . . sex . . . is a bona fide occupational qualification reasonably necessary to the normal operation of that particular business or enterprise."

The District Court rejected the bona fide occupational qualification (bfoq) defense, relying on the virtually uniform view of the federal courts that § 703e provides only the narrowest of exceptions to the general rule requiring equality of employment opportunities. This view has been variously formulated. In *Diaz* v. *Pan American World Airways*, 442 F.2d 385, 388, 3 FEP Cases 337, 339, the Court of Appeals for the Fifth Circuit held that "discrimination based on sex is valid only when the *essence* of the business operation would be undermined by not hiring members of one sex exclusively." (Emphasis in original.) In an earlier case, *Weeks*

v. *Southern Bell Telephone and Telegraph Co.,* 408 F. 228, 235, 1 FEP Cases 656, 661, 70 LRRM 2843, the same court said that an employer could rely on the bfoq exception only by proving "that he had reasonable cause to believe, that is, a factual basis for believing, that all or substantially all women would be unable to perform safely and efficiently the duties of the job involved." See also *Phillips* v. *Martin Marietta Corp.,* 400 U.S. 542, 3 FEP Cases 40. But whatever the verbal formulation, the federal courts have agreed that it is impermissible under Title VII to refuse to hire an individual woman or man on the basis of stereotyped characterizations of the sexes, and the District Court in the present case held in effect that Regulation 204 is based on just such stereotypical assumptions.

We are persuaded—by the restrictive language of § 703e, the relevant legislative history, and the consistent interpretation of the Equal Employment Opportunity Commission—that the bfoq exception was in fact meant to be an extremely narrow exception to the general prohibition of discrimination on the basis of sex.[20] In the particular factual circumstances of this case, however, we conclude that the District Court erred in rejecting the State's contention that Regulation 204 falls within the narrow ambit of the bfoq exception.

The environment in Alabama's penitentiaries is a peculiarly inhospitable one for human beings of whatever sex. Indeed, a federal district court has held that the conditions of confinement in the prisons of the State, characterized by "rampant violence" and a "jungle atmosphere," are constitutionally intolerable. *James* v. *Wallace,* 406 F. Supp. 318, 325 (MD Ala.). The record in the present case shows that because of inadequate staff and facilities, no attempt is made in the four maximum security male penitentiaries to classify or segregate inmates according to their offense or level of dangerousness—a procedure that, according to expert testimony, is essential to effective penalogical administration. Consequently, the estimated 20 percent of the male prisoners who are sex offenders are scattered throughout the penitentiaries' dormitory facilities.

In this environment of violence and disorganization, it would be an oversimplification to characterize Regulation 204 as an exercise in "romantic paternalism." Cf. *Frontiero* v. *Richardson,* 411 U.S. 677, 684, 9 FEP Cases 1253, 1256. In the usual case, the argument that a particular job is too dangerous for women may appropriately be met by the rejoinder that it is the purpose of Title VII to allow the individual woman to make that choice for herself. More is at stake in this case, however, than an individual woman's decision to weigh and accept the risks of

---

[20] In the case of a state employer, the bfoq exception would have to be interpreted at the very least so as to conform to the Equal Protection Clause of the Fourteenth Amendment. The parties do not suggest, however, that the Equal Protection Clause requires more rigorous scrutiny of a State's sexually discriminatory employment policy than does Title VII. There is thus no occasion to give independent consideration to the District Court's ruling that Regulation 204 violates the Fourteenth Amendment as well as Title VII.

employment in a "contact" position in a maximum security male prison.

The essence of a correctional counselor's job is to maintain prison security. A woman's relative ability to maintain order in a male, maximum security, unclassified penitentiary of the type Alabama now runs could be directly reduced by her womanhood. There is a basis in fact for expecting that sex offenders who have criminally assaulted women in the past would be moved to do so again if access to women were established within the prison. There would also be a real risk that other inmates, deprived of a normal heterosexual environment, would assault women guards because they were women. In a prison system where violence is the order of the day, where inmate access to guards is facilitated by dormitory living arrangements, where every institution is understaffed, and where a substantial portion of the inmate population is composed of sex offenders mixed at random with other prisoners, there are few visible deterrents to inmate assaults on women custodians.

The plaintiffs' own expert testified that dormitory housing for aggressive inmates poses a greater security problem than single-cell lockups, and further testified that it would be unwise to use women as guards in a prison where even 10 percent of the inmates had been convicted of sex crimes and were not segregated from the other prisoners. The likelihood that inmates would assault a woman because she was a woman would pose a real threat not only to the victim of the assault but also the basic control of the penitentiary and protection of its inmates and the other security personnel. The employee's very womanhood would thus directly undermine her capacity to provide the security that is the essence of a correctional counselor's responsibility.

There was substantial testimony from experts on both sides of this litigation that the use of women as guards in "contact" positions under the existing conditions in Alabama maximum security male penitentiaries would pose a substantial security problem, directly linked to the sex of the prison guard. On the basis of that evidence, we conclude that the District Court was in error in ruling that being male is not a bona fide occupational qualification for the job of correctional counselor in a "contact" position in an Alabama male maximum security penitentiary.

The judgment is accordingly affirmed in part and reversed in part, and the case is remanded to the District Court for further proceedings consistent with this opinion.

. . .

*It is so ordered.*

MR. JUSTICE MARSHALL, with whom MR. JUSTICE BRENNAN joins, concurring in part and dissenting in part: I agree entirely with the Court's analysis of Alabama's height and weight requirements for prison guards, and with its finding that these restrictions discriminate on the basis of sex in violation of Title VII. Accordingly, I join Parts I and II of the Court's opinion. I also agree with much of the Court's general discussion in Part III of the bona fide occupational qualification exception contained in § 703(e) of Title VII.[1] The Court is unquestionably correct when it holds "that the bfoq exception was in fact meant to be an extremely narrow exception to the general prohibition of discrimination on the basis of sex." *Ante,* at 12, 15 FEP Cases, at 16. See *Phillips* v. *Martin Marietta Corp.,* 400 U.S. 532, 544, 3 FEP Cases 40, 41 (1971) (MARSHALL, J., concurring). I must, however, respectfully disagree with the Court's application of the bfoq exception in this case.

The Court properly rejects two proffered justifications for denying women jobs as prison guards. It is simply irrelevant here that a guard's occupation is dangerous and that some women might be unable to protect themselves adequately. Those themes permeate the testimony of the state officials below, but as the Court holds, "the argument that a particular job is too dangerous for women" is refuted by the "purpose of Title VII to allow the individual woman to make that choice for herself." *Ante,* at 13, 15 FEP Cases, at 16. Some women, like some men, undoubtedly are not qualified and do not wish to serve as prison guards, but that does not justify the exclusion of all women from this employment opportunity. Thus, "[i]n the usual case," *ibid.,* the Court's interpretation of the bfoq exception would mandate hiring qualified women for guard jobs in maximum security institutions. The highly successful experiences of other States allowing such job opportunities, see Briefs *amicus curiae* of the States of California and Washington, confirm that absolute disqualification of women is not, in the words of Title VII, "reasonably necessary to the normal operation" of a maximum security prison.

What would otherwise be considered unlawful discrimination against women is justified by the Court, however, on the basis of the "barbaric and inhumane" conditions in Alabama prisons, conditions so bad that state officials have conceded that they violate the Constitution. See *James* v. *Wallace,* 406 F. Supp. 318, 329, 331 (MD Ala. 1976). To me, this analysis sounds distressingly like saying two wrongs make a right. It is refuted by the plain words of § 706(e). The statute requires that a bfoq be "reasonably necessary to the normal operation of that particular business or enterprise." But no governmental "business" may operate "normally" in violation of the Constitution. Every action of government is constrained by constitutional limitations. While those limits may be violated more frequently than we would wish, no one disputes that the "normal operation" of all government functions takes place within them. A prison system operating in blatant violation of the Eighth Amendment is an exception that should be remedied with all possible speed, as Judge Johnson's comprehensive order in *James* v. *Wallace, supra,* is designed to do. In the meantime, the existence of such violations should not be legitimatized by calling them "normal." Nor should the Court

---

[1] Section 703(e), 42 U.S.C. § 2000e-2(e), provides in pertinent part: ". . . (1) it shall not be an unlawful employment practice for an employer to hire and employ employees . . . on the basis of his . . . sex . . . in those certain instances where . . . sex . . . is a bona fide occupation reasonably necessary to the normal operation of that particular business or enterprise. . . ."

accept them as justifying conduct that would otherwise violate a statute intended to remedy age-old discrimination.

The Court's error in statutory construction is less objectionable, however, than the attitude it displays toward women. Though the Court recognizes that possible harm to women guards is an unacceptable reason for disqualifying women, it relies instead on an equally speculative threat to prison discipline supposedly generated by the sexuality of female guards. There is simply no evidence in the record to show that women guards would create any danger to security in Alabama prisons significantly greater than already exists. All of the dangers—with one exception discussed below—are inherent in a prison setting whatever the gendor of the guards.

The Court first sees women guards as a threat to security because "there are few visible deterrents to inmate assaults on women custodians." *Ante,* at 14, 15 FEP Cases, at 16. In fact, any prison guard is constantly subject to the threat of attack by inmates and "invisible" deterrents are the guard's only real protection. No prison guard relies primarily on his or her ability to ward off an inmate attack to maintain order. Guards are typically unarmed and sheer numbers of inmates could overcome the normal complement. Rather, like all other law enforcement officers, prison guards must rely primarily on the moral authority of their office and the threat of future punishment for miscreants. As one expert testified below, common sense, fairness, and mental and emotional stability are the qualities a guard needs to cope with the dangers of the job. App. 81. Well qualified and properly trained women, no less than men, have these psychological weapons at their disposal.

The particular severity of discipline problems in the Alabama maximum security prisons is also no justification for the discrimination sanctioned by the Court. The District Court found in *James* v. *Wallace, supra,* that guards "must spend all their time attempting to maintain control or to protect themselves." 406 F. Supp., at 325. If male guards face an impossible situation, it is difficult to see how women could make the problem worse, unless one relies on precisely the type of generalized bias against women that the Court agrees Title VII was intended to outlaw. For example, much of the testimony of appellants' witnesses ignores individual differences among members of each sex and reads like "ancient canards about the proper role of women." *Phillips* v. *Martin Marietta Corp., supra,* 400 U.S., at 545, 3 FEP Cases, at 41. The witnesses claimed that women guards are not strict disciplinarians; that they are physically less capable of protecting themselves and subduing unruly inmates; that inmates take advantage of them as they did their mothers, while male guards are strong father figures who easily maintain discipline, and so on.[2] Yet the record shows that the presence of women guards has not led

---

[2] See, e.g., App. 111-12, 117-18, 144, 147, 151-53, 263-64, 290-292, 301-302. The State Commissioner of Corrections summed up these prejudicies in his testimony:

"Q. Would a male that is 5'6", 140 lbs., be able to perform the job of Correctional Counselor in an all male institution?

"A. Well, if he qualifies otherwise, yes.

to a single incident amounting to a serious breach of security in any
Alabama institution.[3] And in any event, "Guards rarely enter the cell
blocks and dormitories." *James* v. *Wallace, supra,* 406 F. Supp., at 325,
where the danger of inmate attacks is the greatest.

It appears that the real disqualifying factor in the Court's view is "[t]he
employee's very womanhood." *Ante,* at 14, 15 FEP Cases, at 17. The Court
refers to the large number of sex offenders in Alabama prisons, and to
"the likelihood that inmates would assault a woman because she was a
woman." *Ibid.* In short, the fundamental justification for the decision is
that women as guards will generate sexual assaults. With all respect, this
rationale regrettably perpetuates one of the most insidious of the old
myths about women—that women, wittingly or not, are seductive sexual
objects. The effect of the decision, made I am sure with the best of intentions, is to punish women because their very presence might provoke
sexual assaults. It is women who are made to pay the price in lost job
opportunities for the threat of depraved conduct by prison inmates.
Once again, "[t]he pedestal upon which women have been placed has . . .
upon closer inspection, been revealed as a cage." *Sail'er Inn, Inc.,* v.
*Kirby,* 5 Cal. 3d 1, 20, 585 P.2d 529, 3 FEP Cases 550 (1971). It is particularly ironic that the cage is erected here in response to feared misbehavior
by imprisoned criminals.[4]

## NOTE

If an employer does not have a similar requirement for women, can he
insist that men wear their hair cut neatly? The courts of appeals have

---

"Q. But a female 5'6", 140 lbs., would not be able to perform all the duties?
"A. No.
"Q. What do you use as a basis for that opinion?
"A. The innate intention between a male and a female. The physical capabilities, the
emotions that go into the psychic make-up of a female vs. the psychic make-up of a male.
The attitude of the rural type inmate we have vs. that of a women. The superior
feeling that a man has, historically, over that of a female." App. 153
Strikingly similar sentiments were expressed a century ago by a justice of this Court
in a case long since discredited:
"I am not prepared to say that it is one of [women's] fundamental rights and
privileges to be admitted into every office and position, including those which require
highly special qualifications and demanding special responsibilities. . . . [I]n my opinion,
in view of the particular characteristics, destiny, and mission of woman, it is within the
province of the legislature to ordain what offices, positions, and callings shall be filled
and discharged by men, and shall receive the benefit of those energies and responsibilities, and that decision and firmness which are presumed to dominate in the sterner
sex." *Bradwell* v. *Illinois,* 16 Wall. 130, 139, 142 (1872) (Bradley, J., concurring).

[3] The Court refers to two incidents involving potentially dangerous attacks on women
in prisons. *Ante,* at 13 n. 22, 15 FEP Cases, at 16. But these did not involve trained corrections Officers; one victim was a clerical worker and the other a student visiting on a
tour.

[4] The irony is multiplied by the fact that enormous staff increases are required by the
District Court's order in *James* v. *Wallace, supra.* This necessary hiring would be a
perfect opportunity for appellants to remedy their past discrimination against women,
but instead the Court's decision permits that policy to continue. Moreover, once conditions are improved in accordance with the *James* order, the problems that the Court
perceives with women guards will be substantially alleviated.

generally rejected the claim. See, for example, *Fagan* v. *National Cash Register Co.*, 481 F.2d 1115, 5 FEP Cases 1335 (1973). "We find ourselves quite unwilling, respecting the male's long hair aspect, to accept as discrimination 'because of sex' the Commission's decision [that it constitutes sex discrimination]." The Court held that such a reading did not comport with the declared objective which Congress sought to achieve.

### (3) *Sexual Favors*

## TOMKINS v. PUBLIC SERVICE ELECTRIC & GAS CO.

*United States Court of Appeals, Third Circuit, 1977*
*568 F.2d 1044, 16 FEP Cases 22*

ALDISERT, Circuit Judge: The question presented is whether appellant Adrienne Tomkins, in alleging that her continued employment with appellee Public Service Electric and Gas Co. [PSE&G] was conditioned upon her submitting to the sexual advances of a male supervisor, stated a cause of action under Title VII of the Civil Rights Act of 1964, as amended, 42 U.S.C. § 2000e et seq. The district court determined that appellant did not state a claim under Title VII, and dismissed her complaint. 422 F. Supp. 553, 13 FEP Cases 1574 (D.N.J. 1976). Taking the allegations of Tomkins' complaint as true, see *Walker, Inc.* v. *Food Machinery*, 382 U.S. 172, 174–75 (1965); *Conley* v. *Gibson*, 355 U.S. 41, 45–46, 9 FEP Cases 439, 442 (1957), we find that a cognizable claim of sex discrimination was made and, accordingly, we reverse the dismissal of the complaint and remand the case to the district court for further proceedings.

### I

Taken as true, the facts set out in appellant's complaint demonstrate that Adrienne Tomkins was hired by PSE&G in April 1971, and progressed to positions of increasing responsibility from that time until August 1973, when she began working in a secretarial position under the direction of a named supervisor. On October 30, 1973, the supervisor told Tomkins that she should have lunch with him in a nearby restaurant, in order to discuss his upcoming evaluation of her work, as well as a possible job promotion. At lunch, he made advances toward her, indicating his desire to have sexual relations with her and stating that this would be necessary if they were to have a satisfactory working relationship. When Tomkins attempted to leave the restaurant, the supervisor responded first by threats of recrimination against Tomkins in her employment, then by threats of physical force, and ultimately by physically restraining Tomkins. During the incident, he told her that no one at PSE&G would help her should she lodge a complaint against him.

Tomkins' complaint alleges that PSE&G and certain of its agents knew or should have known that such incidents would occur, and that they nevertheless "placed [Tomkins] in a position where she would be subjected to the aforesaid conduct of [the supervisor] and failed to take adequate supervisory measures to prevent such incidents from occurring." Amended Complaint, ¶ 24. It further alleged that on the day following the lunch, Tomkins expressed her intention to leave PSE&G as a result of the incident. She agreed to continue work only after being promised a transfer to a comparable position elsewhere in the company. A comparable position did not become available, however, and Tomkins was instead placed in an inferior position in another department. There, she was subjected to false and adverse employment evaluations, disciplinary lay-offs, and threats of demotion by various PSE&G employees. Tomkins maintains that as a result of the supervisor's conduct and the continued pattern of harassment by PSE&G personnel, she suffered physical and emotional distress, resulting in absenteeism and loss of income.

In January 1975, PSE&G fired Tomkins. Following her dismissal, she filed an employment discrimination complaint with the Equal Employment Opportunity Commission, which ultimately issued a Notice of Right to Sue. After Tomkins filed suit in district court, PSE&G moved to dismiss the complaint on various grounds, including failure to state a claim upon which relief may be granted. In addressing the motion, the district court bifurcated the issues raised in the complaint. The court denied the company's motion to dismiss Tomkins' claim of company retaliation against her for complaining about her supervisor's conduct. However, the company's motion to dismiss Tomkins' claim against PSE&G for his actions was granted for failure to state a claim. The latter judgment was determined final by the district court under Rule 54(b), Fed. R. Civ. P., and this appeal followed.

## II

Section 703(a)(1) of Title VII, 42 U.S.C. § 2000e–2(a)(1), provides that "it shall be an unlawful employment practice for an employer . . . to discharge any individual . . . or otherwise to discriminate against any individual with respect to . . . terms, conditions, or privileges of employment because of such individual's . . . sex. . . ." In order to state a claim under this provision, then, it is necessary that Tomkins establish both that the acts complained of constituted a condition of employment, and that this condition was imposed by the employer on the basis of sex.

## A

Tomkins claims that the sexual demands of her supervisor imposed a sex-based "term or condition" on her employment. She alleges that her promotion and favorable job evaluation were made conditional upon her granting sexual favors, and that she suffered adverse job consequences as a result of this incident.[1] In granting appellees' motion to dismiss,

---

[1] [Footnotes numbered as in original.—Ed.] Appellant suggests as an alternate theory of liability that, in addition to prohibiting specific discriminatory acts, Title VII mandates that employees be afforded "a work environment free from the psychological harm

however, the district court characterized the supervisor's acts as "abuse of authority . . . for personal purposes." 422 F. Supp. at 556, 13 FEP Cases at 1576. The court thus overlooked the major thrust of Tomkins' complaint, *i.e.*, that her employer, either knowingly or constructively, made acquiescence in her supervisor's sexual demands a necessary prerequisite to the continuation of, or advancement in, her job.

The facts as alleged by appellant clearly demonstrate an incident with employment ramifications, one within the intended coverage of Title VII.[2] The context within which the sexual advances occurred is itself strong evidence of a job-related condition: Tomkins was asked to lunch by her supervisor for the express purpose of discussing his upcoming evaluation of her work and possible recommendation of her for a promotion. But one need not infer the added condition from the setting alone. It is expressly alleged that the supervisor stated to Tomkins that her continued success and advancement at PSE&G were dependent upon her agreeing to his sexual demands. The demand thus amounted to a condition of employment, an additional duty or burden Tomkins was required by her supervisor to meet as a prerequisite to her continued employment.


B


The issue whether the additional condition was imposed because of Tomkins' gender, as required by Section 703(a)(1), gave rise to various hypotheticals in the briefs and oral argument presented to this court. For example, appellees urge that the supervisor could "just as easily" have sought to satisfy his sexual urges with a male, Appellees' Brief at 8, and thus his actions were not directed only toward the female sex.

Similar to the argument that his acts were merely personal rather than constituting an additional condition of employment, such hypotheticals are irrelevant in the posture in which the appeal reaches this court. It is to the face of the complaint that we must look. And the complaint clearly alleges that Tomkins was discriminated against, "on the basis of her sex," by virtue of her supervisor's actions and PSE&G's acquiescence

---

flowing from an atmosphere of discrimination." Brief for Appellant at 16. Analogizing to EEOC findings of Title VII violations where employees have been subjected to their supervisors' racial epithets and ethnic jokes, *e.g.*, EEOC Decision No. 0679, 4 FEP Cases 441 (1971), appellant contends that the sexual advances and subsequent retaliatory harassment to which she was subjected created an environment of debilitating sexual intimidation constituting a barrier to her employment opportunities. Because we hold that the facts as alleged constitute a sex-based condition of employment in violation of Title VII, we need not pass upon this second theory.

2 Although the specific prohibition against sex discrimination was never the subject of legislative hearings (the word "sex" was added to the 1964 Civil Rights Act's proscriptions and "national origin" during limited House debate), the Supreme Court has taught that the purpose of Congress in enacting Title VII was "the removal of artificial, arbitrary, and unnecessary barriers to employment when the barriers operate invidiously to discriminate on the basis of racial or other impermissible classification." *Griggs* v. *Duke Power Co.*, 401 U.S. 424, 431, 3 FEP Cases 175, 177 (1971).

in those actions. See Amended Complaint, ¶ 39. Specifically, Tomkins averred that PSE&G knew or should have known the facts complained of. Amended Complaint, ¶ 24.[3] Reading the complaint in the light most favorable to Tomkins, the essence of her claim is that her status as a female was the motivating factor in the supervisor's conditioning her continued employment on compliance with his sexual demands.[4]

Cases dealing with the issue presented in this appeal are scarce, and our research has produced no controlling precedent. Reference to certain of the cases is helpful, however, for a discernible pattern emerges from the decisions.

The District of Columbia Circuit was presented with similar facts in Barnes v. Costle, 15 FEP Cases 345, No. 74–2026 (D.C. Cir. July 27, 1977), a Title VII action in which appellant alleged that her job was abolished in retaliation for her refusal to engage in sexual relations with her male supervisor. Plaintiff claimed that in the course of her employment, the supervisor made a number of sexual advances and conditioned any enhancement of her job status on her acquiescing to his sexual demands. Noting appellant's assertion that "she became the target of her superior's sexual desires because she was a woman, and was asked to bow to his demands as the price for holding her job," Slip Opinion at 15, 15 FEP Cases at 351, the Court of Appeals determined that the alleged facts constituted a violation of Title VII, and therefore reversed the district court's grant of summary judgment in favor of defendant.

The Fourth Circuit, in Garber v. Saxon Business Products, 15 FEP Cases 344, No. 76–1610 (4th Cir. Feb. 14, 1977) (per curiam), reversed a district court's grant of a dismissal on similar facts. In the court's view, plaintiff's complaint that she had been terminated for refusing her male superior's sexual demands "allege[d] an employer policy or acquiescence in a practice of compelling female employees to submit to the sexual advances of their male superiors in violation of Title VII." (Slip Opinion

---

[3] PSE&G contends that the supervisor's actions cannot give rise to company liability because he was not acting pursuant to company policy. Whether the incident was company policy or a purely personal incident is a factual determination which this court is not required to make—it is sufficient for our purposes that Tomkins alleged the former.

[4] We would note that, although irrelevant, the situation posed in PSE&G's hypothetical would cause no great concern. Title VII prohibits discrimination against men as well as women. See Rosen v. Public Service Electric and Gas Co., 409 F.2d 775, 1 FEP Cases 708, 70 LRRM 3200 (3d Cir. 1969), 477 F.2d 90, 5 FEP Cases 709 (3d Cir. 1973).
In holding that there was no sex discrimination because "gender lines might as easily been reversed, or even not crossed at all," 422 F. Supp. at 556, 13 FEP Cases 1576, the district court took much too narrow a view of what can constitute sex-based discrimination under Title VII. It is not necessary to a finding of a Title VII violation that the discriminatory practice depend on a characteristic "peculiar to one of the genders," Williams v. Saxbe, 413 F. Supp. 654, 658, 12 FEP Cases 1093, 1097 (D.D.C. 1976), or that the discrimination be directed at all members of a sex; see Sprogis v. United Airlines, 444 F.2d 1194, 3 FEP Cases 621 (7th Cir. 1971), cert. denied, 401 U.S. 491, 4 FEP Cases 37 (1971). It is only necessary to show that gender is a substantial factor in the discrimination, and that if the plaintiff "had been a man she would not have been treated in the same manner," Skelton v. Balzano, 13 FEP Cases 1803, 1807 (D.D.C. 1976); see also Slack v. Havens, 7 FEP Cases 885 (S.D. Cal. 1973), aff'd, 522 F.2d 1091 (9th Cir. 1975); EEOC Decision No. 71–2227, 3 FEP Cases 1245 (1971).

at 1). A similar result was reached in *Williams* v. *Saxbe*, 413 F. Supp. 654, 12 FEP Cases 1093 (D.D.C. 1976) (appeal pending), where it was determined that retaliatory actions of a male supervisor, taken because a female employee declined his sexual advances, constitute an "artificial barrier to employment which was placed before one gender and not the other," 413 F. Supp. at 657, 12 FEP Cases at 1096, and thus sex discrimination violative of Title VII.

Faced with claims that at first appear similar, two district courts reached different results. In *Corne* v. *Bausch and Lomb, Inc.*, 390 F. Supp. 161, 10 FEP Cases 289 (D. Ariz. 1975), *rev'd & remanded on other grounds*, 15 FEP Cases 1370, No. 75–1857 (9th Cir. July 28, 1977), it was held that verbal sexual advances by a male employee to female fellow employees did not constitute actionable sex discrimination under Title VII. *Corne* is distinguishable from the facts before us because plaintiff Corne did not allege that acquiescence in the sexual advances was required as a condition of her employment. Appellant Tomkins, by contrast, clearly alleged such an employment nexus. Also distinguishable from the current appeal is *Miller* v. *Bank of America*, 418 F. Supp. 122, 13 FEP Cases 439 (N.D. Cal. 1976) (appeal pending). Plaintiff Miller alleged that her male supervisor promised her job advancement in return for engaging in sexual relations with him, and subsequently dismissed her when she refused to do so. Not only was it undisputed that defendant bank discouraged such employee misconduct, but plaintiff had failed to avail herself of a bank complaint procedure designed to resolve precisely this sort of complaint. The *Miller* court drew a clear distinction between those facts and a situation where an employer is implicated in a complaint of improper sexual advances:

"[T]here may be situations in which a sex discrimination action can be maintained for an employer's action, or tacit approval, of a personnel policy requiring sex favors as a condition of employment." 418 F. Supp. at 236, 13 FEP Cases at 440.

Although these cases are not dispositive of this appeal, they disclose a pattern of how sexual advances in the employment context do or do not constitute a Title VII violation. The courts have distinguished between complaints alleging sexual advances of an individual or personal nature and those alleging direct employment consequences flowing from the advances, finding Title VII violations in the latter category. This distinction recognizes two elements necessary to find a violation of Title VII: first, that a term or condition of employment has been imposed and second, that it has been imposed by the employer, either directly or vicariously, in a sexually discriminatory fashion. Applying these requirements to the present complaint, we conclude that Title VII is violated when a supervisor, with the actual or constructive knowledge of the employer, makes sexual advances or demands toward a subordinate employee and conditions that employee's job status—evaluation, continued employment, promotion, or other aspects of career development—on a favorable response to those advances or demands, and the employer does not take prompt and appropriate remedial action after acquiring such knowledge.

## IV

We do not agree with the district court that finding a Title VII violation on these facts will result in an unmanageable number of suits and a difficulty in differentiating between spurious and meritorious claims. The congressional mandate that the federal courts provide relief is strong; it must not be thwarted by concern for judicial economy. More significant, however, this decision in no way relieves the plaintiff of the burden of proving the facts alleged to establish the required elements of a Title VII violation. Although any theory of liability may be used in vexatious or bad faith suits, we are confident that traditional judicial mechanisms will separate the valid from the invalid complaints.

The judgment of the district court will be reversed and the cause remanded for further proceedings.

(4) *Pregnancy*

## GENERAL ELECTRIC CO. v. GILBERT

*Supreme Court of the United States, 1976*
*429 U.S. 125, 13 FEP Cases 1657*

MR. JUSTICE REHNQUIST delivered the opinion of the Court.

Petitioner, General Electric Company, provides for all of its employees a disability plan which pays weekly nonoccupational sickness and accident benefits. Excluded from the plan's coverage, however, are disabilities arising from pregnancy. Respondents, on behalf of a class of women employees, brought this action seeking, *inter alia,* a declaration that this exclusion constitutes sex discrimination in violation of Title VII of the Civil Rights Act of 1964, as amended, 42 U.S.C. § 2000e. The District Court for the Eastern District of Virginia, following a trial on the merits, held that the exclusion of such pregnancy-related disability benefits from General Electric's employee disability plan violated Title VII, 375 F. Supp. 367, 7 FEP Cases 796. The Court of Appeals affirmed, 519 F.2d 661, 10 FEP Cases 1201, and we granted certiorari, 423 U.S. 882. We now reverse.

## I

As part of its total compensation package, General Electric provides nonoccupational sickness and accident benefits to all employees under its Weekly Sickness and Accident Insurance Plan (the "Plan") in an amount equal to 60 percent of an employee's normal straight time weekly earnings. These payments are paid to employees who become totally disabled as a result of a nonoccupational sickness or accident. Benefit payments normally start with the eighth day of an employee's total disability (although if an employee is earlier confined to a hospital as a bed patient, benefit payments will start immediately), and continue up to a maximum of 26 weeks for any one continuous period of disability or successive periods of disability due to the same or related causes.

The individual named respondents are present or former hourly paid production employees at General Electric's plant in Salem, Va. Each of these employees was pregnant during 1971 or 1972, while employed by General Electric, and each presented a claim to the company for disability benefits under the Plan to cover the period while absent from work as a result of the pregnancy. These claims were routinely denied on the ground that the Plan did not provide disability benefit payments for any absence due to pregnancy. Respondents thereafter filed individual charges with the EEOC alleging that the refusal of General Electric to pay disability benefits under the Plan for time lost due to pregnancy and childbirth discriminated against her because of sex. Upon waiting the requisite number of days, the instant action was commenced in the District Court. The complaint asserted a violation of Title VII. Damages were sought as well as an injunction directing General Electric to include pregnancy disabilities within the Plan on the same terms and conditions as other nonoccupational disabilities.

Following trial, the District Court made findings of fact, conclusions of law, and entered an order in which it determined that General Electric, by excluding pregnancy disabilities from the coverage of the Plan, had engaged in sex discrimination in violation of § 703(a)(1) of Title VII, 42 U.S.C. § 2000e-2(a)(1). The District Court found that normal pregnancy, while not necessarily either a "disease" or an "accident," was disabling for a period of six to eight weeks, that approximately "ten percent of pregnancies are terminated by miscarriage, which is disabling," and that approximately 10 percent of pregnancies are complicated by diseases which may lead to additional disability. The District Court noted the evidence introduced during the trial, a good deal of it stipulated, concerning the relative cost to General Electric of providing benefits under the Plan to male and female employees, all of which indicated that, with pregnancy-related disabilities excluded, the cost of the Plan to General Electric per female employees was at least as high, if not substantially higher, than the cost per male employee.

The District Court found that the inclusion of pregnancy-related disabilities within the scope of the Plan would "increase G.E.'s [disability benefits plan] costs by an amount which, though large, is at this time undeterminable." 375 F. Supp., at 378, 7 FEP Cases, at 804-805. The District Court declined to find that the present actuarial value of the coverage was equal as between men and women, but went on to decide that even had it found economic equivalence, such a finding would not in any case have justified the exclusion of pregnancy-related disabilities from an otherwise comprehensive nonoccupational sickness and accident disability plan. Regardless of whether the cost of including such benefits might make the Plan more costly for women than for men, the District Court determined that "[i]f Title VII intends to sexually equalize employment opportunity, there must be this one exception to the cost differential defense." 375 F. Supp. at 383, 7 FEP Cases at 808.

The ultimate conclusion of the District Court was that petitioner had discriminated on the basis of sex in the operation of its disability program in violation of Title VII, 375 F. Supp., at 385-86, 7 FEP Cases at 810. An order was entered enjoining petitioner from continuing to exclude pregnancy-related disabilities from the coverage of the Plan, and providing for the future award of monetary relief to individual members of the class affected. Petitioner appealed to the Court of Appeals for the Fourth Circuit, and that court by a divided vote affirmed the judgment of the District Court.

Between the date on which the District Court's judgment was rendered and the time this case was decided by the Court of Appeals, we decided *Geduldig* v. *Aiello,* 417 U.S. 484, 8 FEP Cases 97 (1974), where we rejected a claim that a very similar disability program established under California law violated the Equal Protection Clause of the Fourteenth Amendment because that plan's exclusion of pregnancy disabilities represented sex discrimination. The majority of the Court of Appeals felt that Geduldig was not controlling because it arose under the Equal Protection Clause of the Fourteenth Amendment, and not under Title VII, 519 F.2d, at 666-67, 10 FEP Cases, at 1204-05. The dissenting opinion disagreed with the majority as to the impact of Geduldig, 519 F.2d, at 668-69, 10 FEP Cases, at 1206-1207. We granted certiorari to consider this important issue in the construction of Title VII.

## II

Section 703(a)(1) provides in relevant part that it shall be an unlawful employment practice for an employer

". . . to discriminate against any individual with respect to his compensation, terms, conditions, or privileges of employment, because of such individual's race, color, religion, sex, or national origin," 42 U.S.C. § 2000e-2.

While there is no necessary inference that Congress, in choosing this language, intended to incorporate into Title VII the concepts of discrimination which have evolved from court decisions construing the Equal Protection Clause of the Fourteenth Amendment, the similarities between the congressional language and some of those decisions surely indicates that the latter are a useful starting point in interpreting the former. Particularly in the case of defining the term "discrimination," which Congress has nowhere in Title VII defined, those cases afford an existing body of law analyzing and discussing that term in a legal context not wholly dissimilar from the concerns which Congress manifested in enacting Title VII. We think, therefore, that our decision in *Geduldig* v. *Aiello, supra,* dealing with a strikingly similar disability plan, is quite relevant in determining whether or not the pregnancy exclusion did discriminate on the basis of sex. In *Geduldig*, the disability insurance system was funded entirely from contributions deducted from the wages of participating employees, at a rate of 1 percent of the employee's salary up to an annual maximum of $85. In other relevant respects, the operation of the program was similar to General Electric's disability benefits plan, see 417 U.S., at 487-89, 8 FEP Cases, at 98.

We rejected appellee's Equal Protection challenge to this statutory scheme. We first noted that:

"We cannot agree that the exclusion of this disability from coverage amounts to invidious discrimination under the Equal Protection Clause. California does not discriminate with respect to the persons or groups which are eligible for disability insurance protection under the program. The classification challenged in this case relates to the asserted under-inclusiveness of the set of risks that the State has selected to insure." 417 U.S., at 494, 8 FEP Cases, at 101.

This point was emphasized again, when later in the opinion we noted that:

"[T]his case is thus a far cry from cases like *Reed* v. *Reed*, 404 U.S. 71 (1971), and *Frontiero* v. *Richardson*, 411 U.S. 677, 9 FEP Cases 1253 (1973), involving discrimination based upon gender as such. The California insurance program does not exclude anyone from benefit eligibility because of gender but merely removes one physical condition—pregnancy —from the list of compensable disabilities. While it is true that only women can become pregnant, it does not follow that every legislative classification concerning pregnancy is a sex-based classification like those considered in *Reed, supra,* and *Frontiero, supra*. Normal pregnancy is an objectively identifiable physical condition with unique characteristics. Absent a showing that distinctions involving pregnancy are mere pretexts designed to effect an individous discrimination against the members of one sex or the other, lawmakers are constitutionally free to include or exclude pregnancy from the coverage of legislation such as this on any reasonable basis, just as with respect to any other physical condition.

"The lack of identity between the excluded disability and gender as such under this insurance program becomes clear upon the most cursory analysis. The program divides potential recipients into two groups— pregnant women and nonpregnant persons. While the first group is exclusively female, the second includes members of both sexes." 417 U.S., at 496-97, n. 20, 8 FEP Cases, at 101-102.

The quoted language from *Geduldig* leaves no doubt that our reason for rejecting appellee's equal protection claim in that case was that the exclusion of pregnancy from coverage under California's disability benefits plan was not in itself discrimination based on sex.

. . .

The Court of Appeals was therefore wrong in concluding that the reasoning of *Geduldig* was not applicable to an action under Title VII. Since it is a finding of sex-based discrimination that must trigger, in a

case such as this, the finding of an unlawful employment practice under
§ 703(a)(1), 42 U.S.C. § 2000e-2(a)(1), *Geduldig* is precisely in point in its
holding that an exclusion of pregnancy from a disability benefits plan
providing general coverage is not a gender-based discrimination at all.

There is no more showing in this case than there was in *Geduldig* that
the exclusion of pregnancy benefits is a mere "pretext designed to effect
an indivious discrimination against the members of one sex or the
other." . . . But we have here no question of excluding a disease or disability comparable in all other respects to covered diseases or disabilities
and yet confined to the members of one race or sex. Pregnancy is of course
confined to women, but it is in other ways significantly different from the
typical covered disease or disability. The District Court found that it is
not a "disease" at all, and is often a voluntarily undertaken and desired
condition, 375 F. Supp., at 375, 377, 7 FEP Cases, at 803, 805. . . .

The instant suit was grounded on Title VII rather than the Equal
Protection Clause, and our cases recognize that a prima facie violation
of Title VII can be established in some circumstances upon proof that the
*effect* of an otherwise facially neutral plan or classification is to discriminate against members of one class or another. See *Washington* v.
*Davis,* 426 U.S. 229, 96 S.Ct. 2040, 2051, 12 FEP Cases 1415, 1422 (1976).
For example, in the context of a challenge, under the provisions of § 703
(a)(2), to a facially neutral employment test, this Court held that a prima
facie case of discrimination would be established if, even absent proof of
intent, the consequences of the test were "invidiously to discriminate on
the basis of racial or other impermissible classification," *Griggs* v. *Duke
Power Co.,* 401 U.S. 424, 431, 3 FEP Cases 175, 177 (1971). Even assuming
that it is not necessary in this case to prove intent to establish a prima
facie violation of § 703(a)(1), but cf. *McDonnell Douglas Corp.* v. *Green,*
411 U.S. 792, 802-806, 5 FEP Cases 965, 969-70 (1973), the respondents
have not made the requisite showing of gender-based effects.

As in *Geduldig, supra,* respondents have not attempted to meet the
burden of demonstrating a gender-based discriminatory effect resulting
from the exclusion of pregnancy-related disabilities from coverage. Whatever the ultimate probative value of the evidence introduced before the
District Court on this subject in the instant case, at the very least it
tended to illustrate that the selection of risks covered by the Plan did
not operate, in fact, to discriminate against women. As in *Geduldig,
supra,* we start from the indisputable baseline that "[t]he fiscal and
actuarial benefits of the program . . . accrue to members of both sexes,"
417 U.S., at 497 n. 20, 8 FEP Cases, at 102. We need not disturb the findings of the District Court to note that there is neither a finding, nor was
there any evidence which would support a finding, that the financial
benefits of the Plan "worked to discriminate against any definable group
or class in terms of the aggregate risk protection derived by that group
or class from the program," *id.,* at 496, 8 FEP Cases at 101. The Plan, in
effect (and for all that appears), is nothing more than an insurance package, which covers some risks, but excludes others, see id., at 494, 496-97, 8

FEP Cases, at 100-102. The "package" going to relevant identifiable groups we are presently concerned with—General Electric's male and female employees—covers exactly the same categories of risk, and is facially nondiscriminatory in the sense that "[t]here is no risk from which men are protected and women are not. Likewise, there is no risk from which women are protected and men are not." *Geduldig*, 417 U.S., at 496-97, 8 FEP Cases, at 102. As there is no proof that the package is in fact worth more to men than to women, it is impossible to find any gender-based discriminatory effect in this scheme simply because women disabled as a result of pregnancy do not receive benefits; that is to say, gender-based discrimination does not result simply because an employer's disability benefits plan is less than all inclusive. For all that appears, pregnancy-related disabilities constitute an *additional* risk, unique to women, and the failure to compensate them for this risk does not destroy the presumed parity of the benefits, accruing to men and women alike, which results from the facially evenhanded *inclusion* of risks. . . .

### III

We are told, however, that this analysis of the congressional purpose underlying Title VII is inconsistent with the guidelines of the EEOC, which, it is asserted, are entitled to "great deference" in the construction of the Act, *Griggs, supra*, 401 U.S., at 433-34, 3 FEP Cases at 179; *Phillips* v. *Martin Marietta Corp.*, 400 U.S. 542, 545, 3 FEP Cases 40, 41 (1971) (MARSHALL, J., concurring). The guideline upon which respondents rely most heavily was promulgated in 1972, and states in pertinent part: "Disabilities caused or contributed to by pregnancy, miscarriage, abortion, childbirth, and recovery therefrom are, for all job-related purposes, temporary disabilities and should be treated as such under any health or temporary disability insurance or sick leave plan available in connection with employment. . . ." . . .

. . .

The EEOC guideline in question does not fare well. . . . It is not a contemporaneous interpretation of Title VII, since it was first promulgated eight years after the enactment of that Title. More importantly, the 1972 guideline flatly contradicts the position which the agency had enunciated at an earlier date, closer to the enactment of the governing statute. . . .

. . .

There are also persuasive indications that the more recent EEOC guideline sharply conflicts with other indicia of the proper interpretation of the sex-discrimination provisions of Title VII. The legislative history of Title VII's prohibition of sex discrimination is notable primarily for its brevity. Even so, however, Congress paid especial attention to the provisions of the Equal Pay Act, 29 U.S.C. § 206(d),[21] when it amended

---

[21] [Footnotes numbered as in original.—Ed.] Section 6(d)(1) of the Equal Pay Act, 29 U.S.C. § 206(d)(1), provides, in pertinent part:
"No employer having employees subject to any provisions of this section shall discrimi-

§703(h) of Title VII by adding the following sentence:
"It shall not be an unlawful employment practice under this subchapter for any employer to differentiate upon the basis of sex in determining the amount of the wages or compensation paid or to be paid to employees of such employer if such differentiation is authorized by the provisions of section 206(d) of Title 29." 42 U.S.C. § 2000e-2(h).

This sentence was proposed as the Bennett Amendment to the Senate Bill, 110 Cong. Rec. 13647 (1964), and Senator Humphrey, the floor manager of the bill, stated that the purpose of the amendment was to make it "unmistakably clear" that "differences of treatment in industrial benefit plans, including earlier retirement options for women, may continue in operation under this bill if it becomes law," 110 Cong. Rec. 13663-13664 (1964). Because of this amendment, interpretations of section 6(d) of the Equal Pay Act are applicable to Title VII as well, and an interpretive regulation promulgated by the Wage and Hour Administrator under the Equal Pay Act explicitly states:

"If employer contributions to a plan providing insurance or similar benefits to employees are equal for both men and women, no wage differential prohibited by the equal pay provisions will result from such payments, even though the benefits which accrue to the employees in question are greater for one sex than for the other. The mere fact that the employer may make unequal contributions for employees of opposite sexes in such a situation will not, however, be considered to indicate that the employer's payments are in violation of section 6(d), if the resulting benefits are equal for such employees." 29 CFR § 800.116(d) (1975).

Thus even if we were to depend for our construction of the critical language of Title VII solely on the basis of "deference" to interpretative regulations by the appropriate administrative agencies, we would find ourselves pointed in diametrically opposite directions by the conflicting regulations of the EEOC, on the one hand, and the Wage and Hour Administrator, on the other. Petitioner's exclusion of benefits for pregnancy disability would be declared an unlawful employment practice under § 703(a)(1), but would be declared not to be an unlawful employment practice under § 703(h).

We are not reduced to such total abdication in construing the statute. The EEOC guideline of 1972, conflicting as it does with earlier pronouncements of that agency, and containing no suggestion that some new source of legislative history had been discovered in the intervening eight years, stands virtually alone. Contrary to it are the consistent interpretation of the Wage and Hour Administrator, and the quoted language of

---

nate, within any establishment in which such employees are employed, between employees on the basis of sex by paying wages to employees in such establishment at a rate less than the rate at which he pays wages to employees of the opposite sex in such establishment for equal work on jobs the performance of which requires equal skill, effort, and responsibility, and which are performed under similar working conditions, except where such payment is made pursuant to (i) a seniority system; (ii) a merit system; (iii) a system which measures earnings by quantity or quality of production; or (iv) a differential based on any other factor other than sex. . . ."

Senator Humphrey, the floor manager of Title VII in the Senate. They support what seems to us to be the "plain meaning" of the language used by Congress when it enacted § 703(a)(1).

The concept of "discrimination," of course, was well known at the time of the enactment of Title VII, having been associated with the Fourteenth Amendment for nearly a century, and carrying with it a long history of judicial construction. When Congress makes it unlawful for an employer to "discriminate . . . on the basis of . . . sex . . . ," without further explanation of its meaning, we should not readily infer that it meant something different than what the concept of discrimination has traditionally meant, cf. *Morton* v. *Mancari*, 417 U.S. 535, 549, 8 FEP Cases 105, 111 (1974); *Ozawa* v. *United States, supra*, 260 U.S. 178, 193 (1922). There is surely no reason for any such inference here, see *Gemsco* v. *Walling*, 324 U.S. 244, 260 (1945).

We therefore agree with petitioner that its disability benefits plan does not violate Title VII because of its failure to cover pregnancy-related disabilities. The judgment of the Court of Appeals is

*Reversed.*

. . .

MR. JUSTICE BRENNAN, with whom MR. JUSTICE MARSHALL concurs, dissenting: The Court holds today that without violating Title VII of the Civil Rights Act, 42 U.S.C. § 2000e, a private employer may adopt a disability plan that compensates employees for all temporary disabilities except one affecting exclusively women, pregnancy. I respectfully dissent.
. . .
. . .

## II

*Geduldig* v. *Aiello, supra,* purports to be the starting point for the Court's analysis. There a state-operated disability insurance system containing a pregnancy exclusion was held not to violate the Equal Protection Clause. Although it quotes primarily from one footnote of that opinion at some length, *ante,* at 8-9, 13 FEP Cases, at 1661–_____, the Court finally does not grapple with *Geduldig* on its own terms.
. . .

Thus, *Geduldig* itself obliges the Court to determine whether the exclusion of a sex-linked disability from the universe of compensable disabilities was actually the product of neutral, persuasive actuarial considerations, or rather stemmed from a policy that purposefully downgraded women's role in the labor force. In *Geduldig*, that inquiry coupled with the normal presumption favoring legislative action satisfied the Court that the pregnancy exclusion in fact was prompted by California's legitimate fiscal concerns, and therefore that California did not deny equal protection in effectuating reforms "one step at a time." 417 U.S., at 495, 8 FEP Cases, at 101. But the record in this case makes such deference impossible here. Instead, in reaching its conclusion that a showing of purposeful discrimination has not been made, *ante,* at 10, 13 FEP Cases, at 1662, the Court simply disregards a history of General Electric practices that have served to undercut the employment opportunities of women who become pregnant while employed. Moreover, the Court studiously ignores the undisturbed conclusion of the District Court that General Electric's "discriminatory attitude" toward women was "a motivating factor in its policy," 375 F. Supp. 367, 383, 7 FEP Cases 796, 808 (ED Va. 1974), and that the pregnancy exclusion was neither "neutral on its face" nor "in its intent." Id, at 382, 7 FEP Cases, at 807.

Plainly then, the Court's appraisal of General Electric's policy as a neutral process of sorting risks and "not a gender-based discrimination at all," ante, at 10, 13 FEP Cases, at 1662, cannot easily be squared with the historical record in this case. The Court, therefore, proceeds to a discussion of purported neutral criteria that suffice to explain the lone exclusion of pregnancy from the program. The Court argues that pregnancy is not "comparable" to other disabilities since it is a "voluntary" condition rather than a "disease." Ibid. The fallacy of this argument is that even if "non-voluntariness" and "disease" are to be construed as the operational criteria for inclusion of a disability in General Electric's program, application of these criteria is inconsistent with the Court's gender-neutral interpretation of the company's policy.

For example, the characterization of pregnancy as "voluntary" is not a persuasive factor, for as the Court of Appeals correctly noted, "other than for childbirth disability, [General Electric] has never construed its plan as eliminating all so-called 'voluntary' disabilities," including sport injuries, attempted suicides, venereal disease, disabilities incurred in the commission of a crime or during a fight, and elective cosmetic surgery, 519 F.2d, at 665, 10 FEP Cases, at 1204. Similarly, the label "disease" rather than "disability" cannot be deemed determinative since General Electric's pregnancy disqualification also excludes the 10 percent of pregnancies that end in debilitating miscarriages, 375 F. Supp., at 377, 7 FEP Cases, at 803, the 10 percent of cases where pregnancies are complicated by "diseases" in the intuitive sense of the word, ibid., and cases where women recovering from childbirth are stricken by severe diseases unrelated to pregnancy.

Moreover, even the Court's principal argument for the plan's supposed gender neutrality cannot withstand analysis. The central analytical framework relied upon to demonstrate the absence of discrimination is the principle described in Geduldig: "There is no risk from which men are protected and women are not, . . . [and] no risk from which women are protected and men are not." 417 U.S., at 496-97, cited ante, at 12, 13 FEP Cases, at 1663. In fostering the impression that it is faced with a mere underinclusive assignment of risks in a gender-neutral fashion— that is, all other disabilities are insured irrespective of gender—the Court's analysis proves to be simplistic and misleading. For although all mutually contractible risks are covered irrespective of gender, but see n. 4 supra, the plan also insures risks such as prostatectomies, vasectomies, and circumcisions that are specific to the reproductive system of men and for which there exist no female counterparts covered by the plan. Again, pregnancy affords the only disability, sex-specific or otherwise, that is excluded from coverage. Accordingly, the District Court appropriately remarked:

"[T]he concern of defendants in reference to pregnancy risks, coupled with the apparent lack of concern regarding the balancing of other statistically sex-linked disabilities, buttresses the Court's conclusion that the discriminatory attitude characterized elsewhere in the Court's finding was in fact a motivating factor in its policy." 375 F. Supp., at 383, 7 FEP Cases, at 808.

. . .

MR. JUSTICE STEVENS, dissenting: . . .

Rather, the rule at issue places the risk of absence caused by pregnancy in a class by itself. By definition, such a rule discriminates on account of sex; for it is the capacity to become pregnant which primarily differentiates the female from the male. The analysis is the same whether the rule relates to hiring, promotion, the acceptability of an excuse for absence, or an exclusion from a disability insurance plan. Accordingly, without reaching the questions of motive, administrative expertise, and policy, which MR. JUSTICE BRENNAN so persuasively exposes, or the question of effect to which MR. JUSTICE STEWART and MR. JUSTICE BLACKMUN refer, I conclude that the language of the statute plainly requires the result which the courts of appeals have reached unanimously.

## NASHVILLE GAS CO. v. SATTY

*Supreme Court of the United States, 1977*
*434 U.S. 136, 16 FEP Cases 136*

MR. JUSTICE REHNQUIST delivered the opinion of the Court.

Petitioner requires pregnant employees to take a formal leave of absence. The employee does not receive sick pay while on pregnancy leave. She also loses all accumulated job seniority; as a result, while petitioner attempts to provide the employee with temporary work upon her return, she will be employed in a permanent job position only if no employee presently working for petitioner also applies for the position. The United States District Court for the Middle District of Tennessee held that these policies violate Title VII of the Civil Rights Act of 1965, 78 Stat. 253, as amended, 42 U.S.C. § 2000e *et seq.*, 384 F. Supp. 765, 10 FEP Cases 73 (1974). The Court of Appeals for the Sixth Circuit affirmed. 522 F.2d 850, 11 FEP Cases 1 (1975). We granted certiorari to decide, in light of our opinion last Term in *General Electric Co.* v. *Gilbert*, 429 U.S. 125, 13 FEP Cases 1657 (1976), whether the lower courts properly applied Title VII to petitioner's policies respecting pregnancy.

Two separate policies are at issue in this case. The first is petitioner's practice of giving sick pay to employees disabled by reason of nonoccupational sickness or injury but not to those disabled by pregnancy. The second is petitioner's practice of denying accumulated seniority to female employees returning to work following disability caused by childbirth.[1] We shall discuss them in reverse order.

# I

Petitioner requires an employee who is about to give birth to take a pregnancy leave of indeterminate length. Such an employee does not accumulate seniority while absent, but instead actually loses any job seniority accrued before the leave commenced. Petitioner will not hold the employee's job open for her awaiting her return from pregnancy leave. An employee who wishes to return to work from such leave will be placed in any open position for which she is qualified and for which no individual currently employed is bidding; before such time as a permanent position becomes available, the company attempts to find temporary work for the employee. If and when the employee acquires a permanent position, she regains previously accumulated seniority for purposes of pension, vacation, and the like, but does not regain it for the purpose of bidding on future job openings.

Respondent began work for petitioner on March 24, 1969, as a clerk in its Customer Accounting Department. She commenced maternity leave on December 29, 1972, and gave birth to her child on January 23, 1973. Seven weeks later she sought re-employment with petitioner. The position that she had previously held had been eliminated as a result of bona fide cutbacks in her department. Temporary employment was found for her at a lower salary than she had earned prior to taking leave. While holding this temporary employment, respondent unsuccessfully applied for three permanent positions with petitioner. Each position was awarded to another employee who had begun to work for petitioner before respondent had returned from leave; if respondent had been credited with the seniority that she had accumulated prior to leave, she would have been awarded each of the positions for which she applied. After the temporary assignment was completed, respondent requested, "due to lack of work and job openings," that petitioner change her status from maternity leave to termination in order that she could draw unemployment compensation.

---

1 [Footnotes numbered as in original.—Ed.] Respondent appears to believe that the two policies are indissolubly linked together, and that if one is found to violate Title VII the other must likewise be found to do so. Respondent herself, however, has not taken this tack throughout the course of her lawsuit. In the District Court she attacked not only the two policies at issue before us, but in addition petitioner's requirement that she commence her pregnancy leave five weeks prior to the delivery of her child, the termination of her temporary employment allegedly as retaliation for her complaint regarding petitioner's employment policies, and the lower benefits paid for pregnancy as compared to hospitalization for other causes under a group life, health, and accident policy paid for partly by petitioner and partly by its employees. The District Court concluded that respondent had not proved any of these practices to be violative of Title VII, and respondent did not appeal from that determination. Petitioner appealed from the District Court's conclusion that the two company policies presently in issue violate Title VII.

We conclude that petitioner's policy of denying accumulated seniority to female employees returning from pregnancy leave violates § 703(a)(2) of Title VII, 42 U.S.C. § 2000e–2(a)(2). That section declares it to be an unlawful employment practice for an employer to:

"limit, segregate, or classify his employees or applicants for employment in any way which would deprive or tend to deprive any individual of employment opportunities or otherwise adversely affect his status as an employee because of such individual's . . . sex. . . ."

On its face, petitioner's seniority policy appears to be neutral in its treatment of male and female employees.[2] If an employee is forced to take a leave of absence from his job because of disease or any disability other than pregnancy, the employee, whether male or female, retains accumulated seniority and, indeed, continues to accrue seniority while on leave.[3] If the employee takes a leave of absence for any other reason, including pregnancy, accumulated seniority is divested. Petitioner's decision not to treat pregnancy as a disease or disability for purposes of seniority retention is not on its face a discriminatory policy. "Pregnancy is, of course, confined to women, but it is in other ways significantly different from the typical covered disease or disability." *Gilbert, supra,* at 136, 13 FEP Cases, at 1662.

We have recognized, however, that both intentional discrimination and policies neutral on their face but having a discriminatory effect may run afoul of § 703(a)(2). *Griggs* v. *Duke Power Co.,* 401 U.S. 431, 3 FEP Cases 175 (1971). It is beyond dispute that petitioner's policy of depriving employees returning from pregnancy leave of their accumulated seniority acts both to deprive them "of employment opportunities" and to "adversely affect [their] status as an employee." It is apparent from the previous recitation of the events which occurred following respondent's return from pregnancy leave that petitioner's policy denied her specific employment opportunities that she otherwise would have obtained. Even if she had ultimately been able to regain a permanent position with petitioner, she would have felt the effects of a lower seniority level, with its attendant relegation to less desirable and lower paying jobs, for the remainder of her career with petitioner.

In *Gilbert, supra,* there was no showing that General Electric's policy of compensating for all nonjob-related disabilities except pregnancy favored men over women. No evidence was produced to suggest that men

---

[2] The appearance of neutrality rests in part on petitioner's contention that its pregnancy leave policy is identical to the formal leave of absence granted to employees, male or female, in order that they may pursue additional education. However, petitioner's policy of denying accumulated seniority to employees returning from leaves of absence has not to date been applied outside of the pregnancy context. Since 1962, only two employees have requested formal leaves of absence to pursue a college degree; neither employee has returned to work at petitioner.

[3] The District Court found that even "employees returning from long periods of absence due to non-job related injuries do not lose their seniority and in fact their seniority continues to accumulate while absent." 384 F. Supp., at 768, 10 FEP Cases, at 76. The record reveals that at least one employee was absent from work for 10 months due to a heart attack and yet returned to her previous job at the end of this period with full seniority dating back to her date of hire.

received more benefits from General Electric's disability insurance fund than did women; both men and women were subject generally to the disabilities covered and presumably drew similar amounts from the insurance fund. We therefore upheld the plan under Title VII.

"As there is no proof that the package is in fact worth more to men than to women, it is impossible to find any gender-based discriminatory effect in this scheme simply because women disabled as a result of pregnancy do not receive benefits; that is to say, gender-based discrimination does not result simply because an employer's disability benefits plan is less than all-inclusive. For all that appears, pregnancy-related disabilities constitute an *additional* risk, unique to women, and the failure to compensate them for this risk does not destroy the presumed parity of the benefits, accruing to men and women alike, which results from the facially even-handed *inclusion* of risks." 429 U.S., at 138–40, 13 FEP Cases, at 1663.

Here, by comparison, petitioner has not merely refused to extend to women a benefit that men cannot and do not receive, but has imposed on women a substantial burden that men need not suffer. The distinction between benefits and burdens is more than one of semantics. We held in *Gilbert* that § 703(a)(1) did not require that greater economic benefits be paid to one sex or the other "because of their different roles in the scheme of existence," *Gilbert, supra,* 429 U.S., at 139 n. 17, 13 FEP Cases, at 1663. But that holding does not allow us to read § 703(a)(2) to permit an employer to burden female employees in such a way as to deprive them of employment opportunities because of their different role.

Recognition that petitioner's facially neutral seniority system does deprive women of employment opportunities because of their sex does not end the inquiry under § 703(a)(2) of Title VII. If a company's business necessitates the adoption of particular leave policies, Title VII does not prohibit the company from applying these policies to all leaves of absence, including pregnancy leaves; Title VII is not violated even though the policies may burden female employess. *Griggs, supra,* at 431, 3 FEP Cases, at 177; *Dothard* v. *Rawlinson,* 433 U.S. \_\_\_\_, \_\_\_\_ n. 14, 15 FEP Cases 10, 15 (1977). But we agree with the District Court in this case that since there was no proof of any business necessity adduced with respect to the policies in question that court was entitled to "assume no justification exists." 384 F. Supp., at 771, 10 FEP Cases, at 78.

## II

On the basis of the evidence presented to the District Court, petitioner's policy of not awarding sick-leave pay to pregnant employees is legally indistinguishable from the disability insurance program upheld in *Gilbert, supra.* As in *Gilbert,* petitioner compensates employees for limited periods of time during which the employee must miss work because of a non-job related illness or disability. As in *Gilbert,* the compensation is not extended to pregnancy-related absences. We emphasized in *Gilbert* that exclusions of this kind are not *per se* violations of Title VII: "an exclusion of pregnancy from a disability-benefits plan providing general coverage is not a gender-based discrimination at all." 429 U.S., at 136, 13 FEP Cases, at 1661. Only if a plaintiff through the presentation of other evidence can demonstrate that exclusion of pregnancy from the compensated conditions is a mere "[pretext] designed to effect an invidious discrimination against the members of one sex or the other" does Title VII apply. *Ibid.*

In *Gilbert,* evidence had been introduced indicating that women drew substantially greater sums than did men from General Electric's disability insurance program, even though it excluded pregnancy. *Id.,* at 130–31, nn. 9 and 10, 13 FEP Cases, at 1660. But our holding did not depend on this evidence. The District Court in *Gilbert* expressly declined to find "that the present actuarial value of the coverage was equal as between men and women." We upheld the disability program on the ground "that neither [was] there a finding, nor was there any evidence which would support a finding, that the financial benefits of the Plan 'worked to discriminate against any definable group or class in terms of the aggregate risk protection derived by that group or class from the program.' " *Id.,* at 138, 13 FEP Cases, at 1003. When confronted by a facially neutral plan, whose only fault is underinclusiveness, the burden is on the plaintiff to show that the plan discriminates on the basis of sex in violation of Title VII. *Albemarle Paper Co.* v. *Moody,* 422 U.S. 405, 425, 10 FEP Cases 1181, 1190 (1975); *McDonnell Douglas Corp.* v. *Green,* 411 U.S. 792, 802, 5 FEP Cases 965, 969 (1973).

We again need not decide whether, when confronted by a facially neutral plan, it is necessary to prove intent to establish a prima facie violation of § 703(a)(1). Cf. *McDonnell Douglas Corp., supra,* at 802–806, 5 FEP Cases, at 969–70 (1973). Griggs, supra, held that a violation of § 703(a)(2) can be established by proof of a discriminatory effect. But it is difficult to perceive how exclusion of pregnancy from a disability insurance plan or sick leave compensation program "deprives an individual of employment opportunities" or "otherwise adversely affects his status as an employee" in violation of § 703(a)(2). The direct effect of the exclusion is merely a loss of income for the period the employee is not at work; such an exclusion has no direct effect upon either employment opportunities or job status. Plaintiff's attack in Gilbert, supra, was brought under § 703(a)(1), which would appear to be the proper section of Title VII under which to analyze questions of sick leave or disability payments.

Respondent failed to prove even a discriminatory effect with respect to petitioner's sick-leave plan. She candidly concedes in her brief before this Court that "petitioner's Sick Leave benefit plan is, in and of itself, for all intents and purposes, the same as the Weekly Sickness and Accident Insurance Plan examined in *Gilbert*" and that "if the exclusion of sick pay was the only manner in which respondent had been treated differently by petitioner, *Gilbert* would control." Respondent, however, contends that because petitioner has violated Title VII by its policy respecting seniority following return from pregnancy leave, the sick-leave pay differentiation must also fall.

But this conclusion by no means follows from the premise. Respondent herself abandoned attacks on other aspects of petitioner's employment policies following rulings adverse to her by the District Court, a position scarcely consistent with her present one. We of course recognized in both *Geduldig* v. *Aiello,* 417 U.S. 484, 8 FEP Cases 97 (1974), and in *Gilbert, supra,* that the facial neutrality of an employee benefit plan would not end analysis if it could be shown "that distinctions involving pregnancy are mere pretexts designed to effect an invidious discrimination against the members of one sex or the other. . . ." *Gilbert, supra,* at 135, 13 FEP Cases, at 1661. Petitioner's refusal to allow pregnant employees to retain their accumulated seniority may be deemed relevant by the trier of fact in deciding whether petitioner's sick-leave plan was such a pretext. But it most certainly does not require such a finding by a trier of fact, to say nothing of the making of such a finding as an original matter by this Court.

The District Court sitting as a trier of fact made no such finding in this case, and we are not advised whether it was requested to or not. The decision of the Court of Appeals was not based on any such finding, but instead embodied generally the same line of reasoning as the Court of Appeals for the Fourth Circuit followed in its opinion in *General Electric Co.* v. *Gilbert,* 519 F.2d 661, 10 FEP Cases 1201 (1975). Since we rejected that line of reasoning in our opinion in Gilbert, supra, the judgment of the Court of Appeals with respect to petitioner's sick pay policies must be vacated. That court and the District Court are in a better position than we are to know whether respondent adequately preserved in those courts the right to proceed further in the District Court on the theory which we have just described.[6]

---

[6] Our Brother POWELL in his concurring opinion suggests that we also remand to allow respondent to develop a theory not articulated to us, viz., that petitioner's sick-leave plan is monetarily worth more to men than to women. He suggests that this expansive remand is required because at the time respondent formulated her case "the Court of Appeals uniformly had held that any disability plan that treated pregnancy differently from other disability was *per se* violative of Title VII." *Post,* p. 2. But respondent's complaint was filed in the District Court on July 1, 1974, a pretrial order was entered by that court setting forth the plaintiff's theory and the defendant's theory on August 28, 1974; and the District Court's memorandum and order for judgment was filed on November 4, 1974. The first of the Court of Appeals cases which our Brother POWELL refers to is *Wetzel* v. *Liberty Mutual Insurance Co.,* 511 F.2d 199, 9 FEP Cases 227 (CA3 1975), which was decided on February 11, 1975. See Opinion of BRENNAN, J., dissenting in *General Electric Co.* v. *Gilbert,* 429 U.S. 125, 147, 13 FEP Cases 1657, 1666 (1976). Not only at the time that respondent filed a complaint, but at the time the District Court rendered its decision, *Geduldig* v. *Aiello,* 417 U.S. 484, 8 FEP Cases 97 (1974), had been very recently decided, and the most that can be said on respondent's behalf is that the question of whether the analysis of that case would be carried over to cognate sections of Title VII was an open one. Our opinion in *Gilbert* on this and other issues, of course, speaks for itself; we do not think it can rightly be characterized as so drastic a change in the law as it was understood to exist in 1974 as to enable respondent to raise or reopen issues on remand that she would not under settled principle be otherwise able to do. We assume that the Court of Appeals and the District Court will apply these latter principles in deciding what claims may be open to respondent on remand.

*Affirmed in part, vacated in part, and remanded.*

MR. JUSTICE POWELL, with whom MR. JUSTICE BRENNAN and MR. JUSTICE MARSHALL join, concurring in the result and concurring in part: I join Part I of the opinion of the Court affirming the decision of the Court of Appeals that petitioner's policy denying accumulated seniority for job-bidding purposes to female employees returning from pregnancy leave violates Title VII.[1]

I also concur in the result in Part II, for the legal status under Title VII of petitioner's policy of denying accumulated sick-pay benefits to female employees while on pregnancy leave requires further factual development in light of *General Electric Co.* v. *Gilbert*, 429 U.S. 125, 13 FEP Cases 1657 (1976). I write separately, however, because the Court appears to have constricted unnecessarily the scope of inquiry on remand by holding prematurely that respondent has failed to meet her burden of establishing a prima facie case that petitioner's sick-leave policy is discriminatory under Title VII. This case was tried in the District Court and reviewed in the Court of Appeals before our decision in *Gilbert*. The appellate court upheld her claim in accord with the then uniform view of the courts of appeals that any disability plan that treated pregnancy differently from other disabilities was *per se* violative of Title VII.[2] Since respondent had no reason to make the showing of gender-based discrimination required by *Gilbert*, I would follow our usual practice of vacating the judgment below and remanding to permit the lower court to reconsider its sick-leave ruling in light of our intervening decision.

The issue is not simply one of burden of proof, which properly rests with the Title VII plaintiff, *Albemarle Paper Co.* v. *Moody*, 422 U.S. 405, 425, 10 FEP Cases 1181, 1190 (1975); *McDonnell Douglas Corp.* v. *Green*, 411 U.S. 792, 802, 5 FEP Cases 965, 969 (1973), but of a "full opportunity for presentation of the relevant facts," *Harris* v. *Nelson*, 394 U.S. 286, 298 (1969). Given the meandering course that Title VII adjudication has taken, final resolution of a lawsuit in this Court often has not been possible because the parties or the lower courts proceeded on what was ultimately an erroneous theory of the case. Where the mistaken theory

---

[1] I would add, however, that petitioner's seniority policy, on its face, does not "appear[] to be neutral in its treatment of male and female employees." *Ante*, at 3, 16 FEP Cases, at 138. As the District Court noted below, "only pregnant women are required to take leave and thereby lose job-bidding seniority and no leave is required in other non-work related disabilities. . . ." 384 F. Supp. 765, 771, 10 FEP Cases 73, 78 (MD Tenn. 1974). This mandatory maternity leave is not "identical to the formal leave of absence granted to employees, male or female, in order that they may pursue additional education." *Ante*, at 3 n. 2, 16 FEP Cases, at 138.

[2] See cases cited in *General Electric Co.* v. *Gilbert*, 429 U.S. 125, 147, 13 FEP Cases 1657, 1666 (1976) (BRENNAN, J., dissenting).

Gilbert held that the rationale articulated in *Geduldig* v. *Aiello*, 417 U.S. 484, 8 FEP Cases 97 (1974), involving a challenge on equal protection grounds, also applied to a Title VII claim with respect to the treatment of pregnancy in benefit plans. See 429 U.S., at 133–36, 13 FEP Cases, at 1663–64. Since *Geduldig* itself was silent on the Title VII issue, the Courts of Appeals not unreasonably failed to anticipate the extent to which the *Geduldig* rationale would be deemed applicable in the statutory context. See *Washington* v. *Davis*, 426 U.S. 229, 246–48, 12 FEP Cases 1415 (1976).

is premised on the pre-existing understanding of the law, and where the record as constituted does not foreclose the arguments made necessary by our ruling, I would prefer to remand the controversy and permit the lower courts to pass on the new contentions in light of whatever additional evidence is deemed necessary.

For example, in *Albemarle Paper Co.* v. *Moody, supra,* the Court approved the Court of Appeals' conclusion that the employer had not proved the job relatedness of its testing program, but declined to permit immediate issuance of an injunction against all use of testing in the plant. The Court thought that a remand to the District Court was indicated in part because "[t]he appropriate standard of proof for job relatedness has not been clarified until today," and the plaintiffs "have not until today been specifically apprised of their opportunity to present evidence that even validated tests might be a 'pretext' for discrimination in light of alternative selection procedures available to the Company." 422 U.S., at 436, 10 FEP Cases, at 1194.

Similarly, in *International Bhd. of Teamsters* v. *United States,* 431 U.S. 324, 14 FEP Cases 1514 (1977), we found a remand for further factual development appropriate because the Government had employed an erroneous evidentiary approach that precluded satisfaction of its burden of identifying which nonapplicant employees were victims of the employer's unlawful discrimination and thus entitled to a retroactive seniority award. "While it may be true that many of the nonapplicant employees desired and would have applied for line-driver jobs but for their knowledge of the company's policy of discrimination, the Government must carry its burden of proof, with respect to each specific individual, at the remedial hearings to be conducted by the District Court on remand." *Id.,* at 371, 14 FEP Cases, at 1534. Cf. *Brown* v. *Illinois,* 422 U.S. 590, 613–616 (1975) (POWELL, J., concurring in part).

Here, respondent has abandoned the theory that enabled her to prevail in the District Court and the Court of Appeals. Instead, she urges that her case is distinguishable from *Gilbert:*

"Respondent submits that because the exclusion of sick pay is only one of the many ways in which female employees who experience pregnancy are treated differently by petitioner, the holding in *Gilbert* is not controlling. Upon examination of the overall manner in which female employees who experience pregnancy are treated by petitioner, it becomes plain that petitioner's policies are much more pervasive than the mere under-inclusiveness of the Sickness and Accident Insurance Plan in *Gilbert.*" Brief for the Respondent 10.

At least two distinguishing characteristics are identified by respondent. First, as found by the District Court, only pregnant women are required to take a leave of absence and are denied sick-leave benefits while in all other cases of nonoccupational disability sick-leave benefits are available. 384 F. Supp., at 767, 771, 10 FEP Cases, at 75, 78. Second, the sick-leave policy is necessarily related to petitioner's discriminatory denial of job-bidding seniority to pregnant women on mandatory maternity leave, presumably because both policies flow from the premise that a female employee is no longer in active service when she becomes pregnant.

Although respondent's theory is not fully articulated, she presents a plausible contention, one not required to have been raised until *Gilbert* and not foreclosed by the stipulated evidence of record, see *Gilbert*, 429 U.S., at 130-31, nn. 9 and 10, 13 FEP Cases, at 1659, 1660, or the concurrent findings of the lower courts, see *Village of Arlington Heights* v. *Metropolitan Housing Development Corp.*, 429 U.S. 252, 270 (1977). It is not inconceivable that on remand respondent will be able to show that the combined operation of petitioner's mandatory maternity leave policy and denial of accumulated sick-pay benefits yielded significantly less net compensation for petitioner's female employees than for the class of male employees. A number of the former, but not the latter, endured forced absence from work without sick pay or other compensation. The parties stipulated that between July 2, 1965 and August 27, 1974, petitioner had placed 12 employees on pregnancy leave, and that some of these employees were on leave for periods of two months or more. App. 33. It is possible that these women had not exhausted their sick-pay benefits at the time they were compelled to take a maternity leave, and that the denial of sick pay for this period of absence resulted in a relative loss of net compensation for petitioner's female workforce. Petitioner's male employees, on the other hand, are not subject to a mandatory leave policy, and are eligible to receive compensation in some form for any period of absence from work due to sickness or disability.

In short, I would not foreclose the possibility that the facts as developed on remand will support a finding that "the package is in fact worth more to men than to women." *Gilbert*, 429 U.S., at 138, 13 FEP Cases, at 1613. If such a finding were made, I would view respondent's case as not barred by *Gilbert*. In that case, the Court related: "[t]he District Court noted the evidence introduced at trial, a good deal of it stipulated, concerning the relative cost to General Electric of providing benefits under the Plan to male and female employees, all of which indicated that, with pregnancy-related disabilities excluded, the cost to the plan was at least as high, if not substantially higher, than the cost per male employee." 429 U.S. at 130, 13 FEP Cases, at 1660. The District Court also "found that the inclusion of pregnancy-related disabilities within the scope of the Plan would 'increase G.E.'s (disability benefits plan) costs by an amount which, though large, is at this time undeterminable.' 375 F. Supp., at 378, 7 FEP Cases, at 804–805." *Id.*, at 131, 13 FEP Cases, at 1660. While the District Court declined to make an explicit finding that the actuarial value of the coverage was equal between men and women, it may have been referring simply to the quantum and specificity of proof necessary to establish a "business necessity" defense. See 375 F. Supp. 367, 382–83, 7 FEP Cases 796, 808 (ED Va. 1974). In any event, in *Gilbert* this Court viewed the evidence of record as precluding a prima facie showing of discrimination in "compensation" contrary to § 703(a)(1). "Whatever the ultimate probative value of the evidence introduced before the District Court on this subject . . . at the very least it tended to illustrate that the selection of risks covered by the Plan did not operate, in fact, to discriminate against women." 429 U.S. at 137–38, 13 FEP Cases, at 1663. As the record had developed in *Gilbert*, there was no basis for a remand.

I do not view the record in this case as precluding a finding of discrimination in compensation within the principles enunciated in *Gilbert*.[6] I would simply remand the sick-pay issue for further proceedings in light of our decision in that case.

Mr. Justice Stevens, concurring in the judgment: Petitioner enforces two policies that treat pregnant employees less favorably than other employees who incur a temporary disability. First, they are denied seniority benefits during their absence from work and thereafter; second, they are denied sick pay during their absence. The Court holds that the former policy is unlawful whereas the latter is lawful. I concur in the Court's judgment, but because I believe that its explanation of the legal distinction between the two policies may engender some confusion among those who must make compliance decisions on a day-to-day basis, I advance a separate, and rather pragmatic, basis for reconciling the two parts of the decision with each other and with *General Electric Co.* v. *Gilbert*, 429 U.S. 125, 13 FEP Cases 1657.

The general problem is to decide when a company policy which attaches a special burden to the risk of absenteeism caused by pregnancy is a *prima facie* violation of the statutory prohibition against sex discrimination. The answer "always," which I had thought quite plainly correct,[1] is foreclosed by the Courts holding in *Gilbert*. The answer

---

[6] The Court's opinion at one point appears to read *Gilbert* as holding that a Title VII plaintiff in a § 703(a)(1) case must demonstrate that "exclusion of pregnancy from the compensated conditions is a mere '(pretext).'" *Ante*, at 7, 16 FEP Cases, at 139–40. Later in its opinion, the Court states that we need not decide "whether, when confronted by a facially neutral plan, it is necessary to prove intent to establish a prima facie violation of § 703(a)(1)." Ante, at 8, 16 FEP Cases, at 140. As noted *supra*, n. 1, I cannot assume that petitioner's seniority policy in this case is facially neutral. Moreover, although there may be some ambiguity in the language in *Gilbert*, see concurring opinions of Mr. Justice Stewart and Mr. Justice Blackmun, 429 U.S., at 146, 13 FEP Cases, at 1666, I viewed our decision in that case as grounded primarily on the emphasized fact that no discrimination in compensation as required by § 703(a)(1) had been shown. Indeed, a fair reading of the evidence in *Gilbert* demonstrated that the total compensation of women in terms of disability-benefit plans well may have exceeded that of men. I do not suggest that mathematical exactitude can or need be shown in every § 703(a)(1) case. But essential equality in *compensation* for comparable work is at the heart of § 703(a)(1). In my view, proof of discrimination in this respect would establish a prima facie violation.

[1] "An analysis of the effect of a company's rules relating to absenteeism would be appropriate if those rules referred only to neutral criteria, such as whether an absence was voluntary or involuntary, or perhaps particularly costly. This case, however, does not involve rules of that kind.

"Rather, the rule at issue places the risk of absence caused by pregnancy in a class by itself. By definition, such a rule discriminates on account of sex; for it is the capacity to become pregnant which primarily differentiates the female from the male. The analysis is the same whether the rule relates to hiring, promotion, the acceptability of an excuse for absence, or an exclusion from a disability insurance plan." *General Electric Co.* v. *Gilbert*, 429 U.S. 125, 161–62, 13 FEP Cases 1657, 1673 (Stevens, J., dissenting).

"never" would seem to be dictated by the Court's view that a discrimination against pregnancy is "not a gender-based discrimination at all." [2] The Court has, however, made it clear that the correct answer is "sometimes." Even though a plan which frankly and unambiguously discriminates against pregnancy is "facially neutral," the Court will find it unlawful if it has a "discriminatory effect." [3] The question, then, is how to identify this discriminatory effect.

Two possible answers are suggested by the Court. The Court seems to rely on (a) the difference between a benefit and a burden, and (b) the difference between § 703(a)(2) and § 703(a)(1). In my judgment, both of these differences are illusory.[4] I agree with the Court that the effect of the respondent's seniority plan is significantly different from that of the General Electric disability plan in *Gilbert,* but I suggest that the difference may be described in this way: although the *Gilbert* Court was unwilling to hold that discrimination against pregnancy—as compared with other physical disabilities—is discrimination on account of sex, it may nevertheless be true that discrimination against pregnant or formerly pregnant employees—as compared with other employees—does constitute sex discrimination. This distinction may be pragmatically expressed in terms of whether the employer has a policy which adversely affects a woman beyond the term of her pregnancy leave.

Although the opinion in *Gilbert* characterizes as "facially neutral" a company policy which differentiates between an absence caused by pregnancy and an absence caused by illness, the factual context of *Gilbert* limits the reach of that broad characterization. Under the Court's reasoning, the disability plan in *Gilbert* did not discriminate against pregnant employees or formerly pregnant employees while they were working for the company. If an employee, whether pregnant or nonpregnant, contracted the measles, he or she would receive disability benefits; moreover,

[2] In *Gilbert, id.,* at 136, 13 FEP Cases at 1662, the Court held that "an exclusion of pregnancy from a disability benefits plan providing general coverage is not a gender-based discrimination at all." Consistently with that holding, the Court today states that a "decision not to treat pregnancy as a disease or disability for purposes of seniority retention is not on its face a discriminatory policy." *Ante,* at 4, 16 FEP Cases, at 138.

[3] *Ante,* at 4, 16 FEP Cases, at 138; 429 U.S., at 146, 13 FEP Cases, at 1666 (STEWART and BLACKMUN, JJ., concurring).

[4] Differences between benefits and burdens cannot provide a meaningful test of discrimination since, by hypothesis, the favored class is always benefited and the disfavored class is equally burdened. The grant of seniority is a benefit which is not shared by the burdened class; conversely, the denial of sick pay is a burden which the benefited class need not bear.

The Court's second apparent ground of distinction is equally unsatisfactory. The Court suggests that its analysis of the seniority plan is different because that plan was attacked under § 703(a)(2) of Title VII, not § 703(a)(1). Again, I must confess that I do not understand the relevance of this distinction. It is true that § 703(a)(1) refers to "discrimination" and § 703(a)(2) does not. But the Court itself recognizes that this is not significant since a violation of § 703(a)(2) occurs when a facially neutral policy has a "*discriminatory effect.*" *Ante,* at 4, 16 FEP Cases, at 138 (emphasis added). The Court also suggests that § 703(a)(1) may contain a requirement of intent not present in § 703(a)(2). Whatever the merits of that suggestion, it is apparent that it does not form the basis for any differentiation between the two subparagraphs of § 703 in this case, since the Court expressly refuses to decide the issue. *Ante,* at 8, 16 FEP Cases, at 140.

an employee returning from maternity leave would also receive those benefits. On the other hand, pregnancy, or an illness occurring while absent on maternity leave, was not covered.[5] During that period of maternity leave, the pregnant woman was temporarily cut off from the benefits extended by the Company's plan. At all other times, the woman was treated the same as other employees in terms of her eligibility for the plan's benefits.

The Company's seniority plan in this case has a markedly different effect. In attempting to return to work, the formerly pregnant woman is deprived of all previously accumulated seniority. The policy affects both her ability to re-enter the work force, and her compensation when she does return.[6] The Company argues that these effects are permissible because they flow from its initial decision to treat pregnancy as an unexcused absence. But this argument misconceives the scope of the protection afforded by *Gilbert* to such initial decisions. For the General Electric plan did not attach any consequences to the condition of pregnancy that extended beyond the period of maternity leave. *Gilbert* allowed the employer to treat pregnancy leave as a temporal gap in the full employment status of a woman. During that period, the employer may treat the employee in a manner consistent with the determination that pregnancy is not an illness.[7] In this case, however, the Company's seniority policy has an adverse impact on the employee's status after pregnancy leave is terminated. The formerly pregnant person is permanently disadvantaged as compared to the rest of the work force. And since the persons adversely affected by this policy comprise an exclusively female class, the Company's plan has an obvious discriminatory effect.[8]

Under this analysis, it is clear that petitioner's seniority rule discriminating against formerly pregnant employees is invalid. It is equally clear that the denial of sick pay during maternity leave is consistent with the

---

[5] See *Gilbert*, 429 U.S., at 129 n. 4, 13 FEP Cases, at 1659. Although I have the greatest difficulty with the Court's holding in *Gilbert* that it was permissible to refuse coverage for an illness contracted during maternity leave, I suppose this aspect of *Gilbert* may be explained by the notion that any illness occurring at that time is treated as though it were attributable to pregnancy, and therefore is embraced within the area of permissible discrimination against pregnancy.

[6] *Ante*, at 2, 16 FEP Cases, at 137–38.

[7] These two limitations—that the effect of the employer's policy be limited to the period of the pregnancy leave and that it be consistent with the determination that pregnancy is not an illness—serve to focus the disparate effect of the policy on pregnancy rather than on pregnant or formerly pregnant employees. Obviously, policies which attach a burden to pregnancy also burden pregnant or formerly pregnant persons. This consequence is allowed by *Gilbert*, but only to the extent that the focus of the policy is, as indicated above, on the physical condition rather than the person.

[8] This analysis is consistent with the approach taken by lower courts to post-*Gilbert* claims of pregnancy-based discrimination, which have recognized that *Gilbert* "has nothing to do with foreclosing employment opportunity." *Cook* v. *Arentzen*, 14 E.P.D. ¶ 7544, at 4702, 14 FEP Cases 1643 (CA4 1977); *MacLennan* v. *American Airlines, Inc.*, 46 LW 2215, 15 FEP Cases 1684 (Va. Oct. 21, 1977) (addressing the question of when, if ever, an employer can require an employee to take pregnancy leave). This case does not pose the issue of when an employer may require an employee to take pregnancy leave. *Ante*, at 2 n. 1, 16 FEP Cases, at 137.

*Gilbert* rationale, since the Company was free to withhold those benefits during that period.[9]

As is evident from my dissent in *Gilbert,* I would prefer to decide this case on a simpler rationale. Since that preference is foreclosed by *Gilbert,* I concur in the Court's judgment on the understanding that as the law now stands, although some discrimination against pregnancy—as compared with other physical disabilities—is permissible, discrimination against pregnant or formerly pregnant employees is not.

## (5) *Pension Benefits*

### CITY OF LOS ANGELES v. MANHART

*Supreme Court of the United States, 1978*
*435 U.S. 702, 17 FEP Cases 395*

Mr. Justice Stevens delivered the opinion of the Court.

As a class, women live longer than men. For this reason, the Los Angeles Department of Water and Power required its female employees to make larger contributions to its pension fund than its male employees. We granted certiorari to decide whether this practice discriminated against individual female employees because of their sex in violation of § 703(a)(1) of the Civil Rights Act of 1964, as amended.

For many years the Department has administered retirement, disability, and death benefit programs for its employees. Upon retirement each employee is eligible for a monthly retirement benefit computed as a fraction of his or her salary multiplied by years of service. The monthly benefits for men and women of the same age, seniority, and salary are equal. Benefits are funded entirely by contributions from the employees and the Department, augmented by the income earned on those contributions. No private insurance company is involved in the administration or payment of benefits.

Based on a study of mortality tables and its own experience, the Department determined that its 2,000 female employees, on the average, will live a few years longer than its 10,000 male employees. The cost of a pension for the average retired female is greater than for the average

---

[9] In his concurring opinion, Mr. Justice Powell seems to suggest that, even when the employer's disparate treatment of a pregnant employee is limited to the period of the pregnancy leave, it may still violate Title VII if the Company's rule has a greater impact on one sex than another. *Ante,* at 5–6, 16 FEP Cases, at 145. If this analysis does not require an overruling of *Gilbert* it must be applied with great caution, since the laws of probability would invalidate an inordinate number of rules on such a theory. It is not clear to me what showing, beyond "mathematical exactitude," see Powell, J., concurring, *ante,* at 6–7, n. 6, 16 FEP Cases, at 145, is necessary before this Court will hold that a classification, which is by definition gender-specific, discriminates on the basis of sex. Usually, statistical disparities aid a court in determining whether an apparently neutral classification is, in effect, gender or race specific. Here, of course, statistics would be unnecessary to prove that point. In all events, I agree with the Court that this issue is not presented to us in this case, and accordingly concur in the Court's determination of the proper scope of the remand.

male retiree because more monthly payments must be made to the average women. The Department therefore required female employees to make monthly contributions to the fund which were 14.84 percent higher than the contributions required of comparable male employees. Because employee contributions were withheld from pay checks, a female employee took home less pay than a male employee earning the same salary.

Since the effective date of the Equal Employment Opportunity Act of 1972, the Department has been an employer within the meaning of Title VII of the Civil Rights Act of 1964. See 42 U.S.C. § 2000e. In 1973, respondents brought this suit in the United States District Court for the Central District of California on behalf of a class of women employed or formerly employed by the Department. They prayed for an injunction and restitution of excess contributions.

While this action was pending, the California Legislature enacted a law prohibiting certain municipal agencies from requiring female employees to make higher pension fund contributions than males. The Department therefore amended its plan, effective January 1, 1975. The current plan draws no distinction, either in contributions or in benefits, on the basis of sex. On a motion for summary judgment, the District Court held that the contribution differential violated § 703(a)(1) and ordered a refund of all excess contributions made before the amendment of the plan. The United States Court of Appeals for the Ninth Circuit affirmed.

The Department and various *amici curiae* contend that: (1) the differential in take-home pay between men and women was not discrimination within the meaning of § 703(a)(1) because it was offset by a difference in the value of the pension benefits provided to the two classes of employees; (2) the differential was based on a factor "other than sex" within the meaning of the Equal Pay Act and was therefore protected by the so-called Bennett Amendment; (3) the rationale of *General Electric Co.* v. *Gilbert,* 429 U.S. 125, requires reversal; and (4) in any event, the retroactive monetary recovery is unjustified. We consider these contentions in turn.

## I

There are both real and fictional differences between women and men. It is true that the average man is taller than the average woman; it is not true that the average woman driver is more accident-prone than the average man. Before the Civil Rights Act of 1964 was enacted, an employer could fashion his personnel policies on the basis of assumptions about the differences between men and women, whether or not the assumptions were valid.

It is now well recognized that employment decisions cannot be predicated on mere "stereotyped" impressions about the characteristics of males or females. Myths and purely habitual assumptions about a woman's inability to perform certain kinds of work are no longer acceptable reasons for refusing to employ qualified individuals, or for paying them less. This case does not, however, involve a fictional difference between men and women. It involves a generalization that the parties accept as unquestionably true: women, as a class, do live longer than men. The Department treated its women employees differently from its men employees because the two classes are in fact different. It is equally true, however, that all individuals in the respective classes do not share the characteristic which differentiates the average class representatives. Many women do not live as long as the average man and many men outlive the average woman. The question, therefore, is whether the existence or nonexistence of "discrimination" is to be determined by comparison of class characteristics or individual characteristics. A "stereotyped" answer to that question may not be the same as the answer which the language and purpose of the statute command.

The statute makes it unlawful "to discriminate against any *individual* with respect to his compensation, terms, conditions or privileges of employment, because of such *individual's* race, color, religion, sex, or national origin." 42 U.S.C. § 2000e–2(a)(1) (emphasis added). The statute's focus on the individual is unambiguous. It precludes treatment of individuals as simply components of a racial, religious, sexual, or national class. If height is required for a job, a tall woman may not be refused employment merely because, on the average, women are too short. Even a true generalization about the class is an insufficient reason for disqualifying an individual to whom the generalization does not apply.

That proposition is of critical importance in this case because there is no assurance that any individual woman working for the Department will actually fit the generalization on which the Department's policy is based. Many of those individuals will not live as long as the average man. While they were working, those individuals received smaller paychecks because of their sex, but they will receive no compensating advantage when they retire.

It is true, of course, that while contributions are being collected from the employees, the Department cannot know which individuals will predecease the average woman. Therefore, unless women as a class are assessed an extra charge, they will be subsidized, to some extent, by the class of male employees. It follows, according to the Department, that fairness to its class of male employees justifies the extra assessment against all of its female employees.

But the question of fairness to various classes affected by the statute is essentially a matter of policy for the legislature to address. Congress has decided that classifications based on sex, like those based on national origin or race, are unlawful. Actuarial studies could unquestionably identify differences in life expectancy based on race or national origin, as well as sex. But a statute which was designed to make race irrelevant in the employment market, see *Griggs* v. *Duke Power Co.*, 401 U.S. 424, 436, could not reasonably be construed to permit a take-home pay differential based on a racial classification.

Even if the statutory language were less clear, the basic policy of the statute requires that we focus on fairness to individuals rather than fairness to classes. Practices which classify employees in terms of religion, race, or sex tend to preserve traditional assumptions about groups rather than thoughtful scrutiny of individuals. The generalization involved in this case illustrates the point. Separate mortality tables are easily interpreted as reflecting innate differences between the sexes; but a significant part of the longevity differential may be explained by the social fact that men are heavier smokers than women.

Finally, there is no reason to believe that Congress intended a special definition of discrimination in the context of employee group insurance coverage. It is true that insurance is concerned with events that are individually unpredictable, but that is characteristic of many employment decisions. Individual risks, like individual performance, may not be predicted by resort to classifications proscribed by Title VII. Indeed, the fact that this case involves a group insurance program highlights a basic flaw in the department's fairness argument. For when insurance risks are grouped, the better risks always subsidize the poorer risks. Healthy persons subsidize medical benefits for the less healthy; unmarried workers subsidize the pensions of married workers; [18] persons who eat, drink, or smoke to excess may subsidize pension benefits for persons whose habits are more temperate. Treating different classes of risks as though they were the same for purposes of group insurance is a common practice which has never been considered inherently unfair. To insure the flabby and the fit as though they were equivalent risks may be more common than treating men and women alike; [19] but nothing more than habit makes one "subsidy" seem less fair than the other.[20]

An employment practice which requires 2,000 individuals to contribute more money into a fund than 10,000 other employees simply because each of them is a woman, rather than a man, is in direct conflict with both the

18 [Footnotes numbered as in original.—Ed.] A study of life expectancy in the United States for 1949–1951 showed that 20-year-old men could expect to live to 60.6 years of age if they were divorced. If married, they could expect to reach 70.9 years of age, a difference of more than 10 years. R. Retherford, THE CHANGING SEX DIFFERENTIAL IN MORTALITY 93 (1975).

19 The record indicates, however, that the Department has funded its death benefit plan by equal contributions from male and female employees. A death benefit—unlike a pension benefit—has less value for persons with longer life expectancies. Under the Department's concept of fairness, then, this neutral funding of death benefits is unfair to women as a class.

20 A variation on the Department's fairness theme is the suggestion that a gender-neutral pension plan would itself violate Title VII because of its disproportionately heavy impact on male employees. Cf. Griggs v. Duke Power Co., 401 U.S. 424. This suggestion has no force in the sex discrimination context because each retiree's total pension benefits are ultimately determined by his actual life span; any differential in benefits paid to men and women in the aggregate is thus "based on [a] factor other than sex," and consequently immune from challenge under the Equal Pay Act, 29 U.S.C. § 206(d); cf. n 24, infra. Even under Title VII itself—assuming disparate impact analysis applies to fringe benefits, cf. Nashville Gas Co. v. Satty, No. 75–536, slip op., at 8—the male employees would not prevail. Even a completely neutral practice will inevitably have some disproportionate impact on one group or another. Griggs does not imply, and this Court has never held, that discrimination must always be inferred from such consequences.

language and the policy of the Act. Such a practice does not pass the simple test of whether the evidence shows "treatment of a person in a manner which but for the person's sex would be different." It constitutes discrimination and is unlawful unless exempted by the Equal Pay Act or some other affirmative justification.

## II

Shortly before the enactment of Title VII in 1964, Senator Bennett proposed an amendment providing that a compensation differential based on sex would not be unlawful if it was authorized by the Equal Pay Act, which had been passed a year earlier. The Equal Pay Act requires employers to pay members of both sexes the same wages for equivalent work, except when the differential is pursuant to one of four specified exceptions.[23] The Department contends that the fourth exception applies here. That exception authorizes a "differential based on any other factor other than sex."

The Department argues that the different contributions exacted from men and women were based on the factor of longevity rather than sex. It is plain, however, that any individual's life expectancy is based on a number of factors, of which sex is only one. The record contains no evidence that any factor other than the employee's sex was taken into account in calculating the 14.84 percent differential between the respective contributions by men and women. We agree with Judge Duniway's observation that one cannot "say that an actuarial distinction based entirely on sex is 'based on any other factor other than sex.' Sex is exactly what it is based on." 553 F.2d, at 588.[24]

[23] The Equal Pay Act provides, in part:
"No employer having employees subject to any provisions of this section shall discriminate, within any establishment in which such employees are employed, between employees on the basis of sex by paying wages to employees in such establishment at a rate less than the rate at which he pays wages to employees of the opposite sex in such establishment for equal work on jobs the performance of which requires equal skill, effort, and responsibility, and which are performed under similar working conditions, except where such payment is made pursuant to (i) a seniority system; (ii) a merit system; (iii) a system which measures earnings by quantity or quality of production; or (iv) a differential based on any other factor other than sex: *Provided*, That an employer who is paying a wage rate differential in violation of this subsection shall not, in order to comply with the provisions of this subsection, reduce the wage rate of any employee." 77 Stat. 56–57.
We need not decide whether retirement benefits or contributions to benefit plans are "wages" under the Act, because the Bennett Amendment extends the Act's four exceptions to all forms of "compensation" covered by Title VII. See n. 22, *supra*. The Department's pension benefits, and the contributions that maintain them, are "compensation" under Title VII. Cf. *Peters* v. *Missouri-Pacific R. Co.*, 483 F. 2d 490, 492 n. 3 (CA5 1973), *cert. denied*, 414 U.S. 1002.

[24] The Department's argument is specious because its contribution schedule distinguished only imperfectly between long-lived and short-lived employees, while distinguishing precisely between male and female employees. In contrast, an entirely gender-neutral system of contributions and benefits would result in differing retirement benefits precisely "based on" longevity, for retirees with long lives would always receive more money than comparable employees with short lives. Such a plan would also distinguish in a crude way between male and female pensioners, because of the difference in their average life spans. It is this sort of disparity—and not an explicitly gender-based differential—that the Equal Pay Act intended to authorize.

We are also unpersuaded by the Department's reliance on a colloquy between Senator Randolph and Senator Humphrey during the debate on the Civil Rights Act of 1964. Commenting on the Bennett Amendment, Senator Humphrey expressed his understanding that it would allow many differences in the treatment of men and women under industrial benefit plans, including earlier retirement options for women.[25] Though he did not address differences in employee contributions based on sex, Senator Humphrey apparently assumed that the 1964 Act would have little, if any, impact on existing pension plans. His statement cannot, however, fairly be made the sole guide to interpreting the Equal Pay Act, which had been adopted a year earlier; and it is the 1963 statute, with its exceptions, on which the Department ultimately relies. We conclude that Senator Humphrey's isolated comment on the Senate floor cannot change the effect of the plain language of the statute itself.[26]

## III

The Department argues that reversal is required by *General Electric Co.* v. *Gilbert*, 429 U.S. 125. We are satisfied, however, that neither the holding nor the reasoning of *Gilbert* is controlling.

In *Gilbert* the Court held that the exclusion of pregnancy from an

---

25 "MR. RANDOLPH: Mr. President. I wish to ask of the Senator from Minnesota [Mr. Humphrey], who is the effective manager of the pending bill, a clarifying question on the provisions of title VII.

"I have in mind that the social security system, in certain respects, treats men and women differently. For example, widows' benefits are paid automatically; but a widower qualifies only if he is disabled or if he was actually supported by his deceased wife. Also, the wife of a retired employee entitled to social security receives an additional old age benefit; but the husband of such an employee does not. These differences in treatment as I recall, are of long standing.

"Am I correct, I ask the Senator from Minnesota, in assuming that similar differences of treatment in industrial benefit plans, including earlier retirement options for women, may continue in operation under this bill, if it becomes law?

"MR. HUMPHREY: Yes. That point was made unmistakably clear earlier today by the adoption of the Bennett amendment; so there can be no doubt about it." 110 Cong. Rec. 13663–64 (1964).

26 The administrative constructions of this provision look in two directions. The Wage and Hour Administrator, who is charged with enforcing the Equal Pay Act, has never expressly approved different *employee* contribution rates, but he has said that either equal employer contributions or equal benefits will satisfy the Act. 29 CFR § 800.116(d) (1976). At the same time, he has stated that a wage differential based on differences in the average costs of employing men and women is not based on a "factor other than sex." 29 CFR § 800.151 (1976). The Administrator's reasons for the second ruling are illuminating:

"To group employees solely on the basis of sex for purposes of comparison of costs necessarily rests on the assumption that the sex factor alone may justify the wage differential—an assumption plainly contrary to the terms and purposes of the Equal Pay Act. Wage differentials so based would serve only to perpetuate and promote the very discrimination at which the Act is directed, because in any grouping by sex of the employees to which the cost data relates, the group cost experience is necessarily assessed against an individual of one sex without regard to whether it costs an employer more or less to employ such individual than a particular individual of the opposite sex under similar working conditions in jobs requiring equal skill effort, and responsibility." *Ibid.* To the extent that they conflict, we find that the reasoning of § 800.151 has more "power to persuade" than the *ipse dixit* of § 800.116. Cf. *Skidmore* v. *Swift & Co.*, 323 U.S. 134, 140.

employer's disability benefit plan did not constitute sex discrimination within the meaning of Title VII. Relying on the reasoning in *Geduldig* v. *Aiello,* 417 U.S. 484, the Court first held that the General Electric plan did not involve "discrimination based upon gender as such." [27] The two groups of potential recipients which that case concerned were pregnant women and nonpregnant persons. "While the first group is exclusively female, the second includes members of both sexes." 429 U.S., at 135. In contrast, each of the two groups of employees involved in this case is composed entirely and exclusively of members of the same sex. On its face, this plan discriminates on the basis of sex whereas the General Electric plan discriminated on the basis of a special physical disability.

In *Gilbert* the Court did note that the plan as actually administered had provided more favorable benefits to women as a class than to men as a class.[28] This evidence supported the conclusion that not only had plaintiffs failed to establish a prima facie case by proving that the plan was discriminatory on its face, but they had also failed to prove any discriminatory effect.[29]

In this case, however, the Department argues that the absence of a discriminatory effect on women as a class justifies an employment practice which, on its face, discriminated against individual employees because of their sex. But even if the Department's actuarial evidence is sufficient to prevent plaintiffs from establishing a prima facie case on the theory that the effect of the practice on women as a class was discriminatory, that evidence does not defeat the claim that the practice, on its face, discriminated against every individual woman employed by the Department.[30]

In essence, the Department is arguing that the prima facie showing of

[27] Quoting from the *Geduldig* opinion, the Court stated:
"[T]his case is thus a far cry from cases like *Reed* v. *Reed,* 404 U.S. 71 (1971), and *Frontiero* v. *Richardson,* 411 U.S. 677 (1973), involving discrimination based upon gender as such. The California insurance program does not exclude anyone from benefit eligibility because of gender but merely removes one physical condition—pregnancy—from the list of compensable disabilities." *Id.,* at 134.
After further quotation, the Court added:
"The quoted language from *Geduldig* leaves no doubt that our reason for rejecting appellee's equal protection claim in that case was that the exclusion of pregnancy from coverage under California's disability-benefit plan was not in itself discrimination based on sex." *Id.,* at 135.

[28] See 429 U.S., at 130–31, n. 9.

[29] As the Court recently noted in *Nashville Gas Co.* v. *Satty,* No. 75–536, slip op., at 7, the *Gilbert* holding "did not depend on this evidence." Rather, the holding rested on the plaintiff's failure to prove either facial discrimination or discriminatory effect.

[30] Some *amici* suggest that the Department's discrimination is justified by business necessity. They argue that, if no gender distinction is drawn, many male employees will withdraw from the plan, or even the Department, because they can get a better pension plan in the private market. But the Department has long required equal contributions to its death benefit plan, see n. 19, *supra,* and since 1975 it has required equal contributions to its pension plan. Yet the Department points to no "adverse selection" by the affected employees, presumably because an employee who wants to leave the plans must also leave his job, and few workers will quit because one of their fringe benefits could theoretically be obtained at a marginally lower price on the open market. In short, there has been no showing that sex distinctions are reasonably necessary to the normal operation of the Department's retirement plan.

discrimination based on evidence of different contributions for the respective sexes is rebutted by its demonstration that there is a like difference in the cost of providing benefits for the respective classes. That argument might prevail if Title VII contained a cost justification defense comparable to the affirmative defense available in a price discrimination suit.[31] But neither Congress nor the courts have recognized such a defense under Title VII.[32]

Although we conclude that the Department's practice violated Title VII, we do not suggest that the statute was intended to revolutionize the insurance and pension industries. All that is at issue today is a requirement that men and women make unequal contributions to an employer-operated pension fund. Nothing in our holding implies that it would be unlawful for an employer to set aside equal retirement contributions for each employee and let each retiree purchase the largest benefit which his or her accumulated contributions could command in the open market.[33] Nor does it call into question the insurance industry practice of considering the composition of an employer's work force in determining the probable cost of a retirement or death benefit plan.[34] Finally, we recognize that in a case of this kind it may be necessary to take special care in fashioning appropriate relief.

[31] See 15 U.S.C. § 13(a). Under the Robinson-Patman Act, proof of cost differences justifies otherwise illegal price discrimination; it does not negate the existence of the discrimination itself. See *Federal Trade Commission* v. *Morton Salt Co.*, 334 U.S. 37, 44–45. So here, even if the contribution differential were based on a sound and well recognized business practice, it would nevertheless be discriminatory, and the defendant would be forced to assert an affirmative defense to escape liability.

[32] Defenses under Title VII and the Equal Pay Act are considerably narrower. See, *e.g.*, n. 30, *supra*. A broad cost differential defense was proposed and rejected when the Equal Pay Act became law. Representative Findley offered an amendment to the Equal Pay Act that would have expressly authorized a wage differential tied to the "ascertainable and specific added cost resulting from employment of the opposite sex." 109 Cong. Rec. 9217. He pointed out that the employment of women might be more costly because of such matters as higher turnover and state laws restricting women's hours. *Id.*, at 9205. The Equal Pay Act's supporters responded that any cost differences could be handled by focusing on the factors other than sex which actually caused the differences, such as absenteeism or number of hours worked. The amendment was rejected as largely redundant for that reason. *Id.*, at 9217.

The Senate Report, on the other hand, does seem to assume that the statute may recognize a very limited cost defense, based on "all of the elements of the employment costs of both men and women." S. Rep. No. 176, 88th Cong., 1st Sess., 4. It is difficult to find language in the statute supporting even this limited defense; in any event, no defense based on the *total* cost of employing men and women was attempted in this case.

[33] Title VII and the Equal Pay Act govern relations between employees and their employer, not between employees and third parties. We do not suggest, of course, that an employer can avoid its responsibilities by delegating discriminatory programs to corporate shells. Title VII applies to "any agent" of a covered employer, 42 U.S.C. § 2000e(b), and the Equal Pay Act applies to "any person acting directly or indirectly in the interest of any employer in relation to any employee." 29 U.S.C. § 203(d). In this case, for example, the Department could not deny that the administrative board was its agent after it successfully argued that the two were so inseparable that both shared the city's immunity from suit under 42 U.S.C. § 1983.

[34] Title VII bans discrimination against an "individual" because of "such individual's" sex. 42 U.S.C. § 2000e–2(a)(1). The Equal Pay Act prohibits discrimination "within any establishment," and discrimination is defined as "paying wages to employees . . . at a rate less than the rate at which [the employer] pays employees of the opposite sex" for equal work. 29 U.S.C. § 206(d)(1). Neither of these provisions makes it unlawful to

## IV

The Department challenges the District Court's award of retroactive relief to the entire class of female employees and retirees. Title VII does not require a district court to grant any retroactive relief. A court that finds unlawful discrimination "may enjoin [the discrimination] and order such affirmative action as may be appropriate, which may include, but is not limited to, reinstatement . . . with or without back pay . . . or any other equitable relief as the court deems appropriate." 42 U.S.C. § 2000e–5(g). To the point of redundancy, the statute stresses that retroactive relief "may" be awarded if it is "appropriate."

In *Albemarle Paper Co.* v. *Moody,* 422 U.S. 405, the Court reviewed the scope of a district court's discretion to fashion appropriate remedies for a Title VII violation and concluded that "back pay should be denied only for reasons which, if applied generally, would not frustrate the central statutory purposes of eradicating discrimination throughout the economy and making persons whole for injuries suffered through past discrimination." *Id.,* at 421. Applying that standard, the Court ruled that an award of backpay should not be conditioned on a showing of bad faith. *Id.,* at 422–23. But the *Albemarle* Court also held that backpay was not to be awarded automatically in every case.[35]

The *Albemarle* presumption in favor of retroactive liability can seldom be overcome, but it does not make meaningless the district courts' duty to determine that such relief is appropriate. For several reasons, we conclude that the District Court gave insufficient attention to the equitable nature of Title VII remedies. Although we now have no doubt about the application of the statute in this case, we must recognize that conscientious and intelligent administrators of pension funds, who did not have the benefit of the extensive briefs and arguments presented to us, may well have assumed that a program like the Department's was entirely lawful. The courts had been silent on the question, and the administrative agencies had conflicting views. The Department's failure to act more swiftly is a sign, not of its recalcitrance, but of the problem's complexity. As commentators have noted, pension administrators could reasonably have thought it unfair—or even illegal—to make male employees shoulder more than their "actuarial share" of the pension burden. There is no reason to believe that the threat of a backpay award is needed to cause other administrators to amend their practices to conform to this decision.

Nor can we ignore the potential impact which changes in rules affecting insurance and pension plans may have on the economy. Fifty million Americans participate in retirement plans other than Social Security. The

---

determine the funding requirements for an establishment's benefit plan by considering the composition of the entire force.

[35] Specifically, the Court held that a defendant prejudiced by his reliance on a plaintiff's initial waiver of any backpay claims could be absolved of backpay liability by a district court. *Id.,* at 424. The Court reserved the question whether reliance of a different kind—on state "protective" laws requiring sex differentiation—would also save a defendant from liability. *Id.,* at 423 n. 18.

assets held in trust for these employees are vast and growing—more than $400 billion were reserved for retirement benefits at the end of 1977 and reserves are increasing by almost $50 billion a year. These plans, like other forms of insurance, depend on the accumulation of large sums to cover contingencies. The amounts set aside are determined by a painstaking assessment of the insurer's likely liability. Risks that the insurer foresees will be included in the calculation of liability, and the rates or contributions charged will reflect that calculation. The occurrence of major unforeseen contingencies, however, jeopardizes the insurer's solvency and, ultimately, the insureds' benefits. Drastic changes in the legal rules governing pension and insurance funds, like other unforeseen events, can have this effect. Consequently, the rules that apply to these funds should not be applied retroactively unless the legislature has plainly commanded that result. The EEOC itself has recognized that the administrators of retirement plans must be given time to adjust gradually to Title VII's demands. Courts have also shown sensitivity to the special dangers of retroactive Title VII awards in this field. See *Rosen* v. *Public Serv. Elec. & Gas Co.*, 328 F. Supp. 454, 466–68 (NJ 1971).

There can be no doubt that the prohibition against sex-differentiated employee contributions represents a marked departure from past practice. Although Title VII was enacted in 1964, this is apparently the first litigation challenging contribution differences based on valid actuarial tables. Retroactive liability could be devastating for a pension fund. The harm would fall in large part on innocent third parties. If, as the courts below apparently contemplated, the plaintiffs' contributions are recovered from the pension fund, the administrators of the fund will be forced to meet unchanged obligations with diminished assets. If the reserve proves inadequate, either the expectations of all retired employees will be disappointed or current employees will be forced to pay not only for their own future security but also for the unanticipated reduction in the contributions of past employees.

Without qualifying the force of the *Albemarle* presumption in favor of retroactive relief, we conclude that it was error to grant such relief in this case. Accordingly, although we agree with the Court of Appeals' analysis of the statute, we vacate its judgment and remand the case for further proceedings consistent with this opinion.

MR. JUSTICE BRENNAN took no part in the consideration or decision of this case.

MR. JUSTICE MARSHALL, concurring in part and dissenting in part: I agree that Title VII of the Civil Rights Act of 1964, as amended, forbids petitioners' practice of requiring female employees to make larger contributions to a pension fund than do male employees. I therefore join all of the Court's opinion except Part IV.

I also agree with the Court's statment in Part IV that, once a Title VII violation is found, *Albemarle Paper Co.* v. *Moody*, 422 U.S. 405 (1975), establishes a "presumption in favor of retroactive liability" and that this presumption "can seldom be overcome." *Ante,* at 16. But I do not agree that the presumption should be deemed overcome in this case, especially since the relief was granted by the District Court in the exercise of its discretion and was upheld by the Court of Appeals. I would affirm the decision below and therefore cannot join Part IV of the Court's opinion or the Court's judgment.

. . .

## D. RELIGION

### (1) Sabbatarianism

## TRANS WORLD AIRLINES v. HARDISON

*Supreme Court of the United States, 1977*
*432 U.S. 63, 14 FEP Cases 1697*

MR. JUSTICE WHITE delivered the opinion of the Court.

. . .

Petitioner Trans World Airlines (TWA) operates a large maintenance and overhaul base in Kansas City, Mo. On June 5, 1967, respondent Larry G. Hardison was hired by TWA to work as a clerk in the Stores Department at its Kansas City base. Because of its essential role in the Kansas City operation, the Stores Department must operate 24 hours per day, 365 days per year, and whenever an employee's job in that department is not filled, an employee must be shifted from another department, or a supervisor must cover the job, even if the work in other areas may suffer.

Hardison, like other employees at the Kansas City base, was subject to a seniority system contained in a collective-bargaining agreement that TWA maintains with petitioner International Association of Machinists and Aerospace Workers (IAM). The seniority system is implemented by the union steward through a system of bidding by employees for particular shift assignments as they become available. The most senior employees have first choice for job and shift assignments, and the most junior employees are required to work when the union steward is unable to find enough people willing to work at a particular time or in a particular job to fill TWA's needs.

In the spring of 1968 Hardison began to study the religion known as the Worldwide Church of God. One of the tenets of that religion is that one must observe the Sabbath by refraining from performing any work from sunset on Friday until sunset on Saturday. The religion also proscribes work on certain specified religious holidays.

When Hardison informed Everett Kussman, the manager of the Stores Department, of his religious conviction regarding observance of the Sabbath, Kussman agreed that the union steward should seek a job swap for Hardison or a change of days off; that Hardison would have his religous holidays off whenever possible if Hardison agreed to work the traditional holidays when asked; and that Kussman would try to find Hardison another job that would be more compatible with his religious beliefs. The problem was temporarily solved when Hardison transferred to the 11 p.m.—7 a.m. shift. Working this shift permitted Hardison to observe his Sabbath.

The problem soon reappeared when Hardison bid for and received a transfer from Building 1, where he had been employed, to Building 2, where he would work the day shift. The two buildings had entirely separate seniority lists; and while in Building 1 Hardison had sufficient seniority to observe the Sabbath regularly, he was second from the bottom on the Building 2 seniority list.

In Building 2 Hardison was asked to work Saturdays when a fellow employee went on vacation. TWA agreed to permit the union to seek a change of work assignments for Hardison, but the union was not willing to violate the seniority provisions set out in the collective-bargaining contract, and Hardison had insufficient seniority to bid for a shift having Saturdays off.

A proposal that Hardison work only four days a week was rejected by the company. Hardison's job was essential, and on weekends he was the only available person on his shift to perform it. To leave the position empty would have impaired Supply Shop functions, which were critical to airline operations; to fill Hardison's position with a supervisor or an employee from another area would simply have undermanned another operation; and to employ someone not regularly assigned to work Saturdays would have required TWA to pay premium wages.

When an accommodation was not reached, Hardison refused to report for work on Saturdays. . . .

. . .

## II

The Court of Appeals found that TWA had committed an unlawful employment practice under § 703(a)(1) of the Act. . . .

. . .

In 1967 the EEOC amended its guidelines to require employers "to make reasonable accommodations to the religious needs of employees and prospective employees where such accommodation can be made without undue hardship on the conduct of the employer's business." 29 CFR § 1605.1, 32 Fed. Reg. 10298 (1967). The Commission did not suggest what sort of accommodations are "reasonable" or when hardship to an employer becomes "undue."

This question—the extent of the required accommodation—remained unsettled when this Court affirmed by an equally divided Court the Sixth Circuit's decision in *Dewey* v. *Reynolds Metals Co.,* 429 F.2d 324, 2 FEP Cases 687, 869 (CA6 1970). . . .

In part "to resolve by legislation" some of the issues raised in *Dewey,* 118 Cong. Rec. 706 (1972) (remarks of Sen. Randolph), Congress included the following definition of religion in its 1972 amendments to Title VII:

"The term 'religion' includes all aspects of religious observance and practice, as well as belief, unless an employer demonstrates that he is unable to reasonably accommodate to an employee's or prospective employee's religious observance or practice without undue hardship on the conduct of the employer's business."

Title VII § 701(j). . . . The proponent of the measure, Senator Jennings Randolph, expressed his general desire "to assure that freedom from religious discrimination in the employment of workers is for all time guaranteed by law," 18 Cong. Rec. 705 (1972), but he made no attempt to define the precise circumstances under which the "reasonable accommodation" requirement would be applied.

## III

The Court of Appeals held that TWA had not made reasonable efforts to accommodate Hardison's religious needs. . . .

We disagree. . . .

### A

. . .

The Court of Appeals observed, however, that the possibility of a variance from the seniority system was never really posed to the union. This is contrary to the District Court's findings and to the record. . . . As the record shows, Hardison himself testified that Kussman was willing, but the union was not, to work out a shift or job trade with another employee. App. 76-77.

We shall say more about the seniority system, but at this juncture it appears to us that the system itself represented a significant accommodation to the needs, both religious and secular, of all of TWA's employees. As will become apparent, the seniority system represents a neutral way of minimizing the number of occasions when an employee must work on a day that he would prefer to have off. . . .

### B

We are also convinced, contrary to the Court of Appeals, that TWA cannot be faulted for having failed itself to work out a shift or job swap for Hardison. Both the union and TWA had agreed to the seniority system; the union was unwilling to entertain a variance over the objections of men senior to Hardison. . . .

. . .

Had TWA nevertheless circumvented the seniority system by relieving Hardison of Saturday work and ordering a senior employee to replace him, it would have denied the latter his shift preference so that Hardison could be given his. The senior employee would also have been deprived of his contractual rights under the collective-bargaining agreement.

. . .

Title VII does not contemplate such unequal treatment. . . . It would be anomalous to conclude that by "reasonable accommodation" Congress meant that an employer must deny the shift and job preference of some employees, as well as deprive them of their contractual rights, in order to accommodate or prefer the religious needs of others, and we conclude that Title VII does not require an employer to go that far.

Our conclusion is supported by the fact that seniority systems are afforded special treatment under Title VII itself. Section 703(h) provides in pertinent part:

"Notwithstanding any other provision of this subchapter, it shall not be an unlawful employment practice for an employer to apply different standards of compensation, or different terms, conditions, or privileges of employment pursuant to a bona fide seniority or merit system . . . provided that such differences are not the result of an intention to discriminate because of race, color, religion, sex, or national origin. . . ."

. . .

## C

[T]he Court of Appeals suggested that TWA could have replaced Hardison on his Saturday shift with other available employees through the payment of premium wages. Both of these alternatives would involve costs to TWA, either in the form of lost efficiency in other jobs or as higher wages.

To require TWA to bear more than a *de minimis* cost in order to give Hardison Saturdays off is an undue hardship. . . .

As we have seen, the paramount concern of Congress in enacting Title VII was the elimination of discrimination in employment. In the absence of clear statutory language or legislative history to the contrary, we will not readily construe the statute to require an employer to discriminate against some employees in order to enable others to observe their Sabbath.

*Reversed.*

MR. JUSTICE MARSHALL, with whom MR. JUSTICE BRENNAN joins, dissenting: . . .

Today's decision deals a fatal blow to all efforts under Title VII to accommodate work requirements to religious practices. The Court holds, in essence, that although the EEOC regulations and the Act state that an employer must make reasonable adjustments in his work demands to take account of religious observances, the regulation and Act don't really mean what they say. . . .

## I

. . .

The accommodation issue by definition arises only when a neutral rule of general applicability conflicts with the religious practices of a particular employee. In some of the reported cases, the rule in question has governed work attire; in other cases it has required attendance at some religious function; in still other instances, it has compelled membership in a union; and in the largest class of cases, it has concerned work schedules. . . . In each instance, the question is whether the employee is to be exempt from the rule's demands. To do so will always result in a privilege being "allocated according to religious beliefs," *ante*, at 19, 14 FEP Cases, at 1706. . . .

The point is perhaps best made by considering a not-altogether-hypothetical example. See EEOC Decision No. 71-779, 1973 CCH EEOC Decisions ¶ 6180, 3 FEP Cases 172 (Dec. 21, 1970). Assume that an employer requires all employees to wear a particular type of hat at work in order to make the employees readily identifiable to customers. Such a rule obviously does not, on its face, violate Title VII, and an employee who altered the uniform for reasons of taste could be discharged. But a very different question would be posed by the discharge of an employee who, for religious reasons, insisted on wearing, over her hair a tightly fitted scarf which was visible through the hat. In such a case the employer could accommodate this religious practice without undue hardship—or any hardship at all. Yet as I understand the Court's analysis—and nothing in the Court's response, *ante*, at _____ nn. 14 and 15, 14 FEP Cases, at 1705-1706, is to the contrary—the accommodation would not be required.

. . .

The Court's interpretation of the statute, by effectively nullifying it, has the singular advantage of making consideration of petitioners' constitutional challenge unnecessary. . . . [W]hile important constitutional questions would be posed by interpreting the law to compel employers (or fellow employees) to incur substantial costs to aid the religious observer, not all accommodations are costly, and the constitutionality of the statute is not placed in serious doubt simply because it sometimes requires an exemption from a work rule. Indeed, this Court has repeatedly found no Establishment Clause problems in exempting religious observers from state-imposed duties, *e.g.*, *Wisconsin* v. *Yoder*, 406 U.S. 205, 234-35, n. 22 (1972); *Sherbert* v. *Verner*, 374 U.S. 398, 409, 9 FEP Cases 1152, 1157 (1963); *Zorach* v. *Clauson*, 343 U.S. 306 (1952), even when the exemption was in no way compelled by the Free Exercise Clause, *e.g.*, *Gillette* v. *United States*, 401 U.S. 437 (1971); *Welsh* v. *United States*, 398 U.S. 333, 371-72 (1970) (WHITE, J., dissenting); *Sherbert* v. *Verner.* . . . If the State does not establish religion over non-religion by excusing religious practitioners from obligations owed the State, I do not see how the State can be said to establish religion by requiring employers to do the same with respect to obligations owed the employer. Thus, I think it beyond dispute that the Act does—and, consistently with the First Amendment, can—require employers to grant privileges to religious observers as part of the accommodation process.

## II

[D]id TWA prove that it exhausted all reasonable accommodations, and that the only remaining alternatives would have caused undue hardship on TWA's business? To pose the question is to answer it, for all that the District Court found TWA had done to accommodate respondent's Sabbath observance was that it "held several meetings with [respondent] . . . [and] authorized the union steward to search for someone who would swap shifts." *Hardison* v. *TWA*, 375 F. Supp. 877, 890, 10 FEP Cases 502, 512 (WD Mo. 1974). To conclude that TWA, one of the largest air carriers in the Nation, would have suffered undue hardship had it done anything more defies both reason and common sense.

. . .

[T]hus I do not believe it can be even seriously argued that TWA would have suffered "undue hardship" to its business had it required respondent to pay the extra costs of his replacement, or had it transferred respondent to his former department.

What makes this case most tragic, however, is not that respondent Hardison has been needlessly deprived of his livelihood simply because he chose to follow the dictates of his conscience. Nor is the tragedy of the case exhausted by the impact it will have on thousands of Americans like Hardison who could be forced to live on welfare as the price they must pay for worshipping their God. The ultimate tragedy is that despite Congress' best efforts, one of this Nation's pillars of strength—our hospitality to religious diversity—has been seriously eroded. All Americans will be a little poorer until today's decision is erased.

I respectfully dissent.

## NOTE

Would the company have shown an "undue hardship" if not for its attempts to transfer Hardison? Most federal courts have followed *Hardison* despite differences on the facts. *E.g., Wren* v. *T.I.M.E.-D.C.,* 453 F. Supp. 583 (E.D. Mo. 1978); *Rohr* v. *Western Electric Co.,* 567 F.2d 829 (8th Cir. 1977); *Blakely* v. *Chrysler Corp.,* 407 F. Supp. 1227 (E.D. Mo. 1975), *rev'd sub nom. Chrysler Corp.* v. *Mann,* 561 F.2d 1282 (8th Cir. 1977). In *Jordan* v. *North Carolina National Bank,* 565 F.2d 72 (4th Cir. 1977), *rev'g* 399 F. Supp. 172 (W.D.N.C. 1975), for example, the Fourth Circuit reversed a judgment for the plaintiff even though the trial court had found that the personnel officer had made "no attempts to locate a job for the plaintiff where Saturday work would not be necessary." Most state courts have also failed to protect Sabbatarianism. In *Redmond* v. *GAF Corp.,* however, the Seventh Circuit affirmed a pre-*Hardison* judgment based on a finding that defendant "made no effort to accommodate plaintiff," who had no Sabbatarian conviction, but who had requested time off on Saturdays to attend Bible class. 574 F.2d 897, 903 (7th Cir. 1978.) See also, *Kentuckey Comm'n on Human Rights* v. *Department for Human Resources,* 564 S.W.2d 38 (KY. App. 1978) (*Hardison* "persuasive, if not controlling" on state law question, but finding of "no reasonable effort to accommodate" not clearly erroneous).

(2)  *Union Security*

## MAINE HUMAN RIGHTS COMMISSION
## v. PAPERWORKERS, LOCAL 1361

*Supreme Judicial Court of Maine, 1978*
*383 A.2d 369, 17 FEP Cases 347*

POMERY, Judge: . . .

. . . In the case now before us the interests of a labor union and the interests of Ms. Clarita Michaud regarding discrimination by reason of her religious beliefs and her practices dictated by her religion have come in sharp conflict. It is our responsibility to resolve those conflicts of interest consistent with the intention of the Legislature when it enacted the Maine Act and the intention of the Congress when it enacted the National Labor Relations Act.

. . .

Ms. Clarita Michaud was employed by the defendant Oxford Paper Company (Company) as a laboratory technician since November 1970. In 1974 the Union was certified as the exclusive bargaining representative for a unit which included Ms. Michaud's position. Thereafter on June 1, 1975 the Company and the Union entered into a collective bargaining agreement which contained a union security clause obligating all employees in part to pay periodic union dues of $6.00 per month. Upon written request from the Union, the Company was contractually obligated to discharge an employee for nonpayment of the dues.

Ms. Michaud informed the Union that her religious beliefs as a Seventh-day Adventist precluded her from paying the monthly dues. She did, however, indicate to the Union that she would be willing to pay an amount of money equal to union dues to a charitable organization. This proposal was unacceptable to the Union and pursuant to the collective bargaining agreement it requested on July 17, 1975 that the Company discharge Ms. Michaud.

. . .

### I

The Maine Act declares that
"[i]t shall be unlawful employment discrimination, in violation of this Act, except where based on a bona fide occupational qualification:

"C. For any labor organization . . . to cause or attempt to cause an employer to discriminate against any individual in violation of this section. . . ." 5 M.R.S.A. § 4572(1)(C).

The Union asserts on cross-appeal that this provision is inapplicable to the case at bar, for the Maine Act prohibits only religiously motivated discrimination. Here, however, the Union security provision was applied to all persons in the bargaining unit uniformly, and Ms. Michaud was terminated because she did not pay her union dues, not because of her religion, the Union says.

The Union is not unaware of the seminal United States Supreme Court decision in *Griggs* v. *Duke Power Co.*, 401 U.S. 424, 3 FEP Cases 175 (1971) in which the Court squarely rejected this type of argument in construing Title VII of the Civil Rights Act of 1964, 42 U.S.C. §§ 2000e et. seq. (Federal Act). Writing for a unanimous Court, MR. CHIEF JUSTICE BURGER stated that "Congress directed the thrust of the [Federal] Act to the *consequences* of employment practices, not simply the motivation." *Id*. at 432, 3 FEP Cases at 178. (emphasis in original). The Court found that "[t]he [Federal] Act proscribes not only overt discrimination but also practices that are fair in form, but discriminatory in operation." *Id*. at 431, 3 FEP Cases at 178.

The legislative history of the Maine Act indicates that it was meant to have very broad coverage. Governor Curtis in addressing the first meeting of the Task Force on Human Rights, the commission appointed to draft the Maine Act, set forth a broad mandate. . . . In particular, the Governor asked the Task Force to "consider what possibilities exist for state law to supplement federal legislation or extend its coverage in the area of fair employment practices." *Id*. In submitting the proposed legislation, the Task Force stressed the salutary goals that they envisioned when drafting the Maine Act.

"We should take the lead not only in solving our own problems, whether of social conscience or political history, but also we should take the lead in the nation by showing the way in these areas. . . ."

. . .

In short, we find nothing in the Maine Act which suggests that the Legislature intended it to apply to the limited situation, typically devoid of proof, that an employer or labor organization intends to discriminate. As in *Griggs* v. *Duke Power Co.*, *supra*, the touchstone of our statutory prohibition is whether in fact the disputed practice results in unlawful employment discrimination.

. . .

## II

. . .

Section 3.05 of the Employment Guidelines of the Maine Human Rights Commission (section 3.05) which defines religious discrimination and provides an affirmative defense states:

*"The duty not to discriminate on religious grounds includes an obligation on the part of the employer to make reasonable accommodations to the religious needs of employees and prospective employees where such accommodations can be made without undue hardship to the conduct of the employer's business.* Because of the particularly sensitive nature of refusing to hire or discharging an individual on account of his religious beliefs, the burden of proof that the accommodations required by the

individual's religious needs impose an undue hardship to the conduct of the employer's business, is on the employer." (emphasis supplied).
. . .

Section 3.05 is a virtual carbon copy of the Federal Commission's regulation 29 C.F.R. §1605.1. . . .
. . .

Section 3.05 is a reasonable construction of the Maine Act. The Union complains that there is no statutory indication that the Legislature intended an employer or labor organization to accommodate an individual's religious beliefs to the point of hardship. On the contrary, in the absence of a bona fide occupational qualification, any discharge based upon religion would be a violation of the Act. One of the purposes of section 3.05 is to breathe flexibility into an otherwise airtight prohibition against religous discrimination, by providing that a reasonable accommodation need not be made if it would amount to undue hardship. We find nothing unreasonable in such an interpretation.
. . .

## III

On appeal the Commission alleges insufficient evidence to support the Superior Court's finding that no reasonable accommodation could be made to Ms. Michaud's religious beliefs without undue hardship to the Union. . . .

. . . This ruling disregards a basic tenant [sic] of our guidelines which provides:

"Resolution of such cases depends on *specific factual circumstances* and involves a delicate balancing of an applicant or employee's religious needs with the degree of disruption imposed on the employer's business operation." (emphasis supplied)
Section 3.05, Employment Guidelines of the Maine Human Rights Commission.
Thus although such conclusion may be warranted following an evidentiary hearing, the judgment cannot be reached without an analysis of the specific factual circumstances which were involved.

In finding that an exemption from the Union dues requirement would be an undue hardship as a matter of law, the Court relied upon Section 8(a)(3) of the National Labor Relations Act, 29 U.S.C. §158(a)(3).

Two distinct but interrelated problems potentially arise between our construction of the Maine Act and section 8(a)(3) and other provisions of the National Labor Relations Act, 29 U.S.C. §§151 *et seq.*:

1. Whether a direct conflict exists between the two statutes, and

2. Whether notwithstanding the absence of a direct conflict the National Labor Relations Act has preempted the Commission's state court action.
We have concluded that there is neither a problem of conflict nor preemption that would preclude the relief here sought. . . .

. . . Section 8(a)(3) on its face does not mandate union security agree-

ments; it merely provides "[t]hat nothing in this subchapter, or in any other statute of the United States, shall preclude an employer from making [a union security] agreement with a labor organization. . . ."
. . .

[A]n exemption from the union dues requirement contingent upon payment of an equivalent sum to charity would not substantially undermine the purpose behind a union security clause. Although payment to charity would not directly compensate a union for its services, it does prevent an employee from becoming a "free rider" in the sense of benefitting as a result of union activity on his behalf without paying anything at all. . . .

Nor is a suit under the Maine Act preempted by the enactment of a comprehensive national labor law. . . .

[T]he Union conduct in seeking a discharge for failure to pay union dues is not an unfair labor practice. As such [*San Diego Building Trades Council* v.] *Garmon* [359 U.S. 236 (1959)] is inapplicable.
. . .

On remand the Superior Court should hear testimony and take evidence on whether the Union and the Company without undue hardship can accommodate the religious beliefs of Ms. Michaud by permitting her to pay to a nonreligious charity an equivalent sum of union dues. Among the factors that the court should consider in determining whether to exempt Ms. Michaud is the financial burden to the Union that would result from the loss of her union dues. To require the Union to bear more than a *de minimis* extra cost would be an undue hardship on the Union. *Trans World Airlines, Inc.* v. *Hardison, supra.* In addition, the Court should consider the impact on the morale of the Union members from any such exemption. Although mere grumbling will not suffice, *Draper* v. *United States Pipe & Foundry Co.,* 527 F.2d 515, 11 FEP Cases 1106 (6th Cir. 1975), any adverse effect on Union solidarity should be carefully scrutinized.
. . .

GODFREY, Judge, with whom ARCHIBALD, Judge, concurs, dissenting:
. . . The Maine civil rights statute can be fairly construed to require employers and unions to take steps to accommodate the free exercise of religion as long as the accommodation does not amount to an undue burden on the union and employer. . . .
. . .

[I]n *Anderson* v. *General Dynamics,* 430 F.Supp. 418, 14 FEP Cases 667 (S.D. Cal. 1977), the court examined the federally recognized role of union security agreements and held that the accommodation of giving an amount equal to union dues to charity imposes an undue burden on the union. . . .

In *Trans World Airlines, Inc.* v. *Hardison,* 432 U.S. 63, 14 FEP Cases 1697 (1977), the Supreme Court dealt with a substantially similar accommodation problem. . . . Union security agreements to cover bargaining costs are similar in importance and function to seniority provisions.

Thus, under the Supreme Court's interpretation of undue burden, imposing an exception to such union security agreements imposes an undue burden. Furthermore, to force the union to forego the $72 annual fee would be to impose more than a *de minimis* cost.

The appeal should be denied and the judgment of the Superior Court affirmed.

### (3) *Grooming Codes*

Complaints involving deviations from company dress codes have received less attention than those relating to work schedules and union dues. Conceptually, these cases should be easier to resolve, since they are less likely to involve serious elements of the "discrimination against other employees" condemned by Justice White in *Hardison*. The case law, particularly with regard to beards, is unsettled.

A Jewish chaplain, dismissed from the Air Force because he refused to shave his beard, successfully sued for reinstatement. A district court in Connecticut held that a federal prison regulation against beards was unconstitutional as applied to religious objectors. Requiring "more than a rational relation" to a legitimate purpose, the court rejected the Government's contention that the potential difficulty of identifying an escaped prisoner (who may have shaved his beard) justified the rule. *Moscovitz* v. *Wilkinson*, 432 F.Supp 947 (D. Conn 1977). Cases under Title VII and state nondiscrimination provisions, however, have accepted minimal justifications (*e.g.*, employee morale). *Cupit* v. *Baton Rouge Police Dep't*, 277 So.2d 454, 6 FEP Cases 10 (La.Ct.App. 1973).

As Justice Marshall's dissent in *Hardison* noted, the EEOC sustained the complaint of a nurse who wore a tightly fitted scarf underneath the required nurse's cap. EEOC Dec. 71-779, 3 FEP Cases 172 (1970). The Commission also found for a Muslim woman who was not permitted to wear a long dress, in part because the firm's dress code had not previously been enforced against other "attention-getting clothing." EEOC Dec. 72-2620, 4 FEP Cases 23 (1972). The New York Court of Appeals held that a narcotics rehabilitation officer could be forbidden from wearing "exotic" Sunni Muslim garb, in part because it was "prosyletizing" and might "adversely affect" his charges. *Abdush-Shahid* v. *N.Y. State Narcotics Control Comm'n*, 12 FEP Cases 136 (Sup.Ct.Wchester.Cty. 1975), aff'd, 382 N.Y.2d 813 (App.Div. 1976).

### NOTE

The Ninth Circuit held that an employee established a *prima facie* case of discrimination by proving that work requirements conflicted with a "bona fide" religious belief and that he had notified the employer of the conflict; the employer must then assume the burden of pleading and proving that he had made "reasonable accommodation." *Burns* v. *South-*

*ern Pacific Transp. Co.,* —— F.2d ——, 17 FEP Cases 1648 (9th Cir. 1978).

The substantive trend of the foregoing cases seems to be as follows:

(a) The employer will prevail in scheduling cases if the accommodation conflicts with the seniority rights of other employees or requires that any substantial cost be borne by the employer.

(b) The employee will be excused by union assessments providing his objection is religious and he agrees to donate an equivalent amount to charity.

(c) Only modest deviations from dress codes will be required, unless the requirement appears intentionally discriminatory or perhaps when the employee is a clergyman.

### (4) *Abortions*

Can an employer fire a woman for pregnancy if having an abortion violates her religious convictions? Can an employer fire a woman who has an abortion because it fails to conform to his religious convictions?

Although neither of these questions has been posed under Title VII, a pregnant Air Force officer failed in her constitutional claim that her conviction against abortion required an exemption to the requirement that pregnant officers be decommissioned. The court of appeals found a "compelling state interest," and the case was mooted before appeal. *Struck* v. *Secretary of Defense,* 460 F.2d 1372 (9th Cir. 1971), *cert. vacated, remanding to consider issue of mootness,* 409 U.S. 1071 (1972).

The Health Services Extension Act of 1973 and the National Research Act of 1974 provide religious nondiscrimination provisions regarding private hospitals receiving funds under the Hill-Burton Act. 87 Stat. 33, *codified at* 42 U.S.C. §300a-7(b); 88 Stat. 353, *codified at* 42 U.S.C. §300a-7(c)(1976). Federally funded hospitals and research facilities may not discriminate against personnel because of their "religious beliefs or moral convictions respecting sterilization procedures and abortions," or because they performed or refused to perform these procedures. *Watkins* v. *Mercy Medical Center,* 323 F.2d 959 (4th Cir. 1963). The hospital need not, however, accommodate a member physician by making its facilities and personnel available for abortions. *Id.,* see also §300a-7(a); *Taylor* v. *St. Vincent's Hospital,* 523 F.2d 75, *cert. denied,* 424 U.S. 948 (1976) (constitutional to prohibit any court from finding that funded hospital acts under color of law for purposes of ordering abortions) .

### (5) *Constitutionality of §701(j)*

Prior to the Supreme Court's decision in *Hardison,* the Sixth Circuit considered and sustained the constitutionality of §701(j) against an attack based on the Establishment Clause. *Cummins* v. *Parker Seal Co.,* 516 F.2d 544, 10 FEP Cases 974 (6th Cir. 1975). An equally divided Court affirmed the decision summarily, 429 U.S. 65 (1976), and the majority in *Hardison* explicitly avoided the issue. In *Burns, supra,* reversing a judgment following *Hardison,* the Ninth Circuit refused to permit defendants to raise the constitutionality issue for the first time on appeal.

Is any "accommodation" required by §701(j), no matter how trivial, constitutional? Can a court determine what does (and does not) constitute a "religious" belief? These issues were recently considered by the Western District of Pennsylvania.

## GAVIN v. PEOPLES NATIONAL GAS CO.

*United States District Court, Western District of Pennsylvania, 1979*
*18 FEP Cases 1431*

COHILL, District Judge: . . .
The plaintiff argues that by failing to exempt him from raising and lowering the flag as part of his job duties, the defendant has violated the "reasonable accommodation" requirement of Title VII. The defendant responds that if this is so, the "reasonable accommodation" requirement is unconstitutional. The question for decision, then, is whether the reasonable accommodation provision of Title VII, 42 U.S.C. § 2000e(j), is unconstitutional as applied to the facts of this case.

. . .
A careful review of these cases arising under the Establishment Clause would demonstrate that the question of encouraging religion is often one of balancing legitimate state interests against prohibited results or one of the degree of involvement between church and state. The Supreme Court has established three tests of the constitutionality of statutes challenged under the Establishment Clause. In *Meek* v. *Pittenger,* 421 U.S. 349, 358–59, the Court instructed:
"In judging the constitutionality of the various forms of assistance . . . the District Court applied the three-part test that had been clearly stated, if not easily applied, by this Court in recent Establishment Clause cases. First, the statute must have a secular legislative purpose. Second, it must have a 'primary effect' that neither advances nor inhibits religion. Third, the statute and its administration must avoid excessive government entanglement with religion. . . ."
If a statutory provision fails any of these three tests, it is likely to be violative of the Establishment Clause.

The defendant argues that the legislative enactment challenged here fails all three; it contends that the purpose of the amendment was to advance certain specific religions, that the effect of the amendment is generally to promote religion, and that the amendment fosters the entanglement of the government in religious activity.

There is some indication in the legislative history that the floor amendment which became §701(j) was originally motivated by sectarian impulses. Remarks on the floor of the Senate by Senator Jennings Randolph include these revealing statements:
"I am sure that my colleagues are well aware that there are several reli-

gious bodies—we could call them religious sects; denominational in nature—not large in membership but with certain strong convictions, that believe there should be a steadfast observance of the sabbath and require that the observance of the day of worship, the day of The Sabbath, be other than on Sunday. . . . There are approximately 750,000 men and women who are Orthodox Jews in the U.S. work force who fall in this category of persons I am discussing. There are an additional 425,000 men and women in the work force who are Seventh Day Adventists.

. . .

"[T]here has been a partial refusal at times on the part of employers to hire or continue in employment employees whose religious practices rigidly require them to abstain from work in the nature of hire on particular days. So there has been, because of understandable pressures, such as commitments of a family nature, and otherwise, a dwindling of the membership of some of the religious organizations because of the situation to which I have just directed attention. . . ."

. . .

If the quoted remarks were the sole reason for passage of the "reasonable accommodation" provision, we might agree with the defendant that such passage "abandon[ed] secular purposes in order to put an imprimatur on one religion, or on religion as such, or to favor the adherents of any sect or religious organization" in violation of the Establishment Clause. *Gillette* v. *United States,* 401 U.S. 437, 450 (1971). However, it is arguable that a secular purpose may be inferred from the amendment in light of the larger purposes of Title VII. We noted earlier the continuous tension between the Establishment Clause and the Free Exercise Clause of the First Amendment. The purpose of the religious accommodation amendment may have been to be sure that the Free Exercise Clause had meaning to these workers whose religious beliefs fell outside the norms around which the daily schedules of most businesses were arranged. . . . We recognize that there are valid arguments to be made on both sides of the test of "secular purpose" with this amendment.

Likewise, whether the effect of the amendment is primarily to advance religion is an unsettled question. We also note that in recent Supreme Court cases this second test—secular primary effect—has itself been debated among the justices. . . .

. . .

It is clear from reviewing the cases that individuals of certain religious beliefs have been benefitting under the 1972 amendment. Parenthetically, we would note that this may be because members of certain sects are more knowledgeable of the law, or for any number of reasons. Eventually, the protection of the act may spread to many others. However, it can only spread to individuals who characterize their beliefs or convictions as "religious." If one were an avid sports fan, one could not use that enthusiasm, however intense, to require an accommodation to one's desire to attend a sports event. Many philosophies overlap with religious beliefs: vegetarianism, conscientious objection, pantheism, for example. *Quare:* at what point does a philosophy, a conviction, or a feeling become a religious belief entitled to a "reasonable accommodation"?

. . .

We believe that the defendant has raised serious constitutional challenges to the validity of this amendment under the "purpose" and "effect" tests outlined by the Supreme Court. However, we believe that these questions could better be resolved by an appellate court on an appropriate record, perhaps on a fuller record than that before us now.

. . .

However, the last test, or "helpful signpost," of unconstitutionality directly affects any consideration of this case. This third test is that "the statute and its administration must avoid excessive government entanglement with religion." *Meek* v. *Pittenger,* 421 U.S. 349, 359 (1975). "The test is inescapably one of degree." *Walz* v. *Tax Commission,* 397 U.S. 664, 674 (1970).

The separation of church and state in our society has long required that government take a "hands off" approach to internal church disputes and matters of religious doctrine. *Watson* v. *Jones,* 13 Wall. 679 (1872); *Kedroff* v. *St. Nicholas Cathedral,* 344 U.S. 94 (1952).

. . .

The implication of this conclusion is that under an act prohibiting religious discrimination in employment, only religious beliefs which are part of a recognized creed are protected. But what if two experts were called and they disagreed on what beliefs were acceptable in a given sect? What if there were majority and minority views of what beliefs were acceptable? These are not merely academic questions, because we have before us a complainant who asserts a religious belief which has been questioned by his employer and which has, in a prior proceeding, been adjudicated not to be a valid religious belief. At a minimum, were this case to be tried, we would have to determine whether the belief asserted is to be characterized as a "religious" belief, and whether such a belief, which may be outside the standardized creed of his faith, is protected under the Act. We might well then have to reach the hypothetical questions posed above.

. . .

We hasten to add that we accord all due respect to the plaintiff and to whatever beliefs he holds, religious or otherwise. And it is just because we respect his beliefs and are entrusted with the constitutional responsibility of protecting the free exercise of those beliefs that we fear becoming involved in an adjudication of whether those beliefs are legitimate, or whether they are "religious." We shudder at (and believe the First Amendment would be shaken by) a courtroom scene wherein experts would be cross-examined as to the legitimacy of a specific religious conviction.

Because proceeding to trial on the facts of this case would necessarily lead to an entanglement of this court with religious beliefs, requiring us to abandon the constitutionally-mandated "hands off" attitude in matters of religion and conscience, we find that this amendment cannot constitutionally be applied to the case before us.

[The court concluded that any definition of "religion" broad enough to pass the Establishment Clause would be unconstitutionally vague.]

These "due process" and "establishment" problems are like the blanket which, when pulled up over the head, uncovers the feet. Any legislative definition would make the limits of protection of the act more clear and ease our due process concerns; however, since all definitions are inclusive and exclusive by nature, any legislative or judicial definition of religion invites a First Amendment problem.

These larger questions are more appropriate concerns for appellate courts, and we would invite their review.

. . .

Whatever the ultimate disposition of these larger issues, we are certain we cannot proceed with the case before us without violating either the prohibitions of the Establishment Clause or the due process rights of the defendant. Since no facts are disputed, and since the religious discrimination claim is the only claim of plaintiff over which we have jurisdiction, summary judgment will be entered for the defendant.

## (6) *What Constitutes a Religious Group or Belief?*

The constitutional ban on religious tests, derived from the Free Exercise Clause, also extends to protect atheists. The state may not require an affirmance of "belief in God" as a condition for a license for private employment. *Torcaso* v. *Watkins,* 367 U.S. 488, 494 (1963).

During the debates on the 1964 Act, Congress indicated that Title VII also protects the right "not to believe." Moreover, membership in a self-styled "patriotic organization," in this case the Ku Klux Klan, was held not protected. *Bellamy* v. *Mason's Stores, Inc.,* 508 F.2d 504 (4th Cir. 1974).

Even if not derived from a group, religious "beliefs" or "creeds" may be protected. The discharge of an employee for writing a book criticizing organized religions was found to be illegal. EEOC Dec. 72-1301, 4 FEP Cases 715 (1972). Expression of views on the job, however, is not necessarily protected, especially if these annoy fellow employees or ridicule their beliefs. *Augustine* v. *Anti-Defamation League of B'nai B'rith,* 249 N.W.2d 547, 15 FEP Cases 66 (Wis.Sup.Ct. 1977).

## (7) *Religious Institutions*

### McCLURE v. SALVATION ARMY

*United States Court of Appeals, Fifth Circuit, 1972*

*460 F.2d 553, 4 FEP Cases 490, cert. denied as untimely filed, 409
U.S. 896, 5 FEP Cases 46, rehearing denied, 409 U.S. 1060 (1972)*

COLEMAN, District Judge: . . .

[Mrs. McClure, a minister in the Salvation Army, charged that she was given a lower salary and less preferential assignments than her male counterparts. The district court refused to apply Title VII.]

The language and the legislative history of §702 compel the conclusion that Congress did not intend that a religious organization be exempted from liability for discriminating against its employees on the basis of race, color, sex or national origin with respect to their compensation, terms, conditions or privileges of employment.

This view necessitates consideration of the constitutional issue.

Does the application of the provisions of Title VII to the relationship between The Salvation Army and Mrs. McClure (a church and its minister) violate either of the Religion Clauses of the First Amendment?

. . .

Only in rare instances where a "compelling state interest in the regulation of a subject within the State's constitutional power to regulate" is shown can a court uphold state action which imposes even an "incidental burden" on the free exercise of religion. In this highly sensitive constitutional area " 'only the gravest abuses, endangering paramount interests, give occasion for permissible limitation.' " *Sherbert* v. *Verner*, 374 U.S. 398. . . .

The relationship between an organized church and its ministers is its lifeblood. . . .

. . .

[I]n addition to injecting the State into substantive ecclesiastical matters, an investigation and review of such matters of church administration and government as a minister's salary, his place of assignment and his duty, which involve a person at the heart of any religious organization, could only produce by its coercive effect the very opposite of that separation of church and State contemplated by the First Amendment. As was said by JUSTICE CLARK in *Abington School District* v. *Schempp*, 374 U.S. 203, 10 L.Ed.2d 844 (1963), "the breach of neutrality that is today a trickling stream may all too soon become a raging torrent . . . ."

We find that the application of the provisions of Title VII to the employment relationship existing between The Salvation Army and Mrs. McClure, a church and its minister, would result in an encroachment by the State into an area of religious freedom which it is forbidden to enter by the principles of the free exercise clause of the First Amendment. Yet, "if a serious doubt of constitutionality is raised, it is a cardinal principle that this Court will first ascertain whether a construction of the statute is fairly possible by which the question may be avoided." *Ashwander* v. *Tennessee Valley Authority*, 1936, 297 U.S. 288, 346, 80 L.Ed. 688 (concurring opinion of MR. JUSTICE BRANDEIS).We therefore hold that Congress did not intend, through the nonspecific wording of the applicable provisions of Title VII, to regulate the employment relationship between church and minister. The order of the District Court sustaining The Salvation Army's motion to dismiss the complaint for want of jurisdiction is

*Affirmed.*

## KING'S GARDEN v. FCC

*United States Court of Appeals, District of Columbia Circuit, 1974*
*498 F.2d 51, 7 FEP Cases 1083, cert. denied, 419 U.S. 996,*
*8 FEP Cases 1028 (1974)*

WRIGHT, Circuit Judge: Petitioner is a non-profit, interdenominational, religious, and charitable organization. Its activities include a number of ministries whose basic goal is to "share Christ world wide" (Record at p. 15). Petitioner is also the licensee of Radio Stations KBIQ-FM and KGDN in Edmonds, Washington. In these proceedings it seeks review of an order of the Federal Communications Commission which found that it was discriminating on religious grounds in its employment practices and directed it to submit to the Commission a statement of its future hiring practices and policies. Petitioner relies upon a 1972 amendment to Title VII of the 1964 Civil Rights Act which exempts all activities of any "religious corporation, association, educational institution, or society" from the Act's ban on religious discrimination in employment. [Hereinafter the 1972 exemption.] Before 1972 only the "religious activities" of such organizations had been exempted. . . .

We affirm the Commission rulings. The 1972 exemption is of very doubtful constitutionality, and Congress has given absolutely no indication that it wished to impose the exemption upon the FCC. . . . The limited exemption which the FCC currently recognizes to its own anti-bias rules adequately protects a sectarian licensee's rights under the Communications Act and the First Amendment. Accordingly we uphold the Commission's regulatory scheme as facially sound, while recognizing that its future application will require continuing judicial scrutiny.

## I

The sponsors of the 1972 exemption were chiefly concerned to preserve the statutory power of sectarian schools and colleges to discriminate on religious grounds in the hiring of all of their employees.[6] But the exemption's simple and unqualified terms obviously accomplish far more than this. . . .

---

[6] [Footnotes numbered as in original.—Ed.] Section 702 of the 1964 Civil Rights Act (Pub. L. 88-352, 78 Stat. 255, *former* 42 U.S.C. § 2000e-1) had exempted "educational institution[s]" from all of the Act's employment discrimination rules. Early versions of the legislation which became the Equal Employment Opportunities Act of 1972 deleted this blanket exemption for educational institutions and proposed to add "religious educational institution[s]" to the list of religious organizations which § 702 had exempted as to religious discrimination in "religious activities." See § 3 of S. 2515, 92nd Cong., 1st Sess., Sept. 14, 1971. Senator Allen objected that
"[u]nder the provisions of the bill there would be nothing to prevent an atheist being forced upon a religious school to teach some subject other than theology."
LEGISLATIVE HISTORY OF THE EQUAL OPPORTUNITY ACT OF 1972 844 (Nov. 1972). To remedy this evil the Senators proposed striking the word "religious" from the term "religious activities" used in the provision exempting religious organizations from the ban on sectarian hiring practices. Amendment 809 to S. 2515, LEGISLATIVE HISTORY, *supra*, at 789.

In creating this gross distinction between the rules facing religious and non-religious entrepreneurs, Congress placed itself on collision course with the Establishment Clause. Laws in this country must have a secular purpose and a "primary effect" which neither advances nor inhibits religion. *Committee for Public Education & Religious Liberty* v. *Nyquist,* 413 U.S. 756, 773 (1973). . . .

. . .

It was not, of course, constitutionally required that Congress prohibit religious discrimination in private sector employment. But this having been done, by the Civil Rights Act, the wholesale exemption for religious organizations alone can only be seen as a special preference. Compare *Reitman* v. *Mulkey,* 387 U.S. 369 (1967). The First Amendment demands "neutrality" of treatment between religious and non-religious groups. . . .

## II

Congress' obvious purpose in enacting the 1972 exemption was to constrain the power of the *Equal Employment Opportunities Commission* (EEOC) to regulate *private* religious entities, At the time the exemption was debated the civil rights statute to which it is expressly addressed applied only to private sector employers. The exemption's sponsors were chiefly interested in the employment rights of wholly private educational institutions. Even in their most sweeping statements the sponsors spoke of immunizing only those activities which had traditionally been free of all government regulation:

"Our amendment would strike out the word "religious" and remove religious institutions in all respects from subjugation to the EEOC."

. . .

## III

The question remains whether the FCC's anti-bias rules violate King's Garden's rights under the First Amendment and the Communications Act. It is to protect these rights that the Commission exempts from the ban on sectarian hiring "the employment of persons whose work is . . . connected with the espousal of the licensee's religious views." This general policy is to be particularized on a case-by-case basis:

"[As] there are [job] categories . . . which may be defined differently by each licensee, we do not believe that it is advisable to issue a general declaratory ruling. . . . We have only general information and we are dealing with an area where First Amendment rights are often involved. We believe it would be preferable, therefore, to have specific factual settings presented to us before issuing rulings. . . ."

The challenge here is to the facial adequacy of the exemption. Application of the general exemption policy to a particular job position may raise additional problems, but they are not presently before us.

King's Garden argues that the FCC's exemption is too narrow as to abridge the sect's right of religious association, under the Free Exercise

Clause, and its right, under the First Amendment generally, to broadcast religious views of its choice.

. . .

[I]t may well be that, after it has met its "fairness doctrine" and "personal attack doctrine" obligations and produced some programs of general community interest, King's Garden has the right to give a sectarian tone or perspective to all of its other programming. This right would be infringed if the Commission, in applying its exemption, were to find no "espousal" of "religious views" in a type of programming which King's Garden considered a significant expression of its sectarian viewpoint.

. . .

The Commission has set itself the difficult task of drawing lines between the secular and religious aspects of the broadcasting operations of its sectarian licensees. Though this is a delicate undertaking, it is one which the First Amendment thrusts upon every public body which has dealings with religious organizations. See *Nyquist, supra,* 413 U.S. at 775; *Tilton* v. *Richardson,* 403 U.S. 672, 681 (1971); *Lemon* v. *Kurtzman, supra,* 403 U.S. at 614. The courts have traditionally granted the FCC considerable leeway to work out the difficult First Amendment problems endemic to a system of licensed communications. *Columbia Broadcasting System, supra,* 412 U.S. at 102–103 and 132; *Red Lion, supra,* 395 U.S. at 386–401; *National Broadcasting Co., supra,* 319 U.S. at 227. As presently formulated, the Commission's religious exemption is facially adequate. Problems of application there may be, but they will be questions for another day. Affirmed.

### (8) Harassment

Employers must provide a work environment "free from religious intimidation." In general, employers may not permit supervisors to berate the religious beliefs of their charges or to preach their own religions. Employees may not be required to attend prayer meetings or to participate in religious activities. *Young* v. *Southwestern Savings & Loan Ass'n,* 509 F.2d 140, 10 FEP Cases 522 (5th Cir. 1975). Individuals who resign "as a result of intolerable conditions" are treated as having been constructively discharged for the purposes of bringing charges under Title VII.

### (9) Holidays

## MANDEL v. HODGES

*California Appellate Court, First District, 1976*
*54 Cal. App.3d 596, 12 FEP Cases 627*

RATTIGAN, Judge:
[Jewish state employees brought suit to enjoin the Governor from declaring Good Friday a paid holiday. The trial court made the following "conclusions of law."]

"1. Respondents Department of Public Health and State of California have granted their employees time off from work annually for many years on Good Friday between the hours of 12 noon and 3:00 P.M. without reduction in pay, pursuant to executive order of Respondent Governor acting under the provisions of Government Code Sections 6700 and 18025.

"2. Respondents have failed and refused to grant the same treatment to Petitioner and others similarly situated with regard to Yom Kippur and other religious holidays of religions other than the Christian religion.

"3. The said discretionary power exercised by the Governor in said manner is purportedly pursuant to a delegation of power granted by the State Legislature, but the said Legislature does not itself possess the authority to prefer one religion over another or [to] establish a religion, and therefore cannot confer upon Respondent Governor the power to do so.

"4. Paying of State employees for taking off from work on Good Friday, pursuant to said executive order violates the First Amendment of the United States Constitution because the State, by reason of the Fourteenth Amendment to said Constitution, is prohibited from making any law respecting the establishment of religion; said action further violates Article I, Section 4 of the California Constitution, in that it constitutes discrimination and preference of one religion over others."

. . .

IV.   THE FEDERAL CONSTITUTIONAL QUESTION

As stated in its conclusion of law no. 4 (quoted *supra*) and in the judgment (see fn. 1, *ante*), one of the grounds upon which the trial court invalidated the Governor's Good Friday order was that it violated the Establishment Clause of the First Amendment of the United States Constitution. As the court also indicated in conclusion of law no. 4, the prohibitive effect of the Establishment Clause is made applicable to the several states by operation of the Due Process Clause of the Fourteenth Amendment. (*Cantwall* v. *Connecticut* (1940) 310 U.S. 296, 303-304; *Abington School Dist.* v. *Schempp* (1963) 374 U.S. 203, 215-16.)

Although the Establishment Clause states only that no law shall be made "respecting an establishment of religion" (see fn. 10, *ante*), it has "a secular reach far more penetrating in the conduct of Government than merely to forbid an 'established church.' " (*McCollum* v. *Board of Education* (1948) 333 U.S. 203, 213.) It was "intended to erect 'a wall of separation between church and State.' " (*Everson* v. *Board of Education* (1947) 330 U.S. 1, 16.)

Recognizing that "total separation is not possible in an absolute sense," and that "[s]ome relationship between government and religious organizations is inevitable" (*Lemon* v. *Kurtzman* (1971) 403 U.S. 602, 614), the United States Supreme Court has formulated a tripartite test which a statute must meet before it may be held in conformity with the Establishment Clause, as follows: ". . . [T]he now well-defined three-part test has emerged from our decisions is a product of considerations derived from the full sweep of the Establishment Clause cases. Taken together, these decisions dictate that to pass muster under the Establishment Clause the law in question, first, must reflect a clearly secular legislative purpose, second, must have a primary effect that neither advances nor inhibits religion, and, third, must avoid excessive government entanglement with religion." (*Committee for Public Education* v. *Nyquist* (1973) 413 U.S. 756, 772-73, citations omitted.)

. . .


### (1)   THE GOOD FRIDAY ORDER DOES NOT "REFLECT A CLEARLY SECULAR PURPOSE"

Addressing the trial court's findings that "Good Friday is a wholly religious day," and that "the hours of 12 noon to 3 P.M. on said day have a special significance which is profoundly rooted in Christian theology" (finding no. 13, quoted *supra*), appellants argue that "although time off on Good Friday might have its origins rooted in Christian history, and although Christian sects may derive some indirect benefit from the fact that state employees have time off on Good Friday, this does not prove that the purpose [of the Governor's order] is not as it clearly appears: to provide a necessary period of relaxation and rest from the ordinary routine of work for all state employees."

. . .

The Sunday Closing Law cases are wholly inapposite to the present facts because they hold in effect that a state law prohibiting work on Sunday serves a secular purpose of historical evolution. In contrast, there is no evidence in the present case that the Christian holy day of Good Friday has become secularized in any degree during the course of its long-time observance by Christian sects. The trial court's contrary finding that it *"is a wholly religious* day" (finding no. 13, quoted *supra* [italics added here]), being supported by substantial evidence (see fn. 3, *ante*), is controlling in this respect.

. . .

[T]he Governor's order fails the first aspect of the tripartite test which it must meet in order to "pass muster under the Establishment Clause." (*Committee for Public Education* v. *Nyquist, supra,* 413 U.S. 756 at pp. 772-73.) This failure alone is conclusive of its unconstitutionality: the three aspects of the test are conjunctive, and government action to which it is applied must satisfy each of them in order to withstand constitutional scrutiny. (*Wolman* v. *Essex* (S.D. Ohio 1972) 342 F. Supp. 399, 411 [*affd.* 409 U.S. 808)].) For the reasons next stated in sequence, however, we have concluded that the Governor's order fails the other two aspects of the test as well.

## (2)   THE "PRIMARY EFFECT" OF THE ORDER "ADVANCES RELIGION"

. . .

In the present case, the state action exemplified by the Governor's Good Friday order . . . has *no* "secular purpose" beyond which it may be deemed to have only an *indirect* and *incidental* effect beneficial to the religious institutions." (*Committee for Public Education* v. *Nyquist, supra*, 413 U.S. 756 at p. 775 [italics added].) To the contrary, the order is *directly* "beneficial to religious institutions." Its promulgation by the Governor, and its execution throughout the State office complex, amount to an observance by the State itself (in the sense of its recognition, if not its active ceremonial participation), of the "wholly religious day" which the trial court found Good Friday to be. In the implementation of the order, State employees are given paid time off "for worship." (See text at fn. 11, *ante*.)

The fact—stressed by appellants—that the order does not *require* the employees to "worship" during the three-hour "holiday" is not material. The decisive consideration is that it affords them the opportunity, and actually encourages them, to "worship" if they are so inclined. Under the circumstances, the order is unconstitutional because its "primary effect" is one which "advances religion" within the meaning of the critical test.

. . .

## (3)   THE ORDER CONSTITUTES AN "EXCESSIVE ENTANGLEMENT WITH RELIGION"

. . .

The Governor's order obviously reaches the thousands of State employees who are directly involved by reason of their being given time off from work during the designated three-hour period of Good Friday. It reasonably may—and realistically must—be presumed to reach the countless members of the public who are denied access to State offices by the closure it causes, and by the people of California whose public business is perceptibly interrupted, during the period. There is no reason for these results other than the State's observance of a "wholly religious day" as a holiday, which is the unmistakable effect of the Governor's order as discussed *supra*. Because the "wholly religious" character of the day is exclusively Christian in origin and practice, its observance by the State in our religiously pluralistic society offers a "divisive political potential" which may in itself constitute an even "broader base of entanglement" for constitutional purposes. . . . Under all the circumstances, we perceive in the Governor's order an "excessive government entanglement with religion" whereby it fails the third aspect of the test to which the Establishment Clause subjects it. . . .

## V. THE STATE CONSTITUTIONAL QUESTION

Although appellants have made no point of it, we cannot ignore the trial court's separately-stated conclusion that the annual Good Friday order was invalid upon the distinct ground that it violated article I, section 4, of the California Constitution. (See its conclusion of law no. 4, quoted *supra*.) The history and structure of our national federalist system has both permitted and required the long-standing judicial construction of the California Constitution as a document whose "vitality" and "force" are independent of its federal counterpart. . . .

. . .

When the present judgment was entered, section 4 of article I provided in pertinent part: "The free exercise and enjoyment of religious profession and worship, without discrimination or preference, shall forever be guaranteed in this State. . . ." As re-adopted by vote of the people on November 5, 1974 (in conjunction with its repeal as formerly worded), and as now pertinent, it provides: "Free exercise and enjoyment of religion without discrimination or preference are guaranteed. . . . The Legislature shall make no law respecting an establishment of religion. . . ."

. . . By its express terms, what it mandates is the perpetual guaranty of the "[f]ree exercise and enjoyment" of religion; what it prohibits is "discrimination" against, "or preference" in favor of, one religion as opposed to another.

The Governor's Good Friday order has produced both of the results which the clause prohibits. Because it has appointed an exclusively Christian holy day as a paid "holiday" for all pertinent purposes affecting state offices and employees, it amounts to "discrimination" against all non-Christian religions and "preference" of those which are Christian. The trial court made these effects abundantly clear, in its findings and conclusions, by citing the discriminatory and preferential character of the order with reference to the Jewish religion. (See findings 13, 14 and 15, and conclusion of law no. 2, all as quoted *supra*.)

The court was therefore correct in concluding that the exclusive action in question "further violates Article I, Section 4 of the California Constitution in that it constitutes discrimination and preference of one religion over others." (Conclusion of law no. 4.) The judgment is to be affirmed on this distinct basis.

[In closing, the court suggested that the decision is limited.]

. . . It is addressed exclusively to the State's "holiday" involvement with the "wholly religious" day of Good Friday as described. It does not reach the "holiday" observance of any other day which has religious connotations, past or present. (As to Christmas, for example, see *Allen* v. *Morton* (1973) 495 F.2d 65, 72-74.)

The judgment is affirmed. . . .

# 3. Enforcement Litigation

## A. TIME LIMITATIONS

### OCCIDENTAL LIFE INSURANCE CO. v. EEOC

*Supreme Court of the United States, 1977*
*432 U.S. 355, 14 FEP Cases 1718*

MR. JUSTICE STEWART delivered the opinion of the Court.

In 1972 Congress amended Title VII of the Civil Rights Act of 1964 so as to empower the Equal Employment Opportunity Commission to bring suit in a federal district court against a private employer alleged to have violated the Act. The sole question presented by this case is what time limitation, if any, is imposed on the EEOC power to bring such a suit.

### I

On December 27, 1970, an employee of the petitioner Occidental Life Insurance Company filed a charge with the EEOC claiming that the company had discriminated against her sex.[1] After a fruitless referral to the appropriate state agency, the charge was formally filed with the EEOC on March 9, 1971,[2] and subsequently served on the company. After investigation, the EEOC served proposed findings of fact on the company on February 25, 1972, to which the company in due course filed exceptions. Conciliation discussions between the EEOC and the company began in the summer of 1972. These discussions continued sporadically into 1973, but on September 13 of that year the EEOC determined that conciliation efforts had failed and so notified the company and the original complainant. The latter requested that the case be referred to the General Counsel of the EEOC to bring an enforcement action. On February 22, 1974, approximately three years and two months after the complainant first communicated with the EEOC and five months after conciliation efforts had failed, the EEOC brought this enforcement action in a federal district court.

The District Court granted the company's motion for summary judgment on the ground that the law requires that an enforcement action be

---

[1] [Footnotes numbered as in original.—Ed.] The charge specified that the most recent act of discrimination was on October 1, 1970.
[2] Civil Rights Act of 1964 § 706(b), (d), 78 Stat. 253 (1964); *Love v. Pullman Co.*, 404 U.S. 522, 4 FEP Cases 150.

brought within 180 days of the filing of a charge with the EEOC.[3] Alternatively, the court held that the action was subject to the most appropriate state limitations statute and was therefore barred by the one-year limitation provision of California Code of Civil Procedure § 340(3).[4] The Court of Appeals for the Ninth Circuit reversed, holding that the federal law does not impose a 180-day limitation on the EEOC's authority to sue and that the action is not governed by any state statute of limitations. *EEOC* v. *Occidental Life Insurance Co.*, 535 F.2d 533, 12 FEP Cases 1300.

We granted certiorari, _____ U.S. _____, to consider an important and recurring question regarding Title VII.

## II

As enacted in 1964, Title VII limited the EEOC's function to investigation of employment discrimination charges and informal methods of conciliation and persuasion.[5] The failure of conciliation efforts terminated the involvement of the EEOC. Enforcement could then be achieved, if at all, only if the charging party, or other person aggrieved by the allegedly unlawful practice, initiated a private suit within 30 days after EEOC notification that conciliation had not been successful.[6]

In the Equal Employment Opportunity Act of 1972 [7] Congress established an integrated, multistep enforcement procedure culminating in the EEOC's authority to bring a civil action in a federal court. That procedure begins when a charge is filed with the EEOC alleging that an employer has engaged in an unlawful employment practice. A charge must be filed within 180 days after the occurrence of the allegedly unlawful practice, and the EEOC is directed to serve notice of the charge on the employer within 10 days of filing.[8] The EEOC is then required to investigate the charge and determine whether there is reasonable cause to believe that it is true. This determination is to be made "as promptly as possible and, so far as practicable, not later than one hundred and twenty days from the filing of the charge." [9] If the EEOC finds that there is

---

[3] The 1972 amendments to Title VII were made applicable "with respect to charges pending with the Commission on the date of enactment." Pub. L. No. 92-61 § 14, 86 Stat. 113 (1972). The District Court also held that EEOC enforcement suits, such as this one, based on charges within the coverage of § 14 must be brought within 180 days of March 24, 1972, the effective date of the amendments.

[4] The District Court's decision in *EEOC* v. *Occidental Life Insurance Co.*, No. 74-1698 (MD Cal., Dec. 9, 1974), is not officially reported. It is unofficially reported at 12 FEP Cases 1298.

[5] Civil Rights Act of 1964 § 706(a), 78 Stat. 253 (1964).

[6] *Id.*, § 706(e).

[7] Pub. L. No. 92-261, 86 Stat. 103 (1972), 42 U.S.C. § 2000e *et seq.* (Supp. V.), amending, Civil Rights Act of 1964, 78 Stat. 253. All subsequent citations to Title VII in this opinion are to the 1964 Act as amended.

[8] § 706(e), 42 U.S.C. § 2000e-5(e) (Supp. V). If a charge has been initially filed with or referred to a state or local agency, it must be filed with the EEOC within 300 days after the practice occurred or within 30 days after notice that the state or local agency has terminated its proceeding whichever is earlier. *Ibid.*

[9] § 706(b), 42 U.S.C. § 2000e-5(b) (Supp. V).

reasonable cause it "shall endeavor to eliminate any such unlawful employment practice by informal methods of conference, conciliation, and persuasion." [10] When "the Commission [is] unable to secure . . . a conciliation agreement acceptable to the Commission, the Commission may bring a civil action against any respondent not a government, governmental agency, or political subdivision named in the charge." [11]

The 1972 Act expressly imposes only one temporal restriction on the EEOC's authority to embark upon the final stage of enforcement—the bringing of a civil suit in a federal district court: Under § 706(f)(1), the EEOC may not invoke the judicial power to compel compliance with Title VII until at least 30 days after a charge has been filed. But neither § 706(f) nor any other section of the Act explicitly requires the EEOC to conclude its conciliation efforts and bring an enforcement suit within any maximum period of time.

The language of the Act upon which the District Court relied in finding a limitation that bars the bringing of a lawsuit by the EEOC more than 180 days after a timely charge has been filed with it is found in § 706(f)(1), which provides in relevant part:

"If a charge filed with the Commission , , , is dismissed by the Commission, or within one hundred and eighty days from the filing of such charge or the expiration of any period of reference [from a state agency], whichever is later, the Commission has not filed a civil action under this section . . . , or the Commission has not entered into a conciliation agreement to which the person aggrieved is a party, the Commission . . . , shall so notify the person aggrieved and within ninety days after the giving of such notice a civil action may be brought against the respondent named in the charge (A) by the person claiming to be aggrieved or (B) if such charge was filed by a member of the Commission, by any person whom the charge alleges was aggrieved by the alleged unlawful employment practice."

On its face, § 706(f)(1) provides little support for the argument that the 180-day provision is such a statute of limitations. Rather than limiting action by the EEOC, the provision seems clearly addressed to an alternative enforcement procedure: If a complainant is dissatisfied with the progress the EEOC is making on his or her charge of employment discrimination, he or she may elect to circumvent the EEOC procedures and seek relief through a private enforcement action in a district court. The 180-day limitation provides only that this private right of action does not arise until 180 days after a charge has been filed. Nothing in § 706(f)(1) indicates that EEOC enforcement powers cease if the complainant decides to leave the case in the hands of the EEOC rather than to pursue a private action.

In short, the literal language of § 706(f)(1) simply cannot support a

[10] § 706(b), 42 U.S.C. § 2000e-5(b) (Supp. V).

[11] § 706(f)(1), 42 U.S.C. § 2000e-5(f)(1) (Supp. V). In the case of a government, governmental agency, or political subdivision, the EEOC is required, upon failure of conciliation, to refer the case to the Attorney General who may then bring a civil action. *Ibid.*

determination that it imposes a 180-day time limitation on EEOC enforcement suits. On the contrary, a natural reading of § 706(f)(1) can lead only to the conclusion that it simply provides that a complainant whose charge is not dismissed or promptly settled or litigated by the EEOC may himself bring a lawsuit, but that he must wait 180 days before doing so. After waiting for that period, the complainant may either file a private action within 90 days after EEOC notification or continue to leave the ultimate resolution of his charge to the efforts of the EEOC.

Only if the legislative history of § 706(f)(1) provided firm evidence that the subsection cannot mean what it so clearly seems to say would there be any justification for construing it in any other way. But no such evidence is to be found.

[Discussion of legislative history omitted.]

The legislative history of § 706(f)(1) thus demonstrates that the provision was intended to mean exactly what it seems to say: that an aggrieved person unwilling to await the conclusion of extended EEOC proceedings may institute a private lawsuit 180 days after a charge has been filed. The subsection imposes no limitation upon the power of the EEOC to file suit in a federal court.[21]

### III

The company argues that if the Act contains no limitation on the time during which an EEOC enforcement suit may be brought, then the most analogous state statute of limitations should be applied.[22] Relying on a long line of cases in this Court holding state limitations periods applicable to actions brought under federal statutes, the company contends that California law barred the EEOC from bringing this lawsuit.

When Congress has created a cause of action and has not specified the period of time within which it may be asserted, the Court has frequently inferred that Congress intended that a local time limitation should apply. *E.g., Runyon* v. *McCrary,* 427 U.S. 160, 179-182 (Civil Rights Act of 1866); *Autoworkers* v. *Hoosier Cardinal Corp.,* 383 U.S. 696, 61 LRRM 2545 (Section 301 of the Labor Management Relations Act); *O'Sullivan* v. *Felix,* 233 U.S. 318 (Civil Rights Act of 1871): *Chattanooga Foundry & Pipe Works* v. *Atlanta,* 203 U.S. 390 (Sherman Antitrust Act); *Campbell* v. *Haverhill,* 155 U.S. 610 (Patent Act). This "implied absorption of State statutes of limitation within the interstices of . . . federal enactments is a phase of fashioning remedial details where Congress has not spoken but left matters for judicial determination." *Holmberg* v. *Armbrecht,* 327 U.S. 392, 395.

But the Court has not mechanically applied a state statute of limita-

---

[21] In addition to the Court of Appeals for the Ninth Circuit in the present case, six other courts of appeals have reached this conclusion. [Citations omitted.]

[22] The two courts of appeals that have considered this question have reached differing conclusions. *EEOC* v. *Kimberly-Clark, supra,* at 1359-60, 10 FEP Cases, at 44-45 (state limitations not applicable); *EEOC* v. *Griffin Wheel Co.,* 511 F.2d 456, 10 FEP Cases 531 (CA5) (state limitations applicable to backpay suits only).

tions simply because a limitations period is absent from the federal statute. State legislatures do not devise their limitations periods with national interests in mind, and it is the duty of the federal courts to assure that the importation of state law will not frustrate or interfere with the implementation of national policies. "Although state law is our primary guide in this area, it is not, to be sure, our exclusive guide." *Johnson* v. *Railway Express Agency,* 421 U.S. 454, 465, 10 FEP Cases 817, 821. State limitations periods will not be borrowed if their application would be inconsistent with the underlying policies of the federal statute. *Ibid.; Autoworkers* v. *Hoosier Cardinal Corp., supra.,* at 701; *Board of County Commissioners* v. *United States,* 308 U.S. 343, 352. With these considerations in mind, we turn to the company's argument in this case.

When Congress first enacted Title VII in 1964 it selected "[c]ooperation and voluntary compliance . . . as the preferred means for achieving" the goal of equality of employment opportunities. *Alexander* v. *Gardner Denver Co.,* 415 U.S. 36, 44, 7 FEP Cases 81, 84. To this end, Congress created the EEOC and established an administrative procedure whereby the EEOC "would have an opportunity to settle disputes through conference, conciliation, and persuasion before the aggrieved party was permitted to file a lawsuit." *Ibid.* Although the 1972 amendments provided the EEOC with the additional enforcement power of instituting civil actions in federal courts, Congress preserved the EEOC's administrative functions in § 706 of the amended Act. Thus, under the procedural structure created by the 1972 amendments, the EEOC does not function simply as a vehicle for conducting litigation on behalf of private parties; it is a federal administrative agency charged with the responsibility of investigating claims of employment discrimination and settling disputes, if possible, in an informal, noncoercive fashion. Unlike the typical litigant against whom a statute of limitations might appropriately run, the EEOC is required by law to refrain from commencing a civil action until it has discharged its administrative duties.

In view of the federal policy requiring employment discrimination claims to be investigated by the EEOC and, whenever possible, administratively resolved before suit is brought in a federal court, it is hardly appropriate to rely on the "State's wisdom in setting a limit . . . on the prosecution. . . ." *Johnson* v. *Railway Express Agency, supra* at 464, 10 FEP Cases, at 821. For the "State's wisdom" in establishing a general limitation period could not have taken into account the decision of Congress to delay judicial action while the EEOC performs its administrative responsibilities. See *Order of Railroad Telegraphers* v. *Railway Express Agency, Inc.,* 321 U.S. 342, 348, 14 LRRM 506; *Cope* v. *Anderson,* 331 U.S. 461, 464; *Rawlings* v. *Ray,* 312 U.S. 96, 98. Indeed, the one-year statute of limitations applied by the District Court in this case could under some circumstances directly conflict with the timetable for administrative action expressly established in the 1972 Act.

But even in cases involving no inevitable and direct conflict with the express time periods provided in the Act, absorption of state limitations would be inconsistent with the congressional intent underlying the enactment of the 1972 amendments. Throughout the congressional debates many members of both Houses demonstrated an acute awareness of the enormous backlog of cases before the EEOC and the consequent delays of 18 to 24 months encountered by aggrieved persons awaiting administrative action on their complaints. Nevertheless, Congress substantially increased the workload of the EEOC by extending the coverage of Title VII to state employers, private employers with as few as 15 employees, and nonreligious educational institutions; [26] by transferring the authority to bring pattern or practice suits from the Attorney General to the Commission; and by authorizing the Commission to bring civil actions in the federal courts. It would hardly be reasonable to suppose that a Congress aware of the severe time problems already facing the EEOC would grant that agency substantial additional enforcement responsibilities and at the same time consign its federal lawsuits to the vagaries of diverse state limitations statutes, some as short as one year.

Congress did express concern for the need of time limitations in the fair operation of the Act, but that concern was directed entirely to the initial filing of a charge with the EEOC and prompt notification thereafter to the alleged violator. The bills passed in both the House and the Senate contained short time periods within which charges were to be filed with the EEOC and notice given to the employer. And the debates and reports in both Houses made evident that the statute of limitations problem was perceived in terms of these provisions, rather than in terms of a later limitation on the EEOC's power to sue. That perception was reflected in the final version of the 1972 Act, which requires that a charge must be filed with the EEOC within 180 days of the alleged violation of Title VII, and that the alleged violator must be notified "of the charge (including the date, place and circumstances of the alleged unlawful employment practice) . . . within ten days" thereafter.

The fact that the only statute of limitations discussions in Congress were directed to the period preceding the filing of an initial charge is wholly consistent with the Act's overall enforcement structure—a sequential series of steps beginning with the filing of a charge with the EEOC. Within this procedural framework, the benchmark, for purposes of a statute of limitations, is not the last phase of the multistage scheme, but the commencement of the proceeding before the administrative body.

## IV

The absence of inflexible time limitations on the bringing of lawsuits will not, as the company asserts, deprive defendants in Title VII civil

---

[26] §§ 701(a), (b), 42 U.S.C. §§ 2000e (a), (b) 2000e-1 (Supp. V). The number of state and local governmental employees who would be brought under the jurisdiction of the EEOC was estimated to be more than 10 million. 117 Cong. Rec. 31961 (1971) (remarks of Rep. Perkins); 118 Cong. Rec. 699 (1972) (remarks of Sen. Fannin). The elimination of the exemption for nonreligious educational institutions added an estimated 4.3 million employees. 118 Cong. Rec. 4931 (1972) (remarks of Sen. Cranston).

actions of fundamental fairness or subject them to the surprise and prejudice that can result from the prosecution of stale claims. Unlike the litigant in a private action who may first learn of the cause against him upon service of the complaint, the Title VII defendant is alerted to the possibility of an enforcement suit within 10 days after a charge has been filed. This prompt notice serves, as Congress intended, to give him an opportunity to gather and preserve evidence in anticipation of a court action.

Moreover, during the pendency of EEOC administrative proceedings, a potential defendant is kept informed of the progress of the action. Regulations promulgated by the EEOC require that the charged party be promptly notified when a determination of reasonable cause has been made,[32] 29 CFR § 1601.19b(b), and when the EEOC has terminated its efforts to conciliate a dispute, id., §§ 1601.23, 1601.25.

It is, of course, possible that despite these procedural protections a defendant in a Title VII enforcement action might still be significantly handicapped in making his defense because of an inordinate EEOC delay in filing the action after exhausting its conciliation efforts. If such cases arise the federal courts do not lack the power to provide relief. This Court has said that when a Title VII defendant is in fact prejudiced by a private plaintiff's unexcused conduct of a particular case, the trial court may restrict or even deny backpay relief. *Albemarle Paper Co.* v. *Moody,* 422 U.S. 405, 424-25, 10 FEP Cases 1181, 1190. The same discretionary power "to locate 'a just result' in light of the circumstances peculiar to the case," ibid., can also be exercised when the EEOC is the plaintiff.

The judgment of the Court of Appeals is affirmed.

## ELECTRICAL WORKERS, IUE, LOCAL 790 v. ROBBINS & MYERS, INC.

*Supreme Court of the United States, 1976*
*429 U.S. 229, 13 FEP Cases 1813*

MR. JUSTICE REHNQUIST delivered the opinion of the Court.

Petitioners seek review of a decision of the Court of Appeals for the Sixth Circuit holding that a claim brought by petitioner Dortha Guy under Title VII was barred by her failure to file a charge with the Equal Employment Opportunity Commission (EEOC) within the statutory limitations period. They present three contentions: the existence and utilization of grievance procedures postpones the date on which an allegedly discriminatory firing took place; the existence and utilization of

---

[32] Prompt notice of a reasonable cause determination also serves to cure any deficiencies in the 10-day notice that may result from EEOC amendment of the claimed violation after investigation. See *EEOC* v. *General Electric Co.*, 532 F.2d 359, 366, 12 FEP Cases 21, 25 (CA4); *EEOC* v. *Huttig Sash & Door Co.*, 511 F.2d 453, 455, 10 FEP Cases 529, 531 (CA5); *EEOC* v. *Kimberly-Clark Corp.*, 511 F.2d 1352, 1363, 10 FEP Cases 38, 45 (CA6). See also *NLRB* v. *Fant Milling Co.*, 360 U.S. 301, 44 LRRM 2236; *National Licorice Co.* v. *NLRB*, 309 U.S. 350, 367-69, 6 LRRM 674.

grievance procedures tolls the running of the limitations period which would otherwise begin on the date of the firing; and the 1972 amendments to Title VII, Equal Employment Opportunity Act of 1972, 86 Stat. 103 (Mar. 24, 1972), extending the limitations period from 90 to 180 days, apply to the charge in this case.

## I

Respondent terminated the employment of petitioner Guy on October 25, 1971, and assigned as its reason for doing so her failure to comply with procedures contained in the collective-bargaining agreement pertaining to leaves of absence. Two days later petitioner caused a grievance alleging the "unfair action" of the Company in firing her to be filed on her behalf in accordance with the provisions of the collective-bargaining agreement then in force between petitioner Local 790 of the International Union of Electrical, Radio and Machine Workers (Local 790) and respondent. That agreement's dispute resolution procedure, which is to be commenced within "five (5) working days of the commission of the act originating the grievance," consists of three grievance steps followed by one arbitration step. Guy's grievance was processed through the third step of the grievance procedure where it was denied on November 18, 1971, with the finding that her termination had been in accordance with the provisions of the collective-bargaining agreement.

On February 10, 1972, a date 84 days after the denial of her grievance at the third stage, but 108 days after the date of her discharge, Guy, who is black, filed a charge of racial discrimination with the EEOC directed against both Robbins & Myers and Local 790. The EEOC in due course issued its determination and "right to sue" letter finding that there was "no reason to believe that race was a factor in the decision to discharge" Guy. Her suit in the United States District Court for the Western District of Tennessee under 42 U.S.C. § 2000e-5 was met by a motion to dismiss on the ground, *inter alia*, that it was barred because of her failure to file a charge with the EEOC within 90 days of her discharge, § 706(d), 42 U.S.C. § 2000e-5(d).[1] The District Court dismissed her action,[2] and the Court of Appeals affirmed that judgment by a divided vote, 525 F.2d 124, 11 FEP Cases 641. That court felt that it would be "utterly inconsistent" with our opinions in *Johnson* v. *Railway Express Agency*, 421 U.S. 454, 10 FEP Cases 817 (1975) and in *Alexander* v. *Gardner-Denver Co.*, 415 U.S. 36, 7 FEP Cases 81 (1974) to hold that the pursuit of a contractual grievance procedure operates to toll a Title VII remedy "which the em-

---

[1] [Footnotes numbered as in original.—Ed.] At the time of her discharge, and at the time the charge was filed with the EEOC, § 706(d) stated, in pertinent part: "A charge under subsection (a) of this section shall be filed within ninety days after the alleged unlawful employment practice occurred. . . ." Section 706(d) was renumbered as § 706(e), 42 U.S.C. § 2000e-5(e), as a result of the 1972 amendments to the Act. Whenever § 706(d) is cited in this opinion, it refers to the pre-1972 version of what is now § 706(e).

[2] Guy also alleged a cause of action under 42 U.S.C. § 1981. By order dated May 30, 1974, the District Court dismissed this cause of action because of a failure to meet the applicable Tennessee statute of limitations. No appeal was taken from this decision.

ployee has a right to resort to concurrently." 525 F.2d, at 126, 11 FEP
Cases, at 642. Then, noting the question of the applicability of the 1972
amendments to Title VII raised by the EEOC as *amicus curiae* (also
noting without more that "[s]ince this issue was not raised in the District
Court by any party to the case, we are not required to consider it") the
Court of Appeals stated

"Plaintiff Guy's claim was barred on January 24, 1972. She did not file
her charge with EEOC until February 10, 1972. The amendments to
Title VII, increasing the time within which to file her charge to 180 days,
did not become effective until March 24, 1972. 42 U.S.C. §2000e-5(e). The
subsequent increase of time to file the charge enacted by Congress could
not revive plaintiff's claim which had been previously barred and extinguished." 525 F.2d, at 128, 11 FEP Cases, at 643-44.
The dissenting judge disagreed on this point, believing that the case
should be remanded for consideration of the effect of the 1972 amendments.

We granted certiorari, 425 U.S. 950, to resolve an apparent circuit
conflict on two of these issues: tolling during the pendency of a collective-
bargaining-contract's grievance mechanism, and the applicability of the
1972 amendments to charges filed more than 90 days from the date of
the alleged discriminatory act but less than 180 days before the time the
amendments became effective.

## II

[The Court rejected the first contention.]

## III

We think that petitioners' arguments for tolling the statutory period
for filing a claim with the EEOC during the pendency of grievance or
arbitration procedures under the collective-bargaining contract are virtually foreclosed by our decisions in *Alexander* v. *Gardner-Denver Co.*,
415 U.S. 36, 7 FEP Cases 81 (1974), and in *Johnson* v. *Railway Express
Agency*, 421 U.S. 454, 10 FEP Cases 817 (1975). In *Alexander* we held that
an arbitrator's decision pursuant to provisions in a collective-bargaining
contract was not binding on an individual seeking to pursue his Title
VII remedies in court. We reasoned that the contractual rights under a
collective-bargaining agreement and the statutory right provided by
Congress under Title VII "have legally independent origins and are
equally available to the aggrieved employee," 415 U.S., at 52, 7 FEP
Cases, at 87,[8] and for that reason we concluded that:
"[I]n instituting an action under Title VII, the employee is not seeking
review of the arbitrator's decision. Rather, he is asserting a statutory right

[8] See also *id.*, at 48-49, 7 FEP Cases, at 85-86: "Title VII was designed to supplement,
rather than supplant, existing laws and institutions relating to employment discrimination." We felt that the legislative history was quite clear in this respect, see, *e.g.*, 110
Cong. Rec. 7202, 13650-652 (1964); H. R. 9247, 92d Cong., 1st Sess. (1971); H. R. Rep.
No. 92-238 (1971); S. Rep. No. 415, 92d Cong., 1st Sess., at 24 (1971).

independent of the arbitration process." 415 U.S., at 54, 7 FEP Cases, at 88.

One Term later, we reaffirmed the independence of Title VII remedies from other pre-existing remedies available to an aggrieved employee. In *Johnson* v. *Railway Express Agency,* 421 U.S. 454, 10 FEP Cases 817 (1975), we held that the timely filing of a charge with the EEOC pursuant to § 706 of Title VII did not toll the running of the statute of limitations applicable to an action, based on the same facts, brought under 42 U.S.C. § 1981. In reaffirming the independence of Title VII remedies from other remedies, we noted that such independence might occasionally be a two-edged sword,[9] but "in the face of congressional emphasis upon the existence and independence of the two remedies," we were disinclined "to infer any positive preference for one over the other, without a more definite expression in the legislation Congress has enacted," 421 U.S., at 461, 10 FEP Cases at 820.

Petitioners insist that notwithstanding these decisions, equitable tolling principles should be applied to this case, and that the application of such principles would toll the 90-day period pending completion of the grievance procedures. This is so, they say, because in this case the "policy of repose, designed to protect defendants," *Burnett* v. *New York Central R. Co.,* 380 U.S. 424, 428 (1965), is "outweighed [because] the interests of justice require vindication of the plaintiff's rights," ibid.

But this is quite a different case from *Burnett, supra.*[10] There the plaintiff in an FELA action *had* asserted his FELA claim in the state courts, which had concurrent jurisdiction with the federal courts, but he had the misfortune of filing his complaint in an Ohio state court where venue did not lie under Ohio law. This Court held that such a filing was sufficient to toll the statutory limitations period, even though the state court action was dismissed for improper venue and a new complaint ultimately filed in the United States District Court. The Court said: "Petitioner here did not sleep on his rights but brought an action within the statutory period in a state court of competent jurisdiction. Service of process was made upon the respondent notifying him that petitioner was asserting his cause of action." 380 U.S., at 429.

Here petitioner Guy in the grievance proceedings was not asserting

---

[9] "Conciliation and persuasion through the administrative process [*e.g.,* Title VII], to be sure, often constitute a desirable approach to settlement of disputes based on sensitive and emotional charges of invidious employment discrimination. We recognize, too, that the filing of a lawsuit might tend to deter efforts at conciliation, that lack of success in the legal action could weaken the Commission's efforts to induce voluntary compliance, and that a suit is privately oriented and narrow, rather than broad, in application, as successful conciliation tends to be. But these are the natural effects of the choice Congress has made available to the claimant by its conferring upon his independent administrative and judicial remedies. The choice is a valuable one," *Johnson* v. *Railway Express Agency, supra,* at 461, 10 FEP Cases, at 820.

[10] In no way is this a situation in which a party has "been prevented from asserting" his or her rights, *Burnett* v. *New York Central R. Co., supra,* at 429. There is no assertion that Guy was "prevented" from filing a charge with the EEOC within 90 days of October 25, 1971; indeed, it is conceded and even urged that she could have filed it the following day, had she so wished.

the same statutory claim in a different forum, nor giving notice to respondent of that statutory claim, but was asserting an independent claim based on a *contract* right, *Alexander* v. *Gardner-Denver Co., supra,* at 53-54, 56-58, 7 FEP Cases at 87, 89. *Burnett* cannot aid this petitioner, see *Johnson* v. *Railway Express Agency, supra,* at 467-68, and n. 14, 10 FEP Cases, at 822." [11]

Petitioners advance as a corollary argument for tolling the premise that substantial policy considerations, based on the central role of arbitration in labor-management relations, see *United Steelworkers* v. *American Mfg. Co.,* 363 U.S. 564, 46 LRRM 2423 (1960), *Textile Workers Union* v. *Lincoln Mills,* 353 U.S. 448, 40 LRRM 2113 (1957), also dictate a finding that the Title VII limitations period is tolled in this situation. Similar arguments by the employer in *Alexander* v. *Gardner-Denver Co., supra,* urging the superiority and pre-eminence of the arbitration process were rejected by us in that case, and we find the reasoning of that case controlling in rejecting this claim made by petitioners.

Petitioners also advance a related argument that the danger of possible conflict between the concurrent pursuit of both collective bargaining and Title VII remedies should result in tolling the limitations period for the latter while the former proceeds to conclusion. Similar arguments to these, albeit relating to § 1981 and not to private labor agreements, were, however, raised and rejected in *Johnson, supra.* We think the language we used in that case is sufficient to dispose of this claim:
"it is conceivable, and perhaps almost to be expected, that failure to toll will have the effect of pressing a civil rights complainant who values his § 1981 claim into court before the EEOC has completed its administrative proceeding. One answer to this, although perhaps not a highly satisfactory one, is that the plaintiff in his § 1981 suit may ask the court to stay proceedings until the administrative efforts at conciliation and voluntary compliance have been completed. But the fundamental answer to petitioner's argument lies in the fact—presumably a happy one for the civil rights claimant—that Congress clearly has retained § 1981 as a remedy against private employment discrimination separate from and independent of the more elaborate and time-consuming procedures of Title VII." 421 U.S., at 465-66, 10 FEP Cases, at 821-22.

Petitioners contend at some length that tolling would impose almost no costs, as the delays occasioned by the grievance-arbitration process would be "slight," [12] noting that the maximum delay in invoking the three-stage grievance procedure (although not including the arbitration step) under the collective-bargaining agreement in force in this case would be 35 days.

[11] We concluded in *Johnson* that "[o]nly where there is complete identity of the causes of action will the protections suggested by petitioner necessarily exist and will the courts have an opportunity to assess the influence of the policy of repose inherent in a limitations period," *id.,* at 468 n. 14, 10 FEP Cases, at 822. See n. 14, *infra.*

[12] Petitioners contend that the vast majority of collective-bargaining agreements have stringent time restrictions on the resolution of disputes through the grievance stages, see, *e.g.,* Brief of Petitioner Local 790, at 38-39; see also EEOC Brief *Amicus Curiae,* at 23 n. 13.

But the principal answer to this contention is that Congress has already spoken with respect to what it considers acceptable delay when it established a 90-day limitations period, and gave no indication that it considered a "slight" delay followed by 90 days equally acceptable. In defining Title VII's jurisdictional prerequisites "with precision," *Alexander* v. *Gardner-Denver Co., supra,* at 47, 7 FEP Cases, at 85, Congress did not leave to courts the decision as to which delays might or might not be "slight." [13]

Congress did provide in § 706(d) one exception for this 90-day limitations period, when it provided that the limitations period should run for a maximum additional 120 days when there existed "a state or local law prohibiting the unlawful employment practice alleged and establishing or authorizing a state or local authority to grant or seek relief from such practice or to institute criminal proceedings with respect thereto upon receiving notice thereof," § 706(b). Where Congress has spoken with respect to a claim much more closely related to the Title VII claim than is the contractual claim pursued under the grievance procedure, and then firmly limited the maximum possible extension of the limitations period applicable thereto, we think that all of petitioners' arguments taken together simply do not carry sufficient weight to overcome the negative implication from the language used by Congress, cf. *Johnson* v. *Railway Express Agency, supra,* at 461, 10 FEP Cases, at 820.[14]

[On the third contention, the Court held that the 180-day period was applicable.]

## B.   RELATIONSHIP BETWEEN TITLE VII AND § 1981

### JOHNSON v. RAILWAY EXPRESS AGENCY, INC.

*Supreme Court of the United States, 1975*
*421 U.S. 454, 10 FEP Cases 817*

MR. JUSTICE BLACKMUN delivered the opinion of the Court.

This case presents the issue whether the timely filing of a charge of employment discrimination with the Equal Employment Opportunity

---

[13] Even taken on its own ground, this argument is not unambiguously favorable to petitioners. If the collective-bargaining dispute settlement procedures are as speedy as suggested, no real need for tolling has been shown. In the instant case, for example, at the conclusion of stage three of the grievance procedure, Guy still had 66 days in which to file a charge with the EEOC, and no reason has been advanced as to why this was not ample time.

[14] Adherence to the limitations period assures prompt notification to the employer of a charge of an alleged violation of Title VII, see § 702(b). The grievance process assures no such comparable notice. In the instant case, the grievance alleged only an "unfair action." Even if racial discrimination is explicitly discussed, however, the grievance procedure properly involves only *contractual* questions, and would but fortuitously implicate the Title VII standards, *Alexander v. Gardner-Denver Co., supra,* at 53-54, 56-58, 7 FEP Cases, at 87, 89; see also *Johnson v. Railway Express Agency, supra,* 467-68 n. 14, 10 FEP Cases, at 822. Petitioners' arguments respecting the policies behind private resolution of labor disputes through collective bargaining, moreover, apply equally to

Commission (EEOC), pursuant to § 706 of Title VII of the Civil Rights Act of 1964, 42 U.S.C. § 2000e-5, tolls the running of the period of limitation applicable to an action, based on the same facts, instituted under 42 U.S.C. § 1981.

## I

Petitioner, Willie Johnson, Jr., is a Negro. He started to work for respondent, Railway Express Agency, Inc., now, by change of name, REA Express, Inc. (REA), in Memphis, Tennessee in spring of 1964 as an express handler. On May 31, 1967, while still employed by REA, but now as a driver rather than as a handler, petitioner, with others, timely filed with the EEOC a charge that REA was discriminating against its Negro employees with respect to seniority rules and job assignments. He also charged the respondent unions, Brotherhood of Railway Clerks Tri-State Local and Brotherhood of Railway Clerks Lily of the Valley Local, with maintaining racially segregated memberships (white and Negro respectively). Three weeks later, on June 20, REA terminated petitioner's employment. Petitioner then amended his charge to include an allegation that he had been discharged because of his race.

The EEOC issued its "Final Investigation Report" on December 22, 1967. App. 14a. The report generally supported petitioner's claims of racial discrimination. It was not until more than two years later, however, on March 31, 1970, that the Commission rendered its decision finding reasonable cause to believe petitioner's charges. And 9½ more months went by before the EEOC, on January 15, 1971, pursuant to 42 U.S.C. § 2000e-5 (e), as it then read, gave petitioner notice of his right to institute a Title VII civil action against the respondents within 30 days.[1]

After receiving this notice, petitioner encountered some difficulty in obtaining counsel. The United States District Court for the Western District of Tennessee, on February 12, 1971, permitted petitioner to file the right-to-sue letter with the court's clerk as a complaint, in satisfaction of the 30-day requirement. The court also granted petitioner leave to proceed *in forma pauperis* and it appointed counsel to represent him. On March 18, counsel filed a "Supplemental Complaint" against REA and the two unions, alleging racial discrimination on the part of the defendants, in violation of Title VII of the 1964 Act *and* of 42 U.S.C. § 1981. The unions and REA respectively moved for summary judgment or, in the alternative, for dismissal of all claims.

---

the arbitration stage as they do to the grievance stage, cf. *Emporium Capwell Co.* v. *Western Addition Community Org.*, 420 U.S. 50, 66-67, 9 FEP Cases, 195, 202-203 (1975); *Alexander* v. *Gardner-Denver Co., supra*, at 56, 59-60, 7 FEP Cases, at 88-89, 90; *Boy's Market, Inc.* v. *Retail Clerk's Union*, 398 U.S. 235, 74 LRRM 2257 (1970). Yet, at the arbitration stage the assurance of but a "slight" delay is lacking.

[1] [Footnotes numbered as in original.—Ed.] The applicable statute later was amended to allow a period of 90 days, after issuance of the notice, in which to bring the Title VII action. 42 U.S.C. § 2000e-5(f)(1), as amended by Pub. L. 92-261, § 4(a), 86 Stat. 104, 106 (1972).

The District Court dismissed the § 1981 claims as barred by Tennessee's one-year statute of limitations. Tenn. Code § 28-304. Petitioner's remaining claims were dismissed on other grounds.[3]

In his appeal to the United States Court of Appeals for the Sixth Circuit, petitioner, with respect to his § 1981 claims, argued that the running of the one-year period of limitation was suspended during the pendency of his timely filed administrative complaint with the EEOC under Title VII. The Court of Appeals rejected this argument. . . . Because of an apparent conflict between that ruling and language and holdings in cases from other circuits,[4] we granted certiorari restricted to the limitation issue. We invited the Solicitor General to file a brief as *amicus curiae* expressing the views of the United States. 417 U.S. 929, 8 FEP Cases 95 (1974).

II

A. Title VII of the Civil Rights Act of 1964 was enacted "to assure equality of employment opportunities by eliminating those practices and devices that discriminate on the basis of race, color, religion, sex, or national origin." *Alexander* v. *Gardner-Denver Co.*, 415 U.S. 36, 44, 7 FEP Cases 81, 84 (1974). It creates statutory rights against invidious discrimination in employment and establishes a comprehensive scheme for the vindication of those rights.

Anyone aggrieved by employment discrimination may lodge a charge with the EEOC. That Commission is vested with the "authority to investigate individual charges of discrimination, to promote voluntary compliance with the requirements of Title VII, and to institute civil actions against employers or unions named in a discrimination charge." *Ibid.* Thus, the Commission itself may institute a civil action. 42 U.S.C. (1970 ed., Supp. III) § 2000e-5 (f)(1). If, however, the EEOC is not successful in obtaining "voluntary compliance" and, for one reason or another, chooses not to sue on the claimant's behalf, the claimant, after the passage of 180 days, may demand a right-to-sue letter and institute the Title VII action himself without waiting for the completion of the conciliation procedures. 42 U.S.C. (1970 ed., Supp. III) § 2000e-5(f)(1). See H. R. Rep. No. 238, 92d

---

[3] The District Court also based its dismissal of petitioner's § 1981 claim against REA on the alternative ground that he had failed to exhaust his administrative remedies under the Railway Labor Act, 45 U.S.C. e. 8. App. 102a. The Court of Appeals did not address the exhaustion argument. Inasmuch as we limited our grant of certiorari to the limitation issue, 417 U.S. 929, 8 FEP Cases 95 (1974), we have no occasion here to express a view as to whether a § 1981 claim of employment discrimination is ever subject to a requirement that administrative remedies be exhausted.

The claims against the unions were dismissed on res judicata grounds. App. 101a. The Court of Appeals agreed with that disposition. 489 F.2d 525, 530 n. 1, 7 FEP Cases 486 (CA6 1974). This issue, also, was not included in our grant of certiorari.

[4] See, e.g., *Boudreaux* v. *Baton Rouge Marine Contracting Co.*, 437 F.2d 1011, 1017 n. 16, 3 FEP Cases 99, 103 (CA5 1971); *Macklin* v. *Spector Freight Systems, Inc.*, 156 U.S. App. D.C. 69, 84-85, n. 30, 478 F.2d 979, 994-995 n. 30, 5 FEP Cases 994, 1005-1006 (1973).

Cong., 2d Sess., 12 (1971); *McDonnell Douglas Corp.* v. *Green,* 411 U.S. 792, 5 FEP Cases 965 (1973).

In the claimant's suit, the Federal District Court is empowered to appoint counsel for him, to authorize the commencement of the action without the payment of fees, costs, or security, and even to allow an attorney's fees. 42 U.S.C. (1970 ed., Supp. III) § 2000e-5(f)(1) and 42 U.S.C. § 2000e-5(k). Where intentional engagement in unlawful discrimination is proved, the court may award backpay and order "such affirmative action as may be appropriate." 42 U.S.C. (1970 ed., Supp. III) § 2000e-5(g). The backpay, however, may not be for more than the two-year period prior to the filing of the charge with the Commission. *Ibid.* Some district courts have ruled that neither compensatory nor punitive damages may be awarded in the Title VII suit.

Despite Title VII's range and its design as a comprehensive solution for the problem of invidious discrimination in employment, the aggrieved individual clearly is not deprived of other remedies he possesses and is not limited to Title VII in his search for relief. "[T]he legislative history of Title VII manifests a congressional intent to allow an individual to pursue independently his rights under both Title VII and other applicable state and federal statutes." *Alexander* v. *Gardner-Denver, Co.,* 415 U.S., at 48, 7 FEP Cases at 85. In particular, Congress noted "that the remedies available to the individual under Title VII are coextensive with the indivdual's [sic] right to sue under the provisions of the Civil Rights Act of 1866, 42 U.S.C. § 1981, and that the two procedures augment each other and are not mutually exclusive." H. R. Rep. No. 238, 92d Cong., 1st Sess., 19 (1971). See also S. Rep. No. 415, 92d Cong., 1st Sess., 24 (1971). Later in considering the Equal Employment Opportunity Act of 1972, the Senate rejected an amendment that would have deprived a claimant of any right to sue under § 1981. 118 Cong. Rec. 3371-3373 (1972).

B. Title 42 U.S.C. § 1981, being the present codification of § 1 of the century-old Civil Rights Act of 1866, 14 Stat. 27, on the other hand, on its face relates primarily to racial discrimination in the making and enforcement of contracts. Although this Court has not specifically so held, it is well settled among the federal courts of appeals—and we now join them—that § 1981 affords a federal remedy against discrimination in private employment on the basis of race. An individual who establishes a cause of action under § 1981 is entitled to both equitable and legal relief, including compensatory and, under certain circumstances, punitive damages. See, e.g., *Caperci* v. *Huntoon,* 397 F.2d 799 (CA1), *cert. denied,* 393 U.S. 940 (1968); *Mansell* v. *Saunders,* 372 F.2d 573 (CA5 1967). And a backpay award under § 1981 is not restricted to the two years specified for backpay recovery under Title VII.

Section 1981 is not coextensive in its coverage with Title VII. The latter is made inapplicable to certain employers. 42 U.S.C. § 2000e(b). Also, Title VII offers assistance in investigation, conciliation, counsel, waiver of court costs, and attorneys' fees, items that are unavailable at least under the specific terms of § 1981.

## III

Petitioner, and the United States as *amicus curiae,* concede, as they must, the independence of the avenues of relief respectively available under Title VII and the older § 1981. See *Jones* v. *Alfred H. Mayer Co.,* 392 U.S. 409, 416-417 n. 20 (1968). Further, it has been noted that the filing of a Title VII charge and resort to Title VII's administrative machinery are not prerequisites for the institution of a § 1981 action. . . .

We are satisfied, also, that Congress did not expect that a § 1981 court action usually would be resorted to only upon completion of Title VII procedures and the Commission's efforts to obtain voluntary compliance. Conciliation and persuasion through the administrative process, to be sure, often constitute a desirable approach to settlement of disputes based on sensitive and emotional charges of invidious employment discrimination. We recognize, too, that the filing of a law-suit might tend to deter efforts at conciliation, that lack of success in the legal action could weaken the Commission's efforts to induce voluntary compliance, and that a suit is privately oriented and narrow, rather than broad, in application, as successful conciliation tends to be. But these are the natural effects of the choice Congress has made available to the claimant by its conferring upon him independent administrative and judicial remedies. The choice is a valuable one. Under some circumstances, the administrative route may be highly preferred over the litigatory; under others, the reverse may be true. We are disinclined, in the face of congressional emphasis upon the existence and independence of the two remedies, to infer any positive preference for one over the other, without a more definite expression in the legislation Congress has enacted, as, for example, proscription of a § 1981 action while an EEOC claim is pending.

We generally conclude, therefore, that the remedies available under Title VII and under § 1981, although related, and although directed to most of the same ends, are separate, distinct, and independent. With this base established, we turn to the limitation issue.

## IV

A. Since there is no specifically stated or otherwise relevant federal statute of limitations for a cause of action under § 1981, the controlling period would ordinarily be the most appropriate one provided by state law. . . . For purposes of this case, the one-year limitation period in Tenn. Code § 28-304 clearly and specifically has application.[7] See *Warren* v.

---

[7] In the petition for certiorari it was argued that § 28-304 was inapplicable to petitioner's claim because that statute is limited to claims for damages, whereas petitioner sought injunctive relief as well as backpay. Our limited grant of certiorari foreclosed our considering whether some other Tennessee statute, such as Tenn. Code § 28-309 (six years for an action on a contract) or § 28-310 (10 years on an action not otherwise provided for), might be the appropriate one. We also have no occasion to consider whether Tennessee's express application of the one-year limitation period to federal civil rights actions is an impermissible discrimination against the federal cause of action, see *Republic Pictures Corp.* v. *Kappler,* 151 F.2d 543, 546-547, 5 WH Cases 680 (CA8 1945), *aff'd,* 327 U.S. 757, 5 WH Cases 864 (1946), or whether the enactment of the limitation period after the cause of action accrued, Tenn. Pub. Acts 1961, c. 28, did not touch the pre-existing federal claim.

*Norman Realty Co.,* —— F.2d —— (CA8 1975). The cause of action asserted by petitioner accrued, if at all, not later than June 20, 1967, the date of his discharge. Therefore, in the absence of some circumstance that suspended the running of the limitation period, petitioner's cause of action under § 1981 was time-barred after June 20, 1968, some two and one-half years before petitioner filed his complaint.

B. Respondents argue that the only circumstances that would suspend or toll the running of the limitation period under § 28-304 are those expressly provided under state law. See Tenn. Code §§ 28-106 to 28-115 and 28-301. Petitioner concedes, at least implicitly, that no tolling circumstance described in the State's statutes was present to toll the period for his § 1981 claim. He argues, however, that state law should not be given so broad a reach. He claims that, although the duration of the limitation period is bottomed on state law, it is federal law that governs other limitations aspects, such as tolling, of a § 1981 cause of action. Without launching into an exegesis on the nice distinctions that have been drawn in applying state and federal law in this area,[8] we think it suffices to say that petitioner has overstated his case. Indeed, we may assume that he would argue vigorously in favor of applying state law if any of the Tennessee tolling provisions could be said to assist his cause.[9]

Any period of limitation, including the one-year period specified by § 28-304, is understood fully only in the context of the various circumstances that suspend it from running against a particular cause of action. Although any statute of limitations is necessarily arbitrary, the length of the period allowed for instituting suit inevitably reflects a value judgment concerning the point at which the interests in favor of protecting valid claims are outweighed by the interests in prohibiting the prosecution of stale ones. In virtually all statutes of limitation the chronological length of the limitation period is interrelated with provisions regarding tolling, revival, and questions of application. In borrowing a state period of limitation for application to a federal cause of action, a federal court is relying on the State's wisdom in setting a limit, and exceptions thereto, on the prosecution of a closely analogous claim.

There is nothing anomalous or novel about this. State law has been followed in a variety of cases that raised questions concerning the overtones and details of application of the state limitation period to the federal cause of action. . . . Nor is there anything peculiar to a federal civil rights action that would justify special reluctance in applying state law. Indeed, the express terms of 42 U.S.C. § 1988[10] suggest that the contrary is true.

---

[8] See generally Hill, *State Procedural Law in Federal Nondiversity Litigation,* 69 HARV. L. REV. 66 (1955).

[9] At oral argument petitioner advanced just such a proposition with respect to the applicability of Tennessee's saving statute, Tenn. Code § 28-106. Tr. of Oral Arg. 14. See also Petition for Cert. 21 n. 27.

[10] Title 42, U.S.C. § 1988 provides:
"The jurisdiction in civil and criminal matters conferred on the district courts by the provisions of this chapter and Title 18, for the protection of all persons in the United States in their civil rights, and for their vindication, shall be exercised and enforced in

C. Although state law is our primary guide in this area, it is not, to be sure, our exclusive guide. As the Court noted in *Auto Workers* v. *Hoosier Corp.*, 383 U.S., at 706-707, considerations of state law may be displaced where their application would be inconsistent with the federal policy underlying the cause of action under consideration.

Petitioner argues that a failure to toll the limitation period in this case will conflict seriously with the broad remedial and humane purposes of Title VII. Specifically, he urges that Title VII embodies a strong federal policy in support of conciliation and voluntary compliance as a means of achieving the statutory mandate of equal employment opportunity. He suggests that failure to toll the statute on a § 1981 claim during the pendency of an administrative complaint in the EEOC would force a plaintiff into premature and expensive litigation that would destroy all chances for administrative conciliation and voluntary compliance.

We have noted this possibility above and, indeed, it is conceivable, and perhaps almost to be expected, that failure to toll will have the effect of pressing a civil rights complainant who values his § 1981 claim into court before the EEOC has completed its administrative proceeding.[11] One answer to this, although perhaps not a highly satisfactory one, is that the plaintiff in his § 1981 suit may ask the court to stay proceedings until the administrative efforts at conciliation and voluntary compliance have been completed. But the fundamental answer to petitioner's argument lies in the fact—presumably a happy one for the civil rights claimant— that Congress clearly has retained § 1981 as a remedy against private employment discrimination separate from and independent of the more elaborate and time consuming procedures of Title VII. Petitioner freely concedes that he could have filed his § 1981 action at any time after his cause of action accrued; in fact, we understand him to claim an unfettered right so to do. Thus, in a very real sense, petitioner has slept on his § 1981 rights. The fact that his slumber may have been induced by faith in the adequacy of his Title VII remedy is of little relevance inasmuch as the two remedies are truly independent. Moreover, since petitioner's Title VII court action now also appears to be time-barred because of the peculiar procedural history of this case, petitioner, in effect, would have us extend the § 1981 cause of action well beyond the life of even his Title VII cause of action. We find no policy reason that excuses petitioner's

---

conformity with the laws of the United States, so far as such laws are suitable to carry the same into effect; but in all cases where they are not adapted to the object, or are deficient in the provisions necessary to furnish suitable remedies and punish offenses against law, the common law, as modified and changed by the constitution and statutes of the State wherein the court having jurisdiction of such civil or criminal cause is held, so far as the same is not inconsistent with the Constitution and laws of the United States, shall be extended to and govern the said courts in the trial and disposition of the cause, and, if it is of a criminal nature, in the infliction of punishment on the party found guilty."

11 We are not unmindful of the significant delays that have attended administrative proceedings in the EEOC. See, e.g., *Chromcraft Corp.* v. *EEOC*, 465 F.2d 745, 4 FEP Cases 1085 (CA5 1972); *Equal Employment Opportunity Comm.* v. *E. I. duPont deNemours & Co.*, 373 F.Supp. 1321, 1329, 7 FEP Cases 759 (Del 1974).

failure to take the minimal steps necessary to preserve each claim independently.

. . .

The judgment of the Court of Appeals is affirmed.

*It is so ordered.*

MR. JUSTICE MARSHALL, with whom MR. JUSTICE DOUGLAS and MR. JUSTICE BRENNAN join, concurring in part and dissenting in part.

. . .

Congress' failure to include a built-in limitations period in § 1981 does not automatically warrant "an imprimatur on state law" and sanction the borrowing of both the effect as well as the duration from state law. *United Auto Workers* v. *Hoosier Cardinal Corp.,* 383 U.S., at 709 (WHITE, J., dissenting); *Holmberg* v. *Armbrecht,* 327 U.S., at 394-395; *Board of County Comm'rs* v. *United States,* 308 U.S. 343 (1939). It is well settled that when federal courts sit to enforce federal rights, they have an obligation to apply federal equity principles:

"When Congress leaves to the federal courts the formulation of remedial details, it can hardly expect them to break with historic principles of equity in the enforcement of federally-created equitable rights." *Holmberg* v. *Armbrecht,* 327 U.S., at 395.

See also *Moviecolor Ltd.* v. *Eastman Kodak Co.,* 288 F.2d 80 (CA2), *cert. denied,* 368 U.S. 821 (1961).

The effect to be given the borrowed statute is thus a matter of judicial implication. Simply stated, we must determine whether the national policy considerations favoring the continued availability of the § 1981 cause of action outweigh the interests protected by the State's statute of limitations. . . .

I

Title VII and now § 1981 both express the federal policy against discriminatory employment practices. *Emporium Capwell Co.* v. *WACO,* 420 U.S. ——, ——, 9 FEP Cases 195 (1975); *Alexander* v. *Gardner-Denver Co.,* 415 U.S. 36, 44, 7 FEP Cases 81 (1974); *McDonnell Douglas Corp.* v. *Green,* 411 U.S. 792, 800, 5 FEP Cases 965 (1973); *Griggs* v. *Duke Power Co.,* 401 U.S. 424, 429-430, 3 FEP Cases 175 (1971). As we have recently observed, "legislative enactments in this area have long evinced a general intent to accord parallel or overlapping remedies against discrimination." *Alexander* v. *Gardner-Denver Co.,* 415 U.S. at 47, 7 FEP Cases at 85. It is this general legislative intent that must guide us in determining whether congressional purpose with respect to a particular statute is effectuated by tolling the statute of limitations.

. . .

In *Alexander* v. *Gardner-Denver, supra,* we examined the relationship between compulsory arbitration and litigation under Title VII, a relationship analogous to that between the EEOC factfinding and conciliation process and litigation under § 1981, and accommodated both avenues of redress. The reasoning leading to that result is equally compelling here. Forced compliance with a short statute of limitations during the pendency of a charge before the EEOC would discourage and/or frustrate recourse to the congressionally favored policy of conciliation, *Alexander* v. *Gardner-Denver,* 415 U.S., at 44, and "the possibility of voluntary compliance or settlement of Title VII claims would thus be reduced, and the result could well be more litigation, not less." *Id.,* at 59, 7 FEP Cases, at 90. Cf. *American Pipe & Const. Co.* v. *Utah,* 414 U.S. 538, 555-556 (1974).

Congressional effort, with the 1972 amendments, to strengthen the administrative remedy by increasing EEOC's ability to conciliate complaints is frustrated by the majority's requirement that an employee file the § 1981 action prior to the conclusion of the Title VII conciliation efforts in order to avoid the bar of the statute of limitations.[1] Legislative pains to avoid unnecessary and costly litigation by making the informal, investigatory and conciliatory offices of EEOC readily available to victims of unlawful discrimination cannot be squared with the formal mechanistic requirement of early filing for the technical purpose of tolling a limitations statute. In sum the federal policies weigh strongly in favor of tolling.

## II

Examination of the purposes served by the statute of limitations indicates that they would not be frustrated by adoption of the tolling rule. Statutes of limitations are designed to insure fairness to defendants by preventing the revival of stale claims in which the defense is hampered by lost evidence, faded memories and disappearing witnesses, and to avoid unfair surprise. None of these factors exist here.

Respondents were informed of the petitioner's grievances through the complaint filed with the Commission and conciliation negotiations. The charge filed with the EEOC and the § 1981 claim arise out of the same factual circumstances. The petitioner in this case diligently pursued the informal procedures before the Commission and adhered to the congressional preference for conciliation prior to litigation. Now, when Johnson asserts his right to proceed with litigation under § 1981 after his good faith, albeit unnecessary, compliance with Title VII procedures, the majority interposes the bar of the Tennessee statute of limitations which clearly was not designed to include such cases.[2]

---

[1] Loss of the § 1981 cause of action would deprive the aggrieved employee of the opportunity to recover punitive damages and more ample backpay.

[2] Under the Court's no-tolling principle petitioner's discharge on June 20, 1967, activated the statute which subsequently ran on June 20, 1968—two years prior to his receipt of the right to sue letter. The majority suggests that even if the statute were tolled during the consideration of the EEOC charge and the initial court proceedings, petitioner's Title VII action may be time-barred because of the unusual procedural history of the case, requiring the Court to extend his § 1981 claim beyond that arising out of Title VII. But our limited grant of certiorari forecloses consideration of the timeliness of the Title VII claim.

In my judgment, following the anti-tolling position of the Court to its logical conclusion produces an inequitable result. Aggrieved employees will be forced into simultaneously prosecuting premature § 1981 actions in the federal courts. In essence, the litigant who first explores conciliation prior to resort to litigation must file a duplicative claim in the District Court on which the court will either take no action until the Title VII proceedings are concluded or proceed in frustration of the EEOC attempts to conciliate. No federal policy considerations warrant this waste of judicial time and derogation of the conciliation process.

Adoption of the tolling principle, however, protects the federal interest in both preserving multiple remedies for employment discrimination and in the proper function of the limitations statute. As a normal consequence tolling works to suspend the operation of a statute of limitations during the pendency of an event or condition. . . .

. . . The federal policy in favor of continuing availability of multiple remedies for persons subject to employment discrimination is inconsistent with the majority's decision not to suspend the operation of the statute. As long as the claim arising under § 1981 is essentially limited to the Title VII claim, staleness and unfair surprise disappear as justification for applying the statute.[3] Additionally, the difference in statutory origin for the right asserted under the EEOC charge and the subsequent § 1981 suit is of no consequence since the claims are essentially equivalent in substance. . . .

## C. CLASS ACTIONS

## EAST TEXAS MOTOR FREIGHT SYSTEM, INC. v. RODRIGUEZ

*Supreme Court of the United States, 1977*
*431 U.S. 395, 14 FEP Cases 1505*

MR. JUSTICE STEWART delivered the opinion of the Court.

These cases, like *International Brotherhood of Teamsters* v. *United States, ante,* at _____, 14 FEP Cases at 1514, involve alleged employment discrimination on the part of an employer and unions in the trucking industry. The employer, East Texas Motor Freight System, Inc., is a common carrier that employs city and over-the-road, or "line" truck drivers. The company has a "no-transfer" policy, prohibiting drivers from transferring between terminals or from city driver to line-driver

---

In any event this case reflects no departure from the normal rule of tolling. Consistent with the common understanding that tolling entails a suspension rather than an extension of a period of limitations, petitioner is allowed whatever time remains under the applicable statute, as well as the benefit of any state savings statute. Under Tenn. Code Ann. § 28-106 an action dismissed without prejudice may be reinstituted within a year of dismissal. The filing here falls well within that time frame.

[3] Where there are differences between the § 1981 claim and the Title VII complaint, the district courts could easily limit the tolling to those portions of the § 1981 claim that overlapped with the Title VII allegations. Cf. *EEOC* v. *Louisville & Nashville R. Co.,* 505 F.2d 610, 617, 8 FEP Cases 1316 (CA5 1974); *Sanchez* v. *Standard Brands,* 431 F.2d 455, 466, 2 FEP Cases 788, 912 (CA5 1970).

jobs.[1] In addition, under the applicable collective-bargaining agreements between the company and the unions, competitive seniority runs only from the date an employee enters a particular bargaining unit, so that a line driver's competitive seniority does not take into account any time he may have spent in other jobs with the company.[2]

The respondents brought this suit against the company and the unions in a federal district court, challenging the above practices. Although their complaint denominated the cause as a class action, they did not move for class certification in the trial court. After a two-day hearing the court dismissed the class allegations of the complaint and decided against the individual respondents on the merits. The Court of Appeals for the Fifth Circuit reversed, after itself certifying what it considered an appropriate class and holding that the no-transfer rule and the seniority system violated the statutory rights of that class under 42 U.S.C. § 1981 and Title VII of the Civil Rights Act of 1964, 78 Stat. 253, as amended, 42 U.S.C. § 2000e *et seq.* (1970 ed. and Supp. V). *Rodriguez* v. *East Texas Motor Freight,* 505 F.2d 40, 8 FEP Cases 1246. This Court granted certiorari to review the judgment of the Court of Appeals, 425 U.S. 990.

## I

The respondents are three Mexican-Americans who initiated this litigation as the named plaintiffs, Jesse Rodriguez, Sadrach Perez, and Modesto Herrera. They were employed as city drivers at the company's San Antonio terminal, and were members of Teamsters Local Union 657 and of the Southern Conference of Teamsters. There was no line-driver operation at the San Antonio terminal, and the respondents stipulated that they had not been discriminated against when they were first hired. In August of 1970, some years after they were hired, each of them applied in writing for a line-driver job. In accord with its no-transfer policy, the company declined to consider these applications on their individual merits. The respondents then filed complaints with the Equal Employment Opportunity Commission, and after receiving "right to sue" letters from the Commission, see 42 U.S.C. § 2000e-5(e), they brought this lawsuit.

According to the complaint, the suit was brought on behalf of the named plaintiffs and all Negroes and Mexican-Americans who had been denied equal employment opportunities with the company because of their race or national origin. The complaint specifically alleged "that the appropriate class should consist of all defendant's East Texas Motor Freight's Mexican-American and Black in-city drivers included in the collective-bargaining agreement entered into between East Texas Motor

---

1 [Footnotes numbered as in original.—Ed.] Under this policy a city driver must resign his job and forfeit all seniority in order to be eligible for a line-driver job. He gets no priority over other line-driver applicants by virtue of formerly having been with the company, and if he fails to become a line driver he is not automatically entitled to be restored to his city job.

2 For a fuller description of a similar seniority system, see *International Brotherhood of Teamsters* v. *United States, ante,* at 17, 14 FEP Cases, at 1522.

Freight and the Southern Conference of Teamsters covering the State of Texas. Additionally that such class should properly be composed of all Mexican-American and Black applicants for line driver positions with East Texas Motor Freight . . . from July 2, 1965 [the effective date of Title VII] to present." [3]

Despite the class allegations in their complaint, the plaintiffs did not move prior to trial to have the action certified as a class action pursuant to Fed. Rule Civ. Proc. 23, and no such certification was made by the District Judge. Indeed, the plaintiffs had stipulated before trial that "the only issue presently before the Court pertaining to the company is whether the failure of the Defendant East Texas Motor Freight to consider Plaintiffs' line driver applications constituted a violation of Title VII and 42 U.S.C. § 1981." And the plaintiffs confined their evidence and arguments at trial to their individual claims. The defendants responded accordingly, with much of their proof devoted to showing that Rodriguez, Perez, and Herrera were not qualified to be line drivers.

Following trial, the District Court dismissed the class-action allegations. It stressed the plaintiffs' failure to move for a prompt determination of the propriety of class certification, their failure to offer evidence on that question, their concentration at the trial on their individual claims, their stipulation that the only issue to be determined concerned the company's failure to act on their applications, and the fact that, contrary to the relief the plaintiffs sought, see n. 3, *supra,* a large majority of the membership of Local 657 had recently rejected a proposal calling for the merger of city-driver and line-driver seniority lists with free transfer between jobs.[4]

The District Court also held against the named plaintiffs on their individual claims. It ruled that the no-transfer policy and the seniority system were proper business practices, neutrally applied, and that the company had not discriminated against the plaintiffs or retaliated against them for filing charges with the EEOC. The court further found that "[n]one of the plaintiff employees could satisfy all of the qualifications for a road driver position according to the company manual due to age or weight or driving record. . . . The driving, work, and/or physical records of the plaintiffs are of such nature that only casual consideration

[3] In addition to attacking the legality of the company's no-transfer and seniority policies, the complaint charged that the company excluded Negroes and Mexican-Americans from line-driver jobs, and that it had discharged plaintiff Perez and harassed plaintiff Rodriguez in retaliation for their having filed charges with the EEOC. The Southern Conference of Teamsters and Teamsters Local 657 were charged with participating in the exclusion of minority persons from line-driver jobs, acquiescing in the company's other discriminatory practices, and entering into collective-bargaining agreements that perpetuated the discrimination against Mexican-Americans and Negroes and erected "dual lines of seniority." In addition to other relief, the plaintiffs demanded that the company "merge its line-driver and city-driver seniority lists so as to provide for a singular seniority system based solely on an employee's anniversary date with the company."

[4] The large majority of the members of Local 657 at the meeting that rejected the proposal were Mexican-American or Negro city drivers, negating any possibility that the vote was controlled by white persons or by line drivers.

need be given to determine that the plaintiffs cannot qualify to become road drivers."

The Court of Appeals for the Fifth Circuit reversed. With respect to the propriety of the class action, the appellate court discounted entirely the plaintiffs' failure to move for certification. Determination of the class nature of a suit, the court ruled, is a "responsibility [that] falls to the court." 505 F.2d at 50, 8 FEP Cases, at 1252. Although the plaintiffs had acknowledged on appeal that only their individual claims had been tried, and had requested no more than that the case be remanded to the trial court for consideration of the class-action allegations, the Court of Appeals itself certified a class consisting of all of the company's Negro and Mexican-American city drivers covered by the applicable collective-bargaining agreements for the State of Texas. Stating that "the requirements of Rule 23(a) must be read liberally in the context of suits brought under Title VII and Section 1981," *ibid.*, the court found that the named plaintiffs could "fairly and adequately protect the interests of the class." The court minimized the antagonism between the plaintiffs and other city drivers with respect to the complaint's demand that seniority lists be merged, since "[t]he disagreement . . . concerned only the proper remedy; there was no antagonism with regard to the contention that the defendants practiced discrimination against the plaintiff class." *Id.*, at 51, 8 FEP Cases, at 1254.[5]

After certifying the class, the Court of Appeals went on to find class-wide liability against the company and the union on the basis of the proof adduced at the trial of the individual claims. Contrary to the understanding of the judge who had tried the case, the appellate court determined that the trial had proceeded "as in a class action," with the acquiescence of the judge and the defendants. *Id.*, at 52, 8 FEP Cases, at 1254.[6] The parties' stipulation that the only issue before the trial court concerned the company's failure to consider the named plaintiff's applications for line-driver jobs was discounted as no more than "an attempt to eliminate some confusion in the exposition of evidence at trial." *Ibid.*

Accordingly, the Court of Appeals concluded, upon the trial record, that the company had discriminated against Negroes and Mexican-Americans in hiring line drivers, that the company's no-transfer rule and seniority system perpetuated the past discrimination and were not justified by business necessity, that the company's requirement of three years of immediately prior line-haul experience was an illegal employ-

---

[5] The court also stated that possible antagonism could be cured by tailoring the award of relief, but it did not suggest how such tailoring could be accomplished short of doing what it in fact did: awarding retroactive seniority to discriminatees and ignoring the named plaintiffs' separate demand that the seniority lines be merged.

[6] The Court of Appeals apparently concluded on the basis of a colloquy appearing in the trial transcript that the parties and the trial judge understood the trial to concern the class claims as well as the individual claims. 505 F.2d, at 52, and n. 14, 8 FEP Cases, at 1254. This was contrary to the understanding of the trial judge as reflected in his findings. Moreover, as the full colloquy reveals, the trial judge ruled that evidence concerning general company practice would be admitted not because of the class allegations, but only because it was probative with respect to the plaintiffs' individual claims.

ment qualification, and that the unions had violated Title VII and 42 U.S.C. § 1981 by "their role in establishing separate seniority rosters that failed to make allowance for minority city drivers who had been discriminatorily relegated to city driver jobs." 505 F.2d, at 61, 8 FEP Cases, at 1262. The Court of Appeals did not disturb the trial court's finding that none of the named plaintiffs was qualified to be a line driver; rather, it held only that that finding had been "premature," because each plaintiff, as a member of the class, would be entitled to have his application considered on the merits when future line-driver vacancies arose.[7]

## II

It is our conclusion that on the record before it the Court of Appeals plainly erred in declaring a class action and in imposing upon the petitioners classwide liability. In arriving at this conclusion we do not reach the question whether a Court of Appeals should ever certify a class in the first instance. For it is inescapably clear that the Court of Appeals in any event erred in certifying a class in this case, for the simple reason that it was evident by the time the case reached that court that the named plaintiffs were not proper class representatives under Fed. Rule Civ. Proc. 23(a).[8]

In short, the trial court proceedings made clear that Rodriguez, Perez, and Herrera were not members of the class of discriminatees they purported to represent. As this Court has repeatedly held, a class representative must be part of the class and "possess the same interest and suffer the same injury" as the class members. *Schlesinger* v. *Reservists Committee To Stop the War,* 418 U.S. 208, 216. See, *e.g., Kremens* v. *Bartley,* 431 U.S. ——, —— n.12; *Sosna* v. *Iowa,* 419 U.S. 393, 403; *Rosario* v. *Rockefeller,* 410 U.S. 752, 759 n. 9; *Hall* v. *Beals,* 396 U.S. 45, 49; *Bailey* v. *Patterson,* 369 U.S. 31, 32–33. The District Court found upon abundant evidence that these plaintiffs lacked the qualifications to be hired as line drivers.[9] Thus, they could have suffered no injury as a result of the

---

[7] The Court of Appeals ordered that all class members be given an opportunity to transfer to line-driver jobs with retroactive seniority to be determined under the Fifth Circuit's "qualification date" principle. See *International Brotherhood of Teamsters, ante,* at 6-7, 14 FEP Cases at 1518.

[8] Rule 23(a) provides:

"(a) Prerequisites to a Class Action. One or more members of a class may sue or be sued as representative parties on behalf of all only if (1) the class is so numerous that joinder of all members is impracticable, (2) there are questions of law or fact common to the class, (3) the claims or defenses of the representative parties are typical of the claims or defenses of the class, and (4) the representative parties will fairly and adequately protect the interests of the class."

[9] Jesse Rodriguez did not have prior over-the-road experience with a truck line. His record as a city driver included at least three accidents and at least five personal injuries. Modesto Herrera had been involved in at least three accidents and seven injuries, resulting in much time lost from work. He had received four warning letters from the company, of which three concerned abnormally low productivity. Sadrach Perez had been fired from his city-driver job by the time of suit. The District Court found that on occasion Perez had claimed to be totally and permanently disabled and had then returned to work, and that customers had complained of his disrespect and discourteousness. The company had placed at least four warning letters in his file before discharging

alleged discriminatory practices, and they were, therefore, simply not eligible to represent a class of persons who did allegedly suffer injury. Furthermore, each named plaintiff stipulated that he had not been discriminated against with respect to his initial hire. In the light of that stipulation they were hardly in a position to mount a classwide attack on the no-transfer rule and seniority system on the ground that these practices perpetuated past discrimination and locked minorities into the less desirable jobs to which they had been discriminatorily assigned.

Apart from the named plaintiffs' evident lack of class membership, the record before the Court of Appeals disclosed at least two other strong indications that they would not "fairly and adequately protect the interests of the class." [10] One was their failure to move for class certification prior to trial. Even assuming, as a number of courts have held, that a district judge has an obligation on his own motion to determine whether an action shall proceed as a class action, see, *e.g.*, *Senter* v. *General Motors Corp.*, 532 F.2d 511, 520–21, 12 FEP Cases 451, 458 (CA6); *Garrett* v. *City of Hamtramck*, 503 F.2d 1236, 1243 (CA6); *Castro* v. *Beecher*, 459 F.2d 725, 731, 4 FEP Cases 700, 705 (CA1), the named plaintiffs' failure to protect the interests of class members by moving for certification surely bears strongly on the adequacy of the representation that those class members might expect to receive. See, *e.g.*, *Nance* v. *Union Carbide Corp.*, 540 F.2d 718, 722–25, 13 FEP Cases 231, 234–36 (CA4), *cert. pending*, Nos. 76-828, 76-834; *Danner* v. *Phillips Petroleum Co.*, 447 F.2d 159, 164, 3 FEP Cases 858, 862 (CA5); *Beasley* v. *Kroehler Mfg. Co.*, 406 F.Supp. 926, 931, 13 FEP Cases 93, 97 (N.D. Tex.); *Walker* v. *Columbia University*, 62 F.R.D. 63, 64, 7 FEP Cases 100, 101 (SDNY); *Glodgett* v. *Betit*, 368 F.Supp. 211, 214 (Vt.); *Herbst* v. *Able*, 45 F.R.D. 451, 453 (SDNY). Another factor, apparent on the record, suggesting that the named plaintiffs were not appropriate class representatives was the conflict between the vote by members of the class rejecting a merger of the city and line-driver collective-bargaining units,[11] and the demand in the plaintiffs' complaint for just such a merger. See, *e.g.*, *Hansberry* v. *Lee*, 311 U.S. 32, 44–45.

---

him, referring to his failure to make deliveries, poor production, absence from work, and violation of instructions and company policy. More than 10 customers had notified the company that they would refuse freight if Perez was sent to deliver it and would refuse to give up freight if Perez was sent to receive it. An arbitration committee convened in connection with Perez' discharge had decided in the company's favor.

In light of this evidence, the District Court's finding that none of the respondents was qualified to be a line driver was not clearly erroneous. Nor was this finding in any way "premature." The trial had concerned the company's failure to consider the respondents' individual line-driver applications, and the plaintiffs had requested backpay and transfer with carryover seniority in addition to other relief. Even assuming, *arguendo*, that the company's failure even to consider the applications was discriminatory, the company was entitled to prove at trial that the respondents had not been injured because they were not qualified and would not have been hired in any event. See, *e.g.*, *International Brotherhood of Teamsters, supra*, at 42 n. 53, 14 FEP Cases, at 1533. Cf. *Mt. Healthy City School District Board of Education* v. *Doyle*, 429 U.S. 274, 285-287.

10 See Fed. Rule Civ. Proc 23(a), quoted in n. 8, *supra*.

11 See *supra*, at _____, 14 FEP Cases, at 1507.

We are not unaware that suits alleging racial or ethnic discrimination are often by their very nature class suits, involving classwide wrongs. Common questions of law or fact are typically present. But careful attention to the requirements of Fed. Rule Civ. Proc. 23 remains nonetheless indispensable. The mere fact that a complaint alleges racial or ethnic discrimination does not in itself ensure that the party who has brought the lawsuit will be an adequate representative of those who may have been the real victims of that discrimination.

For the reasons we have discussed, the District Court did not err in denying the individual relief or in dismissing the class allegations of the respondents' complaint.[12] The judgment of the Court of Appeals is, accordingly, vacated, and the cases are remanded to that court for further proceedings consistent with this opinion.[13]

*It is so ordered.*

## UNITED AIR LINES v. McDONALD

*Supreme Court of the United States, 1977*
*432 U.S. 385, 14 FEP Cases 1711*

Mr. Justice Stewart delivered the opinion of the Court.

Rule 24 of the Federal Rules of Civil Procedure requires that an application to intervene in federal litigation must be "timely." In this case a motion to intervene was filed promptly after the final judgment of a district court, for the purpose of appealing the court's earlier denial of class action certification. The question presented is whether this motion was "timely" under Rule 24.

Until November 7, 1968, United Airlines required its female stewardesses to remain unmarried as a condition of employment; no parallel restriction was imposed on any male employees, including male stewards

---

[12] Obviously, a different case would be presented if the District Court had certified a class and only later had it appeared that the named plaintiffs were not class members or were otherwise inappropriate class representatives. In such a case, the class claims would have already been tried, and, provided the initial certification was proper and decertification not appropriate, the claims of the class members would not need to be mooted or destroyed because subsequent events or the proof at trial had undermined the named plaintiffs' individual claims. See, *e.g., Franks* v. *Bowman*, 424 U.S. 747, 752-57, 12 FEP Cases 549, 551-53; *Moss* v. *Lane Co.*, 471 F.2d 853, 855-56, 5 FEP Cases 376, 377-78 (CA4). Where no class has been certified, however, and the class claims remain to be tried, the decision whether the named plaintiffs should represent a class is appropriately made on the full record, including the facts developed at the trial of the plaintiffs' individual claims. At that point, as the Court of Appeals recognized in this case, "there [are] involved none of the imponderables that make the [class action] decision so difficult early in litigation." 505 F.2d, at 51, 8 FEP Cases, at 1254. See also *Cox* v. *Babcock & Wilcox Co.*, 471 F.2d 13, 15-16, 5 FEP Cases 374, 375-76 (CA4).

[13] The union petitioners, in Nos. 75-651 and 75-715, also attack the judgments entered against them in *Herrera* v. *Yellow Freight System, Inc.*, 505 F.2d 66, 8 FEP Cases 1266 (CA5), and *Resendis* v. *Lee Way Motor Freight, Inc.*, 505 F.2d 69, 8 FEP Cases 1268 (CA5). The judgments against the unions in those related cases are also vacated, and the cases are remanded to the Court of Appeals for further consideration in light of this opinion and our opinion in *International Brotherhood of Teamsters* v. *United States, ante*, at _____, 14 FEP Cases at 1514.

and cabin flight attendants.[1] This "no-marriage rule" resulted in the termination of the employment of a large number of stewardesses, and in turn spawned a good deal of litigation.

One of the first challenges to this rule was brought by Mary Sprogis, who filed timely charges with the Equal Employment Opportunity Commission in August 1966, contending that her discharge constituted sex discrimination in violation of Title VII of the Civil Rights Act of 1964. 42 U.S.C. § 2000(e) *et seq.* (1970 & Supp. V). The EEOC found reasonable cause to believe that United's policy was illegal, and issued a "right to sue letter." [2] Sprogis then filed a timely individual action in a federal district court, and the court agreed that the no-marriage rule violated Title VII. 308 F.Supp. 959, 2 FEP Cases 432 (ND Ill.). United took an interlocutory appeal under 28 U.S.C. § 1292(b) on the issue of liability, and the Court of Appeals for the Seventh Circuit affirmed the finding of sex discrimination. 444 F.2d 1194, 3 FEP Cases 621.

While the appeal in the *Sprogis* case was pending, the present action was filed in the same District Court by Carol Romasanta, a United stewardess who had been discharged in 1967 because of her marriage. She too had filed charges with the EEOC, leading to a finding of cause to believe that the no-marriage rule violated Title VII and the issuance of a right to sue letter. Romasanta then promptly filed the present suit as a class action on behalf of herself and all other United stewardesses discharged because of the no-marriage rule. Another United stewardess, Brenda Altman, was later permitted to intervene as a named plaintiff.

Several months later, the District Court granted United's motion to strike the complaint's class allegations, ruling that the class could properly consist of only those stewardesses who, upon the loss of their employment because of marriage, had filed charges under either a fair employment statute or United's collective-bargaining agreement. As thus defined, the class numbered not more than 30 and in the court's view did not satisfy the numerosity requirement of Rule 23(a)(1) of the Federal Rules of Civil Procedures.[3] As part of its order, however, the District Court allowed 12 married stewardesses who had protested the termination of their employment to intervene as additional parties plaintiff. Pursuant to 28 U.S.C. § 1292(b), the District Court certified for appeal its order striking the class allegations, but the Court of Appeals declined to accept this interlocutary appeal.[4]

1 [Footnotes numbered as in original.—Ed.] See generally *Sprogis* v. *United Air Lines, Inc.*, 444 F.2d 1194, 1197-1201, 3 FEP Cases 621, 623-26 (CA7).

2 The relevant statutory provision at that time, 42 U.S.C. § 2000e-5(e) (1970), stated that if within 30 days after a charge was filed with the Commission or within 30 days after expiration of a period of reference of the charge to a state or local fair employment agency, the Commission had been unable to secure voluntary compliance, the EEOC "shall so notify the person aggrieved and a civil action may, within thirty days thereafter, be brought" by the charging party. The period was extended to 90 days in 1972. *Id.*, § 2000e-5(f)(1) (Supp. V).

3 Rule 23(a)(1) lists as one prerequisite to maintenance of a class action that "the class is so numerous that joinder of all members is impracticable."

4 In the Seventh Circuit, a denial of class certification is an interlocutory order not reviewable as of right until after entry of final judgment. *Anschul* v. *Sitmar Cruises, Inc.*,

The litigation proceeded as a joint suit on behalf of the original and the intervening plaintiffs, and the court ultimately determined that those plaintiffs not yet reinstated in their jobs were entitled to that remedy, and that every plaintiff was entitled to backpay. To aid in determining the amount of each backpay award, the court appointed as a special master the same person who had performed a similar task in the *Sprogis* litigation.[5] Following guidelines adopted in *Sprogis,* the parties eventually agreed upon the amounts to be awarded each plaintiff, and upon consummation of this agreement the trial court entered a judgment of dismissal on October 3, 1975.

The specific controversy before us arose only after the entry of that judgment. The respondent, a former United stewardess, had been discharged in 1968 on account of the no-marriage rule. She was thus a putative member of the class as defined in the original Romasanta complaint. Knowing that other stewardesses had challenged United's no-marriage rule, she had not filed charges with the EEOC or a grievance under the collective-bargaining agreement.[6]

After learning that a final judgment had been entered in the Romasanta suit, and that despite their earlier attempt to do so the plaintiffs did not now intend to file an appeal challenging the District Court's denial of class certification, she filed a motion to intervene for the purpose of appealing the District Court's adverse class determination order. Her motion was filed 18 days after the District Court's final judgment, and thus was well within the 30-day period for an appeal to be taken.[7] The District Court denied the motion, stating:

"Well, in my judgment, gentlemen, this is five years now this has been in litigation, and this lady has not seen fit to come in here and seek relief from this Court in any way during that period of time, and litigation must end. I must deny this motion. Of course, that is an appealable order itself, and if I am in error then the Court of Appeals can reverse me and we will grant a hearing, but in my judgment this is too late to come in."

---

544 F.2d 1364 (CA7). Even were we to assume *arguendo* that the Seventh Circuit is wrong in not recognizing the so-called death knell doctrine, which permits immediate appeal of adverse class determinations where the claims are so small that individual suits are uneconomical, appeal before final judgment would not have been available in this lawsuit, for the individual claims were sufficiently large to permit the action to proceed, as it did, on an individual basis. See generally 7A C. Wright & A. Miller, FEDERAL PRACTICE AND PROCEDURE: Civil, § 1802, at 271-77 (1972); *id.,* at 129-30 (Supp. 1977).

5 In *Sprogis,* following affirmance by the Court of Appeals of the District Court's finding of liability, the case was remanded for further proceedings. The special master appointed by the District Court recommended that the plaintiff be awarded over $10,000 in damages, the District Court approved that award, and the Court of Appeals affirmed. See *Sprogis* v. *United Air Lines, Inc.,* 517 F.2d 387, 389-90, 392, 10 FEP Cases 1249, 1250, 1252-53.

6 As the opinion in *Albemarle Paper Co.* v. *Moody,* 422 U.S. 405, 10 FEP Cases 1181, makes clear, full relief under Title VII "may be awarded on a class basis . . . without exhaustion of administrative procedures by the unnamed class members." *Id.,* at 414 n. 8, 10 FEP Cases, at 1186. See also *Franks* v. *Bowman Transportation Co.,* 424 U.S. 747, 771, 12 FEP Cases 549, 558.

7 See Fed Rule App. Proc. 4(a).

The respondent promptly appealed the denial of intervention as well as the denial of class certification to the Court of Appeals for the Seventh Circuit. The appellate court reversed, holding that the District Court had been wrong in believing that the motion to intervene was untimely under Rule 24(b),[8] and had also erred in refusing to certify the class as described in the Romasanta complaint—a class consisting of all United stewardesses discharged because of the no-marriage rule, whether or not they had formally protested the termination of their employment. *Romasanta* v. *United Airlines, Inc.,* 437 F.2d 915, 13 FEP Cases 1437.

United's petition for certiorari did not seek review of the determination that its no-marriage rule violated Title VII, nor did it contest the merits of the Court of Appeals' decision on the class certification issue. Instead, it challenged only the Court of Appeals' ruling that the respondent's post-judgment application for intervention was timely. We granted the petition, —— U.S. ——, to consider that single issue.

In urging reversal, United relies primarily upon *American Pipe and Construction Co.* v. *Utah,* 414 U.S. 538. That case involved a private antitrust class action that had been filed 11 days short of the expiration of the statutory limitations period.[9] The trial court later denied class certification because the purported class did not satisfy the numerosity requirement of Rule 23(a)(1).[10] Neither the named plaintiffs nor any unnamed member of the class appealed that order, either then or at any later time. Eight days after entry of the order, a number of the putative class members moved to intervene as plaintiffs, but the trial court denied the motions as untimely. This Court ultimately reversed that decision, ruling that in those circumstances "the commencement of the original class suit tolls the running of the statute for all purported members of the class who make timely motions to intervene after the court has found the suit inappropriate for class action status." 414 U.S., at 553. Since 11 days remained when the statute of limitations again began to run after denial of class certification, and the motions to intervene as plaintiffs were filed only eight days after that denial, they were timely. *Id.,* at 560–61.

It is United's position that, under *American Pipe,* the relevant statute of limitations began to run after the denial of class certification in the Romasanta action. United thus reasons that the respondent's motion to intervene was time-barred, and in support of this position makes alternative arguments based on two different statutory periods of limitations prescribed by Title VII.[11]

---

[8] In relevant part, Rule 24(b) provides:
"Upon timely application anyone may be permitted to intervene in an action . . . when an applicant's claim or defense and the main action have a question of law or fact in common. . . . In exercising its discretion the court shall consider whether the intervention will unduly prejudice the adjudication of the rights of the original parties."

[9] See 414 U.S., at 541-542.

[10] See n. 3, *supra*.

[11] A person complaining of employment discrimination is ordinarily required to file a charge with the EEOC within 180 days of the occurrence of the discriminatory act. 42 U.S.C. § 2000e-5(e) (Supp. V). Once the administrative process has been exhausted and

This argument might be persuasive if the respondent had sought to intervene in order to join the named plaintiffs in litigating her individual claim based on the illegality of United's no-marriage rule, for she then would have occupied the same position as the intervenors in *American Pipe*. But the later motion to intervene in this case was for a wholly different purpose. That purpose was to obtain appellate review of the District Court's order denying class action status in the Romasanta lawsuit,[12] and the motion complied with, as it was required to, the time limitation for lodging an appeal prescribed by Fed. Rule App. Proc. 4 (a). Success in that review would result in the certification of a class, the named members of which had complied with the statute of limitations; the respondent is a member of that class against whom the statute had not run at the time the class action was commenced.

The lawsuit had been commenced by the timely filing of a complaint for classwide relief, providing United with "the essential information necessary to determine both the subject matter and size of the prospective litigation. . . ." *American Pipe, supra,* at 555.[13] To be sure, the case was "stripped of its character as a class action" upon denial of certification by the District Court. Advisory Committee's Note on the 1966 Amendments to Rule 23, 28 U.S.C. App., p. 7767. But "it does not . . . follow that the case must be treated as if there never was an action brought on behalf of absent class members." *Philadelphia Electric Company* v. *Anaconda American Brass Co.,* 43 F.R.D. 452, 461 (ED Pa.). The District Court's refusal to certify was subject to appellate review after final judgment at the behest of the named plaintiffs, as United concedes.[14] And

---

the EEOC sends the complainant a right to sue letter, a civil action in federal district court must be filed within 90 days of receipt of the right to sue letter. Id., § 2000e-5(f)(1), discussed in n. 2, *supra*. Since nearly three years passed after the adverse class determination before the respondent took any action, under United's theory her action is time-barred whichever of the two limitations periods is thought to be the relevant one.

[12] Cf. Shapiro, *Some Thoughts on Intervention Before Courts, Agencies, and Arbitrators,* 81 HARV. L. REV. 721, 727 (1968) ("It is both feasible and desirable to break down the concept of intervention into a number of litigation rights and to conclude that a given person has one or some of these rights but not all.").

[13] The unlawful discrimination alleged in the complaint—enforcement of the no-marriage rule—was plainly part of a uniform companywide policy that had been applied to all stewardesses. See also S. Rep. No. 92-415, p. 27 (1971) ("Title VII actions are by their very nature class complaints"), cited in *Albemarle Paper Co.* v. *Moody,* 422 U.S. 405, 414 n. 8, 10 FEP Cases 1181, 1186.

[14] See, *e.g., Share* v. *Air Properties G. Inc.,* 538 F.2d 279, 283 (CA9); *Zenith Laboratories, Inc.* v. *Carter-Wallace, Inc.,* 530 F.2d 508, 512 (CA3); *Penn* v. *San Juan Hospital, Inc.,* 528 F.2d 1181, 1188-90 (CA10); *Bailey* v. *Ryan Stevedoring Co.,* 528 F.2d 551, 553-54, 12 FEP Cases 1026, 1027-28 (CA5); *Wright* v. *Stone Container Corp.,* 524 F.2d 1058, 1061-63, 11 FEP Cases 1322, 1323-24 (CA8); *Paton* v. *La Prade,* 524 F.2d 862, 874-75 (CA3); *Haynes* v. *Logan Furniture Mart, Inc.,* 503 F.2d 1161, 1162-65 (CA7); *Galvan* v. *Levine,* 490 F.2d 1255, 1260-62 (CA2); *Roberts* v. *Union Co.,* 487 F.2d 387, 6 FEP Cases 1153 (CA6); *Esplin* v. *Hirschi,* 402 F.2d 94 (CA10).

United argues that it was unfairly surprised when after having settled the case with all of the original and intervening plaintiffs it nonetheless faced an appeal, and suggests that the negotiation of settlements will be impeded if post-judgment intervention like the respondent's is permitted. The characterization of the resolution of the Romasanta action as a "settlement" could be slightly misleading. It is of course true that opposing counsel agreed upon a disposition that resulted in dismissal of the complaints. But that

since the named plaintiffs had attempted to take an interlocutory appeal from the order of denial at the time the order was entered, there was no reason for the respondent to suppose that they would not later take an appeal until she was advised to the contrary after the trial court had entered its final judgment.

The critical fact here is that once the entry of final judgment made the adverse class determination appealable, the respondent quickly sought to enter the litigation. In short, as soon as it became clear to the respondent that the interests of the unnamed class members would no longer be protected by the named class representatives she promptly moved to intervene to protect those interests.[15]

United can hardly contend that its ability to litigate the issue was unfairly prejudiced simply because an appeal on behalf of putative class members was brought by one of their own, rather than by one of the original named plaintiffs. And it would be circular to argue that an unnamed member of the putative class was not a proper party to appeal, on the ground that her interests had been adversely determined in the trial court. United was put on notice by the filing of the Romasanta complaint of the possibility of classwide liability, and there is no reason why Mrs. McDonald's pursuit of that claim should not be considered timely under the circumstances here presented.

Our conclusion is consistent with several decisions of the federal courts permitting post-judgment intervention for the purpose of appeal.[16] The

---

agreement came only after the District Judge had granted motions by some plaintiffs for partial summary judgment, and, there was never any question about United's liability in view of the *Sprogis* decision. All that remained to be determined was the computation of backpay, and the guiding principles for that computation had been established in *Sprogis*. The "settlement" ultimately reached merely applied those principles to the claims in this case.

The respondent's motion to intervene was filed less than three weeks after the "settlement" was incorporated in the District Court's final judgment, and necessarily "concern[ed] the same evidence, memories, and witnesses as the subject matter of the original class suit." *American Pipe*, 414 U.S., at 562 (Blackmun, J., concurring). There is no reason to believe that in that short period of time, United discarded evidence or was otherwise prejudiced.

15 A rule requiring putative class members who seek only to appeal from an order denying class certification to move to intervene shortly after entry of that order would serve no purpose. Intervention at that time would only have made the respondent a superfluous spectator in the litigation for nearly three years, for the denial of class certification was not appealable until after final judgment, see n. 4, *supra*. Moreover, such a rule would induce putative class members to file protective motions to intervene to guard against the possibility that the named representatives might not appeal from the adverse class determination. Cf. *American Pipe, supra*, at 553. The result would be the very "multiplicity of activity which Rule 23 was designed to avoid." Id., at 551. Cf. *Franks* v. *Bowman Transportation Co.*, 424 U.S. 747, 757 n. 9, 12 FEP Cases 549, 553.

16 A case closely in point is *American Brake Shoe & Foundry Co.* v. *Interborough Rapid Transit Co.*, 3 F.R.D. 162 (SDNY). That case involved a plan for reorganization of the Interborough Rapid Transit Company and for its consolidation with the Manhattan Elevated Railway. Mannheim, an owner of a series of bonds in the Manhattan Railway, had participated in the District Court not merely representing his own interests but also acting as "attorney in fact" for other owners of the bonds. After the District Court had approved the plan as fair and equitable, and had subsequently ordered its implementation, Mannheim filed a notice of appeal. He then decided to abandon the appeal and to seek to surrender his bonds pursuant to the terms of the plan. One of the other holders of the same series of bonds, for whom Mannheim had

critical inquiry in every such case is whether in view of all the circumstances the intervenor acted promptly after the entry of final judgment. Cf. *NAACP* v. *New York,* 413 U.S. 345, 366. Here, the respondent filed her motion within the time period in which the named plaintiffs could have taken an appeal. We therefore conclude that the Court of Appeals was correct in ruling that the respondent's motion to intervene was timely filed and should have been granted.

*Affirmed.*

MR. JUSTICE STEVENS took no part in the consideration or decision of this case.

MR. JUSTICE POWELL, with whom The Chief Justice and MR. JUSTICE WHITE join, dissenting.

## D. CONSENT DECREES

## EATON v. COURTAULDS OF NORTH AMERICA

*United States Court of Appeals, Fifth Circuit, 1978*
*578 F.2d 87, 17 FEP Cases 1767*

GEE, Circuit Judge: This appeal revolves around the interpretation of one section of a consent decree entered into by the parties and accepted by the district court in 1973.

The consent decree in question settled the claims of a group of black employees who had initiated an action under Title VII of the 1964 Civil Rights Act. 42 U.S.C. §2000e, *et seq.,* against Courtaulds of North America and against the local and national units of the Textile Workers Union of America. Among other things, the black employees had contended that the defendants maintained a discriminatory promotional

---

been acting as attorney in fact, then moved to intervene for the purpose of prosecuting an appeal on behalf of herself and all other nonsurrendering bondholders. Noting that it is "essential in the administration of our system of justice, that litigants should have their day in court" and that the motion was filed within the time in which an appeal might have been brought, the District Court ruled that the motion to intervene was timely. *Id.,* at 164.

The decision in *Pellegrino* v. *Nesbit,* 203 F.2d 463 (CA9), is also similar to the case at bar. There a corporation had filed an action against corporate officers under § 16(b) of the Securities Exchange Act of 1934, 15 U.S.C. § 78p(b), for recovery of short-swing profits. The District Court entered judgment for the defendants, and when the corporation failed to appeal, a shareholder sought to intervene for the purpose of appealing from the District Court decision. The Court of Appeals, reversing the District Court, ruled that the motion was timely and intervention should have been permitted. *Id.,* at 465-66.

Post-judgment intervention for the purpose of appeal has been found to be timely even in litigation that is not representative in nature, and in which the intervenor might therefore be thought to have a less direct interest in participation in the appellate phase. See, *e.g., Hodgson* v. *United Mine Workers,* 153 U.S. App. D.C. 407, 417-19, 473 F.2d 118, 129, 81 LRRM 2689; *Smuck* v. *Hobson,* 132 U.S. App. D.C. 372, 378-79, 408 F.2d 175, 181-82; *Zuber* v. *Allen,* 387 F.2d 862, discussed in *Hobson* v. *Hanson,* 44 F.R.D. 18, 29-30, n. 10 (DC); *Wolpe* v. *Poretsky,* 79 U.S. App. D.C. 141, 144, 144 F.2d 505, 508; *United States Casualty Company* v. *Taylor,* 64 F.2d 521, 526-27 (CA4).

Insofar as the motions to intervene in these cases were made within the applicable time for filing an appeal, they are consistent with our opinion and judgment in the present case.

and seniority system. This, they said, was due in part to the past practice of segregated job classifications under which black employees had been placed in undesirable labor classifications only; although by the time of the lawsuit black employees had gained the right to transfer, they could do so only at the cost of their seniority. This in turn was because under the collective bargaining agreement between the union and Courtaulds, seniority was reckoned by service within particular sections or "lines of progression," rather than by an employee's total length of service with the company. When one departed one "line" to enter another, then he began in the new "line" with no seniority, and that regardless of how long he had been employed at the *plant*.

Whatever the truth of those allegations, the parties did arrive at the 1973 settlement agreement that purported, among other things, to solve these problems of seniority. For seniority purposes the agreement set out special provisions for an "Affected Class" of 57 named black employees who had been hired in the "labor section" before October 21, 1968, and provided that, subject to certain specific limitations, the "Affected Class" members would be entitled to what was called "Court Seniority" in connection with promotions, demotions and layoffs. This "Court Seniority" was defined by the employee's length of continuous service with Courtaulds.

The present controversy concerns the application of the settlement agreement's "Court Seniority" clauses in the context of a reduction in force. The paragraphs under dispute are the following:
"[VII.]D. 1. When members of the Affected Class compete with each other or with employees not of the Affected Class as to layoff, demotion and recall, Court Seniority shall be the applicable seniority for such purposes and may be utilized by Affected Class employees and any other employees so competing. Court Seniority for the purposes of demotion, layoff and recall shall not be lost by failure either to bid or to accept an entry level job as is set forth in preceding Paragraph 'C'.

"2. Subject to the express exception in Paragraph III. (F) above, an Affected Class employee or any other person can only use his Court Seniority in case of demotion, layoff or recall *from his position in the line of progression in which he is as of the date of this Settlement Agreement downward to the entry job in that same line of progression*. He can at no time use Court Seniority to jump from section to section or from department to department."
(Emphasis added.)

The entire case hinges on the referent of the prepositional clause beginning with "in which" in the emphasized portion: if this clause modified "position," one result emerges; but if it modifies "line of progression," it has quite a different meaning. At the time this controversy arose the company and the union read the "in which" clause to modify "position." On this reading the company could, at the time of a layoff, bump each Affected Class employee back to the position he had occupied at the time of the 1973 agreement, and the employee could only apply his Court Seniority to avoid further drops in position. Each of the appellants had transferred to the Spinning Department prior to the 1973 settlement, and each had used his Court Seniority in that line of progression to advance to a job position higher than that to which he would have advanced under ordinary section seniority. But when a reduction in force occurred in 1974 the company, applying its interpretation of paragraph VII.D.2. of the agreement, bumped each plaintiff back to his pre-settlement position in the Spinning Department.

The plaintiffs contested this procedure, arguing that it was based on a misreading of paragraph D.2. They contend that the "in which" clause modifies "line of progression" rather than "position." On this reading the Affected Class members, in case of a reduction in force, should be able to apply Court Seniority to protect themselves in the new positions they have attained as a result of the settlement, without first being bumped back by section seniority to their pre-settlement positions. The company's interpretation, they argue, turns paragraph D.2. into an exception that virtually swallows the rule of Court Seniority as applied to layoffs by paragraph D.1. Upon their demotions the plaintiffs filed grievances. These were denied, and an arbitrator decided in favor of the company, unaccountably finding no ambiguity in the disputed clause.[1]

Meanwhile, appellants applied to the district court for a declaration of their rights and enforcement of the settlement agreement. The district court, like the arbitrator, determined that the phrase in question was not ambiguous and that the defendants' interpretation was correct.

We reverse. We note preliminarily that we are not bound by the clearly erroneous standard of review of Federal Rule of Civil Procedure 52(a).[2] The Supreme Court has said that "since consent decrees and orders have many of the attributes of ordinary contracts, they should be construed

---

1 [Footnotes numbered as in original.—Ed.] These matters were referred to arbitration in accordance with Article IX of the settlement agreement, which provides that "any dispute or disagreement arising under this Settlement Agreement involving matters governed by the Collective Bargaining Agreement as it may be modified by the Settlement Agreement shall be referred for resolution to the grievance process provided by the Collective Bargaining Agreement in effect at the time in question . . ." This article does not explicitly make the arbitrator's decision binding on the parties; moreover, the settlement agreement explicitly provides that the district court—which initially heard the litigation and accepted the settlement—was to retain jurisdiction over the agreement. We think that the district court correctly treated this enforcement action as one requiring de novo review by the court. Such review appears to be contemplated by the settlement agreement. In addition, while the settlement agreement casts the case in a different light from an initial Title VII action, there are certain analogies to such an action. Here, too, the appellants' nondiscrimination rights are governed in large part by a legal document, here the settlement agreement, that is independent of the collective bargaining agreement. Deferral to the arbitrator's decision would raise at least some of the same difficulties that could be raised in deferral to arbitration in a Title VII suit, due for example to the different nature of the arbitration forum and possible conflicts of interest between the grievants and their union representatives in arbitration proceedings. See *Alexander* v. *Gardner-Denver Co.*, 415 U.S. 36, 55–60, 39 L.Ed.2d 147, 7 FEP Cases 81 (1974).

2 Since this issue involves interpretation of the language of an existing settlement, rather than the initial acceptance of a consent decree as fair to the parties, the district court's exercise of discretion is not in question, and we do not review for abuse of discretion.

basically as contracts," *United States* v. *ITT Continental Baking Co.,* 420 U.S. 223, 236, 43 L.Ed.2d 148 (1975), and this Court has observed that the contractural aspects of a consent decree exist "chiefly . . . in regard to disputes concerning what the parties actually consented to as reflected by the judgment in question." *United States* v. *Kellum,* 523 F.2d 1284, 1287 (5th Cir. 1975). The present issue thus should clearly be treated as a matter of contractual interpretation. It has been frequently stated, however, that the interpretation of the written language of a contract is a matter of law and is reviewable as such. See, *e.g., First National Bank of Miami* v. *Insurance Co. of North America,* 495 F.2d 519 (5th Cir. 1974); C. Wright & A. Miller, FEDERAL PRACTICE & PROCEDURES CIVIL, §2588. The reason was stated in our opinion in *Illinois Central Railroad Co.* v. *Gulf, Mobile & Ohio Railroad Co.,* 308 F.2d 374, 375 (5th Cir. 1962): "Since this Court is in as good position to interpret the . . . written contract as was the district court, we cannot rely upon the clearly erroneous rule, but must ourselves construe the contract without any presumption in favor of the judgment of the district court."

Thus, our review of the district court's interpretation of the consent decree's language is comparable to review of a district court's contract interpretation and is not restricted by the clearly erroneous rule of F.R.Civ.P. 52(a); the matter may rather be considered afresh by this court as a matter of law. See *Kimbell Foods, Inc.* v. *Republic National Bank,* 557 F.2d 491 (5th Cir. 1977).

If possible, we are required to analyze a contract's meaning by its language without resort to extrinsic considerations. This is because the language of an agreement, unless ambiguous, represents the parties' intention. *Kimbell, supra* at 496. Of settlement agreements in particular, the Supreme Court has said that:

"[T]he agreement reached normally embodies a compromise; in exchange for the saving of cost and elimination of risk, the parties each give up something they might have won had they proceeded with the litigation. Thus the *decree* itself cannot be said to have a purpose; rather the *parties* have purposes, generally opposed to each other, and the resultant decree embodies as much of those opposing purposes as the respective parties have the bargaining power and skill to achieve. For these reasons, the scope of a consent decree must be discerned within its four corners, and not by reference to what might satisfy the purposes of one of the parties to it."

*United States* v. *Armour & Co.,* 402 U.S. 673, 681–82, 29 L.Ed.2d 256 (1971). Where ambiguities exist in the language of a consent decree, the court may turn to other "aids to construction," such as other documents to which the consent decree refers, as well as legal materials setting the context for the use of particular terms. *ITT Continental Baking, supra,* 420 U.S. at 238–43.

We are puzzled by the district court's stated view that the syntactically opaque language of clause VII.D.2 is "not ambiguous," but we think that the district court was correct in attempting to construe this clause in the light of other portions of the agreement. We disagree, however, with the district court's ultimate construction of the phrase. That interpretation focused on the opening clause of paragraph VII.D.2, "Subject to the express exception in Paragraph III.(F). . . ." This clause refers to the ten named members of the Affected Class who had not yet transferred at the time the settlement agreement went into effect; paragraph III.F entitled them to transfer within thirty days after the settlement without forfeiting Court Seniority in the new section. The district court reasoned that since this group of ten employees was excepted from the operation of paragraph VII.D.2, these ten had full Court Seniority for purposes of demotion, as provided in paragraph VII.D.1, whereas the other members of the Affected Class had only the restricted Court Seniority of paragraph VII.D.2; that is, they could be bumped back to their immediate pre-settlement positions before Court Seniority applied. Thus, the court said, the exception clause removed any ambiguity in paragraph D.2, since it meant that the general Court Seniority of paragraph D.1 had at least some applicability, namely to the ten employees who had not transferred prior to the settlement.

This argument is unconvincing. It assumes the very point at issue, *i.e.*, that the "in which" clause modifies "position" rather than "line of progression" and that consequently all but the expected ten of the 57 Affected Class members could indeed be bumped back to their pre-settlement positions before Court Seniority would apply. Moreover, the argument is even less appealing when paragraphs VII.D.2 and 2 are read together and in the context of the entire agreement.

To recapitulate, paragraph VII.D.1 provides in general language that Court Seniority is to apply in case of layoff, demotion and recall of the 57 Affected Class members. The next paragraph is VII.D.2, the paragraph in dispute here. In the main it deals with the subject of section transfers by Affected Class members. The first clause refers to the ten named Affected Class members who had not yet transferred and reserves to them the right to transfer one time without loss of Court Seniority; [3] the last sentence states that Court Seniority may not be used to jump from section to section.

Sandwiched between these two phrases dealing with transfers is the language at issue. The appellants argue, we think compellingly, that their reading of the language is the natural and appropriate reading, since it also relates to section transfers, *i.e.*, if the "in which" clause refers to "Line of progression," the clause in question merely restricts the use of full Court Seniority to those who refrain from transferring after the date of the settlement. The appellees' reading, on the other hand, would have the disputed clause shift abruptly from the subject of section transfers to an entirely different subject, namely the bumping back to a baseline

---

[3] It seems apparent that this provision was intended to permit the laggards to escape from the undesirable lines as their more enterprising brethren already had. That it should intend to put them on a par is understandable; that the clause should be intended to reward their timidity is not.

job of all but ten of the 57 Affected Class members. We think it highly unlikely that the parties would have placed so severe a restriction on the use of Court Seniority, by all but a few of the Affected Class members, in the middle of a paragraph that ostensibly deals with intersectional transfers. Nor does the decree as a whole give any hint of a reason why the ten who have not yet transferred should be awarded full Court Seniority in the event of demotions, whereas their brethren would not— particularly when paragraph VII.D.1 appears on its face to give equal rights to all 57 of the Affected Class members. Thus, we think that the appellees' reading of the language is highly artificial.

The Supreme Court has cautioned against the use of such "strained" constructions of settlement agreements. *United States* v. *Atlantic Refining Co.*, 360 U.S. 19, 22, 3 L.Ed.2d 1054 (1959); see also *Hughes* v. *United States*, 342 U.S. 353, 96 L.Ed. 394 (1952). The natural reading of paragraph VII.D.2 is as a restriction on intersectional transfers; thus, the "in which" clause should be read to modify "line of progression" so that all 57 members of the Affected Class are entitled to full Court Seniority in the event of demotion or layoff, subject of course to the transfer restrictions of paragraph D.2 and any further restrictions embodied elsewhere in the settlement.

Because of our reading of the language of the decree, we do not reach appellants' further contentions as to modification of the decree.

We reverse and remand for further proceedings consistent with this opinion.

Reversed and Remanded.

LYNNE, Senior District Judge, dissenting: This appeal involves only tangentially the familiar right-remedy dichotomy inherent in cases arising under Title VII of the Civil Rights Act of 1964.[1] Primarily, appellants contend for reversal that the district judge misconstrued the terms of a consent decree,[2] entered on the 11th day of January, 1973, in concluding that it had not been violated by defendants. I would affirm.

As of the date of the consent decree, Mr. Freddie Eaton (Eaton) and Mr. Willie Sullivan (Sullivan), both black employees of defendant in its textile manufacturing plant in Mobile, Alabama, each occupied job number 3 (from the bottom) in the Spinning Line of Progression. Thereafter, each advanced to job number 6 therein. Shortly prior to November 26, 1974, in the course of a reduction in force, defendant company, by applying the seniority provisions of its contract[3] with the union[4] as the

[1] 42 U.S.C. § 2000e, *et seq.*

[2] On May 10, 1971, 13 named employees brought a Title VII class action against defendants, company and union, broadly claiming racial discrimination in employment. On December 4, 1972, the parties submitted to the court a proposed settlement agreement subscribed by able counsel. Having analyzed the agreement and found it to be fair, adequate, reasonable and not the product of collusion between the parties, the district judge expressly approved it on January 11, 1973. Thus, the settlement agreement became in fact and in law a consent decree.

[3] Sometimes referred to as contract seniority.

[4] Textile Workers Union of America, AFL-CIO.

bargaining representative of its employees rolled back Eaton and Sullivan to the position of Utility Operators (job number 3).

There followed grievances, denied by the company, arbitration, which resulted in vindication of the company's position, and, finally, a motion filed with the court for "declaration of rights and enforcement of the decree," which was denied, engendering this appeal. The focus at each of these stages was on the following provisions of Section VII of the decree:

"D.1. When members of the affected class compete with each other or with employees not of the affected class as to layoff, demotion and recall, Court Seniority shall be the applicable seniority for such purposes and may be utilized by affected class employees and any other employees so competing. Court Seniority for the purposes of demotion, layoff and recall shall not be lost by failure either to bid or to accept an entry level job as is set forth in preceding Paragraph 'C.'

"2. Subject to the express exception in Paragraph III.(F) above, an affected class employee or any other person can only use his Court Seniority in the case of demotion, layoff or recall *from his position in the line of progression in which he is as of the date of his Settlement Agreement downward to the entry job in that same line of progression.* He can at no time use Court Seniority to jump from section to section or from department to department." (Emphasis added.)

As though it were a simple exercise in syntax, the parties mightily contest the juxtaposition of the prepositional phrase, "in which he is as of the date of this Settlement Agreement," to the nouns, "position" and "line" [of progression].

The arbitrator held that there was no ambiguity present in Paragraph 2 of the decree and that neither Eaton nor Sullivan "had the right to use the expanded court or plant-wide seniority to compete with all others at the time of layoff but rather had to wait until they reached their base job possessed 'as of the date of this Settlement Agreement' before utilizing the Court Seniority."

I do not disagree that ambiguity is present in the naked language quoted above. However, the conscientious district judge did not mechanically or casually accept the result of the arbitration award. There is implicit in his well-reasoned opinion that he recognized that there is indeed ambiguity when Paragraphs VII(D)(1) and VII(D)(2) are read *in pari materia*. He resolved this patent ambiguity by reference to the concluding language of Paragraph III(F) of the decree and reasoned that the introductory clause of Paragraph VII(D)(2), which refers to Paragraph III(F), removes any ambiguity between the *unrestricted* use of Court Seniority under Paragraph VII(D)(1) and the *restricted* use of Court Seniority under Paragraph VII(D)(2).

I agree that the clearly erroneous rule is not to be applied in reviewing the judgment of the district court. It is the settled rule in this circuit that: "Since this Court is in as good position to interpret the 190–page written contract as was the district court, we cannot rely upon the clearly erroneous rule, but must ourselves construe the contract without any presumption in favor of the judgment of the district court." Rule 52(a), Federal Rules of Civil Procedure, 28 U.S.C.A.; *Galena Oaks Corporation* v. *Scofield,* 5 Cir., 1954, 218 F.2d 217; *Illinois Central Railroad Co.* v. *Gulf, Mobile & Ohio R. Co.,* 308 F.2d 374, 375 (5th Cir. 1962).

The governing rule of construction of a consent decree was stated by the Supreme Court in *United States* v. *Armour & Co.,* 402 U.S. 673, 681–82, 29 L.Ed.2d 256 (1971);

"Consent decrees are entered into by parties to a case after careful negotiation has produced agreement on their precise terms. The parties waive their right to litigate the issues involved in the case and thus save themselves the time, expense, and inevitable risk of litigation. Naturally, the agreement reached normally embodies a compromise; in exchange for the saving of cost and elimination of risk, the parties each give up something they might have won had they proceeded with the litigation. Thus the *decree* itself cannot be said to have a purpose; rather the *parties* have purposes, generally opposed to each other, and the resultant decree embodies as much of those opposing purposes as the respective parties have the bargaining power and skill to achieve. *For these reasons, the scope of a consent decree must be discerned within its four corners and not be reference to what might satisfy the purposes of one of the parties to it.* Because the defendant has, by the decree, waived his right to litigate the issues raised, a right guaranteed to him by the Due Process Clause, the conditions upon which he has given that waiver must be respected, and the instrument must be construed as it is written, and not as it might have been written had the plaintiff established his factual claims and legal theories in litigation." (Emphasis added; footnote omitted).

After careful review of the consent decree, aided by the briefs and oral arguments of able and experienced counsel, I cannot say that the district judge erred in the construction he placed upon the terms of such decree after critical analysis.

My profound disagreement with the opinion for the Court arises from the rigidity of its mandate that, upon remand, the district judge, stripped of his discretion, must construe ambiguous language precisely as this Court prefers. I could understand a remand which proceeds upon the premise that the consent decree is ambiguous; the ambiguity must be recognized, and it must be resolved forthrightly. How? Appropriately, the Court, relying upon *I.T.T. Continental Baking Co.,* note 9, *infra,* replies: "Where ambiguities exist in the language of a consent decree, the court may turn to other 'aids to construction,' such as other documents to which the consent decree refers, as well as legal materials setting the context for the use of particular terms," yet the Court, without resort to such other aids, proceeds to a construction which is apparently binding upon the district court. I must confess that "[t]he more you explain it, the less I understand it."

I respectfully dissent.

## E. ATTORNEY'S FEES

## CHRISTIANSBURG GARMENT CO. v. EEOC

*Supreme Court of the United States, 1978*
*434 U.S. 412, 16 FEP Cases 502*

MR. JUSTICE STEWART delivered the opinion of the Court.

Section 706(k) of Title VII of the Civil Rights Act of 1964 provides: "In any action or proceeding under this title the court, in its discretion, may allow the prevailing party . . . a reasonable attorney's fee. . . ." [1] The question in this case is under what circumstances an attorney's fee should be allowed when the defendant is the prevailing party in a Title VII action—a question about which the federal courts have expressed divergent views.

### I

Two years after Rosa Helm had filed a Title VII charge of racial discrimination against the petitioner Christiansburg Garment Company (the company), the Equal Employment Opportunity Commission notified her that its conciliation efforts had failed and that she had the right to sue the company in federal court. She did not do so. Almost two years later, Congress enacted the 1972 Amendments to Title VII.[2] Section 14 of these Amendments authorized the Commission to sue in its own name to prosecute "charges pending with the Commission" on the effective date of the Amendments. Proceeding under this section, the Commission sued the company, alleging that it had engaged in unlawful employment practices in violation of the Act. The company moved for summary judgment on the ground, *inter alia,* that the Rosa Helm charge had not been "pending" before the Commission when the 1972 Amendments took effect. The District Court agreed, and granted summary judgment in favor of the company. *Equal Employment Opportunity Commission v. Christiansburg Garment Co., Inc.,* 376 F. Supp. 1067 (WD Va.).[3]

---

[1] [Footnotes numbered as in original.—Ed.] "In any action or proceeding under this subchapter the court, in its discretion, may allow the prevailing party, other than the Commission or the United States, a reasonable attorney's fee as part of the costs, and the Commission and the United States shall be liable for costs the same as a private person." 78 Stat. 261, 42 U.S.C. § 2000e–5(k).

[2] Pub. L. 92–261, 86 Stat. 103.

[3] The Commission argued that charges as to which no private suit had been brought as of the effective date of the Amendments remained "pending" before the Commission so long as the complaint had not been dismissed and the dispute had not been resolved through conciliation. The Commission supported its construction of § 14 with references to the legislative history of the 1972 Amendments.

The District Court concluded that when Rosa Helm was notified in 1970 that conciliation had failed and that she had a right to sue the company, the Commission had no further action legally open to it, and its authority over the case terminated on that date. Section 14's reference to "pending" cases was held "to be limited to charges still in the process of negotiation and conciliation" on the effective date of the 1972 Amendments. 376 F. Supp., at 1074, 7 FEP Cases, at 1239.

The District Court rejected on the merits two additional grounds advanced by the company in support of its motion for summary judgment.

The company then petitioned for the allowance of attorney's fees against the Commission pursuant to § 706(k) of Title VII. Finding that "the Commission's action in bringing the suit cannot be characterized as unreasonable or meritless," the District Court concluded that "an award of attorney's fees to petitioner is not justified in this case." [4] A divided Court of Appeals affirmed, 550 F.2d 949, 14 FEP Cases 262, and we granted certiorari to consider an important question of federal law, _____ U.S. _____.

## II

It is the general rule in the United States that in the absence of legislation providing otherwise, litigants must pay their own attorneys' fees. *Alyeska Pipeline Co.* v. *Wilderness Society*, 421 U.S. 240, 10 FEP Cases 826. Congress has provided only limited exceptions to this rule "under selected statutes granting or protecting various federal rights." *Id.*, at 260. Some of these statutes make fee awards mandatory for prevailing plaintiffs; [5] others make awards permissive but limit them to certain parties, usually prevailing plaintiffs.[6] But many of the statutes are more flexible, authorizing the award of attorneys' fees to either plaintiffs or defendants, and entrusting the effectuation of the statutory policy to the discretion of the district courts.[7] Section 706(k) of Title VII of the Civil Rights Act of 1964 falls into this last category, providing as it does that a district court may in its discretion allow an attorney's fee to the prevailing party.

In *Newman* v. *Piggie Park Enterprises*, 390 U.S. 400, the Court considered a substantially identical statute authorizing the award of attorney's fees under Title II of the Civil Rights Act of 1964.[8] In that case the plaintiffs had prevailed, and the Court of Appeals had held that they should be awarded their attorneys' fees "only to the extent that the respondents' defenses had been advanced 'for purposes of delay and not in good faith.' " *Id.*, at 401. We ruled that this "subjective standard" did not properly effectuate the purposes of the counsel-fee provision of Title II.

---

[4] The opinion of the District Court dealing with the motion for attorney's fees is not officially reported, but appears at 12 FEP Cases 533.

[5] See, *e.g.*, the Clayton Act, 38 Stat. 731, 15 U.S.C. § 15; the Fair Labor Standards Act of 1938, 52 Stat. 1069, as amended, 29 U.S.C. § 216(b); Packers and Stockyards Act, 42 Stat. 165, 7 U.S.C. § 210(f); the Truth in Lending Act, 82 Stat. 157, 15 U.S.C. § 1640(a); and the Merchant Marine Act of 1936, 49 Stat. 2015, 46 U.S.C. § 1227.

[6] See, *e.g.*, the Privacy Act of 1974, 88 Stat. 1897, 5 U.S.C. § 552a(g)(2)(B); Fair Housing Act of 1968, 82 Stat. 88, 42 U.S.C. § 3612(c).

[7] See, *e.g.*, Trust Indenture Act of 1939, 53 Stat. 1171, 15 U.S.C. § 77ooo(e); Securities Exchange Act of 1934, 48 Stat. 889, 897, 15 U.S.C. §§ 78i(e), 78r(a); Federal Water Pollution Prevention and Control Act of 1972, 86 Stat. 888, 33 U.S.C. § 1365(d); Clean Air Act Amendments of 1970, 84 Stat. 1706, 42 U.S.C. § 1857h-2(d); Noise Control Act of 1972, 86 Stat. 1244, 42 U.S.C. § 4911(d).

[8] "In any action commenced pursuant to this subchapter, the court, in its discretion, may allow the prevailing party, other than the United States, a reasonable attorney's fee as part of the costs, and the United States shall be liable for costs the same as a private person." 42 U.S.C. § 2000a–3(b).

Relying primarily on the intent of Congress to cast a Title II plaintiff in the role of "a 'private attorney general,' vindicating a policy that Congress considered of the highest priority," we held that a prevailing plaintiff under Title II "should ordinarily recover an attorney's fee unless special circumstances would render such an award unjust." *Id.*, at 402. We noted in passing that if the objective of Congress had been to permit the award of attorneys' fees only against defendants who had acted in bad faith, "no new statutory provision would have been necessary," since even the American common-law rule allows the award of attorneys' fees in those exceptional circumstances. *Id.*, at 402 n. 4.[9]

In *Albemarle Paper Co.* v. *Moody*, 422 U.S. 405, 10 FEP Cases 1181, the Court made clear that the *Piggie Park* standard of awarding attorney's fees to a successful plaintiff is equally applicable in an action under Title VII of the Civil Rights Act. *Id.*, at 415, 10 FEP Cases, at 1186. See also *Northcross* v. *Memphis Board of Education*, 412 U.S. 427, 428. It can thus be taken as established, as the parties in this case both acknowledge, that under § 706(k) of Title VII a prevailing *plaintiff* ordinarily is to be awarded attorney's fees in all but special circumstances.[10]

## III

The question in the case before us is what standard should inform a district court's discretion in deciding whether to award attorney's fees to a successful *defendant* in a Title VII action. Not surprisingly, the parties in addressing the question in their briefs and oral arguments have taken almost diametrically opposite positions.[11]

The company contends that the *Piggie Park* criterion for a successful plaintiff should apply equally as a guide to the award of attorney's fees to a successful defendant. Its submission, in short, is that every prevailing defendant in a Title VII action should receive an allowance of attorney's fees "unless special circumstances would render such an award unjust." [12]

The respondent Commission, by contrast, argues that the prevailing defendant should receive an award of attorney's fees only when it is found that the plaintiff's action was brought in bad faith. We have concluded that neither of these positions is correct.

[9] The propriety under the American common-law rule of awarding attorney's fees against a losing party who has acted in bad faith was expressly reaffirmed in *Alyeska Pipeline Co.* v. *Wilderness Society*, 421 U.S., at 258–259.

[10] *Chastang* v. *Flynn & Emrich Co.*, 541 F.2d 1040, 1045, 12 FEP Cases 1533, 1537 (CA4) (finding "special circumstances" justifying no award to prevailing plaintiff); *Carrion* v. *Yeshiva Univ.*, 535 F.2d 722, 727, 13 FEP Cases 1521, 1525–26 (CA2); *Johnson* v. *Georgia Highway Express, Inc.*, 488 F.2d 714, 716, 7 FEP Cases 1, 2–3 (CA5); *Parham* v. *Southwestern Bell Telephone Co.*, 433 F.2d 421, 429–30, 2 FEP Cases 1017, 1024 (CA8).

[11] Briefs by *amici* have also been filed in support of each party.

[12] This was the view taken by Judge Widener, dissenting in the Court of Appeals, 550 F.2d, at 952, 14 FEP Cases, at 264. At least two other federal courts have expressed the same view. *EEOC* vs. *Bailey Co., Inc.*, 563 F.2d 439, 456, 15 FEP Cases 972, 986 (CA6); *United States* v. *Allegheny-Ludlum Industries, Inc.*, 558 F.2d 742, 744, 15 FEP Cases 583, 584 (CA5).

## A

Relying on what it terms "the plain meaning of the statute," the company argues that the language of § 706(k) admits of only one interpretation: "A prevailing defendant is entitled to an award of attorney's fees on the same basis as a prevailing plaintiff." But the permissive and discretionary language of the statute does not even invite, let alone require, such a mechanical construction. The terms of § 706(k) provide no indication whatever of the circumstances under which either a plaintiff *or* a defendant should be entitled to attorney's fees. And a moment's reflection reveals that there are at least two strong equitable considerations counselling an attorney's fee award to a prevailing Title VII plaintiff that are wholly absent in the case of a prevailing Title VII defendant.

First, as emphasized so forcefully in *Piggie Park*, the plaintiff is the chosen instrument of Congress to vindicate "a policy that Congress considered of the highest priority." 390 U.S., at 402. Second, when a district court awards counsel fees to a prevailing plaintiff, it is awarding them against a violator of federal law. As the Court of Appeals clearly perceived, "these policy consideration which support the award of fees to a prevailing plaintiff are not present in the case of a prevailing defendant." 550 F.2d, at 951, 14 FEP Cases, at 263. A successful defendant seeking counsel fees under § 706(k) must rely on quite different equitable considerations.

But if the company's position is untenable, the Commission's argument also misses the mark. It seems clear, in short, that in enacting § 706(k) Congress did not intend to permit the award of attorney's fees to a prevailing defendant only in a situation where the plaintiff was motivated by bad faith in bringing the action. As pointed out in *Piggie Park*, if that had been the intent of Congress, no statutory provision would have been necessary, for it has long been established that even under the American common-law rule attorney's fees may be awarded against a party who has proceeded in bad faith.[13]

Furthermore, while it was certainly the policy of Congress that Title VII plaintiffs should vindicate "a policy that Congress considered of the highest priority," *Piggie Park, supra,* 390 U.S., at 402, it is equally certain that Congress entrusted the ultimate effectuation of that policy to the adversary judicial process, *Occidental Life Insurance Co.* v. *EEOC,* 432 U.S. _____, 14 FEP Cases 1718. A fair adversary process presupposes both a vigorous prosecution and a vigorous defense. It cannot be lightly assumed that in enacting § 706(k), Congress intended to distort that process by giving the private plaintiff substantial incentives to sue, while foreclosing to the defendant the possibility of recovering his expenses in

---

· 13 See n. 9, *supra.* Had Congress provided for attorneys' fee awards only to successful plaintiffs, an argument could have been made that the congressional action had preempted the common-law rule, and that, therefore, a successful defendant could not recover attorney's fees even against a plaintiff who had proceeded in bad faith. Cf. *Byram Concretanks, Inc.* v. *Warren Concrete Products Company of New Jersey,* 374 F.2d 649, 651 (CA3). But there is no indication whatever that the purpose of Congress in enacting § 706(k) in the form that it did was simply to foreclose such an argument.

resisting even a groundless action unless he can show that it was brought in bad faith.

## B

The sparse legislative history of § 706(k) reveals little more than the barest outlines of a proper accommodation of the competing considerations we have discussed. The only specific reference to § 706(k) in the legislative debates indicates that the fee provision was included to "make it easier for a plaintiff of limited means to bring a meritorious suit." [14] During the Senate floor discussions of the almost identical attorney's fee provision of Title II, however, several Senators explained that its allowance of awards to defendants would serve "to deter the bringing of lawsuits without foundation," [15] "to discourage frivolous suits," [16] and "to diminish the likelihood of unjustified suits being brought." [17] If anything can be gleaned from these fragments of legislative history, it is that while Congress wanted to clear the way for suits to be brought under the Act, it also wanted to protect defendants from burdensome litigation having no legal or factual basis. The Court of Appeals for the District of Columbia Circuit seems to have drawn the maximum significance from the Senate debates when it concluded:

"[From these debates] two purposes for § 706(k) emerge. First, Congress desired 'to make it easier for a plaintiff of limited means to bring a meritorious suit.' . . . But second, and equally important, Congress intended to 'deter the bringing of lawsuits without foundation' by providing that the 'prevailing party'—be it plaintiff or defendant—could obtain legal fees." *Grubbs* v. *Butz,* 548 F.2d 973, 975, 13 FEP Cases 245, 246–47.

The first federal appellate court to consider what criteria should govern the award of attorney's fees to a prevailing Title VII defendant was the Court of Appeals for the Third Circuit in *United States Steel Corporation* v. *United States,* 519 F.2d 359, 10 FEP Cases 1106. There a district court had denied a fee award to a defendant that had successfully resisted a Commission demand for documents, the court finding that the Commission's action had not been " 'unfounded, meritless, frivolous, or vexatiously brought.' " 519 F.2d, at 363, 10 FEP Cases, at 1108. The Court of Appeals concluded that the District Court had not abused its discretion in denying the award. *Id.,* at 365, 10 FEP Cases, at 1109. A similar standard was adopted by the Court of Appeals for the Second Circuit in *Carrion* v. *Yeshiva University,* 535 F.2d 722, 13 FEP Cases 1521. In upholding an attorney's fee award to a successful defendant, that court stated that such awards should be permitted "not routinely, not simply because he succeeds, but only where the action brought is found to be

[14] Remarks of Senator Humphrey, 110 Cong. Rec. 12724 (1964).
[15] Remarks of Senator Lausche, 110 Cong. Rec. 13668 (1964).
[16] Remarks of Senator Pastore, 110 Cong. Rec. 14214 (1964).
[17] Remarks of Senator Humphrey, 110 Cong. Rec. 6534 (1964).

unreasonable, frivolous, meritless, or vexatious." *Id.*, at 727, 13 **FEP** Cases, at 1525.[18]

To the extent that abstract words can deal with concrete cases, we think that the concept embodied in the language adopted by these two Courts of Appeals is correct. We would qualify their words only by pointing out that the term "meritless" is to be understood as meaning groundless or without foundation, rather than simply that the plaintiff has ultimately lost his case, and that the term "vexatious" in no way implies that the plaintiff's subjective bad faith is a necessary prerequisite to a fee award against him. In sum, a district court may in its discretion award attorney's fees to a prevailing defendant in a Title VII case upon a finding that the plaintiff's action was frivolous, unreasonable or without foundation, even though not brought in subjective bad faith.

In applying these criteria, it is important that a district court resist the understandable temptation to engage in *post-hoc* reasoning by concluding that, because a plaintiff did not ultimately prevail, his action must have been unreasonable or without foundation. This kind of hindsight logic could discourage all but the most airtight claims, for seldom can a prospective plaintiff be sure of ultimate success. No matter how honest one's belief that he has been the victim of discrimination, no matter how meritorious one's claim may appear at the outset, the course of litigation is rarely predictable. Decisive facts may not emerge until discovery or trial. The law may change or clarify in the midst of litigation. Even when the law or the facts appear questionable or unfavorable at the outset, a party may have an entirely reasonable ground for bringing suit.

That § 706(k) allows fee awards only to *prevailing* private plaintiffs should assure that this statutory provision will not in itself operate as an incentive to the bringing of claims that have little chance of success.[19] To take the further step of assessing attorneys' fees against plaintiffs simply because they do not finally prevail would substantially add to the risks inhering in most litigation and would undercut the efforts of Congress to promote the vigorous enforcement of the provisions of Title VII. Hence, a plaintiff should not be assessed his opponent's attorney's fees unless a court finds that his claim was frivolous, unreasonable, or groundless, or that the plaintiff continued to litigate after it clearly became so. And, needless to say, if a plaintiff is found to have brought or continued such a claim in *bad faith,* there will be an even stronger basis for charging him with the attorney's fees incurred by the defense.[20]

---

[18] At least three other Circuits are in general agreement. See *Bolton* v. *Murray Envelope Corp.*, 553 F.2d 881, 884 n. 2, 15 FEP Cases 478, 480 (CA5); *Grubbs* v. *Butz*, _____ U.S. App. D.C. _____, 548 F.2d 973, 975–76, 13 FEP Cases 245, 247; *Wright* v. *Stone Container Corp.*, 524 F.2d 1058, 1063–64, 11 FEP Cases 1322, 1325 (CA8).

[19] See remarks of Senator Miller, 110 Cong. Rec. 14214 (1964), with reference to the parallel attorney's fee provision in Title II.

[20] Initially, the Commission argued that the "costs" assessable against the Government under § 706(k) did not include attorney's fees. See, *e.g.,* *United States Steel Corp.* v. *United States*, 519 F.2d 359, 362, 10 FEP Cases 1106, 1107–1108 (CA3); *Van Hoomissen* v. *Xerox Corp.*, 503 F.2d 1131, 1132–33, 8 FEP Cases 725, 726 (CA9). But the courts of

## IV

In denying attorney's fees to the company in this case, the District Court focused on the standards we have discussed. The Court found that "the Commission's action in bringing suit cannot be characterized as unreasonable or meritless" because "the basis upon which petitioner prevailed was an issue of first impression requiring judicial resolution" and because the "Commission's statutory interpretation of § 14 of the 1972 amendments was not frivolous." The Court thus exercised its discretion squarely within the permissible bounds of § 706(k). Accordingly, the judgment of the Court of Appeals upholding the decision of the District Court is affirmed.

### F. FEDERAL EMPLOYEE SUITS

## CHANDLER v. ROUDEBUSH

*Supreme Court of the United States, 1976*
*425 U.S. 840, 12 FEP Cases 1368*

MR. JUSTICE STEWART delivered the opinion of the Court.

In 1972 Congress extended the protection of Title VII of the Civil Rights Act of 1964, 78 Stat. 253, as amended 42 U.S.C. § 2000e *et seq.* (1970 ed. Supp. IV), to employees of the Federal Government. A principal

---

appeals rejected this position and, during the course of appealing this case, the Commission abandoned its contention that it was legally immune to adverse fee awards under § 706(k). 550 F.2d, at 951, 14 FEP Cases, at 263.

It has been urged that fee awards against the Commission should rest on a standard different from that governing fee awards against private plaintiffs. One *amicus* stresses that the Commission, unlike private litigants, needs no inducement to enforce Title VII since it is required by statute to do so. But this distinction between the Commission and private plaintiffs merely explains why Congress drafted § 706(k) to preclude the recovery of attorney's fees by the Commission; it does not support a difference in treatment among private and government plaintiffs when a prevailing defendant seeks to recover his attorney's fees. Several courts and commentators have also deemed significant the Government's greater ability to pay adverse fee awards compared to a private litigant. See *e.g., United States Steel Corp.* v. *United States,* 519 F.2d, at 364 n. 24, 10 FEP Cases, at 1109 (CA3); Heinsz, *Attorney's Fee For Prevailing Title VII Defendants: Toward a Workable Standard,* 8 TOLEDO L. REV. 259, 290 (1977); Comment, *Title VII, Civil Rights Act of 1964: Standards for Award of Attorney's Fees to Prevailing Defendants,* 1976 WIS. L. REV. 207, 228. We are informed, however, that such awards must be paid from the Commission's litigation budget, so that every attorney's fee assessment against the Commission will inevitably divert resources from the agency's enforcement of Title VII. See 46 Comp. Gen. 98, 100 (1966); 38 Comp. Gen. 343, 344–345 (1958). The other side of this coin is the fact that many defendants in Title VII claims are small- and moderate-size employers for whom the expense of defending even a frivolous claim may become a strong disincentive to the exercise of their legal rights. In short, there are equitable considerations on both sides of this question. Yet § 706(k) explicitly provides that "the Commission and the United States shall be liable for costs the same as a private person." Hence, although a district court may consider distinctions between the Commission and private plaintiffs in determining the reasonableness of the Commission's litigation efforts, we find no grounds for applying a different general standard whenever the Commission is the losing plaintiff.

goal of the amending legislation, the Equal Employment Opportunity Act of 1972, Pub. L. 92-261, 86 Stat. 103, was to eradicate " 'entrenched discrimination in the Federal service,' " *Morton* v. *Mancari,* 417 U.S. 535, 547, 8 FEP Cases 105, 109, by strengthening internal safeguards and by according "[a]ggrieved [federal] employees or applicants . . . the full rights available in the courts as are granted to individuals in the private sector under title VII." [1] The issue presented by this case is whether the 1972 Act gives federal employees the same right to a trial *de novo* of employment discrimination claims as "private sector" employees enjoy under Title VII.

## I

The petitioner, Mrs. Jewell Chandler, is a Negro. In 1972 she was employed as a Claims Examiner by the Veterans Administration. In August of that year she applied for a promotion to the position of Supervisory Claims Examiner. Following a selection procedure she was designated as one of three finalists for the position. The promotion was awarded to a Filipino-American male. The petitioner subsequently filed a complaint with the Veterans Administration alleging that she had been denied the promotion because of unlawful discrimination on the basis of sex and race. After an administrative hearing on the claim, the presiding complaints examiner submitted proposed findings to the effect that the petitioner had been discriminated against on the basis of sex but not race and recommended that she be given a retroactive promotion to the position for which she had applied. The Agency rejected the proposed finding of sex discrimination as not "substantiated by the evidence," and accordingly granted no relief.[2] The petitioner filed a timely appeal to the Civil Service Commission Board of Appeals and Review, which affirmed the Agency's decision.

Within 30 days after receiving notice of the Commission's decision, the petitioner brought the present suit in a federal district court under § 717 (c) of the Civil Rights Act of 1964, as amended, 42 U.S.C. 2000e-16(c) (1970 ed. Supp. IV). After moving unsuccessfully for summary judgment, she initiated discovery proceedings by filing notice of two depositions and a request for the production of documents. The respondents moved for an order prohibiting discovery on the ground that the judicial action authorized by § 717(c) is limited to a review of the administrative record. The petitioner opposed the motion, asserting that she had a right under § 717(c) to a plenary judicial trial *de novo*. The District Court adopted the holding of the United States District Court for the District of Columbia in *Hackley* v. *Johnson,* 360 F. Supp. 1247, 6 FEP Cases 79, *rev'd sub nom. Hackley* v. *Roudebush,* _____ U.S. App. D.C. _____, 520 F.2d 108,

---

1 [Footnotes numbered as in original.—Ed.] S. Rep. No. 92-415, 92nd Cong., 1st Sess. 16 (1971) (hereinafter cited as Senate Report).

2 The Veterans Administration accepted the examiner's proposed finding of no race discrimination.

11 FEP Cases 487, that a "trial *de novo* is not required [under § 717(c)] in all cases" and that review of the administrative record is sufficient if "an absence of discrimination is affirmatively established by the clear weight of the evidence in the record. . . ." 360 F. Supp., at 1252, 6 FEP Cases at 83.[3] Applying this standard of review, the District Court determined that "the absence of discrimination is firmly established by the clear weight of the administrative record" and granted summary judgment in favor of the respondents. The Court of Appeals affirmed the judgment, agreeing with the District Court's ruling that § 717(c) contemplates not a trial *de novo* but the "intermediate scope of inquiry expounded in *Hackley* v. *Johnson*. . . ." 515 F.2d 251, 255, 10 FEP Cases 689, 691 (CA9). We granted certiorari to resolve a conflict among the circuits concerning the nature of the judicial proceeding provided by § 717(c).[4] 423 U.S. 821.

## II

We begin with the language of the statute. Section 717(c), 42 U.S.C. § 2000e-16(c), states that within 30 days after notice of final adverse administrative action on a federal employee's discrimination complaint by either the employing agency or the Civil Service Commission (in the event a permissive appeal is taken), or after 180 days of delay by the agency or the Commission, the employee "may file a civil action as provided in section 2000e-5 of this title, in which civil action the head of the department, agency, or unit, as appropriate, shall be the defendant." Section 717(d), 42 U.S.C. § 2000e-16(d), goes on to specify that "[t]he provisions of section 2000e-5(f) through (k) of this title, as applicable shall govern civil actions brought hereunder."

Section 2000e-5 (§ 706 of the Civil Rights Act of 1964) authorizes the Equal Employment Opportunity Commission (EEOC) to bring "civil actions" on behalf of private sector employees in Federal District Court.[5] Alternatively, § 706(f)(1) of the Act, 42 U.S.C. § 2000e-5(f)(1), authorizes an individual employee to sue on his own behalf if a specified period of delay has elapsed or if the Commission has declined to represent him on the basis of its initial determination that "there is not reasonable cause to believe that the charge is true. . . ." § 706(b), 42 U.S.C. § 2000e-5(b).

---

[3] The District Court in Hackley had held that even if that "exacting standard" were not met, a full trial *de novo* would not necessarily be required. Rather a district could, "in its discretion, as appropriate, remand, take testimony to supplement the administrative record, or grant the plaintiff relief on the administrative record." *Hackley* v. *Johnson*, 360 F. Supp., at 1252, 6 FEP Cases, at 83.

[4] Four courts of appeals have held that § 717(c) gives federal employees the right to a trial *de novo* in the district court. [Citations omitted.] Three other courts of appeals have held that federal employees are not generally entitled to trials *de novo*. [Citations omitted.]

[5] The Attorney General for the United States is given responsibility for instituting Title VII civil actions on behalf of employees of state governments, governmental agencies, or political subdivisions. § 706(f)(1), 42 U.S.C. § 2000e-5(f)(1).

Sections 706(f) through (k), 42 U.S.C. §§ 2000e-5(f) through (k), provide specific rules and guidelines for private sector "civil actions."

It is well established that § 706 of the Civil Rights Act of 1964 accords private sector employees the right to *de novo* consideration of their Title VII claims. *Alexander* v. *Gardner-Denver Co.*, 415 U.S. 36, 7 FEP Cases 81; *McDonnell Douglas Corp.* v. *Green*, 411 U.S. 792, 798-99, 5 FEP Cases 965, 968; *Norman* v. *Missouri Pacific Railroad*, 414 F.2d 73, 75 n. 2, 1 FEP Cases 863, 864, 71 LRRM 2940 (CA8). The "employee's statutory right to a trial *de novo* under Title VII [of the Civil Rights Act of 1964]. . . ." *Alexander* v. *Gardner-Denver Co.*, 415 U.S., at 38, 7 FEP Cases, at 82, embodies a congressional decision to "vest federal courts with plenary powers to enforce the [substantive] requirements [of Title VII]. . . ." *Id.,* at 47, 7 FEP Cases, at 85.

The 1972 amendments to the 1964 Act added language to § 706 which reflects the *de novo* character of the private sector "civil action" even more clearly than did the 1964 version.[6] Section 706(f)(4), 42 U.S.C. § 2000e-5(f)(4), for instance, requires the chief judge of the district in which a "civil action" is pending to "immediately . . . designate a judge in such district to hear and determine the case." The judge so designated must "assign the case for hearing at the earliest practicable date. . . ." § 706 (f)(5), 42 U.S.C. § 2000e-5(f)(5). If the case has not been "scheduled . . . for trial within one hundred and twenty days after issue has been joined," then the designated judge may appoint a special master to hear it. *Ibid.* And, as under the 1964 version, if the district court "finds" that the respondent has intentionally committed an unlawful employment practice, then the court may order appropriate relief. § 706(g), 42 U.S.C. § 2000e-5(g). The terminology employed by Congress—"assign the case for hearing," "scheduled for trial," "finds"—indicates clearly that the "civil action" to which private sector employees are entitled under the amended version of Title VII is to be a trial *de novo.*

Since federal sector employees are entitled by § 717(c) to "file a civil action as provided in Section 2000e-5" and since the civil action provided in 2000e-5 is a trial *de novo,* it would seem to follow syllogistically that federal employees are entitled to a trial *de novo* of their employment discrimination claims. The Court of Appeals, however, held that a contrary result was indicated by the words "as applicable" in § 717(d) and by the legislative history of § 717, and in support of that position the Government further argues that routine *de novo* trials of federal employees' claims would clash with the 1972 Act's delegation of enforcement responsibilities to the Civil Service Commission and would contravene this Court's view that "*de novo* review is generally not to be presumed." *Consolo* v. *Federal Maritime Commission*, 383 U.S. 607, 619 n. 17.

## A. *The Meaning of the Phrase "As Applicable"*

The opinion of the District Court for the District of Columbia in *Hackley* v. *Johnson, supra,* relied on by the Court of Appeals here, ex-

---

6 Civil Rights Act of 1964, Title VII, § 706, 78 Stat. 259-261.

pressed the view that the phrase "as applicable" in § 717(d) evidences a congressional intent to restrict or qualify the right to a *de novo* proceeding granted by § 717(c). 360 F. Supp., at 1252 n. 9, 6 FEP Cases, at 82. A careful reading of § 717(d) and the provisions to which it refers indicates, however, that the phrase was intended merely to reflect the fact that certain provisions in §§ 706(f) through (k) pertain to aspects of the Title VII enforcement scheme that have no possible relevance to judicial proceedings involving federal employees.

. . .

The most natural reading of the phrase "as applicable" in § 717(d) is that it merely reflects the inapplicability of provisions in §§ 706(f) through (k) detailing the enforcement responsibilities of the EEOC and the Attorney General.[7] We cannot, therefore, agree with the view expressed by the District Court in *Hackley* v. *Johnson, supra,* and relied on by the Court of Appeals here, that Congress used the words "as applicable" to voice its intent to disallow trials *de novo* by aggrieved federal employees who have received prior administrative hearings. As the Court of Appeals for the District of Columbia Circuit held in reversing *Hackley* v. *Johnson, supra,* such an interpretation of the phrase "as applicable" would require a strained and unnatural reading of §§ 706(f) through 706(k). *Hackley* v. *Roudebush, supra,* 520 F.2d at 121, 11 FEP Cases, at 496-97. This Court pointed out in *Lynch* v. *Alworth-Stephens Co.,* 267 U.S. 364, 370, that " 'the plain, obvious and rational meaning of a statute is always to be preferred to any curious, narrow, hidden sense that nothing but the exigency of a hard case and the ingenuity and study of an acute and powerful intellect would discover.' " To read the phrase "as applicable" in § 717(d) as obliquely qualifying the federal employee's right to a trial *de novo* under § 717(c) rather than as merely reflecting the inapplicability to § 717(c) actions of provisions relating to the enforcement responsibilities of the EEOC or the Attorney General would violate this elementary canon of construction.

## B. *Legislative History*

The legislative history of the 1972 amendments reinforces the plain meaning of the statute and confirms that Congress intended to accord federal employees the same right to a trial *de novo* as is enjoyed by private sector employees and employees of state governments and political subdivisions under the amended Civil Rights Act of 1964.

[Discussion of legislative history omitted.]

In short, the bills reported out of the Senate and the House committees and the accompanying reports reveal a thorough and meticulous consideration of the question whether an administrative agency or a court should be given primary adjudicative responsibility for particular categories of Title VII complaints and an unambiguous choice to grant federal employees the right to plenary trials in the federal district courts.

---

[7] See *Hackley* v. *Roudebush, supra,* 520 F.2d, at 119-20, 11 FEP Cases, at 495-96.

. . .

Senator Dominick reiterated the theme of remedial disparity through-out the floor debates, arguing for equal treatment of private sector and federal sector complainants: Since the latter were entitled to plenary adjudication of their claims by a federal district court, rather than mere appellate review on a substantial evidence basis following agency adjudication, he contended, the former should be treated similarly.

. . .

Since the federal employee provisions of the Senate bill were eventually adopted by the conference committee and passed by Congress, the legislative history of that bill is the most helpful on the issue presented here. The sequence of debate, amendment and Senate passage of S. 2515 shows unmistakably that the Senate decided to provide both private and federal sector employees the adjudicative mechanism which the Senate committee had advocated for federal, but not private sector, employees. No changes were made or even proposed with respect to the committee's choice to allow federal employees judicial trials rather than "substantial evidence" review of administrative dispositions of their discrimination claims. On the contrary, it was the federal sector *de novo* procedure which served as the model for Senator Dominick's proposed alteration of private sector enforcement provisions. The passage of the Dominick amendment and the subsequent approval of S. 2515 by the Senate achieved the parity which Senator Dominick had advocated—judicial trial *de novo* for private as well as federal employees.

The Court of Appeals held that "the district judge faced with a demand for a trial *de novo* is entitled to determine, at a pretrial conference or otherwise, why the plaintiff believes that a trial *de novo* is necessary," 515 F.2d at 255, 10 FEP Cases, at 691-92, and concluded that the petitioner had presented "nothing before the district court to indicate that a useful purpose would be served by having a trial *de novo.*" *Ibid.* This approach substantially parallels the holding in *Hackley* v. *Johnson, supra,* that

"[t]he trial *de novo* is not required in all cases. The District Court is required by the Act to examine the administrative record with utmost care. If it determines that an absence of discrimination is affirmatively established by the clear weight of the evidence in the record, no new trial is required. If this exacting standard is not met, the Court shall, in its discretion, as appropriate, remand, take testimony to supplement the administrative record, or grant the plaintiff relief on the administrative record." 360 F. Supp., at 1252, 6 FEP Cases, at 83.

Nothing in the legislative history indicates that the federal sector "civil action" was to have this chameleon-like character, providing fragmentary *de novo* consideration of discrimination claims where "appropriate," 360 F. Supp., at 1252, 6 FEP Cases, at 83, and otherwise providing record review. On the contrary, the options which Congress considered were entirely straightforward. It faced a choice between record review of agency action based on traditional appellate standards and trial *de novo* of Title VII claims. The Senate committee selected trial *de novo* as the proper means for resolving the claims of federal employees. The Senate broadened the category of claims entitled to trial *de novo* to include those of private sector employees, and the Senate's decision to treat private and federal sector employees alike in this respect was ratified by the Congress as a whole.

## BROWN v. GSA

*Supreme Court of the United States, 1976*
*425 U.S. 820, 12 FEP Cases 1361*

MR. JUSTICE STEWART delivered the opinion of the Court.

The principal question presented by this case is whether § 717 of the Civil Rights Act of 1964 provides the exclusive judicial remedy for claims of discrimination in federal employment.

The petitioner, Clarence Brown, is a Negro who has been employed by the General Services Administration since 1957. He is currently classified in grade GS-7 and has not been promoted since 1966. In December 1970 Brown was referred, along with two white colleagues, for promotion to grade GS-9 by his supervisors. All three were rated "highly qualified," and the promotion was given to one of the white candidates for the position. Brown filed a complaint with the GSA Equal Employment Opportunity Office alleging that racial discrimination had biased the selection process. That complaint was withdrawn when Brown was told that other GS-9 positions would soon be available.

Another GS-9 position did become vacant in June 1971, for which the petitioner along with two others was recommended as "highly qualified." Again a white applicant was chosen. Brown filed a second administrative complaint with the GSA Equal Employment Opportunity Office. After preparation and review of an investigative report, the GSA Regional Administrator notified the petitioner that there was no evidence that race had played a part in the promotion. Brown requested a hearing, and one was held before a complaints examiner of the Civil Service Commission. In February 1973, the examiner issued his findings and recommended decision. He found no evidence of racial discrimination; rather he determined that Brown had not been advanced because he had not been "*fully* [*sic*] cooperative."

The GSA rendered its final decision in March 1973. The Agency's Director of Civil Rights informed Brown by letter of his conclusion that considerations of race had not entered the promotional process. The Director's letter told Brown that if he chose, he might carry the administrative process further by lodging an appeal with the Board of Appeals and Review of the Civil Service Commission and that, alternatively, he could file suit within 30 days in federal district court.

Forty-two days later Brown filed suit in a federal district court. The complaint alleged jurisdiction under Title VII of the Civil Rights Act of

1964, 42 U.S.C. § 2000e *et seq.*, "with particular refernce to" § 717; under 28 U.S.C. § 1331 (general federal question jurisdiction); under the Declaratory Judgment Act, 28 U.S.C. §§ 2201, 2202 (1970); and under the Civil Rights Act of 1866, as amended, 42 U.S.C. § 1981 (1970).

. . .

The primary question in this litigation is not difficult to state: Is § 717 of the Civil Rights Act of 1964, as added by § 11 of the Equal Employment Opportunity Act of 1972, 42 U.S.C. § 2000e-16, the exclusive individual remedy available to a federal employee complaining of job-related racial discrimination? But the question is easier to state than it is to resolve. Congress simply failed explicitly to describe § 717's position in the constellation of antidiscrimination law. We must, therefore, infer congressional intent in less obvious ways. As Chief Justice Marshall once wrote for the Court, "[w]here the mind labours to discover the design of the legislature, it seizes everything from which aid can be derived. . . ." *Fisher* v. *Blight,* 2 Cranch 358, 386 (1805).

Title VII of the Civil Rights Act of 1964 forbids employment discrimination based on race, color, religion, sex, or national origin. 42 U.S.C. §§ 2000e-2 to 2000e-3. Until it was amended in 1972 by the Equal Employment Opportunity Act, however, Title VII did not protect federal employees. 42 U.S.C. § 2000e(b). Although federal employment discrimination clearly violated both the Constitution, *Bolling* v. *Sharpe,* 347 U.S. 497 (1954), and statutory law, 5 U.S.C. § 7151, before passage of the 1972 Act, the effective availability of either administrative or judicial relief was far from sure. Charges of racial discrimination were handled parochially within each federal agency. A hearing examiner might come from outside the agency, but he had no authority to conduct an independent examination, and his conclusions and findings were in the nature of recommendations that the agency was free to accept or reject.[5] Although review lay in the Board of Appeals and Review of the Civil Service Commission, Congress found "skepticism" among federal employees "regarding the Commission's record in obtaining just resolutions of complaints and adequate remedies. This has discouraged persons from filing complaints with the Commission for fear that it will only result in antagonizing their supervisors and impairing any hope of future advancement."

If administrative remedies were ineffective, judicial relief from federal employment discrimination was even more problematic before 1972. Although an action seeking to enjoin unconstitutional agency conduct would lie, it was doubtful that backpay or other compensatory relief for employment discrimination was available at the time that Congress was considering the 1972 Act. For example, in *Gnotta* v. *United States,* 415 F.2d 1271, 2 FEP Cases 111, the Court of Appeals for the Eighth Circuit had held in 1969 that there was no jurisdictional basis to support the plaintiff's suit alleging that the Corps of Engineers had discriminatorily

[5] [Footnotes numbered as in original.—Ed.] S. Rep. No. 92-415, 92d Cong., 1st Sess., 14 (1971).

refused to promote him. Damages for alleged discrimination were held beyond the scope of the Tucker Act, 28 U.S.C. § 1346, since no express or implied contract was involved. 415 F.2d, at 1278, 2 FEP Cases, at 116. And the plaintiff's cause of action under the Administrative Procedure Act, 5 U.S.C. § 701-706, and the Mandamus Act, 28 U.S.C. § 1361, was held to be barred by sovereign immunity, since his claims for promotion would necessarily involve claims against the Treasury.

[Citations omitted.]

Concern was evinced during the Hearings before the Committees of both Houses over the apparent inability of federal employees to engage the judicial machinery in cases of alleged employment discrimination. . . . Thus, the Senate Report observed, "[t]he testimony of the Civil Service Commission notwithstanding, the Committee found that an aggrieved Federal employee does not have access to the courts. In many cases, the employee must overcome a U.S. Government defense of sovereign immunity or failure to exhaust administrative remedies with no certainty as to the steps required to exhaust such remedies. Moreover, the remedial authority of the Commission and the courts has also been in doubt." S. Rep. No. 92-415, 92d Cong., 1st Sess., 16 (1971). Similarly, the House Committee stated, "[t]here is serious doubt that court review is available to the aggrieved Federal employee. Monetary restitution or back pay is not attainable. In promotion situations, a critical area of discrimination, the promotion is often no longer available." H.R. Rep. No. 92-238, 92d Cong., 1st Sess., 25 (1971).

. . .

The legislative history thus leaves little doubt that Congress was persuaded that federal employees who were treated discriminatorily had no effective judicial remedy. And the case law suggests that conclusion was entirely reasonable. Whether that understanding of Congress was in some ultimate sense incorrect is not what is important in determining the legislative intent in amending the 1964 Civil Rights Act to cover federal employees. For the relevant inquiry is not whether Congress correctly perceived the then state of the law, but rather what its perception of the state of the law was.

This unambiguous congressional perception seems to indicate that the congressional intent in 1972 was to create an exclusive, pre-emptive administrative and judicial scheme for the redress of federal employment discrimination. We need not, however, rest our decision upon this inference alone. For the structure of the 1972 amendment itself fully confirms the conclusion that Congress intended it to be exclusive and preemptive.

Section 717 of the Civil Rights Act of 1964, as added by § 11 of the Equal Employment Opportunity Act of 1972, 42 U.S.C. § 2000e-16, proscribes federal employment discrimination and establishes an administrative and judicial enforcement system. Section 717(a) provides that all personnel actions affecting federal employees and applicants for federal employment "shall be made free from any discrimination based on race, color, religion, sex, or national origin."

Sections 717(b) and (c) establish complementary administrative and judicial enforcement mechanisms designed to eradicate federal employment discrimination. Subsection (b) delegates to the Civil Service Commission full authority to enforce the provisions of subsection (a) "through appropriate remedies, including reinstatement or hiring of employees with or without back pay," to issue "rules, regulations, orders and instructions as it deems necessary and appropriate" to carry out its responsibilities under the Act, and to review equal employment opportunity plans that are annually submitted to it by each agency and department.

Section 717(c) permits an aggrieved employee to file a civil action in a federal district court to review his claim of employment discrimination. Attached to that right, however, are certain preconditions. Initially, the complainant must seek relief in the agency that has allegedly discriminated against him. He then may seek further administrative review with the Civil Service Commission or, alternatively, he may, within 30 days of receipt of notice of the agency's final decision, file suit in federal district court without appealing to the Civil Service Commission. If he does appeal to the Commission, he may file suit within 30 days of the Commission's final decision. In any event, the complainant may file a civil action if, after 180 days from the filing of the charge or the appeal, the agency or Civil Service Commission has not taken final action.

Sections 706(f) through (k), 42 U.S.C. § 2000e-5(f) to 2000e-5(1), which are incorporated "as applicable" by § 717(d), govern such issues as venue, the appointment of attorneys, attorney fees, and the scope of relief. Section 717(e), finally, retains within each governmental agency "primary responsibility to assure nondiscrimination in employment. . . ."

The balance, completeness, and structural integrity of § 717 are inconsistent with petitioner's contention that the judicial remedy afforded by § 717(c) was designed merely to supplement other putative judicial relief. His view fails, in our estimation, to accord due weight to the fact that unlike these other supposed remedies, § 717 does not contemplate merely judicial relief. Rather, it provides for a careful blend of administrative and judicial enforcement powers. Under the petitioner's theory, by perverse operation of a type of Gresham's Law, § 717, with its rigorous administrative exhaustion requirements and time limitations, would be driven out of currency were immediate access to the courts under other, less demanding statutes permissible. The crucial administrative role that each agency together with the Civil Service Commission was given by Congress in the eradication of employment discrimination would be eliminated "by the simple expedient of putting a different label on [the] pleadings." *Preiser* v. *Rodriguez*, 411 U.S. 475, 489-90 (1973). It would require the suspension of disbelief to ascribe to Congress the design to allow its careful and thorough remedial scheme to be circumvented by artful pleading.

The petitioner relies upon our decision in *Johnson* v. *Railway Express*

*Agency, Inc.,* 421 U.S. 454, 10 FEP Cases 817 (1975), for the proposition that Title VII did not repeal preexisting remedies for employment discrimination. In *Johnson* the Court held that in the context of *private employment* Title VII did not preempt other remedies. But that decision is inapposite here. In the first place, there were no problems of sovereign immunity in the context of the *Johnson* case. Second, the holding in *Johnson* rested upon the explicit legislative history of the 1964 Act which " 'manifests a congressional intent to allow an individual to pursue independently his rights under both Title VII and other applicable state and federal statutes.' " *Id.,* at 459, 10 FEP Cases, at 819, quoting *Alexander* v. *Gardner-Denver Co.,* 415 U.S. 36, 48, 7 FEP Cases 81, 85 (1974). Congress made clear "that the remedies available to the individual under Title VII are co-extensive with the indiv[i]dual's right to sue under the provisions of the Civil Rights Act of 1866, 42 U.S.C. § 1981, and that the two procedures augment each other and are not mutually exclusive.' " *Id.,* quoting H.R. Rep. No. 92-238, p. 19 (1971). See also *Jones* v. *Alfred H. Mayer Co.,* 392 U.S. 409, 415-17 (1968). There is no such legislative history behind the 1972 amendments. Indeed, as indicated above, the congressional understanding was precisely to the contrary.

. . .

We hold, therefore, that since Brown failed to file a timely complaint under § 717(c), the District Court properly dismissed the case. Accordingly, the judgment is affirmed.

*It is so ordered.*

MR. JUSTICE MARSHALL took no part in the consideration of this case.

MR. JUSTICE STEVENS, with whom MR. JUSTICE BRENNAN joins, dissenting: . . .

As the legislative history discussed in *Chandler* v. *Roudebush,* _____ U.S. _____. 12 FEP Cases 1368, demonstrates, Congress intended federal employees to have the same rights available to remedy racial discrimination as employees in the private sector. Since the law is now well settled that victims of racial discrimination in the private sector have a choice of remedies and are not limited to Title VII, federal employees should enjoy parallel rights. The reasoning which governed the decisions in *Johnson, supra,* n. 1, and *Alexander, supra,* n. 1, applies with equal force to federal employees. There is no evidence, either in the statute itself or in its history, that Congress intended the 1972 amendment to be construed differently from the basic statute.

The fact that Congress incorrectly assumed that federal employees would have no judicial remedy if § 717 had not been enacted undermines rather than supports the Court's conclusion that Congress intended to repeal or amend laws that it did not think applicable. Indeed, the General Subcommittee on Labor of the House Committee on Education and Labor rejected an amendment which would have explicitly provided that § 717 would be the exclusive remedy for federal employees. In sum, the legislative history of § 717 discloses a clear intent to provide federal employees with rights that parallel those available to employees in the private sector, no evidence of an intention to make the remedy exclusive, and the rejection of an amendment which would have so provided.

The burden of persuading us that we should interpolate such an important provision into a complex, carefully drafted statute is a heavy one. Since that burden has not been met, I would simply read the statute as Congress wrote it.

# 4. The Executive Order Program and Affirmative Action

## A. THE EXECUTIVE POWER

### (1) *Historical and Legislative Background*

Excerpts From EQUAL EMPLOYMENT OPPORTUNITY COMMISSION, LEGISLATIVE HISTORY OF TITLES VII AND XI OF THE CIVIL RIGHTS ACT OF 1964 (1968)

Adoption of the Civil Rights Act of 1964, with its Title VII equal employment opportunity provisions, culminated a drive begun many years before. It was a drive that gained fruition first in the area of government employment and much later in the area of government contract employment.

But efforts to enact federal legislation to deal with equal employment opportunity on a broad basis, some of which extended back into the 1940's, had been stymied in Congress. The only successes in legislating in this area had been achieved in the states.

### Government Employment

Until the New Deal period of the 1930's, action by the federal government relating to employment discrimination was largely confined to government employees. The Civil Service Act of 1883, for example, sought to establish the principle of "merit employment." One of the first regulations issued under the law outlawed religious discrimination in federal employment. (The Pendleton Act [Civil Service Act], 22 Stat. 403, 1883, 5 U.S.C. ch. 12, 1958; U.S. Civil Service Commission, Rule VIII, 1883)

In 1940, a Civil Service rule forbade racial, as well as religious, discrimination in federal employment. (Executive Order 8587, 5 Fed. Reg. 445, 1940) Then, when Congress adopted the Ramspeck Act, extending the coverage of the Civil Service Act and amending the Classification Act of 1923, the principle of "equal rights for all" in classified federal employment was established. The Act declared:

"In carrying out the provisions of this title, and the provisions of the Classification Act of 1923, as amended, there shall be no discrimination against any person, or with respect to the position held by any person, on account of race, creed, or color." (Ramspeck Act, 54 Stat. 1211, 1940, Title I, 5 U.S.C. sec. 631a, 1958)

431

New Deal Legislation

In the 1930's during the early New Deal period, a policy of equal opportunity in employment and training financed by federal funds was established by congressional and executive action. The policy extended not only to direct federal employment and employment by government contractors, but to employment and training opportunities provided by grant-in-aid programs as well.

The principle of equal job opportunity first was enunciated by Congress in the Unemployment Relief Act of 1933. It provided:

"That in employing citizens for the purpose of this Act no discrimination shall be made on account of race, color, or creed." (Unemployment Relief Act of 1933, 48 Stat. 22)

Many of the laws passed under the New Deal contained similar provisions. If the laws themselves did not bar discrimination, the policy of nondiscrimination was enunciated by the executive branch. Regulations issued under the National Industrial Recovery Act and the laws providing for public low-rent housing and defense housing programs, for example, forbade discrimination based on race, color, or religion. (National Industrial Recovery Act of 1933, Title II, 48 Stat. 200; 44 C.F.R. sec. 265-33, 1938)

Although these pronouncements amounted to unequivocal declarations by the legislative and executive branches, they were of limited effect in most instances. In practice, they amounted to little more than expressions of policy. There were no standards by which discrimination could be determined, and machinery and sanctions for enforcement were rare.

### EXPERIENCE DURING WORLD WAR II

The inclusion of nondiscrimination provisions in laws providing for federally financed training programs continued after the outbreak of World War II. Despite these provisions, leaders of the Negro community contended that Negroes still were being denied federally financed training for defense jobs. They threatened a Negro march on Washington.

The First FEPC

On June 25, 1941, President Roosevelt issued Executive Order 8802 establishing a five-man Fair Employment Practice Committee. The Committee was set up as an independent agency responsible solely to the President. The executive order declared the following to be the government's policy:

"To encourage full participation in the national defense program by all citizens of the United States, regardless of race, creed, color, or national origin, in the firm belief that the democratic way of life within the nation can be defended successfully only with the help and support of all groups within its borders." (Executive Order 8802, 6 Fed. Reg. 3109, 1941)

Broad in scope, the order applied to all defense contracts, to employment by the federal government, and to vocational and training programs administered by federal agencies. The FEPC was authorized to receive and investigate complaints of discrimination, to take "appropriate steps" to redress valid grievances, and to recommend to federal agencies and to the President whatever measures it deemed necessary and proper to carry out the purposes of the order.

The FEPC, nevertheless, had its weaknesses. It had a staff of only eight members, and it lacked direct enforcement powers. So it concentrated on drafting policies and conducting public hearings throughout the country.

The later transfer of the FEPC to the War Manpower Commission deprived it of its autonomy. A dispute with the Chairman of the Manpower Commission led to the resignation of several members of the FEPC, and the Committee, in effect, suspended operations early in 1943.

## The Second FEPC

Later in 1943, President Roosevelt issued Executive Order 9346 establishing a new Fair Employment Practices Committee and declaring it to be the policy of the government to promote the fullest utilization of manpower and to eliminate employment discrimination. (Executive Order 9346, 8 Fed. Reg. 7183, 1943)

A broader jurisdiction than that of its predecessor was given to the new FEPC. It extended to all employment by government contractors (not merely those in defense industries), recruitment and training for war production, and employment by the federal government. Moreover, its authority with regard to labor unions was extended to include discrimination in membership as well as in employment.

The second FEPC was much better staffed than its predecessor. Its budget permitted it to employ a staff of nearly 120 and to open 15 field offices. In its three years of existence, it processed approximately 8,000 complaints and conducted 30 public hearings. It still lacked power, however, to enforce its decisions except by negotiation, moral suasion, and the pressure of public opinion. Its authority expired at the end of June 1946.

### GOVERNMENT CONTRACTS

From 1946 until 1964, the principal government efforts to eliminate racial and religious discrimination in employment were in the area of government contracts. A major step was taken by President Truman in 1951 when he issued a series of executive orders directing certain government agencies to include nondiscrimination clauses in their contracts.

## The Truman Committee

On December 3, 1951, Truman issued Executive Order 10308 creating the Committee on Government Contract Compliance. It was an 11-member group composed of representatives of industry, the public, and the five principal government contracting agencies. (16 Fed. Reg. 12303, 1951)

After studying the effectiveness of the existing program, the Committee made more than 20 recommendations for improving the program. Many were aimed at the establishment of effective enforcement procedures for the nondiscrimination clause.

## The Eisenhower Committee

On August 13, 1953, President Eisenhower issued an order replacing the Truman Committee with the President's Committee on Government Contracts—a 15-member group composed of representatives of industry, labor, government, and the public. (Executive Order 10479, 18 Fed. Reg. 4899, 1953)

The Eisenhower Committee was given the following duties:

1. To make recommendations to contracting agencies for improving nondiscrimination provisions in government contracts.

2. To serve as a clearing house for complaints alleging violation of the nondiscrimination clauses.

3. To encourage and assist with educational programs by nongovernmental groups.

Once again, however, the Committee had no power to enforce its recommendations. It had to rely on the procurement agencies to adjust complaints, although a report on the disposition of each complaint had to be made to the Committee.

## The Kennedy Committee

The policy of nondiscrimination by government contractors was given teeth under the Kennedy Administration. In Executive Order 10925 issued on March 6, 1961, President Kennedy created a new President's Committee on Equal Employment Opportunity charged with the responsibility of effectuating equal employment opportunity both in government employment and in employment on government contracts. (26 Fed. Reg. 1977, 1961)

There was a dramatic break with the past under the new order. While earlier orders had imposed an obligation on contractors not to discriminate on the basis of race, creed, color, or national origin, the Kennedy order also required the contractors to take affirmative action to make the policy effective.

Government contractors were required to do the following:

1. Not to discriminate against any employee or job applicant because of race, creed, color, or national origin.

2. To take affirmative action to ensure that applicants are employed and employees are treated during their employment without regard to race, creed, color, or national origin.

3. To state in all solicitations or advertisements for employees that all qualified applicants will receive consideration without regard to race, creed, color, or national origin.

4. To advise each labor union with which they deal of their commitments under the order.

5. To include the obligations under the order in every subcontract or purchase order, unless specifically exempted.

6. To comply with all provisions of the order and the rules and regulations issued by the Committee; to furnish all information and reports required by the Committee; to permit access to books, records, and accounts for the purpose of investigation to ascertain compliance.

7. To file regular compliance reports describing hiring and employment practices.

## Enforcement

The new order had teeth in it. In addition to requiring contractors to file compliance reports, it gave the Committee specific enforcement powers. To assure compliance, the Committee was authorized to do the following:

1. Publish the names of noncomplying contractors and unions.

2. Recommend suits by the Justice Department to compel compliance.

3. Recommend criminal actions by the Justice Department against contractors who furnish false information.

4. Terminate the contract of a noncomplying employer.

5. Forbid the contracting agencies to enter into new contracts with contractors who have discriminated unless they can demonstrate that they have changed their policies.

The most effective method of achieving compliance, however, was the "plan for progress"—described by the Committee as a procedure for effecting compliance through cooperation. At the time the Civil Rights Act was passed, there were more than 200 large companies operating under such plans. They require the contractor to set up effective recruitment programs to give members of minority groups equal opportunity of employment.

## Program Broadened

Under Executive Order 11114 issued by President Kennedy on June 22, 1963, the no-discrimination requirement was extended to all construction contracts paid for in whole or in part with funds obtained from the federal government or borrowed on the credit of the government pursuant to a grant, contract, loan, insurance, or guarantee. It also was extended to contracts undertaken pursuant to any federal program involving such a grant, contract, loan, insurance, or guarantee.

On February 13, 1964, President Johnson issued Executive Order 11141 declaring a federal policy under which federal supply contractors and subcontractors are forbidden (1) to discriminate because of age in hiring, promoting, or discharging employees, or in connection with working conditions or privileges, and (2) to specify an age limit in help-wanted ads. Both prohibitions are subject to a qualification permitting discrimination based upon a bona fide occupational qualification, retirement plan, or statutory requirement.

Discrimination by Unions

The Committee set up by President Kennedy was directed to use its best efforts to get unions to cooperate with and comply in the implementation of the executive orders, but the Committee had no direct means of compelling compliance by unions. The obligation not to discriminate runs from the contractor to the government.

The standards and compliance procedures for apprenticeship under federal programs were issued in December 1963. . . .

### (2)  OFCCP 1965–1978: The Age of Administrative Evolution

A great many changes took place, primarily through administrative evolution, between 1965 and 1978 when President Carter's reorganization went into effect. The following overview was taken from an OFCCP Basic Compliance Training Course which was in use for the training of compliance personnel immediately prior to the 1978 reorganization.

## A BRIEF HISTORY OF CONTRACT COMPLIANCE*
. . .

On September 24, 1965, President Johnson issued Executive Order 11246. The new Executive Order established a new administrative arrangement with the Secretary of Labor, rather than a Presidential Committee, charged with supervising and coordinating the activities of the contracting agencies. The contracting agencies maintained primary responsibility for obtaining compliance. The Secretary of Labor was empowered to issue regulations implementing the Order, investigate complaints, conduct compliance reviews, hold hearings and impose sanctions. The Secretary was also given authority to direct contracting agencies to conduct such complaint investigations, compliance reviews, hold hearings and impose sanctions as he deemed necessary for implementation of the Order. The Office of Federal Contract Compliance was established in the Office of the Secretary of Labor on October 5, 1965, to administer the new Executive Order. The Secretary of Labor has delegated the authority for carrying out the responsibilities under such order to the Director of the Office of Federal Contract Compliance. The Director of OFCC has delegated some authority to contracting Federal agencies to enforce contract compliance regulation; but this authority is to be exercised only under the Director's general guidance and control.

Under Executive Order 11246, a Federal contractor is now required to include in each contract a seven-point equal opportunity clause in which the employer agrees not to discriminate against anyone in the

---

* This excerpt was taken from a very elaborate set of materials prepared by Pacifica Consultants for OFCCP and the contents thereof are the property of OFCCP. Originally designated Office of Federal Contract Compliance, the agency was renamed Office of Federal Contract Compliance Programs on June 17, 1975. Both acronyms—OFCC and OFCCP—are used herein. The most recent description of OFCCP may be found in Chapter 1 and REFERENCE SUPPLEMENT—DISCRIMINATION IN EMPLOYMENT.

hiring process or during employment on the basis of race, color, creed, or national origin. In 1967, Executive Order 11246 was amended by Executive Order 11375 to "prohibit discrimination in employment because of race, color, religion, sex or national origin." (The effect of the amendment was to eliminate "creed" as prohibited criteria, but add "religion" and "sex.") In addition, the contractor also agrees to take "affirmative action" to ensure that applicants are employed, and that employees are treated during their employment, without regard to their race, color, religion, sex, or national origin. Some contracts are not required to contain the equal opportunity clause. For exemptions from the requirement, refer to 41 CFR 60-1.5.

### AFFIRMATIVE ACTION REQUIREMENTS

OFCC regulations issued May 1, 1968, explained for the first time the meaning of the affirmative action requirement and also required each Federal contractor with 50 or more employees, and a Federal contract of $50,000 or more to develop for each of its establishments a written plan of affirmative action. These regulations were supplemented on February 5, 1970, by adding an entirely new part amending and clarifying the sections of the regulation on affirmative action.

This addition to the regulations, referred to as Order 4, stated that any contractor required to develop affirmative action compliance programs had not complied fully with the Executive Order until a program was developed and found acceptable by using standards and guidelines of Order 4. Order 4 set forth three basic requirements and eight additional guidelines for affirmative action compliance programs. The three basic obligations imposed on the contractors were (1) to perform an analysis of minority utilization in all job categories, (2) establish goals and a timetable to correct deficiencies, and (3) develop data collection systems and reporting plans documenting progress in achieving affirmative action goals. These general affirmative requirements were clarified and expanded by a second set of regulations, issued in 1970 and significantly revised in 1971. The second set of regulations, Revised Order 4, required contractors for the first time to include women in affirmative action programs. In addition, Revised Order 4 introduced the requirements that contractors remedy the effects of past discrimination experienced by incumbent employees. Finally, the regulation established a procedure to be followed by Federal agencies prior to imposing sanctions for failure to comply with affirmative action requirements (41 CFR 60-2.2 (1974)).

In October of 1971, OFCC issued the Testing and Selection Order (41 CFR 60-3). This Order required that if tests and other selection procedures used by contractors caused an adverse impact on minorities or women, then such tests and other procedures must be shown to be job related (valid).

The Testing Order was amended in January of 1974 to add specific documentation requirements for elements to be included in studies of job relatedness (validity) of selection procedures. In December of 1976 the Testing Order was replaced by the Federal Executive Agency Guidelines on Employee Selection Procedures (41 CFR 60-3), a joint document of the Departments of Labor and Justice and the Civil Service Commission. The new Guidelines lay out more specific requirements for validity studies done by contractors, while taking into account changes in the field of personnel psychology since the Testing Order was issued in 1971.

In March 1972, OFCC instructed the compliance agencies to implement a review procedure called Order 14. The compliance agencies objected to certain aspects of the order and formed an Interagency Committee on Order 14 to make recommendations to OFCC.

Revised Order 14 was issued to the compliance agencies by the Secretary of Labor in January 1973. Compliance agencies were critical of Revised Order 14 and they felt that the confidentiality provisions of the order would seriously inhibit the review process. By July 1974, OFCC had issued a substantially improved version of Revised Order 14. The order instructed the compliance agencies routinely to select contractors for review and delineated the various aspects and steps of the review process.

In September 1974, OFCC and EEOC signed a Memorandum of Understanding which provided that all Executive Order complaints would be referred to EEOC. This Memorandum superseded a similar agreement signed on May 20, 1970, which was never fully implemented. The 1970 Memorandum provided that OFCC and EEOC would routinely exchange information concerning pending investigations, employers under investigation, as well as outstanding and resolved complaints or charges. The only provision even partially carried out was that which stipulated that complaints filed with OFCC would be deemed EEOC charges and would be promptly transmitted to EEOC. In practice, OFCC directed the compliance agencies to refer to EEOC individual complaints, but not those alleging systemic or class-wide discrimination.

The 1974 agreement, like the one in 1970, provided that the agencies would exchange data on outstanding Title VII charges and Executive Order compliance reviews, as well as information concerning specific respondents. Each agency also agreed to notify the other before conducting an investigation or compliance review. In addition the 1974 agreement provided for each agency (1) to notify the other before issuing a debarment notice or instituting a Title VII lawsuit, and (2) to coordinate their efforts with regard to industry-wide projects. The 1974 memorandum did not alter the practice of handling complaints between the two agencies. The complaints received by OFCCP that allege class or systemic discrimination are usually investigated under the auspices of OFCCP, while complaints alleging individual discrimination are generally referred to EEOC.

## OFCC ORGANIZATION AND STAFFING

When Executive Order 11246 was initially implemented in 1965, OFCCP was established in the Office of the Secretary of Labor, thus providing the opportunity for a close link between the OFCC program and the Secretary. However, in 1969 OFCCP was transferred from the Office of the Secretary to the Wage and Labor Standards Administration, which subsequently underwent reorganizations and became known as the Employment Standards Administration (ESA).

ESA is headed by an Assistant Secretary who directs four separate offices, the Wage and Hour Division, the Women's Bureau, Office of Workers' Compensation Programs, and OFCCP. All four office heads serve as Deputy Assistant Secretaries to the Assistant Secretary for Employment Standards, who approves all activities of the four units.

OFCCP's activities are also indirectly overseen by the Office of the Solicitor of Labor, which has responsibility for all legal activities of the Department. The Solicitor's office routinely reviews all OFCCP proposed guidelines and regulations and has played an important role in influencing OFCCP policies.

There have been a number of reorganizations within OFCCP's Washington office since its transfer to ESA.

OFCCP underwent a major reorganization in January 1974 in order to increase its ability to monitor the supply and service contract compliance program. See Figure I.

## 1. *Policy Guidance*

The OFCCP develops rules and regulations to be issued by the Secretary of Labor and orders of a specific nature that are issued directly by the Director, OFCCP. It also establishes policy to resolve specific compliance programs, as well as approaches, systems and procedures for adherence by compliance agencies and contractors alike in meeting program requirements.

Other issuances include implementing instructions, interpretations and specific guidance on a case-by-case basis. These issuances take the form of written directives which flow from the Director, OFCCP, to the Agency Contract Compliance Officer. Some examples of basic issuances are the obligations of Government Contractors and Subcontractors; Revised Order No. 4, which contains standards and enforcement procedures for the Affirmative Action requirements; Sex Discrimination Guidelines and Testing Guidelines. . . .

### a. Post Compliance Review Audit

The post compliance review audit is a process under which the OFCCP, applying selective criteria, routinely requests copies of standard compliance review reports and contractor's affirmative action compliance programs and supporting materials from the agencies for review and evaluation. This process enables OFCCP to determine whether the policies are producing the results intended, the need for any alteration of existing policies, the need for policy interpretation and clarification, and/or the need for technical assistance.

### b.   On-Site Compliance Review Audit

The on-site compliance review audit is a process under which OFCCP participates with compliance agencies in the actual conduct of an on-site compliance review. The purpose of the on-site compliance review audit as it relates to policy development is to validate the conclusions arrived at in the post compliance review audit.

### c.   Special Directed Compliance Review

The special directed compliance review is a joint OFCCP/agency undertaking in which OFCCP assumes the policy leadership in the agency compliance review. Where complex or critical issues are identified, for example, through the post compliance review audit and/or the on-site compliance review audit for which there is no existing policy, the OFCCP arranges a joint OFCCP/Agency compliance review during which it pursues whatever compliance and enforcement operations that may be necessary on a joint basis.

## 2.   *Agency Program Evaluation*

The OFCCP program evaluation activity operates on both a continuing and an annual basis. As an ongoing matter where routine or non-pattern type deficiencies in the agencies' systems and procedures are identified, the matter is communicated in writing to the agency contract compliance officer with specific recommendations concerning measures to be instituted for program improvement.

Where major or pattern type agency capability or implementation problems cannot be fully identified and corrected, the agency audit process is used.

In addition an annual formal program evaluation report is forwarded to each compliance agency. In response, a proposed program plan is developed by each agency and forwarded to the Director, OFCCP, for approval.

### a.   Agency Audit

The agency audit is a process under which the OFCCP conducts an on-site examination of the compliance agency's systems and procedures for achieving compliance by government contractors with the Executive Order and implementing regulations. Under this process the OFCCP determines whether the major problems identified derive from specific elements of the agency's management practices and policies.

### b.   Formal Agency Program Evaluation

The formal agency evaluation is an annual process under which the OFCCP assesses the performance of each agency against the general program direction contained in the annual Program Guidance Memorandum (PGM) and its supplements, and against individual office directives, policy and program guides provided throughout the fiscal year. A formal program evaluation report is prepared on each compliance agency.

### c.    Compliance Agency Program Plan Requirement

In response to the formal annual evaluation, each agency prepares for the approval of OFCCP its proposed program plan for the ensuing fiscal year.

## 3.    Program Leadership

Program leadership is an inherent feature of the OFCCP's responsibility to administer Executive Order 11246 on behalf of the Secretary of Labor. OFCCP's leadership is most often reflected in those processes involving special directed compliance reviews, OFCCP compliance reviews, the program guidance memorandum, high impact programs, operating activities in the construction industry, and training.

### a.    OFCCP Compliance Reviews

An OFCCP Compliance Review is a compliance review directed by OFCCP under an informal understanding with the appropriate compliance agency, or where absolutely necessary, under an assumption of jurisdiction. The purpose of an OFCCP Compliance Review is to resolve cases and issues in limited and unusual circumstances in which the matters demonstrably cannot be handled by the compliance agency.

Examples of such circumstances are:

(1) Situations in which the compliance agency requests or otherwise demonstrates the need for technical assistance.

(2) Compliance activities involving contractors, who by virtue of their non-compliance posture, have attracted widespread public attention or the attention of national minority and women's groups or congressional and other groups.

(3) Cases of joint interest between OFCCP, the Equal Employment Opportunity Commission and/or the Department of Justice, or other Federal EEO enforcement agencies.

(4) Cases of flagrant compliance agency enforcement deficiencies.

### b.    High Impact Programs

High Impact Programs consist of activities conducted by agencies under the general leadership of OFCCP to reach conciliation agreements or negotiate model affirmative action compliance programs with Federal contractors on a corporate-wide, industry-wide or area-wide basis. The process includes: (1) the selection of one or more industries, corporations, or geographical areas which present common patterns of employment discrimination or underutilization of minorities and women; (2) the conduct of compliance reviews of a representative sample of contractor facilities within the industry, corporation or geographical area; (3) the preparation of a model conciliation agreement or affirmative action program to correct the compliance problems disclosed during the compliance reviews; and (4) negotiations with industry or corporate officials to adopt and implement the agreement or affirmative action program at each of their establishments.

THE COMPLIANCE AGENCIES

Section 60-1.6 of Chapter 60 Title 41 of the Code of Federal Regulations (41 CFR 60-1.6) assigns each compliance agency the primary responsibility for achieving compliance with the Executive Order. In implementing this responsibility, the agencies are required by the Order to abide by the rules and regulations and orders of the Secretary of Labor.

There are 16 Federal Departments, Agencies and Authorities which are designed by the Director of OFCCP to perform certain Federal contract compliance functions. They are:

1 Department of Agriculture (USDA)
2 Energy Research Development Administration (ERDA)
3 Department of Commerce
4 Department of Defense (DOD)
5 Environmental Protection Agency (EPA)
6 General Services Administration (GSA)
7 Department of Health, Education, and Welfare (DHEW)
8 Department of Interior
9 Department of Housing and Urban Development (HUD)
10 Department of Justice (LEAA)
11 Small Business Administration (SBA)
12 Tennessee Valley Authority (TVA)
13 Department of Transportation (DOT)
14 Department of Treasury
15 Veterans Administration (VA)
16 National Aeronautics and Space Administration (NASA)

In the future these agencies will be consolidated to eleven units. The purpose of this is to improve OFCCP's management of the compliance program.

## SIC Code Assignment

These Federal compliance agencies are assigned compliance responsibility for contracts by OFCCP on the basis of Standard Industrial Classification (SIC) codes. SIC codes are numerical classifications in a coding system developed by the Office of Management and Budget for use in classifying establishments by principal industry activity. NASA, TVA, LEAA, and SBA are not responsible for any SIC codes but are responsible for construction contracts let by these agencies.

## SIC Code Exceptions

a. The Department of Interior is assigned the compliance responsibility for all contractors in the State of Alaska, including the construction industry.

b. Government-owned and contractor operated plants (GOCO's) of the Energy Research Development Administration and the Department of Defense are assigned to those agencies respectively, regardless of industry identification.

c. Regardless of industry identification, the Department of Transportation (DOT) is assigned compliance responsibility for all contractor facilities in the Washington National Airport and Dulles International Airport, both of which are owned by the Federal Government and administered by the Federal Aviation Administration.

## Agency Compliance Responsibility

The agencies' compliance and enforcement processes are developed pursuant to 41 CFR 60-1.6 that requires each agency to develop and implement a comprehensive compliance program subject to the approval of OFCCP. This program must provide for the appointment of a contract compliance officer who reports directly to the head of the agency and who has overall responsibility for compliance and enforcement operations. Fifteen (15) of the compliance agencies have regional and/or area offices. Only one compliance agency (USDA) does not have field operations and conducts its compliance reviews and related activities directly from the headquarters level.

A compliance review is to begin with a request for copies of the affirmative action compliance program and supporting documentation, including the work-force analysis. The compliance agency is permitted to conduct a review on the premises of the contractor at the outset if the review is being conducted prior to the award of a contract. This review must be conducted in a relatively short period of time. Another exception to this desk audit requirement is provided for complaint investigations.

In conducting the off-site desk audit, the EOS must analyze the current composition of the contractor's work force to identify those job titles in which minorities and/or women are either underrepresented or concentrated, and those job titles or job groups where underutilization exists. Since discrimination may occur in placing minorities and/or women only in particular job titles, the result may be underrepresentation in some jobs and concentration in others.

Once identified, these job titles are to be the principal focus of the review. For each such "focus job title" with a substantial concentration of minorities and women, the reviewer is instructed to identify those "specific" jobs wherein the minority and female incumbents could have been denied placement, promotion, or transfer due to discrimination.

Further analysis of these incumbent employees, who may constitute an affected class, is to be conducted during the review on the premises of the contractor. Prior to the on-site review, the agency is to inform the contractor that it must provide detailed listings of these employees for onsite investigation by the agency's representatives.

For each "focus job title" in which underutilization exists, the EOS is to determine whether the contractor's affirmative action compliance program goals are sufficient and whether its past performance in meeting these goals has been adequate. While goals must be set for the purpose of ultimately eliminating underutilization, the contractor should further establish annual rates of hiring and promoting women and minorities. These objectives must be the maximum rates that can be achieved by good faith recruitment and training programs and "must not be lower than the percentage rate set in the ultimate goal."

In addition to the analysis of the contractor's work force, the EOS must review data on applicant flow and hiring rates to determine whether there is a lower rate of job offers to and hiring of minorities or women with regard to the focus job titles. If a lower rate is found to have occurred, then the EOS must ask the contractor to provide, during the on-site review, an analysis showing the reasons for rejecting all of the applicants in the sample data. The EOS should conduct a similar review of promotion, transfer and termination practices. Analysis of recruitment, hiring, selections and placement patterns is to be based on 100 applicants or 10 percent of all applicants, whichever number is greater, within the organizational unit where the focus job titles exist.

If a contractor believes that data requested for off-site analysis are not relevant to its compliance status, it may request a ruling from the agency's Contract Compliance Officer. This ruling, which must be made within 10 days, may be appealed to the Director of OFCCP. However, the information in question must be provided to the compliance review officer off-site pending a final ruling by the OFCCP Director, which also must be made within 10 days. If the desk audit review reveals that the contractor has not demonstrated a reasonable effort to comply with Revised Order No. 4, the agency may immediately issue a Show Cause Notice without conducting an on-site review. The agency may also forego the on-site review if it determines that the contractor's affirmative action compliance program conforms with Revised Order No. 4 and if an on-site review has been conducted within the preceding two years.

Prior to the initiation of the on-site review, the EOS is to send a letter to the contractor listing the information which must be available on-site. If sample data on applicant flow, promotions, transfers, and terminations were not submitted previously, the contractor must provide this data for on-site analysis.

During the on-site review, the EOS should survey the community concerning the contractor and labor force  conditions, determine the nature and extent of the employer's government contracts, inspect the facilities to ascertain if EEO posters are displayed, and interview management

FIGURE I

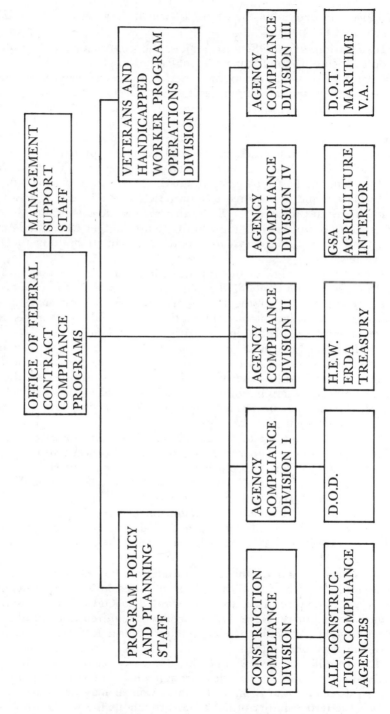

employees to determine the extent to which they are aware of and play a role in EEO policies.

In addition, the EOS must review the contractor's job application process, including completing the analysis of applicant flow data. At this stage, the EOS should determine whether the selection processes used in hiring and promoting employees has an adverse impact on applicants identifiable by race, sex or ethnic group. If the entire selection process has an adverse impact, the EOS must determine which of the selection procedures in the process has produced the adverse impact. The EOS must then determine whether the contractor has prepared an adequate study validating the selection standard according to OFCCP Guidelines. If the standard has not been validated, the contractor must take steps to validate it and be required to eliminate or alter its use. If a validation study has been prepared, the EOS must review the evidence to determine whether it complies with the requirements of OFCCP's Guidelines. If questions arise, the agency can submit the validation study to OFCCP for review.

If the on-site review of the applicant flow data reveals that minorities and women are not applying for jobs with the contractor in proportion to their representation in the labor force, the EOS must investigate the contractor's recruitment methods and sources, and whether his recruitment practices are attracting minorities and/or females.

Further, the EOS must prepare a final analysis of hires, promotion, transfer, and termination of women and minorities compared with such rates for nonminorities and males. The EOS must also review the wages and salaries of a sampling of employees in selected job titles to determine whether minorities or women hold positions paying lower rates than other positions with similar duties.

Moreover, during the on-site review, the EOS must prepare an analysis of focus job titles in which there are substantial concentrations of minorities and women. These employees may constitute an affected class.

At the completion of the on-site review, the EOS is to hold an "exit conference" with the contractor's officials. The purpose of the conference is to solicit from the contractor commitments to take specific corrective action for apparent violations identified during the course of the compliance review, which "should be contained in a written conciliation agreement."

Upon completion of the exit conference, the EOS must prepare a written report according to the format required in Revised Order No. 14. This report does not have to be forwarded to OFCCP, but is subject to review by that office. However, the agency is required to forward a coding sheet to OFCCP before the contractor's affirmative action compliance program may be accepted.

The compliance review and the affirmative action requirement for Federal Contractors are vehicles through which the years of job discrimination directed towards minorities and women may be overcome.

It is the responsibility of the EOS throughout the review process to be keenly aware that the basic purpose underlying the compliance review is to insure that minorities and women are given equal opportunities; and where no affirmative action/good faith efforts are taken by employers, the economic upgrading of minorities and women in the country grows at a very slow pace. The EOS's job is to help create opportunities; the compliance process is the tool used to accomplish that goal.

## NOTE

For descriptive material on the programs which have been established under the various executive orders of the Presidents dealing with employment discrimination, see: "Employment," 1961 U.S. COMMISSION ON CIVIL RIGHTS REPORT NO. 3; NORGREN AND HILL, TOWARD FAIR EMPLOYMENT (1964); and M. SOVERN, LEGAL RESTRAINTS ON RACIAL DISCRIMINATION (1966). See also: "Federal Civil Rights Enforcement Efforts," Reports of the U.S. Commission on Civil Rights, 1969-1974, the chapters on the Office of Contract Compliance. For comments, see: Jones, *To Rouse "A Slumbering Giant"—Government Contracting and Equal Employment Initiatives for the 1970's*, LABOR LAW DEVELOPMENTS (1971) at 151; Jones, *Contract Compliance in Phase II—The Dawning of the Age of Enforcement*, 4 GEORGIA L. REV. 756 (1970); INDUSTRIAL & LABOR RELATIONS REV., Vol. 29, No. 4 (1976), Report of Conference Evaluating the Office of Contract Compliance.

The details of the contractual obligations under the executive order will emerge in the cases and materials throughout this chapter. It seems reasonable that enforcement of those obligations, whatever they might be, would be subject to ordinary contract concepts in law. Of course, the Government, by rule or otherwise, could provide special procedures for the enforcement of these special obligations, but unless and until such procedures are provided, it does not seem unreasonable that parties subject to the executive order would resort to available principles of law. In this next section we explore efforts to apply general contract law to these problems.

## B.   ENFORCING THE CONTRACTUAL OBLIGATION

(1)  *Requiring the Contractor to Comply*

### FARMER v. PHILADELPHIA ELECTRIC CO.
*U.S. Court of Appeals, Third Circuit, 1964*
*329 F.2d 3, 1 FEP Cases 36*

GANEY, Circuit Judge: This is an appeal from an order of the District Court dismissing the complaint. Since diversity of citizenship of the parties does not exist here, the threshold question is whether that court had jurisdiction under 28 U.S.C.A. § 1331(a).[1] The case appears to be the first of its kind in the Federal courts.

In substance the complaint, filed September 13, 1962, makes the following averments: By an Executive Order, duly issued pursuant to the Constitution and enabling legislation of Congress, and by rules and regulations concerning procurement duly promulgated by the General Services Administration, it is provided that all government contracts shall contain a provision setting forth that "in the performance of the work under the contract, the contractor will not discriminate against any employee during employment . . . because of race, creed, color, or national origin . . . ." Since 1951, the defendant entered into certain contracts containing a nondiscrimination clause with the United States. In November of 1954, plaintiff was injured while working as a lineman for the defendant. The latter, after assigning him to light work duty for awhile in accordance with its prior announced policy, ordered him to return to lineman duty although he was physically unable to perform that type of work. When he declined to report to work as a lineman, the defendant terminated his employment on August 18, 1958. Paragraph 13 of the complaint states:

"13. Defendant has failed and neglected to perform the condition of the said contract with the United States of America in that it has discriminated against the plaintiff because of his race and color in refusing to place plaintiff upon light duty status while it has tendered such permanent status to employees of white color or of the Caucasian race."

Claiming a federal right as a third-party beneficiary of certain contracts between the United States and defendant, he demands compensatory and punitive damages from defendant for physical and emotional injury, loss of job opportunity, loss of constitutional rights and of his natural rights as a human being, as a result of defendant's discriminatory action.

[The Court traces the history of the executive order program to date, which is omitted.]

Plaintiff asserts that the matter in controversy here arises under the Constitution or laws of the United States within the meaning of 28 U.S.C.A. § 1331(a). This assertion is not frivolous. Under the holding of *Bell* v. *Hood,* 327 U.S. 678, 685, 66 S.Ct. 773, 90 L.Ed. 939 (1946), and *Wheeldin* v. *Wheeler,* 373 U.S. 647, 649, 83 S.Ct. 1441, 10 L.Ed.2d 605 (1963), we must conclude that on the face of the complaint the District Court had jurisdiction.

Does the matter here arise under the Constitution or laws of the United States within the meaning of 28 U.S.C.A. § 1331(a)? Among other reasons, the Constitution and its amendments were adopted to limit the exercise of certain powers by Governmental officials, both National and State, so that certain individual rights would not be disturbed by them. However,

---

1 [Footnotes numbered as in original—Ed.] The Act of March 3, 1875, § 1, 18 Stat. 470, was the first statute conferring jurisdiction on the federal courts in cases involving a "federal question." The wording of that statute has been substantially preserved in the present Act. See Wright, FEDERAL COURTS (Handbook Series, 1963), § 17.

the complaint does not assert any claim against anyone acting under, or color of, Governmental authority, but one against a private corporate employer. Hence the matter in controversy is not one arising under the Constitution.

Does it arise under the laws of the United States? [7] Plaintiff maintains that the authority to issue the applicable executive orders in question stems from subsections (a) and (c) of § 205 of the Federal Property and Administrative Services Act of 1949. There are instances when the President issues proclamations and orders, and governmental agencies promulgate rules and regulations, pursuant to a mandate or a delegation of authority from Congress. In such instances the proclamations, orders, rules and regulations have the force and effect of laws.[8] Subsections (a) and (c) of the Federal Property and Administrative Services Act of 1949, 63 Stat. 389, 40 U.S.C.A. § 486(a) and (c) provide:

"(a) The President may prescribe such policies and directives, not inconsistent with the provisions of this chapter [Chapter 10 of Title 40], . . . chapter 4 of Title 41 . . . as he shall deem necessary to effectuate the provisions of said chapters, which policies and directives shall govern the Administrator and executive agencies in carrying out their respective functions hereunder."

"(c) The Administrator shall prescribe such regulations as he deems necessary to effectuate his functions under this chapter [Chapter 10 of Title 40], . . . chapter 4 of Title 41 . . . and the head of each executive agency shall cause to be issued such orders and directives as such head deems necessary to carry out such regulations."

Chapter 10 of Title 40 is concerned with the procurement, utilization, management and disposal of property by government agencies. The purpose of Chapter 4 of Title 41 is to facilitate the procurement of property and services for the government by uniform procedures.

Defendant does not contend that the requiring of non-discrimination provisions in government contracts is beyond the power of Congress. See *Youngstown Sheet & Tube Co.* v. *Sawyer,* 343 U.S. 579, 588, 72 S.Ct. 863, 96 L.Ed. 1153 (1952). Nor does it maintain that the executive orders and regulations were issued without statutory authority. In view of the above quoted subsections of § 205 and the declaration of policy by Congress in § 2 of the Defense Production Act of 1950, and its amendments, 50 U.S.C.A. App. § 2062, we have no doubt that the applicable executive orders and regulations have the force of law.[9] See *Lichter* v.

---

[7] The District Court did not find it necessary to answer this question. In viewing the complaint as stating a cause of action under common-law contract principles and applying the test of *Gully* v. *First National Bank,* 299 U.S. 109, 112, 57 S.Ct. 96, 81 L.Ed. 70 (1936), it concluded that "the Executive Order does not create a right which is an essential element of plaintiff's cause of action." 215 F.Supp. 729, 731 (E.D.Pa. 1963).

[8] *Hampton, Jr. & Co.* v. *United States,* 276 U.S. 394, 48 S.Ct. 348, 72 L.Ed. 624 (1928); *United States* v. *Gilbertson,* 111 F.2d 978, 980 (C.A.7, 1940); *Belden* v. *Chase,* 150 U.S. 674, 698, 14 S.Ct. 264, 37 L.Ed. 1218 (1893); *Maryland Casualty Co.* v. *United States,* 251 U.S. 342, 349, 40 S.Ct. 155, 64 L.Ed. 297 (1920).

[9] An argument to the contrary, although not advocated by him, is summed up by Robert S. Pasley in an article on *The Nondiscrimination Clause in Government Contracts,* 43 VA.LAW REV. 837 (1957). At p. 857 of the article, he states: "Congress has

*United States,* 334 U.S. 742, 785, 68 S.Ct. 1294, 92 L.Ed. 1694 (1948);
*United States* v. *Excel Packing Co.,* 210 F.2d 596 (C.A.10 1954), cert.
denied, 348 U.S. 817, 75 S.Ct. 28, 99 L.Ed. 664. However, the matter
does not end here for we still must determine whether a violation of the
nondiscrimination provisions by a party, a private corporation, to the
contract gives the plaintiff a right to bring a civil action in the Federal
courts for damages sustained as a result of that violation. No statute in
terms confers a private remedy. Plainly the executive orders do not
expressly provide for one. Nor do they, in our opinion, do so by implication. The history of the executive orders on the subject from 1951 to
the present all point to the conclusion that the enforcement of the nondiscrimination provisions in Government contracts has been entrusted
to one or more of the Governmental agencies with the assistance of a
committee appointed by the President. The only provisions of any order
mentioning court proceedings are paragraphs (b) and (c) of § 312 dealing
with sanctions and penalties in Executive Order 10925. These paragraphs
provide that the contracting agency or the Committee recommend to the
Department of Justice that appropriate proceedings "within the limitations of applicable law" be brought against noncomplying contractors
and that criminal proceedings be brought against those furnishing false
information to a contracting agency or to the Committee. Paragraph (f)
of § 312 of the Order states:

"(f) Under rules and regulations prescribed by the committee, each
contracting agency shall make reasonable efforts within a reasonable
time limitation to secure compliance with the contract provisions of this
order *by methods of conference, conciliation, mediation, and persuasion*
before proceedings shall be instituted under paragraph (b) of this section,
or before a contract shall be terminated in whole or in part under paragraph (d) of this section for failure of a contractor or subcontractor to
comply with the contract provisions of this order."

Section 307 of this Order in pertinent part provides:

"Each contracting agency shall be primarily responsible for obtaining
compliance with the rules, regulations, and orders of the Committee
with respect to contracts entered into by such agency . . . . All contracting agencies shall comply with the Committee's rules in discharging
their primary responsibility for securing compliance with the provisions

---

expressly refused to continue the FEPC and has declined to enact antidiscriminatory
legislation. For the executive to attempt to reach the same result by indirection,
through the Government contract device, is an [invalid] attempt to legislate where
Congress has refused to do so."

In addition, Congress has not directly appropriated any money for carrying out the
policies announced in the executive orders. A report by the Committee on Government
Contracts notes that attempts to secure some form of Congressional sanction for the
program failed in the 1958-59 session and were defeated at both the regular and special
sessions in 1960. See SEVENTH ANNUAL REPORT (1961), pp. 6, 9. The Act of May 3, 1945,
59 Stat. 134, 31 U.S.C. § 691, the only legislation specifically cited in Executive Order
14079 as authority for issuing the order, is merely a general appropriation measure for
making appropriation to executive departments and agencies available to defray the cost
of interdepartmental committees.

of contracts and otherwise with the terms of this Executive order and of the rules, regulations, and orders of the Committee pursuant hereto. . . . They are further directed to appoint or designate . . . compliance officers. It shall be the duty of such officers to seek compliance with the objectives of this order *by conference, conciliation, mediation, or persuasion.*" (Italics ours)

The regulations of the President's Committee on Equal Employment Opportunity, issued under Executive Order 10925, 26 F.R. 6585 (July 1961), 41 CFR, § 60-1.24(b)(2), state in part:

"If the investigation [made by the contracting agency] indicates the existence of an apparent violation of the nondiscrimination provisions, the matter should be resolved by informal means whenever possible." When informal means are unsuccessful, 41 CFR, § 60-1.24(b)(3) provides that the appropriate sanction or penalty may be imposed. However, the intention of the Committee to maintain control over the imposition of such sanctions and penalties is shown by the provision that

"The contracting agency shall not impose any sanction or penalty under Section 312 of the Order, except under subsection (d) of that section relating to contract termination, without prior approval of the Committee . . . ."

Further, § 60-1.29 of 41 CFR provides that no case shall be referred to the Department of Justice for legal action without ten days' notice to the contractor "affording him an opportunity to comply with the provisions of the Order . . . .", and that

"In addition, the contracting agency shall make reasonable efforts to persuade the contractor to comply with the Order and to take such corrective action as may be appropriate."

As far as we have been able to ascertain, the Department of Justice has not instituted any proceeding in any court against any noncomplying contractor to enforce the nondiscrimination provisions of a Government contract.

The history of the orders, the rules and regulations made pursuant to them, and the actual practice in the enforcement of the nondiscrimination provisions are all strong persuasive evidence, it seems to us, that court action as a remedy was to be used only as a last resort, and that the threat of a private civil action to deter contractors from failing to comply with the provisions was not contemplated by the orders.[10] As a matter

[10] According to the 1953 Report by the President's Committee on Government Contract Compliance, appointed by Harry S. Truman, that Committee considered but recommended against the possibility of allowing suit by the injured employees and applicants or the insertion in Government contracts of a provision conferring "third-party beneficiary" rights upon them.

An excellent comprehensive Note on State enforcement of antidiscrimination legislation by administrative commissions, 74 HARV.L.REV. (1961), states at p. 528:

"Antidiscrimination commissions serve a unique function in the American legal and governmental framework. It is the basic assumption of the statutes, in some specifically stated, that individuals have a personal civil right to equal treatment. Although most other personal rights are enforceable only by an aggrieved individual's initiation of a court action in which he must bear the cost and inconvenience of the proceedings, the importance of equal treatment to the general welfare gives the state a special interest

of fact, the words "breach of the provision" or "unlawful" do not appear in any of them.

We know of no announced overriding federal common law permitting a right of action by an employee against his employer for the latter's failure to comply with the nondiscrimination provision in a government contract.

In any event, §§ 12.806-5 to 12.806-8 of the Armed Services Procurement Regulations, 25 F.R. 14275 (December 31, 1960), 32 CFR, Part 1 to 39 (1961), §§ 12.806-5 to 12.806-8, provided for the filing and processing of complaints for the alleged noncompliance with the provisions of the nondiscrimination clause with the appropriate military department.[11] The President's Committee on Equal Employment Opportunity has promulgated similar regulations. See 26 F.R. 6588-89 (July 1961), 41 CFR, Rev'd January 1963, §§ 60.1.20 to 60.1.27. However, there is no allegation in the complaint that plaintiff has filed a complaint with any Governmental contracting agency, military or civilian, or with the President's Committee. Though it requests damages for an alleged wrongful discharge because of plaintiff's refusal to obey an assertedly discriminatory order by his employer, the complaint does not rule out a challenge to the validity of his discharge and the seeking of reinstatement, with or without back pay under a light duty status, as an alternative item for relief. There has been no showing of impending harm or any inadequacy of the contracting agencies of the President's Committee to give plaintiff adequate relief so as to permit short circuiting the administrative process. Cf. *Aircraft & Diesel Equipment Corp.* v. *Hirsch,* 331 U.S. 752, 67 S.Ct. 1493, 91 L.Ed. 1796 (1947), and *Slocum* v. *Delaware,* L. & W. R. Co., 339 U.S. 239, 244, 70 S.Ct. 577, 94 L.Ed. 795 (1950). We believe that the doctrine of "exhaustion of administrative remedies" should at least be applied here, and that plaintiff be required to file a complaint with an appropriate contracting agency or with the President's Committee before being permitted to seek the aid of a Federal district court. However, whether a district court could then entertain jurisdiction is not here decided.

Whether the application of the doctrine of exhaustion of administrative remedies precludes bringing a suit for wrongful discharge or for damages pursuant to a state antidiscrimination statute independent of the provisions of a contract, we need not decide here. However, we may point out that in the case of *Colorado Anti-Discrimination Commission* v. *Continental Air Lines, Inc.,* 372 U.S. 714, 724, 83 S.Ct. 1022, 10 L.Ed. 2d 84 (1963), although the Supreme Court did not reach the question whether an executive order foreclosed state legislation on the subject of antidiscrimination, the Court did say at page 725 of its Opinion in 372

---

in vindicating the rights of complainants. Since the enforcement of an individual's right will have a broad educative effect on the community, the state has also an interest of its own as strong as the complainant's. By replacing the ineffective civil or criminal suit with administrative investigation and enforcement, it is able to ensure that both objectives are realized."

[11] Also see 32 CFR (1963 Supp.) §§ 12.806-6 to 12.806-8.

U.S., at page 1028 of 83 S.Ct., 10 L.Ed.2d 84: "It is impossible for us to believe that the Executive intended for its orders to regulate air carrier discrimination among employees so persuasively as to preempt state legislation intended to accomplish the same purpose."

For the reasons stated, the order of the District Court and the judgment entered thereon granting defendant's motion to dismiss the complaint will be affirmed.

## FARKAS v. TEXAS INSTRUMENT, INC.

*U.S. Court of Appeals, Fifth Circuit, 1967*
*375 F.2d 629, 1 FEP Cases 890, cert. denied, 389 U.S. 977 (1967)*

TUTTLE, Chief Judge: Appellant, a naturalized citizen of the United States, is a native of Romania. He was employed as an engineer by the defendant Texas Instrument, Inc. from June, 1962 until his discharge in May, 1963. The complaint asserts that the defendants, Texas Instrument, Inc., and Ling-Temco-Vought, Inc., were prime contractors operating under federal government contracts containing certain provisions, required to be included therein by an Executive Order issued by the President, which forbade the defendants from discriminating against any employee or applicant for employment in connection with the performance of their contracts on the basis, inter alia, of national origin. In substance, appellant claims that his discharge from Texas Instrument was motivated by discrimination based upon his national origin, that Ling-Temco-Vought refused to hire him for the same reason, and that the two defendants engaged in a conspiracy to prevent him from securing employment by the use of certain methods described as "blackball" tactics.

Appellant asserts jurisdiction under 23 U.S.C.A. § 1331, the federal question statute, and 28 U.S.C.A. § 1343, providing for jurisdiction of "any civil action authorized by law to be commenced by any person . . . because of the deprivation of any right or privilege of a citizen of the United States by any act done in furtherance of any conspiracy mentioned in section 1985 of Title 42 . . . ." The trial judge dismissed the complaint for failure to state a claim within the jurisdiction of the district court. We agree that the complaint must be dismissed, but not for want of jurisdiction.

### I

We consider first the claims of discriminatory discharge and refusal to hire.

[Quote of Executive Order No. 10925 is omitted.—Ed.]

B. This brings us to the question whether a private civil action is a permissible method of enforcing the antidiscrimination provisions of Executive Order No. 10925. This question was considered in *Farmer* v. *Philadelphia Electric Co.*, 329 F.2d 3 (3rd Cir. 1964).

[Excerpts from the *Farmer* decision are omitted—Ed.] . . .

Were there an absence of any remedy save that which might be fashioned under the general jurisdiction of the federal courts, the inference would be strong that that jurisdiction was intended to be invoked to give vitality to the contractual assurances of nondiscrimination given pursuant to the Order. But this is not the case. The path was open to appellant under the Order to lay his complaint before the President's Committee on Equal Employment Opportunity. 41 C.F.R. §§ 60.1.20-27. He alleges that he has availed himself of this opportunity, but that the Committee refused him relief. In light of the Order's emphasis on administrative methods of obtaining compliance with the required contractual provisions, and its narrowly limited reference to judicial enforcement thereof, we conclude that that refusal is final. See *Switchmen's Union* v. *National Mediation Board*, 320 U.S. 297, 64 S.Ct. 95, 88 L.Ed. 61 (1943). Accordingly, the claims predicated upon breach of contractual nondiscrimination provisions must be dismissed on the merits for failure to state a cause of action upon which relief can be granted.

## II

We turn now to the claimed conspiracy. The complaint alleges that "at various times subsequent to his discharge by Defendant Texas Instrument, Inc., said Defendant knowingly, intentionally and unlawfully combined with other persons, firms and corporations to deprive the Plaintiff of the equal protection of the laws and of equal privileges and immunities under the laws and his rights as a citizen of the United States by preventing the Plaintiff from obtaining and securing employment, and in causing the Plaintiff to be pressured, threatened, harassed and intimidated by local law enforcement officers who were caused to follow the Plaintiff about and subject him to unreasonable and unwarranted surveillance and interrogation, all under the color of state law and authority, and injuring the Plaintiff in person and property for lawfully attempting to enforce his rights to the equal protection of the laws." Appellant's contention is that by these actions, the defendants have violated 42 U.S.C. §§ 1985(2) and (3).

Original jurisdiction over actions brought to recover damages resulting from such violations is committed to the district courts by 28 U.S.C. § 1343. Clearly, appellant has *attempted* to state a right based on Sections 1343 and 1985. His federal claim is neither immaterial to the relief sought nor, in our judgment, wholly insubstantial. Thus, under *Bell* v. *Hood,* supra, the district court had jurisdiction to determine the question whether the allegations of conspiracy in appellant's complaint stated a federally-granted cause of action. *Congress of Racial Equality* v. *Clemmons,* 323 F.2d 54 (5th Cir. 1963).

On the merits, the difficulty with appellant's claim is that it nowhere contains the essential allegations of state action. As we said in *Clemmons,* supra, "It is still the law that the Fourteenth Amendment and the statutes enacted pursuant to it, including 42 U.S.C.A., § 1985, apply only where there is state action." Id. at 62.

Appellant does allege that the defendants furnished false information to local and federal authorities (including the federal officer sent to investigate the complaint filed by appellant pursuant to Executive Order No. 10925), and that they caused local law enforcement officers to "subject him to unwarranted and unreasonable surveillance and interrogation."

In one sense, of course, these allegations do show involvement by officials "acting under color of state law." But these alleged activities are not the sort of "state action" with which § 1985 is concerned. Appellant alleges that local law enforcement officers were caused to subject him to unreasonable and unwarranted surveillance and interrogation, but he does not allege that the persons *responsible* for this alleged invasion of his rights were acting under color of state law. In fact, he alleges that the defendants, both private corporations, caused these actions to be taken. As we said in *Dinwiddie* v. *Brown*, 230 F.2d 465 (5th Cir. 1956):

"This is not to deny that if state officers conspire with private individuals in such a way as to defeat or prejudice a litigant's rights in state court, that would amount to a denial of equal protection of the laws by persons acting under color of state law. *It is another matter, however, where they act wholly within their official responsibilities and do not intentionally cooperate in any fraudulent scheme.* In such a case, the tort is solely that of the private individuals, and redress of the wrong rests with the state courts." Id. at 469. (Emphasis added.)

The allegations of conspiracy, then, do not state a cause of action upon which relief can be granted, and the complaint should therefore have been dismissed for that reason.

For the reasons stated, the judgment of dismissal is

*Affirmed.*

## LEWIS v. WESTERN AIRLINES, INC.

*United States District Court, Northern District of California, 1974*
*379 F. Supp. 684, 8 FEP Cases 373*

WOLLENBERG, District Judge: Plaintiffs seek to maintain this action for employment discrimination against Western Airlines and several employees of the federal government charged with ensuring compliance by Western Airlines with federal anti-discrimination laws. The complaint alleges causes of action under Title VII of the Civil Rights Act of 1964, 42 U.S.C. §§ 2000e *et seq.*, Executive Order 11246, as amended, 3 C.F.R. 169 (1974), 28 U.S.C. § 1361, plus 42 U.S.C. §§ 1981, 1983, 1985, and 1986. Defendant Western Airlines moves for a more definite statement, F.R.Civ.P. Rule 12(e), and to dismiss the third claim for relief, which alleges a cause of action under Executive Order 11246.

### More Definite Statement

Plaintiffs' allegation in Paragraph 50 of the complaint, that they have exhausted all available administrative remedies with respect to the third claim for relief, is sufficient to enable Defendants to file responsive pleadings. This is all that is required by F.R.Civ.P. Rule 12(e), *E.E.O.C.* v. *Bartenders International Union AFL-CIO*, 6 FEP Cases 208, No. C-73-0518 RFP (N.D. Cal. June 22, 1973); *E.E.O.C.* v. *Pick Memphis Corp.*, 5 FEP Cases 1310, 5 E.P.D. ¶ 8471 (W.D. Tenn. 1973), and, accordingly, the motion for a more definite statement will be denied.

### Dismiss Third Claim for Relief

Whether Plaintiffs may maintain a private cause of action under Executive Order 11246 is a question which has not been considered by the Court of Appeals of this Circuit. The regulatory scheme of the Executive Order essentially prohibits employers holding government contracts from engaging in unlawful employment discrimination and requires them to adopt and implement affirmative action programs calculated to eliminate whatever vestiges of employment discrimination may remain in their operations.[1] It was recently held in *Legal Aid Society of Alameda County* v. *Brennan*, —— F.Supp. ——, 8 FEP Cases 178 (N.D. Cal. filed June 20, 1974), that Executive Order 11246 may be the basis of a private action seeking an order that the appropriate agency of the federal government enforce the provisions of the Executive Order and of regulations issued pursuant to it (hereinafter "Regulations"). The present case presents the different question whether such an action may be brought directly against the contractor believed to be in violation of the Executive Order.

In *Farkas* v. *Texas Instrument, Inc.*, 375 F.2d 629, 1 FEP Cases 890, 71 LRRM 3154 (5th Cir., 1967), a case frequently cited as authority for denying a cause of action under the Executive Order, the Court concluded that the history and text of Executive Order 10925, a predecessor of Executive Order 11246, suggest that no private right of enforcement through a civil action was contemplated by its enactment. The Court's position in *Farkas* was that certain administrative remedies were provided by Executive Order 10925 and by regulations issued pursuant to it, that these remedies were intended to be exclusive, and that once they were exhausted, the aggrieved person was without further recourse. 375 F.2d at 633. The Court cited as authority *Farmer* v. *Philadelphia Electric Co.*, 329 F.2d 3, 1 FEP Cases 36, 55 LRRM 2685 (3d Cir. 1964), and *Switchmen's Union* v. *National Mediation Board*, 320 U.S. 297, 13 LRRM 616 (1943).

---

[1] [Footnotes numbered as in original.—Ed.] Following is a summary of the terms and procedures for enforcement of the Executive Order established by the President and by the Secretary of Labor pursuant to Section 201 of the Executive Order, 3 C.F.R. 169, 170 (1974). The text of the Executive Order is found at 3 C.F.R. 169 (1974), and the Regulations appear at 41 C.F.R. § 60-1.1 *et seq.* (1973).

Executive Order 11246 seeks to ensure that employers holding government contracts hire their employees without regard to race, color, religion, sex or national origin. 41 C.F.R. § 60-1.1 (1973). To implement this goal, the Executive Order incorporates into every government contract, except those exempted by Section 204 of the Executive Order, 3 C.F.R. 169, 172 (1974) and 41 C.F.R. § 60-1.5 (1973), as a matter of law the equal opportunity clause set out in Section 202 of the Executive Order, 3 C.F.R. 169, 170-71 (1974); see 41 C.F.R. §§ 60-1.4(a) and (b) (1973). The equal opportunity clause prohibits discrimination in hiring and in the conditions of employment and requires employers to take affirmative action to ensure that their operations are free from

In *Farmer*, the court presented at length their view that Executive Order 10925 does not create a private right of action for its enforcement. The court concluded, however, that, having failed to exhaust the administrative remedies provided by the Executive Order, plaintiff was therefore barred from maintaining the action: "[W]hether a district court could then [after administrative remedies were exhausted] entertain jurisdiction is not here decided". 329 F.2d at 10, 1 FEP Cases at 41, 55 LRRM at 2690. The question of a private right of action, posed by the present lawsuit, was therefore expressly reserved by the court in *Farmer*. *Switchmen's Union* will be discussed, *infra*.

The Supreme Court has held that "[a]ll constitutional questions aside, it is for Congress to determine how the rights which it creates shall be enforced [citation omitted]. In such a case the specification of one remedy

---

the effects of the proscribed discrimination. The purpose, scope and content of the required affirmative action programs are set out in detail in Revised Order No. 4 issued by the Secretary of the Department of Labor. 41 C.F.R. §§ 60-2.1, *et seq.* (1973). The Executive Order and the Regulations provide certain sanctions and, to some extent, attempt to prescribe the procedure for imposing these sanctions when employers fail to comply with the equal opportunity clause.

The Executive Order assigns to the Secretary of Labor responsibility for ensuring compliance with the equal opportunity clause, Section 203 of the Executive Order, 3 C.F.R. 169, 170 (1974), and the Secretary of Labor delegated this function to the Director of the Office of Federal Contracts Compliance, (hereinafter "the Director") who remains under the Secretary's supervision. 41 C.F.R. § 60-1.2 (1973). The Director designates various agencies in the executive department of the federal government as "Compliance Agencies" and supervises their work. These Compliance Agencies are charged with ensuring compliance with the equal opportunity clause. 41 C.F.R. § 60-1.3(d) (1973).

Under the Executive Order and the Regulations, there are two procedures for detecting violations of the equal opportunity clause, and these share a common set of sanctions which may be imposed. See Sections 206(a) and (b) of the Executive Order, 3 C.F.R. 169, 172-73 (1974), and the Regulations at 41 C.F.R. §§ 60-1.20 and 60-1.21 (1973). The Regulations require compliance reviews of employers to be made regularly by the Compliance Agencies or by the Director to ensure that the equal opportunity clause is being implemented. 41 C.F.R. § 60-1.20(c) (1973). An employee or prospective employee who suspects an employer is violating the equal employment clause of its contract may file a complaint with the appropriate agency or with the Director, and this complaint must be promptly investigated. 41 C.F.R. §§ 60-1.21 to 60-1.24(b) (1973). When, as a result of either a compliance review pursuant to 41 C.F.R. § 60-1.20 (1973) or pursuant to the investigation of a complaint made pursuant to 41 C.F.R. §§ 60-1.21 to 60-1.23 (1973), it is determined that an employer is violating the equal opportunity clause of his contract, the Director may act directly or authorize the appropriate agency to cancel, terminate or suspend the employer's government contracts, to bar the employer from receiving further contracts, or to "impose such other sanctions as are authorized by the order." 41 C.F.R. § 60-1.24(c)(3) (1973). The term "other sanctions" refers specifically to sections 209(a)(2) and (a)(3) of the Executive Order, 3 C.F.R. 169, 173-74 (1974), which authorize the Secretary of Labor, who, pursuant to 41 C.F.R. § 60-1.27 (1973), has authorized the Director, to

(2) Recommend to the Department of Justice that in cases in which there is substantial or material violation of the [equal opportunity clause], appropriate proceedings be brought to enforce [that clause], including the enjoining, within the limitations of applicable law, of organizations, individuals, or groups who prevent directly or indirectly . . . compliance with the provisions of this Order.

(3) Recommend to the Equal Employment Opportunity Commission or the Department of Justice that appropriate proceedings be instituted under Title VII of the Civil Rights Act of 1964.

No such action may be taken unless the employer under investigation has been afforded the opportunity for a hearing pursuant to 41 C.F.R. § 60-1.26 (1973). 41 C.F.R. § 60-1.24(c)(3) (1973).

normally excludes another. [citations omitted.]" *Switchmen's Union* v. *National Mediation Board,* 320 U.S. 297, 301, 13 LRRM 616 (1943). Because of the "narrowly limited reference to judicial enforcement" contained in the terms of the Executive Order,[2] the Fifth Circuit, citing *Switchmen's Union, supra,* refused to recognize a private cause of action under the Executive Order, *Farkas* v. *Texas Instrument, supra.* Both *Switchmen's Union* and *Farkas,* though, were decided before *Data Processing Service* v. *Camp,* 397 U.S. 150 (1970), and *Barlow* v. *Collins,* 397 U.S. 159 (1970).

*Data Processing Service* v. *Camp, supra,* and *Barlow* v. *Collins, supra,* hold that an individual may bring a civil action to enforce or challenge a federal regulatory statute or regulation, even if the statute or regulation does not specifically confer such a right of action, provided the individual can show he has a personal interest in the outcome of the litigation which is within the zone of interests sought to be protected by the statute or regulation in question. In *Data Processing Service* and in *Barlow* the administrative actions under review challenged agency action and named a representative of the federal agency as a defendant. The same is true of *Abbott Laboratories* v. *Gardner,* 387 U.S. 136 (1967), on which plaintiffs here also rely. In *Euresti* v. *Stenner,* 458 F.2d 1115 (10th Cir. 1972), however, plaintiff brought a class action against a hospital administrator to force a hospital that was receiving federal funds pursuant to the Hill-Burton Act, 42 U.S.C. §§ 291, *et seq.,* to comply with the terms of the Act requiring that a reasonable portion of the services of a hospital receiving federal funds be made available to indigent persons. Citing *Barlow* v. *Collins, supra,* Justice Clark, sitting by designation and writing for the Tenth Circuit, held that plaintiffs had standing to maintain a private action to enforce the Hill-Burton Act, which does not expressly provide for such an action, because the hospital was operating under a contract "explicitly incorporating the federal statutory obligation" and because the plaintiffs were within the zone of interests intended to be protected by the statute and were directly affected by its violation. 458 F.2d at 1118-19. Executive Order 11246 and the Regulations expressly incorporate as a matter of law into the government's contracts with Defendant Western Airlines the equal opportunity clause mandated by the Executive Order. 3 C.F.R. 169, 170-71 (1974); 41 C.F.R. §§ 60-1.4(a) and (b) (1973). The Executive Order is specific regarding sanctions which may be imposed on employers failing to comply with the provisions of the equal opportunity clause. Section 209(a) of the Executive Order, 3 C.F.R. 169, 173-74 (1974).

Defendant's reliance on *Switchmen's Union* and on the more recent Court of Appeals cases which have likewise relied upon *Switchmen's Union* is misplaced. Plaintiffs in *Switchmen's Union* sought judicial review of the decision by the National Mediation Board that the Brotherhood of Railroad Trainmen would represent the yardmen employed by certain railroads. In deciding whether judicial review of an administrative

---

[2] Sections 209(a)(2) and (a)(3), 3 C.F.R. 169, 173-74 (1974).

decision is available when it is not expressly provided by the statute in question, the Court stated that the nature of the problem and the history of the relevant statute are of great importance. 320 U.S. at 301. Proceeding to consider the nature of the problem and the history of the statute, the Court found that in fashioning the procedures for determining which labor union would be the bargaining representative for a group of the workers, Congress was faced with a highly delicate and controversial problem, one which if not resolved with every appearance of care and judiciousness each time it arose, could impair the National Mediation Board's ability to carry out its other obligations. 320 U.S. at 302-03. Having come this far, the Court concluded:

"Where Congress took such great pains to protect the Mediation Board in its handling of an explosive problem, we cannot help but believe that if Congress had desired to implicate the federal judiciary and to place on the federal courts the burden of having the final say on any aspect of the problem, it would have made its desire plain."
320 U.S. at 303, 16 LRRM at 619.

The situations in *Euresti* v. *Stenner, supra,* and the present case are clearly distinct from that in *Switchmen's Union.* The necessity on which the Court rested its decision in *Switchmen's Union* is absent in the present case. In *Switchmen's Union* the Court examined the language and history of the statute in question and were able to conclude that Congress intended the administrative remedy it fashioned so carefully to be exclusive. 320 U.S. at 305. Unlike in *Switchmen's Union,* there is here no delicate situation which will jeopardize other important national policies if not handled in precisely the manner provided in the Secretary of Labor's Regulations. In promulgating the Executive Order and Regulations, the President and Secretary of Labor were not confronted by an "explosive problem" which possibly could cause even greater problems if not handled in a particular way. Even the Regulations, however, do not contemplate that their approach to the problem of employment must be exclusive.[3] On the contrary, in their determination to eliminate employment discrimination, which itself is responsible for great social problems, Congress, the President, and many states have provided numerous remedies, usually with the provision that they are not meant to repeal whatever other remedies might exist. . . .

Implying a private right of action from a statute or Executive Order should not become a device to undercut effective administrative remedies established by Congress or pursuant to an Executive Order. To maintain a cause of action against Defendant Western Airlines, Plaintiffs will have to show, as they have pleaded, that they have exhausted whatever administrative remedies were reasonably available. The only relief Plaintiffs seek directly under the Executive Order [4] is an injunction compelling the

[3] "The rights and remedies of the Government hereunder are not exclusive and do not affect rights and remedies provided elsewhere by law, regulation, or contract. . . ." 41 C.F.R. § 60-1.1 (1973).

[4] Other relief sought is available under Title VII of the Civil Rights Act of 1964, *supra,* and other statutes.

Secretary of Labor, the Director of the Office of Federal Contracts Compliance, and the Federal Aviation Administration to comply with their mandate under the Executive Order and the Regulations. A writ of mandate is available to provide this relief. *Legal Aid Society of Alameda County* v. *Brennan, supra.* Because Western Airlines' interests are integrally involved in this proceeding and would be substantially affected by the relief Plaintiffs seek under the Executive Order, it is a proper party to this action. F.R.Civ.P. Rule 19(a)(2).

*Switchmen's Union* being inapposite here, this Court having concluded that the principles announced in *Data Processing Service* and *Barlow* and applied in *Euresti* v. *Stenner* should control, and Western Airlines' interests being basic to this lawsuit, it is proper that Defendant Western Airlines be a party in this lawsuit. Accordingly, Defendant's motion to dismiss the third claim for relief is hereby denied.

## NOTES

1. On an unsuccessful effort to require the Federal Government, as employer, to abide by the executive order, see *Gnotta* v. *U.S.,* 415 F.2d 1271, 2 FEP Cases 111 (8th Cir. 1969), *cert. denied,* 397 U.S. 934, 2 FEP Cases 451 (1970).

2. See also *Penn* v. *Schlesinger,* 497 F.2d 907, 8 FEP Cases 453 (5th Cir. 1974), *reversing en banc,* 490 F.2d 700, 6 FEP Cases 1109 (5th Cir. 1973), cert. filed October 23, 1974.

(2) *Prohibiting Interference With the Contract*

## UNITED STATES v. LOCAL 189, UNITED PAPERMAKERS AND PAPERWORKERS AND CROWN ZELLERBACH CORPORATION

*U.S. District Court, Eastern District of Louisiana, New Orleans Division, 1968*

*282 F. Supp. 39*

Action by United States against local union and its parent and employer for relief for violation of Civil Rights Act and from interference with implementation of executive order forbidding racial discrimination in employment opportunities by government contractors. . . .

ORDER

HEEBE, District Judge: This cause having come on for hearing on the motion of the United States for a preliminary injunction against the defendants, as well as a trial on the merits of the complaints of the United States and the plaintiff-intervenors, Anthony Hill, David Johnson, Sr., and Local 189a, United Papermakers and Paperworkers, for permanent injunctive relief;

IT IS NOW THE ORDER OF THE COURT that, for the reasons assigned, the relief sought be, and the same is hereby, GRANTED to the following extent:

(a) The defendants Crown Zellerbach Corporation and Local 189, United Papermakers and Paperworkers, AFL-CIO, CLC, and United Papermakers and Paperworkers, AFL-CIO, CLC, their officers, agents, employees, servants and all persons and organizations in active concert or participation with them, are hereby ENJOINED and RESTRAINED, pending the further orders of this Court, from discriminating against the Negro employees of the defendant Crown Zellerbach Corporation's paper mill at Bogalusa, Louisiana, in violation of Title VII of the Civil Rights Act of 1964, and in particular, the defendants are hereby ORDERED to ABOLISH forthwith the system of "job seniority" and any other seniority system designed to discriminate against the Negro employees at said plant or having the effect of so discriminating, insofar as such systems may apply to the promotion, demotion, or selection for training of Negro employees hired prior to January 16, 1966 in competition with employees of the opposite race; and the said defendants are ORDERED to ESTABLISH, with respect to such promotions, demotions and selection for training, and in the place of such "job seniority" or similar systems, a system of "mill seniority" as follows:

(1) Total mill seniority (i.e., the length of continuous service in the mill) alone shall determine who the "senior" bidder or employee is for purposes of permanent or thirty-day promotions, or for purposes of demotion, in all circumstances in which one or more of the competing employees is a Negro employee hired prior to January 16, 1966;

(2) For jobs which operate only one shift per day, promotions to fill casual or vacation vacancies will be made on the same basis as permanent and thirty-day promotions;

(3) For jobs which operate more than one shift per day, promotions because of casual or vacation vacancies will be awarded to the senior (as determined in (1) above) qualified man on the shift and/or machine where the vacancy exists;

(4) Promotions and demotions above shall not affect persons who have formal written waivers in effect at that time. Persons promoted shall go around a waived position in any job slot, and persons demoted shall likewise go around such a position on the way down;

(5) Qualified employees shall be selected for training on the same basis as for promotion described above.

The provisions of this decree pertaining to the implementation by the defendants of a system of "mill seniority" shall be placed into effect within ten days from the entry of this order; prior to the implementation of the said "mill seniority" system, the defendants are ENJOINED and RESTRAINED from interfering and failing to comply with the agreement of March 19, 1967, as modified by the agreements of June 16, 1967 and January 3, 1968, between the defendant Crown Zellerbach Corporation and the Office of Federal Contract Compliance of the United States Department of Labor.

(b) The defendant Local 189, United Papermakers and Paperworkers, AFL-CIO, CLC, and United Papermakers and Paperworkers, AFL-CIO, CLC, their officers, agents, members, employees, servants, and all persons and organizations in active concert or participation with them, are EN-JOINED and RESTRAINED, pending the further orders of this Court, from interfering with or hindering, by striking, threatening to strike, or otherwise, the compliance by the defendants with the foregoing provisions of this order.

REASONS

We find, as a matter of fact, (1) that Crown and the white local actively engaged, prior to January 1966, in a pervasive pattern of discrimination against the Negro employees at Crown's Bogalusa paper mill with respect to employment opportunities of promotion, demotion and selection for training; (2) that the continuation of the "job seniority" system, or any seniority system which incorporates job seniority as a substantial factor in promotion, demotion and selection for training, operates, because of the situation engendered by the pervasive past discrimination by the defendants at Crown's Bogalusa paper mill, to effectively presently discriminate against Negro employees at the mill whenever Negro employees hired prior to January 1966 compete against white employees for promotion, demotion or selection for training; (3) that a system of "mill seniority," as defined in the Collective Bargaining Agreement between Crown and the local unions presently in force at the Bogalusa plant, would not have such a continuing discriminatory effect against the Negro employees; and (4) that "job seniority," as a consideration in the promotion and demotion of employees within a particular line of progression and in the selection of employees for training, is not necessitated by safety or efficiency factors, nor for any other reason is "job seniority" objectively a better or more desirable basis than "mill seniority" for promotion, demotion or selection for training of employees within the context of the present lines of progression in force at Crown's Bogalusa paper mill.

As a matter of law, we hold that this Court has jurisdiction of this action under 42 U.S.C. § 2000e-6 (b) and 28 U.S.C. § 1331 and § 1345, and that discrimination against Negroes with respect to employment opportunities at this mill is properly subject to attack by the government pursuant not only to Title VII of the Civil Rights Act of 1964,[1] but also under

---

1 [Footnotes numbered as in original—Ed.] The parties have stipulated that Crown is an employer within the meaning of 42 U.S.C. § 2000e(b) and is engaged in an industry affecting commerce within the meaning of 42 U.S.C. § 2000e(h), and that Local 189 and its parent union are labor organizations within the meaning of 42 U.S.C. § 2000e(d) and are engaged in an industry affecting commerce within the meaning of 42 U.S.C. 2000e(e).

§ 209 of Executive Order 11246.[2] That order, like the order in *Farkas* v. *Texas Instrument, Inc.,* 375 F.2d 629, 632 (5th Cir. 1967), is to be accorded the force and effect of statutory law.

. . .

The white local is not immune from suit or injunctive process of this Court by reason of the general terms of the Norris-LaGuardia Act, 29 U.S.C. § 101 et seq. Even prior to the enactment of Title VII, the Supreme Court had held that racial discrimination by a union was not sanctioned or protected from corrective court orders by the Norris-LaGuardia Act. *Virginian R. Co.* v. *System Federation No. 40,* 300 U.S. 515, 57 S.Ct. 592, 81 L.Ed. 789 (1937); *Graham* v. *Brotherhood of Locomotive Firemen & Enginemen,* 338 U.S. 232, 70 S.Ct. 14, 94 L.Ed. 22 (1949); *Brotherhood of Railroad Trainmen* v. *Howard,* 343 U.S. 768, 774, 72 S.Ct. 1022, 96 L.Ed. 1283 (1952). These decisions were not predicated on any peculiarity in the antidiscrimination provisions of the Railway Labor Act, *Textile Workers Union of America* v. *Lincoln Mills of Ala.,* 353 U.S. 448, 458, 77 S.Ct. 923, 1 L.Ed.2d 972 (1957), and we find the holdings of these cases equally applicable to the provisions of Title VII and Executive Order 11246. Merely because § 706 of Title VII, 42 U.S.C. § 2000c-5 (h), (authorizing private suits for the correction of Title VII violations), contains an express exemption from the anti-injunction provisions of the Norris-LaGuardia Act, while § 707, 42 U.S.C. § 2000e-6, (authorizing civil actions by the Attorney General), does not, fails to influence our holding. Section 707 provides, in the broadest possible language, for the protection of Title VII rights by suit by the Attorney General seeking "permanent or temporary injunction, restraining order or other order against the person or persons responsible . . . as [may be] necessary to insure the *full enjoyment* of [Title VII] rights." (emphasis supplied) 42 U.S.C. § 2000e-6 (a). This language cannot be read to prohibit the remedy against unions which may be responsible for Title VII violations. Title VII read as a whole forbids such a restrictive interpretation. Section 2000e(a) defines "person" to include "one or more individuals, *labor unions,* . . . ; § 2000e-2(c) specifically lists the acts of labor organizations which constitute "unlawful employment practices" under Title VII; § 2000e-2(c) (3) makes it unlawful for a labor organization "to cause or attempt to cause an employer to discriminate against an individual in violation of [Title VII]." To hold injunctive remedies against such unlawful union practices available to individuals under § 706 and not to the Attorney General seeking to correct what will usually be much more serious and pervasive "patterns or practices of resistance" under § 707 would be inconsistent and irrational, and destructive to the national achievement of the basic aims of Title VII.

---

[2] The parties have stipulated that "Since at least 1961, the defendant, Crown, has supplied materials under government contracts and subcontracts, which contain equal employment opportunity clauses similar to or the same as those appearing [in] the Executive Order 11246 and Executive Order 10925, to the extent required by those orders."

It is undisputed—in fact, the ultimate facts compelling the conclusion have been stipulated by all parties—that prior to May 1964 Crown followed an active program of discrimination in employment opportunities against its Negro employees at its Bogalusa plant, and that not until January 1966 were considerations of race fully obliterated with respect to the job opportunities of the employees at the plant. Although not equally responsible for this situation, the white local was in good measure at fault: the discrimination against Negro employees was possible because Local 189 was all white, and Negro employees excluded from that local had an organization of their own, Local 189a; discrimination was arranged by the device of granting "jurisdiction" over the more attractive lines of progression and the more lucrative jobs to the white local.

. . .

"Job seniority" is certainly not *inherently* prejudicial to Negroes; there is nothing about "job seniority" systems themselves to make them necessarily offensive; nor do we think "mill seniority" necessarily a better system. It is not the job seniority system in and of itself, but rather the continuous discrimination practiced by the defendants within the framework of that system, which now requires that the system be abolished in this case. Within the framework of a "job seniority" system, Negro employees have been forced into the inferior lines of progression and the less desirable jobs. The defendants claim that active discrimination against Negroes has now ceased. But the fact that Negroes who, under the present liberalized policy, have only recently entered formerly white progression lines are forced to compete with white employees for promotion on the basis of "job seniority" continues, in each case of such competition, the discriminatory effect of the long history of the relegation of those Negroes to other, less desirable lines.

We cannot accept the Union's contention that such discrimination is not prohibited by Title VII and that Title VII cannot be used in any way to alter or affect seniority systems. Where a seniority system has the effect of perpetuating discrimination, and concentrating or "telescoping" the effect of past years of discrimination against Negro employees into the *present* placement of Negroes in an inferior position for promotion and other purposes, that present result is prohibited, and a seniority system which operates to produce that present result must be replaced with another system. We agree wholeheartedly with the conclusion in *Quarles* v. *Philip Morris, Inc.*, 279 F.Supp. 505 (E.D.Va. 1968), that present discrimination cannot be justified under Title VII simply because Title VII refers to an effective date and because present discrimination is caused by conditions in the past. "Congress did not intend to freeze an entire generation of Negro employees into discriminatory patterns that existed before the act." *Quarles*, supra, at 516.

. . .

We do not deny, by our present order, the right of Crown to urge some other equally acceptable system, if there be any, by which to control the flow of employee promotion and demotion, or the right of Local 189 to bargain for any such system. But we cannot permit the plaintiffs herein to remain without a remedy to present and continuing discrimination merely because the remedy called for involves matters which may be subject to the bargaining efforts of unions. Title VII provides for the correction of discriminatory practices by any remedial order which may be necessary; the scope of the remedy is not restricted to matters outside the jurisdiction of labor organizations. 42 U.S.C. § 2000e-6. Should an acceptable system other than "mill seniority" be proposed by any interested party, nothing herein would prohibit the Union from bargaining for it or Crown from implementing it, subject, of course, to the approval of the Court.

## NOTES

1. See also, *U.S.* v. *Papermakers and Paperworkers, Local 189,* 301 F. Supp. 906, 1 FEP Cases 820 (E.D. La. 1969), in which, among other things, the Court granted a permanent injunction against the defendants: "Crown Zellerbach Corp. Local 189, United Papermakers and Paperworkers, AFL-CIO, CLC, and the United Papermakers and Paperworkers, AFL-CIO, CLC, their officers, agents, employees, servants, and all other persons and organizations in active concerts or participation with them, are hereby permanently enjoined and restrained from discriminating against the Negro employees of the defendant, Crown Zellerbach Corp. papermill at Bogalusa, Louisiana, in violation of Title VII of the Civil Rights Act of 1964, in violation of the obligations imposed pursuant to Executive Order No. 11246, . . ." *Aff'd,* 416 F.2d 980, 1 FEP Cases 875 (5th Cir. 1969), *rehearing denied per curiam,* 416 F.2d 980; *cert. denied,* 397 U.S. 919, 2 FEP Cases 426 (1970).

2. See also *Todd* v. *Joint Apprenticeship Committee,* 223 F.Supp. 12 (N.D. Ill. 1963), *vacated as moot,* 332 F.2d 243 (7th Cir. 1964), *cert. denied,* 379 U.S. 899 (1964), 58 LRRM 2496.

3. For other examples of the Government's efforts to prevent interference with the contractual obligations, see *U.S.* v. *Building & Construction Trades Council of St. Louis,* 271 F.Supp. 447, 1 FEP Cases 897 (D.C. Mo. 1966); *U.S.* v. *Sheet Metal Workers Local 36,* 280 F.Supp. 719, 1 FEP Cases 387 (D.C. Mo. 1968).

## (3) *Requiring the Government to Act*

## ETHRIDGE v. RHODES

*U.S. District Court, Southern District of Ohio, Eastern Division, 1967*
*268 F. Supp. 83, 1 FEP Cases 185*

KINNEARY, District Judge: This is a class action for declaratory and injunctive relief brought by plaintiffs . . . [against certain state officials]. . . .

The Amended Complaint alleges that defendants, as duly elected and appointed officials of the State of Ohio, are about to enter into contracts for the construction of the Medical Basic Sciences Building on the campus of The Ohio State University, at Columbus. Plaintiffs seek to enjoin the State of Ohio from entering into such contracts on the ground that such action will be a deprivation, under color of state law, of their privileges and immunities as citizens of the United States as secured to them by the equal protection and due process clauses of the Fourteenth Amendment to the Constitution of the United States and Title 42, United States Code, Sections 1981 and 1983. It is charged that this activity violates these provisions inasmuch as it represents a continuation of state participation in a pattern of discrimination against plaintiffs, and the class they represent, in access to job opportunities on construction projects financed by federal and state funds, solely on the basis of their race.

. . .

Bids from contractors were received by the State of Ohio for the construction of the Medical Basic Sciences Building, and after review, contracts were sent to at least four contractors for their signatures. While these contracts have been signed and returned by the contractors and have not been signed by state officials, a declaration of intention to sign them has been made by state officials.

At least one of the contractors who has signed such a contract refused to submit a "responsive bid," that is, one containing the following assurance in compliance with the antidiscrimination provisions of the defendant Governor's executive order dealing with construction contracts:

### ASSURANCE

The undersigned hiring source, in response to the Executive Order issued by Governor James A. Rhodes on June 15, 1966, as amended December 30, 1966, hereby gives its assurance to ——— as follows:

(1) Admission to the full referral facilities of this hiring source, both as to apprentices and journeymen, is open on equal terms to all qualified persons without discrimination based on race, color, religion, national origin or ancestry.

(2) (a) From July 1, 1966, through December 31, 1966, the apprenticeship program of this hiring source will select all qualified applicants for apprenticeship training without regard to race, color, religion, national origin or ancestry.

(b) From January 1, 1967 through December 31, 1967, this hiring source will comply with each legally imposed requirement of clause (5) (b) of the Governor's Executive Order dated June 15, 1966, as amended December 30, 1966.

(c) After January 1, 1968, this hiring source will comply with every legally imposed requirement of clause (5)(c) of the said Governor's Executive Order.

Clause 5 of the Executive Order reads as follows:

(5) He and his subcontractors have received assurance in writing (*in the form appended hereto as Appendix B*) from each hiring source, including labor unions (which assurance, where appropriate, was authorized by vote of its membership) that

(a) Commencing July 1, 1966, and continuing through December 31, 1966, said hiring source's apprenticeship program will select all qualified applicants for apprenticeship training without regard to race, color, religion, national origin or ancestry.

(b) Commencing January 1, 1967, and continuing through December 31, 1967, said hiring source will have in its apprentice group and refer for employment without discrimination, both whites and non-whites (*including negroes*) or in the alternative, said hiring source shall be deemed to have waived any right to be a recruitment source with respect to every twentieth employee hired and shall likewise be deemed to have consented that every twentieth employee of the craft referred by said hiring source, *counting both apprentices and journeymen, may be recruited from another source for any employment derived from such bidder's bid, pledges and commitments, and report of assurances received.*

(c) After January 1, 1968, said hiring source will have in its apprentice and journeymen groups, and refer for employment without discrimination, both whites and non-whites (*including negroes*) or in the alternative, it shall be deemed to have waived its right to be a recruitment source for every fifteenth employee hired and shall likewise be deemed to have consented that every fifteenth employee of the craft referred by said hiring source, *counting both apprentices and journeymen,* may be recruited from another source *for any employment derived from such bidder's bid, pledges and commitments, and report of assurances received.*
Upon discovering that no responsive bids were submitted in the category of heating, ventilating and air conditioning, defendant Gienow requested and received from defendant Rhodes a waiver of application of the assurances requirement to this contract.

. . .

Defendants are aware that a number of unions have not referred Negroes for employment on the construction of other buildings erected by the State of Ohio on the campus of The Ohio State University. Defendants know to a certainty that many of the unions which will be used as labor sources by the proposed contractors on the Medical Basic Sciences Building project do not now have any Negro members. And the defendants also know that union officials responsible for admission to these unions have been persistently "out" or unavailable to Negroes who seek membership in such unions. Thus, the evidence presented establishes defendants' knowledge of a pattern of discrimination against Negroes, solely on the basis of their race, as to admission and referral by certain of the craft unions which will be used as labor sources for this project. There is, in addition, uncontroverted proof that no steps have been taken by the responsible union officials to correct such inequities. . . .

The Fourteenth Amendment proscription of racial discrimination does not extend to the acts of non-governmental persons such as union officials. Civil Rights Cases, 109 U.S. 3, 3 S.Ct. 18, 27 L.Ed. 835 (1883). However, when a state has become a joint participant in a pattern of racially discriminatory conduct by placing itself in a position of interdependence with private individuals acting in such a manner—that is, the proposed contractors acting under contract with unions that bar Negroes—this constitutes a type of "state action" proscribed by the Fourteenth Amendment. . . . Thus, as in the instant suit, where a state through its elected and appointed officials, undertakes to perform essential governmental functions—herein, the construction of facilities for public education—with the aid of private persons, it cannot avoid the responsibilities imposed on it by the Fourteenth Amendment by merely ignoring or failing to perform them. *Ibid.*

Plaintiffs have correctly asserted jurisdiction under § 1983. This statute is intended to allow redress against official representatives of the state who abuse their positions. It was enacted as a means for enforcing the provisions of the Fourteenth Amendment against those who act as officials of the State, whether they act in accordance with their authority or misuse it. . . .

The officials of the State of Ohio, through the testimony of the defendant, Director of Public Works, have displayed a shocking lack of concern over the realities of this whole situation and the inevitable discrimination that will result from entering into and performing under the proposed contracts with the proposed contractors. This Director testified that non-discrimination is just another provision of the contract, and his best solution for correcting discrimination, if and when it occurs, is to invoke the sanctions of the performance bond. This solution is totally inadequate for the elimination of the pattern of discrimination that has been allowed to exist. Defendants' failure to assure qualified minority workers equal access to job opportunities on public construction projects by acquiescing in the discriminatory practices of contractors and craft unions clearly falls within the proscription of the Fourteenth Amendment, and a cause of action is stated under § 1983. In a venture, such as this one, where the state as a governmental entity becomes a joint participant with private persons, the restrictions of the Fourteenth Amendment apply not only to the actions of the state but also to the acts of its private partners—the contractors—and the state is bound to affirmatively insure compliance with the constitutional provisions. . . . Since this section imposes civil liability, proof of a "specific intent to deprive a person of a federal right" is not required as under the criminal civil rights statutes. . . .

We come next to the question of the procedural availability of the injunction remedy in this case. The plaintiffs are here seeking an extraordinary remedy. It must be established that the threatened injury is irreparable and that no other adequate remedy exists. . . .

Defendants assert that the threatened injury is not irreparable and that an injunction is not the only adequate remedy because Title 42, United States Code, Section 2000e-1-15, and Ohio Rev. Code, ch. 4112, provide a remedy for the specific injury set out in the Complaint. It is alleged that through the commissions set up by these statutes and judicial enforcement of their orders, any person found to have been discriminated against could gain access to labor organizations and be awarded a back pay differential for the pecuniary damages suffered through the discriminatory exclusions from work on the project. However, it is quite apparent from the evidence presented that the threatened injury is not fully reparable through the utilization of the procedures set out in both the federal and state statutes.

Moreover, while the statutory provisions may serve to redress the pecuniary damage resulting from discrimination, they do not take a single step toward mending the psychological damage to both the party discriminated against and others in the class he represents. It is evident from the testimony of the several sociologists who appeared as witnesses in this case that discrimination in the area of employment stunts the educational and technical potential development of the class subject to such inequities. This Court is also mindful of the evidence submitted by experts in cases dealing with discrimination in others areas of life. Such evidence pointed out that segregation and discrimination not only denote inferiority of the class discriminated against, but also retard the development of that class, and that in cases in which this type of activity receives the sanction of the government, the impact is even greater. . . .

Injuries of this kind are not subject to any sort of monetary valuation. Thus, the pecuniary awards allowed under the federal and state statutes provide no adequate remedy.

Apart from the question of the reparability of discrimination by money damages, the Director of the Ohio State Civil Rights Commission testified that the Commission has been ineffectual in remedying discrimination in the craft unions. The Director further testified that even with the powers available to the Commission, the case by case approach which must be followed by that body results in too long a delay before any meaningful steps will be made toward eliminating discrimination. In view of the requirement that the state administrative remedy be sought before use of the federal administrative remedy, Title 42, United States Code, Section 2000e-5(b) (See Senate Discussion, June 4, 1964) the delay in administration is compounded. Thus, the federal administrative remedy also lacks any sort of speedy effectiveness.

. . .

[The court's order enjoined the state from entering into contracts with employers unwilling to execute the required assurance, or who had binding "hiring hall" contracts with discriminatory unions.]

# HADNOTT v. LAIRD

*U.S. Court of Appeals, District of Columbia Circuit, 1972*
*463 F.2d 304, 4 FEP Cases 374*

WILKEY, Circuit Judge:

Plaintiffs appeal from an order of the District Court dismissing an action for injunctive and declaratory relief against the Secretary of Defense and the Administrator of the General Services Administration. Plaintiffs brought the action on their own behalf and "on behalf of all black employees, applicants for employment, and prospective applicants for employment at the southern facilities" of eleven paper product companies having supply contracts with Defense and GSA, alleging that the rights of plaintiffs (and the class they represent) had been violated under the due process clause of the Fifth Amendment by the failure of the Government to enforce the companies' contractual agreements for nondiscrimination. The action sought an injunction against the two government officials, preventing the award of any future contracts and requiring the termination of the existing ones until all alleged racially discriminatory employment practices should be eliminated. The District Court dismissed the action on two grounds, sovereign immunity and the failure of the plaintiffs to exhaust their administrative remedies. Without reaching the first, we affirm on the latter ground.

## I.

The facts are stated fully in the published opinion [1] of the able trial judge. Executive Order 11246, last in the series of Presidential orders directed at eliminating discrimination, requires that every government contract include specific provisions binding the contractor not to discriminate against any employee or applicant because of race, color, creed, or national origin, and to take affirmative action to insure that nondiscrimination is a reality. The penalties for violating these contractual obligations include contract cancellation, termination, or suspension, and ineligibility for future government contracts.

The overall enforcement of these nondiscriminatory contract obligations is entrusted not to the specific contracting agencies themselves (although they have primary responsibility for obtaining compliance), but to the Secretary of Labor. Aside from the contracts with his own Department, he has no special interest in any particular contract or contractor, but independently has the specific duty to see that the nondiscriminatory provisions are enforced with all government contractors. To carry out his responsibility the Secretary has created the Office of Federal Contract Compliance and promulgated detailed regulations, which among other things, establish a complete procedure under which any employee or applicant for employment may complain of discriminatory practices by a government contractor.[2] Following a complaint

---

1 [Footnotes numbered as in original—Ed.] 317 F. Supp. 379 (1970).
2 41 C.F.R. § 60-1.21-.23.

the regulations require prompt investigation to determine if there has been a violation of the equal opportunity clause. In accord with the usual common sense principle of avoiding litigation where possible, if investigation indicates a violation, the preferred solution is for the offending contractor to take immediate corrective steps. If the contractor disputes the existence of violations, he is given a hearing, at which time the complainants or witnesses offered by them may be heard.[3] If after hearing a violation is determined, the penalties authorized by the Executive Order may be imposed.[4]

At the time of oral argument, out of the eleven companies involved here, with three the Government had reached new affirmative action agreements correcting violations found by the investigation, compliance reviews had been conducted and were being analyzed to determine the existence of violation in four instances, and the remaining four companies were scheduled for compliance reviews in the near future.[5]

II.

Although administrative action under Executive Order 11246 has been and is taking place, yet nowhere in the record is it asserted that any specific one of the plaintiffs has filed a complaint against one of the

[3] 41 C.F.R. § 60-1.26(b) (1) (2) reads as follows:

"(b) *Formal hearings*—(1) General *procedure*. The Director or the agency head, with the approval of the Director, may convene formal hearings pursuant to Subpart B of this part. Such hearings shall be conducted in accordance with procedures prescribed by the Director or the agency head. Reasonable notice of a hearing shall be sent by registered mail, return receipt requested, to the last known address of the prime contractor or subcontractor complained against. Such notice shall contain the time and place of hearing, a statement of the provisions of the order and regulations pursuant to which the hearing is to be held, and a concise statement of the matters pursuant to which the action furnishing the basis of the hearing has been taken or is proposed to be taken. Copies of such notice shall be held before a hearing officer designated by the Director or an agency head. Each party shall have the right to counsel, a fair opportunity to present evidence and argument and to cross-examine. Wherever a formal hearing is based in whole or in part on matters subject to the collective bargaining agreement and compliance may necessitate a revision of such agreement, any labor organization which is signatory to the agreement shall have the right to participate as a party. Any other person or organization shall be permitted to participate upon a showing that such person or organization has an interest in the proceedings and may contribute materially to the proper disposition thereof. The hearing officer shall make his proposed findings and conclusions upon the basis of the record before him.

"(2) *Cancellation, termination, and debarment*. No order for cancellation or termination of existing contracts or subcontracts or for disbarment from further contracts or subcontracts pursuant to section 209 of the order shall be made without affording the prime contractor or subcontractor an opportunity for a hearing. . . ."

41 C.F.R. § 60-2.2(c) (1) reads as follows:

"(1) If the contractor fails to show good cause for his failure or fails to remedy that failure by developing and implementing an acceptable affirmative action program within 30 days, the compliance agency, upon the approval of the Director, shall issue a notice of proposed cancellation or termination of existing contracts or subcontracts and debarment from future contracts and subcontracts pursuant to § 60-1.26(b), giving the contractor 10 days to request a hearing. If a request for hearing has not been received within 10 days from such notice, such contractor will be declared ineligible for future contracts and current contracts will be terminated for default."

[4] C.F.R. § 60-1.24, 60-1.26, 60-1.27.

[5] While the Senate Committee on Labor and Public Welfare stated, in its recommendations for the bill to improve the Equal Employment Opportunity Commission

named companies and invoked the procedure provided by Executive Order 11246 and the implementing regulations.[6] There is thus no showing by plaintiffs that they have asserted before and been denied rights by the OFCC. Instead, plaintiffs argue, first, that it would be fruitless for them to do so and, second, that because they are asserting constitutional rights they cannot be required to do so before resorting to the federal court.

A.

As to the usefulness of plaintiffs resorting to the administrative procedure set up to achieve precisely the results which plaintiffs desire in this case, i.e., either strict compliance with equal employment opportunity requirements or the debarment of the offending companies from government contracts, we are of the opinion that plaintiffs will never know the result until they try.[7] Plaintiffs have a variety of excuses as to why pursuing the prescribed administrative route instead of leaping into court with a constitutional claim would be a waste of their time.

1. Principally plaintiffs claim that in the instances where the investigation has been made and completed, and corrective action taken pursuant to a new, specific affirmative action agreement, the companies are still in violation. If this is true, there is nothing to preclude the

---

which the Senate passed on 2 October 1970, as noted by the plaintiffs,
". . . [T]he committee also believes that an adequate job of providing equal employment opportunity has not, and is not, being provided through the Federal procurement function. There has been far too much nonpublic discussion and negotiation and far too few understandable results. In many instances the [Labor] Department's claim that something major happened, when measured against the demonstration that something actually happened, is grossly lacking in the clarity the the public and minorities can understand.
"In short, OFCC is still suffering from a paucity of credible achievements. . . ."
(S. Rep. No. 91-1137, Equal Employment Opportunities Act (1970), 20), the committee nonetheless "decided not to recommend such changes in the existing legislative structure at the present time" (*Id.*), thus leaving the federal contract compliance function with the OFCC rather than "overburdening" the Equal Employment Opportunity Commission with it. See also Hearings on S. 2453 Before the Subcommittee on Labor of the Senate Committee on Labor and Public Welfare, 91st Cong., 1st Sess. 37, 38, 92-98, 100, 114, 168-69, 194.

6 See 317 F.Supp. 379, 385, n. 5.

7 Our dissenting colleague accepts the position of plaintiffs that the administrative, including Title VII, remedies available do not provide "any realistic possibility for the relief plaintiffs seek," adding that under these administrative procedures "the government participates in the form of judge or mediator, but a declaration of governmental duties and responsibilities is not contemplated by such procedures." First, considering that Congress and the Executive Branch labored long and hard to create just these procedures, we are reluctant to hold that all this was in vain because these remedies do not provide "any realistic possibility for the relief plaintiffs seek" in precisely those situations for which they were designed. At least we would not so hold on the showing made by plaintiffs here. Secondly, in the absence of final administrative action on plaintiffs' applications here, how can anyone be certain that a judicial declaration of governmental duties and responsibilities is required at all? In the interest of avoiding unnecessary, or duplicitous, governmental action, particularly in the light of the crowded dockets confronting the judiciary at present, it would appear most sensible for the court to await final administrative action here before proceeding, if the need to do so still remains.

plaintiffs from filing another complaint making such factual assertions as they think can be established, and calling for a hearing on such complaint in which the plaintiffs and witnesses offered by them may be allowed to participate.

2. Plaintiffs further assert that neither Executive Order 11246 nor the regulations provide an absolute right to the complainants or witnesses offered by them to participate in such hearings, but the regulations do provide that if there is a hearing the individual complainant may participate in the administrative hearing, if he can show he has an interest in the proceeding and may contribute materially to the proper disposition thereof.[8] *Rosado* v. *Wyman,* 397 U.S. 397, 90 S.Ct. 1207, 25 L.Ed.2d 442 (1970), should not discourage plaintiffs. As the trial court pointed out:
"There the Department of Health, Education and Welfare had 'no procedures whereby welfare recipients may trigger and participate in the Department's review of state welfare programs.' (397 U.S., at 406, 90 S.Ct. at 1215.) Such is not the case here."[9]

3. Plaintiffs further assert that in some (but not all) of the instances where revised contractual obligations have been put into effect following the compliance investigation triggered by the show-cause order, the new contracts have been refused to the plaintiffs on the grounds that these agreements are confidential. Whether this is true or not, we would assume that if a complaint were filed by the plaintiffs in regard to any one of these companies in this situation, the contract provisions would be a matter of relevant evidence at the hearing.

In the present posture of this case the plaintiffs came into the United States District Court without any administrative record whatsoever, for the apparent reason that plaintiffs had never pursued a complaint, if they had filed any in the first instance,[10] under the administrative procedures provided under Executive Order 11246 and the regulations pursuant thereto.[11] Administrative action should be pursued in cases like this one in view of the comprehensive administrative remedies available to the plaintiffs. Finality would be obtained by plaintiffs themselves presenting and pursuing complaints with the OFCC at whatever stage of the compliance agreement process.[12] We cannot say with

[8] 41 C.F.R. § 60-1.26(b).

[9] 317 F.Supp., at 385.

[10] See note 6, *supra.*

[11] We are unable to appreciate plaintiffs' argument that pursuing their administrative remedy somehow involves much more labor on their part. Under a complaint filed with the Office of Federal Contract Compliance all plaintiffs need establish is that the accused company is in violation. Under the action brought in the District Court the plaintiffs by their own theory must establish (1) that the accused company is in violation, and that (2) the appropriate government officials have not taken required action. In the OFCC proceeding there is provision for appointed counsel for each complainant, 41 C.F.R. § 60-1.26(b), in addition to the reasonably expected action of the enforcement officials.

Similarly, under a Title VII court action directed against the companies, discussed under III *infra,* comparative advantages would accrue to plaintiffs.

[12] The plaintiffs' grievances might arise at any one of three stages: (1) Before any

exactitude what will occur if the plaintiffs go to the Office of Federal Contract Compliance and file a complaint in each of the eleven instances which they cited to the District Court and now cite to this court. But we are assured that one of several things will happen: (1) the Office of Federal Contract Compliance may actually reject the complaint on the ground that the matter has already been investigated, compliance assured, and the matter closed; (2) the OFCC may accept the complaint, reopen the investigation, but deny plaintiffs any role in such investigation by offering testimony or otherwise; or (3), the OFCC may reopen the investigation, conduct an open hearing, in which plaintiffs are allowed to participate. In either eventuality, the plaintiffs will have definite administrative action to which to point when they then come into the United States District Court for review under the provisions of the Administrative Procedure Act.[13]

**B.**

Turning now to plaintiffs' second argument against the applicability of the exhaustion doctrine here, the plaintiffs contend that whether their resort to administrative remedies would be useless or useful, they are not relegated to administrative remedies, but can seek redress originally in the federal courts for alleged violation of their constitutional

---

OFCC consideration or action with respect to plaintiffs' complaints; (2) During OFCC consideration or action; or (3) After OFCC consideration and action, in the form either of a finding of no discriminatory practices or acceptance by a company or companies of a compliance agreement, which plaintiffs find is insufficient or not being enforced. In any of these cases, complainants should at first attempt to make full use of the administrative remedies explicitly designed to provide the kind of relief which they seek here—elimination of discriminatory practices on the part of companies. *Having once fully but unsuccessfully pursued the available administrative remedies, plaintiffs would have exhausted them and they would pose no bar to judicial consideration of the plaintiffs' complaints.*

13 Plaintiffs beg a further inadequacy, that they are not assured that the Administrative Procedure Act would give them judicial review of administrative action taken pursuant to regulations promulgated under an Executive Order, in contrast to statute. This bugaboo would seem to have been exercised by *Service* v. *Dulles*, 354 U.S. 363, 77 S.Ct. 1152, 1 L.Ed.2d 1403 (1957).

While the plaintiffs assert that there have been only three instances in the entire history of the OFCC program in which formal hearings were instituted for the purpose of debarring a government contractor (In Matter of Timken Roller Bearing Co., OFCC Docket No. 100-68; In Matter of Allen-Bradley Co., OFCC Docket No. 101-68; and In Matter of Bethlehem Steel Co., OFCC Docket No. 102-68), and that no contract has ever been cancelled, such hearings and subsequent debarment are not, of course, the only manner in which final administrative action may be obtained before judicial consideration is appropriate.

The dissent's assertion that filing a new complaint would merely be fruitless is not warranted in view of the scenario which we envision here. In the event that any of the three possible courses of action described above results, the plaintiffs will have final administrative action and will not have to bear the additional burden of asserting that the specific administrative remedies provided for the very situations involved here are meaningless. In addition, the statement by the dissent that the plaintiffs have been denied an opportunity to present their evidence is incorrect; in the first place, they may be able to present it before the OFCC. In the event they are not asked to do so and receive an adverse decision there, they may seek judicial review again, but this time with the advantage of having final administrative action to which they can point.

rights by government officials. However, the Supreme Court cases cited by plaintiffs and the dissent here in support of this theory do not involve federal officials but do involve state or other non-federal officers, and furthermore were brought against such officials under the Civil Rights Act.[14]

Aside from the fact that plaintiffs' theory is not supported in the cases cited, there are several affirmative reasons why plaintiffs should not be allowed to bring the action originally against these federal officials on this constitutional ground.

First, if the existence of Executive Order 11246 and the implementing regulations providing administrative enforcement of a nondiscrimination policy with government contractors is completely meaningless, it follows—and plaintiffs on oral argument candidly so agreed[15]—that

---

[14] McNeese v. Board of Education, 373 U.S. 668, 83 S.Ct. 1433, 10 L.Ed.2d 622 (1963); Monroe v. Pape, 365 U.S. 167, 81 S.Ct. 473, 5 L.Ed.2d 492 (1961); Damico v. California, 389 U.S. 416, 88 S.Ct. 526, 19 L.Ed.2d 647 (1967). See also 317 F. Supp. 379, 385 (1970). The dissent, in addition to the above-cited Supreme Court cases, cites Chisley v. Richland Parish School Board, 448 F.2d 1251 (5th Cir. 1971), and Hobbs v. Thompson, 448 F.2d 456 (5th Cir. 1971), for the proposition that "the requirement of exhaustion is rapidly disappearing from that area of our jurisprudence dealing with the vindication of constitutional rights." This overlooks the fact, however, that the two Fifth Circuit cases he cites, as well as the three Supreme Court cases referred to above, are concerned with the question of the necessity for exhausting state judicial or administrative remedies prior to seeking relief in the federal courts. Chisley involved a teacher's complaint that he had been dismissed solely because of his race, and the Fifth Circuit therein held that exhaustion of either state judicial or state administrative remedies was not a prerequisite to invoking the federal right provided by the Civil Rights Act of 1871. In Hobbs, involving a challenge to a provision prohibiting city firemen from taking an active part in primary elections and other political activities, the Fifth Circuit reached the same result with respect to the necessity of exhausting state judicial remedies before seeking federal relief under the 1871 Civil Rights Act. In addition, the dissent's reliance on United States v. Frazer, 317 F.Supp. 1079 (M.D.Ala.1970), for the proposition that the basic legal issue in that case and the one at bar is the same, is misplaced. As Judge Johnson himself recognized in Frazer, the remedy provided by Title VII, available to plaintiffs here, "defines the term 'employer' in such a manner as to exclude states or political subdivisions." (317 F.Supp., at 1082). The petitioners in the instant case have a range of administrative remedies carefully articulated by Congress and the Executive Branch to provide precisely the relief they seek, a situation vastly different from that confronting the petitioner, the United States, in Frazer.

[15] The taped transcript of the oral argument reveals the following:
THE COURT: . . . If there were no Executive Order 11246 I take it you would still be here today . . .
PLAINTIFFS' COUNSEL [Mr. Sobol]: Yes, sir.
THE COURT: . . . arguing your constitutional right.
PLAINTIFF'S COUNSEL: Precisely.
THE COURT: Then this means that, to follow it along, in the absence of Executive Order 11246, making this a distinctive case, the theory—your constitutional theory—would still be valid, that you could come into court and ask the court to prohibit any government agency [from] making purchases from any company that was in its conduct violating the Constitution.
PLAINTIFFS' COUNSEL: I would narrow our proposition a little—that the Government knew in its [the company's] employment practices was violating the Constitution. We don't reach the broader case.
. . .
THE COURT: Or, that the Government knew that the company had employment practices which violated the law.
PLAINTIFFS' COUNSEL: Yes, sir.
THE COURT: . . . That if the Government continues dealing with it, the company

whenever a government contractor is allegedly violating any other federal statute, then an original action in a federal court to compel the government department to cease doing business with the private company would lie as a means of enforcement of the statute (or constitutional provision) being violated. To read the due process clause as containing the remedy of government contract cancellation, available to be invoked by an aggrieved private party is a bit unprecedented. Unprecedented, and likewise fraught with the possibility of complete disruption of the usual procedures for statutory enforcement.

And unnecessary. Executive Order 11246, plus supporting comprehensive regulations, was tailored to afford a specific remedy for any violation of the due process clause by racial discrimination committed by government contractors. There is no need to construe the due process clause as containing any particular remedy and being virtually self-executing. The remedy provided by Executive Order 11246 is precisely what the plaintiffs seek here, and directed against the type violators, government contractors, by whose actions plaintiffs may be really aggrieved.

Finally, in view of plaintiffs' constitutional claims advanced in the instant case and the availability of alternate judicial and administrative remedies, it would be particularly inappropriate for this court to involve itself with such constitutional claims at this point. Involvement might well be unnecessary, if the plaintiffs pursued the range of alternatives available to them described above and immediately hereafter. As the Supreme Court stated in *Aircraft & Diesel Corp.* v. *Hirsch*:

"[T]he very fact that constitutional issues are put forward constitutes a strong reason for not allowing this suit either to anticipate or to take the place of [a final alternative judicial or administration procedure]. When that has been done, it is possible that nothing will be left of appellant's claim, asserted both in this proceeding and in this cause, concerning which it will have basis for complaint."[16]

III.

Our conclusion that plaintiffs should not be permitted to initiate an original court action, demanding the remedy of government contract termination with all companies found racially discriminating in employment practices, with the remedy derived directly from the due process clause, is reinforced by the existence of still another remedy to vindicate their rights unresorted to by plaintiffs. Recognizing that Title VII of the Civil Rights Act of 1964 is not an exclusive remedy,[17] and that the

---

in violation of law, under the Constitution you can come in and ask the court to prohibit such government dealings.
THE COURT: All right.
PLAINTIFFS' COUNSEL: Yes sir. Thank you very much.

[16] 331 U.S. 752, at 772, 67 S.Ct. 1493, at 1503, 91 L.Ed. 1796 (1947).

[17] Local 12, *United Rubber Workers* v. *NLRB*, 368 F.2d 12 (5th Cir. 1966), cert. denied, 389 U.S. 837, 88 S.Ct. 53, L.Ed.2d 99 (1967); *Waters* v. *Wisconsin Steel Works*, 427 F2d 476 (7th Cir 1970); *Sanders* v. *Dobbs House, Inc.*, 431 F.2d 1097 (5th Cir. 1970); and Section 706 (b) of the Civil Rights Act of 1964, 42 U.S.C. § 2000e-5 (b).

action is brought directly against the offending company rather than against government officials as plaintiffs have done here, still, if plaintiffs are interested in securing equal employment opportunities with private companies instead of litigating with government officials, this is precisely the purpose for which Title VII was designed.[18]

Indeed, two of the named plaintiffs have filed complaints with the Equal Employment Opportunity Commission, but, as the District Court noted,[19] they have not taken the next steps requisite to instituting civil actions against the companies. Whereas these two or any of the named plaintiffs, or any other employee or applicant, could file charges with the EEOC, and in the court if voluntary compliance were not secured by the Commission, they have not done so. Such Title VII suits may be class actions under Rule 23, F.R.Civ.P.[20] If the charges are proved, all the class plaintiffs can obtain complete relief from the asserted discriminatory employment practices. In so doing, plaintiffs could have the assistance of court-appointed counsel and bring the action without paying the usual fees.[21]

The manifest disinterest of plaintiffs in pursuing the effective remedies provided by Congress and the Executive can be explained only by their desire to create a hitherto unfound construction and implicit remedy in the Fifth Amendment due process clause, i.e., private party class actions to compel government officials to terminate contracts with private companies having racially discriminatory practices without the benefit of any enabling statute or administrative procedure. To do so would be unwise, unprecedented, and in complete disregard of the carefully thought out remedies provided by both Congress and the Executive to vindicate plaintiffs' rights. The dismissal by the District Court is

*Affirmed.*

JOHNSON, Chief District Judge (dissenting): I respectfully dissent.

This action was brought against Melvin R. Laird as Secretary of Defense and Robert L. Kunzig as Administrator of the General Services Administration. The complaint sought (1) a declaratory judgment that the award of contracts by the defendants to racially discriminating companies and the failure to enforce the companies' contractual commitments to nondiscrimination have involved the federal government in discriminatory employment practices which thereby have violated plaintiffs' right to due process under the Fifth Amendment, and (2) an

18 In fact, the Senate has recently passed and the House now has before it legislation which would expand the power of the EEOC by permitting it to seek injunctive relief itself in the federal district courts against those it finds to be engaging in discriminatory employment practices. H.R. 1746, 92d Cong., 2d Sess. as amended and passed Senate, 22 February 1972; 118 Cong.Rec. S2302-2306 (daily ed. 22 February 1972).

19 317 F.Supp., at 387.

20 *Oatis* v. *Crown Zellerbach Corporation,* 398 F.2d 496 (5th Cir. 1968); *Miller* v. *International Paper Company,* 408 F.2d 283 (5th Cir. 1969).

21 42 U.S.C. §§ 2000e-5(e) (k). We do not hold that plaintiffs must allege and prove that they themselves have been discriminated against. It is sufficient if they allege and prove discrimination against any members of the class they purport to represent.

injunction prohibiting the defendants from awarding any further governmental contracts to the discriminating companies and requiring the cancellation or termination of existing contracts with these companies until such time as the discriminatory practices have been eliminated. Despite the clear import of this prayer for relief, the majority would relegate the plaintiffs to the pursuit of what I consider to be wholly inadequate administrative procedures.

There is no doubt that plaintiffs' ultimate goal is the end of what they allege are the racially discriminatory hiring and employment practices of the companies mentioned in this action. This case is a direct attempt to achieve that end. Here plaintiffs seek a declaration of the government's duty affirmatively to secure nondiscriminatory policies among governmental contractors who are being economically sustained by government contracts and public funds.

In my judgment the majority has mis-stated plaintiffs' case by characterizing it as seeking "either strict compliance with equal employment opportunity requirements or the disbarment of the offending companies from government contracts." Rather, the fundamental thrust of plaintiffs' action seeks a judicial declaration outlining the extent to which government officials who contract with companies that engage in racially discriminatory hiring and promotion practices must undertake to end racial discrimination by these companies. To put it more succinctly, plaintiffs are saying that these government officials have failed to fulfill their constitutional duty to contract with only nondiscriminatory companies and have thereby subsidized and continue to subsidize with federal funds widespread, blatant and continuing racial discrimination. Plaintiffs are seeking a judicial declaration of basic constitutional rights.

Neither administrative remedies under Executive Order 11246 nor those available under Title VII provide any realistic possibility for the relief plaintiffs seek. Those avenues are for the resolution of employee-employer conflict. Certainly under either procedure the government participates in the form of judge or mediator, but a declaration of governmental duties and responsibilities is not contemplated by such procedures. It may be that administrative remedies are available to government officials to force offending companies to cease such invidious practices. This fact, however, does not mean that the victims of such practices cannot litigate their rights in the federal judicial system.

Even assuming that the majority is correct that plaintiffs could theoretically gain relief through these administrative procedures, there is a strong contervailing consideration which suggests that such relegation in this case is neither required nor appropriate. It is that the requirement of exhaustion is rapidly disappearing from that area of our jurisprudence dealing with the vindication of constitutional rights. See *Damico* v. *California*, 339 U.S. 416, 88 S.Ct. 526, 19 L.Ed.2d 647 (1967); *McNeese* v. *Board of Education*, 373 U.S. 668, 83 S.Ct. 1433, 10 L.Ed.2d 622 (1963); *Monroe* v. *Pape*, 365 U.S. 167, 81 S.Ct. 473, 5 L.Ed.2d 492

(1961); *Chisley* v. *Richland Parish School Board,* 448 F.2d 1251 (5th Cir. 1971); *Hobbs* v. *Thompson,* 448 F.2d 456 (5th Cir. 1971).

I get the impression that the majority may be saying that federal officials are less obligated than their state counterparts to obey the Constitution; certainly, they are no more immune for their violations. See *Bolling* v. *Sharpe,* 347 U.S. 497, 500, 74 S.Ct. 693, 98 L.Ed. 884 (1954). While substantially different from a factual standpoint, the basic legal issue involved in *United States of America by John N. Mitchell, Attorney General* vs. *John S. Frazer, as Director, Alabama Personnel Department,* 317 F. Supp. 1079 (M.D.Ala.1970), regarding the duty of government officials to protect the rights of citizens against infringement by organizations being subsidized with federal funds, is substantially the same. In *United States* v. *Frazer,* the Court determined that the United States was subsidizing various programs that were being administered by the defendant State of Alabama officials. After making a finding of discrimination on the basis of race in hiring and promotional practices on the part of State officials, the Court observed, among other things, that:

"... Failure on the part of any of these Government officials to take legal action in the event that racial discrimination does exist would constitute dereliction of official duty.

"... Here, the United States is seeking to enforce the terms and conditions which Congress expressly imposed upon the expenditure of federal funds. To put it another way, the United States is merely attempting to enforce the express terms and conditions which the State of Alabama agreed to meet in receiving federal funds. . . ."

In the case now before this Court, the only difference is that here the plaintiffs are the ones being discriminated against by the organizations receiving federal funds through various contracts with the United States government being administered by the defendants.

As for the fact that this case is brought under the Fifth Amendment, rather than 42 U.S.C. § 1983, the majority has simply stated a distinction without a difference. Since § 1983 applies only to state action, it is unavailable for challenges to federal officers. More fundamentally, the proper consideration for whether exhaustion is necessary is the similarity of the rights sought to be protected and the reasoning which justifies dispensing with administrative remedies, not the identity of the jurisdictional provision. The crucial factor is that in this case, as in the prior cases, the plaintiffs are seeking protection of or a declaration concerning basic constitutional rights allegedly infringed upon by government officials. There is no sound reason for concluding that an administrative agency is better equipped or more competent than the federal judiciary to determine the merits of plaintiffs' claims.

The majority has also failed to respond adequately to plaintiffs' contention that the administrative remedies are ineffective and unavailing. For example, it is clear from a reading of the regulations that under either the Executive Order or Title VII, the plaintiffs could file complaints against the offending companies. This would not, however, guarantee plaintiffs the right to participate in the agency proceedings, although they may be permitted to do so. They have no control whatever over the investigation or prosecution of the action. They must file the complaint and then hope for the best. I find this case sufficiently similar to *Rosado* v. *Wyman,* 397 U.S. 397, 90 S.Ct. 1207, 25 L.Ed.2d 442 (1970), to render exhaustion inappropriate.

In addition, past practice demonstrates that without a judicial declaration of their duties under the Constitution, the defendant federal officials are unlikely to take the action plaintiffs desire. Plaintiffs alleged that as to at least four of the 11 firms involved here, the OFCC has investigated and found the companies to be discriminating. Yet no action has been taken. Administrative hearings have been held and the defendant officials continue to deal and contract with the discriminating companies. The majority says that if the companies are still violating, then a new complaint can be filed. The mere suggestion of such redundancy, however, points out the fruitlessness of the action.

In sum, it seems to me to be highly ironic that this Court is relegating a claim of constitutional violation by federal officials to other federal administrators despite the fact that the administrators have already exhibited their disinterest in safeguarding plaintiffs' rights. It may be that the Fifth Amendment does not require the cancellation of contracts made by government officials with discriminating companies. Plaintiffs, however, have been denied an opportunity to present their evidence since the case went out in the district court without a hearing. I would remand the case for a hearing of the merits.

## NOTE

Where the statute, or in this case the executive order, is silent on the rights of those affected to seek judicial assistance, what should the courts' response be when efforts are made to secure relief? See *e.g. Implied Rights of Action to Enforce Civil Rights: The Case for a Sympathetic View,* 87 YALE L. J. 1378 (1978), and *Implied Private Actions Under Federal Statutes—The Emergence of a Conservative Doctrine,* 18 WILLIAM & MARY L. REV. 429 (1976).

## LEGAL AID SOCIETY OF ALAMEDA COUNTY v. BRENNAN

*United States District Court, Northern District of California, 1974*
*381 F. Supp. 125, 8 FEP Cases 178*

ZIRPOLI: District Judge: Executive Order 11246, issued September 24, 1965, requires companies that hold federal contracts to:
"take affirmative action to ensure that applicants are employed, and that employees are treated during employment without regard to their race, color, religion, sex or national origin. . . ."

This case involves important questions concerning the enforcement of this executive order and the scope of judicial review of individual governmental agencies' actions taken in its enforcement. Plaintiffs move for partial summary judgment and an order requiring the United States Department of Agriculture [USDA] and the persons within the USDA responsible for enforcing the executive order to refrain from approving affirmative action programs of contractors assigned to the USDA in Alameda County, California, which do not comply with the regulations that set out the requirements of an adequate affirmative action program. Before considering the narrow questions presented by this motion, it is necessary to review the history of this litigation, the executive order and regulations at issue, and consider defendants' objections to the court's jurisdiction.

I. Plaintiffs' original complaint filed in this action in February, 1973, contained four claims for relief, seeking: (1) to compel defendants to release information on the ethnic composition of the work forces of the Alameda County contractors subject to Executive Order 11246; (2) to require the USDA to disclose the affirmative action programs and compliance review reports of Alameda County contractors assigned to the USDA for enforcement purposes; (3) to require defendants responsible for these programs within the USDA to enforce the requirements of Executive Order 11246 and the regulations and orders issued pursuant to the executive order; and (4) to direct the Secretary of Labor and the Director of the Office of Federal Contract Compliance [OFCC], who delegated enforcement responsibility to the USDA, to require the USDA to comply with the executive order and corresponding regulations.

Named as defendants were Peter J. Brennan, Secretary of the Department of Labor, who is responsible for the overall administration of Executive Order 11246, and who is required to "adopt such rules and regulations and issue such orders as he deems necessary and appropriate to achieve the purposes" of the executive order; Philip J. Davis, Director of the OFCC, to whom the responsibility for enforcing the executive order has been delegated; Earl L. Butz, Secretary of the USDA, to which primary enforcement responsibility for federal contractors engaged in farming, the provision of agricultural services, suppliers of food and kindred products, tobacco manufacturers, and certain businesses in the wholesale food trade have been assigned; and finally William Gladden, Chief of the Contract Compliance Division of the USDA's Office of Equal Opportunity, who is ultimately responsible for enforcement within the USDA.

Plaintiffs originally included the Alameda Legal Aid Society, a federally funded law project which represents low income minority persons in Alameda County, California, and which has a compliance project designed specifically to secure the enforcement of laws relating to equal employment opportunity; the director of the project; four unemployed minority persons who have sought employment at businesses which come within the compliance requirements of the executive order and regulations issued thereunder; and the Western Regional Job Council, an unincorporated association in Oakland, California, whose primary concern is the employment of minority persons.

With respect to the third and fourth claims for relief, plaintiffs contend that defendants have failed to enforce Executive Order 11246 and the regulations issued pursuant to it in two respects: (1) they have failed to undertake any review whatsoever of the affirmative action programs of the majority of federal contractors, and (2) that where they have reviewed programs, they have approved ones which fail to comply with the executive order and regulations. Their motion for partial summary judgment deals only with the second contention.

These claims were previously the subject of defendants' motions to dismiss for lack of subject matter jurisdiction and failure to state a claim upon which relief can be granted on the grounds of sovereign immunity, nonreviewability of discretionary agency action, and failure of plaintiffs to exhaust their administrative remedies. These motions were denied by the court May 31, 1973, but they have since been renewed by defendants, and their arguments are discussed more fully below.

Following the denial of defendants' motions to dismiss, plaintiffs obtained the affirmative action programs of some 27 USDA assigned contractors in Alameda County which were reviewed and approved during the period from August, 1972, through January, 1973. Following receipt of these programs, plaintiffs reviewed them and sent the USDA a lengthy and detailed memorandum specifying their claims that the programs as approved were in violation of the applicable regulations, specifically Revised Order Number 4, 41 C.F.R. Part 60-2 (1973), entitled, "Affirmative Action Programs." When no response was made, plaintiffs discussed the issues raised with an attorney from the Department of Labor. Finally, after waiting over two months, plaintiffs brought the motion for partial summary judgment now pending before the court. As initially presented, the motion sought to restrain the USDA from approving affirmative action programs that are not in compliance with Executive Order 11246 and the regulations issued thereunder. A nationwide scope of relief was requested.

. . .

II. It is important to distinguish at the outset that the basis of this action is not the claims of individuals against specific contractors for failure to employ them in a certain job; rather it is an action seeking relief in the nature of mandamus to require federal officers to perform specific and clearly defined duties mandated by Executive Order 11246 and the regulations promulgated pursuant to the executive order.

Defendants argue that a mandamus action is inappropriate here under either the mandamus statute, 28 U.S.C. § 1361, or the Administrative Procedure Act, 5 U.S.C. §§ 701-706, because the acts which plaintiffs seek to compel are committed to the discretion of the agencies involved, because this action is barred by the doctrine of sovereign immunity, and because Executive Order 11246 does not create a private cause of action.

Defendants' principal contention is that Executive Order 11246 is not mandated by any Act of Congress or the Constitution, which therefore makes all federal agency actions taken pursuant to its discretionary and nonreviewable. On the other hand, executive orders clearly carry the force and effect of law if they are issued pursuant to constitutional or statutory authority. This particular executive order and its direct antecedents have consistently been held to be based on statutory authority resting with the President to provide for procurement, utilization, and management of government property. . . .

. . .

Hence, the court concludes that Executive Order 11246 was issued pursuant to constitutional and statutory authority, and has the full force and effect of law. It is axiomatic that regulations issued pursuant to such an executive order also carry the force and effect of law. . . .

Next, defendants urge that whatever effect these regulations have, approval and review of federal contractors' affirmative action programs are not mandatory, but discretionary duties, which are unenforceable in a mandamus-type proceeding.

This argument is amply refuted by the language of the regulations themselves. As noted above, Executive Order 11246 requires companies having federal contracts to:

"take affirmative action to ensure that applicants are employed, and that employees are treated during employment without regard to their race, color, religion, sex, or national origin."

§ 201(1), 3 C.F.R. 169, 170 (1974). The requirements of this "affirmative action" are spelled out in detail in regulations issued by the OFCC, which also set forth the responsibilities of the enforcement agency. . . .

As pointed out by the District of Columbia circuit in *Adams* v. *Richardson,* 480 F.2d 1159 (D.C. Cir. 1973), the agency discretion exception to the general rule that agency action is reviewable is a narrow one, applicable only where the statute and regulations are so broadly drawn there is no law to apply. *Id.* at 1161-62. Executive Order 11246 and the regulations issued thereunder provide detailed and specific guidance to determine the required content of affirmative action programs, and even these regulations have been further explicated by the OFCC.

Furthermore, the appropriate compliance agency response is provided for in affirmative and mandatory language, as set out above. Under these circumstances, defendants are charged with an enforceable legal duty to disapprove affirmative action programs which do not comply with Revised Order Number 4.

Nevertheless, defendants argue the actions taken by the OFCC and the USDA are not reviewable in this court because this is an unconsented suit against the United States and barred by the doctrine of sovereign immunity. *Larson* v. *Domestic & Foreign Corp.,* 337 U.S. 682 (1949). *Dugan* v. *Rank,* 372 U.S. 609, at 620 (1963), states the doctrine as follows:

"The general rule is that a suit is against the sovereign if 'the judgment sought would expend itself on the public treasury or domain, or interfere with the public administration,' or if the effect of the judgment would be 'to restrain the government from acting, or to compel it to act.' " (citations omitted)

Therefore, this suit is barred by the doctrine of sovereign immunity unless it falls within one of the exceptions recognized by these same cases. Plaintiffs' main contention is that the OFCC and the USDA officers have taken improper action and failed to act where clearly required to do so by regulations having the force and effect of law in approving programs which violate the requirements of Revised Order Number 4. Such a claim clearly falls within the ultra vires exception to the bar of sovereign immunity. As stated in *Larson*:

"[w]here the officer's powers are limited by statute, his actions beyond those limitations are considered individual and not sovereign actions. The officer is not doing the business which the sovereign has empowered him to do or he is doing it in a way which the sovereign has forbidden. His actions are *ultra vires* his authority and therefore may be made the object of specific relief."
337 U.S. at 689.

Since plaintiffs allege that the federal defendants have violated a plain legal duty imposed by valid regulations properly issued, and since whatever burden which might be imposed on the federal officials involved is outweighed by the gains anticipated through vigorous enforcement of Executive Order 11246, the court has jurisdiction to review the challenged actions of these government officials on the merits pursuant to 5 U.S.C. §§ 701-706; 28 U.S.C. § 1361; and 28 U.S.C. § 1331. . . .

Finally, defendants argue that the executive order does not create a private right of action against either government officials or private contractors, relying on *Blaze* v. *Moon,* 440 F.2d 1348, 3 FEP Cases 347 (5th Cir. 1971); *Gnotta* v. *United States,* 415 F.2d 1271, 2 FEP Cases 111 (8th Cir. 1969), *cert. denied,* 397 U.S. 934, 2 FEP Cases 451 (1970); *Farkas* v. *Texas Instrument, Inc., supra; Farmer* v. *Philadelphia Electric Co.,* 329 F.2d 3, 1 FEP Cases 36, 55 LRRM 2685 (3d Cir. 1964); and *CORE* v. *Commissioner,* 270 F.Supp. 537, 1 FEP Cases 497, 68 LRRM 2243 (D.Md. 1967). These cases were private suits by individuals seeking relief from or employment with specific government contractors, using various theories employing Executive Order 11246. The present action, however, is a suit against the officials of the federal compliance agencies to require them to comply with their statutory enforcement duties. See *Adams* v. *Richardson, supra.* None of the plaintiffs in this action seeks a particular job with a specific contractor. Indeed, the action is solely directed against federal officials vested with enforcement duties under Executive Order 11246. Without indicating any approval of the holdings in those cases cited by defendants, they are simply inapplicable to this action.

III. Defendants also argue that plaintiffs have failed to exhaust their administrative remedies set out in 41 C.F.R. § 60-1.21 *et seq.* (1973). The regulations in question provide that, "[a]ny employee of any contractor or applicant for employment with such contractor may, . . . file in writing a complaint of alleged discrimination in violation of the equal opportunity clause." 41 C.F.R. § 60-1.21 (1973). The regulations go on to prescribe the proper place to file the complaint, § 60-1.22, its contents,

§ 60-1.23, procedures for investigating and informally resolving the complaint, § 60-1.24, hearings in appropriate cases, § 60-1.26, and authority where necessary to impose the sanctions described in subsections 209(a) (1), (5), and (6) of Executive Order 11246, which include cancellation of government contracts, 41 C.F.R. § 60-1.27 (1973). See also 41 C.F.R. § 60-1.26(b)(2)(v) (1973). It is undisputed that none of the named plaintiffs have filed such complaints against any of the 29 contractors whose affirmative action programs are before the court.

Defendants' argument, however, is based on a misconception of the nature of this action which was discussed previously in considering defendants' claim that no private right of action exists under the executive order. Plaintiffs have steadfastly insisted, and the court is persuaded, that the crux of this action is not complaints of specific acts of discrimination against the named private contractors; rather it is based upon the failure of the federal compliance agencies to require federal contractors to undertake meaningful affirmative action in the employment of minorities and women. The complaint procedure outlined above is designed only to deal with complaints by individuals against the actions of specific companies. The regulations contain no administrative procedures for challenging the actions of the federal enforcement agencies themselves. There are no remedies for plaintiffs to exhaust in this area.

Nevertheless, plaintiffs did file an extensive memorandum with exhibits attached with defendants on September 5, 1973, to which defendants have made no direct response. The memorandum specifically presented plaintiffs' claims that the 27 (now 29) affirmative action programs were deficient in virtually every significant respect. These claims form the substance of plaintiffs' subsequently noticed motion for summary judgment, to which the court now turns.

IV. The essence of plaintiffs' motion for partial summary judgment is that each of the 29 affirmative action programs approved by the USDA in Alameda County during the period from August, 1972, to January, 1973, was in violation of the legal requirements for such programs as set out in the applicable regulations, particularly Revised Order Number 4, 41 C.F.R. Part 60-2 (1973).

Since defendants admit that the affirmative action programs of all 29 contractors were initially reviewed and approved by the USDA during the period specified above, the remaining issues before the court are: (1) whether the programs so approved were in substantial compliance with Revised Order Number 4, and (2) if not, whether the failure of the USDA to enforce the regulations and orders issued pursuant to Executive Order 11246 is excusable, precluding entry of summary judgment and the relief sought by plaintiffs.

Plaintiffs have made a thorough and convincing showing that each of the 29 affirmative action programs approved by the USDA for Alameda County contractors is in violation of the regulations in one or more of the following respects: (1) they contain inadequate utilization analyses which are designed to show each job category in which the contractor is deficient in the utilization of minority persons and women, 41 C.F.R. § 60-2.11 (1973); (2) they fail to establish adequate goals and timetables designed to correct each deficiency within the minimum period necessary, 41 C.F.R. §§ 60-2.10, 60-2.12 & 60-1.20(b) (1973); and (3) they fail to include additional ingredients required by Revised Order Number 4, 41 C.F.R. § 60-2.13 (1973).

. . .

V. In conclusion, therefore, to the extent that the material facts with regard to plaintiffs' motion for partial summary judgment consist of the affirmative action programs themselves which were approved by the USDA, there is no factual dispute. The USDA does not seriously contest plaintiffs' claim that the 29 programs it approved in Alameda County were not in compliance with even the most fundamental requirements of Revised Order Number 4.

The course of the USDA's actions subsequent to the filing of this case further substantiate plaintiffs' claims that the USDA approved flagrantly inadequate affirmative action programs. After plaintiffs questioned the propriety of the USDA's initial approvals, the USDA and OFCC began a review of the 29 Alameda County contractors' affirmative action programs. By mid-March, 1974, this review resulted in issuance of eight show cause notices and six conciliation meetings were conducted. Thus, even the USDA, upon closer analysis, recognized that its earlier approvals were in error. Ordinarily, this subsequent review activity would be an encouraging sign indicating that future compliance with the mandates of Revised Order Number 4 might be achieved without judicial intervention. However, the affidavit of William Gladden, *supra,* shows that these auspicious developments have been achieved only by distorting the USDA's entire review program. Since February, 1972, only three show cause orders have been directed by the USDA to companies unrelated to the 29 Alameda County contractors whose programs are the subject of this litigation; all the show cause orders issued in 1974 have been issued to the Alameda County contractors. Hence, this distortion of the USDA's efforts cannot be taken to demonstrate that the previous course of pro forma review of affirmative action programs so amply demonstrated by plaintiffs will not continue in the future when the attention directed by this lawsuit is removed.

Therefore, injunctive relief is appropriate as a means of assuring compliance by defendants with their own regulations, and necessary because there is a clear danger that the illegal and improper approvals of non-complying affirmative action programs will continue unless defendants are restrained from repetition of their past unlawful review, and because there is no adequate remedy at law or any remedy of any kind whatsoever which can correct defendants' actions.

Accordingly, the court will direct entry of partial summary judgment in favor of plaintiffs regarding the 29 Alameda County contractors whose programs were previously approved by the USDA. Defendants Butz and Gladden will be restrained from approving affirmative action programs which do not contain adequate utilization analyses, goals and timetables, and action oriented programs. These defendants will be further ordered to rescind their approval of those affirmative action programs of contractors that plaintiffs have shown to contain serious and demonstrably inadequate elements required by Revised Order Number 4 and to institute enforcement proceedings against those companies. Finally, to insure compliance with the court's mandate, until further order of the court defendants will be required to submit to the court and counsel for plaintiffs copies of any additional affirmative action programs approved by the USDA for Alameda County contractors along with supporting papers within 15 days of their approval.

Plaintiffs shall submit findings and an appropriate order in accordance with the court's ruling.

## UNITED STATES v. DUQUESNE LIGHT CO.

*United States District Court, Western District of Pennsylvania, 1976*
*423 F.Supp. 507, 13 FEP Cases 1608*

HUBERT I. TEITELBAUM, District Judge: This is an action brought by the United States against the Duquesne Light Company of Pittsburgh to enforce the contractual obligations imposed by Executive Order No. 11246, as amended (3 C.F.R. 169 et seq.). The Executive Order provides that all (non-exempt) contractors with the government agree to engage in non-discriminatory employment practices as part of their contractual obligations.

The complaint alleges that Duquesne Light is a government contractor subject to Executive Order 11246, and that the company has utilized employment practices which discriminate against blacks and women in violation of the Executive Order and the regulations promulgated thereunder. The government seeks, *inter alia*, injunctive relief against Duquesne Light, including compensatory payments (back pay) to black and female employees of the defendant company and to black and female applicants who were rejected for employment.

The case is presently before the Court on Duquesne Light's motion under Rule 12 of the Federal Rules of Civil Procedure to dismiss those portions of the complaint which seek an award of back pay for persons allegedly discriminated against in employment by defendant on the basis of race or sex, and who continue to suffer the current effects of such alleged discrimination; in addition, defendant contends that the instant suit should be dismissed as to its Shippingport Atomic Power Station on grounds that a 30-day show cause notice was not issued by the Federal Energy Research and Development Administration regarding that facility. For reasons noted briefly below, defendant's motion will be denied.

Defendant initially contends that there exists no congressional or constitutional authority for an executive decision to secure [in a breach of contract action] back pay for the victims of racial or sexual discrimination practiced in the past by government contractors. A similar issue was decided in *Contractor's Ass'n* v. *Secretary of Labor*, 442 F.2d 159, 3 **FEP** Cases 395 (3rd Cir. 1971). In that case, plaintiffs challenged the validity of affirmative action programs instituted by the Secretary of Labor under the auspices of Executive Order 11246. The Court of Appeals held that statutory authority for the programs could be found in § 205(a) of the Federal Property and Administrative Services Act of 1949, 40 U.S.C. § 486 (a) [hereinafter "FPASA"].[1] This section empowers the President to take measures to implement the basic policy of the Act, which is to establish an "economical and efficient" system for government procurement of property and services.[2] The affirmative action programs before the Court in *Contractor's Ass'n* were found to be in furtherance of the policy underlying the FPASA because:

". . . it is in the interest of the United States in all procurement to see that its supplier is not over the long run increasing its costs and delaying its programs by excluding from the labor pool available workmen." 442 F.2d at 170, 3 FEP Cases at 402.

Similarly, the President may believe that the availability of restitutionary relief, by providing an incentive to eliminate discriminatory employment practices, would decrease government costs as effectively as would affirmative action programs of the type upheld in *Contractor's Ass'n*. The Court is not concerned with the validity of such a theory; whether *vel non* a backpay order would further the purposes of the Act is a question to be determined by the President under § 205(a) of the FPASA. Here, where the question is the authority of the executive to enact a program, it is enough for the Court to say that neither the language nor the policy of the statute is contradicted by a suit for restitutionary relief.[3]

As an alternative ground for its decision, the Court in *Contractor's Ass'n* stated that the Executive Order could be supported by the inherent authority of the President, regardless of whether statutory authorization could be found. 442 F.2d. at 171, 3 FEP Cases at 403. Whether the authority be inherent or statutory, it would include the right to seek a back-pay order for the reasons stated above.

Having decided that statutory and constitutional authority for the executive to seek restitutionary relief from government contractors

---

[1] [Footnotes numbered as in original.—Ed.] The text of § 205(a) reads: "the President may prescribe such policies and directives, not inconsistent with the provisions of this Act, as he shall deem necessary to effectuate the provisions of said Act, which policies and directives shall govern the Administrator and executive agencies in carrying out their respective functions hereunder." 40 U.S.C. § 486(a) (1970).

[2] 40 U.S.C. § 471 (1970).

[3] Duquesne contends that Congress intended the Civil Rights Act of 1964, and the 1972 amendments to it, 42 U.S.C. § 2000a, et seq. (1970) to be the exclusive source of restitutionary remedies for discriminatory employment practices. The same argument was advanced and rejected with respect to affirmative action programs in *Contractor's Ass'n*. Having examined the relevant portions of the Civil Rights Act and its legislative history, 110 Cong. Rec. 2575, 13650-52, 118 Cong. Rec. 3367-70, 3371-73, 3959-65, this Court finds no support for the contention that Congress intended Title VII to be exclusive of other sources of restitutionary relief. See *Contractor's Ass'n, supra*, at 171-74, 3 FEP Cases at 403-405.

allegedly guilty of discriminatory employment practices does exist, we turn to the question of whether Executive Order 11246 itself and the regulations issued pursuant thereto allow the government to enforce the provisions of the Order by means of an action for, *inter alia,* back pay.

The sanctions and penalties available for the enforcement of the Executive Order are listed in § 209(a) thereof. Under this section, contracts with non-complying contractors may be cancelled or they may be continued upon condition that the contractor comply with the Executive Order in the future. A non-complying contractor may be barred from entering into future contracts with the government. Also, the Secretary of Labor may "[r]ecommend to the Equal Employment Opportunity Commission or to the Department of Justice that appropriate proceedings be instituted under Title VII of the Civil Rights Act of 1964." [4] Nowhere in the Executive Order or its accompanying regulations is a back-pay order specifically mentioned. This should not, however, be interpreted, by negative implication, as a statement of an intention to exclude a back-pay order as a sanction available to remedy violations of the Executive Order. Section 209(a)(2) allows the Secretary of Labor to:

"Recommend to the Department of Justice that, in cases in which there is a material or substantial violation of the contractual provisions set forth in Section 202 of this Order, *appropriate proceedings* be brought to enforce those provisions, including the enjoining, within the limits of applicable law, of organizations, individuals, or groups who prevent directly or indirectly, compliance with the provisions of this Order." (Emphasis added.)

By its reference to "appropriate proceedings," § 209(a)(2) confers on the government discretion to invoke the equitable powers of this Court. Absent a [congressional] limitation upon those powers, the government may seek any remedy which will effectuate the purposes of the Order, provided only that the government is constitutionally or statutorily empowered to request such relief. That this Court has the equitable power to grant, and that the government has authority to seek restitutionary relief are established propositions. *Mitchell* v. *DeMario Jewelry,* 361 U.S. 288, 14 WH Cases 416 (1959); *Porter* v. *Warner Co.,* 328 U.S. 395 (1945). This Court therefore decides that the Executive Order does permit the government to request restitutionary relief.[5]

[4] 3 C.F.R. at 173.

[5] Duquesne Light seeks to avoid the above result by pointing out that this is an action for breach of contract and that general principles of contract law do not permit the relief sought by the government. The government is here seeking restitution; not for itself, but for the victims of past discrimination allegedly practiced by defendant. Duquesne admits that a promisee (the government here) may sue to enforce the provisions of a contract designed to benefit a third-party beneficiary. But Duquesne denies that discriminatees are third-party beneficiaries of the Executive Order. Duquesne also argues that a promisee seeking to enforce contract provisions in favor of a third-party beneficiary is entitled only to specific performance and is not entitled to recover damages.

Were this an ordinary contract action the Court would be constrained to delve more deeply into the issues of contract law presented by the defendant. But while this action is ostensibly brought in contract, it is in actuality an attempt to enforce a statutorily-authorized administrative program. Executive Order 11246, while enacted pursuant to

Section 209(b) of Executive Order 11246 provides that:

"Under rules and regulations prescribed by the Secretary of Labor, each contracting agency shall make reasonable efforts within a reasonable time limitation to secure compliance with the contract provisions of this Order by methods of conference, conciliation, mediation and persuasion before proceedings shall be instituted under sub-section (a)(2) of this section. . . ."

Under the authority granted him by § 209(b), the Secretary has issued 41 C.F.R. § 60-2.2, providing that:

"Immediately upon finding that a contractor has no affirmative action program or has deviated sustantially from an approved affirmative action program or that his program is not acceptable, the contracting officer, the compliance agency representative or the representative of the Office of Federal Contract Compliance, whichever has made such a finding, shall notify officials of the appropriate compliance agency and the office of Federal Contract Compliance of such fact. The compliance agency shall issue a notice to the contractor giving him 30 days to show cause why enforcement proceedings under Section 209(b) [sic—"(a)"] of Executive Order 11246, as amended, should not be instituted.
. . .
"(2) During the 'show cause' period of 30 days every effort shall be made by the compliance agency through conciliation, mediation, and persuasion to resolve the deficiencies which led to the determination of non-responsibility. . . ."

The defendant maintains numerous contracts with the government, most of which are with the General Services Administration (GSA). Duquesne also maintains a contract with the government relating to the operation of its Shippingport Atomic Power Station (SAPS). Unlike the other contracts, this contract is not with GSA but with the Pittsburgh Naval Reactors Office (PNRO) of the Energy Research and Development Administration (ERDA). Duquesne concedes that a "show cause" order effective to satisfy the requirements of 41 C.F.R. § 60-2.2 was issued by GSA. It argues, however, that the SAPS facility may not be brought into this action because ERDA, the compliance agency for SAPS, has not issued a "show cause" notice, even though, as stated in the complaint (the allegations of which must be regarded as true for the purpose of this motion), the GSA notice referred to the SAPS facility and ERDA participated in attempts to secure voluntary compliance with Executive Order 11246.

The Court is persuaded by the government's arguments that the notice requirements of 41 C.F.R. § 60-2.2 were satisfied. The "show cause" notice may not have gone out under ERDA's letterhead, but the GSA "show cause" notice and ERDA's participation in attempts to seek voluntary compliance with the Executive Order substantially satisfied the notice requirements.

---

the authorization given the President in the FPASA, is intended to effectuate the government policy, indeed the constitutional command, against invidious discrimination. The remedies available to enforce such a measure should not be limited to those discernible by reference to ordinary principles of contract law.

The Court also questions the need for a "show cause" notice to be issued before the government can commence judicial proceedings—the full text of § 60-2.2 apparently contemplates that a "show cause" notice is required as a condition before holding an *administrative* hearing leading to the concellation of contracts or debarment from future contracts. But having decided that the requirements of § 60-2.2 were substantially adhered to, the Court need not reach the issue of whether a "show cause" notice must issue before judicial enforcement of the Executive Order is possible. See *United States* v. *Mississippi Power and Light Co.,* _____ F. Supp. _____, 10 FEP Cases 1084 (S.D. Miss., April 21, 1975); *United States* v. *New Orleans Public Service, Inc.,* _____ F. Supp. _____, 8 FEP Cases 1089 (E.D. La., Nov. 13, 1974).

An appropriate Order will be entered in accordance with this memorandum.

### ORDER

AND Now, to-wit, this 30th day of November, 1976, in consideration of the foregoing memorandum of decision in the above-captioned case, IT IS ORDERED that defendant's motion to partially dismiss the government's complaint be and the same is hereby denied.

It appearing to the Court that the government has filed an amended complaint joining as defendants the unions which represent Duquesne employees, IT IS FURTHER ORDERED that the defendant company's motion to dismiss the complaint for failure to join indispensable parties be and the same is hereby denied as moot.

## NOTES

1. See also *National Association for the Advancement of Colored People* v. *Federal Power Commission,* 96 S. Ct. 1806, 12 FEP Cases 1251 (May 19, 1976).

In this case the NAACP and several other organizations representing blacks, Spanish-speaking Americans, and females petitioned the FPC for the issuance of a rule requiring equal employment opportunity and non-discrimination in the employment practices of those organizations which the Federal Power Commission regulates. The FPC refused to initiate the rule-making proceedings, asserting that it had no jurisdiction to adopt such a rule. On petition for review, the court of appeals, while agreeing that the FPC lacked power to prescribe personnel practices in detail and to act upon personnel complaints, held that the FPC had "power to take into account, in the performance of its regulatory function, including licensing and rate review, evidence that the regulatee is a demonstrated discriminator in its employment relations." The Supreme Court granted certiorari and determined that the FPC's duty to advance the "public interest" did not afford any basis for its prohibiting regulatees from engaging in discriminatory employment practices. It held that the "public interest" in the Federal Power Act and in the Natural Gas Act required the FPC to promote the orderly production of supplies of electric energy and natural gas at just and reasonable rates but did not constitute a directive to that Commission to seek to eradicate employment discrimination. The Supreme Court held, however, that the FPC is authorized to consider the consequences of discriminatory employment practices of its regulatees insofar as such consequences might be directly related to the establishment of just and reasonable rates in the public interest. To the extent that discriminatory employment practices of regulatees could be demonstrably quantified by judicial decree or final action of an administrative agency to show that illegal duplicative or unnecessary labor costs are demonstrably the product of such discrimination, the Federal Power Commission should disallow them.

This case is an example of creative use of the rule-making authority of administrative agencies as a vehicle to secure review of employment discrimination practices although the plaintiffs were less than totally successful in their efforts to require the agency to adopt rules. See also *Office of Communications of United Church of Christ* v. *FCC*, 359 F.2d 994 (D.C. Cir. 1966).

2. See *Timken Company* v. *Vaughan*, 12 FEP Cases 1140 (D.C. N.D. Ohio, May 3, 1976), for a case in which the company debarred from further government contracts with the United States or agencies thereof by an order of the Department of Defense sued for declaratory judgment and injunctive relief against such debarment. The court held that the U.S. Defense Department's determination of noncompliance with Executive Order 11246 was subject to review by a federal district court under the Administrative Procedures Act, and that such debarment orders were subject to be set aside if arbitrary, capricious, or abusive of discretion, or if the agency failed to meet statutory procedures of constitutional requirements. The district court reversed the decision of the Defense Department on grounds that its factual determinations were not supported by substantial evidence.

3. See also *Savannah Printing Union* v. *Union Camp Corp.*, 350 F. Supp. 632, 5 FEP Cases 670 (D.C. Ga. 1972), on the conflict between layoff provisions of a collective bargaining agreement and Executive Order 11246. Modifications in layoff provisions were ordered although the provisions were "neutral on their face." Compare *Jersey Central Power & Light Co.* v. *IBEW*, 508 F.2d 687, 9 FEP Cases 117 (3rd Cir. 1975), *vacated and remanded*, 425 U.S. 987, 12 FEP Cases 1335 (1976).

## (4)  Limits on Governmental Action

## UNITED STATES v. NEW ORLEANS PUBLIC SERVICE, INC.

### United States Court of Appeals, Fifth Circuit, 1977
### 553 F.2d 459, 14 FEP Cases 1734

AINSWORTH, Circuit Judge: Appellant, New Orleans Public Service, Inc. (hereinafter NOPSI), appeals from an adverse decision of the district court holding that NOPSI is a government contractor subject to Executive Order 11246,[1] and permanently enjoining NOPSI from failing and refusing to comply with the Order, as amended, and the implementing rules and regulations. Questions as the force, coverage and enforcement of the Executive Order are involved. The principal issue today before us is whether a public utility which, under a city permit, enjoys a local monopoly in the sale of electricity and a near-monopoly in the sale of natural gas and which sells such energy to the Government in substantial amount can be required by the Government to comply with the equal opportunity obligations of Executive Order 11246, even though the utility has not agreed to be so bound. We hold that the Government can compel such a utility to follow the Order; however, we disagree with the district court as to the appropriate remedy.

Executive Order 11246 prohibits employment discrimination by government contractors. The Order was issued by President Johnson in 1965, and requires that all covered government contracts contain a nondiscrimination clause, including an agreement to take affirmative action to achieve the equal opportunity goals of the Executive Order's mandate. *Id.* § 202.

NOPSI is a public utility which produces, distributes and sells electric power to consumers located in that part of New Orleans, Louisiana, on the east bank of the Mississippi River, and sells and distributes natural gas to consumers throughout the city. The company sells its gas and electricity pursuant to indeterminate permits,[2] like franchises, issued by the City Council of New Orleans. NOPSI is the only company with indeterminate permits to supply New Orleans with gas, and the east bank of the city with electricity. If any New Orleans consumer (including the Federal Government) on the east bank wishes to buy electric service, the consumer must purchase from NOPSI. NOPSI also provides most of the natural gas service to consumers (including the Federal Government) throughout the city, and in those cases where companies receive their

---

[1] [Footnotes numbered as in original.—Ed.] 30 Fed. Reg. 12319 (1965), 3 C.F.R. 339 (1964-1965 Compilation), as amended by Exec. Order No. 11375, 32 Fed. Reg. 14303 (1967), 3 C.F.R. 406 (1969), 42 U.S.C.A. § 2000e note (1974), superseded in part (irrelevant for purposes herein) by Exec. Order No. 11478, 34 Fed. Reg. 12985 (1969), 3 C.F.R. 133 (1969 Compilation), 42 U.S.C.A. § 2000e note (1974).

[2] Under an indeterminate permit, the company is granted the right to supply such services indefinitely, but the grantor City Council retains the right to buy the utility operation from the company, thus terminating the permit.

gas from other sources, NOPSI has agreed to the arrangement and has built and maintained the transmission line connecting the company with the parish boundary. The federal agencies which buy electricity from NOPSI are on the east bank, and have no alternative source of electric power. NOPSI is regulated by the City Council, which in 1973 granted the company rate increases for its electric and natural gas services to customers.

A number of federal agencies and installations in New Orleans are major purchasers of electricity and natural gas from NOPSI. In 1973 NOPSI supplied such federal users with nearly $2 million worth of electricity utility service, and with more than $2,680,000 worth of electric and natural gas utility services combined. There are nine federal agencies which at the present time and during the period 1965-1973 each have received over $10,000 annually in combined gas and electric services from NOPSI: some of those each have received more than $50,000 in such utility services annually. The biggest user, the Michoud Assembly Facility (hereinafter Michoud) of the National Aeronautics and Space Administration (hereinafter NASA), alone received approximately $1.4 million worth of electricity and natural gas in 1973. The agencies are billed monthly and pay for the services on a regular basis.

According to the district court opinion, NOPSI supplies the Government with utility services pursuant to various contractual arrangements. The court found that NOPSI is supplying 22 federal agencies under written agreements. Some of those contracts predated the Executive Order, but the court found that they were modified by, *inter alia,* the 1973 revised rate schedules which were approved by the City Council; were applied to the particular contract by NOPSI; and were accepted, through payment, by the agency. A few of those contracts contained nondiscrimination clauses required by earlier Executive Orders. In the case of two agencies in the group, the Government had sent NOPSI a proposed new contract, containing the nondiscrimination clause required by Executive Order 11246, but NOPSI rejected the proposed contract on the ground that the clause was unsatisfactory. Other contracts were signed in 1972 or on dates not specified by the district court opinion and were modified by the revised rate schedules in 1973.

In addition, the district court found that NOPSI is supplying six other federal agencies pursuant to contracts which were not formal, written agreements. Some of those contracts, for example, were based on letter requests from the federal agencies; another was based on an oral agreement.

Somewhat more complicated is the relationship between NOPSI and NASA's Michoud facility. Disagreement in that relationship precipitated the instant litigation. NOPSI supplied Michoud with electricity and natural gas under a written contract between the utility and the space agency which was signed in 1965 and terminated according to its own terms in June 1970. That contract contained an equal opportunity clause which was required by Executive Order 10925, the predecessor of Executive Order 11246. The contract also contained a limitation clause restricting the scope of the contract to the Michoud operations. Because of the NASA-NOPSI relationship involving utilities service at Michoud, the Government has tried in the past to review NOPSI's compliance with Executive Order 11246, but NOPSI has resisted on the ground that it was not covered by the Order. Attempts between the Government and NOPSI to negotiate a new utilities contract for Michoud broke down, with the Government unwilling to agree to a scope limitation like that in the 1965 contract, and NOPSI unwilling to agree to an equal opportunity clause without such a limitation. Nevertheless, NASA asked NOPSI to continue supplying Michoud, and NOPSI has continued to do so even though the formal contract has expired, subject to the rate schedules set out by NOPSI at the time of the termination of the written contract. The district court, after surveying the preceding facts, held that a contract existed between NASA and NOPSI.[3]

The Government's efforts to conduct a compliance review of NOPSI began in 1969, and further unsuccessful attempts were made through 1972. This action was initiated by the Government through the Justice Department in 1973 to compel NOPSI's compliance with the Executive Order. After holding that NOPSI was covered by the Order, the district court permanently enjoined the utility from failing or refusing to comply with the Order and implementing regulations. The injunction reached NOPSI's refusal to allow the Government to conduct compliance reviews of NOPSI, and authorized the parties to begin discovery. In addition, the court retained continuing jurisdiction to effectuate NOPSI's full compliance with the Executive Order.

### I. THE VALIDITY AND APPLICABILITY OF THE EXECUTIVE ORDER

. . .

For purposes of the instant case, the critical—and disputed—provision of the federal contract compliance program is found in the Secretary of Labor's regulations, 41 C.F.R. § 60-1, as amended by 42 Fed.Reg. 3254, et seq. (1977), and states:

"(e) *Incorporation by operation of the Order.*—By operation of the Order, the equal opportunity clause shall be considered to be a part of every contract and subcontract required by the Order and the regulations in this part to include such a clause whether or not it is physically incorporated in such contracts and whether or not the contract between the agency and the contractor is written."

§ 60-1.4(e)[5] Cf. *id.* § 60-1.4(d) (incorporation by reference). The "equal

---

[3] The facts indicating the circumstances under which NOPSI supplied energy to the various government agencies are laid out fully in the district court's opinion, and are incorporated herein except insofar as they indicate specific contractual arrangements between NOPSI and the Government. The long-standing seller-purchaser relationship indisputedly makes NOPSI a government contractor, and further contractual underpinning is unnecessary for our holding.

[5] We note that, although certain changes in the regulations have occurred as a result of the 1977 amendments, the result we reach today would be the same whether or not

opportunity clause" referred to in the regulation is the nondiscrimination clause set forth in the Executive Order. "Contract" means any "government contract," and "government contract" is defined to include "any agreement or modification thereof between any contracting agency and any person for the furnishing of supplies or services." *Id.* § 60-1.3. The term "services," as used in the regulation, includes utility services. Id. Executive Order 11246 states in section 202 that the Order applies to every government contract entered into after the effective date unless the contract is specifically exempted under section 204. No such exemption is applicable in the instant case.[6] Therefore, assuming no problems concerning the Order's basic validity or its application herein, NOPSI is clearly subject to the requirements of the program.

B. NOPSI'S ARGUMENT

NOPSI argues that the Executive Order and the regulations do not give the Labor Department's Office of Federal Contract Compliance— the agency which administers the Executive Order—authority to compel the company to fulfill the affirmative action obligations of the program. In support of its position, NOPSI offers three arguments which speak to the validity of the regulations as herein applied, from the point of view of both executive power and general contract law.

First, NOPSI points out that it did not seek the Government's business or any government contracts. NOPSI contends that the relevant judicial decisions on the Executive Order all involved employers that sought the Government's business, e.g., by bidding for government contracts, or were unquestionably government contractors, and that each case therefore presented an element of consent which is here lacking. Second, the company argues that it has consistently refused to accept the Order's affirma-

---

the new regulations were in effect. Furthermore, we would apply the current version of the regulations in any event, since this appeal involves both a program requiring present compliance by NOPSI and a continuing injunctive order of the district court. The language of the provision cited in the accompanying text reflects a minor change. The Labor Department's comments state:
"The effect of the change in § 60-1.4(e) is to make it clear that, consistent with the intent of the Secretary and with existing case law, the equal opportunity clause is considered a part of all nonexempt contracts, including unwritten contracts. . . ." 42 Fed. Reg. 3454 (1977).

6 Section 204 of the Order provides that the Secretary of Labor may grant an exemption to a specific contract because of "special circumstances," or may exempt "facilities of a contractor which are in all respects separate and distinct from activities of the contractor related to the performance of the contract: *Provided,* That such an exemption will not interfere with or impede the effectuation of the purposes of this Order. . . ."
No such exemption has been granted to NOPSI. Section 204(3) also provides for a class exemption, by rule or regulation, for contracts involving less than specified amounts of money. A contract which exceeds $10,000 (or a contract of a government contractor having an aggregate total of government contracts within a twelve-month period in excess of $10,000) is not exempt under section 204(3) from the requirements of the nondiscrimination clause. 41 C.F.R. 60-1.5, 42 Fed. Reg. 3454, 3459 (1977). Therefore, NOPSI is a nonexempt contractor. The effective date of the Order causes no problem since the case involves a contractual relationship which, in particular instances, has been renewed or modified by the parties since such effective date. See discussion *infra.*

tive action obligation. This argument, related to the first, assumes the necessity of NOPSI's consent in order for the company to be bound by the nondiscrimination clause. Third, NOPSI contends that it is not furnishing energy to the Government pursuant to any contract, but instead is supplying such energy pursuant to its franchises, granted by the City, which require NOPSI to provide power to all consumers who request it. Under that argument, NOPSI's status as a City franchisee precludes its having the status of a Federal Government contractor, given the fact that NOPSI has refused to accede to the contract terms required by the Government. Accordingly, NOPSI and amicus Mississippi Power & Light Company, appellant in No. 75-2590, 5 Cir., 1977, slip opinion p. 3610, _____ F.2d _____, 14 FEP Cases 1730, the companion case which we also decided today, challenge the application of the Executive Order both on the ground that it conflicts with the contractual principle of consent, and that it is action taken without authority from Congress.

C. THE PROGRAM'S FORCE AND EFFECT

The starting point of our analysis is the well-established proposition that the Order has the force and effect of law.

[The court's discussion of authorities supporting the validity of the Executive Order program is omitted.]

. . . However, Congress not only has refused to circumscribe the role of the Office of Federal Contract Compliance in combating employment discrimination, but has indicated a concern for the efficacy of such efforts and an intent that they would continue. The regulation in controversy is an integral part of a long-standing program which Congress has recognized and approved. We have no difficulty, therefore, in finding congressional authorization for the provision.[8] It follows that the application

---

[8] NOPSI argues that application of the Executive Order herein contravenes the principle in *Youngstown Sheet & Tube Co.* v. *Sawyer,* 343 U.S. 579 (1952), in which the Supreme Court held that President Truman's seizure of the steel mills was unlawful. In *Youngstown,* however, Congress had refused to authorize governmental seizure of property as was therein attempted. Therefore, the President had acted in the face of that congressional decision and in the absence of any other power authorizing his action. See 343 U.S. at 585-89. The instant case is thus distinguishable, since the Executive acted here pursuant to congressional authorization. The application of the Order today before us falls within the first category of executive power—that of maximum power—which Justice Jackson identified in his concurring opinion in *Youngstown,* 343 U.S. at 635-37; see *Contractors Ass'n, supra,* 442 F.2d at 168-71, 3 FEP Cases at 401-403. Furthermore, the analogy to a seizure is manifestly imprecise.

At oral argument, NOPSI also cited *NAACP* v. *FPC,* 425 U.S. 662, 12 FEP Cases 1251 (1976), in which the Supreme Court held that the Federal Power Commission did not have authority under the Federal Power Act and the Natural Gas Act to issue a rule prohibiting discriminatory employment practices by the agency's regulatees. However, *FPC* does not aid appellant's position. The opinion does not hold that an agency cannot issue regulations concerning affirmative action, assuming the agency has a statutory basis for doing so, nor does it suggest that issuance of such regulations is prohibited unless Congress has authorized the agency to promulgate them. Furthermore, the Court did hold that the *FPC* indirectly could regulate discriminatory employment practices by its regulatees, to the extent that such practices demonstrably affected a regulatee company's labor costs. *Id.,* 425 U.S. at 666-70, 12 FEP Cases at 1253-54. Therefore, under *FPC,* a government agency can regulate discriminatory employment prac-

of the Order to NOPSI is also authorized, for such action requires no extension of the regulation's coverage. The regulation incorporating by operation of the Order the nondiscrimination clause into every government contract would be a dead letter if the Government could not apply it to a government contractor like NOPSI, merely because the company refused to consent.

Although no circuit has confronted the precise legal issue today before us, we find the *Contractors Ass'n* case to be a very persuasive precedent. There the Third Circuit specifically considered the validity of the Philadelphia Plan, relating to minority hiring in federally-assisted construction projects, which was promulgated pursuant to Executive Order 11246. The court upheld the Plan, on the ground that it was within the implied authority of the President. Insofar as the Philadelphia Plan was instituted to implement the mandate of the Executive Order in a particular geographic area and industry, the court's holding clearly flowed from a view that the Executive Order program itself was valid, at least with respect to federally-assisted construction contracts. Moreover, in language on all fours, the Third Circuit specifically stated that Executive imposition of nondiscrimination contract provisions (including an affirmative action clause) in the Government procurement area is action pursuant to the express or implied authorization of Congress. 442 F.2d at 170, 3 FEP Cases at 403.

In response to the argument that a decision for the Government in this case would go beyond the Third Circuit's holding in *Contractors Ass'n*, we believe that our decision today fits within that precedent and, in fact, approves a more confined power than did the *Contractors Ass'n* court. We here impose the nondiscrimination obligation on a company which,

---

tices to the extent that such discrimination is related directly to the agency's functions. That principle should be read in light of *Rosetti Contracting* and *Northeast Constr.*, which involve the Executive Order herein and require only a loose relationship between the noneconomic objective, *i.e.*, regulating employment discrimination, and the procurement function. *Rosetti Contracting, supra*, 508 F.2d at 1045 n. 18, 9 FEP Cases at 178; *Northeast Constr., supra*, 485 F.2d at 760-61, 5 FEP Cases at 751-52. We also note *Mississippi Power & Light's* citation of *Hampton* v. *Mow Sun Wong*, 426 U.S. 88, 12 FEP Cases 1377 (1976), apparently to rebut the proposition that Congress ratifies executive orders by subsequently recognizing their existence and making reference to them. However, to the extent that the Supreme Court addressed this issue in *Mow Sun Wong*, the opinion turned on the particular facts in controversy. That case involved, *inter alia*, the question whether acquiescence by the Executive and Congress in a Civil Service Commission policy imposing a citizenship requirement on federal employees was sufficient to give the Commission rule the same support as an express statutory or presidential command. The Court held that neither appropriations acts nor executive orders in which Congress and the President, respectively, had considered the policy and spoken to it in some fashion could fairly be read as evidencing either approval or disapproval of the policy by either branch. *Id.*, 426 U.S. at 104-14, 12 FEP Cases at 1383-88. The opinion makes clear, though, that the legislative history and executive orders there in dispute could arguably be taken either way, *i.e.*, they might be read as evidencing either disapproval or approval, and it was that ambiguity which gave rise to the Court's statement. Thus, *Mow Sun Wong* is clearly distinguishable from the case at bar. The legislative history behind the program today before us lacks such ambiguity as dictated the *Mow Sun Wong* result. Furthermore, the cited case lacked the clear directive from the Executive—by Executive Order—which is the very source of the program we confront and uphold herein.

as a public utility, holds City-granted franchises and, pursuant thereto, (1) enjoys special economic advantages, including a monopoly, and (2) sells directly to the Government. To so apply the provision is far easier, in our judgment, than to apply it, as in *Contractors Ass'n* to a mere bidder for federally-assisted construction project contracts. The ease of application is a function of both the Government's legal power and the utility's economic power in their direct contractual relationship.

### E. CONTRACT LAW

The second aspect of NOSPI's attack on the Executive Order as herein applied focuses on contract law. The company contends that its lack of consent to be bound by the nondiscrimination clause distinguishes the prior cases involving the validity of the Order. Whatever, if any, authorization exists for the program is vitiated when, as here, it is imposed on a nonconsenting public utility, the company argues, because the contractual consent principle is violated. We disagree.

We find that the absence of NOPSI's consent to the Executive Order is not determinative, and does not render the prior caselaw distinguishable. Furthermore, we reject the company's contention that NOPSI is not a government contractor.

Government contracts are different from contracts between ordinary parties. See *M. Steinthal & Co.* v. *Seamans,* 1971, 147 U.S.App.D.C. 221, 455 F.2d 1289, 1304. See also Vaketta & Wheeler, *A Government Contractor's Right to Abandon Performance,* 65 Geo.L.J. 27 (1976). The Government has the unrestricted power to determine those with whom it will deal, and to fix the terms and conditions upon which it will make needed purchases. *Perkins* v. *Lukens Steel Co.,* 310 U.S. 113, 127, 1 WH Cases 54 (1940); *Southern Ill. Bldrs. Ass'n* v. *Ogilvie,* S.D.Ill., 1971, 327 F. Supp. 1154, 3 FEP Cases 571, *aff'd,* 471 F.2d 680, 5 FEP Cases 229 (7 Cir., 1972); cf. *King* v. *Smith,* 392 U.S. 309 (1968); Vacketta & Wheeler, *supra.* Agreement to such conditions is unnecessary: where regulations apply and require the inclusion of a contract clause in every contract, the clause is incorporated into the contract, even if it has not been expressly included in a written contract or agreed to by the parties. *M. Steinthal, supra,* at 1304; *J. W. Bateson Co.* v. *United States,* 1963, 162 Ct.Cl. 566, 569; *G. L. Christian, supra,* 312 F.2d at 424; see *Russell Motor Car Co.* v. *United States,* 261 U.S. 514 (1923). See also *De Laval Steam Turbine Co.* v. *United States,* 284 U.S. 61 (1931); *College Point Boat Corp.* v. *United States,* 267 U.S. 12 (1925).[9]

A contractual relationship obviously exists between NOPSI and the Government, notwithstanding the company's attempt to disclaim government-contractor status. This contractual relationship exists by virtue of

---

[9] A contract between the Government and one of its contractors need not be in writing in order to be enforceable. See, *e.g.,* Pattern, *Government Contracts—Are They Enforceable If Not in Writing?,* 7 Pub. Contract L.J. 232 (1975). Similarly, the applicability of the Executive Order to NOPSI does not depend upon the existence of a formal written contract. We do not say today that no such contract exists between NOPSI and the Government, since resolution of that question is unnecessary to our holding.

the fact that the company sells millions of dollars worth of utility services to various agencies of the Federal Government, and has done so for many years. The district court's extensive factual findings as to particular contracts aids us in this determination; however, we would reach it even in the absence of any oral or written agreements to particular terms, because the relationship so clearly reflects a contract.

Furthermore, we cannot understand how NOPSI seriously can deny status as a government contractor for the reason that it is supplying utility services to the Government pursuant to local franchises which require the company to furnish such energy to all consumers who request it. That the company services customers under local franchises does not negate the obvious fact that NOPSI renders such services to individual customers pursuant to contracts, whether written or parol, and whether explicit or implicit in the parties' course of dealing.

NOPSI's status as a public utility, operating under local franchises granted by the City of New Orleans, and providing services to the United States, renders the utility's express consent unnecessary in light of the Executive Order. Acceptance of the benefits of the local franchises subjected NOPSI to the obligations attached thereto. Cf. *Almeida-Sanchez* v. *United States,* 413 U.S. 266, 271 (1973). When NOPSI undertook to satisfy those obligations by selling energy to the Government, the company did so according to the terms imposed by the Government.[10]

NOPSI implies, in addition, that because of its public-utility status, imposition of the Executive Order's requirements would be unfair. The unfairness, the company suggests, stems from NOPSI's lack of choice as to whether to accept the Government's business. However, the fact that NOPSI is a public utility militates strongly in *favor* of allowing the Government to impose the obligations of the Executive Order on the company. NOPSI's franchises give it a local monopoly in the sale of electricity and a near-monopoly in the sale of natural gas. A monopolistic government supplier, unlike a seller in an ordinary market, has the economic power to resist the Executive Order. In the situation under consideration, the Government needs to buy electric energy in the New Orleans area. If NOPSI were allowed to prevail in its contentions, the Government would have to either acquiesce or else go without necessary services. Obviously, a local utility cannot force such a dilemma upon the Government. Otherwise, a valid and important nationwide federal program set in place by the President over a third of a century ago, continued by every one of his successors, approved by Congress and applicable to all government contractors, could be nullified by any seller with a monopoly in a service, supply or property needed by the Government,

10 We are not inferring here any implied or constructive agreement by NOPSI to the terms of the Executive Order. Our holding is dictated by (1) the sale by the company of energy to the Government, *and* (2) the fact that such sale of services was made by a company which, under City franchises, enjoyed a local monopoly in such services needed by the Government. The presence of both those elements triggered the regulation, 41 C.F.R. § 60-1.4(e), and thus, the application of the program's obligations by operation of the Order.

just by virtue of the seller's economic position. Here, NOPSI's monopoly exists only because of local legislative action. The supremacy clause of the Constitution obviously cannot countenance such a result. We hold, therefore, that the Government can compel NOPSI to comply with the equal opportunity obligations of Executive Order 11246, even though the company has not expressly consented to be bound by that Order.

## II. NOPSI'S FOURTH AMENDMENT CONTENTIONS

NOPSI next contends that the Executive Order and implementing regulations violate the fourth amendment when applied to a public utility which does not seek to do business with the Government and has not consented to the provisions of the Order. This argument parallels the company's central contention in the case, and is similarly without merit.

[The discussion of the Fourth Amendment issue is omitted. See *Barlow's v. Marshall*, 436 U.S. 307 (1978).] [12]

## III. THE DISTRICT COURT'S INJUNCTIVE ORDER

We turn finally to NOPSI's disagreement with the district court's injunctive order. The company argues that the court lacked jurisdiction to issue that order, under which the court retained jurisdiction over this action for the purpose of enforcing the substantive provisions of the Executive Order.

We hold that, the district court having found NOPSI to be covered by the Executive Order, the task of obtaining NOPSI's compliance with the program should be left to the Government's own administrative compliance processes. Accordingly, we modify that part of the district court's

[12] *Mississippi Power & Light* argues that the Executive Order's provision for Government access to a contractor's books and records is unconstitutional because: (1) the provision is without statutory authorization, and (2) it does not contain a procedure for judicial review. The argument about lack of statutory authorization is without merit in light of the pattern of congressional approval for the Executive Order program which we found in section I of this opinion. The argument about lack of judicial review is also without merit since, in the setting of the instant controversy, it is purely hypothetical. Here there has been no attempt to obtain access by force to the company's records without judicial approval; in fact, there has been ample judicial review in these proceedings of the Government's attempt to conduct a compliance review of NOPSI.

Since oral argument, *Mississippi Power & Light* has called our attention to *Brennan* v. *Gibson's Products, Inc.*, E.D. Tex., 1976, 407 F. Supp. 154, *appeal docketed*, No. 76-1526 (5 Cir. Feb. 27, 1976), a case in which a three-judge court held that an attempt by Department of Labor officials to conduct a warrantless inspection of a business, pursuant to the Occupational Safety and Health Act of 1970, violated the Fourth Amendment. However, *Gibson's Prods.* does not deter us from the conclusion we have reached. As the three-judge court pointed out, the company involved there was not licensed and had no history of close regulation, and the statutory provisions which appeared to authorize the search were not limited to such businesses, but instead embraced "the whole spectrum of unrelated and disparate activities which compose private enterprise in the United States." *Id.*, 407 F. Supp. at 161-62. Furthermore, there was no reason to believe that the thing sought to be controlled by the regulatory system before the court existed in the area to be searched. *Id.* at 162. Therefore, *Gibson's Prods.* is manifestly distinguishable from both the instant case and those cases upon which we have relied.

opinion which retained jurisdiction over this suit and which dictated a mandate of injunction clearly contemplating substantive enforcement of the Executive Order. Our decision is based on equitable considerations, and should not be read as holding that the district court lacked jurisdiction in any respect for its ruling. Resolution of NOPSI's objections to the court's injunctive order is therefore unnecessary to our holding; however, we proceed to dismiss all of the company's present objections in order that they may not be interposed again as obstacles to enforcement of the program herein.

NOPSI makes two major arguments in this regard. The first is that the Government has failed to follow the procedural requirements of the Executive Order and implementing regulations. NOPSI alleges that the Government was required to proceed by conciliation and persuasion, but instead chose to pursue litigation in its compliance strategy. In addition, NOPSI contends that the Government has failed to afford the company a hearing mandated under the program. In support of these assertions, NOPSI relies on a number of regulatory provisions. We need not respond to each assertion specifically, in view of the fact that the Government's attempts to conduct a voluntary compliance review of NOPSI date back to 1969.

The regulations now in effect [13] provide for the institution of administrative or judicial enforcement proceedings in response to violations of the Executive Order. Violations may be found, based upon, *inter alia,*

"(iv) a contractor's refusal to submit an affirmative action program; (v) a contractor's refusal to allow an on-site compliance review to be conducted; (vi) a contractor's refusal to supply records or other information as required by these regulations . . . or (vii) any substantial or material violation or the threat of [such] a . . . violation of the contractual provisions of the Order, or of the rules or regulations issued pursuant thereto."

41 C.F.R. § 60-1.26(a)(1). The district court found such a violation. The regulations further provide that whenever the Director of the Office of Federal Contract Compliance has reason to believe that there exists the threat or fact of violation of the Order or regulations, the Director "may institute administrative enforcement proceedings . . . *or* refer the matter to the Department of Justice to enforce the contractual provisions of the Order, to seek injunctive relief . . . and to seek such additional relief, including back pay, as may be appropriate. *There are no procedural prerequisites to a referral to the Department of Justice* by the Director, and *such referrals may be accomplished without proceeding through the conciliation procedures* in this chapter, *and a referral may be made at any stage in the procedures* under this chapter."

*Id.* § 60-1.26(a)(2) (emphasis added).

The preceding regulation plainly rebuts NOPSI's first contention.[14]

---

13 See note 5 *supra.*

14 As to NOPSI's argument that the Government was required to proceed by conciliation and persuasion, we think that the facts described at the outset of our opinion

And the regulation also refutes NOPSI's second major assertion, which is that the Justice Department cannot bring judicial proceedings to enforce the provisions of the Executive Order until the OFCC or the compliance agency (here the General Services Administration) has first exhausted the administrative procedures of the program. Two more observations are in order as to the exhaustion argument. First, the cases cited by NOPSI in support of that contention involve private actions and are, therefore, inapposite to the situation where the Government itself has decided to pursue judicial litigation in enforcing Executive Order 11246.[15] Second, while we recognize that, as NOPSI argues, substantial arguments can be mustered for application of the exhaustion doctrine, we nevertheless have no reason to read an exhaustion requirement into a program which clearly and deliberately provides judicial enforcement as an alternative to administrative enforcement, and which explicitly rejects procedural prerequisites to judicial enforcement.

Despite our conclusion that the district court had both the jurisdiction and the power to direct by injunctive order NOPSI's compliance, we conclude that the enforcement function in this case would be better carried out administratively by the compliance agencies. This decision is reached in the exercise of our equitable discretion, for "the manner, means and method for resolving" this dispute must be devised under "inherent equitable principles." *R. L. Johnson* v. *Goodyear Tire & Rubber Co.*, 5 Cir., 1974, 491 F.2d 1364, 1367, 7 FEP Cases 627, 629.[16] In light of our holding that NOPSI is covered by the Executive Order and has violated it, our primary mission at this point, of course, is to render such relief as is necessary and appropriate to effectuate the mandate of the Executive Order as fully and expeditiously as possible. However, the relief imposed should not "run against the grain of fundamental fairness which should hopefully be the outcome of any equitable decree." *Id*. at 1379, 7 FEP Cases at 638. In the particular setting of this case, where NOPSI has never agreed to be bound by the Order, we believe that fundamental fairness requires that the Government, armed this time with court's opinion, now obtain the company's voluntary compliance before calling for the support of our injunctive powers.

---

indicate that such efforts took place. In addition, we find no conflict between 41 C.F.R. § 60-1.26(a)(2) and section 209(b) of the Executive Order. While section 209(b) directs the contracting agency to make reasonable efforts to achieve by conciliation and persuasion, those efforts are to be made pursuant to the regulations issued by the Secretary of Labor. *Id*. Thus, section 60-1.26(a)(2) qualifies the Government's responsibilities under section 209(b) of the Order, rather than vice versa, and the two provisions can be read consistently.

15 For example, to the extent that the exhaustion argument is rooted in notions of deference to the administrative process and the administrative agency, the argument has no bearing in the instant context.

16 *Johnson* is one of the cases cited by the Government for the proposition that the district court's retention of jurisdiction and injunctive order were justified. While those cases indicate that the district court had the authority to take the action which it took —a conclusion we do not dispute—they in no way suggest that the district court's injunctive order was required in the circumstances before us. Since we have concluded that our remedial task will best effectuate the Executive Order, discussion of those cases is unnecessary.

Other equitable factors support this result. The basic approach of the Executive Order program, as implemented, is enforcement by Executive agencies, in particular the Department of Labor, even though the Order itself provides the judicial enforcement alternative in section 209(a)(2). The Executive has expertise, which this court lacks, in the administration of the program, and that expertise can profitably be brought to bear on the problem at bar. Further, we see no reason to burden our scarce judicial resources with the task of supervising the enforcement of the federal contract compliance program, unless such judicial enforcement becomes necessary.

Our decision today is not an invitation to further delay by NOPSI in complying with the Executive Order. Such delay would be intolerable. In its brief, NOPSI states:

"If a court of final appellant (sic) resort upholds the District Court determination that NOPSI is a government contractor notwithstanding its refusal to consent to the contractual equal opportunity provisions of Executive Order 11246, the General Services Administration and the OFCC should then be afforded the opportunity to work with NOPSI in developing an appropriate affirmative action program, if indeed one is found necessary . . . ."

Brief for Appellant at 46-47.[17] That statement underlies the remedial approach which we today require. We assume, based on the quoted passage, NOPSI's good faith in complying with the Order, given our holding that the company is covered by it.

To restate our decision, then, the appropriate government compliance agency—whether OFCC or GSA—may proceed by administrative action to obtain NOPSI's compliance with the Executive Order. Though we are removing the injunctive mandate of the district court, our decision contemplates good faith negotiations between the parties, and certain issues decided herein are precluded from further negotiation. The company cannot any longer dispute its coverage under the Executive Order, nor can the company attempt to nullify the effect of the Order's application by demanding limitation-of-scope language in any contract or proposed affirmative action program that would restrict the impact of the Order. Moreover, NOPSI has no valid Fourth Amendment objections to the Government's demands for access either to the company's facilities or to the company's books and records, nor can NOPSI further delay or resist compliance by insisting on merely technical or unnecessary procedural niceties.

The Government may proceed at once in enforcing the Executive Order by administrative action. The parties are advised that, having fashioned our relief on the assumption of NOPSI's good faith in complying with our decision herein, this court will look with disfavor on any future attempts to delay compliance.

---

[17] NOPSI's statement suggests the possibility that an affirmative action program might not be found necessary. We read the regulations, however, to require a written affirmative action program. See 41 C.F.R. § 60-1.40(a).

Modified and Affirmed.

CLARK, Circuit Judge, dissenting: The decisive question in both this case and *United States* v. *Mississippi Power & Light Co.,* _____ F.2d _____, 14 FEP Cases 1730, slip opinion p. 3610 (5th Cir. 1977), which we also decide today, is whether the federal government may impose a substantial contract obligation on a public utility simply because that utility supplies energy to federal installations as required by state law and the terms of its state or municipal franchise. The majority answers in the affirmative. I respectfully disagree.

# I

In order to determine whether New Orleans Public Service, Inc. [NOPSI], or Mississippi Power & Light Co. [MP&L] must comply with a comprehensive equal opportunity clause despite their explicit refusals to subject themselves to it, three issues must be resolved. First, was the issuance of the Executive Order which requires the clause be included in every federal contract a valid exercise of Presidential power? Second, what relation must exist between a person and the federal government before that person is subject to the dictates of the equal opportunity clause by operation of the Executive Order? And third, does the requisite relation exist between the federal government and either NOPSI or MP&L. Since the resolution of the second and third issues furnishes a sufficient ground for my decision of this case, I do not reach the constitutional puzzles presented by the first.[1]

. . .

# II

Had the court adopted the position of this dissent, the effectiveness of the Executive Order as a tool for eliminating discrimination in employment would not have been destroyed. The vast majority of those supplying goods and services to the federal government are not under a pre-existing legal obligation to do so, but rather are contractors within the meaning of the Order. Nothing said here would affect the applicability of the provisions of the equal opportunity clause to them. Nor would such a decision leave public utilities at liberty to treat their employees as they pleased. There are a plethora of state and federal measures designed to eliminate discriminatory employment practices to which they are subject.

I do not dissent to defend discriminatory employment practices. But when the government has chosen to attack them through the mechanism of inserting a nondiscrimination clause in its contracts rather than by enacting a statute, there are limits to what it can accomplish. Those limits

---

[1] For the purpose of this dissent, I make two assumptions. The first is that the Executive Order is valid and possesses the force and effect of law. The second is that the Secretary of Labor did not exceed the rulemaking authority granted him by the Executive Order when he issued 41 C.F.R. § 60-1.4(e) (1976), as amended, 42 Fed. Reg. 3454, 3459 (1977), which incorporates the equal opportunity clause into all non-exempt government contracts by operation of the Executive Order.

have been exceeded here. The majority makes a mistake when it allows the government to forge ahead to a desirable end by means that stand the law of contracts on its head.

## NOTE

Following a determination that the Occupational Safety and Health Act, which authorized the Secretary of Labor's agents to search any employment facility subject to the Act for safety violations, was unconstitutional, the Supreme Court vacated and remanded *NOPSI* and *Mississippi Power & Light* for reconsideration in the light of its decision in *Marshall* v. *Barlow's, Inc.,* 436 U.S. 307 (1978).

For a discussion of problems raised by the NOPSI case see *Imposition of Affirmative Action Obligations on Nonconsenting Government Contractors,* 91 HARV. L. REV. 506 (1977).

## UNIROYAL, INC. v. MARSHALL

*United States Court of Appeals, Seventh Circuit, 1978*
*579 F.2d 1060, 17 FEP Cases 1207*

MARSHALL, District Judge: In this appeal, we are asked to decide whether Executive Order 11246, which prohibits discriminatory employment practices by all government contractors, grants sufficient rulemaking authority to the Department of Labor to permit the use of pre-hearing discovery techniques and administrative subpoenas in administrative enforcement proceedings. Appellant Uniroyal, Inc., brought this collateral pre-enforcement action in the district court challenging these procedures. The district court denied Uniroyal's motion for a preliminary injunction and granted summary judgment for the government. We affirm upon the limited ground that plaintiffs' action was premature because of the "long settled rule of judicial administration that no one is entitled to judicial relief, for a supposed or threatened injury, until the prescribed administrative remedy has been exhausted." *Myers* v. *Bethlehem Corp.,* 303 U.S. 41, 51, 1A LRRM 575 (1938); *Frey* v. *CEA,* 547 F.2d 46 (7th Cir. 1976).

Uniroyal, Inc., a manufacturer of chemical, rubber and plastic products, holds numerous contracts with the federal government. All government contractors are required by Executive Order 11246 (the Order) to include in each contract a clause which obligates them to take affirmative action to ensure that employees are treated without regard to race, color, sex, religion or national origin. See 41 C.F.R. § 60-1.4. The Order is administered by the Secretary of the Department of Labor (the Secretary), who is authorized to issue implementation rules and regulations. Under these regulations, the Secretary has delegated his enforcement responsibilities to the Office of Federal Contract Compliance Programs (OFCCP). 41 C.F.R. § 60-1.2.

Specific responsibility for monitoring a contractor's compliance with the Order is entrusted to a compliance agency, which conducts periodic reviews to determine whether the contractor is adhering to the terms of the equal opportunity clause in his contract. 41 C.F.R. § 60-1.3 and § 60-1.20. In the case of Uniroyal, the compliance agency is the Department of the Interior (Interior). In January, 1976 Interior conducted an on-site review of Uniroyal's Mishawaka, Indiana plant and found a number of deficiencies in its adherence to the terms of its contract. These included the failure to supply complete and accurate data to Interior investigators, the failure to identify areas in the work force where women and minorities were underrepresented, the failure to set goals and timetables for an affirmative action program, and the assignment of women and minorities to lower-paying jobs than those held by male and white employees of comparable qualifications and seniority. Interior gave Uniroyal thirty days to show cause why contract termination and debarment proceedings should not be initiated.

Over the next several months, repeated attempts were made to reach a negotiated settlement of the dispute. Those efforts proved unproductive, and in July, 1976 the Director of OFCCP issued a formal complaint which commenced the administrative enforcement proceeding. Uniroyal denied the charges of non-compliance with the Order, and the case was set for a hearing before an administrative law judge.

Formal pre-hearing discovery began in November, 1976, when the government filed interrogatories and requests for production of documents. The implementing regulations, which were promulgated in 1972 and 1977, authorize an array of pre-hearing discovery devices, including interrogatories, requests for admissions, requests to produce documents, requests to enter and inspect property, and depositions on oral examination. 41 C.F.R. § 60-30.9 through § 60-30.11. Over the next eight months, the government filed about fifteen discovery requests, including deposition notices directed to six Uniroyal officials. Uniroyal filed two discovery requests of its own during this period.

While the government has responded to Uniroyal's discovery requests, Uniroyal in turn has been largely uncooperative and dilatory. By securing several extensions of time, it delayed its response to the government's requests for more than three months. When it did respond, Uniroyal refused to supply large blocks of information, contending that the requested information was irrelevant, confidential, beyond the scope of the proceeding, or physically unavailable. The government subsequently procured several orders from the administrative law judge compelling Uniroyal to provide more complete answers. Uniroyal was still unwilling to accommodate, and on May 10, 1977 it raised for the first time the contention that the Secretary of Labor lacked authority to issue the pre-hearing discovery rules. It asked the administrative law judge to bar discovery and vacate the prior orders. In turn, the government moved for an order terminating Uniroyal's present contracts and declaring Uniroyal ineligible for future contracts due to its failure to engage in discovery.

The administrative law judge denied Uniroyal's motions to preclude discovery, stating that an administrative proceeding was not the proper forum to test the validity of the rules. Uniroyal has appealed this interlocutory ruling to the Secretary of Labor, and that appeal is still pending. The judge also enlarged the scope of a hearing scheduled for June 28, 1977 to consider evidence on whether Uniroyal's refusal to engage in prehearing discovery and its defiance of the judge's discovery orders constituted a violation of Executive Order 11246 and grounds for imposing sanctions, including contract termination. Finally, the judge ruled that unless the company answered outstanding requests to admit and interrogatories prior to the upcoming hearing, those requests would be deemed admitted.

One week before the scheduled June 28 hearing, Uniroyal filed its instant complaint in the district court against three government officials charged with administering the Order,[1] seeking to bar enforcement of the OFCCP's pre-hearing discovery rules. The challenged rules are published at 41 C.F.R. § 60-30.1 (last sentence), which provides that the Federal Rules of Civil Procedure shall control in the absence of a specific provision, § 60-30.9 through § 60-30.11, which authorize pre-hearing discovery, and § 60-30.17, which authorizes the issuance of administrative subpoenas to compel the attendance of witnesses and the production of documents at hearings. In its complaint, Uniroyal asserted that the rules were invalid because they were not expressly authorized by the Administrative Procedure Act, 5 U.S.C. § 701 *et seq.*, by Executive Order 11246, or by its statutory fountainhead, the Federal Property and Administrative Services Act of 1949, 40 U.S.C. § 486. Uniroyal also claimed that the government's efforts to terminate its contracts for non-compliance with the rules deprived it of property rights protected by the due process clause of the Fifth Amendment. In its prayer for relief, Uniroyal sought to enjoin the defendants from holding the scheduled administrative hearing and from imposing any sanctions for Uniroyal's non-compliance with pretrial discovery requests. It also sought a declaration that the discovery rules were an impermissible and unconstitutional exercise of defendants' authority.

The district court entered an *ex parte* temporary restraining order on June 22, resulting in the cancellation of the June 28 administrative hearing. However, that order was subsequently dissolved, and on August 15 the district court denied plaintiff's motion for a preliminary injunction and entered summary judgment in favor of the defendants.[2] The court

---

1 [Footnotes numbered as in original.—Ed.] Those officials are F. Ray Marshall, Secretary of the Department of Labor, Weldon J. Rougeau, Director of OFCCP, and Cecil D. Andrus, Secretary of the Department of the Interior.

2 Following the dismissal of Uniroyal's court action, the administrative hearing was rescheduled and eventually took place in November, 1977. Evidence was presented on the issue of sanctions for Uniroyal's refusal to engage in pre-hearing discovery. On June 14, 1978, we were advised by Uniroyal that on April 11, 1978, the administrative law judge issued a Recommended Decision recommending to the Secretary that Uniroyal's present contract be cancelled and that Uniroyal be declared ineligible for future government contracts due to its refusal to comply with the government's discovery

rested its ruling on several grounds. First, Uniroyal failed to show that it would suffer irreparable injury if a preliminary injunction were denied, since it was in no danger of losing government contracts prior to the completion of the scheduled administrative hearing. Second, Uniroyal had failed to exhaust the administrative procedures specified in its contracts with the government, because the issue of discovery sanctions was still pending before the administrative law judge. Third, the case met none of the requirements for pre-enforcement review of agency action, and therefore was not ripe for judicial decision. Finally, the regulations were valid, since they were lawful contract terms and were not in conflict with or in excess of their underlying authority.

On October 17, 1977 this court denied Uniroyal's motion for an injunction pending appeal in which it sought an order restraining defendants from proceeding with any administrative hearing until we ruled on Uniroyal's appeal.

On appeal, Uniroyal challenges each of the reasons offered by the district court. Because we agree with the district court that Uniroyal is precluded from maintaining its action because of its failure to exhaust an available administrative remedy, we affirm without reaching the merits of the validity of the rules.

The exhaustion doctrine is intended to defer judicial review until controversies have been channeled through the complete administrative process. The exhaustion requirement serves to avoid collateral, dilatory action of the likes of the instant action and to ensure the efficient, uninterrupted progression of administrative proceedings and the effective application of judicial review. It provides an agency with an opportunity "to correct its own errors, to afford the parties and the courts the benefit of [the agency's] experience and expertise, and to compile a [factual] record which is adequate for judicial review." *Weinberger* v. *Salfi*, 422 U.S. 749, 765 (1975).

Under a strict application of this principle, Uniroyal must await the final decision of the Secretary of Labor before obtaining judicial review. The applicable regulations provide that interlocutory rulings of the administrative law judge are not appealable to the Secretary until the administrative law judge transfers the case to the Secretary. § 60-30.19(b). Before those rulings become final, the administrative law judge must issue his recommended findings, conclusions and decision, and certify the record to the Secretary. § 60-30.27. After the parties are given an opportunity to file exceptions to the administrative law judge's ruling, the Secretary issues a final decision, which is then subject to judicial review. 5 U.S.C. § 704.

In the present case, the administrative proceeding has reached the hearing stage, and the administrative law judge has entered his recommended decision which is now pending before the Secretary. Thus the agency action is not final, and is ordinarily not reviewable.

---

requests and the administrative law judge's orders in respect thereto. The Recommended Decision is now pending before the Secretary on review.

Recognizing the premature character of its judicial challenge, Uniroyal seeks to place its lawsuit within one of the exceptions to the exhaustion doctrine. Emphasizing that the exhaustion doctrine should be applied with due regard for its purposes, see *McKart* v. *United States,* 395 U.S. 185, 193 (1969), Uniroyal first contends that those purposes are not served when the agency is faced with purely legal issues concerning the scope of its statutory authority. In such cases, the issues will not be better framed and more amenable to judicial resolution after agency action, since no factual determinations, discretionary decisions, or expert judgments are required.

In *Jewel Companies, Inc.* v. *F.T.C.,* 432 F.2d 1155 (7th Cir. 1970), this court allowed an "inherently legal attack" on an agency's statutory authority prior to the issuance of its final order. Plaintiffs sought to enjoin the FTC from pursuing its administrative complaint under the Robinson-Patman Act, 15 U.S.C. § 13(c). They raised four claims that the FTC had acted outside its statutory authority in issuing the complaint. This court held that only one claim qualified for immediate judicial review —*i.e.,* that one of the Commissioners who voted to issue the complaint had misconstrued the statutory standard for initiating a prosecution under the Act. In reaching that holding, the court stated that "[t]he question raised is inherently a legal one and does not involve any factual determinations." 432 F.2d at 1159. This language supports the conclusion that administrative remedies may be bypassed when pure questions of law are presented, and one of this court's later opinions has read *Jewel* this broadly. *Borden, Inc.* v. *FTC,* 495 F.2d 785, 787 (7th Cir. 1974).

However, the *Jewel* opinion required more than the mere presence of a question of statutory interpretation. The court also examined the nature of the procedural error asserted to determine whether it would be subject to judicial review after final agency action. If the error could not be rectified after administrative proceedings were concluded, or if the scope of judicial review was too narrow to encompass the claim, application of the exhaustion doctrine would unfairly prevent the plaintiffs from receiving meaningful judicial consideration of their claims. *Skinner & Eddy Corp.* v. *United States,* 249 U.S. 557 (1919). The *Jewel* plaintiffs confronted this spectre of inadequate judicial review, since "the court of appeals would only decide whether the final order [was] supported by the evidence and would not question the authority of the Commission in issuing the complaint." 432 F.2d at 1159.

Uniroyal does not have a similar barrier to judicial review here. Prior to the administrative hearing, the administrative law judge rejected its claim that the pre-hearing discovery rules exceeded the agency's statutory authority, reasoning that such issues are inappropriate in an administrative forum. But Uniroyal has appealed that ruling to the Secretary, and the regulations provide for review of such rulings by the Secretary after the administrative law judge has issued his administrative decision. § 60-30.19(b). Assuming that the Secretary eventually issues a final order adverse to Uniroyal on this preliminary ruling, it may be questioned on judicial review. 5 U.S.C. § 704. Uniroyal therefore has adequate judicial remedies to test its theories of statutory construction.

Additional reasons support the application of the exhaustion doctrine to questions of law. Federal courts should accord great deference to an agency's construction of its authorizing statute. *Udall* v. *Tallman*, 380 U.S. 1, 16 (1965). Although the administrative law judge has repudiated his function as statutory interpreter, the Secretary has not taken a similar position, since the administrative proceedings have not yet reached his domain. When they do, ". . . more light may be thrown on the [Secretary's] statutory and practical justifications for the regulation." *Toilet Goods Ass'n* v. *Gardner*, 387 U.S. 158, 166 (1967). When these justifications become apparent, a reviewing court can better assess the issue of statutory authority.

Furthermore, this court has been reluctant to intervene in administrative proceedings to upset orders dealing with the discovery of documents, despite the presence of issues of statutory construction. In *Frey* v. *CEA*, 547 F.2d 46 (7th Cir. 1976), the exhaustion doctrine was applied to dismiss a claim that parties to disciplinary hearings before the Commodity Exchange Authority (CEA) have a statutory right to prehearing discovery. The plaintiffs had been charged with misconduct in the trading of commodities, and sought subpoenas from the CEA to secure the records and testimony of certain traders. The administrative law judge denied the requests for pre-hearing discovery, finding no statutory or constitutional basis for such requests but reserved the right to allow the production of the requested documents during the hearing if their relevance became apparent. Before the hearing began, the plaintiffs filed a complaint for declaratory and injunctive relief, claiming that the refusal to allow pre-hearing discovery violated their rights to due process of law, threatened to irreparably harm the quality of their defense at the hearing, and violated their clear statutory rights to pre-hearing discovery.

In reversing the district court's grant of injunctive relief, the court found that several considerations demonstrated the premature nature of judicial review. First, the administrative proceedings had not even progressed to a hearing, and a real possibility existed that a favorable order would moot plaintiffs' claims, or that the administrative law judge would adopt procedures during the hearing to ensure an adequate production of documents. Second, even if the order were unfavorable, judicial review would later be available to test plaintiffs' rights to discovery. Third, although a failure to exhaust administrative procedures can generally be excused by the threat of irreparable injury, litigation expenses were insufficient injury by themselves to warrant early judicial intervention. Finally, the agency's failure to allow discovery did not fall within the exception allowing a bypass of administrative remedies where "the agency has clearly violated a right secured by statute or agency regulation." 547 F.2d at 50. The statutory provisions and regulations relied on by the plaintiffs were susceptible to a narrow reading which would exclude authorization for pre-hearing discovery. The court therefore refused to permit judicial review of the administrative law judge's interlocutory order denying discovery.

It is significant that although the *Frey* plaintiffs raised legal issues which turned predominantly, if not entirely, on matters of statutory and regulatory construction, the court required exhaustion unless the legal rights conferred by those provisions were "clearly violated." In the present case, Uniroyal raises similar legal issues, although their arguments support defensive rather than offensive challenges to discovery procedures. We will show, for the following reasons, that Uniroyal's claim of a statutory exemption from discovery is not clearer than the *Frey* plaintiffs' claim of a statutory entitlement to discovery.

Relying on § 555 of the Administrative Procedure Act, Uniroyal first proposes that there must be express statutory authority for pre-hearing discovery and administrative subpoenas to be available to federal agencies. Section 555 provides that no investigative act, demand, or subpoena may be issued or enforced except as "authorized by law." Uniroyal next advances the theory that the general rulemaking powers of the Secretary are insufficient to support discovery powers. Section 201 of Executive Order 11246 authorizes the Secretary to promulgate such rules and regulations "as he deems necessary and appropriate to achieve the purposes thereof." For a regulation to be valid, it must be within the scope of the Executive Order. *Contractors Ass'n of Eastern Pennsylvania* v. *Secretary of Labor*, 442 F.2d 159, 175, 3 FEP Cases 395, 407 (3d Cir. 1971), *cert. denied*, 404 U.S. 854, 3 FEP Cases 1030. Two sections of the Order form relevant guides to the scope of the Secretary's discovery powers. Section 202(5) requires government contractors to furnish all information and reports required by the Order and its implementing regulations. It also directs that the contractor ". . . will permit access to his books, records, and accounts by the contracting agency and the Secretary of Labor for purposes of investigation to ascertain compliance with such rules, regulations and orders." Section 208 of the Order authorizes the Secretary to hold hearings "for compliance, enforcement, or educational purposes."

Seeing a distinction between the investigatory discovery mentioned in § 202 and the pre-hearing discovery sought here, Uniroyal contends that the Secretary's discovery powers are extinguished once an investigation matures into a formal administrative complaint and is set for a hearing. Because the Order is silent on the contractor's duty to furnish information once the pre-hearing and hearing process has begun, Uniroyal says no such obligation exists, and the Secretary's discovery rules therefore violate the APA requirement of express statutory authorization.

We do not believe Uniroyal has demonstrated that the Secretary's pre-hearing discovery rules so clearly exceed the bounds of the Executive Order that immediate judicial intervention is required. Uniroyal can point to no section of the Order with which those regulations are in explicit conflict. The APA requirement of legal authorization does not clearly require *express* statutory authority. The Secretary has broad rulemaking authority, and the Order gives him broad power both to engage in fact-gathering during the investigative stage to ascertain compliance, and to hold enforcement hearings to prosecute violations discovered during those investigations. For the Secretary to adopt discovery rules in the gap between an investigation and a hearing does not clearly expand the agency's powers. The burden on the company producing documents appears to be the same whether it is complying with an investigative demand under § 202(5) of the Order, or a discovery request under the pre-hearing discovery regulations. Furthermore, the courts are divided on the scope of powers conferred by general rulemaking authority. Compare *Federal Maritime Comm'n* v. *Anglo-Canadian Shipping Co.*, 335 F.2d 255 (9th Cir. 1964) (pre-hearing discovery rule allowing production of documents must be expressly authorized by Congress and cannot be founded on general rulemaking statute) with *National Petroleum Refiners Ass'n* v. *FTC*, 482 F.2d 672 (D.C. Cir. 1973) (substantive rulemaking authority to define unfair and deceptive practices can be based on a general rulemaking statute). In reviewing the case law on this issue, the court in *National Petroleum Refiners* noted that "overwhelming judicial support [has been] given to expansive agency readings of statutory rulemaking authorizations that are not flatly inconsistent with other statutory provisions, . . ." and explained that stricter standards requiring express legislative authorization have only been applied to "novel assertions of agency powers." 482 F.2d at 691. Given the detailed enforcement scheme and broad investigative powers established by Executive Order 11246, we see nothing clearly novel or objectionable about the Secretary's pre-hearing discovery regulations. Consequently, there is insufficient cause to disrupt the administrative proceedings prior to a final agency decision.

For the foregoing reasons the judgment is Affirmed.

On June 14, 1978 Uniroyal renewed its motion for an injunction pending our decision on the merits, which this court had denied on October 17, 1977. The new ground asserted for such relief is the April 11, 1978 Recommended Decision of the administrative law judge which is adverse to Uniroyal. See Note 2, *supra*. That Recommended Decision is now pending on review before the Secretary. In light of our decision affirming the district court's judgment we see no basis upon which we could or should grant injunctive relief pending appeal. Accordingly, the renewed motion is Denied.

## NOTE

For a case involving disclosure of affirmative action plans, see *Chrysler Corp.* v. *Schlesinger*, 565 F.2d 1172, 15 FEP Cases 1217 (3rd Cir. 1977), *vacated and remanded sub nom. Chrysler Corp.* v. *Brown*, _____ U.S. _____, 19 FEP Cases 475 (1979).

## C.  AFFIRMATIVE ACTION CONCEPTS

Executive Order 10925, the Kennedy order, contained two elements of great significance which distinguished it from its predecessors: (1) the affirmative action requirement, and (2) the specification, in the order, of sanctions for violations, which in prior executive orders were there only by implication.

By far the most significant conceptual innovation in the civil rights field is the use of affirmative action. In the Kennedy order this remedial concept, ordinarily utilized as a remedy after determination of fault, is imposed as a condition of doing government business. The assurance of affirmative action to facilitate equal employment opportunity is an undertaking *in addition* to the undertaking not to discriminate on the basis of race, creed, color, or national origin.

Specific inclusion of the sanctions to be imposed for violation of the contractual commitment clearly signaled a governmental intention, or pretention as history has revealed it, to enforce the obligations.

The affirmative action concept was conceived as a response during the Eisenhower Administration to a criticism of the President's committee programs in the final report of the committee chaired by then Vice President Nixon. That report advised as follows: "Overt discrimination . . . is not as prevalent as is generally believed. To a greater degree, *the indifference of employers to establishing a positive policy* of nondiscrimination hinders qualified applicants and employees from being hired and promoted on the basis of equality." (Emphasis in original.) This sound advice regarding the nature of discrimination was not duplicated with recommendations regarding the nature of administrative organizations which could most effectively pursue the goals of affirmative action.

Before the potential of the affirmative action concept of the executive order could be effectively implemented, it was necessary for the governmen to come to grips with the use of numbers. Numbers raised the spectre of quotas and the fear that any use of goals or timetables would be declared illegal. The principal case in which these issues are joined follows.

### CONTRACTORS ASSN. OF EASTERN PENNSYLVANIA v. SECRETARY OF LABOR

*U.S. Court of Appeals, Third Circuit, 1971*
*442 F.2d 159, 3 FEP Cases 395, affirming 311 F. Supp. 1002 (E.D. Pa. 1970)*

GIBBONS, Circuit Judge:

The original plaintiff, the Contractors Association of Eastern Pennsylvania (the Association) and the intervening plaintiffs,[1] construction con-

1 [Footnotes numbered as in original—Ed.] James D. Morrissey, Inc.; The Conduit & Foundation Corp.; Glasgow, Inc.; Buckley & Company; The Nyleve Company; Erb Engineering & Constr. Co.; Perkins, Kanak, Foster, Inc.; and Lansdowne Constructors, Inc.

tractors doing business in the Philadelphia area (the Contractors), appeal from an order of the district court which denied their motion for summary judgment, granted the motion of the federal defendants [2] to dismiss the Association complaint for lack of standing, and granted the cross-motion of the federal defendants for summary judgment.[3] When deciding these motions, the district court had before it the Association's verified complaint, a substantially identical complaint of the contractors, the affidavits of Vincent G. Macaluso and Ward McCreedy on behalf of the federal defendants which identified certain relevant documents, a stipulation by the parties as to certain facts, and two affidavits of Howard G. Minckler on behalf of the plaintiffs.

The complaint challenges the validity of the Philadelphia Plan, promulgated by the federal defendants under the authority of Executive Order No. 11246.[4] That Plan is embodied in two orders issued by officials of the United States Department of Labor, dated June 27, 1969 and September 23, 1969 respectively. . . . In summary, they require that bidders on any federal or federally assisted construction contracts for projects in a five-county area around Philadelphia,[5] the estimated total cost of which exceeds $500,000, shall submit an acceptable affirmative action program which includes specific goals for the utilization of minority manpower in six skilled crafts: ironworkers, plumbers and pipefitters, steamfitters, sheetmetal workers, electrical workers, and elevator construction workers.

Executive Order No. 11246 requires all applicants for federal assistance to include in their construction contracts specific provisions respecting fair employment practices, including the provision:

"The contractor will take affirmative action to ensure that applicants are employed, and that employees are treated during employment, without regard to their race, color, religion, sex or national origin." [6]

The Executive Order empowers the Secretary of Labor to issue rules and regulations necessary and appropriate to achieve its purpose. On June 27, 1969 Assistant Secretary of Labor Fletcher issued an order implementing the Executive Order in the five-county Philadelphia area. The order required bidders, prior to the award of contracts, to submit "acceptable affirmative action" programs "which shall include specific goals of minority manpower utilization." The order contained a

[2] The Secretary of Labor, George P. Shultz; The Assistant Secretary of Labor, Arthur A. Fletcher; The Director, Office of Federal Contract Compliance, John L. Wilks; The Secretary of Agriculture, Clifford M. Hardin.

[3] An additional defendant, the General State Authority of the Commonwealth of Pennsylvania, has not participated in this appeal.

[4] 30 Fed. Reg. 12319 (Sept. 24, 1965), as amended by Exec. Order No. 11375, 32 Fed. Reg. 14303 (Oct. 13, 1967), 3 C.F.R. 406 (1969), 42 U.S.C.A. § 2000(e) (1970), superseded in part by Exec. Order No. 11478, 34 Fed. Reg. 12985 (Aug. 8, 1969), 3 C.F.R., 1969 Comp. 133, 42 U.S.C. § 2000(e) (1970).

[5] Encompassing Bucks, Chester, Delaware, Montgomery and Philadelphia Counties in Pennsylvania.

[6] § 202(1). This wording comes from Exec. Order No. 11375, see note 4 supra, and represents a minor change from the original designed to parallel the classes of discrimination prohibited by Title VII of the Civil Rights Act of 1964, 42 U.S.C. § 2000(e) et seq.

finding that enforcement of the "affirmative action" requirement of Executive Order No. 11246 had posed special problems in the construction trades.[7] Contractors and subcontractors must hire a new employee complement for each job, and they rely on craft unions as their prime or sole source for labor. The craft unions operate hiring halls. "Because of the exclusionary practices of labor organizations," the order finds "there traditionally has been only a small number of Negroes employed in these seven trades."[8] The June 27, 1969 order provided that the Area Coordinator of the Office of Federal Contract Compliance, in conjunction with the federal contracting and administering agencies in the Philadelphia area, would determine definite standards for specific goals in a contractor's affirmative action program. After such standards were determined, each bidder would be required to commit itself to specific goals for minority manpower utilization. The order set forth factors to be considered in determining definite standards, including: [specifics of order omitted—Ed.]

The order of September 23, 1969 specified that on each invitation to bid each bidder would be required to submit an affirmative action program. The order further provided:

"4. No bidder will be awarded a contract unless his affirmative action program contains goals falling within the range set forth . . . above . . .

. . .

"6. The purpose of the contractor's commitment to specific goals as to minority manpower utilization is to meet his affirmative action obligations under the equal opportunity clause of the contract. This commitment is not intended and shall not be used to discriminate against any qualified applicant or employee. Whenever it comes to the bidder's attention that the goals are being used in a discriminatory manner, he must report it to the Area Coordinator of the Office of Federal Contract Compliance of the U.S. Department of Labor in order that appropriate sanction proceedings may be instituted.

. . .

"8. The bidder agrees to keep such records and file such reports relating to the provisions of this order as shall be required by the contracting or administering agency."

In November, 1969, the General State Authority of the Commonwealth of Pennsylvania issued invitations to bid for the construction of an earth dam on Marsh Creek in Chester County, Pennsylvania. Although this dam is a Commonwealth project, part of the construction cost, estimated at over $3,000,000 is to be funded by federal monies under a program

---

[7] Recognition of this problem antedated the present Plan. Under the Philadelphia Pre-Award Plan, which was put into effect on November 30, 1967 by the Philadelphia Federal Executive Board, each apparent low bidder was required to submit a written affirmative action program assuring minority group representation in eight specified trades as a precondition to qualifying for a construction contract or subcontract. This predecessor Plan was suspended due to an Opinion letter by the Comptroller General stating that it violated the principles of competitive bidding. 48 Comp. Gen. 326 (1968).

[8] The Order of June 27, 1969 listed "roofers and waterproofers" among the trades underrepresented by minority craftsmen. The order of September 23, 1969 dropped this category from the list, leaving the six trades previously named.

administered by the Department of Agriculture.[9] The Secretary of Agriculture, one of the federal defendants, as a condition for payment of federal financial assistance for the project, required the inclusion in each bid of a Philadelphia Plan Commitment in compliance with the order of September 23, 1969. On November 14, 1969, the General State Authority issued on addendum to the original invitation for bids requiring all bidders to include such a commitment in their bids. It is alleged and not denied that except for the requirement by the Secretary of Agriculture that the Philadelphia Plan Commitment be included, the General State Authority would not have imposed such a requirement on bidders.

The Association consists of more than eighty contractors in the five-county Philadelphia area who regularly employ workers in the six specified crafts, and who collectively perform more than $150,000,000 of federal and federally assisted construction in that area annually. Each of the contractor plaintiffs is a regular bidder on federal and federally assisted construction projects. The complaint was filed prior to the opening of bids on the Marsh Creek dam. It sought injunctive relief against the inclusion of a Philadelphia Plan Commitment requirement in the invitation for bids. By virtue of a stipulation that the General State Authority would issue a new and superseding invitation for bids if the district court held the Plan to be unlawful, the parties agreed that bids could be received without affecting the justiciability of the controversy. Bids were received on January 7, 1970. One of the intervening contractor plaintiffs submitted a low bid and appeared at the time of the district court decision to be entitled to an award of the contract.

The complaints of the Association and the contractors refer to the fact that the Comptroller General of the United States has opined that the Philadelphia Plan Commitment is illegal and that disbursement of federal funds for the performance of a contract containing such a promise will be treated as unlawful.[10] The plaintiffs point out that the withholding of funds after a contractor has commenced performance would have catastrophic consequences, since contractors depend upon progress payments, and are in no position to complete their contracts without such payments. They allege that the Philadelphia Plan is illegal and void for the following reasons:

1. It is action by the Executive branch not authorized by the constitution or any statute and beyond Executive power.
2. It is inconsistent with Title VII of the Civil Rights Act of 1964.[11]

[9] Federal assistance was authorized under the Watershed Protection and Flood Prevention Act, 16 U.S.C. § 1001 et seq.

[10] Comp. Gen. Op., Letter to Sec. of Labor George P. Shultz, August 5, 1969, 115 CONG. REC. 17,201-04 (daily ed. Dec. 18, 1969). The Comptroller General had objected to earlier efforts at implementing the "affirmative action" aspect of Exec. Order No. 11246 on the ground that these plans failed to inform prospective bidders of definite minimum standards for acceptable programs. In his negative opinion letter in response to the original Philadelphia Pre-Award Plan, he had also adverted to the possibility of conflict with Title VII of the Civil Rights Act of 1964. See note 7 supra. The Title VII objections became the heart of the opinion of August 5, 1969 which challenged the validity of the Revised Philadelphia Plan.

[11] 42 U.S.C. § 2000 (e) et seq.

3. It is inconsistent with Title VI of the Civil Rights Act of 1964.[12]
4. It is inconsistent with the National Labor Relations Act.[13]
5. It is substantively inconsistent with and was not adopted in procedural accordance with Executive Order No. 11246.
6. It violates the process because
   a) it requires contradictory conduct impossible of consistent attainment;
   b) it unreasonably requires contractors to undertake to remedy an evil for which the craft unions, not they, are responsible;
   c) it arbitrarily and without basis in fact singles out the five-county Philadelphia area for discriminatory treatment without adequate basis in fact or law; and
   d) it requires quota hiring in violation of the Fifth Amendment.

The federal defendants moved both to dismiss the complaint under Rule 12(b)(1), Fed. R. Civ. P. and for summary judgment under Rule 56(b) Fed. R. Civ. P. They asserted that the plaintiffs lacked standing and that they were entitled to judgment as a matter of law. The plaintiffs moved for summary judgment. The district court held that the Association lacked standing to maintain the suit, that the Contractors had such standing, and that the Plan was valid. It granted summary judgment for the federal defendants, and the plantiffs appeal.

### STANDING

The district court's holding that the Association lacked standing to sue was handed down prior to that of the Supreme Court in *Association of Data Processing Service Orgs., Inc.* v. *Camp,* 397 U.S. 150 (1970), and in the light of that decision and the more recent decision in *Citizens to Preserve Overton Park, Inc.* v. *Volpe,* 39 U.S.L.W. 4287 (U.S. March 2, 1971), is at least doubtful. We need not reach this issue, however, since the Contractor plaintiffs who as bidders are directly impacted by the requirement that they agree in their bid to comply with the Plan, clearly have standing. *Abbott Laboratories* v. *Gardner,* 387 U.S. 136 (1967). All plaintiffs have been represented by the same attorney, and the presence or absence of the Association as a plaintiff has no practical significance.

### EXECUTIVE POWER

The plaintiffs contend that the Philadelphia Plan is social legislation of local application enacted by the Executive without the benefit of statutory or constitutional authority. They point out, probably correctly, that the Plan imposes on the successful bidder on a project of the Commonwealth of Pennsylvania record keeping and hiring practices which violate Pennsylvania law.[14] If the Plan was adopted pursuant to a valid

[12] 42 U.S.C. § 2000(d) et seq.
[13] 29 U.S.C. § 151 et seq.
[14] The Pennsylvania Human Relations Act, 43 P.S. § 951 et seq. (Supp. 1970, specifically prohibits an employer from keeping any record of or using any form of application with respect to the race, color, religion, ancestry, sex or national origin of an applicant for employment. 43 P.S. § 955(b)(1). The Act also prohibits the use of a

exercise of Presidential power its provisions would, of course, control over local law. See *United States* v. *City of Chester,* 144 F.2d 415, 420 (3d Cir. 1944); cf. *United States* v. *Allegheny County,* 322 U.S. 174, 183 (1944); *Panhandle Oil Co.* v. *Knox,* 277 U.S. 218, 221 (1928). But, say the plaintiffs, where there is neither statutory authorization nor constitutional authority for the Executive action, no substantive federal requirements may be imposed upon a contract between the Commonwealth and its contractor.

The district court's answer is that the federal government "has the unrestricted power to fix the terms, conditions and those with whom it will deal." [15] For this proposition it cites *Perkins* v. *Lukens Steel Co.,* 310 U.S. 113 (1940) and *King* v. *Smith,* 392 U.S. 309, 333 (1968). Neither case is in point, however on the issue of Executive as distinguished from federal power. *King* v. *Smith* held that the Alabama substitute father regulation was inconsistent with the Social Security Act, 42 U.S.C. § 606 (a), and points out that the federal government may impose the terms and conditions upon which its money allotments may be disbursed. The conditions referred to were imposed by Congress, not by the Executive branch. *Perkins* v. *Lukens Steel Co.* interprets the Public Contracts Act of June 30, 1936 [16] which requires that sellers to the federal government pay prevailing minimum wages. It holds that an administrative determination of prevailing wages in a given industry made by the Secretary of Labor is not subject to judicial review on behalf of a potential seller.[17] The opinion contains the language:
"Like private individuals and businesses, the Government enjoys the unrestricted power to produce its own supplies, to determine those with whom it will deal, and to fix the terms and conditions upon which it will make needed purchases." [18]
The quoted language refers to federal power exercised pursuant to a statutory mandate. The case is not in point on the issue of Executive power absent such a mandate.

The federal defendants and several amici [19] contend that Executive power to impose fair employment conditions incident to the power to

quota system for employment based on the same criteria. 32 P.S. § 955(b)(3). The record keeping prohibition may be of limited force due to certain requirements of Title VII of the Civil Rights Act of 1964. 42 U.S.C. § 2000(e)-8(c). Moreover, we do not know how the Pennsylvania courts or the Pennsylvania Human Relations Commission would react to a scheme of "benign" quota hiring.

[15] 311 F. Supp. 1002, 1011 (E.D. Pa. 1970).

[16] 49 Stat. 2036-39, 41 U.S.C. §§ 35-45.

[17] The actual holding of *Perkins* was subsequently nullified by Congress. 66 Stat. 308 (1952), 41 U.S.C. § 43(a). See 4 K. Davis, ADMINISTRATIVE LAW § 28.06 (1958).

[18] 310 U.S. at 127.

[19] Amici favoring the Plan include the City of Philadelphia, the Urban League of Philadelphia, Wives for Equal Employment Opportunity, the Lawyers' Committee for Civil Rights Under Law, and the N.A.A.C.P. Appearing as amici in opposition to the Plan are the Building and Construction Trades Dep't, AFL-CIO, the Building and Construction Trades Council of Philadelphia and Vicinity, AFL-CIO, the General Building Contractors Ass'n, Inc., the National Electrical Contractors Ass'n, and the Associated General Contractors of America.

contract has been upheld in this Circuit and in the Fifth Circuit. They cite *Farmer* v. *Philadelphia Electric Company,* 329 F.2d 3 (3d Cir. 1964 and *Farkas* v. *Texas Instrument, Inc.,* 375 F.2d 629 (5th Cir.), cert. denied, 389 U.S. 977 (1967). Both cases discussed the Executive Order program for achieving fair employment in the context of Government contracts rather than federally assisted state contracts, and both assumed the validity of the Executive Order then applicable.[20] Both cases held that even assuming the validity of the Executive Order, it did not give rise to a private cause of action for damages by a party subjected to discrimination. Discussion of the validity of the Executive Order was in each case dictum. Moreover, both *Farmer* and *Farkas* refer to 40 U.S.C. § 486(a) as the source of the Executive power to issue the order. That subsection authorizes the President to prescribe such policies and directives as he deems necessary to effectuate the provisions of Chapter 10 of Title 40 [21] and Chapter 4 of Title 41.[22] These chapters deal with procurement of Government property and services, not with federal assistance programs. Thus even if *Farmer* and *Farkas* were holdings rather than dicta as to Executive power, the holdings would not reach the instant case. The validity of the Executive Order program as applied to the construction industry in state government contracts by virtue of federal assistance has not been litigated, so far as we have been able to determine, in any case reaching the courts of appeals.[23] Certainly no case has arisen which considers Executive power to impose, by virtue of federal assistance, contract terms in a state construction contract which are at variance with state law.

The limitations of Executive power have rarely been considered by the courts. One of those rare instances is *Youngstown Sheet & Tube Co.* v. *Sawyer,* 343 U.S. 579 (1952). From the six concurring opinions and one dissenting opinion in that case, the most significant guidance for present purposes may be found in that of Justice Jackson:

"We may well begin by a somewhat oversimplified grouping of practical situations in which a President may doubt, or others may challenge, his powers, and by distinguishing roughly the legal consequences of this factor of relativity.

"1. When the President acts pursuant to an express or implied authorization of Congress, his authority is at its maximum, for it includes all that he possesses in his own right plus all that Congress can delegate. In these circumstances, and in these only, may he be said (for what it may be worth) to personify the federal sovereignty. If his act is held unconstitutional under these circumstances, it usually means that the Federal Government as an undivided whole lacks power. A seizure executed by the President pursuant to an Act of Congress would be supported by the

[20] Exec. Order No. 10925, 26 Fed. Reg. 1977 (March 6, 1961), 3 C.F.R., 1961 Comp. 86.
[21] Management and Disposal of Government Property.
[22] Procurement Procedures.
[23] But cf. *Weiner* v. *Cuyahoga Community College,* 19 Ohio St. 2d 35, 249 N.E.2d 907 (1969), cert. denied, 396 U.S. 1004 (1970); *Ethridge* v. *Rhodes,* 268 F. Supp. 83 (S.D. Ohio 1967).

strongest of presumptions and the widest latitude of judicial interpretation, and the burden of persuasion would rest heavily on any who might attack it.

"2. When the President acts in absence of either a congressional grant or denial of authority, he can only rely upon his own independent powers, but there is a zone of twilight in which he and Congress may have concurrent authority, or in which its distribution is uncertain. Therefore congressional inertia, indifference or quiescence may sometimes, at least as a practical matter, enable, if not invite, measures on independent presidential responsibility. In this area, any actual test of power is likely to depend on the imperatives of events and contemporary imponderables rather than on abstract theories of law.

"3. When the President takes measures incompatible with the expressed or implied will of Congress, his power is at its lowest ebb, for then he can rely only upon his own constitutional powers minus any constitutional powers of Congress over the matter. Courts can sustain exclusive presidential control in such a case only by disabling the Congress from acting upon the subject. Presidential claim to a power at once so conclusive and preclusive must be scrutinized with caution, for what is at stake is the equilibrium established by our constitutional system." [24]

Plaintiffs contend that the Philadelphia Plan in inconsistent with the will of Congress expressed in several statutes. We deal with these statutory contents hereinafter. Thus for the moment we may set to one side consideration of Justice Jackson's third category, and turn to category (1), action expressly or impliedly authorized, and category (2), action in which the President has implied power to act in the absence of congressional preemption. To determine into which category the Philadelphia Plan falls a review of Executive Orders in the field of fair employment practices is helpful. [History of Executive Orders omitted.—Ed.]

. . .

. . . In the area of Government procurement Executive authority to impose non-discrimination contract provisions falls in Justice Jackson's first category: action pursuant to the express or implied authorization of Congress.

Exec. Order No. 10925 [41] signed by President Kennedy on March 6, 1961, among other things enlarged the notice requirements and specified that the President's Committee on Equal Employment Opportunity could by rule, regulation or order impose sanctions for violation. Coverage still extended only to federal government contracts. Significantly for purposes of this case, however, the required contract language was amended to add the provision:

"The Contractor will take affirmative action to ensure that applicants are employed, and that employees are treated during employment, without regard to their race, creed, color, or national origin." [42]

The Philadelphia Plan is simply a refined approach to this "affirmative

[24] 343 U.S. at 635-38 (footnotes omitted).
[41] 26 Fed. Reg. 1977, 3 C.F.R., 1959-63 Comp. 448.
[42] Id., pt. III, § 301(1).

action" mandate. Applied to federal procurement the affirmative action clause is supported by the same Presidential procurement authority that supports the non-discrimination clause generally.

The most significant change in the Executive Order program for present purposes occurred on June 22, 1963 when the President signed Executive Order No. 11114,[13] which amended Executive Order No. 10925 by providing that the same non-discrimination contract provisions heretofore required in all federal procurement contracts must also be included in all federally assisted construction contracts. By way of Executive Order No. 11246 [14] issued in 1965. President Johnson trans-ferred to the Secretary of Labor the functions formerly specified in Executive Order Nos. 10925 and 11114, and he continued both the affirmative action requirement and the coverage of federally assisted construction contracts.

While all federal procurement contracts must include an affirmative action covenant,[15] the coverage on federally assisted contracts has been extended to construction contracts only. This choice is significant, for it demonstrates that the Presidents were not attempting by the Executive Order program merely to impose their notions of desirable social legislation on the states wholesale. Rather, they acted in the one area in which discrimination in employment was most likely to affect the cost and the progress of projects in which the federal government had both financial and completion interests. In direct procurement the federal government has a vital interest in assuring that the largest possible pool of qualified manpower be available for the accomplishment of its projects. It has the identical interest with respect to federally assisted construction projects. When the Congress authorizes an appropriation for a program of federal assistance, and authorizes the Executive branch to implement the program by arranging for assistance to specific projects, in the absence of specific statutory regulations it must be deemed to have granted to the President a general authority to act for the protection of federal interests. In the case of Executive Order Nos. 11246 and 11114 three Presidents have acted by analogizing federally assisted construction to direct federal procurement. If such action has not been authorized by Congress (Justice Jackson's first category), at the least it falls within the second category. If no congressional enactments prohibit what has been done, the Executive action is valid. Particularly is this so when Congress, aware of Presidential action with respect to federally assisted construction projects since June of 1963, has continued to make appropriations for such projects. We conclude, therefore, that unless the Philadelphia Plan is prohibited by some other congressional enactment, its inclusion as a precondition for federal assistance was within the implied authority of the

[43] 28 Fed. Reg. 6485, 3 C.F.R., 1959-63 Comp. 774.
[44] See note 4 supra.
[45] Section 204 of Exec. Order No. 11246 provides that the Secretary of Labor may exempt certain contracts and purchase orders from the requirements of the order because of special circumstances in the national interest and that he may by rule or regulation exempt certain classes of contracts (1) to be performed outside the United States, (2) for standard commercial supplies or raw materials, (3) involving insubstantial amounts of money or workers, or (4) involving subcontracts below a specified tier.

President and his designees. We turn, then to a consideration of the statutes on which plaintiffs rely.

## THE CIVIL RIGHTS ACT OF 1964

Plaintiffs suggest that by enacting Title VII of the Civil Rights Act of 1964, 42 U.S.C. § 2000e et seq, which deals comprehensively with discrimination in employment, Congress occupied the field. The express reference in that statute to Executive Order No. 10925 or any other Executive Order prescribing fair employment practices for Government contractors, 42 U.S.C. § 2000e-8(d), indicates, however, that Congress contemplated continuance of the Executive Order program. Moreover we have held that the remedies established by Title VII are not exclusive. *Young* v. *International Telephone & Telegraph Co.,* —— F.2d —— (3d Cir. 1971).

But while Congress has not prohibited Presidential action in the area of fair employment on federal or federally assisted contracts, the Executive is bound by the express prohibitions of Title VII. The argument most strenuously advanced against the Philadelphia Plan is that it requires action by employers which violates the Act. Plaintiffs point to § 703(j), 42 U.S.C. § 2000e-2(j):
"Nothing contained in this subchapter shall be interpreted to require any employer . . . [or] labor organization . . . to grant preferential treatment to any individual or to any group because of the race . . . of such individual or groups on account of an imbalance which may exist with respect to the total number or percentage of persons of any race . . . employed . . . in comparison with the total number or percentage of persons of such race . . . in the available work force in any community . . . or other area."
The Plan requires that the contractor establish specific goals for utilization of available minority manpower in six trades in the five-county area. Possibly an employer could not be compelled, under the authority of Title VII, to embrace such a program, although § 703(j) refers to percentages of minorities in an area work force rather than percentages of minority tradesmen in an available trade work force. We do not meet that issue here, however, for the source of the required contract provision is Executive Order No. 11246. Section 703(j) is a limitation only upon Title VII, not upon any other remedies, state or federal.

Plaintiffs, and more particularly the union amici, contend that the Plan violates Title VII because it interferes with a bona fide seniority system. Section 703(h), 42 U.S.C. § 2000(e)-2(h), provides:
"Notwithstanding any other provision of this subchapter, it shall not be an unlawful employment practice for an employer to employ different standards of compensation, or different terms, conditions, or privileges of employment pursuant to a bona fide seniority or merit system . . ."
The unions, it is said, refer men from the hiring halls on the basis of seniority, and the Philadelphia Plan interferes with this arrangement since few minority tradesmen have high seniority. Just as with § 703(j), how-

ever, § 703(h) is a limitation only upon Title VII, not upon any other remedies.[46]

Plaintiffs contend that the Plan, by imposing remedial quotas, requires them to violate the basic prohibitions of Section 703(a), 42 U.S.C. § 2000 (e)-2(a):

"It shall be an unlawful employment practice for an employer—

(1) to fail or refuse to hire . . . any individual . . . because of such individual's race . . . or

(2) to . . . classify his employees in any way which would deprive . . . any individual of employment opportunities . . . because of such individual's race . . ."

Because the Plan requires that the contractor agree to specific goals for minority employment in each of the six trades and requires a good faith effort to achieve those goals, they argue, it requires (1) that they refuse to hire some white tradesmen, and (2) that they classify their employees by race, in violation of § 703(a). This argument rests on an overly simple reading both of the Plan and of the findings which led to its adoption.

The order of September 23, 1969 contained findings that although overall minority group representation in the construction industry in the five-county Philadelphia area was thirty per cent, in the six trades representation was approximately one per cent. It found, moreover, that this obvious underrepresentation was due to the exclusionary practices of the unions representing the six trades. It is the practice of building contractors to rely on union hiring halls as the prime source for employees. The order made further findings as to the availability of qualified minority tradesmen for employment in each trade, and as to the impact of an affirmative action program with specific goals upon the existing labor force. The Department of Labor found that contractors could commit to the specific employment goals "without adverse impact on the existing labor force." Some minority tradesmen could be recruited, in other words, without eliminating job opportunities for white tradesmen.

To read Section 703(a) in the manner suggested by the plaintiffs we would have to attribute to Congress the intention to freeze the status quo and to foreclose remedial action under other authority designed to overcome existing evils. We discern no such intention either from the language of the statute or from its legislative history. Clearly the Philadelphia Plan is color-conscious. Indeed the only meaning which can be attributed to the "affirmative action" language which since March of 1961 has been included in successive Executive Orders is that Government contractors must be color-conscious. Since 1941 the Executive Order program has recognized that discriminatory practices exclude available

---

[46] This same subsection refers to ability tests. The Supreme Court recently in *Griggs* v. *Duke Power Co.*, 39 U.S.L.W. 4317 (U.S. Mar. 8, 1971) considered the extent to which such tests are permissible. The Court said:
"But Congress directed the thrust of the Act to the *consequences* of employment practices, not simply the motivation." 39 U.S.L.W. at 4319.
It held that the tests must be job related. Nor can seniority make permanent the effects of past discrimination. *Local 189, United Papermakers & Paperworkers* v. *United States*, 416 F.2d 980 (5th Cir. 1969), cert. denied, 397 U.S. 919 (1970); *Quarles* v. *Philip Morris, Inc.*, 279 F.Supp. 505 (E.D. Va. 1968).

minority manpower from the labor pool. In other contexts color-consciousness has been deemed to be an appropriate remedial posture. *Porcelli* v. *Titus,* 302 F. Supp. 726 (D.N.J. 1969) aff'd, 431 F.2d 1254 (3d Cir. 1970); *Norwalk CORE* v. *Norwalk Redevelopment Agency,* 395 F.2d 920, 931 (2d Cir. 1968); *Offermann* v. *Nitkowsky,* 378 F.2d 22, 24 (2d Cir. 1967). It has been said respecting Title VII that "Congress did not intend to freeze an entire generation of Negro employees into discriminatory patterns that existed before the Act." *Quarles* v. *Philip Morris, Inc., supra,* 279 F. Supp. at 514. The *Quarles* case rejected the contention that existing, nondiscriminatory seniority arrangements were so sanctified by Title VII that the effects of past discrimination in job assignments could not be overcome.[47] We reject the contention that Title VII prevents the President acting through the Executive Order program from attempting to remedy the absence from the Philadelphia construction labor of minority tradesmen in key trades.

What we have said about Title VII applies with equal force to Title VI of the Civil Rights Act of 1964, 42 U.S.C. § 2000(d) et seq. That Title prohibits racial and other discrimination in any program or activity receiving federal financial assistance.[48] This general prohibition against discrimination cannot be construed as limiting Executive authority in defining appropriate affirmative action on the part of a contractor.

We hold that the Philadelphia Plan does not violate the Civil Rights Act of 1964.

### THE NATIONAL LABOR RELATIONS ACT

The June 27, 1969 order, par. 8(b) provides:

"It is no excuse that the union with which the contractor has a collective bargaining agreement failed to refer minority employees. Discrimination in referral for employment, even if pursuant to provisions of a collective bargaining agreement, is prohibited by the National Labor Relations Act and the Civil Rights Act of 1964. It is the longstanding uniform policy of OFCC that contractors and subcontractors have a responsibility to provide equal employment opportunity if they want to participate in federally involved contracts. To the extent they have delegated the responsibility for some of their employment practices to some other organization or agency which prevents them from meeting their obligations pursuant to Executive Order 11246, as amended, such contractors cannot be considered to be in compliance with Executive Order 11246, as amended, or the implementing rules, regulations and orders."

The union amici vigorously contend that the Plan violates the National Labor Relations Act by interfering with the exclusive union referral sys-

[47] The federal courts in overcoming the effects of past discrimination are expressly authorized in Title VII to take affirmative action. 42 U.S.C. § 2000(e)-5(g). See *Vogler* v. *McCarty,* 294 F. Supp. 368 (E.D. La. 1968), aff'd *sub. nom. International Ass'n Heat & Frost I. & A. Wkrs. v. Vogler,* 407 F.2d 1047 (5th Cir. 1969).

[48] Section 604 of Title VI, 42 U.S.C. § 2000(d)-3, states that nothing in the Title authorizes agency action under the Title with respect to employment practices of any employer, except where federal assistance is primarily aimed at providing employment. However, since the Philadelphia Plan does not purport to derive its authorization from Title VI, this section does not affect its validity.

tems to which the contractors have in collective bargaining agreements bound themselves. Exclusive hiring hall contracts in the building and construction industry are validated by Section 8(f) of the National Labor Relations Act, 29 U.S.C. § 158(f). In *Teamsters Local 357* v. *NLRB,* 365 U.S. 667 (1961), the Supreme Court held that the National Labor Relations Board could not proscribe exclusive hiring hall agreements as illegal per se since Congress had not chosen to prohibit hiring halls. It is argued that the President is attempting to do what the Supreme Court said the National Labor-Relations Board could not do—prohibit a valid hiring hall agreement. Of course collective bargaining agreements which perpetuate the effects of past discrimination are unlawful under Title VII. *Local 189, United Papermakers & Paperworkers* v. *United States, supra; United States* v. *Sheet Metal Workers, Local 36,* 416 F.2d 123, 132 (8th Cir. 1969). The findings of past discrimination which justified remedial action in these cases were made in judicial proceedings, however. See 42 U.S.C. § 2000e-5(g). The amici contend that the Assistant Secretary's nonjudicial finding of prior exclusionary practices is insufficient to support the Plan's implied requirement that the contractor look to other sources for employees if the unions fail to refer sufficient minority group members.

It is clear that while hiring hall arrangements are permitted by federal law they are not required. Nothing in the National Labor Relations Act purports to place any limitation upon the contracting power of the federal government. We have said hereinabove that in imposing the affirmative action requirement on federally assisted construction contracts the President acted within his implied contracting authority. The assisted agency may either agree to do business with contractors who will comply with the affirmative action covenant, or forego assistance. The prospective contractors may either agree to undertake the affirmative action covenant, or forego bidding on federally assisted work. If the Plan violates neither the Constitution nor federal law, the fact that its contractual provisions may be at variance with other contractual undertakings of the contractor is legally irrelevant. Factually, of course, that variance is quite relevant. Factually it is entirely likely that the economics of the marketplace will produce an accommodation between the contract provisions desired by the unions and those desired by the source of the funds. Such an accommodation will be no violation of the National Labor Relations Act.

The absence of a judicial finding of past discrimination is also legally irrelevant. The Assistant Secretary acted not pursuant to Title VII but pursuant to the Executive Order. Regardless of the cause, exclusion from the available labor pool of minority tradesmen is likely to have an adverse effect upon the cost and completion of construction projects in which the federal government is interested. Even absent a finding that the situation found to exist in the five-county area was the result of deliberate past discrimination, the federal interest in improving the availability of key tradesmen in the labor pool would be the same. While a court must find intentional past discrimination before it can require affirmative action under 42 U.S.C. § 2000e-5(g), that section imposes no restraint upon the measures which the President may require of the beneficiaries of federal assistance. The decision of his designees as to the specific affirmative action which would satisfy the local situation did not violate the National Labor Relations Act and was not prohibited by 42 U.S.C. § 2000e-5(g).

### CONSISTENCY WITH EXECUTIVE ORDER NO. 11246

The plaintiffs argue that the affirmative action mandate of § 202 of Executive Order No. 11246 is limited by the more general requirement in the same section. "The contractor will not discriminate against any employee or applicant for employment because of race, creed, color, or national origin." They contend that properly construed the affirmative action referred to means only policing against actual present discrimination, not action looking toward the employment of specific numbers of minority tradesmen.

Section 201 of the Executive Order provides:

"The Secretary of Labor shall be responsible for the administration of Parts II [government contracts] and III [Federal assistance] of this Order and shall adopt such rules and regulations and issue such orders as he deems necessary and appropriate to achieve the purposes thereof."

Acting under this broad delegation of authority the Labor Department in a series of orders of local application made it clear that it interpreted "affirmative action" to require more than mere policing against actual present discrimination.[49] Administrative action pursuant to an Executive Order is invalid and subject to judicial review if beyond the scope of the Executive Order. *Peters* v. *Hobby,* 349 U.S. 331 (1955). But the courts should give more than ordinary deference to an administrative agency's interpretation of an Executive Order or regulation which it is charged to administer. *Udall* v. *Tallman,* 380 U.S. 1 (1965); *Bowles* v. *Seminole Rock & Sand Co.,* 325 U.S. 410, 413 (1945). The Attorney General has issued an opinion that the Philadelphia Plan is valid,[50] and the President has continued to acquiesce in the interpretation of the Executive Order made by his designee. The Labor Department interpretation of the affirmative action clause must, therefore, be deferred to by the courts.

Plaintiffs also contend that the signing of the June 27, 1969 and September 23, 1969 orders by an assistant secretary rather than by the Secretary of Labor makes those orders procedurally invalid. Here they rely on § 401 which provides:

"The Secretary of Labor may delegate to any officer, agency, or employee in the Executive branch of the Government, any function or duty of the Secretary under Parts II and III of this Order, except authority to promulgate rules and regulations of a general nature."

[49] See United States Commission on Civil Rights. The Federal Civil Rights Enforcement at 167-72 (1970).

[50] Att'y. Gen. Op., Letter to Sec. of Labor Shultz, Sept. 22, 1969, 115 Cong. Rec. 17,204-06 (daily ed. Dec. 18, 1969).

The Plan, they say, is a rule or regulation of a general nature, and could have been issued only by the Secretary. In the first place the Plan is not general. It is based upon findings as to the available construction manpower in a specific labor market. Moreover, the interpretation of § 401 made by the administrator requires the same deference from the courts as is required toward his other interpretations of the order. We will not second guess his delegation to the Assistant Secretary of the duty of enforcing the affirmative action covenant.

### THE DUE PROCESS CONTENTIONS

Plaintiffs urge that the Plan violates the Due Process Clause of the Fifth Amendment in several ways.

First, they allege that it imposes on the contractors contradictory duties impossible of attainment. This impossibility arises, they say, because the Plan requires both an undertaking to seek achievement of specific goals of minority employment and an undertaking not to discriminate against any qualified applicant or employee, and because a decision to hire any black employee necessarily involves a decision not to hire a qualified white employee. This is pure sophistry. The findings in the September 23, 1969 order disclose that the specific goals may be met, considering normal employee attrition and anticipated growth in the industry, without adverse effects on the existing labor force. According to the order the construction industry has an essentially transitory labor force and is often in short supply in key trades. The complaint does not allege that these findings misstate the underlying facts.

Next the plaintiff urge that the Plan is arbitrary and capricious administrative action, in that it singles out the contractors and makes them take action to remedy the situation created by acts of past discrimination by the craft unions. They point to the absence of any proceedings under Title VII against the offending unions, and urge that they are being discriminated against. This argument misconceives the source of the authority for the affirmative action program. Plaintiffs are not being discriminated against. They are merely being invited to bid on a contract with terms imposed by the source of the funds. The affirmative action covenant is no different in kind than other covenants specified in the invitation to bid. The Plan does not impose a punishment for past misconduct. It exacts a covenant for present performance.

Some amici urge that selection of the five-county Philadelphia area was arbitrary and capricious and without basis in fact. The complaint contains a conclusive allegation to this effect. No supporting facts are alleged. It is not alleged, for example, that the specific goals for minority manpower utilization would be different if more or fewer counties were to be included in the September 23, 1969 order. The union amici do question the findings made by the Assistant Secretary of Labor, but the complaint, fairly read, does not put these findings in issue. We read the allegation with respect to the five-county area as putting in issue the legal authority of the Secretary to impose a specific affirmative action requirement in any separate geographic area. The simple answer to this contention is that federally assisted construction contracts are performed at specific times and in specific places. What is appropriate affirmative action will vary according to the local manpower conditions prevailing at the time.

Finally, the plaintiffs urge that the specific goals specified by the Plan are racial quotas prohibited by the equal protection aspect of the Fifth Amendment. See *Shapiro* v. *Thompson,* 394 U.S. 618, 641-42 (1969); *Schneider* v. *Rush,* 377 U.S. 163 (1964); *Bolling* v. *Sharpe,* 347 U.S. 497 (1954). The Philadelphia Plan is valid Executive action designed to remedy the perceived evil that minority tradesmen have not been included in the labor pool available for the performance of construction projects in which the federal government has a cost and performance interest. The Fifth Amendment does not prohibit such action.

One final point. The plaintiffs contend that although there were cross-motions for summary judgment the district court, while it should have entered summary judgment in their favor, could not properly enter summary judgment against them. Several amici press this point on appeal even more strenuously than do plaintiffs. They contend that neither the finding of past discrimination by the craft unions made in the June 27, 1969 order nor the statistical findings as to availability of minority tradesmen, employee attrition, and industry growth made in the September 23, 1969 order should be accepted as true.

The federal defendants conceded in the district court that the affidavit of Mr. Macaluso, to which copies of both orders were attached, was offered not for the truth of the underlying facts but only to identify the orders. This concession was not significant for the decision on the motions under Rule 12(b)(1) and Rule 56(b). The complaint to which the motions by the federal defendants was addressed nowhere challenges the factual underpinnings of the specific goals set forth in the September 23, 1969 order. Rather the complaint makes a legal attack upon the power of the Department of Labor to impose these goals as contractual commitments. Read generously the complaint can be construed to challenge the administrative procedures followed by the Assistant Secretary in determining these goals. We have dealt hereinabove with that challenge insofar as it questions compliance with the procedure specified in Executive Order No. 11246. Insofar as the complaint challenges on broader administrative law grounds the method by which the Assistant Secretary assembled the data for the September 23, 1969 order, we hold that public hearings after notice were an appropriate means for the administrative agency to obtain the information needed for informed judgment. Cf. *Shannon* v. *Department of Housing & Urban Development,* —— F.2d —— (3d Cir. 1971). No public hearing was held prior to the issuance of the June 27, 1969 order, which contains the Assistant Secretary's finding of past exclusionary union practices. He relied upon published data, however, which itself may have been sufficient to justify administrative action leading to the specification of contract provisions. We need not decide that issue, however, for in our view the data in the September 23, 1969 order revealing the percentages of utilization of minority group tradesmen in the six trades compared with the availability of such tradesmen in the five-county area, justified issuance of the order without regard to a finding as to the cause of the situation. The federal interest is in maximum availability of construction tradesmen for the projects in which the federal government has a cost and completion interest. A finding as to the historical reason for the exclusion of available tradesmen from the labor pool is not essential for federal contractual remedial action.

The judgment of the district court will be affirmed.

## NOTES

1. See also, *State of Washington* v. *Baugh Construction Co.* 312 F. Supp. 598 (W.D. Wash. 1969) 2 FEP Cases 271. Cf. *Porcelli* v. *Titus,* 431 F.2d 1254 (3rd Cir. 1970) 2 FEP Cases 1024.

2. As 1970 drew to a close, construction programs of the Office of Federal Contract Compliance, which consumed substantial amounts of the professional staff time of the small organization, had evolved two basic approaches to the continuing problems of the Equal Employment Opportunity in the construction industry. The first to emerge was the so-called, "imposed plan" typified by the revised Philadelphia Plan. The second approach was the "home town" solution which was first typified by the Chicago Plan.

The "home town" approach is the fruit of negotiations among the concerned interests in a given community. It generally involves the construction industry representatives, the affected labor unions, and representatives of the minority community. It may also include some participation from local public officials and technical assistance from the Office of Federal Contract Compliance. The "home town" approach has been endorsed by the AFL-CIO and is obviously the preferred approach of the Department of Labor. However, both have been attacked as non-productive with particular criticism that the "home town" plans are facades behind which discrimination as usual continues to operate.

3. For general discussions of the constitutionality of the EEO Executive Order, see Speck, *Enforcement of Non-Discrimination Requirements for Government Contract Work,* 63 COLUM. L. REV. 243 (1963); See Powers, *Federal Procurement and Equal Employment Opportunity,* 29 LAW AND CONTEM. PROB. 468 (1964); Price, *The Affirmative Action Concept of Equal Employment Opportunity,* 16 LAB. L.J. 603 (1965).

4. The *Weiner* decision cited in the principal case was the first decision squarely confronting the issue of the compatibility of affirmative action plans with Title VII. The dissenting opinion of Chief Justice Taft summarizes the position of opponents of such measures:

"As stated in the majority's statement of the case, 'the invitation for bids on the contract contained specifications which required the contractor to submit an *Affirmative Action Plan* intended to "have the *result of assuring* that there is minority group representation in all trades on the job and in all phases of the work" ' and 'Reliance's bid was formally rejected by the College for failure to include submission of' such a plan.

"I fail to perceive any distinction between such a 'Plan intended to "have the *result of assuring* ... minority group representation" ' and a guarantee of such representation. Counsel for the College conceded that such a guarantee would be a discrimination against others that is prohibited by the Civil Rights Act of 1964 (Section 2000e-2[j], Title 42, U.S. Code).

"Likewise, the majority opinion concedes that '[t]he establishment of a quota of employment of any particular minority would . . . be discriminatory in violation of' that Act. Certainly, such an unlawful establishment of a quota would necessarily be a part of any '*Affirmative Action Plan* intended to "have the *result of assuring* that there is minority group representation in all trades on the job and in all phases of the work." ' "

5. A union whose membership would be adversely affected by an employer's loss of government contracts due to discrimination in employment practices is entitled to participation in the compliance hearing. See *Crown Zellerbach Corp.* v. *Wirtz*, 281 F. Supp. 337, 1 FEP Cases 274 (D.C. D.C. 1968); see also *U.S.* v. *Carpenters Local 169*, 457 F.2d 210, 4 FEP Cases 85 (7th Cir. 1972).


## ASSOCIATED GENERAL CONTRACTORS OF MASS., INC. v. ALTSHULER

*United States Court of Appeals, First Circuit, 1973*
*490 F.2d 9, 6 FEP Cases 1013*

COFFIN, Chief Judge: This is an appeal from a judgment sustaining, as constitutional and in accord with state law, certain contract requirements imposed by the Commonwealth of Massachusetts upon contractors engaged in publicly funded construction work at Boston State College. Appellants are thirteen individual construction companies, now engaged in construction of public buildings for the Commonwealth, and a membership corporation comprised of one hundred forty-five general contracting firms which together perform approximately 80 per cent of all construction in the Commonwealth. Each of the appellants was a prospective bidder for the Boston State College contract.

In relevant part, § 1B of the contract requires that the contractor

". . . maintain on his project, which is located in an area in which there are high concentrations of minority group persons, a not less than twenty percent ratio of minority employee man hours to total employee man hours in each job category. . . ."

Section V, ¶ 3, of the contract provides, however, that the contractor must hire only "competent" workers. The Secretary of Transportation and Construction for the Commonwealth, who is charged with enforcing the contract provisions, interprets this to mean that § 1B requires the hiring of only "qualified" workers. The district court has interpreted the contract in the same way.

The contract also requires that the contractor engage in special referral procedures as well as traditional referral methods, cooperate with a Liaison Committee composed of various representatives from community groups, make weekly compliance reports to the Liaison Committee and the Massachusetts Commission Against Discrimination (M.C.A.D.), and permit the M.C.A.D. access to books, records, and accounts containing employment information.

The contract further stipulates that the M.C.A.D. will investigate any alleged non-compliance with the contract terms and notify the contractor of both its findings and recommendations as to how he might comply with the terms. If the contractor fails to accept the recommendations and in addition the M.C.A.D. determines that the contractor has not taken "every possible measure to achieve compliance", the M.C.A.D. will report its findings to the Bureau of Construction and recommend that specific sanctions be imposed. Before imposing any sanctions, however, pursuant to the Commonwealth's Administrative Procedures Act, M.G.L.A. c. 30A §§ 10, 11 and according to the Secretary of Transportation and Construction, the Bureau will provide the contractor with notice of the findings and a hearing in which he may challenge them.

Because the federal government pays a portion of the construction costs of the Boston State project, contractors are also required to accept federal bid conditions, promulgated by the United States Secretary of Labor pursuant to § 201 of Executive Order No. 11246 (30 F.R. 12319, as amended, 32 F.R. 14303; 34 F.R. 12985) and 41 C.F.R. 60. The specific contractual elements of the federal bid conditions are derived from the Boston Area Construction Program (the Boston Plan), a "hometown" equal employment opportunity plan prepared by the local construction industry in cooperation with the Department of Labor. Unlike the Commonwealth's § 1B, the federal Boston Plan sets area-wide percentage objectives for minority hiring within each trade, rather than percentage goals for each project. Under the Boston Plan the responsibility for fulfilling the objectives does not lie with the individual contractor; he merely agrees to hire whatever minority workers are referred to him by the trades unions in the course of the plan's operation. Moreover, while § 1B requires that contractors take "every possible measure" to comply with the contract terms, the Boston Plan necessitates merely a "good faith" effort by the contractor. A fourth point of difference between the two plans is that the Boston Plan places the burden of proving non-compliance upon the government agency, while § 1B places the burden of proving compliance, once non-compliance has been alleged, upon the contractor himself.

Appellants challenge the constitutionality of § 1B of the contract requirements imposed by the Commonwealth on three grounds: They contend, first, that § 1B varies so significantly from the federal bid conditions of the Boston Plan that it violates the Supremacy Clause of Article

VI; second, that § 1B imposes a fixed racial hiring quota which violates the Equal Protection clause of the Fourteenth Amendment; and finally, that § 1B permits the imposition of sanctions without proper notice or an opportunity to be heard, in violation of the Due Process clause of the Fourteenth Amendment. Appellants also contend, pursuant to the pendent jurisdiction of this court, that § 1B involves the M.C.A.D. in activities which go beyond the scope of its enabling legislation.

I. In order to deal with appellants' first contention, that § 1B violates the Supremacy Clause because the federal Boston Plan must necessarily preempt § 1B, it is necessary to set out the context in which this case arises.

We note at the outset that the construction industry has been particularly slow, throughout the nation, to open itself to racial minorities.[1] For this reason, in 1967 the federal government launched pilot plans in several cities designed to increase minority employment on federally funded construction projects by way of "affirmative action" programs. Executive Order 11246, under which the Secretary of Labor was authorized to promulgate such programs,[3] required that contractors "take affirmative action to ensure that applicants are employed . . . without regard to race. . . ." Affirmative action itself was defined as "specific steps to guarantee equal employment opportunity keyed to the problems and needs of members of minority groups, including, when there are deficiencies, the development of specific goals and time tables. . . ."[4]

After several different affirmative action programs had been implemented, with varying degrees of success,[5] in 1970 the government permitted particular communities to develop their own "hometown" affirmative action programs.[6] If the Secretary of Labor approved the plans,[7] the plans would receive federal funding, and local contractors who complied

---

[1] [Footnotes numbered as in original.—Ed.] See MARSHALL, THE NEGRO AND ORGANIZED LABOR, 118-28 (1965); Hill, *The Racial Practices of Organized Labor: The Contemporary Record in The Negro and the American Labor Movement* 313-314 (J. Jacobson, ed., 1968).

As of May 19, 1970, only 11.8% of the 1.1 million members of the construction unions in America were members of racial minorities. The higher the skilled union, the smaller the percentage of minority workers becomes: 38.3% of construction laborers are members of racial minorities, while 5.1% of electrical workers, and 2.1% of plumbers. Equal Employment Opportunity Commission Release No. 70-15 (May 19, 1970).

[3] Under the Secretary of Labor's regulations, the Director of the Office of Contract Compliance (O.F.C.C.) has full authority to implement the policies of the Secretary. Thus, the position of the O.F.C.C. is analogous to that of the Commonwealth's Bureau of Construction.

[4] 41 C.F.R. § 60. 1.40(a) (Supp. 1970).

[5] Plans have been promulgated for Philadelphia, Washington, D.C., St. Louis, Atlanta, and Camden, N.J. See 41 C.F.R. 60.5, 69.6, 60.8, and 38 F.R. 21533 (Aug. 10, 1973). Such "imposed" plans operate only on the contractors; they do not require, and typically do not have, the cooperation of the unions involved.

[6] There are now approximately forty-seven hometown plans finally approved by the O.F.C.C., including approximately twenty-nine federally funded training programs.

[7] The O.F.C.C. determines the adequacy of the hometown plan by considering such factors as (1) the minority population of the area to be covered by the plan; (2) the minority manpower utilization in the industry (on a trade by trade basis); (3) the availability of minorities for employment; (4) the need and availability of training programs; and (5) the projected growth and attrition factors of the area industry in the near future.

with them would thereby comply with the mandate of Executive Order 11246.[8]

The Boston Plan emerged from negotiations between representatives of buildings trades unions, contractors, and minority communities in the Boston area, and was approved by the Secretary of Labor in the fall of 1970. Although it fulfilled its first year goal of training and placing three hundred sixty minority workers, relationships with the minority community representatives deteriorated to the extent that the Department of Labor withheld second year funding until a revised plan could be negotiated. The new plan, beginning operations in January, 1972, did not have the participation of representatives of Boston's minority communities.[9] In addition, although put into effect two years after the original Boston Plan had commenced, the revised plan retained the same minority employment goal as that of the original plan.

At about the same time as the revised Boston Plan was put into effect, the Commonwealth began an inquiry of its own into the need for a separate state affirmative action program. The inquiry revealed that despite the existence of the federal Boston Plan, minority membership in all of the nineteen participating unions amounted to less than four per cent of union membership, while minorities comprised approximately twenty-three per cent of the population of Boston. Since virtually all of the contractors who engage in state funded projects rely upon these predominantly white unions for workers, minority employment in the construction trades continued to be extremely low. The Commonwealth also determined that the Boston Plan had no provision for the collection of reliable data on the actual number of hours worked by minority workers placed on construction jobs. Finally, in the opinion of the Commonwealth's Office of Transportation and Construction, the Boston Plan lacked adequate enforcement machinery.[10] On the basis of these findings the Commonwealth concluded that the federal Boston Plan had not gone far enough, and that a separate, state affirmative action program was required for construction projects in which state funds were committed.

The contract for the construction of Boston State College is the first to incorporate both the Commonwealth's own § 1B bid conditions, promul-

---

[8] For any trades or contractors not participating in the hometown plan, Part II of the federal bid conditions sets forth mandatory affirmative action requirements for each individual contractor, generally paralleling those of the hometown plan. The principal distinction with respect to Parts I and II of the bid conditions is that the obligations under Part II are individual obligations that run to a contractor's own work forces, with each contractor responsible for its own training program. Under Part I (the hometown plan), the minority hiring goals are obligations of the trade, and it is the administrative committee of the hometown plan that assigns fair share goals to the individual contractors.

[9] The United States Department of Labor is now funding a subcontract with the Recruiting and Training Program (formerly the Workers Defense League), a minority organization which is providing recruiting, training, and referrals for the Boston Plan.

[10] The Commonwealth was also of the view that it is desirable to concentrate minority employment in the trade in projects in or near minority neighborhoods. Thus, the Commonwealth contends that its plan is not designed simply for the purpose of increasing minority employment but also for altering the geographic distribution of placements.

gated under authority of the Governor's Executive Order No. 74, and the federal Boston Plan bid conditions. The Assistant Secretary of Transportation and Construction for the Commonwealth has determined that there exist adequate journeymen, apprentices, and trainees within Boston's minority community to provide at least twenty per cent of the work force for the project, as well as for other projects anticipated in the area.[11] It is estimated that the total work force required for the Boston State Project will vary between forty-seven and one hundred fifty persons; contractors on the project must therefore take "every possible measure" to employ between ten and thirty qualified minority workers.

Appellants contend that because the Commonwealth's § 1B affirmative action program places different requirements upon contractors than those of the Boston Plan, the two are in conflict, and that the state plan must therefore be declared invalid. Appellants point out, most particularly, that under § 1B, contractors must bear the burden of showing that they have taken "every possible measure" to comply, whereas under the Boston Plan, they must have made merely a "good faith effort" and the burden of showing non-compliance rests with the government agency. They also stress that the record keeping and referral requirements of § 1B are more onerous than those of the Boston Plan.

In deciding whether state regulations should be invalidated because they conflict with federal law, courts have tended to examine both the possibility of broad conflict in "purposes and objectives" between the two schemes, *Hines* v. *Davidowitz*, 312 U.S. 52, 67 (1940), and the likelihood of specific conflict in the implementation of the two programs.

Clearly, the broad purposes which lay behind the federal Boston Plan and the Commonwealth's § 1B are congruent. Affirmative action, defined in the President's Executive Order as ". . . steps to guarantee equal employment . . . including . . . the development of specific goals and time tables . . ." has the same meaning as affirmative action as defined in the Governor's Executive Order: ". . . positive and aggressive measures to insure equal opportunity." Both plans envisage minority hiring goals as a means of achieving equal opportunity.

Nothing in the President's Executive Order requires that affirmative action taken under the Order be uniform throughout the country, nor does it necessitate that the federal government be the source for every program. An important aspect of federal implementation is the development of "hometown" plans, conceived and developed by local contractor's unions, and minority representatives. And in at least one instance the federal government has relied upon a plan originally conceived by state officials for their own state funded contracts. See *Illinois Builders Ass'n* v. *Ogilvie*, 327 F.Supp. 1154, 3 FEP Cases 571 (S.D. Ill. 1971), *aff'd*, 471 F.2d 680, 5 FEP Cases 229 (7th Cir. 1972).

Nor is there any indication that the federal government has intended to preempt this field. Federal preemption should not be presumed, absent

---

[11] The district court found that the minority populations of neighborhoods in which the Commonwealth's plan is to be applied is approximately 40%.

"a clear manifestation of intention" to preempt the field. . . . The President's Executive Order merely requires that contractors take some "affirmative action" and directs the Secretary of Labor to "use his best efforts" through "state and local agencies" as well as federal agencies. The Secretary of Labor has stated, as amicus curiae, that the federal program is not meant to preempt state programs such as the Commonwealth's § 1B. And congressional policy in this area, as expressed in Title VII of the Civil Rights Act of 1964, the statute most closely analogous to the President's Executive Order, is clearly one of encouraging state cooperation and initiative in remedying racial discrimination. Title VII, 42 U.S.C. § 2000h-4 expressly disclaims any intent to preempt state action. . . .

Even if there is no conflict between the purposes and objectives of the two schemes, the state plan might still be invalid if there is a showing of "such actual conflict between the two schemes of regulation that both cannot stand in the same area. . . ." . . . While we acknowledge that § 1B may be more demanding than the Boston Plan, and may well involve higher administrative costs, there is no reason to suppose that contractors could not comply with both at the same time. By complying with § 1B's minority hiring goals on projects funded by both the state and the federal government, contractors would also comply with the Boston Plan's goals. The reporting requirements are different for the two plans, but this merely necessitates the filing of two different sets of reports.

The only place where the two plans might be found slightly incompatible is in the area of trade union referrals. Recognizing that union reluctance to admit minorities to apprenticeship programs has been one primary reason for the small percentage of minorities in the construction trades,[12] the Boston Plan focuses upon encouraging area-wide minority recruitment into the unions, and therefore does not alter the patterns of contractor reliance upon the unions for referrals. The Commonwealth's § 1B, however, facilitates referrals from sources other than the unions by providing alternative mechanisms for recruiting minority workers.

We think, however, that there is little likelihood that § 1B would discourage union initiative in training and recruiting minorities. The Commonwealth's program will operate on a small scale, only within neighborhoods with a high minority population; the contractors for the Boston College project are required to employ approximately thirty minority workers. The federal Boston Plan is designed to train and place three hundred sixty minority workers each year drawn from all over the state. Therefore, despite the Commonwealth's program, building trades unions will be obligated to continue their efforts at recruiting minority workers and referring them to contractors. Furthermore, the Commonwealth's program does not prohibit union referrals. It merely provides other sources for referrals. Thus, § 1B might actually induce a stepped-up program of union recruitment if the unions are desirous of maintaining contractor reliance upon union referrals.

[12] See *Employment and Manpower Problems in the Cities: Implications of the Reports of the National Advisory Commission on Civil Disorders,* Hearing Before the Joint Economic Comm., 90th Cong., 2d Sess. at 38 (1968).

We conclude, therefore, that § 1B presents no challenge to the Supremacy Clause.

II. Appellant's second contention, that the Commonwealth's § 1B imposes a fixed racial hiring quota which violates the Equal Protection clause of the Fourteenth Amendment, presents a more difficult issue, the implications of which stretch far beyond this particular dispute.

The first Justice Harlan's much quoted observation that "the Constitution is colorblind . . . [and] does not . . . permit any public authority to know the race of those entitled to be protected in the enjoyment of such rights", *Plessy* v. *Ferguson*, 163 U.S. 537, 554 (1896) (dissenting opinion) has come to represent a long-term goal. It is by now well understood, however, that our society cannot be completely colorblind in the short term if we are to have a colorblind society in the long term. After centuries of viewing through colored lenses, eyes do not quickly adjust when the lenses are removed. Discrimination has a way of perpetuating itself, albeit unintentionally, because the resulting inequalities make new opportunities less accessible. Preferential treatment is one partial prescription to remedy our society's most intransigent and deeply rooted inequalities.

Intentional, official recognition of race has been found necessary to achieve fair and equal opportunity in the selection of grand juries, *Brooks* v. *Beto*, 336 F.2d 1 (5th Cir. 1966); tenants for public housing, *Otero* v. *New York City Housing Authority*, 42 LW 2185 (2d Cir. Sept. 12, 1973); *Norwalk CORE* v. *Norwalk Redevelopment Agency*, 395 F.2d 920 (2d Cir. 1968); *Gautreaux* v. *Chicago Housing Authority*, 304 F.Supp. 736 (N.D. Ill. 1969); school administrators, *Porcelli* v. *Titus*, 431 F.2d 1254, 2 FEP Cases 1024 (3d Cir. 1970); and children who are to attend a specific public school, *Swann* v. *Charlotte-Mechlenburg Board of Education*, 402 U.S. 1 (1971).

The intentional, official recognition of race in the selection of union members or construction workers has been constitutionally tested and upheld in two contexts. The first is where courts have ordered, pursuant to Title VII of the Civil Rights Act of 1964, 42 U.S.C. §2000e-5(g), remedial action for past discrimination. In fulfilling their "duty to render a decree which will so far as possible eliminate the discriminatory effects of the past . . .", *Louisiana* v. *United States*, 380 U.S. 145, 154 (1965), courts have ordered unions to grant immediate membership to a number of minority applicants, *United States* v. *Wood, Wire, and Metal Lathers International Union, Local No. 46*, 471 F.2d 408, 5 FEP Cases 318 (2d Cir. 1973), *cert. denied*, 41 LW 3645, 5 FEP Cases 1122 (U.S. June 12, 1973); to begin an affirmative minority recruitment program, *United States* v. *Sheet Metal Workers International Ass'n, Local No. 36*, 416 F.2d 123, 2 FEP Cases 127 (8th Cir. 1969); to match normal referrals with minority referrals until a specific objective has been obtained, *Heat and Frost Workers, Local 53* v. *Vogler*, 407 F.2d 1047, 1 FEP Cases 577 70 LRRM 2257 (5th Cir. 1969); or to take on a certain number of minority apprentices for each class of workers, *United States* v. *Ironworkers Local 86*, 443 F.2d 544, 3 FEP Cases 496 (9th Cir. 1971), *cert. denied*, 404 U.S. 984, 4 FEP

Cases 37 (1971). Courts have also ordered employers to hire minority employees up to thirty per cent of the total work force, *Stamps* v. *Detroit Edison*, 6 FEP Cases 612, 42 LW 2200 (E.D. Mich. Oct. 2, 1973); to hire one minority worker every time two white workers were hired, up to a certain number, *Carter* v. *Gallagher*, 452 F.2d 315, 4 FEP Cases 121 (8th Cir. 1971), *cert. denied*, 406 U.S. 950, 4 FEP Cases 771 (1972); and in our own *Castro* v. *Beecher*, 459 F.2d 725, 4 FEP Cases 1223 (1972), we ordered that black and Spanish-speaking applicants for police positions, who had failed to measure up to a constitutionally impermissible set of hiring standards, be given priority in future hiring.

The second context in which race has been recognized as a permissible criterion for employment is where courts have upheld federal affirmative action programs against challenges under the Equal Protection clause or under the anti-preference provisions of Title VII of the Civil Rights Act of 1964, 42 U.S.C. § 2000-2(j). Recognizing that the discretionary power of public authorities to remedy past discrimination is even broader than that of the judicial branch, see *Swann* v. *Charlotte-Mechlenburg*, *supra* at 16; cf. *Katzenbach* v. *Morgan*, 384 U.S. 641, 653 (1966), courts have upheld the specific percentage goals and time tables for minority hiring found in the Philadelphia Plan, *Contractors Ass'n of Eastern Pennsylvania* v. *Secretary of Labor*, 311 F.Supp. 1002, 2 FEP Cases 472 (E.D. Pa. 1970), *aff'd*, 442 F.2d 159, 3 FEP Cases 395 (3d Cir. 1971), *cert. denied*, 404 U.S. 854, 3 FEP Cases 1030 (1971), the Cleveland Plan, *Weiner* v. *Cuyahoga Community College District*, 19 Ohio St.2d 35, 249 N.E. 2d 907, 908, 2 FEP Cases 30 (1969), *cert. denied*, 396 U.S. 1004, 2 FEP Cases 337 (1970), the Newark Plan, *Joyce* v. *McCrane*, 320 F.Supp. 1284, 3 FEP Cases 111 (D. N.J. 1970), and the Illinois Ogilvie Plan, *Southern Illinois Builders Ass'n* v. *Ogilvie*, 327 F.Supp. 1154, 3 FEP Cases 571 (S.D. Ill. 1971), *aff'd*, 471 F.2d 680, 5 FEP Cases 229 (7th Cir. 1972).

Despite ample precedent for using race as a criterion of selection where the goal is equal opportunity, we approach its use in the present case with care. This marks the first time, to our knowledge, that a court has been asked to sanction a plan for hiring a specific percentage of minority workers that requires an employer to take "every possible measure" to reach the goal on each job site, and places upon him the burden of proving compliance, under threat of serious penalties if that burden is not sustained. It is but a short step from these requirements to a demand that an employer give an absolute percentage preference to members of a racial minority, regardless of their qualifications and without consideration for their availability within the general population. The Commonwealth's affirmative action plan forces us to address a fundamental question: are there constitutional limits to the means by which racial criteria may be used to remedy the present effects of past discrimination and achieve equal opportunity in the future?

There are good reasons why the use of racial criteria should be strictly scrutinized and given legal sanction only where a compelling need for remedial action can be shown. *Norwalk CORE* v. *Norwalk Redevelop-*

*ment Agency,* 395 F.2d 920, 931-32 (2d Cir. 1969). Government recognition and sanction of racial classifications may be inherently divisive, reinforcing prejudices, confirming perceived differences between the races, and weakening the government's educative role on behalf of equality and neutrality. [13] It may also have unexpected results, such as the development of indicia for placing individuals into different racial categories. Once racial classifications are imbedded in the law, their purpose may become perverted: a benign preference under certain conditions may shade into a malignant preference at other times.[14] Moreover, a racial preference for members of one minority might result in discrimination against another minority, a higher proportion of whose members had previously enjoyed access to a certain opportunity.

In the present instance, there is no question that a compelling need exists to remedy serious racial imbalance [15] in the construction trades, particularly in Roxbury, Dorchester, and South End, where minorities constitute approximately forty per cent of the population, and yet only about four per cent of the membership of buildings trades unions, and where there has been a long history of racial discrimination in those unions. Such an imbalance within the relatively lucrative, highly visible, and expanding construction trades undermines efforts at achieving equal opportunity elsewhere in the economy and contributes to racial tensions.[16]

Even where a long history of discrimination and continuing racial imbalance compels the remedial use of racial criteria, however, the means chosen to implement the compelling interest should be reasonably related to the desired end. See *Contractors Ass'n of Eastern Pennsylvania* v. *Secretary of Labor, supra,* 311 F.Supp. at 1011; cf. *McLaughlin* v. *Florida,* 379 U.S. 184, 193 (1964). A program which included unrealistic minority hiring goals might impose an unreasonable burden on the employer and upon qualified workers who were denied jobs because they were not members of the racial minority. Unrealistically high goals are likely, in addition, to foment racial tensions and to prompt employers to circumvent the rules.

A program of affirmative action might be considered to impose unrealistic and unreasonable hiring goals if it included a racial preference

---

[13] See Kaplan, *Equal Justice in an Unequal World; Equality for the Negro—The Problem of Special Treatment,* 61 Nw. U. L. Rev. 363 (1966).

[14] For example, a preference for induction into the armed services might appear to some to be a positive opportunity for training and steady work, yet might also appear at other times or to other people to be a somewhat negative opportunity.

[15] Based upon information revealed in the depositions of several union officials, and other statistical information such as the "Equal Employment Opportunity Local Union Reports", the district court concluded that racial imbalance does exist in the Boston construction trades and such imbalance is the result of past discriminatory practices on the part of many "entities" in that industry. Such inferences from statistical showings of racial imbalance are permitted. See, e.g., *Carter* v. *Gallagher,* 452 F.2d 315, 323, 4 FEP Cases 121 (8th Cir. 1971); *Parham* v. *Southwestern Bell Telephone,* 433 F.2d 421, 426, 2 FEP Cases 1017 (8th Cir. 1970); *Jones* v. *Lee Way Motor Freight,* 431 F.2d 245, 247, 2 FEP Cases 895 (10th Cir. 1970).

[16] If, at some future time, racial balance were to be achieved in Boston's construction trades, we assume that there would no longer exist a compelling need for remedial action, and the use of such racial criteria would no longer be warranted.

that could not be fulfilled, or could be fulfilled only by taking on workers who were unqualified for the trainee, apprentice, or journeyman status for which they were hired. Equal opportunity is an elusive concept, but at its core it carries the simple mandate that opportunities should be open to all on the basis of competence alone. Thus, it would be consistent with the goal of equal opportunity to give first priority to members of a minority that had previously been denied equal opportunity, if those members were otherwise as qualified as were qualified members of the majority population. In order that this special treatment be meaningful, of course, there should be equal opportunity to gain the training necessary to qualify.[17]

While § 1B says nothing about hiring "qualified" minority workers, § V, ¶ 3 of the same contract requires that the contractor hire only "competent" workers. The district court has interpreted § 1B in light of § V, ¶ 3, to require that the twenty per cent minority employees of § 1B be "qualified" for the status to which they were assigned. The Commonwealth's Secretary of Transportation and Construction, who is charged with implementing these provisions, has interpreted § 1B in the same way.

Appellants maintain, however, that the goal of twenty per cent minority workers on each construction site, combined with the contractor's burden of proving that he has taken "every possible measure to achieve compliance" with the goal, will necessarily move the contractor to hire unqualified minority workers, rather than run the risk of incurring sanctions. While we think that this is an unwarranted concern, given that the Boston State College project will require approximately thirty minority workers, we concede that, in principle, a high percentage goal for minority hiring combined with a high burden of proving compliance might create the likelihood that unqualified workers would be hired.

Despite the fact that the Secretary of Transportation and Construction alleges that the twenty per cent goal was based upon an assessment of current availability of minority journeymen, apprentices, and trainees, courts are ill equipped to judge the accuracy of such assessments. It becomes important, therefore, that affirmative action plans, such as the Commonwealth's § 1B, contain fair procedures for contractors to make a showing that insufficient qualified minority workers are available. Thus, any reasonable program designed to remedy racial imbalance must incorporate the necessary elements of due process. So long as contractors receive notice and a meaningful opportunity to challenge any allegations of non-compliance and prove that they have taken whatever efforts are required of them to comply, it is less important that a particular percentage goal might be slightly optimistic or unrealistic, given current availability of qualified minority workers.

Appellants' contention that § 1B violates the Equal Protection clause is therefore intimately tied to their contention that § 1B, in violation of the Due Process clause, permits the imposition of sanctions without

---

[17] Thus, presumably, to be "qualified" for a training program would require less competence than to be "qualified" for apprenticeship or journeyman status.

proper notice or an opportunity to be heard, an issue to which we now turn.

III.  Appellants' due process claim concerns § 1B.2 of the contract provisions, which states, *inter alia,* that ". . . the Commission (M.C.A.D.) shall make a final report on non-compliance, and recommend to the Bureau [of Construction] the imposition of one or more of the sanctions listed below. . . . [T]he Bureau shall impose one or more of the following sanctions, as it may deem appropriate. . . ."

The M.C.A.D.'s determination of non-compliance is made *ex parte.* Contractors are notified of the findings and given an opportunity to take specific steps which would, in the opinion of the M.C.A.D., bring them into compliance, but contractors are not permitted to challenge the findings of non-compliance at this juncture.

The Bureau of Construction is required, pursuant to the Commonwealth's Administrative Procedure Act, M.G.L.A. c. 30A §§ 10, 11, to hold a hearing before any penalties may be imposed on the contractors for non-compliance. What is in dispute is the scope of this hearing. Appellants maintain that § 1B.2 allows, at most, a challenge to the particular sanction which the M.C.A.D. has recommended, in favor of what might be contended to be a more appropriate sanction, but not a challenge to the truth of the M.C.A.D.'s basic findings of non-compliance. If appellants' interpretation of § 1B.2 were correct, their due process claim would have some merit because contractors would be subject to serious penalties, such as debarment from participation in state contracts for three years, without having had an opportunity to contest the findings on which the imposition of the penalty was based. . . .

We do not think, however, that § 1B.2 must necessarily be interpreted to require such a narrowing of the scope of the administrative hearing. The contract states that the Bureau "shall impose" one of the sanctions only "as it may deem appropriate to attain full and effective enforcement." It would seem perfectly consistent with this mandate for the Bureau to determine for itself that the contractor had in fact taken "every possible measure" to achieve compliance, despite the findings of the M.C.A.D. to the contrary, and that any sanction would be inappropriate. The presumption of constitutionality customarily accorded state statutes, e.g., *United States* v. *Carolene Products,* 304 U.S. 144, 152 (1938), would dictate that we apply this interpretation. The Supreme Judicial Court of Massachusetts has, moreover, construed certain other Commonwealth statutes, facially lacking express provisions for notice and hearing, as impliedly calling for such due process requirements. . . .

The Commonwealth's Secretary of Transportation and Construction has given the foregoing interpretation to § 1B.2, and has stipulated that no sanctions may be imposed against a contractor until he has had a full hearing before officials of the Bureau of Construction in which he may challenge any findings of non-compliance by the M.C.A.D. Since the Secretary is entrusted with interpretation and implementation of the contract provisions, his view is at least entitled to "respectful consideration", *Fox*

v. *Standard Oil Co.*, 294 U.S. 87, 96 (1935). We see no reason not to accept his interpretation in this case, *Law Students Research Council* v. *Wadmond*, 401 U.S. 154, 162 (1971), and indeed condition our holding on the consistent application of this interpretation. We conclude, therefore, that § 1B so construed does not violate the Due Process clause of the Fourteenth Amendment.

Since contractors are provided with notice and a full opportunity to contest allegations of non-compliance, they may thereby show that insufficient qualified minority workers were available. Therefore, in light of our preceding analysis, we find that § 1B does not violate the Equal Protection clause of the Fourteenth Amendment.

IV. Appellants' final contention, which comes within the compass of our pendant jurisdiction, is that the Commonwealth's § 1B program involves the M.C.A.D. in activities that are prohibited by the anti-preference clause of M.G.L.A. c. 151B, § 4. This clause provides in relevant part, that ". . . nothing contained in this chapter or in any rule or regulation issued by the Commission [M.C.A.D.] shall be interpreted as requiring any employer, employment agency or labor organization to grant preferential treatment to any individual or to any group because of the race . . . of such individual or group. . . ."

The anti-preference clause has not been interpreted by Massachusetts courts. The district court determined, however, that the statute is inapplicable to activities of the M.C.A.D. carried on pursuant to § 1B for two reasons. The first is that the anti-preference clause applies only to regulations issued by the M.C.A.D., while under § 1B the M.C.A.D. merely investigates and makes recommendations under regulations promulgated by the Secretary of Transportation and Construction. The second reason is that, contrary to the assertions of appellants, the clause applies only to authority vested in the statute itself, while the authority for § 1B stems from the Governor's Executive Order No. 74 and from M.G.L.A. c. 6A § 24 and c. 149 § 44A, both of which provide for the acceptance or the rejection of bids. We agree with this analysis.

In addition, we would point to the way in which federal courts have dealt with the anti-preference provision of Title VII of the Civil Rights Act of 1964, 42 U.S.C. § 2000e-2(j), which is analogous to the Commonwealth's anti-preference clause. In *United States* v. *I.B.E.W. Local 38*, 428 F.2d 144, 2 FEP Cases 716 (6th Cir. 1970), *cert. denied*, 400 U.S. 943, 2 FEP Cases 1121 (1970), the court construed that provision to mean that an employer was not required to grant preferential treatment to minorities merely because of racial imbalance on his work force, but that some preference might be required to remedy the present effects of past discrimination. "Any other interpretation would allow complete nullification of the stated purpose of the Civil Rights Act of 1964". *Id.* at 149-50, 2 FEP Cases 720. See also *Carter* v. *Gallagher, supra.*

It is undisputed that past racial discrimination in Boston's construction trades is in large part responsible for the present racial imbalance. Given this fact, we find it difficult to conceive that Massachusetts would interpret its own anti-preference provision in such a way as to prohibit programs designed to remedy that imbalance.

We conclude, therefore, that the Commonwealth's § 1B is violative of neither state law nor the federal Constitution.

*Affirmed.*

## NOTES

1. The issues of conflict of laws as well as the "two contexts" within which the quota controversy arises are adequately canvassed in the two preceding cases. As of fall 1978, the Supreme Court of the United States had not reviewed an employment case precisely raising these issues. But see *United States* v. *Montgomery County Board,* 395 U.S. 225 (1971), in which the Court sustained a 12-percent goal of faculty and staff integration to secure a unitary school system.

2. For a variety of comments on the goals/quotas of the Philadelphia Plan, see Note, *The Philadelphia Plan: Equal Employment Opportunity in the Construction Trades,* 6 COLUM. J. LAW & SOCIAL PROBLEMS 187 (1970); Jones, *The Bugaboo of Employment Quotas,* 1970 WIS. L. REV. 341; Comment, *The Philadelphia Plan: A Study in the Dynamics of Executive Power,* 39 U.CHI.L.REV. 752(1972).

### D.  AFFIRMATIVE ACTION OR IMPERMISSIBLE PREFERENCES— THE CONTINUING CONFLICTS

In the preceding cases we have considered challenges to affirmative action programs which were *imposed* upon nonconsenting contractors. The following cases illustrate problems with voluntary or "quasi-voluntary" implementation of affirmative action plans.

## EEOC v. AMERICAN TELEPHONE & TELEGRAPH CO.

*United States Court of Appeals, Third Circuit, 1977*
*556 F.2d 167, 14 FEP Cases 1211*

GIBBONS, Circuit Judge: This is an appeal by three labor unions: the Communications Workers of America (CWA), the Telephone Coordinating Council TCC-1, International Brotherhood of Electrical Workers (IBEW), and the Alliance of Independent Telephone Unions (Alliance) (hereinafter referred to collectively as the intervening defendants). The order below denied their motions to modify a consent decree, dismissed the motion of CWA for a preliminary injunction against continued implementation of an affirmative action override provided for by the decree, and granted the motion of the plaintiffs and the original defendants for the entry of a supplemental injunctive order. The plaintiffs are the Equal Employment Opportunity Commission (EEOC), the Secretary of Labor, and the United States. Their complaint, filed on January 18, 1973, charged violations of the Fair Labor Standards Act, of Title VII of the Civil Rights Act of 1964, and of Executive Order 11246. The defendant is the American Telephone and Telegraph Company (AT&T), appearing for itself and on behalf of its associated telephone companies in the Bell System. On the same day that the complaint was filed AT&T answered, denying the violations alleged. However, it simultaneously approved and consented to a decree which embodied and was designed to enforce a negotiated agreement under which AT&T undertook to implement a model affirmative action program. That program was designed to overcome the effects of past employment discrimination in the Bell System with respect to women, blacks, and other minorities. The intervening defendants contend that the consent decree, as originally agreed to and as supplemented, conflicts with provisions of collective bargaining agreements between them and AT&T, and otherwise unlawfully invades rights of their members respecting competitive seniority in transfer and promotion.[1] We affirm.

## I. THE CONSENT DECREE

In November 1970, AT&T filed with the Federal Communications Commission (FCC) a proposed tariff which would increase interstate telephone rates. Before that filing was acted on, EEOC filed with the FCC a petition requesting that the increase be denied because AT&T's operating companies were engaged in system-wide discrimination against women and minorities. The FCC initiated a special proceeding to consider the charges, holding 60 days of hearings in 1971 and 1972. A number of organizations intervened in support of the EEOC. While the hearings progressed, settlement negotiations took place between AT&T and the government parties, which eventually led to the termination of the FCC special proceeding and the entry of the Consent Decree. Although the Alliance of Independent Telephone Unions did not participate in negotiating the Consent Decree, the IBEW did participate, and CWA was invited to do so but remained deliberately aloof. 365 F. Supp. at 1108, 1109, 6 FEP Cases at 645.

The Bell System is one of the largest employers in the United States. Traditionally, its operating companies have been organized along departmental lines. The plant department has been responsible for installa-

---

1 [Footnotes numbered as in original.—Ed.] The decision appealed from is reported. *Equal Employment Opportunity Commission* v. *American Telephone & Telegraph Company,* 419 F. Supp. 1022, 13 FEP Cases 392 (E.D. Pa. 1976). The prior history of this protracted litigation may be gleaned from *Equal Employment Opportunity Commission* v. *American Telephone & Telegraph Company,* 506 F.2d 735, 9 FEP Cases 53 (3d Cir. 1974) *affirming in part and remanding in part* 356 F. Supp. 1105, 6 FEP Cases 643 (E.D. Pa. 1973). In that case, we recognized that CWA would have standing to intervene as a defendant to protect its existing collective bargaining agreements. Thereafter CWA, IBEW and Alliance moved for and were granted leave to intervene as defendants for the purpose of seeking modification of the consent decree.

tion and maintenance of physical facilities such as central office equipment, transmission lines, and subscriber telephones. The traffic department has been responsible for putting calls through, operator assistance, information, and related services. The commercial department has handled subscriber sales and billing. The accounting department has performed the bookkeeping and accounting functions. Until at least the late 1960's, Bell System hiring practices generally followed departmental lines. The plant department, in which craft jobs predominated, was traditionally a male preserve, while female employees were generally employed as operators, bookkeepers, or in other clerical occupations in the traffic and commercial departments. Pay scales at both entry and higher levels in the plant department were, and remain, higher than for employees with comparable length of service in the other departments. Transfers from the traffic or commercial departments were possible, but there was a general policy of slotting a transferred employee in at the next higher pay rate than that last enjoyed in the previous position. Since traffic and commercial employees had lower starting rates at each step of the wage progression schedule, that policy resulted in a transferee to the plant department receiving a lower rate of pay than would an employee performing the same job who had been hired on the same date, but had started in the plant department. These hiring practices resulted in a concentration of males and females in certain classifications. Moreover, there was an imbalance between the racial and ethnic composition of the work forces of many operating companies and the racial and ethnic makeup of their available labor markets. The intervening defendants do not dispute that past patterns and practices were discriminatory, nor do they dispute that the present work force in many Bell System departments still reflects those past patterns and practices.

The Consent Decree directs the Bell System Companies to establish goals and intermediate targets to promote the full utilization of all race, sex, and ethnic groups in each of fifteen job classifications. The intermediate targets, set annually, reflect the representation of such groups in the external labor market in relevant pools for each operating company's work force. The intermediate targets are the major prospective remedies in the Consent Degree. When any Bell Company is unable to achieve or maintain its intermediate target, applying normal selection standards, it is required by the decree to depart from those standards in selecting candidates for promotional opportunities. It must then pass over candidates with greater seniority or better qualifications in favor of members of the underrepresented group who are at least "basically qualified." Without this affirmative action override, the greater time in title of incumbent members of the over-represented race, sex, or ethnic group would inevitably reduce the opportunity for advancement of the underrepresented groups and would perpetuate the effects of the former discrimination. The affirmative action override applies, however, only to minority *promotional* opportunity. A promotion under the override does not result in any increase in competitive seniority for purposes of layoff or rehire, as to which the collective bargaining agreements control.[2] The life of the decree is six years, ending on January 17, 1979. It provides that AT&T may bargain collectively with collective bargaining representatives for alternative provisions which would also comply with federal law. No such alternative provisions have been presented to the district court.

## II. THE SUPPLEMENTAL ORDER

In an interim report on compliance with the Consent Decree it appeared that in a number of specific categories the Bell Companies fell short of attaining intermediate targets promulgated for 1973. The government plaintiffs and AT&T jointly moved for the entry of a supplemental order aimed at remedying these deficiencies and assuring future achievement of targets and goals. The supplemental order provides that unmet targets shall be carried forward in certain establishments and job classifications. For a two month period ending on October 24, 1976 some Bell Companies were required to make all placements in affected job classifications from groups as to which their targets had not been met. The supplemental order also provides for the creation of a Bell System Affirmative Action Fund and its expenditure on projects which will advance the objects of the decree. It also articulates the understanding of the parties that while the original Consent Decree was not intended to supplant the collective bargaining agreements, to the extent that any provisions of the latter would prevent the achievement of the affirmative action targets and goals, the decree controlled. The carry-forward provisions of the supplemental order do not enlarge the Bell Companies' total affirmative action obligations under the Consent Decree, nor do they extend its life.

## III. BELL SYSTEM PROMOTIONAL SENIORITY

Since the only alleged conflict between the collective bargaining agreements and the Consent Decree and supplemental order relates to promotional seniority, our starting point is a description of bargained-for promotional practices. The contracts between AT&T and each of the intervening defendants are not identical. As to each intervening defendant there are also variations, in contracts with specific operating companies, negotiated locally to reflect local conditions and practices. However, a common feature of all the agreements is that seniority for all purposes is

[2] The Consent Decree, Part A, § III-C provides:
"Net credited service shall be used for determining layoff and related force adjustments and recall to jobs where nonmanagement female and minority employees would otherwise be laid off, affected or not recalled. Collective bargaining agreements or Bell Company practices shall govern the confines of the group of employees being considered. Provided, however, vacancies created by layoff and related force adjustments shall not be considered vacancies for purposes of transfer and promotion under this Section."

determined by "net credited service" in any department in the Bell System. It is also common to provide that in selecting employees for promotion, other factors being equal, the Company will promote the employee with the greatest net credited service. However, it is clear that the company has not bargained to the union any role in the determination of employee qualifications. Some agreements refer to "the employee whom Company finds is best qualified." Others speak of "ability, aptitude, attendance, physical fitness for the job, and proximity to the assignment." Some agreements even qualify the seniority-equal qualification language by language to the effect that "[n]othing in this paragraph shall be construed to prevent Company from promoting employees for unusually meritorious service or exceptional ability." Although their approach to the alleged conflict between Consent Decree and their collective bargaining agreements is not identical the intervening defendants agree that the bargained-for promotional system is a merit selection system. Management determines the employee best qualified in its judgment, but seniority decides the issue where two employees are considered by management to be equally qualified. The effect of the affirmative action override, then, where and when it operates, is to eliminate from consideration those employees who would normally have been selected under pre-decree practice. The decree provides for selecting, from the under-utilized group of persons, those who in the judgment of management are "basically qualified." Although the briefs of the intervening defendants stress the issue of competitive seniority, the real dispute is less over seniority, which under the contracts would only be determinative in cases of equal qualification, as over the departure from the "best qualified" criterion. The continued operation of that criterion would, of course, significantly confine promotions within departmental lines, as has been the past practice, since experience in the department will always be a significant factor in an employee's qualification level. By executing the Consent Decree AT&T has agreed, in the instances in which the affirmative action override applies, to limit its bargained-for management prerogative of determining the employee best qualified for promotion, so long as it promotes a basically qualified applicant from an under-represented group. The unions urge that it may not do so without illegally breaching their collective bargaining agreements and the rights of some of the employees they represent.

## IV.  THE UNION CONTENTIONS

Claiming standing as representatives of their members and by virtue of the conflict between the affirmative action override and the collective bargaining agreements, the intervenor unions attack the Consent Decree on a number of grounds. Some of these grounds transcend the issue of the purported conflict between the decree and the collective bargaining agreements. They recognize that in making their broad-gauged challenge they may be acting inconsistently with the best interests of some of the persons whom they represent in the collective bargaining process, but point out that the potential conflict is inherent in the collective bargaining relationship. See *Emporium Capwell Co.* v. *Western Addition Community Organization,* 420 U.S. 50, 9 FEP Cases 195 (1975). Since the unions object to the claimed inconsistency between the decree and the promotional seniority provisions of their contracts, they have standing to assert all grounds of invalidity of the decree which would result in the elimination of that conflict. Moreover they are appropriate representatives of their members within the standing test of *Sierra Club* v. *Morton,* 405 U.S. 727 (1972). Thus we will consider each of their statutory and constitutional challenges, as well as the contention that entry of the decree was an abuse of the district court's discretion.

A.  THE CONSENT DECREE AND THIRD PARTY INTERESTS

The unions contended in the district court, and contend somewhat less vigorously here, that it was improper in a Consent Decree to award relief affecting third party rights. That objection is meritless. To the extent that third party rights in which the unions are interested have been affected, they were allowed to intervene and be heard in this case. They do not dispute the factual predicate of the decree, the prior patterns and practices of discrimination. If this were a litigated judgment the fact that they and their members did not cause the discrimination would not prevent relief affecting third parties. See *Franks* v. *Bowman Transp. Co.,* 424 U.S. 747, 778, 12 FEP Cases 549, 561 (1976). At best, in a fully litigated case, they would be entitled to be heard only on the appropriateness of the remedy. They have been heard on that aspect of the case. Class actions frequently affect the interests of persons who are before the court only by virtue of the opting out provisions of Fed. R. Civ. P. 23(c). We have approved the settlement of those actions even over the objection of class members who think additional relief should have been granted. *E.g., Bryan* v. *Pittsburgh Plate Glass Co.,* 494 F.2d 799, 7 FEP Cases 822 (3d Cir.), *cert. denied,* 419 U.S. 900, 8 FEP Cases 1007 (1974); *Ace Heating & Plumbing Company* v. *Crane Company,* 453 F.2d 30 (3d Cir. 1971).

These cases hold that approval of such a settlement, arrived at after negotiations between the defendant and the class representative, will be reversed only if the court abused its discretion in approving it. There is, of course, a difference between approving a settlement benefitting a plaintiff class whose representative negotiated it, and approving a settlement imposing burdens on an unrepresented class of defendants. The recognition of that difference was the very reason why in *Equal Employment Opportunity Commission* v. *American Telephone & Telegraph Company, supra,* 506 F.2d at 741-42, 9 FEP Cases at 58, we held that CWA could move to intervene as a defendant. Following intervention the unions were permitted a full opportunity to convince the court that the relief AT&T had agreed to went beyond that required to remedy the violation. The posture of the case before us is, for all practical purposes, that of a fully litigated decree.

## B.  THE § 703 CONTENTION

Advancing essentially the same argument that we expressly rejected in *United States* v. *Int'l Union of Elevator Const.*, 538 F.2d 1012, 1019, 13 FEP Cases 81, 87 (3d Cir. 1976), the intervening defendants urge that §§ 703(a), 703(h) and 703(j) of Title VII, 42 U.S.C. §§ 2000e-2(a), (h), (j), prohibit the district court from providing for an affirmative action plan containing interim targets and goals, and prohibit an affirmative action override. As we noted in *Elevator Constructors,* that argument is foreclosed by *Franks* v. *Bowman Transp. Co., supra,* 424 U.S. at 757-62, 12 FEP Cases at 553-55. Even the Justices who wrote separately in *Franks* acknowledged that § 703 is not a statutory limitation upon the remedial authority conferred on the district courts by § 706(g), 42 U.S.C. § 2000e-5(g).

## C.  THE § 706(G) CONTENTIONS

The intervening defendants also urge several separate challenges to the decree, based on their interpretation of § 706(g). The first of these is that the section prohibits quota remedies, and that the interim targets and goals of the Consent Decree amount to such a remedy. That challenge is also foreclosed by *Elevator Constructors, supra,* and we will not repeat the analysis of the legislative history of the 1972 amendments to Title VII upon which we relied in rejecting it.[3]

The unions contend that *Elevator Constructors* is distinguishable in that it did not deal with competitive seniority but only with new hires. In one sense that is true, for the case dealt with a remedy in an industry where employers relied upon a hiring hall and a transitory work force. But the blunt fact is that the union membership quota remedy we approved in *Elevator Constructors* did involve competitive seniority with respect to referrals from a hiring hall. 538 F.2d at 1017-18, 13 FEP Cases at 86. More significant than our decision in the hiring hall context, however, is the Supreme Court's holding in *Franks* v. *Bowman Transp. Co., supra,* that a change in competitive seniority is a permissible § 706(g) remedy. We are not free to reconsider the issue. Even if we were we do not think it is appropriately presented in this case, since the decree actually preserves layoff and rehire competitive seniority, and only modifies the method of selection for promotion and transfer. It affects not all seniority rights, but only some. And among two equally basically qualified under-represented group applicants, for example, the seniority provisions would still operate, even with respect to promotion and transfer.

The unions' major challenge to the decree, however, is that in all our prior Title VII remedy cases, and in those in the Supreme Court as well, the remedy provided relief only in favor of identifiable victims of specific past discrimination. They contend that § 706(g) proscribes any decree, even in a class action, which would permit relief to a minority group member who could not so identify himself.

[3] 538 F.2d 1012, 1019-20, 13 FEP Cases 81, 87-88.

The intervenor defendants misread our prior authority. Nothing in the decree which we approved in *Elevators Constructors* limited its applicability to blacks who had applied and been rejected for membership in the union. The decree ran to the benefit of the *class* of persons found to have been underutilized by virtue of a discriminatory pattern or practice. Moreover, the contention ignores the fact that in this case the United States sued to enforce Executive Order No. 11246. In *Contractors Ass'n of Eastern Pa.* v. *Secretary of Labor*, 442 F.2d 159, 3 FEP Cases 395 (3d Cir. 1971), we held that the Executive Order was a valid effort by the government to assure utilization of all segments of society in the available labor pool for government contractors, entirely apart from Title VII. Certainly that broader governmental interest is sufficient in itself to justify relief directed at classes rather than individual victims of discrimination. It is undisputed that the Bell System is a major governmental contractor.

We could rest on *Elevator Constructors* and *Contractors of Eastern Pa.* as controlling precedents in this Circuit. However, since it seems likely that review will be sought in the Supreme Court it is appropriate that we discuss the merits of the unions' contention that § 706(g) proscribes class relief to classes which may contain persons who are not identifiable victims of specific discrimination.

Before doing so, we note that even if we were to accept the unions' position on § 706(g), this decree would have a large scope of valid operation. The chief charge is that for years Bell System hiring practices steered certain classes of persons into certain departments. Any member of the affected class who became a Bell System employee during the time the practices operated was affected by them, at least to the extent that he or she was not informed that employment opportunities might exist in other departments. We do not think that Congress, in enacting Title VII, intended that § 706(g) remedies be available only to those knowledgeable enough and militant enough to have demanded and been refused what was not in fact available. All who became employees while the challenged employment practices operated were individual victims of the practice. Thus the unions' objection only goes to the possibility that some minority group members, hired after the offending practices ceased, might be able to take advantage of the affirmative action override. No record was made in the district court, by the intervening defendants or anyone else, to establish whether there is a significant number of such persons. Recognizing that there are thousands of class members who could validly be protected, even on the unions' construction of § 706(g), we would find it extremely difficult to set aside the decree in the absence of such a record. The district court in framing a remedy could certainly balance the possibility that some recent hires who were not affected by the offending prior practices might be advantaged against the practicality that the decree had to be simple enough in operation to achieve its main purpose. Thus, we would not reverse even if we agreed with the intervening defendants' interpretation of § 706(g).

That interpretation rests upon the last sentence of that subsection: "[n]o order of the court shall require the admission or reinstatement of an individual as a member of a union, or the hiring, reinstatement, or promotion of an individual as an employee, or the payment to him of any back pay, if such individual was refused admission, suspended, or expelled, or was refused employment or advancement or was suspended or discharged for any reason other than discrimination on account of race, color, religion, sex, or national origin or in violation of section 2000e-3(a) of this title."

The unions urge that any relief going beyond class members who can show that they, rather than the class to which they belong, have been discriminated against is proscribed.

The last sentence in § 706(g) must be read in light of the settled construction of the rest of the section. That settled construction is that once a prima facie showing is made that an employer has engaged in a practice which violates Title VII, the burden shifts to it to prove that there is a benign justification or explanation.[4] The last sentence of § 706(g) says precisely that. Obviously, an employer can meet an individual charge by showing that although that individual was a member of the disadvantaged class he was also a thief, or a drunk or an incompetent, and was for such a reason denied employment or promotion. But the sentence does not speak at all to the showing that must be made by individual suitors, or class representatives on behalf of class members, or the EEOC on behalf of class members. The sentence merely preserves the employer's defense that the non-hire, discharge, or non-promotion was for a cause other than discrimination. Nothing in the Consent Decree prevents AT&T from asserting that defense with respect to individual applicants for promotion, and it is difficult to see what interest the unions have in it.

The sparse legislative history available on the bills which became Title VII confirm our interpretation of the sentence. In H.R. 7152, what is now § 706(g) appeared as § 707(e). A section-by-section analysis contained in H.R. Rep. No. 914, 88th Cong. 1st Sess. (1964), states of the latter:

"[n]o *order of the court may require the* admission or reinstatement of an individual as a member of the union or the hiring, reinstatement, or *promotion of an individual* as an employee or payment of any back pay *if the individual was refused* admission, suspended, or separated, or was refused employment or *advancement,* or was suspended or discharged *for cause."* EEOC, Legislative History of Titles VII and XI of Civil Rights Act of 1964 (hereinafter referred to as "Legislative History"), p. 2029 (emphasis supplied).

"For cause" clearly refers to an employer's defense. H.R. 7152 went directly to the floor of the Senate, where major changes were made.

---

[4] *United States* v. *Int'l Union of Elevator Const.,* 538 F.2d 1012, 1017 & n. 8, 13 FEP Cases 81, 85 (3d Cir. 1976). See *Franks* v. *Bowman Transp., Co.,* 424 U.S. 747, 772, 12 FEP Cases 549, 559 (1976). Cf. *Albemarle Paper Co.* v. *Moody,* 422 U.S. 405, 425, 10 FEP Cases 1181, 1190 (1975); *McDonnell Douglas Corp.* v. *Green,* 411 U.S. 792, 802, 5 FEP Cases 965, 969 (1973).

None, however, substantively affected § 707(e) except that sex was included among the proscribed bases of discrimination, and the section was renumbered to § 706(g). Confirming the Senate's understanding that the last sentence merely preserved the employers' defense is the comparative analysis of the Senate and House bills printed in the Congressional Record on June 9, 1964:

## "House Version

"11. No order of court shall require the admission or reinstatement of an individual to a labor organization or the hiring, reinstatement, promotion of an individual by an employer if the labor organization or employer took action for any reason other than discrimination on account of race, color, religion, or national origin."

## "Senate Version

"11. Same, except 'sex' was included. (This had been unintentionally omitted in House bill.) Also, court action in this regard was prohibited where an individual opposed, made a charge, testified, assisted, or participated in an investigation, hearing or proceeding of an unlawful employment practice of an employer, employment agency, or labor organization." Legislative History at 3027.

The intervening defendants rely on what they consider to be contrary indications in an explanatory memorandum on § 707(e) by Senators Clark and Case. Legislative History at 3044. We place no reliance on this ambiguous reference, since the section-by-section analysis quoted above is a more authoritative indication of congressional understanding. We also note that in considering the 1972 amendments to Title VII, Congress rejected the Ervin no-quota amendment to the 1972 Act. It did so after specific discussion of *United States* v. *Ironworkers Local 86*, 443 F.2d 544, 3 FEP Cases 496 (9th Cir.), *cert. denied*, 404 U.S. 984, 4 FEP Cases 37 (1971). The Ironworkers remedy, like that in our *Elevator Constructors case, supra,* included a new membership provision not limited to identifiable victims of specific past discrimination. As we pointed out in the latter case, the solid rejection of the Ervin amendment confirmed the prior understanding by Congress that an affirmative action quota remedy in favor of a class is permissible. 538 F.2d at 1019-20, 13 FEP Cases at 87-88. We are reinforced in our conclusion that class relief, without regard to the victim status of every class member, is appropriate by the firm consensus in the courts of appeals upon the lawfulness of class-based hiring preferences and membership goals.[5]

[5] E.g., *United States* v. *Elevator Constructors Local 5, supra; Rios* v. *Steamfitters Local 638,* 501 F.2d 622, 8 FEP Cases 293 (2d Cir. 1974); *United States* v. *Wood Lathers Local 46,* 471 F.2d 408, 5 FEP Cases 318 (2d Cir.), *cert. denied,* 412 U.S. 939, 5 FEP Cases 1122 (1973); *United States* v. *N.L. Indus. Inc.,* 479 F.2d 354, 5 FEP Cases 823 (8th Cir. 1973); *NAACP* v. *Beecher,* 504 F.2d 1017, 8 FEP Cases 855 (1st Cir. 1974), *cert. denied,* 421 U.S. 910, 10 FEP Cases 555 (1975); *United States* v. *IBEW Local 38,* 428 F.2d 144, 2 FEP Cases 716 (6th Cir.), *cert. denied,* 400 U.S. 943, 2 FEP Cases 1121 (1970); *Morrow* v.

We find meritless the proposal that we distinguish, for purposes of the availability of class action relief, between new hires and those already employed. Nothing in the language of the last sentence of § 706(g), upon which the intervening defendants base their individualized remedies argument, suggests such a distinction. Class action relief is equally available to both new hires and employees. The only distinction between the two classes is that in considering a seniority or promotion remedy, a court of equity must take into account expectations of other incumbent employees. But those incumbent employees will be affected identically by a remedy in favor of identifiable victims of specific discrimination as by a remedy which includes employee members not so identifiable. The impact on incumbent employees goes to the scope rather than the availability of class relief.[6]

Summarizing, none of the intervenors' interpretations of § 706(g), urged upon us a prohibitions against the intermediate targets, the employment goals, or the affirmative action override, persuade us.

## D. ABUSE OF DISCRETION

We turn then to the contention that even assuming the existence of statutory authority, the district court abused its discretion in refusing to grant the unions' motions to modify the Consent Decree, and in entering the Supplemental Order. As with equitable remedies generally, the scope of relief is a matter entrusted in the first instance to the trial court. As the Supreme Court has made plain, however

". . . that discretion imports not the court's ' "inclination, but . . . its

---

*Crisler,* 491 F.2d 1053, 7 FEP Cases 586 (5th Cir.), *cert. denied,* 419 U.S. 895, 8 FEP Cases 1007 (1974); *Southern Illinois Builders Ass'n* v. *Ogilvie,* 471 F.2d 680, 5 FEP Cases 229 (7th Cir. 1972); *United States* v. *Ironworkers Local 86,* 443 F.2d 544, 3 FEP Cases 496 (9th Cir.), *cert. denied,* 404 U.S. 984, 4 FEP Cases 37 (1971); *Patterson* v. *American Tobacco Co.,* 535 F.2d 257, 12 FEP Cases 314 (4th Cir.), *cert. denied,* 45 LW 3350, 13 FEP Cases 808 (U.S. Nov. 2, 1976) (Nos. 76-46, 76-56). Cf. *Albemarle Paper Co.* v. *Moody,* 422 U.S. 405, 414 n. 8, 10 FEP Cases 1181, 1188 (1976):
"The petitioners also contend that no backpay can be awarded to those unnamed parties in the plaintiff class who have not themselves filed charges with the EEOC. We reject this contention. The Courts of Appeals that have confronted the issue are unanimous in recognizing that backpay may be awarded on a class basis under Title VII without exhaustion of administrative procedures by the unnamed class members. See, e.g., *Rosen* v. *Public Service Electric & Gas Co.,* 409 F.2d 775, 780, 1 FEP Cases 708, 711-712, 70 LRRM 3200 (CA3 1969), and 477 F.2d 90, 95-96, 5 FEP Cases 709, 712 (CA3 1973); *Robinson* v. *Lorillard Corp.,* 444 F.2d 791, 802, 3 FEP Cases 653, 661 (CA4 1971); *United States* v. *Georgia Power Co.,* 474 F.2d 906, 919-921, 5 FEP Cases 587, 596-597 (CA5 1973); *Head* v. *Timken Roller Bearing Co., supra,* at 876; *Bowe* v. *Colgate-Palmolive Co.,* 416 F.2d 711, 719-721, 2 FEP Cases 121, 126-127 (CA7 1969); *United States* v. *N.L. Industries, Inc.* 479 F.2d 354, 378-379, 5 FEP Cases 823, 843 (CA8 1973). The Congress plainly ratified this construction of the Act in the course of enacting the Equal Employment Act of 1972, Pub. L. 92-261, 86 Stat. 103."

[6] See, *e.g., Ostapowicz* v. *Johnson,* 541 F.2d 394, 13 FEP Cases 517 (3d Cir. 1976), *cert. denied,* 45 LW 3463, 14 FEP Cases 266 (U.S. January 11, 1977); *Erie Human Relations Comm'n* v. *Tullio,* 493 F.2d 371, 7 FEP Cases 477 (3d Cir. 1974): *Commonwealth* v. *O'Neill,* 473 F.2d 1029, 5 FEP Cases 713 (3d Cir. 1973) (per curiam) *(en banc); Kirkland* v. *New York State Dept. of Correctional Serv.,* 520 F.2d 420, 430, 11 FEP Cases 38, 45 (2d Cir. 1975), *cert. denied,* 45 LW 3249, 13 FEP Cases 962 (U.S. October 5, 1976).

judgment; and its judgment is to be guided by sound legal principles." '
Discrction is vested not for purposes of 'limit[ing] appellate review of
trial courts, or . . . invit[ing] inconsistency and caprice,' but rather to
allow the most complete achievement of the objectives of Title VII that
is attainable under the facts and circumstances of the specific case. 422
U.S., at 421, 10 FEP Cases at 1188. Accordingly the District Court's denial
of any form of seniority remedy must be reviewed in terms of its effect
on the attainment of the Act's objectives under the circumstances presented by this record." *Franks* v. *Bowman Transp. Co., supra,* 424 U.S. at
770-71, 12 FEP Cases at 558.

In *Franks,* the Court reviewed the denial rather than the award of relief,
but it is equally relevant to the scope of appellate review of the award
of relief as well. As we pointed out in Part IV A, *supra,* this case comes
to us after actual litigation by the intervening defendants over the scope
of relief. Thus it is closer, procedurally, to *Franks* v. *Bowman, supra,* than
to *Bryan* v. *Pittsburgh Plate Glass Co., supra,* and *Kober* v. *Westinghouse
Electric Corp.,* 480 F.2d 240, 247-50, 5 FEP Cases 1166, 1171-73 (3d Cir.
1973), in which we reviewed settlements objected to by plaintiff class
members. But whether we apply the standard of appellate review for
litigated Title VII cases or that for review of settlements, considerable
deference must be accorded the decision of the trial judge as a remedy.

The intervening defendants do not dispute that past hiring practices
violated the law, that the makeup of the work force in many Bell System
departments reflects the present effects of those past practices, or that continuance of the "best qualified" criterion for promotion, by rewarding
experience in a given department, would tend to perpetuate those effects.
Nor have they urged (except in their general attacks against all affirmative action targets and goals) that relating the targets and goals to
minority representation in the available work force was error. They do
contend that other means of attaining those goals might have been
resorted to, and might be equally effective. But the decree preserves for
the unions the opportunity to bargain collectively for such alternative
means. The district court gave careful consideration to all the union's
objections, and struck an appropriate balance between the integrity of
the collective bargaining process and the necessity for effective relief.
The affirmative action override was not applied across the board, but only
when necessary to bring particular work units into compliance. The intermediate targets and the goals remain subject to periodic review and adjustment. The decree is short lived. It makes no intrusion upon competitive seniority for layoffs or rehires. In the circumstances we cannot
say that the court abused its discretion.

### E.  CONSTITUTIONAL CHALLENGES

Finally, the intervening defendants challenge the decree on the ground
that any court-imposed remedy requiring a quota, target or goal defined
in terms of sex, race or national origin violates the due process clause

of the fifth amendment. In its broadest reach, this argument is that any class action remedy for discrimination against minorities is unconstitutional, for any such remedy of necessity defines the protected class. We are not asked to go quite that far. The unions do not object to the provisions of the decree prohibiting employment discrimination in the future. Their objection is to the provisions for overcoming the effects of past practices. We have rejected the same constitutional arguments against affirmative action remedies in the past. *United States* v. *Int'l Union of Elevator Const., supra,* 538 F.2d at 1018, 13 FEP Cases at 86; *Erie Human Relations Comm'n* v. *Tullio, supra; Contractors Ass'n of Eastern Pa.* v. *Secretary of Labor, supra,* 442 F.2d at 176, 3 FEP Cases at 408. See *Oburn* v. *Shapp,* 521 F.2d 142, 149, 11 FEP Cases 58, 63 (3d Cir. 1975) (GARTH, J.). The intervening defendants would have us distinguish these cases because they did not involve competitive seniority, and thus did not involve contractual interests of other employees. We pointed out above that *Elevator Constructors* did involve competitive seniority. But in any event the proposed distinction is unavailing. *Franks* v. *Bowman Transp. Co., supra,* holds that the contractual interest of an employee in competitive seniority must yield to an appropriate Title VII remedy. See 424 U.S. at 778, 12 FEP Cases at 560-61. Federal statutory remedies need not be color blind or sex unconscious.[7]

We recognize that the remedy adopted by the district court can operate to the disadvantage of members of groups which have not previously been discriminated against compared to members of sex or racial groups previously subject to discrimination who have not themselves been discriminated against. The remedy thus constitutes federal action which classifies by membership in a sex or racial group, and must be held invalid under the equal protection guarantee inherent in the due process clause of the Fifth Amendment unless it can be shown that the interest in making the classification is sufficiently great.

The standard applied by the Court in evaluating that interest has differed somewhat for sex as opposed to racial classifications. Racial classifications are subject to strict scrutiny: the federal "purpose or interest" must be "both constitutionally permissible and substantial," and the "use of the classification" must be " 'necessary . . . to the accomplishment' of [the] purpose or the safeguarding of [the] interest." *In re Griffiths,* 413 U.S. 717, 721-22 (1973) (footnotes omitted). On the other hand, "classifications by gender must serve important governmental objectives and must be substantially related to achievement of those objectives." *Craig* v. *Boren,* 429 U.S. 190, 197 (December 20, 1976). The

---

[7] Our conclusion is strengthened by the Supreme Court's recent decision in *United Jewish Organization of Williamsburgh, Inc.* v. *Carey,* 430 U.S. 444 (March 1, 1977). There, the Court held that racial quotas could permissibly be used to effect legislative reapportionment pursuant to a constitutional federal statute. The claims of discrimination by petitioners were unavailing where the racial reapportionment was designed to remedy the effects of past discrimination. See also *Franks* v. *Bowman Transp. Co., supra,* 424 U.S. at 775 & n. 35, 12 FEP Cases at 560; *United States* v. *Bethlehem Steel Corp.,* 446 F.2d 652, 663, 3 FEP Cases 589, 596 (2d Cir. 1971); *Vogler* v. *McCarty, Inc.,* 451 F.2d 1236, 1238-39, 4 FEP Cases 12, 14 (5th Cir. 1971).

present classifications are permissible in the case of race, and are thus permissible a fortiori with respect to sex.

The federal interest in the present case is that of remedying the effect of a particular pattern of employment discrimination upon the balance of sex and racial groups that would otherwise have obtained— an interest distinct from that of seeing that each individual is not disadvantaged by discrimination, since it centers on the distribution of benefits among groups. This purpose is "substantial" within the meaning of *In re Griffiths, supra,*[8] where the Supreme Court said that "a State does have a substantial interest in the qualifications of those admitted to the practice of law . . ." 413 U.S. at 725. The governmental interest in having all groups fairly represented in employment is at least as substantial, and since that interest is substantial [9] the adverse effect on third parties is not a constitutional violation. Moreover, the same exclusion of such members could conceivably result from remedies afforded to individual victims of discrimination. This remedy operates no differently. Furthermore, as we noted above, the affirmative action override is necessary to the practical accomplishment of the remedial goal.

It will doubtless be possible to detail, and thus to employ remedies other than quotas, for many individual instances of discrimination. But it is also true that much discrimination cannot be proved through evidence of individual cases, even though a prima facie case can be made out on the basis of statistical or other evidence. It will, for example, be nearly impossible to show that individuals were deterred from applying for hiring or promotion, or from attempting to meet the prerequisites for advancement, because of their well-founded belief that a particular employer would not deal fairly with members of their particular sex or racial group. Moreover, even apart from problems of proof, goals and quotas are necessary to counteract the effects of discriminatory practices because some victims of discrimination no longer seek the job benefits which they were discriminatorily denied. In such cases, quotas are needed to counteract the effect of discriminatory practices upon the balance of sex and racial groups that would otherwise have obtained.

The use of employment goals and quotas admittedly involves tensions with the equal protection guarantee inherent in the due process clause of the Fifth Amendment. But the remedy granted by the district court is permissible because it seems reasonably calculated to counteract the detrimental effects a particular, identifiable pattern of discrimination has had upon the prospects of achieving a society in which the distribution

[8] The Court said in footnote 9 of its opinion that: "The state interest required has been characterized as 'overriding,' [*McLaughlin* v. *Florida,* 379 U.S. 184, 196 (1964)]; *Loving* v. *Virginia,* 388 U.S. 1, 11 (1967); 'compelling,' *Graham* v. *Richardson* [403 U.S. 365, 375 (1971)]; 'important,' *Dunn* v. *Blumstein,* 405 U.S. 330, 343 (1972), or "substantial," *ibid.* We attribute no particular significance to these variations in diction."

[9] See findings in House Judiciary Committee Report on H.R. 7152, reprinted in E.E.O.C., Legislative History of Titles VII and XI of Civil Rights Act of 1964 at 2018.

of jobs to basically qualified members of sex and racial groups is not affected by discrimination.

The judgment appealed from will be affirmed.

## STEELWORKERS v. WEBER

*Supreme Court of the United States, 1979*

_____ *U.S.* _____, *20 FEP Cases 1*

MR. JUSTICE BRENNAN delivered the opinion of the Court.

Challenged here is the legality of an affirmative action plan—collectively bargained by an employer and a union—that reserves for black employees 50 percent of the openings in an in-plant craft training program until the percentage of black craft workers in the plant is commensurate with the percentage of blacks in the local labor force. The question for decision is whether Congress, in Title VII of the Civil Rights Act of 1964 as amended, 42 U.S.C. § 2000e, left employers and unions in the private sector free to take such race-conscious steps to eliminate manifest racial imbalances in traditionally segregated job categories. We hold that Title VII does not prohibit such race-conscious affirmative action plans.

### I

In 1974 petitioner United Steelworkers of America (USWA) and petitioner Kaiser Aluminum & Chemical Corporation (Kaiser) entered into a master collective-bargaining agreement covering terms and conditions of employment at 15 Kaiser plants. The agreement contained, *inter alia,* an affirmative action plan designed to eliminate conspicuous racial imbalances in Kaiser's then almost exclusively white craft work forces. Black craft hiring goals were set for each Kaiser plant equal to the percentage of blacks in the respective local labor forces. To enable plants to meet these goals, on-the-job training programs were established to teach unskilled production workers—black and white—the skills necessary to become craft workers. The plan reserved for black employees 50 percent of the openings in these newly created in-plant training programs.

This case arose from the operation of the plan at Kaiser's plant in Gramercy, La. Until 1974 Kaiser hired as craft workers for that plant only persons who had had prior craft experience. Because blacks had long been excluded from craft unions,[1] few were able to present such credentials. As a consequence, prior to 1974 only 1.83 percent (five out of 273) of the skilled craft workers at the Gramercy plant were black, even though the work force in the Gramercy area was approximately 39 percent black.

---

[1] [Footnotes numbered as in original.—Ed.] Judicial findings of exclusion from crafts on racial grounds are so numerous as to make such exclusion a proper subject for judicial notice. See, *e.g., United States* v. *International Union of Elevator Constructors,*

Pursuant to the national agreement Kaiser altered its craft hiring prac-tice in the Gramercy plant. Rather than hiring already trained outsiders, Kaiser established a training program to train its production workers to fill craft openings. Selection of craft trainees was made on the basis of seniority, with the proviso that at least 50 percent of the new trainees were to be black until the percentage of black skilled craft workers in the Gramercy plant approximated the percentage of blacks in the local labor force. See 415 F. Supp. 761, 764.

During 1974, the first year of the operation of the Kaiser-USWA affirma-tive action plan, 13 craft trainees were selected from Gramercy's produc-tion work force. Of these, 7 were black and 6 white. The most junior black selected into the program had less seniority than several white production workers whose bids for admission were rejected. Thereafter one of those white production workers, respondent Brian Weber, instituted this class action in the United States District Court for the Eastern District of Louisiana.

The complaint alleged that the filling of craft trainee positions at the Gramercy plant pursuant to the affirmative action program had resulted in junior black employees receiving training in preference to more senior white employees, thus discriminating against respondent and other simi-larly situated white employees in violation of §§ 703(a) [2] and (d) [3] of Title VII. The District Court held that the plan violated Title VII, entered a judgment in favor of the plaintiff class, and granted a perma-nent injunction prohibiting Kaiser and the USWA "from denying plain-

---

538 F.2d 1012 (CA3 1976); *Associated General Contractors of Massachusetts* v. *Altshuler,* 490 F.2d 9 (CA1 1973); *Southern Illinois Builders Association* v. *Ogilve,* 471 F.2d 680 (CA7 1972); *Contractors Association of Eastern Pennsylvania* v. *Secretary of Labor,* 442 F.2d 159 (CA3 1971); *Local 53 of International Association of Heat & Frost, etc.* v. *Vogler,* 407 F.2d 1047 (CA5 1969); *Buckner* v. *Goodyear,* 339 F. Supp. 1108 (ND Ala. 1972), *aff'd without opinion,* 476 F.2d 1287 (CA5 1973). See also United States Commis-sion on Civil Rights, THE CHALLENGE AHEAD: EQUAL OPPORTUNITY IN REFERRAL UNIONS 58–94 (1976) (summarizing judicial findings of discrimination by craft unions); G. Myrdal, AN AMERICAN DILEMMA (1944) 1079–1124; R. Marshall and V. Briggs, THE NEGRO AND APPRENTICESHIP (1967); S. Spero and A. Harris, THE BLACK WORKER (1931); United States Commission on Civil Rights, EMPLOYMENT 97 (1961); State Advisory Com-mittee, United States Commission on Civil Rights, 50 STATES REPORT 209 (1961); Marshall, "The Negro in Southern Unions," in THE NEGRO AND THE AMERICAN LABOR MOVEMENT (ed. Jacobson, Anchor 1968) p. 145; App., 63, 104.

[2] Section 703(a), 42 U.S.C. § 2000e–2(a), provides:
"(a) It shall be an unlawful employment practice for an employer—
"(1) to fail or refuse to hire or to discharge any individual, or otherwise to discrimi-nate against any individual with respect to his compensation, terms, conditions, or privileges of employment, because of such individual's race, color, religion, sex, or national origin; or
"(2) to limit or classify his employees or applicants for employment in any way which would deprive or tend to deprive any individual of employment opportunities or other-wise adversely affect his status as an employee, because of such individual's race, color, religion, sex, or national origin."

[3] Section 703(d), 42 U.S.C. § 2000e–2(d), provides:
"It shall be an unlawful employment practice for any employer, labor organization, or joint labor-management committee controlling apprenticeship or other training or retraining, including on-the-job training programs to discriminate against any individ-ual because of his race, color, religion, sex, or national origin in admission to, or em-ployment in, any program established to provide apprenticeship or other training."

tiffs, Brian F. Weber and all other members of the class, access to on-the-job training programs on the basis of race." 415 F. Supp. 761 (1976). A divided panel of the Court of Appeals for the Fifth Circuit affirmed, holding that all employment preferences based upon race, including those preferences incidental to bona fide affirmative action plans, violated Title VII's prohibition against racial discrimination in employment. 563 F.2d 216 (1978). We granted certiorari. _____ U.S. _____ (1979). We reverse.

## II

We emphasize at the outset the narrowness of our inquiry. Since the Kaiser-USWA plan does not involve state action, this case does not present an alleged violation of the Equal Protection Clause of the Constitution. Further, since the Kaiser-USWA plan was adopted voluntarily, we are not concerned with what Title VII requires or with what a court might order to remedy a past proven violation of the Act. The only question before us is the narrow statutory issue of whether Title VII *forbids* private employers and unions from voluntarily agreeing upon bona fide affirmative action plans that accord racial preferences in the manner and for the purpose provided in the Kaiser-USWA plan. That question was expressly left open in *McDonald* v. *Santa Fe Trail Trans. Co.*, 427 U.S. 273, 281 n. 8 (1976) which held, in a case not involving affirmative action, that Title VII protects whites as well as blacks from certain forms of racial discrimination.

Respondent argues that Congress intended in Title VII to prohibit all race-conscious affirmative action plans. Respondent's argument rests upon a literal interpretation of §§ 703(a) and (d) of the Act. Those sections make it unlawful to "discriminate . . . because of . . . race" in hiring and in the selection of apprentices for training programs. Since, the argument runs, *McDonald* v. *Santa Fe Trans. Co., supra,* settled that Title VII forbids discrimination against whites as well as blacks, and since the Kaiser-USWA affirmative action plan operates to discriminate against white employees solely because they are white, it follows that the Kaiser-USWA plan violates Title VII.

Respondent's argument is not without force. But it overlooks the significance of the fact that the Kaiser-USWA plan is an affirmative action plan voluntarily adopted by private parties to eliminate traditional patterns of racial segregation. In this context respondent's reliance upon a literal construction of §§ 703(a) and (d) and upon *McDonald* is misplaced. See *McDonald* v. *Santa Fe Trail Trans. Co., supra,* at 281 n. 8. It is a "familiar rule, that a thing may be within the letter of the statute and yet not within the statute, because not within its spirit, nor within the intention of its makers." *Holy Trinity Church* v. *United States,* 143 U.S. 457, 459 (1892). The prohibition against racial discrimination in §§ 703(a) and (d) of Title VII must therefore be read against the background of the legislative history of Title VII and the historical context from which the Act arose. See *Train* v. *Colorado Public Interest Research Group,* 426 U.S. 1, 10 (1976); *Woodworkers* v. *NLRB,* 386 U.S. 612, 620 (1967);

*United States* v. *American Trucking Assns.*, 310 U.S. 534, 543–544 (1940). Examination of those sources makes clear that an interpretation of the sections that forbade all race-conscious affirmative action would "bring about an end completely at variance with the purpose of the statute" and must be rejected. *United States* v. *Public Utilities Comm'n*, 345 U.S. 295, 315 (1953). See *Johansen* v. *United States*, 343 U.S. 427, 431 (1952); *International Union* v. *Juneau Spruce Corp.*, 342 U.S. 237, 243 (1952); *Texas & Pacific R. Co.* v. *Abilene Oil Co.*, 204 U.S. 426 (1907).

Congress' primary concern in enacting the prohibition against racial discrimination in Title VII of the Civil Rights Act of 1964 was with "the plight of the Negro in our economy." 110 Cong. Rec. 6548 (remarks of Sen. Humphrey). Before 1964, blacks were largely relegated to "unskilled and semi-skilled jobs." *Id.*, at 6548 (remarks of Sen. Humphrey); *id.*, at 7204 (remarks of Sen. Clark); *id.*, at 7279–7280 (remarks of Sen. Kennedy). Because of automation the number of such jobs was rapidly decreasing. See 110 Cong. Rec., at 6548 (remarks of Sen. Humphrey); *id.*, at 7204 (remarks of Sen. Clark). As a consequence "the relative position of the Negro worker [was] steadily worsening. In 1947 the non-white unemployment rate was only 64 percent higher than the white rate; in 1962 it was 124 percent higher." *Id.*, at 6547 (remarks of Sen. Humphrey). See also *id.*, at 7204 (remarks of Sen. Clark). Congress considered this a serious social problem. As Senator Clark told the Senate:

"The rate of Negro unemployment has gone up consistently as compared with white unemployment for the past 15 years. This is a social malaise and a social situation which we should not tolerate. That is one of the principal reasons why this bill should pass." *Id.*, at 7220.

Congress feared that the goals of the Civil Rights Act—the integration of blacks into the mainstream of American society—could not be achieved unless this trend were reversed. And Congress recognized that that would not be possible unless blacks were able to secure jobs "which have a future." *Id.*, at 7204 (remarks to Sen. Clark). See also *id.*, at 7279–7280 (remarks of Sen. Kennedy). As Senator Humphrey explained to the Senate.

"What good does it do a Negro to be able to eat in a fine restaurant if he cannot afford to pay the bill? What good does it do him to be accepted in a hotel that is too expensive for his modest income? How can a Negro child be motivated to take full advantage of integrated educational facilities if he has no hope of getting a job where he can use that education? *Id.*, at 6547.

. . .

"Without a job, one cannot afford public convenience and accommodations. Income from employment may be necessary to further a man's education, or that of his children. If his children have no hope of getting a good job, what will motivate them to take advantage of educational opportunities." *Id.*, at 6552.

These remarks echoed President Kennedy's original message to Congress upon the introduction of the Civil Rights Act in 1963.

"There is little value in a Negro's obtaining the right to be admitted to hotels and restaurants if he has no cash in his pocket and no job." *Id.,* at 11159.

Accordingly, it was clear to Congress that "the crux of the problem [was] to open employment opportunities for Negroes in occupations which have been traditionally closed to them," *id.,* at 6548 (remarks of Sen. Humphrey), and it was to this problem that Title VII's prohibition against racial discrimination in employment was primarily addressed.

It plainly appears from the House Report accompanying the Civil Rights Act that Congress did not intend wholly to prohibit private and voluntary affirmative action efforts as one method of solving this problem. The Report provides:

"No bill can or should lay claim to eliminating all of the causes and consequences of racial and other types of discrimination against minorities. There is reason to believe, however, that national leadership provided by the enactment of Federal legislation dealing with the most troublesome problems *will create an atmosphere conducive to voluntary or local resolution of other forms of discrimination.*" H.R. Rep. No. 914, 88th Cong., 1st Sess. (1963), at 18. (Emphasis supplied.)

Given this legislative history, we cannot agree with respondent that Congress intended to prohibit the private sector from taking effective steps to accomplish the goal that Congress designed Title VII to achieve. The very statutory words intended as a spur or catalyst to cause "employers and unions to self-examine and to self-evaluate their employment practices and to endeavor to eliminate, so far as possible, the last vestiges of an unfortunate and ignominious page in this country's history," *Albemarle* v. *Moody,* 422 U.S. 405, 418 (1975), cannot be interpreted as an absolute prohibition against all private, voluntary, race-conscious affirmative action efforts to hasten the elimination of such vestiges.[4] It would be ironic indeed if a law triggered by a Nation's concern over centuries of racial injustice and intended to improve the lot of those who had "been excluded from the American dream for so long," 110 Cong. Rec., at 6552 (remarks of Sen. Humphrey), constituted the first legislative prohibition of all voluntary, private, race-conscious efforts to abolish traditional patterns of racial segregation and hierarchy.

Our conclusion is further reinforced by examination of the language and legislative history of § 703(j) of Title VII.[5] Opponents of Title VII

---

[4] The problem that Congress addressed in 1964 remains with us. In 1962 the nonwhite unemployment rate was 124 percent higher than the white rate. See 110 Cong. Rec. 6547 (remarks of Sen. Humphrey). In 1978 the black unemployment rate was 129 percent higher. See MONTHLY LABOR REVIEW, U.S. Department of Labor Bureau of Labor Statistics 78 (Mar. 1979).

[5] Section 703(j) of Title VII, 42 U.S.C. § 2000e–2(j), provides:

"Nothing contained in this subchapter shall be interpreted to require any employer, employment agency, labor organization, or joint labor-management committee subject to this subchapter to grant preferential treatment to any individual or to any group because of the race, color, religion, sex, national origin of such individual or group on account of an imbalance which may exist with respect to the total number or per-

raised two related arguments against the bill. First, they argued that the
Act would be interpreted to *require* employers with racially imbalanced
work forces to grant preferential treatment to racial minorities in order to
integrate. Second, they argued that employers with racially imbalanced
work forces would grant preferential treatment to racial minorities, even
if not required to do so by the Act. See 110 Cong. Rec. 8618–8619 (remarks of Sen. Sparkman). Had Congress meant to prohibit all race-
conscious affirmative action, as respondent urges, it easily could have
answered both objections by providing that Title VII would not require
or *permit* racially preferential integration efforts. But Congress did not
choose such a course. Rather Congress added § 703(j) which addresses
only the first objection. The section provides that nothing contained in
Title VII "shall be interpreted to *require* any employer . . . to grant
preferential treatment . . . to any group because of the race . . . of such
. . . group on account of" a defacto racial imbalance in the employer's
work force. The section does *not* state that "nothing in Title VII shall be
interpreted to *permit*" voluntary affirmative efforts to correct racial imbalances. The natural inference is that Congress chose not to forbid all
voluntary race-conscious affirmative action.

The reasons for this choice are evident from the legislative record.
Title VII could not have been enacted into law without substantial support from legislators in both Houses who traditionally resisted federal
regulation of private business. Those legislators demanded as a price for
their support that "management prerogatives and union freedoms . . . be
left undisturbed to the greatest extent possible." H.R. Rep. No. 914, 88th
Cong., 1st Sess., Pt. 2 (1963), at 29. Section 703(j) was proposed by Senator
Dirksen to allay any fears that the Act might be interpreted in such a way
as to upset this compromise. The section was designed to prevent § 703
of Title VII from being interpreted in such a way as to lead to undue
"Federal Government interference with private businesses because of
some Federal employee's ideas about racial balance or imbalance." 110
Cong. Rec., at 14314 (remarks of Sen. Miller).[6] See also *id.*, at 9881

---

centage of persons of any race, color, religion, sex, or national origin employed by any
employer, referred or classified for employment by an employment agency or labor
organization, or admitted to, or employed in, any apprenticeship or other training
program, in comparison with the total number or percentage of persons of such race,
color, religion, sex, or national origin in any community, State, section, or other area,
or in the available work force in any community, State, section, or other area."

Section 703(j) speaks to substantive liability under Title VII, but it does not preclude
courts from considering racial imbalance as evidence of a Title VII violation. See
*Teamsters* v. *United States*, 431 U.S. 324, 339–340, n. 20 (1977). Remedies for substantive
violations are governed by § 706(g), 42 U.S.C. §2000e–5(g).

[6] Title VI of the Civil Rights Act of 1964, considered in *University of California
Regents* v. *Bakke*, 438 U.S. 265 (1978), contains no provision comparable to § 703(j).
This is because Title VI was an exercise of federal power over a matter in which the
Federal Government was already directly involved: the prohibitions against race-based
conduct contained in Title VI governed "program[s] or activit[ies] receiving Federal
financial assistance." 42 U.S.C. § 2000d. Congress was legislating to assure federal funds
would not be used in an improper manner. Title VII, by contrast, was enacted
pursuant to the Commerce power to regulate purely private decisionmaking and was

(remarks of Sen. Allott); *id.*, at 10520 (remarks of Sen. Carlson); *id.*, at 11471 (remarks of Sen. Javits); *id.*, at 12817 (remarks of Sen. Dirksen). Clearly, a prohibition against all voluntary, race-conscious, affirmative action efforts would disserve these ends. Such a prohibition would augment the powers of the Federal Government and diminish traditional management prerogatives while at the same time impeding attainment of the ultimate statutory goals. In view of this legislative history and in view of Congress' desire to avoid undue federal regulation of private businesses, use of the word "require" rather than the phrase "require or permit" in § 703(j) fortifies the conclusion that Congress did not intend to limit traditional business freedom to such a degree as to prohibit all voluntary, race-conscious affirmative action.[7]

We therefore hold that Title VII's prohibition in §§ 703(a) and (d) against racial discrimination does not condemn all private, voluntary, race-conscious affirmative action plans.

### III

We need not today define in detail the line of demarcation between permissible and impermissible affirmative action plans. It suffices to hold that the challenged Kaiser-USWA affirmative action plan falls on the permissible side of the line. The purposes of the plan mirror those of the statute. Both were designed to break down old patterns of racial segregation and hierarchy. Both were structured to "open employment oppor-

---

not intended to incorporate and particularize the commands of the Fifth and Fourteenth Amendments. Title VII and Title VI, therefore, cannot be read *in pari materia*. See 110 Cong. Rec. 8315 (1964) (remarks of Sen. Cooper). See also *id.*, at 11615 (remarks of Sen. Cooper).

[7] Respondent argues that our construction of § 703 conflicts with various remarks in the legislative record. See, *e.g.*, 110 Cong. Rec. 7213 (Sens. Clark and Case); *id.*, at 7218 (Sens. Clark and Case); *id.*, at 6549 (Sen. Humphrey); *id.*, at 8921 (Sen. Williams). We do not agree. In Senator Humphrey's words, these comments were intended as assurances that Title VII would not allow establishment of systems "to *maintain* racial balance in employment." *id.*, at 11848. They were not addressed to temporary, voluntary, affirmative action measures undertaken to eliminate manifest racial imbalance in traditionally segregated job categories. Moreover, the comments referred to by respondent all preceded the adoption of § 703(j), 42 U.S.C. § 2000e-2(j). After § 703(j) was adopted congressional comments were all to the effect that employers would not be *required* to institute preferential quotas to avoid Title VII liability, see, *e.g.*, *id.*, at 12819 (remarks of Sen. Dirksen); *id.*, at 13079–13080 (remarks of Sen. Clark); *id.*, at 15876 (remarks of Rep. Lindsay). There was no suggestion after the adoption of § 703(j) that wholly voluntary, race-conscious, affirmative action efforts would in themselves constitute a violation of Title VII. On the contrary, as Representative MacGregor told the House shortly before the final vote on Title VII:

"Important as the scope and extent of this bill is, it is also vitally important that all Americans understand what this bill does not cover.

"Your mail and mine, your contacts and mine with our constituents, indicates a great degree of misunderstanding about this bill. People complain about . . . preferential treatment or quotas in employment. There is a mistaken belief that Congress is legislating in these areas in this bill. When we drafted this bill we excluded these issues largely because the problems raised by these controversial questions are more properly handled at a governmental level closer to the American people and by communities and individuals themselves." 110 Cong. Rec. 15893 (remarks of Rep. MacGregor).

tunities for Negroes in occupations which have been traditionally closed to them." 110 Cong. Rec. 6548 (remarks of Sen. Humphrey).[8]

At the same time the plan does not unnecessarily trammel the interests of the white employees. The plan does not require the discharge of white workers and their replacement with new black hires. Cf. *McDonald* v. *Santa Fe Trail Trans. Co., supra.* Nor does the plan create an absolute bar to the advancement of white employees; half of those trained in the program will be white. Moreover, the plan is a temporary measure; it is not intended to maintain racial balance, but simply to eliminate a manifest racial imbalance. Preferential selection of craft trainees at the Gramercy plant will end as soon as the percentage of black skilled craft workers in the Gramercy plant approximates the percentage of blacks in the local labor force. See 415 F. Supp. 761, 763.

We conclude, therefore, that the adoption of the Kaiser-USWA plan for the Gramercy plant falls within the area of discretion left by Title VII to the private sector voluntarily to adopt affirmative action plans designed to eliminate conspicuous racial imbalance in traditionally segregated job categories.[9] Accordingly, the judgment of the Court of Appeals for the Fifth Circuit is

*Reversed.*

MR. JUSTICE POWELL and MR. JUSTICE STEVENS took no part in the consideration or decision of this case.

MR. JUSTICE BLACKMUN, concurring: While I share some of the misgivings expressed in MR. JUSTICE REHNQUIST's dissent, *post,* concerning the extent to which the legislative history of Title VII clearly supports the result the Court reaches today, I believe that additional considerations, practical and equitable, only partially perceived, if perceived at all, by the 88th Congress, support the conclusion reached by the Court today, and I therefore join its opinion as well as its judgment.

I

In his dissent from the decision of the United States Court of Appeals for the Fifth Circuit, Judge Wisdom pointed out that this case arises from a practical problem in the administration of Title VII. The broad prohibition against discrimination places the employer and the union on what he accurately described as a "high tightrope without a net beneath them." 563 F.2d 216, 230. If Title VII is read literally, on the one hand they face liability for past discrimination against blacks, and on the other they face

---

[8] See n. 1, *supra.* This is not to suggest that the freedom of an employer to undertake race-conscious affirmative action efforts depends on whether or not his effort is motivated by fear of liability under Title VII.

[9] Our disposition makes unnecessary consideration of petitioners' argument that their plan was justified because they feared that black employees would bring suit under Title VII if they did not adopt an affirmative action plan. Nor need we consider petitioners' contention that their affirmative action plan represented an attempt to comply with Executive Order 11246.

liability to whites for any voluntary preferences adopted to mitigate the effects of prior discrimination against blacks.

In this case, Kaiser denies prior discrimination but concedes that its past hiring practices may be subject to question. Although the labor force in the Gramercy area was approximately 39 percent black, Kaiser's work force was less than 15 percent black, and its craft work force was less than 2 percent black. Kaiser had made some effort to recruit black painters, carpenters, insulators, and other craftsmen, but it continued to insist that those hired have five years prior industrial experience, a requirement that arguably was not sufficiently job-related to justify under Title VII any discriminatory impact it may have had. See *Parson* v. *Kaiser Aluminium & Chemical Corp.*, 575 F.2d 1374, 1389 (CA5 1978), *cert. denied*, _____ U.S. _____ (1979). The parties dispute the extent to which black craftsmen were available in the local labor market. They agree, however, that after critical reviews from the Office of Federal Contract Compliance, Kaiser and the Steelworkers established the training program in question here and modeled it along the lines of a Title VII consent decree later entered for the steel industry. See *United States* v. *Allegheny-Ludlum Industries, Inc.*, 517 F.2d 826 (CA5 1976). Yet when they did this, respondent Weber sued, alleging that Title VII prohibited the program because it discriminated against him as a white person and it was not supported by a prior judicial finding of discrimination against blacks.

Respondents' reading of Title VII, endorsed by the Court of Appeals, places voluntary compliance with Title VII in profound jeopardy. The only way for the employer and the union to keep their footing on the "tightrope" it creates would be to eschew all forms of voluntary affirmative action. Even a whisper of emphasis on minority recruiting would be forbidden. Because Congress intended to encourage private efforts to come into compliance with Title VII, see *Alexander* v. *Gardner-Denver Co.*, 415 U.S. 36, 44 (1974), Judge Wisdom concluded that employers and unions who had committed "arguable violations" of Title VII should be free to take reasonable responses without fear of liability to whites. 563 F.2d., at 230. Preferential hiring along the lines of the Kaiser program is a reasonable response for the employer, whether or not a court, on these facts, could order the same step as a remedy. The company is able to avoid identifying victims of past discrimination, and so avoids claims for backpay that would inevitably follow a response limited to such victims. If past victims should be benefited by the program, however, the company mitigates its liability to those persons. Also, to the extent that Title VII liability is predicated on the "disparate effect" of an employer's past hiring practices, the program makes it less likely that such an effect could be demonstrated. Cf. *County of Los Angeles* v. *Davis*, _____ U.S. _____, _____ (1979) (hiring could moot a past Title VII claim). And the Court has recently held that work force statistics resulting from private affirmative action were probative of benign intent in a "disparate treatment" case. *Furnco Construction Corp.* v. *Waters*, 438 U.S. 567, 579–580 (1978).

The "arguable violation" theory has a number of advantages. It responds to a practical problem in the administration of Title VII not anticipated by Congress. It draws predictability from the outline of present law, and closely effectuates the purpose of the Act. Both Kaiser and the United States urge its adoption here. Because I agree that it is the soundest way to approach this case, my preference would be to resolve this litigation by applying it and holding that Kaiser's craft training program meets the requirement that voluntary affirmative action be a reasonable response to an "arguable violation" of Title VII.

## II

The Court, however, declines to consider the narrow "arguable violation" approach and adheres instead to an interpretation of Title VII that permits affirmative action by an employer whenever the job category in question is "traditionally segregated." *Ante,* at 13, and n. 9. The sources cited suggest that the Court considers a job category to be "traditionally segregated" when there has been a societal history of purposeful exclusion of blacks from the job category, resulting in a persistent disparity between the proportion of blacks in the labor force and the proportion of blacks among those who hold jobs within the category.*

"Traditionally segregated job categories," where they exist, sweep far more broadly than the class of "arguable violations" of Title VII. The Court's expansive approach is somewhat disturbing for me because, as Mr. Justice Rehnquist points out, the Congress that passed Title VII probably thought it was adopting a principle of nondiscrimination that would apply to blacks and whites alike. While setting aside that principle can be justified where necessary to advance statutory policy by encouraging reasonable responses as a form of voluntary compliance that mitigates "arguable violations," discarding the principle of nondiscrimination where no countervailing statutory policy exists appears to be at odds with the bargain struck when Title VII was enacted.

---

* The jobs in question here include those of carpenter, electrician, general repairman, insulator, machinist, and painter. App. 165. The sources cited, *ante,* at 2 n. 1, establish, for example, that although 11.7 percent of the United States population in 1970 was black, the percentage of blacks among the membership of carpenters' unions was only 3.7 percent. For painters, the percentage was 4.9, and for electricians, 2.6. United States Commission on Civil Rights, THE CHALLENGE AHEAD: EQUAL OPPORTUNITY IN REFERRAL UNIONS 274, 281 (1976). Kaiser's Director of Equal Opportunity Affairs testified that, as a result of discrimination in employment and training opportunity, blacks were underrepresented in skilled crafts "in every industry of the United States, and in every area of the United States." App. 90. While the parties dispute the cause of the relative underrepresentation of blacks in Kaiser's craft work force, the Court of Appeals indicated that it thought "the general lack of skills among available blacks" was responsible. 563 F.2d, at 224 n. 13. There can be little doubt that any lack of skill has its roots in purposeful discrimination of the past, including segregated and inferior trade schools for blacks in Louisiana, United States Commission on Civil Rights, 50 STATES REPORT 209 (1961); traditionally all-white craft unions in that State, including the electrical workers and the plumbers, *id.,* at 208; union nepotism, *Local 53; Asbestos Workers* v. *Vogler,* 407 F.2d 1047 (CA5 1969); and segregated apprenticeship programs, R. Marshall and V. Briggs, THE NEGRO AND APPRENTICESHIP 27 (1967).

A closer look at the problem, however, reveals that in each of the principal ways in which the Court's "traditionally segregated job categories" approach expands on the "arguable violations" theory, still other considerations point in favor of the broad standard adopted by the Court, and make it possible for me to conclude that the Court's reading of the statute is an acceptable one.

A.  The first point at which the Court departs from the "arguable violations" approach is that it measures an individual employer's capacity for affirmative action solely in terms of a statistical disparity. The individual employer need not have engaged in discriminatory practices in the past. While, under Title VII, a mere disparity may provide the basis for a prima facie case against an employer, *Dothard* v. *Rawlinson,* 433 U.S. 321, 329–331 (1977), it would not conclusively prove a violation of the Act. *Teamsters* v. *United States,* 431 U.S. 324, 339–340, n. 20 (1977); see § 703(j), 42 U.S.C. § 2000e–2(j). As a practical matter, however, this difference may not be that great. While the "arguable violation" standard is conceptually satisfying, in practice the emphasis would be on "arguable" rather than on "violation." The great difficulty in the District Court was that no one had any incentive to prove that Kaiser had violated the Act. Neither Kaiser nor the Steelworkers wanted to establish a past violation, nor did Weber. The blacks harmed had never sued and so had no established representative. The Equal Employment Opportunity Commission declined to intervene, and cannot be expected to intervene in every case of this nature. To make the "arguable violation" standard work, it would have to be set low enough to permit the employer to prove it without obligating himself to pay a damage award. The inevitable tendency would be to avoid hairsplitting litigation by simply concluding that a mere disparity between the racial composition of the employer's work force and the composition of the qualified local labor force would be an "arguable violation," even though actual liability could not be established on that basis alone. See Note, 57 N.C. L. REV. 695, 714–719 (1979).

B.  The Court also departs from the "arguable violation" approach by permitting an employer to redress discrimination that lies wholly outside the bounds of Title VII. For example, Title VII provides no remedy for pre-Act discrimination, *Hazelwood School District* v. *United States,* 433 U.S. 299, 309–310 (1977); yet the purposeful discrimination that creates a "traditionally segregated job category" may have entirely predated the Act. More subtly, in assessing a prima facie case of Title VII liability, the composition of the employer's work force is compared to the composition of the pool of workers who meet valid job qualifications. *Hazelwood,* 433 U.S., at 308, and n. 13; *Teamsters* v. *United States,* 431 U.S., at 339–340, and n. 20 (1977). When a "job category" is traditionally segregated, however, that pool will reflect the effects of segregation, and the Court's approach goes further and permits a comparison with the composition of the labor force as a whole, in which minorities are more heavily represented.

Strong considerations of equity support an interpretation of Title VII that would permit private affirmative action to reach where Title VII itself does not. The bargain struck in 1964 with the passage of Title VII guaranteed equal opportunity for white and black alike, but where Title VII provides no remedy for blacks, it should not be construed to foreclose private affirmative action from supplying relief. It seems unfair for respondent Weber to argue, as he does, that the asserted scarcity of black craftsmen in Louisiana, the product of historic discrimination, makes Kaiser's training program illegal because it ostensibly absolves Kaiser of all Title VII liability. Brief for Respondents 60. Absent compelling evidence of legislative intent, I would not interpret Title VII itself as a means of "locking in" the effects of segregation for which Title VII provides no remedy. Such a construction, as the Court points out, *ante*, at 9, would be "ironic," given the broad remedial purposes of Title VII.

The dissent, while it focuses more on what Title VII does not require than on what Title VII forbids, cites several passages that appear to express an intent to "lock in" minorities. In mining the legislative history anew, however, the dissent, in my view, fails to take proper account of our prior cases that have given that history a much more limited reading than that adopted by the dissent. For example, in *Griggs* v. *Duke Power Co.*, 401 U.S. 424, 434–436, and n. 11 (1971), the Court refused to give controlling weight to the memorandum of Senators Clark and Case which the dissent now finds so persuasive. See *post*, at 21–24. And in quoting a statement from that memorandum that an employer would not be "permitted . . . to prefer Negroes for future vacancies," *post*, at 22, the dissent does not point out that the Court's opinion in *Teamsters* v. *United States*, 431 U.S. 324, 349–351 (1977), implies that that language is limited to the protection of established seniority systems. Here seniority is not in issue because the craft training program is new and does not involve an abrogation of pre-existing seniority rights. In short, the passages marshaled by the dissent are not so compelling as to merit the whip hand over the obvious equity of permitting employers to ameliorate the effects of past discrimination for which Title VII provides no direct relief.

### III

I also think it significant that, while the Court's opinion does not foreclose other forms of affirmative action, the Kaiser program it approves is a moderate one. The opinion notes that the program does not afford an absolute preference for blacks, and that it ends when the racial composition of Kaiser's craft work force matches the racial composition of the local population. It thus operates as a temporary tool for remedying past discrimination without attempting to "maintain" a previously achieved balance. See *University of California Regents* v. *Bakke*, 438 U.S. 265, 342 n. 17 (1978) (BRENNAN, WHITE, MARSHALL, and BLACKMUN, JJ.). Because the duration of the program is finite, it perhaps will end even before the "stage of maturity when action along this line is no longer necessary." *Id.*, at 403 (BLACKMUN, J.). And if the Court has misperceived the political will, it has the assurance that because the question is statutory Congress may set a different course if it so chooses.

MR. CHIEF JUSTICE BURGER, dissenting: The Court reaches a result I would be inclined to vote for where I a Member of Congress considering a proposed amendment of Title VII. I cannot join the Court's judgment, however, because it is contrary to the explicit language of the statute and arrived at by means wholly incompatible with long-established principles of separation of powers. Under the guise of statutory "construction," the Court effectively rewrites Title VII to achieve what it regards as a desirable result. It "amends" the statute to do precisely what both its sponsors and its opponents agreed the statute was *not* intended to do.

...

MR. JUSTICE REHNQUIST, with whom THE CHIEF JUSTICE joins, dissenting: In a very real sense, the Court's opinion is ahead of its time: it could more appropriately have been handed down five years from now, in 1984, a year coinciding with the title of a book from which the Court's opinion borrows, perhaps subconsciously, at least one idea. Orwell describes in his book a governmental official of Oceania, one of the three great world powers, denouncing the current enemy, Eurasia, to an assembled crowd:

"It was almost impossible to listen to him without being first convinced and then maddened. . . . The speech had been proceeding for perhaps twenty minutes when a messenger hurried onto the platform and a scrap of paper was slipped into the speaker's hand. He unrolled and read it without pausing in his speech. Nothing altered in his voice or manner, or in the content of what he was saying, but suddenly the names were different. Without words said, a wave of understanding rippled through the crowd. Oceania was at war with Eastasia! . . . The banners and posters with which the square was decorated were all wrong! . . .

"[T]he speaker had switched from one line to the other actually in mid-sentence, not only without a pause, but without even breaking the syntax." G. Orwell, NINETEEN EIGHTY-FOUR, 182–183 (1949).

Today's decision represents an equally dramatic and equally unremarked switch in this Court's interpretation of Title VII.

The operative sections of Title VII prohibit racial discrimination in employment *simpliciter*. Taken in its normal meaning, and as understood by all Members of Congress who spoke to the issue during the legislative debates, see *infra*, at _____, this language prohibits a covered employer from considering race when making an employment decision, whether the race be black or white. Several years ago, however, a United States District Court held that "the dismissal of white employees charged with misappropriating company property while not dismissing a similarly charged Negro employee does not raise a claim upon which Title VII relief may be granted." *McDonald* v. *Santa Fe Trail Tranps. Co.*, 427 U.S. 273, 278 (1976). This Court unanimously reversed, concluding from the "uncontradicted legislative history" that "Title VII prohibits racial discrimination against the white petitioners in this case upon the same standards as would be applicable were they Negroes. . . ." 427 U.S., at 280.

We have never wavered in our understanding that Title VII "prohibits *all* racial discrimination in employment, without exception for any particular employees." *Id.,* at 283 (emphasis in original). In *Griggs* v. *Duke Power Co.,* 401 U.S. 424, 429 (1971), our first occasion to interpret Title VII, a unanimous court observed that "[d]iscriminatory preference, for any group, minority or majority, is precisely and only what Congress has proscribed." And in our most recent discussion of the issue, we uttered words seemingly dispositive of this case: "It is clear beyond cavil that the obligation imposed by Title VII is to provide an equal opportunity for *each* applicant regardless of race, without regard to whether members of the applicant's race are already proportionately represented in the work force." *Furnco Construction Corp.* v. *Waters,* 438 U.S. 567, _____ (1978) (emphasis in original).[1]

Today, however, the Court behaves much like the Orwellian speaker earlier described, as if it had been handed a note indicating that Title VII would lead to a result unacceptable to the Court if interpreted here as it was in our prior decisions. Accordingly, without even a break in syntax, the Court rejects "a literal construction of § 703(a)" in favor of newly discovered "legislative history," which leads it to a conclusion directly contrary to that compelled by the "uncontradicted legislative history" unearthed in *McDonald* and our other prior decisions. Now we are told that the legislative history of Title VII shows that employers are free to discriminate on the basis of race: an employer may, in the Court's words, "trammel the interests of white employees" in favor of black employees in order to eliminate "racial imbalance." *Ante,* at 12. Our earlier interpretations of Title VII, like the banners and posters decorating the square in Oceania, were all wrong.

As if this were not enough to make a reasonable observer question this Court's adherence to the oft-stated principle that our duty is to construe rather than rewrite legislation, *United States* v. *Rutherford,* slip op., at 9 (June _____, 1979), the Court also seizes upon § 703(j) of Title VII as an independent, or at least partially independent, basis for its holding. Totally ignoring the wording of that section, which is obviously addressed to those charged with the responsibility of interpreting the law rather than those who are subject to its proscriptions, and totally ignoring the months of legislative debates preceding the section's introduction and passage, which demonstrate clearly that it was enacted to prevent precisely what occurred in this case, the Court infers from § 703(j) that "Congress chose not to forbid all voluntary race-conscious affirmative action." *Ante,* at 10.

Thus, by a *tour de force* reminiscent not of jurists such as Hale, Holmes, and Hughes, but of escape artists such as Houdini, the Court eludes clear statutory language, "uncontradicted" legislative history, and uniform precedent in concluding that employers are, after all, permitted to con-

---

[1] Our statements in *Griggs* and *Furnco Construction,* patently inconsistent with today's holding, are not even mentioned, much less distinguished, by the Court.

sider race in making employment decisions. It may be that one or more of the principal sponsors of Title VII would have preferred to see a provision allowing preferential treatment of minorities written into the bill. Such a provision, however, would have to have been expressly or impliedly excepted from Title VII's explicit prohibition on all racial discrimination in employment. There is no such exception in the Act. And a reading of the legislative debates concerning Title VII, in which proponents and opponents alike uniformly denounced discrimination in favor of, as well as discrimination against, Negroes, demonstrates clearly that any legislator harboring an unspoken desire for such a provision could not possibly have succeeded in enacting it into law.

# I

Kaiser opened its Gramercy, La., plant in 1958. Because the Gramercy facility had no apprenticeship or in-plant craft training program, Kaiser hired as craft workers only persons with prior craft experience. Despite Kaiser's efforts to locate and hire trained black craftsmen, few were available in the Gramercy area, and as a consequence, Kaiser's craft positions were manned almost exclusively by whites. In February 1974, under pressure from the Office of Federal Contract Compliance to increase minority representation in craft positions at its various plants,[2] and hoping to deter the filing of employment discrimination claims by minorities, Kaiser entered into a collective-bargaining agreement with the United Steelworkers of America (Steelworkers) which created a new on-the-job craft training program at 15 Kaiser facilities, including the Gramercy plant. The agreement required that no less than one minority applicant be admitted to the training program for every nonminority applicant until the percentage of blacks in craft positions equaled the percentage of blacks

[2] The Office of Federal Contract Compliance (OFCC), subsequently renamed the Office of Federal Contract Compliance Programs (OFCCP), is an arm of the Department of Labor responsible for ensuring compliance by government contractors with the equal employment opportunity responsibilities established by Executive Order 11246, 30 Fed. Reg. 12319 (1965), as amended by Executive Order 11375, 32 Fed. Reg. 14303 (1967), and by Executive Order 12086, 43 Fed. Reg. 46501 (1978).

Executive Order 11246 requires all applicants for federal contracts to refrain from employment discrimination and to "take affirmative action to ensure that applicants are employed, and that employees are treated during employment, without regard to their race, color, religion, sex or national origin." § 202(j), 3 CFR § 169 (1974), reprinted following 42 U.S.C. § 2000e (1970). The Executive Order empowers the Secretary of Labor to issue rules and regulations necessary and appropriate to achieve its purpose. He, in turn, has delegated most enforcement duties to the OFCC. See 41 CFR § 60–20.1 et seq.; 41 CFR § 60–2.24.

The affirmative action program mandated by 41 CFR § 60–2 (Revised Order No. 4) for nonconstruction contractors requires a "utilization" study to determine minority representation in the work force. Goals for hiring and promotion must be set to overcome any "underutilization" found to exist.

The OFCC employs the "power of the purse" to coerce acceptance of its affirmative action plans. Indeed, in this case, "the district court found that the 1974 collective-bargaining agreement reflected less of a desire on Kaiser's part to train black craft workers than a self-interest in satisfying the OFCC in order to retain lucrative government contracts." 563 F.2d 216, 226 (CA5 1977).

in the local work force.[3] Eligibility for the craft training programs was to be determined on the basis of plant seniority, with black and white applicants to be selected on the basis of their relative seniority within their racial group.

Brian Weber is white. He was hired at Kaiser's Gramercy plant in 1969. In April 1974 Kaiser announced that it was offering a total of nine positions in three on-the-job training programs for skilled craft jobs. Weber applied for all three programs, but was not selected. The successful candidates—five black and four white applicants—were chosen in accordance with the 50 percent minority admission quota mandated under the 1974 collective-bargaining agreement. Two of the successful black applicants had less seniority than Weber.[4] Weber brought the instant class action[5] in the United States District Court for the Eastern District of Louisiana, alleging that use of the 50 percent minority admission quota to fill vacancies in Kaiser's craft training programs violated Title VII's prohibition on racial discrimination in employment. The District

---

[3] The pertinent portions of the collective-bargaining agreement provide: "It is further agreed that the Joint Committee will specifically review the minority representation in the existing Trade, Craft and Assigned Maintenance classifications, in the plants set forth below, and, where necessary, establish certain goals and time tables in order to achieve a desired minority ratio:

"[Gramercy Works listed, among others]

"As apprentice and craft jobs are to be filled, the contractual selection criteria shall be applied in reaching such goals; at a minimum, not less than one minority employee will enter for every non-minority employee entering until the goal is reached unless at a particular time there are insufficient available qualified minority candidates. . . .

. . .

"The term 'minority' as used herein shall be as defined in EEOC Reporting Requirements." 415 F. Supp. 761, 763 (ED La. 1976).

The "Joint Committee" subsequently entered into a "Memorandum of Understanding" establishing a goal of 39 percent as the percentage of blacks that must be represented in each "craft family" at Kaiser's Gramercy plant. Id., at 764. The goal of 39 percent minority representation was based on the percentage of minority workers available in the Gramercy area.

Contrary to the Court's assertion, it is not at all clear that Kaiser's admission quota is a "temporary measure . . . not intended to maintain racial imbalance." Ante, at 13. Dennis E. English, industrial relations superintendent at the Gramercy plant, testified at trial:

"Once the goal is reached of 39 percent, or whatever the figure will be down the road, I think it's subject to change, once the goal is reached in each of the craft families, at that time, we will then revert to a ratio of what that precentage is, if it remains at 39 percent and we attain 39 percent someday, we will then continue placing trainees in the program at that percentage. The idea, again, being to have a minority representation in the plant that is equal to that representation in the community work force population." App. 69.

[4] In addition to the April programs, the company offered three more training programs in 1974 with a total of four positions available. Two white and two black employees were selected for the programs, which were for "Air Conditioning Repairman" (one position), "Carpenter-Painter" (two positions), and "Insulator" (one position). Weber sought to bid for the insulator trainee position, but he was not selected because that job was reserved for the most senior qualified black employee. App. 46.

[5] The class was defined to include the following employees:

"All persons employed by Kaiser Aluminum & Chemical Corporation at its Gramercy, Louisiana, works who are members of the United Steelworkers of America, AFL–CIO Local 5702, who are not members of a minority group, and who have applied for or were eligible to apply for on-the-job training programs since February 1, 1974." 415 F. Supp., at 763.

Court and the Court of Appeals for the Fifth Circuit agreed, enjoining further use of race as a criterion in admitting applicants to the craft training programs.[6]

## II

Were Congress to act today specifically to prohibit the type of racial discrimination suffered by Weber, it would be hard pressed to draft language better tailored to the task than that found in § 703(d) of Title VII:

"It shall be an unlawful employment practice for any employer, labor organization, or joint labor-management committee controlling apprenticeship or other training or retraining, including on-the-job training programs to discriminate against any individual because of his race, color, religion, sex, or national origin in admission to, or employment in, any program established to provide apprenticeship or other training." 43 U.S.C. § 2000e–2(d).

Equally suited to the task would be § 703(a)(2), which makes it unlawful for an employer to classify his employees "in any way which would deprive or tend to deprive any individual of employment opportunities or otherwise adversely affect his status as an employee, because of such individ-

---

[6] In upholding the District Court's injunction, the Court of Appeals affirmed the District Court's finding that Kaiser had not been guilty of any past discriminatory hiring or promotion at its Gramercy plant. The court thus concluded that this finding removed the instant case from this Court's line of "remedy" decisions authorizing fictional seniority in order to place proven victims of discrimination in as good a position as they would have enjoyed absent the discriminatory hiring practices. See *Franks* v. *Bowman Transp. Co.*, 424 U.S. 747 (1976). "In the absence of prior discrimination," the Court of Appeals observed, "a racial quota loses its character as an equitable *remedy* and must be banned as an unlawful racial *preference* prohibited by Title VII, §§ 703(a) and (d). Title VII outlaws preferences for any group, minority or majority, if based on race or other impermissible classifications, but it does not outlaw preferences favoring victims of discrimination." 563 F.2d, at 224 (emphasis in original). Nor was the Court of Appeals moved by the claim that Kaiser's discriminatory admission quota is justified to correct a lack of training of Negroes due to past societal discrimination: "Whatever other effects societal discrimination may have, it has had—by the specific finding of the court below, *no effect* on the seniority of any party here." *Id.*, at 226 (emphasis in original). Finally, the Court of Appeals rejected the argument that Kaiser's admission quota does not violate Title VII because it is sanctioned, indeed compelled, by Executive Order 11246 and regulations issued by the OFCC mandating affirmative action by all government contractors. See n. 2, *supra*. Citing *Youngstown Sheet & Tube Co.* v. *Sawyer*, 343 U.S. 579 (1952), the court concluded that "[i]f Executive Order 11246 mandates a racial quota for admission to on-the-job training by Kaiser, *in the absence of any prior hiring or promotion discrimination,* the Executive Order must fall before the direct congressional prohibition [of § 703(d)]." *Id.*, at 227 (emphasis in original).

Judge Wisdom, in dissent, argued that "[i]f an affirmative action plan, adopted in a collective bargaining agreement, is a reasonable remedy for an *arguable* violation of Title VII, it should be upheld." *Id.*, at 230. The United States, in its brief before this Court, and MR. JUSTICE BLACKMUN, *ante*, at _____, largely adopt Judge Wisdom's theory, which apparently rests on the conclusion that an employer is free to correct *arguable* discrimination against his black employees by adopting measures that he *knows* will discriminate against his white employees.

ual's race, color, religion, sex, or national origin." 42 U.S.C. § 2000e–2(a)(2).[7]

Entirely consistent with these two express prohibitions is the language of §703(j) of Title VII, which provides that the Act is not to be interpreted "to require any employer . . . to grant preferential treatment to any individual or to any group because of the race . . . of such individual or group" to correct a racial imbalance in the employer's work force. 42 U.S.C. § 2000e–2(j).[8] Seizing on the word "require," the Court infers that Congress must have intended to "permit" this type of racial discrimination. Not only is this reading of § 703(j) outlandish in the light of the flat prohibitions of §§ 703(a) and (d), but, as explained [in] Part III, it is totally belied by the Act's legislative history.

Quite simply, Kaiser's racially discriminatory admission quota is flatly prohibited by the plain language of Title VII. This normally dispositive fact,[9] however, gives the Court only momentary pause. An "interpretation" of the statute upholding Weber's claim would, according to the Court, " 'bring about an end completely at variance with the purpose of the statute.' " *Ante,* at 6, quoting *United States* v. *Public Utilities Comm'n,* 345 U.S. 295, 315 (1953). To support this conclusion, the Court calls upon the "spirit" of the Act, which it divines from passages in Title VII's legislative history indicating that enactment of the statute was prompted by Congress' desire "to open employment opportunities for Negroes in occupations which [had] been traditionally closed to them." *Ante,* at 8, quoting 110 Cong. Rec. 6548 (1964) (remarks of Sen. Humphrey).[10] But the legislative history invoked by the Court to avoid the

---

[7] Section 703(a)(1) provides the third express prohibition in Title VII of Kaiser's discriminatory admission quota:

"It shall be an unlawful employment practice for an employer—

"(1) to fail or refuse to hire or to discharge an individual, or otherwise to discriminate against any individual with respect to his compensation, terms, conditions, or privileges of employment, because of such individual's race, color, religion, sex, or national origin. . . ." 42 U.S.C. § 2000e–2(a)(1).

[8] The full text of § 703(j), 42 U.S.C. § 2000e–2(j), provides as follows:

"(j) Nothing contained in this subchapter shall be interpreted to require any employer, employment agency, labor organization, or joint labor-management committee subject to this subchapter to grant preferential treatment to any individual or to any group because of the race, color, religion, sex, or national origin of such individual or group on account of an imbalance which may exist with respect to the total number or percentage of persons of any race, color, religion, sex or national origin employed by any employer, referred or classified for employment by any employment agency or labor organization, admitted to membership or classified by any labor organization, or admitted to, or employed in, any apprenticeship or other training program, in comparison with the total number or percentage of persons of such race, color, religion, sex, or national origin in any community, State, section, or other area, or in the available work force in any community, State, section, or other area."

[9] "If the words are plain, they give meaning to the act, and it is neither the duty nor the privilege of the courts to enter speculative fields in search of a different meaning.

". . . [W]hen words are free from doubt they must be taken as the final expression of the legislative intent, and are not to be added to or subtracted from by considerations drawn . . . from any extraneous source." *Caminetti* v. *United States,* 242 U.S. 470, 490 (1917).

[10] In holding that Title VII cannot be interpreted to prohibit use of Kaiser's racially discriminatory admission quota, the Court reasons that it would be "ironic" if a law

plain language of §§ 703(a) and (d) simply misses the point. To be sure, the reality of employment discrimination against Negroes provided the primary impetus for passage of Title VII. But this fact by no means supports the proposition that Congress intended to leave employers free to discriminate against white persons.[11] In most cases, "[l]egislative history . . . is more vague than the statute we are called upon to interpret." *United States* v. *Public Utilities Comm'n,* 345 U.S. 295, 321 (1954) (Jackson, J., concurring). Here, however, the legislative history of Title VII is as clear as the language of §§ 703(a) and (d), and it irrefutably demonstrates that Congress meant precisely what it said in §§ 703(a) and (d) —that *no* racial discrimination in employment is permissible under Title VII, not even preferential treatment of minorities to correct racial imbalance.

---

inspired by the history of racial discrimination in employment against blacks forbade employers from voluntarily discriminating against whites in favor of blacks. I see no irony in a law that prohibits *all* voluntary racial discrimination, even discrimination directed at whites in favor of blacks. The evil inherent in discrimination against Negroes is that it is based on an immutable characteristic, utterly irrelevant to employment decisions. The characteristic becomes no less immutable and irrelevant, and discrimination based thereon becomes no less evil, simply because the person excluded is a member of one race rather than another. Far from ironic, I find a prohibition on all preferential treatment based on race as elementary and fundamental as the principle that "two wrongs do not make a right."

[11] The only shred of legislative history cited by the Court in support of the proposition that "Congress did not intend wholly to prohibit private and voluntary affirmative action efforts," *ante,* at 8, is the following excerpt from the Judiciary Committee Report accompanying the civil rights bill reported to the House:

"No bill can or should lay claim to eliminating all of the causes and consequences of racial and other types of discrimination against minorities. There is reason to believe, however, that national leadership provided by the enactment of Federal legislation dealing with the most troublesome problems *will create an atmosphere conducive to voluntary or local resolution of other forms of discrimination.*" H.R. Rep. No. 914, 88th Cong., 1st Sess., 18 (1963) (hereinafter H.R. Rep.), quoted *ante,* at 8.

The Court seizes on the italicized language to support its conclusion that Congress did not intend to prohibit voluntary imposition of racially discriminatory employment quotas. The Court, however, stops too short in its reading of the House Report. The words immediately following the material excerpted by the Court are as follows:

"It is, however, possible and necessary for the Congress to enact legislation which prohibits and provides the means of terminating *the most serious types of discrimination.* This H.R. 7152, as amended, would achieve in a number of related areas. It would reduce discriminatory obstacles to the exercise of the right to vote and provide means of expediting the vindication of that right. It would make it possible to remove the daily affront and humiliation involved in discriminatory denials of access to facilities ostensibly open to the general public. It would guarantee that there will be no discrimination upon recipients of Federal financial assistance. It would prohibit discrimination in employment, and provide means to expedite termination of discrimination in public education. It would open additional avenues to deal with redress of denials of equal protection of the laws on account of race, color, religion, or national origin by State or local authorities." H.R. Rep., at 18 (emphasis added).

When thus read in context, the meaning of the italicized language in the Court's excerpt of the House Report becomes clear. By dealing with "the most serious types of discrimination," such as discrimination in voting, public accommodations, employment, etc., H.R. 7152 would hopefully inspire "voluntary or local resolution of other forms of discrimination," that is, forms other than discrimination in voting, public accommodations, employment, etc.

One can also infer from the House Report that the Judiciary Committee hoped that federal legislation would inspire voluntary elimination of discrimination against minority groups other than those protected under the bill, perhaps the aged and handicapped to name just two. In any event, the House Report does not support the Court's

### III

In undertaking to review the legislative history of Title VII, I am mindful that the topic hardly makes for light reading, but I am also fearful that nothing short of a thorough examination of the congressional debates will fully expose the magnitude of the Court's misinterpretation of Congress' intent.

[Mr. Rehnquist's review of the legislative history is omitted.]

### IV

Reading the language of Title VII, as the Court purports to do, "against the background of [its] legislative history . . . and the historical context from which the Act arose," *ante,* at 6, one is led inescapably to the conclusion that Congress fully understood what it was saying and meant precisely what it said. Opponents of the civil rights bill did not argue that employers would be permitted under Title VII voluntarily to grant preferential treatment to minorities to correct racial imbalance. The plain language of the statute too clearly prohibited such racial discrimination to admit of any doubt. They argued, tirelessly, that Title VII would be interpreted by federal agencies and their agents to require unwilling employers to racially balance their work forces by granting preferential treatment to minorities. Supporters of H.R. 7152 responded, equally tirelessly, that the Act would not be so interpreted because not only does it not require preferential treatment of minorities, it does not *permit* preferential treatment of any race for any reason. It cannot be doubted that the proponents of Title VII understood the meaning of their words, for "[s]eldom has similar legislation been debated with greater consciousness for the need for 'legislative history' or with greater care in the making thereof, to guide the courts in interpreting and applying the law." Title VII: Legislative History, at 444.

To put an end to the dispute, supporters of the civil rights bill drafted and introduced § 703(j). Specifically addressed to the opposition's charge, § 703(j) simply enjoins federal agencies and courts from interpreting Title VII to require an employer to prefer certain racial groups to correct imbalances in his work force. The section says nothing about voluntary preferential treatment of minorities because such racial discrimination is plainly proscribed by §§ 703(a) and (d). Indeed, had Congress intended to except voluntary, race-conscious preferential treatment from the blanket prohibition on racial discrimination in §§ 703(a) and (d), it surely could have drafted language better suited to the task than § 703(j). It knew how. Section 703(i) provides:

---

proposition that Congress, by banning racial discrimination in employment, intended to permit racial discrimination in employment.

Thus, examination of the House Judiciary Committee's report reveals that the Court's interpretation of Title VII, far from being compelled by the Act's legislative history, is utterly without support in that legislative history. Indeed, as demonstrated in Part III, *infra,* the Court's interpretation of Title VII is totally refuted by the Act's legislative history.

"Nothing contained in [title VII] shall apply to any business or enterprise on or near an Indian reservation with respect to any publicly announced employment practice of such business or enterprise under which a preferential treatment is given to any individual because he is an Indian living on or near a reservation." § 703(i), 42 U.S.C. § 2000e–2(i).

## V

Our task in this case, like any other case involving the construction of a statute, is to give effect to the intent of Congress. To divine that intent, we traditionally look first to the words of the statute and, if they are unclear, then to the statute's legislative history. Finding the desired result hopelessly foreclosed by these conventional sources, the Court turns to a third source—the "spirit" of the Act. But close examination of what the Court proffers as the spirit of the Act reveals it as the spirit animating the present majority, not the Eighty-eighth Congress. For if the spirit of the Act eludes the cold words of the statute itself, it rings out with unmistakable clarity in the words of the elected representatives who made the Act law. It is *equality*. Senator Dirksen, I think, captured that spirit in a speech delivered on the floor of the Senate just moments before the bill was passed:

"[T]oday we come to grips finally with a bill that advances the enjoyment of living; but, more than that, it advances the equality of opportunity.

"I do not emphasize the word 'equality' standing by itself. It means equality of opportunity in the field of education. It means equality of opportunity in the field of employment. It means equality of opportunity in the field of participation in the affairs of government. . . .

"That is it.

"Equality of opportunity, if we are going to talk about conscience, is the mass conscience of mankind that speaks in every generation, and it will continue to speak long after we are dead and gone." 110 Cong. Rec. 14510 (1964).

There is perhaps no device more destructive to the notion of equality than the *numerus clausus*—the quota. Whether described as "benign discrimination" or "affirmative action," the racial quota is nonetheless a creator of castes, a two-edged sword that must demean one in order to prefer another. In passing Title VII Congress outlawed *all* racial discrimination, recognizing that no discrimination based on race is benign, that no action disadvantaging a person because of his color is affirmative. With today's holding, the Court introduces into Title VII a tolerance for the very evil that the law was intended to eradicate, without offering even a clue as to what the limits on that tolerance may be. We are told simply that Kaiser's racially discriminatory admission quota "falls on the permissible side of the line." *Ante,* at 12. By going not merely *beyond,* but directly *against* Title VII's language and legislative history, the Court has sown the wind. Later courts will face the impossible task of reaping the whirlwind.

# UNITED STATES v. EAST TEXAS MOTOR FREIGHT SYSTEM

*United States Court of Appeals, Fifth Circuit, 1977*
*564 F.2d 179, 16 FEP Cases 163*

WYATT, Senior District Judge: These are separate appeals by the United States and by the Equal Employment Opportunity Commission (EEOC) from orders filed on May 21, 1975, and on June 26, 1975, in the United States District Court for the Northern District of Texas (Honorable Sarah T. Hughes, District Judge). There is a cross appeal by defendant International Brotherhood of Teamsters, Chauffeurs, Warehousemen and Helpers of America ("the Union") from the order of May 21, 1975.

## 1.

The action was commenced on June 29, 1972 by the Attorney General in the name of the United States as plaintiff. It was said to be brought to enforce provisions of Title VII of the Civil Rights Act of 1964 (42 U.S.C. § 2000e and following) and certain obligations imposed by Executive Order No. 11246 (30 F.R. 12319). As to Title VII, the action was authorized by 42 U.S.C. § 2000e-6(a).

The defendants named were: East Texas Motor Freight ("ET"), the Union, and International Association of Machinists and Aerospace Workers ("Machinists"). Machinists defaulted by filing no answer and for purposes of this appeal may be disregarded.

ET is an extensive common carrier of motor freight. The Union through local union affiliates represents a majority of ET employees. The local union affiliates and ET are parties to collective bargaining agreements, approved by the Union.

The claim was that ET as a policy and practice discriminated against blacks and persons of Spanish origin and that the collective bargaining agreements with the Union by their seniority provisions prevented transfer to better jobs of minorities, who could not carry their seniority for bidding and for layoffs. Thus, it was said that the seniority provisions of the Union agreements perpetuated the past discrimination.

ET has over-the-road (OTR) truck drivers, who drive between terminals in different cities, and city drivers, who drive only in and about the city in which their assigned terminal is located. OTR drivers have the better and higher paid jobs and the minorities were said to have been excluded from this category by ET.

The United States and ET entered into a proposed consent decree which was approved by the District Court and signed on February 18, 1974, and filed on February 19, 1974. The Union did not consent to the decree; it opposed the entry of that decree.

The consent decree settled all issues between the United States and ET. It provided for elimination of discriminatory practices and for various forms of affirmative action by ET. It did not affect seniority provisions of union agreements but left these for resolution after trial of the issues between the United States and the Union. As part of the consent decree ET paid $175,000 in back pay to members of the affected class.

A proposed pretrial order, signed by counsel for plaintiff United States, for ET, and for the Union was filed on May 17, 1974. By order of the District Court, filed May 22, 1974, this proposal became "a formally adopted pretrial order." From this order and from all else, it was evident that the issue to be tried between the plaintiff and the Union was whether the seniority provisions of the collective bargaining agreements between the Union and ET violated Title VII and the Executive Order because they perpetuated the effects of the discrimination practiced by ET. The plaintiff asked that this issue be resolved in its favor, that an award of back pay be made against the Union, and that (despite the agreements between ET and the Union) "full company seniority carryover" be awarded to members of the affected class transferring under provisions of the consent decree. The Union opposed all this, and defended the seniority provisions.

By order filed January 24, 1975, EEOC was substituted as a party plaintiff for the United States as to all Title VII aspects of the action. This was in accordance with 42 U.S.C. § 2000e-6(d). The United States was left in the action as a party plaintiff as to those aspects of the action relating to Executive Order 11246.

The trial was before the District Court without a jury, beginning on April 21, 1975 and ending, after interruptions, on May 6, 1975. The adversaries were the United States and EEOC on the one hand, and the Union on the other. ET continued as a party to the action but claimed that the consent decree removed it as an active litigant.

The District Court on May 21, 1975, signed and filed an "order," which is also a memorandum opinion and from which these appeals are taken.

The District Court found that the "seniority system" in the collective bargaining agreements was a barrier to the movement of minorities to the desirable OTR jobs. The District Court awarded "seniority relief" in specified respects, in disregard of the contract seniority provisions, and directed that the parties make "any necessary revisions in seniority under the applicable collective bargaining agreements." The District Court denied any back pay award against the Union on the ground that under the consent decree the affected class had already been "fully compensated."

The two plaintiffs then moved to amend the May 21, 1975, order so as to award back pay against the Union and to expand the seniority rights to be granted.

By order with memorandum opinion, filed June 26, 1975, the District Court denied the motion to amend, leaving the May 21, 1975, order to stand as filed. The denial of back pay against the Union was rested, however, on a different ground: that the employer was principally responsible for the discrimination.

These appeals followed.

2.

When the appeals were reached for argument in April 1977, it appeared that certiorari had been granted by the Supreme Court in cases whose decision would have a significant bearing on the disposition of the appeals in the case at bar. The cases then pending in the Supreme Court were (1) *International Brotherhood of Teamsters* v. *United States* and *T.I.M.E. — DC* v. *United States* (consolidated; *cert. granted* May 24, 1976, 425 U.S. 990; referred to in short as the "Teamsters" case) and (2) *East Texas Motor Freight System, Inc.* v. *Rodriguez* and two other cases (*cert. granted* May 24, 1976, 425 U.S. 990; referred to in short as the "Rodriguez" case).

The decisions in *Teamsters* and *Rodriguez* were handed down on May 31, 1977. The opinion and result in *Rodriguez* are not relevant to the issues here on appeal. The *Teamsters* opinion, 431 U.S. 324, 14 FEP Cases 1514, and result are highly relevant here and must be examined.

3.

In the *Teamsters* case, the employer company was a motor freight carrier, the Union was the same as here, the discrimination charged against the company was the same as that charged here, and the seniority system embodied in contracts with the Union was the same seniority system in the union agreements here in suit.

The seniority system set out in the union contracts has, as a principal feature, seniority by bargaining unit. An OTR driver is in an OTR driver bargaining unit; a city driver is in a city driver bargaining unit. Transfer from city driving to OTR driving means loss of all seniority, thus discouraging transfers and thereby perpetuating prior discrimination.

The Supreme Court in the *Teamsters* case held that Section 703(h) of Title VII (42 U.S.C. § 2000e-2(h)) made it lawful to apply a seniority system even where "it may perpetuate pre-Act discrimination" (14 FEP Cases at 1526). The seniority system must be "bona fide" (42 U.S.C. § 2000e-2(h)) but in the case at bar it was conceded that the union contracts were "neutral on their face" and that no contention was made by the government that they were "negotiated for a discriminatory purpose" (App. 88, 89).

As to post-Act discrimination, the Supreme Court ruled, in *Teamsters* and in *United Air Lines* v. *Evans,* 431 U.S. 553, 14 FEP Cases 1510, that its perpetuation by a seniority system did not make the system unlawful but that by timely action retroactive seniority relief for individual employees could be secured.

The conclusion in Teamsters was that "the Union's conduct in agreeing to and maintaining the [seniority] system did not violate Title VII" (14 FEP Cases at 1527).

In ordering the cases remanded to the District Court, the Supreme Court in Teamsters established principles for guidance as to retroactive seniority. No employee who suffered discrimination before the effective date of the Act (July 2, 1965) can be given any relief. No employee can be given retroactive seniority to a date earlier than the effective date of the Act.

But employees who suffered from discrimination after the effective date of the Act can, on the necessary showing, obtain seniority relief within the principles of *Franks* v. *Bowman Transportation Co.*, 424 U.S. 747, 12 FEP Cases 549 (1976). The kind and character of showing on a number of points, as well as the burden of proof in some instances are explained in the *Teamsters* opinion.

### 4.

In the light of the opinion in *Teamsters*, it is clear that under Title VII the District Court correctly decided two of the matters about which the plaintiffs originally urged reversal: (a) there can be no monetary award against the Union, and (b) use of the Union's grievance procedure in the collective bargaining agreements for one of the steps in resolving seniority disputes was a proper exercise of discretion (in that it was held that those agreements did not violate Title VII). The plaintiffs concede that the back pay claim is eliminated by the *Teamsters* decision because it was based on Title VII; their appeal in this respect was "withdrawn" (Supplemental Brief, p. 2). As will later be seen, plaintiffs continue to urge that the Executive Order will support the award of retroactive seniority relief.

It appears that, as indicated before, even after the *Teamsters* decision some retroactive seniority relief can properly be granted to "individual employees" under Title VII (14 FEP Cases at 1527), if the necessary showing of post-Act discrimination is made and other evidence adduced. The difficulty on the present record is that the case was not tried as to individual employees and no distinction was made as to pre-Act and post-Act discrimination as to them. As counsel for plaintiffs explained at one point: ". . . we have not put up proof on trial specifically for them, but it is also true, as the Court of Appeals for the Fifth Circuit has held in *United States* versus *Time DC* just recently, it would be ridiculous because of the very nature of a Title 7 lawsuit to put on proof on each and every specific individual" (Minutes, October 3, 1975 hearing, p. 18). All this, of course, has been changed by the *Teamsters* decision.

It is apparent that on the record before it, the District Court, not then having the benefit of the *Teamsters* opinion, made no attempt to separate pre-Act and post-Act discrimination. The order of May 21, 1975, shows this by its terms. Moreover, in their supplemental brief (p. 9) the plaintiffs concede that about 75 percent of the retroactive seniority dates mandated below were for dates before the effective date of the Act, a result clearly against part of the decision in *Teamsters*, 14 FEP Cases at 1527.

In this state of affairs, as to all claims under Title VII, we are required to affirm the orders appealed from to the extent that they deny any money award against the Union and to the extent that they provide for use of the grievance procedure of the union contracts as a step in the resolution of retroactive seniority disputes for individual employees; in all other respects, the orders appealed from must be vacated and the action remanded to the District Court for further proceedings consistent with the principles laid down in the *Teamsters* opinion and consistent with this opinion.

5.

It remains to consider whether the claims of plaintiffs based on Executive Order 11246 require a different result. The argument for plaintiffs, after the *Teamsters* decision, is that the award of seniority rights by the District Court should be sustained on the basis of the Executive Order but at the same time should be modified to reflect the points made by plaintiffs on their appeal taken before the *Teamsters* decision. The argument is presented by both plaintiffs but since plaintiff EEOC was made a party only with respect to Title VII aspects, only the United States as plaintiff appears to have standing to urge the Executive Order. We do not dwell on this point but will continue to refer to both plaintiffs.

The Executive Order imposes obligations on government contractors and subcontractors designed to eliminate employment discrimination of the same sort to which Title VII is directed. The order is authorized by the broad grant of procurement authority. 40 U.S.C. § 486(a).

As the complaint makes clear, it is only ET which is a government contractor or subcontractor; the union is neither.

The Secretary of Labor is responsible for the administration of the Executive Order.

6.

There seems to be no authority in the Executive Order for any action against a labor union except a union "engaged in work under government contracts" and as to such a union the action authorized is for violation of Title VI or Title VII and this only after "best efforts" to cause cooperation (Sec. 207). It is not claimed that the Union here was "engaged in work under government contracts" and, of course, if it were, only a Title VII action would be authorized.

7.

There are "sanctions and penalties" provided in the Executive Order (Sec. 209(a)) but none of these support the present argument of plaintiffs.

Section 209(a)(3) authorizes the Secretary to recommend action under Title VII but as to labor unions this must refer to those "engaged in work under government contracts" and thus does not refer to the Union here. But even if this section did refer to the Union defendant, it would not support any present argument for plaintiffs because the authority is for a Title VII action only.

Section 209(a)(2) authorizes the Secretary, where there are violations of contractual provisions, to recommend proceedings to enforce those provisions. There are no contractual provisions to be enforced against the Union here, which is not a government contractor nor subcontractor. The section does speak of enjoining "organizations" etc. who "prevent compliance with the provisions of this Order." There is no claim in the complaint nor elsewhere that the Union has prevented or attempted to prevent compliance with the Executive Order. But even if an action against the Union under the Executive Order were authorized, it would necessarily be an action to enforce contract provisions by way of damages or an injunction; nothing in the Order suggests any authority to direct retroactive seniority benefit to third party discriminatees.

8.

This Court has ruled that the Executive Order has the force and effect of law and that there may be judicial proceedings to enforce its provisions against a government contractor. *United States* v. *New Orleans Public Service, Inc.,* 553 F.2d 459, 14 FEP Cases 1734, *petition for rehearing en banc denied,* 559 F.2d 30 (1977) (5th Cir. 1977; the "Nopsi case"). In *Nopsi,* however, the sole defendant was a supplier of services to the government—a public utility supplier—which had declined to accept the contract provision of the Executive Order. This Court, in a divided decision, held that the utility was nonetheless a government contractor. While the Executive Order was thus held applicable, the Court directed that enforcement be carried out in the first instance by administrative, not judicial, action. This was because of the following principle: "The basic approach of the Executive Order program, as implemented, is enforcement by executive agencies, in particular the Department of Labor, even though the Order itself provides the judicial enforcement alternative in Section 209(a)(2)" (553 F.2d at 474, 14 FEP Cases at 1747). There is nothing in the *Nopsi* decision to support the present argument of plaintiffs as to a labor union which is not a government contractor.

9.

If we assume, however, that the Executive Order does authorize an action against the Union to award retroactive seniority relief to individual employees, then the issue is whether a bona fide seniority system is lawful under Title VII (by virtue of Section 703(h) of Title VII) but unlawful under the Executive Order.

The plaintiffs argue that the obligations on government contractors under the Executive Order are "above and beyond" those imposed on employers by Title VII because the Executive Order contains no provision similar to Section 703(h) of Title VII (Supplemental Brief, p. 11). This is an argument never made until after the *Teamsters* decision.

The argument cannot be accepted because Congress has declared for a policy that a bona fide seniority system shall be lawful. The Executive may not, in defiance of such policy, make unlawful—or penalize—a bona fide seniority system. *Youngstown Co.* v. *Sawyer,* 343 U.S. 579, 587-589 (1952). This Court, in the recent Nopsi decision (above cited), recognized that an order of the Executive has the force of law only "if it is not in conflict with an express statutory provision" (553 F.2d at 465, 14 FEP Cases at 1739). Section 703(h) of Title VII is such a provision. The authorities cited by plaintiffs, to whatever extent applicable, are before the Teamsters decision and are made obsolete by that decision.

The Supreme Court made it clear in Teamsters that parties to seniority agreements could not be required to subordinate their rights to those of pre-Act discriminatees because this would be "a perversion of the congressional purpose" (14 FEP Cases at 1526). The Court added: "Congress did not intend to make it illegal for employees with vested seniority rights to continue to exercise those rights, even at the expense of pre-Act discriminatees" (14 FEP Cases at 1526). The quoted language is not based on any specific words in Title VII but on the fixed intent of Congress and the policy behind that intent.

Moreover, the Supreme Court in *Teamsters* (14 FEP Cases at 1531) emphasized earlier decisions that Title VII courts had been given broad equitable powers so as to enable them to give the "most complete relief possible." In this context, relief was limited to identified individual victims for whom the necessary showing could be made. If such relief is the "most complete . . . possible," the Executive Order could scarcely be interpreted to demand more.

### 10.

The Supreme Court itself gives a fairly strong indication that the principles in *Teamsters* are not to be limited to claims under Title VII. In *Sabala* v. *Western Gillette, Inc.,* 516 F.2d 1251, 11 FEP Cases 98 (5th Cir. 1975), a similar situation to that at bar, claims against the employer were under both Title VII and 42 U.S.C. § 1981 but those against the unions were "on Section 1981 exclusively" (516 F.2d at 1254, 11 FEP Cases at 101). This Court granted relief against employer and unions; both employer and unions petitioned for certiorari. After the *Teamsters* decision, the Supreme Court granted the petition of the *unions* (as well as that of the employer), vacated the judgment of this Court and remanded to this Court "for further consideration in light of" the *Teamsters* decision. _____ U.S. _____, 14 FEP Cases 1686 (1977). This Court then considered it "appropriate for the District Court, in the first instance, to reconsider its decision in light of" the *Teamsters* decision in the Supreme Court and remanded to the District Court for that purpose. 559 F.2d 282, 283, 15 FEP Cases 1809 (5 Cir. 1977).

### 11.

There is a cross-appeal by the Union to be considered.

The first point on the cross-appeal is said to be error in the District Court in respect of seniority relief by provision for a class rather than on an individual basis. What has already been said as to the effect of the *Teamsters* decision on the appeal of plaintiffs disposes of this point. The orders appealed from are being vacated as to the seniority relief granted by the District Court and the Union cross-appellant on remand may urge its contention before that Court in the light of the *Teamsters* decision.

The second point on the cross-appeal is that the local unions were indispensable parties. This argument by the Union (international) was rejected by this Court in *T.I.M.E.-DC*, 517 F.2d 299, at 310-11, 11 FEP Cases 66, at 73-74; the Supreme Court made no comment on the matter.

The third point on the cross-appeal is that the Union (international) was not a proper party because it had no sufficient connection with the collective bargaining agreements containing the seniority provisions. This Court held to the contrary in *TIME-DC*, already cited, and the Supreme Court stated that the Union (referring to this cross-appellant) "will properly remain in this litigation as a defendant. . . ." 431 U.S. at 356, 14 FEP Cases at 1527 fn. 43.

The orders appealed from are affirmed to the extent that they deny any money award against the Union, to the extent that they provide for use of the grievance procedure of the union contracts as a step in the resolution of retroactive seniority benefits for individual employees, to the extent that they reflect a decision that the local unions are not indispensable parties, and to the extent that they find the Union (the international) a proper party defendant. The orders appealed from are in other respects vacated and the cause remanded to the District Court for further proceedings in the light of *International Brotherhood of Teamsters* v. *United States*, 431 U.S. 324, 14 FEP Cases 1514 (1977), of other relevant decisions of the Supreme Court and of this Court rendered since the trial of this case, and of this opinion. The parties should be free to submit new evidence subject to such limitations as the District Court may appropriately impose.

AFFIRMED IN PART; VACATED AND REMANDED IN PART.


## NOTE

In *Fullilove* v. *Kreps*, 584 F.2d 600 (CA 2 1978), the Court of Appeals affirmed a lower court decision sustaining the constitutionality of the Public Works Employment Act of 1977. The Act mandated that at least 10 percent of any grant for public works be set aside for minority business enterprises. The court held, among other things, that the Government's interest in overcoming disadvantages resulting from past discrimination in employment on account of race is sufficiently compelling to justify a remedy requiring racial preferences and the Supreme Court granted certiorari (47 USLW 3760 (May 21, 1979)) and will review the case in the 1979 Term of Court.

# 5. EEO and Labor Relations Laws

## A. DUTY OF FAIR REPRESENTATION

### STEELE v. LOUISVILLE & NASHVILLE RAILROAD CO.

*Supreme Court of the United States, 1944*
*323 U.S. 192, 15 LRRM 708*

MR. CHIEF JUSTICE STONE delivered the opinion of the Court.

The question is whether the Railway Labor Act, 48 Stat. 1185, 45 U.S.C. §§ 151 *et seq.*, imposes on a labor organization, acting by authority of the statute as the exclusive bargaining representative of a craft or class of railway employees, the duty to represent all the employees in the craft without discrimination because of their race, and, if so, whether the courts have jurisdiction to protect the minority of the craft or class from the violation of such obligation.

. . .

The allegations of the bill of complaint, so far as now material, are as follows: Petitioner, a Negro, is a locomotive fireman in the employ of respondent Railroad, suing on his own behalf and that of his fellow employees who, like petitioner, are Negro firemen employed by the Railroad. Respondent Brotherhood, a labor organization, is, as provided under § 2, Fourth of the Railway Labor Act, the exclusive bargaining representative of the craft of firemen employed by the Railroad and is recognized as such by it and the members of the craft. The majority of the firemen employed by the Railroad are white and are members of the Brotherhood, but a substantial minority are Negroes who, by the constitution and ritual of the Brotherhood, are excluded from its membership. As the membership of the Brotherhood constitutes a majority of all firemen employed on respondent Railroad, and as under § 2, Fourth the members because they are the majority have the right to choose and have chosen the Brotherhood to represent the craft, petitioner and other Negro firemen on the road have been required to accept the Brotherhood as their representative for the purposes of the Act.

On March 28, 1940, the Brotherhood, purporting to act as representative of the entire craft of firemen, without informing the Negro firemen or giving them opportunity to be heard, served a notice on respondent Railroad and on twenty other railroads operating principally in the southeastern part of the United States. The notice announced the Brotherhood's desire to amend the existing collective bargaining agreement in such manner as ultimately to exclude all Negro firemen from the service. By established practice on the several railroads so notified only white firemen can be promoted to serve as engineers, and the notice proposed that only "promotable," i.e., white, men should be employed as firemen or assigned to new runs or jobs or permanent vacancies in established runs or jobs.

On February 18, 1941, the railroads and the Brotherhood, as representative of the craft, entered into a new agreement which provided that not more than 50 percent of the firemen in each class of service in each seniority district of a carrier should be Negroes; that until such percentage should be reached all new runs and all vacancies should be filled by white men; and that the agreement did not sanction the employment of Negroes in any seniority district in which they were not working. The agreement reserved the right of the Brotherhood to negotiate for further restrictions on the employment of Negro firemen on the individual railroads. On May 12, 1941, the Brotherhood entered into a supplemental agreement with respondent Railroad further controlling the seniority rights of Negro firemen and restricting their employment. The Negro firemen were not given notice or opportunity to be heard with respect to either of these agreements which were put into effect before their existence was disclosed to the Negro firemen.

Until April 8, 1941, petitioner was in a "passenger pool," to which one white and five Negro firemen were assigned. These jobs were highly desirable in point of wages, hours and other considerations. Petitioner had performed and was performing his work satisfactorily. Following a reduction in the mileage covered by the pool, all jobs in the pool were, about April 1, 1941, declared vacant. The Brotherhood and the Railroad, acting under the agreement, disqualified all the Negro firemen and replaced them with four white men, members of the Brotherhood, all junior in seniority to petitioner and no more competent or worthy. As a consequence petitioner was deprived of employment for sixteen days and then was assigned to more arduous, longer, and less remunerative work in local freight service. In conformity to the agreement, he was later replaced by a Brotherhood member junior to him, and assigned work on a switch engine, which was still harder and less remunerative, until January 3, 1942. On that date, after the bill of complaint in the present suit had been filed, he was reassigned to passenger service.

. . .

The Supreme Court of Alabama took jurisdiction of the cause but held on the merits that petitioner's complaint stated no cause of action. . . . It thought that the Brotherhood was empowered by the statute to enter into the agreement of February 18, 1941, and that by virtue of the statute the Brotherhood has power by agreement with the Railroad both to create the seniority rights of petitioners and his fellow Negro employees and to destroy them. It construed the statute, not as creating the relationship of principal and agent between the members of the craft and the Brotherhood, but as conferring on the Brotherhood plenary authority to treat with the Railroad and enter into contracts fixing rates of pay and working conditions for the craft as a whole without any legal obligation or duty to protect the rights of minorities from discrimination or unfair treatment, however gross. Consequently it held that neither the Brotherhood nor the Railroad violated any rights of petitioner or his fellow Negro employees by negotiating the contracts discriminating against them.

. . .

Section 2, Second, requiring carriers to bargain with the representative so chosen, operates to exclude any other from representing a craft. *Virginian R. Co.* v. *System Federation, supra* [300 U.S. 545]. The minority members of a craft are thus deprived by the statute of the right, which they would otherwise possess, to choose a representative of their own, and its members cannot bargain individually on behalf of themselves as to matters which are properly the subject of collective bargaining. *Order of Railroad Telegraphers* v. *Railway Express Agency,* 321 U.S. 342, and see under the like provisions of the National Labor Relations Act *J. I. Case Co.* v. *Labor Board,* 321 U.S. 332, and *Medo Photo Supply Corp.* v. *Labor Board,* 321 U.S. 678.

. . .

Unless the labor union representing a craft owes some duty to represent non-union members of the craft, at least to the extent of not discriminating against them as such in the contracts which it makes as their representative, the minority would be left with no means of protecting their interests or, indeed, their right to earn a livelihood by pursuing the occupation in which they are employed. While the majority of the craft chooses the bargaining representative, when chosen it represents, as the Act by its terms makes plain, the craft or class, and not the majority. The fair interpretation of the statutory language is that the organization chosen to represent a craft is to represent all its members, the majority as well as the minority, and it is to act for and not against those whom it represents. It is a principle of general application that the exercise of a granted power to act in behalf of others involves the assumption toward them of a duty to exercise the power in their interest and behalf, and that such a grant of power will not be deemed to dispense with all duty toward those for whom it is exercised unless so expressed.

We think that the Railway Labor Act imposes upon the statutory representative of a craft at least as exacting a duty to protect equally the interests of the members of the craft as the Constitution imposes upon a legislature to give equal protection to the interests of those for whom it legislates. Congress has seen fit to clothe the bargaining representative with powers comparable to those possessed by a legislative body both to create and restrict the rights of those whom it represents, cf. *J. I. Case Co.* v. *Labor Board supra,* 335, but it has also imposed on the representative a corresponding duty. We hold that the language of the Act to which we have referred, read in the light of the purposes of the Act, expresses the aim of Congress to impose on the bargaining representative of a craft or class of employees the duty to exercise fairly the power conferred upon it in behalf of all those for whom it acts, without hostile discrimination against them.

This does not mean that the statutory representative of a craft is barred from making contracts which may have unfavorable effects on some of the members of the craft represented. Variations in the terms of the contract based on differences relevant to the authorized purposes of the contract in conditions to which they are to be applied, such as differences in seniority, the type of work performed, the competence and skill with which it is performed, are within the scope of the bargaining representation of a craft, all of whose members are not identical in their interest or merit. . . . Without attempting to mark the allowable limits of differences in the terms of contracts based on differences of conditions to which they apply, it is enough for present purposes to say that the statutory power to represent a craft and to make contracts as to wages, hours and working conditions does not include the authority to make among members of the craft discriminations not based on such relevant differences. Here the discriminations based on race alone are obviously irrelevant and invidious. Congress plainly did not undertake to authorize the bargaining representative to make such discriminations. . . .

The representative which thus discriminates may be enjoined from so doing, and its members may be enjoined from taking the benefit of such discriminatory action. No more is the Railroad bound by or entitled to take the benefit of a contract which the bargaining representative is prohibited by the statute from making. In both cases the right asserted, which is derived from the duty imposed by the statute on the bargaining representative, is a federal right implied from the statute and the policy which it has adopted. It is the federal statute which condemns as unlawful the Brotherhood's conduct. . . .

We conclude that the duty which the statute imposes on a union representative of a craft to represent the interests of all its members stands on no different footing and that the statute contemplates resort to the usual judicial remedies of injunction and award of damages when appropriate for breach of that duty.

The judgment is accordingly reversed and remanded for further proceedings not inconsistent with this opinion.

*Reversed.*

## B.  Discrimination as an Unfair Labor Practice

## UNITED PACKINGHOUSE, FOOD AND ALLIED WORKERS INT'L UNION v. NLRB

*United States Court of Appeals, District of Columbia Circuit, 1969*
*416 F.2d 1126, 73 LRRM 2095, cert. denied, 396 U.S. 903 (1969)*

. . .

III.  We turn now to the question: can an employer's policy and practice of invidious discrimination against its employees on account of race or national origin violate Section 8(a)(1) of the National Labor Relations Act? When established as hereinafter discussed, we answer this question in the affirmative and remand this part of the case to the Board for further proceedings.[12]

Preliminarily, we find that the area of racial discrimination is not new to the Board. Although we have found no cases in which an employer's policy of discrimination as such was alleged to be a violation of the Act there is a history of union discrimination coming within the Board's jurisdiction.

That history begins with holdings by the Supreme Court that unions have a statutory duty of "fair representation," first under the Railway Labor Act, later under the National Labor Relations Act.

. . .

The Board adopted the Court-enunciated doctrine of fair representation and found that its violation is a union unfair labor practice under the NLRA.

. . .

*Local No. 12, United Rubber etc. Workers,* 150 NLRB 312 (1964), *enforced,* 5 Cir., 368 F.2d 12 (1966), *cert. denied,* 389 U.S. 837 (1967). The Fifth Circuit enforced the Board's order in *Rubber Workers,* upholding its determination that violation of the duty of fair representation is an unfair labor practice.

. . .

Thus it is apparent that the Board has not felt itself unable to examine charges of union racial discrimination to determine whether they are true, and if true, what the effect is on the discriminated employees. No reason appears why employer discrimination is exempt from Board scrutiny.[13]

In order to hold that employer racial discrimination violates Section 8(a)(1) it must be found that such discrimination is not merely unjustified, but that it interferes with or restrains discriminated employees from exercising their statutory right to act concertedly for their own aid or protection, as guaranteed by Section 7 of the Act. To be sure, Section 7 rights are not to be taken narrowly. That section protects concerted

---

[12] [Footnotes numbered as in original.—Ed.] The posture of this case leads us to order a remand on this issue. The unfair labor practice hearing against the company included a charged violation of § 8(a)(5) for failure to bargain about racial discrimination. However, the Board's General Counsel explicitly did not proceed on a theory that the discrimination itself violated § 8(a)(1). As noted, evidence indicating racial discrimination was produced to aid in finding whether there was a § 8(a)(5) bargaining violation. Thus the matter of the company's racial policies was litigated and the Examiner found, and the Board agreed, that the company did practice racial discrimination. We think, however, that in fairness to the company it should have an opportunity to have the matter more fully litigated, with notice that the question of a § 8(a)(1) violation is specifically to be determined. Thus the case is remanded to the Board to conduct such a hearing.

[13] The Board has examined employer racial discrimination in another context. It has held that an employer violates the Act if, during an election to certify a union, the employer makes flagrant appeals to racial prejudice in an attempt to defeat the union. See, *e.g., Sewell Manufacturing Co.,* 138 NLRB 66 (1962).

activity by workers to alleviate oppressive working conditions, regardless of whether their activity is channeled through a union, through collective bargaining, or through some other means.

. . .

And racially integrated working conditions are valid objects for employee action. *NLRB* v. *Tanner Motor Livery, Ltd.*, 9 Cir., 349 F.2d 1 (1965). The right to act concertedly for mutual aid obviously includes the right to act freely, without employer compulsion or deterrence against such activity. Thus in the context of employer racial discrimination the question reduces to whether that discrimination inhibits its victims from asserting themselves against their employer to improve their lot.

We find that an employer's invidious discrimination on account of race or national origin has such an effect. This effect is twofold: (1) racial discrimination sets up an unjustified clash of interests between groups of workers which tends to reduce the likelihood and the effectiveness of their working in concert to achieve their legitimate goals under the Act; and (2) racial discrimination creates in its victims an apathy or docility which inhibits them from asserting their rights against the perpetrator of the discrimination. *We find that the confluence of these two factors sufficiently deters the exercise of Section 7 rights as to violate Section 8(a)(1).*

The first effect is obvious—racial discrimination sets apart the white from the Negro (and Latin American) workers. The principle of "divide and conquer" is older than the history of labor relations in this country, but that does not lessen its application here. The white workers expend their energy against the Negroes, the latter resent the whites, and neither group sees that sometimes their interests might be better served by joint action against their common employer. When white employees may suffer from upgrading the positions of Negroes, the employer's policy of discrimination inevitably sets group against group, thus frustrating the possibility of effective concerted action.

Gunnar Myrdal, in his study AN AMERICAN DILEMMA (1944), noted this factor in employment race relations:

"When once the white workers' desires for social prestige become mobilized against the Negroes . . ., when they have come to look upon Negroes as different from themselves and consequently do not feel a common labor solidarity with them, 'economic interests' also will back up discrimination. . . . To give white workers a monopoly on all promotions is, of course, to give them a vested interest in job segregation.

. . .

The Board does not dispute Myrdal's findings. Rather, it points to other discriminations in employment, such as that based on seniority; it suggests the conflicting interests resulting from a seniority system cannot support a Section 8(a)(1) charge. This argument misses the point. First, the seniority distinction may be reasonably justified, whereas here the basis for discrimination is not only unjustified but in fact illegal. Second, we are not holding that all discrimination, even where unjustified, is by itself sufficient to make out a violation. Rather, as noted in Note 15, *supra*, it is the conjunction of the unreasonable and illegal discrimination with the induced docility in the discriminated group which is the basis of our unfair labor practice holding.

The conclusion that racial discrimination may impede its victims in asserting their rights seems inescapable. This docility stems from a number of factors—fear, ignorance of rights, and a feeling of low self-esteem engendered by repeated second class treatment because of race or national origin. Discrimination in employment is no different in this respect than discrimination in other spheres. In its historic decision in *Brown* v. *Board of Education of Topeka*, 347 U.S. 483, 494 (1954), the Supreme Court stated:

". . . **To separate [Negroes] from others of similar age and qualifica-**tions solely because of their race generates a feeling of inferiority as to their status in the community that may affect their hearts and minds in a **way unlikely ever to be undone. . . .**"

This docility has been recognized by union leaders, businessmen, government officials and psychologists. Thus George Meany, president of the AFL-CIO, referred to the reluctance of Negro employees to file complaints under fair employment practices laws because of the fear of retaliation which accompanies racial discrimination. Senate and House hearings on equal employment bills are laced with references to the degradation, disillusionment, lack of motivation, and lessening of incentive to improve which result from racial discrimination in employment. The Civil Rights Commission has shown the debilitating effect of menial labor on Negroes, and has pointed up the reluctance of those Negroes to ask for improvement. Psychological studies have pointed out the psychologically debilitating effects of discrimination in general, and Dr. Kenneth B. Clark, especially in his book DARK GHETTO (1965), has shown how discrimination-induced self-hatred in Negro inhabitants of slums, due in good part to discrimination in employment, creates a feeling of inferiority and lack of motivation to assert themselves to change their condition. In all this, discrimination in employment thus establishes, or reinforces the effect of discrimination in other areas—an inhibition to act for change.

Finally, this docility has been demonstrated by the record in this case. The Trial Examiner found explicitly that the policy of discrimination had this effect. His decision noted:

"**The great sense of inferiority of the 'Mexican' in the area . . . was** shown by answers on cross-examination of the chairman of the negotiating committee, Fernando Gonzales. Although by his demeanor he impressed me as one of the natural leaders of the Latin group of employees, an impression corroborated by his selection as chairman of the negotiating committee, he was not inclined to stand up for his rights when, the morning after the first bargaining session, which he had attended, he was sent out into the cold to perform the 'flagging' job. Asked on cross-examination if he asked why he was being sent out there, Gonzales replied, '**You don't ask questions there, sir; you only do what you are told.**' . . .

"This same sense of inferiority and docility on the part of the 'Mexican' group was further disclosed through the testimony of Polo Arias . . . [After being transferred to a lower-paying job] he did not ask why . . . [He testified] 'in a company like that you don't ask questions, you just do what they tell you.' Elaborating, a little later he repeated the substance of this answer, and added: '. . . I am a grown man and I know, you know, what you are supposed to do and what you are not supposed to do, even if you have got the right to do it.' He added that he knew he would not gain anything by asking.
. . .

"It is clear on this record, and I conclude, that the only reason Respondent paid Ruiz $1.50 an hour for seven months while he was doing a $1.80 job which five or six Anglos were concurrently paid $1.80 for performing, was because Respondent considered Ruiz and the other minority employees as docile, cheap labor, and in order to keep them in this condition of servitude. . . ."

In the light of these considerations, we conclude that an employer's policy and practice of invidious discrimination on account of race or national origin is a violation of Section 8(a)(1). For the reasons noted above, the case is remanded to the Board for hearings on whether the company here has such a policy and practice. If the Board finds that the company does, the Board shall order an appropriate remedy.

*Order affirmed; case remanded*
*for further proceedings.*

PRETTYMAN, Senior C. J.: I concur in the remand for hearings and findings. As I see it, Section 8(a)(1) of this statute makes illegal any act, policy, or program of an employer which interferes with, restrains or coerces employees in the exercise of rights given them by Section 7 of the Act. In the matter before us the complainant alleged that this employer has such a policy and program. In that situation the Board should receive the evidence and make findings. In my judgment it makes no difference what the program is called or how it is catalogued; if, in fact, by its use the employer interferes with, restrains or coerces his employees in the exercise of Section 7 rights, it is an unfair labor practice and is prohibited. I think it is neither necessary nor advisable for us at this time to explore in depth the possibilities of a program such as complainant depicts; I think we should await a finding of the facts. My brethren think otherwise. I concur in the result.

## NOTES

1. On remand, the Board found the evidence insufficient to justify a finding of racial discrimination. 194 NLRB No. 3 (1972) (Member Jenkins dissenting).

2. If bargaining on a discrimination issue produces a clause to be voted on by the union membership, is it appropriate to permit minority group members within the local union a "veto power" with regard to such a clause?

3. If parties to a collective agreement adopt an antidiscrimination clause less stringent than the requirements of a local ordinance, what course should be followed by an arbitrator deciding a grievance proceeding brought under the clause? See W. Gould, *Non-Governmental Remedies for Employment Discrimination*, 20 SYRACUSE L. REV. 865 (1969).

4. In *Jubilee Mfg. Co.*, 82 LRRM 1482, the Board refused to apply the *Packinghouse Workers* theory to a case involving sex discrimination on the grounds that Section 7 rights were not interfered with.

## C.  REMEDIES AGAINST UNIONS WHICH DISCRIMINATE

### NLRB v. GLASS BOTTLE BLOWERS ASS'N, LOCAL 106

*United States Court of Appeals, Sixth Circuit, 1975*

*520 F.2d 693, 89 LRRM 3020*

PHILLIPS, Chief Judge: This case presents the question of whether a labor union with a bargaining relationship in a plant commits an unfair labor practice by maintaining two different locals segregated on the basis of sex and by segregated processing of grievances. The National Labor Relations Board, in a badly split decision, answered this question in the affirmative, and ordered the merger of the two segregated Local Unions. The decision of the Board is reported at 210 N.L.R.B. No. 131 (1974).

We enforce the order of the Board.

Locals 106 and 245 of the Glass Blowers Association, AFL-CIO, (Locals or Local Unions) serve as joint bargaining representatives for the production and maintenance employees of Owens-Illinois, Inc., at its plant in Columbus, Ohio. In 1949 the parent International Union, the Glass Bottle Blowers Association, AFL-CIO (International Union), entered into a contract with Owens-Illinois. From the outset of this contractual relationship there have been two separate locals which service the agreement: Local 106, which confines its membership to men, and Local 245, which confines its membership to women. There are approximately 800 male employees and approximately 370 female employees.

In 1968 or early in 1969, the Company agreed with the two Locals and the International Union to merge the seniority list of its employees and to eliminate previous inequities as to job availability based on sex. Thereafter positions no longer were designated as men's or women's jobs and were to be open to bidding by all employees in the plant who were physically capable of performing the work, without regard to sex. However, the Local Unions continued to segregate their memberships and the processing of grievances by sex.

The constitution and by-laws of the International Union contain no provisions for discrimination on the basis of sex.

The collective bargaining agreement for 1973-74 was negotiated by a joint bargaining committee composed of representatives of both Locals and the International Union and was ratified at a joint membership meeting of the two Local Unions.

The Administrative Law Judge found, in effect, that the male and female employees received equal, though separate, treatment and therefore there was no violation.

Rejecting the decision of the Administrative Law Judge the Board found that the Local Unions violated § 8(b)(1)(A) of the Act by maintaining segregated memberships, by separately processing grievances of male and female unit members and by refusing to process grievances because of the sex and union membership of employees. The Local Unions were ordered to cease and desist from the unfair labor practices found. The Board ordered the Local Unions to merge; to admit to membership and process the grievance of any unit employee, upon request, without regard to sex; and to post appropriate notices. The majority opinion of the Board expressed the following conclusions:

"We cannot accept [The Administrative Law Judge's] reasoning. Separate but equal treatment on the basis of sex is as self-contradictory as separate but equal on the basis of race."[4]
In both areas separation in and of itself connotes and creates inequalities. Not only can separating females from males solely because of sex generate a feeling of inferiority among the females as to their work status, since the policy of separation is usually interpreted as reflecting the inferiority of the females, but also it can, as set forth below, adversely affect the working conditions of both groups solely because of the difference in sex.

For example, since, as mentioned previously, a grievance affects both male and female employees regardless of which Local processes the grievance, the employees whose Local did not process a grievance merely because of the grievant's sex are nonetheless bound by the outcome of the other Local's processing of the grievance. These employees have therefore, solely because of sex, been denied a voice in the resolution of matters affecting their working conditions.

Indeed, Respondent's sexual discrimination serves no useful purpose. The collective-bargaining agreement applies equally to all employees and makes no distinctions based on sex or local memberships. All jobs are open to both sexes. There are, thus, no special circumstances to justify the separate processing of grievances or the maintenance of separate locals.

Accordingly, we find that Respondents by maintaining locals whose memberships are restricted by sex and by refusing to process grievances because of the sex of the employees and their nonmembership in each of Respondents, respectively, restrained and coerced employees in the exercise of their Section 7 rights in violation of Section 8(b)(1)(A) of the Act.[5]

[4] [Footnotes numbered as in original.—Ed.] *Cf. Brown* v. *Board of Education,* 347 U.S. 483, in which the Supreme Court held that segregation of children in public schools solely on the basis of race was "inherently unequal."

[5] Chairman Miller would make clear that he views the violation herein as arising out of Respondent's failure fairly to represent the employees, in that separate but allegedly

We agree with the conclusion of the Board.

"Undoubtedly questions of statutory interpretation, especially when arising in the first instance in judicial proceedings, are for the courts to resolve, giving appropriate weight to the judgment of those whose special duty is to administer the questioned statute. . . . But where the question is one of specific application of a board statutory term in a proceeding in which the agency administering the statute must determine it initially, the reviewing court's function is limited." (Citations omitted.) *NLRB* v. *Hearst Publications, Inc.*, 322 U.S. 111, 130–31 (1944).

Giving the decision of the Board its proper weight, we agree that the maintenance of local unions, segregated by sex, and segregated handling of grievances, are unfair labor practices on the part of the Local Unions which restrain or coerce employees in the exercise of their § 7 rights.

Although the Local Unions assert that the majority of the women employees prefer to keep their separate union because it gives them "clout," it was stipulated that:

"Certain women employees included within the unit designated under Article 3 of the collective bargaining agreement had requested membership in Local 106 at various times in October of 1971, and November of 1971, and such requests were denied or refused by Local 106."

The President of Local 106 testified that certain women employees in the unit had requested admission to Local 106 and that their requests had been denied. On at least one occasion some men employees requested and were granted permission to attend a meeting of Local 245.

Even assuming that a majority or even all the women in the unit preferred a separate union to attain "clout," and this is not clear from the record, we hold that the Board was justified in concluding that this would not provide a defense for the refusal of the joint bargaining representatives to admit to membership or to process the grievances of any unit employee, upon request, without regard to sex. In *NLRB* v. *Allis-Chalmers Mfg. Co.*, 388 U.S. 175, 180 (1967), the Supreme Court said:

"National labor policy has been built on the premise that by pooling their economic strength and acting through a labor organization freely chosen by the majority, the employees of an appropriate unit have the most effective means of bargaining for improvements in wages, hours, and working conditions."

The rights of minorities are not forfeited by the merger of the Local Unions. These rights are protected by the duty imposed on the bargaining agent to represent fairly all employees in the unit.

---

equal representation is not fair representation, as the Chairman understands the meaning of that term as used in *Miranda Fuel Company, Inc.*, 140 NLRB 181, and *Local No. 12, United Rubber, Cork Linoleum & Plastic Workers of America, AFL–CIO (The Business League of Gadsden)*, 150 NLRB 312, enfd, 368 F.2d 12 (C.A. 5), cert. denied, 389 U.S. 837. Although a majority of the Board, including the Chairman, held, in *Jubilee Manufacturing Company*, 202 NLRB No. 2, that employer discrimination on account of sex does not per se violate Sec. 8(a)(1), there was no union respondent and thus no issue of fair representation posed in that case. As this Board said in *Miranda, supra*, at p. 185, ". . . labor organizations, because they do represent employees, have statutory obligations to employees which employers do not."

The Unions contend that the Board's directive of a merger of the two Locals is an improper remedial order. We recognize that the statute prohibits the Board from interfering in local union affairs. Section 8(b)(1)(A) states that the section "shall not impair the right of a labor organization to prescribe its own rules with respect to the acquisition or retention of membership therein." However, we conclude that the ordering of a merger of the two Local Unions, under the facts and circumstances of this case, does not constitute an unauthorized interference in local union affairs. It is well settled that the Board's discretion in formulating appropriate remedial relief is broad and that the scope of judicial review is narrow. See *Fibreboard Paper Products Corp.* v. *NLRB*, 379 U.S. 203, 216 (1964); see also *NLRB* v. *Gissel Packing Co.*, 395 U.S. 575, 612 n. 32 (1969); *Virginia Electric & Power Co.* v. *NLRB*, 319 U.S. 533, 539–40 (1943); *Decaturville Sportswear Co.* v. *NLRB*, 406 F.2d 886, 888–89 (6th Cir. 1969).

Enforcement is granted.


## FARMER v. HOTEL WORKERS, LOCAL 1064

*U.S. District Court, Eastern District of Michigan, 1978*
*99 LRRM 2166*

THORNTON, Senior District Judge: This is an action for violation of the duty of fair representation pursuant to Section 301 of the Labor-Management Relations Act of 1947 (29 U.S.C. § 185), and for violation of civil rights pursuant to Title VII of the Civil Rights Act of 1964 (42 U.S.C. § 2000e, *et seq.*). Trial was had to the Court commencing October 13, 1976 and terminating November 24, 1976. Based on the entire record in this case, including all the evidence adduced at the trial and argument presented by counsel for the respective parties, the Court makes the following Findings of Fact and Conclusions of Law.

### FINDINGS OF FACT

1. The plaintiffs and plaintiff's decedent in this action — Minnie Farmer, Hyardis Chambers, Shirley Wooton and Frances Ratliff — are all white females who are or were employed by Automatic Retailers of America (hereinafter ARA Services, Inc.) at its Great Lakes Steel Division in an around Ecorse, Michigan, and are or were members in good standing of defendant Local 1064, United Catering, Restaurant, Bar and Hotel Workers, R.W.D.S.U., AFL-CIO (hereinafter Local 1064) during the period of their employment with ARA Services, Inc., and its predecessor, Slater Systems of Maryland, Inc.;

2. Defendant Local 1064, United Catering, Restaurant, Bar and Hotel Workers, R.W.D.S.U., AFL-CIO, is a labor organization and has been since January 12, 1955, the certified bargaining agent for the non-supervisory employees of ARA Services, Inc.'s Great Lakes Steel Division

(Exhibit 4); the present force of approximately fifty (50) non-supervisory employees at the Great Lakes Steel Division of ARA Services, Inc. comprises only one of approximately seventy-two (72) separate "units" into which Local 1064 as a whole is divided (Exhibit 88, Exhibit 138). The total membership of Local 1064 at the present time is approximately two thousand (2,000) members (Testimony of Local 1064 General Secretary, Paul Domeny).

. . .

19. The revolutionary change in the nature of the food service operation as the result of vending machine service required the creation of several new classifications within the Local 1064 bargaining unit: these new classifications were first reflected in the collective bargaining agreement effective January 21, 1962. . . .

. . .

21. The decision of ARA Services, Inc. in 1961-62 to consider only its male employees and applicants for employment for selection and training for the newly-created vending serviceman classification was readily conceded by its then Midwest Regional Operations Manager, Frank C. Sands; a number of factors, . . . suggest that defendant Local 1064, if not an active supporter of the company's decision in this respect, at least did nothing whatsoever to oppose it. Thus, while the company based its decision as to which male employees to train for vending servicemen upon seniority . . . , the company and Local 1064 apparently ignored the fact that all but three of the thirty-eight most senior employees in the bargaining unit in 1962 were females . . . ; in fact, the most senior male selected for vending service training in 1962 was twenty-fourth in order of seniority within the bargaining unit;

. . .

41. Since . . . , Local 1064 has not taken one . . . grievance to arbitration on behalf of any employee within the Great Lakes Steel-Ford Motor Co. Rouge area bargaining units (testimony of Paul Domeny), this despite the fact that female members of the unit, including but not limited to the plaintiffs, have actively filed grievances during the period since 1963, complaining *inter alia* of both sex discrimination and their exclusion from the higher-paying and longer-houred jobs within the bargaining unit (testimony of Hyardis Chambers, Shirley Wooton, Minnie Farmer, Paul Domeny and Faye Baumgartner; Deposition of Frances Ratliff; Exs. 52, 58, 62, 80, 83, 84, 85, 86, 87, 93, 94, 97, 98, 103, 104, 105, 110, 114, 116, 133, 134, 136, 137, 139, 140, 141, 142). Notwithstanding the fact that Local 1064 General Secretary Paul Domeny or its attorney, William Mazey, decided in at least a half-dozen instances that particular grievances of plaintiffs were sufficiently meritorious, significant and likely to be successful at arbitration to warrant a recommendation or request for arbitration (testimony of Paul Domeny; Exs. 78, 79, 81, 85) , the grievances were either settled or withdrawn without the grievant's knowledge or contrary to her desires and with but one possible exception, did not result in the grievant's receipt of any monetary relief (back pay) . . . ;

while none of the plaintiffs ever attempted to invoke the provisions of the Local 1064 by-laws which provided for the filing of charges against a member or officer (although not an employee or attorney), it was at least initially due to their inability to secure a copy of the union's constitution and by-laws (testimony of Hyardis Chambers, Minnie Farmer); in addition, on the two occasions upon which the plaintiffs specifically sought the assistance of the International Union in resolving problems at the local level, their requests were summarily denied. . . .

. . .

### CONCLUSIONS OF LAW

. . .

## Duty of Fair Representation

2. As the exclusive representative of the non-supervisory employees of ARA Services, Inc.'s Great Lakes Steel Division (and its predecessors), defendant Local 1064 has the obligation to represent plaintiffs (and plaintiff's decedent) "fairly and impartially" and "to make an honest effort to serve the interests of all . . . members [of the bargaining unit] without hostility to any." *Humphrey* v. *Moore,* 375 U.S. 335, 342, 55 LRRM 2031 (1964); *Ford Motor Co.* v. *Huffman,* 345 U.S. 330, 337-38, 31 LRRM 2548 (1953); *Wallace Corp.* v. *NLRB,* 323 U.S. 248, 255, 15 LRRM 697 (1944); defendant Local 1064's obligation in this respect extends not only to the enforcement of the collective bargaining agreement through the fair and impartial processing of grievances, but also to the fair representation of all segments of the bargaining unit during the negotiation of the collective bargaining agreement itself. *Vaca* v. *Sipes,* 386 U.S. 171, 177, 64 LRRM 2369 (1967); *Hines* v. *Anchor Motor Freight, Inc.,* 424 U.S. 554, 564, 91 LRRM 2481 (1976);

3. Although a labor organization such as defendant Local 1064 is neither expected nor required to represent each member of the bargaining unit, completely to his/her satisfaction, it breaches the duty of fair representation owed to each and every member when its conduct toward any member of the bargaining unit, or to a segment thereof, becomes arbitrary, discriminatory or in bad faith. *Vaca* v. *Sipes, supra* at 171; *Ford Motor Co.* v. *Huffman, supra* at 338; consequently, a union must conform its behavior to each of three separate standards: first, it must treat all factions and segments of its membership without hostility or discrimination; next, the broad discretion of the union in asserting the rights of its individual members must be exercised in complete good faith and honesty; finally, the union must avoid arbitrary conduct. Each of these requirements represents a distinct and separate obligation and, therefore, bad faith is not an indispensable element of every claim that a labor organization has breached its duty of fair representation. *Ruzicka* v. *General Motors Corp.* 523 F.2d 306, 309-10. . . .

4. While an action for breach of the duty of fair representation will normally be entertained only following unsuccessful resort to the internal

procedures of the union's constitution and by-laws, the failure of the plaintiffs here to exhaustively pursue their internal remedies is excused by their inability for a substantial period to secure an up-to-date copy of Local 1064's constitution and by-laws and the inadequacy and futility of the procedures set forth in those by-laws, once they became known. . . . Given both the absence of any local constitutional provision under which plaintiffs could have secured any relief other than the censure of the local union officers and the lack of any satisfactory response to plaintiffs' entreaties to the International Union in 1963 and 1970, it cannot realistically be said that there was available from the union, at either the local or international level, a remedy which was neither uncertain nor futile. . . .

5. Defendant Local 1064 breached the duty of fair representation owed to each of the plaintiffs by negotiating and entering into collective bargaining agreements, the provisions of which were not adequately explained to the membership prior to ratification and/or varied from the terms explained and which:

(a) resulted in transfers between and promotions within job classifications which perpetuated the sexually discriminatory hiring and assignment patterns for which Slater System Maryland, Inc. and ARA Services, Inc. were initially responsible;

(b) relegated the plaintiffs and the vast majority of female employees to the fewer-houred, lower-paying classification of vending machine attendant while their less senior male counterparts were competing for the six and seven day per week, higher paying vending machine serviceman jobs;

(c) compensated the plaintiffs and the vast majority of the female employees who were likewise assigned to the vending machine attendant's classification at a substantially lower rate than the largely male classifications of vending machine serviceman and truck driver, even though the jobs involved comparable responsibilities as indicated in the contractually established job descriptions; and

(d) provided substantial step increases and raises in the hourly rates paid to the largely male classifications of vending machine repairman, serviceman and truck driver between 1962 and 1970 and comparably smaller increases, if any, to the virtually all female classification of vending machine attendant.

The conclusion that defendant Local 1064 breached its duty of fair representation in negotiating the afore-described provisions is reinforced not only by the circumstances under which the contracts were ratified (See e.g., Ex. 121) and the refusal of more than one of the plaintiffs to sign the resulting collective bargaining agreements as a member of the negotiating committee (Ex. 12), but by the fact that a majority of the membership on three successive occasions voted in favor of contractual demands which were precisely the reverse of those negotiated (Exs. 42, 45, 50, 51, 54, 59, 63); *Vaca* v. *Sipes*, 386 U.S. 171, 177, 64 LRRM 2369 (1967); *Barton Brands, Ltd.* v. *NLRB*, 529 F.2d 793, 798–800, 91 LRRM 2241

(7th Cir. 1976); *Goodin* v. *Clinchfield R.R.*, 229 F.2d 578, 37 LRRM 2515 (6th Cir.), *cert. denied*, 351 U.S. 953, 38 LRRM 2160 (1956);

6. Defendant Local 1064 also breached the duty of fair representation owed to each of the plaintiffs by arbitrarily failing and/or refusing to arbitrate and/or compromise on terms satisfactory to them, grievances arising under the collective bargaining agreement. *Ruzicka* v. *General Motors Corp.*, 523 F.2d 306, 90 LRRM 2497, *rehearing denied*, 528 F.2d 912, 91 LRRM 3054 (6th Cir. 1975). While a labor organiziation does not automatically breach its statutory duty when, contrary to an individual grievant's wishes, it settles or otherwise resolves a grievance short of arbitration, the arbitrary refusal or unexplained failure of defendant Local 1064 to favorably resolve or arbitrate plaintiffs' grievances of admitted merit is plainly violative of its duty of fair representation. *Ruzicka* v. *General Motors Corp., supra; Ruggirello* v. *Ford Motor Co.*, 411 F. Supp. 758, 760, 92 LRRM 2228 (E.D. Mich. 1976); cf., *Curth* v. *Faraday, Inc.*, 401 F. Supp. 678, 681, 90 LRRM 2735 (E.D. Mich. 1975).

. . .

8. As a result of defendant Local 1064's breach of the duty of fair representation as to each of the plaintiffs and plaintiff Ratliff's decedent, each is entitled to damages attributable to the union's failure to fairly represent them. *Czosek* v. *O'Mara*, 397 U.S. 25, 28–29, 73 LRRM 2481 (1970); *Vaca* v. *Sipes, supra* at 196–98; where the union's breach of the duty of fair representation involves only a failure to process an employee's grievance, the damages attributable solely to the employer's breach of contract giving rise to the grievance are not chargeable to the union and damages attributable to the union's conduct are usually *de minimis*. *Vaca* v. *Sipes, supra* at 197; *Richardson* v. *Communications Workers of America*, 443 F.2d 974, 981, 77 LRRM 2566 (8th Cir. 1971), *cert. denied*, 414 U.S. 818, 84 LRRM 2421 (1973); *DeArroyo* v. *Sindicato de Trabajadores Packinghouse, supra* at 289–90. However, where as in the case at bar, the union's refusal to represent its members(s) results also from its wrongful participation in the breach of contract or from the negotiation of arbitrary and discriminatory contractual provisions, then the union may be held jointly and severally liable with the company or its liability for damages may be apportioned to the extent that it shares responsibility for the whole of such damage. *Jones* v. *Trans World Airlines, supra* at 798; *Petersen* v. *Rath Packing Co.*, 461 F.2d 312, 316, 80 LRRM 2833 (8th Cir. 1972); *Richardson* v. *Communications Workers of America, supra* at 982.

9. Appropriate damages for the union's breach of the duty of fair representation normally include damages for lost earnings (the difference between the amount actually earned by each of the plaintiffs within the limitations period and the amount each would have earned if employed in the higher-paying serviceman's classification from the date of earliest eligibility), the difference in vacation pay to which each of the plaintiffs would be entitled as a result of the difference between actual and lost earnings, the difference between the amount plaintiffs Chambers, Farmer

and Ratliff actually received in workmen's compensation and the amount each would have received had their awards been based instead upon earnings as a vending serviceman, and any other compensatory, "make-whole" relief. *St. Clair* v. *Local U. No. 515 of Int. Bro. of Teamsters,* 422 F.2d 128, 132, 73 LRRM 2048 (6th Cir. 1969); *Jones* v. *Trans World Airlines, Inc., supra* at 798–99; *Thompson* v. *Bro. of Sleeping Car Porters,* 367 F.2d 489, 63 LRRM 2111 (4th Cir. 1966), *cert. denied,* 386 U.S. 960, 64 LRRM 2574 (1967); *Central of Ga. Ry.* v. *Jones,* 229 F.2d 648, 37 LRRM 2435 (5th Cir.), *cert. denied,* 352 U.S. 848, 38 LRRM 2716 (1956);

10. While consequential damages sustained as a secondary result of the union's failure to represent are not generally awarded in fair representation actions (*St. Clair* v. *Local U. No. 515 of Int. Bro. of Teamsters, supra* at 132), the courts have recognized that damages for emotional and mental distress may be appropriate in exceptional circumstances such as those here, where Local 1064 engaged in harassment and ridicule of the plaintiffs. . . . Finally, plaintiffs are entitled to a reasonable attorney's fee and other costs and expenses (parking, transportation, filing and deposition costs, etc.) which were incurred by them in the prosecution of their claims against both ARA Services, Inc. and Local 1064, costs which they would not have incurred but for the union's breach of its duty to represent them fairly and in good faith. . . .

## NOTES

1. Should the doctrine of fair representation be more strictly applied in the area of discrimination based on a Title VII prohibited categorization? Consider the discussion in *Alexander* v. *Gardner Denver, infra,* concerning Congress's intent for the federal courts to exercise control over Title VII and the discussion of the arbitration process and Title VII.

2. In *Archie* v. *Chicago Truck Drivers,* 99 LRRM 2582 (7th Cir. 1978), the Seventh Circuit held that a black employee's charge of breach of the duty of fair representation did not have to prove bad faith on the part of the union. The court held that a showing of arbitrariness alone would be enough.

3. In *Smallwood* v. *National Can Co.,* 583 F.2d 419, 18 FEP Cases 709 (9th Cir. 1978), the circuit court upheld a district court's finding that a union had retaliated against a black employee who had filed an employment discrimination action against the employer. The employee claimed the union had denied him resinstatement in the union in violation of section 704(a) of Title VII. The union issued a permanent injunction, restraining the union "from denying Smallwood membership or retalitating against him in any other way." Smallwood also received attorney's fees and costs. Could this case also be viewed as a breach of the duty of fair representation? Is it an unfair labor practice?

# HANDY ANDY, INC. v. TEAMSTERS, LOCAL 657

*National Labor Relations Board, 1977*
*228 NLRB No. 59, 94 LRRM 1354*

Before NLRB: MURPHY, Chairman; FANNING, JENKINS, PENELLO, and WALTHER, Members. . . .

The employer's sole objection to the issuance of a certification to the Union is that

"[t]he Union . . . practices invidious discrimination by engaging in practices such as excluding persons from membership on the basis of race, alienage or national origin and/or is shown to have a propensity to fail to represent employees fairly."

The Employer contends that the Union's alleged discriminatory practices preclude it from being certified as an exclusive bargaining representative, citing *Bekins Moving & Storage Co. of Florida, Inc., supra.* As evidence in support of its objection, the Employer relies primarily upon several decisions by the United States Court of Appeals for the Fifth Circuit. In these cases, the court held, inter alia, that certain seniority provisions of the National Master Freight Agreement, to which the Union is a party together with various employers (but not the Employer herein), were unlawful because they perpetuated the effects of the employers' past discrimination. Consequently, the court found that the Union, by being party to such an agreement, had violated Title VII of the Civil Rights Act of 1964.

The Employer's reliance on *Bekins* is based on the majority's holding in that case that the Board is constitutionally required to consider issues raised by an objection grounded on alleged invidious discrimination prior to issuance of a Board certification of representative. As the majority noted in *Bekins,* however, the question of whether a labor organization's invidious discrimination constitutes objectionable conduct warranting withholding certification was a novel issue and one on which the Supreme Court has not ruled. We now conclude that the policies of the Act are better effectuated by considering allegations that a labor organization practices invidious discrimination in appropriate unfair labor practice rather than representation proceedings. Accordingly, for the reasons set forth hereafter, the *Bekins* decision is overruled.

In our view neither the Fifth Amendment to the Constitution nor the National Labor Relations Act, as amended, requires the Board to resolve questions of alleged invidious discrimination by a labor organization before it may lawfully certify the union as the exclusive bargaining representative of employees in an appropriate unit. Indeed, it appears to us that the contrary is true; namely, that the Board is not authorized to withhold certification of a labor organization duly selected by a majority of the unit employees. In so holding, we are fully cognizant of our continuing obligation under the statute to police the conduct of certified unions as it relates to their duty of fair representation. Issues relating to

whether a union engages in unlawful race, sex, or other invidious forms
of discrimination have historically been considered by the Board in the
context of unfair labor practice proceedings. Such a proceeding, for the
reasons discussed below, continues to be the appropriate vehicle for resolving such issues and for devising the appropriate remedies for unlawful
discrimination including revocation of certification. This route recognizes
the substantive and procedural differences between representation and
unfair labor practice proceedings and affords the charged party the full
panoply of due process of law without at the same time denying or delaying the employees' right to the services of their designated bargaining
agent.

The majority in *Bekins* concluded that precertification consideration
of alleged invidious discrimination by labor organizations is required by
the Fifth Amendment to the Constitution because the Board may not
lawfully bestow its certification upon a union which in fact discriminates
on the basis of such considerations. The majority stated that, under the
principle enunciated by the Supreme Court in *Shelley* v. *Kraemer* and
subsequent cases, were the Board, as a Federal agency, to confer the
benefits of certification on a labor organization which practices unlawful
discrimination "the power of the Federal Government would surely appear to be sanctioning, and indeed furthering, the continued practice of
such discrimination, thereby running afoul of the due process clause of
the fifth amendment."

The foregoing statement misconstrues the "state action" doctrine as
defined in *Shelley* v. *Kraemer, supra,* and its progeny. In *Shelley,* petitioners were blacks seeking to buy property covered by private restrictive
covenants which prohibited occupancy of the covered premises by persons
"not of the Caucasian race." The state courts had enforced the covenants
and, consequently, had found that petitioner could not obtain valid title.
The Supreme Court held that the agreement, standing alone, did not
violate any constitutional right of petitioners, emphasizing that:

"[T]he principle has become firmly embedded in our constitutional
law that the action inhibited by the [equal protection clause] of the
Fourteenth Amendment is only such action as may fairly be said to be
that of the States. That Amendment erects no shield against merely
private conduct, however discriminatory or wrongful." [Footnote omitted].

The Court concluded, however, that enforcement of the covenants by
state courts was state action subject to the equal protection clause. In so
concluding, the Court commented:

"It is clear that but for the *active intervention* of the state courts,
supported by the full panoply of state power, petitioners would have been
free to occupy the properties in question without restraint.

"These are not cases . . . in which the States have merely abstained
from action, leaving private individuals free to impose such discriminations as they see fit. Rather, these are *cases in which the States have made
available to such individuals the full coercive power of government to
deny to petitioners, on the grounds of race or color, the enjoyment of*

*property rights* in premises which petitioners are willing and financially able to acquire and which the grantors are willing to sell." [Emphasis supplied.]

Thus, the prohibited state action in *Shelley* v. *Kraemer* was the *affirmative enforcement* by the State of a private agreement to discriminate.

Similarly, in *Peterson et al.* v. *City of Greenville,* 10 blacks were arrested for trespassing after refusing to leave a segregated lunch counter. In reversing their convictions, the Supreme Court noted that a local ordinance requiring segregation at lunch counters had removed the decision to segregate from the sphere of private choice, and thus sufficiently involved the State in the counter manager's discrimination to violate the equal protection clause. Thus, the case stands for the principle that a governmental body which *requires* a private party to discriminate runs afoul of the Fifth or Fourteenth Amendments.

The governmental action doctrine, as applied to statutes and regulations, was further expanded in *Reitman* v. *Mulkey* to extend to mere "authorization" of private discrimination. In that case, an amendment to the California state constitution, which prohibited any governmental agency within the State from abridging the absolute discretion of any property owner to sell or lease, or to refuse to sell or lease, his property to anyone for any reason, was declared unconstitutional. Although purporting to remain neutral on the question of private racial discrimination in housing, the amendment repealed two open housing statutes, and erected a barrier to attaining any such legislation in the future. The Court held that, taken in the context of the conditions and attitudes of its passage, the amendment "was intended to authorize, and does authorize, racial discrimination in the housing market." Thus, the prohibited state action in *Reitman* was *authorization* by the State of private discrimination.

Finally, in *Moose Lodge No. 107* v. *Irvis,* a state liquor control agency, in granting liquor licenses, promulgated numerous regulations with which licensees had to comply. One of these required that "[e]very club licensee shall adhere to all of the provisions of its Constitution and By-laws." *Moose Lodge* had a provision in its constitution which denied membership to blacks. The trial court had relied on the pervasive regulation of the club's activity by the liquor control board in ruling that the agency was sufficiently implicated with the discriminating club to violate the fourteenth amendment. But the Court, in analyzing the amount of government involvement necessary to raise constitutional issues, rejected the trial court's reasoning, noting that "[h]owever detailed this type of regulation may be in some particulars, it cannot be said to in any way *foster* or *encourage* racial discrimination." (Emphasis supplied.) The Court held that only one regulation which had the effect of specifically requiring the club to discriminate was sufficiently involved with the private club's racially discriminatory policy to run afoul of the Constitution. None of the other regulations governing the operation of *Moose Lodge* were so entwined with the racial policies as to trigger the equal protection clause.

because they did not specifically support the racial discrimination. . . .
. . .

We recognize, of course, that certification of a labor organization confers substantial benefits. The Board does not, however, by certifying a labor organization, place its imprimatur on all the organization's activity, lawful or otherwise. On the contrary, a certification is neither more nor less than an acknowledgment that a majority of the employees in an appropriate bargaining unit have selected the union as their exclusive bargaining representative. The choice of representative is made by the employees, and may not be exercised by this Board. . . .

Clearly, certification does not constitute enforcement or even approval of a labor organization's activities, and should not be construed as "state action" restricted by the Fifth Amendment.
. . .

. . . The Act and the Board's implementation of it can hardly be said to be "significantly involved" in the union's discrimination, since the duty of fair representation in its various forms *specifically prohibits* a union from practicing unlawful discrimination under the authority of the Act. Therefore, the Board, while it may extend the Act's protection to the union, is not involved in the union's discriminatory activities, a requirement of the governmental action doctrine.
. . .

A logical consequence of the *Bekins* constitutional determination is the conclusion that in their respective areas of authority the Federal agencies have overlapping responsibility for remedying any invidious discrimination by private parties. For example, one might argue that the Interstate Commerce Commission may not constitutionally approve a route of a common carrier which engages in discriminatory hiring practices or that the Securities and Exchange Commission is prohibited from approving a prospectus of a corporation which engages in such practices. This argument was recently rejected by the Supreme Court in *National Association for the Advancement of Colored People* v. *Federal Power Commission,* in which the Court held that the FPC does not have the authority to promulgate rules prohibiting its regulatees from engaging in discriminatory employment practices, but that the Commission does have authority to consider the consequences of employment discrimination in performing its mandated regulatory functions. . . .
. . .

Not only does the *Bekins* approach impair the national labor policy favoring collective bargaining, but it is ineffective in implementing an antidiscrimination policy. Denying certification and bargaining orders to discriminating unions may seem to be an effective sanction as the status of bargaining representative is the source of a union's power. However, many unions have no need of Board aid to gain or keep the position of bargaining representative. Most unions do not resort to certification elections to establish their majority status, and many unions which are certified would not be harmed by losing their certifications. Entrenched unions, which already have well-established bargaining relationships with employers, need no aid from the Board in maintaining their positions. Powerful unions, which can make effective use of such traditional self-help remedies as striking and picketing to force employers to bargain, have no need for bargaining orders. These powerful and entrenched unions are the ones with the least natural incentive to lower racial barriers, because they do not have to worry about attracting votes at representation elections as the weaker unions must. Thus the *Bekins* remedies fail to reach those unions likely to be the worst offenders. In addition, *Bekins,* by increasing the duration of representation cases, would create problems in applying Section 8(b)(7)(C) to picketing by unions whose representational eligibility is being litigated or has been denied by the Board. To prevent a union found ineligible for certification from engaging in recognitional picketing and thereby to secure the representative status unavailable through the Board's usual representation case processes, and to prevent the prospect of a series of election petitions followed by recognitional picketing, the Board would be under pressure to disregard the literal language of Section 8(b)(7)(C) by making any recognitional picketing by an ineligible union a violation of that section.

Also, under the majority *Bekins* holding, a labor organization could be denied certification upon the mere presumption that it will fail to discharge its responsibility to represent employees in *this* unit fairly solely because it has failed to represent employees fairly in some *other* bargaining unit, rather than on proof of such dereliction as to unit employees in a revocation proceeding. In fact, the Employer herein, in seeking to prevent the issuance of certification, relies upon discriminatory provisions in the Union's contracts in other bargaining units with other employers, contracts to which this Employer has never been a party and which were found to be unlawful solely because they perpetuated the other employers' past discrimination. For the Board to conclude that there will be further unlawful conduct solely on the basis of such evidence is directly contrary to our longstanding policy. Traditionally, as is true of virtually all court and administrative determinations, the Board's findings and remedies apply only to the particular parties before us.

The *Bekins* holding further would lead to anomalous situations such as that where an employer exercises exclusive control over hiring, resulting in the total absence of female and black employees in the unit, yet it is argued that this situation constitutes evidence of the union's propensity to practice discrimination and certification of the union would perpetuate this condition. In these circumstances it would be ludicrous to excuse the employer from its bargaining obligation.

. . .

We conclude that our statutory function of eliminating invidious discrimination of labor organizations is best served by scrutinizing their activities when they are subject to our adversary procedures and remedial orders. Indeed, the Board has long utilized unfair labor practice procedures to consider allegations of invidious discrimination by labor organizations and employers which interferes with Section 7 rights. We have done so with respect to unions by policing their conduct *vis-a-vis* the employees in units they represent through our power to remedy a labor organization's breach of its duty of fair representation. This doctrine was first enunciated by the Board in *Miranda Fuel Company, Inc.*:

"Section 7 thus gives employees the right to be free from unfair or irrelevant or invidious treatment by their exclusive bargaining agent in matters affecting their employment. This right of employees is a statutory limitation on statutory bargaining representatives, and we conclude that Section 8(b)(1)(A) of the Act accordingly prohibits labor organizations, when acting in a statutory representative capacity, from taking action against any employee upon considerations or classifications which are irrelevant, invidious, or unfair." [Footnote omitted.]

This doctrine of the duty of fair representation was derived from the Supreme Court's decision in three companion cases: *Steele* v. *Louisville & Nashville Railroad Co.; Tunstall* v. *Brotherhood of Locomotive Firemen & Enginemen;* and *Wallace Corporation* v. *N.L.R.B. In Steele* and *Tunstall,* both of which involved racial discrimination by a union which was statutory representative under the Railway Labor Act, the Court concluded that such a representative "cannot rightly refuse to perform the duty, which is inseparable from the power of representation conferred upon it, to represent the entire membership of the craft." In *Wallace,* which did not involve race discrimination, the Court held that the same duty of fair representation was required of bargaining representatives selected under the National Labor Relations Act.

The duty of fair representation has become the touchstone of the Board's concern with invidious discrimination by unions. For example, it is well established that a labor organization's rejection of an employee's grievance solely because of his or her race breaches the duty of fair representation and violates Section 8(b)(1)(A), 8(b)(2), and 8(b)(3) of the Act. Similarly, we have held that a union's refusal to process grievances filed to protest an employer's segregated plant facilities constitutes a violation of Section 8(b)(1)(A).

In *Galveston Maritime Association, Inc.,* the Board held, again relying on the duty of fair representation, that a union's maintenance of a collective-bargaining agreement which allocated work on the basis of race violated Section 8(b)(1)(A), 8(b)(2), and 8(b)(3) of the Act. The Board premised the 8(b)(2) violation on its conclusion that the establishment, maintenance, and enforcement of discriminatory work quotas based on irrelevant, invidious, and unfair considerations of race and union membership discriminated against employees in violation of Section 8(a)(3) of the Act and that, by causing an employer to so discriminate, a union violates Section 8(b)(2). In holding that the work allocation violated Section 8(b)(3), the Board concluded that "a labor organization's duty to bargain collectively includes the duty to represent fairly," on grounds that collective-bargaining agreements which discriminate invidiously are not lawful under the Act and therefore do not meet the good faith requirements of Section 8(d).

The duty of fair representation is not limited to present discrimination, but is also breached by union policies which perpetuate past discrimination. Thus, in *Houston Maritime Association*, the union had a policy prior to September 1963 of refusing to accept black applicants for membership. In the latter part of that month, the union adopted a policy of closing its register of applicants and refusing to accept any further applications regardless of the applicant's race. In addition to finding that the union's new policy violated Section 8(b)(1)(A) and Section 8(b)(2) of the Act as an attempt to perpetuate past discrimination, the Board found that the employers who had participated in the pattern of unlawful conduct had thereby violated Section 8(a)(1) and (3).

While these cases clearly illustrate that we provide a remedy for breach of the duty of fair representation, thereby protecting employees from invidious discrimination by their bargaining representative, other remedies for a union's unlawful discrimination are also available. For example, we have held that a union commits unfair labor practices by attempting to force an employer to continue discriminatory practices even though no breach of the duty of fair representative is involved. Additionally, the Board has, in appropriate cases, revoked the certification of unions which engage in unlawful invidious discrimination.

As the foregoing discussion indicates, the Board has long recognized its obligation to consider issues concerning discrimination on the basis of race, sex, national origin, or other unlawful, invidious, or irrelevant reasons when they are raised in an appropriate context, and we shall continue to do so.

However, on the basis of all the foregoing, although we neither approve nor condone discriminatory practices on the part of unions, we hereby overrule *Bekins* as we conclude that the holding of that case is neither mandated by the Constitution nor by the Act and is destructive of the policies embodied in Section 9(c) of the Act. We further conclude that issues such as those raised by the Employer herein are best considered in the context of appropriate unfair labor practice proceedings. We do so on the basis of the paramount importance of avoidance of delay in representation cases, the procedural safeguards afforded in unfair labor practice proceedings which are not available in representation proceedings, the somewhat different purposes served by Section 8 and Section 9 of the Act, and the fact that effective procedures already exist for litigation of the type of discrimination alleged by the Employer herein.

We therefore overrule the Employer's objection and shall certify the Union as the representative of the employees in the unit found appropriate above.

. . .

JENKINS, Member, dissenting. . . .

In an attempt to rationalize their conclusion that the due process clause of the fifth amendment does not prohibit the Board's certification of a discriminating union, my colleagues assert that the view of the majority in *Bekins* that certification of a discriminating union violates constitutional restrictions misconstrued the Supreme Court delineation of the scope of prohibited state action. After reviewing a number of cases in which the Supreme Court held state action involved with invidious discrimination exceeded constitutional bounds, my colleagues state that such an involvement is found in circumstances, among others, where the government authorized private discrimination or fostered and encouraged private discrimination. They conclude, however, that certification of a discriminating union does not sufficiently involve the Board in the union's invidiously discriminatory practices to render its action unconstitutional because "a certification is neither more nor less than an acknowledgement that a majority of the employees in an appropriate bargaining unit have selected the union as their exclusive bargaining representative" and does not authorize the union to engage in discrimination.

This evaluation of the Board's involvment in the union's discriminatory practices is a patent understatement of the significant effects of certification. By certification the union becomes the statutory bargaining agent with statutory rights. Improper interference with the selection of the bargaining representative is the violation of "public, not private, rights." *Virginia Electric & Power Co.* v. *NLRB*, 319 U.S. 533, 543, 12 LRRM 739 (1943). The usual form of certification of representative provides that the "labor organization is the exclusive representative of all the employees in the . . . appropriate unit for the purposes of collective bargaining in respect to rates of pay, wages, hours of employment, or other conditions of employment." The invidious discrimination of a discriminating union is practiced in the very areas to which the certification as representative relates. As previously noted, certification of a union confers the exclusive right to represent all employees in the bargaining unit, the right to be free from challenge for a year, and a presumption that its majority status continues after a year. Without the Board's certification a labor organization does not enjoy the right of a statutory bargaining agent. Obviously, a union's status as the statutory bargaining agent enhances its position with respect to both the employer and the unit employees. By certifying a union which excludes blacks or women from membership or segregates them in a separate local, the Board directs the employer to bargain exclusively with this discriminating union as representative of the excluded or segregated blacks or women. Minorities do not have a protected right, separate from the certified representative, to engage in concerted activities to protest discrimination by their employer. *Emporium Capwell Co.* v. *Western Addition Community Organization*, 420 U.S. 50, 9 FEP Cases 195 (1975). Certification is thus an integral part of the representation function in which the union practices discrimination and is patently direct participation and assistance by a Government agency, contrary to constitutional strictures, in the union's discriminatory representation. Accordingly, "[w]hen a governmental agency recognizes such a union to be the bargaining representative it significantly becomes a willing participant in the union's discriminatory practices." *Mansion House, supra,* 473 F.2d at 473. The Board's conferring the status of statutory bargaining agent upon a union which engages in invidious discrimination clearly fosters and supports the union's discriminatory practices and this constitutes the Board's involvement in them under the standards which my colleagues acknowledge but contend are not applicable here. As the Supreme Court stated in *Burton* v. *Wilmington Parking Authority, supra,* where the state authority merely leased space in a public building to a private restaurant which denied service to blacks, there existed "that degree of state participation and involvement in discriminatory action which it was the design of the Fourteenth Amendment to condemn."

The Board's decisions holding breach of the duty of fair representation to be an unfair labor practice, with which I of course fully agree, are no substitute for the disqualification of a discriminating union in a representation proceeding. The Fifth Amendment does not permit a Government agency to provide the instrument for practicing discrimination merely because at some uncertain future date the Board may have an opportunity to terminate this discrimination in unfair labor practice proceedings set in motion by the charges of private parties if the General Counsel decides to file a complaint. The Board cannot initiate unfair labor practice proceedings. Moreover, for a variety of reasons, such proceedings may never be instituted notwithstanding the discriminatory exclusion of minorities from the union or from employment in the certified unit.

The effect of a union's exclusion of blacks or women from membership or their segregation in separate locals may discourage them from seeking or retaining employment with an employer who is compelled by the Board's certification to bargain exclusively with the discriminating union. An employer confronted with a certification may find it expedient to enter into a collective-bargaining agreement with a union which excludes blacks or women from employment. In these situations, the possibility of invidious discrimination being raised as an unfair labor practice is minimized or eliminated. The certification of the Board thus serves as an instrument for the perpetuation of invidious discriminatory practices. It is clear to me, therefore, that the due process clause of the fifth amendment requires that certification be denied whenever the evidence establishes that the labor organization's representation in the unit for which it requests certification will be infected with invidious discrimination.

## BELL & HOWELL CO. v. NLRB

*U.S. Court of Appeals, District of Columbia Circuit, 1979*
*100 LRRM 2192*

BAZELON, Circuit Judge: Petitioner Bell & Howell Co. (Bell & Howell) challenges an order of the National Labor Relations Board (NLRB) requiring Bell & Howell to bargain with Local 399, Operating Engineers (Local 399) as collective bargaining representative for Bell & Howell's stationary engineers at its Lincolnwood, Illinois facility.

Bell & Howell contends that it is not obligated to bargain with Local 399 because Local 399 allegedly discriminates against women in its membership policy and benefit plans. . . . We affirm the Board's decision that Bell & Howell violated § § 8(a)(5) and (1) of the Act.[1]

. . .

Initially, we must determine whether Bell & Howell has standing to challenge the Board's certification of Local 399 where the challenge is based on Local 399's alleged discrimination against women. The Board, relying on *Virginian Ry. Co.* v. *System Federation 40,* contends that an employer lacks standing to assert the constitutional rights of its employees as a defense to the statutory obligation to bargain with the employees' chosen representative.

The economic consequences of a bargaining order to an employer appear sufficient to establish "injury in fact," the element of standing mandated by the case or controversy requirement of Article III. An employer who has been found guilty of an unfair labor practice and has been ordered to bargain is also a "person aggrieved" within the meaning of § 10(f) of the Act. Therefore, the employer is also well within the ambit of the statutory authorization to seek review.

Normally, however, one who properly invokes the jurisdiction of a federal court "has standing to seek redress for injuries done him, but may not seek redress for injuries to others." *Moose Lodge No. 107* v. *Irvis,* 407 U.S. 163, 166 (1972). In challenging Local 399's certification, Bell & Howell did not allege that Local 399's discriminatory policies have or will cause any harm to Bell & Howell (*e.g.,* by preventing Bell & Howell from hiring female stationary engineers or causing Bell & Howell to violate statutes prohibiting discrimination against women.)

The barrier against asserting the rights of third parties does not appear to be rooted in Article III itself, but rather is a prudential doctrine designed to limit unnecessary decisions of constitutional questions. The rule against allowing a party to assert the constitutional rights of third persons has been relaxed in certain situations, particularly where the third party's interest might otherwise go unprotected.

Whether in this case the interest would otherwise go unprotected depends on precisely how the "interest" at stake is defined. If the interest is

---

[1] [Footnotes numbered as in original.—Ed.] In *NLRB* v. *Mansion House Center Management Co.,* 473 F.2d 471, 82 LRRM 2608 (8th Cir. 1973), the court held that an employer may introduce evidence of a union's racially discriminatory policies as a defense to a charge that the employer refused to bargain with the union in violation of § 8(a)(5). The court, noting the constitutional problems that might arise should the Board make its "remedial machinery" available to a discriminatory union, held that: "the claim of racial discrimination allegedly practiced by a union seeking recognition as a representative bargaining unit under the act is a relevant area of inquiry for the Board when the defense is appropriately raised before the Board upon a company's refusal to bargain."
*Id.* at 474. For the reasons that appear more fully herein, we are compelled to disagree with that conclusion.

in eliminating the union's discriminatory practices, there are alternative means of achieving this goal under both the LMRA (once the union has been certified) and Title VII, and under both provisions the action can be brought by the victim of discrimination. If, on the other hand, the interest is in preventing certification of a discriminatory union, there may be no adequate alternative to allowing the employer to raise the issue. The right of a dissenting unit member, or an individual outside the unit, to intervene in a representation proceeding in order to raise the discrimination issue is questionable. Moreover, even if such an individual could intervene, the nonreviewability of certification decisions might insulate from judicial review any Board decision in favor of the union.[19]

We think certification in itself is sufficiently important that the constitutionality of the practice announced in *Handy Andy* should not be insulated from review. Our conclusion is reinforced by a concern that if the Board's certification of a discriminatory union violates the Fifth Amendment, then our enforcement of a bargaining order with such a union might equally violate the Fifth Amendment. We are mindful of the Court's observation in *Shelley* v. *Kraemer,* 334 U.S. 1, 22 (1948): "[t]he Constitution confers upon no individual the right to demand action by the State which results in the denial of equal protection of the laws to other individuals." We must therefore decide whether granting enforcement of this bargaining order would deny equal protection to those who are the victims of union discrimination, particularly where those persons might otherwise be precluded from challenging the constitutionality of the order on their own behalf.

We thus conclude that Bell & Howell has standing to raise the constitutional rights of victims of discrimination in this case. Although *Virginian Railway* implies a contrary result, that case was decided prior to a series of cases elaborating the "jus tertii" doctrine and also preceded the Supreme Court decisions holding that court enforcement of private discrimination constitutes state action in violation of the Fourteenth Amendment.

## B. SECTION 9(c)(1) OF THE LMRA

Section 9(c)(1) of the LMRA provides, *inter alia:* "If the Board finds . . . [that] a question of representation exists, it *shall* direct an election by secret ballot and *shall* certify the results thereof." . . .

. . .

A refusal to certify a union chosen by a majority in the unit thus can be justified only in the most compelling circumstances, when certification would conflict with other significant goals of the Act. In this case Bell & Howell argues that the vital national commitment to eradicate employment discrimination justifies denying certification to Local 399.

---

[19] We need not decide whether an individual discriminated against by the union could bring an action in district court challenging the certification under *Leedom* v. *Kyne,* 358 U.S. 184, 43 LRRM 2222 (1958). See note 6 *supra.*

Although other federal agencies have primary responsibilities for carrying out the national anti-discrimination policy, Bell & Howell correctly observes that the Board too has a role in promoting this goal. The Board already implements this policy as an aspect of enforcing the union's statutory duty of fair representation. A union violates its duty of fair representation when it takes advantage of its monopoly position as exclusive bargaining representative to discriminate invidiously against employees or potential employees on the basis of race or sex. Breach of this duty may violate §§ 8(b)(1)(A), b(2) and b(3) of the Act, and subjects the offending union to Board-imposed sanctions as well as private causes of action.

It is by no means certain that the interpretation of the LMRA urged by Bell & Howell would substantially further anti-discrimination goals in a manner consistent with the other policies of the LMRA. First, denying certification or withholding a bargaining order from a discriminatory union may be an ineffective remedy for union discrimination. These sanctions will have no effect on unions that are strong enough to establish collective bargaining relationships with employers without recourse to the Board.

Second, these sanctions are at odds with the remedial focus of the Board's authority. At best, denying certification or withholding a bargaining order will prevent future discrimination in the unit that the union seeks to represent. That sanction provides no remedy for those who are already victims of the union's discrimination. Yet, it is well settled that the Board's principal remedial power is to "make whole" employees who have been injured by violations of the LMRA.

Finally, to give the Board responsibility for investigating allegations of past union discrimination that occurred outside the unit for which the union seeks certification would unnecessarily duplicate the functions of the EEOC. The broader scope of the EEOC's investigative and remedial authority, its expertise in detecting subtle and complex forms of discrimination, and its single-purpose anti-discrimination mission combine to make the EEOC a preferable vehicle for eliminating union discrimination.

In contrast to denial of certification before the union becomes exclusive bargaining representative, sanctions based on violations of the duty of fair representation are more likely to be effective in providing a remedy for victims of discrimination, in a manner more consonant with the other underlying policies of the LMRA. The duty of fair representation applies to all exclusive bargaining representatives, not simply to those who use the Board's electoral or remedial machinery. Complaints that the union has violated its duty of fair representation are more likely to be brought by the individuals who are the victims of discrimination. This appropriately focuses the Board's inquiry on the union's conduct in a particular bargaining unit, easing the Board's fact-finding activities. When the complaint is brought by a victim of discrimination, the Board can tailor its order to redress specific instances of discrimination, making the victims whole, and, at the same time, providing more protection for the employees' right of self-determination. If remedies for discrimination are imposed only after the collective bargaining relationship is established, the employer cannot use allegations of discrimination as a pretext to frustrate or delay the employees' right to select their representative.

In sum, we conclude that nothing in the LMRA, interpreted in light of the purposes of the Act, requires the NLRB to consider allegations of discrimination prior to certifying a victorious union, at least where the proffered evidence of discrimination relates to past union misconduct outside the bargaining unit that the union seeks to represent.

## NOTES

1. In *NLRB* v. *Mansion House Center Management Corp.*, 473 F.2d 471, 9 FEP Cases 358 (8th Cir. 1973), the Eighth Circuit held that the NLRB improperly issued a bargaining order on behalf of a union guilty of racial discrimination. The court held that the order involved the Board in racial discrimination in violation of the Fifth Amendment.

2. There has been much discussion of the relationship between Title VII and NLRA rights and remedies. For contrasting views, see Meltzer, *The National Labor Relations Act and Racial Discrimination: The More Remedies the Better?*, 42 U. CHI. L. REV. 1 (1974); *The Inevitable Interplay of Title VII and the National Labor Relations Act and New Rule for the NLRB*, 123 U. PENN. L. REV. 158 (1974).

### D. SELF-HELP FOR RACIAL DISCRIMINATION

### NLRB v. SUMTER PLYWOOD CORP.

*United States Court of Appeals, Fifth Circuit, 1976*
*535 F.2d 917, 14 FEP Cases 191*

GOLDBERG, Circuit Judge: The National Labor Relations Board (the Board) petitions this Court for enforcement of its order that Sumter Plywood (the Company) bargain collectively with the Southern Council of Industrial Workers, United Brotherhood of Carpenters and Joiners of America, AFL-CIO (the Union). The Company, as respondent, argues that enforcement should be denied because of alleged improprieties on the part of the Union in its organizational campaign. . . .

### I. PROCEDURAL BACKGROUND

The Company is engaged in the manufacture and sale of plywood and lumber products in Livingston, Alabama. Pursuant to the Union's representation petition and after an organizational campaign to be discussed below, an election was held among the workers at the Company on

November 16, 1972. The unit, stipulated to be appropriate, included approximately 241 eligible voters, 204 of whom were black. The tally showed 156 votes for the Union and 77 against, with only four ballots challenged or void.

. . .

## C. THE RACIAL ORIENTATION OF THE CAMPAIGN

. . . When racial considerations have been injected into a representation campaign by the party which prevails in the election, this Court in some circumstances will cast a burden on that party to establish that the racial message was truthful and germane, "and where there is doubt as to whether the total conduct of such party is within the described bounds, the doubt will be resolved against him." *NLRB* v. *Bancroft Mfg. Co., supra,* 516 F.2d at 440–41, quoting *Sewell Mfg. Co.,* 1962, 138 NLRB 66, 71–72. From *Bancroft* and the authorities relied upon therein, it appears that the major concern in this regard is that workers of one race not be persuaded to vote for or against a Union on the basis of invidious prejudices they might have against individuals of another race. Clearly, some statements regarding the effect that a Union might have on the workers of a particular race can be acceptable.

As with the objection relating to the statement about signing cards, there was never a formal hearing on this issue of racial taint. Thus even if we conclude that the facts found by the Board were not sufficient for the election to be invalidated as tainted by racial considerations, we still must face the question of whether the proffered evidence was sufficient to require a formal hearing on the issue. In the context of the racial taint issue here, the two questions are substantially the same, since the Company bases its arguments largely on the incidents found to be facts by the Regional Director. In reviewing the Board's refusal to order a formal hearing, we assume as true any further allegations made by the Company which are supported by the proffer of specific evidence.

*Bancroft* indicates that the reversal of burden of persuasion occurs if the racial remarks "form the core or theme of the campaign," or if the statements are racially inflammatory. 516 F.2d at 442. If neither condition obtains, the injection of racial considerations should be reviewed under the familiar standards applicable to other types of alleged improprieties. *Id.* We will examine, then, the incidents cited by the Company and noted in the Regional Director's initial Report on Objections, to determine if the evidence and specific allegations could support a finding that racial considerations either formed the core or theme of the campaign, or, though not central, were nevertheless "inflammatory."

The electorate, as we have noted, was overwhelmingly black—204 out of 241 eligible voters. The charges leveled by the Company at the Union's attempt to woo this electorate can be grouped roughly into one alleged sin of omission—the exclusion of whites from the campaign—and one alleged sin of commission—the Union's affirmative "appeal to racial hatred and prejudice." Respondent's Brief at 19.

Statements of white workers reviewed by the Regional Director in his investigation indicated that some of the Union's black organizers specifically avoided giving to whites the campaign material that the organizers distributed to blacks at the plant gate. One white worker who was handed a campaign handbill testified to circumstances which made the distribution of the literature to him seem unintentional. These white workers stated that they were never invited to join the Union or to attend any Union meetings, and that they knew of no white workers who were so invited. The Union organizational meetings were, with the exception of a white Union organizer, attended only by blacks. One Union organizer admitted that he had not contacted any whites during the campaign.

Other evidence before the Regional Director indicated that whites were not totally excluded from the campaign. One white Union organizer stated that he had contacted a number of white employees early in the campaign. White employees were included in the Union's mailing of campaign materials shortly before the election.[10]

The allegations of the Company and the evidence before the Regional Director are sufficient for us to conclude that the Union's campaign evinced only a minimal interest in the white voters. The Board, at oral argument, conceded that this was a fair characterization of the campaign. This concentration on voters of one race, to the relative exclusion of voters of the other, is disturbing and is not to be condoned, but we feel that it is not enough in itself to invalidate the election, at least in the absence of any indication either that whites were absolutely excluded or that leading Union organizers deliberately promoted a policy of excluding workers of one race from the campaign. That the Union's appeal in this case was predominately to blacks does not in itself tell us either that race was the theme of the campaign, or that the Union's appeal was inflammatory. Rather, we think the racial one-sidedness of the Union's effort should be given the analytical effect in our review of intensifying the scrutiny with which we regard the incidents of the Union's "appeal to race hatred" cited by the Company.

The Union's major literary effort in the campaign was an eleven page pamphlet which contained two cartoons arguably racial in tone. One depicted "Uncle Tom" as one of the hurdles that must be crossed on the road to unionism; the other depicted a black man being kicked out of a welfare office, saying "I hope this don't happen to my brothers." The remainder of the pamphlet is classic campaign rhetoric—a color-blind extolment of the virtues of unionism.

At two of the Union's organizing meetings, a local black politician spoke to the all black audience, told them "black people should stick

[10] [Footnotes numbered as in original.—Ed.] The Company argues that this mailing to whites should be discounted as a demonstration of even-handedness, since the *Excelsior* mailing list given the Union by the Company did not specify the race of the employees, and thus the Union could not feasibly contact only the blacks. See *Excelsior Underwear, Inc.*, 1966, 156 NLRB 1236. If it had been the intent of the Union to limit its campaign exclusively to blacks, however, the Union could simply have eschewed the colorblind mailing which obviously would reach whites, and concentrated instead on other more individualized forms of information dissemination.

together," and urged them to register to vote. Sylvester Hicks, a major Union organizer, responded to a black employee's complaint about the paucity of black secretaries and supervisors in the plant by saying that blacks had been under slavery for 100 years, but that the Union could help. At another meeting, Hicks said "something about black people being behind for a long time." A statement from one black employee alleged that she had been called a "white mouth" by one of the Union's representatives after she indicated that she would not support the Union.

The Company also presented evidence to the Regional Director to the effect that "black power" bumper stickers appeared on some employee cars about three weeks before the election, and that employees on occasion would exchange a clenched fist salute. The black employees in one department developed a pro-Union cheer a few days before the election which included this "black power" salute.

Upon these allegations and this evidence the Company grounded its charge that the Union improperly injected racial considerations into the campaign. Despite the heightened suspicion with which we regard these incidents, because of the relatively exclusive concentration of the campaign upon blacks, we must conclude that racial considerations did not form the "core or theme" of the Union's campaign, and that the racial messages authored by the Union were not "inflammatory."

The bulk of the campaign literature consisted of colorblind unionist appeals. The challenged cartoons are patently inoffensive. The term "Uncle Tom" certainly connotes some racial message, but it also connotes an economic one—the desire for a break with the tradition of economic dependency. As to the objection regarding the black male being booted from the welfare office, we can only note that the era of the invisibility of blacks in illustrative media has passed. The Company's assumption that a white figure would evince no racial message, whereas a black figure constitutes an appeal to racial hatred, is an assumption grounded in a past all too recent, but nonetheless past. Downtrodden workers are ubiquitous in Union organizing propaganda, and in choosing a color for the illustrations here, we cannot expect the Union to have been unmindful that the electorate was almost 85 percent black.

Nothing in the record indicates that the local politician's exhortation that "black people should stick together" was anything other than an appeal for the employees' votes for him in the general election. Hick's statements to the all black audiences represented an attempt to equate black economic betterment with unionism, but could not be construed as an effort to set blacks against whites or to suggest that blacks were entitled to greater rights than whites.

The black power salutes and bumper stickers indicate only that supporters of the Union identified betterment of the conditions of blacks with a victory of the Union in the election.[17] They do not indicate that

---

[17] There is no suggestion that the Union was officially involved in the black power salutes and bumper stickers, and so we could deny enforcement because of this conduct only if it "disrupted the voting procedure or destroyed the atmosphere necessary to the exercises of a free choice in the representation election." *NLRB* v. *Golden-Age*

the Union campaign was grounded on a black versus white emotionalism. The "white mouth" comment and the few other random incidents with racial overtones suggest perhaps that some supporters of the Union attempted to capitalize on black resentment against previous white oppression by associating anti-unionism with that white oppression. Even under searching scrutiny, however, these few alleged incidents in the context of the entire organizing campaign cannot be seen to rise from *de minimis* to "central" or "inflammatory" stature.

Our review of the evidence, then, leaves us in agreement with the Regional Director, who after a thorough examination into the allegations concluded as follows:

". . . [T]he evidence considered as a whole does not reveal the kind of appeals to racial prejudice, on matters unrelated to the election issues, which make it impossible for employees to exercise the franchise in a sober and informed manner. The Employer presented no evidence of overt appeals to racial prejudice that would tend to engender racial hatred. An overwhelming majority of the employees in the unit were black; the [Union] directed its campaign primarily toward these employees; and because of the general election in which white and black candidates were opposing each other, race was an issue in Sumter County in November, 1972. Certainly, many of the employees were interested in their status as black individuals. It appears from the evidence that [the Union] raised the issue of race in an effort to show that it could bring economic benefits to Negro workers rather than in an effort to inflame racial hatred with irrelevant and unrelated matters."

In one sense discussed above, this case is more difficult than *Bancroft, supra.* We do not have available here a factor which served to buttress our decision to uphold the election there:

"This campaign was waged in a bargaining unit which was 57 percent white and 43 percent black. As a matter of common sense, any attempt by the Union to set black against white would have been suicidal, for the Union could successfully organize these plants only by forging a harmonious racial amalgam. . . .

". . . [Racially oriented statements by Union organizers] were . . . in the nature of asides addressed to a particular group of employees in the context of a campaign aimed at securing the adherence of all employees to the Union. . . ."

516 F.2d at 442, 443.

As noted, the unit at Sumter Plywood was 85 percent black, so "commonsense" cannot guide us in the absence of other factors as to the wisdom *vel non* of a racist campaign.[18] We have looked carefully at the evidence, however, and find that no showing has been made that the campaign was racist. The real thrust of the *Bancroft* rationale, then, applies equally well to this case:

---

*Beverage Co.,* 5 Cir. 1969, 415 F.2d 26, 32 n. 5. See also *Bush Hog, Inc.,* 5 Cir. 1969, 420 F.2d 1266, 1268–69; *Hobco Mfg. Co.,* 1967, 164 NLRB 862.

[18] The racially oriented campaign approved in *Baltimore Luggage, supra* note 9, was conducted in a unit of 144 employees, 134 of whom were black. 387 F.2d at 745.

". . . [T]here is no evidence here that the Union told blacks that they ought to dominate the Union or enjoy benefits unavailable to their fellow workers. There is no evidence that the Union sought to incite blacks against whites; at no time were there either acts or threats of interracial violence, and there is certainly nothing to indicate that the black employees were less favorably disposed toward the Company than were their white co-workers, either before or after the remarks in question. In this case there was no racially-oriented campaign; the vast bulk of the literature on both sides was devoted to the economic issues ordinarily found in representation contests: whether the Union or the Company would ensure the highest wages, the best pension plans, the firmest job security. . . .

". . . [T]his record does not disclose that the disputed statements had an inflammatory effect on the black employees."
516 F.2d at 442–43.

Comparing the racially-oriented statements in this case with those permitted, though not condoned, in *Bancroft,* we find that the statements there were more difficult to excuse. Slyvester Hicks was also the Union organizer in *Bancroft,* and there he told black employees that "if the blacks did not stay together as a group and the Union lost the election, all the blacks would be fired." *Id.* at 440. Other statements and rumors from Union people attributed to the specific employer in *Bancroft* an antiblack animus. The racially oriented remarks in our case do not go so far, either in disregard of facts or in specific insinuations about the employer involved.

The racial messages delivered by the Union here, then, neither formed the core of the campaign, nor were inflammatory, and, in part because these messages dealt largely with subjective matters, it is difficult to characterize the messages as "misrepresentations." A final factor strongly supports our decision not to deny enforcement—the election result was 156 to 77 in favor of the Union. With that majority, a significantly stronger showing of improper consideration of race than was proffered here would be required for us to negate the Board's decision to uphold the election or to remand to the Board for a hearing on the issue.

We emphasize that our decision in *Bancroft* and our decision today, contrasted with *Sewell,* do not reflect a direct racial double standard. In *Sewell* the white employer in Mississippi sought to defeat the Union's 1961 organizing effort by repeatedly stressing to his all-white workforce that the Union was pro-integration. He even circulated a picture of a white Union organizer "dancing with a [black] lady friend." See 138 NLRB at 66–67. Clearly, such messages were not germane to any of the real issues in the Union's campaign, and could only have had the effect of inflaming racial prejudices in an already racially troubled time and place.

This decision and *Bancroft* apply the neutral principle that some degree of "consciousness-raising" will be permitted in union organizing campaigns among ethnic groups which have historically been economically disadvantaged, as long as the ethnic message becomes neither the core of the campaign nor inflammatory. For such groups, the call to ethnic pride and unity has a strong claim to congruence with the Union's traditional call to economic betterment. This cannot be said of appeals to the "ethnic pride" of historically advantaged groups.

## EMPORIUM CAPWELL CO. v. WESTERN ADDITION COMMUNITY ORGANIZATION

*Supreme Court of the United States, 1975*
*420 U.S. 50, 9 FEP Cases 195*

Opinion of the Court by MR. JUSTICE MARSHALL, announced by MR. CHIEF JUSTICE BURGER.

This case presents the question whether, in light of the national policy against racial discrimination in employment, the National Labor Relations Act protects concerted activity by a group of minority employees to bargain with their employer over issues of employment discrimination. The National Labor Relations Board held that the employees could not circumvent their elected representative to engage in such bargaining. The Court of Appeals for the District of Columbia Circuit reversed and remanded, holding that in certain circumstances the activity would be protected, 485 F.2d 917, 83 LRRM 2738. Because of the importance of the issue to the administration of the Act, we granted certiorari. . . . We now reverse.

I.  The Emporium Capwell Company (the Company) operates a department store in San Francisco. At all times relevant to this case it was a party to the collective-bargaining agreement negotiated by the San Francisco Retailer's Council, of which it was a member, and the Department Store Employees Union (the Union) which represented all stock and marking area employees of the Company. The agreement, in which the Union was recognized as the sole collective-bargaining agency for all covered employees, prohibited employment discrimination by reason of race, color, creed, national origin, age, or sex, as well as union activity. It had a no-strike or lockout clause, and it established grievance and arbitration machinery for processing any claimed violation of the contract, including a violation of the antidiscrimination clause.[1]

On April 3, 1968, a group of Company employees covered by the agreement met with the Secretary-Treasurer of the Union, Walter Johnson,

---

[1] [Footnotes numbered as in original.—Ed.] Section 5(B) provided:
"Any act of any employer, representative of the Union, or any employee that is interferring with the faithful performance of this agreement, or a harmonious relationship between the employers and the UNION, may be referred to the Adjustment Board for such action as the Adjustment Board deems proper, and is permissive within this agreement."
Section 36(B) established an Adjustment Board consisting of three union and three management members. Section 36(C) provided that if any matter referred to the Adjustment Board remained unsettled after seven days, either party could insist that the dispute be submitted to final and binding arbitration.

to present a list of grievances including a claim that the Company was discriminating on the basis of race in making assignments and promotions. The union official agreed to take certain of the grievances and to investigate the charge of racial discrimination. He appointed an investigating committee and prepared a report on the employees' grievances, which he submitted to the Retailer's Council and which the Council in turn referred to the Company. The report described "the possibility of racial discrimination" as perhaps the most important issue raised by the employees and termed the situation at the Company as potentially explosive if corrective action were not taken. It offered as an example of the problem the Company's failure to promote a Negro stock employee regarded by other employees as an outstanding candidate but a victim of racial discrimination.

Shortly after receiving the report, the Company's labor relations director met with Union representatives and agreed to "look into the matter" of discrimination and see what needed to be done. Apparently unsatisfied with these representations, the Union held a meeting in September attended by Union officials, Company employees, and representatives of the California Fair Employment Practices Committee (FEPC) and the local antipoverty agency. The Secretary-Treasurer of the Union announced that the Union had concluded that the Company was discriminating, and that it would process every such grievance through to arbitration if necessary. Testimony about the Company's practices was taken and transcribed by a court reporter, and the next day the Union notified the Company of its formal charge and demanded that the joint union-management Adjustment Board be convened "to hear the entire case."

At the September meeting some of the Company's employees had expressed their view that the contract procedures were inadequate to handle a systemic grievance of this sort; they suggested that the Union instead begin picketing the store in protest. Johnson explained that the collective agreement bound the Union to its processes and expressed his view that successful grievants would be helping not only themselves but all others who might be the victims of invidious discrimination as well. The FEPC and antipoverty agency representatives offered the same advice. Nonetheless, when the Adjustment Board meeting convened on October 16, James Joseph Hollins, Tom Hawkins, and two other employees whose testimony the Union had intended to elicit refused to participate in the grievance procedure. Instead, Hollins read a statement objecting to reliance on correction of individual inequities as an approach to the problem of discrimination at the store and demanding that the president of the Company meet with the four protestants to work out a broader agreement for dealing with the issue as they saw it. The four employees then walked out of the hearing.

Hollins attempted to discuss the question of racial discrimination with the Company president shortly after the incidents of October 16. The president refused to be drawn into such a discussion but suggested to Hollins that he see the personnel director about the matter. Hollins, who had spoken to the personnel director before, made no effort to do so again. Rather, he and Hawkins and several other dissident employees held a press conference on October 22 at which they denounced the store's employment policy as racist, reiterated their desire to deal directly with "the top management" of the Company over minority employment conditions, and announced their intention to picket and institute a boycott of the store. On Saturday, November 2, Hollins, Hawkins, and at least two other employees picketed the store throughout the day and distributed at the entrance handbills urging consumers not to patronize the store.[2] Johnson encountered the picketing employees, again urged them to rely on the grievance process, and warned that they might be fired for their activities. The picketers, however, were not dissuaded, and they continued to press their demand to deal directly with the Company president.[3]

On November 7, Hollins and Hawkins were given written warnings that a repetition of the picketing or public statements about the Company could lead to their discharge.[4] When the conduct was repeated the following Saturday, the two employees were fired.

[2] The full text of the handbill read:
"* * BEWARE * * * * BEWARE * * * * BEWARE * * EMPORIUM SHOPPERS 'Boycott Is On' 'Boycott Is On'
"For years at The Emporium black, brown, yellow and red people have worked at the lowest jobs, at the lowest levels. Time and time again we have seen intelligent, hard working brothers and sisters denied promotions and respect.
"The Emporium is a 20th Century colonial plantation. The brothers and sisters are being treated the same way as our brothers are being treated in the slave mines of Africa.
"Whenever the racist pig at The Emporium injures or harms a black sister or brother, they injure and insult all black people. THE EMPORIUM MUST PAY FOR THESE INSULTS. Therefore, we encourage all of our people to take their money out of this racist store, until black people have full employment and are promoted justly through out The Emporium.
"We welcome the support of our brothers and sisters from the churches, unions, sororities, fraternities, social clubs, Afro-American Institute, Black Panther Party, W.A.C.O. and the Poor Peoples Institute."
[3] Johnson testified that Hollins "informed me that the only one they wanted to talk to was Mr. Batchelder [the Company president] and I informed him that we had concluded negotiations in 1967 and I was a spokesman for the union and represented a few thousand clerks and I have never met Mr. Batchelder. . . ." App. 76.
[4] The warning given to Hollins read:
"On October 22, 1968, you issued a public statement at a press conference to which all newspapers, radio, and TV stations were invited. The contents of this statement were substantially the same as those set forth in the sheet attached. This statement was broadcast on Channel 2 on October 22, 1968 and Station KDIA.
"On November 2nd you distributed copies of the attached statement to Negro customers and prospective customers, and to other persons passing by in front of The Emporium.
"These statements are untrue and are intended to and will, if continued, injure the reputation of The Emporium.
"There are ample legal remedies to correct any discrimination you may claim to exist. Therefore, we view your activities as a deliberate and unjustified attempt to injure your employer.
"This is to inform you that you may be discharged if you repeat any of the above acts or make any similar public statement."
That given to Hawkins was the same except that the first paragraph was not included. App. 106.

Respondent Western Addition Community Organization, a local civil rights association of which Hollins and Hawkins were members, filed a charge against the Company with the National Labor Relations Board. The Board's General Counsel subsequently issued a complaint alleging that in discharging the two the Company had violated § 8(a)(1) of the National Labor Relations Act, 29 U.S.C. § 158(a)(1). After a hearing the NLRB Trial Examiner found that the discharged employees had believed in good faith that the Company was discriminating against minority employees, and that they had resorted to concerted activity on the basis of that belief. He concluded, however, that their activity was not protected by § 7 of the Act, and that their discharges did not, therefore, violate § 8(a)(1).

The Board, after oral argument, adopted the findings and conclusions of its Trial Examiner and dismissed the complaint. 192 NLRB 173, 77 LRRM 1669. Among the findings adopted by the Board was that the discharged employees' course of conduct

"was no mere presentation of a grievance, but nothing short of a demand that the [Company] bargain with the picketing employees for the entire group of minority employees." [5]

The Board concluded that protection of such an attempt to bargain would undermine the statutory system of bargaining through an exclusive, elected representative, impede elected unions' efforts at bettering the working conditions of minority employees "and place on the Employer an unreasonable burden of attempting to placate self-designated representatives of minority groups while abiding by the terms of a valid bargaining agreement and attempting in good faith to meet whatever demands the bargaining representative put forth under that agreement."[6]

On respondent's petition for review the Court of Appeals reversed and remanded. The court was of the view that concerted activity directed against racial discrimination enjoys a "unique status" by virtue of the national labor policy against discrimination, as expressed in both the

[5] 192 NLRB, at 185. The evidence marshaled in support of this finding consisted of Hollins' meeting with the Company president in which he said that he wanted to discuss the problem perceived by minority employees; his statement that the picketers would not desist until the president treated with them; Hawkins' testimony that their purpose in picketing was to "talk to the top management to get better conditions"; and his statement that they wanted to achieve their purpose through "group talk and through the president if we could talk to him," as opposed to use of the grievance-arbitration machinery.

[6] The Board considered but stopped short of resolving the question of whether the employees' invective and call for a boycott of the Company bespoke so malicious an attempt to harm their employer as to deprive them of the protection of the Act. The Board decision is therefore grounded squarely on the view that a minority group member may not by-pass the Union and bargain directly over matters affecting minority employees, and not at all on the tactics used in this particular attempt to obtain such bargaining.

Member Jenkins dissented on the ground that the employees' activity was protected by § 7 because it concerned the terms and conditions of their employment. Member Brown agreed but expressly relied upon his view that the facts revealed no attempt to bargain "but simply to urge [the Company] to take action to correct conditions of racial discrimination which the employees reasonably believed existed at The Emporium." 192 NLRB, at 179.

NLRA, see *United Packinghouse Workers Union* v. *NLRB,* 416 F.2d 1126, 70 LRRM 2489, *cert. denied,* 396 U.S. 903, 72 LRRM 2658 (1969), and in Title VII of the Civil Rights Act of 1964, 42 U.S.C. § 2000e *et seq.,* and that the Board had not adequately taken account of the necessity to accommodate the exclusive bargaining principle of the NLRA to the national policy of protecting action taken in opposition to discrimination from employer retaliation. The court recognized that protection of the minority group concerted activity involved in this case would interfere to some extent with the orderly collective-bargaining process, but it considered the disruptive effect on that process to be outweighed where protection of minority activity is necessary to full and immediate realization of the policy against discrimination. In formulating a standard for distinguishing between protected and unprotected activity, the majority held that the "Board should inquire, in cases such as this, whether the union was actually remedying the discrimination to the *fullest extent possible by the most expedient and efficacious means.* Where the union's efforts fall short of this high standard, the minority group's concerted activity cannot lose its section 7 protection." [8] Accordingly, the court remanded the case for the Board to make this determination and, if it found in favor of the employees, to consider whether their particular tactics were so disloyal to their employer as to deprive them of § 7 protection under our decision in *NLRB* v. *Local Union No. 1229,* 346 U.S. 464, 33 LRRM 2183 (1953).

II.  Before turning to the central questions of labor policy raised by this case, it is important to have firmly in mind the character of the underlying conduct to which we apply them. As stated, the Trial Examiner and the Board found that the employees were discharged for attempting to bargain with the Company over the terms and conditions of employment as they affected racial minorities. Although the Court of Appeals expressly declined to set aside this finding, respondent has devoted considerable effort to attacking it in this Court, on the theory that the employees were attempting only to present a grievance to their employer within the meaning of the first proviso to § 9(a). We see no occasion to disturb the finding of the Board. . . . The issue, then, is whether such attempts to engage in separate bargaining are protected by § 7 of the Act or proscribed by § 9(a).

## A

Section 7 affirmatively guarantees employees the most basic rights of industrial self-determination, "the right to self-organization, to form, join, or assist labor organizations, to bargain collectively through representatives of their own choosing, and to engage in other concerted activities for

---

[8] 485 F.2d, at 931 (emphasis in original). We hasten to point out that it had never been determined in any forum, at least as of the time that Hollins and Hawkins engaged in the activity for which they were discharged, that the Company had engaged in any discriminatory conduct. The Board found that the employees believed that the Company had done so, but that no evidence introduced in defense of their resort to self-help supported this belief.

the purpose of collective bargaining or other mutual aid or protection," as well as the right to refrain from these activities. These are, for the most part, collective rights, rights to act in concert with one's fellow employees; they are protected not for their own sake but as an instrument of the national labor policy of minimizing industrial strife "by encouraging the practice and procedure of collective bargaining" 29 U.S.C. § 151.

Central to the policy of fostering collective bargaining, where the employees elect that course, is the principle of majority rule. See *NLRB* v. *Jones & Laughlin Steel Corp.*, 301 U.S. 1, 1 LRRM 703 (1937). If the majority of a unit chooses union representation, the NLRA permits them to bargain with their employer to make union membership a condition of employment, thereby imposing their choice upon the minority. 29 U.S.C. §§ 157, 158(a)(3). In establishing a regime of majority rule, Congress sought to secure to all members of the unit the benefits of their collective strength and bargaining power,[13] in full awareness that the superior strength of some individuals or groups might be subordinated to the interest of the majority. . . .

. . .

In vesting the representatives of the majority with this broad power Congress did not, of course, authorize a tyranny of the majority over minority interests. First, it confined the exercise of these powers to the context of a "unit appropriate for the purposes of collective bargaining," i.e., a group of employees with a sufficient commonality of circumstances to ensure against the submergence of a minority with distinctively different interests in the terms and conditions of their employment. . . . Second, it undertook in the 1959 Landrum-Griffin amendments, 73 Stat. 519, to assure that minority voices are heard as they are in the functioning of a democratic institution. Third, we have held, by the very nature of the exclusive bargaining representative's status as representative of all unit employees, Congress implicitly imposed upon it a duty fairly and in good faith to represent the interests of minorities within the unit. . . . And the Board has taken the position that a union's refusal to process grievances against racial discrimination, in violation of that duty, is an unfair labor practice. . . . Indeed, the Board has ordered a union implicated by a collective bargaining agreement in discrimination with an employer to propose specific contractual provisions to prohibit racial discrimination. . . .

## B

Against this background of long and consistent adherence to the principle of exclusive representation tempered by safeguards for the protection of minority interests, respondent urges this Court to fashion a limited exception to that principle; employees who seek to bargain separately with their employer as to the elimination of racially discriminatory

---

[13] In introducing the bill that became the NLRA, Senator Wagner said of the provisions establishing majority rule, "Without them the phrase 'collective bargaining' is devoid of meaning, and the very few unfair employers are encouraged to divide their workers against themselves." 79 Cong. Rec. 2371, I Leg. Hist. of the NLRA 1313 (1935).

employment practices peculiarly affecting them,[15] should be free from the constraints of the exclusivity principle of § 9(a). Essentially because established procedures under Title VII or, as in this case, a grievance machinery, are too time-consuming, the national labor policy against discrimination requires this exception, respondent argues, and its adoption would not unduly compromise the legitimate interests of either unions or employers.[16]

Plainly, national labor policy embodies the principles of nondiscrimination as a matter of highest priority, *Alexander* v. *Gardner-Denver Co.,* 415 U.S. 36, 47, 7 FEP Cases 81 (1974), and it is a commonplace that we must construe the NLRA in light of the broad national labor policy of which it is a part. . . . These general principles do not aid respondent, however, as it is far from clear that separate bargaining is necessary to help eliminate discrimination. Indeed, as the facts of this case demonstrate, the proposed remedy might have just the opposite effect. The collective-bargaining agreement in this case prohibited without qualification all manner of invidious discrimination and made any claimed violation a grievable issue. The grievance procedure is directed precisely at determining whether discrimination has occurred. That orderly determination, if affirmative, could lead to an arbitral award enforceable in court. Nor is there any reason to believe that the processing of grievances is inherently limited to the correction of individual cases of discrimination. Quite apart from the essentially contractual question of whether the Union could grieve against a "pattern or practice" it deems inconsistent with the nondiscrimination clause of the contract, one would hardly expect an employer to continue in effect an employment practice that routinely results in adverse arbitral decisions.[19]

[15] As respondent conceded at oral argument, the rule it espouses here would necessarily have equal application to any identifiable group of employees—racial or religious groups, women, etc.—that reasonably believed themselves to be the object of invidious discrimination by their employer. Tr. of Oral Arg. 30-31. As seemingly limited by the Court of Appeals, however, such a group would have to give their elected representative an opportunity to adjust the matter in some way before resorting to self-help.

[16] Our analysis of respondent's argument in favor of the exception makes it unnecessary either to accept or reject its factual predicate, viz. that the procedures now established for the elimination of discrimination in employment are too cumbersome to be effective. We note, however, that the present record provides no support for the proposition. Thus, while respondent stresses the fact that Hollins and Hawkins had brought their evidence of discrimination to the Union in April 1968 but did not resort to self-help until the following October, it overlooks the fact that although they had been in contact with the state FEPC they did not file a charge with that agency or the EEOC. Further, when they abandoned the procedures to which the Union was bound because they thought "the Union was sort of putting us off and on and was going into a lot of delay that we felt was unnecessary," App. 26, it was at the very moment that the Adjustment Board had been convened to hear their testimony.

[19] "The processing of disputes through the grievance machinery is actually a vehicle by which meaning and content are given to the collective bargaining agreement," *United Steelworkers of America* v. *Warrior & Gulf Navigation Co.,* 363 U.S. 574, 581, 46 LRRM 2416 (1960); hence "the common law of the shop." *Id.,* at 580, quoting Cox, *Reflections Upon Labor Arbitration,* 72 HARV. L. REV. 1482, 1489 (1959).

The remarks of Union Secretary-Treasurer Johnson in response to the suggestion that the Union abandon the grievance-arbitration avenue in favor of economic

The decision by a handful of employees to bypass the grievance procedure in favor of attempting to bargain with their employer, by contrast,
may or may not be predicated upon the actual existence of discrimination.
An employer confronted with bargaining demands from each of several
minority groups would not necessarily, or even probably, be able to agree
to remedial steps satisfactory to all at once. Competing claims on the
employer's ability to accommodate each group's demands, e.g., for reas-
signments and promotions to a limited number of positions, could only
set one group against the other even if it is not the employer's intention
to divide and overcome them. Having divided themselves, the minority
employees will not be in position to advance their cause unless it be by
recourse *seriatim* to economic coercion, which can only have the effect of
further dividing them along racial or other lines.[20] Nor is the situation
materially different where, as apparently happened here, self-designated
representatives purport to speak for all groups that might consider themselves to be victims of discrimination. Even if in actual bargaining the
various groups did not perceive their interests as divergent and further
subdivide themselves, the employer would be bound to bargain with them
in a field largely preempted by the current collective-bargaining agreement with the elected bargaining representative. In this case we do not
know precisely what form the demands advanced by Hollins, Hawkins,
et al. would take, but the nature of the grievance that motivated them
indicates that the demand would have included the transfer of some
minority employees to sales areas in which higher commissions were
paid.[21] Yet the collective-bargaining agreement provided that no employee
would be transferred from a higher-paying to a lower-paying classification
except by consent or in the course of a layoff or reduction in force. The
potential for conflict between the minority and other employees in this
situation is manifest. With each group able to enforce its conflicting
demands—the incumbent employees by resort to contractual processes
and the minority employees by economic coercion—the probability of
strife and deadlock, is high; the likelihood of making headway against
discriminatory practices would be minimal. . . .

---

coercion are indicative. "I informed them," he testified, "what an individual wanted
to do on their own they could do, but I wasn't going to engage in any drama, but I
wanted some orderly legal procedures that would have some long lasting effect."
192 N.L.R.B., at 182.

[20] The Company's Employer Information Report EEO-1 to the EEOC for the period
during which this dispute arose indicates that it had employees in every minority
group for which information was required. Among sales workers alone it recorded
male and female employees who were Negro, Oriental, and Spanish-surnamed. Court
of Appeals App. 230. In addition, the Union took the position that older employees
were also being discriminated against.

[21] At the Board hearing Hollins and Hawkins advanced as a basis for their belief
that the Company was discriminating in assignments and promotions their own survey, "Briefing on Conditions, The Case of No Black or Minority Such as, Chinese,
Filipino, or Any Others in High Commission Areas," Gen. Counsel Ex. 10, Court of
Appeals App. 167, 169. This document reproduced in part in this Court, states,
"We demand selling personnel of the following Racial groups to be infiltrated into
the following high commission selling areas. Black, Mexicans, Chinese, Filipinos,
etc." A number of such departments of the store is then listed. App. 18.

What has been said here in evaluating respondent's claim that the policy against discrimination requires § 7 protection for concerted efforts at minority bargaining has obvious implications for the related claim that legitimate employer and union interests would not be unduly compromised thereby. The court below minimized the impact on the Union in this case by noting that it was not working at cross-purposes with the dissents, and that indeed it could not do so consistent with its duty of fair representation and perhaps its obligations under Title VII. As to the Company, its obligations under Title VII are cited for the proposition that it could have no legitimate objection to bargaining with the dissidents in order to achieve full compliance with that law.

This argument confuses the employees' substantive right to be free of racial discrimination with the procedures available under the NLRA for securing these rights. Whether they are thought to depend upon Title VII or have an independent source in the NLRA, they cannot be pursued at the expense of the orderly collective-bargaining process contemplated by the NLRA. The elimination of discrimination and its vestiges is an appropriate subject of bargaining, and an employer may have no objection to incorporating into a collective bargaining agreement the substance of his obligation not to discriminate in personnel decisions; the Company here has done as much, making any claimed dereliction a matter subject to the grievance-arbitration machinery as well as to the processes of Title VII. But that does not mean that he may not have strong and legitimate objections to bargaining on several fronts over the implementation of the right to be free of discrimination for some of the reasons set forth above. Similarly, while a union cannot lawfully bargain for the establishment or continuation of discriminatory practices, . . . it has a legitimate interest in presenting a united front on this as on other issues and in not seeing its strength dissipated and its statute denigrated by sub-groups within the unit separately pursuing what they see as separate interests. When union and employer are not responsive to their legal obligations, the bargain they have struck must yield *pro tanto* to the law, whether by means of conciliation through the offices of the EEOC, or by means of federal court enforcement at the instance of either that agency or the party claiming to be aggrieved.

Accordingly, we think neither aspect of respondent's contention in support of a right to short-circuit orderly, established processes for eliminating discrimination in employment is well-founded. The policy of industrial self-determination as expressed in § 7 does not require fragmentation of the bargaining unit along racial or other lines in order to consist with the national labor policy against discrimination. And in the face of such fragmentation, whatever its effect on discriminatory practices, the bargaining process that the principle of exclusive representation is means to lubricate could not endure unhampered.

III. Even if the NLRA, when read in the context of the general policy against discrimination, does not sanction these employees' attempt to bargain with the Company, it is contended that it must do so if a specific element of that policy is to be preserved. The element in question is the congressional policy of protecting from employer reprisal employee efforts to oppose unlawful discrimination, as expressed in § 704(a) of Title VII. . . . Since the discharged employees here had, by their own lights, "opposed" discrimination, it is argued that their activities "fell plainly within the scope of," and their discharges therefore violated, § 704(a).[24] The notion here is that if the discharges did not also violate § 8(a)(1) of NLRA, then the integrity of § 704(a) will be seriously undermined. We cannot agree.

Even assuming that § 704(a) protects employees' picketing and instituting a consumer boycott of their employer,[25] the same conduct is not necessarily entitled to affirmative protection from the NLRA. Under the scheme of that Act, conduct which is not protected concerted activity may lawfully form the basis for the participants' discharge. That does not mean that the discharge is immune from attack on other statutory grounds in an appropriate case. If the discharges in this case are violative of § 704(a) of Title VII, the remedial provisions of that title provide the means by which Hollins and Hawkins may recover their jobs with back pay, 42 U.S.C. § 2000e-5(g).

Respondent objects that reliance on the remedies provided by Title VII is inadequate effectively to secure the rights conferred by Title VII. There are indeed significant differences between proceedings initiated under Title VII and an unfair labor practice proceeding. Congress chose to encourage voluntary compliance with Title VII by emphasizing conciliatory procedures before federal coercive powers could be invoked. Even then it did not provide the EEOC with the power of direct enforcement, but

[24] This argument as advanced by respondent is somewhat weakened by its context of insistence that the discharged employees were not seeking to bargain with the Company. The same argument is made in the amicus curiae brief of the National Association for the Advancement of Colored People on the assumption, however, that bargaining—over the issue of racial discrimination alone—was their objective. In light of our declination to upset the finding to that effect, we take the argument as the amicus makes it. NAACP Br. 9-14.

[25] The question of whether § 704(a) is applicable to the facts of this case is not as free from doubt as the respondent and amicus would have it. In its brief the NLRB argues that § 704(a) is directed at protecting access to the EEOC and federal courts. Pettway v. American Cast Iron Pipe Co., 411 F.2d 998, 71 LRRM 2347, 1 FEP Cases 752 (CA5 1969). We have previously had occasion to note that "[n]othing in Title VII compels an employer to absolve and rehire one who has engaged in . . . deliberate, unlawful activity against it." McDonnell Douglas Corp. v. Green, 411 U.S. 792, 803, 5 FEP Cases 965, 969 (1973). Whether the protection afforded by § 704(a) extends only to the right of access or well beyond it, however, is not a question properly presented by this case. Nor is it an appropriate question to be answered in the first instance by the NLRB. Questions arising under Title VII must be resolved by the means that Congress provided for that purpose.

In the course of arguing for affirmance of the decision below, under which the NLRB would be called upon to evaluate the effectiveness of a union's efforts to oppose employer discrimination in the bargaining unit, respondent takes the position that the Board is well-equipped by reason of experience and perspective to play a major role in the process of eliminating discrimination in employment. The Board-enforced duty of fair representation, it is noted, has already exposed it to the problems that inhere in detecting and deterring racial discrimination within unions. What is said above does not call into question either the capacity or the propriety of the Board's sensitivity to questions of discrimination. It pertains, rather, to the proper allocation of a particular function—adjudication of claimed violations of Title VII—that Congress has assigned elsewhere.

made the federal courts available to the agency or individual to secure compliance with Title VII. See *Alexander* v. *Gardner-Denver Co., supra,* 415 U.S., at 44-45. 7 FEP Cases at 84. By contrast, once the General Counsel of the NLRB decides to issue a complaint, vindication of the charging party's statutory rights becomes a public function discharged at public expense, and a favorable decision by the Board brings forth an administrative order. As a result of these and other differences, we are told that relief is typically available to the party filing a charge with the NLRB in a significantly shorter time, and with less risk, than obtains for one filing a charge with the EEOC.

Whatever its factual merit, this argument is properly addressed to the Congress and not to this Court or the NLRB. In order to hold that employer conduct violates §8(a)(1) of the NLRA *because* it violates § 704(a) of Title VII, we would have to override a host of consciously made decisions well within the exclusive competence of the legislature. This obviously, we cannot do.

*Reversed.*

MR. JUSTICE DOUGLAS, dissenting.

The Court's opinion makes these union members—and others similarly situated—prisoners of the union. The law, I think, was designed to prevent that tragic consequence. Hence, I dissent.

. . .

The law should facilitate the involvement of unions in the quest for racial equality in employment, but it should not make the individual a prisoner of the union. While employees may reasonably be required to approach the union first, as a kind of "exhaustion" requirement before resorting to economic protest, cf. *NLRB* v. *Tanner Motor Livery,* 419 F.2d 216, 72 LRRM 2866 (CA9 1969), they should not be under continued inhibition when it becomes apparent that the union response is inadequate. The Court of Appeals held that the employees should be protected from discharge unless the Board found on remand that the union had been prosecuting their complaints "to the fullest extent possible, by the most expeditious means." I would not disturb this standard. Union conduct can be oppressive even if not made in bad faith. The inertia of weak-kneed, docile union leadership can be as devastating to the cause of racial equality as aggressive subversion. Continued submission by employees to such a regime should not be demanded.

I would affirm the judgment below.

## NOTE

See *NLRB* v. *Owners Maintenance,* 581 F.2d 44 (2nd Cir. 1978).

In a case not dealing with any Title VII issues, the court discussed and distinguished *Emporium Capwell.* The case dealt with two employees who were fired because they were alleged to have made false statements on their employment applications. After filing grievances, the two employees distributed leaflets on the sidewalk in front of the employer's entrance. This activity was found to be protected activity. The court said that in *Emporium* the employer "repudiated" the grievance process, while in the case before the court, "the goal of the leafletting campaign was not separate bargaining but the enlistment of support for the employees' rights in the grievance proceeding."

## E.   INTEGRATION OF ARBITRATION WITH STATUTORY REMEDIES

### ALEXANDER v. GARDNER-DENVER CO.

*Supreme Court of the United States, 1974*
*415 U.S. 36, 7 FEP Cases 81*

MR. JUSTICE POWELL delivered the opinion of the Court.

This case concerns the proper relationship between federal courts and the grievance-arbitration machinery of collective-bargaining agreements in the resolution and enforcement of an individual's rights to equal employment opportunities under Title VII of the Civil Rights Act of 1964, 42 U.S.C. § 2000e *et seq.* Specifically, we must decide under what circumstances, if any, an employee's statutory right to a trial *de novo* under Title VII may be foreclosed by prior submission of his claim to final arbitration under the nondiscrimination clause of a collective-bargaining agreement.

I.   In May 1966, petitioner Harrell Alexander, Sr., a black, was hired by respondent Gardner-Denver Company (the "company") to perform maintenance work at the company's plant in Denver, Colorado. In June 1968, petitioner was awarded a trainee position as a drill operator. He remained at that job until his discharge from employment on September 29, 1969. The company informed petitioner that he was being discharged for producing too many defective or unusable parts that had to be scrapped.

On October 1, 1969, petitioner filed a grievance under the collective-bargaining agreement in force between the company and petitioner's union, Local No. 3029 of the United Steelworkers of America (the "union"). The grievance stated: "I feel I have been unjustly discharged and ask that I be reinstated with full seniority and pay." No explicit claim of racial discrimination was made.

Under Art. 4 of the collective-bargaining agreement, the company retained "the right to hire, suspend or discharge [employees] for proper cause." Art. 5, § 2 provided, however, that "there shall be no discrimination against any employee on account of race, color, religion, sex, national origin, or ancestry," and Art. 23, § 6(a) stated that "[n]o employee will be discharged, suspended or given a written warning notice except for just cause." The agreement also contains a broad arbitration clause covering "differences aris[ing] between the Company and the Union as to the meaning and application of the provisions of this Agreement" and "any trouble aris[ing] in the plant." Disputes were to be submitted to a multistep grievance procedure, the first four steps of which involved negotiations between the company and the union. If the dispute remained unresolved, it was to be remitted to compulsory arbitration. The company and the union were to select and pay the arbitrator, and his decision was to be "final and binding upon the Company, the Union, and any employee or employees involved." The agreement further provided that "[t]he arbitrator shall not amend, take away, add to, or change any of the provisions of this Agreement, and the arbitrator's decision must be based solely on an interpretation of the provisions of this Agreement." The parties also agreed that there "shall be no suspension of work" over disputes covered by the grievance-arbitration clause.

The union processed petitioner's grievance through the above machinery. In the final prearbitration step, petitioner raised, apparently for the first time, the claim that his discharge resulted from racial discrimination. The company rejected all of petitioner's claims, and the grievance proceeded to arbitration. Prior to the arbitration hearing, however, petitioner filed a charge of racial discrimination with the Colorado Civil Rights Commission, which referred the complaint to the Equal Employment Opportunity Commission on November 5, 1969.

At the arbitration hearing on November 20, 1969, petitioner testified that his discharge was the result of racial discrimination and informed the arbitrator that he had filed a charge with the Colorado Commission because he "could not rely on the union." The union introduced a letter in which petitioner stated that he was "knowledgeable that in the same plant others have scrapped an equal amount and sometimes in excess, but by all logical reasoning I . . . have been the target of preferential discriminatory treatment." The union representative also testified that the company's usual practice was to transfer unsatisfactory trainee drill operators back to their former positions.

On December 30, 1969, the arbitrator ruled that petitioner had been "discharged for just cause." He made no reference to petitioner's claim of racial discrimination. The arbitrator stated that the union had failed to produce evidence of a practice of transferring rather than discharging trainee drill operators who accumulated excessive scrap, but he suggested that the company and the union confer on whether such an arrangement was feasible in the present case.

On July 25, 1970, the Equal Employment Opportunity Commission determined that there was not reasonable cause to believe that a violation of Title VII of the Civil Rights Act of 1964, 42 U.S.C. § 2000e et seq., had occurred. The Commission later notified petitioner of his right to institute a civil action in .federal court within 30 days. Petitioner then filed the present action in the United States District Court for the District of Colorado, alleging that his discharge resulted from a racially discriminatory employment practice in violation of § 703(a)(1) of the Act. See 42 U.S.C. § 2000e-2(a)(1).

The District Court granted respondent's motion for summary judgment and dismissed the action. 346 F.Supp. 1012, 4 FEP Cases 1205 (1971). The court found that the claim of racial discrimination had been submitted to the arbitrator and resolved adversely to petitioner.[4] It then held that petitioner, having voluntarily elected to pursue his grievance to final arbitration under the nondiscrimination clause of the collective-bargaining agreement, was bound by the arbitral decision and thereby precluded from suing his employer under Title VII. The Court of Appeals for the Tenth Circuit affirmed *per curiam* on the basis of the District Court's opinion. 466 F.2d 1209, 4 FEP Cases 1210 (1972).

We granted petitioner's application for certiorari. 410 U.S. 925 (1973). We reverse.

II. Congress enacted Title VII of the Civil Rights Act of 1964, 42 U.S.C. § 2000e *et seq.*, to assure equality of employment opportunities by eliminating those practices and devices that discriminate on the basis of race, color, religion, sex or national origin. *McDonnell Douglas Corp.* v. *Green,* 411 U.S. 792, 800, 5 FEP Cases 965 (1973); *Griggs* v. *Duke Power Co.,* 401 U.S. 424, 429-430, 3 FEP Cases 175 (1971). Cooperation and voluntary compliance were selected as the preferred means for achieving this goal. To this end, Congress created the Equal Employment Opportunity Commission and established a procedure whereby existing State and local equal employment opportunity agencies, as well as the Commission, would have an opportunity to settle disputes through conference, conciliation, and persuasion before the aggrieved party was permitted to file a lawsuit. In the Equal Employment Opportunity Act of 1972, Pub. L. 92-261, 86 Stat. 103, Congress amended Title VII to provide the Commission with further authority to investigate individual charges of discrimination, to promote voluntary compliance with the requirements of Title VII, and to institute civil actions against employers or unions named in a discrimination charge.

Even in its amended form, however, Title VII does not provide the Commission with direct powers of enforcement. The Commission cannot adjudicate claims or impose administrative sanctions. Rather, final responsibility for enforcement of Title VII is vested with federal courts. The Act authorizes courts to issue injunctive relief and to order such affirmative action as may be appropriate to remedy the effects of unlawful employment practices. 42 U.S.C. § 2000e-5(f) and (g). Courts retain these broad remedial powers despite a Commission finding of no reasonable cause to believe that the Act has been violated. *McDonnell Douglas Corp.* v. *Green, supra,* 411 U.S., at 798-799, 5 FEP Cases 965. Taken together, these provisions make plain that federal courts have been assigned plenary powers to secure compliance with Title VII.

In addition to reposing ultimate authority in federal courts, Congress gave private individuals a significant role in the enforcement process of Title VII. Individual grievants usually initiate the Commission's investi-

---

4 [Footnotes numbered as in original.—Ed.] In reaching this conclusion, the District Court relied on petitioner's deposition acknowledging that he had raised the racial discrimination claim during the arbitration hearing. 346 F.Supp. 1012, 1014, 4 FEP Cases 1205.

gatory and conciliatory procedures. And although the 1972 amendment to Title VII empowers the Commission to bring its own actions, the private right of action remains an essential means of obtaining judicial enforcement of Title VII. 42 U.S.C. § 2000e-5(f)(1). In such cases, the private litigant not only redresses his own injury but also vindicates the important congressional policy against discriminatory employment practices. . . .

Pursuant to this statutory scheme, petitioner initiated the present action for judicial consideration of his rights under Title VII. The District Court and the Court of Appeals held, however, that petitioner was bound by the prior arbitral decision and had no right to sue under Title VII. Both courts evidently thought that this result was dictated by notions of election of remedies and waiver and by the federal policy favoring arbitration of labor disputes, as enunciated by this Court in *Textile Workers Union* v. *Lincoln Mills*, 353 U.S. 448, 40 LRRM 2113 (1957), and the *Steelworkers Trilogy*.[6] See also *Boys Markets, Inc.* v. *Retail Clerks Union*, 398 U.S. 235, 74 LRRM 2257 (1970); *Gateway Coal Co.* v. *United Mine Workers of America, et al.*, —— U.S. ——, 85 LRRM 2049 (1974). We disagree.

III. Title VII does not speak expressly to the relationship between federal courts and the grievance-arbitration machinery of collective-bargaining agreements. It does, however, vest federal courts with plenary powers to enforce the statutory requirements; and it specifies with precision the jurisdictional prerequisites that an individual must satisfy before he is entitled to institute a lawsuit. In the present case, these prerequisites were met when petitioner (1) filed timely a charge of employment discrimination with the Commission, and (2) received and acted upon the Commission's statutory notice of the right to sue. 42 U.S.C. §§ 2000e-5(b), (e), and (f). See *McDonnell Douglas Corp.* v. *Green, supra,* 411 U.S., at 798. There is no suggestion in the statutory scheme that a

---

[6] *United Steelworkers of America* v. *American Mfg. Co.*, 363 U.S. 564, 46 LRRM 2414 (1960); *United Steelworkers of America* v. *Warrior & Gulf Navigation Co.*, 363 U.S. 574, 46 LRRM 2416 (1960); *United Steelworkers of America* v. *Enterprise Wheel & Car Corp.*, 363 U.S. 593, 46 LRRM 2423 (1960). In *Textile Workers Union* v. *Lincoln Mills, supra,* this Court held that a grievance-arbitration provision of a collective-bargaining agreement could be enforced against unions and employers under § 301 of the Labor Management Relations Act, 29 U.S.C. § 185. The Court noted that the congressional policy, as embodied in § 203(d) of the LMRA, 29 U.S.C. § 173(d), was to promote industrial peace and that the grievance-arbitration provision of a collective agreement was a major factor in achieving this goal. *Id.*, at 455. In the *Steelworkers Trilogy,* the Court further advanced this policy by declaring that an order to arbitrate will not be denied "unless it may be said with positive assurance that the arbitration clause is not susceptible of an interpretation that covers the asserted dispute." *United Steelworkers of America* v. *Warrior & Gulf Navigation Co.*, 363 U.S. 564, 582-583, 46 LRRM 2414, 2419 (1960). The Court also stated that "so far as the arbitrator's decision concerns construction of the contract, the courts have no business overruling him because their interpretation of the contract is different from his." *United Steelworkers of America* v. *Enterprise Wheel & Car Corp.*, 363 U.S. 593, 599, 46 LRRM 2423, 2426 (1960). And in *Republic Steel Co.* v. *Maddox*, 379 U.S. 650, 58 LRRM 2193 (1965), the Court held that grievance-arbitration procedures of a collective bargaining agreement must be exhausted before an employee may file suit to enforce contractual rights.

For the reasons stated in Parts III, IV, and V of this opinion, we hold that the federal policy favoring arbitration does not establish that an arbitrator's resolution of a contractual claim is dispositive of a statutory claim under Title VII.

prior arbitral decision either forecloses an individual's right to sue or divests federal courts of jurisdiction.

In addition, legislative enactments in this area have long evinced a general intent to accord parallel or overlapping remedies against discrimination.[7] In the Civil Rights Act of 1964, 42 U.S.C. § 2000e et seq., Congress indicated that it considered the policy against discrimination to be of the "highest priority." Newman v. Piggie Park Enterprises, Inc., supra, 390 U.S., at 402. Consistent with this view, Title VII provides for consideration of employment-discrimination claims in several forums. See 42 U.S.C. § 2000e-5(b) (EEOC); 42 U.S.C. § 2000e-5(c) (State and local agencies); 42 U.S.C. § 2000e-5(f) (federal courts). And, in general, submission of a claim to one forum does not preclude a later submission to another.[8] See 42 U.S.C. §§ 2000e-5(b) and (f); McDonnell Douglas Corp. v. Green, supra. Moreover, the legislative history of Title VII manifests a congressional intent to allow an individual to pursue independently his rights under both Title VII and other applicable state and federal statutes. The clear inference is that Title VII was designed to supplement, rather than supplant, existing laws and institutions relating to employment discrimination. In sum, Title VII's purpose and procedures strongly suggest that an individual does not forfeit his private cause of action if he first pursues his grievance to final arbitration under the nondiscrimination clause of a collective-bargaining agreement.

In reaching the opposite conclusion, the District Court relied in part on the doctrine of election of remedies. That doctrine, which refers to situations where an individual pursues remedies that are legally or factually inconsistent, has no application in the present context. In submitting his grievance to arbitration, an employee seeks to vindicate his contractual right under a collective-bargaining agreement. By contrast, in filing a lawsuit under Title VII, an employee asserts independent statutory rights accorded by Congress. The distinctly separate nature of these contractual and statutory rights is not vitiated merely because both were violated as a result of the same factual occurrence. And certainly no inconsistency results from permitting both rights to be enforced in their respectively appropriate forums. The resulting scheme is somewhat analogous to the procedure under the National Labor Relations Act as amended, where disputed transactions may implicate both contractual and statutory rights. Where the statutory right underlying a particular claim may not be abridged by contractual agreement, the Court has recognized that consideration of the claim by the arbitrator as a contractual dispute under the collective-bargaining agreement does not preclude subsequent consideration of the claim by the National Labor Relations Board as an unfair labor practice charge or as a petition for clarification of the union's

---

[7] See, e.g., 42 U.S.C. § 1981 (Civil Rights Act of 1866); 42 U.S.C § 1983 (Civil Rights Act of 1871).

[8] For example, Commission action is not barred by "findings and orders" of state or local agencies. See 42 U.S.C. §2000e-5(b). Similarly, an individual's cause of action is not barred by a Commission finding of no reasonable cause to believe that the Act has been violated. See 42 U.S.C. § 2000e-5(f); McDonnell Douglas Corp. v. Green, supra.

representation certificate under the Act. *Carey* v. *Westinghouse Corp.*, 375 U.S. 261, 55 LRRM 2042 (1964). Cf. *Smith* v. *Evening News Assn.*, 371 U.S. 195, 51 LRRM 2646 (1962). There, as here, the relationship between the forums is complementary since consideration of the claim by both forums may promote the policies underlying each. Thus, the rationale behind the election of remedies doctrine cannot support the decision below.[14]

We are also unable to accept the proposition that petitioner waived his cause of action under Title VII. To begin, we think it clear that there can be no prospective waiver of an employee's rights under Title VII. It is true, of course, that a union may waive certain statutory rights related to collective activity, such as the right to strike. *Mastro Plastics Corp.* v. *NLRB*, 350 U.S. 270, 37 LRRM 2587 (1956); *Boys Markets, Inc.* v. *Retail Clerks Union*, 398 U.S. 235, 74 LRRM 2257 (1970). These rights are conferred on employees collectively to foster the processes of bargaining and properly may be exercised or relinquished by the union as collective-bargaining agent to obtain economic benefits for unit members. Title VII, on the other hand, stands on plainly different ground; it concerns not majoritarian process, but an individual's right to equal employment opportunities. Title VII's strictures are absolute and represent a congressional command that each employee be free from discriminatory practices. Of necessity, the rights conferred can form no part of the collective-bargaining process since waiver of these rights would defeat the paramount congressional purpose behind Title VII. In these circumstances, an employee's rights under Title VII are not susceptible to prospective waiver. . . .

The actual submission of petitioner's grievance to arbitration in the present case does not alter the situation. Although presumably an employee may waive his cause of action under Title VII as part of a voluntary settlement,[15] mere resort to the arbitral forum to enforce contractual rights constitutes no such waiver. Since an employee's rights under Title VII may not be waived prospectively, existing contractual rights and remedies against discrimination must result from other concessions already made by the union as part of the economic bargain struck with the em-

---

[14] Nor can it be maintained that election of remedies is required by the possibility of unjust enrichment through duplicative recoveries. Where, as here, the employer has prevailed at arbitration, there of course can be no duplicative recovery. But even in cases where the employee has first prevailed, judicial relief can be structured to avoid such windfall gains. See, e.g., *Oubichon* v. *North American Rockwell Corp.*, 482 F.2d 569, 6 FEP Cases 171 (CA9 1973); *Bowe* v. *Colgate-Palmolive Co.*, 416 F.2d 711, 2 FEP Cases 121 (CA7 1971). Furthermore, if the relief obtained by the employee at arbitration were fully equivalent to that obtainable under Title VII, there would be no further relief for the court to grant and hence no need for the employee to institute suit.

[15] In this case petitioner and respondent did not enter into a voluntary settlement expressly conditioned on a waiver of petitioner's cause of action under Title VII. In determining the effectiveness of any such waiver, a court would have to determine at the outset that the employee's consent to the settlement was voluntary and knowing. In no event can the submission to arbitration of a claim under the nondiscrimination clause of a collective-bargaining agreement constitute a binding waiver with respect to an employee's rights under Title VII.

ployer. It is settled law that no additional concession may be exacted from any employee as the price for enforcing those rights. *J. I. Case Co.* v. *Labor Board*, 321 U.S. 332, 338-339, 14 LRRM 501 (1944).

Moreover, a contractual right to submit a claim to arbitration is not displaced simply because Congress also has provided a statutory right against discrimination. Both rights have legally independent origins and are equally available to the aggrieved employee. This point becomes apparent through consideration of the role of the arbitrator in the system of industrial self-government.

As the proctor of the bargain, the arbitrator's task is to effectuate the intent of the parties. His source of authority is the collective-bargaining agreement, and he must interpret and apply that agreement in accordance with the "industrial common law of the shop" and the various needs and desires of the parties. The arbitrator, however, has no general authority to invoke public laws that conflict with the bargain between the parties:

"[A]n arbitrator is confined to interpretation and application of the collective bargaining agreement; he does not sit to dispense his own brand of industrial justice. He may of course look for guidance from many sources, yet his award is legitimate only so long as it draws its essence from the collective bargaining agreement. When the arbitrator's words manifest an infidelity to his obligation, courts have no choice but to refuse enforcement of the award." *United Steelworkers of America* v. *Enterprise Wheel & Car Corp.*, 363 U.S., at 597, 46 LRRM, at 2425.

If an arbitral decision is based "solely on the arbitrator's view of the requirements of enacted legislation," rather than on an interpretation of the collective-bargaining agreement, the arbitrator has "exceeded the scope of his submission," and the award will not be enforced. *Ibid*. Thus the arbitrator has authority to resolve questions of contractual rights, and this authority remains regardless whether certain contractual rights are similar to, or duplicative of, the substantive rights secured by Title VII.

IV. The District Court and the Court of Appeals reasoned that to permit an employee to have his claim considered in both the arbitral and judicial forums would be unfair since this would mean that the employer, but not the employee, was bound by the arbitral award. In the District Court's words, it could not "accept a philosophy which gives the employee two strings to his bow when the employer has only one." 346 F.Supp., at 1019, 4 FEP Cases, at 1209. This argument mistakes the effect of Title VII. Under the *Steelworker's Trilogy,* an arbitral decision is final and binding on the employer and employee, and judicial review is limited as to both. But in instituting an action under Title VII, the employee is not seeking review of the arbitrator's decision. Rather, he is asserting a statutory right independent of the arbitration process. An employer does not have "two strings to his bow" with respect to an arbitral decision for the simple reason that Title VII does not provide employers with a cause of action against employees. An employer cannot be the victim of discriminatory employment practices. *Oubichon* v. *North American Rockwell Corp.*, 482 F.2d 569, 573, 6 FEP Cases 171 (CA9 1973).

The District Court and the Court of Appeals also thought that to permit a later resort to the judicial forum would undermine substantially the employer's incentive to arbitrate and would "sound the death knell for arbitration clauses in labor contracts." 346 F.Supp., at 1019, 4 FEP Cases, at 1209. Again, we disagree. The primary incentive for an employer to enter into an arbitration agreement is the union's reciprocal promise not to strike. . . . It is not unreasonable to assume that most employers will regard the benefits derived from a no-strike pledge as outweighing whatever costs may result from according employees an arbitral remedy against discrimination in addition to their judicial remedy under Title VII. Indeed, the severe consequences of a strike may make an arbitration clause almost essential from both the employees and the employer's perspective. Moreover, the grievance-arbitration machinery of the collective-bargaining agreement remains a relatively inexpensive and expeditious means for resolving a wide range of disputes, including claims of discriminatory employment practices. Where the collective-bargaining agreement contains a nondiscrimination clause similar to Title VII, and where arbitral procedures are fair and regular, arbitration may well produce a settlement satisfactory to both employer and employee. An employer thus has an incentive to make available the conciliatory and therapeutic process of arbitration which may satisfy an employee's perceived need to resort to the judicial forum, thus saving the employer the expense and aggravation associated with a lawsuit. For similar reasons, the employee also has a strong incentive to arbitrate grievances, and arbitration may often eliminate those misunderstandings or discriminatory practices that might otherwise precipitate resort to the judicial forum.

V. Respondent contends that even if a preclusion rule is not adopted, federal courts should defer to arbitral decisions on discrimination claims where: (i) the claim was before the arbitrator; (ii) the collective-bargaining agreement prohibited the form of discrimination charged in the suit under Title VII; and (iii) the arbitrator has authority to rule on the claim and to fashion a remedy.[17] Under respondent's proposed rule, a court would grant summary judgment and dismiss the employee's action if the above conditions were met. The rule's obvious consequence in the present case would be to deprive the petitioner of his statutory right to attempt to establish his claim in a federal court.

At the outset, it is apparent that a deferral rule would be subject to many of the objections applicable to a preclusion rule. The purpose and procedures of Title VII indicate that Congress intended federal courts to exercise final responsibility for enforcement of Title VII; deferral to arbitral decisions would be inconsistent with that goal. Furthermore, we have long recognized that "the choice of forums inevitably affects the scope of the substantive right to be vindicated." *U.S. Bulk Carriers* v. *Arguelles*, 400 U.S. 358, 359-360, 76 LRRM 2161, 2164 (1971) (Harlan, J., concur-

---

[17] Brief of Respondent, at 37. Respondent's proposed rule is analogous to the NLRB's policy of deferring to arbitral decisions on statutory issues in certain cases. See *Spielberg Manufacturing Co.*, 112 NLRB 1080, 1082, 36 LRRM 1152 (1955).

ring). Respondent's deferral rule is necessarily premised on the assumption that arbitral processes are commensurate with judicial processes and that Congress impliedly intended federal courts to defer to arbitral decisions on Title VII issues. We deem this supposition unlikely.

Arbitral procedures, while well suited to the resolution of contractual disputes, makes arbitration a comparatively inappropriate forum for the final resolution of rights created by Title VII. This conclusion rests first on the special role of the arbitrator, whose task is to effectuate the intent of the parties rather than the requirements of enacted legislation. Where the collective-bargaining agreement conflicts with Title VII, the arbitration must follow the agreement. To be sure, the tension between contractual and statutory objectives may be mitigated where a collective-bargaining agreement contains provisions facially similar to those of Title VII. But other facts may still render arbitral processes comparatively inferior to judicial processes in the protection of Title VII rights. Among these is the fact that the specialized competence of arbitrators pertains primarily to the law of the shop, not the law of the land. . . . Parties usually choose an arbitrator because they trust his knowledge and judgment concerning the demands and norms of industrial relations. On the other hand, the resolution of statutory or constitutional issues is a primary responsibility of courts, and judicial construction has proven especially necessary with respect to Title VII, whose broad language frequently can be given meaning only by reference to public law concepts.

Moreover, the fact-finding process in arbitration usually is not equivalent to judicial fact-finding. The record of the arbitration proceedings is not as complete; the usual rules of evidence do not apply; and rights and procedures common to civil trials, such as discovery, compulsory process, cross-examination, and testimony under oath, are often severely limited or unavailable. . . . And as this Court has recognized, "[a]rbitrators have no obligation to the court to give their reasons for an award." *United Steelworkers of America* v. *Enterprise Wheel & Car Corp.*, 363 U.S. 593, at 598, 46 LRRM 2423, at 2425. Indeed, it is the informality of arbitral procedure that enables it to function as an efficient, inexpensive, and expeditious means for dispute resolution. This same characteristic, however, makes arbitration a less appropriate forum for final resolution of Title VII issues than the federal courts.[19]

---

[19] A further concern is the union's exclusive control over the manner and extent to which an individual grievance is presented. See *Vaca* v. *Sipes*, 386 U.S. 171, 64, LRRM 2369 (1967); *Republic Steel Co.* v. *Maddox*, 379 U.S. 650, 58 LRRM 2193 (1965). In arbitration, as in the collective-bargaining process, the interests of the individual employee may be subordinated to the collective interests of all employees in the bargaining unit. See *J. I. Case Co.* v. *Labor Board*, 321 U.S. 332, 14 LRRM 501 (1944). Moreover, harmony in interest between the union and the individual employee cannot always be presumed, especially where a claim of racial discrimination is made. See, e.g., *Steele* v. *Louisville & N. R. Co.*, 323 U.S. 192, 15 LRRM 708 (1944); *Tunstall* v. *Brotherhood of Locomotive Firemen*, 323 U.S. 210, 15 LRRM 715 (1944). And a breach of the union's duty of fair representation may prove difficult to establish. See *Vaca* v. *Sipes, supra; Humphrey* v. *Moore,* 375 U.S. 335, 342, 348-351, 55 LRRM 2031. In this respect, it is noteworthy that Congress thought it necessary to afford the protections of Title VII against unions as well as employers. See 52 U.S.C. $ 2000e-(c).

It is evident that respondent's proposed rule would not allay these concerns. Nor are we convinced that the solution lies in applying a more demanding deferral standard, such as that adopted by the Fifth Circuit in *Rios* v. *Reynolds Metals Co.,* 467 F.2d 54, 5 FEP Cases 1 (1972).[20] As respondent points out, a standard that adequately insured effectuation of Title VII rights in the arbitral forum would tend to make arbitration a procedurally complex, expensive, and time-consuming process. And judicial enforcement of such a standard would almost require courts to make *de novo* determinations of the employees' claims. It is uncertain whether any minimal savings in judicial time and expense would justify the risk to vindication of Title VII rights.

A deferral rule also might adversely affect the arbitration system as well as the enforcement scheme of Title VII. Fearing that the arbitral forum cannot adequately protect their rights under Title VII, some employees may elect to bypass arbitration and institute a lawsuit. The possibility of voluntary compliance or settlement of Title VII claims would thus be reduced, and the result could well be more litigation, not less.

We think, therefore, that the federal policy favoring arbitration of labor disputes and the federal policy against discriminatory employment practices can best be accommodated by permitting an employee to pursue fully both his remedy under the grievance-arbitration clause of a collective-bargaining agreement and his cause of action under Title VII. The federal court should consider the employee's claim *de novo*. The arbitral decision may be admitted as evidence and accorded such weight as the court deems appropriate.[21]

The judgment of the Court of Appeals is                           *Reversed.*

[20] In *Rios*, the court set forth the following deferral standard:
"First, there may be no deference to the decision of the arbitrator unless the contractual right coincides with rights under Title VII. Second, it must be plain that the arbitrator's decision is in no way violative of the private rights guaranteed by Title VII, nor of the public policy which inheres in Title VII. In addition, before deferring, the district court must be satisfied that (1) the factual issues before it are identical to those decided by the arbitrator; (2) the arbitrator had power under the collective agreement to decide the ultimate issue of discrimination; (3) the evidence presented at the arbitral hearing dealt adequately with all factual issues; (4) the arbitrator actually decided the factual issues presented to the court; (5) the arbitration proceeding was fair and regular and free of procedural infirmities. The burden of proof in establishing these conditions of limitation will be upon the respondent as distinguished from the claimant." 467 F.2d, at 58, 5 FEP Cases, at 4. For a discussion of the problems posed by application of the Rios standard, see Note, *Judicial Deference to Arbitrators' Decisions in Title VII Cases,* 26 STAN. L. REV. 421 (1974).

[21] We adopt no standards as to the weight to be accorded an arbitral decision, since this must be determined in the court's discretion with regard to the facts and circumstances of each case. Relevant factors include the existence of provisions in the collective-bargaining agreement that conform substantially with Title VII, the degree of procedural fairness in the arbitral forum, adequacy of the record with respect to the issue of discrimination, and the special competence of particular arbitrators. Where an arbitral determination gives full consideration to an employee's Title VII rights, a court may properly accord it great weight. This is especially true where the issue is solely one of fact, specifically addressed by the parties and decided by the arbitrator on the basis of an adequate record. But courts should ever be mindful that Congress, in enacting Title VII, thought it necessary to provide a judicial forum for the ultimate resolution of discriminatory employment claims. It is the duty of courts to assure the full availability of this forum.

## NOTE

1. *Collyer Insulated Wire,* 192 NLRB 837 (1971), is the leading case on the NLRB's deferral to an arbitrator's decision in a case that also arguably violated a labor statute. The Board felt it was consistent with federal law to allow the matter to be directed by the grievance machinery. Is this consistent with *Gardner-Denver?* The Supreme Court favorably discussed the *Collyer* case in dictum in a case decided after *Gardner-Denver.* See *William E. Arnold Co.* v. *Carpenters District Council,* 417 U.S. 12, 16-17 (1974). The Court seemed not to notice any problem with *Gardner-Denver.*

Is there some reason Title VII claims should be treated differently from claims under the National Labor Relations Act? Does *Gardner-Denver's* discussion of the special nature of Title VII claims provide the answer?

2. If the courts are to decide Title VII questions, should any weight be given to the arbitrator's decision? Reconsider footnote 21. Should the arbitrator's expertise in handling Title VII claims make any difference?

3. Suppose a group of minority employees bring an employment discrimination action against their employer. The employer, the employees, and the union enter into a consent decree. The decree states that any disputes as to interpretation are to be settled by an arbitrator. A dispute arises and the arbitrator rules against the employees. Under *Gardner-Denver,* should the employees be able to receive a new interpretation of the decree in court? See *Eaton* v. *Courtaulds of North America, Inc.,* 578 F.2d 87 (5th Cir. 1978). Note especially footnote 1.

4. The rationale of *Gardner-Denver* has found application in other areas. See *Garner* v. *Giarrusso,* 571 F.2d 1330 (5th Cir. 1978) (police officer's Title VII claims of employment discrimination could be heard in district court even though they had been brought before City Civil Service Commission). Cf. *Brown* v. *GSA,* 425 U.S. 820, 12 FEP Cases 1361 (1976) (the Court per Stewart held that in claims of discrimination in federal employment, Section 717 of the Civil Rights Act of 1964 was the sole remedy available).

## TIPLER v. E. I. duPONT deNEMOURS & CO.

*United States Court of Appeals, Sixth Circuit, 1971*

*443 F.2d 125, 3 FEP Cases 540*

WILLIAM E. MILLER, Circuit Judge: This action is based on Title VII of the Civil Rights Act of 1964. It comes before us upon a discretionary appeal from a denial of appellant's motion to reconsider the Court's prior adverse ruling on a motion for summary judgment. Plaintiff-appellee, a Negro laborer who had been employed by defendant-appellant for ten years, successfully participated in a union election which ousted appellant's white foreman from a position of leadership in a 95 percent black union. Appellee and three other black employees were subsequently discharged from employment with appellant on May 5, 1967. Appellant contends that these employees were fired for cause, especially for leaving work early on the day of their discharge.

On May 8, 1967, appellee filed a Charge of Discrimination with the Equal Employment Opportunity Commission (EEOC), alleging that his discharge was racially motivated, that appellant discriminated against Negroes in both the physical conditions of employment and the opportunities for promotion, and that he had been punished for advocating his rights as an employee. After appellee amended his charge of discrimination to include general allegations of racial discrimination and the EEOC conducted an investigation, a Notice of Rights to Sue was issued on August 19, 1969, based upon the EEOC's findings of reasonable cause to believe that appellant had violated Title VII of the Civil Rights Act of 1964, 42 U.S.C. §§ 2000e *et seq.*

Two days later on May 10, 1967, appellee filed a claim for unemployment compensation with the Tennessee State Department of Employment Security. Finding that appellee was not discharged for misconduct within the meaning of the applicable Tennessee statute, the appeals tribunal of the Tennessee Employment Security Department reversed a preliminary determination and allowed appellee's claim.

On May 11, 1967, appellee filed a charge with the National Labor Relations Board (NLRB), alleging in general terms that he had been fired in violation of Sections 8(a)(1)[2] and 8(a)(3)[3] of the National Labor Relations Act. In an amended charge he specified that appellant had discharged him because of his union activities. Following an extended evidentiary hearing, the NLRB Trial Examiner found that appellee was dismissed for cause and not because of the personal vengeance of appellant's foreman, and recommended that appellee's claim be dismissed. The NLRB accepted the Trial Examiner's findings and recommendation.

Pursuant to the EEOC's authorization, appellee then filed suit in the United States District Court for the Western District of Tennessee, Western Division, seeking an injunction against future racially discriminatory practices, reinstatement and back pay, and general relief. He alleged that his discharge was based on racial motivations and his active opposition to appellant's unlawful employment practices. He further charged that appellee discriminated against Negro employees in the provision of restrooms, eating facilities, coffee breaks and opportunities for promotion, in violation of Title VII of the Civil Rights Act of 1964.

Appellant filed a motion for summary judgment on the issues of appellee's discharge, reinstatement and back pay. The motion, alleging

---

[2] [Footnotes numbered as in original.—Ed.] Section 8(a)(1) of the National Labor Relations Act reads: "(a) It shall be an unfair labor practice for an employer . . . (1) to interfere with, restrain, or coerce employees in the exercise of the rights guaranteed in section 157 of this title [dealing with the right of employees to organize and join labor organizations, to bargain collectively, etc.]" 29 U.S.C. § 158(a)(1).

[3] Section 8(a)(3) of the National Labor Relations Act reads in pertinent part: "(a) It shall be an unfair labor practice for an employer . . . (3) by discrimination in regard to hire or tenure of employment or any term or condition of employment to encourage or discourage membership in any labor organization. . . ." *Id.* § 158(a)(3).

collateral estoppel and res judicata, judicial estoppel, lack of standing, and a variance between the EEOC charge and the judicial complaint, was denied. Appeal is from the denial of a motion to reconsider.[4]

## I. COLLATERAL ESTOPPEL AND RES JUDICATA

Appellant first argues that the appellee is precluded by res judicata and collateral estoppel from asserting that he was discharged because of racial prejudice since the cause of his discharge was previously litigated by the NLRB. We do not agree.

Although frequently confused, res judicata and collateral estoppel are different theories which often lead to the same result. These rules have been distinguished in the following manner:

". . . application of the doctrine of res judicata necessitates an identity of causes of action, while the invocation of collateral estoppel does not. Each doctrine, on the other hand, requires that, as a general rule, both parties to the subsequent litigation must be bound by the prior judgment. The essence of collateral estoppel by judgment is that some question or fact in dispute has been judicially and finally determined by a court of competent juridiction between the same parties or their privies. Thus the principle of such an estoppel may be stated as follows: Where there is a second action between parties, or their privies, who are bound by a judgment rendered in a prior suit, but the second action involves a different claim, cause, or demand, the judgment in the first suit operates as a collateral estoppel as to, but only as to, those matters or points which were in issue or controverted and upon the determination of which the initial judgment necessarily depended." 1B Moore's Federal Practice ¶ 0.441[2], at 3777 (footnotes omitted).

Neither collateral estoppel nor res judicata is rigidly applied. Both rules are qualified or rejected when their application would contravene an overriding public policy or result in manifest injustice. . . .

It is now accepted that both res judicata and collateral estoppel can be applicable to decisions of administrative agencies acting in a judicial capacity. . . .

Despite the possible applicability of these doctrines to administrative decisions, in the instant action it would be inappropriate to apply either. The issue here is whether appellee's dismissal was in violation of Title VII of the Civil Rights Act of 1964. The NLRB decision, on the other hand, dealt with an alleged violation of the National Labor Relations Act. Although these two acts are not totally dissimilar, their differences significantly overshadow their similarities. *Pettway* v. *American Cast Iron Pipe Co.*, 411 F.2d 998 (5th Cir. 1969). See Comment, 44 N.Y.U.L. Rev. 404 (1969). Absent a special consideration, a determination arising solely under one statute should not automatically be binding when a similar question arises under another statute. See *Title* v. *Immigration and Naturalization Service*, 322 F.2d 21, 25 n. 11 (9th Cir. 1963); 2 K. Davis,

---

[4] The District Judge granted a discretionary appeal pursuant to 28 U.S.C. § 1292(b).

ADMINISTRATIVE LAW TREATISE § 18.04, at 577–78 (1958); cf. *Commissioner of Internal Revenue* v. *Sunnen*, 333 U.S. 591, 601–602 (1948). This is because the purposes, requirements, perspective and configuration of different statutes ordinarily vary. This case provides an excellent example of the differences in two statutes. Racial discrimination in employment is an unfair labor practice that violates Section 8(a)(1) of the National Labor Relations Act if the discrimination is unjustified and interferes with the affected employees' right to act concertedly for their own aid or protection. *United Packinghouse, Food & Allied Workers International Union* v. *National Labor Relations Board*, 416 F.2d 1126, 1135, *cert. denied*, 396 U.S. 903 (1969). In contrast, racial discrimination in employment is prohibitied by Title VII without reference to the effect on the employees' right to unite. Hence, certain discriminatory practices that are valid under the National Labor Relations Act may be invalid under Title VII. See *Taylor* v. *Armco Steel Corp.*, 429 F.2d 498 (5th Cir. 1970). See generally, Fuchs & Ellis, *Title VII: Relationship and Effect on the National Labor Relations Board*, 7 B.C.IND. & COM.L.REV. 575, 597–600 (1966).

As a result of the variant standards of these statutes, the NLRB hearing did not adequately consider the factors necessary for a Title VII violation. The Trial Examiner was primarily concerned with the question whether the appellee's union activities led to his discharge.[5] This is understandable considering that the Trial Examiner was only investigating a possible violation of the National Labor Relations Act. Consequently, he did not fully explore the racial aspects of the case before him.[6] Had he done so, he may have been acting beyond the scope of his authority since certain acts of racial discrimination are not within the ambit of the National Labor Relations Act, even though they are proscribed by Title VII. Considering the differences in these two acts, it would be anomalous if a finding under one should preclude a determination under the other, absent special considerations.

The legislative history of Title VII supports this conclusion. During the debate in Congress over Title VII, Senator Clark introduced a letter from the Attorney General indicating that Title VII does not prevent an individual from proceeding under both Title VII and the National Labor Relations Act. 110 Cong.Rec. 7207 (1964). Similarly, the United States Senate rejected a proposed amendment which would have made Title VII the exclusive means of relief for most discriminatory employment prac-

---

[5] The Trial Examiner's final conclusion stated: ". . . I conclude and find that, Tipler's participation in or association with intraunion disputations with Shinault [appellant's foreman] played no role in Jackson's decision [to fire the appellee] and that his decision would have been the same if Tipler had had no dispute with Shinault." Exhibit C–5, page 12.

[6] It is interesting to note that during the NLRB hearing appellant's attorney objected to the introduction of evidence of racial discrimination. When Tipler told that he would have been fired had he used certain restroom facilities, appellant's counsel stated: "I will object to this. This has nothing to do with union activities. He is bringing out race. I think it is inflammatory and prejudicial and I don't see any relevancy to it." Exhibit C–8, page 44.

tices. 110 Cong.Rec. 13650–52 (1964). This action is some evidence at least that Congress, realizing the differences between Title VII and other statutes directly or indirectly proscribing racial discrimination in employment, did not intend for a decision under one such provision to bar automatically a suit under another statutory scheme.

This Court's recent decision in *Dewey* v. *Reynolds Metals,* 429 F.2d 324 (6th Cir. 1970), *cert. granted,* 400 U.S. 1008 (1971), does not contradict this conclusion. *Dewey* held that a Title VII action could not be brought after the grievance had been finally adjudicated by the binding arbitration procedures required by the collective bargaining contract. This result was the product of a fear that a contrary result would "destroy the efficacy of arbitration." *Id.* at 332. In the case before us, however, no such overriding policy considerations are present, for no binding arbitration was required. Therefore, the special circumstances upon which *Dewey* was based are not relevant here.

## II.  JUDICIAL ESTOPPEL

Appellant also argues that appellee is precluded by the doctrine of judicial estoppel from asserting in this action that his discharge was racially motivated since he had twice previously maintained under oath that his discharge was the product of union activities. Despite the seeming inconsistency in appellee's positions, a consideration of the context of the union activities indicates that the inconsistency is of form rather than substance. Allegations of racial motivation were inherent in the appellee's complaints to the NLRB [7] and the Tennessee State Department of Employment Security. Appellee's union activity, asserted before both agencies as the cause of his discharge, was clearly the product of racial tension and hostility. In that intraunion fight, the overwhelming number of black members successfully replaced the union's white leadership with a slate composed of blacks. Appellant's foreman was one of the deposed white union officials. In this context, it is not inconsistent for appellee to assert that his discharge at the suggestion of the white foreman was the result of either union activity or racial considerations, or both.

## III.  STANDING

Appellant further alleges that appellee has no standing to challenge the alleged discriminatory practices since he is no longer an employee of the appellant. This contention is contrary to the clear weight of authority. In *Johnson* v. *Georgia Highway Express, Inc.,* 417 F.2d 1122 (5th Cir. 1969), for example, the Court permitted a former employee, allegedly fired for racial reasons, to maintain a class action consisting of an "across

---

[7] Appellant himself noted the "racial overtones in the issues litigated before the N.L.R.B." Brief of Appellant, p. 8. As the result of this aspect of the case, appellant described appellee's claim before the NLRB as an allegation of discharge "for unlawful reasons relating to his intraunion, racially oriented power struggle." *Id.* at 9.

the board" attack on discrimination. See also *Carr* v. *Conoco Plastics, Inc.,* 423 F.2d 57 (5th Cir. 1970); *Wilson* v. *Monsanto Co.,* 315 F. Supp. 977 (E.D.La.1970) (job applicant); *Kemp* v. *General Electric Co.,* 60 L.C. ¶ 9238 (N.D.Ga.1969) (discharged employees); *Gunn* v. *Layne & Bowler, Inc.,* 56 L.C. & ¶ 9088 (W.D.Tenn.1967) (discharged employee). But cf. *Colbert* v. *H-K Corp.,* 295 F. Supp. 1091 (N.D.Ga.1968). It is to be noted that although the present action is not labelled a class action, it "is perforce a sort of class action for fellow employees similarly situated." *Jenkins* v. *United Gas Corp.,* 400 F.2d 28, 33 (5th Cir. 1968). See also *Blue Bell Boots, Inc.* v. *Equal Employment Opportunity Commission,* 418 F.2d 355 (6th Cir. 1969). Appellant's black employees will benefit if appellee's position is upheld in the District Court, for part of his complaint seeks general relief against a wide range of past and present allegedly discriminatory practices. Considering the class aspects of this action, the District Court should take necessary precautions to protect the interests of the parties who will be affected by the action.

IV.  SCOPE OF EEOC CHARGE

Finally, appellant contends that appellee cannot raise the issue in the courts that he was discharged for his active opposition to appellant's unlawful employment practices because this allegation was not included within his EEOC charge.

Before deciding this question, it is necessary to establish several general principles. First, this Court has recognized that Title VII of the Civil Rights Act of 1964 should not be construed narrowly. *Blue Bell Boots, Inc.* v. *Equal Employment Opportunity Commission,* 418 F.2d 355, 358 (6th Cir. 1969). In addition, charges of discrimination filed before the EEOC will generally be filed by lay complainants who are unfamiliar with the niceties of pleading and are acting without assistance of counsel. *Graniteville Company* v. *Equal Employment Opportunity Commission,* 438 F.2d 32 (4th Cir. 1971). As a result, federal courts should not allow procedural technicalities to preclude Title VII complaints. *Sanchez* v. *Standard Brands, Inc.,* 431 F.2d 455 (5th Cir. 1970). When this approach is applied to the determination of whether a judicial complaint encompasses the EEOC charge, it is clear that the exact wording of the charge of discrimination need not "presage with literary exactitude the judicial pleading which may follow." *Id.* at 465. Rather, the complaint in the judicial proceedings is only limited to the scope of the EEOC investigation reasonably expected to grow out of the charge of discrimination. *Id.* at 466; *King* v. *Georgia Power Co.,* 295 F. Supp. 943 (N.D.Ga.1968).

In the case at bar it is true that neither the original nor amended charge of discrimination stated precisely that appellee was discharged for his active opposition to appellant's alleged unlawful employment practices. The original charge of discrimination did allege, however, that appellee was punished for asserting his rights as an employee. In addition, among other contentions, the amended charge of discrimination stated that appellant discriminated against Negroes by terminating appellee's employment without justification. We read these charges as sufficient to include the allegation that appellee was discharged for his active opposition to appellant's unlawful employment practices. The fact that a judicial complaint alleges a more detailed and refined contention than that contained in the charge of discrimination does not mean that the former was not included in the latter.

Appellant cites two cases in support of his position. Neither is controlling. *Oatis* v. *Crown Zellerbach Corp.*, 398 F.2d 496 (5th Cir. 1968), was specifically rejected by the Fifth Circuit as authority on the question presented here. *Sanchez* v. *Standard Brands, Inc.*, 431 F.2d 455, 466 (5th Cir. 1970). Similarly, *Colbert* v. *H-K Corp.*, 295 F. Supp. 1091 (N.D.Ga. 1968), does not support appellant's contention. In that case the District Court held that the judicial complaint must only be *"related* to the charge filed with the EEOC." *Id.* at 1093 (emphasis added). The necessary relationship is clearly present in the case at bar.

Affirmed.

# 6. Equal Pay

## A. Substantial Equality—Remedies

## LAFFEY v. NORTHWEST AIRLINES

*United States Court of Appeals, District of Columbia Circuit, 1976*
*567 F.2d 429, 13 FEP Cases 1067*

Spottswood W. Robinson, III, Circuit Judge: Northwest Airlines (NWA) appeals from a judgment of the District Court declaring certain of its personnel policies violative of the Equal Pay Act of 1963 and Title VII of the Civil Rights Act of 1964, and granting injunctive and monetary relief. The principal practice in issue here is the payment to women employed as stewardesses of salaries lower than those paid to men serving as pursers for work found by the court to be substantially equal. Others are the provision to stewardesses of less desirable layover accommodations and allowances for maintenance of uniforms, and the imposition of weight restrictions upon stewardesses only. In varying respects and degrees NWA challenges findings of fact and conclusions of law on these matters, as well as the propriety of the remedial measures adopted.

On careful review of the extensive record on appeal, we sustain the District Court's adjudications on all substantive questions of statutory infringement. We also uphold most but not all of the court's specifications on relief. Thus we affirm the judgment in part, vacate it in part and remand the case to the District Court for further proceedings.

### I. History of the Employment Practices

#### A. Stewardess and Purser Positions

Between 1927 and 1947, all cabin attendants employed on NWA's aircraft were women, whom NWA classified as "stewardesses." In 1947, when the company initiated international service, it established a new cabin-attendant position of "purser," and for two decades thereafter adhered to an undeviating practice of restricting purser jobs to men alone. In implementation of this policy, NWA created another strictly all-male cabin-attendant classification—"flight service attendant"—to serve as a training and probationary position for future pursers. NWA has

maintained a combined seniority list for pursers and flight service attendants, on which seniority as pursers accrued to flight service attendants
immediately upon assumption of their duties as such, and a separate
seniority list for stewardesses. From 1951 until 1967, flight service attendants had a contractual right to automatic promotion to purser vacancies
in the order of their seniority.

It was not until 1967, when a new collective bargaining agreement
was negotiated, that stewardesses first became contractually eligible to
apply for purser positions. During negotiations on the issue, NWA, for
both the 1967 agreement and another in 1970, rejected an additional
union proposal that stewardesses, like flight service attendants, be allowed
to progress to purser slots according to seniority, stating that the company
"prefers males and intends to have them." The company has also insisted
upon the right of "selectivity" in choosing which stewardesses might become pursers, and has imposed other restrictions on stewardesses seeking
purser vacancies which had not previously been laid on flight service
attendants.

Company policy had been to fill purser openings by hiring "men off
the street" and training them for a short time, after which notices of
purser vacancies would be posted. Following the 1967 collective bargaining agreement affording stewardesses access to these jobs, however, NWA
hired five male purser-applicants without ever posting notices of the
vacancies. In 1970, after three years of ostensibly open admission to purser
status, NWA had 137 male cabin attendants—all as pursers—and 1,747
female cabin attendants—all but one as stewardesses.

The sole female purser at that time was Mary P. Laffey, who bid for
a purser vacancy in 1967, after nine years' service as a stewardess. Although that purser position was scheduled to be filled in November,
1967, processing of her application was delayed assertedly for the reason
that NWA needed to administer new tests to purser applicants. These
tests had never previously been used in selecting pursers, and during the
interim between Ms. Laffey's application and her appointment NWA
hired two male pursers without benefit of any tests. Finally, in June,
1968, Ms. Laffey became a purser, but was placed on the bottom rung
of the purser-salary schedule and received less than her income as a
senior stewardess.

## B. STEWARDESS AND PURSER DUTIES

On this appeal, NWA does not challenge holdings by the District Court
that Title VII was violated by NWA's refusal to hire female pursers.
Rather, the appeal focuses primarily on whether the payment of unequal
salaries to stewardesses and pursers, while occupying positions as such,
implicates Title VII and the Equal Pay Act. The purser wage scale
ranges from 20 to 55 percent higher than salaries paid to stewardesses of
equivalent seniority. The Equal Pay Act forbids this pay differential
unless greater skill, effort or responsibility is required to perform purser
duties. Title VII likewise proscribes inferior sex-based compensation plans

for women and, additionally, extends its protection to ban conditions of employment imposed discriminatorily upon women employees.

### (1) *Flight Assignments*

In gauging whether NWA's pursers and stewardesses performed equal work, the District Court analyzed in great detail NWA's flight operations and its usage of the three different categories of cabin attendants. NWA flies diverse itineraries, which affect the type of personnel assigned to the flight, and which are categorized by particular terminology. In brief, "pure domestic commercial flights" are regularly-scheduled commercial flights which begin and end in the United States, and do not continue to the Orient. Other commercial flights originate in one city in the United States, fly to an intermediate destination in the United States, and then on to the Orient; and the intra-United States portions of such trips are known as "domestic segments of international flights." "Trans-pacific commercial flights" are regularly-scheduled flights between Anchorage, Seattle, Honolulu and Tokyo; while "commercial interport flights" are regularly scheduled flights between Tokyo and other Asian cities. "Military air charters" are flights contracted with the United States Government to provide regularly-scheduled military air charter service.

Pure domestic commercial flights are, with some exceptions, served exclusively by stewardesses and flight service attendants. Pursers are ordinarily utilized on interport flights, transpacific commercial flights, domestic segments of international flights, and on all types of charters, military or otherwise, including pure domestic flights. Since 1967, the company has also maintained a crew of stewardesses with proficiency in one or more foreign languages, who are assigned to certain international flights.

NWA schedules a different cabin-attendant crew on each flight segment; one crew will fly the domestic segment, another will take over for the transpacific link, and still a third is used on the interport portion. Pursers and stewardesses bid separately, according to seniority, for monthly schedules.

### (2) *Overall Evaluation*

Probing beneath the different titles, bidding schedules and salaries, the District Court made extensive factual findings comparing the work actually done by pursers and stewardesses, and held it to be essentially equal when considered as a whole. For example, pursers are assigned to the first-class section of the aircraft, which has a smaller passenger load per cabin attendant and a correspondingly more leisurely work pace as compared with the chores inherited by stewardesses assigned to the tourist-class section. The hourly work load also tends to be greater on the "short hop" domestic schedules than on the longer international flights.

Duties performed do not differ significantly in nature as between pursers and stewardesses. All must check cabins before departure, greet and seat passengers, prepare for take-off, and provide in-flight food, beverage and general services. All must complete required documentation, maintain cabin cleanliness, see that passengers comply with regulations and deplane passengers. The premier responsibility of any cabin attendant is to insure the safety of passengers during an emergency, and cabin attendants all must possess a thorough knowledge of emergency equipment and procedures on all aircraft. All attendants also must be knowledgeable in first aid techniques and must be able to handle the myriad of medical problems that arise in flight. Food service varies greatly between flights, but pursers engage in no duties that are not also performed on the same or another flight by stewardesses. Another important duty—building goodwill between NWA and its passengers—depends on the poise, tact, friendliness, good judgment and adaptability of every cabin attendant, male or female.

### (3) Domestic and International Flights

The District Court found that when pursers are scheduled on pure domestic flights, their duties are identical to those of stewardesses functioning as "senior cabin attendants"—the most senior purser, or the most senior stewardess on flights with no purser. A substantial percentage of NWA's overall utilization of pursers is on pure domestic flights and domestic segments of international flights. Similarly, a substantial percentage of the company's use of pursers is their assignment to military air charter flights. Many pursers fly flights of these types exclusively for months or years at a time.

Although, as NWA argues, after January, 1971, pursers as a group have spent more nights away from home than do stewardesses, the District Court found that these longer trips "do not constitute substantially dissimilar working conditions from those of other cabin attendants":
"More consecutive days away from home also means more consecutive days at home during the month. The preferences of cabin attendants in this regard are highly subjective—some prefer one long trip a month, while others prefer shorter trips; . . . . Because ground time is not counted toward flight time, purser schedules (encompassing longer flights) entail fewer actual hours of work. . . ."

### (4) Documentation Tasks

With respect to documentation responsibilities, the District Court found that pursers and stewardesses have different, but comparable, duties. Stewardesses alone sell liquor, and are alone required to complete inventory and sales records, and beverage usage reports. On flights carrying tax-free liquor, customs inventory forms must be completed both by stewardesses and pursers, and all cabin attendants are subject to discipline for error. On all flights, the senior cabin attendant and the senior in tourist—the senior stewardess in the tourist class—must make appropriate entries in the log book, and also prepare an inflight-service report, seating charts, accident reports and other diverse documents.

Pursers are responsible for administering international quarantine procedures for passengers, crew and cargo. As the requirements vary from port to port, pursers must keep their knowledge current in order to comply with applicable regulations. These duties, however, are not required on all flights to which pursers are assigned, such as on pure domestic flights on which pursers perform no documentation duties, and on certain domestic segments on which such purser duties are minimal. To boot, pursers are instructed to carry out their international documentation responsibilities at times when no significant passenger service is required, and other cabin attendants perform all other necessary services during those times. The District Court found that "the documentary duties described which are . . . assigned only to pursers involved no greater skill, effort or responsibility than the stewardess job."

## (5) *Stewardess and Purser Responsibilities*

The District Court also examined another general, more intangible, duty advanced by NWA as a factor rendering the purser job different in kind from the stewardess position. The company's cabin service manual states that the senior purser on a flight will always be considered the senior cabin attendant and as such must coordinate the activities of the other attendants, and is to be held "responsible and accountable" for the proper rendering of service on that flight. But the manual further provides that if no purser is scheduled, the most senior stewardess will serve as senior flight attendant and will similarly be charged with co-ordination of cabin service, although she is accountable only for the conduct of service in the section of the aircraft in which she works, responsibility for the remainder being placed on the senior attendant in the other section of the aircraft.

Senior cabin attendants, be they purser or stewardess, have a number of supervisory duties. These include monitoring and, where necessary, correcting the work of other cabin attendants; determining the times of meals and movie showings; shifting cabin attendants from section to section to balance workloads; and giving pre-departure briefings on emergency equipment and procedures. On large planes, even if a purser in the first-class section is designated the senior cabin attendant, the senior in tourist shoulders these same burdens in her section of the aircraft—overseeing the great majority of passengers and cabin attendants. Stewardesses and pursers alike are subject to disciplinary action if they fail to carry out their "supervisory responsibilities."

There is, however, no merit system maintained to reward those who "supervise" better than others; all pursers and all stewardesses are on uniform, separate wage scales, regardless of whether—or how well—an individual performs.

NWA asserts that it hired, trained and promoted male pursers in the belief that they would exercise leadership and be "responsible and accountable for the entire cabin service staff," whereas stewardesses functioning as senior cabin attendants on particular flights would be re-

sponsible for coordination of cabin service on the entire flight but would be "accountable" only for the manner of service in their assigned sections of the aircraft. The District Court found that, in practice, this distinction between levels of responsibility and accountability is illusory:
"Only in the purser's formal relationship with the Company does his accountability differ from the nonpurser senior cabin attendant and that difference is derived from status rather than as a function of the job. . . ."
The court found, moreover, that the senior cabin attendant's duties are not substantially greater than the ordinary cabin attendant's function:
". . . Cabin service attendants are employed to serve and protect Company passengers. The 'Supervisory' functions of senior cabin attendants— whether purser or stewardess—are less important than, and require no greater skill, effort or responsibility, than the other functions assigned to all cabin attendants."

## C. THE DISTRICT COURT'S CONCLUSIONS

Careful evaluation of the facts comprehensively found led the District Court to conclude that NWA had discriminated against women cabin attendants on the basis of sex, in violation of Title VII and the Equal Pay Act, by compensating stewardesses and pursers unequally for equal work on "jobs the performance of which requires equal skill, effort and responsibility and which are performed under similar working conditions." More specifically the court found that NWA had discriminated in "willfull violation" of the Equal Pay Act (a) by paying female stewardesses lower salaries and pensions than male pursers; (b) by providing female cabin attendants less expensive and less desirable layover accommodations than male cabin attendants; (c) by providing to male but not to female cabin attendants a uniform-cleaning allowance; and (d) "by paying Mary P. Laffey a lower salary as a purser than it pays to male pursers with equivalent length of cabin attendant service." All of these same actions were held by the District Court also to be violations of Title VII. . . .

On this appeal, NWA challenges the District Court's central ruling that disparate compensation for equal work violates Title VII additionally to the Equal Pay Act. It attacks also the court's holding that stewardesses and pursers are entitled to equal pay, and the corollary finding that stewardesses who became pursers were improperly denied credit for their stewardess seniority on the purser seniority list. The company also disputes the court's conclusion that Title VII was violated by its policies regarding cleaning allowances and layover accommodations. Lastly, it objects to the remedial measure adopted by the court to cure the conceded violation as to weight restrictions. These contentions, in turn, we now examine.

## II. THE APPLICABLE STATUTES

By the Equal Pay Act, adopted in 1963 as an addition to the Fair Labor Standards Act of 1938, Congress ordained:

"No employer having employees subject to any provisions of this section shall discriminate . . . between employees on the basis of sex by paying wages to employees . . . at a rate less than the rate at which he pays wages to employees of the opposite sex . . . for equal work on jobs the performance of which requires equal skill, effort, and responsibility and which are performed under similar working conditions, except where such payment is made pursuant to (i) a seniority system; (ii) a merit system; (iii) a system which measures earnings by quantity or quality of production; or (iv) a differential based on any other factor other than sex. . . ."

By Title VII, Congress has also decreed, with exceptions not immediately relevant, that

"[i]t shall be an unlawful employment practice for an employer—

"(1) to fail or refuse to hire or to discharge any individual, or otherwise to discriminate against any individual with respect to his compensation, terms, conditions, or privileges of employment, because of such individual's race, color, religion, sex, or national origin; or

"(2) to limit, segregate, or classify his employees or applicants for employment in any way which would deprive or tend to deprive any individual of employment opportunities or otherwise adversely affect his status as an employee, because of such individual's race, color, religion, sex, or national origin."

It is by these standards that objections to the substantive features of the District Court's judgment are to be gauged on this appeal.

## A. INTERRELATIONSHIP OF THE STATUTES

NWA argues that the two statutes, read in *para materia,* do not authorize monetary relief premised upon both legislative schemes for the same act of paying disparate wages. It is said that while the Equal Pay Act permits a statutory class action to secure equal pay for equal work by employees of different sexes, Title VII's guaranty of nondiscriminatory "compensation" applies only to such minority groups as are not covered by the Equal Pay Act.

NWA further contends that the District Court was inconsistent in finding transgressions of both statutes. The argument in this connection may be summarized briefly. If the purser and stewardess jobs are "equal," and thus support the court's holding of an Equal Pay Act violation, the company's refusal to permit women to become pursers does not deprive them of advancement opportunities—because the jobs are equal—and thus there can be no encroachment upon Title VII. Conversely, if the purser job is superior, there is no infringement of the Equal Pay Act although access to that position has unlawfully been denied to women under Title VII. NWA does not challenge the court's finding that Title VII was dishonored by the exclusion of female employees from the purser position, but the company does contest the conclusion that the comparability of that position and the stewardess position brings the salary differential between pursers and stewardesses into collision with the Equal Pay Act.

We reject these approaches. The District Court's finding that NWA's purser and stewardess jobs are essentially equal in duties and responsibilities is not logically inconsistent with the court's conclusions that NWA impinged on Title VII by blocking the entry of women into the purser category. Although, as the District Court determined, the two jobs require equal "skill, effort, and responsibility" so as to command equivalent salaries under the Equal Pay Act, any statutorily-unexempted sex-based barrier to obtaining a particular job is forbidden by Title VII. Among the options withheld by Title VII from an employer are those which "limit . . . or classify his employees or applicants for employment in any way which would deprive or tend to deprive any individual of employment opportunities . . . because of such individual's . . . sex . . ." Notwithstanding, NWA classified its cabin attendants more prominently as all-female stewardesses and all-male pursers, and barred women applicants from the ranks of the latter though capable through existing employment and accrued experience with NWA to meet all of its purser-criteria save sex. That plainly was outlawed by Title VII as a sex-founded deprivation of employment opportunities, not the least of which were the superior emoluments which NWA bestowed on the purser position.

Nor do we doubt that the same set of facts may form the basis for redress under both Title VII and the Equal Pay Act if the requirements of each are separately satisfied and the claimant does not reap overlapping relief for the same wrong. Unless foreclosed by the statutory language or history, nothing to rob aggrieved parties of the freedom to select among multiple remedies for separate though concurrent statutory violations is apparent.

Title VII rights are independent of the rights created by other statutes, and where remedies coincide the claimant should be allowed to utilize whichever avenue of relief is desired. This would seem to be the clearer for claimants under Title VII which, as the Supreme Court held in *Alexander* v. *Gardner-Denver*, was intended to "supplement, rather than supplant existing laws . . . relating to employment." The Court has also noted that the legislative history of Title VII "manifests a congressional intent to allow an individual to pursue independently his rights under Title VII and other applicable state and federal statutes." During the preenactment debates, Congress rejected a proposed amendment which would have made Title VII the exclusive remedy for the unlawful employment practices it covers, and thereby evinced a congressional purpose to leave open other modes of relief available to victims of discriminatory employment practices.

Although Title VII reaches farther than the Equal Pay Act to protect groups other than those sex-based classes and to proscribe discrimination in many facets of employment additional to compensation, nowhere have we encountered an indication that Title VII was intended either to supplant or be supplanted by the Equal Pay Act in the relatively small area in which the two are congruent. On the contrary, we are satisfied that the provisions of both acts should be read in *pari materia*, and neither should be interpreted in a manner that would undermine the other. In *Orr* v. *Frank R. MacNeill & Son, Inc.*, the Fifth Circuit declared that "[t]he sex discrimination provision of Title VII of the Civil Rights Act of 1964 must be construed in harmony with the Equal Pay Act of 1963." We agree, and we now so hold.

Moreover, the language of Title VII itself explicitly declares that it is unlawful for an employer to offer an employee discriminatory "compensation . . . because of such individual's . . . sex." The legislative history of Title VII yields no hint that the guaranty of nondiscriminatory compensation was extended only to minority groups not embraced within the Equal Pay Act. Indeed, Title VII refers specifically to the Equal Pay Act and states that a sex-predicated wage differential is immune from attack under Title VII only if it comes within one of the four enumerated exceptions to the Equal Pay Act. This, then, focuses our inquiry once again upon whether the District Court correctly found that the employee-litigants had overcome the factors urged by NWA as proof that the stewardess and purser jobs were unequal, or whether NWA had sustained an affirmative defense under one of the Equal Pay Act's exceptions permitting limited instances of disparate pay for equal work.

. . .

### III. THE EQUAL PAY ACT CLAIMS

As the Third Circuit has said, the Equal Pay Act
"was intended as a broad charter of women's rights in the economic field. It sought to overcome the age-old belief in women's inferiority and to eliminate the depressing effects on living standards of reduced wages for female workers and the economic and social consequences which flow from it." [*Schultz* v. *Wheaton Glass Co.*, 421 F.2d 259, 9 FEP Cases 502 (3rd Cir.), *cert. denied*, 398 U.S. 905, 9 FEP Cases 1408 (1970).]
And as the Supreme Court has declared,
"Congress' purpose in enacting the Equal Pay Act was to remedy what was perceived to be a serious and *endemic* problem of employment discrimination in private industry—the fact that the wage structure of 'many segments of American industry has been based on an ancient but outmoded belief that a man, because of his role in society, should be paid more than a woman even though his duties are the same.' S. Rep. No. 176, 88th Cong., 1st Sess., 1 (1963). The solution adopted was quite simple in principle: to require that 'equal work will be rewarded by equal wages.' " [*Corning Glass Works* v. *Brennan, supra.*]

### A. THE GUIDING PRINCIPLES

An Equal Pay Act claimant must show that her salary was lower than that paid by the employer to "employees of the opposite sex . . . for equal work on jobs the performance of which requires equal skill, effort, and responsibility, and which are performed under similar working conditions." The claimant bears the onus of demonstrating that the work unequally recompensed was "equal" within the meaning of the Act. Once this has been done, the claimant will prevail unless the employer asserts as an affirmative defense that the wage differential is justified under one of the four exceptions enumerated in the Act—"(i) a seniority system; (ii) a merit system; (iii) a system which measures earnings by quantity or quality of production; or (iv) a differential based on any other factor other than sex." If one or more of these defenses is invoked, the employer bears the burden of proving that his policies fall within an exempted area. This interpretation of the procedural mechanics of the Equal Pay Act comports with the construction of other provisions of the Fair Labor Standards Act, of which the Equal Pay Act is a part, by which statutory exceptions and exemptions are considered matters of affirmative defense to be proven by the employer.

One of the more frequent controversies aroused by the Equal Pay Act has involved litigants' attempts to demonstrate that jobs with different titles and descriptions are in reality equal in their calls upon the job-holders. The contest often necessitates an assessment of the significance of differences in job demands advanced by the employer to show that the jobs are not equal. For "[it] is now well settled that the jobs need not be identical in every respect before the Equal Pay Act is applicable"; the phrase "equal work" does not mean that the jobs must be identical, but merely that they must be "substantially equal." A wage differential is justified only if it compensates for an appreciable variation in skill, effort or responsibility between otherwise comparable job work activities.

The Department of Labor has promulgated an extensive series of regulations [123] to guide the "application of the equal pay standard, [which] is not dependent on job classifications or titles but depends rather on actual job requirements and performance. . . ." One regulation states:
"Congress did not intend that inconsequential differences in job content would be a valid excuse for payment of a lower wage to an employee of one sex than to an employee of the opposite sex if the two are performing equal work on essentially the same job in the same establishment."
Another points out that "[I]nsubstantial or minor differences in the degree or amount of skill, or effort, or responsibility required for the performance of jobs will not render the equal pay standard inapplicable."

These regulations are entitled to "great deference" by the courts in applying the Equal Pay Act to given factual situations.[127] Courts have consistently held that differences in the duties respectively assigned male and female employees must be "evaluated as part of the entire job." [128] Thus,

---

123 [Footnotes numbered as in original.—Ed.] 29 C.F.R. §§ 800.114-800.166 (1975).

127 See *Hodgson* v. *Corning Glass Works*, 474 F.2d 226, 232, 9 FEP Cases 806, 810 (2d Cir. 1973); *aff'd*, 417 U.S. 188, 41 L.Ed.2d 1, 9 FEP Cases 919 (1974); *Brennan* v. *Prince William Hosp. Corp.*, *supra* note 105, 503 F.2d at 287-88 n. 5, 9 FEP Cases at 982; *Brennan* v. *City Stores, Inc.*, 479 F.2d 235, 239-420, 9 FEP Cases 846, 850 (5th Cir. 1973). See also *National Automatic Laundry & Cleaning Council* v. *Shultz*, 143 U.S. App. D.C. 274, 282, 443 F.2d 689, 702, 19 WH Cases 984 (1971).

128 See, *e.g.*, *Brennan* v. *Prince William Hosp. Corp.*, *supra* note 105, 503 F.2d at 290, 9 FEP Cases at 984.

if in the aggregate the jobs require substantially similar skills, efforts and responsibilities, the work will be adjudged equal despite minor variations.[129]

When there is a disparity between salaries paid men and women for similar positions bearing different titles—such as pursers and stewardesses —the courts have scrutinized the evidence to discern whether the salary differential is justified by heterogeneous duties.[130] Another regulation of the Department of Labor states in relevant part,

"[i]n determining whether job differences are so substantial as to make jobs unequal, it is pertinent to inquire whether and to what extent significance is given to such differences in setting the wage levels for such jobs. Such an inquiry may . . . disclose that apparent differences between jobs have not been recognized as relevant for wage purposes. . . ."

An employer cannot justify a pay differential by mere assumptions on career-orientation, the duration or probable length of working time, or a supposed respect for male authority and leadership. Moreover, "training programs which appear to be available only to employees of one sex will . . . be carefully examined to determine whether such programs are, in fact, bona fide." [133]

An employer must show a consistent pattern of performance of additional duties in order to demonstrate that added duties are genuinely the motivating factor for the substantially higher pay. It is not sufficient that an increased workload might hypothetically have commanded a higher salary if it is not in fact the basis for a significantly greater wage. The employer may not fabricate an after-the-fact rationalization for a sex-based pay difference. "[T]he semblance of [a] valid job classification system may not be allowed to mask the existence of wage discrimination based on sex." [134]

Often, evidence superficially purporting to justify greater pay as compensation for added work is found upon close examination to have in-

---

[129] 29 C.F.R. §§ 800.126, 800.130(c). See, e.g., Brennan v. Prince William Hosp. Corp., supra note 105, 503 F.2d at 290, 291, 9 FEP Cases at 984; Hodgson v. American Bank of Commerce, supra note 121, 447 F.2d at 421-23, 9 FEP Cases at 680-81; Hodgson v. Brookhaven Gen. Hosp., supra note 100, 436 F.2d at 724-26, 9 FEP Cases at 582-84.

[130] See, e.g., Hodgson v. Brookhaven Gen. Hosp., supra note 100 ("orderlies" and "nurses aides").

[133] 29 C.F.R. § 800.148. See also Hodgson v. Behrens Drug Co., 475 F.2d 1041, 1046-47, 9 FEP Cases 816, 820 (5th Cir.), cert. denied, 414 U.S. 822, 9 FEP Cases 1408 (1973); Hodgson v. Security Nat'l Bank, 460 F.2d 57, 60-61, 9 FEP Cases 761, 764 (8th Cir. 1972) (reversing a lower court decision which ruled that a male-dominated bank management training program was bona fide); Hodgson v. Fairmont Supply Co., supra note 116, 454 F.2d at 498-99, 9 FEP Cases at 712 (reversing a District Court finding which had upheld a sex-based sales training program); Shultz v. First Victoria Nat'l Bank, supra note 118, 420 F.2d at 655-57, 9 FEP Cases at 501-502 (male-dominated executive training programs" for bank tellers did not constitute a factor "other than sex" which would permit a pay differential where female tellers were never included in the training program).

[134] Brennan v. Prince William Hosp. Corp., supra note 105, 503 F.2d at 285-86, 9 FEP Cases at 980. See also, Shultz v. Wheaton Glass Co., supra note 100, 421 F.2d at 265, 9 FEP Cases at 507; Hodgson v. Brookhaven Gen. Hosp., supra note 100, 436 F.2d at 723 n. 3, 9 FEP Cases at 581-82; Hodgson v. American Bank of Commerce, supra note 121, 447 F.2d at 422-23, 9 FEP Cases at 681; Shultz v. First Victoria Nat'l Bank, supra note 118, 420 F.2d at 655, 9 FEP Cases at 499-500.

consistencies which render its evidentiary value weaker. Where, for example, all male employees receive greater pay but only some perform the extra tasks allegedly justifying that pay, a reasonable inference is that maleness—not the added chores—is the basis for the higher wage. This is particularly true if the duties are of peripheral importance and the increase in pay is substantial.[135] Moreover, if some women without added compensation render the same extra performance that purportedly justified the pay differential favoring men, the inference becomes even stronger that the duties are irrelevant to the wage setting.[136] Similar evidence of discriminatory wage patterns is to be found where women are paid only for the amount of time actually spent on the extra work, but men are uniformly paid at the higher rate regardless of whether or not they are doing the work.[137] Additionally the Fourth Circuit has found corroborative evidence that higher pay is not related to extra duties when "qualified female employees are not given the opportunity to do the extra work." [138] The conclusion to be drawn, when any of these inconsistent patterns exists, is that

"[d]espite claims to the contrary, the extra tasks were found to be make-weights. This left sex—which in this context refers to the availability of women at lower wages than men—as the one discernible reason for the wage differential. That, however, is precisely the criterion for setting wages that the Act prohibits." [139]

## B. THE CASE AT BAR

Applying these principles to the instant case, we perceive no error in the District Court's conclusion that the alleged differences in occupational duties proffered by NWA to justify the higher wage paid to pursers do not demonstrate that the stewardess and purser jobs are disparate. The court found that there is a uniform pay-scale for pursers which exceeds the pay-scale for stewardesses; and that these contrasting schemes are uncorrelated with pursers' and stewardesses' respective employment bur-

---

135 *Shultz* v. *Wheaton Glass Co., supra* note 100, 421 F.2d at 263-64, 9 FEP Cases at 504-505; *Hodgson* v. *Fairmont Supply Co., supra* note 116, 454 F.2d at 493, 9 FEP Cases at 708; *Hodgson* v. *Behrens Drug Co., supra* note 133, 475 F.2d at 1047, 9 FEP Cases at 821; *Brennan* v. *Prince William Hosp. Corp., supra* note 105, 503 F.2d at 285-86, 9 FEP Cases at 981; *Hodgson* v. *Miller Brewing Co.,* 457 F.2d 221, 225 n. 8, 9 FEP Cases 726, 729 (7th Cir. 1972); *Shultz* v. *American Can Co.-Dixie Prods., supra* note 116, 424 F.2d at 360-62, 9 FEP Cases at 526-27.

136 See *Brennan* v. *Prince William Hosp. Corp., supra* note 105, 503 F.2d at 288, 9 FEP Cases at 983-84; *Hodgson* v. *Behrens Drug Co., supra* note 133, 475 F.2d at 1047, 9 FEP Cases at 822; *Hodgson* v. *Montana State Bd. of Educ.,* 336 F. Supp. 524, 525, 9 FEP Cases 715, 716-17 (D. Mont. 1972).

137 *Shultz* v. *American Can Co.-Dixie Prods., supra* note 116, 424 F.2d at 360-61, 9 FEP Cases at 527.

138 *Brennan* v. *Prince William Hosp. Corp., supra* note 105, 503 F.2d at 286, 9 FEP Cases at 981, citing *Shultz* v. *Wheaton Glass Co., supra* note 100.

139 *Brennan* v. *Prince William Hosp. Corp., supra* note 105, 503 F.2d at 286, 9 FEP Cases at 981, citing *Brennan* v. *City Stores, Inc., supra* note 127, 479 F.2d at 241 n. 12, 9 FEP Cases at 850 and *Hodgson* v. *Brookhaven Gen. Hosp., supra* note 100, 436 F.2d at 726, 9 FEP Cases at 584.

dens. Pursers flying exclusively on domestic routes with no international documentation obligations are compensated evenly with pursers on international flights, despite the company's insistence that the onus of international flying is one of the explanations of the greater purser salary. To be sure, stewardesses who staff international flights do receive a foreign-flying supplement, but pursers' pay remains 20 to 35 percent larger than that of stewardesses of comparable seniority engaging solely in international travel.

Pursers consistently assigned to flights on which they do not function as the senior cabin attendant receive the same salary as those flying constantly in that capacity, while stewardesses rendering like service derive no supplemental income. A greater mantle of supervisory responsibility supposedly inherent in the position of senior cabin attendant thus does not exonerate the extra compensation awarded pursers. In fact, stewardesses' supervisory labors may exceed those of pursers. The more junior cabin attendants who need more supervision are relegated by the seniority flight-bidding system to the tourist-class section of the least desirable domestic flights, and the probability is that a stewardess acting as senior cabin attendant or senior-in-tourist will be charged with training as well as normal supervision. Pursers, possessing the more popular flights, are positioned in the first-class section with the more senior stewardesses, who require little or no supervision. The District Court further found that "a substantial percentage of the Company's overall utilization of pursers consisted of their assignment . . . exclusively, for months or years at a time," to flights on which their functions are "identical" to or "less demanding" than stewardesses' tasks.

In sum, stewardesses are confined to the same lower salaries whether or not flying as the senior cabin attendant, regardless of how taxing the service on their flights may be, and irrespective of the performance of documentation work. Pursers, at all times and under all conditions, received substantially superior salaries. This evidence leads convincingly to the conclusion that the contrast in pay is a consequence of the historical willingness of women to accept inferior financial rewards for equivalent work—precisely the out-moded practice which the Equal Pay Act sought to eradicate.

Nor can NWA reasonably contend that it gives pursers higher salaries because, as a group, they discharge extra duties more frequently than stewardesses, and thus for accounting convenience are recompensed equally. As the District Court found, the company "maintains records which enable it to determine what flight a given cabin attendant has flown each day, the position held each day, and the time spent by that cabin attendant each day." [151] But as the court further found, "[t]hese records enable the Company to pay cabin attendants different amounts for different portions of their monthly service. Flight service attendants temporarily filling pursers vacancies are paid the purser rate

[151] *Laffey* v. *Northwest Airlines, supra* note 1, 366 F. Supp. at 788-89, 6 FEP Cases at 922-23 (Find. 81).

only while flying as pursers. Stewardesses flying international receive the 'foreign flying' supplement only for the hours spent on the international flight. Permanently assigned pursers receive the purser rate . . . whether or not they are filling the purser position on the flight and irrespective of the kind of flight, domestic, foreign or interport. Except for the 'foreign flying supplement' all stewardesses of a given longevity receive the same salary, irrespective of the nature of the flights or the position occupied on the flight." [152]

The records would facilitate the ascertainment of differential salaries for dissimilar portions of the monthly service if in fact the activities purportedly justifying the larger salary were really the reason for the added compensation.

It is not legally appropriate to accord stewardesses salary increments only when they serve as the senior cabin attendant. We have pointed to the inconsistencies between occupational tasks and rewards to underscore our conviction that the District Court properly concluded that any greater duties demanded of pursers is not the foundation for their higher pay.[153]

---

[152] *Id.*

[153] It is argued that pursers are salaried higher because they must function under more onerous working conditions—in that they are confined to a more restricted bidding schedule and are assigned to more foreign flights. However, stewardesses with foreign language proficiency are confined to an even more restricted bidding schedule and yet they are paid at the rate applicable to other stewardesses. *Laffey* v. *Northwest Airlines, supra* note 1, 366 F. Supp. at 778, 6 FEP Cases at 914 (Find. 44). And foreign flying stewardesses are assigned to more foreign flights but receive only the same flying supplement that all stewardesses get for any foreign flying. Id. Moreover, pursers realize substantially higher pay than do stewardesses engaged in foreign flying. Therefore, NWA cannot justify the increased purser-pay on the basis of more restricted bidding schedules or more extensive foreign flying since stewardesses subjected to these same circumstances are nevertheless paid considerably less.

More importantly, NWA cannot support the higher pay on the ground that pursers and stewardesses perform their jobs under different working conditions. In *Corning Glass Works* v. *Brennan, supra* note 111, 417 U.S. at 202-203, 9 FEP Cases at 924-925, the Supreme Court defined "working conditions" as a term having a "different and much more specific meaning" than "a layman might . . . assume." Only "surroundings"—such as toxic chemicals or fumes regularly encountered by a worker—and "hazards"—such as those which pose the risk of severe physical injury—are encompassed within the meaning of "working conditions." The District Court's finding that stewardesses and pursers perform under similar working conditions is thus amply supported in the record.

NWA also asserts on appeal that even if the District Court was correct in holding that the jobs of stewardess and purser are equal, at least part of the compensation received by pursers falls within an exception to the Act as payment made pursuant to "a differential based on any other factor other than sex." 29 U.S.C. § 206(d)(1)(iv) (1970). NWA contends that one factor other than sex is foreign flying; it points out that since stewardesses on foreign flights get a foreign flying supplement, at least that portion of purser salary rests on a factor other than sex. The counter-argument advanced is that the exception to the Act is an affirmative defense which NWA has waived because it was never pleaded. We need not resolve this issue, however, since even if NWA properly raised the defense, it has not shouldered its burden of proving it.

The District Court implicitly found that the purser salary is not based on foreign flying, when it found that a "substantial percentage of the Company's overall utilization of pursers consisted of their assignment to pure domestic flights or to the domestic segments of international flights," *Laffey* v. *Northwest Airlines, supra* note 1, 366 F. Supp. at 787, 6 FEP Cases at 921 (Find. 73), and that pursers received the same pay regardless of whether they were engaged in foreign flying. *Id.* at 788-89, 6 FEP Cases at 922-23 (Find. 81). Consequently, NWA did not substain its burden of proving that part

In no way does this detract from the court's finding that the senior-cabin-attendant function was a mission that did not alter the basic equality of all cabin attendant jobs:

"The 'supervisory' functions of Senior cabin attendants—whether purser or stewardess—are less important than, and require no greater skill, effort or responsibility, than the other functions assigned to all cabin attendants."

We cannot say that this finding is clearly erroneous, and it follows that all cabin attendants perform equal work and are legally entitled to places on equal salary scales. Although the senior cabin attendant is "responsible" for the cabin crew during the flight, the Secretary of Labor's regulations define job responsibility in terms of the degree of employee accountability for job performance. At the trial of this case, witnesses testified that both pursers and stewardesses are disciplined substantially less for unsatisfactory performance as senior cabin attendant than for subpar passenger service. And although the company imposes rigorous sanctions on cabin attendants charged with misconduct affecting customer relations, its records disclose only one instance of disciplinary action against a purser for failure to adequately monitor the work of other cabin attendants. This strongly suggests that the provision of high quality service to passengers—exacted of all cabin attendants—is the most important undertaking for which the company compensates pursers and stewardesses. The increased responsibility borne by the more senior personnel in both classifications is rewarded by larger salaries given to those on the upper rungs of the pay ladder, and this will continue with a combined stewardess-purser salary scale.

In a similar case, the Fifth Circuit reversed a finding that a salary differential between male and female bank tellers was justified by the men's supposedly greater managerial role in "supervising the cashing of checks, helping the other tellers balance out, and generally acting as troubleshooters when unusual or difficult problems arose." [156] The court found it "doubtful at best that such small, insignificant additional duties can ever serve as a justification for the differential evidenced in the Bank's wage figures." [157] We affirm the District Court's findings that NWA purser and stewardess positions are substantially equal within the intent of the Equal Pay Act and demand financial response at the purser-level of recompense. [158]

---

of the purser salary was intended as compensation for foreign flying and was not "an added payment based on sex." *Corning Glass Works* v. *Brennan, supra* note 111, 417 U.S. at 204, 9 FEP Cases at 925.

[156] *Hodgson* v. *American Bank of Commerce, supra* note 121, 447 F.2d at 422, 9 FEP Cases at 680.

[157] *Id.*

[158] Once the stewardess position is found to be equal work to that of purser, not only must access to the job of purser be granted to women, but women who remain stewardesses must also be given pay equal to pursers'. The wage rates for male employees cannot be reduced to achieve equality, because the proviso to 29 U.S.C. § 206(d)(1) insures that in fashioning a remedy, "an employer who is paying a wage rate differential in violation of this subsection shall not, in order to comply with the provisions of this subsection, reduce the wage rate of any employee." 29 U.S.C. § 206(d)(1) (1970).

[Omitted.]

The District Court's judgment is devoted in substantial measure to remediation of violations found, under either the Equal Pay Act or Title VII, with respect to sex-based differentials in salaries, pensions, lay-over lodgings furnished and uniform-maintenance allowances.[188] In each category, the judgment effects an equalization upward [189] by mandating for female employees the same treatment that NWA had theretofore afforded male employees, [190] and enjoins sex discrimination in any significant aspect of employment of cabin attendants [191] in the future.[192] The judgment also awards backpay [193] under the Equal Pay Act to each "Equal Pay Act plaintiff" [194] for the three-year period preceding the filing of that plaintiff's written consent to joinder in the suit as a claimant therefore; [195] it similarly grants backpay under Title VII to each "Title VII plaintiff" [196] for the period commencing two years prior to the filing of the first charge with the Equal Employment Opportunity Commission,[197] terminating, however, for each employee who is also an Equal Pay Act plaintiff at the beginning of her Equal Pay Act recovery period.[198] NWA complains that some of these provisions go too far, and affected employees insist that the relief granted on these subjects does not extend far enough.

---

[188] *Laffey* v. *Northwest Airlines, supra* note 1, 374 F. Supp. at 1382-90, 7 FEP Cases at 689-93.

[189] As we have heretofore observed, see note 158 supra, the Equal Pay Act forbids attempted compliance with its provisions by "equalization" through a downward revision of pay. 29 U.S.C. § 206(d)(1) (1970). See *Corning Glass Works* v. *Brennan, supra* note 111, 417 U.S. at 206-207, 9 FEP Cases at 926.

[190] *Laffey* v. *Northwest Airlines, supra* note 1.

[191] The judgment defines "cabin attendants" as "all American-based employees of [NWA] whose principal duties consist of providing in-flight cabin service, whether denominated stewardess, pursuer, flight service attendant, steward, or otherwise." *Id.* at 1384, 7 FEP Cases at 689.

[192] *Id.* at 1385, 7 FEP Cases at 689-90.

[193] Grouped as backpay, though addressed discretely, are cabin attendants' salaries, pensions, the value of lodgings furnished and allowances for uniform-maintenance. *Id.* at 1385-87, 7 FEP Cases at 689-91.

[194] "Equal Pay Act plaintiff(s)" in the judgment are "all female cabin attendants employed by [NWA] who filed timely written consents with this Court, in accordance with 29 U.S.C. § 256 [1970], to become parties plaintiff with respect to the Equal Pay Act aspects of this lawsuit." *Id.* at 1384, 7 FEP Cases at 689.

[195] *Id.* at 1385-86, 7 FEP Cases at 689-90.

[196] "Title VII plaintiff(s)" under the judgment are "all female cabin attendants employed by [NWA] at any time on or after July 2, 1965, excluding only those who filed timely elections with this Court to be excluded from this lawsuit in its entirety." Id. at 1384, 7 FEP Cases at 689.

[197] See Part V(C) *infra*.

[198] *Laffey* v. *Northwest Airlines, supra* note 1, 374 F. Supp. at 1386-87, 7 FEP Cases at 690.

A. PERIOD OF BACKPAY RECOVERY UNDER THE EQUAL PAY ACT

Congress has imposed time limits upon the initiation of employee suits under the Equal Pay Act for either backpay or liquidated damages. The relevant statute specifies that any such action

"may be commenced within two years after the cause of action accrued, and . . . shall be forever barred unless commenced within two years after the cause of action accrued, except that a cause of action arising out of a willful violation may be commenced within three years after the cause of action accrued. . . ." [199]

The District Court found NWA's Equal Pay violation "willful" within the meaning of this provision [200] and awarded the Equal Pay Act plaintiffs [201] backpay [202] for three-year periods preceding the filing of timely written consents.[203] NWA contends that retrospection of its backpay liability for periods exceeding two years is an erroneous application of the statute. The core argument, as we understand, is that the statutory word "willfull" connotes an unwholesome state of mind said to be absent in this case, particularly since in an independent ruling the District Court denied liquidated damages upon a finding that NWA's sex-discriminatory policies were pursued in good faith.[204]

(1) *The Standard for Determining Willfulness*

The suit-limitation provision does not undertake to define "willfull" on its own, nor have we encountered elsewhere in companion legislation any definition seemingly referable to that provision.[205] Courts wrestling with its facial ambiguity have usually subscribed to one or the other of two divergent views. Some, notably in the Fifth Circuit, read "willful" as requiring nothing more than knowledge of the possible applicability of the governing statute to the conduct eventually held to be legally wanting.[206] "Stated most simply," says the Court of Appeals for that Circuit, "we think the test should be: Did the employer know the [statute] was in the picture." [207] Other courts take a differently worded

---

[199] 29 U.S.C. § 255(a) (1970).

[200] *Laffey* v. *Northwest Airlines, supra* note 1, 374 F. Supp. at 1390, 7 FEP Cases at 688.

[201] See note 194 *supra.*

[202] See note 193 *supra.*

[203] See note 194 *supra* and accompanying text.

[204] We discuss that finding in Part V-B *infra.*

[205] See note 230 *infra.*

[206] *Brennan* v. *Heard*, 491 F.2d 1, 3, 21 WH Cases 601 (5th Cir. 1974); *Brennan* v. *J. M. Fields, Inc.*, 488 F.2d 443, 448, 9 FEP Cases 894, 897 (5th Cir. 1973), *cert. denied*, 419 U.S. 881, 9 FEP Cases 1408 (1974); *Brennan* v. *General Motors Acceptance Corp.*, 482 F.2d 825, 828-29, 21 WH Cases 187 (5th Cir. 1973); *Coleman* v. *Jiffy June Farms, Inc.*, 458 F.2d 1138, 1142, 20 WH Cases 630 (5th Cir. 1971), *cert. denied*, 409 U.S. 948, 20 WH Cases 937 (1972).

[207] *Coleman* v. *Jiffy June Farms, Inc., supra* note 206, 458 F.2d at 1142, 20 WH Cases at 631.

approach: [208] "[W]illful," declares one, "retains its traditional meaning that violations of the Act must be deliberate, voluntary and intentional." [209] NWA urges upon us still another meaning: that "willfull" requires bad purpose as an element of the violation.

Under some statutes, particularly those directed at conduct involving moral turpitude, an act is "willfull" only if done malevolently, wickedly or criminally.[210] Under other types of statutes, it suffices that the act was performed consciously and voluntarily, rather than inadvertently or accidentally.[211] Betwixt these two formulations, "willfull" has been given various other meanings,[212] although shades of difference ofttimes diminish when the probe extends beneath the surface.[213] Because of its inherent instability, only the most careful consideration of the term "willfull" in its legislative context can provide satisfactory assurance that eventually it will take on its proper cast.[214] And so it does here.

The suit-limitation provision in its original form was part of the congressional response to an "existing emergency" [215] three decades ago. In 1946, the Supreme Court had held that employees were entitled to portal-to-portal pay under the Fair Labor Standards Act.[216] In 1947, Congress declared that allowance of claims therefore would create "wholly unexpected liabilities, immense in amount and retroactive in operation," [217] and enacted legislation to deal with the situation.[218] A limitation period of two years for all claims [219] was designed specifically to eliminate differences arising from "the varying and extended periods of time for which, under the laws of the several States, potential retroactive liability may be imposed upon employers. . . ." [220] Its aim thus was to establish

---

208 *Hodgson* v. *Unified School Dist.*, 21 WH Cases 574, 577 (D. Kan. 1973); *Boll* v. *Federal Reserve Bank*, 365 F. Supp. 637, 648-49, 21 WH Cases 876 (E.D. Mo. 1973), *aff'd*, 497 F.2d 335, 21 WH Cases 886 (1974); *Brennan* v. *Westinghouse Credit Corp.*, 21 WH Cases 871, 875-76 (E.D. Tenn. 1973). See also *Dunlop* v. *New Jersey*, 522 F.2d 504, 518, 22 WH Cases 478 (3d Cir. 1975); *Hodgson* v. *Cactus Craft of Arizona*, 481 F.2d 464, 467, 21 WH Cases 145 (9th Cir. 1973); *Hodgson* v. *Barge, Waggoner & Sumner, Inc.*, 377 F. Supp. 842, 845, 21 WH Cases 6 (M.D. Tenn. 1972), *aff'd*, 477 F.2d 598, 21 WH Cases 9 (6th Cir. 1973).

209 *Brennan* v. *Westinghouse Credit Corp.*, *supra* note 208, 21 WH Cases at 876.

210 *E.g.*, *Spurr* v. *United States*, 174 U.S. 728, 734-35 (1899).

211 *E.g.*, *Nabob Oil Co.* v. *United States*, 190 F.2d 478, 480, 10 WH Cases 318 (10th Cir.), *cert. denied*, 342 U.S. 876, 10 WH Cases 465 (1951).

212 See, *e.g.*, *United States* v. *Murdock*, 290 U.S. 389, 394-95 (1933).

213 "It is only in very few criminal cases that 'willfull' means 'done with a bad purpose.' Generally, it means 'no more than that the person charged with the duty knows what he is doing. It does not mean that, in addition, he must suppose that he is breaking the law.'" *Townsend* v. *United States*, 68 App. D.C. 223, 229, 95 F.2d 352, 358, *cert. denied*, 303 U.S. 664 (1938).

214 See *Spies* v. *United States*, 317 U.S. 492, 497 (1943).

215 29 U.S.C. § 251 (1970).

216 *Anderson* v. *Mt. Clemens Pottery Co.*, 328 U.S. 680, 6 WH Cases 83 (1946).

217 29 U.S.C. § 251 (1970).

218 The legislation was the Portal-to-Portal Act of 1947, Act of May 14, 1947, ch. 52, 61 Stat. 84, as amended, 29 U.S.C. §§ 251 *et seq.* (1970). See also *Steiner* v. *Mitchell*, 350 U.S. 247, 253, 12 WH Cases 750 (1956).

219 Act of May 14, 1947, ch. 52, § 6, 61 Stat. 87.

220 Act of May 14, 1947, ch. 52, § 1, 61 Stat. 84, 29 U.S.C. § 251.

for employee recoveries a nationally uniform cutoff point, whether for purposeful or innocent transgressions of the Act.

The limitation period continued at two years until enactment of the Fair Labor Standards Amendments of 1966.[221] During the process leading to that legislation, an effort was made to enlarge the limitation period to three years for any type of violation, for reasons expressed by the then Secretary of Labor:

"The lengthening of the statute of limitations to three years will allow workers more time to familiarize themselves with their legal right to back wages and thus improve enforcement of the Act. The short statute of limitations gives competitive advantage to violators and penalizes many workers in the collection of wages legally due. The Federal Criminal Statute runs for three years or more. The existing two-year period under [the Fair Labor Standards Act] is also shorter than that allowed creditors of employees to collect money owed for food and rent bills." [222]

As the bill emerged from committee, however, the limitation provision appeared in its current form.[223] The period had been lengthened to three years for a "willfull violation," but for others it remained at two.[224] We have not uncovered any clear-cut statement in the legislative history as to why the extension to three years was thus encumbered. There is ample room, however, for an informed belief that, with the amendments' broad expansion of the Act's coverage [225] and resultant concern over the effect on the small businessman,[226] an unqualified increase of the limitation period would bear too heavily upon an inevitably larger group of exclusively inadvertent violators.[227]

Be that as it may, the important consideration is the absence from the legislative history of any visible movement to impart criminal-law precepts of moral culpability into the statutory scheme as a condition to accountability for a civil wrong. There is nothing to suggest that the congressional effort either in 1947 or 1966 was the exaction of a penalty, to which moral culpability would be highly relevant. On the contrary, the implication is almost irresistible that the objective consistently was the erection of a bulwark to extensive liability, and to economic hardships that would follow. Because in 1947 Congress feared a crisis from enforcement of an unexpected multitude of newly-arising claims, and

[221] Pub. L. No. 89-901, 80 Stat. 830 (1966).

[222] Hearings on H.R. 8259 Before the General Subcommittee on Labor of the Committee on Education and Labor 7 (1965) (statement of Secretary Wirtz).

[223] S. Rep. No. 1487, 89th Cong., 2d Sess. 36, 69 (1966); H.R. Rep. No. 1366, 89th Cong., 2d Sess. 46, 77 (1966).

[224] See text supra at note 199.

[225] See S. Rep. No. 1487, 89th Cong., 2d Sess. 1-4 (1966); H.R. Rep. No. 1366, 89th Cong., 2d Sess. 4-10 (1966).

[226] "The proposed coverage brings small local business immediately into coverage. There are no exact figures on how many retail establishments would be affected by the bill, but there are definite indications that the number is substantial. . . . Businessmen state that they will have to reduce their work forces substantially and even then will be faced with the grave problem of whether or not they can remain in business." S. Rep. No. 1487, 89th Cong., 2d Sess. 76-77 (statement of Senator Fannin).

[227] See note 226 supra.

because in 1966 the coverage of the Act was being greatly widened to encompass a host of enterprises never before subjected, it seems evident that on each occasion Congress wished to insure that those who were unwittingly intercepted by the Act were not impacted with a three-year statute of limitations. These circumstances undergird the unlikelihood that "willfull," in this rule, was intended to exact bad purpose on the employer's part—rather than simply a lesser factor reducing the employer's predicament to something less than a wholly unanticipated prospect of late-found liability—as a precondition to an extra year's recovery.

It seems also significant that the requirement of willfullness is not one which must be met in order that there be liability, but rather is one to be satisfied before there can be expanded liability. The nonwillful character of a violation of the Act does not defeat recovery, although it does confine the period therefore to two years, and a willful violation lengthens the period merely by another year. An employer out of compliance, but not willfully so, is spared the burden of recompense beyond a period of two years; an employer willfully out of compliance, despite his willfulness is spared beyond a period of three years. The relatively small difference between the two- and three-year periods tends to question any notion that the distinguishing criterion was to be moral rather than intellectual culpability. Since a morally innocent employer is nonetheless liable for two years, one may ask why a "willfull" violator's accountability is for only one year more if the term is to imply wicked purpose.

We realize, of course, that a lighter burden would subject a good many employers to the extra year of liability notwithstanding that their violations may represent little or no more than an erroneous interpretation of the statutory requirements. On the other hand, employers as a class occupy a much superior position vis-a-vis their employees to ascertain the effect of the law upon their business policies and practices. Even where the closeness of the question of the statute's applicability hampers or forestalls absolute decisional accuracy, there is no good reason for translating the employer's error into a loss of pay for the employee.

Atop all else, the Equal Pay Act and the Fair Labor Standards Act, of which the former is a part, undoubtedly are remedial statutes, as such to be liberally construed in favor of their intended beneficiaries.[228] In light of this, as well as the historical backdrop against which we must view this legislation, we could not readily attribute to Congress a purpose to impose upon employee-claimants the much heavier burden -- sometimes, perhaps, a well-nigh impossible burden — of proving an iniquitous employer state-of-mind as a prerequisite to a backpay recovery for the third year. We reject, then, a definition of "willfull" in the suit-limitation provision which would demand proof that the employer entertained a bad purpose or an evil intent. At the same time, we need not go so far as to hold that a violation is willful merely because from the employer's

---

[228] *E.g., Corning Glass Works* v. *Brennan, supra* note 111, 417 U.S. at 208, 9 FEP Cases at 927. *Coles* v. *Penny,* _____ U.S. App. D.C. _____, _____, 531 F.2d 609, 615, 12 FEP Cases 1785, 1790 (1976).

viewpoint the statute was in the picture.[229] Nor need we undertake to precisely define "willfull" for cases closer than the one at bar.[230] We think that at the very least the employer's noncompliance is "willfull" when he is cognizant of an appreciable possibility that he may be subject to the statutory requirements and fails to take steps reasonably calculated to resolve the doubt.[231] We think, too, that the same conclusion follows when an equally aware employer consciously and voluntarily charts a course which turns out to be wrong.[232] Beyond these holdings, we need not venture now.

## (2) *The Decision on NWA*

The District Court expressly found NWA's multifold violations of the Equal Pay Act to be "willful".[233] The court explained:

"The Equal Pay Act violation was willful in that [NWA] was fully aware of the Equal Pay Act and adopted a deliberate and knowing course of conduct despite its awareness. The Court does not find an intentional, bad faith, attempt to evade the law. The judgment of [NWA] that its conduct would not be found to be in violation of the Equal Pay Act has been found to be in error. The conduct of [NWA] in the exercise of that judgment was willful." [234]

This finding is fully binding upon us unless "clearly erroneous." [235] NWA does not say that the finding lacks evidentiary support in the record, nor could it. An official of NWA testified by deposition that since 1963 the company was aware of the Equal Pay Act, was generally familiar with its provisions, and had internally reviewed it for its possible

[229] As one commentator has observed, "[s]ince virtually every employer knows of the possible applicability of [the Fair Labor Standards Act] to his business, the practical effect of this interpretation is to eliminate the two year statute of limitations from the act. If this were the result Congress intended, it would not have drafted the statute so that the two year period is the rule and the three year period is the exception." Richards, *Monetary Awards in Equal Pay Act Litigation*, 29 ARK. L. REV. 328, 338 (1975).

[230] NWA contends that "willful," in the suit-limitation provision takes on the interpretation given the same work in the criminal provision of the Fair Labor Standards Act, 29 U.S.C. § 216(a) (1970). We do not agree that the criminal construction is to be imparted into the civil provision simply because both provisions are part of the same statute. The purposes of the two sections are entirely different; one punishes as criminal certain specified conduct while the other subserves a policy to which punishment is entirely foreign. Compare *Corning Glass Works* v. *Brennan, supra* note 111, 417 U.S. at 207, 9 FEP Cases at 926. In any event, under § 216's definition of "willful," "[i]t is sufficient if the act was deliberate, voluntary and intentional as distinguished from one committed through inadvertence, accidentally or by ordinary negligence." *Nabob Oil Co.* v. *United States, supra* note 211, 190 F.2d at 480, 10 WH Cases at 319. We reach no different conclusion in this case by that definition. See note 232 *infra* and accompanying text. Compare *Coleman* v. *Jiffy June Farms, Inc., supra* note 206, 458 F.2d at 1142.

[231] Compare *Brennan* v. *Heard, supra* note 206, 491 F.2d at 3.

[232] In situations of that sort, "the act [is] deliberate, voluntary and intentional as distinguished from one committed through inadvertence, accidentally or by ordinary negligence." See note 230 *supra*.

[233] *Laffey* v. *Northwest Airlines, supra* note 1, 374 F. Supp. at 1390, 7 FEP Cases at 688.

[234] *Id.*

[235] Fed. R. Civ. P. 52(a).

application to the company.[236] NWA understood the Act's central provision that male and female employees cannot be paid differently for performing substantially the same work, and considered its own policies respecting cabin attendants in that light.[237] The company concluded that the Act was inapplicable because it felt that the purser and stewardess jobs were substantially different.[238] Even after the filing of charges with the Equal Employment Opportunity Commission and the subsequent filing of this lawsuit, NWA continued to adhere to that position.[239] No written memorandum on the subject was prepared or received by the company, although it may have been provided oral advisories by a trade association.[240] The witness had no recollection that NWA ever conferred with outside counsel on the subject, and he did not specifically mention any sort of legal advice at all.[241] We have not been referred to, nor have we discovered, any other evidence bearing on the subject. We think the witness' testimony amply sustains the District Court's finding that NWA "was fully aware of the Equal Pay Act and adopted a deliberate and knowing course of conduct despite its awareness." [242]

NWA asserts, however, that the facts found are legally insufficient to enable the conclusion that the violation was "willfull." It argues for an interpretation of the term which would require bad purpose or evil intent,[243] which the District Court's findings disclaimed.[244] We have declined acceptance of that definition of willfulness,[245] and in our view of the most that willfulness involves [246] we are satisfied that the necessary elements are present here. NWA not only knew of the Equal Pay Act and its content but also correctly understood its prohibition on different salary levels for men and women performing substantially similar work. With little or nothing beyond internal consideration by laymen—even after the present legal challenge got under way—the company consciously though erroneously concluded that its treatment of pursers and stewardesses was unaffected by the Act. We deem that sufficient to comprise willfulness; in the District Court's words, "[t]he conduct of the Company in the exercise of that judgment was willful." [247] For reasons already extensively articulated,[248] we agree.

It is also contended by NWA that the District Court was logically inconsistent in finding that the Equal Pay Act violation occurred in good

236 J. App. 1477-78.
237 J. App. 1478.
238 J. App. 1478-79.
239 J. App. 1479.
240 J. App. 1477-78.
241 J. App. 1477-78.
242 See text *supra* at note 234.
243 See text *supra* at note 210.
244 See text *supra* at note 234.
245 See text *supra* at notes 229-32.
246 See note 230 *supra*.
247 See text *supra* at note 234.
248 See text *supra* at notes 214-32.

faith [249] and in also finding that the violation was willful. This claim is of a piece with NWA's insistence that willfulness is inextricably tied to bad purpose.[250] We have said that it is not; [251] we have equated willfulness, rather, with conduct which is conscious and voluntary in character.[252] It follows that a practice may be deliberate, and thus willful, notwithstanding motivation that is honest. Even if NWA pursued in good faith the policies which the District Court held to be unlawful, its conduct was willful within the meaning of the limitation provision.

## B. GOOD FAITH

To each affected employee, an employer infringing the Equal Pay Act is statutorily liable, in consequence of its interrelationship with the Fair Labor Standards Act,[253] not only for unpaid compensation but also for "an additional equal amount as liquidated damages." [254] The predicate for the latter imposition is the reality that "[t]he retention of a workman's pay may well result in damages too obscure and difficult of proof for estimate other than by liquidated damages." [255] Originally mandatory in its provision,[256] the statutory provision on liquidated damages was amended in 1947 to confer discretion on the courts to deny otherwise awardable liquidated damages in whole or part when satisfied that the employer acted or omitted action "in good faith and that he had reasonable grounds for believing that his act or omission was not a violation. . . ." [257] In the instant case, the District Court so found:

"[NWA] did have reasonable grounds for belief that it was not violating the Equal Pay Act. While this court has found as fact that the jobs of purser and stewardess are in fact equal, it was not unreasonable for the Company to have believed otherwise. Five factors support this conclusion: The traditional practice of the Company in treating the positions as unequal, the general industry practice to the same effect, the acquiescence of the stewardess' bargaining representative in this arrangement, the absence of any grievances or even suggestions from stewardesses to the contrary prior to the present controversy, and the absence of any clear legal precedent or guideline precisely in point." [258]

---

249 See Part V(B) *infra.*

250 See text *supra* at note 243.

251 See text *supra* at notes 214-32.

252 See text *supra* at notes 229-32.

253 See note 88 *supra* and accompaning text.

254 "Any employer who violates the provisions of [the Fair Labor Standards Act] shall be liable to the employee or employees affected in the amount of the unpaid minimum wages, or unpaid overtime compensation, as the case may be, and in an additional equal amount as liquidated damages." 29 U.S.C. § 216(b) (1970).

255 *Overnight Motor Transp. Co.* v. *Missel,* 316 U.S. 572, 583-84, 2 WH Cases 47 (1942).

256 See text *infra* at notes 264-70.

257 "[I]f the employer shows to the satisfaction of the court that the act or omission giving rise [to the violation] was in good faith and that he had reasonable grounds for believing that his act or omission was not a violation of [the Act] as amended, the court may, in its sound discretion, award no liquidated damages or award any amounts thereof not to exceed the amount specified in" § 216(b), *supra* note 254. 29 U.S.C. § 260 (1970).

258 *Laffey* v. *Northwest Airlines, supra* note 1, 374 F. Supp. at 1390, 7 FEP at 688.

The good faith of which the Act speaks is "an honest intention to ascertain what the . . . Act requires and to act in accordance with it." [259] That necessitates a subjective inquiry.[260] The statutory call for reasonable grounds for a belief in compliance with the Act imposes a requirement additional to good faith,[261] and one that involves an objective standard.[262] Any assessment of an employer's good faith or grounds for his belief in the legal propriety of his conduct is necessarily a finding of fact, to be disturbed on appeal only if clearly erroneous.[263] In the case at bar, however, it is clear enough that the District Court relied on factors not supportive of its conclusion. Accordingly, we must remand for redetermination of the issue.

The current version of the liquidated damages provision was enacted in response to the Supreme Court's "lament" in *Overnight Motor Transportation* v. *Missel* [264] of the then mandatory nature of the judicial duty respecting liquidated damages.[265] In that case, the fact that an employer was not exempt from the Fair Labor Standards Act's coverage did not plainly emerge until after the employment in question had ended. The Court expressed sympathy for the employer but concluded nevertheless:

"Perplexing as [the employer's] problem may have been, the difficulty does not warrant shifting the burden to the employee. The wages were specified for him by the statute, and he was no more at fault than the employer. The liquidated damages for failure to pay the minimum wages . . . are compensation, not a penalty or punishment by the Government . . . The retention of a workman's pay may well result in damages too obscure and difficult of proof for estimate other than by liquidated damages." [266]

Congress reacted by an amendment conferring the present discretion on the courts to limit or deny liquidated damages if the employer could meet the "substantial burden" [267] of proving that his failure to comply was in good faith and also was predicated on reasonable grounds for a belief that he was in compliance.[268] If the employer cannot convince the

---

259 *Addison* v. *Huron Stevedoring Corp.*, 204 F.2d 88, 93, 11 WH Cases 312 (2d Cir.), *cert. denied*, 346 U.S. 877, 11 WH Cases 682 (1953).

260 *Id.* at 93.

261 *Id.* See also note 268 *infra.*

262 *Addison* v. *Huron Stevedoring Corp.*, *supra* note 259, 204 F.2d at 93.

263 Fed. R. Civ. P. 52(a); *Addison* v. *Huron Stevedoring Corp.*, *supra* note 259; *Hodgson* v. *Miller Brewing Co.*, *supra* note 135, 457 F.2d at 228, 9 FEP Cases at 731; *Day & Zimmerman* v. *Reed*, 168 F.2d 356, 360, 7 WH Cases 1040 (8th Cir. 1948); *Lassiter* v. *Guy F. Atkinson Co.*, 176 F.2d 984, 993, 21 A.L.R.2d 1313, 9 WH Cases 126 (9th Cir. 1949).

264 *Supra* note 255.

265 Portal-to-Portal Act, H.R. Rep. No. 71, at 7-8 (1947).

266 316 U.S. at 583-84, 2 WH Cases at 52.

267 *Rothman* v. *Publicker Indus., Inc.*, 201 F.2d 618, 620, 11 WH Cases 242 (3d Cir. 1953).

268 29 C.F.R. § 790.22(b) (1975) provides:
"The conditions prescribed as prerequisites to [the court's denial of liquidated damages] are two: (1) The employer must show to the satisfaction of the court that the act or

court in these respects, an award of liquidated damages remains mandatory; [269] and even if the employer's presentation is persuasive the court
may still exercise its discretion to grant liquidated damages totally or
partially.[270]

Examined against this background, the reasons given by the District
Court for disallowing liquidated damages betray their legal inadequacy.[271]
That an employer and others in the industry have broken the law for a
long time without complaints from employees is plainly not the reasonable ground to which the statute speaks.[272] Nor is it enough that it appear
that the employer probably did not act in bad faith; he must affirmatively
establish that he acted both in good faith and on reasonable grounds.[273]
That duty is accentuated here, where the prevalence of sex-discrimination
litigation against the airline industry [274] naturally prompts the question
whether NWA should reasonably have known that neither its own tradition, the industry custom nor the employees' silence was a reliable in-

---

omission giving rise to such action was in good faith; and (2) he must show also, to
the satisfaction of the court, that he had reasonable grounds for believing that his
act or omission was not a violation of the Fair Labor Standards Act . . . If, . . . the
employer does not show to the satisfaction of the court that he has met the two conditions mentioned above, the court is given no discretion by the statute, and it continues
to be the duty of the court to award liquidated damages." (Footnote omitted.)
*Rothman* v. *Publicker Indus., Inc., supra* note 267, 201 F.2d at 620, 11 WH Cases at
244 (under the Portal-to-Portal Act, a delinquent employer seeking to escape payment
of liquidated damages has "a plain and substantial burden of persuading the court
that his failure to obey the [Fair Labor Standards Act] was both in good faith and
predicated upon such reasonable grounds that it would be unfair to impose upon him
more than a compensatory verdict."). See also *Wright* v. *Carrig,* 275 F.2d 448, 14 WH
Cases 492 (4th Cir. 1960); *McClanahan* v. *Matthews,* 440 F.2d 320, 322-23, 26 A.L.R.
Fed. 598, 19 WH Cases 1051 (6th Cir. 1971). Cf. *National Automatic Laundry & Cleaning Council* v. *Shultz, supra* note 127, 143 U.S. App. D.C. at 282 & n. 6, 443 F.2d at 697
& n. 6, and see generally Richards, *Monetary Awards in Equal Pay Act Litigation,* 29
ARK. L. REV. 328, 347-54 (1975).

269 *McClanahan* v. *Matthews, supra* note 268, 440 F.2d at 323, 19 WH Cases at 1052;
*Thomas* v. *Louisiana,* 348 F. Supp. 792, 20 WH Cases 927 (W.D. La. 1972); 29 C.F.R.
§ 790.22(b) (1974); *contra, Baird* v. *Wagoner Transp. Co.,* 18 WH Cases 597 (W.D. Mich.
1968), *aff'd,* 425 F.2d 407, 19 WH Cases 450 (6th Cir.), *cert. denied,* 400 U.S. 829, 19
WH Cases 712 (1970).

270 *McClanahan* v. *Matthews, supra* note 268, 440 F.2d at 322-24, 19 WH Cases at
1052.

271 The court's ruling on liquidated damages has been characterized as one "of
particular interest and very doubtful correctness." Richards, *Monetary Awards in
Equal Pay Act Litigation,* 29 ARK. L. REV. 328, 352 (1975). The degree to which Congress' 1947 modification may have changed the character of liquidated damages from
compensatory to punitive allowances is a matter we need not now decide. See generally
*id.* at 348-50; *Russell* v. *American Tobacco Co.,* 528 F.2d 357, 366, 11 FEP Cases 395,
402 (4th Cir. 1975), *cert. denied,* _____ U.S. _____, 12 FEP Cases 1090 (1976).

272 See note 268 *supra.*

273 See note 268 *supra.*

274 *E.g., Pond* v. *Braniff Airways,* 500 F.2d 161, 8 FEP Cases 659 (5th Cir. 1974);
*Airline Stewards & Stewardess' Ass'n, Local 550,* v. *American Airlines,* 490 F.2d 636, 6
FEP Cases 1197 (7th Cir. 1973), *cert. denied,* 416 U.S. 993, 7 FEP Cases 1160 (1974);
*Sprogis* v. *United Airlines,* 444 F.2d 1194, 3 FEP Cases 621 (7th Cir.), *cert. denied,* 404
U.S. 991, 4 FEP Cases 37 (1971); *Gerstle* v. *Continental Airlines,* 358 F. Supp. 545, 5
FEP Cases 976 (D. Colo. 1973); *Cooper* v. *Delta Airlines,* 274 F. Supp. 781, 1 FEP
Cases 241, 66 LRRM 2489 (E.D. La. 1967); *DeFiguieredo* v. *Trans World Airlines,* 322
F. Supp. 1384, 3 FEP Cases 143 (S.D.N.Y. 1971); *Maguire* v. *Trans World Airlines,* 55
F.R.D. 48, 9 FEP Cases 760 (S.D.N.Y. 1972).

dicium of the demands of the law.[275] We need not inquire whether business custom or employee acquiescence might in particular circumstances explain why an otherwise punctilious employer did not investigate his situation more thoroughly, for in any event they do not provide a reasonable foundation for a positive belief that in fact there is compliance.

We share with the District Court the view that ambiguous or complex legal requirements may provide reasonable grounds for an employer's good faith but erroneous belief that he is in conformity with the Act.[276] Indeed, just that sort of employer-predicament was the concern of Congress when it enacted the 1947 amendments.[277] But legal uncertainty, to assist the employer's defense, must pervade and markedly influence the employer's belief; merely that the law is uncertain does not suffice. While the District Court cited the absence of precise legal guidelines as a factor indicating reasonableness on NWA's part, it made no finding that that condition actually led NWA to believe that it was in compliance with the Equal Pay Act. Furthermore, even when the court finds good faith and a reasonable basis, it retains discretion to award liquidated damages.[278] We cannot say that the District Court's decision to deny such damages would have been reached had it known that any of the five factors upon which it relied would not survive scrutiny.[279]

---

[275] Employee silence is very different from an absence of complaint by Department of Labor officials following examination of the employer's system. See *Retail Store Employees Union, Local 400* v. *Drug Fair Community Drug Co.*, 307 F. Supp. 473, 479-80, 19 WH Cases 305 (D.D.C. 1969); *Hodgson* v. *Barge, Wagoner & Sumner, Inc.*, supra note 208, 377 F. Supp. at 1845.

[276] *Van Dyke* v. *Bluefield Gas Co.*, 210 F.2d 620, 12 WH Cases 10 (4th Cir.), cert. denied, 347 U.S. 1014, 12 WH Cases 188 (1954); *General Elec. Co.* v. *Porter*, 208 F.2d 805, 11 WH Cases 736 (9th Cir. 1953); *Harp* v. *Continental/Moss-Gordin Gin Co.*, 259 F. Supp. 198, 18 WH Cases 319 (M.D. Ala. 1966), aff'd, 386 F.2d 995, 18 WH Cases 321 (5th Cir. 1967); *Kelly* v. *Ballard*, 298 F. Supp. 1301, 18 WH Cases 847 (S.D. Cal. 1969); *Bauler* v. *Pressed Steel Car Co.*, 81 F. Supp. 172, 8 WH Cases 55 (N.D. Ill. 1948), aff'd, 182 F.2d 357, 9 WH Cases 416 (2d Cir. 1950); *Peperissa* v. *Coren-Indik, Inc.*, 298 F. Supp. 34, 18 WH Cases 819 (E.D. Pa. 1969).
On the other hand, maintenance of a practice of "highly questionable legality" constitutes bad faith. *Albemarle Paper Co.* v. *Moody*, supra note 174, 422 U.S. at 422, 10 FEP Cases at 1189. Lack of reasonable grounds has also been found where an employer waited for an impending Supreme Court decision on the validity of amending legislation, *Thomas* v. *Louisiana*, supra note 269, 348 F. Supp. at 796; where a Supreme Court decision in another case had made it clear that the employer's defense was not valid, *King* v. *Board of Educ.*, 435 F.2d 295, 298, 19 WH Cases 778 (7th Cir. 1970), cert. denied, 402 U.S. 908, 19 WH Cases 1018 (1971); where the employer continued a course of conduct after inspectors indicated that it violated the Act, *American Newspaper Guild* v. *Republican Publishing Co.*, 8 WH Cases 140, aff'd, 172 F.2d 943, 8 WH Cases 598 (1st Cir. 1949); where the employer claimed that he did not know the details of the job in issue, *Day & Zimmerman* v. *Reid*, supra note 263, 168 F.2d at 359-360.

[277] See text supra at notes 264-70.

[278] See note 270 supra and accompanying text.

[279] In *Crago* v. *Rockwell Mfg. Co.*, 301 F. Supp. 743, 19 WH Cases 55 (W.D. Pa. 1969), it was held that "[a]lthough defendant did not do all that might have been done by a reasonable employer in determining whether it was in compliance with the Act, such as securing from its legal department a reliable opinion incident to plaintiff's employment, and again seeking the advice of the Wage and Hour Division, this circumstance does not preclude defendant from protection under [the liquidated damages provision]." *Id.* at 748. The court then found that the defendant had acted in good faith on reasonable grounds to believe it was not violating the Act, but still awarded partial liquidated

## B. SIMILAR WORKING CONDITIONS

## CORNING GLASS WORKS v. BRENNAN

*Supreme Court of the United States, 1974*
*94 S. Ct. 2223, 9 FEP Cases 919*

MR. JUSTICE MARSHALL delivered the opinion of the Court.

These cases arise under the Equal Pay Act of 1963, 29 U.S.C. § 206(d)(1), which added to the Fair Labor Standards Act the principle of equal pay for equal work regardless of sex. The principal question posed is whether Corning Glass Works violated the Act by paying a higher base wage to male night shift inspectors than it paid to female inspectors performing the same tasks on the day shift, where the higher wage was paid in addition to a separate night shift differential paid to all employees for night work. In No. 73-29, the Court of Appeals for the Second Circuit, in a case involving several Corning plants in Corning, New York, held that this practice violated the Act, 474 F.2d 226, 20 WH Cases 1114 (1973). In No. 73-695, the Court of Appeals for the Third Circuit, in a case involving a Corning plant in Wellsboro, Pennsylvania, reached the opposite conclusion. 480 F.2d 1254, 21 WH Cases 140 (1973). We granted certiorari and consolidated the cases to resolve this unusually direct conflict between two circuits. 414 U.S. 1110. Finding ourselves in substantial agreement with the analysis of the Second Circuit, we affirm in No. 73-29 and reverse in No. 73-695.

I. Prior to 1925, Corning operated its plants in Wellsboro and Corning only during the day, and all inspection work was performed by women. Between 1925 and 1930, the company began to introduce automatic production equipment which made it desirable to institute a night shift. During this period, however, both New York and Pennsylvania law prohibited women from working at night. As a result, in order to fill inspector positions on the new night shift, the company had to recruit male employees from among its male day workers. The male employees so transferred demanded and received wages substantially higher than those paid to women inspectors engaged on the two day shifts.[3] During this

---

damages "representing plaintiff's loss of use of the overtime compensation due him. . . ." *Id.*

The employee litigants also complain that the provision of the judgment on liquidated-damages is ambiguous in one respect and deficient in another. Since we are remanding the matter of liquidated damages in toto for reconsideration by the District Court, to which any further grievance by either side may be addressed, we do not pass on these contentions on this appeal.

[3] [Footnotes numbered as in original.—Ed.] Higher wages were demanded in part because the men had been earning more money on their day shift jobs than women were paid for inspection work. Thus, at the time of the creation of the new night shift, female day shift inspectors received wages ranging from 20 to 30 cents per hour. Most of the men designated to fill the newly created night shift positions had been working in the blowing room where the lowest wage rate was 48 cents per hour and where additional incentive pay could be earned. As night shift inspectors these men received 53 cents per hour. There is also some evidence in the record that additional compensation was necessary because the men viewed inspection jobs as "demeaning" and as "women's work."

same period, however, no plant-wide shift differential existed and male employees working at night, other than inspectors, received the same wages as their day shift counterparts. Thus a situation developed where the night inspectors were all male,[4] the day inspectors all female, and the male inspectors received significantly higher wages.

In 1944, Corning plants at both locations were organized by a labor union and a collective-bargaining agreement was negotiated for all production and maintenance employees. This agreement for the first time established a plant-wide shift differential,[5] but this change did not eliminate the higher base wage paid to male night inspectors. Rather, the shift differential was superimposed on the existing difference in base wages between male night inspectors and female day inspectors.

Prior to the June 11, 1964, effective date of the Equal Pay Act, the law in both Pennsylvania and New York was amended to permit women to work at night. It was not until some time after the effective date of the Act, however, that Corning initiated efforts to eliminate the differential rates for male and female inspectors. Beginning in June 1966, Corning started to open up jobs on the night shift to women. Previously separate male and female seniority lists were consolidated and women became eligible to exercise their seniority, on the same basis as men, to bid for the higher paid night inspection jobs as vacancies occurred.

On January 20, 1969, a new collective-bargaining agreement went into effect, establishing a new "job evaluation" system for setting wage rates. The new agreement abolished for the future the separate base wages for day and night shift inspectors and imposed a uniform base wage for inspectors exceeding the wage rate for the night shift previously in effect. All inspectors hired after January 20, 1969, were to receive the same base wage, whatever their sex or shift. The collective-bargaining agreement further provided, however, for a higher "red circle" rate for employees hired prior to January 20, 1969, when working as inspectors on the night shift. This "red circle" rate served essentially to perpetuate the differential in base wages between day and night inspectors.

The Secretary of Labor brought these cases to enjoin Corning from violating the Equal Pay Act and to collect back wages allegedly due female employees because of past violations. Three distinct questions are presented: (1) Did Corning ever violate the Equal Pay Act by paying male night shift inspectors more than female day shift inspectors? (2) If so, did Corning cure its violation of the Act in 1966 by permitting women to work as night shift inspectors? (3) Finally, if the violation was not remedied in 1966, did Corning cure its violation in 1969 by equalizing day and night inspector wage rates but establishing higher "red circle" rates for existing employees working on the night shift?

[4] A temporary exception was made during World War II when manpower shortages caused Corning to be permitted to employ women on the steady night shift inspection jobs at both locations. It appears that women night inspectors during this period were paid the same higher night shift wages earned by the men.

[5] The shift differential was originally three cents an hour for the afternoon shift and five cents an hour for the night shift. It has been increased to 10 and 16 cents per hour respectively.

II. Congress' purpose in enacting the Equal Pay Act was to remedy what was perceived to be a serious and endemic problem of employment discrimination in private industry—the fact that the wage structure of "many segments of American industry has been based on an ancient but outmoded belief that a man, because of his role in society, should be paid more than a woman, even though his duties are the same." S. Rept. No. 176, 88th Cong., 1st Sess. (1963), at 1. The solution adopted was quite simple in principle: to require that "equal work be rewarded by equal wages." *Ibid.*

The Act's basic structure and operation are similarly straightforward. In order to make out a case under the Act, the Secretary must show that an employer pays different wages to employees of opposite sexes "for equal work on jobs the performance of which requires equal skill, effort, and responsibility, and which are performed under similar working conditions." Although the Act is silent on this point, its legislative history makes plain that the Secretary has the burden of proof on this issue, as both of the courts below recognized.

The Act also establishes four exceptions—three specific and one a general catch-all provision—where different payment to employees of opposite sexes "is made pursuant to (i) a seniority system; (ii) a merit system; (iii) a system which measures earnings by quantity or quality of production; or (iv) a differential based on any other factor other than sex." Again, while the Act is silent on this question, its structure and history also suggest that once the Secretary has carried his burden of showing that the employer pays workers of one sex more than workers of the opposite sex for equal work, the burden shifts to the employer to show that the differential is justified under one of the Act's four exceptions. All of the many lower courts that have considered this question have so held, and this view is consistent with the general rule that the application of an exemption under the Fair Labor Standards Act is a matter of affirmative defense on which the employer has the burden of proof.

The contentions of the parties in this case reflect the Act's underlying framework. Corning argues that the Secretary has failed to prove that Corning ever violated the Act because day shift work is not "performed under similar working conditions" as night shift work. The Secretary maintains that day shift and night shift work are performed under "similar working conditions" within the meaning of the Act.[13] Although the Secretary recognizes that higher wages may be paid for night shift work, the Secretary contends that such a shift differential would be based

---

[13] The Secretary also advances an argument that even if night and day inspection work is assumed not to be performed under similar working conditions, the differential in base wages is nevertheless unlawful under the Act. The additional burden of working at night, the argument goes, was already fully reflected in the plantwide shift differential, and the shifts were made "similar" by payment of the shift differential. This argument does not appear to have been presented to either the Second or the Third Circuit, as the opinions in both cases reflect an assumption on the part of all concerned that the Secretary's case would fail unless night and day inspection work was found to be performed under similar working conditions. For this reason, and in view of our resolution of the "working condition" issue, we have no occasion to consider and intimate no views on this aspect of the Secretary's argument.

upon a "factor other than sex" within the catch-all exception to the Act and that Corning has failed to carry its burden of proof that its higher base wage for male night inspectors was in fact based on any factor other than sex.

The courts below relied in part on conflicting statements in the legislative history having some bearing on this question of statutory construction. . . .

. . .

. . . [In hearings, industry representatives] repeatedly urged that the bill be amended to include an exception for job classification systems, or otherwise to incorporate the language of job evaluation into the bill. Thus Corning's own representative testified:

"Job evaluation is an accepted and tested method of obtaining equity in wage relationship.

"A great part of industry is committed to job evaluation by past practice and by contractual agreement as the basis for wage administration. " 'Skill' alone, as a criterion, fails to recognize other aspects of the job situation that affect job worth.

"We sincerely hope that this committee in passing language to eliminate wage differences based on sex alone, will recognize in its language the general role of job evaluation in establishing equitable rate relationships." [18]

We think it plain that in amending the Act's definition of equal work to its present form, the Congress acted in direct response to these pleas. Spokesmen for the amended bill stated, for example, during the House debates:

"The concept of equal pay for jobs demanding equal skill has been expanded to require also equal effort, responsibility, and similar working conditions. These factors are the core of all job classification systems. They form a legitimate basis for differentials in pay." [19]

Indeed, the most telling evidence of congressional intent is the fact that the Act's amended definition of equal work incorporated the specific language of the job evaluation plan described at the hearings by Corning's own representative— that is, the concepts of "skill," "effort," "responsibility," and "working conditions."

Congress' intent, as manifested in this history, was to use these terms to incorporate into the new federal act the well-defined and well-accepted principles of job evaluation so as to ensure that wage differentials based upon bona fide job evaluation plans would be outside the purview of the Act. The House Report emphasized:

"This language recognizes there are many factors which may be used to measure the relationships between jobs and which establish a valid basis for a difference in pay. These factors will be found in a majority of the job classification systems. Thus, it is anticipated that a bona fide job classification system that does not discriminate on the basis of sex will

[18] Senate Hearings, supra, n. 15, at 98; House Hearings, supra, n. 15, at 234.
[19] 109 Cong. Rec. 9195 (Representative Frelinghuysen). See also H. Rep. No. 309, supra, at 8.

serve as a valid defense to a charge of discrimination." H. R. Rep., *supra*, at 3.

It is in this light that the phrase "working conditions" must be understood, for where Congress has used technical words or terms of art, "it [is] proper to explain them by reference to the art or science to which they [are] appropriate." . . .

While a layman might well assume that time of day worked reflects one aspect of a job's "working conditions" the term has a different and much more specific meaning in the language of industrial relations. As Corning's own representative testified at the hearings, the element of working conditions encompasses two subfactors: "surroundings" and "hazards." "Surroundings" measure the elements, such as toxic chemicals or fumes, regularly encountered by a worker, their intensity, and their frequency. "Hazards" take into account the physical hazards regularly encountered, their frequency, and the severity of injury they can cause. This definition of "working conditions" is not only manifested in Corning's own job evaluation plans but is also well accepted across a wide range of American industry.[21]

Nowhere in any of these definitions is time of day worked mentioned as a relevant criterion. The fact of the matter is that the concept of "working conditions," as used in the specialized language of job evaluation systems, simply does not encompass shift differentials. Indeed while Corning now argues that night inspection work is not equal to day inspection work, all of its own job evaluation plans, including the one now in effect, have consistently treated them as equal in all respects, including working conditions.[22] And Corning's Manager of Job Evaluation testified in No. 73-29 that time of day worked was not considered to be a "working condition." Significantly, it is not the Secretary in this case who is trying to look behind Corning's bona fide job evaluation system to require equal pay for jobs which Corning has historically viewed as unequal work. Rather, it is Corning which asks us to differentiate between jobs which the company itself has always equated. We agree with the Second Circuit that the inspection work at issue in this case, whether performed during the day or night, is "equal work" as that term is defined in the Act.

[21] See Belcher, WAGE AND SALARY ADMINISTRATION 271-274, 278, 287-289 (1955); II United States Dept. of Labor, DICTIONARY OF OCCUPATIONAL TITLES 656 (3d ed. 1965); United States Civil Service Comm'n, JOB GRADING SYSTEM FOR TRADES AND LABOR ORGANIZATIONS, F.P.M. Supp. 512-1, at A3-3.

[22] Pursuant to its 1944 collective-bargaining agreement, Corning adopted a job classification system developed by its consultants, labelled the SJ&H plan, which evaluated inspector jobs on the basis of "general schooling," "training period," "manual skill," "versatility," "job knowledge," "responsibility," and "working conditions." Under this evaluation, the inspector jobs, regardless of shift, were found equal in all respects, including "working conditions," which were defined as the "surrounding conditions (wet, heat, cold, dust, grease, noises, etc.) and physical hazards (bruises, cuts, heavy lifting, fumes, slippery floors, machines, chemicals, gases, bodily injuries, etc.) to which employees are unavoidably subjected while performing the duties."

A new plan, put into effect in 1963-1964 and called the CGW plan, also found no significant differences in the duties performed by men and women inspectors and awarded the same point values for skill, effort, responsibility, and working conditions, regardless of shift.

This does not mean, of course, that there is no room in the Equal Pay Act for nondiscriminatory shift differentials. Work on a steady night shift no doubt has psychological and physiological impacts making it less attractive than work on a day shift. The Act contemplates that a male night worker may receive a higher wage than a female day worker, just as it contemplates that a male employee with 20 years seniority can receive a higher wage than a woman with two years seniority. Factors such as these play a role under the Act's four exceptions—the seniority differential under the specific seniority exception, the shift differential under the catchall exception for differentials "based on any other factor other than sex."

The question remains, however, whether Corning carried its burden of proving that the higher rate paid for night inspection work, until 1966 performed solely by men, was in fact intended to serve compensation for night work, or rather constituted an added payment based upon sex. We agree that the record amply supported the District Court's conclusion that Corning had not sustained its burden of proof.[26] As its history revealed, "the higher night rate was in large part the product of the generally higher wage level of male workers and the need to compensate them for performing what were regarded as demeaning tasks." 474 F.2d, at 233, 20 WH Cases 1118. The differential in base wages originated at a time when no other night employees received higher pay than corresponding day workers and it was maintained long after the company instituted a separate plant-wide shift differential which was thought to compensate adequately for the additional burdens of night work. The differential arose simply because men would not work at the low rates paid women inspectors, and it reflected a job market in which Corning could pay women less than men for the same work. That the company took advantage of such a situation may be understandable as a matter of economics, but its differential nevertheless became illegal once Congress enacted into law the principle of equal pay for equal work.

III. We now must consider whether Corning continued to remain in violation of the Act after 1966 when, without changing the base wage rates for day and night inspectors, it began to permit women to bid for jobs on the night shift as vacancies occurred. It is evident that this was more than a token gesture to end discrimination, as turnover in the night shift inspection jobs was rapid. The record in No. 73-29 shows, for example, that during the two-year period after June 1, 1966, the date women were first permitted to bid for night inspection jobs, women took 152 of the 278 openings, and women with very little seniority were able to obtain positions on the night shift. Relying on these facts, the com-

---

[26] This question, as well as the questions discussed in Part III, *infra*, were considered by the District Court and the Court of Appeals only in No. 73-29, and not in 73-695, since in the latter case the courts below concluded that the Secretary had failed to prove that night and day shift inspection work was performed under similar working conditions. We deal with these issues, then, only on the basis of the record in No. 73-29. To the extent that there are any differences in the records in these two cases on factual matters relating to these questions, we leave it to the District Court and the Court of Appeals in No. 73-695 to resolve these questions in the first instance, on the basis of the record created in that case.

pany argues that it ceased discriminating against women in 1966, and was no longer in violation of the Equal Pay Act.

But the issue before us is not whether the company, in some abstract sense, can be said to have treated men the same as women after 1966. Rather, the question is whether the company remedied the specific violation of the Act which the Secretary proved. We agree with the Second Circuit, as well as with all other circuits that have had occasion to consider this issue, that the company could not cure its violation except by equalizing the base wages of female day inspectors with the higher rates paid the night inspectors. This result is implicit in the Act's language, its statement of purpose, and its legislative history.

. . .

The company's final contention—that it cured its violation of the Act when a new collective-bargaining agreement went into effect on January 20, 1969—need not detain us long. While the new agreement provided for equal base wages for night or day inspectors hired after that date, it continued to provide unequal base wages for employees hired before that date, a discrimination likely to continue for some time into the future because of a large number of laid-off employees who had to be offered re-employment before new inspectors could be hired. After considering the rather complex method in which the new wage rates for employees hired prior to January 1969 were calculated and the company's stated purpose behind the provisions of the new agreement, the District Court in No. 73-29 concluded that the lower base wage for day inspectors was a direct product of the company's failure to equalize the base wages for male and female inspectors as of the effective date of the Act. We agree it is clear from the record that had the company equalized the base wage rates of male and female inspectors on the effective date of the Act, as the law required, the day inspectors in 1969 would have been entitled to the same higher "red circle" rate the company provided for night inspectors.[29] We therefore conclude that on the facts of this case, the company's continued discrimination in base wages between night and day workers, though phrased in terms of a neutral factor other than sex, nevertheless

---

[29] The January 1969 agreement provided an 8% or 20¢ per hour across-the-board wage increase, applied to the pre-January 1969 base wage and made retroactive to November 4, 1968. The contract also instituted new "job evaluation" wage rates for various positions. In the case of inspectors, the new "job evaluation" rate was higher than the retroactively increased base wage of day shift inspectors but was lower than the retroactively increased base wage of night shift inspectors. The contract further provided that where the job evaluation was less than the current rate for the job— that is, less than the retroactively increased old rate—employees hired before January 20, 1969, would continue to be paid the old rate, through "red circle" protection. Thus, the day shift inspectors received the new job evaluation rate, while the night shift inspectors continued to receive the higher "red circled" night shift base wage. Had the company complied with the law and equalized up the base wages of day shift inspectors prior to 1969, the retroactively increased base wage of day shift inspectors would have been the same as the retroactively increased rate of night shift inspectors, and the day shift inspectors would have been entitled to the same "red circle" protection granted the night shift inspectors, since that retroactively increased rate was higher than the new job evaluation rate.

operated to perpetuate the effects of the company's prior illegal practice of paying women less than men for equal work. . . .

The judgment in No. 73-29 is affirmed. The judgment in No. 72-695 is reversed and the case remanded to the Court of Appeals for further proceedings consistent with this opinion.

*It is so ordered.*

MR. JUSTICE STEWART took no part in the consideration or decision of these cases.

The CHIEF JUSTICE, MR. JUSTICE BLACKMUN, and MR. JUSTICE REHNQUIST dissent. . . .

# 7. Age

## A.  Bona Fide Occupational Qualification

## HODGSON v. GREYHOUND LINES, INC.

*United States Court of Appeals, Seventh Circuit, 1974*
*499 F.2d 859, 7 FEP Cases 817*

SWYGERT, Chief Judge: Defendant-appellant, Greyhound Lines, Inc., appeals from a finding that its maximum hiring age policy for applicants for the position of driver of intercity passenger buses violated the Age Discrimination in Employment Act of 1967, 29 U.S.C. §§ 621, *et seq.* Pursuant to that policy Greyhound declines to consider applications for intercity bus drivers from those individuals thirty-five years of age or older.[2]

The Government contends that Greyhound's hiring policy violates section 4(a)(1) of the Act, 29 U.S.C. § 623(a)(1), which makes it unlawful "to fail or refuse to hire . . . any individual . . . because of such individual's age." In addition the Government charges that Greyhound's maximum hiring age violates section 4(a)(2) of the Act, 29 U.S.C. § 623(a) (2), which prohibits efforts "to limit, segregate, or classify . . . employees in any way which would deprive . . . any individual of employment opportunities or otherwise adversely affect his status as an employee, because of such individual's age." Also the Government claims that Greyhound's advertisements indicating age differentiation in employment is forbidden by section 4(e) of the Act, 29 U.S.C. § 623(e).

Greyhound, although admitting the employment and advertising practices charged by the Government, denies that such practices violate the Act in that it is contended that Greyhound's actions are exempted from the Act's proscriptions. Under section 4(f) (1) of the Act, 29 U.S.C. § 623 (f)(1), an employer may differentiate as to age without violating the Act if age is shown to be a "bona fide occupational qualification reasonably necessary to the normal operation of the particular business. . . ." Greyhound contends that its maximum age hiring policy is premised on considerations of public safety and as such constitutes a "bona fide occupational qualification."

At trial Greyhound urged that abolition of its maximum age hiring policy with respect to intercity bus drivers would increase the likelihood of risk of harm due to driver failure and thereby concomitantly impede

---

[2] [Footnotes numbered as in original.—Ed.] The Act prohibits age discrimination with respect to those persons age forty to sixty-five. 9 U.S.C. § 631.

Greyhound's efforts for safety. The trial judge held that Greyhound had failed to meet its "burden of demonstrating that its policy of age limitation is reasonably necessary to the normal and safe operation of its business." In making this determination the trial judge stated:

"[T]he defendant's policy is not founded on the 'factual basis' for its belief that 'all or substantially all [applicants over age 40] . . . would be unable to perform safely and efficiently the duties of the job involved.' . . ."

I. The standard for the burden of proof placed on Greyhound by the trial judge was taken from the Fifth Circuit's decision in *Weeks* v. *Southern Bell Telephone & Telegraph Co.*, 408 F.2d 228, 1 FEP Cases 656, 70 LRRM 2843 (5th Cir. 1969). In that case the telephone company was faced with a charge of sex discrimination for refusing to consider the application of a woman for the position of switchman. As an affirmative defense the telephone company claimed that the sex of an applicant for the position of switchman was a bona fide occupational qualification because of the allegedly strenuous activity of lifting of weights in excess of thirty pounds occasionally required in fulfilling the job of switchman. In discussing the burden of proof cast upon the telephone company the court stated:

"[W]e hold that in order to rely on the bona fide occupational qualification exception an employer has the burden of proving that he had reasonable cause to believe, that is, a factual basis for believing, that all or substantially all women would be unable to perform safely and efficiently the duties of the job involved." 408 F.2d at 235, 1 FEP Cases at 661, 70 LRRM at 2848.

The Court denied the telephone company a bona fide occupational qualification exemption, holding that the company had failed to meet its burden of proof. The court declined to indulge in an assumption, "on the basis of a 'stereotyped characterization' that few or no women can safely lift thirty pounds, while all men are treated as if they can." 408 F.2d at 235, 236, 1 FEP Cases at 661, 70 LRRM at 2848.

Although the standard for the burden of proof annunciated in *Weeks* may properly be applicable to the circumstances of that sex discrimination case, we find its application inappropriate in the instant action. Unlike *Weeks,* our concern goes beyond that of the welfare of the job applicant and must include consideration of the well-being and safety of bus passengers and other highway motorists. In fashioning the standard of proof in *Weeks,* the Fifth Circuit was not confronted with a situation where the lives of numerous persons are completely dependant on the capabilities of the job applicant. Accordingly, we find that decision is of no avail in formulating the standard of proof to be imposed in the instant case.

A more pertinent case is the Fifth Circuit's decision in *Diaz* v. *Pan American World Airways, Inc.*, 442 F.2d 385, 3 FEP Cases 337 (5th Cir. 1971). In *Diaz* Pan American airline was charged with a violation of the 1964 Civil Rights Act because of its refusal to hire male flight cabin attendants solely because of their sex. As an affirmative defense Pan American argued that being a female was a "bona fide occupational qualification" for the position of flight cabin attendant. In an effort to carry its burden of proof, Pan American produced evidence demonstrating: that females were superior in performing the nonmechanical aspects of the job such as reassuring anxious passengers and providing personalized service; that passengers preferred female attendants (the basic psychological reasons for such preference); and that the actualities of the hiring process would make it more difficult to find those few males suitable to attend to the psychological needs of passengers.

In analyzing the standard of proof required of Pan American to establish a "bona fide occupational qualification reasonably necessary to the normal operation of that particular business or enterprise," the Fifth Circuit construed the word "necessary" in the Act to require:

"[T]hat we apply a business *necessity* test, not a business *convenience* test. That is to say, discrimination based on sex is valid only when the *essence* of the business operation would be undermined by not hiring members of one sex exclusively." (Emphasis in original.) 442 F.2d at 388, 3 FEP Cases at 339.

The court proceeded to characterize the essence of the normal operation of an airline stating that: "The primary function of an airline is to transport passengers safely from one point to another." 442 F.2d at 388, 3 FEP Cases at 339. In the court's view Pan American could not establish that the employment of male cabin attendants would have any impact on its ability to provide safe transportation and accordingly the court rejected Pan American's defense of bona fide occupational qualification. Pan American's basis for excluding male applicants, that they could not cater to the psychological needs of the passengers as adequately as females, was found merely "tangential to the essence of the business involved." 442 F.2d at 388, 3 FEP Cases at 339.

Similar to the airline industry, the essence of Greyhound's business is the safe transportation of its passengers. Thus we deem it necessary that Greyhound establish that the essence of its operations would be endangered by hiring drivers over forty years of age. To that end we note the decision in *Spurlock* v. *United Airlines, Inc.*, 475 F.2d 216, 5 FEP Cases 17 (10th Cir. 1972), where, in addressing itself to the validity of preemployment job qualifications for the position of airline pilot alleged to discriminate against Blacks, the Tenth Circuit stated:

"When a job requires a small amount of skill and training and the consequences of hiring an unqualified applicant are insignificant, the courts should examine closely any pre-employment standard or criteria which discriminate against minorities. In such a case, the employer should have a heavy burden to demonstrate to the court's satisfaction that his employment criteria are job-related. On the other hand, when the job clearly requires a high degree of skill and the economic and human risks involved in hiring an unqualified applicant are great, the employer bears a correspondingly lighter burden to show that his employment criteria are job-related. Cf. 29 C.F.R. § 1607.5(c)(2)(iii). The job of airline flight officer is clearly such a job. United's flight officers pilot aircraft worth as much as $20 million and transport as many as 300 passengers per flight. The risks involved in hiring an unqualified applicant are staggering. The public interest clearly lies in having the most highly qualified persons available to pilot airliners. The courts, therefore, should proceed with great caution before requiring an employer to lower his pre-employment standards for such a job." 475 F.2d at 219, 5 FEP Cases at 19.

As reflected in the *Spurlock* decision, a public transportation carrier, such as Greyhound, entrusted with the lives and well-being of passengers, must continually strive to employ the most highly qualified persons available for the position of intercity bus driver for the paramount goal of a bus carrier is safety. Due to such compelling concerns for safety, it is not necessary that Greyhound show that all or substantially all bus-driver applicants over forty could not perform safely. Rather, to the extent that the elimination of Greyhound's hiring policy may impede the attainment of its goal of safety, it must be said that such action undermines the essence of Greyhound's operations. Stated differently, Greyhound must demonstrate that it has a rational basis in fact to believe that elimination of its maximum hiring age will increase the likelihood of risk of harm to its passengers. Greyhound need only demonstrate however a minimal increase in risk of harm for it is enough to show that elimination of the hiring policy might jeopardize the life of one more person than might otherwise occur under the present hiring practice.

II. In an effort to satisfy its burden of proof, Greyhound produced an array of evidence to substantiate its claim for a bona fide occupational qualification. That evidence included testimony by transportation industry officials, former high-ranking officials of the Interstate Commerce Commission, and Greyhound officers. The testimony of these officials, although persuasive in view of their accumulated experience in the transportation industry, is not of itself sufficient to establish a bona fide occupational qualification. In our view we find more compelling Greyhound's evidence relating to: the rigors of the extra-board work assignments; the degenerative physical and sensory changes in a human being brought on by the aging process which begins in the late thirties in the life of a person; and the statistical evidence reflecting, among other things, that Greyhound's safest driver is one who has sixteen to twenty years of driving experience with Greyhound and is between fifty and fifty-five years of age, an optimum blend of age and experience with Greyhound which could never be attained in hiring an applicant forty years of age or over. This compelling evidence in combination with the general testimony of the transportation industry officials adequately demonstrates Greyhound has a rational basis in fact to believe that elimination of its maximum hiring age will increase the likelihood of risk of harm to the well-being of its passengers and others.

At the outset we note that the thrust of Greyhound's contention and supporting evidence is that the human body undergoes physical and sensory changes beginning around age thirty-five and that these degenerative changes, caused by aging, have a detrimental impact on driving skills. Moreover, these changes are not detectable by a physical examination. The Government admits that these degenerative changes do occur, but contends that they do not affect driving skills because the driver between forty and sixty-five years of age compensates for these changes through increased maturity and driving experience. In addition the Government claims that even though a physical examination of applicants between forty and sixty-five might not detect degenerative changes impairing driving ability, any such infirmities will be detected during the course of the other elaborate functional and psychological examinations conducted by Greyhound in screening intercity driver applicants.

The medical testimony on behalf of the Government reflects the gravamen of the Government's challenge to Greyhound's hiring practice. According to the Government's medical witnesses an applicant forty to sixty-five years of age should be judged on the basis of his "functional age," that is, his ability and capacity to do the job, rather than his chronological age. When the testimony of the medical experts on both sides is considered, however, it is not clear that functional age is readily or practicably determinable. Moreover, the Government's medical witnesses seemingly admit that chronological age is at least an indicator of driving ability. Even assuming that Greyhound's examinations of driving skills other than the physical examination can adequately screen out degenerative disabilities occasioned by age in the forty to sixty-five age bracket, it is questionable whether Greyhound could practicably scrutinize the continued fitness of such drivers on a frequent and regular basis.

We come now to the nub of Greyhound's contention that its maximum hiring age policy is a bona fide occupational qualification reasonably necessary to mainstay the safety of its operations. Greyhound urges that the impact of the aging process will be magnified by the rigorous physical and mental demands of the extra-board work assignment system to which all new drivers between the ages of forty to sixty-five would be assigned under its seniority system. There are two work categories into which Greyhound bus drivers are classified. The first is the regular run driver who operates those schedules published in Greyhound's timetables. The regular runs are generally regarded by the drivers as more desirable and require the least strenuous work. These runs are bid by the drivers on the basis of a seniority system established in collective bargaining agreements. The remaining work is performed by the group of drivers referred to as extra-board drivers. A newly hired driver, regardless of age or prior experience, goes to the bottom of the seniority list where he is available for assignments from the extra-board. In general the new driver will remain on the extra-board for a period of ten to forty years depending upon the seniority list in the territory in which he is employed.

While on the extra-board the driver is on call twenty-four hours a day, seven days a week with as little as two hours' notice, to take runs that the more senior regular run drivers do not operate. Often these operations involve odd and irregular hours and, frequently, long charter trips outside the territory served by the regular routes of Greyhound, that may last up to thirty days.

At trial there was testimony to the effect that Greyhound's extra-board work is particularly physically and mentally demanding and that it places an unusual amount of emotional stress on the driver and is often disruptive of the driver's routine of living. One of the redeeming aspects of the operation of the extra-board and the seniority system, however, is that it rewards the driver by giving him an opportunity, as he grows older, to solicit the work that he feels he is best qualified to perform. In the earlier years of a driver's employment he is not able to do that for he must accept whatever work is not performed by the regular drivers. The seniority system is highly advantageous as presently constituted for it allows the older, more experienced driver to compensate for his aging by selecting the more attractively and easily performed work.

Greyhound contends that even though an applicant between age forty and sixty-five may satisfactorily perform on the driver qualification examinations so that at the outset he would be entitled to employment, there is no way of telling how safely he will perform for a sustained period of time given the fact that he will be assigned to the arduous tasks involved on the extra-board at a time when his body begins to undergo degenerative changes due to the aging process. The statistical evidence produced by Greyhound lends support to its belief that elimination of the maximum hiring age will increase the risk of harm to its passengers. The evidence demonstrates that the rigors of the extra-board are such that extra-board drivers, even with the advantage of youth, experience twice as many accidents per million miles driven than that incurred by regular run drivers, namely, 9.79 accidents per million miles as compared with 4.3 accidents per million miles for regular run drivers. With respect to the effect of the aging process on the safety records of Greyhound's drivers, the statistical evidence establishes that despite the offsetting benefits derived through increased experience as a Greyhound driver, the driver accident rate begins to increase at age fifty-five. Likewise, the statistical evidence isolating driver experience illustrates that as a driver's experience with Greyhound increases his accident rate correspondingly decreases, but that this rate reverses and begins to increase after twenty-six years of experience concomitant with the period during which the aging process is operative. In addition, the statistical evidence establishes that Greyhound's safest driver is fifty-five years of age and has sixteen years of experience as a Greyhound driver—two qualities which newly hired drivers between ages forty and sixty-five would never be able to attain during their tenure at Greyhound.

Besides the foregoing statistical evidence, Greyhound directs our attention to a 1972 study sponsored by the Bureau of Motor Carrier Safety of the United States Department of Transportation which supports certain of Greyhound's claims regarding the likely physical and mental capabilities of newly hired drivers age forty to sixty-five on the extra board. The study indicates that its testing results "are consistent with the hypothesis that older drivers become fatigued more quickly and consequently experience [a] greater proportion of accidents after prolonged driving than younger drivers." Similar to Greyhound's experience, the study showed that the percentage of accidents decreased substantially as the bus or truck driver's age increased from age thirty to the age group forty-one to forty-five but then generally increased from the forty-one to forty-five age group to fifty-six years of age. The study's accident analysis indicated that older drivers tend to experience proportionally more of their accidents after about five hours on the road than do younger drivers. The study summary concludes that the "adverse effects of prolonged driving were evidently more pronounced for older drivers (aged forty-five or more) than for younger drivers" and that "older drivers generally showed an earlier decline in psychophysiological arousal than the younger ones and dropped to a lower absolute level of arousal."

With respect to the evidence adduced by Greyhound the Government argues that it constitutes mere conjecture and generalized opinion testimony and is not objective data, demonstrating the inability to cope with the demands of the extra-board. The Government concurs in the district court's holding that Greyhound has failed to establish a "factual basis" for its position. We cannot agree. In our view Greyhound's position as to the potential increase of risk of harm which would be incurred by the elimination of its maximum hiring age is well-founded and grounded on an adequate factual basis. Greyhound need not establish its belief to the certainty demanded by the Government and the district court for to do so would effectively require Greyhound to go so far as to experiment with the lives of passengers in order to produce statistical evidence pertaining to the capabilities of newly hired applicants forty to sixty-five years of age. Greyhound has amply demonstrated that its maximum hiring age policy is founded upon a good faith judgment concerning the safety needs of its passengers and others. It has established that its hiring policy is not the result of an arbitrary belief lacking in objective reason or rationale.

The judgment of the district court is reversed.


## HOUGHTON v. McDONNELL DOUGLAS CORP.

*United States Court of Appeals, Eighth Circuit, 1977*
*553 F.2d 561, 14 FEP Cases 1594*

Tom C. Clark, Associate Justice: Appellant Phillip W. Houghton brought this age discrimination action against McDonnell Douglas Corporation (the Company) following his removal at the age of 52, from the position of Chief Production Test Pilot and his subsequent termination from the Company's employ. He sued for reinstatement to his former position, an injunction against future discrimination, reimbursement of lost wages, liquidated damages, counsel fees and costs. The District Court found that age is a bona fide occupational qualification (BFOQ) for test pilots and that Houghton was properly terminated due to his inability to adjust to the new non-flying position offered him, thus denying him any relief. Houghton and the Secretary of Labor, who had intervened in the suit, have appealed. We find that the BFOQ is not a controlling test, under the facts here, and that Houghton was improperly terminated from his position as Chief Production Test Pilot. We, therefore, reverse the judgment and remand it for a new trial in accordance with this opinion.

. . . Houghton was hired by the Company in 1946 as an assistant aerodynamicist and in ten years was the Chief Production Test Pilot, a position he held until December, 1972. In July, 1971, the Company found it necessary to reduce its pilot staff due to declining production rate, and it decided to do so by age. Houghton, as the oldest test pilot in the Company's history, and two other test pilots who were ages 48 and 46, were transferred from flight status. The Company had no set age policy for the transfer of test pilots to nonflying positions, relying solely on "intuitive judgment."

Houghton was offered a choice of placement either in the Flight Safety or Flight Simulation Departments. However, after interviews with the appropriate department managers, he decided that both positions were "very clearly . . . a large step downward . . . in job appeal, job status [and salary]." He advised the Company that neither was acceptable and sought outside employment but failed. He returned to the Company and assumed his former position without flight duties but this, too, was not satisfying. In November, 1972, he was offered a place in the Space Shuttle Simulation Program but rejected it for similar reasons. Ultimately, Houghton was terminated in December of 1972 for nonproductivity.

. . . The Company admitted that Houghton was removed from flight status solely because of his age, but asserted that age was a BFOQ for test pilots under § 4(f)(1) of the Act.

. . . In support of its case, the Company called two experts who believed that age is an appropriate BFOQ for production test pilots, based on their studies reflecting the physiological and psychological changes that accompany the aging process in the general population. However, each conceded that changes in the aging process occur at diverse rates and varying degrees in different persons. . . .

. . . The evidence was, in our judgment, insufficient to support an inference of diminished ability among older pilots to adequately perform their work.

Moreover, statistical studies reveal that the accident rate of professional pilots decreases with age. The former Director of Aerospace Safety for the United States Air Force testified that the major cause of accidents is poor pilot judgment, a factor which experience alone can remedy. Further, less than one percent of all aircraft accidents are traceable to medical disability, and of this one percent, the most frequent culprit is gastroenteritis which bears no relationship to age.

Additional documentary evidence indicates that the Air Force, Navy, NASA and the FAA do not restrict healthy pilots in their fifties from flying supersonic aircraft.

Despite this mountain of evidence against the Company's position, the District Court entered a judgment in its favor, finding that age had been satisfactorily proven as a BFOQ for test pilots. While we find no quarrel *per se* with the BFOQ test, we do not believe it controls here. Houghton's ability to continue to qualify as a test pilot must be judged under the provisions of the Act, including § 4(f)(1). In our view, the Company did not meet the burden imposed by the latter section.

. . . Here, however, the Company's evidence was of a general nature applicable only to the general population. In this regard, it shed little light on the relative capabilities of test pilots as a group to adequately perform their tasks beyond a certain age. Houghton's evidence, however, was of a specialized nature, showing age changes are much slower among test pilots as a group than among the general population. . . . [E]ven the Company doctors found Houghton in excellent physical condition, and we note a total absence of evidence which would indicate he was not capable of performing test pilot functions.

. . .

We note that Houghton claims he was "constructively discharged." However, a constructive discharge generally takes place when an employer makes working conditions so intolerable that the employee is forced to quit. *Young* v. *Southwestern Savings & Loan Ass'n,* 509 F.2d 140, 144, 10 FEP Cases 522, 525 (5th Cir. 1975). Houghton did not resign. The motivating cause of his discharge was his insistence upon his statutory right under the Act. This in itself is an illegal motivating factor on the part of the Company. *Brennan* v. *Maxey's Yamaha, Inc.,* 513 F.2d 179, 181, 22 WH Cases 213 (8th Cir. 1975). His illegal transfer from flight status, in the face of his insistence upon his statutory rights, was the root cause of his severance. He is thus entitled to relief.

. . . If on remand it is found that Houghton is still physically capable of safely and effectively performing the duties of Chief Production Test Pilot, he must be reinstated in that position, awarded such damages as he has suffered by reason of his discharge, and other relief, including attorney fees, to which he is entitled. In calculating damages, the District Court should appropriately consider the substantially lesser salary Houghton would have earned in the position offered him by the Company and such other factors as it deems relevant.

## B.   Reasonable Factors Other Than Age

### MASTIE v. GREAT LAKES STEEL CORP.

*U.S. District Court, Eastern District of Michigan, 1976*
*424 F. Supp. 1299, 14 FEP Cases 952*

Ralph B. Guy, District Judge: Plaintiffs, Frank Mastie and Kenneth Seymour, brought this action pursuant to the Federal Age Discrimination in Employment Act of 1967 (ADEA), 29 U.S.C. 620, *et seq.,* Public Law 90-202, claiming discrimination on the basis of age. . . .

. . .

Plaintiffs, Mastie and Seymour, commenced employment with defendant Great Lakes Steel Corporation on November 1, 1935, and March 10, 1936, respectively. . . . Mastie also worked at the No. 3 slab yard at the 96 inch mill at various times from 1947 to 1971. . . . Seymour worked primarily at the 96 inch mill; however, at times, he also worked in temporary assignments at the 80 inch mill in the No. 5 and No. 6 slab yards. . . .

. . .

In 1971, Great Lakes Steel decided to terminate operations at the 96 inch hot mill. The 96 inch mill had become obsolete and also more costly to operate than more modern mills in current operation. As a matter of fact, as soon as the 80 inch mill was installed in 1961, it was contemplated that the 96 inch mill would eventually be phased out of operation. However, the testimony at trial indicated that the decision to shut down the 96 inch mill was first orally communicated to Rees, manager of the entire hot mill operations from 1968 to 1972, by Burt Fishley, Rees' supervisor, sometime during the spring of 1971. . . .

. . .

Prior to the curtailment of operations on the 96 inch mill, Rees commenced an evaluation process which encompassed all the supervisory employees then employed at the 96 and 80 inch mills. . . .

. . .

. . . [T]he company sought to place the employees displaced from the 96 inch mill as best they could. . . . After evaluating the relative supervisory capabilities of the nineteen employees and transferring employees to available and open positions, Mastie and Seymour were the only two employees who had not been given new positions with the defendant. . . . [A]fter the normally heavy vacation season was over in September, both Mastie and Seymour were asked to take early retirement under one of the defendant's retirement programs; or, in the alternative, to take a position as a rank and file employee in the defendant's steel mill. As became apparent to the plaintiffs, however, the retirement benefits available to them would exceed the compensation available as an hourly rank and file employee and, as a result, the plaintiffs refused defendant's offer to return to the rank and file classification.

. . .

There is no dispute by defendant that at the time plaintiffs were involuntarily retired both were within the protected class under the ADEA. Also, both plaintiffs' ages put them among the oldest, although not the oldest, of the nineteen employees the company could properly consider in filling the available foremen positions at the time. After being involuntarily terminated, the plaintiffs sought relief from various state and federal agencies authorized to administrate the respective age discrimination laws therein. There is no contention made by defendant that plaintiffs have failed to exhaust administrative remedies as provided in 29 U.S.C. § 626(d).

Plaintiffs, in essence, rely on the theory that since they were within the protected class of employees for the ADEA, were terminated from their positions while younger employees were retained, and maintained a certain plateau of ability exceeding the minimum required for the positions in which they could have been placed, that, as a result, their age was "a" factor in the defendant's decision to terminate them. Alternatively, and in support of the above theory, the plaintiffs contend that there was an economic advantage to the defendant in terminating them as opposed to younger employees since they were paid more than younger retained employees and also that their early retirement permitted defendant to avoid higher pension payments had plaintiffs retired at an older age. Since this economic advantage relates in substantial part to the plaintiffs' ages, it is alleged that a decision based on this economic factor amounts to prohibited activity under the ADEA. Lastly, it is contended that statistical evidence establishes that defendant made its decision to terminate plaintiffs on the basis of their ages.

Defendant, in response to plaintiffs' arguments, contends that plaintiffs were terminated as a result of the curtailment of operations at the 96 inch mill and the bona fide judgment of the management personnel at Great Lakes Steel that plaintiffs had the least ability and potential relative to the other employees evaluated at the time. . . .

## A. AGE DISCRIMINATION IN GENERAL

Age discrimination in employment has been characterized as unique from race, sex or national origin discrimination. The legislative history is punctuated with references to the special nature of age discrimination. Typical in this regard is the testimony of Willard Wirtz, Secretary of Labor in 1967, before the House Subcommittee investigating the need and scope of age discrimination legislation:
"I would suggest this kind of discrimination is entirely different from racial discrimination; the root of racial discrimination is purely bigotry. This is not true here."
. . .
The Act was never intended to be a panacea for all older workers terminated or not offered employment by an employer. This position is best illustrated by the Statement of Findings and Purpose in the Act itself:
"(a) The Congress hereby finds and declares that—
. . .
"(2) the setting of arbitrary age limits regardless of potential for job performance has become a common practice, and certain otherwise desirable practices may work to the disadvantage of older persons;
. . .
"(b) It is therefore the purpose of this Act to promote employment of older persons based on their ability rather than age; to prohibit arbitrary age discrimination in employment; to help employers and workers find ways of meeting problems arising from the impact of age on employment." 29 U.S.C. § 621.

Thus, the Act was designed only to attack those employers' personnel policies and practices which arbitrarily classified employees or potential employees on the basis of age and did not seek to affect employer decisions based on individual assessments of a person's abilities, capabilities and potential.

. . .

However, not every personnel decision by an employer which results in differential treatment of individuals in the protected class is a violation of the Act. The Act permits certain practices and policies which are not contrary to the general purpose of the Act:

"(f) It shall not be unlawful for an employer, . . . —

"(1) to take any action otherwise prohibited under subsections (a), (b), (c), or (e) of this section where age is a bona fide occupational qualification reasonably necessary to the normal operation of the particular business, or where the differentiation is based on reasonable factors other than age. . . ." 29 U.S.C. § 624(f).

It was the considered judgment of Congress that instances may arise where it would be necessary for an employer arbitrarily to impose age restrictions; however, where an employer makes such an attempt, the burden of proof is on the employer to establish that exceptional circumstances exist justifying such a policy, see 29 C.F.R. § 860.102(b) and § 860.103(e). On the other hand, an employer need not rely on these defenses where the differential treatment of an individual in the protected class results from an individual assessment as opposed to an arbitrary determination of that person's performance or potential. See *Laugesen* v. *Anaconda Co.*, 510 F.2d 307, 313, 10 FEP Cases 567, 571 (CA 6 1975). Under these circumstances, the employee must prove that the determining factor in the employer's individual evaluation of the employee was tainted by the employee's age.

### B. BURDEN OF PROOF

The burden of proof applied to age discrimination litigation has been held to be identical to that promulgated for Title VII litigation by the United States Supreme Court in *McDonnell Douglas* v. *Green*, 411 U.S. 792, 5 FEP Cases 965 (1973). See *Wilson* v. *Sealtest Foods*, 501 F.2d 84, 8 FEP Cases 749 (CA 5 1974). . . . As noted by the Sixth Circuit in *Laugesen, supra,* however, the applicability of the *McDonnell Douglas* standard to a discharge age discrimination case is not at all clear. . . .

. . . Although plaintiff can preclude a directed verdict in the defendant's favor by establishing a prima facie case, this does not relieve the plaintiff of the responsibility of proving discrimination by the preponderance of the evidence. In other words, a prima facie case of discrimination is not synonymous with establishing discrimination by a preponderance of the evidence.

It is a rare defendant, however, that will not present evidence that its action was motivated by nondiscriminatory reasons. As a matter of fact, a defendant who fails to present a defense in response to a plaintiff's prima facie case will in all likelihood be found to have violated the ADEA. The burden placed upon the defendant, therefore, is the burden of going forward with the evidence of its defense. . . . Although the *Bittar* court [512 F.2d 582 (CA 5 1974)] was technically correct in its holding that only the burden of going forward shifts to a defendant after a plaintiff's prima facie case has been established, the practical distinction between the burden of going forward with the evidence and the burden of proof to establish a nondiscrimination reason for the action taken is, in many instances, a distinction without substance.

. . .

### f. TEST FOR SUFFICIENCY OF EVALUATION PROCESS

Prior courts have held that an employer can satisfy its burden of objectivity for terminating employees following a reduction in operations by establishing that it conducted and relied on a thorough evaluation process of the employees affected. . . .

The court concludes that the defendant in this case did undertake a concerted and genuine effort to evaluate the employees in the evaluated group and that these evaluations were conducted impartially, conscientiously and without any intention to do anyone an injustice. . . .Thus, plaintiffs have failed in their first theory for establishing a case of age discrimination.

### 2. HIGHER COST OF EMPLOYMENT

Plaintiff's second theory for establishing a case of age discrimination is that they were terminated because the cost of their employment to the defendant was higher than for younger employees retained and thus, since the higher labor cost had a direct relationship to the plaintiff's ages, the defendant violated the ADEA. Cost differentials in employment have been denominated as the real rather than imagined reasons for discrimination against the aged. Higher employment costs may result from increased direct compensation or benefit programs, higher training costs, and higher costs brought about by the diminished productivity of older persons resulting from reduced ability or physical disabilities.

In the instant case, plaintiffs argue that defendant benefitted financially from their termination. First, plaintiffs contend that they were receiving the highest monthly salaries of the employees in the evaluation group. However, Defendant's Exhibit No. 8 reveals that Mastie's and Seymour's monthly salary as of August 1, 1971, ranked fifth and tenth, respectively, among the nineteen employees included in the evaluated group. It is, therefore, clear that the defendant was not arbitrarily seeking to terminate those employees receiving the highest rate of pay. . . .

Second, plaintiffs contend that their termination permitted the company to forego higher pension contributions for them. . . .

Although the court is convinced by the testimony presented at trial that the plaintiffs' monthly pension benefits would have been greater had they retired at a later age, there was substantial disagreement and confusion relative to whether the company's retirement of any other employee in the evaluated group would cost the company more or less in terms of contributions to the pension fund. On the one hand, there was testimony presented by Mr. Rogerson, indicating that if an employee younger than plaintiffs had been retired, it would have cost the company more in pension contributions; whereas, there was also testimony that after an employee reaches 60 years of age the employee's pension benefits increase at a substantially greater rate than at less than 60 years of age. However, it is also clear that if the company had retired a younger employee in the evaluated group who had not yet worked the requisite number of years for vesting of the retirement program, retirement of this employee would result in *no* additional pension costs to the company. Thus, it is entirely conceivable and consistent with plaintiffs' cost theory that the defendant would rather terminate its younger employees whose pension benefits had not vested. Through a constant turnover of personnel, the company could eliminate costly pension contributions which the plaintiffs argue are significant enough to have motivated the company to force them into early retirement.

. . .

The legislative history does not expressly deal with the issue of higher costs associated with older employees except that there was general consensus among those testifying at the House and Senate Subcommittee Hearings on the Age Act that higher out of pocket costs are associated with the employment of older employees. However, certain inferences can be drawn from the legislative history which may shed some light on this issue. For example, Senator George Smathers stated that if the Age Act was interpreted to require employers to hire and employ older workers and provide them with the same fringe benefits as younger workers, regardless of cost, that employers would be provided with a ready justification for refusing to hire and employ older workers, namely, the higher costs of their employment. To eradicate this perceived difficulty that could arise, Senator Smathers proposed the following amendment to the Age Act:

"(g) Nothing in this Act shall be construed to make unlawful the varying of coverage under any pension, retirement, or insurance plan or any plan for providing medical or hospital benefits or benefits for work injuries, where such variance is necessary to prevent the employer's being required to pay more for coverage of an employee than would be required to provide like coverage for his other employees."

. . . Significantly, the regulation speaks in terms of "general assertions" rather than "individual assertions" of higher employment costs for older workers. The absence of any discussion in this regulation relative to individual assessments and differentiations on the basis of costs creates, in this court's view, a strong negative implication that the Labor Department interprets the Act as authorizing differentiations on the basis of individual assessments of higher costs for older workers. The court readily concludes that an employer's arbitrary and across-the-board pronouncement that older workers are more expensive to employ than younger workers would be a flagrant violation of the Act.

Thus, even if the court were to assume that the cost of retaining plaintiffs would have been greater for the defendant than for other younger employees in the evaluated group, a conclusion the court finds unnecessary in light of its other findings, the court interprets the ADEA as permitting an employer to consider employment costs where such consideration is predicated upon an individual as opposed to a general assessment that the older worker's cost of employment is greater than for other workers.

### 3. use of statistics

. . .

Institutional, psychological, economic and physiological restraints to employing the aged suggest that statistics might not be a reliable indicator of an employer's compliance with the Act's proscriptions. . . . [T]he court finds . . . that age discrimination is not identical to either race or sex discrimination and thus the same principles governing the use of statistics in those types of cases should not be applied across the board to age cases. On this basis, precedents citing the extensive use of statistics in race discrimination cases are inapposite, although statistics may be helpful in conjunction with other evidence in developing a prima facie case.

### D. age as "a" or "determining" factor

. . .

The court finds that on the basis of the legislative history, Labor Department regulations and authoritative case law, the proper interpretation of the Act is that age must be a "determining" factor in an employer's personnel policies or practices before a violation of the Act occurs. The Senate report to Congress relative to the proposed Age Act states:

"The purpose of this legislation, simply stated, is to insure that age, within the limits prescribed herein, is not a determining factor in a refusal to hire."

. . . most significantly, the Sixth Circuit in *Laugesen* v. *Anaconda, supra,* after citing Labor Department Regulation 29 C.F.R. § 860. 103(c) and the general law relative to proximate cause in tort, expressed the following conclusion on the appropriate instruction that should have been given the jury in that case:

"However expressed, we believe it was essential for the jury to understand from the instructions that there could be more than one factor in the decision to discharge him and that he was nevertheless entitled to recover if one such factor was his age *and* if in fact it made a difference in determining whether he was to be retained or discharged. This is so even though the need to reduce the employee force generally was also a strong, and perhaps even more compelling, reason." (emphasis added) 510 F.2d at 317, 10 FEP Cases at 574.

## Conclusion

The court is not unsympathetic to the plight of the older workers in today's rapidly developing economy. However, the ADEA was never intended as an all encompassing cure for the employment ills of the nation's aged population. To the extent that the Age Act does not reach sufficiently the important and significant problems faced by the aged, further Congressional action in this area may be desirable. However, it is not this or any court's duty of function to distort the intention and meaning of a Congressional statute, albeit one broadly denominated as remedial civil rights legislation.

In essence, the court finds that plaintiffs have failed to establish a case of age discrimination by a preponderance of the evidence.

## C.   RETIREMENT

### THE COST OF GROWING OLD: BUSINESS NECESSITY AND THE AGE DISCRIMINATION IN EMPLOYMENT ACT*

*85 Yale Law Journal 565 (1979)*

. . .

. . . The ADEA was not intended to force employers to cease operations or absorb overwhelming economic losses, and Congress has elsewhere exhibited sensitivity to employer personnel cost problems. The protection from discrimination afforded to competent older workers under the Act must at some point be balanced against an employer's possibly valid claim of business necessity.

### III.  A STANDARD FOR REVIEW OF COST-BASED DISCHARGES

The less-detrimental-alternative standard, as developed in Title VII caselaw, encourages a search for alternatives to the challenged personnel practice that can accomplish the employer's business purpose with less harmful effects on the protected group. The standard assumes that at some point an employer's business purpose may become sufficiently compelling to override a predictable disparate impact on the protected group. This standard is well-suited to the current dilemma under the ADEA. When the practice challenged is termination of one or more competent older employees, a decrease in the number of workers discharged is one obvious indicator of a "less detrimental" result. In addition, when the business purpose is cost reduction, a court can compare different alternatives as means to this end.

The less-detrimental-alternative standard typically would come into play in the following situation: for reasons of austerity, the employer has terminated workers within a job category or classification who would be more costly to retain than other equally competent workers within the same category; and the discharged ADEA complainants have demonstrated a disparate impact that was predictable in light of previous length-of-service pay increases.

## A. EMPLOYER'S "SUBSTANTIAL COST" BURDEN

An employer should be required to prove the magnitude of his economic problems before a court in effect consents to overlook the fact that age made a difference in the implementation of his austerity program. Because a predictably disparate impact is only tolerated as a result of an employer's economic self-interest, the deference traditionally accorded to an avowal of that self-interest is not appropriate. To maintain such deference would tacitly encourage employers to act on business motivations that are clearly discriminatory.

In addition, the discriminatory impact being challenged is not strictly "job-related" as that term has been understood in an employment discrimination context. What is at stake is not a performance-related occupational qualification but rather a purely economic consideration. When a showing of economic need is the sole explanation for a certain discriminatory effect, the employer should have a threshold burden of persuading the trier of fact as to the substantiality of that need.

. . .

## B. PLAINTIFF'S "REASONABLE ALTERNATIVES" BURDEN

The ADEA endorses efforts to devise workable remedies that minimize the discriminatory impact of employment practices. Once an employer has established a substantial cost problem to which a reduction in personnel certainly bears a reasonable relation, the question becomes whether discharge of costlier employees is an unavoidable response to the problem. Requiring the employer himself to provide an answer would yield a limited range of alternative responses, and also pose the significant problem of negative proof. Encouraging a court to propose particular alternatives would involve the judiciary directly in making complex and far-reaching business judgments that may be considerably beyond its competence. The plaintiff, as the party whose interest lies in alternatives to discharge, is in the best position to present a wide range of alternatives.

At the same time, in order to protect employers from the harassment of interminable frivolous proposals, the plaintiff's burden should be to present only reasonable alternatives. A fair amount of specificity will be demanded of employers in determining the substantiality of economic need, and a plaintiff should have to set forth a comparably detailed alternative proposal. There is a limited range of reasonable alternatives to a reduction-in-force, and a private plaintiff need not rely solely on creative imagination to suggest how they might be applied, individually or in combination, to the evidence before him.

One alternative that might produce an abatement of costs comparable to that achieved through a reduction-in-force is a comprehensive adjustment in the salary structure. The plaintiff might propose a reappraisal of job categories based on what each category is actually worth, with pay rates adjusted to reflect a single level or narrow range of compensation for each classification. Such a scheme would affect disproportionately those with the longest service, but it would preserve employment security. Pay rates might also be reduced across the board so that the wages of all employees in the relevant unit or division would be scaled down.

When pay rate reductions are inappropriate, one or more other alternatives may be more suitable. Work sharing, achieved through either a reduced work week or alternating periods of work, may yield substantial cost savings. The right to displace or "bump" a less senior worker, based on seniority within one or several closely related job categories, would reduce cost with minimal disruption of operations, and would also be easy to administer. A shift to incentive pay practices would control future costs by tying individual pay rates closely to actual production. There is also the option of requiring employers to offer discharged employees other jobs within the organization as these become available, or to provide meaningful assistance in their search for jobs elsewhere.

## C. EMPLOYER'S BURDEN TO REJECT LESS DETRIMENTAL ALTERNATIVES

If the plaintiff advances alternatives with a less detrimental impact, the employer must demonstrate that such alternatives would be inadequate from a cost perspective. In particular, an employer will have to show not simply that the less discriminatory alternative, which may well involve a more pervasive disruption of the status quo, costs more to implement, but that the cost differential is a substantial one. In light of the expressed congressional opposition to citing cost as a reason for not hiring older workers, a less than substantial cost should not excuse a failure to retain them.

## Conclusion

The ADEA protects competent older workers from discriminatory employment decisions, however indirect or unintentional the discrimination. At some point, this protection must be balanced against an employer's legitimate economic imperatives. The employer's desire to reduce his business costs will continue to receive judicial recognition under the ADEA. But even the most critical cost considerations need not be addressed through age-related categories. If courts will make clear that alternatives less detrimental than salary-related discharge are the preferred response under the ADEA, employers may elect to pursue a more conciliatory approach and may incidentally avoid the costs of litigation.

Such a judicial emphasis should serve to strengthen the employment protection to which older workers are entitled under the Act.

## UNITED AIR LINES v. McMANN

*Supreme Court of the United States, 1977*
*434 U.S. 192, 16 FEP Cases 146*

MR. CHIEF JUSTICE BURGER, delivered the opinion of the Court.

The question presented in this case is whether, under the Age Discrimination in Employment Act of 1967, retirement of an employee over his objection and prior to reaching age 65 is permissible under the provisions of a bona fide retirement plan established by the employer in 1941 and joined by the employee in 1964. We granted certiorari to resolve a conflict between the holdings of the Fifth Circuit in *Brennan* v. *Taft Broadcasting Co.*, 500 F.2d 212 (1974), and the Fourth Circuit now before us. See *Zinger* v. *Blanchette*, 549 F.2d 901 (CA3 1977), *petition for cert. filed*, April 7, 1977 (No. 76–1375).

### I

The operative facts were stipulated by the parties in the District Court and are not controverted here. McMann joined United Air Lines, Inc. in 1944, and continued as an employee until his retirement at age 60 in 1973. Over the years he held various positions with United and at retirement held that of technical specialist-aircraft systems. At the time McMann was first employed, United maintained a formal retirement income plan it had inaugurated in 1941, in which McMann was eligible to participate, but was not compelled to join. He voluntarily joined the plan in January of 1964. The application form McMann signed showed the normal retirement age for participants in his category was 60 years.

McMann reached his 60th birthday on January 23, 1973, and was retired on February 1, 1973, over his objection. He then filed a notice of intent to sue United for violation of the Act pursuant to 29 U.S.C. § 626(d). Although he received an opinion from the Department of Labor that United's plan was bona fide and did not appear to be a subterfuge to evade the purposes of the Act, he brought this suit.

McMann's suit in the District Court seeking injunctive relief, reinstatement and backpay alleged his forced retirement was solely because of his age and was unlawful under the Act. United's response was that McMann was retired in compliance with the provisions of a bona fide retirement plan which he had voluntarily joined. On facts as stipulated, the District Court granted United's motion for summary judgment.

In the Court of Appeals it was conceded the plan was bona fide "in the sense that it exists and pays benefits." But McMann, supported by a brief *amicus curiae* filed in that court by the Secretary of Labor, contended the enforcement of the age 60 retirement provision, even under a bona fide plan instituted in good faith in 1941, was a subterfuge to evade the Act.

The Court of Appeals agreed, holding that a pre-age 65 retirement falls within the meaning of "subterfuge" unless the employer can show that the "early retirement provision . . . has some economic or business purpose other than arbitrary age discrimination." *McMann* v. *United Air Lines, Inc.,* 542 F.2d 217, 221 (1976). The Court of Appeals remanded the case to the District Court to allow United an opportunity to show an economic or business purpose and United sought review here.

We reverse.

## II

Section 2(b) of the Age Discrimination in Employment Act of 1967 recites that its purpose is
"to promote employment of older persons based on their ability rather than age; to prohibit arbitrary age discrimination in employment; to help employers and workers find ways of meeting problems arising from the impact of age on employment." 29 U.S.C. § 621(b).
Section 4(a)(1) of the Act makes it unlawful for an employer
"to discharge any individual or otherwise discriminate against any individual with respect to his compensation, terms, conditions, or privileges of employment, because of such individual's age. . . ." 29 U.S.C. § 623 (a)(1).
The Act covers individuals between ages 40 and 65, 29 U.S.C. § 631, but does not prohibit all enforced retirements prior to age 65; some are permitted under § 4(f)(2) which provides:
"It shall not be unlawful for an employer . . . or labor organization to observe the terms of a bona fide seniority system or any bona fide employee benefit plan such as a retirement, pension, or insurance plan which is not a subterfuge to evade the purposes of this [Act], except that no such employee benefit plan shall excuse the failure to hire any individual. . . ." 29 U.S.C. § 623(f)(2). See *infra,* at 6–10.

McMann argues the term "normal retirement age" is not defined in the plan other than in a provision that "A Participant's Normal Retirement Date is the first day of the month following his 60th birthday." From this he contends normal retirement age does not mean mandatory or compelled retirement at age 60, and United therefore did not retire him "to observe the terms" of the plan as required by § 4(f)(2). As to this claim, however, we accept the analysis of the plan by the Court of Appeals, Fourth Circuit:
"While the meaning of the word 'normal' in this context is not free from doubt, counsel agreed in oral argument on the manner in which the plan is operated in practice. The employee has no discretion whether to continue beyond the 'normal' retirement age. United legally may retain employees such as McMann past age 60, but has never done so; its policy has been to retire all employees at the 'normal' age. Given these facts, we conclude that *for purposes of this decision, the plan should be regarded*

*as one requiring retirement at age 60 rather than one permitting it at the option of the employer."* 542 F.2d, at 219. (Emphasis supplied.)

...

. . . In light of the facts stipulated by the parties and found by the District Court, we also accept the Court of Appeals' view as to the meaning of "normal."

In *Brennan* v. *Taft Broadcasting Co., supra,* at 215, the Fifth Circuit held that establishment of a bona fide retirement plan long before enactment of the Act, "eliminat[ed] any notion that it was adopted as a subterfuge for evasion." In rejecting the *Taft* reasoning, the Fourth Circuit emphasized that it distinguished between the Act and the *purposes* of the Act. The distinction relied on is untenable because the Act is the vehicle by which its purposes are expressed and carried out; it is difficult to conceive of a subterfuge to evade the one which does not also evade the other.

McMann argues that § 4(f)(2) was not intended to authorize involuntary retirement before age 65, but was only intended to make it economically feasible for employers to hire older employees by permitting the employers to give such older employees lesser retirement and other benefits than provided for younger employees. We are persuaded that the language of § 4(f)(2) was not intended to have such a limited effect.

In *Zinger* v. *Blanchette,* 549 F.2d 901 (1977), *petition for cert. filed,* April 7, 1977 (No. 76–1375), the Third Circuit had before it both the *Taft* and *McMann* decisions. It accepted *McMann's* distinction between the Act and its purposes, which, in this setting, we do not, but nevertheless concluded:

"The primary purpose of the Act is to prevent age discrimination in *hiring* and *discharging* workers. There is, however, a clear, measurable difference between outright discharge and retirement, a distinction that cannot be overlooked in analyzing the Act. While discharge without compensation is obviously undesirable, retirement on an adequate pension is generally regarded with favor. A careful examination of the legislative history demonstrates that, while cognizant of the disruptive effect retirement may have on individuals, Congress continued to regard retirement plans favorably and chose therefore to legislate only with respect to discharge." 549 F.2d, at 905. (Emphasis supplied.)

The dissent relies heavily upon the legislative history, which by traditional canons of interpretation is irrelevant to an unambiguous statute. However, in view of the recourse to the legislative history we turn to that aspect to demonstrate the absence of any indication of congressional intent to undermine the countless bona fide retirement plans existing in 1967 when the Act was passed. Such a pervasive impact on bona fide existing plans should not be read into the Act without a clear, unambiguous expression in the statute.

When the Senate Subcommittee was considering the bill, the then Secretary of Labor, Willard Wirtz, was asked what effect the Act would have on existing pension plans. His response was:

"It would be my judgment . . . that the effect of the provisions in 4(f)(2) [of the original bill] . . . is to protect the application of almost all plans which I know anything about. . . . It is intended to protect retirement plans." Hearings on S. 830 before the Subcommittee on Labor of the Senate Committee on Labor and Public Welfare, 90th Cong., 1st Sess., at 53 (1967).

When the present language of § 4(f)(2) was later proposed by amendments, Mr. Wirtz again commented that established pension plans would be protected. Hearings on H. R. 4221 before the General Subcommittee on Labor of the House Committee on Education and Labor, 90th Cong., 1st Sess., at 40 (1967).

. . .

The true intent behind § 4(f)(2) was not lost on the representatives of organized labor; they viewed it as protecting an employer's right to require pre-65 retirement pursuant to a bona fide retirement plan and objected to it on that basis. The legislative director for the AFL-CIO testified:

"We likewise do not see any reason why the legislation should, as is provided in section 4(f)(2) of the Administration bill, permit involuntary retirement of employees under 65. . . . Involuntary retirement could be forced, regardless of the age of the employee, subject only to the limitation that the retirement policy or system in effect may not be merely a subterfuge to evade the Act." Senate Hearings, *supra*, at 96.

In order to protect workers against involuntary retirement, the AFL-CIO suggested an "Amendment to Eliminate Provision Permitting Involuntary Retirement From the Age Discrimination in Employment Act, and to Substitute Therefor Provision Safeguarding Bona Fide Seniority or Merit Systems," which would have deleted any reference to retirement plans in the exception. *Id.* at 100. This amendment was rejected.

But as noted in *Zinger,* 549 F.2d, at 907, the exemption of benefit plans remained in the bill as enacted notwithstanding Labor's objection, and the Labor proposed exemption for seniority systems was added. There is no basis to view the final version of § 4(f)(2) as an acceptance of Labor's request that the benefit plan provision be deleted; the plain language of the statute shows it is still there, albeit in different terms.

Also added to the section when it emerged from the Senate Subcommittee is the language "except that no such employee benefit plan shall excuse the failure to hire any such individual." Rather than reading this addendum as a redundancy as does the dissent, *post,* at 5, and 5 n. 5, it is clear this is the result of Senator Javits' concern that observance of existing retirement plan terms might discourage hiring of older workers. *Supra,* at 8. Giving meaning to each of these provisions leads inescapably to the conclusion they were intended to permit observance of the mandatory retirement terms of bona fide retirement plans, but that the existence of such plans could not be used as an excuse not to hire any person because of age.

There is no reason to doubt that Secretary Wirtz fully appreciated the difference between the Administration and Senate bills. He was aware of Senator Javits' concerns, and knew the Senator sought to amend the original bill to focus on the *hiring* of older persons notwithstanding the existence of pension plans which they might not economically be permitted to join. See Senate Hearings, *supra,* at 40. Senator Javits' view was enacted into law making it possible to employ such older persons without compulsion to include them in pre-existing plans.

The dissent misconceives what was said in the Senate debate. The dialogue between Senators Javits and Yarborough, the minority and majority managers of the bill, respectively, is set out below and clearly shows awareness of the continued vitality of pre-age 65 retirements.

### III

In this case, of course, our function is narrowly confined to discerning the meaning of the statutory language; we do not pass on the wisdom of fixed mandatory retirements at a particular age. So limited we find nothing to indicate Congress intended wholesale invalidation of retirement plans instituted in good faith before its passage, or intended to require employers to bear the burden of showing a business or economic purpose to justify bona fide pre-existing plans as the Fourth Circuit concluded. In ordinary parlance, and in dictionary definitions as well, a subterfuge is a scheme, plan, stratagem or artifice of evasion. In the context of this statute, "subterfuge" must be given its ordinary meaning and we must assume Congress intended it in that sense. So read, a plan established in 1941, if bona fide, as is conceded here, cannot be a subterfuge to evade an Act passed 26 years later. To spell out an intent in 1941 to evade a statutory requirement not enacted until 1967 attributes, at the very least, a remarkable prescience to the employer. We reject any such *per se* rule requiring an employer to show an economic or business purpose in order to satisfy the subterfuge language of the Act.

Accordingly, the judgment of the Court of Appeals is reversed and the case is remanded for further proceedings consistent with this opinion.

*Reversed.*

. . .

Mr. Justice White, concurring in the judgment:

### I

While I agree with the Court and with Mr. Justice Stewart that Mc-Mann's forced retirement at age 60 pursuant to United's retirement income plan does not violate the Age Discrimination in Employment Act, 29 U.S.C. § 621 *et seq.,* I disagree with the proposition that this bona fide plan necessarily is made lawful under § 4(f)(2) of the Act, 29 U.S.C. § 623(f)(2), merely because it was adopted long before the Act's passage. Even conceding that the retirement plan could not have been a subterfuge to evade the purposes of the Act when it was adopted by

United in 1941, I believe that the decision by United to continue the mandatory aspects of the plan after the Act became effective in 1968 must be separately examined to determine whether it is proscribed by the Act.

The legislative history indicates that the exception contained within § 4(f)(2) "applies to new and *existing* employee benefit plans, and to both the establishment and *maintenance* of such plans." H. R. Rep. No. 805, 90th Cong., 1st Sess., 4 (1967); S. Rep. No. 723, 90th Cong., 1st Sess., 4 (1967) (emphasis added). This statement in both the House and Senate reports demonstrates that there is no magic in the fact that United's retirement plan was adopted prior to the Act, for not only the plan's establishment but also its maintenance must be scrutinized. For that reason, unless United was legally bound to continue the mandatory retirement aspect of its plan, its decision to continue to require employees to retire at age 60 after the Act became effective must be viewed in the same light as a post-Act decision to adopt such a plan.

No one has suggested in this case that United did not have the legal option of altering its plan to allow employees who desired to continue working beyond age 60 to do so; at the most it has been concluded that United simply elected to apply its retirement policy uniformly. See *ante*, at 4. Because United chose to continue its mandatory retirement policy beyond the effective date of the Act, I would not terminate the inquiry with the observation that the plan was adopted long before Congress considered the age discrimination act but rather would proceed to what I consider to be the crucial question: does the Act prohibit the mandatory retirement pursuant to a bona fide retirement plan of an employee before he reaches age 65? My reading of the legislative history, set out in Part II of the Court's opinion, convinces me that it does not.

. . .

### III

In this case, the Fourth Circuit recognized the fact that United's retirement plan is "bona fide" in the sense that it provides McMann with substantial benefits. The court, however, viewed as separate and additional the requirement that the plan not be a subterfuge to evade the purposes of the Act. I find no support in the legislative history for the interpretation of that language as requiring "some economic or business purpose." 542 F.2d 217, 221 (CA4 1976). Rather, as I read the history, Congress intended to exempt from the Act's prohibition all retirement plans—even those whose only purpose is to terminate the services of old workers—as long as the benefits they pay are not so unreasonably small as to make the "retirements" nothing short of discharges.

What little discussion there was in Congress concerning the meaning of the § 4(f)(2) exception indicates that the no-subterfuge requirement was merely a restatement of the requirement that the plan be bona fide. See 113 Cong. Rec. 31255 (1967). It is significant that the subterfuge language was contained in the original Administration bill, for that version was recognized as being "intended to protect retirement plans." See *ante,* at 7. Because all retirement plans necessarily make distinctions based on age, I fail to see how the subterfuge language, which was included in the original version of the bill and was carried all the way through, could have been intended to impose a requirement which almost no retirement plan could meet. For that reason I would interpret the § 4(f)(2) exception as protecting actions taken pursuant to a retirement plan which is designed to pay substantial benefits.

Because the Court relies exclusively upon the adoption date of United's retirement plan as a basis for concluding that McMann's forced retirement was not unlawful, I cannot join its opinion. Instead, I would adopt the approach taken by the Third Circuit in *Zinger* v. *Blanchette,* 549 F.2d 901 (CA3 1977), *petition for cert. filed,* April 7, 1977 (No. 76–1375), and would hold that his retirement was valid under the Act, not because the retirement plan was adopted by United prior to the Act's passage, but because the Act does not prohibit involuntary retirements pursuant to bona fide plans.

MR. JUSTICE MARSHALL, with whom MR. JUSTICE BRENNAN joins, dissenting: Today the Court, in its first encounter with the Age Discrimination in Employment Act of 1967, Pub. L. 90–202, 81 Stat. 602, 29 U.S.C. § 621 *et seq.,* sharply limits the reach of that important law. In apparent disregard of settled principles of statutory construction, it gives an unduly narrow interpretation to a congressional enactment designed to remedy arbitrary discrimination in the workplace. Because I believe that the Court misinterprets the Act, I respectfully dissent.

But for § 4(f)(2) of the Act, 29 U.S.C. § 623(f)(2), petitioner's decision to discharge respondent because he reached the age of 60 would violate § 4(a)(1), 29 U.S.C. § 623(a)(1). This latter section makes it unlawful for an employer "to fail or refuse to hire or to discharge or otherwise discriminate against any individual [between 40 and 65] with respect to his compensation, terms, conditions, or privileges of employment, because of such individual's age."

The language used in § 4(a)(1) tracks the language of § 703(a)(1) of the Civil Rights Act of 1964, 42 U.S.C. § 2000e–2(a)(1). This section has been interpreted as forbidding involuntary retirement when improper criteria, such as race or sex, are used in selecting those to be retired. With reference to the statutory language, courts have reasoned that forced retirement is "tantamount to a discharge." *Bartmess* v. *Drewrys U.S.A., Inc.,* 444 F.2d 1186, 1189 (CA7), *cert. denied,* 404 U.S. 939 (1971), or that the employer requiring retirement is "discriminat[ing] against" the retired employee "with respect to . . . [a] condition . . . of employment," see *Peters* v. *Missouri Pacific Railroad Co.,* 483 F.2d 490, 492 n. 3 (CA5), *cert. denied,* 414 U.S. 1002 (1973); *Rosen* v. *Public Service Electric & Gas Co.,* 477 F.2d 90, 94–95 (CA3 1973); *Bartmess* v. *Drewrys U.S.A., Inc., supra,* 444 F.2d, at 1188–89.

Given these constructions of § 703(a)(1) of the Civil Rights Act and the absence of any indication that Congress intended § 4(a)(1) of the Age

Discrimination in Employment Act to be interpreted differently, I would construe the identical language of the two statutes in an identical manner. The question that remains is whether § 4(f)(2) sanctions this otherwise unlawful act. That section provides:

"It shall not be unlawful for an employer . . . to observe the terms of a bona fide seniority system or any bona fide employee benefit plan such as a retirement, pension, or insurance plan, which is not a subterfuge to evade the purposes of [the Act]. . . ."

The opinion of the Court assumes that this language is clear on its face. *Ante,* at 3, 6. I cannot agree with this premise. In my view, the statutory language is susceptible of at least two interpretations, and the only reading consonant with congressional intent would preclude involuntary retirement of employees covered by the Act.

On this latter reading, § 4(f)(2) allows different treatment of older employees only with respect to the benefits paid or available under certain employee benefit plans, including pension and retirement plans. Alternatively, the section may be read, as the Court has, also to permit involuntary retirement of older employees prior to age 65 pursuant to a pension or retirement benefit plan. *Ante,* at 3. The critical question, then, is whether the phrase "employee benefit plan," as used by Congress here to include a "retirement, pension or insurance plan," encompasses only the rules defining what benefits retirees receive, or whether it also encompasses rules mandating retirement at a particular age.

. . .

The Court's analysis of the legislative history establishes that the primary purpose of the Act was to facilitate the hiring of old workers. I have no quarrel with that proposition. Understanding this primary purpose, however, aids not at all in determining whether Congress also intended to prohibit forced retirement of those already employed. The Court's analysis of the legislative history on this issue, *ante,* at 6–9, on which MR. JUSTICE WHITE relies, *ante,* at 2–3, is unpersuasive, since it relies primarily on references to an exception that was not enacted.

There can be no question, that had Congress enacted § 4(f)(2) in the form in which it was proposed by the Administration, forced retirement would be permissible. That section of the initial bill quite specifically allowed such retirement. It provided:

"It shall not be unlawful for an employer . . . to separate involuntarily an employee under a retirement policy or system where such policy or system is not merely a subterfuge to evade the purposes of this Act. . . ." S. 830, H. R. 4221. § 4(f)(2), 90th Cong., 1st Sess.

Thus the remarks of . . . on which the Court relies . . . quite properly reflect that the bill as it then existed would have authorized involuntary retirement. But the present benefit-plan exception to the § 4(a) prohibition on age discrimination differs significantly from that contained in the original bill. The specific authorization for involuntary retirement was deleted. That this deletion was made may of itself suggest that

Congress concluded such an exception was unwise; a review of the legislative history strongly supports this view.

. . .

Any doubt as to the correctness of reading the Act to prohibit forced retirement is dispelled by considering the anomaly that results from the Court's contrary interpretation. Under §§ 4(a) and 4(f)(2), see n. 5, *supra*, it is unlawful for an employer to refuse to hire a job applicant under the age of 65 because of his age. If, as the Court holds, involuntary retirement before age 65 is permissible under § 4(f)(2), the individual so retired has a simple route to regain his job: he need only reapply for the vacancy created by his retirement. As a new applicant, the individual plainly cannot be denied the job because of his age. And as someone with experience in performing the tasks of the "vacant" job he once held, the individual likely will be better qualified than any other applicant. Thus the individual retired one day would have to be hired the next. We should be loathe to attribute to Congress an intention to produce such a bizarre result,

One final reason exists for rejecting the Court's broad interpretation of the Act's exemption. The Age Discrimination in Employment Act is a remedial statute designed, in the Act's own words, "to promote employment of older persons based on their ability rather than age; to prohibit arbitrary age discrimination in employment; [and] to help employers and workers find ways of meeting problems arising from the impact of age on employment." § 1(b), 29 U.S.C. § 621(b). It is well settled that such legislation should "be given a liberal interpretation . . . [and] exemptions from its sweep should be narrowed and limited to effect the remedy intended." *Piedmont & Northern R. Co.* v. *ICC,* 286 U.S. 299, 311–12 (1932). See also, *e. g., Phillips* v. *Walling,* 324 U.S. 490, 493 (1945). To construe the § 4(f)(2) exemption broadly to authorize involuntary retirement when no statement in the Committee reports or by the Act's floor managers or sponsors in the debates supports that interpretation flouts this fundamental principle of construction.

The mischief the Court fashions today may be short lived. Both the House and Senate have passed amendments to the Act. 123 Cong. Rec. H9984–9985 (Daily ed. Sept. 23, 1977); *id.,* at S17303 (Daily ed. Oct. 19, 1977). The amendments to § 4(f)(2) expressly provide that the involuntary retirement of employees shall not be permitted or required pursuant to any employee benefit plan. Thus, today's decision may have virtually no prospective effect. But the Committee reports of both Houses make plain that, properly understood, the existing Act already prohibits involuntary retirement, and that the amendment is only a clarification necessitated by court decisions misconstruing congressional intent. H. R. Rep. No. 95–527, 95th Cong., 1st Sess. (1977), at 5–6; *id.,* at 27 (additional views of Rep. Weiss, quoting statement of Sen. Javits) ; S. Rep. No. 95–493, 95th Cong., 1st Sess. (1977), at 9–10. Because the Court today has also misconstrued congressional intent and has thereby deprived many older workers of the protection which Congress sought to afford, I must dissent.

## ZINGER v. BLANCHETTE

*United States Court of Appeals, Third Circuit, 1977*
*549 F.2d 901, 14 FEP Cases 497*

WEIS, Circuit Judge: Acknowledging the inexorable march of time but unwilling to leave his employment before the customary age of 65, the plaintiff contests his involuntary retirement one year earlier. He contends that an agreement by his employer preceding the formation of the Penn Central Railroad and the Age Discrimination in Employment Act both proscribe his premature retirement. Consequently, he seeks to augment his pension to what it would have been had he remained in service until he reached 65. Though he argues vigorously, we conclude that he cannot prevail on either of his contentions and, therefore, we must affirm the district court's judgment for the defendants.

Only months before his sixty-fifth birthday and despite his protests, the Penn Central Transportation Company retired plaintiff Zinger, making him eligible for pension benefits from several sources, including the Railroad Retirement Fund. However, these payments total $834.12 less per year than he would have received had he continued to work for Penn Central until age 65.

. . .

. . . In 1962, the Pennsylvania Railroad also adopted an "Interim Pension Policy" to pay benefits to those employees retiring before 65, when payments began under the Railroad Retirement Act.

In the preliminary negotiations for the Pennsylvania and New York Central merger, management agreed with the unions to provide extensive job protection for their members. . . .

On April 5, 1965, the chairman of the board of the Pennsylvania Railroad sent a letter addressed to "PRR Supervisors, Managers, and Officers" explaining some effects of the merger. Mr. Zinger was one of the persons who received this communication. In the body of the letter, the chairman wrote:

"You will note from Section I, [of the attachment] which applies to you, that non-agreement supervisors, managers, and officers will be offered continued employment until they retire, . . . ."

The attached document, captioned "Personnel Policy for Merger of the Pennsylvania and New York Central Railroads Applying to Supervisors, Managers, Officers and other Employees Not Subject to Agreement with Unions," listed two classifications of personnel not subject to the union agreement: "I. Supervisors, Managers, and Officers" and "II. Other Employees Not Subject to Agreements with Unions." Paragraph E under the first category read:

"The company may elect to retire any such person between ages 60 and 65 and he, as well as any such person over 60 years of age who is unwilling to relocate or accept a position in a new field of endeavor, will be provided interim pension allowances . . ."

. . .

In the district court, plaintiff asked for injunctive relief and damages, asserting that as a "non-agreement employee" he could not be involuntarily retired. In addition, he alleged that the early retirement plan violated the Age Discrimination in Employment Act of 1967, 29 U.S.C. § § 621 *et seq.* The district court rejected both contentions, and entered judgment for the defendants.

Plaintiff's position, as we understand it, is that, as a salaried employee of the railroad, he was entitled to the benefits of the protective agreement approved by the ICC as a condition of the merger. . . .

. . .

. . . [T]he agreement states, "[a]n employee shall not be regarded as deprived of employment or placed in a worse position . . . in case of his . . . retirement. . . ."

. . .

After a careful review of the evidence, we find nothing to show that the protective agreement, even if it covers plaintiff, prohibits the early retirement on a pension otherwise permitted by company policy.

Since he has failed to prove any breach of the protective agreement, we need not decide whether the plaintiff would be considered an "employee" within the terms of the statute or the ICC order. . . . What evidence there is in this case tends to show an intention to exclude, but since the record is not as complete as it might be, we think it better practice not to issue a definitive ruling. . . .

## II.

Disposition of the protective agreement issue, however, does not end the case. As an alternative, Zinger contends that the Penn Central program authorizing involuntary retirement between the ages of 60 and 65 violates the Age Discrimination in Employment Act of 1967, 29 U.S.C. § § 621 *et seq.* He asserts that the early retirement provision, although bona fide, is a "subterfuge" and, hence, not within the exception described in 29 U.S.C. § 623(f):

"It shall not be unlawful for an employer, employment agency, or labor organization—

. . .

"(2) to observe the terms of a bona fide seniority system or any bona fide employee benefit plan such as a retirement, pension, or insurance plan, which is not a subterfuge to evade the purposes of this Act, except that no such employee benefit plan shall excuse the failure to hire any such individual."

The railroad argues that since the early retirement plan predated the Act, it cannot be considered a subterfuge. We believe this chronological argument lacks merit and the mere fact that the plan was in existence before the Act was passed is not determinative. The statute speaks of evading the *"purposes"* of the Act—not the Act itself. Thus, a seniority practice or employee benefit plan effective long before the enactment of the statute could, nevertheless, be opposed to its purposes and thus be a subterfuge. . . .

Plaintiff's contention is that the Act proscribes involuntary retirement before 65. In a far reaching decision, *McMann* v. *United Air Lines, Inc., supra,* the Court of Appeals for the Fourth Circuit held that the Act, by implication, outlaws all programs providing for involuntary retirement before age 65, whether at the company's option or under mandatory provisions. However, in *Brennan* v. *Taft Broadcasting Co., supra,* the Fifth Circuit held that a bona fide plan providing benefits upon involuntary retirement at age 60 was not a subterfuge and therefore permissible under the Act.

Confronted with diametrically different interpretations by two highly respected courts, we must independently examine the Act and its legislative history.

. . .

The primary purpose of the Act is to prevent age discrimination in hiring and discharging workers. There is, however, a clear, measureable difference between outright discharge and retirement, a distinction that cannot be overlooked in analyzing the Act. While discharge without compensation is obviously undesirable, retirement on an adequate pension is generally regarded with favor. A careful examination of the legislative history demonstrates that, while cognizant of the disruptive effect retirement may have on individuals, Congress continued to regard retirement plans favorably and chose therefore to legislate only with respect to discharge.

. . . As referred to committee, both Senate and House Bills provided: "Sec. 4(f) It shall not be unlawful . . .

"(2) to separate involuntarily an employee under a retirement policy or system where such policy or system is not merely a subterfuge to evade the purposes of this Act."

. . .

. . . Representatives of organized labor expressed reservations about § 4(f)(2) at the subcommittee hearings in both houses. . . .

However, the union representatives were not successful in their efforts to remove the retirement provision from the bill, although the protection for seniority systems which they advocated was incorporated in the same section of the Act.

While the present form of § 4(f)(2) differs slightly from its original form in the Senate and House bills, we do not regard the difference as important. . . .

. . .

The former Secretary of Labor obviously thought that bona fide retirement programs permitting involuntary retirement before age 65 were exempted from the Act. The interpretive bulletin, 29 C.F.R. § 860.110, issued by the Department of Labor soon after enactment of the statute reads:

[T]he Act authorizes involuntary retirement irrespective of age, provided that such retirement is pursuant to the terms of a retirement or pension plan meeting the requirements of section 4(f)(2). . . .
"(b) This exception does not apply to the involuntary retirement before 65 of employees *who are not participants in the employer's retirement or pension program.* . . .

The bulletin demonstrates the Secretary's recognition of the difference between retirement with and without a pension; the financial effect of the latter being the same as outright discharge. . . . In the report of January 31, 1976, Secretary Brennan articulated the department's position:
"[R]etirements [before 65] are unlawful unless the mandatory retirement provision: (1) is contained in a bona fide pension or retirement plan, (2) is required by the terms of the plan and is not optional, and (3) is essential to the plan's economic survival or to some other legitimate purpose—i.e., is not in the plan for the sole urpose [sic] of moving out older workers, which purpose has now been made unlawful by the ADEA."
. . .

. . . [T]he Secretary's latter day position is not only contrary to that taken by his predecessor contemporaneously with the consideration and passage of the Act, but also to the views of the Congressional committees which declined that proposal when it was forthrightly presented to them. Thus, rather than proposing an amendment to Congress, as Congress had instructed, the Secretary seeks to change the Act by court decision or administrative fiat.
. . .

We leave to congressional consideration the broad policy questions underlying the desirability of regulating the minimum age for compensated involuntary retirement. Factors such as the population's gradually increasing average age and the proper methods of insuring the stability of the Social Security Plan may argue for an even higher retirement age. On the other hand, unemployment prevalent among younger members of society and a developing trend to distribute available employment by the use of a four day work week pull in the opposite direction. Further, the enactment of the Pension Reform Act of 1974 may be an important factor, concerned as it is with the financial stability of retirement plans and transferability of benefits.
. . . Congress may well decide that prudence dictates a tentative, experimental approach. It is not the function of the courts to accelerate that process when Congress unquestionably is acting within its proper scope.
. . . To summarize, involuntary retirement pursuant to a bona fide plan that is not a subterfuge but which requires or permits retirement at age 60 at the option of the employer is not unlawful.
Accordingly, the plaintiff's contentions must fail, and the judgment of the district court will be affirmed.

# 8. National Origin and Alienage

## A. Title VII and §1981

### ESPINOZA v. FARAH MANUFACTURING CO.

*Supreme Court of the United States, 1973*
*414 U.S. 86, 6 FEP Cases 933*

Mr. Justice Marshall delivered the opinion of the Court.

This case involves interpretation of the phrase "national origin" in Title VII of the Civil Rights Act of 1964. Petitioner Cecilia Espinoza is a lawfully admitted resident alien who was born in and remains a citizen of Mexico. She resides in San Antonio, Texas, with her husband, Rudolfo Espinoza, a United States citizen. In July, 1969, Mrs. Espinoza sought employment as a seamstress at the San Antonio division of respondent Farah Manufacturing Company. Her employment application was rejected on the basis of a long-standing company policy against the employment of aliens. After exhausting their administrative remedies with the Equal Employment Opportunity Commission, Petitioners commenced this suit in the District Court alleging that respondent had discriminated against Mrs. Espinoza because of her "national origin" in violation of § 703 of Title VII, 42 U.S.C. § 2000e-2(a) (1). The District Court granted petitioners' motion for summary judgment, holding that a refusal to hire because of lack of citizenship constitutes discrimination on the basis of "national origin." 343 F.Supp. 1205, 4 FEP Cases 929. The Court of Appeals reversed, concluding that the statutory phrase "national origin" did not embrace citizenship. 462 F.2d 1331, 4 FEP Cases 931. We granted the writ to resolve this question of statutory construction, 411 U.S. 946, and now affirm.

Section 703 makes it "an unlawful employment practice . . . for an employer to fail or refuse to hire . . . any individual . . . because of such individual's race, color, religion, sex, or national origin." Certainly the plain language of the statute supports the result reached by the Court of Appeals. The term "national origin" on its face refers to the country where a person was born, or, more broadly, the country from which his or her ancestors came.

The statute's legislative history, though quite meager in this respect, fully supports this construction. The only direct definition given the phrase "national origin" is the following remark made on the floor of the House of Representatives by Congressman Roosevelt, Chairman of the House Subcommittee which reported the bill: "It means the country from which you or your forebears come from. You may come from Poland, Czechoslovakia, England, France, or any other country." 110 Cong. Rec. 2548-49 (1964). We also note that an earlier version of § 703 had referred to discrimination because of "race, color, religion, national origin, or *ancestry*." H.R. 7152. 88th Cong. 1st Sess. § 804, Oct. 2, 1963 (Comm. print) (emphasis added). The deletion of the word "ancestry" from the final version was not intended as a material change, see H.R. Rep. No. 914, 88th Cong. 1st Sess. (1963), at 87, suggesting that the terms "national origin" and "ancestry" were considered synonymous.

There are other compelling reasons to believe that Congress did not intend the term "national origin" to embrace citizenship requirements. Since 1914, the Federal Government itself, through Civil Service Commission regulations, has engaged in what amounts to discrimination against aliens by denying them the right to enter competitive examination for federal employment. Executive Order No. 1997 (1914); see 5 U.S.C. § 3301; 5 CFR § 388.101 (1972). But it has never been suggested that the citizenship requirement for federal employment constitutes discrimination because of national origin, even though since 1943, various executive orders have expressly prohibited discrimination on the basis of national origin in federal governmental employment. See, e.g., Exec. Order 9346, 8 Fed. Reg. 7183 (1943); Exec. Order 11478, 34 Fed. Reg. 12985 (1969).

Moreover, § 701(b) of Tit. VII, in language closely paralleling § 703, makes it "the policy of the United States to insure equal employment opportunities for Federal employees without discrimination because of . . . national origin. . . ." Civil Rights Act of 1964, P.L. 88-352, § 701(b), 78 Stat. 254, reenacted P.L. 89-554, 80 Stat. 523 (1966), 5 U.S.C. 7151. The legislative history of that section reveals no mention of any intent on Congress' part to reverse the long-standing practice of requiring federal employees to be United States citizens. To the contrary, there is every indication that no such reversal was intended. Congress itself has on several occasions since 1964 enacted statutes barring aliens from federal employment. The Treasury, Postal Service, and General Appropriations Act of 1973, for example, provides that "no part of any appropriation contained in this or any other Act shall be used to pay compensation of any officer or employee of Government of the United States . . . unless such person is a citizen of the United States." P.L. 92-351, § 602, 86 Stat. 471 (1972). See also P.L. 91-144, § 502, 83 Stat. 336-337 (1970); P.L. 91-439, § 502, 84 Stat. 902 (1970).

To interpret the term "national origin" to embrace citizenship requirements would require us to conclude that Congress itself has repeatedly flouted its own declaration of policy. This Court cannot lightly find such a breach of faith. See *Bate Refrigerator Co.* v. *Sulzberger,* 157 U.S. 1, 38 (1895). So far as federal employment is concerned, we think it plain that Congress has assumed that the ban on national origin discrimination in § 701(b) did not affect the historical practice of requiring citizenship as a condition of employment. See *First National Bank* v. *Missouri,* 263 U.S. 640, 658 (1924). And there is no reason to believe Congress intended the term "national origin" in § 703 to have any broader scope. Cf. *King* v. *Smith*, 392 U.S. 309, 330-331 (1961).

Petitioners have suggested that the statutes and regulations discriminating against noncitizens in federal employment are unconstitutional under the Due Process Clause of the Fifth Amendment. We need not address that question here, for the issue presented in this case is not whether Congress has the power to discriminate against aliens in federal employment, but rather, whether Congress intended to prohibit such discrimination in private employment. Suffice it to say that we cannot conclude Congress would at once continue the practice of requiring citizenship as a condition of federal employment and, at the same time, prevent private employers from doing likewise. Interpreting § 703 as petitioners suggest would achieve the rather bizarre result of preventing Farah from insisting on United States citizenship as a condition of employment while the very agency charged with enforcement of Tit. VII would itself be required by Congress to place such a condition on its own personnel.

. . .

Finally, petitioners seek to draw support from the fact that Tit. VII protects all individuals from unlawful discrimination, whether or not a citizen of the United States. We agree that aliens are protected from discrimination under the Act. That result may be derived not only from the use of the term "any individual" in § 703, but also as a negative inference from the exemption in § 702, which provides that Tit. VII "shall not apply to an employer with respect to the employment of aliens outside any State. . . ." 42 U.S.C. §2000e-1. Title VII was clearly intended to apply with respect to the employment of aliens inside any State.[8]

The question posed in the present case, however, is not whether aliens are protected from illegal discrimination under the Act, but what kinds of discrimination the Act makes illegal. Certainly it would be unlawful for an employer to discriminate against aliens because of race, color, religion, sex, or national origin—for example, by hiring aliens of Anglo-Saxon background but refusing to hire those of Mexican or Spanish ancestry. Aliens are protected from illegal discrimination under the Act, but nothing in the Act makes it illegal to discriminate on the basis of citizenship or alienage.

We agree with the Court of Appeals that neither the language of the Act, nor its history, nor the specific facts of this case indicate that respondent has engaged in unlawful discrimination because of national origin.[9]

*Affirmed.*

[8] Title VII of the Civil Rights Act of 1964 protects all individuals, both citizens and noncitizens, domiciled or residing in the United States, against discrimination on the basis of race, color, religion, sex, or national origin."
29 CFR § 1606.1(c) (1972).

[9] Petitioners argue that respondent's policy of discriminating against aliens is prohibited by 42 U.S.C. § 1982 which provides: "All citizens of the United States shall have the same right, in every State and Territory, as is enjoyed by white citizens thereof to inherit, purchase, lease, sell, hold, and convey real and personal property." This issue was neither raised before the courts below nor presented in the petition for a writ of certiorari. Accordingly we express no views thereon.

# GUERRA v. MANCHESTER TERMINAL CORP.

*United States Court of Appeals, Fifth Circuit, 1974*
*498 F.2d 641, 8 FEP Cases 433*

GOLDBERG, Circuit Judge: In this case we face again the difficult problem of harmonizing and synchronizing overlapping statutory methods for combatting employment discrimination. We face also the question whether the protective umbrella supplied by the federal civil rights laws is broad enough to cover those who claim discrimination based on their status as aliens. Two of the three defendants—the union local and the union international—appeal various portions of a generally adverse decision by the district court. We affirm in part, reverse in part, and remand for further proceedings.

## I. The Scenario—Triple Feature

Most of the important details in the controversy are undisputed, the parties having submitted stipulated facts to the court below on cross-motions for summary judgment. From October 24, 1960, to January 10, 1967, plaintiff-appellee Guerra, a Mexican citizen lawfully residing in Houston, Texas, as a registered alien, worked for defendant Manchester Terminal Corporation [Terminal]. During this entire period Guerra maintained his family in Mexico. Employees at Terminal's Houston facility worked in either the Cotton Compress and Warehouse Department [Compress] or the Dock and Commodity Department [Dock]. Initially Guerra worked in Compress, but in 1963 he was transferred to Dock, where he performed satisfactorily.

Defendant Local 1581, International Longshoremen's Association [Local], represents Terminal's employees in each department. A single labor agreement covers employees in both departments, and provides higher rates of pay for all eleven job classifications in Dock than for any of the forty job classifications in Compress. At the time of the events from which this litigation arose, Local limited its membership to United States citizens and to those who had declared their intention to become citizens. Guerra was not a member although most of the members were Mexican-Americans or Mexican Nationals.

As a result of contract negotiations during the summer of 1965, Terminal agreed to hire its employees through the union hiring hall and to give preference to United States citizens. In addition, the bargaining agreement extended hospitalization benefits to both the worker and his family for those employed in Dock, but limited the benefits to the worker alone for those in Compress. The union membership then voted to establish a hiring hall referral system under which the more desirable jobs in Dock went first to United States citizens, then to Mexican citizens with families residing in the United States. Any jobs open thereafter would go to Mexican citizens who, like Guerra, kept their families in Mexico.

On September 7, 1965, Terminal transferred Guerra from Dock back to Compress. This action, taken because of union insistence, triggered the litigation that is now before this Court. Guerra was told that he could not have permanent employment in Dock until he either became a United States citizen or moved his family from Mexico to the United States, and his place in Dock was taken by a Mexican-American with more seniority. Guerra continued to work in Compress until he voluntarily left Terminal's employ in 1967.

. . .

Guerra alleged that various policies and practices followed by defendants discriminated against him and other Mexican Nationals on the basis of national origin in violation of rights secured by Title VII of the Civil Rights Act of 1964, 42 U.S.C. § 2000e *et seq.*, and by the Civil Rights Act of 1866, 42 U.S.C. § 1981.[1] He sought declaratory and injunctive relief as well as back pay and attorneys' fees. By final order entered on November 6, 1972, the district court held that defendants had engaged in an illegal discriminatory practice.[2] After a March 1973 hearing on damages, the court (1) permanently enjoined all the defendants from giving job preferences based on the citizenship of an employee or the residence of the employee's family; (2) permanently enjoined defendants Local and International from requiring United States citizenship as a condition of membership in the union; (3) imposed back pay liability on defendants Local and International, jointly and severally; and (4) ordered all defendants to pay reasonable attorneys fees and costs.

## II. Title VII Claim

In *Espinoza* v. *Farah Manufacturing Co.*, this Court held that an employer's refusal to hire an applicant because of her lack of United States citizenship did not fall within the prohibition of Title VII of the Civil Rights Act of 1964 against employment discrimination on the basis of national origin, 42 U.S.C. § 2000e-2(a)(1) (1970). On the authority of *Espinoza* the court below concluded that plaintiff-appellee Guerra was not entitled to relief under Title VII, reasoning that any discrimination against Guerra turned on his status as an alien and on the foreign residence of his family rather than on his national origin.

After the district court's decision, the Supreme Court affirmed our decision in *Espinoza, Espinoza* v. *Farah Manufacturing Co.*, 1973, 414 U.S. 86, 94 S.Ct. 334, 38 L.Ed.2d 287, 6 FEP Cases 933. The Court did note that Title VII protected aliens otherwise within its coverage from discrimination based on race, color, religion, sex, or national origin, and that a citizenship requirement might be unlawful if it were "but one part of a wider scheme of unlawful national origin discrimination" or had "the

---

[1] [Footnotes numbered as in original.—Ed.] Guerra also alleged violations of the duty of fair representation owed to himself and the class, and invoked the court's jurisdiction pursuant to 29 U.S.C. § 151 *et seq.* The court did not pass on that portion of the complaint, and none of the parties has mentioned it on this appeal.

[2] *Guerra* v. *Manchester Terminal Corp.*, S.D.Tex.1972, 350 F.Supp. 529, 5 FEP Cases 181; noted in 8 TEXAS INT'L L.J. 403 (1973) and 6 VAND.J. TRANSNAT'L L. 660 (1973).

purpose or effect of discriminating on the basis of national origin." 414 U.S. at 92, 94 S.Ct. at 338, 38 L.Ed.2d at 293, 6 FEP Cases at 935. The Court concluded, however, that Title VII did not apply to discrimination based solely on lack of United States citizenship. Like Mrs. Espinoza, appellee Guerra has failed to demonstrate that he suffered from discrimination based on his national origin rather than on his status as an alien. We therefore affirm the district court's denial of relief under Title VII.

### III. Section 1981 Claim: Limitations

Appellants make a broad-based attack on the district court's treatment of the portion of the case resting on 42 U.S.C. § 1981. We consider first the argument that Guerra's § 1981 claim was barred by limitations.

. . .

### IV. Section 1981 Claim: Other Issues

Appellants also challenge the district court's decision on Guerra's § 1981 claim as a matter of statutory interpretation and on the merits. They argue that § 1981 is not applicable to aliens; that a suit based on the statute requires a showing of state action; and that Guerra failed to demonstrate that he was the victim of an act of discrimination within the prohibition of § 1981.[26] We need not linger long over these arguments.

Noting that the statutes that now appear as 42 U.S.C. § 1981 and § 1982 had their origin in section one of the Civil Rights Act of 1866,[27] appellants cite a number of cases for the proposition that both provisions are limited to remedying racial discrimination. It is hardly open to dispute that the 1866 Act "was designed to do just what its terms suggest: to prohibit all racial discrimination, whether or not under color of law, with respect to the rights enumerated therein. . . ." *Jones* v. *Alfred H. Mayer Co.,* 1966, 392 U.S. 409, 436, 88 S.Ct. 2186, 2201, 20 L.Ed.2d 1189, 1205. See *Georgia* v. *Rachel,* 1966, 384 U.S. 780, 86 S.Ct. 1783, 16 L.Ed.2d 925. Moreover, the Supreme Court has indicated that one modern derivative of the Act, 42 U.S.C. § 1982, is aimed at racial discrimination affecting the right to purchase or lease property. *Jones* v. *Alfred H. Mayer Co., supra.* It does not necessarily follow that § 1981, another modern derivative, is also so limited.

In the first place, as the detailed study of the legislative history by the able district judge below demonstrates,[28] subsequent congressional action explicitly broadened the language of the portion of the 1866 Act that has become § 1981 to include "all persons" [29] in order to bring aliens within

[26] 42 U.S.C. § 1981 provides:
"All persons within the jurisdiction of the United States shall have the same right in every State and Territory to make and enforce contracts, to sue, be parties, give evidence, and to the full and equal benefit of all laws and proceedings for the security of persons and property as is enjoyed by white citizens, and shall be subject to like punishment, pains, penalties, taxes, licenses, and exactions of every kind, and to no other."

[27] Act of April 9, 1866, ch. 31, § 1, 14 Stat. 27.

[28] 350 F.Supp. at 533, 536, 5 FEP Cases at 183-185.

[29] As it has since its passage, the statute that is now 42 U.S.C. 1982 applies to "all citizens":

its coverage.[30] It is unnecessary to repeat the district court's legislative summary here. We have been unable to detect any significant flaws in the analysis, and we adopt that portion of the district court's opinion as our own. More important, as the district court also noted, the Supreme Court has explicitly indicated that this statute applies to aliens. *Takahashi* v. *Fish and Game Commission*, 1948, 334 U.S. 410, 419, 68 S.Ct. 1138, 92 L.Ed. 1478, 1487. As recently as 1971 the Court, referring to 42 U.S.C. § 1981, noted that, "The protection of this statute has been held to extend to aliens as well as to citizens." *Graham* v. *Richardson*, 403 U.S. 365, 377, 91 S.Ct. 1848, 1855, 29 L.Ed.2d 534, 545.[31]

Apparently conceding the possibility that § 1981 might apply to aliens, appellants next turn to the legislative history for support of their argument that the statute offers protection only against state action.[32] Whatever the merits of appellants' legislative archaeology, the decision of this Court clearly foreclose their argument. We held in *Sanders* v. *Dobbs Houses, Inc.*, 5 Cir. 1970, 431 F.2d 1097, 2 FEP Cases 942, that § 1981 extends to private discrimination in employment, and we have reaffirmed Judge Clark's cogent *Sanders* opinion many times since. . . .

---

"All citizens of the United States shall have the same right, in every State and Territory, as is enjoyed by white citizens thereof to inherit, purchase, lease, sell, hold, and convey real and personal property."

30 See Comment, *Is Section 1981 Modified by Title VII of the Civil Rights Act of 1964?*, 1970 DUKE L.J. 1223, 1237-38.

31 *Takahashi* was a challenge to a World War II inspired state statute forbidding the issuance of commercial fishing licenses to aliens ineligible for citizenship. *Graham* was a challenge to state actions conditioning welfare benefits on the possession of United States citizenship or on residence as an alien within the United States for a certain number of years. In both cases the Court held that the statutes denied aliens the equal protection of the laws guaranteed them under the Fourteenth Amendment. Accord, *Sugarman* v. *Dougall*, 1973, 413 U.S. 634, 93 S.Ct. 2842, 37 L.Ed.2d 853, 5 FEP Cases 1152.

Various lower courts have also concluded that 1981, or its antecedents, applies to noncitizens as well as citizens. *Roberto* v. *Hartford Fire Ins. Co.*, 7 Cir. 1949, 177 F.2d 811, 814, *cert. denied*, 339 U.S. 920, 70 S.Ct. 622, 94 L.Ed. 1343; *Lopez* v. *The White Plains Housing Authority*, S.D.N.Y.1972, 355 F.Supp. 1016, 1026; *Mohamed* v. *Parks*, D.Mass. 1973, 352 F.Supp. 518, 5 FEP Cases 594; *League of Academic Women* v. *Regents of University of California*, N.D.Cal.1972, 343 F.Supp. 636, 4 FEP Cases 808.

32 Implicit in appellants' position we sense the suggestion that Congress could not have constitutionally extended § 1981 to cover private discrimination against aliens. Because the 1866 Act was passed pursuant to the Thirteenth Amendment, any modern offspring of that statute, e.g., 42 U.S.C. § 1982, could reach private discrimination. By contrast, though the original source for § 1981 may have been the 1866 Act, the genesis of the "all citizens" language according to the Revisors' Historical Note was the Civil Rights Act of 1870. See *Tillman* v. *Wheaton-Haven Rec. Assn.*, 1973, 410 U.S. 431, 439 and n. 11, 93 S.Ct. 1090, 35 L.Ed.2d 403, 410 and n. 11. Since legislative history and Supreme Court decisions, e. g., *Strauder* v. *West Virginia*, 1880, 100 U.S. 303, 25 L.Ed. 664, indicate that the 1870 Act rested on the Fourteenth Amendment, any of its descendants must apply only against state action. Thus, though § 1981 might reach both private and public discrimination based on race, constitutionally it can reach only public discrimination based on alienage. We respectfully decline to embrace that *reductio ad absurdum*. Whatever constitutional foundation motivated the legislators who extended § 1981's predecessor to aliens, the Supreme Court has on several occasions suggested that authority to do so could be found in Congress's exclusive constitutional power over immigration and naturalization. *Graham* v. *Richardson, supra*, 403 U.S. at 377, 91 S.Ct. 1848, 29 L.Ed.2d at 544-545; *Takahashi* v. *Fish and Game Comm'n, supra*, 334 U.S. at 419, 68 S.Ct. 1138, 92 L.Ed. at 1487. See *Truax* v. *Raich*, 1915, 239 U.S. 33, 42, 36 S.Ct. 7, 60 L.Ed. 131, 135.

As their final line of defense appellants offer the argument that no act of discrimination within the prohibition of § 1981 occurred. Assuming *arguendo* that § 1981 reaches private discrimination against aliens, they insist that under the work referral system in effect at Manchester Terminal Corporation Guerra's transfer was not based on his alienage. As they see it, family residence, not citizenship, was the primary distinction drawn among workers: "The important inquiry is whether Guerra would have been transferred because of alienage if his family had resided in the United States and the answer to that is a simple no." Brief for Appellants at 11.

Appellants have sought refuge behind a semantic Maginot Line. The relevant inquiry in the case *sub judice* is whether Guerra would have been transferred because of his family's residence if he had been a United States citizen, and the answer to that is a simple no.[34] To be sure, the immediate obstacle between Guerra and the preferred Dock job was his family's residence in Mexico; but the obstacle was placed in his path because of his Mexican citizenship. That other Mexican citizens, those with families residing in the United States, could and did overcome the obstacle does not alter the basic fact that only noncitizens of the United States were put to the test.[35] Appellants may have softened the lines drawn by the citizenship requirement by distinguishing between classes of noncitizens; the difference in treatment nonetheless rested in the first instance of citizenship. That is exactly the sort of employment practice prohibited by 42 U.S.C. § 1981.[36]

## B. State Employment

### AMBACH v. NORWICK

*Supreme Court of the United States, 1979*
_____ U.S. _____, *19 FEP Cases 467, revs'g Norwick v. Nyquist,*
*417 F. Supp. 913, 14 FEP Cases 585*

Mr. Justice Powell delivered the opinion of the Court.

This case presents the question whether a State, consistently with the Equal Protection Clause of the Fourteenth Amendment, may refuse to

---

[34] As plaintiff-appellee notes, if family residence had really been the touchstone, the order of priority for jobs in Dock would have been first preference to those with families residing in the United States, second preference to all others.

[35] Nor is it relevant here that Guerra was the only employee actually displaced by the new hiring preference rule.

[36] Given a union composed predominantly of Mexican-Americans and Mexican Nationals intending to become United States citizens, we recognize the unlikelihood that Guerra's transfer resulted from his national origin, particularly since his place was taken by a Mexican-American. As to appellants' suggestion, Brief at 9, that Guerra lost his job to a man with more seniority, the stipulated facts in this case are that Guerra was transferred because he is a Mexican citizen whose family resides in Mexico.

employ as elementary and secondary school teachers aliens who are eligible
for United States citizenship but who refuse to seek naturalization.

## I

New York Education Law § 3001(3) forbids certification as a public
school teacher of any person who is not a citizen of the United States,
unless that person has manifested an intention to apply for citizenship.[1]
The Commissioner of Education is authorized to create exemptions from
this prohibition, and has done so with respect to aliens who are not yet
eligible for citizenship.[2] Unless a teacher obtains certification, he may not
work in a public elementary or secondary school in New York.[3]

Appellee Norwick was born in Scotland and is a subject of Great
Britain. She has resided in this country since 1965 and is married to a
United States citizen. Appellee Dachinger is a Finnish subject who came
to this country in 1966 and also is married to a United States citizen. Both
Norwick and Dachinger currently meet all of the educational requirements New York has set for certification as a public school teacher, but
they consistently have refused to seek citizenship in spite of their eligibility to do so. Norwick applied in 1973 for a teaching certificate covering
nursery school through sixth grade, and Dachinger sought a certificate
covering the same grades in 1975.[4] Both applications were denied because

---

[1] [Footnotes numbered as in original—Ed.] The statute provides:
"No person shall be employed or authorized to teach in the public schools of this
state who is:
"3. Not a citizen. The provisions of this subdivision shall not apply, however, to an
alien teacher now or hereafter employed provided such teacher shall make due application to become a citizen and thereafter within the time prescribed by law shall
become a citizen. The provisions of this subdivision shall not apply after July first,
nineteen hundred sixty-seven, to an alien teacher employed pursuant to regulations
adopted by the Commissioner of Education permitting such employment." N. Y.
Educ. Law § 3001 (3).
The statute contains an exception for persons who are ineligible for United States
citizenship solely because of an oversubscribed quota. Id., § 3001-a. Because this statutory provision is in all respects narrower than the exception provided by regulation,
see n. 2, infra, as a practical matter it has no effect.
The State does not certify the qualifications of teachers in the private schools,
although it does require that such teachers be "competent." N. Y. Educ. Low § 3204(2)
(McKinney 1970). Accordingly, we are not presented with the question of, and express
no view as to, the permissibility of a citizenship requirement pertaining to teachers
in private schools.

[2] The following regulation governs here:
"Citizenship. A teacher who is not a citizen of the United States or who has not declared intention of becoming a citizen may be issued a provisional certificate providing
such teacher has the appropriate educational qualifications as defined in the regulations and (1) possesses skills or competencies not readily available among teachers
holding citizenship, or (2) is unable to declare intention of becoming a citizen for valid
statutory reasons." 8 N. Y. Code of Rules and Regulations § 80.2(i).

[3] Certification by the Commissioner of Education is not required of teachers at state
institutions of higher education and the citizenship restriction accordingly does not
apply to them. Brief for Appellants 13 n. *

[4] At the time of her application Norwick had not yet met the post-graduate educational requirements for a permanent certificate and accordingly applied only for a
temporary certificate, which also is governed by § 3001 (3). She since has obtained the
necessary graduate degree for full certification. Dachinger previously had obtained a
temporary certificate, which had lapsed at the time of her 1975 application. The

of appellees' failure to meet the requirements of § 3001(3). Norwick then filed this suit seeking to enjoin the enforcement of § 3001(3), and Dachinger obtained leave to intervene as a plaintiff.

A three-judge District Court was convened pursuant to 28 U.S.C. § 2281. Applying the "close judicial scrutiny" standard of *Graham* v. *Richardson,* 403 U.S. 365, 372 (1971), the court held that § 3001(3) discriminated against aliens in violation of the Equal Protection Clause. 417 F. Supp. 913 (SDNY 1976). The court believed that the statute was overbroad, because it excluded all resident aliens from all teaching jobs regardless of the subject sought to be taught, the alien's nationality, the nature of the alien's relationship to this country, and the alien's willingness to substitute some other sign of loyalty to this Nation's political values, such as an oath of allegiance. *Id.,* at 921. We noted probable jurisdiction over the State's appeal, 436 U.S. 902 (1978), and now reverse.

## II

### A

The decisions of this Court regarding the permissibility of statutory classifications involving aliens have not formed an unwavering line over the years. State regulation of the employment of aliens long has been subject to constitutional constraints. In *Yick Wo* v. *Hopkins,* 118 U.S. 356 (1886), the Court struck down an ordinance which was applied to prevent aliens from running laundries, and in *Truax* v. *Raich,* 239 U.S. 33 (1915), a law requiring at least 80 percent of the employees of certain businesses to be citizens was held to be an unconstitutional infringement of an alien's "right to work for a living in the common occupations of the community . . . ."*Id.,* at 41. At the same time, however, the Court also has recognized a greater degree of latitude for the States when aliens were sought to be excluded from public employment. At the time *Truax* was decided, the governing doctrine permitted States to exclude aliens from various activities when the restriction pertained to "the regulation or distribution of the public domain, or of the common property or resources of the people of the State, . . ." *Id.,* at 39. Hence, as part of a larger authority to forbid aliens from owning land, *Frick* v. *Webb,* 263 U.S. 326 (1923); *Webb* v. *O'Brien,* 263 U.S. 313 (1923); *Porterfield* v. *Webb,* 263 U.S. 225 (1923); *Terrace* v. *Thompson,* 263 U.S. 197 (1923); *Blythe* v. *Hinkley,* 180 U.S. 333 (1901); *Hauenstein* v. *Lynham,* 100 U.S. 483 (1880), harvesting wildlife, *Patsone* v. *Pennsylvania,* 232 U.S. 138 (1914); *McCready* v. *Virginia,* 94 U.S. 391 (1877), or maintaining an inherently dangerous enterprise, *Clarke* v. *Deckebach,* 274 U.S. 392 (1927), States permissibly could exclude aliens from working on public construction projects, *Crane* v. *New York,* 239 U.S. 195 (1915), and, it appears, from engaging in any form of public employment at all, see *Truax,* at 40.

---

record does not indicate whether Dachinger previously had declared an intent to obtain citizenship or had obtained the temporary certificate because of some applicable exception to the citizenship requirement.

Over time, the Court's decisions gradually have restricted the activities from which States are free to exclude aliens. The first sign that the Court would question the constitutionality of discrimination against aliens even in areas affected with a "public interest" appeared in *Oyama* v. *California,* 332 U.S. 633 (1948). The Court there held that statutory presumptions designed to discourage evasion of California's ban on alien landholding discriminated against the citizen children of aliens. The same Term, the Court held that the "ownership" a State exercises over fish found in its territorial waters "is inadequate to justify California in excluding any or all aliens who are lawful residents of the State from making a living by fishing in the ocean off its shores while permitting all others to do so." *Takahashi* v. *Fish & Game Comm'n,* 334 U.S. 410, 421 (1948). This process of withdrawal from the former doctrine culminated in *Graham* v. *Richardson,* 403 U.S. 365 (1971), which for the first time treated classifications based on alienage as "inherently suspect and subject to close judicial scrutiny." *Id.,* at 372. Applying *Graham,* this Court has held invalid statutes that prevented aliens from entering a State's classified civil service, *Sugarman* v. *Dougall,* 413 U.S. 634 (1973), practicing law, *In re Griffiths,* 413 U.S. 717 (1973), working as an engineer, *Examining Bd.* v. *Flores de Otero,* 426 U.S. 572 (1976), and receiving state educational benefits, *Nyquist* v. *Mauclet,* 432 U.S. 1 (1977).

Although our more recent decisions have departed substantially from the public interest doctrine of *Truax's* day, they have not abandoned the general principle that some state functions are so bound up with the operation of the State as a governmental entity as to permit the exclusion from those functions of all persons who have not become part of the process of self-government. In *Sugarman,* we recognized that a State could, "in an appropriately defined class of positions, require citizenship as a qualification for office." We went on to observe:

"Such power inheres in the State by virtue of its obligation, already noted above, 'to preserve the basic conception of a political community.' . . . And this power and responsibility of the State applies, not only to the qualifications of voters, but also to persons holding state elective or important nonelective executive, legislative, and judicial positions, for officers who participate directly in the formulation, execution, or review of broad public policy perform functions that go to the heart of representative government." *Id.,* at 647 (citation omitted).

The exclusion of aliens from such governmental positions would not invite as demanding scrutiny from this Court. *Id.,* at 648. See also *Nyquist* v. *Mauclet,* supra, at 11; *Perkins* v. *Smith,* 370 F. Supp. 134 (Md. 1974), aff'd, 426 U.S. 913 (1976).

Applying the rational basis standard, we held last Term that New York could exclude aliens from the ranks of its police force. *Foley* v. *Connelie,* 435 U.S. 291 (1978). Because the police function fulfilled "a most fundamental obligation of government to its constituency" and by necessity cloaked policemen with substantial discretionary powers, we viewed the police force as being one of this appropriately defined classes of positions for which a citizenship requirement could be imposed. *Id.*, at 297. Accordingly, the State was required to justify its classification only "by a showing of some rational relationship between the interest sought to be protected and the limiting classification." *Id.*, at 296.

The rule for governmental functions, which is an exception to the general standard applicable to classifications based on alienage, rests on important principles inherent in the Constitution. The distinction between citizens and aliens, though ordinarily irrelevant to private activity, is fundamental to the definition and government of a State. The Constitution itself refers to the distinction no less than 11 times, see *Sugarman* v. *Dougall, supra*, at 651–652 (REHNQUIST, J., dissenting), indicating that the status of citizenship was meant to have significance in the structure of our government. The assumption of that status, whether by birth or naturalization, denotes an association with the polity which, in a democratic republic, exercises the powers of governance. See *Foley* v. *Connelie, supra*, at 295. The form of this association is important: an oath of allegiance or similar ceremony cannot substitute for the unequivocal legal bond citizenship represents. It is because of this special significance of citizenship that governmental entities, when exercising the functions of government, have wider latitude in limiting the participation of noncitizens.[5]

B

In determining whether, for purposes of equal protection analysis, teaching in public schools constitutes a governmental function, we look to the role of public education and to the degree of responsibility and discretion teachers possess in fulfilling that role. See *id.*, at 297. Each of these considerations supports the conclusion that public school teachers may be regarded as performing a task "that go[es] to the heart of representative government." *Sugarman* v. *Dougall, supra*, at 647.[6]

---

[5] That the significance of citizenship has constitutional dimensions also has been recognized by several of our decisions. In *Trop* v. *Dulles,* 356 U.S. 86 (1958), a plurality of the Court held that the expatriation of an American citizen constituted cruel and unusual punishment for the crime of desertion in time of war. In *Afroyim* v. *Rusk,* 387 U.S. 253 (1967), the Court held that the Constitution forbade Congress from depriving a person of his citizenship against his will for any reason.

[6] The dissenting opinion of MR. JUSTICE BLACKMUN, in reaching an appropriate conclusion, appears to apply a different analysis from that employed in our prior decisions. Rather than consider whether public school teachers perform a significant government function, the inquiry mandated by *Foley* v. *Connelie,* 435 U.S. 291 (1978), and *Sugarman* v. *Dougall,* 413 U.S. 634 (1973), the dissent focuses instead on the general societal importance of primary and secondary school teachers both public and private. Thus the dissent on the one hand depreciates the importance of New York's citizenship requirement because it is not applied to private school teachers, and on the other hand argues that the role teachers perform in our society is no more significant than that filled by attorneys. This misses the point of *Foley* and *Sugarman.* New York's citizenship requirement is limited to a governmental function because it applies only to teachers employed by and acting as agents of the State. The Connecticut statute held unconstitutional in *In re Griffiths,* 413 U.S. 717 (1973), by contrast, applied to all attorneys, most of whom do not work for the government. The exclusion of aliens from access to the bar implicated the right to pursue a chosen occupation, not access to public employment. Cf. *Nyquist* v. *Mauclet,* 432 U.S. 1, 15–16, n. * (1977) (POWELL, J.,

Public education, like the police function, "fulfills a most fundamental obligation of government to its constituency." *Foley,* at 297. The importance of public schools in the preparation of individuals for participation as citizens, and in the preservation of the values on which our society rests, long has been recognized by our decisions:

"Today, education is perhaps the most important function of state and local governments. Compulsory school attendance laws and the great expenditures for education both demonstrate our recognition of the importance of education to our democratic society. It is required in the performance of our most basic public responsibilities, even service in the armed forces. It is the very foundation of good citizenship. Today it is a principal instrument in awakening the child to cultural values, in preparing him for later professional training, and in helping him to adjust normally to his environment." *Brown* v. *Board of Education,* 347 U.S. 483, 493 (1954).

See also *Keyes* v. *School Dist. No. 1,* 413 U.S. 189, 246 (1973) (POWELL, J., concurring); *San Antonio Ind. School Dist.* v. *Rodriguez,* 411 U.S. 1, 29–30 (1973); *Wisconsin* v. *Yoder,* 406 U.S. 205, 213 (1972); *id.,* at 238–239 (WHITE, J., concurring) ; *Abington School Dist.* v. *Schempp,* 374 U.S. 203, 230 (1963) (BRENNAN, J., concurring); *Adler* v. *Board of Education,* 342 U.S. 485, 493 (1952); *McCollum* v. *Board of Education,* 333 U.S. 203, 212 (1948) (Frankfurter, J., concurring); *Pierce* v. *Society of Sisters,* 268 U.S. 510 (1925); *Meyer* v. *Nebraska,* 262 U.S. 390 (1923); *Interstate Consolidated Street R. Co.* v. *Massachusetts,* 207 U.S. 79 (1907).[7] Other authorities have perceived public schools as an "assimilative force" by which diverse and conflicting elements in our society are brought together on a broad but common ground. See, *e.g.,* J. Dewey, DEMOCRACY AND EDUCATION 26 (1929); N. Edwards & H. Richey, THE SCHOOL IN THE AMERICAN SOCIAL ORDER 623–624 (1963). These perceptions of the public schools as inculcating fundamental values necessary to the maintenance of a democratic political system have been confirmed by the observations of social scientists. See R. Dawson & K. Prewitt, POLITICAL SOCIALIZATION 146–167 (1969); R. Hess & J. Torney, THE DEVELOPMENT OF POLITICAL ATTITUDES IN CHILDREN 114, 158–171, 217–220 (1967); V. O. Key, PUBLIC OPINION AND AMERICAN DEMOCRACY 323–343 (1961).[8]

---

dissenting). The distinction between a private occupation and a government function was noted expressly in *Griffiths:*

"Lawyers do indeed occupy professional positions of responsibility and influence that impose on them duties correlative with their vital right of access to the courts. Moreover, by virtue of their professional aptitudes and natural interests, lawyers have been leaders in government throughout the history of our country. Yet, they are not officials of government by virtue of being lawyers." 413 U.S., at 729.

7 As *San Antonio Ind. School Dist.* v. *Rodriguez, supra,* recognized, there is no inconsistency between our recognition of the vital significance of public education and our holding that access to education is not guaranteed by the Constitution. *Id.,* at 30–35.

8 The curricular requirements of New York's public school system reflect some of the ways a public school system promotes the development of the understanding that is prerequisite to intelligent participation in the democratic process. The schools are required to provide instruction "to promote a spirit of patriotic and civic service and obligation and to foster in the children of the state moral and intellectual qualities

Within the public school system, teachers play a critical part in developing students' attitude toward government and understanding of the role of citizens in our society. Alone among employees of the system, teachers are in direct, day-to-day contact with students both in the classrooms and in the other varied activities of a modern school. In shaping the students' experience to achieve educational goals, teachers by necessity have wide discretion over the way the course material is communicated to students. They are responsible for presenting and explaining the subject matter in a way that is both comprehensible and inspiring. No amount of standardization of teaching materials or lesson plans can eliminate the personal qualities a teacher brings to bear in achieving these goals. Further, a teacher serves as a role model for his students, exerting a subtle but important influence over their perceptions and values. Thus, through both the presentation of course materials and the example he sets, a teacher has an opportunity to influence the attitudes of students toward government, the political process, and a citizen's social responsibilities.[9] This influence is crucial to the continued good health of a democracy.[10]

Furthermore, it is clear that all public school teachers, and not just those responsible for teaching the courses most directly related to government, history, and civic duties, should help fulfill the broader functions of the public school system.[11] Teachers, regardless of their specialty, may be called upon to teach other subjects, including those expressly dedicated

---

which are essential in preparing to meet the obligations of citizenship in peace or in war, . . ." N. Y. Educ. L. § 801 (1) (McKinney 1970). Flag and other patriotic exercises also are prescribed, as loyalty is a characteristic of citizenship essential to the preservation of a country. *Id.*, § 802. In addition, required courses include classes in civics, United States and New York history, and principles of American government. *Id.*, § 3204 (3)(a)(1), (2).

Although private schools also are bound by most of these requirements, the State has a stronger interest in ensuring that the schools it most directly controls, and for which it bears the cost, are as effective as possible in teaching these courses.

[9] Although the findings of scholars who have written on the subject are not conclusive, they generally reinforce the commonsense judgment, and the experience of most of us, that a teacher exerts considerable influence over the development of fundamental social attitudes in students, including those attitudes which in the broadest sense of the term may be viewed as political. See *e.g.*, R. Dawson & K. Prewitt, POLITICAL SOCIALIZATION 158–167 (1969); R. Hess & J. Torney, THE DEVELOPMENT OF POLITICAL ATTITUDES: IN CHILDREN 162–163, 217–218 (1967). Cf. Note, *Aliens' Right to Teach: Political Socialization and the Public Schools,* 85 YALE L. J. 90, 99–104 (1975).

[10] Appellees contend that restriction of an alien's freedom to teach in public schools is contrary to principles of diversity of thought and academic freedom embodied in the First Amendment. See also Note, *supra,* n. 8, at 106–109. We think the attempt to draw an analogy between choice of citizenship and political expression or freedom of association is wide of the mark, as the argument would bar any effort by the State to promote particular values and attitudes toward government. Section 3001 (3) does not inhibit appellees from expressing freely their political or social views or from associating with whomever they please. Cf. *Givhan* v. *Western Line Consol. School Dist,* _____ U.S. _____, _____ (1979); *Mt. Healthy City School Dist.* v. *Doyle,* 429 U.S. 274 (1977); *Pickering* v. *Board of Education,* 391 U.S. 563 (1968). Nor are appellees discouraged from joining with others to advance particular political ends. Cf. *Shelton* v. *Tucker,* 364 U.S. 479 (1957). The only asserted liberty of appellees withheld by the New York statute is the opportunity to teach in the State's schools so long as they elect not to become citizens of this country. This is not a liberty that is accorded constitutional protection.

[11] At the primary school level, for which both appellees sought certification, teachers are responsible for all of the basic curriculum.

to political and social subjects.[12] More importantly, a State properly may regard all teachers as having an obligation to promote civic virtues and understanding in their classes, regardless of the subject taught. Certainly a State also may take account of a teacher's function as an example for students, which exists independently of particular classroom subjects. In light of the foregoing considerations, we think it clear that public school teachers come well within the "governmental function" principle recognized in *Sugarman* and *Foley*. Accordingly, the Constitution requires only that a citizenship requirement applicable to teaching in the public schools bears a rational relationship to a legitimate state interest. See *Massachusetts Board of Retirement* v. *Murgia*, 427 U.S. 307, 314 (1976).

### III

As the legitimacy of the State's interest in furthering the educational goals outlined above is undoubted, it remains only to consider whether § 3001(3) bears a rational relationship to this interest. The restriction is carefully framed to serve its purpose, as it bars from teaching only those aliens who have demonstrated their unwillingness to obtain United States citizenship.[13] Appellees, and aliens similarly situated, in effect have chosen to classify themselves. They prefer to retain citizenship in a foreign country with the obligations it entails of primary duty and loyalty.[14] They have rejected the open invitation extended to qualify for eligibility to teach by applying for citizenship in this country. The people of New York, acting through their elected representatives, have made a judgment that citizenship should be a qualification for teaching the young of the State in the public schools, and § 3001(3) furthers that judgment.[15]

*Reversed.*

[12] In New York, for example, all certified teachers, including those in the secondary schools, are required to be available for up to five hours of teaching a week in subjects outside their specialty. 8 N. Y. Code of Rules & Regulations § 80.2 (c).

[13] See n. 2, *infra*.

[14] As our cases have emphasized, resident aliens pay taxes, serve in the armed forces, and have made significant contributions to our country in private and public endeavors. See *In re Griffiths*, 413 U.S. 717, 722 (1973); *Sugarman* v. *Dougall*, 413 U.S. 634, 645 (1973); *Graham* v. *Richardson*, 403 U.S. 365, 376 (1971). No doubt many of them, and we do not exclude appellees, would make excellent public school teachers. But the legislature, having in mind the importance of education to state and local governments, see *Brown* v. *Board of Education*, 347 U.S. 483, 493 (1954), may determine eligibility for the key position in discharging that function on the assumption that *generally* persons who are citizens, or who have not declined the opportunity to seek United States citizenship, are better qualified than are those who have elected to remain aliens. We note in this connection that regulations promulgated pursuant to § 3001 (3) do provide for situations where a particular alien's special qualifications as a teacher outweigh the policy primarily served by the statute. See 8 N. Y. Code of Rules & Regulations § 80.2 (i)(1). The State informs us, however, that the authority conferred by this regulation has not been exercised. Brief for Appellant 7 n. *.

[15] Appelles argue that the State cannot rationally exclude aliens from teaching positions and yet permit them to vote for and sit on certain local schools boards. We note, first, that the State's legislature has not expressly endorsed this policy. Rather, appellants as an administrative matter have interpreted the statute governing New York City's unique community school boards, N. Y. Educ. Law § 2590–c (McKinney Supp. 1978–1979), to permit aliens who are the parents of public school students to participate in these boards. See App. 27, 29. We also may assume, without having to decide, that there is a rational basis for a distinction between teachers and board

MR. JUSTICE BLACKMUN, with whom MR. JUSTICE BRENNAN, MR. JUSTICE MARSHALL, and MR. JUSTICE STEVENS join, dissenting: Once again the Court is asked to rule upon the constitutionality of one of New York's many statutes that impose a requirement of citizenship upon a person before that person may earn his living in a specified occupation.[1] These New York statutes, for the most part, have their origin in the frantic and overreactive days of the first World War when attitudes of parochialism and fear of the foreigner were the order of the day. This time we are concerned with the right to teach in the public schools of the State, at the elementary and secondary levels, and with the citizenship requirement that N.Y. Educ. Law § 3001.3 (McKinney), quoted by the Court, at 1 n. 1, imposes.[2]

As the Court acknowledges, *ante*, at 3, its decisions regarding the permissibility of statutory classifications concerning aliens "have not formed an unwavering line over the years."[3] Thus, just last Term, in *Foley* v. *Connelie*, 435 U.S. 291 (1978), the Court upheld against equal protection challenge the New York statute limiting appointment of members of the state police force to citizens of the United States. The touchstone, the Court indicated, was that citizenship may be a relevant qualification for fulfilling " 'important nonelective executive, legislative, and judicial positions' held by 'officers who participate directly in the formulation, execution, or review of broad public policy.' " *Id.*, at 296, quoting *Sugarman* v. *Dougall*, 413 U.S. 634, 647 (1973). For such positions, a State need show only some rational relationship between the interest sought to be protected and the limiting classification. Police, it then was felt, were clothed with authority to exercise an almost infinite variety of discretionary powers that could seriously affect members of the public. 435 U.S., at 297. They thus fell within the category of important officers who participate directly in the execution of "broad public policy." The Court was persuaded that citizenship bore a rational relationship to the special demands of police positions, and that a State therefore could constitutionally confine that public responsibility to citizens of the United States. *Id.*, at 300. The propriety of making citizenship a qualification for a narrowly defined class of positions was also recognized, in passing, in *Sugarman* v. *Dougall*, 413 U.S., at 647, and in *Nyquist* v. *Mauclet*, 432 U.S. 1, 11 (1977).

members based on their respective responsibilities. Although possessing substantial responsibility for the administration of the schools, board members teach no classes, and rarely if ever are known or identified by the students.

[1] One of the appellees in *Nyquist* v. *Mauclet*, 432 U.S. 1 (1977), submitted a list of the New York statutes that required citizenship, or a declaration of intent to become a citizen, for no fewer than 37 occupations. Brief for Appellee Mauclet, O. T. 1976, No. 76–208, pp. 19–22, nn. 8–44, inclusive. Some of those statutes have been legislatively repealed or modified, or judicially invalidated. Others are still in effect. Among the latter are those relating to the occupations of inspector, certified shorthand reporter, funeral director, masseur, physical therapist, and animal technician.

[2] This particular citizenship requirement had its origin in 1918 N. Y. Laws, ch. 158, effective Apr. 4, 1918.

[3] "To be sure, the course of decisions protecting the employment rights of resident aliens has not been an unswerving one." *In re Griffiths*, 413 U.S. 717, 720 (1973).

On the other hand, the Court frequently has invalidated a state provision that denies a resident alien the right to engage in specified occupational activity: *Yick Wo* v. *Hopkins,* 118 U.S. 356 (1886) (ordinance applied so as to prevent Chinese subjects from engaging in the laundry business); *Truax* v. *Raich,* 239 U.S. 33 (1915) (statute requiring an employer's work force to be composed of not less than 80 percent "qualified electors or native-born citizens"); *Takahashi* v. *Fish & Game Comm'n,* 334 U.S. 410 (1948) (limitation of commercial fishing licenses to persons not "ineligible to citizenship"); *Sugarman* v. *Dougall, supra* (New York statute relating to permanent positions in the "competitive class" of the state civil service); *In re Griffiths,* 413 U.S. 717 (1973) (the practice of law); *Nelson* v. *Miranda,* 413 U.S. 902 (1973), summarily affirming 351 F. Supp. 735 (Ariz. 1972) (social service worker and teacher); *Examining Board* v. *Flores de Otero,* 426 U.S. 572 (1976) (the practice of civil engineering). See also *Nyquist* v. *Mauclet, supra* (New York statute barring certain resident aliens from state financial assistance for higher education).

Indeed, the Court has held more than once that state classifications based on alienage are "inherently suspect and subject to close judicial scrutiny." *Graham* v. *Richardson,* 403 U.S. 365, 372 (1971). See *Examining Board* v. *Flores de Otero,* 426 U.S., at 601–602; *In re Griffiths,* 413 U.S., at 721; *Sugarman* v. *Dougall,* 413 U.S., at 642; *Nyquist* v. *Mauclet,* 432 U.S., at 7. And "[a]lienage classifications by a State that do not withstand this stringent examination cannot stand." *Ibid.*

There is thus a line, most recently recognized in *Foley* v. *Connelie,* between those employments that a State in its wisdom constitutionally may restrict to United States citizens, on the one hand, and those employments, on the other, that the State may not deny to resident aliens. For me, the present case falls on the *Sugarman-Griffiths-Flores de Otero-Mauclet* side of that line, rather than on the narrowly isolated *Foley* side.

We are concerned here with elementary and secondary education in the public schools of New York State. We are not concerned with teaching at the college or graduate levels. It seems constitutionally absurd, to say the least, that in these lower levels of public education a Frenchman may not teach French or, indeed, an Englishwoman may not teach the grammar of the English language. The appellees, to be sure, are resident "aliens" in the technical sense, but there is not a word in the record that either appellee does not have roots in this country or is unqualified in any way, other than the imposed requirement of citizenship, to teach. Both appellee Norwick and appellee Dachinger have been in this country for over 12 years. Each is married to a United States citizen. Each currently meets all the requirements, other than citizenship, that New York has specified for certification as a public school teacher. Tr. of Oral Arg. 4.[4] Each is willing, if required, to subscribe to an oath to support the Constitutions

---

[4] Appellee Norwick is a *summa cum laude* graduate of a Massachusetts college and received an A average in full-time graduate work in the State University of New York at Albany. She has taught both in this country and in Great Britain.

of the United States and of New York.[5] Each lives in an American community, must obey its laws, and must pay all of the taxes citizens are obligated to pay. Appellees, however, have hesitated to give up their respective British and Finnish citizenships, just as lawyer Fre Le Poole Griffiths, the subject of *In re Griffiths, supra,* hesitated to renounce her Netherlands citizenship, although married to a citizen of the United States and a resident of Connecticut.

But the Court, to the disadvantage of appellees, crosses the line from *Griffiths* to *Foley* by saying, *ante,* at 6, that the "distinction between citizens and aliens, though ordinarily irrelevant to private activity, is fundamental to the definition and government of a State." It then concludes that public school teaching "constitutes a governmental function," *ante,* at 7, and that public school teachers may be regarded as performing a task that goes "to the heart of representative government." *Ibid.* The Court speaks of the importance of public schools in the preparation of individuals for participation as citizens, and in the preservation of the values on which our society rests.[6] After then observing that teachers play a critical part in all this, the Court holds that New York's citizenship requirement is constitutional because it bears a rational relationship to the State's interest in furthering these educational goals.

I perceive a number of difficulties along the easy road the Court takes to this conclusion:

First, the New York statutory structure itself refutes the argument. Section 3001.3, the very statute at issue here, provides for exceptions with respect to alien teachers "employed pursuant to regulations adopted by the commissioner of education permitting such employment." Section 3001-a provides another exception for persons ineligible for United States citizenship because of oversubscribed quotas. Also, New York is unconcerned with any citizenship qualification for teachers in the private schools of the State, even though the record indicates that about 18 percent of the pupils at the elementary and secondary levels attend private schools. The education of those pupils seems not to be inculcated with something less than what is desirable for citizenship and what the Court calls an influence "crucial to the continued good health of a democracy." *Ante,* at 9. The State apparently, under § 3001.3, would not hesitate to employ an alien teacher while he waits to attain citizenship, even though he may fail ever to attain it. And the stark fact that the State permits some aliens to sit on certain local school boards, N.Y. Educ. Law § 2590-c.4

---

Appellee Dachinger is a *cum laude* graduate, with a major in German, of Lehman College, a unit of the City University of New York, and possesses a Master's degree in Early Childhood Education from that institution. She has taught at a day care center in the Bronx.

Each appellee, thus, has received and excelled in educational training the State of New York itself offers.

[5] See *In re Griffiths,* 413 U.S., at 726 n. 18.

[6] One, of course, can agree with this observation. One may concede, also, that public schools are an " 'assimilative force' by which diverse and conflicting elements in our society are brought together on a broad but common ground," *ante,* at 8, and that the inculcation of fundamental values by our public schools is necessary to the maintenance of a democratic political system.

(McKinney) (Supp. 1978–1979), reveals how shallow and indistinct is New York's line of demarcation between citizenship and noncitizenship. The Court's attempted rationalization of this fact, *ante,* at 12 n. 14, hardly extinguishes the influence school board members, including these otherwise "disqualified" resident aliens, possess in school administration, in the selection of faculty, and in the approval of textbooks and instructional materials.

Second, the New York statute is all-inclusive in its disqualifying provisions: "No person shall be employed or authorized to teach in the public schools of the state who is . . . [n]ot a citizen." It sweeps indiscriminately. It is "neither narrowly confined nor precise in its application," nor limited to the accomplishment of substantial state interests. *Sugarman* v. *Dougall,* 413 U.S., at 643. See Note, *Aliens' Right to Teach: Political Socialization and the Public Schools,* 85 YALE L. J. 90, 109–111 (1975).

Third, the New York classification is irrational. Is it better to employ a poor citizen-teacher than an excellent resident alien teacher? Is it preferable to have a citizen who has never seen Spain or a Latin American country teach Spanish to eighth graders and to deny that opportunity to a resident alien who may have lived for 20 years in the culture of Spain or Latin America? The State will know how to select its teachers responsibly, wholly apart from citizenship, and can do so selectively and intelligently.[7] That is the way to accomplish the desired result. An artificial citizenship bar is not a rational way. It is, instead, a stultifying provision. The route to "diverse and conflicting elements" and their being "brought together on a broad but common ground," which the Court so emphasizes, *ante,* at 8, is hardly to be achieved by disregarding some of the diverse elements that are available, competent, and contributory to the richness of our society and of the education it could provide.

Fourth, it is logically impossible to differentiate between this case concerning teachers and *In re Griffiths* concerning attorneys. If a resident alien *may not* constitutionally be barred from taking a state bar examination and thereby becoming qualified to practice law in the courts of a State, how is one to comprehend why a resident alien *may* constitutionally be barred from teaching in the elementary and secondary levels of a

---

[7] In *In re Griffiths* the Court significantly has observed:

"Connecticut has wide freedom to gauge on a case-by-case basis the fitness of an applicant to practice law. Connecticut can, and does, require appropriate training and familiarity with Connecticut law. Apart from such tests of competence, it requires a new lawyer to take both an 'attorney's oath' to perform his functions faithfully and honestly and a 'commissioner's oath' to 'support the constitution of the United States, and the constitution of the state of Connecticut.' Appellant has indicated her willingness and ability to subscribe to the substance of both oaths, and Connecticut may quite properly conduct a character investigation to insure in any given case 'that an applicant is not one who "swears to an oath *pro forma* while declaring or manifesting his disagreement with or indifference to the oath." *Bond* v. *Floyd,* 385 U.S. 116, 132.' *Law Students Research Council* v. *Wadmond,* 401 U.S., at 164. Moreover, once admitted to the bar, lawyers are subject to continuing scrutiny by the organized bar and the courts. In addition to discipline for unprofessional conduct, the range of post-admission sanctions extends from judgments for contempt to criminal prosecutions and disbarment. In sum, the Committee simply has not established that it must exclude all aliens from the practice of law in order to vindicate its undoubted interest in high professional standards." 413 U.S., at 725–727 (footnotes omitted).

State's public schools? One may speak proudly of the role model of the teacher, of his ability to mold young minds, of his inculcating force as to national ideals, and of his profound influence in the impartation of our society's values. Are the attributes of an attorney any the less? He represents us in our critical courtroom controversies even when citizenship and loyalty may be questioned. He stands as an officer of every court in which he practices. He is responsible for strict adherence to the announced and implied standards of professional conduct, to the requirements of evolving ethical codes, and for honesty and integrity in his professional and personal life. Despite the almost continuous criticism leveled at the legal profession, he, too, is an influence in legislation, in the community, and in the role model figure that the professional person enjoys.[8] The Court specifically recognized this in *In re Griffiths:*

"Lawyers do indeed occupy professional positions of responsibility and influence that impose on them duties correlative with their vital right of access to the courts. Moreover, by virtue of their professional aptitudes and natural interests, lawyers have been leaders in government throughout the history of our country." 413 U.S., at 729.[9]

If an attorney has a constitutional right to take a bar examination and practice law, despite his being a resident alien, it is impossible for me to see why a resident alien, otherwise completely competent and qualified, as these appellees concededly are, is constitutionally disqualified from teaching in the public schools of the great State of New York. The District Court expressed it well and forcefully when it observed that New York's exclusion "seems repugnant to the very heritage the State is seeking to inculcate." 417 F. Supp. 913, 922 (SDNY 1976).

I respectfully dissent.

---

[8] See also *Stockton* v. *Ford,* 11 How. 232, 247 (1851); *Hickman* v. *Taylor,* 329 U.S. 495, 514–515 (1947) (concurring opinion); *Schware* v. *Board of Bar Examiners,* 353 U.S. 232, 247 1957) (concurring opinion); *In re Sawyer,* 360 U.S. 622, 668 (1959) (dissenting opinion); J. Story, MISCELLANEOUS WRITINGS, VALUE AND IMPORTANCE OF LEGAL STUDIES, 503–549 (W. Story ed., 1972); H. Stone, *The Public Influence of the Bar,* 48 Harv. L. Rev. 1 (1934); W. Brennan, Jr., THE RESPONSIBILITIES OF THE LEGAL PROFESSION (1967); A. de Tocqueville, DEMOCRACY IN AMERICA 321–331 (Schocken ed. 1961); J. Rogers, "The Lawyer in American Public Life," in MORRISON FOUNDATION LECTURES 40, 61 (1940).

[9] In order to keep attorneys on the nongovernmental side of the classification line, the Court continued:
"Yet, they are not officials of government by virtue of being lawyers. Nor does the status of holding a license to practice law place one so close to the core of the political process as to make him a formulator of government policy." 413 U.S., at 719.

## C. FEDERAL EMPLOYMENT

## HAMPTON v. WONG

*Supreme Court of the United States, 1976*
*426 U.S. 88, 12 FEP Cases 1377*

MR. JUSTICE STEVENS delivered the opinion of the Court.

Five aliens, lawfully and permanently residing in the United States, brought this litigation to challenge the validity of a policy, adopted and enforced by the Civil Service Commission and certain other federal agencies, which excludes all persons except American citizens and natives of Samoa from employment in most positions subject to their respective jurisdiction. . . .

### I

Each of the five plaintiffs was denied federal employment solely because of his or her alienage. They were all Chinese residents of San Francisco and each was qualified for an available job.

. . .

We granted certiorari to decide the following question presented by the petition:

"Whether a regulation of the United States Civil Service Commission that bars resident aliens from employment in the federal competitive civil service is constitutional."

We now address that question.

### II

Petitioner's have chosen to argue on the merits of a somewhat different question. In their brief, the petitioners rephrased the question presented as "Whether the Civil Service Commission's regulation . . . is within the constitutional powers of Congress and the President and hence not a constitutionally forbidden discrimination against aliens."

This phrasing of the question assumes that the Commission regulation is one that was mandated by the Congress, the President, or both. On this assumption, the petitioners advance alternative arguments to justify the discrimination as an exercise of the plenary federal power over immigration and naturalization. First, the petitioners argue that the equal protection aspect of the Due Process Clause of the Fifth Amendment is wholly inapplicable to the exercise of federal power over aliens, and therefore no justification for the rule is necessary. Alternatively, the petitioners argue that the Fifth Amendment imposes only a slight burden of justification on the Federal Government, and that such a burden is easily met by several factors not considered by the District Court or the Court of Appeals. Before addressing these arguments, we first discuss certain limitations which the Due Process Clause places on the power of the Federal Government to classify persons subject to its jurisdiction.

The federal sovereign, like the States, must govern impartially. The concept of equal justice under law is served by the Fifth Amendment's guarantee of due process, as well as by the Equal Protection Clause of the Fourteenth Amendment. Although both Amendments require the same type of analysis, see *Buckley* v. *Valeo* (Jan. 30, 1976, slip op., at 87), the Court of Appeals correctly stated that the two protections are not always coextensive. Not only does the language of the two Amendments differ, but more importantly, there may be overriding national interests which justify selective federal legislation that would be unacceptable for an individual State. On the other hand, when a federal rule is applicable to only a limited territory, such as the District of Columbia, or an insular possession, and when there is no special national interest involved, the Due Process Clause has been construed as having the same significance as the Equal Protection Clause.

In this case we deal with a federal rule having nationwide impact. The petitioners correctly point out that the paramount federal power over immigration and naturalization forecloses a simple extension of the holding in *Sugarman* as decisive of this case. We agree with the petitioners' position that overriding national interests may provide a justification for a citizenship requirement in the federal service even though an identical requirement may not be enforced by a State.

...

In this case the petitioners have identified several interests which the Congress or the President might deem sufficient to justify the exclusion of noncitizens from the federal service. They argue, for example, that the broad exclusion may facilitate the President's negotiation of treaties with foreign powers by enabling him to offer employment opportunities to citizens of a given foreign country in exchange for reciprocal concessions—an offer he could not make if those aliens were already eligible for federal jobs. Alternatively, the petitioners argue that reserving the federal service for citizens provides an appropriate incentive to aliens to qualify for naturalization and thereby participate more effectively in our society. They also point out that the citizenship requirement has been imposed in the United States with substantial consistency for over 100 years and accords with international law and the practice of most foreign countries. Finally, they correctly state that the need for undivided loyalty in certain sensitive positions clearly justifies a citizenship requirement in at least some parts of the federal service, and that the broad exclusion serves the valid and administrative purpose of avoiding the trouble and expense of classifying those positions which properly belong in executive or sensitive categories.[24]

The difficulty with all of these arguments except the last is that they do not identify any interest which can reasonably be assumed to have influenced the Civil Service Commission, the Postal Service, the General Service Administration, or the Department of Health, Education, and

[24] We note, however, that the petitioners do not rely on the District Court's reasoning that the regulation might be justified as serving the economic security of United States citizens. Our discussion of the "special public interest" doctrine in *Sugarman* v. *Dougall*, 413 U.S. 634, 643-645, 5 FEP Cases 1152, 1155-1156, no doubt explains the petitioners' failure to press this argument in this case. We have no occasion, therefore, to decide when, if ever, that doctrine might justify federal legislation.

Welfare in the administration of their respective responsibilities or, specifically, in the decision to deny employment to the respondents in this litigation. We may assume with the petitioners that if the Congress or the President has expressly imposed the citizenship requirement, it would be justified by the national interest in providing an incentive for aliens to become naturalized, or possibly even as providing the President with an expendable token for treaty negotiating purposes; but we are not willing to presume that the Chairman of the Civil Service Commission, or any of the other original defendants, was deliberately fostering an interest so far removed from his normal responsibilities. Consequently, before evaluating the sufficiency of the asserted justification for the rule, it is important to know whether we are reviewing a policy decision made by Congress and the President or a question of personnel administration determined by the Civil Service Commission.

<h2 style="text-align:center">IV</h2>

It is the business of the Civil Service Commission to adopt and enforce regulations which will best promote the efficiency of the federal civil service. That agency has no responsibility for foreign affairs, for treaty negotiations, for establishing immigration quotas or conditions of entry, or for naturalization policies. Indeed, it is not even within the responsibility of the Commission to be concerned with the economic consequences of permitting or prohibiting the participation by aliens in employment opportunities in different parts of the national market. On the contrary, the Commission performs a limited and specific function.

The only concern of the Civil Service Commission is the promotion of an efficient federal service.[47] In general it is fair to assume that its goal would be best served by removing unnecessary restrictions on the eligibility of qualified applicants for employment. With only one exception, the interests which the petitioners have put forth as supporting the Commission regulation at issue in this case are not matters which are properly the business of the Commission. That one exception is the administrative desirability of having one simple rule excluding all noncitizens when it is manifest that citizenship is an appropriate and legitimate requirement for some important and sensitive positions. Arguably, therefore, administrative convenience may provide a rational basis for the general rule.

For several reasons that justification is unacceptable in this case. The Civil Service Commission, like other administrative agencies, has an obligation to perform its responsibilities with some degree of expertise, and to make known the reasons for its important decisions. There is nothing in the record before us, nor in matter of which we may properly take judicial notice, to indicate that the Commission actually made any considered evaluation of the relative desirability of a simple exclusionary rule on the one hand, or the value to the service of enlarging the pool of eligible employees on the other. Nor can we reasonably infer that the administrative burden of establishing the job classifications for which citizenship is an appropriate requirement would be a particularly onerous task for an expert in personnel matters; indeed, the Postal Service apparently encountered no particular difficulty in making such a classification. Of greater significance, however, is the quality of the interest at stake. Any fair balancing of the public interest in avoiding the wholesale deprivation of employment opportunities caused by the Commission's indiscriminate policy, as opposed to what may be nothing more than a hypothetical justification, requires rejection of the argument of administrative convenience in this case.[48]

In sum, assuming without deciding that the national interests identified by the petitioners would adequately support an explicit determination by Congress or the President to exclude all noncitizens from the federal service, we conclude that those interests cannot provide an acceptable rationalization for such a determination by the Civil Service Commission. The impact of the rule on the millions of lawfully admitted resident aliens is precisely the same as the aggregate impact of comparable state rules which were invalidated by our decision in *Sugarman*. By broadly denying this class substantial opportunities for employment, the Civil Service Commission rule deprives its members of an aspect of liberty. Since these residents were admitted as a result of decisions made by the Congress and the President, implemented by the Immigration and Naturalization Service acting under the Attorney General of the United States,[49] due process requires that the decision to impose that deprivation of an important liberty be made either at a comparable level of government or, if it is to be permitted to be made by the Civil Service Commission, that it be justified by reasons which are properly the concern of that agency. We hold that § 338.101(a) of the Civil Service Commission Regulations has deprived these respondents of liberty without due process of law and is therefore invalid.

The judgment of the Court of Appeals is

*Affirmed.*

MR. JUSTICE BRENNAN, with whom MR. JUSTICE MARSHALL joins, concurring: I join the Court's opinion with the understanding that there are reserved the equal protection questions that would be raised by congressional or Presidential enactment of a bar on employment of aliens by the Federal Government.

MR. JUSTICE REHNQUIST, with whom THE CHIEF JUSTICE, MR. JUSTICE WHITE, and MR. JUSTICE BLACKMUN join, dissenting.

---

[48] We find no merit in the Government's argument that a more discriminating rule would inevitably breed litigation which in turn would enhance the administrative burden. For even though the argument of administrative convenience may not support a total exclusion, it would adequately support a rather broad classification of positions reflecting the considered judgment of an agency expert in personnel matters. For the classification itself would demonstrate that the Commission had at least considered the extent to which the imposition of the rule is consistent with its assigned mission.

[49] See 8 U.S.C. § 1103.

## NOTE

The Supreme Court decided the above case on June 1, 1976. On September 2, 1976, President Ford issued Executive Order 11935, 41 Fed. Reg. 37301, which added to Civil Service Rule VII, 5 CFR Part 7, the following new section:

"Section 7.4 Citizenship.

"(a) No person shall be admitted to competitive examination unless such person is a citizen or national of the United States.

"(b) No person shall be given any appointment in the competitive service unless such person is a citizen or national of the United States.

"(c) The Commission may, as an exception to this rule and to the extent permitted by law, authorize the appointment of aliens to positions in the competitive service when necessary to promote the efficiency of the service in specific cases or for temporary appointments."

In *Mow Sun Wong* v. *Hampton*, 435 F. Supp. 37 (1977), the President's exclusion of aliens was upheld for the reasons suggested by the Supreme Court. The same result was reached in *Vergara* v. *Hampton*, 581 F.2d 1281 (7th Cir. 1978).

# 9. The Handicapped

## A. Federal Legislation

### REHABILITATING THE REHABILITATION ACT OF 1973 *

*58 Boston University Law Review 247 (1978)*

#### I. introduction

The Rehabilitation Act of 1973 [1] represents a comprehensive federal response to the plight of the nation's handicapped.[2] The Act makes significant contributions in four distinct areas. First, in an attempt to promote "comprehensive and continuing State plans . . . for providing vocational rehabilitation services to handicapped individuals," the Act provides for federal coordination of and monetary assistance to state vocational rehabilitation programs. Second, the Act encourages novel research on both the state and federal level into the myriad problems experienced by the handicapped. Third, the Act establishes several new and innovative federal programs, such as a National Center for Deaf-Blind Youths and Adults and federal mortgage insurance for rehabilitation facilities.

The fourth major contribution of the Rehabilitation Act of 1973 is embodied in sections 503 [8] and 504,[9] which together have far-reaching

---

* Reprinted by permission. Copyright © 1978 by Boston University Law Review.

[1] [Footnotes numbered as in original.—Ed.] 29 U.S.C. §§ 701-794 (Supp. III 1973).

[2] Estimates of the number of handicapped persons within the United States vary. The U.S. Department of Labor recently fixed the number conservatively at twenty million. Employment Standards Administration, U.S. Dep't of Labor, Fact Sheet: *Who Are the Handicapped?* Another commentator estimates that the number is closer to twelve million. Note, *Abroad in the Land: Legal Strategies to Effectuate the Rights of the Physically Disabled*, 61 Geo. L. Rev. 1501, 1501 n. 2 (1973).

[8] 29 U.S.C. § 793(a) (Supp. III 1973). Section 503(a) provides in part: "Any contract in excess of $2,500 entered into by any Federal department or agency for the procurement of personal property and nonpersonal services (including construction) for the United States shall contain a provision that, in employing persons to carry out such contract the party contracting with the United States shall take affirmative action to employ and advance in employment qualified handicapped individuals." *Id.* This provision also applies to subcontracts in excess of $2500 entered into by a prime contractor for the purpose of carrying out the federal contract. *Id.*

[9] *Id.* § 794. Section 504 provides in part: "No otherwise qualified handicapped individual in the United States . . . shall, solely by reason of his handicap, be excluded from the participation in, be denied the benefits of, or be subjected to discrimination under any program or activity receiving Federal financial assistance." *Id.*

ramifications for large segments of the general public as well as for handicapped people. Section 503 provides that every employer doing business with the federal government under a contract for more than $2500 must take affirmative action to accommodate qualified handicapped individuals in all phases of employment. Section 504 prohibits discrimination against any qualified handicapped individual by any "recipient" [10] of federal financial assistance.

. . .

## II.   SECTIONS 503 AND 504

### A. ADMINISTRATIVE HISTORY

In January 1974, an executive order delegated to the Secretary of Labor the authority to prescribe and enforce rules and regulations implementing section 503.[11] Regulations promulgated pursuant to this authority became effective on June 11, 1974.[12] Under the regulations, the Department of Labor's Office of Federal Contract Compliance Programs (OFCCP) is solely responsible for the enforcement of section 503 and its regulations.

Section 504's administrative history is more brief. The executive branch did not delegate its section 504 rulemaking authority until April 28, 1976.[15] The delegation of authority provided that federal departments and agencies possessing the power to provide federal financial assistance —labeled the "compliance agencies"—should promulgate and enforce rules and regulations consistent with the standards and procedures established by the Secretary of Health, Education and Welfare. Twelve months later, the Secretary of HEW signed the first—and, to date, the only— section 504 regulations,[18] which became effective on June 3, 1977.[19]

### B. COVERAGE PREREQUISITES

Section 503 and section 504 both specify two requirements that must be satisfied in order to establish coverage. First, both sections protect only "qualified handicapped individuals." [20] Regulations under the two sections define a "handicapped individual" as any person who:

---

[10] A "recipient" is any state or its subdivision, agency, institution, organization, or person who receives federal financial assistance, either directly from the Federal Government or through another recipient. 42 Fed. Reg. 22,678 (1977) (to be codified in 45 C.F.R. § 84.3(f)).

[11] Exec. Order No. 11,758, 39 Fed. Reg. 2075 (1974), *reprinted in* 29 U.S.C. § 701 app., at 2069 (Supp. IV 1974).

[12] 39 Fed. Reg. 20,566 (1974).

[15] Exec. Order No. 11,914, 3 C.F.R. 117 (1977).

[18] Secretary Califano signed the regulations on April 28, 1977. 42 Fed. Reg. 22,677 (1977). Secretary Califano offered several reasons for the delay: (1) insufficient congressional guidance regarding the issues raised by section 504; (2) a change in the presidential administration; and (3) reluctance to sign the regulations without first ensuring that the regulations adequately addressed the legitimate needs of the handicapped. U.S. Dep't of Health, Education and Welfare, HEW News 7-8 (Apr. 28, 1977).

[19] 42 Fed. Reg. 22,676 (1977).

[20] Compare 29 U.S.C. § 793(a) (Supp. III 1973) with *id.* § 794.

"(1) has a physical or mental impairment which substantially limits one or more of such person's major life activities, (2) has a record of such impairment or (3) is regarded as having such an impairment." [21]

Thus, under both sections, "handicapped individual" is broadly defined to include not only persons who have an actual present impairment,[22] but also persons who have a history of or have been misclassified as having had a handicap.[23] Moreover, the definition protects all those who are perceived as having a handicap, regardless of whether an impairment actually exists.[24]

However, section 503 and section 504 necessarily have different definitions of the term "qualified." Section 503 by its terms only covers job applicants and employees of an employer who holds a section 503 contract. For employers covered by section 503, the regulations define a "qualified" handicapped individual as a handicapped person "who is capable of performing a particular job, with reasonable accommodation to his or her handicap." Section 504 defines "qualified" similarly in the employment context, but the section's broader coverage requires a defini-

---

[21] 41 C.F.R. § 60-741.2 (1977) (section 503); 42 Fed. Reg. 22,678 (1977) (to be codified in 45 C.F.R. § 84.3(j)(1)) (section 504). Major life activities include, but are not limited to, ambulation, learning, socialization and employment. 41 C.F.R. § 60-741 app. A, at 441 (1977) (section 503); 42 Fed. Reg. 22,678 (1977) (to be codified in 45 C.F.R. § 84.3 (j)(2)(ii)) (section 504). The definition contained in the regulations is identical to the statutory definition. 29 U.S.C. § 706(6) (Supp. IV 1974).

Prior to 1974, the Rehabilitation Act defined "handicapped individual" as a person who had a physical or mental disability that "substantially impaired" the individual's employability, and who could "reasonably be expected to benefit in terms of employability from vocational rehabilitation services." Rehabilitation Act of 1973, § 7(6), 87 Stat. 355 (1973). Thus, a handicapped person was covered by the statute only if rehabilitation services could improve that person's "employability." Because rehabilitation services often cannot improve the severely handicapped person's "employability," this definition of "handicapped" excluded from the Act's coverage those persons most in need of the Act's protection—the severely handicapped. The 1974 Amendments to the Rehabilitation Act provided a new and broader definition of handicapped individual, see text accompanying this note, which clearly encompasses the severely handicapped.

[22] Two of the more controversial impairments are alcoholism and drug addiction. See *Caring for the Disabled*, Boston Herald American, July 14, 1977, at 12, col. 6. The United States Attorney General recently issued an opinion concluding that alcoholics and drug addicts are covered by both sections of the Act. Letter from Attorney General Griffin Bell to HEW Secretary Califano (Apr. 12, 1977). The Departments of Labor and HEW have taken steps to implement this opinion. Office of Information, U.S. Dep't of Labor, Labor News (July 6, 1977) (section 503), . . . 42 Fed. Reg. 22,686 (1977) (to be codified in 45 C.F.R. § 84 app. A, n. 3) (section 504).

[23] 41 C.F.R. § 60-741 app. A, at 441-42 (1977) (section 503); 42 Fed. Reg. 22,678 (1977) (to be codified in 45 C.F.R. § 84.3(j)(2)(iii)) (section 504). This portion of the definition encompasses, for example, persons who have previously had a mental illness, a heart attack, or cancer. See 41 C.F.R. § 60-741 app. A, at 441-42 (1977) (section 503); 42 Fed. Reg. 22,686 (1977) (to be codified in 45 C.F.R. § 84 app. A, n. 3) (section 504). The actual handicap need not continue to exist. If the person has a "record of such impairment," sections 503 and 504 both protect the individual. 41 C.F.R. § 60-741 app. A, at 741 (1977) (section 503); 42 Fed. Reg. 22,678 (1977) (to be codified in 45 C.F.R. § 84.3(j)(2) (iii)) (section 504).

[24] 41 C.F.R. § 60-741 app. A, at 442 (1977) (section 503); 42 Fed. Reg. 22,678 (1977) (to be codified in 45 C.F.R. § 84.3(j)(2)(iv)) (section 504). The regulations recognize that other people's perceptions may themselves constitute a "physical or mental impairment that substantially limits major life activities. . . ." 42 Fed. Reg. 22,678 (1977) (to be codified in 45 C.F.R. § 84.3(j)(2)(iv)(B)).

tion of "qualified" handicapped individuals in other contexts as well. For example, because the Department of Health, Education and Welfare extends federal financial assistance to educational institutions, section 504 regulations must also define "qualified handicapped individual" with reference to educational assistance.

The second prerequisite to coverage under section 503 and section 504 identifies those parties who owe a statutory duty to qualified handicapped individuals. Section 503 imposes obligations only upon employers who satisfy three requirements. First, the employer must hold a federal contract.[29] Second, the contract must be for the procurement of personal property and nonpersonal services, including construction contracts.[30] Third, the contractual amount must exceed $2500. In contrast, section 504 applies to every recipient of federal financial assistance, regardless of the amount of assistance received. Although section 503 applies only to holders of federal contracts, section 504 applies to recipients of grants, loans, contracts and other forms of financial assistance.

## C. LEGAL OBLIGATIONS

Although section 504 regulates areas not covered by section 503, both sections prescribe conduct within the area of employment practices.[35] In this context, the two sections impose upon the employer different legal obligations. Section 503 requires a covered employer to take "affirmative

[29] 41 C.F.R. §60-741.3(a)(1) (1977). The term "contractor" also includes a subcontractor who otherwise satisfies the jurisdictional prerequisites. *Id.* § 60-741.2.

[30] *Id.* § 60-741.2. The term "government contract" does not include either agreements in which the contracting parties stand in an employer-employee relationship, or "federally assisted contracts." *Id.* The regional offices of the OFCCP find it particularly difficult to interpret this provision of the regulations. Interview with Margaret Joyce, Employment Opportunity Specialist for Region I of the OFCCP, in Boston, Mass. (Jan. 13, 1978).

Based upon the "federally assisted contract" exception, the Department of Labor's solicitor for Region I opined that federal money disbursed to a local housing authority by the Department of Housing and Urban Development pursuant to a Consolidated Annual Contributions Contract did not constitute a section 503 contract. *Id.*

[35] 41 C.F.R. § 60-741 (1977) (section 503); 42 Fed. Reg. 22,680-81 (1977) (to be codified in 45 C.F.R. §§ 84.11-.14) (section 504). Handicapped persons have had great difficulty finding gainful employment. Studies demonstrate that the unemployment rates for the handicapped are significantly higher than the national rate. Employment Standards Administration, *supra* note 2; Note, *supra* note 2, 61 GEO. L. REV. at 1512 n. 78. Although handicaps may limit a person's employability, see text accompanying note 100 *infra*, many employers also have misconceptions regarding handicapped job applicants and employees that further constrict the job opportunities available to a handicapped person. Note, *supra* note 2, 12 COLUM. J.L. & SOC. PROB. at 458 nn. 6 & 7; Note, *supra* note 2, 61 GEO. L. REV. at 1513 & nn. 81-84. Professors ten Broek and Matson identified hostility and condescension as the two predominant employer attitudes that foster these misconceptions, ten Broek & Matson, *The Disabled and the Law of Welfare*, 54 CALIF. L. REV. 809, 809-16 (1966). An employer's typical fears include a belief that the employer's insurance premiums will increase, that considerable expense will be necessary in order to make accommodations for the handicapped, that safety records will be jeopardized, that handicapped employees will demand special privileges, and that handicapped workers will perform inadequately. Wolfe, *Disability Is No Handicap for duPont*, THE ALLIANCE REVIEW (Winter 1973-1974) (U.S. Dep't of Labor reprint). A study conducted by the duPont Corporation indicates that these concerns are overstated or unfounded. *Id.*

action" in the employment of handicapped individuals. Section 504 prohibits "discrimination" against qualified handicapped individuals but imposes no additional affirmative action obligation. Thus, the question whether federal money received is covered by section 503 or by section 504 may determine both the existence and the extent of the legal obligation owed by the employer.

An employer's obligations under section 503 depend upon the contractual amount involved. If the contractual amount is less than or equal to $2500, section 503 does not in any way regulate the employer's conduct. If the contract exceeds $2500, section 503 imposes varying obligations. Section 503 regulations incorporate into every covered contract an affirmative action clause.[40] The clause requires the performance of several specific duties [41] and imposes upon an employer a general obligation to comply with all section 503 regulations. Section 503 regulations also compel an employer to make a "reasonable accommodation" to the handicap of an employee unless the employer can demonstrate that the accommodation "would impose an undue hardship on the conduct of the contractor's business." Additionally, an employer is required to review his personnel procedures to ensure that such procedures give careful and thorough consideration to the job qualifications of applicants and employees known to be handicapped. The contractor must also review all physical and mental job requirements to make certain that, to the extent that these requirements disqualify otherwise qualified handicapped individuals, such requirements are job-related and "consistent with business necessity and the safe performance of the job." Finally, the employer is not permitted to reduce the compensation of a qualified handicapped individual because of the individual's possible outside source of disability insurance or benefit.[46]

If the federal contract in question exceeds $50,000 and is held by an employer with fifty or more employees, section 503 regulations impose additional obligations. In this case, the employer must develop and maintain a written "affirmative action program," setting forth the employer's

[40] Id. § 60-741.23. The clause is deemed to be a part of the contract, regardless of whether it is expressly included in the document. Id. The contracting parties may incorporate the clause by reference. Id. § 60-741.22. Paragraph (f) of the affirmative action clause, reprinted in id. § 60-741.4, requires the covered contractor to include the affirmative action clause in every covered subcontract.

[41] Paragraph (d) of the affirmative action clause, reprinted in id. § 60-741.4, requires the contractor to post conspicuous notices as prescribed by the OFCCP. Paragraph (e) of the affirmative action clause, reprinted in id. § 60-741.4, requires the contractor to inform each union with which the employer has a collective bargaining agreement that the contractor-employer has legal obligations under the Act.

[46] Id. § 60-741.6(e). However, federal law does not require that employers always pay handicapped workers wages equal to the wages that must be paid to nonhandicapped workers. 29 U.S.C. § 214(c) (1970); 29 C.F.R. § 525 (1975). Thus, severely handicapped persons working in sheltered workshops usually do not receive federal minimum wages. Employment Standards Administration/Employment & Training Administration, 1 Sheltered Workshop Study: A Nationwide Report on Sheltered Workshops and Their Employment of Handicapped Individuals 64-95 (1977). See generally id. at 16-20. But cf. 41 C.F.R. § 60-741.6(j) (1977) (contracts with sheltered workshops do not substitute for affirmative action within the contractor's own workforce).

policies and practices with regard to handicapped applicants and employees.[47] The contractor is required to review and update the affirmative action program annually,[48] and this program is also subject to review by the OFCCP.[49]

Section 504 requirements are somewhat different. Within the employment context, the duties owed to qualified handicapped individuals under section 504 are similar to those duties owed under section 503. For example, section 504 requires that the employer make a "reasonable accommodation" to handicapped applicants and employees and defines the accommodations that must be made in terms nearly identical to those contained in the section 503 regulations. However, section 504 imposes no additional requirements on recipients of larger sums of money, and section 504 regulations thus impose no written affirmative action program obligation similar to that imposed under section 503.[51]

## D. ENFORCEMENT PROCEDURES AND REMEDIES

The OFCCP is wholly responsible for enforcing section 503, regardless of which federal department or agency awarded the contract. In contrast, each department or agency providing federal financial assistance is responsible for enforcing section 504 with respect to the projects and programs funded by that particular agency.

Sections 503 and 504 each utilize a complaint process, whereby any person who believes he was deprived of rights granted by the Act may file a complaint with the appropriate compliance agency. Aside from setting

[47] C.F.R. § 60-741.5 (1977). The contractor-employer must develop a written affirmative action program for each facility. *Id.* § 60-741.5(a). The contractor may request the Director of the OFCCP to "waive" the requirement for any of the contractor's facilities that are "in all respects separate and distinct from" federal contract work. *Id.* § 60-741.3(a)(5); see text accompanying notes 111-12 *infra.* Absent a waiver, the contractor must develop the written affirmative action program within 120 days of the commencement of a contract that exceeds $50,000. 41 C.F.R. § 60-741.5(a) (1977).

[48] 41 C.F.R. § 60-741.5(b) (1977). Unless the contractor holds other federal contracts that satisfy the $50,000 jurisdictional prerequisite, the legal obligation to maintain the written affirmative action program expires when the contract is completed. See *id.* § 60-741.3(a)(2).

[49] The OFCCP may review an affirmative action program after receiving some indication that the program either does not exist or is inadequate. See *e.g., id.* §§ 60-741.26(a), .28(a). Recently, however, one regional office of the OFCCP instituted a program whereby the office routinely contacted a contractor shortly after receiving notice that the contractor had been awarded a contract exceeding $50,000. This program is designed to prevent violations of the Act before they occur. Interview with Margaret Joyce, *supra* note 30.

[51] The two sets of regulations also differ in several other respects. Although section 503 regulations require only that the contractor review the job requirements to ensure that the requirements are "job related and . . . consistent with business necessity and the safe performance of the job," 41 C.F.R. § 60-741.6(c)(1) (1977), section 504 regulations provide that the contractor's use of an employment test or other selection criterion is valid only if "alternative . . . tests or criteria that do not screen out . . . as many handicapped persons are not shown by the Director [of HEW's Office for Civil Rights] to be available." 42 Fed. Reg. 22,680 (1977) (to be codified in 45 C.F.R. § 84.13(a)(2)). Additionally, section 503 regulations require a more extensive review of personnel policies than the section 504 regulations require. Compare 41 C.F.R. § 60-741.5 (1977) with 42 Fed. Reg. 22,680 (1977) (to be codified in 45 C.F.R. § 84.11(a)(3)).

forth procedures with which the complainant must comply,[54] both sections state a preference for informal resolution of a complaint whenever possible [55] and grant to compliance agencies the powers necessary to investigate the complaint.[56] Under both sections, the time at which the right to judicial review attaches is unclear.[57] The possible existence of

[54] For example, the complaint must be filed within 180 days of the alleged violation. 41 C.F.R. § 60-741.26(a) (1977) (section 503); 42 Fed. Reg. 22,685 (1977) (to be codified in 45 C.F.R. § 84.61) (incorporating by reference 45 C.F.R. § 80.7(b) (1976)) (section 504). Section 503 regulations authorize an extension of the filing date for "good cause shown." 41 C.F.R. § 60-741.26(a) (1977). The OFCCP looks to at least two factors to determine whether the complainant has demonstrated good cause. First, using only the information supplied by the complainant, the OFCCP tries to evaluate the respondent's efforts to inform handicapped persons of the respondent's affirmative action obligations. Second, the OFCCP determines whether the complainant has made a "good faith effort" to pursue his legal rights. A good faith effort generally includes retaining a lawyer, exercising collective bargaining grievance procedures, and filing a complaint with either a state agency or a different federal agency. Interview with Margaret Joyce, *supra* note 30. Section 504 regulations also authorize extensions, although they do not state what test must be met in order to justify an extension. 42 Fed. Reg. 22,685 (1977) (to be codified in 45 C.F.R. § 84.61) (incorporating by reference 45 C.F.R. § 80.7 (1976)).

[55] Compare 41 C.F.R. § 60-741.28(a) (1977) with 42 Fed. Reg. 22,685 (1977) (to be codified in 45 C.F.R. § 84.61) (incorporating by reference 45 C.F.R. § 80.7(d) (1976)). Often, an employer's collective bargaining agreement will contain procedures for informal resolution of complaints. Section 503 regulations require that, when the complainant is an employee of a contractor who has an internal grievance procedure, the OFCCP must initially refer the complaint to the respondent's grievance procedure. 41 C.F.R. § 60-741.26(b) (1977). If no agreement that is satisfactory to the complainant has been reached within sixty days, then the OFCCP should resume the investigation. *Id.*

Most collective bargaining agreements include a provision for binding arbitration of those complaints that are not resolved by less formal procedures, U.S. Bureau of Labor Statistics, Dep't of Labor, Bull. No. 1822, Characteristics of Agreements Covering 1,000 Workers or More 64 (1974), and courts almost routinely affirm the arbitrator's award. See *United Steelworkers* v. *Enterprise Wheel & Car Corp.*, 363 U.S. 593 (1960). However, arbitration awards resulting from complaints alleging violations of the Rehabilitation Act should be upheld only if the complainant finds the award satisfactory. See 41 C.F.R. § 60-741.26(b) (1977). Thus, a union's decision not to arbitrate a handicapped member's grievance, see, *e.g.*, *Vaca* v. *Sipes*, 386 U.S. 171 (1967), would no longer be binding upon the complainant.

[56] Compare, *e.g.*, 41 C.F.R. § 60-741.53 (1977) with 42 Fed. Reg. 22,685 (1977) (to be codified in 45 C.F.R. § 84.61) (incorporating by reference 45 C.F.R. § 80.6(c) (1976)) (right of access to contractor's or recipient's records during normal business hours); and 41 C.F.R. § 60-741.51 (1977) with 42 Fed. Reg. 22,685 (1977) (to be codified in 45 C.F.R. § 84.61) (incorporating by reference 45 C.F.R. § 80.7(e) (1976)) (right to protect from future discrimination any person who files a complaint, testifies, assists, or otherwise participates in any activity relating to administration of the Act).

[57] Presumably, the Administrative Procedure Act, 5 U.S.C. §§ 551-706 (1970), will govern this question. Under this act, "final agency action for which there is no other adequate remedy in a court [is] subject to judicial review." *Id.* § 704. Therefore, the determinative question is when an action by the OFCCP is "final." For example, under section 503 regulations, if the OFCCP's investigation results in a determination that no violation exists, or if the OFCCP after finding a violation "decides not to initiate administrative or legal proceedings," 41 C.F.R. § 60-741.26(g)(1) (1977), then the complainant has a right to appeal to the Director of the OFCCP. *Id.* The question whether such an appeal is necessary before judicial review attaches has not yet arisen. For a brief analysis of the problems involved in determining the right to judicial review under the Rehabilitation Act, see Note, *Lowering the Barriers to Employment of the Handicapped: Affirmative Action Obligations Imposed on Federal Contractors*, 81 DICK. L. REV. 174, 189-90 (1977).

Courts are divided on the issue whether section 503 creates a private cause of action independent of the right of judicial review. Compare *Drennon* v. *Philadelphia Gen.*

additional administrative enforcement methods available to the OFCCP under section 503 [58] and to the compliance agencies under section 504 is also unsettled.

The remedies for a violation of section 503 include withholding of progress payments, termination of a federal contract and debarment from the receipt of future federal contracts. Moreover, the section 503 regulations authorize additional judicial remedies,[63] including injunctive relief. Although the range of remedies available under section 504 regulations is still unsettled, section 504 does correspond to section 503 in authorizing

---

*Hosp.*, 428 F. Supp. 809 (E.D. Pa. 1977); *Duran v. City of Tampa*, 14 Empl. Prac. Dec. ¶ 7799 (M.D. Fla. 1977), with *Rogers v. Frito-Lay, Inc.*, 433 F. Supp. 200 (N.D. Tex. 1977); *Wood v. Diamond Tel. Co.*, 440 F. Supp. 1003 (D. Del. 1977). See also Wright, *Equal Treatment of the Handicapped by Federal Contractors*, 26 EMORY L.J. 65, 89-96 (1977). On the other hand, courts appear more consistent in holding that section 504 creates a private cause of action. *E.g.*, *Leary v. Crapsey*, 566 F.2d 863 (2d Cir. 1977); *Lloyd v. Regional Transp. Auth.*, 548 F.2d 1277 (7th Cir. 1977); *Gurmankin v. Costanzo*, 14 Empl. Prac. Dec. ¶ 7519 (3d Cir. 1977). Several explanations may underlie this conclusion. First, the language of section 504 is virtually identical to that found in other civil rights statutes under which courts have found a private cause of action. This similarity of language may support the inference that Congress intended to grant a private right of action under section 504. See 120 Cong. Rec. 30,534 (1974). Second, because no regulations existed under section 504 until recently, a private cause of action would not displace any administrative process and, indeed, may well be the only available method of enforcing section 504. However, as other federal departments and agencies promulgate section 504 regulations, this rationale for finding a section 504 cause of action may lose its validity.

58 The national OFCCP has developed a new enforcement method called a "directed review." The directed review is designed to determine whether those contractors that are subject to the written affirmative action requirement have fulfilled their responsibilities in this regard. Directed reviews are scheduled to commence in 1978. Interview with Margaret Joyce, *supra* note 30.

63 *Id.* § 60-741.28(b).

The OFCCP recently issued the first five administrative complaints under the section 503 regulations. U.S. Dep't of Labor, Labor News (Sept. 27, 1977); U.S. Dep't of Labor, Labor News (July 18, 1977). Judicial enforcement of administrative remedies has not yet been necessary; nor has a district court had occasion to fashion supplementary judicial remedies.

Although back pay is not specifically authorized by section 503 regulations, it would almost certainly be an available judicial remedy. Back pay may be necessary in order to ensure effective relief. See *Albemarle Paper Co. v. Moody*, 422 U.S. 405, 417-18 (1975). Such awards are available to other protected groups under similar circumstances. See, *e.g.*, *id.* (back pay awarded to an "affected class" under Title VII of the Civil Rights Act of 1964); *United States v. Duquesne Light Co.*, 13 Fair Empl. Prac. Cas. 1608 (W.D. Pa. 1976) (back pay awarded under Executive Order 11,246 Program); *Bishop v. Jeleff Assoc.*, 398 F. Supp. 579 (D.D.C. 1974) (back pay awarded under Age Discrimination in Employment Act). Moreover, conciliation agreements between the agency and the parties to a complaint often include back pay awards. See *e.g.*, U.S. Dep't of Labor Labor News 3 (July 18, 1977); U.S. Dep't of Labor, Labor News (Jan. 10, 1976).

Compensatory damages are not specifically authorized by the regulations but should be awarded if back pay alone would not constitute a sufficient remedy. There is less justification for allowing an award of punitive damages. Although an award of punitive damages is not specifically prohibited under the regulations, such an award would not significantly aid enforcement of the Act; nor would such an award be necessary to compensate the complainant. However, courts have divided on the issue whether punitive damages are available under statutes that are similar in intent to the Rehabilitation Act. See, *e.g.*, *Jackson v. Illinois Cent. Gulf R.R.*, 14 Empl. Prac. Dec. ¶ 7784 (S.D. Ala. 1977) (punitive damages not available under the Age Discrimination in Employment Act); *Dean v. American Security Ins. Co.*, 429 F. Supp. 3 (N.D. Ga. 1976) (punitive damages available under the Age Discrimination in Employment Act).

the withholding or termination of, or the debarment from the future receipt of, federal financial assistance.

## III.   CURRENT ISSUES UNDER SECTION 503

The OFCCP has encountered several problems concerning section 503's applicability to various respondent-employers. Additionally, the OFCCP has not yet resolved precisely which handicapped persons are protected by section 503. The enforcement of section 504 will eventually raise many of these same issues. Because the OFCCP has already attempted to develop solutions under section 503, this Note will analyze these issues in lights of those attempts.

. . .

### B.   COVERAGE OVER THE COMPLAINANT

The determination whether a particular complainant is covered by section 503 raises several issues. Section 503 protects only "qualified handicapped individuals," [84] and the regulations define such an individual as a handicapped person who is capable of performing a particular job with reasonable accommodations to his or her handicap. However, neither section 503 nor the implementing regulations suggests a methodology for determining whether a particular job applicant or employee comes within this definition. Additionally, although the language of section 503 limits coverage to those handicapped employees and job applicants actually carrying out the federal contract, the regulations promulgated under section 503 extend coverage to *all* handicapped job applicants and employees of the covered contractor. Therefore, the regulations appear to exceed the scope of the Act.

### 1. Defining "Qualified Handicapped Individual"

According to the section 503 regulations, a "qualified" handicapped individual is a "handicapped individual" who is "capable of performing a particular job" with "reasonable accommodations" to his or her handicap.

Although the severely handicapped person will be relatively easy to recognize, an employer may have more difficulty identifying those people whose impairment is less severe but to whom the employer may still owe a duty. Section 503 regulations authorize several procedures for determining whether a person meets the definition of "handicapped individual." For example, the contractor-employer may require a medical examination, or may request that the applicant or employee submit medical documentation to support the claim that a "handicap" exists.[88] Yet the

---

[84] 29 U.S.C. § 793(a) (Supp. III 1973).

[88] *Id.* § 60-741.7(b). Nothing in the regulations prohibits the employer from giving a preemployment examination. *Id.* § 60-741.6(c)(3). Except in three situations, *id.* §§ 60-741.6(c)(3)(i)-(3)(iii), this preemployment examination must be kept confidential.

regulations provide no guidance with regard to how to determine whether a handicapped person is also "qualified" for the purposes of section 503 —whether the handicapped person is "capable of performing a particular job with reasonable accommodations to his or her handicap."

A case by case analysis is the only feasible method of determining whether a handicapped person is "qualified" within the meaning of the section. Other civil rights programs utilize a goal-timetable approach to implement antidiscrimination policies in the employment context. For example, the Executive Order 11,246 Program imposes upon federal contractor-employers an affirmative action requirement with regard to women and minorities.[90] Under the Program's goal-timetable approach,[91] the contractor groups jobs by similarity of job content, compensation and potential for advancement. The executive order regulations then require the contractor-employer to identify those "job groups" in which, for example, women are underutilized. One useful indicator of underutilization is a statistical comparison between the availability, within the contractor's labor market, of women who are capable of performing the jobs within the job group and the contractor's actual employment of women within that job group.[93] If the labor market availability rate for qualified women significantly exceeds the contractor's actual employment rate of women within the job group, the statistical comparison indicates that women are underutilized within that job group. Once underutilization is established,[94] the Executive Order Program regulations require the contractor to set significant goals and timetables for correcting this under-

---

Section 503 regulations also require that contractors who are subject to the written affirmative action program requirements "invite all applicants and employees who believe themselves covered by the Act and who wish to benefit under the affirmative action program to identify themselves. . . ." *Id.* § 60-741.5(c)(1). The invitation must state that the information is voluntarily provided, that it will be kept confidential, and that refusal to provide the information will not subject the applicant or employee to adverse treatment. *Id. See also id.* § 60-741 app. B., at 442.

[90] Exec. Order No. 11,246, § 202, 3 C.F.R. 339, 340-41 (1964-1965 Compilation). Many of the employers covered under the Executive Order Program also have legal obligations under section 503. For example, contractors holding a federal contract that exceeds $50,000 and having more than fifty employees must develop a written affirmative action program with regard to women and minorities. 41 C.F.R. § 60-2.1 (1977). Thus, every employer who must develop a written affirmative action program for the handicapped, *id.* § 60-741.5, must also establish a written affirmative action action program for women and minorities. *Id.* § 60-2.1.

[91] 41 C.F.R. § 60-2.12 (1977). The goals and timetables are part of the Executive Order Program's written affirmative action program. For a general commentary on the use of goals and timetables, see Office of Fed. Contract Compliance Programs, *supra* note 13, at 69-95.

[93] *Id.* § 60-2.11(b)(2). The state or local employment security agencies group the data by "standard metropolitan statistical areas" (SMSAs). One of the problems with SMSA data is that the relevant labor market, and thus the availability rates, may vary depending on the job in question. Although an employer may hire laborers from only the local labor market, he or she may make a nationwide search for technical or executive positions. Interview with E. William Richardson, Assistant Regional Administrator for Region I of the OFCCP, in Boston, Mass. (Jan. 6, 1978).

[94] The statistical comparison only indicates possible underutilization. The compliance agent will probably have to go "on site" and make a further investigation at the contractor's facility. *See* 41 C.F.R. § 60-60.3(b) (1977).

utilization. These goals and timetables reflect, among other factors, the labor market availability rate of qualified women and the turnover rate within the job group.

The assumption underlying the use of goals and timetables is that sex or race does not itself disqualify a person from performing a particular job. This assumption can be invalid, however, when the relevant factor is handicap; the existence of a handicap may well disqualify an individual from performing a particular job. Moreover, because handicaps differ in degree as well as in kind, the development of labor market availability data for the handicapped is technically and economically unfeasible. Consequently, the goal-timetable approach will identify neither the availability nor the underutilization of the handicapped.[99] A case by case analysis thus appears to be the most appropriate and realistic method for determining whether a handicapped person is "qualified" for protection under the Act.

Section 503 regulations also require a contractor-employer to make a "reasonable accommodation"[100] to a handicapped individual's impairment. Accordingly, the case by case determination whether a handicapped individual is qualified should involve a three-part inquiry. First, the contractor must measure the abilities of the handicapped person against the job requirements. If the handicapped person is capable of performing the job, he or she is a "qualified" handicapped individual.[101] However, if the handicapped individual is incapable of performing the job, the contractor must make a second inquiry to ascertain whether any potential accommodations would enable the handicapped individual to perform the job. If no such accommodation is possible, the handicapped person is not "qualified." If one or more accommodations would allow the handicapped individual to perform the job, a third inquiry must be made to determine whether any of these potential accommodations would be "reasonable." If any of these potential accommodations is "reasonable"—that is, the accommodation would impose no "undue hardship" on the contractor's business—the handicapped individual is "qualified."[103]

[99] The inability to compile availability data for the handicapped also explains the different enforcement procedures under the Executive Order 11,246 Program and section 503, respectively. The OFCCP enforces the Executive Order Program primarily through the "compliance review" process. See text accompanying notes 124-27 infra. This process depends largely upon a type of statistical data that cannot be compiled with reference to the handicapped. See text accompanying note 98 supra. Thus, the OFCCP necessarily depends primarily on the more individualized complaint process to enforce the Rehabilitation Act.

[100] 41 C.F.R. § 60-741.2 (1977). Because an action that would constitute an accommodation for a person with one type of handicap might actually be a hindrance to a person with a different type of handicap, the contractor must consider accommodations on an individualized basis. See ten Broek, supra note 2, at 861.

[101] Some employers misperceive the issue to be whether the handicapped individual is more qualified than the other job applicants. Interview with Margaret Joyce, supra note 30.

[103] But see Note, Affirmative Action Toward Hiring Qualified Handicapped Individuals, 49 So. CAL. L. REV. 785, 813-26 (1976). This Note disagrees with the proposition that "reasonable" accommodations should be measured according to the capabilities of the employer and argues that "reasonableness" should instead be assessed on a societal basis. Id. at 814-15.

2. Scope of Section 503 Coverage Over Qualified Handicapped Individuals

Section 503 requires contractors to take affirmative action in employing persons who will carry out federal contracts. The regulations, however, extend protection to *all* handicapped employees and job applicants of covered federal contractors, including those persons who do not work under the federal contract. These regulations arguably extend coverage of handicapped individuals beyond the scope authorized by the language of section 503. Congress undoubtedly possesses the power to protect—as the regulations purport to do—handicapped individuals who do not work on any federal contract.[106] Whether Congress actually intended such broad coverage under section 503 remains unresolved.

The legislative history of section 503 does not reveal Congress' intent with regard to the scope of that section's coverage.[107] Nor has any court addressed the issue. At least two practical considerations arguably support the OFCCP's position that the regulations are valid. First, a distinction between those employees who work on a federal contract and those who do not is difficult to make. For example, in a large manufacturing plant, an assembler may produce an item that is sold both to the federal government and on the open market; similarly, a bookkeeper will usually do work related to both federal and nonfederal contracts. Second, although an employee does not directly "carry out" a federal contract, the contract may be an indirect source of his or her position. For example, a large federal contract may subsidize other corporate ventures that would not by themselves generate sufficient income to justify their continued existence. Thus, many incidental jobs may depend upon the existence of the federal contract.

Two co-authors have agreed with the OFCCP and concluded that the regulations are valid. These commentators argue that the section 503 regulations simply create a "presumption that all employees of a federal contractor are in some way engaged in furthering performance of the federal contract." This presumption is based not only on the Act itself, but also the reality that "the massive task of ascertaining which employees

---

106 See, *e.g.*, Vietnam Era Veterans' Readjustment Assistance Act of 1974, § 402, 38 U.S.C. § 2012 (Supp. IV 1974); Age Discrimination in Employment Act, 29 U.S.C. §§ 621(a)(4), 623 (1970).

107 The level of federal financial participation was the most controversial feature of the Act. President Nixon vetoed two federal bills that preceded the current Act because the bills were "fiscally irresponsible." 119 Cong. Rec. 5880-81, 9597 (1973). After the Senate unsuccessfully attempted to override the second veto, *id.* at 10,822-23, Congress and the President agreed upon a compromise bill that eventually became the Rehabilitation Act of 1973. S. 1875, 93d Cong., 1st Sess. (1973). President Ford vetoed the 1974 Amendments to the Act, citing fiscal concerns as a factor influencing his decision, 120 Cong. Rec. 36,850-51 (1974), but Congress overrode his veto by an overwhelming majority. *Id.* at 36,621-22 (House vote); *id.* at 36,882 (Senate vote). Because the political controversy surrounding the Rehabilitation Act did not focus upon section 503, the legislative history of the Act sheds no light on the issue whether Congress intended that section 503 extend coverage as broadly as the section 503 regulations purport to do. See S. Rep. No. 318, 93d Cong., 1st Sess., *reprinted in* [1973] 2 U.S. Code Cong. & Ad. News 2076, 2079-82.

have an effect on the performance of a particular federal contract would be beyond the capabilities of the Department of Labor." The commentators argue that the "waiver procedures" found in the section 503 regulations constitute a means by which an employer may rebut this presumption of coverage. Under those procedures, the Director of the OFCCP may, at the contractor's request, waive section 503 coverage with respect to any of the contractor's facilities that the Director finds to be "in all respects separate and distinct from activities . . . related to the performance of the [federal] contract."

The language of section 503, however, does not support this analysis of the OFCCP's position. Section 503 unambiguously extends coverage only to handicapped individuals who "carry out such [a federal] contract." The section 503 waiver regulation applies only if a contractor's *facilities* are separate and distinct from federal contract work. The waiver provision simply does not refer to those employment responsibilities that are separate and distinct from the federal contract work; thus, this provision should not give rise to any presumption concerning the scope of section 503. For example, if the contractor requests a waiver for one of his facilities and the Director of the OFCCP finds that a single employee at that facility is engaged in federal contract work, the Director may deny the waiver because the facility is not "in all respects separate and distinct from" federal contract work. However, this denial of waiver to the facility does not address the issue whether section 503 protects *all* the handicapped employees at that facility, or only the single handicapped employee at that facility who is actually performing federal contract work.

The coverage dilemma should be resolved by promulgating new regulations or by reading into the existing regulations a different procedure by which the covered contractor may rebut the presumption that all of the contractor's employees are "carrying out" the federal contract. The regulations promulgated under the McNamara-O'Hara and Walsh-Healey Acts illustrate how such a rebuttable presumption would work. Both those acts provide that covered federal contractors must pay minimum standards of compensation to employees engaged in the federal contract work. Although the regulations create a presumption that all of a covered contractor's employees are engaged in work under the federal contract, they also allow the employer to rebut the presumption by presenting affirmative proof to the contrary. Such an approach would be appropriate in the context of section 503. This construction would reconcile the scope of coverage under the section 503 regulations with the language of section 503 itself and would eliminate the administrative difficulty of determining which employees are covered by section 503.

## SENATE REPORT NO. 93-1297

### 93rd Cong., 1st Sess. (1974)

. . .

In order to embody this underlying intent, section 111(a) of the Senate amendment to H.R. 14225 added a new definition of "handicapped individual" for the purposes of titles IV and V of the Act as follows:

"Any person who (A) has a physical or mental impairment which substantially limits such person's functioning or one or more of such person's major life activities, (B) has a record of such an impairment, or (C) is regarded as having such an impairment."

The Conference agreement on H.R. 14225, and this identical original bill, deletes from clause (A) the language "such person's functioning or" as redundant.

The amended defintion eliminates any reference to employment and takes cognizance of the fact that handicapped persons are discriminated against in a number of ways. First, they are discriminated against when they are, in fact, handicapped (this is similar to discrimination because of race and sex). Second, they are discriminated against because they are classified or labeled, correctly or incorrectly, as handicapped (this has no direct parallel in either race or sex discrimination, although racial and ethnic factors may contribute to misclassification as mentally retarded). Third, they are discriminated against if they are regarded as handicapped, regardless of whether they are in fact handicapped (this has a parallel in race discrimination where a person is regarded as being of a minority group even though, in fact, he or she is not).

Clause (A) in the new definition eliminates any reference to employment and makes the definition applicable to the provision of Federally-assisted services and programs. Clause (B) is intended to make clearer that the coverage of sections 503 and 504 extends to persons who have recovered—in whole or in part—from a handicapping condition, such as a mental or neurological illness, a heart attack, or cancer and to persons who were classified as handicapped (for example, as mentally ill or mentally retarded) but who may be discriminated against or otherwise be in need of the protection of sections 503 and 504.

Clause (C) in the new definition clarifies the intention to include those persons who are discriminated against on the basis of handicap, whether or not they are in fact handicapped, just as title VI of the Civil Rights Act of 1964 prohibits discrimination on the ground of race, whether or not the person discriminated against is in fact a member of a racial minority. This subsection includes within the protection of sections 503 and 504 those persons who do not in fact have the condition which they are perceived as having, as well as those persons whose mental or physical condition does not substantially limit their life activities and who thus are not technically within clause (A) in the new definition. Members of both of these groups may be subjected to discrimination on the basis of their being regarded as handicapped.

The new definition applies to section 503, as well as to section 504, in order to avoid limiting the affirmative action obligation of a Federal contractor to only that class of persons who are eligible for vocational rehabilitation services. It should be noted, however, that the affirmative action obligation cannot be fulfilled by the expediency of hiring or limiting services to persons marginally or previously handicapped or persons "regarded as" handicapped. Rather, an acceptable affirmative action program must be aimed at the entire class of employable handicapped persons, with particular attention to those who are presently, actually, and significantly handicapped. This standard parallels the obligation of a Federal contractor under Executive Order No. 11246 to employ persons who might be discriminated against on the basis of national origin: the obligation extends to all ethnic groups within the available applicant pool and cannot be fulfilled selectively by hiring persons from only one ethnic group. Where applicable, section 504 is intended to include a requirement of affirmative action as well as a prohibition against discrimination.

## SOUTHEASTERN COMMUNITY COLLEGE v. DAVIS

*Supreme Court of the United States, 1979*
_____ *U.S.* _____, *47 USLW 4689*

Mr. Justice Powell delivered the opinion of the Court.

This case presents a matter of first impression for this Court: Whether § 504 of the Rehabilitation Act of 1973, which prohibits discrimination against an "otherwise qualified handicapped individual" in federally funded programs "solely by reason of his handicap," forbids professional schools from imposing physical qualifications for admission to their clinical training programs.

### I

Respondent, who suffers from a serious hearing disability, seeks to be trained as a registered nurse. During the 1973–1974 academic year she was enrolled in the College Parallel program of Southeastern Community College, a state institution that receives federal funds. Respondent hoped to progress to Southeastern's Associate Degree Nursing program, completion of which would make her eligible for state certification as a registered nurse. In the course of her application to the nursing program, she was interviewed by a member of the nursing faculty. It became apparent that respondent had difficulty understanding questions asked, and on inquiry she acknowledged a history of hearing problems and dependence on a hearing aid. She was advised to consult an audiologist.

On the basis of an examination at Duke University Medical Center, respondent was diagnosed as having a "bilateral, sensori-neural hearing loss." App. 127a. A change in her hearing aid was recommended, as a result of which it was expected that she would be able to detect sounds "almost as well as a person would who has normal hearing." App. 127a–128a. But this improvement would not mean that she could discriminate among sounds sufficiently to understand normal spoken speech. Her lip-reading skills would remain necessary for effective communication:

"While wearing the hearing aid, she is well aware of gross sounds occurring in the listening environment. However, she can only be responsible for speech spoken to her, when the talker gets her attention and allows her to look directly at the talker." App. 128a.

Southeastern next consulted Mary McRee, Executive Director of the North Carolina Board of Nursing. On the basis of the audiologist's report, McRee recommended that respondent not be admitted to the nursing program. In McRee's view, respondent's hearing disability made it unsafe for her to practice as a nurse.[1] In addition, it would be impossible for respondent to participate safely in the normal clinical training program, and those modifications that would be necessary to enable safe participation would prevent her from realizing the benefits of the program: "To adjust patient learning experiences in keeping with [respondent's] hearing limitations could, in fact, be the same as denying her full learning to meet the objectives of your nursing programs." App. 132a–133a.

After respondent was notified that she was not qualified for nursing study because of her hearing disability, she requested reconsideration of the decision. The entire nursing staff of Southeastern was assembled, and McRee again was consulted. McRee repeated her conclusion that on the basis of the available evidence, respondent "has hearing limitations which could interfere with her safely caring for patients." App. 139a. Upon further deliberation, the staff voted to deny respondent admission.

Respondent then filed suit in the United States District Court for the Eastern District of North Carolina, alleging both a violation of § 504 of the Rehabilitation Act of 1973, 87 Stat. 394, as amended, 29 U.S.C. § 794,[2] and a denial of equal protection and due process. After a bench

---

[1] [Footnotes numbered as in original.—Ed.] McRee also wrote that respondent's hearing disability could preclude her practicing safely in "any setting" allowed by "a license as L[icensed] P[ractical] N[urse]." App. 132a. Respondent contends that inasmuch as she already was licensed as a practical nurse, McRee's opinion was inherently incredible. But the record indicates that respondent had "not worked as a practical nurse except to do a little bit of night duty," App. 32a, and had not done that for several years before applying to Southeastern. Accordingly, it is at least possible to infer that respondent in fact could not work safely as a practical nurse in spite of her license to do so. In any event, we note the finding of the District Court that "a Licensed Practical Nurse, unlike a Licensed Registered Nurse, operates under constant supervision and is not allowed to perform medical tasks which require a great degree of technical sophistication." 424 F. Supp. 1341, 1342–1343 (EDNC 1976).

[2] The statute provides in full:
"No otherwise qualified handicapped individual in the United States, as defined in Section 706(6) of this title, shall, solely by reason of his handicap, be excluded from the participation in, or be denied the benefits of, or be subjected to discrimination under any program or activity receiving Federal financial assistance *or under any program or activity conducted by any Executive agency or by the United States Postal Service. The head of each such agency shall promulgate such regulations as may be necessary to carry out the amendments to this section made by the Rehabilitation, Comprehensive Services, and Developmental Disabilities Act of 1978. Copies of any proposed regulation shall be submitted to appropriate authorizing committees of the Congress, and such regulation may take effect no earlier than the thirtieth day after the date on which such regulation is so submitted to such committees.*"
The italicized portion of the section was added by § 119 of the Rehabilitation, Comprehensive Services, and Developmental Disabilities Act of 1978, 92 Stat. 2982. Respondent asserts no claim under this portion of the statute.

trial, the District Court entered judgment in favor of Southeastern. 424 F. Supp. 1341 (1976). It confirmed the findings of the audiologist that even with a hearing aid respondent cannot understand speech directed to her except through lipreading, and further found that,

"[I]n many situations such as an operation room, intensive care unit, or post-natal care unit, all doctors and nurses wear surgical masks which would make lip-reading impossible. Additionally, in many situations a Registered Nurse would be required to instantly follow the physician's instructions concerning procurement of various types of instruments and drugs where the physician would be unable to get the nurse's attention by other than vocal means." Id., at 1343.

Accordingly, the Court concluded that:

"[Respondent's] handicap actually prevents her from safely performing in both her training program and her proposed profession. The trial testimony indicated numerous situations where [respondent's] particular disability would render her unable to function properly. Of particular concern to the court in this case is the potential danger to future patients in such situations." Id., at 1345.

Based on these findings, the District Court concluded that respondent was not an "otherwise qualified handicapped individual" protected against discrimination by § 504. In its view, "[o]therwise qualified, can only be read to mean otherwise able to function sufficiently in the position sought in spite of the handicap, if proper training and facilities are suitable and available." Ibid. Because respondent's disability would prevent her from functioning "sufficiently" in Southeastern's nursing program, the Court held that the decision to exclude her was not discriminatory within the meaning of § 504.[3]

On appeal, the Court of Appeals for the Fourth Circuit reversed. 574 F.2d 1158 (1978). It did not dispute the District Court's findings of fact, but held that the Court had misconstrued § 504. In light of administrative regulations that had been promulgated while the appeal was pending, see 42 Fed. Reg. 22676 (May 4, 1977),[4] the appellate court believed that § 504 required Southeastern to "reconsider plaintiff's application for admission to the nursing program without regard to her hearing ability." Id., at 1160. It concluded that the District Court had erred in taking respondent's handicap into account in determining whether she was "otherwise qualified" for the program, rather than confining its inquiry to her "academic and technical qualifications." Id., at 1161. The Court of Appeals also suggested that § 504 required "affirmative conduct" on the part

---

[3] The District Court also dismissed respondent's constitutional claims. The Court of Appeals affirmed that portion of the order, and respondent has not sought review of this ruling.

[4] Relying on the plain language of the Act, the Department of Health, Education, and Welfare (HEW) at first did not promulgate any regulations to implement § 504. In a subsequent suit against HEW, however, the United States District Court for the District of Columbia held that Congress had intended regulations to be issued and ordered HEW to do so. Cherry v. Mathews, 419 F. Supp. 922 (1976). The ensuing regulations currently are embodied in 45 CFR pt. 84.

of Southeastern to modify its program to accommodate the disabilities of applicants, "even when such modifications become expensive." *Id.,* at 1162.

Because of the importance of this issue to the many institutions covered by § 504, we granted certiorari. 439 U.S. _____ (1979). We now reverse.[5]

## II

This is the first case in which this Court has been called upon to interpret § 504. It is elementary that "[t]he starting point in every case involving the construction of a statute is the language itself." *Blue Chip Stamps* v. *Manor Drug Stores,* 421 U.S. 723, 756 (1975) (POWELL, J., concurring); see *Greyhound Corp.* v. *Mt. Hood Stages, Inc.,* 437 U.S. 322, 330 (1978); *Santa Fe Industries, Inc.* v. *Green,* 430 U.S. 462, 472 (1977). Section 504 by its terms does not compel educational institutions to disregard the disabilities of handicapped individuals or to make substantial modifications in their programs to allow disabled persons to participate. Instead, it requires only that an "otherwise qualified handicapped individual" not be excluded from participation in a federally funded program "solely by reason of his handicap," indicating only that mere possession of a handicap is not a permissible ground for assuming an inability to function in a particular context.[6]

The court below, however, believed that the "otherwise qualified" persons protected by § 504 include those who would be able to meet the requirements of a particular program in every respect except as to limitations imposed by their handicap. See 574 F.2d, at 1160. Taken literally, this holding would prevent an institution from taking into account any

---

[5] In addition to challenging the construction of § 504 by the Court of Appeals, Southeastern also contends that respondent cannot seek judicial relief for violations of that statute in view of the absence of any express private right of action. Respondent asserts that whether or not § 504 provides a private action, she may maintain her suit under 42 U.S.C. § 1983. In light of our disposition of this case on the merits, it is unnecessary to address these issues and we express no views on them. See *Norton* v. *Mathews,* 427 U.S. 524, 529–531 (1976); *Moor* v. *County of Alameda,* 411 U.S. 693, 715 (1973); *United States* v. *Augenblick,* 393 U.S. 348, 351–352 (1969).

[6] The Act defines "handicapped individual" as follows:

"The term 'handicapped individual' means any individual who (A) has a physical or mental disability which for such individual constitutes or results in a substantial handicap to employment and (B) can reasonably be expected to benefit in terms of employability from vocational rehabilitation services provided pursuant to subchapters I and III of this chapter. For the purposes of subchapters IV and V of this chapter, such term means any person who (A) has a physical or mental impairment which substantially limits one or more of such person's major life activities, (B) has a record of such an impairment, or (C) is regarded as having such an impairment." Section 7 of the Rehabilitation Act of 1973, 87 Stat. 359, as amended, 88 Stat. 1619, 89 Stat. 2, 29 U.S.C. § 706(6).

This definition comports with our understanding of § 504. A person who has a record of or is regarded as having an impairment may at present have no actual incapacity at all. Such a person would be exactly the kind of individual who could be "otherwise qualified" to participate in covered programs. And a person who suffers from a limiting physical or mental impairment still may possess other abilities that permit him to meet the requirements of various programs. Thus it is clear that Congress included among the class of "handicapped" persons covered by § 504 a range of individuals who could be "otherwise qualified." See S. Rep. No. 1297, 93d Cong., 2d Sess., 38–39 (1974).

limitation resulting from the handicap, however disabling. It assumes, in effect, that a person need not meet legitimate physical requirements in order to be "otherwise qualified." We think the understanding of the District Court is closer to the plain meaning of the statutory language. An otherwise qualified person is one who is able to meet all of a program's requirements in spite of his handicap.

The regulations promulgated by the Department of Health, Education, and Welfare (HEW) to interpret § 504 reinforce, rather than contradict, this conclusion. According to these regulations, a "[q]ualified handicapped person" is, "[w]ith respect to postsecondary and vocational education services, a handicapped person who meets the academic and technical standards requisite to admission or participation in the [school's] education program or activity. . . ." 45 CFR § 84.3(k)(3) (1978). An explanatory note states:

"The term 'technical standards' refers to *all* nonacademic admissions criteria that are essential to participation in the program in question." 45 CFR pt. 84, App. A, at p. 405 (emphasis supplied).

A further note emphasizes that legitimate physical qualifications may be essential to participation in particular programs.[7] We think it clear, therefore, that HEW interprets the "other" qualifications which a handicapped person may be required to meet as including necessary physical qualifications.

## III

The remaining question is whether the physical qualifications Southeastern demanded of respondent might not be necessary for participation in its nursing program. It is not open to dispute that, as Southeastern's Associate Degree Nursing program currently is constituted, the ability to understand speech without reliance on lipreading is necessary for patient safety during the clinical phase of the program. As the District Court found, this ability also is indispensable for many of the functions that a registered nurse performs.

Respondent contends nevertheless that § 504, properly interpreted, compels Southeastern to undertake affirmative action that would dispense with the need for effective oral communication. First, it is suggested that respondent can be given individual supervision by faculty members whenever she attends patients directly. Moreover, certain required courses

[7] The note states:
"Paragraph (k) of § 84.3 defines the term 'qualified handicapped person.' Throughout the regulation, this term is used instead of the statutory term 'otherwise qualified handicapped person.' The Department believes that the omission of the word 'otherwise' is necessary in order to comport with the intent of the statute because, read literally, 'otherwise' qualified handicapped persons include persons who are qualified except for their handicap, rather than in spite of their handicap. Under such a literal reading, a blind person possessing all the qualifications for driving a bus except sight could be said to be 'otherwise qualified' for the job of driving. Clearly, such a result was not intended by Congress. In all other respects, the terms 'qualified' and 'otherwise qualified' are intended to be interchangeable." 45 CFR pt. 84, App. A, at p. 405.

might be dispensed with altogether for respondent. It is not necessary, she argues, that Southeastern train her to undertake all the tasks a registered nurse is licensed to perform. Rather, it is sufficient to make § 504 applicable if respondent might be able to perform satisfactorily some of the duties of a registered nurse or to hold some of the positions available to a registered nurse.[8]

Respondent finds support for this argument in portions of the HEW regulations discussed above. In particular, a provision applicable to post-secondary educational programs requires covered institutions to make "modifications" in their programs to accommodate handicapped persons, and to provide "auxiliary aids" such as sign-language interpreters.[9] Respondent argues that this regulation imposes an obligation to ensure full participation in covered programs by handicapped individuals and, in particular, requires Southeastern to make the kind of adjustments that would be necessary to permit her safe participation in the nursing program.

We note first that on the present record it appears unlikely respondent could benefit from any affirmative action that the regulation reasonably

---

[8] The court below adopted a portion of this argument:

"[Respondent's] ability to read lips aids her in overcoming her hearing disability; however, it was argued that in certain situations such as in an operating room environment where surgical masks are used, this ability would be unavailing to her.

"Be that as it may, in the medical community, there does appear to be a number of settings in which the plaintiff could perform satisfactorily as an RN, such as in industry or perhaps a physician's office. Certainly [respondent] could be viewed as possessing extraordinary insight into the medical and emotional needs of those with hearing disabilities.

"If [respondent] meets all the other criteria for admission in the pursuit of her RN career, under the relevant North Carolina statutes, N.C. Gen. Stat. §§ 90–158, et seq., it should not be foreclosed to her simply because she may not be able to function effectively in all the roles which registered nurses may choose for their careers." 574 F.2d 1158, 1161 n. 6 (CA4 1978).

[9] This regulation provides in full:

"(a) *Academic requirements.* A recipient [of federal funds] to which this subpart applies shall make such modifications to its academic requirements as are necessary to ensure that such requirements do not discriminate or have the effect of discriminating, on the basis of handicap, against a qualified handicapped applicant or student. Academic requirements that the recipient can demonstrate are essential to the program of instruction being pursued by such student or to any directly related licensing requirement will not be regarded as discriminatory within the meaning of this section. Modifications may include changes in the length of time permitted for the completion of degree requirements, substitution of specific courses required for the completion of degree requirements, and adaptation of the manner in which specific courses are conducted.

. . .

"(d) *Auxiliary aids.* (1) A recipient to which this subpart applies shall take such steps as are necessary to ensure that no handicapped student is denied the benefits of, excluded from participation in, or otherwise subjected to discrimination under the education program or activity operated by the recipient because of the absence of educational auxiliary aids for students with impaired sensory, manual, or speaking skills.

"(2) Auxiliary aids may include taped texts, interpreters or other effective methods of making orally delivered materials available to students with hearing impairments, readers in libraries for students with visual impairments, classroom equipment adapted for use by students with manual impairments, and other similar services and actions. Recipients need not provide attendants, individually prescribed devices, readers for personal use or study, or other devices or services of a personal nature." 45 CFR § 84.44.

could be interpreted as requiring. Section 84.44(d)(2), for example, explicitly excludes "devices or services of a personal nature" from the kinds of auxiliary aids a school must provide a handicapped individual. Yet the only evidence in the record indicates that nothing less than close, individual attention by a nursing instructor would be sufficient to ensure patient safety if respondent took part in the clinical phase of the nursing program. See 424 F. Supp., at 1346. Furthermore, it also is reasonably clear that § 84.44(a) does not encompass the kind of curricular changes that would be necessary to accommodate respondent in the nursing program. In light of respondent's inability to function in clinical courses without close supervision, Southeastern with prudence could allow her to take only academic classes. Whatever benefits respondent might realize from such a course of study, she would not receive even a rough equivalent of the training a nursing program normally gives. Such a fundamental alteration in the nature of a program is far more than the "modification" the regulation requires.

Moreover, an interpretation of the regulations that required the extensive modifications necessary to include respondent in the nursing program would raise grave doubts about their validity. If these regulations were to require substantial adjustments in existing programs beyond those necessary to eliminate discrimination against otherwise qualified individuals, they would do more than clarify the meaning of § 504. Instead, they would constitute an unauthorized extension of the obligations imposed by that statute.

The language and structure of the Rehabilitation Act of 1973 reflect a recognition by Congress of the distinction between the evenhanded treatment of qualified handicapped persons and affirmative efforts to overcome the disabilities caused by handicaps. Section 501(b), governing the employment of handicapped individuals by the Federal Government, requires each federal agency to submit "an affirmative action program plan for the hiring, placement, and advancement of handicapped individuals. . . ." These plans "shall include a description of the extent to which and methods whereby the special needs of handicapped employees are being met." Similarly, § 503(a), governing hiring by federal contractors, requires employers to "take affirmative action to employ and advance in employment qualified handicapped individuals. . . ." The President is required to promulgate regulations to enforce this section.

Under § 501(c) of the Act, by contrast, state agencies such as Southeastern are only "encourage[d] . . . to adopt such policies and procedures." Section 504 does not refer at all to affirmative action, and except as it applies to federal employers it does not provide for implementation by administrative action. A comparison of these provisions demonstrates that Congress understood accommodation of the needs of handicapped individuals may require affirmative action and knew how to provide for it in those instances where it wished to do so.[10]

---

[10] Section 115(a) of the Rehabilitation Act of 1978 added to the 1973 Act a section authorizing grants to state units for the purpose of providing "such information and

Although an agency's interpretation of the statute under which it operates is entitled to some deference, "this deference is constrained by our obligation to honor the clear meaning of a statute, as revealed by its language, purpose and history." *International Brotherhood of Teamsters v. Daniel*, 439 U.S. _____, _____ n. 20 (1979). Here neither the language, purpose, nor history of § 504 reveals an intent to impose an affirmative action obligation on all recipients of federal funds.[11] Accordingly, we hold that even if HEW has attempted to create such an obligation itself, it lacks the authority to do so.

## IV

We do not suggest that the line between a lawful refusal to extend affirmative action and illegal discrimination against handicapped persons always will be clear. It is possible to envision situations where an insistence on continuing past requirements and practices might arbitrarily deprive genuinely qualified handicapped persons of the opportunity to participate in a covered program. Technological advances can be expected to enhance opportunities to rehabilitate the handicapped or otherwise to

---

technical assistance (including support personnel such as interpreters for the deaf) as may be necessary to assist those entities in complying with this Act, particularly the requirements of section 504." 92 Stat. 2971, codified at 29 U.S.C. § 775. This provision recognizes that on occasion the elimination of discrimination might involve some costs; it does not imply that the refusal to undertake substantial changes in a program by itself constitutes discrimination. Whatever effect the availability of these funds might have on ascertaining the existence of discrimination in some future case, no such funds were available to Southeastern at the time respondent sought admission to its nursing program.

11 The Government, in a brief *amicus curiae* in support of respondent, cites a report of the Senate Committee on Labor and Public Welfare on the 1974 amendments to the 1973 Act and several statements by individual Members of Congress during debate on the 1978 amendments, some of which indicate a belief that § 504 requires affirmative action. See Brief for the Government as *Amicus Curiae* 44–50. But these isolated statements by individual Members of Congress or its committees, all made after the enactment of the statute under consideration, cannot substitute for a clear expression of legislative intent at the time of enactment. *Quern* v. *Mandley*, 436 U.S. 725, 736 n. 10 (1978); *Los Angeles Dept. of Water & Power* v. *Manhart*, 435 U.S. 702, 714 (1978). Nor do these comments, none of which represents the will of Congress as a whole, constitute subsequent "legislation" such as this Court might weigh in construing the meaning of an earlier enactment. Cf. *Red Lion Broadcasting Co.* v. *FCC*, 395 U.S. 367, 380–381 (1969).

The Government also argues that various amendments to the 1973 Act contained in the Rehabilitation Act of 1978 further reflect Congress' approval of the affirmative action obligation created by HEW's regulations. But the amendment most directly on point undercuts this position. In amending § 504, Congress both extended that section's prohibition of discrimination to "any program or activity conducted by any Executive agency or by the United States Postal Service" and authorized administrative regulations to implement only *this amendment*. See n. 2, *supra*. The fact that no other regulations were mentioned supports an inference that no others were approved.

Finally, we note that the assertion by HEW of the authority to promulgate any regulations under § 504 has been neither consistent nor longstanding. For the first three years after the section was enacted, HEW maintained the position that Congress had not intended any regulations to be issued. It altered its stand only after having been enjoined to do so. See n. 4, *supra*. This fact substantially diminishes the deference to be given to HEW's present interpretation of the statute. See *General Electric Co.* v. *Gilbert*, 429 U.S. 125, 143 (1976).

qualify them for some useful employment. Such advances also may enable attainment of these goals without imposing undue financial and administrative burdens upon a State. Thus situations may arise where a refusal to modify an existing program might become unreasonable and discriminatory. Identification of those instances where a refusal to accommodate the needs of a disabled person amounts to discrimination against the handicapped continues to be an important responsibility of HEW.

In this case, however, it is clear that Southeastern's unwillingness to make major adjustments in its nursing program does not constitute such discrimination. The uncontroverted testimony of several members of Southeastern's staff and faculty established that the purpose of its program was to train persons who could serve the nursing profession in all customary ways. See, e.g., App. 35a, 52a, 53a, 71a, 74a. This type of purpose, far from reflecting any animus against handicapped individuals, is shared by many if not most of the institutions that train persons to render professional service. It is undisputed that respondent could not participate in Southeastern's nursing program unless the standards were substantially lowered. Section 504 imposes no requirement upon an educational institution to lower or to effect substantial modifications of standards to accommodate a handicapped person.[12]

One may admire respondent's desire and determination to overcome her handicap, and there well may be various other types of service for which she can qualify. In this case, however, we hold that there was no violation of § 504 when Southeastern concluded that respondent did not qualify for admission to its program. Nothing in the language or history of § 504 reflects an intention to limit the freedom of an educational institution to require reasonable physical qualifications for admission to a clinical training program. Nor has there been any showing in this case that any action short of a substantial change in Southeastern's program would render unreasonable the qualifications it imposed.

## V

Accordingly, we reverse the judgment of the court below, and remand for proceedings consistent with this opinion.

*So ordered.*

---

[12] Respondent contends that it is unclear whether North Carolina law requires a registered nurse to be capable of performing all functions open to that profession in order to obtain a license to practice, although McRee, the Executive Director of the state Board of Nursing, had informed Southeastern that the law did so require. See App. 138a–139a. Respondent further argues that even if she is not capable of meeting North Carolina's present licensing requirements, she still might succeed in obtaining a license in another jurisdiction.

Respondent's argument misses the point. Southeastern's program, structured to train persons who will be able to perform all normal roles of a registered nurse, represents a legitimate academic policy, and is accepted by the State. In effect it seeks to ensure that no graduate will pose a danger to the public in any professional role he or she might be cast. Even if the licensing requirements of North Carolina or some other State are less demanding, nothing in the Act requires an educational institution to lower its standards.

## TRAGESER v. LIBBIE REHABILITATION CENTER

*United States Court of Appeals, Fourth Circuit, 1978*
*18 FEP Cases 1141, cert. denied, 47 USLW 3814 (1979)*

BUTZNER, Circuit Judge: Novella H. Trageser appeals the district court's dismissal of her complaint alleging that the termination of her employment at Libbie Rehabilitation Center constituted handicap discrimination in violation of § 504 of the Rehabilitation Act of 1973, the fifth and fourteenth amendments to the Constitution, and 42 U.S.C. § 1983. We affirm because § 120(a) of the Comprehensive Rehabilitation Services Amendments of 1978 forecloses her claim under the Rehabilitation Act of 1973, and lack of governmental action precludes recovery on the other grounds.

### I

Libbie, a private corporation, operates a nursing home for profit in Richmond, Virginia. It receives substantial income from the state and federal governments in the form of Medicare, Medicaid, Veterans Administration, and welfare payments. The purpose of these payments is to compensate for treatment of specified patients who are entitled to the benefits. The home is subject to inspection by the Virginia Department of Health.

Trageser, a registered nurse, was hired in 1971 and promoted to director of nurses in 1975. Her sight is impaired by a condition known as retinitis pigmentosa, which is hereditary and progressive.

On April 28, 1976, the certification officer from the Virginia Department of Health conducted a regular inspection of the nursing home. The inspector told the administrator of the home that Trageser's eyesight had deteriorated since the last inspection and asked what the home intended to do about it. The administrator relayed these comments to the board of directors. At its meeting on June 7, 1976, the board resolved to dismiss her. Upon learning of this decision, Trageser resigned.

Trageser then brought this action seeking reinstatement, back pay, and an injunction against payment of federal financial assistance to the home unless she was reinstated. The district court treated the termination of her employment as tantamount to discharge, but it granted Libbie's motion to dismiss the complaint for failure to state a claim upon which relief could be granted. See *Trageser* v. *Libbie Rehabilitation Center*, 16 E.P.D. ¶ 8117, 17 FEP Cases 938 (E.D. Va. 1977).

### II

Trageser bases her claim on § 504 of the Rehabilitation Act of 1973 [1] which provides as follows:

---

[1] [Footnotes numbered as in original.—Ed.] 29 U.S.C.A. § 794 (1975).

"No otherwise qualified handicapped individual in the United States . . . shall, solely by reason of his handicap, be excluded from the participation in, be denied the benefits of, or be subjected to discrimination under any program or activity receiving Federal financial assistance."

In § 120(a) of the Comprehensive Rehabilitation Services Amendments of 1978, Congress added, among other provisions, § 505(a)(2)[2] which states:

"The remedies, procedures, and rights set forth in title VI of the Civil Rights Act of 1964 shall be available to any person aggrieved by any act or failure to act by any recipient of Federal assistance or Federal provider of such assistance under § 504 of this Act."

Title VI contains the prototype of § 504 of the Rehabilitation Act. See *Lloyd* v. *Regional Transportation Authority*, 548 F.2d 1277, 1280 and n. 9 (7th Cir. 1977). Section 601 of Title VI[3] provides as follows:

"No person in the United States shall, on the ground of race, color, or national origin, be excluded from participation in, be denied the benefits of, or be subjected to discrimination under any program or activity receiving Federal financial assistance."

The broad prohibition of § 601 is, however, qualified by § 604,[4] which creates the following limitation:

"Nothing contained in this subchapter shall be construed to authorize action under this subchapter by any department or agency with respect to any employment practice of any employer, employment agency, or labor organization except where a primary objective of the Federal financial assistance is to provide employment."[5]

Although § 604 expressly curtails the authority of federal departments and agencies, it also restricts private suits. Thus, because of § 604, Title VI does not provide a judicial remedy for employment discrimination by institutions receiving federal funds unless (1) providing employment is a primary objective of the federal aid,[6] or (2) discrimination in employment necessarily causes discrimination against the primary beneficiaries of the federal aid.[7]

Title VII of the Civil Rights Act of 1964[8] provides the primary statutory remedies for racial and ethnic discrimination in employment. Rec-

---

[2] Act of November 6, 1978, Pub. L. No. 95–602, § 120(a), H.R. Conf. Rep. No. 95–1780 on H.R. 12467, 95th Cong., 2d Sess. 29 (1978), 124 Cong. Rec. H12675 (daily ed., Oct. 12, 1978) (to be codified as 29 U.S.C. § 795(a)(2)).

[3] 42 U.S.C. § 2000d.

[4] 42 U.S.C. § 2000d–3.

[5] The § 604 restriction on enforcement of fair employment practices is tempered in appropriate cases by availability of the remedies of Title VII of the Civil Rights Act of 1964, 42 U.S.C. § 2000e, *et seq.*, and of 42 U.S.C. § 1983.

[6] See, *e.g.*, *Quiroz* v. *City of Santa Ana*, 17 E.P.D. ¶ 8631 at p. 7221, 18 FEP Cases 1138 at p. 1140 (C.D. Calif. 1978); *Feliciano* v. *Romney*, 363 F. Supp. 656, 672 (S.D. N.Y. 1973).

[7] See *Caulfield* v. *Board of Education*, 583 F.2d 605, 17 E.P.D. ¶ 8600 at p. 7078, 18 FEP Cases 7 (2d Cir. 1978); *United States* v. *Jefferson County Board of Education*, 372 F.2d 836, 883 (5th Cir. 1966).

[8] 42 U.S.C. § 2000e, *et seq.*

ognizing this, Congress supplemented the Rehabilitation Act by including in § 120(a) of the 1978 amendments a new subsection 505(a)(1) [9] which
makes the pertinent remedies, procedures, and rights of Title VII available to federal employees who complain of handicap discrimination in
employment in violation of § 501 of the Rehabilitation Act.[10] Congress
also could have utilized Title VII to define the rights and remedies of a
person in Trageser's position who must rely on § 504. Instead, for employees of private institutions receiving federal financial aid, § 120(a) of
the 1978 amendments makes available only the remedies, procedures, and
rights of Title VI, which, as we have noted above, contains the restriction
of § 604. The distinction that § 120(a) draws between the relief available
to federal employees and that available to employees of private institutions receiving federal assistance could not have been inadvertent. We
therefore conclude that we must apply the limitation contained in § 604
of Title VI to § 504 of the Rehabilitation Act in literal compliance with
§ 120(a) of the 1978 amendments.[11]

We cannot accept Trageser's contention that the 1978 amendments are
inapplicable to her 1976 dismissal. We must decide this case in accordance with the law as it exists at the time we render our decision " 'unless
doing so would result in manifest injustice or there is statutory direction
or legislative history to the contrary.' " *Cort* v. *Ash*, 422 U.S. 66, 76–77
(1975). In the absence of legislative history to the contrary, the explicit
incorporation of § 604 of Title VI simply confirms a plausible reading
of § 504 as originally enacted. See, *e.g.*, Guy, *The Developing Law on
Equal Employment Opportunity for the Handicapped: An Overview and
Analysis of the Major Issues*, 7 U. BALT. L. REV. 183, 207 (1978). We
therefore find no manifest injustice in applying the amendments to illu-
minate this case which was pending when they were enacted.

A private action under § 504 to redress employment discrimination
therefore may not be maintained unless a primary objective of the federal financial assistance is to provide employment. There has been no
such allegation in this case; nor could there be one. Viewing the complaint in the light most favorable to Trageser, in compliance with Federal
Rule of Civil Procedure 12(b)(6), we nevertheless hold that she cannot
prevail on her § 504 claim.[12]

[9] Section 505(a)(1) (to be codified as 29 U.S.C. § 795(a)(1)) provides in pertinent part:
"The remedies, procedures, and rights set forth in section 717 of the Civil Rights Act
of 1964 . . . including the application of sections 706(f) through 706(k) . . . shall be
available, with respect to any complaint under section 501 of this Act, to any employee
or applicant for employment aggrieved by the final disposition of such complaint, or by
the failure to take final action on such complaint."

[10] 29 U.S.C. § 791.

[11] The Secretary of Health, Education, and Welfare has promulgated regulations to
implement § 504 of the Rehabilitation Act of 1973. See 45 C.F.R. Part 84 (1977). He
has not, however, had an opportunity to conform those regulations to the 1978 amendments incorporating § 604 of Title VI.

[12] Trageser's reliance on *Davis* v. *Southeastern Community College*, 574 F.2d 1158,
1159 (4th Cir. 1978), is misplaced. That was not an employment discrimination case.
She also relies on several § 504 employment discrimination cases, decided prior to the
1978 amendments. See, *e.g.*, *Drennon* v. *Philadelphia General Hospital*, 428 F. Supp.

## III

Trageser also based her complaint on 42 U.S.C. § 1983, the fourteenth amendment, and the equal protection component of the due process clause in the fifth amendment. We conclude, however, that the district court correctly granted Libbie's motion to dismiss these claims.

Section 1983 requires Trageser to show that Libbie acted under color of either a state law or regulation or a state-enforced custom. *Adickes* v. *S. H. Kress & Co.*, 398 U.S. 144, 148, 161–69 (1970). To establish a denial of equal protection of the laws in violation of the fifth and fourteenth amendments, Trageser is required to do more than merely allege governmental regulation of the nursing home. She must demonstrate that Libbie's ostensibly private conduct was in reality an act of either the state or federal government. There must exist "a sufficiently close nexus between the State and the challenged action of the regulated entity so that the action of the latter may be fairly treated as that of the State itself." *Jackson* v. *Metropolitan Edison Co.*, 419 U.S. 345, 351 (1974). To satisfy this requirement, Trageser relies on (1) Libbie's receipt of public funds and (2) the state inspector's role in Libbie's decision to dismiss her.

Libbie did not participate in the Hill-Burton construction program which "subjects hospitals to an elaborate and intricate pattern of governmental regulations, both state and federal." See *Simkins* v. *Moses H. Cone Memorial Hospital*, 323 F.2d 959, 964 (4th Cir. 1963). Consequently, our decision in Simkins which detected state action in the operation of participating hospitals does not control here. Moreover, we have previously held that the receipt of Medicaid funds does not convert private medical care to state action. *Walker* v. *Pierce*, 560 F.2d 609 (4th Cir. 1977). For similar reasons, we decline to ascribe state action to Libbie's receipt of Medicare and Veterans Administration benefits.

To show state action, Trageser also relies on the query of the state inspector who, noting that her eyesight had deteriorated, asked what Libbie intended to do about it. The inspector did not include this observation about Trageser among the deficiencies found at the home, and Trageser does not allege that the state would or could impose any sanctions on Libbie if it continued to employ her. Libbie's subsequent decision to dismiss her, therefore, cannot be considered an action of the state itself. See *Jackson* v. *Metropolitan Edison Co.*, 419 U.S. 345, 351 (1974).

Consequently, neither Libbie's receipt of patients' benefits nor Virginia's regulation of the home constitutes state action sufficient to sustain the § 1983 and constitutional claims.

The judgment of the district court is affirmed.

---

809, 814–16, 14 FEP Cases 1385, 1390–91 (E.D. Pa. 1977); Gurmankin v. Costanzo, 411 F. Supp. 982, 989, 12 FEP Cases 1057, 1062 (E.D. Pa. 1976), aff'd on other grounds, 556 F.2d 184, 14 FEP Cases 1359 (3d Cir. 1977) (dicta). These cases, however, did not address the application of § 604 of Title VI.

# DAVIS v. BUCHER

*U.S. District Court, Eastern District of Pennsylvania, 1978*
*451 F. Supp. 791, 17 FEP Cases 918*

CAHN, District Judge: Plaintiffs have brought this action on behalf of themselves and others similarly situated to challenge the hiring practices of the City of Philadelphia (hereinafter "City") regarding job applicants with prior histories of drug abuse. The named plaintiffs, Woolworth Davis, Salvatore D'Elia, and Herbert Sims, Jr., claim they were denied employment solely on the basis of former drug use, without regard to their qualifications, present rehabilitative status or the nature of the job for which they had applied. Defendants are various City officials entrusted with the authority to develop and implement employment practices.

Plaintiffs allege that the hiring policy of the City of Philadelphia unlawfully discriminates against former drug abusers in violation of the Equal Protection Clause and the Due Process Clause of the United States Constitution. The plaintiffs also allege violations of the Federal Rehabilitation Act of 1973, 29 U.S.C. § 794, and the Civil Rights Act of 1871, 42 U.S.C. § 1983.

Plaintiffs have moved for summary judgment and class certification. The City has not opposed the class certification motion but has contested the merits of plaintiffs' legal claims. After careful consideration of the contentions of the parties and an independent review of the appropriateness of class certification, I grant both motions.

## FACTS

Since this is a summary judgment motion, I base my decision on undisputed facts and view these facts in the light most favorable to the party opposing the motion. The affidavits, depositions, and documentary evidence establish the following facts.

At various times, plaintiffs filed job applications with the City of Philadelphia. Plaintiff Davis reported for a medical examination on January 27, 1977, at the Municipal Medical Dispensary after having been notified by the City that he had been selected for the next class of firemen. (Davis affidavit, Par. 5–7.) During the examination the physician noticed a scar. Davis explained that during a four month period in 1972 he had used nonnarcotic amphetamines injected intravenously, but that he had not engaged in drug use since that time. The doctor agreed that the scar was old. (Davis Affidavit, Par. 3, 8.) Nevertheless, plaintiff was told that he could not be employed in any city job because the City would not hire anyone with a past drug history. It is undisputed that but for the scar on plaintiff's forearm and his admission of prior drug use, plaintiff Davis would have been hired as a fireman with the Philadelphia Fire Department. (Davis Affidavit, Par. 10, 11.)

Salvatore D'Elia is a former narcotics addict who has been enrolled in a methadone program. (D'Elia Affidavit, Par. 2.) Random urine samples required by federal law showed that he was using no drugs other than methadone. (D'Elia Affidavit, Par. 8.) D'Elia applied for a position with the City of Philadelphia under Title II of the Comprehensive Employment and Training Act (CETA), 29 U.S.C. 841, *et seq.* (D'Elia Affidavit, Par. 10.) He was referred for employment to both the Museum of Art as a security guard and the Philadelphia Civic Center as a laborer. On both occasions he was denied employment because of his history of drug use. (D'Elia Affidavit, Par. 11–12.) Next he was referred for a job as a physical property maintenance worker. He was accepted for employment and sent to the dispensary for a medical examination. At this time he was again rejected because of his former drug use. (D'Elia Affidavit, Par. 15.) Thus, on three separate occasions he was refused employment solely on the basis of his drug history.[1]

Plaintiff Herbert Sims is a former user of morphine and heroin. He took these drugs near the end of his two year tour of duty with the armed services. (Sims Affidavit, Par. 2.) He has been totally drug free since 1975. (Sims Affidavit, Par. 3–4.) Sims was accepted for employment by the Department of Streets subject to his passing a medical examination. (Sims Affidavit, Par. 7–8.) At the examination, plaintiff was told that pursuant to city personnel policy he was rejected for employment because of his admitted former drug abuse. (Sims Affidavit Par. 9.)

The facts, as demonstrated by the undisputed affidavits, show that Davis, D'Elia, and Sims are rehabilitated. They were all fully qualified for the positions for which they applied. At oral argument, counsel for the defense stipulated that but for the old scars and admissions of prior drug use the applicants would have been hired by the City of Philadelphia.[2]

### DISCUSSION

## I. THE SUMMARY JUDGMENT MOTION

### A. *The City's Policy Regarding Employment of Substance Abusers*

The City's policy concerning employment of narcotic substance abusers has been interpreted by the medical dispensary staff (Lawler deposition at pp. 10, 13–20, 17–19) to include past or present drug use, abuse, or addiction. According to the City, the policy is grounded in the City Civil Service Regulations 8.0233:

"The Director may refuse to examine an applicant or may disqualify a candidate at any time prior to appointment either during or after an

---

[1] [Footnotes numbered as in original.—Ed.] In early November, 1977, plaintiff was sent by the CETA office for an interview by the Department of Streets. Plaintiff was hired as a physical property maintenance worker and was sent for another physical examination. He passed the examination and the examining physician made no mention of his prior drug use.

[2] Three other persons who are not party to this litigation except as potential class members submitted affidavits establishing that they too were denied employment solely because of their prior drug use. Counsel for the City has not contested that this was the basis for their denial of employment.

examination . . . who is addicted to the intemperate use of intoxicating liquors, or the use of harmful drugs, . . ."

and 10.0910:

"The name of an eligible shall be removed from an eligible list for any of the following reasons: . . . Addiction to the intemperate use of intoxicating liquors or to the use of harmful drugs."

and in Section XIV of "Procedures & Policies Regarding Medical Examination":

"Generally, emotional instability, immaturity, psychosis, alcoholism, or drug addiction, are disqualifying for all positions."

The medical examination through which this policy is enforced is the last stage in the process of screening job applicants. The purpose of the medical examination is to determine whether a job applicant is medically qualified for the position for which he has applied. (Lawler Deposition at p. 7.) Counsel for the City has represented that the medical examiners have the discretion to overlook past drug use as a disqualifying characteristic for city employment. Counsel stipulates, however, that this discretion was not exercised with respect to the plaintiffs and the three nonparty affiants in the instant case and that an absolute bar to employment due to former drug use was imposed. In excluding plaintiffs from employment because of past drug use, the medical dispensary staff did not consider whether such a history of substance abuse medically disqualified a person from performing a particular job. At least with respect to the named plaintiffs and the three nonparty affiants, the effect of the City's policy was that, once it was revealed a prospective employee formerly used drugs, he would not be employed.

### B. Defendant's Policy Is Violative of § 504 of the Rehabilitation Act, 1973, 29 U.S.C. § 794

Plaintiffs claim that former drug addicts fall within the protection of the Rehabilitation Act of 1973, 29 U.S.C. § 701 et seq. (hereinafter "Act") and that the Act provides them with a remedy for the discrimination alleged here. Section 504 of the Act provides in pertinent part:

"No otherwise qualified handicapped individual in the United States, . . . shall, solely by reason of his handicap, be excluded from the participation in, be denied the benefits of, or be subject to discrimination under any program or activity receiving Federal financial assistance."

29 U.S.C. § 794. The City contends that Congress did not intend drug addicts to be included within the definition of handicapped for purposes of § 504. However, although there are no cases on point, I am persuaded that the clear words of the statute do encompass drug addiction.

29 U.S.C. § 706(b) defines a handicapped individual as:

"[A]ny person . . . who (a) has a physical or mental impairment which substantially limits one or more of such person's major life activities, (b) has a record of such impairment, or (c) is regarded as having such an impairment."

It is undisputed that drug addiction substantially affects an addict's ability to perform major life activities, defined by Department of Health, Education and Welfare regulations supplementing the Act, 42 Fed. Reg. 22686 *et seq.* (May 4, 1977) (hereinafter "the Regulations") as "caring for one's self, performing manual tasks, walking, seeing, hearing, speaking, breathing, learning, and working." Regulations § 84.2(j)(2)(ii). Furthermore, prior addiction and drug use clearly fall within the definition of having a "record of such impairment," 29 U.S.C. § 706(6)(c), as defined in § 84.2(j)(2)(iii) of the Regulations.[3]

Counsel for the City might reasonably have argued, absent any indication to the contrary, that Congress must have intended to differentiate drug use from other physical and mental handicaps because (1) it is a handicap voluntarily created by the handicapped person; and (2) drug possession and use are generally illegal and Congress could not have wished to compensate users for criminal activity. This argument, however, loses all force in view of the Department of Health, Education and Welfare analysis of the Act accompanying the Regulations. The analysis, at 42 Fed. Reg. 22686 (May 4, 1977) directly addresses and disposes of the issue of whether drug addicts are encompassed by the Act.

"The Secretary has carefully examined the issue and has obtained a legal opinion from the Attorney General. That opinion concludes that drug addiction and alcoholism are 'physical or mental impairments' within the meaning of section 7(6) of the Rehabilitation Act of 1973, as amended, and that drug addicts and alcoholics are therefore handicapped for purposes of section 504 if their impairment substantially limits one of their major life activities. The Secretary therefore believes that he is without authority to exclude these conditions from the definition. There is a medical and legal consensus that alcoholism and drug addiction are diseases although there is disagreement as to whether they are primarily mental or physical. In addition, while Congress did not focus specifically on the problems of drug addiction and alcoholism in enacting section 504, the committees that considered the Rehabilitation Act of 1973 were made aware of the Department's long-standing practice of treating addicts and alcoholics as handicapped individuals eligible for rehabilitation services under the Vocational Rehabilitation Act."

The conclusion that Congress intended to include past drug users within the protections of the Act is reasonable as a matter of public policy as well. Drug addiction is a serious public problem. It is therefore not surprising that Congress would wish to provide assistance for those who have overcome their addiction and give some support and incentive for those who are attempting to overcome it. The HEW regulations including drug addicts as handicapped individuals for purposes of § 504

---

[3] The HEW analysis of the regulations states:

"Under the definition of 'record' in paragraph (j)(2)(iii), persons who have a history of a handicapping condition but no longer have the condition, as well as persons who have been incorrectly classified as having such a condition, are protected from discrimination under section 504. Frequently occurring examples of the first group are persons with histories of mental or emotional illness, heart disease, or cancer. . . ."

merely recognize these realities. I therefore conclude that persons with histories of drug use, including present participants in methadone maintenance programs, are "handicapped individuals" within the meaning of the statutory and regulatory language.

The City treats drug users as if they were handicapped, yet discriminates against them. The Regulations provide that even pre-employment inquiries into handicaps are prohibited for purposes other than to determine "an applicant's ability to perform job-related functions." Regulations § 84.14(a). Although plaintiffs had met the requirements of all selection criteria except the medical examination, they were disqualified at the very final stage of the hiring process solely because of their former drug abuse. Furthermore, plaintiffs submitted uncontested evidence that persons with a history of substance abuse, and in particular ex-heroin addicts, could be employed successfully. (Affidavit of Thomas W. Collins, par. 14; Woody Affidavit, par. 29–34; Dodson Affidavit, par. 11.) See also *Beazer* v. *New York City Transit Authority,* 399 F. Supp. 1032, 1037, 1048–49, 1058 (S.D. N.Y. 1975), *aff'd,* 558 F.2d 97, 17 FEP Cases 226 (2d Cir. 1977). Thus, by virtue of the absolute exclusion from consideration for city employment, the City denied them the benefits of a program receiving federal financial assistance (*e.g.* CETA funds) in direct violation of the Act.[4]

---

[4] I emphasize, however, that the statute and regulation apply only to discrimination against qualified handicapped persons solely by reason of their handicap. If in any individual situation it can be shown that a particular addiction or prior drug use prevents successful performance of a job, the applicant need not be provided the employment opportunity in question. As stated in the HEW analysis of the Act:

"The Secretary wishes to reassure recipients that inclusion of addicts and alcoholics within the scope of the regulation will not lead to the consequences feared by many commenters. It cannot be emphasized too strongly that the statute and the regulation apply only to discrimination against qualified handicapped persons solely by reason of their handicap. The fact that drug addiction and alcoholism may be handicaps does not mean that these conditions must be ignored in determining whether an individual is qualified for services or employment opportunities. On the contrary, a recipient may hold a drug addict or alcoholic to the same standard of performance and behavior to which it holds others, even if any unsatisfactory performance or behavior is related to the person's drug addiction or alcoholism. In other words, while an alcoholic or drug addict may not be denied services or disqualified from employment solely because of his or her condition, the behavioral manifestations of the condition may be taken into account in determining whether he or she is qualified.

"With respect to the employment of a drug addict or alcoholic, if it can be shown that the addiction or alcoholism prevents successful performance of the job, the person need not be provided the employment opportunity in question. For example, in making employment decisions, a recipient may judge addicts and alcoholics on the same basis it judges all other applicants and employees. Thus, a recipient may consider—for all applicants including drug addicts and alcoholics—past personnel records, absenteeism, disruptive, abusive, or dangerous behavior, violations of rules and unsatisfactory work performance. Moreover, employers may enforce rules prohibiting the possession or use of alcohol or drugs in the work-place, provided that such rules are enforced against all employees."

42 Fed. Reg. 22686 (May 4, 1977). In this case, however, the City concedes that prior drug abuse and/or present maintenance on methadone are factors which alone do not detract from an applicant's qualifications.

# NOTE

In 1978 Congress amended the definition:

"(B) Subject to the second sentence of this subparagraph, the term 'handicapped individual' means, for purposes of titles IV and V of this Act, any person who (i) has a physical or mental impairment which substantially limits one or more of such person's major life activities, (ii) has a record of such an impairment, or (iii) is regarded as having such an impairment. For purposes of sections 503 and 504 as such sections relate to employment, such term does not include any individual who is an alcoholic or drug abuser whose current use of alcohol or drugs prevents such individual from performing the duties of the job in question or whose employment, by reason of such current alcohol or drug abuse, would constitute a direct threat to property or the safety of others." Pub. L. No. 95-602, 29 U.S.C.A. § 706(7)(B).

The Committee Report contained the following explanation:

### ALCOHOLICS AND DRUG ABUSERS

"H.R. 12467, as amended, also adopted an amendment by Representative John Erlenborn which would exclude alcoholics and drug abusers in need of rehabilitation from the definition of 'handicapped individual.' This amendment only applies, however, for the purposes of section 503 and 504 as they relate to employment discrimination. Active alcoholics and drug abusers would still be eligible for rehabilitation services.

"The committee emphasizes that an individual with a record of alcohol or drug abuse or who is regarded as being an individual who is an alcoholic or drug abuser may still be protected by the provisions of sections 503 and 504 if he or she is not in need of rehabilitation. This protects otherwise qualified self-reformed or rehabilitated alcoholics or drug abusers from unreasonable discrimination."

See 1978 U.S. Code Cong. and Adm. News, p. 7312.

## B.  STATE LEGISLATION

## CONNECTICUT GENERAL LIFE INSURANCE CO. v. DEPARTMENT OF INDUSTRY, LABOR & HUMAN RELATIONS

*Wisconsin Supreme Court, 1979*
*18 FEP Cases 1447*

BEILFUSS, Chief Justice: DILHR found the complainant had a "drinking problem," concluded it was a handicap and that the employer discharged the complainant because of his handicap contrary to Wisconsin's

Fair Employment Act.[1] A make-whole order was issued and is the subject of this appeal.

The dispositive issues as we view them are whether the evidence is sufficient to support the findings, and whether the findings of fact and conclusions of law are adequate. We conclude they are not and reverse.

On August 3, 1973, Gerald F. Bachand, the claimant, was discharged by petitioner-appellant Connecticut General Life Insurance Company. Bachand had been with Connecticut General in various positions in branch offices in several cities for over five years. At the time of his discharge he was an assistant manager in the company's Racine office, a position he had occupied since his promotion and transfer to the branch approximately one year earlier. The appellant-employer maintains that Bachand was fired for his unsatisfactory job performance. The respondent DILHR concluded that Bachand was discharged because of a handicap. The trial court affirmed this finding by DILHR.

George Bachand filed a complaint with DILHR on August 29, 1973, alleging discrimination and unlawful discharge by his former employer, the appellant Connecticut General Life Insurance Company, because of a handicap. The charge was routinely handled by a DILHR field representative. On the basis of her investigations, on May 15, 1974 an initial determination was made that there was probable cause to believe Connecticut General had discriminated against Bachand because of a handicap in violation of sec. 111.31–111.37, Stats. The department's conciliation effort over the next several months undertaken pursuant to sec. 111.36(3) proved unsuccessful, and on December 5, 1974 the matter was certified for hearing.

Notice of hearing dated April 30, 1975 was given the parties. Connecticut General responded on May 8, 1975, with an answer denying any unlawful discrimination on its part and alleging that Bachand was legitimately terminated for not properly discharging his duties, for acting beyond the scope of his authority and for having a disruptive influence on the other personnel in the office. In addition, it asserted affirmative defenses: first, that the complaint failed to state facts sufficient to constitute a cause of action; second, that alcoholism was not a handicap within the meaning of sec. 111.32 of the Wisconsin Fair Employment Act; third, that even if alcoholism were to be so classified, appellant's action in discharging Bachand was legitimated by the terms of the exemption in sec. 111.32(5)(f) since Bachand's drinking problem prevented him from adequately fulfilling his job-related responsibilities.

On June 5, 1975, a hearing was held on the complaint before a DILHR hearing examiner. Complainant George Bachand and Robert Strom, Regional Claims Manager of appellant company and Bachand's former supervisor, were the principal witnesses at the hearing. In addition, Kendra Piotrowski, office supervisor of the Racine branch, testified on behalf of the company, corroborating certain aspects of Strom's testimony.

---

1 [Footnotes numbered as in original.—Ed.] Sec. 111.31 *et seq.*, Stats.

George Bachand testified he worked for appellant company for more than five years. He joined the company as a junior claims representative, received several promotions and ultimately rose to the position of Assistant Manager of the company's Racine office—the position he occupied at the time of his termination. The company's annual progress evaluation reports ranked him as a satisfactory employee who met or exceeded company standards and had good potential. Strom himself had given Bachand a satisfactory rating seven months before deciding to discharge him. To the best of Bachand's knowledge, there had been no complaints from policyholders about the manner in which he handled their accounts.

In sharp contrast to Bachand's testimony, Strom testified that Bachand's work was frequently inconsistent and untimely throughout the entire time he had been with the Racine office. There had been many situations where Strom had received complaints from disgruntled policyholders that calls had not been returned or things had been delayed past promised or due dates. However, no written warnings had been given to Bachand. Kendra Piotrowski corroborated Strom's evaluation. She testified that files referred to Bachand were delayed "quite frequently." None of her staff wanted to submit work to Bachand for his approval for fear they would not get it back. From the end of 1972 on, Ms. Piotrowski would frequently report to Strom that Bachand was not doing his work.

The testimony at the hearing also revealed that the events which immediately preceded and allegedly triggered Bachand's termination were also in dispute. Bachand testified that he voluntarily admitted himself to DePaul Rehabilitation Hospital, a rehabilitation hospital for alcoholics and drug addicts, for a period of approximately one month from April 29, 1973 to May 26, 1973. He informed his supervisor Strom two days prior to his admittance. At this time Strom was very supportive; he told Bachand that he had been doing a good job and was generally encouraging. On his return Bachand essentially resumed the same duties as before, with the additional management of a new project involving the computerization of Long Term Disability (LTD) benefit policies.

On May 30, 1973, just four days after his release from DePaul, Bachand and Strom had a meeting. According to Bachand's testimony, at this meeting Strom "informed me that the personnel department told him to tell me that if I had one slip I'd be placed on disability retirment." Strom in his testimony denied making that statement. Strom also asked to receive Bachand's medical records and a written statement from his treating psychiatrist indicating what he could and could not do. Bachand testified that the usual post-sick leave procedure was simply to provide a "certification" for work letter from the physician. At the end of June, Bachand left for vacation. At this time there was no indication that the LTD project was falling behind. On July 10, 1973, shortly after returning from his vacation, he received a letter signed by Strom placing him on "demand performance." In a meeting the following day, Strom explained that this was due to the fact that the LTD computer conversion project had fallen seriously behind in his absence and had required extensive overtime work by other employees to meet the scheduled deadline. Approximately twenty days after being placed on probation Bachand received a termination letter effective August 3, 1973.

Bachand contends that his loss of favor with the company from the time his drinking problem became known to his ultimate firing, his previous satisfactory work record, and the lack of substantial reasons for termination cited by the company justify the conclusion that he was discharged because of his handicap.

Strom's testimony concerning the two-month period between Bachand's return from sick leave and his ultimate termination was very different. Strom testified that Bachand totally failed to implement the LTD program before leaving for vacation and consequently left the entire unit without direction during his absence. Strom also testified that Bachand neglected an important account, the White Pin Corporation, by failing to make timely return telephone calls. Furthermore, he improperly injected himself into personnel problems, contrary to their express agreement, and caused serious upset among the staff. Bachand had earlier testified that the White Pin calls had been returned in two days and that any involvement he had in personnel matters was at Mr. Strom's specific request. With respect to the demand for medical reports, Strom testified that he had followed routine procedure for lengthy disability and hospitalization cases. He further testified that while he did in fact read the medical records, they did not influence his discharge decision. Strom also stated that he considered the twenty-day probationary period sufficient in Bachand's case, although the average demand performance period was about sixty days. He also testified that Bachand was not terminated because of his drinking problem but because of his unsatisfactory job performance, citing specifically the LTD program, the White Pin affair, and interference in personnel problems.

After the hearing, recommended findings, conclusions, order and relief were made and duly served on the parties. Timely exceptions were filed on behalf of the company. Oral argument on the recommended decision was had before the commission of the department on October 28, 1975. The recommended findings and conclusions of the hearing examiner were adopted by the commission without exception. The relevant findings are as follows:

"...

"4. On April 29, 1973 Complainant voluntarily entered the DePaul Rehabilitation Hospital for treatment of a drinking problem which he had had for the previous ten years.

"...

"9. Respondent terminated Complainant on July 31, 1973 purportedly for mishandling personnel matters and undue delay in returning a client's call.

"10. Previous to Complainant's hospitalization he had received periodic ratings by management personnel of Respondent, and all his ratings were satisfactory or better."

Significantly, the recommended and adopted findings contained no specific finding that Bachand's "drinking problem" was—or had been diagnosed as—alcoholism.

The conclusions of law provide in pertinent part:

" . . .

"2. Complainant is handicapped within the meaning of the Act. *Chicago, Milwaukee, St. Paul & Pacific Railroad* v. *Department of Industry, Labor and Human Relations*, 62 Wis.2d 392, 8 FEP Cases 938 (1974).

"3. Respondent terminated Complainant because Complainant's drinking problem became known when he sought treatment for it.

"4. Respondent has failed to carry its burden of establishing that Complainant was physically or otherwise unable to efficiently perform at the standard set by his employer the duties of the job."

The recommended order and relief of the hearing examiner was also adopted, with certain modifications not material to the questions raised in the proceeding. The final order, issued on November 5, 1975, provided in part:

"a. Respondent shall cease and desist from discriminating against the Complainant because of his handicap.

"b. Respondent shall immediately offer to reinstate Complainant to his former position or its substantial equivalent with full seniority and other rights to which he would have been entitled had he not been terminated.

"c. Respondent shall immediately clear Complainant's employment record of any derogatory comments related to his drinking problem that it may contain.

"d. Respondent shall immediately make Complainant whole for any losses in pay and benefits he has suffered by reason of the unlawful discharge. . . ."

On December 2, 1976, a petition for judicial review of the department's order was filed in the Circuit Court for Dane County by petitioner-appellant company, seeking reversal on the ground that the department's decision was arbitrary and capricious and unsupported by substantial evidence in view of the entire record as submitted.

An order affirming the decision and order of the department was entered in the Circuit Court for Dane County on December 4, 1976. JUDGE TORPHY, JR., in a memorandum decision set forth the court's reasoning. Support for the court's initial conclusion that a "drinking problem" constituted a handicap under the Fair Employment Act was derived from three sources: the language of this court in *Chicago, M., St. P. & P. R.R. Co.* v. *ILHR Dept.*, 62 Wis.2d 392, 396, 215 N.W.2d 443, 8 FEP Cases 938 (1974); the legislative policy the Act was designed to further; and common knowledge that alcoholism can operate to make achievement unusually difficult. It is apparent from the language of the decision that the court took "drinking problem" to mean "alcoholism."

The court's conclusion that the decision was supported by substantial evidence was based on a review of the record. With specific respect to Bachand's alleged alcoholism, the court declared, "The evidence certainly supported the finding that the employe had a drinking problem."

The legislature of this state has enacted a Fair Employment Act which prohibits discrimination in the hiring, firing and promotion of employees because of age, race, creed, color, handicap, sex, and national ancestry or origin. The Act is contained in ch. 111 of the statutes and the parts pertinent to the issues before us are as follows:

"SUBCHAPTER II

"FAIR EMPLOYMENT

"111.31 *Declaration of policy.* (1) The practice of denying employment and other opportunities to, and discriminating against, properly qualified persons by reason of their age, race, creed, color, handicap, sex, national origin or ancestry, is likely to foment domestic strife and unrest, and substantially and adversely affect the general welfare of a state by depriving it of the fullest utilization of its capacities for production. The denial by some employers, licensing agencies and labor unions of employment opportunities to such persons solely because of their age, race, creed, color, handicap, sex, national origin or ancestry, and discrimination against them in employment, tends to deprive the victims of the earnings which are necessary to maintain a just and decent standard of living, thereby committing grave injury to them.

"(2) It is believed by many students of the problem that protection by law of the rights of all people to obtain gainful employment, and other privileges free from discrimination because of age, race, creed, color, handicap, sex, national origin or ancestry, would remove certain recognized sources of strife and unrest, and encourage the full utilization of the productive resources of the state to the benefit of the state, the family and to all the people of the state.

"(3) In the interpretation and application of this subchapter, and otherwise, it is declared to be the public policy of the state to encourage and foster to the fullest extent practicable the employment of all properly qualified persons regardless of their age, race, creed, color, handicap, sex, national origin or ancestry. This subchapter shall be liberally construed for the accomplishment of this purpose."

"111.32 *Definitions.* When used in this subchapter:

". . .

"(5)(a) 'Discrimination' means discrimination because of age, race, color, handicap, sex, creed, national origin or ancestry, by an employer or licensing agency individually or in concert with others, against any employe or any applicant for employment or licensing, in regard to his hire, tenure or term, condition or privilege of employment or licensing.

. . .

". . .

"(c) Nothing in this subsection shall be construed to prevent termination of the employment of any person physically or otherwise unable to perform his duties, . . .

". . .

"(f) It is discrimination because of handicap:

"1. For an employer, labor organization, licensing agency or other person to refuse to hire, employ, admit or license, or to bar or to terminate from employment, membership or licensure any individual, or to discriminate against any individual in promotion, compensation or in terms, conditions or privileges of employment unless such handicap is reasonably related to the individual's ability adequately to undertake the job-related responsibilities of that individual's employment, membership or licensure."

Analysis of the questions raised by the parties in this case is difficult by the lack of clarity and precision in the findings and conclusions of the hearing examiner. Before reaching the matters argued both by the parties and by the Amicus Curiae, the threshold issue whether the findings made by the department are sufficiently definite and certain must be decided. Review of the department's decision and of the record of the hearing reveals that they are not.

Ch. 227, Stats., sets out the standards for an agency decision. Sec. 227.10 (formerly sec. 227.13) declares as follows:

"227.10 *Decisions*. Every decision of an agency following a hearing shall be in writing accompanied by findings of fact and conclusions of law. The findings of fact shall consist of a concise and separate statement of the ultimate conclusions upon each material issue of fact without recital of evidence."

The necessity of providing a clear statement of findings was recently reiterated by this court in *Edmonds* v. *Board of Fire & Police Commrs.,* 66 Wis.2d 337, 225 N.W.2d 575 (1975). While the court was not speaking specifically of the requirements of ch. 227 since the body in question was the Board of Fire & Police Commissioners of the City of Milwaukee and not a state agency, its language is apropos.

We do not mean to state that the statutory standards for agency decisions in ch. 227, Stats., have been given a rigid and inflexible cast. Where the evidence is clear and convincing, this court, or the trial court, can supply a finding of fact—missing from the agency decision—where it might be required. And a mislabeled finding will be treated by the reviewing court as what it is rather than as what it is called. Nonetheless, sec. 227.10 (and its predecessor sec. 227.13) has been interpreted to require remand when an administrative body has omitted necessary factual findings or when the factual basis for the decision is otherwise uncertain and unclear in cases where the evidence in the record is inconclusive or totally lacking, thus making it impossible for the court to supply the necessary finding on review. *Consolidated Const. Co., Inc.* v. *Casey,* 71 Wis.2d 811, 819, 238 N.W.2d 758 (1976), and *Edmonds, supra,* 66 Wis.2d at 349.

In the present case the department's decision contains only three statements—one classed as a finding of fact, two as conclusions of law—which specifically relate to Bachand's alleged handicap:

"4. On April 29, 1973 Complainant voluntarily entered the DePaul

Rehabilitation Hospital for treatment of a drinking problem which he
had had for the previous ten years."

"2. Complainant is handicapped within the meaning of the Act.
*Chicago, Milwaukee, St. Paul & Pacific Railroad* v. *Department of Industry, Labor and Human Relations,* 62 Wis.2nd, 392, 8 FEP Cases 938
(1974).

"3. Respondent terminated Complainant because Complainant's drinking problem became known when he sought treatment for it."

These statements do not reveal what the department actually understood
Bachand's handicap to be. Nowhere in the decision is the term "drinking
problem" expressly explained. Nor can it be inferred from the language
of the findings and conclusions as a whole that the department implicitly
equated the vague expression "drinking problem" with the medical term
"alcoholism." The trial court's automatic assumption to that effect was
unjustified.

The term "drinking problem" can mean different things to many persons. It has been used in common parlance to denote everything from
chronic alcoholism to an occasional secret second Sunday sherry. Used,
as it is here by the department, without explanation or elaboration, the
phrase conveys very little denotative meaning. It is an unfortunate choice
of words for a summary of factual findings and legal conclusions because
it can very well be used to avoid or at least to blur a clear statement of
one's actual meaning.

The evidence in the hearing record is equally unenlightening and inconclusive. The only testimony regarding Bachand's problem is that of
Bachand himself. He described his "drinking problem" in the following
way:

"I went to DePaul Rehabilitation Hospital on April 29, 1973.

". . .

". . . DePaul Rehabilitation Hospital is a rehabilitation hospital for
alcoholics and drug addicts.

". . .

"I had a history of drinking for ten years prior to that. The frequency
increased. The amount didn't increase but I was drinking more often
during the week. I was waking up in the mornings feeling tense; some
mornings I had the shakes. My drinking was confined to night. I never
drank on the job. It was just around 10:00 o'clock and thereafter. I had
a history of insomnia and at first I thought it was a panacea and it turned
out to be worse."

No medical evidence was received concerning the exact nature and
severity of Bachand's condition. The appellant company attempted to
offer Bachand's medical record in evidence. Complainant Bachand objected to the admittance of the documents, claiming they were both irrelevant and highly confidential. The objection was sustained and the
medical records were excluded.

To further cloud matters, Bachand's counsel made reference to Bach-
and's "alcoholism problem" several times in questioning. In addition

Bachand in his original complaint to DILHR used the term "alcoholism" to describe his alleged handicap. However, there is simply not enough evidence in the record and in the language of the department's decision for this court to hold that the department rested its conclusion that Bachand was handicapped on the fact that his drinking problem constituted alcoholism. The evidence is also insufficient to allow the court in this review to formulate a clear definition—short of alcoholism—of a "drinking problem" handicap. Indeed, to attempt to do so in view of the department's expertise in the area and in light of the fact that this is an important case of first impression would be inappropriate.[5]

If the department's use of the phrase "drinking problem" is construed to mean "alcoholism"—as the amicus curiae and the trial court assume and as the appellant puts forward as one possible interpretation—an additional difficulty arises. Alcoholism is a disease. Its diagnosis is a matter of expert medical opinion proved by a physician and not by a layman. *State* v. *Freiberg*, 35 Wis.2d 480, 101, 151 N.W.2d 1 (1967).

Our opinion in *Chicago, M., St. P. R.R. Co.* v. *ILHR Dept.*, 62 Wis.2d 392, 215 N.W.2d 443, 8 FEP Cases 938 (1974), is cited as authority for the proposition that Bachand was a handicapped person. We do not construe it as such. In that case the handicapped employee suffered from the medically diagnosed disease of asthma which did not affect his ability to perform the tasks assigned. In this case "drinking problem" is not defined nor even the extent of Bachand's problem. Nor do we know whether his drinking was volitional or non-volitional, nor whether it had progressed to medically definable alcoholism. If his drinking was volitional it hardly can be classified as a handicap within the meaning of our anti-discrimination statute. No medical testimony was presented in this case. A conclusion that Bachand's handicap was alcoholism without competent evidence of a medical diagnosis to that effect would be error.

We do not mean to infer that the substantive issue involved in this case is not an important one. It is. ". . . [I]t cannot be denied that the destructive use of alcoholic beverages is one of our principal social and public health problems." *Powell* v. *Texas*, 392 U.S. 514, 526–27 (1968). Alcohol is "not just 'one more' drug of dependence—it's *the major and original drug of dependence and addiction*." Vol. 3, *Contemporary Drug Problems*, "Alcohol-the All-American Drug of Choice," p. 101, 105 (1974).

It is because the matter here is a serious one of first impression that clarity and certainty in the department's decision are of critical importance. It cannot be concluded with any degree of certainty from the language of the decision and the meager and inconclusive evidence in the record that the department understood Bachand's drinking problem to be something other than alcoholism and based its legal conclusion upon an implicit finding to that effect. Nor would the court be justified in making the alternative assumption, i.e., that the factual foundation of the decision that Bachand was handicapped rested on an unexpressed

---

[5] Cf. *Consolidated Const. Co.* v. *Casey, supra,* 71 Wis. 2d at 818.

finding that Bachand's drinking problem did in fact constitute the disease
of alcoholism. The latter assumption would be particularly inappropriate
if made without benefit of expert opinion on the complex medical and
social questions involved because it might well operate to foreclose consideration of the important advantages in providing treatment, assistance
and legal protection for those who misuse alcohol before the medically
diagnosable disease stage is reached.[6]

The findings and conclusions of the Department of Industry, Labor
and Human Relations are insufficiently clear and certain to satisfy the
provisions of sec. 227.10, Stats. It cannot be ascertained from the decision
or from the evidence in the record whether the conclusion that Bachand
was handicapped rested on the fact that his drinking problem constituted
the disease of alcoholism or an undefined—and on this record undefinable
—condition short of that. The case must be remanded to the department
for more specific findings.

The department may conduct additional hearings if in its discretion
such hearings are necessary or desirable.

*By the Court.* Judgment reversed and remanded for further proceedings
not inconsistent with this opinion.

## CHRYSLER OUTBOARD CORP. v. DEPARTMENT OF INDUSTRY, LABOR & HUMAN RELATIONS

*Wisconsin Circuit Court, Dane County, 1976*

*14 FEP Cases 344*

MICHAEL B. TORPHY, JR., Circuit Judge: This matter is before the
Court on a petition for review of an order of the Department of Industry,
Labor and Human Relations (hereafter Department) dated December 23,
1975. In its Findings of Fact and Conclusions of Law the Department
found that the petitioner, Chrysler Outboard Corp. (hereafter Chrysler),
discriminated against the complainant on the basis of a handicap when
it refused to hire him due to his admission that he had acute lymphocytic
leukemia.

Chrysler admits that it refused to hire the complainant because of his
disease on the recommendation of its medical consultant, Michael J.
Malley, M.D. Dr. Malley based his recommendation on his assessment
that, due to complainant's disease, he ran a high risk of infection from
normal or minor injury, a risk of prolonged recuperation from such
injuries or infections, and a risk of complications from such injuries or
the disease itself, all of which would cause much lost time. In addition
Chrysler stated that it took into consideration the higher costs of insuring
the complainant, as required by their union contract.

---

6 Cf. Block, ALOHOLISM—ITS FACETS AND PHASES, 27 (1965); Davies, "Is Alcoholism
Really a Disease," Vol. 3, *Contemporary Drug Problems* 197, 210 (1974); 83 HARV. L.
REV. 739, *The "Disease Concept of Alcoholism"*; AMER. J. PSYCHIAT, 129.2, August
1972, *Criteria for the Diagnosis of Alcoholism.*

The issue before the Court is whether the Department could find and conclude that Chrysler committed a discriminatory practice within the meaning of the Wisconsin Fair Employment Act by refusing to hire the complainant because he suffers from acute lymphocytic leukemia.

The Department's findings of fact are conclusive if supported by substantial evidence, *Chicago, M., St. P. & P. R.R. Co. v. ILHR Dept.* (1974), 62 Wis.2d 392, 396, 215 N.W.2d 443, 8 FEP Cases 938, 940, and its conclusions of law will be affirmed if not without reason nor inconsistent with the purpose of the Act; *City of Milwaukee v. Wisconsin Employment Relations Commission* (1975), 71 Wis.2d 309, 239 N.W.2d 63, 91 LRRM 3019.

The petitioner alleges that the Department erred in concluding that the complainant's disease constituted a handicap within the meaning of the Fair Employment Act. Petitioner's arguments evidence a lack of understanding of the use of the word "handicap" in Wisconsin Statutes and case law. "Handicap" is not defined in terms of an individual's reduced ability to physically perform a specific job function. In fact, sec. 111.32 (5)(f), Wis. Stats. specifically states that an employer is not required to hire an applicant ". . . who because of a handicap is physically or otherwise unable to efficiently perform, at the standards set by the employer, the duties required in that job."

In *Chicago M., St. P. & P. R.R. Co. v. ILHR Dept.* (1974), 62 Wis.2d 392, 398, 215 N.W.2d 443, 8 FEP Cases 938, 940, the Wisconsin Supreme Court defined handicap as ". . . a disadvantage that makes achievement unusually difficult; esp.: a physical disability that limits the capacity to work." In that case the Court approved a Department conclusion that the complainant's history of asthma constituted a handicap. If an employee's illness or defect makes it more difficult for him to find work, then it certainly operates to make achievement unusually difficult. The petitioner's refusal to hire the complainant in the instant case because of his illness is a classic example of how such an illness operates as a handicap. Complainant's illness clearly constitutes a "handicap" within the meaning of the Wisconsin Fair Employment Act.

Chrysler also alleges that the Department erred in finding that it discriminated against the complainant on the basis of handicap by refusing to hire him. The petitioner argues that its decision not to hire the complainant, based on the recommendation of its medical consultant, was a sound business decision in view of the higher risk of absenteeism and increased insurance costs and was therefore not discriminatory. Once again the petitioner misapprehends the intent of the statute. An employer's refusal to hire a person solely on the basis of a handicap operates to discriminate against him regardless of the intent of the employer.

The Act prohibits discrimination in employment in the broadest sense and the only exceptions are written right into the statute. Section 111.32 (5)(f), Wis. Stats. provides:

"The prohibition against discrimination because of handicap does not apply to failure of an employer to employ or retain as an employe any person who because of a handicap is physically or otherwise unable to efficiently perform, at the standards set by the employer, the duties required in that job. An employer's exclusion of a handicapped employe from life or disability coverage, or reasonable restriction of such coverage, shall not constitute discrimination."

At no point in this case did Chrysler contend that the complainant was unable to perform, at the standards set by the employer, the duties required by the job. Instead the petitioner based its decision on the risk of future absenteeism and the higher insurance costs. Neither of these factors constitute a legal basis for discriminating against the complainant. The statute is written in the present tense. The petitioner's contention that the complainant may at some future date be unable to perform the duties of the job is immaterial. In addition, although the statute does permit some discrimination in insurance coverage offered to a handicapped employee, it does not permit an employer to discriminate in hiring on the basis of increased insurance costs.

In summary, the Department's conclusions of law in this case are reasonable and carry out the intent and purpose of the Act. The findings of fact are neither arbitrary nor capricious and are founded on substantial evidence. Accordingly, the order of the Department dated December 23, 1975, is affirmed.

# 10. EEO and the Constitution

## A. PURPOSEFUL DISCRIMINATION AND VETERANS' PREFERENCE

### PERSONNEL ADMINISTRATOR OF MASSACHUSETTS v. FEENEY

*Supreme Court of the United States, 1979*

*_____ U.S. _____, 47 USLW 4650*

MR. JUSTICE STEWART delivered the opinion of the Court.

This case presents a challenge to the constitutionality of the Massachusetts Veterans Preference Statute, Mass. Gen. Laws, ch. 31, § 23, on the ground that it discriminates against women in violation of the Equal Protection Clause of the Fourteenth Amendment. Under ch. 31, § 23, all veterans who qualify for state civil service positions must be considered for appointment ahead of any qualifying nonveterans. The preference operates overwhelmingly to the advantage of males.

The appellee Helen B. Feeney is not a veteran. She brought this action pursuant to 42 U.S.C. § 1983 alleging that the absolute preference formula established in ch. 31, § 23 inevitably operates to exclude women from consideration for the best Massachusetts civil service jobs and thus unconstitutionally denies them the equal protection of the laws.[2] The three-judge District Court agreed, one judge dissenting. *Anthony v. Commonwealth of Massachusetts*, 415 F. Supp. 485 (1976).[3]

The District Court found that the absolute preference afforded by Massachusetts to veterans has a devastating impact upon the employment opportunities of women. Although it found that the goals of the prefer-

---

[2] [Footnotes numbered as in original.—Ed.] No statutory claim was brought under Title VII of the Civil Rights Act of 1964, 42 U.S.C. § 2000e *et seq*. Section 712 of the Act, 42 U.S.C. § 2000e–11, provides that "nothing in this subchapter shall be construed to repeal or modify any federal, State, territorial or local law creating special rights or preference for veterans." The parties have evidently assumed that this provision precludes a Title VII challenge.

[3] The appellee's case had been consolidated with a similar action brought by Carol B. Anthony, a lawyer whose efforts to obtain a civil service Counsel I position had been frustrated by ch. 31, § 23. In 1975, Massachusetts exempted all attorney positions from the preference, 1975 Mass. Acts, ch. 134, and Anthony's claims were accordingly found moot by the District Court. *Anthony v. Commonwealth of Massachusetts*, 415 F. Supp. 485, 495.

ence were worthy and legitimate and that the legislation had not been enacted for the purpose of discriminating against women, the court reasoned that its exclusionary impact upon women was nonetheless so severe as to require the State to further its goals through a more limited form of preference. Finding that a more modest preference formula would readily accommodate the State's interest in aiding veterans, the court declared ch. 31, § 23 unconstitutional and enjoined its operation.

Upon an appeal taken by the Attorney General of Massachusetts, this Court vacated the judgment and remanded the case for further consideration in light of our intervening decision in *Washington* v. *Davis,* 426 U.S. 229. *Feeney* v. *Commonwealth of Massachusetts,* 434 U.S. 1977. The *Davis* case held that a neutral law does not violate the Equal Protection Clause solely because it results in a racially disproportionate impact; instead the disproportionate impact must be traced to a purpose to discriminate on the basis of race. 426 U.S., at 238–244.

Upon remand, the District Court, one judge concurring and one judge again dissenting, concluded that a veterans' hiring preference is inherently nonneutral because it favors a class from which women have traditionally been excluded, and that the consequences of the Massachusetts absolute preference formula for the employment opportunities of women were too inevitable to have been "unintended." Accordingly, the court reaffirmed its original judgment. *Feeney* v. *Commonwealth of Massachusetts,* 451 F. Supp. 143. The Attorney General again appealed to this Court pursuant to 28 U.S.C. § 1253, and probable jurisdiction of the appeal was noted. _____ U.S. _____.

## I
## A

The Federal Government and virtually all of the States grant some sort of hiring preference to veterans.[6] The Massachusetts preference, which is loosely termed an "absolute lifetime" preference, is among the most generous.[7] It applies to all positions in the State's classified civil service,

---

[6] The first comprehensive federal veterans' statute was enacted in 1944. Veterans' Preference Act of 1944, ch. 287, 58 Stat. 387. The Federal Government has, however, engaged in preferential hiring of veterans, through official policies and various special laws, since the Civil War. See, *e.g.,* Res. of March 3, 1865, No. 27, 13 Stat. 571 (hiring preference for disabled veterans). See generally The Provision of Federal Benefits for Veterans, An Historical Analysis of Major Veterans' Legislation, 1862–1954, Committee Print No. 171, 84th Cong., 1st Sess. (House Comm. on Vets. Affairs, Dec. 28, 1955) 258–265. For surveys of state veterans' preference laws, many of which also date back to the late 19th century, see State Veterans' Laws, Digest of State Laws Regarding Rights, Benefits and Privileges of Veterans and Their Dependents, House Committee on Veterans' Affairs, 91st Cong., 1st Sess. (1969); Fleming & Shanor, *Veterans Preferences in Public Employment: Unconstitutional Gender Discrimination?,* 26 EMORY L. J. 13 (1977).

[7] The forms of veterans' hiring preferences vary widely. The Federal Government and approximately 41 States grant veterans a point advantage on civil service examinations, usually 10 points for a disabled veteran and 5 for one who is not disabled. See Fleming & Shanor, *supra* n. 6, 26 EMORY L. J., at 17, and n. 12 (citing statutes). A few offer only tie-breaking preferences. *Id.* n. 14 (citing statutes). A very few States, like Massachusetts, extend absolute hiring or positional preferences to qualified veterans. *Id.* n. 13. See,

which constitute approximately 60 percent of the public jobs in the State. It is available to "any person, male or female, including a nurse," who was honorably discharged from the United States Armed Forces after at least 90 days of active service, at least one day of which was during "wartime." Persons who are deemed veterans and who are otherwise qualified for a particular civil service job may exercise the preference at any time and as many times as they wish.

Civil service positions in Massachusetts fall into two general categories, labor and official. For jobs in the official service, with which the proofs in this action were concerned, the preference mechanics are uncomplicated. All applicants for employment must take competitive examinations. Grades are based on a formula that gives weight both to objective test results and to training and experience. Candidates who pass are then ranked in the order of their respective scores on an "eligible list." Ch. 31, § 23 requires, however, that disabled veterans, veterans, and surviving spouses and surviving parents of veterans be ranked—in the order of their respective scores—above all other candidates.[10]

Rank on the eligible list and availability for employment are the sole factors that determine which candidates are considered for appointment to an official civil service position. When a public agency has a vacancy, it requisitions a list of "certified eligibles" from the state personnel division. Under formulas prescribed by civil service rules, a small number of candidates from the top of an appropriate list, three if there is only one vacancy, are certified. The appointing agency is then required to choose from among these candidates. Although the veterans' preference thus does not guarantee that a veteran will be appointed, it is obvious that the preference gives to veterans who achieve passing scores a well-nigh absolute advantage.

## B

The appellee has lived in Dracut, Mass. most of her life. She entered the workforce in 1948, and for the next 14 years worked at a variety of jobs in the private sector. She first entered the state civil service system

---

*e.g.*, N.J. Stat. Ann. 11: 27–4 (West 1977); S.D. Comp. Laws Ann. § 33–3–1 (1968); Utah Code Ann. § 34–30–11; Wash. Rev. Code §§ 41.04.010, 73.16.010 (1976).

10 Ch. 131, § 23 provides in full:

"The names of persons who pass examination for appointment to any position classified under the civil service shall be placed upon the eligible lists in the following order:

"(1) Disabled veterans . . . in the order of their respective standing; (2) veterans in the order of their respective standing; (3) persons described in section 23 B [the widow or widowed mother of a veteran killed in action or who died from a service-connected disability incurred in wartime service and who has not remarried] in the order of their respective standing; (4) other applicants in the order of their respective standing. Upon receipt of a requisition, names shall be certified from such lists according to the method of certification prescribed by the civil service rules. A disabled veteran shall be retained in employment in preference to all other persons, including veterans."

A 1977 amendment extended the dependents' preference to "surviving spouses," and "surviving parents." 1977 Mass. Acts, 1977, ch. 815.

in 1963, having competed successfully for a position as Senior Clerk Stenographer in the Massachusetts Civil Defense Agency. There she worked for four years. In 1967 she was promoted to the position of Federal Funds and Personnel Coordinator in the same Agency. The Agency, and with it her job, was eliminated in 1975.

During her 12-year tenure as a public employee, Ms. Feeney took and passed a number of open competitive civil service examinations. On several she did quite well, receiving in 1971 the second highest score on an examination for a job with the Board of Dental Examiners, and in 1973 the third highest on a test for an Administrative Assistant position with a mental health center. Her high scores, however, did not win her a place on the certified eligible list. Because of the veterans' preference, she was ranked sixth behind five male veterans on the Dental Examiner list. She was not certified, and a lower scoring veteran was eventually appointed. On the 1973 examination, she was placed in a position on the list behind 12 male veterans, 11 of whom had lower scores. Following the other examinations that she took, her name was similarly ranked below those of veterans who had achieved passing grades.

Ms. Feeney's interest in securing a better job in state government did not wane. Having been consistently eclipsed by veterans, however, she eventually concluded that further competition for civil service positions of interest to veterans would be futile. In 1975, shortly after her civil defense job was abolished, she commenced this litigation.

## C

The veterans' hiring preference in Massachusetts, as in other jurisdictions, has traditionally been justified as a measure designed to reward veterans for the sacrifice of military service, to ease the transition from military to civilian life, to encourage patriotic service, and to attract loyal and well-disciplined people to civil service occupations.[12] See, e.g., Hutcheson v. Director of Civil Service, 361 Mass. 480, 281 N.E. 2d 53 (1973). The Massachusetts law dates back to 1884, when the State, as part of its first civil service legislation, gave a statutory preference to civil service applicants who were Civil War veterans if their qualifications were equal to those of nonveterans. 1884 Mass. Acts, ch. 320, § 16. This tie-breaking provision blossomed into a truly absolute preference in 1895, when the State enacted its first general veterans preference law and exempted veterans from all merit selection requirements. 1895 Mass. Acts, ch. 501, § 2. In response to a challenge brought by a male nonveteran,

---

[12] Veterans' preference laws have been challenged so often that the rationale in their support has become essentially standardized. See, e.g., Koelfgen v. Jackson, 355 F. Supp. 243 (Minn. 1972), summarily aff'd 410 U.S. 976; August v. Bronstein, 369 F. Supp. 190 (SDNY 1974), summarily aff'd, 417 U.S. 901; Rios v. Dillman, 499 F.2d 329 (CA5 1974); cf. Mitchell v. Cohen, 333 U.S. 411, 419 n. 12. See generally Blumberg, De Facto and De Jure Sex Discrimination Under the Equal Protection Clause: A Reconsideration of the Veterans' Preference in Public Employment, 26 BUFFALO L. REV. 3 (1977). For a collection of early cases, see Annot., Veterans' Preference Laws, 161 A.L.R. 494 (1946).

this statute was declared violative of state constitutional provisions guaranteeing that government should be for the "common good" and prohibiting hereditary titles. *Brown* v. *Russell,* 166 Mass. 14 (1896).

The current veterans' preference law has its origins in an 1896 statute, enacted to meet the state constitutional standards enunciated in *Brown* v. *Russell.* That statute limited the absolute preference to veterans who where otherwise qualified. 1896 Mass. Acts, ch. 517, § 2. A closely divided Supreme Judicial Court, in an advisory opinion issued the same year, concluded that the preference embodied in such a statute would be valid. *Opinion of the Justices,* 166 Mass. 589 (1896). In 1919, when the preference was extended to cover the veterans of World War I, the formula was further limited to provide for a priority in eligibility, in contrast to an absolute preference in hiring. 1919 Mass. Acts, ch. 150, § 2. See *Corliss* v. *Civil Service Comm'rs,* 242 Mass. 61. In *Mayor of Lynn* v. *Comm'r of Civil Service,* 269 Mass. 410, 414, the Supreme Judicial Court, adhering to the views expressed in its 1896 advisory opinion, sustained this statute against a state constitutional challenge.

Since 1919, the preference has been repeatedly amended to cover persons who served in subsequent wars, declared or undeclared. See 1943 Mass. Acts, ch. 194; 1949 Mass. Acts, ch. 642, § 2 (World War II); 1954 Mass. Acts, ch. 627 (Korea); 1968 Mass. Acts, ch. 531, § 1 (Vietnam). The current preference formula in ch. 31, § 23 is substantially the same as that settled upon in 1919. This absolute preference—even as modified in 1919—has never been universally popular. Over the years it has been subjected to repeated legal challenges, see *Hutcheson* v. *Director of Civil Service, supra* (collecting cases), criticism by civil service reform groups, see, *e.g.,* Report of the Massachusetts Committee on Public Service on Initiative Bill Relative to Veterans' Preference, S. No. 279 (Feb. 1926); Report of Massachusetts Special Commission on Civil Service and Public Personnel Administration 37–43 (June 15, 1967) (hereinafter 1967 Report), and in 1926 to a referendum in which it was reaffirmed by a majority of 51.9 percent. See 1967 Report, *supra,* at 38. The present case is apparently the first to challenge the Massachusetts' veterans' preference on the simple ground that it discriminates on the basis of sex.[16]

## D

The first Massachusetts veterans' preference statute defined the term "veterans" in gender-neutral language. See 1896 Mass. Acts, ch. 517, § 2 ("any person" who served in the United States army or navy), and subsequent amendments have followed this pattern, see, *e.g.,* 1919 Mass. Acts,

---

[16] For cases presenting similar challenges to the veterans' preference laws of other States, see *Ballou* v. *State Department of Civil Service,* 75 N.J. 365, 382 F.2d 1118 (1978) (sustaining New Jersey absolute preference); *Feinerman* v. *Jones,* 356 F. Supp. 252 (MD Pa. 1973) (sustaining Pennsylvania point preference); *Branch* v. *DuBois,* 418 F. Supp. 1128 (ND Ill. 1976) (sustaining Illinois modified point preference); *Wisconsin Nat'l Organization for Women* v. *Wisconsin,* 417 F. Supp. 978 (WD Wis. 1976) (sustaining Wisconsin point preference).

ch. 150, § 1 ("any person" who served . . . ); 1954 Mass. Acts, ch. 531, § 1 ("any person, male or female, including a nurse"). Women who have served in official United States military units during wartime, then, have always been entitled to the benefit of the preference. In addition, Massachusetts, through a 1943 amendment to the definition of "wartime service," extended the preference to women who served in unofficial auxiliary woman's units. 1943 Mass. Acts, ch. 194.

When the first general veterans' preference statute was adopted in 1896, there were no women veterans.[18] The statute, however, covered only Civil War veterans. Most of them were beyond middle age, and relatively few were actively competing for public employment. Thus, the impact of the preference upon the employment opportunities of nonveterans as a group and women in particular was slight.

Notwithstanding the apparent attempts by Massachusetts to include as many military women as possible within the scope of the preference, the statute today benefits an overwhelmingly male class. This is attributable in some measure to the variety of federal statutes, regulations, and policies that have restricted the numbers of women who could enlist in the United States Armed Forces,[21] and largely to the simple fact that women

[18] Small numbers of women served in combat roles in every war before the 20th century in which the United States was involved, but usually unofficially or disguised as men. See Binken and Bach, WOMEN AND THE MILITARY 5 (1977). Among the better-known are Molly Pitcher (Revolutionary War); Deborah Sampson (Revolutionary War), and Lucy Brewer (War of 1812). Passing as one "George Baker," Brewer served for three years as a gunner on the U.S.S. Constitution ("Old Ironsides") and distinguished herself in several major naval battles in the War of 1812. See Laffin, WOMEN IN BATTLE 116–122 (1967).

[21] The Army Nurse Corps, created by Congress in 1901, was the first official military unit for women, but its members were not granted full military rank until 1944. See M. Binkin and S. Bach, WOMEN AND THE MILITARY 4–21 (1977) (hereinafter Binkin and Bach); M. E. Treadwell, THE WOMEN'S ARMY CORPS 6 (Dept. of Army, Office of Chief of Military History, 1954) (hereinafter Treadwell). During World War I, a variety of proposals were made to enlist women for work as doctors, telephone operators and clerks, but all were rejected by the War Department. See ibid. The Navy, however, interpreted its own authority broadly to include a power to enlist women as Yeoman F's and Marine F's. About 13,000 women served in this rank, working primarily at clerical jobs. These women were the first in the United States to be admitted to full military rank and status. See Treadwell 10.

Official military corps for women were established in response to the massive personnel needs of the Second World War. See generally Binkin and Bach; Treadwell. The Women's Army Auxiliary Corps (WAAC)—the unofficial predecessor of the Women's Army Corps (WAC)—was created on May 14, 1942, followed two months later by the WAVES (Women Accepted for Voluntary Emergency Service). See Binkin and Bach 7. Not long after, the U.S. Marine Corps Women's Reserve and the Coast Guard Women's Reserve (SPAR) were established. See ibid. Some 350,000 women served in the four services; some 800 women also served as Women's Airforce Service Pilots (WASPS). Ibid. Most worked in health care, administration, and communications; they were also employed as airplane mechanics, parachute riggers, gunnery instructors, air traffic controllers, and the like.

The authorizations for the women's units during World War II were temporary. The Women's Armed Services Integration Act of 1948, 62 Stat. 356–375, established the women's services on a permanent basis. Under the Act, women were given regular military status. However, quotas were placed on the numbers who could enlist; 62 Stat. 357, 360–361 (no more than 2 percent of total enlisted strength); eligibility requirements were more stringent than those for men, and career opportunities were limited. Binken and Bach 11–12. During the 1950's and 1960's, enlisted women constituted little

have never been subjected to a military draft. See generally M. Binkin and S. Bach, WOMEN AND THE MILITARY 4–21 (1977).

When this litigation was commenced, then, over 98 percent of the veterans in Massachusetts were male; only 1.8 percent were female. And over one-quarter of the Massachusetts population were veterans. During the decade between 1963 and 1973 when the appellee was actively participating in the State's merit selection system, 47,005 new permanent appointments were made in the classified official service. Forty-three percent of those hired were women, and, 57 percent were men. Of the women appointed, 1.8 percent were veterans, while 54 percent of the men had veteran status. A large unspecified percentage of the female appointees were serving in lower paying positions for which males traditionally had not applied. On each of 50 sample eligible lists that are part of the record in this case, one or more woman who would have been certified as eligible for appointment on the basis of test results were displaced by veterans whose test scores were lower.

At the outset of this litigation the State conceded that for "many of the permanent positions for which males and females have competed" the veterans' preference has "resulted in a substantially greater proportion of female eligibles than male eligibles" not being certified for consideration. The impact of the veterans' preference law upon the public employment opportunities of women has thus been severe. This impact lies at the heart of the appellee's federal constitutional claim.

## II

The sole question for decision on this appeal is whether Massachusetts, in granting an absolute lifetime preference to veterans, has discriminated against women in violation of the Equal Protection Clause of the Fourteenth Amendment.

## A

The Equal Protection Guarantee of the Fourteenth Amendment does not take from the States all power of classification. *Massachusetts Bd. of Retirement* v. *Murgia,* 427 U.S. 307, 314. Most laws classify, and many affect certain groups unevenly, even though the law itself treats them no differently from all other members of the class described by the law. When the basic classification is rationally based, uneven effects upon particular groups within a class are ordinarily of no constitutional concern. *New York Transit Authority* v. *Beazor,* _____ U.S. _____; *Jefferson* v. *Hackney,* 406 U.S. 535, 548. Cf. *James* v. *Valtierra,* 402 U.S. 137. The

---

more than 1 percent of the total force. In 1967, the 2 percent quota was lifted, Act of Nov. 8, 1967, Pub. L. 90–130, § 1(b), 81 Stat. 376, and in the 1970's many restrictive policies concerning women's participation in the military have been eliminated or modified. See generally Binken and Bach, *supra.* In 1972, women still constituted less than 2 percent of the enlisted strength. *Id.,* at 14. By 1975, when this litigation was commenced, the percentage had risen to 4.0 percent. *Ibid.*

calculus of effects, the manner in which a particular law reverberates in a society, is a legislative and not a judicial responsibility. *Dandridge* v. *Williams*, 397 U.S. 471; *San Antonio Bd. of Education* v. *Rodriguez*, 411 U.S. 1. In assessing an equal protection challenge, a court is called upon only to measure the basic validity of the legislative classification. *Barrett* v. *Indiana*, 229 U.S. 26, 29–30; *Railway Express Co.* v. *New York*, 336 U.S. 106. When some other independent right is not at stake, see, *e.g., Shapiro* v. *Thompson*, 394 U.S. 618, and when there is no "reason to infer antipathy," *Vance* v. *Bradley*, _____ U.S. _____, it is presumed that "even improvident decisions will eventually be rectified by the democratic process. . . ." *Ibid.*

Certain classifications, however, in themselves supply a reason to infer antipathy. Race is the paradigm. A racial classification, regardless of purported motivation, is presumptively invalid and can be upheld only upon an extraordinary justification. *Brown* v. *Board of Education*, 347 U.S. 483; *MacLaughlin* v. *Florida*, 379 U.S. 184. This rule applies as well to a classification that is ostensibly neutral but is an obvious pretext for racial discrimination. *Yick Wo* v. *Hopkins*, 118 U.S. 356; *Guinn* v. *United States*, 238 U.S. 347; cf. *Lane* v. *Wilson*, 307 U.S. 268; *Gomillion* v. *Lightfoot*, 364 U.S. 339. But, as was made clear in *Washington* v. *Davis*, 426 U.S. 229, and *Village of Arlington Heights* v. *Metropolitan Housing Development Corp.*, 429 U.S. 252, even if a neutral law has a disproportionately adverse effect upon a racial minority, it is unconstitutional under the Equal Protection Clause only if that impact can be traced to a discriminatory purpose.

Classifications based upon gender, not unlike those based upon race, have traditionally been the touchstone for pervasive and often subtle discrimination. *Caban* v. *Muhammed*, _____ U.S. _____, _____ (dissenting opinion). This Court's recent cases teach that such classifications must bear a "close and substantial relationship to important governmental objectives," *Craig* v. *Boren*, 429 U.S. 190, 197, and are in many settings unconstitutional. *Reed* v. *Reed*, 404 U.S. 71; *Frontiero* v. *Richardson*, 411 U.S. 677; *Weinberger* v. *Wiesenfeld*, 420 U.S. 636; *Craig* v. *Boren, supra; Califrano* v. *Goldfarb*, 430 U.S. 199; *Orr* v. *Orr*, _____ U.S. _____; *Caban* v. *Muhammed*, _____ U.S. _____. Although public employment is not a constitutional right, *Massachusetts Bd. of Retirement* v. *Murgia, supra,* and the States have wide discretion in framing employee qualifications, see, *e.g., New York Transit Authority* v. *Beazer*, _____ U.S. _____, these precedents dictate that any state law overtly or covertly designed to prefer males over females in public employment would require an exceedingly persuasive justification to withstand a constitutional challenge under the Equal Protection Clause of the Fourteenth Amendment.

## B

The cases of *Washington* v. *Davis, supra,* and *Village of Arlington Heights* v. *Metropolitan Housing Development Corp., supra,* recognize that when a neutral law has a disparate impact upon a group that has historically been the victim of discrimination, an unconstitutional purpose may still be at work. But those cases signalled no departure from the settled rule that the Fourteenth Amendment guarantees equal laws, not equal results. *Davis* upheld a job-related employment test that white people passed in proportionately greater numbers than Negroes, for there had been no showing that racial discrimination entered into the establishment or formulation of the test. *Arlington Heights* upheld a zoning board decision that tended to perpetuate racially segregated housing patterns, since, apart from its effect, the board's decision was shown to be nothing more than an application of constitutionally neutral zoning policy. Those principles apply with equal force to a case involving alleged gender discrimination.

When a statute gender-neutral on its face is challenged on the ground that its effects upon women are disproportionably adverse, a two-fold inquiry is thus appropriate. The first question is whether the statutory classification is indeed neutral in the sense that it is not gender-based. If the classification itself, covert or overt, is not based upon gender, the second question is whether the adverse effect reflects invidious gender-based discrimination. See *Village of Arlington Heights* v. *Metropolitan Housing Authority, supra,* at 226. In this second inquiry, impact provides an "important starting point," *id.,* _____, but purposeful discrimination is "the condition that offends the Constitution." *Swann* v. *Board of Education,* 402 U.S. 1, 16.

It is against this background of precedent that we consider the merits of the case before us.

## III

### A

The question whether ch. 31, § 23 establishes a classification that is overtly or covertly based upon gender must first be considered. The appellee has conceded that ch. 31, § 23 is neutral on its face. She has also acknowledged that state hiring preferences for veterans are not *per se* invalid, for she has limited her challenge to the absolute lifetime preference that Massachusetts provides to veterans. The District Court made two central findings that are relevant here: first, that ch. 31, § 23 serves legitimate and worthy purposes; second, that the absolute preference was not established for the purpose of discriminating against women. The appellee has thus acknowledged and the District Court has thus found that the distinction between veterans and nonveterans drawn by ch. 31, § 23 is not a pretext for gender discrimination. The appellee's concession and the District Court's finding are clearly correct.

If the impact of this statute could not be plausibly explained on a neutral ground, impact itself would signal that the real classification made by the law was in fact not neutral. See *Washington* v. *Davis, supra,* 426 U.S., at 242; *Village of Arlington Heights* v. *Metropolitan Housing Authority, supra,* 429 U.S., at 266. But there can be but one answer to the question whether this veteran preference excludes significant numbers of women from preferred state jobs because they are women or because they are nonveterans. Apart from the fact that the definition of "veterans" in the statute has always been neutral as to gender and that Massachusetts has consistently defined veteran status in a way that has been inclusive of women who have served in the military, this is not a law that can plausibly be explained only as a gender-based classification. Indeed, it is not a law that can rationally be explained on that ground. Veteran status is not uniquely male. Although few women benefit from the preference, the nonveteran class is not substantially all-female. To the contrary, significant numbers of nonveterans are men, and all nonveterans—male as well as female—are placed at a disadvantage. Too many men are affected by ch. 31, § 23 to permit the inference that the statute is but a pretext for preferring men over women.

Moreover, as the District Court implicitly found, the purposes of the statute provide the surest explanation for its impact. Just as there are cases in which impact alone can unmask an invidious classification, cf. *Yick Wo* v. *Hopkins, supra,* there are others, in which—notwithstanding impact—the legitimate noninvidious purposes of a law cannot be missed. This is one. The distinction made by ch. 31, § 23, is, as it seems to be, quite simply between veterans and nonveterans, not between men and women.

## B

The dispositive question, then, is whether the appellee has shown that a gender-based discriminatory purpose has, at least in some measure, shaped the Massachusetts veterans' preference legislation. As did the District Court, she points to two basic factors which in her view distinguish ch. 31, § 23 from the neutral rules at issue in the *Washington* v. *Davis* and *Arlington Heights* cases. The first is the nature of the preference, which is said to be demonstrably gender-biased in the sense that it favors a status reserved under federal military policy primarly to men. The second concerns the impact of the absolute lifetime preference upon the employment opportunities of women, an impact claimed to be too inevitable to have been unintended. The appellee contends that these factors, coupled with the fact that the preference itself has little if any relevance to actual job performance, more than suffice to prove the discriminatory intent required to establish a constitutional violation.

### 1

The contention that this veterans' preference is "inherently non-neutral" or "gender-biased" presumes that the State, by favoring veterans, intentionally incorporated into its public employment policies the panoply of sex-based and assertedly discriminatory federal laws that have prevented all but a handful of women from becoming veterans. There are two serious difficulties with this argument. First, it is wholly at odds with the District Court's central finding that Massachusetts has not offered a preference to veterans for the purpose of discriminating against women. Second, it cannot be reconciled with the assumption made by both the appellee and the District Court that a more limited hiring preference for veterans could be sustained. Taken together, these difficulties are fatal.

To the extent that the status of veteran is one that few women have been enabled to achieve, every hiring preference for veterans, however modest or extreme, is inherently gender-biased. If Massachusetts by offering such a preference can be said intentionally to have incorporated into its state employment policies the historical gender-based federal military personnel practices, the degree of the preference would or should make no constitutional difference. Invidious discrimination does not become less so because the discrimination accomplished is of a lesser magnitude.[23] Discriminatory intent is simply not amenable to calibration. It either is a factor that has influenced the legislative choice or it is not. The District Court's conclusion that the absolute veterans' preference was not originally enacted or subsequently reaffirmed for the purpose of giving an advantage to males as such necessarily compels the conclusion that the State intended nothing more than to prefer "veterans." Given this finding, simple logic suggests that an intent to exclude women from significant public jobs was not at work in this law. To reason that it was, by describing the preference as "inherently non-neutral" or "gender-biased," is merely to restate the fact of impact, not to answer the question of intent.

To be sure, this case is unusual in that it involves a law that by design is not neutral. The law overtly prefers veterans as such. As opposed to the written test at issue in *Davis,* it does not purport to define a job related characteristic. To the contrary, it confers upon a specifically described group—perceived to be particularly deserving—a competitive head start. But the District Court found, and the appellee has not disputed, that this legislative choice was legitimate. The basic distinction between veterans and nonveterans, having been found not gender-based, and the goals of the preference having been found worthy, ch. 31 must be analyzed as is any other neutral law that casts a greater burden upon women as a group than upon men as a group. The enlistment policies of the armed services may well have discriminated on the basis of sex. See *Frontiero* v. *Richardson,* 411 U.S. 677; cf. *Schlesinger* v. *Ballard,* 419 U.S. 498. But the history of discrimination against women in the military is not on trial in this case.

2

The appellee's ultimate argument rests upon the presumption, common to the criminal and civil law, that a person intends the natural

---

[23] This is not to say that the degree of impact is irrelevant to the question of intent. But it is to say that a more modest preference, while it might well lessen impact and, as the State argues, might lessen the effectiveness of the statute in helping veterans, would not be any more or less "neutral" in the constitutional sense.

and foreseeable consequences of his voluntary actions. Her position was well stated in the concurring opinion in the District Court: "Conceding . . . that the goal here was to benefit the veteran, there is no reason to absolve the legislature from awareness that the means chosen to achieve this goal would freeze women out of all those state jobs actively sought by men. To be sure, the legislature did not wish to harm women. But the cutting-off of women's opportunities was an inevitable concomitant of the chosen scheme—as inevitable as the proposition that if tails is up, heads must be down. Where a law's consequences are *that* inevitable, can they meaningfully be described as unintended?" 451 F. Supp. 143, 151.

This rhetorical question implies that a negative answer is obvious, but it is not. The decision to grant a preference to veterans was of course "intentional." So, necessarily, did an adverse impact upon nonveterans follow from that decision. And it cannot seriously be argued that the legislature of Massachusetts could have been unaware that most veterans are men. It would thus be disingenuous to say that the adverse consequences of this legislation for women were unintended, in the sense that they were not volitional or in the sense that they were not foreseeable.

"Discriminatory purpose," however, implies more than intent as volition or intent as awareness of consequences. See *United Jewish Organizations* v. *Carey,* 430 U.S. 144, 179 (concurring opinion).[24] It implies that the decisionmaker, in this case a state legislature, selected or reaffirmed a particular course of action at least in part "because of," not merely "in spite of," its adverse effects upon an identifiable group.[25] Yet nothing in the record demonstrates that this preference for veterans was originally devised or subsequently re-enacted because it would accomplish the collateral goal of keeping women in a stereotypic and predefined place in the Massachusetts Civil Service.

To the contrary, the statutory history shows that the benefit of the preference was consistently offered to "any person" who was a veteran. That benefit has been extended to women under a very broad statutory definition of the term veteran. The preference formula itself, which is the

[24] Proof of discriminatory intent must necessarily usually rely on objective factors, several of which were outlined in *Villiage of Arlington Heights* v. *Metropolitan Housing Authority,* 429 U.S. 252, 266. The inquiry is practical. What a legislature or any official entity is "up to" may be plain from the results its actions achieve, or the results they avoid. Often it is made clear from what has been called, in a different context, "the give and take of the situation." *Cramer* v. *United States,* 325 U.S. 1, 32–33. (Jackson, J.)

[25] This is not to say that the inevitability or foreseeability of consequences of a neutral rule has no bearing upon the existence of discriminatory intent. Certainly, when the adverse consequences of a law upon an identifiable group are as inevitable as the gender-based consequences of ch. 31, § 23, a strong inference that the adverse effects were desired can reasonably be drawn. But in this inquiry—made as it is under the Constitution—an inference is a working tool, not a synonym for proof. When as here, the impact is essentially an unavoidable consequence of a legislative policy that has in itself always been deemed to be legitimate, and when, as here, the statutory history and all of the available evidence affirmatively demonstrate the opposite, the inference simply fails to ripen into proof.

focal point of this challenge, was first adopted—so it appears from this record—out of a perceived need to help a small group of older Civil War veterans. It has since been reaffirmed and extended only to cover new veterans. When the totality of legislative actions establishing and extending the Massachusetts veterans' preference are considered, see *Washington* v. *Davis, supra,* 426 U.S., at 242, the law remains what it purports to be: a preference for veterans of either sex over nonveterans of either sex, not for men over women.

IV

Veterans' hiring preferences represent an awkward—and, many argue, unfair—exception to the widely shared view that merit and merit alone should prevail in the employment policies of government. After a war, such laws have been enacted virtually without opposition. During peacetime they inevitably have come to be viewed in many quarters as un democratic and unwise.[28] Absolute and permanent preferences, as the troubled history of this law demonstrates, have always been subject to the objection that they give the veteran more than a square deal. But the Fourteenth Amendment "cannot be made a refuge from ill-advised . . . laws." *District of Columbia* v. *Brooke,* 214 U.S. 138, 150. The substantial edge granted to veterans by ch. 31, § 23 may reflect unwise policy. The appellee, however, has simply failed to demonstrate that the law in any way reflects a purpose to discriminate on the basis of sex.

The judgment is reversed, and the case is remanded for further proceedings consistent with this opinion.

MR. JUSTICE STEVENS, with whom MR. JUSTICE WHITE joins, concurring: While I concur in the Court's opinion, I confess that I am not at all sure that there is any difference between the two questions posed at pp. 16–17, *ante.* If a classification is not overtly based on gender, I am inclined to believe the question whether it is covertly gender-based is the same as the question whether its adverse effects reflect invidious gender-based discrimination. However the question is phrased, for me the answer is largely provided by the fact that the number of males disadvantaged by Massachusetts' Veterans Preference (1,867,000) is sufficiently large—and sufficiently close to the number of disadvantaged females (2,954,000)—to refute the claim that the rule was intended to benefit males as a class over females as a class.

MR. JUSTICE MARSHALL, with whom MR. JUSTICE BRENNAN joins, dissenting: Although acknowledging that in some circumstances, discriminatory intent may be inferred from the inevitable or foreseeable impact of a statute, *ante,* at 22 n. 25, the Court concludes that no such intent has been established here. I cannot agree. In my judgment, Massachusetts'

---

[28] See generally Veterans' Preference Oversight Hearings before Subcomm. on Civil Service, 95th Cong., 1st Sess. (1977); Report of Comptroller General, Conflicting Con gressional Policies: Veterans' Preference and Apportionment vs. Equal Employment Opportunity (Sept. 29, 1977).

choice of an absolute veterans' preference system evinces purposeful gender-based discrimination. And because the statutory scheme bears no substantial relationship to a legitimate governmental objective, it cannot withstand scrutiny under the Equal Protection Clause.

I

The District Court found that the "prime objective" of the Massachusetts Veterans Preference Statute, Mass. Gen. Laws, ch. 31, § 23, was to benefit individuals with prior military service. 415 F. Supp. 485, 497 (Mass. 1976). See 451 F. Supp. 143, 145 (Mass. 1978). Under the Court's analysis, this factual determination "necessarily compels the conclusion that the state intended nothing more than to prefer 'veterans.' Given this finding, simple logic suggests than an intent to exclude women from significant public jobs was not at work in this law." *Ante,* at 20. I find the Court's logic neither simple nor compelling.

That a legislature seeks to advantage one group does not, as a matter of logic or of common sense, exclude the possibility that it also intends to disadvantage another. Individuals in general and lawmakers in particular frequently act for a variety of reasons. As this Court recognized in *Arlington Heights* v. *Metropolitan Housing Development Corp.,* 429 U.S. 252, 265 (1977), "[r]arely can it be said that a legislature or administrative body operating under a broad mandate made a decision motivated by a single concern." Absent an omniscience not commonly attributed to the judiciary, it will often be impossible to ascertain the sole or even dominant purpose of a given statue. See *McGinnis* v. *Royster,* 410 U.S. 263, 276–277 (1973); Ely, *Legislative and Administrative Motivation in Constitutional Law,* 79 YALE L. J. 1205, 1214 (1970). Thus, the critical constitutional inquiry is not whether an illicit consideration was the primary or but-for cause of a decision, but rather whether it had an appreciable role in shaping a given legislative enactment. Where there is "proof that a discriminatory purpose has been *a* motivating factor in the decision. . . . judicial deference is no longer justified." *Arlington Heights* v. *Metropolitan Housing Corp., supra,* at 265–266 (emphasis added).

Moreover, since reliable evidence of subjective intentions is seldom obtainable, resort to inference based on objective factors is generally unavoidable. See *Beer* v. *United States,* 425 U.S. 130, 148–149, n. 4 (1976) (MARSHALL, J., dissenting); cf. *Palmer* v. *Thompson,* 403 U.S. 217, 224–225 (1971); *United States* v. *O'Brien,* 391 U.S. 367, 383–384 (1968). To discern the purposes underlying facially neutral policies, this Court has therefore considered the degree, inevitability, and foreseeability of any disproportionate impact as well as the alternatives reasonably available. See *Monroe* v. *Board of Commissioners,* 391 U.S. 450, 459 (1968); *Goss* v. *Board of Education,* 373 U.S. 683, 688–689 (1963); *Gomillion* v. *Lightfoot,* 364 U.S. 339 (1960); *Griffin* v. *Illinois,* 351 U.S. 12, 17 n. 11 (1956). Cf. *Albemarle Paper Co.* v. *Moody,* 422 U.S. 405, 425 (1975).

In the instant case, the impact of the Massachusetts statute on women is undisputed. Any veteran with a passing grade on the civil service exam must be placed ahead of a nonveteran, regardless of their respective scores. The District Court found that, as a practical matter, this preference supplants test results as the determinant of upper-level civil service appointments. 415 F. Supp., at 488–489. Because less than 2 percent of the women in Massachusetts are veterans, the absolute preference formula has rendered desirable state civil service employment an almost exclusively male prerogative. 451 F. Supp., at 151 (CAMPBELL, J., concurring).

As the District Court recognized, this consequence followed foreseeably, indeed inexorably, from the long history of policies severely limiting women's participation in the military.[1] Although neutral in form, the statute is anything but neutral in application. It inescapably reserves a major sector of public employment to "an already established class which, as a matter of historical fact, is 98 percent male." Ibid. Where the foreseeable impact of a facially neutral policy is so disproportionate, the burden should rest on the State to establish that sex-based considerations played no part in the choice of the particular legislative scheme. Cf. Castaneda v. Partida, 430 U.S. 482 (1977); Washington v. Davis, 426 U.S. 229, 241 (1976); Alexander v. Louisiana, 405 U.S. 625, 532 (1972); see generally Brest, Palmer v. Thompson: An Approach to the Problem of Unconstitutional Legislative Motive, 1971 SUP. CT. L. REV. 95, 123.

Clearly, that burden was not sustained here. The legislative history of the statute reflects the Commonwealth's patent appreciation of the impact the preference system would have on women, and an equally evident desire to mitigate that impact only with respect to certain traditionally female occupations. Until 1971, the statute and implementing civil service regulations exempted from operation of the preference any job requisitions "especially calling for women." 1954 Mass. Acts, ch. 627, § 5. See also 1896 Mass. Acts, ch. 517, § 6; 1919 Mass. Act, ch. 150, § 2; 1945 Mass. Acts, ch. 725, § 2(e); 1965 Mass. Acts, ch. 53, § 2; ante, at 8–9, nn. 13, 14. In practice, this exemption, coupled with the absolute preference for veterans, has created a gender-based civil service hierarchy, with women occupying low grade clerical and secretarial jobs and men holding more

---

[1] See 415 F. Supp. 485, 490, 495–499 (Mass. 1976); 451 F. Supp. 143, 145, 148 (Mass. 1978). In addition to the 2 percent quota on women's participation in the armed forces, see ante, at 12 n. 21, enlistment and appointment requirements have been more stringent for females than males with respect to age, mental and physical aptitude, parental consent, and educational attainment. M. Binkin and S. Bach, WOMEN AND THE MILITARY (1977) (hereinafter Binkin and Bach); Note, The Equal Rights Amendment and the Military, 82 YALE L. J. 1533, 1539 (1973). Until the 1970's, the armed forces precluded enlistment and appointment of women, but not men, who were married or had dependent children. See 415 F. Supp., at 490; App. 85; Exs. 98, 99, 103, 104. Sex-based restrictions on advancement and training opportunities also diminished the incentives for qualified women to enlist. See Binkin and Bach 10–17; Beans, Sex Discrimination in the Military, 67 MILIT. L. REV. 19, 59–83 (1979). Cf. Schlesinger v. Ballard, 419 U.S. 498, 508 (1975).

Thus, unlike the employment examination in Washington v. Davis, 426 U.S. 229 (1976), which the Court found to be demonstrably job-related, the Massachusetts preference statute incorporates the results of sex-based military policies irrelevant to women's current fitness for civilian public employment. See 415 F. Supp., at 498–499.

responsible and remunerative positions. See 415 F. Supp., at 488; 451 F. Supp., at 148 n. 9.

Thus, for over 70 years, the Commonwealth has maintained, as an integral part of its veteran's preference system, an exemption relegating female civil service applicants to occupations traditionally filled by women. Such a statutory scheme both reflects and perpetuates precisely the kind of archaic assumptions about women's roles which we have previously held invalid. See *Orr* v. *Orr*, ____ U.S. ____ (1979); *Califano* v. *Goldfarb*, 430 U.S. 199, 210–211 (1977); *Stanton* v. *Stanton*, 421 U.S. 7, 14 (1975); *Weinberger* v. *Wiesenfeld*, 420 U.S. 636, 645 (1975). Particularly when viewed against the range of less discriminatory alternatives available to assist veterans,[2] Massachusett's choice of a formula that so severely restricts public employment opportunities for women cannot reasonably be thought gender-neutral. Cf. *Albemarle Paper Co.* v. *Moody, supra,* at 425. The Court's conclusion to the contrary—that "nothing in the record" evinces a "collateral goal of keeping women in a stereotypic and predefined place in the Massachusetts Civil Service," *ante,* at 22—displays a singularly myopic view of the facts established below.[3]

## II

To survive challenge under the Equal Protection Clause, statutes reflecting gender-based discrimination must be substantially related to the achievement of important governmental objectives. See *Califano* v. *Webster*, 430 U.S. 313, 316–317 (1977); *Craig* v. *Boren*, 429 U.S. 190, 197 (1976); *Reed* v. *Reed*, 404 U.S. 71, 76 (1971). Appellants here advance three interests in support of the absolute preference system: (1) assisting veterans in their readjustment to civilian life; (2) encouraging military enlistment; and (3) rewarding those who have served their country. Brief for Appellants 24. Although each of those goals is unquestionably legitimate, the "mere recitation of a benign compensatory purpose" cannot of itself insulate legislative classifications from constitutional scrutiny. *Weinberger* v. *Wiesenfeld, supra,* at 648. And in this case, the Commonwealth has failed to establish a sufficient relationship between its objectives and the means chosen to effectuate them.

---

[2] Only four States afford a preference comparable in scope to that of Massachusetts. See Fleming and Shanor, *Veterans' Preferences and Public Employment: Unconstitutional Gender Discrimination?*, 26 EMORY L. J. 13, 17 n. 13 (1977) (citing statutes). Other States and the Federal Government grant point or tie-breaking preferences that do not foreclose opportunities for women. See *id.,* at 13, and nn. 13, 14; *ante,* at 4 n. 7; Hearings Before the Subcommittee on Civil Service of the House Committee on Post Office and Civil Service, 95th Cong., 1st Sess., 4 (1977) (statement of Alan Campbell, Chairman, U.S. Civil Service Commission).

[3] Although it is relevant that the preference statute also disadvantages a substantial group of men, see *ante,* at 1 (STEVENS, J., concurring), it is equally pertinent that 47 percent of Massachusetts men over 18 are veterans, as compared to 0.8 percent of Massachusetts women. App. 83. Given this disparity, and the indicia of intent noted at pp. 4–5, *supra,* the absolute number of men denied preference cannot be dispositive, especially since they have not faced the barriers to achieving veteran status confronted by women. See n. 1, *supra.*

With respect to the first interest, facilitating veterans' transition to civilian status, the statute is plainly overinclusive. Cf. *Trimble* v. *Gordon,* 430 U.S. 762, 770–772 (1971); *Jiminez* v. *Weinberger,* 417 U.S. 628, 637 (1974). By conferring a permanent preference, the legislation allows veterans to invoke their advantage repeatedly, without regard to their date of discharge. As the record demonstrates, a substantial majority of those currently enjoying the benefits of the system are not recently discharged veterans in need of readjustment assistance.[4]

Nor is the Commonwealth's second asserted interest, encouraging military service, a plausible justification for this legislative scheme. In its original and subsequent re-enactments, the statute extended benefits retroactively to veterans who had served during a prior specified period. See *ante,* at 8–9. If the Commonwealth's "actual purpose" is to induce enlistment, this legislative design is hardly well-suited to that end. See *Califano* v. *Webster, supra,* at 317; *Weinberger* v. *Wiesenfeld, supra,* at 648. For I am unwilling to assume what appellants made no effort to prove, that the possibility of obtaining an *ex post facto* civil service preference significantly influenced the enlistment decisions of Massachusetts residents. Moreover, even if such influence could be presumed, the statute is still grossly overinclusive in that it bestows benefits on men drafted as well as those who volunteered.

Finally, the Commonwealth's third interest, rewarding veterans, does not "adequately justify the salient features" of this preference system. *Craig* v. *Boren,* 429 U.S., at 202. See *Orr* v. *Orr,* _____ U.S., at _____. Where a particular statutory scheme visits substantial hardship on a class long subject to discrimination, the legislation cannot be sustained unless "carefully tuned to alternative considerations." *Trimble* v. *Gordon, supra,* at 772. See *Caban* v. *Mohammed,* _____ U.S. _____ n. 13 (1979); *Mathews* v. *Lucas,* 427 U.S. 495 (1976). Here, there are a wide variety of less discriminatory means by which Massachusetts could effect its compensatory purposes. For example, a point preference system, such as that maintained by man States and the Federal Government, see n. 2, *supra,* or an absolute preference for a limited duration, would reward veterans without excluding all qualified women from upper level civil service positions. Apart from public employment, the Commonwealth, can, and does, afford assistance to veterans in various ways, including tax abatements, educational subsidies, and special programs for needy veterans. See Mass. Gen. Laws Ann., ch. 59, § 5 (West Supp. 1979); Mass. Gen. Laws Ann., ch. 69, §§ 7, 73 (West Supp. 1979); and Mass. Gen. Laws Ann., chs. 115, 115A (West Supp. 1978). Unlike these and similar benefits, the costs of which are distributed across the taxpaying public generally, the Massachusetts statute exacts a substantial price from a discrete group of individuals who have long been subject to employment discrimination,[5]

---

[4] The eligibility lists for the positions Ms. Feeney sought included 95 veterans for whom discharge information was available. Of those 95 males, 64 (67%) were discharged prior to 1960. App. 106, 150–151, 169–170.

[5] See *Frontiero* v. *Richardson,* 411 U.S. 677, 689 n. 23 (1973); *Kahn* v. *Shevin,* 416 U.S. 351, 353–354 (1974); United States Bureau of the Census, Current Population Reports,

and who, "because of circumstances totally beyond their control, have [had] little if any chance of becoming members in the preferred class." 415 F. Supp., at 499. See n. 1, *supra.*

In its present unqualified form, the Veteran's Preference Statute precludes all but a small fraction of Massachusetts women from obtaining any civil service position also of interest to men. See 451 F. Supp., at 151 (Campbell, J., concurring). Given the range of alternatives available, this degree of preference is not constitutionally permissible.

I would affirm the judgment of the court below.

## NOTE

In *Davis* v. *Passman,* 47 USLW 4643 (June 5, 1979), a U.S. Congressman dismissed petitioner, a female, from the position of deputy administrative assistant for the stated reason "that it was essential that the understudy to my Administrative Assistant be a man." The Supreme Court, 5-to-4, sustained a cause of action for sex discrimination based upon the Due Process Clause of the Fifth Amendment and the general federal question jurisdiction of 28 U.S.C. § 1331(a).

Since Passman was no longer a Congressman, the majority did not discuss the question of equitable relief, but held that damages would constitute an appropriate remedy. The case was remanded to determine (1) whether the Speech and Debate Clause of the Constitution provided a congressional immunity and, if not, (2) whether, under the Equal Protection component of the Due Process Clause, "important governmental objectives" are served by the gender-based employment of congressional staff.

Chief Justice Burger and Justice Powell wrote vigorous dissenting opinions based largely on separation of powers doctrine. Justice Stewart's dissent emphasized the importance of the Speech and Debate Clause issue. Justice Rehnquist concurred in all dissents.

## B. Due Process and Irrebuttable Presumption

### CLEVELAND BOARD OF EDUCATION v. LaFLEUR

*Supreme Court of the United States, 1974*
*414 U.S. 632, 6 FEP Cases 1253*

Mr. Justice Stewart delivered the opinion of the Court.

The respondents in No. 72-777 and the petitioner in No. 72-1129 are female public school teachers. During the 1970-1971 school year, each informed her local school board that she was pregnant; each was com-

---

No. 107, Money Income and Poverty Status of Families and Persons in the United States: 1976 (Advance Report) (Table 7) (Sept. 1977).

pelled by a mandatory maternity leave rule to quit her job without pay several months before the expected birth of her child. These cases call upon us to decide the constitutionality of the school boards' rules.
. . .

By acting to penalize the pregnant teacher for deciding to bear a child, overly restrictive maternity leave regulations can constitute a heavy burden on the exercise of these protected freedoms. Because public school maternity leave rules directly affect "one of the basic civil rights of man," *Skinner* v. *Oklahoma*, at 541, the Due Process Clause of the Fourteenth Amendment requires that such rules must not needlessly, arbitrarily, or capriciously impinge upon this vital area of a teacher's constitutional liberty. The question before us in these cases is whether the interests advanced in support of the rules of the Cleveland and Chesterfield County School Boards can justify the particular procedures they have adopted.

The school boards in these cases have offered two essentially overlapping explanations for their mandatory maternity leave rules. First, they contend that the firm cut-off dates are necessary to maintain continuity of classroom instruction, since advance knowledge of when a pregnant teacher must leave facilitates the finding and hiring of a qualified substitute. Secondly, the school boards seek to justify their maternity rules by arguing that at least some teachers become physically incapable of adequately performing certain of their duties during the latter part of pregnancy. By keeping the pregnant teacher out of the classroom during these final months, the maternity leave rules are said to protect the health of the teacher and her unborn child, while at the same time assuring that students have a physically capable instructor in the classroom at all times.

It cannot be denied that continuity of instruction is a significant and legitimate educational goal. Regulations requiring pregnant teachers to provide early notice of their condition to school authorities undoubtedly facilitate administrative planning toward the important objective of continuity. But as the Court of Appeals for the Second Circuit noted in *Green* v. *Waterford Board of Education*, 472 F.2d 629, 635, 5 FEP Cases 443, 447:

"Where a pregnant teacher provides the Board with a date certain for commencement of leave, however, that value [continuity] is preserved; an arbitrary leave date set at the end of the fifth month is no more calculated to facilitate a planned and orderly transition between the teacher and a substitute than is a date fixed closer to confinement. Indeed, the latter . . . would afford the Board more, not less, time to procure a satisfactory long-term substitute." (Footnote omitted.)

Thus, while the advance notice provisions in the Cleveland and Chesterfield County rules are wholly rational and may well be necessary to serve the objective of continuity of instruction, the absolute requirements of termination at the end of the fourth or fifth month of pregnancy are not. Were continuity the only goal, cut-off dates much later during pregnancy would serve as well or better than the challenged rules, providing that ample advance notice requirements were retained. Indeed, continuity would seem just as well attained if the teacher herself were allowed to choose the date upon which to commence her leave, at least so long as the decision were required to be made and notice given of it well in advance of the date selected.

In fact, since the fifth or sixth months of pregnancy will obviously begin at different times in the school year for different teachers, the present Cleveland and Chesterfield County rules may serve to hinder attainment of the very continuity objectives that they are purportedly designed to promote. For example, the beginning of the fifth month of pregnancy for both Mrs. LaFleur and Mrs. Nelson occurred during March of 1971. Both were thus required to leave work with only a few months left in the school year, even though both were fully willing to serve through the end of the term. Similarly, if continuity were the only goal, it seems ironic that the Chesterfield County rule forced Mrs. Cohen to leave work in mid-December 1970 rather than at the end of the semester in January, as she requested.

We thus conclude that the arbitrary cut-off dates embodied in the mandatory leave rules before us have no rational relationship to the valid state interest of preserving continuity of instruction. As long as the teacher is required to give substantial advance notice of her condition, the choice of firm dates later in pregnancy would serve the boards' objectives just as well, while imposing a far lesser burden on the women's exercise of constitutionally protected freedom.

The question remains as to whether the fifth and sixth month cut-off dates can be justified on the other ground advanced by the school boards —the necessity of keeping physically unfit teachers out of the classroom. There can be no doubt that such an objective is perfectly legitimate, both on educational and safety grounds. And, despite the plethora of conflicting medical testimony in these cases, we can assume *arguendo* that at least some teachers become physically disabled from effectively performing their duties during the latter stages of pregnancy.

The mandatory termination provisions of the Cleveland and Chesterfield County rules surely operate to insulate the classroom from the presence of potentially incapacitated pregnant teachers. But the question is whether the rules sweep too broadly. See *Shelton* v. *Tucker,* 364 U.S. 479. That question must be answered in the affirmative, for the provisions amount to a conclusive presumption that every pregnant teacher who reaches the fifth or sixth month of pregnancy is physically incapable of continuing. There is no individualized determination by the teacher's doctor—or the school board's—as to any particular teacher's ability to continue at her job. The rules contain an irrebuttable presumption of physical incompetency, and that presumption applies even when the medical evidence as to an individual woman's physical status might be wholly to the contrary.

. . .

. . . While the medical experts in these cases differed on many points, they unanimously agreed on one—the ability of any particular pregnant woman to continue at work past any fixed time in her pregnancy is very much an individual matter. Even assuming *arguendo* that there are some women who would be physically unable to work past the particular cut-off dates embodied in the challenged rules, it is evident that there are large numbers of teachers who are fully capable of continuing work for longer than the Cleveland and Chesterfield County regulations will allow. Thus, the conclusive presumption embodied in these rules, like that in *Vlandis,* is neither "necessarily nor universally true," and is violative of the Due Process Clause.

The school boards have argued that the mandatory termination dates serve the interest of administrative convenience, since there are many instances of teacher pregnancy, and the rules obviate the necessity for case-by-case determinations. Certainly, the boards have an interest in devising prompt and efficient procedures to achieve their legitimate objectives in this area. But, as the Court stated in *Stanley* v. *Illinois,* at 656:

"[T]he Constitution recognizes higher values than speed and efficiency. Indeed, one might fairly say of the Bill of Rights in general, and the Due Process Clause in particular, that they were designed to protect the fragile values of a vulnerable citizenry from the overbearing concern for efficiency and efficacy that may characterize praiseworthy government officials no less, and perhaps more, than mediocre ones." (Footnote omitted.)

While it might be easier for the school boards to conclusively presume that all pregnant women are unfit to teach past the fourth or fifth month or even the first month, of pregnancy, administrative convenience alone is insufficient to make valid what otherwise is a violation of due process of law. The Fourteenth Amendment requires the school boards to employ alternative administrative means, which do not so broadly infringe upon basic constitutional liberty, in support of their legitimate goals.

We conclude, therefore, that neither the necessity for continuity of instruction nor the state interest in keeping physically unfit teachers out of the classroom can justify the sweeping mandatory leave regulations that the Cleveland and Chesterfield County School Boards have adopted. While the regulations no doubt represent a good-faith attempt to achieve a laudable goal, they cannot pass muster under the Due Process Clause of the Fourteenth Amendment, because they employ irrebuttable presumptions that unduly penalize a female teacher for deciding to bear a child.

In addition to the mandatory termination provisions, both the Cleveland and Chesterfield County rules contain limitations upon a teacher's eligibility to return to work after giving birth. Again, the school boards offer two justifications for the return rules—continuity of instruction and the desire to be certain that the teacher is physically competent when she returns to work. As is the case with the leave provisions, the question is not whether the school board's goals are legitimate, but rather whether the particular means chosen to achieve those objectives unduly infringe upon the teachers' constitutional liberty.

Under the Cleveland rule, the teacher is not eligible to return to work until the beginning of the next regular school semester following the time when her child attains the age of three months. A doctor's certificate attesting to the teacher's health is required before return; an additional physical examination may be required at the option of the school board.

The respondents in No. 72-777 do not seriously challenge either the medical requirements of the Cleveland rule or the policy of limiting eligibility to return to the next semester following birth. The provisions concerning a medical certificate or supplemental physical examination are narrowly drawn methods of protecting the school board's interest in teacher fitness; these requirements allow an individualized decision as to teacher's condition, and thus avoid the pitfalls of the presumptions inherent in the leave rules. Similarly, the provision limiting eligibility to return to the semester following delivery is a precisely drawn means of serving the school board's interest in avoiding unnecessary changes in classroom personnel during any one school term.

The Cleveland rule, however, does not simply contain these reasonable medical and next-semester eligibility provisions. In addition, the school board requires the mother to wait until her child reaches the age of three months before the return rules begin to operate. The school boards have offered no reasonable justification for this supplemental limitation, and we can perceive none. To the extent that the three months provision reflects the school board's thinking that no mother is fit to return until that point in time, it suffers from the same constitutional deficiencies that plague the irrebuttable presumption in the termination rules. The presumption, moreover, is patently unnecessary, since the requirement of a physician's certificate or a medical examination fully protects the school's interests in this regard. And finally, the three month provision simply has nothing to do with continuity of instruction, since the precise point at which the child will reach the relevant age will obviously occur at a different point throughout the school year for each teacher.

Thus, we conclude that the Cleveland return rule, insofar as it embodies the three months age provision, is wholly arbitrary and irrational, and hence violates the Due Process Clause of the Fourteenth Amendment. The age limitation serves no legitimate state interest, and unnecessarily penalizes the female teacher for asserting her right to bear children.

We perceive no such constitutional infirmities in the Chesterfield County rule. In that school system, the teacher becomes eligible for reemployment upon submission of a medical certificate from her physician; return to work is guaranteed no later than the beginning of the next school year following the eligibility determination. The medical certificate is both a reasonable and narrow method of protecting the school board's interest in teacher fitness, while the possible deferring of return until the next school year serves the goal of preserving continuity of instruction. In short, the Chesterfield County rule manages to serve the legitimate state interests here without employing unnecessary presumptions that broadly burden the exercise of protected constitutional liberty.

For the reasons stated, we hold that the mandatory termination provisions of the Cleveland and Chesterfield County maternity regulations violate the Due Process Clause of the Fourteenth Amendment, because of their use of unwarranted conclusive presumptions that seriously burden the exercise of protected constitutional liberty. For similar reasons, we hold the three months' provision of the Cleveland return rule unconstitutional.

. . .

## GURMANKIN v. COSTANZO

*United States Court of Appeals, Third Circuit, 1977*
*556 F.2d 184, 14 FEP Cases 1359*

GIBBONS, Circuit Judge: In these appeals we review two injunctive orders entered by the district court in an action charging that the defendants, officials of the Philadelphia School District, discriminated against the plaintiff, Judith Gurmankin, because she is a blind person.[1] Ms. Gurmankin is an English teacher. She holds a Professional Certificate from the Pennsylvania Department of Education as a teacher of Comprehensive English in Pennsylvania Public Schools. In 1969 she attempted to obtain employment in the Philadelphia School District. At that time the District's medical and personnel policy excluded blind teachers from teaching sighted students in the public schools. Applicants who were certified as having a "chronic or acute physical defect," including blindness, were prevented from taking the Philadelphia Teachers Examination. Ms. Gurmankin was examined by the District's Director of Medical Services, and rejected for any position teaching sighted students because of her blindness. Ms. Gurmankin persisted in her attempts to take the examination and with the assistance of counsel at Community Legal Services, Inc., in the spring of 1974 she was admitted, and passed.

When her name was reached on the eligibility list the District offered her several positions, none of which she accepted, because they were not accompanied by an agreement that she would be afforded seniority as of the time she should properly have been admitted to the examination. Ms. Gurmankin filed this suit in November 1974, and on March 31, 1976 the district court ruled in her favor. The court ordered defendants to offer her employment

"as a secondary school English teacher, with seniority rights and all other rights accruing to a secondary school English teacher commencing employment in September, 1970. Specifically, the plaintiff is to have the same rights under the School District's teacher transfer policy as a teacher who commenced employment in September, 1970."

---

[1] [Footnotes numbered as in original.—Ed.] The district court opinion is reported. *Gurmankin* v. *Costanzo,* 411 F. Supp. 982 (E.D. Pa. 1976).

The effect of this injunction was to require her employment, with a September 1970 seniority date. The court reserved decision on class aspects of the litigation and on back pay and attorney's fees.

Both the defendants and Ms. Gurmankin appealed from the injunction. The defendants contend that no order should have been entered. Ms. Gurmankin contends that the court fixed a seniority date later than that to which she was entitled. The defendants attempted unsuccessfully to obtain a stay pending appeal.

Despite the absence of a stay, ten months after the injunction issued Ms. Gurmankin still was not employed by the District as an English teacher. Several offers of employment had been made to her, but she rejected them as not reflecting the seniority awarded her by the court. In January, 1977, she filed a motion to amend the injunction. She contended that the District had offered her only the least attractive schools in the system, while teachers with less seniority were placed in more attractive schools. The court permitted limited discovery on that contention, found it to be meritorious, and concluded:

"The School District's continued refusal over the past ten months to place Ms. Gurmankin in an appropriate position has prevented the court's order from accomplishing its purpose. Moreover, the School District has indicated that it will not make any further offers to the plaintiff unless compelled by court order. This court is under a duty to insure that its orders provide full and adequate relief, and if an order is inadequate, it should be modified accordingly."

It then amended the injunction to provide:

"Within thirty (30) days of the date of this order, the defendants shall provide the plaintiff with a position as an English teacher at one of the six schools designated by plaintiff in Plaintiff's Supplemental Interrogatory, or at some other school acceptable to the plaintiff."

From this order the defendants again appealed, and again unsuccessfully sought a stay. The appeals were consolidated. In each we affirm.

## I. THE ORIGINAL INJUNCTION

The defendants contend that the court erred in finding a due process violation in the District's pre–1974 policy of refusing to allow blind persons to take the Philadelphia Teachers Examination. They also contend that an award of seniority is beyond the equitable powers of a federal court. Ms. Gurmankin defends the injunction not only for the constitutional reasons on which the district court relied, but also on equal protection grounds and on a statutory supremacy ground. The statutory supremacy argument refers to § 504 of the Rehabilitation Act of 1973, P.L. 93–112, 87 Stat. 357, 29 U.S.C. § 794:

"[n]o otherwise qualified handicapped individual in the United States, as defined in section 706(6) of this title, shall, solely by reason of his handicap, be excluded from participation in, be denied the benefits of, or be subjected to discrimination under any program or activity receiving Federal financial assistance."

It was apparently in response to this statute that in 1974 the District changed its policy and permitted Ms. Gurmankin to take the examination.[2] If the statutory supremacy claim would suffice to sustain the injunction we would be obliged to rest on it rather than reach the due process ground on which the district court relied.[3] But as that court noted, the Rehabilitation Act of 1973 did not become effective until December, 1973. P.L. 93–112, § 500(a), 29 U.S.C. § 790(a). Ms. Gurmankin concedes that it would not apply to pre–1974 injuries. The same would appear to be true of the later Pennsylvania statutes.[4] The seniority relief afforded by the injunction is designed to remedy pre–1974 discrimination. Thus, that relief requires that we consider the district court's constitutional holding.

Relying on *Cleveland Board of Education* v. *LaFleur*, 414 U.S. 632, 6 FEP Cases 1253 (1974), the court held that the District policy of preventing blind teachers from teaching sighted students created an irrebuttable presumption that blind persons could not be competent teachers, in violation of due process. In *LaFleur* the Supreme Court ruled that mandatory leaves for pregnant teachers, five months before the birth of their children created an irrebuttable presumption of physical incompetency to teach after the fourth month of pregnancy. The court held that denying pregnant teachers the opportunity to present evidence of continued competency violated due process. The challenge was not to the requirement that teachers be sufficiently healthy for the rigors of the classroom, but to the denial of the opportunity to show that they were. In this case, as well, Gurmankin's complaint is not addressed to the requirement that Philadelphia teachers pass a qualifying examination, which she eventually passed, but rather to the pre–1974 denial of the opportunity to demonstrate her competency. We agree with the district court that *Cleveland Board of Education* v. *LaFleur, supra,* controls. The refusals by the District to permit her to take the examination violated due process by subjecting Ms. Gurmankin to an irrebuttable presumption that her blindness made her incompetent to teach sighted students.

In *LaFleur,* of course, the court dealt with employed teachers, and thus with some continued expectation of employment based on state law. Ms. Gurmankin had no contract of employment, but she had an expectation, based on state law, of being admitted to the qualifying examination. In July 1970 she was issued a Professional Certificate, No. 190–34–3597, by the Pennsylvania Department of Education, certifying her as a qualified teacher of Comprehensive English. Under the rules of the Philadel-

---

[2] See also Act of December 19, 1974, P.L. 966, No. 318, amending the Pennsylvania Human Relations Act, 43 P.S. §§ 952–955 (1975 Cum. Supp.) to prohibit discrimination in employment because of a "non-job related handicap or disability." The district court opinion does not deal with any possible pendent state law claim, probably because initial proceedings under the Pennsylvania statute must be filed before an administrative agency. 43 P.S. § 960.

[3] *Hagans* v. *Lavine*, 415 U.S. 528 (1974).

[4] See n. 2, *supra.*

phia School District this certificate was the only requirement for entrance to the examination. She was, by virtue of the irrebuttable presumption of incompetency, deprived of the opportunity to take it between 1970 and 1974. The right to take the examination is a right arising under state law, and its deprivation in an arbitrary manner violated due process.

The District urges that even if we agree that there was a due process violation, the trial court lacked the power to cure it by the award of rightful place seniority. It distinguishes cases such as *Franks* v. *Bowman Transp. Co.*, 424 U.S. 747, 12 FEP Cases 549 (1976) and *United States* v. *Int'l Union of Elevator Constructors*, 538 F.2d 1012, 13 FEP Cases 81 (3d Cir. 1976) as confined solely to remedies for violations of Title VII of the Civil Rights Act of 1964. 42 U.S.C. § 2000e *et seq*. But the language of Title VII in § 706(g), 42 U.S.C. § 2000e–5(g), on which the courts have relied in affording seniority relief is merely ". . . any other equitable relief as the court deems appropriate." There is no distinction in the law of equitable remedies between suits brought under Title VII and suits brought in reliance on 42 U.S.C. § 1983, or directly on the Fourteenth Amendment.
"[W]here federally protected rights have been invaded, it has been the rule from the beginning that courts will be alert to adjust their remedies so as to grant the necessary relief."
*Bell* v. *Hood*, 327 U.S. 678, 684 (1946); *Bivens* v. *Six Unknown Federal Narcotics Agents*, 403 U.S. 388, 392 (1971). The equitable relief of an award of a retroactive seniority date was, on the record before us, entirely appropriate.


## C. EQUAL PROTECTION


### NYC TRANSIT AUTHORITY v. BEAZER

*Supreme Court of the United States, 1979*
_____ U.S. _____, 19 FEP Cases 149, revs'g 558 F.2d 97,
17 FEP Cases 226 (1977)

MR. JUSTICE STEVENS delivered the opinion of the Court.
The New York Transit Authority refuses to employ persons who use methadone. The District Court found that this policy violates the Equal Protection Clause of the Fourteenth Amendment. In a subsequent opinion, the court also held that the policy violates Title VII of the Civil Rights Act of 1964. The Court of Appeals affirmed without reaching the statutory question. The departure by those courts from the procedure normally followed in addressing statutory and constitutional questions in the same case, as well as concern that the merits of these important questions had been decided erroneously, led us to grant certiorari. _____ U.S. _____. We now reverse.

The Transit Authority (TA) operates the subway system and certain bus lines in New York City. It employs about 47,000 persons, of whom many—perhaps most—are employed in positions that involve danger to themselves or to the public. For example, some 12,300 are subway motormen, towermen, conductors, or bus operators. The District Court found that these jobs are attended by unusual hazards and must be performed by "persons of maximum alertness and competence." 399 F. Supp. 1033, 1052. Certain other jobs, such as operating cranes and handling high voltage equipment, are also considered "critical," or "safety sensitive," while still others, though classified as "noncritical," have a potentially important impact on the overall operation of the transportation system.[2]

TA enforces a general policy against employing persons who use narcotic drugs. The policy is reflected in Rule 11 (b) of TA's Rules and Regulations.

"Employees must not use, or have in their possession, narcotics, tranquilizers, drugs of the Amphetamine group or barbiturate derivatives or paraphernalia used to administer narcotics or barbiturate derivatives, except with the written permission of the Medical Director—Chief Surgeon of the System."

Methadone is regarded as a narcotic within the meaning of Rule 11(b). No written permission has even been given by TA's Medical Director for the employment of a person using methadone.[3]

The District Court found that methadone is a synthetic narcotic and a central nervous system depressant. If injected into the blood stream with

[2] [Footnotes numbered as in original.—Ed.]
Thus, about 13,400 employees are involved in the maintenance of subway cars, buses, track, tunnels, and structures. Another 5,600 work in subway stations, and over 2,000 are engaged in office tasks that include the handling of large sums of money. TA hires about 3,000 new employees each year.

[3] By its terms, Rule 11(b) does not apply to persons who formerly used methadone or any other drug, and the District Court did not find that TA had any general policy covering former users. On the contrary, the court found that "[t]he situation is not entirely clear with respect to the policy of the TA regarding persons who have successfully concluded participation in a methadone program." 399 F.Supp., at 1036.
Although it did not settle the question of what policy TA enforces in this respect, the District Court included former users in the plaintiff class. It then afforded them relief from any blanket exclusionary policy that TA *might* enforce, although, again, the supporting factual findings were admittedly "not [based on] a great deal" of evidence. *Id.*, at 1051.
TA contends that the meager evidence received at trial on the "former users" issue was insufficient to support either the class or relief determinations made with respect to those persons. We go further. As far as we are aware there was no evidence offered at trial, and certainly none relied upon by the District Court, that TA actually refused employment to any former user entitled to relief under the injunction ordered by that court. (As we point out in n. 12, infra, the one named plaintiff, Frazier, who was a former user when the complaint was filed was clearly a *current* user at the time he first applied for a job with TA and may well have been properly perceived as a current user when he next applied, notwithstanding his assertion of successful completion during the intervening three weeks. In any case, he had not completed a full year of methadone maintenance and could therefore be excluded under the District Court's injunction.)
It follows that neither the findings of fact, nor the record evidence, squarely presents any issue with respect to former users that must be resolved in order to dispose of this litigation. And, of course, it is those findings and that evidence, rather than statements of the parties on appeal and even off-hand and clearly erroneous charac-

a needle, it produces essentially the same effects as heroin.[4] Methadone has been used legitimately in at least three ways—as a pain killer, in "detoxification units" of hospitals as an immediate means of taking addicts off of heroin,[5] and in long range "methadone maintenance programs" as part of an intended cure for heroin addiction. See 21 CFR § 310.304(b) (1978). In such programs the methadone is taken orally in regular doses for a prolonged period. As so administered, it does not produce euphoria or any pleasurable effects associated with heroin; on the contrary, it prevents users from experiencing those effects when they inject heroin, and also alleviates the severe and prolonged discomfort otherwise associated with an addict's discontinuance of the use of heroin.

About 40,000 persons receive methadone maintenance treatment in New York City, of whom about 26,000 participate in the five major public or semipublic programs,[6] and 14,000 are involved in about 25 private programs.[7] The sole purpose of all these programs is to treat the addiction of persons who have been using heroin for at least two years.

---

terizations of the findings and evidence by the Court of Appeals, see opinion of MR. JUSTICE POWELL, *post*, at 2–3, 19 FEP Cases, at 159, that determine the issues properly before this Court. A policy excluding all former users would be harder to justify than a policy applicable only to persons currently receiving treatment. A court should not reach out to express an opinion on the constitutionality of such a policy unless necessary to adjudicate a concrete dispute between adverse litigants. We shall therefore confine our consideration to the legality of TA's enforcement of its Rule 11(b) against *current* users of methadone.

[4] "Heroin is a narcotic which is generally injected into the bloodstream by a needle. It is a central nervous system depressant. The usual effect is to create a 'high'—euphoria, drowsiness—for about thirty minutes, which then tapers off over a period of about three or four hours. At the end of this time the heroin user experiences sickness and discomfort known as 'withdrawal symptoms.' There is intense craving for another shot of heroin, after which the cycle starts over again. A typical addict will inject heroin several times a day." 399 F.Supp., at 1038.

[5] The District Court found that detoxification is accomplished "by switching a heroin addict to methadone and gradually reducing the doses of methadone to zero over a period of about three weeks. The patient thus detoxified is drug free. Moreover, it is hoped that the program of gradually reduced doses of methadone leaves him without the withdrawal symptoms, or the 'physical dependence' on a narcotic." 399 F.Supp., at 1038.

[6] "The five major public or semi-public methadone maintenance programs in New York City are:
"(1) Beth Israel program . . . with 33 clinics treating 7100 patients:
"(2) A program administered by the City of New York with 39 clinics treating 12,400 patients (hereafter referred to as 'the City program');
"(3) A program administered by the Bronx State Hospital and the Albert Einstein College of Medicine, with 7 clinics treating about 2400 patients;
"(4) A program operated by the Addiction Research and Treatment Center (ARTC) with 6 clinics treating about 1200 patients; and
"(5) A program operated by the New York State Drug Abuse Control Commission (DACC), with 8 clinics treating about 1100 patients.
"The total number of patients treated in public or semi-public programs is about 26,000. It appears that these programs are financed almost entirely by federal, state and city funds." 399 F.Supp., at 1040.

[7] "[V]ery little specific information was provided [at trial] regarding the private clinics." 399 F.Supp., at 1046. What evidence there was indicated that those clinics were likely to be less successful and less able to provide accurate information about their clients than the public clients. Id., at 1046, 1050.

Methadone maintenance treatment in New York is largely governed by regulations promulgated by the New York Drug Abuse Control Commission. Under the regulations, the newly accepted addict must first be detoxified, normally in a hospital. A controlled daily dosage of methadone is then prescribed. The regulations require that six doses a week be administered at a clinic, while the seventh day's dose may be taken at home. If progress is satisfactory for three months, additional doses may be taken away from the clinic, although throughout most of the program, which often lasts for several years, there is a minimum requirement of three clinic appearances a week. During these visits, the patient not only receives his doses but is also counseled and tested for illicit use of drugs.[8]

The evidence indicates that methadone is an effective cure for the physical aspects of heroin addiction. But the District Court also found "that many persons attempting to overcome heroin addiction have psychological or lifestyle problems which reach beyond what can be cured by the physical taking of doses of methadone." 399 F. Supp., at 1039. The crucial indicator of successful methadone maintenance is the patient's abstinence from the illegal or excessive use of drugs and alcohol. The District Court found that the risk of reversion to drug or alcohol abuse declines dramatically after the first few months of treatment. Indeed, "the strong majority" of patients who have been on methadone maintenance for at least a year are free from illicit drug use.[9] But a significant number are not. On this critical point, the evidence relied upon by the District Court reveals that even among participants with more than 12 months' tenure in methadone maintenance programs, the incidence of drug and alcohol abuse may often approach and even exceed 25 percent.[10]

---

[8] Although the United States Food and Drug Administration has also issued regulations in this area, 21 CFR §§ 291.501, 291.505 (1978), the New York State regulations are as or more stringent and thus effectively set the relevant standards for the authorized methadone maintenance programs involved in this case. Under those regulations, in-clinic ingestion of methadone must be observed by staff members, NYCRR § 2021.13 (b), and must occur with a frequency of six days a week during the first three months, no less than three days a week thereafter through the second year of treatment, and two days a week thereafter. *Id.*, § 2021.13 (a)(1). Tests are required to prevent hoarding of take-home doses, excessive use of methadone, and illicit use of other drugs or alcohol, any of which, if found, can result in increased clinic-visit frequency or in termination from the program. *Id.*, §§ 2021.13 (c) (2), 2021.13 (g). The programs are also required to include "a comprehensive range of rehabilitative services on-site under professional supervision," *id.*, § 2021.13(3), although participation in many of these services is voluntary and irregular.

[9] "I conclude from all the evidence that the strong majority of methadone maintained persons are successful, at least after the initial period of adjustment, in keeping themselves free of the use of heroin, other illicit drugs, and problem drinking." 399 F.Supp., at 1047.

[10] Thus, for example:
"Dr. Trigg of Beth Israel testified that about 5,000 out of the 6,500–7,000 patients in his clinics have been on methadone maintenance for a year or more. He further testified that 75 percent of this 5,000 are free from illicit drug use." 399 F.Supp., at 1046. Similarly, although the figures may be somewhat higher for the City and Bronx State Hospital programs, only 70 percent of the ARTC patients with a year's tenure or more were found to be free from illicit drug or alcohol use. It is reasonable to infer from this evidence that anywhere from 20 to 30 percent of those who have been on maintenance for over a year have drug or alcohol problems.

This litigation was brought by the four respondents as a class action on behalf of all persons who have been, or would in the future be, subject to discharge or rejection as employees of TA by reason of participation in a methadone maintenance program. Two of the respondents are former employees of TA who were dismissed while they were receiving methadone treatment.[11] The other two were refused employment by TA, one both shortly before and shortly after the successful conclusion of his methadone treatment,[12] and the other while he was taking methadone.[13] Their complaint alleged that TA's blanket exclusion of all former heroin addicts receiving methadone treatment was illegal under the Civil Rights Act of 1866, 42 U.S.C. § 1981, Title VII of the Civil Rights Act of 1964, 42 U.S.C. § 2000 et seq., and the Equal Protection Clause of the Fourteenth Amendment.

The trial record contains extensive evidence concerning the success of methadone maintenance programs, the employability of persons taking methadone, and the ability of prospective employers to detect drug abuse or other undesirable characteristics of methadone users. In general, the District Court concluded that there are substantial numbers of methadone users who are just as employable as other members of the general population and that normal personnel screening procedures—at least if augmented by some method of obtaining information from the staffs of methadone programs—would enable TA to identify the unqualified applicants on an individual basis. 399 F. Supp., at 1048–1051. On the other hand, the District Court recognized that at least one-third of the persons receiving methadone treatment—and probably a good many more—would unquestionably be classified as unemployable.[14]

11 Respondent Beazer was dismissed in November 1971 when his heroin addiction became known to TA and shortly after he enrolled in a methadone maintenance program; he successfully terminated his treatment in November 1973. Respondent Reyes began his methadone treatment in 1971 and was dismissed by TA in 1972. At the time of trial, in 1975, he was still participating in a methadone program.

12 Respondent Frasier was on methadone maintenance for only five months, from October 1972 until March 1973. TA refused to employ him as a bus operator in March 1973 and as a bus cleaner in April 1973. Frasier did not participate in a methadone program for even half a year. Moreover, he tested positively for methadone use at the time of his March application and only a few weeks before his April application was rejected under Rule 11(b). See 399 F.Supp., at 1034; App., at 32A. Under these circumstances, the District Court's characterization of Frazier as a "former" user at the time he applied, and its inclusion of Frazier in the group of "tenured" methadone users for whom it felt relief was appropriate under the Equal Protection Clause, see n. 32, infra, are without apparent justification.

13 Respondent Diaz entered a methadone maintenance program in December 1968 and was still receiving treatment at the time of trial. He was refused employment as a maintenance helper in 1970.

14 The District Court summarized the testimony concerning one of the largest and most successful public programs:

"The witnesses from the Beth Israel program testified that about one-third of the patients in that program, after a short period of adjustment, need very little more than the doses of methadone. The persons in this category are situated fairly satisfactorily with respect to matters such as family ties, education and jobs. Another one-third of the patients at Beth Israel need a moderate amount of rehabilitation service, including vocational assistance, for a period of several months or about a year. A person in this category may, for instance, have finished high school, but may have a long heroin history and no employment record. A final one-third of the patients at Beth

After extensively reviewing the evidence, the District Court briefly stated its conclusion that TA's methadone policy is unconstitutional. The conclusion rested on the legal proposition that a public entity "cannot bar persons from employment on the basis of criteria which have no rational relation to the demand of the job to be performed." 399 F. Supp., at 1057. Because it is clear that substantial numbers of methadone users are capable of performing many of the jobs at TA, the court held that the Constitution will not tolerate a blanket exclusion of all users from all jobs.

The District Court enjoined TA from denying employment to any person solely because of participation in a methadone maintenance program. Recognizing, however, the special responsibility for public safety borne by certain TA employees and the correlation between longevity in a methadone maintenance program and performance capability, the injunction authorized TA to exclude methadone users from specific categories of safety sensitive positions and also to condition eligibility on satisfactory performance in a methadone program for at least a year. In other words, the court held that TA could lawfully adopt general rules excluding all methadone users from some jobs and a large number of methadone users from all jobs.

Almost a year later the District Court filed a supplemental option allowing respondents to recover attorney's fees under 42 U.S.C. § 2000e-5(k). This determination was premised on the court's additional holding that TA's drug policy violated Title VII. Having already concluded that the blanket exclusion was not rationally related to any business needs of TA, the court reasoned that the statute is violated if the exclusionary policy has a discriminatory effect against blacks and Hispanics. That effect was proven, in the District Court's view, by two statistics: (1) of the employees referred to TA's medical consultant for suspected violation of its drug policy, 81 percent are black or Hispanic; (2) between 62 percent and 65 percent of all methadone maintained persons in New York City are black or Hispanic. 414 F. Supp. 277, 278–279, 15 FEP Cases 1065, 1066. The Court, however, did not find that TA's policy was motivated by any bias against blacks or Hispanics; indeed, it expressly found that the policy was not adopted with a discriminatory purpose. *Id.*, at 279, 15 FEP Cases, at 1066.

The Court of Appeals affirmed the District Court's constitutional holding. While it declined to reach the statutory issue, it also affirmed the award of attorney's fees under the aegis of the recently enacted Civil Rights Attorney's Fee Awards Act of 1976, 42 U.S.C. § 1988, which provides adequate support for an award of legal fees to a party prevailing on a constitutional claim.

After we granted certiorari, Congress amended the Rehabilitation Act of 1973, 29 U.S.C. § 700 *et seq.*, to prohibit discrimination against a class

---

Israel need intensive supportive services, are performing in the program marginally, and either will be discharged or will be on the brink of discharge." 399 F.Supp., at 1048.

of "handicapped individuals" that arguably includes certain former drug
abusers and certain current users of methadone. Pub. L. 95-251, 95th
Cong., 2d Sess. Respondents argue that the amendment now mandates at
least the prospective relief granted by the District Court and the Court
of Appeals and that we should therefore dismiss the writ as improvidently
granted. We are satisfied, however, that we should decide the constitutional question presented by the petition. Before doing so, we shall discuss
(1) the effect of the Rehabilitation Act on this case; and (2) the error in
the District Court's analysis of Title VII.

## I

Respondents contend that the recent amendment to § 7(6) of the Rehabilitation Act proscribes TA's enforcement of a general rule denying
employment to methadone users.[16] Even if respondents correctly interpret
the amendment, and even if they have a right to enforce that interpretation,[17] the case is not moot since their claims arose even before the act
itself was passed,[18] and they have been awarded monetary relief.[19] Moreover, the language of the statute, even after its amendment, is not free of
ambiguity,[20] and no administrative or judicial opinions specifically considering the impact of the statute on methadone users have been called to

[16] Section 504 of the Rehabilitation Act, 29 U.S.C. § 794, provides:
"No otherwise qualified handicapped individual in the United States, as defined
in section 706 (6) of this title, shall, solely by reason of his handicap, be excluded from
the participation in, be denied the benefits of, or be subjected to discrimination under
any program or activity receiving Federal financial assistance."
It is stipulated that the TA receives federal financial assistance.
    In relevant part, § 7(6) of the Act, 29 U.S.C. § 706(6), as amended, provides:
"The term 'handicapped individual' . . . means any person who (A) has a physical
or mental impairment which substantially limits one or more of such person's major
life activities, (B) has a record of such an impairment, or (C) is regarded as having
such an impairment.
    ". . . For purpose of sections 503 and 504 as such sections relate to employment, such
term does not include any individual who is an alcoholic or drug abuser whose current
use of alcohol or drugs prevents such individual from performing the duties of the
job in question or whose employment, by reason of such current alcohol or drug abuse,
would constitute a direct threat to property or the safety of others."
[17] The question whether a cause of action on behalf of handicapped persons may
be implied under § 504 of the Rehabilitation Act will be addressed by this Court in
Southeastern Community College v. Davis. No. 78–711, cert. granted Jan. 8, 1979.
[18] The latest act of alleged discrimination cited in respondents' complaint occurred
in April 1973, while the Act was passed on September 26, 1973. Pub. L. 93–112. Title V,
and the amendment to § 7(6) went into effect in November 6, 1978.
[19] See n. 17, supra.
[20] In order for the District Court's findings to bring the respondent class conclusively wthin the Act, we would have to find that denying employment to a methadone
user because of that use amounts to excluding an "otherwise qualified handicapped
individual . . . solely by reason of his handicap." Among other issues, this would
require us to determine (1) whether heroin addicts or current methadone users qualify
as "handicapped individual[s]"—i.e., whether that addiction or use is (or is perceived as) a "physical impairment which substantially limits one or more . . . major
life functions"; (2) whether methadone use prevents the individual "from performing
the duties of the job" or "would constitute a direct threat to property or the safety
of others"; and (3) whether the members of the respondent class are "otherwise
qualified"—the meaning of which phrase is at issue in Southeastern Community
College v. Davis, No. 78–711, cert. granted Jan. 8, 1979.

our attention. Of greater importance, it is perfectly clear that however we might construe the Rehabilitation Act, the concerns that prompted our grant of certiorari would still merit our attention.[21] We therefore decline to give the statute its first judicial construction at this stage of the litigation.

## II

Although respondents have consistently relied on both statutory and constitutional claims, the lower courts focused primarily on the latter. Thus when the District Court decided the Title VII issue, it did so only as an afterthought in order to support an award of attorneys fees; the Court of Appeals did not even reach the Title VII issue. We do not condone this departure from settled federal practice. "If there is one doctrine more deeply rooted than any other in the process of constitutional adjudication, it is that we ought not to pass on questions of constitutionality . . . unless such adjudication is unavoidable." *Spector Motor Co.* v. *McLaughlin,* 323 U.S. 101, 105. Before deciding the constitutional question, it was incumbent on those courts to consider whether the statutory grounds might be dispositive. Whatever their reason for not doing so,[23] we shall first dispose of the Title VII issue.[24]

[21] See ante, at n. 1 and accompanying text. Respondents may exaggerate the degree to which the recent amendment altered the law as it existed when we granted certiorari. Even before the Court of Appeals heard argument in this case, in fact, the Attorney General of the United States had issued an interpretation of the Act as it then existed which concluded that the Act "does in general prohibit discrimination against alcoholics and drug addicts in federally-assisted programs. . . ." Opinion of the Honorable Griffin B. Bell, Attorney General of the United States to Honorable Joseph A. Califano, Secretary, Department of Health, Education, and Welfare, April 12, 1977. Respondents brought this interpretation to our attention before we granted certiorari. Brief in Opposition to Certiorari, at A5–A6.

[23] Respondents suggest that the lower courts properly reached the constitutional issue first because only under the Equal Protection Clause could all of the class members, including white methadone users (who presumably do not have standing in this case under Title VII or § 1981) obtain all of the relief including backpay, sought in their complaint. In addition, they point to TA's argument that Title VII and § 1981 are unconstitutional insofar as they authorize relief against a state subdivision without any direct allegation or proof of intentional discrimination. Cf. *Fitzpatrick* v. *Bitzer,* 427 U.S. 445, 12 FEP Cases 1586; *National League of Cities* v. *Usery,* 426 U.S. 833, 22 WH Cases 1064; *Washington* v. *Davis,* 426 U.S. 229, 12 FEP Cases 1415; *Fry* v. *United States,* 421 U.S. 542, 22 WH Cases 284; *Katzenbach* v. *Morgan,* 384 U.S. 641. Under this latter point, it is argued that the District Court quite properly decided to address the constitutionality of a municipal agency's hiring practices before addressing the constitutionality of two Acts of Congress.

Whatever the theoretical validity of respondents' explanations for the actions of the District Court and the Court of Appeals, the fact remains that we are forced to speculate about what motivated them because they never explained their haste to address a naked constitutional issue despite the presence in the case of alternative statutory theories. It also bears noting that in its second opinion the District Court *did* decide that TA's policy violated a federal statute, and its decision, without addressing any constitutional issue, provided a statutory basis for virtually all of the relief that it ultimately awarded. Had it confronted the issue, therefore, it presumably would have concluded that it could have decided the case without addressing the constitutional issue on which it initially decided the case.

[24] The failure of the Court of Appeals to address the statutory issue decided by the District Court does not, of course, prevent this Court from reaching the issue. Cf. *Regents of the University of California* v. *Bakke,* 438 U.S. 265, 17 FEP Cases 1000.

The District Court's findings do not support its conclusion that TA's regulation prohibiting the use of narcotics, or its interpretation of that regulation to encompass users of methadone, violated Title VII of the Civil Rights Act.

A prima facie violation of the Act may be established by statistical evidence showing that an employment practice has the effect of denying the members of one race equal access to employment opportunities. Even assuming that respondents have crossed this threshold, when the entire record is examined it is clear that the two statistics on which they and the District Court relied do not prove a violation of Title VII.[25]

First, the District Court noted that 81 percent of the employees referred to TA's medical director for suspected violation of its narcotics rule were either black or Hispanic. But respondents have only challenged the rule to the extent that it is construed to apply to methadone users, and that statistic tells us nothing about the racial composition of the employees suspected of using methadone.[26] Nor does the record give us any information about the number of black, Hispanic, or white persons who were dismissed for using methadone.

---

We conclude that it is appropriate to reach the issue in this case, rather than remanding it to the Court of Appeals, because it was fully aired before the District Court, it involves the application of settled legal principals to uncontroversial facts, and it has been carefully briefed in this Court without any of the parties even suggesting the possibility of a remand.

Moreover, our treatment of the Title VII claim also disposes of the § 1981 claim without need of a remand. Although the exact applicability of that provision has not been decided by this Court, it seems clear that it affords no greater substantive protection than Title VII.

[25] "Statistics are . . . competent in proving employment discrimination. We caution only that statistics are not irrefutable; they come in infinite variety and, like any other kind of evidence, they may be rebutted. In short, their usefulness depends on all the surrounding facts and circumstances." *Teamsters* v. *United States*, 431 U.S. 324, 339–340, 14 FEP Cases 1514, 1520–1521 (footnote omitted).

From the time they filed their complaint until their submissions to this Court, respondents have relied on statistics to demonstrate the discriminatory *effect of* TA's methadone policy. They have never attempted to present a discriminatory *purpose* case and would be hard pressed to do so in the face of the District Court's explicit finding that no animus motivated TA in establishing its policy, 414 F.Supp., at 279, 15 FEP Cases, at 1066, and in the face of TA's demonstration in forms filed with the Equal Employment Opportunity Commission that the percentage of blacks and Hispanics in its work force is well over twice that of the percentage in the work force in the New York metropolitan area.

Because of our conclusion on the merits of respondents' Title VII claim, we need not address the constitutional challenge made by TA to Title VII insofar as it authorizes relief against a municipal agency under the circumstances of this case. See n. 23, *supra*.

[26] Indeed, it is probable that none of the employees comprising this 81 percent were methadone users. The parties stipulated that:

"TA employees showing physical manifestations of drug abuse *other than* the definite presence of morphine or *methadone* or other illicit drug in the urine are referred to [the medical director] for consultation. . . ." App., at 86A (emphasis added).

In view of this stipulation and the District Court's finding that few if any physical manifestations of drug abuse characterize methadone maintained persons, 399 F.Supp., at 1042–1045, it seems likely that such persons would not be included in the statistical pool referred to by the District Court. It should also be noted that when the dissent refers to the rejection of almost 5 percent of all applicants "due to the rule," *post*, at 3, 19 FEP Cases, at 161, the reference is to all narcotics users rather than to methadone users. The record does not tell us how many methadone users were rejected.

Second, the District Court noted that about 63 percent of the persons in New York receiving methadone maintenance in *public* programs—i.e., 63 percent of the 65 percent of all New York City methadone users who are in such programs[27]—are black or Hispanic. We do not know, however, how many of these persons ever worked or sought to work for TA. This statistic therefore reveals little if anything about the racial composition of the class of TA job applicants and employees receiving methadone treatment. More particularly, it tells us nothing about the class of otherwise-qualified applicants and employees who have participated in methadone maintenance programs for over a year—the only class improperly excluded by TA's policy under the District Court's analysis. The record demonstrates, in fact, that the figure is virtually irrelevant because a substantial portion of the persons included in it are either unqualified for other reasons—such as the illicit use of drugs and alcohol[28]—or have received successful assistance in finding jobs with employers other than TA.[29] Finally, we have absolutely no data on the 14,000 methadone users in the *private* programs, leaving open the possibility that the percentage of blacks and Hispanics in the class of methadone users is not significantly greater than the percentage of those minorities in the general population of New York City.[30]

At best, respondents' statistical showing is weak; even if it is capable of establishing a prima facie case of discrimination, it is assuredly rebutted by TA's demonstration that its narcotics rule (and the rule's application

[27] The statistic relied upon by the District Court was derived from a study of methadone patients prepared by a researcher at Rockefeller University based upon data supplied by the public methadone clinics in New York. In that the District Court admittedly received virtually no evidence about the private clinics, their funding, and their participants, see *ante,* at n. 7, there is no basis for assuming that the Rockefeller University statistic is applicable to participants in the private programs.

[28] To demonstrate employability, the District Court referred to a study indicating that 34 to 59 percent of the methadone users who have been in a maintenance program for a substantial period of time are unemployed. The evidence was inconclusive with respect to all methadone users. 399 F.Supp., at 1047. However, the director of the second largest program in New York testified that only 33 percent of the entire methadone patient population in that program were employable. Trial Transcript, January 10, 1975, at 345. On the statistics relating to illicit use of drugs and alcohol, see *ante,* at 7, 19 FEP Cases at 152.

[29] Although "a statistical showing of disproportionate impact need not always be based on an analysis of the characteristics of actual applicants," *Dothard* v. *Rawlinson,* 433 U.S. 321, 330, 15 FEP Cases 10, 14, "evidence showing that the figures for the general population might not accurately reflect the pool of qualified job applicants" undermines the significance of such figures. *Teamsters* v. *United States, supra,* 431 U.S., at 340 n. 20, 14 FEP Cases, at 1521.

[30] If all of the participants in private clinics are white, for example, then only about 40 percent of all methadone users would be black or Hispanic—compared to the 36.3 percent of the total population of New York that was black or Hispanic as of the 1970 census. Assuming instead that the percentage of those minorities in the private programs duplicates their percentage in the population of New York City, the figures would still only show that 50 percent of all methadone users are black or Hispanic compared to 36.3 percent of the population in the metropolitan area. (The 20 percent figure relied upon by the dissent refers to blacks and Hispanics in the work force, rather than in the total population of the New York metropolitan area. The reason the total-population figure is the appropriate one is because the 63 percent figure relied upon by respondents refers to methadone users in the population generally and not just those in the work force.)

to methadone users) is "job related." [31] The District Court's express finding that the rule was not motivated by racial animus forecloses any claim in rebuttal that it was merely a pretext for intentional discrimination. 414 F. Supp., at 279, 15 FEP Cases, at 1066. We conclude that respondents failed to prove a violation of Title VII. We therefore must reach the constitutional issue.

## III

The Equal Protection Clause of the Fourteenth Amendment provides that no State shall "deny to any person within its jurisdiction the equal protection of the laws." The Clause announces a fundamental principle: the State must govern impartially. Generally rules that apply evenhandedly to all persons within the jurisdiction unquestionably comply with this principle. Only when a governmental unit adopts a rule that has a special impact on less than all the persons subject to its jurisdiction does the question whether this principle is violated arise.

In this case, TA's Rule 11(b) places a meaningful restriction on all of its employees and job applicants; in that sense the rule is one of general applicability and satisfies the equal protection principle without further inquiry. The District Court, however, interpreted the rule as applicable to the limited class of persons who regularly use narcotic drugs, including methadone. As so interpreted, we are necessarily confronted with the question whether the rule reflects an impermissible bias against a special class.

Respondents have never questioned the validity of a special rule for all users of narcotics. Rather, they originally contended that persons receiving methadone should not be covered by that rule; in other words, they should not be included within a class that is otherwise unobjectionable. Their constitutional claim was that methadone users are entitled to be treated like most other employees and applicants rather than like other users of narcotics. But the District Court's findings unequivocally establish that there are relevant differences between persons using methadone regularly and persons who use no narcotics of any kind.[32]

[31] Respondents recognize, and the findings of the District Court establish, that TA's legitimate employment goals of safety and efficiency require the exclusion of all users of illegal narcotics, barbituates, and amphetamines, and of a majority of all methadone users. See *supra*, at n. 4; 6 and nn. 9–10, 19 FEP Cases, at 152; 8 and n. 14, 19 FEP Cases, at 152–153; n. 28. The District Court also held that those goals require the exclusion of all methadone users from the 25 percent of its positions that are "safety sensitive." See *ante*, at 9, 19 FEP Cases, at 153. Finally, the District Court noted that those goals are significantly served by—even if they do not require TA's rule as it applies to all methadone users including those who are seeking employment in non-safety sensitive positions. See *infra*, at nn. 33, 37. The record thus demonstrates that TA's rule bears a "manifest relationship to the employment in question." *Griggs* v. *Duke Power Co.*, 401 U.S. 424, 432, 3 FEP Cases 175, 178. See *Albemarle Paper Co.* v. *Moody*, 422 U.S. 405, 425, 10 FEP Cases 1181, 1190. Whether or not respondents' weak showing was sufficient to establish a prima facie case, it clearly failed to carry respondents' ultimate burden of proving a violation of Title VII.

[32] The District Court found that methadone is a narcotic. See 399 F.Supp., at 1038. See also *id.*, at 1044 ("The evidence is that, during the time patients are being brought

Respondents no longer question the need, or at least the justification, for special rules for methadone users. Indeed, they vigorously defend the District Court's opinion which expressly held that it would be permissible for TA to have a special rule denying methadone users any employment unless they had been undergoing treatment for at least a year, and another special rule denying even the most senior and reliable methadone users any of the more dangerous jobs in the system.

The constitutional defect in TA's employment policies, according to the District Court, is not that TA has special rules for methadone users, but rather that *some* members of the class should have been exempted from *some* requirements of the special rules. Left intact by its holding are rules requiring special supervision of methadone users to detect evidence of drug abuse, and excluding them from high-risk employment. Accepting those rules, the District Court nonetheless concluded that employment in nonsensitive jobs could not be denied to methadone users who had progressed satisfactorily with their treatment for one year, and who, when examined individually, satisfied TA's employment criteria. In short, having recognized that disparate treatment of methadone users simply because they are methadone users is permissible—and having excused TA from an across-the-board requirement of individual consideration of such persons—the District Court construed the Equal Protection Clause as requiring TA to adopt additional and more precise special rules for that special class.

But any special rule short of total exclusion that TA might adopt is likely to be less precise—and will assuredly be more costly[33]—than the

---

up to their constant dosage of methadone (a period of about six weeks), there may be complaints of drowsiness, insomnia, excess sweating, constipation, and perhaps some other symptoms."). Moreover, every member of the class of methadone users was formerly addicted to the use of heroin. None is completely cured; otherwise, there would be no continuing need for treatment. All require some measure of special supervision, and all must structure their weekly routines around mandatory appearances at methadone clinics. The clinics make periodic checks as long as the treatment continues in order to detect evidence of drug abuse. Employers must review, and sometimes verify, these checks; since the record indicates that the information supplied by treatment centers is not uniformally reliable, see n. 7, *supra*, the employer has a special and continuing responsibility to review the condition of these persons.

In addition, a substantial percentage of persons taking methadone will not successfully complete the treatment program. The findings do not indicate with any precision the number who drop out, or the number who can fairly be classified as unemployable, but the evidence indicates that it may well be a majority of those taking methadone at any given time. See nn. 14 and 28, *supra*.

[33] The District Court identified several significant screening procedures that TA would have to adopt specially for methadone users if it abandoned its rule. For example, the court noted that current methadone users (but no other applicants) would have to:

"demonstrate that they have been on a reliable methadone program for a year or more; that they have faithfully abided by the rules of the program; [and] that, according to systematic tests and observations, they have been free of any illicit drug or alcohol abuse for the entire period of treatment excluding a possible adjustment period. . . ." 399 F.Supp., at 1049.

The District Court also recognized that verifying the above demonstrations by the methadone user would require special efforts to obtain reliable information from, *and about,* each of the many different methadone maintenance clinics—a task that it

one that it currently enforces. If eligibility is marked at any intermediate point—whether after one year of treatment or later—the classification will inevitably discriminate between employees or applicants equally or almost equally apt to achieve full recovery.[34] Even the District Court's opinion did not rigidly specify one year as a constitutionally mandated measure of the period of treatment that guarantees full recovery from drug addiction.[35] The uncertainties associated with the rehabilitation of heroin addicts precluded it from identifying any bright line marking the point at which the risk of regression ends.[36] By contrast, the "no drugs" policy now enforced by TA is supported by the legitimate inference that as long as a treatment program (or other drug use) continues, a degree of uncertainty persists.[37] Accordingly, an employment policy that postpones eligibility until the treatment program has been completed, rather than accepting an intermediate point on an uncertain line, is rational. It is

---

recognized could be problematic in some cases. 399 F.Supp., at 1050, see *ante*, at n. 7. Furthermore, once it hired a methadone user, TA would have a continuing duty to monitor his progress in the maintenance program and would have to take special precautions against his promotion to any of the safety-sensitive positions from which the District Court held he may be excluded.

The dissent is therefore repeatedly mistaken in attributing to the District Court a finding that TA's "normal screening process without additional effort" would suffice in the absence of the "no drugs" rule. *Id.*, at 9 n. 10, 19 FEP Cases, at 164. See *id.*, at 5, 9, 19 FEP Cases, at 163, 164. Aggravating this erroneous factual assumption is a mistaken legal proposition advanced by the dissent—that TA can be faulted for failing to prove the unemployability of "successfully maintained methadone users." *Id.*, at 6–7, 19 FEP Cases, at 163. Aside from the misallocation of the burden of proof that underlies this argument, it is important to note, see *id.*, at 7, 19 FEP Cases, at 163, that TA *did* prove that 20 to 30 percent of the class afforded relief by the District Court are *not* "successfully maintained," and hence are assuredly not employable. Even assuming therefore that the percentage of employable persons in the remaining 70 percent is the same as that in the class of TA applicants who do not use methadone, it is respondents who must be faulted for failing to prove that the offending 30 percent could be excluded as cheaply and effectively in the absence of the rule.

34 It may well be, in fact, that many methadone users who have been in programs for something less than a year are actually more qualified for employment than many others who have been in a program for longer than a year.

35 "The TA is not prevented from making reasonable rules and regulations about methadone maintained persons—such as requiring satisfactory performance in a program for a period of time such as a year. . . ." 399 F.Supp., at 1058.

36 These uncertainties are evident not only in the District Court's findings but also in legislative consideration of the problem. See *Marshall* v. *United States*, 414 U.S. 417, 425–427.

37 The completion of the program also marks the point at which the employee or applicant considers himself cured of drug dependence. Moreover, it is the point at which the employee/applicant no longer must make regular visits to a methadone clinic, no longer has access to free methadone that might be hoarded and taken in excessive and physically disruptive doses, and at which a simple urine test—as opposed to a urine test followed up by efforts to verify the bona fides of the subject's participation in a methadone program, and of the program itself—suffices to prove compliance with TA's rules.

Respondents argue that the validity of these considerations is belied by TA's treatment of alcoholics. Although TA refuses to hire new employees with drinking problems, it continues in its employ a large number of persons who have either been found drinking on the job or have been deemed unfit for duty because of prior drinking. These situations give rise to discipline but are handled on an individual basis. But the fact that TA has the resources to expend on one class of problem employees does not by itself establish a constitutional duty on its part to come up with resources to spend on all classes of problem employees.

neither unprincipled nor invidious in the sense that it implies disrespect for the excluded subclass.

At its simplest, the District Court's conclusion was that TA's rule is broader than necessary to exclude those methadone users who are not actually qualified to work for TA. We may assume not only that this conclusion is correct but also that it is probably unwise for a large employer like TA to rely on a general rule instead of individualized consideration of every job applicant. But these assumptions concern matters of personnel policy that do not implicate the principle safeguarded by the Equal Protection Clause.[38] As the District Court recognized, the special classification created by TA's rule serves the general objectives of safety and efficiency.[39] Moreover, the exclusionary line challenged by respondents "is not one which is directed 'against' any individual or category of persons, but rather it represents a policy choice . . . made by that branch of Government vested with the power to make such choices." *Marshall* v. *United States*, 414 U.S. 417, 428. Because it does not circumscribe a class of persons characterized by some unpopular trait or affiliation, it does not create or reflect any special likelihood of bias on the part of the ruling majority.[40] Under these circumstances, it is of no constitutional significance that the degree of rationality is not as great with respect to certain

[38] The District Court also concluded that TA's rule violates the Due Process Clause because it creates an "irrebutable presumption" of unemployability on the part of methadone users. 399 F.Supp., at 1057. Respondents do not rely on the due process argument in this Court, and we find no merit in it.

[39] "[L]egislative classifications are valid unless they bear no rational relationship to the State's objectives. *Massachusetts Bd. of Retirement* v. *Murgia*, [427 U.S. 307, 314, 12 FEP Cases 1569, 1572]. State legislation 'does not violate the Equal Protection Clause merely because the classifications [it makes] are imperfect.' *Dandridge* v. *Williams*, 397 U.S. 471, 485." *Washington* v. *Yakima Indian Nation*, _____ U.S. _____, _____ (slip op., at 38). See also *Vance* v. *Bradley*, 439 U.S. _____, _____, 19 FEP Cases 1, 7, quoting *Phillips Chemical Co.* v. *Dumas School District*, 361 U.S. 376, 385. ("Even if the classification involved here is to some extent both under- and over-inclusive, and hence the line drawn by Congress imperfect, it is nevertheless the rule that in a case like this 'perfection is by no means required.' ").

[40] Since *Barbier* v. *Connolly*, 113 U.S. 27, the Court's equal protection cases have recognized a distinction between "invidious discrimination," *id.*, at 31—i.e., classifications drawn "with an evil eye and an unequal hand" or motivated by "a feeling of antipathy" against, a specific group of residents. *Yick Wo* v. *Hopkins*, 118 U.S. 356, 373–374; *Soon Hing* v. *Crowley*, 113 U.S. 703, 710; see also *Quong Wing* v. *Kirkendall*, 223 U.S. 59; *Holden* v. *Hardy*, 169 U.S. 366, 398—and those special rules that "are often necessary for general benefits [such as] supplying water, preventing fires, lighting streets, opening parks, and many other objects." *Barbier, supra*, 113 U.S., at 31. See also *Washington* v. *Davis*, 426 U.S., 229, 239–241, 12 FEP Cases 1415, 1421–1422. Quite plainly, TA's Rule 11(b) was motivated by TA's interest in operating a safe and efficient transportation system rather than by any special animus against a specific group of persons. Cf. 414 F.Supp., at 279, 15 FEP Cases, at 1066. Respondents recognize this valid general motivation, as did the District Court, and for that reason neither challenges TA's rule as it applies to *all* narcotic users, or even to *all* methadone users. Because respondents merely challenge the rule insofar as it applies to *some* methadone users, that challenge does not even raise the question whether the rule falls on the "invidious" side of the *Barbier* distinction. Accordingly, there is nothing to give rise to a presumption of illegality and to warrant our especially "attentive judgment." Cf. *Truax* v. *Corrigan*, 257 U.S. 312, 327.

ill-defined subparts of the classification as it is with respect to the classification as a whole. *Mathews* v. *Diaz*, 426 U.S. 67, 83–84.[41]

No matter how unwise it may be for TA to refuse employment to individual car cleaners, track repairmen, or bus drivers simply because they are receiving methadone treatment, the Constitution does not authorize a Federal Court to interfere in that policy decision. The judgment of the Court of Appeals is

*Reversed.*

MR. JUSTICE POWELL, concurring in part and dissenting in part: The opinion of the Court addresses, and sustains, the policy of the Transit Authority under its Rule 11 (b) only insofar as it applies to employees and applicants for employment who *"are receiving methadone treatments"* (emphasis supplied). *Ante*, at 3 n. 3, and 24, 19 FEP Cases, at 151 and 158. I concur in the opinion of the Court holding that there is no violation of the Equal Protection Clause or Title VII when the Authority's policy is applied to employees or applicants who are currently on methadone.

But in my view the question presented by the record and opinions of the courts below is not limited to the effect of the rule on present methadone users. Indeed, I have thought it conceded by all concerned that the Transit Authority's policy of exclusion extended beyond the literal language of Rule 11 (b) to persons currently free of methadone use but who had been on the drug within the previous five years. The District Court was unsure whether all past users were excluded but indicated that the policy of exclusion covered at least persons who had been free of methadone use for less than five years. 399 F. Supp. 1032, 1036 (1975).[1] The Court of Appeals for the Second Circuit was unequivocal. It understood that the rule constituted a "blanket exclusion from employment of all persons participating in or having successfully completed methadone maintenance programs." 558 F.2d 97, 99, 17 FEP Cases 226, 227 (1977).

Petitioners' brief in this Court states, in effect, that the Authority will consider only applicants for employment who have been free of a drug problem for "at least five years":

"[T]he Authority will give individual consideration to people with a past history of drug addiction including those who have completed either a

---

[41] "When a legal distinction is determined, as no one doubts there may be, between night and day, childhood and maturity, or any other extremes, a point has to be fixed or a line has to be drawn, or gradually picked out by successive decisions, to mark where the change takes place. Looked at by itself without regard to the necessity behind it the line or point seems arbitrary. It might as well or nearly as well be a little more to one side or the other. But when it is seen that a line or point there must be, and that there is no mathematical or logical way of fixing it precisely, the decision of the legislature must be accepted unless we can say that it is very wide of any reasonable mark." *Louisville Gas Co.* v. *Coleman*, 277 U.S. 32, 41 (HOLMES, J., dissenting).

[1] The District Court also noted that the Authority "contends that it cannot afford to take what it considers the risks of employing *present* or *past* methadone maintained persons, except possibly those who have been successfully withdrawn from methadone for several years." 399 F.Supp. 1032, 1052 (SDNY 1975) (emphasis supplied).

drug free or a methadone maintenance program, and who have been completely drug free and have had a stable history for at least five years."
Brief for Petitioners 5.

There was a similar recognition of the Authority's policy in the petition
for a writ of certiorari.[2]

Despite this unanimity among the parties and courts below as to the
question presented, the Court today simply chooses to limit its decision
to the policy with respect to employees and applicants currently receiving
methadone treatment. The explanation given is that "neither the findings
of fact nor the record evidence squarely presents any issue with respect to
former users that must be resolved in order to dispose of this litigation."
*Ante,* at 2–3, n. 3, 19 FEP Cases, at 151. But the only support the Court
cites for this statement is a lack of proof as to the policy's actual application. In light of the express admission of the Transit Authority to the
District Court that the policy extended to at least some former users,[3]
evidence of the past application of the policy was irrelevant to the fashion
ing of prospective relief.[4]

I conclude that the Court has decided only a portion of the case
presented, and has failed to address what it recognizes as the more difficult
issue. *Ante,* at 2–3, n. 3, 22, and n. 37, 19 FEP Cases, at 150–151, 158. We
owe it to the parties to resolve all issues properly presented, rather than to
afford no guidance whatever as to whether former drug and methadone
users may be excluded from employment by the Authority. I agree with
the courts below that there is no rational basis for an absolute bar against
the employment of persons who have completed successfully a methadone

[2] In petitioners' Statement of the Case the affected class was said to include former
addicts "who are participants in or *have completed* a methadone maintenance program." Pet. for Cert. 4 (emphasis supplied).
  The brief for respondents similarly described the Transit Authority's policy:
"The Transit Authority's blanket denial of employment to fully rehabilitated heroin
addicts who are being or ever have been treated in methadone maintenance programs
violates the Equal Protection and Due Process Clauses of the Fourteenth Amendment."
Brief for Respondents 59.

[3] See, e.g., 3 Court of Appeals App. 1106a–1112a.

[4] The Court seems to imply that because the Transit Authority's policy with respect
to former methadone users had not been invoked against any of the named plaintiffs,
it was improper for the District Court to certify a class of former users who would
be affected by the policy. *Ante,* at 2-3, n. 3, 7 n. 12, 19 FEP Cases, at 150–151, 152.
Even if one were to consider it proper for this Court to disregard the District Court's
explicit finding that plaintiff Frasier "was rejected because of his *former* methadone
use," 399 F.Supp., at 1034 (emphasis supplied), the Court overlooks the further finding
that:
"[I]t is unquestioned that there are many methadone maintenance patients who successfully withdraw from methadone and stay clear of drug abuse thereafter. Plaintiff
Beazer is such a person, having ceased using methadone almost two years ago. . . .
There is no rational reason for maintaining an absolute bar against the employment
of these persons regardless of their individual merit." *Id.,* at 1051.
It is clear that Beazer both was a proper representative of the class of former users
and was interested in Transit Authority employment, inasmuch as reinstatement was
part of the relief he sought. In light of the Transit Authority's unequivocal policy of
not employing persons in Beazer's position, it was unnecessary for him to engage
in the futile ritual of reapplying for employment after terminating his methadone
use in order to have standing to attack the policy.

maintenance program and who otherwise are qualified for employment. See *Vance* v. *Bradley*, 439 U.S. ____, ____, 19 FEP Cases 1 (1979); *Massachusetts Bd. of Retirement* v. *Murgia*, 427 U.S. 307, 314, 12 FEP Cases 1569, 1572 (1976); *San Antonio Ind. School Dist.* v. *Rodriguez*, 411 U.S. 1, 40 (1973). I therefore would affirm the judgment below with respect to the class of persons who are former methadone users.

MR. JUSTICE BRENNAN, dissenting: I would affirm for the reasons stated in Part I of MR. JUSTICE WHITE's dissenting opinion.

MR. JUSTICE WHITE, with whom MR. JUSTICE MARSHALL joins, dissenting: Although the Court purports to apply settled principles to unique facts, the result reached does not square with either Title VII or the Equal Protection Clause. Accordingly, but respectfully, I dissent.

I

As an initial matter, the Court is unwise in failing to remand the statutory claims to the Court of Appeals. The District Court decided the Title VII issue only because it provided a basis for allowing attorney's fees. 414 F. Supp. 277, 278, 15 FEP Cases 1605 (SDNY 1976). The Court of Appeals did not deal with Title VII, relying instead on the intervening passage of the Civil Rights Attorney's Fees Award Act of 1976,[1] which authorized the award of fees for success on the equal protection claim today held infirm by the Court. 588 F.2d 97, 99–100, 17 FEP Cases 226, 228 (CA2 1977). In such circumstances, on finding that we disagree with the judgment of the Court of Appeals as to the constitutional question, we would usually remand the unexplored alternative basis for relief.[2] E.g., *Vermont Yankee Nuclear Power Corp.* v. *NRDC*, 435 U.S. 519, 549 (1978). And see *Village of Arlington Heights* v. *Metropolitan Housing Dev. Corp.*, 429 U.S. 252, 271 (1977), which involved nearly identical circumstances. That course would obviate the need for us to deal with what the Court considers to be a factual issue or at least would provide assistance in analyzing the issue.

Because the Court has decided the question, however, I must express my reservations about the merits of that decision. In a disparate impact hiring case such as this, the plaintiff must show that the challenged practice excludes members of a protected group in numbers disproportionate to their incidence in the pool of potential employees.[3] Respondents made

[1] 42 U.S.C. § 1988.

[2] The Court finds it inappropriate to remand because the Title VII question "was fully aired before the District Court . . . involves the application of settled legal principles to uncontroversial facts, and . . . has been carefully briefed in this Court without any of the parties even suggesting the possibility of a remand." *Ante*, at 14 n. 24, 19 FEP Cases, at 155. The Court is able to overturn the Title VII judgment below, however, only after reversing some of the District Court's key findings of fact, which the parties strongly contest, on grounds that were not aired at all in the District Court or the Court of Appeals. See *infra*, at 2 n. 4, 4, and n. 6, 19 FEP Cases, at 160 and 161.

[3] See *ante*, at 14, 19 FEP Cases, at 155; *Dothard* v. *Rawlinson*, 433 U.S. 321, 329, 15 FEP Cases 10, 14 (1977). The failure to hire is not "because of" race, color, religion,

out a sufficient, though not strong prima facie case by proving that about 63 percent of those using methadone in the New York City area are black or Hispanic and that only about 20 percent of the relevant population as a whole belongs to one of those groups.[4] I think it fair to conclude, as the District must have, that blacks and Hispanics suffer three times as much from the operation of the challenged rule excluding methadone users as one would expect from a neutral practice. Thus, excluding those who are or have been in methadone programs "operate[s] to render ineligible a markedly disproportionate number" of blacks and Hispanics. *Griggs* v. *Duke Power Co.*, 401 U.S. 424, 429, 3 FEP Cases 175, 177 (1971).

In response to this, the Court says that the 63 percent statistic was not limited to those who worked for or sought to work for petitioners and to those who have been successfully maintained on methadone, and that it does not include those in private clinics. *Ante*, at 15–17, 19 FEP Cases at 155–156. I suggest, in the first place, that these attacks on facially valid statistics should have been made in the District Court and the Court of Appeals, see *Dothard* v. *Rawlinson*, 433 U.S. 321, 331, 15 FEP Cases 10, 15 (1977); the first contention was not even made in this Court. It also seems to me that petitioners have little to complain about insofar as the makeup of the applicant pool is concerned since they refused on grounds of irrelevancy to allow discovery of the racial background of the applicants denied employment pursuant to the methadone rule.

In any event, I cannot agree with the Court's assertions that this evidence "reveals little if anything," "tells us nothing," and is "virtually irrelevant." *Ante*, at 15–16, 19 FEP Cases, at 155–156.[5] There is not a shadow of doubt that methadone users do apply for employment with petitioner, and because 63 percent of all methadone users are black or Hispanic, there is every reason to conclude that a majority of methadone users who apply are also from these minority groups. Almost 5 percent of all applicants are rejected due to the rule, and undoubtedly many black

---

sex, or national origin if the adverse relationship of the challenged practice to one of those factors is purely a matter of chance—a statistical coincidence. See *Griggs* v. *Duke Power Co.*, 401 U.S. 424, 430, 3 FEP Cases 175, 177 (1971); Civil Rights Act of 1964, § 703(a), 42 U.S.C. § 2000e–2(a). Beyond the statistically significant relationship between race and participation in methadone programs shown by the figures here, respondents introduced direct evidence that the high frequency of minorities among the disqualified group was not just a chance aberration. See nn. 7 and 15, *infra*.

[4] The Court asserts that the proper percentage is 36.3. Respondents relied upon the 1970 census figures for the New York Standard Metropolitan Statistical Area Work force: 15.0 percent black and 5.1 percent Hispanic. Petitioners accept the 20 percent figure. Brief for Petitioners 53. And the District Court apparently did so also. No matter which figure is correct, there is still a disparate impact.

[5] The Court quotes *Teamsters* v. *United States*, 431 U.S. 324, 340 n. 20, 14 FEP Cases 1514, 1521 (1977), to the effect that " 'evidence showing that the figures for the general population might not accurately reflect the pool of qualified job applicants' undermines the significance of such figures." *Ante*, at 16–17, n. 29, 19 FEP Cases, at 156. Petitioners have not put on such "evidence"; we have only the Court's hypotheses, facially unlikely ones at that. Under the Federal Rules of Evidence, to be admissibly relevant, evidence must tend to establish a material fact. This evidence does that, and by definition unrebutted probative evidence on *the* material fact is sufficient to make out a prima facie case.

and Hispanic methadone users are among those rejected. Why would proportionally fewer of them than whites secure work with petitioner absent the challenged practice? The Court gives no reason whatsoever for rejecting this sensible inference, and where the inference depends so much on local knowledge, I would accept the judgment of the District Court rather than purport to make an independent judgment from the banks of the Potomac. At the very least, as I have said, I would seek the views of the Court of Appeals.

The Court complains that even if minority groups make up 63 percent of methadone-user applicants this statistic is an insufficient indicator of the composition of the group found by the District Court to have been wrongly excluded—that is, those who have been successfully maintained for a year or more. I cannot, however, presume with the Court that blacks or Hispanics will be less likely than whites to succeed on methadone. I would have thought the presumption, until rebutted, would be one of an equal chance of success, and there has been no rebuttal.

Finally, as to the racial composition of the patients at private clinics, I note first that the District Court found that "[b]etween 62 percent and 65 percent of methadone maintained persons in New York City are black and Hispanic . . . ." 414 F. Supp., at 279, 15 FEP Cases, at 1606. The finding was for the total population, not just for public clinics. Even assuming that the Court wishes to overturn this finding of fact as clearly erroneous, I see no support for doing so. The evidence from the Methadone Information Center at Rockefeller University indicated that 61 percent of all patients in the metropolitan area were black or Puerto Rican (with 5.85 percent undefined). This was based on a 1,400 patient sample, which, according to the Center, "was drawn on a random basis and very accurately reflects the *total population* for Metropolitan New York City" (emphasis supplied). There is no reason to believe that this study, which in its reporting of the total number of patients of all races included both public and private clinics, did not include private programs in its racial composition figures.[6] And even if everyone in the

6 Petitioners suggest that the evidence did not include private clinics since the Center does not receive information from them. Had this objection been raised in the District Court as it should have been, respondents would have had the opportunity to remove any doubt about whether the evidence included private programs. Moreover, in support of their suggestion, petitioners rely upon two isolated statements that do not directly discuss the study in question. Dr. Lukoff testified that the private clinics report to the FDA but not to the "Rockefeller Institute register," and he estimated that there were about 1,500 patients in such unreporting clinics. Tr. (Jan. 9, 1975) 252 (emphasis supplied). Dr. Dole, a professor at Rockefeller University and senior physician at the University Hospital, testified that "the methadone data center . . . maintains the computerized inventory on all 40,000 patients in treatment" and that "[a]ll of the known programs report, I presume." Tr. (Jan. 7, 1975) 114 (emphasis supplied). He did testify that "[t]he most detailed documentation comes from the major public" programs, which "comprise about 25,000 out of the 40,000" methadone patients. As to the remaining patients, his program still had "simpl[e] registry information. . . ." *Id.*, at 115–116. In short, the majority's unsupported effort to undermine the District Court's findings of fact merely establishes the wisdom of either remanding or, on the Court's evident assumption that the Court of Appeals would have affirmed the Title VII judgment, abiding by the "two-court rule."

private clinics were white, a highly unlikely assumption at best,[7] the challenged rule would still automatically exclude a substantially greater number of blacks and Hispanics than would a practice with a racially neutral effect.

With all due respect, I would accept the statistics as making a prima facie case of disparate impact. Obviously, the case could have been stronger, but this Court is unjustified in displacing the District Court's acceptance of uncontradicted, relevant evidence. Perhaps sensing that, the Court goes on to say that if such a prima facie showing was made it was rebutted by the fact that the rule is "job related."

Petitioners had the burden of showing job relatedness. They did not show that the rule results in a higher quality labor force, that such a labor force is necessary, or that the cost of making individual decisions about those on methadone was prohibitive. Indeed, as shown in the equal protection discussion infra, petitioners have not come close to showing that the present rule is "demonstrably a reasonable measure of job performance." *Griggs, supra,* at 436, 3 FEP Cases, at 180. No one could reasonably argue that petitioners have made the kind of showing demanded by *Griggs* or *Albemarle Paper Co.* v. *Moody,* 422 U.S. 405, 10 FEP Cases 1181 (1975). By petitioners' own stipulation, see n. 14, infra, this employment barrier was adopted "without meaningful study of [its] relationship to job-performance ability." *Griggs, supra,* at 431, 3 FEP Cases, at 178. As we stated in *Washington* v. *Davis,* 426 U.S. 229, 247, 12 FEP Cases 1415, 1422 (1976), Title VII "involves a more probing judicial review of, and less deference to, the seemingly reasonable acts of administrators and executives than is appropriate under the Constitution . . . ." Therefore, unlike the majority, *ante,* at 17–18, n. 31, 19 FEP Cases, at 156, I think it insufficient that the rule as a whole has some relationship to employment so long as a readily identifiable and severable part of it does not.

## II

I also disagree with the Court's disposition of the Equal Protection claim in light of the facts established below. The District Court found that the evidence conclusively established that petitioners exclude from employment all persons who are successfully on methadone maintenance —that is, those who after one year are "free of the use of heroin, other illicit drugs, and problem drinking," 399 F. Supp., at 1047—and those who have graduated from methadone programs and remain drug-free for less than five years;[8] that past or present successful methadone mainte-

---

[7] The evidence before the District Court established that 80 percent of heroin addicts in the New York City metropolitan area, the source of clients for both public and private methadone clinics, are black or Hispanic.

[8] Because the rule is unwritten in relevant part, there is confusion about its scope. The Court asserts that it does not exclude those who formerly used methadone, and that the District Court "did not settle the question of what policy TA enforces in this respect. . . ." *Ante,* at 3 n. 3, 19 FEP Cases, at 151. In fact, however, petitioners openly admit that they automatically exclude former methadone users unless they "have been completely drug free and have had a stable history for at least five years."

nance is not a meaningful predictor of poor performance or conduct in most job categories; that petitioners could use their normal employee-screening mechanisms to separate the successfully maintained users from the unsuccessful; and that petitioners do exactly that for other groups that common sense indicates might also be suspect employees.[9] Petitioners did not challenge these factual conclusions in the Court of Appeals, but that court nonetheless reviewed the evidence and found that it overwhelmingly supported the District Court's findings. 557 F.2d at 99, 17 FEP Cases, at 227. It bears repeating, then, that both the District Court and the Court of Appeals found that those who have been maintained on methadone for at least a year and who are free from the use of illicit drugs and alcohol can easily be identified through normal personnel procedures and, for a great many jobs, are as employable as and present no more risk than applicants from the general population.

Though petitioners' argument here is primarily an attack upon the fact-finding below, the Court does not directly accept that thesis. Instead, it

---

Brief for Petitioners 5. And I quote the District Court's actual findings which in context is unlike that described by the majority:

"It is clear that a relatively recent methadone user would be subject to the blanket exclusionary policy. However, the TA has indicated that there might be some flexibility with respect to a person who had once used methadone, but had been free of such use for a period of five years or more." 399 F.Supp. 1032, 1036 (SDNY 1975).

The Court finds no "concrete dispute between adverse litigants" over the former users policy because no former user is entitled to relief under the District Court's injunction. *Ante,* at 3 n. 3, 19 FEP Cases, at 151. But respondent Frasier is a former user, see *id.,* at 7 n. 12, 19 FEP Cases, at 152, and the District Court expressly granted him relief, including backpay from the time he was rejected as a recent former methadone user. App. to Pet. for Cert. 77a–78a. The Court says the District Court erred in finding as facts that Frasier was using no narcotics in April 1973 and that petitioners refused to hire him solely because of his prior, apparently successful methadone treatment. As I read the facts as recited by the Court, the District Court was clearly correct, but in any event petitioners have not preserved this argument in the Court of Appeals or here. See Defendants' Proposed Findings of Fact 6–7 (filed Oct. 18, 1974) (Frasier "purportedly" graduated successfully from [a] methadone program on March 19, 1973, and, though otherwise eligible, was rejected due to "his drug history" on April 2, 1973). See also *ante,* at 3 n. 4, 19 FEP Cases, at 159 (POWELL, J., dissenting in relevant part.)

The Court apparently reads the District Court's injunction as protecting only those persons who had been in methadone programs for a year or longer before they were cured. It is incredible that the "District Court would have punished those persons able to triumph over heroin addiction in less than a year. And the context of the District Court's order, combined with the grant of relief to respondent Frasier, makes it clear that the court intended to protect, and had good reason to do so, *all* former methadone users as well as those current users who have been successfully maintained for more than a year.

9 Respondents presented numerous top experts in this field and large employers with former heroin users treated with methadone. Both sides rested after six days of trial, but the District Court demanded nine more days of further factual development, and an eight-hour inspection of petitioners' facilities, because it did not believe that the evidence could be so one-sidedly in respondents' favor. The court correctly realized its responsibility in a public law case of this type to demand the whole story before making a constitutional ruling. See Chayes, *The Role of the Judge in Public Law Litigation,* 89 HARV. L. REV. 1281 (1976). The District Court called six witnesses of its own, and it chose them primarily because they had written articles on methadone maintenance that petitioners asserted had shown the unreliability of that method of dealing with heroin addiction. It also correctly expressed its refusal to base its judgment on shifting medical opinions.

concludes that the District Court and the Court of Appeals both misapplied the Equal Protection Clause. On the facts as found, however, one can reach the Court's result only if that Clause imposes no real constraint at all in this situation.

The question before us is the rationality of placing successfully maintained or recently cured persons in the same category as those just attempting to escape heroin addiction or who have failed to escape it rather than in with the general population.[10] The asserted justification for the challenged classification is the objective of a capable and reliable work force, and thus the characteristic in question is employability. "Employability," in this regard, does not mean that any particular applicant, much less every member of a given group of applicants, will turn out to be a model worker. Nor does it mean that no such applicant will ever become or be discovered to be a malingerer, thief, alcoholic, or even heroin addict. All employers take such risks. Employability, as the District Court used it in reference to successfully maintained methadone users, means only that the employer is no more likely to find a member of that group to be an unsatisfactory employee than he would an employee chosen from the general population.

Petitioners had every opportunity, but presented nothing to negative the employability of successfully maintained methadone users as distinguished from those who were unsuccessful. Instead, petitioners, like the Court, dwell on the methadone failures—those who quit the programs or who remain but turn to illicit drug use. The Court, for instance, makes much of the drug use of many of those in methadone programs, including those who have been in such programs for more than one year. *Ante*, at 6, and n. 10, 19 FEP Cases, at 152. But this has little force since those persons are not "successful," can be and have been identified as such, see *id.*, at 5, 19 FEP Cases, at 151,[11] and, despite the Court's efforts to put them there, see *id.*, at 21 n. 33, 19 FEP Cases, at 157, are not within the protection of the District Court's injunction. That 20 to 30 percent are unsuccessful after one year in a methadone program tells us nothing about the employability of the successful group, and it is the latter category of applicants that the District Court and the Court of Appeals held to be unconstitutionally burdened by the blanket rule disqualifying them from employment.

The District Court and the Court of Appeals were therefore fully justified in finding that petitioners could not reasonably have concluded that the protected group is less employable than the general population and that excluding it "has no rational relation to the demands of the jobs

---

[10] The rule's treatment of those who succeed is at issue here, since the District Court effectively amended the complaint to allege discrimination against that subgroup, see Fed. Rule Civ. Proc. 15(b), and implicitly found no constitutional violation with respect to others burdened by the practice.

[11] The evidence indicates that poor risks will shake out of a methadone-maintenance program within six months. 399 F.Supp., at 1048–1049. It is a measure of the District Court's caution that it set a one-year standard.

to be performed." [12] 399 F. Supp., at 1057. In fact, the Court assumes that petitioners' policy is unnecessarily broad in excluding the successfully maintained and the recently cured, *ante,* at 22, 19 FEP Cases, at 158, and that a member of that group can be selected with adequate precision. *Id.,* at 5, 19 FEP Cases, at 151. Despite this, the validity of the exclusion is upheld on the rational basis of the uninvolved portion of the rule, that is, that the rule excludes many who are less employable. But petitioners must justify the distinction between groups, not just the policy to which they have attached the classification. The purpose of the rule as a whole is relevant only if the classification within the rule serves the purpose, but the majority's assumption admits that is not so.

Justification of the blanket exclusion is not furthered by the statement that "any special rule short of total exclusion . . . is likely to be less precise" than the current rule. *Id.,* at 20, 19 FEP Cases, at 157. If the rule were narrowed as the District Court ordered, it would operate more precisely in at least one respect, for many employable persons would no longer be excluded. Nor does the current rule provide a "bright line," for there is nothing magic about the point five years after treatment has ended. There is a risk of "regression" among those who have never used methadone, and the Court cannot overcome the District Court's finding that a readily ascertainable point exists at which the risk has so decreased that the maintained or recently cured person is generally as employable as anyone else. [13]

Of course, the District Court's order permitting total exclusion of all methadone users maintained for less than one year, whether successfully or not, would still exclude some employables and would to this extent be overinclusive. "Overinclusiveness" as to the primary objective of employability is accepted for less successful methadone users because it fulfills a secondary purpose and thus is not "overinclusive" at all. See *Vance* v. *Bradley,* 439 U.S. ____, ____, 19 FEP Cases 1, 7 (1979). Although many of those who have not been successfully maintained for a year are employable, as a class they, unlike the protected group, are not as employable as the general population. Thus, even assuming the bad risks could be identified, serving the end of employability would require unusual efforts to determine those more likely to revert. But that legitimate secondary goal is not fulfilled by excluding the protected class: The District Court found that the fact of successful participation for one year could be

---

[12] A major sponsor of the recent amendments to the Rehabilitation Act, see *ante,* at 10–11, and n. 16, 19 FEP Cases, at 153–154, described the congressional determination behind them as being that a public employer "cannot assume that a history of alcoholism or drug addiction, including a past addiction currently treated by methadone maintenance, poses sufficient danger in and of itself to justify exclusion [from employment]. Such an assumption would have no basis in fact. . . ." 124 Cong. Rec. S19002 (Sen. Williams) (Oct. 14, 1978).

[13] Though a person free of illicit drug use for one year might subsequently revert, those who have graduated from methadone programs might do so also, and the Court apparently believes that the employment exclusion could not constitutionally be extended to them. See *ante,* at 3 n. 3, and 22 n. 37, 19 FEP Cases, at 151 and 158. See also *ante,* at 3–4, 19 FEP Cases, at 159–160 (POWELL, J., dissenting in relevant part).

discovered through petitioners' normal screening process without additional effort and, I repeat, that those who meet that criterion are no more likely than the average applicant to turn out to be a poor employee.[14] Accordingly, the rule's classification of successfully maintained persons as dispositively different from the general population is left without any justification and, with its irrationality and invidiousness thus uncovered, must fall before the Equal Protection Clause.[15]

[14] Since the District Court found as a fact that the bad risks could be culled from this group through the normal processing of employment applications, the only possible justification for this rule is that it eliminates applications in which petitioners would invest some time and effort before finding the person unemployable. The problem, however, is that not everyone in the general population is employable. Thus, if vacancies are to be filled, individualized hiring decisions must be made in any event.

The fact of methadone use must be determined somehow, so all applications must at least be read, and petitioners require all applicants under 35, and many existing employees, to submit to urinalysis. Reading the applications may disclose not only the fact of methadone use by also whether the person has certain educational or other qualifications and whether he or she has had a stable employment experience or any recent job-related difficulties.

The Court says that petitioners would be burdened by having to verify that a methadone applicant was successful in his program. But the program itself verifies that fact, and the District Court found that all petitioners would have to do is get in touch with the program, and that "this is essentially no different from obtaining relevant references for other types of applicants." 399 F.Supp., at 1050 n. 3. A number of expert witnesses testified that the methadone clinics have far more information about their patients than personnel officers could ordinarily hope to acquire. The Court fears that some of the programs might not be reliable, but the District Court found that most are and ruled that petitioners do not have to hire any applicant "where there is reason to doubt the reliability of "the information furnished by the applicant's clinic. Id., at 1058; accord, id., at 1050 n. 3. Consequently, I see no error at all, much less clear error, in the District Court's finding of fact that petitioners "can perform this screening for methadone maintenance patients in basically the same way as in the case of other prospective employees." Id., at 1048; accord, id., at 1037 and 1050 n. 3.

As to supervision of those who are hired, the fact that they present no greater risk than any other employee eliminates the need for any special supervision, except perhaps a notation on their personnel files that they need not be assigned to safety-sensitive positions. The District Court found as a fact that petitioners' methods of monitoring all their employees "can be used for persons on methadone maintenance just as they are used for other persons. . . ." Id., at 1037.

[15] I have difficulty also with the Court's easy conclusion that the challenged rule was "[q]uite plainly" not motivated "by any special animus against a specific group of persons." Ante, at 23 n. 40, 19 FEP Cases, at 158. Heroin addiction is a special problem of the poor, and the addict population is composed largely of racial minorities that the Court has previously recognized as politically powerless and historical subjects of majoritarian neglect. Persons on methadone maintenance have few interests in common with members of the majority, and thus are unlikely to have their interests protected, or even considered, in governmental decisionmaking. Indeed, petitioners stipulated that "[o]ne of the reasons for the . . . drug policy is the fact that [petitioners] feel[ ] an adverse public reaction would result if it were generally known that [petitioners] employed persons with a prior history of drug abuse, including persons participating in methadone maintenance programs." App. 83A. It is hard for me to reconcile that stipulation of animus against former addicts with our past holdings that "a bare . . . desire to harm a politically unpopular group cannot constitute a legitimate governmental interest." U. S. Dept. of Agriculture v. Moreno, 413 U.S. 528, 534 (1973). On the other hand, the afflictions to which petitioners are more sympathetic, such as alcoholism and mental illness, are shared by both white and black, rich and poor.

Some weight should also be given to the history of the rule. See Village of Arlington Heights v. Metropolitan Housing Dev. Corp., 429 U.S. 252, 267–268 (1977). Petitioners

Finally, even were the District Court wrong, and even were successfully maintained persons marginally less employable than the average applicant,[16] the blanket exclusion of only these people, when but a few are actually unemployable and when many other groups have varying numbers of unemployable members, is arbitrary and unconstitutional. Many persons now suffer from or may again suffer from some handicap related to employability.[17] But petitioners have singled out respondents—unlike exoffenders, former alcoholics and mental patients, diabetics, epileptics, and those currently using tranquilizers, for example—for sacrifice to this at best ethereal and likely nonexistent risk of increased unemployability. Such an arbitrary assignment of burdens among classes that are similarly situated with respect to the proferred objectives is the type of invidious choice forbidden by the Equal Protection Clause.[18]

---

admit that it was not the result of a reasoned policy decision and stipulated that they had never studied the ability of those on methadone maintenance to perform petitioners' jobs. Petitioners are not directly accountable to the public, are not the type of official body that normally makes legislative judgments of fact such as those relied upon by the majority today, and are by nature more concerned with business efficiency than with other public policies for which they have no direct responsibility. Cf. *Hampton* v. *Mow Sun Wong*, 426 U.S. 88, 103, 12 FEP Cases 1377, 1382–1383 (1976). But see *ante*, at 23, 19 FEP Cases, at 158. Both the State and City of New York, which do exhibit those democratic characteristics, hire persons in methadone programs for similar jobs.

These factors together strongly point to a conclusion of invidious discrimination. The Court, however, refuses to view this rule as one circumscrib[ing] a class of persons characterized by some unpopular trait or affiliation," *id.*, at 23, 19 FEP Cases, at 158, because it is admittedly justified as applied to many current and former heroin addicts. Because the challenged classification unfairly burdens only a portion of all heroin addicts, the Court reasons that it cannot possibly have been spurred by animus by the "ruling majority." All that shows, however, is that the characteristic in question is a legitimate basis of distinction in some circumstances; heroin addiction is a serious affliction that will often affect employability. But sometimes antipathy extends beyond the facts that may have given rise to it, and when that happens the "stereotyped reaction may have no rational relationship—other than pure prejudicial discrimination—to the stated purpose for which the classification is being made." *Mathews* v. *Lucas*, 427 U.S. 495, 520–521 (1976) (dissenting opinion) (footnote omitted). That is the case here.

16 The District Court found that the only common physical effects of methadone maintenance are increases in sweating, insomnia, and constipation, and a decrease in sex drive. 399 F.Supp., at 1044–1045. Those disabilities are unfortunate but are hardly related to inability to be a subway janitor. This Court hints that the employability of even those successfully being maintained on methadone might be reduced by their obligation to appear at their clinics three times a week. *Ante*, at 19 n. 32, 19 FEP Cases, at 157. But all employees have outside obligations, and petitioners have neither argued nor proven that this particular duty would interfere with work.

The District Court did find that a possible but rare effect of methadone is minor impairment of abilities "required for the performance of potentially hazardous tasks, such as driving a car or operating machinery," 399 F.Supp., at 1045, and the court exempted from the relief ordered such positions as subway motorman which require "unique sensitivity." *Id.*, at 1052. But this does not make rational the blanket exclusion from all jobs, regardless of the qualifications required.

17 The District Court found, and petitioners have not challenged, that current problem drinkers present more of an employment risk than do respondents. Petitioners do not automatically discharge employees who are found to have a drinking problem. 399 F.Supp., at 1058.

18 The Court argues that "the fact that [petitioners have] the resources to expend on one class of problem employees does not by itself establish a constitutional duty

## D. Homosexuals

## SINGER v. U.S. CIVIL SERVICE COMMISSION

*United States Court of Appeals, Ninth Circuit, 1976*
*530 F.2d 247, 12 FEP Cases 208*

JAMESON, District Judge: This is an appeal from a summary judgment of dismissal of an action brought by John F. Singer, plaintiff-appellant, against the United States Civil Service Commission and certain of its officials, defendants-appellees, seeking declaratory and injunctive relief and damages for termination of Singer's employment because of his homosexual conduct. The district court held that there was "substantial evidence in the administrative record to support the findings and conclusions" of the Civil Service Commission. Both sides rely upon excerpts from that record, and particularly statements of the Commission and its officials. Accordingly we set forth the record in some detail.

### FACTUAL BACKGROUND

On August 2, 1971, Singer was hired by the Seattle Office of the Equal Employment Opportunity Commission (EEOC) as a clerk typist. Pursuant to 5 C.F.R. § 315.801 *et seq.*, he was employed for one year on probationary status, subject to termination if "his work performance or conduct during this period (failed) to demonstrate his fitness or his qualifications for continued employment" (§ 315.804).[1] At the time he was hired Singer informed the Director of EEOC that he was a homosexual.

On May 12, 1972, an investigator for the Civil Service Commission sent a letter to Singer inviting him "to appear voluntarily for an interview to comment upon, explain or rebut adverse information which has come to the attention of the Commission" as a result of its investigation to determine Singer's "suitability for employment in the competitive Federal service." The interview was set for May 19. Singer appeared at the appointed time with his counsel. Singer was advised that the investigation

---

on [their] part to come up with resources to spend on all classes of problem employees." *Ante,* at 22 n. 37, 19 FEP Cases, at 158. If respondents were demanding to have the benefit of a rehabilitation program extended to them, petitioners could perhaps argue for freedom to deal with only one problem at a time due to limited resources. See *Williamson* v. *Lee Optical Co.,* 348 U.S. 483, 489 (1955). In that situation, the lack of resources, or the desire to experiment in a limited field, might be a legitimate objective explaining the classification. But respondents are not asking for special, beneficial treatment; they are asking why they should be absolutely excluded from the opportunity to compete for petitioners' jobs.

[1] [Footnotes numbered as in original.—Ed.] § 315.804 provides for notice in writing as to why a probationer is "being separated and the effective date of the action. The information in the notice as to why the employee is being terminated shall, as a minimum, consist of the agency's conclusions as to the inadequacies of his performance or conduct."

by the Commission disclosed that "you are homosexual. You openly professes that you are homosexual and you have received wide-spread publicity in this respect in at least two states." Specific acts were noted, which may be summarized as follows:

(1) During Singer's previous employment with a San Francisco mortgage firm Singer had "flaunted" his homosexuality by kissing and embracing a male in front of the elevator in the building where he was employed and kissing a male in the company cafeteria;

(2) The San Francisco Chronicle wrote an article on Singer in November of 1970 in which he stated his name and occupation and views on "closet queens";

(3) At the Seattle EEOC office Singer openly admitted being "gay" and indicated by his dress and demeanor that he intended to continue homosexual activity as a "way of life";

(4) On September 20, 1971, Singer and another man applied to the King County Auditor for a marriage license, which was eventually refused by the King County Superior Court; [2]

(5) As a result of the attempt to obtain the marriage license Singer was the subject of extensive television, newspaper and magazine publicity;

(6) Articles published in the Seattle papers of September 21, 1971 included Singer's identification as a typist employed by EEOC and quoted Singer as saying, in part, that he and the man he sought to marry were "two human beings who happen to be in love and want to get married for various reasons";

(7) Singer was active as an "organizer, leader and member of the Board of Directors of the Seattle Gay Alliance, Inc."; his name accompanied by (his) "place of employment appeared as one of the individuals involved in the planning and conducting of a symposium presented by the Seattle Gay Community"; he appeared in a radio "talk show" and displayed homosexual advertisements on the windows of his automobile;

(8) Singer sent a letter to the Civil Service Commission about a planned symposium on employment discrimination stating in part, "I work for the E.E.O.C., and am openly Gay. . . ."

Singer was offered an opportunity to comment "regarding these matters." He did not do so. On May 22 his counsel by letter requested a citation to the Civil Service regulations under which the investigation was proceeding and any regulation related to his alleged unsuitability for employment. In a response dated May 23 the Commission stated that its authority was found in Rule 5, Section 5.2 of the Civil Service Rules and Regulations; and that the "suitability standards in Section 731.201 of the Commission's regulations" cite as disqualifying factors: "Criminal, infamous, dishonest, immoral, or notoriously disgraceful conduct."

---

[2] The order was appealed. In *Singer* v. *Hara*, 11 Wash. App. 247, 522 P.2d 1187 (1974), the Court of Appeals of Washington affirmed the Superior Court and held that the Washington statutory prohibition against same-sex marriages did not violate any constitutional right. A petition for review was denied by the Supreme Court of Washington.

Singer and his counsel were given a further opportunity to appear on Wednesday, May 24, to make a statement or give further information. Instead an affidavit was presented dated May 26 in which Singer stated that (1) he had read the investigative report; (2) the identification of his employment as a typist for the EEOC (6 above) was done by the newspaper without his "specific authorization"; (3) the use of his place of employment with respect to the symposium (7 above) was "not specifically authorized" by him and "was done without (his) knowledge or consent"; and (4) he saw nothing in the report "which in any way indicates that my conduct has been in violation of regulations pertaining to federal employees."

By letter dated June 26, 1972, the Chief of the Investigations Division of the Seattle office of the Civil Service Commission notified Singer that by reason of his "immoral and notoriously disgraceful conduct" he was disqualified under Section 731.201(b) of the Civil Service Regulations (5 CFR § 731.201(b)) and that his agency had been directed to separate him from the service.[3]

Singer appealed the decision. Following the submission of briefs, the Hearing Examiner, on September 14, 1972, upheld the decision of the Chief of the Investigations Division. In advising Singer that instructions for his removal were being renewed, the Examiner reviewed the virtually unrefuted charges against Singer and continued in part:

"In reaching a decision on your appeal, careful consideration has been given to the written representations and evidence submitted in your behalf by Attorney Christopher E. Young on September 7, 1972, in lieu of an opportunity for personal appearance afforded to you on that date. In pertinent part, these representations contend that your supervisor and co-workers have experienced no complaint with your performance or conduct on the job,[4] and that your removal will not promote the efficiency of the service. The appellate representations otherwise disagree with the Commission's determination that homosexual conduct is immoral in nature and does not meet requirements of suitability for the Federal service, contending that such actions based on an individual's

---

[3] The reasons for the Commission's conclusion were set forth in the letter as follows:
"The information developed by the investigation, taken with your reply, indicate that you have flaunted and broadcast your homosexual activities and have sought and obtained publicity in various media in pursuit of this goal. . . . Your activities in these matters are those of an advocate for a socially repugnant concept.
". . . In determining that your employment will not promote the efficiency of the service, the Commission has considered such pertinent factors as the potential disruption of service efficiency because of the possible revulsion of other employees to homosexual conduct and/or their apprehension of homosexual advances and solicitations; the hazard that the prestige and authority of a Government position will be used to foster homosexual activity, particularly among youth; the possible use of Government funds and authority in furtherance of conduct offensive to the mores and law of our society; and the possible embarrassment to, and loss of public confidence in, your agency and the Federal civil service."
[4] In an evaluation report, Singer had been rated by his supervisor as "superior" or "very good" in various categories of job performance. A letter from his co-workers expressed the opinion that Singer had been a competent employee and that their experience with him had been "educational and positive."

personal sexuality and sexual activities are violative of constitutional rights of privacy and free speech.

"However, there is more to the 'efficiency of the service' than the proper performance of assigned duties. The immoral and notoriously disgraceful conduct which is established by the evidence in your case, in our view, does have a direct and material bearing upon your fitness for Federal employment. Activities of the type you have engaged in, which has not been limited to activity conducted in private, are such that general public knowledge thereof would reflect discredit upon the Federal government as your employer, impeding the efficiency of the service by lessening general public confidence in the fitness of the government to conduct the public business with which it is entrusted. The federal government, like any employer, may be judged by the character and conduct of the persons in its employ, and it will promote the efficiency of the service to remove from its employ any individual whose detrimental influence will detract from that efficiency."

Singer appealed to the United States Civil Service Commission, Board of Appeals and Review. In a decision and order dated December 1, 1972, the Board affirmed the decision of the Regional Office dated September 14, 1972, saying in part:

"There is evidence in the file which indicated that appellant's actions establish that he has engaged in immoral and notoriously disgraceful conduct, openly and publicly flaunting his homosexual way of life and indicating further continuance of such activities. Activities of the type he has engaged in are such that general public knowledge thereof reflects discredit upon the Federal Government as his employer, impeding the efficiency of the service by lessening general public confidence in the fitness of the Government to conduct the public business with which it is entrusted."

On December 29, 1972, Singer filed this action on behalf of himself and other persons similarly situated, seeking injunctive and declaratory relief. The complaint was later amended to include a prayer for damages and an order restoring Singer to his Civil Service position. Summary judgment of dismissal with prejudice was entered on March 29, 1974.

### CONTENTIONS OF PARTIES

Appellant contends that he was discharged because of his status as a homosexual without the Commission showing any "rational nexus" between his homosexual activities and the efficiency of the service, in violation of the Due Process Clause of the Fifth Amendment; and that he has been denied freedom of expression and the right to petition the Government for redress of grievances, in violation of the First Amendment. The Commission argues that appellant's discharge as a probationary employee was not arbitrary, capricious, an abuse of discretion, or unconstitutional; that appellant was not discharged because of his status as a homosexual; and that appellant's repeated flaunting and advocacy of a controversial lifestyle, with substantial publicity in which he was identified as an employee of EEOC, provided a rational basis for the Commission's conclusion as to "possible embarrassment to, and loss of public confidence in (the) agency and the Federal Civil Service."

In considering these contentions, we are concerned with recent developments of the law in four related areas: (1) the extent of judicial review of agency decisions; (2) the extent of the Government's prerogative to regulate the conduct of its employees; (3) the constitutional rights of probationary employees; and (4) the dismissal of government employees for homosexual activities.

### SCOPE OF REVIEW OF AGENCY ACTION

While the concept of the scope of review of agency action in the discharge of government employees has broadened in recent years, it is still narrow. *Dennis* v. *Blount,* 497 F.2d 1305, 1309 (9 Cir. 1974). The applicable rule was well summarized in *Toohey* v. *Nitzo,* 429 F.2d 1332, 1334 (9th Cir. 1970):

"Dismissal from federal employment is largely a matter of executive agency discretion. Particularly is this true during the probationary period. The scope of judicial review is narrow. Assuming that statutory procedures meet constitutional requirements, the court is limited to a determination of whether the agency substantially complied with its statutory and regulatory procedures, whether its factual determinations were supported by substantial evidence, and whether its action was arbitrary, capricious or an abuse of discretion." [5]

### RIGHT OF GOVERNMENT TO CONTROL CONDUCT AND SPEECH OF EMPLOYEES

As with scope of review of action of government agencies, courts are increasingly re-examining and considering . . . to what extent the Government's prerogative to employ or discharge permits it to regulate conduct of its employees" which might otherwise violate constitutional rights. *Meehan* v. *Macy,* 392 F.2d 822, 832 (1968).[6] It is well established, however, that the Government as an employer has interests in regulating the speech of its employees "that differ significantly from those it possesses in connection with regulation of the speech of the citizenry in general." The problem is to arrive at the proper balance between the interests of the employee, as a citizen, and the interest of the Government, as an employer, "in promoting the efficiency of the public service it performs

---

[5] See also *Seebach* v. *Cullen,* 338 F.2d 663 (9 Cir. 1964), *cert. denied,* 380 U.S. 972 (1965); *Frommhagen* v. *Klein,* 456 F.2d 1391, 1393 (9 Cir. 1972).

[6] Judge Leventhal noted further:

"As Government services multiply, the liberties of Government employees come to be the liberties of an increasing and substantial portion of the citizenry, and are accordingly given increased recognition. There is a reverse side to the coin: With mounting provision of increased and increasingly indispensable services rendered by Government employees, the public weal demands administration that is effective and disciplined, and not beset by turmoil and anarchy."

through its employees." *Pickering* v. *Board of Education,* 391 U.S. 563, 568 (1968).

## STATUS OF PROBATIONARY EMPLOYEE

As a probationary employee appellant had no right *per se* to continued employment.[7] However, even though a person has no "right" to a valuable governmental benefit and "even though the government may deny him the benefit for any number of reasons," it "may not deny a benefit to a person on a basis that infringes his constitutionally protected interests—especially his interest in freedom of speech." *Perry* v. *Sindermann,* 408 U.S. 593, 597 (1972). Moreover, while the Civil Service Commission has wide discretion in determining what reasons may justify removal of federal employees, that discretion is not unlimited. Due process limitations in determining what reasons justify removal may apply to those whose employment is not protected by statute.

It is clear that the Civil Service Commission complied with the statutory and regulatory procedures in its investigation of appellant's conduct and in his dismissal. It is clear also that the dismissal was not based upon unfounded and unsupported charges. Appellant in effect admitted the truth of the charges.[8] The sole question is whether the action of the Commission in dismissing appellant on the basis of the admitted charges was arbitrary and capricious, an abuse of discretion, and in violation of appellant's constitutional rights.

## DISMISSAL FOR HOMOSEXUAL ACTIVITIES

With the foregoing principles and trends in mind, we turn to those cases which have considered homosexual activities as a basis for dismissal of Civil Service employees. The leading case is *Norton* v. *Macy,* 417 F.2d 1161, 9 FEP Cases 1382 (1969) (opinion by JUDGE BAZELON, with JUDGE WRIGHT concurring and JUDGE TAMM dissenting), where a protected civil servant sought review of his discharge for "immoral conduct" and for possessing personality traits which rendered him "unsuitable for further Government employment." The employee was "competent" and doing "very good" work. He was dismissed solely because he had made an off-duty homosexual advance. The Commission found that this act amounted to "immoral, indecent, and disgraceful conduct," resulting in possible embarrassment to the employing agency. Relying on the First Amendment and the Due Process Clause the court held that the dismissal could not be sustained on the grounds relied on by the Commission, in that the employer agency had not demonstrated any "rational basis" for its conclusion that discharge would "promote the efficiency of the service."

---

[7] See *Board of Regents* v. *Roth,* 408 U.S. 564 (1972); *Jenkins* v. *U.S. Post Office,* 475 F.2d 1256 (9th Cir. 1973). It is clear also that a probationary employee has "fewer procedural rights than permanent employees in the competitive service." *Sampson* v. *Murray,* 415 U.S. 61, 81 (1974).

[8] In his affidavit Singer stated, however, that he had not specifically authorized some of the newspaper publicity.

The court noted, however, that homosexual conduct cannot be ignored as a factor in determining fitness for federal employment since it might "bear on the efficiency of the service in a number of ways." More specifically the court said: "If an employee makes offensive overtures while on the job, or if his conduct is notorious, the reactions of other employees and of the public with whom he comes in contact in the performance of his official functions may be taken into account. Whether or not such potential consequences would justify removal, they are at least broadly relevant to 'the efficiency of the service.' " 417 F.2d at 1166, 9 FEP Cases at 1386.

The court concluded in *Norton*, 417 F.2d. at 1167, 9 FEP Cases at 1386, that:

"A reviewing court must at least be able to discern some reasonably foreseeable, specific connection between an employee's potentially embarrassing conduct and the efficiency of the service. Once the connection is established, then it is for the agency and the Commission to decide whether it outweighs the loss to the service of a particular competent employee.

"In the instant case appellee has shown us no such specific connection. Indeed, on the record appellant is at most an extremely infrequent offender, who neither openly flaunts nor carelessly displays his unorthodox sexual conduct in public.[9] Thus, even the potential for the embarrassment the agency fears is minimal. We think the unparticularized and unsubstantiated conclusion that such possible embarrassment threatens the quality of the agency's performance is an arbitrary ground for dismissal."

*Norton* v. *Macy* was construed by another panel of the Court of Appeals for the District of Columbia, in *Gayer* v. *Schlessinger*, 490 F.2d 740 (1973), in an opinion by Judge Fahy with Judge Leventhal concurring, and Judge Robb concurring in part and dissenting in part.[10] The court concluded regarding *Norton* "Thus the court said [in part] that a rational connection between an employee's homosexual conduct and the efficiency of the service may exist" justifying agency personnel action. 490 F.2d at 750. The court noted (n. 21 p. 750) that judicial opinion on the issue was not unanimous since in *Anonymous* v. *Macy*, 398 F.2d 317, 318 (5 Cir. 1968), the court rejected the contention that homosexual acts of

[9] In a footnote the court noted that there was "no evidence that (Norton) was ever engaged in any offensive conduct in public. His private conduct came to light only through police investigation tactics of at least questionable legality." 417 F.2d at 1167, n. 27.

[10] In *Gayer* the court considered three cases in which the district court had set aside the revocation of security clearance for homosexuals. Appellant relies upon two of those cases, *Wentworth* v. *Laird*, D.C., 348 F. Supp. 1153 (1972), and *Gayer* v. *Laird*, D.C., 332 F. Supp. 169 (1971). While the Court of Appeals affirmed the district court, it did so on the ground that in *Wentworth* the Hearing Examiner and Appeals Board had relied on answers to questions which were in violation of an executive order and thus impermissible, and in the second case the scope of examination was excessive. The orders were affirmed without prejudice to further proceedings by the Government consistent with the court's opinion. The third case *(Gayer)* was remanded to the administrative level to afford the employee an opportunity to respond to questions held proper, suspension to be sustained in case of his failure to answer the questions.

employees do not affect the efficiency of the service and may not be the basis of discharge.[11] The court in *Gayer* concluded that, "As in other decisions of importance the bearing of particular conduct . . . must be left to a rational appraisal based on relevant facts"; that the determination of the government agency should be "explained in such manner that a reviewing court may be able to discern whether there is a rational connection between the facts relied upon and the conclusions drawn"; that some deference must be accorded the decision of the agency; and that the "degree of this deference must be the result of a nice but not— easily—definable weighing of the ingredients of which the particular case is comprised." 490 F.2d at 750-51.

In *Society for Individual Rights, Inc.* v. *Hampton,* 63 F.R.D. 399 (N.D.Cal. 1973), an organization of homosexual persons and a discharged employee brought an action to "challenge the United States Civil Service Commission's policy as stated in Federal Personnel Manual Supplement (Int.) 731–71 of excluding from government employment all persons who have engaged in or solicited others to engage in homosexual acts." [12] The court found that the decision of the Board of Appeals and Review was "based solely upon the fact that plaintiff is presently a homosexual person and the Commission's view that the employment of such persons will bring the government service into 'public contempt.'" Following *Norton* v. *Macy,* the court held that the "Commission can discharge a person for immoral behavior only if that behavior actually impairs the efficiency of the service," and that the Commission had not met, or even tried to meet, this standard. 63 F.R.D. at 401. The court accordingly ordered reinstatement of the discharged employee and that the Commission "forthwith cease excluding or discharging from government service any homosexual person whom the Commission would deem unfit for government employment solely because the employment of such a person in the government service might bring that service into the type of public contempt which might reduce the government's ability to perform the public business with the essential respect and confidence of the citizens which it serves." 63 F.R.D. at 402.

The court recognized, however, that "granting this relief will not interfere with the power of the Commission to dismiss a person for homosexual conduct in those circumstances where more is involved than the Commission's unparticularized and unsubstantiated conclusion that possible embarrassment about an employee's homosexual conduct threatens the quality of the government's performance. Thus, although the overbroad rule stated in Federal Personnel Manual Supplement (Int.) 731–71

---

[11] The court also considered the effect of prior decisions of the D.C. Circuit Court in *Adams* v. *Laird,* 420 F.2d 230 (1969), *cert. denied,* 397 U.S. 1039 (1970); *Dew* v. *Halaby,* 317 F.2d 582 (1973), *petition for cert. dismissed,* 379 U.S. 951 (1964); and *Scott* v. *Macy,* 402 F.2d 644 (1968), both majority and dissenting opinions.

[12] The manual read in pertinent part:
"*Homosexuality and Sexual Perversion*—Persons about whom there is evidence that they have engaged in or solicited others to engage in homosexual or sexually perverted acts with them, without evidence of rehabilitation, are not suitable for Federal employment."

*supra,* n. 1, cannot be enforced, the Commission is free to consider what particular circumstances might justify dismissing an employee for charges relating to homosexual conduct." [13] 63 F.R.D. at 401.

## CHANGES IN CIVIL SERVICE REGULATIONS AND PERSONNEL MANUAL

At oral argument counsel called attention to changes in the Personnel Manual following *Society for Individual Rights* v. *Hampton,* which were set forth in a bulletin issued December 21, 1973,[14] and also to amendments to the Civil Service Regulations relating to Suitability Disqualification, which became effective July 2, 1975,[15] following rule making proceedings initiated on December 3, 1973. The bulletin issued on December 21, 1973, was not made a part of the record in this case, and it does not appear that it was called to the attention of the district court. The new regulations were adopted subsequent to the entry of judgment and during the pendency of this appeal. Our decision in this case is based on the record before the district court and the regulations and guidelines in effect when appellant's contract was terminated.[16]

## REASON FOR TERMINATION OF EMPLOYMENT

We conclude from a review of the record in its entirety that appellant's employment was not terminated because of his status as a homosexual or because of any private acts of sexual preference. The statements of the Commission's investigation division, hearing examiner, and Board

[13] Notice of appeal was given, but the appeal was later dismissed on motion of the Civil Service Commission.

[14] The bulletin called attention to the opinion in *Hampton,* noting that it was a class action and applicable to all federal employees. The Commission, therefore, instructed those "engaged in suitability evaluation" as follows:

"Accordingly, you may not find a person unsuitable for Federal employment merely because that person is a homosexual or has engaged in homosexual acts, nor may such exclusion be based on a conclusion that a homosexual person might bring the public service into public contempt. You are, however, permitted to dismiss a person or find him or her unsuitable for Federal employment where the evidence establishes that such person's homosexual conduct affects job fitness—excluding from such consideration, however, unsubstantiated conclusions concerning possible embarrassment to the Federal service."

[15] 5 C.F.R. Part 73, relating to Suitability Disqualification, was substantially amended. In the provision listing reasons for disqualification, the word "immoral" was deleted, Section 731.202(b), as amended reading in part: "(2) Criminal, dishonest, infamous or notoriously disgraceful conduct." The "Suitability Guidelines for Federal Employment" was revised to conform to the new regulations. The amended guidelines for determining "Infamous or Notoriously Disgraceful Conduct" reads in part:

"Individual sexual conduct will be considered under the guides discussed above. Court decisions require that persons not be disqualified from Federal employment solely on the basis of homosexual conduct. The Commission and agencies have been enjoined not to find a person unsuitable for Federal employment solely because that person is homosexual or has engaged in homosexual acts. Based upon these court decisions and outstanding injunction, while a person may not be found unsuitable based on unsubstantiated conclusions concerning possible embarrassment to the Federal service, a person may be dismissed or found unsuitable for Federal employment where the evidence establishes that such person's sexual conduct affects job fitness."

[16] We do not imply that the amended regulations and guidelines would require a different result under the facts of this case.

of Appeals make it clear that the discharge was the result of appellant's "openly and publicly flaunting his homosexual way of life and indicating further continuance of such activities," while identifying himself as a member of a federal agency. The Commission found that these activities were such that "general public knowledge thereof reflects discredit upon the Federal Government as his employer, impeding the efficiency of the service by lessening public confidence in the fitness of the Government to conduct the public business with which it was entrusted."

This case is factually distinguishable from *Norton* v. *Macy* and the other cases discussed *supra,* involving, private sexual acts and considering situations where there was no showing that the discharge would "promote the efficiency of the service." It is apparent from their statements that the Commission and its officials appreciated the requirement of *Norton* v. *Macy,* decided three years earlier, that the discharge of a homosexual must be justified by a finding that his conduct affected the efficiency of the service. As noted *supra, Norton* v. *Macy* recognized that notorious conduct and open flaunting and careless display of unorthodox sexual conduct in public might be relevant to the efficiency of the service. The Commission set forth in detail the specified conduct upon which it relied in determining appellant's unsuitability for continued employment in the competitive Federal service. We are able to discern "a rational connection between the facts relied upon and the conclusions drawn" (*Gayer* v. *Schlessinger, supra*) and agree with the district court that there was substantial evidence to support the findings and conclusions of the Civil Service Commission.

### FIRST AMENDMENT RIGHTS

With respect to appellant's contention that his First Amendment rights have been violated, appellant relies on two cases which deserve comment. The first of these cases, *Gay Students Org. of University of New Hampshire* v. *Bonner,* 509 F.2d 652 (1 Cir. 1974), did not involve public employment, but rather the validity of a regulation prohibiting a homosexual organization from holding social activities on the campus. The court concluded that "The GSO's efforts to organize the homosexual minority, 'educate' the public as to its plight, and obtain for it better treatment from individuals and from the government . . . represent but another example of the associational activity unequivocally singled out for protection in the very 'core' of association cases decided by the Supreme Court." [17] In holding that "conduct may have a communicative content sufficient to bring it within the ambit of the First Amendment, the Court also recognized that "[c]ommunicative conduct is subject to regulation as to 'time, place and manner' in the furtherance of a substantial governmental interest, so long as the restrictions imposed are only so broad as required in order to further the interest and are unre-

[17] Citing, *inter alia, NAACP* v. *Button,* 371 U.S. 415 (1963); *NAACP* v. *Alabama ex rel. Patterson,* 357 U.S. 449 (1958).

lated to the content and subject matter of the message communicated."
509 F.2d at 660.

In *Acanfora* v. *Board of Education of Montgomery County*, 491 F.2d
498 (4 Cir. 1974), the Board had transferred Acanfora to a nonteaching
position when they found that he was a homosexual. The Board's action
was upheld on the ground that Acanfora had deliberately withheld from
his application information relating to his homosexuality. In holding,
however, that Acanfora's public statements on homosexuality were protected by the First Amendment, the court recognized the balancing test
set forth in *Pickering* v. *Board of Education, supra,* and continued:

"At the invitation of the Public Broadcasting System, Acanfora appeared with his parents on a program designed to help parents and homosexual children cope with the problems that confront them. Acanfora
also consented to other television, radio, and press interviews. The tran-
scripts of the television programs, which the district court found to be
typical of all the interviews, disclose that he spoke about the difficulties
homosexuals encounter, and, while he did not advocate homosexuality,
he sought community acceptance. He also stressed that he had not, and
would not, discuss his sexuality with the students.

"In short, the record discloses that press, radio and television commentators considered homosexuality in general, and Acanfora's plight in
particular, to be a matter of public interest about which reasonable
people could differ, and Acanfora responded to their inquiries in a
rational manner. There is no evidence that the interviews disrupted the
school, substantially impaired his capacity as a teacher, or gave the
school officials reasonable grounds to forecast that these results would
flow from what he said. We hold, therefore, that Acanfora's public statements were protected by the first amendment and that they do not just
justify either the action taken by the school system or the dismissal of
his suit." 491 F.2d at 500.

*Bonner* and *Acanfora* are factually distinguishable. Neither involved
the open and public flaunting or advocacy of homosexual conduct.
Applying the balancing test of *Pickering* v. *Board of Education,* the
Commission could properly conclude that under the facts of this case,
the interest of the Government as an employer "in promoting the efficiency of the public service" outweighed the interest of its employee in
exercising his First Amendment Rights through publicly flaunting and
broadcasting his homosexual activities.

Affirmed.

## NOTE

The decision of the court of appeals was vacated and remanded for
consideration in light of the position asserted by the Solicitor General.
429 U.S. 1034, 14 FEP Cases 203 (1977). See FPM Supplement 731-1 (1975)
for the Civil Service guidelines for determining suitability for federal
employment.

For cases involving the discharge of homosexuals from the military, see *Matlovich* v. *Secretary of the Air Force,* 18 FEP Cases 1061 (1978), and *Berg* v. *Claytor,* 18 FEP Cases 1068 (1978).

In *Gaylord* v. *Tacoma School District No. 10,* 88 Wash.2d 286, 559 P.2d 1340 (1977), *cert. denied,* 434 U.S. 879 (1977), the Washington Supreme Court upheld the discharge of a homosexual on grounds of immorality and impairment of fitness to teach.

In *Doe* v. *Commonwealth's Attorney,* 425 U.S. 901 (1976), the Court, without any argument or stating any reasons, summarily affirmed a three-judge court's dismissal of a challenge to Virginia's sodomy law. The three-judge court divided 2 to 1. Justices Brennan, Marshall, and Stevens would have set the case for oral argument. In his opinion in *Carey* v. *Population Services Int'l,* 451 U.S. 678 (1977), Justice Brennan stated that the court "has not yet definitively answered the difficult question whether and to what extent the Constitution prohibits state statutes regulating [private consensual sexual] behavior among adults." Justice Rehnquist, on the other hand, citing *Doe* v. *Commonwealth's Attorney,* asserted that "the facial constitutional validity of criminal statutes prohibiting certain consensual acts has been 'definitively' established."

# Table of Cases

Cases presented in text or partial text are in italic type. Other cases—those discussed or merely cited—are in roman type. References are to pages.

# Topical Index